CONTEMPORARY CRIMINAL PROCEDURE:

COURT DECISIONS FOR LAW ENFORCEMENT

by
Larry E. Holtz

10TH EDITION

QUESTIONS ABOUT THIS PUBLICATION?

For CUSTOMER SERVICE ASSISTANCE concerning replacement pages, shipments, billing, reprint permission, or other matters,

please call Customer Service Department at 800-833-9844
email *customer.support@lexisnexis.com*
or visit our interactive customer service website at *www.lexisnexis.com/printcdsc*

For EDITORIAL **content questions** concerning this publication,

email: *LEpublications@lexisnexis.com*

For **information on other LEXISNEXIS MATTHEW BENDER publications**,

please call us at 877-461-8801
or visit our online bookstore at *www.lexisnexis.com/bookstore*

ISBN: 978-1-4224-2616-6

© 2008 Matthew Bender & Company, Inc., a member of the LexisNexis Group.

 LexisNexis®

Matthew Bender & Company, Inc.
Editorial Offices
P.O. Box 7587
Charlottesville, VA 22906-7587
800-446-3410
www.lexisnexis.com

Product Number 7489812

(Pub. 74898)

PREFACE

Contemporary **Criminal Procedure: Court Decisions for Law Enforcement** has been created exclusively for the modern law enforcement or criminal justice practitioners operating in either the federal or state system. It presents a new and innovative approach to the study of constitutional criminal procedure and provides a quick reference to the pertinent classical and current judicial decisions which directly affect the day-to-day activity of the professional law enforcement and criminal justice communities.

The majority of cases presented come from the United States Supreme Court and the United States Circuit Courts of Appeal. Additionally, in recognition of the present proclivity of many state courts to depart from the federal rule—relying on their own state constitutions to afford their citizens enhanced protection to their privacy interests—we have identified some key areas where a State might so depart.

This text, therefore, serves two purposes. First, it removes the guesswork in, and tedious search for, "today's" law. The quick-reference format should prove invaluable not only for officers in the field but also for attorneys in court who need an instant answer (and the case law which supports that answer) to a criminal procedure problem.

This text also has been organized as a college text, offering those who teach criminal procedure, criminal law, or general police science courses, a current, clear and concise approach to the law of arrest, search and seizure, investigative detentions (stop and frisk), motor vehicle stops, and fire-scene procedures. This material constitutes Part I, and includes chapters one through ten. Part II, incorporating chapters eleven through thirteen, explores the legal issues surrounding interviews, confessions and *Miranda*, identification procedures, and the Sixth Amendment rights to counsel and confrontation. Because no discussion of contemporary criminal procedure would be complete without reference to the issues surrounding the possession and distribution of dangerous illegal drugs, Part III, chapter fourteen, has been included for the purpose of highlighting the problems law enforcement officials face when they must establish an individual's possession of illegal drugs, or his possession with the intent to distribute them. Finally, Part IV, chapter fifteen, presents the recent cases which have been handed down in the area of law-enforcement liability.

Each of the principal cases presented consists of a court decision which has been analyzed, dissected, and restructured into a question and answer format. The **Question** presented, which is the general issue (or one of the issues) in the case, is placed at the beginning of the case, directly under the case name and citation. The **Answer** to the question represents the holding of the case, *i.e.*, the "rule of law," and immediately follows the question presented. Immediately following the answer is the court's analysis, or the **Rationale** behind the rule of law. The Notes which follow many of the principal cases further explore the particular subject area, and illustrate classical and current variations of the principal theme.

As we all know, the most well-settled aspect of criminal procedure is its continuous change and development. Therefore, to keep this text truly "contemporary," updated editions will be available annually.

iii

THE AUTHOR

Larry E. Holtz received his Bachelor of Arts Degree in Criminal Justice from Temple University, Philadelphia, Pennsylvania, graduating *Summa Cum Laude*. In December of 1988, he received his *Juris Doctorate* from Temple University School of Law, graduating in the top ten percent of his class.

Formerly a Sergeant of Detectives with the Atlantic City Police Department, a Deputy Attorney General and an assistant county prosecutor, Mr. Holtz is presently an attorney specializing in police administrative matters, the Municipal Prosecutor for several towns in the southern New Jersey area, and the Executive Director of Holtz Learning Centers, Ltd. He is also a certified police instructor, providing training at numerous police training academies in New Jersey and Pennsylvania, and is an Adjunct Professor of Law at Widener University School of Law, Wilmington, Delaware, and an Adjunct Professor of Criminal Justice at Rowan University, Glassboro, New Jersey.

Mr. Holtz is the author of the *New Jersey Law Enforcement Handbook*, the *Pennsylvania Law Enforcement Handbook, Criminal Evidence for Law Enforcement Officers*, and *Investigative and Operational Report Writing*. He is published in the *Pennsylvania Law Journal-Reporter*, the *Journal of Criminal Law and Criminology*, and the *Dickinson Law Review*. In addition, he is the co-author of the *Texas Law Enforcement Handbook* and the *Supervision of Police Personnel Study Guide*.

Mr. Holtz is a member of the Bar in New Jersey, Pennsylvania, and the District of Columbia.

> NO POLICE PROCEDURES SHOULD BE
> CHANGED, ALTERED, OR MODIFIED
> PURSUANT TO THE MATERIAL
> FOUND HEREIN BEFORE CONSULTING
> WITH YOUR LOCAL PROSECUTOR, DISTRICT
> ATTORNEY, STATE ATTORNEY GENERAL OR
> UNITED STATES ATTORNEY.

HOLTZ LEARNING CENTERS

As the Executive Director of Police Training for Holtz Learning Centers, Ltd., Mr. Holtz provides a wide variety of basic and advanced training to law enforcement officials in New Jersey and Pennsylvania. His seminars cover such topics as (1) The Laws of Arrest, Search and Seizure (basic and advanced); (2) Criminal and Motor Vehicle Law Updates; (3) Interviews, Confessions and *Miranda*; (4) Kinetic Reading (designed to supercharge one's reading speed, comprehension and memory); (5) Investigative and Operational Report Writing; and (6) Principles of Police Supervision and Management. In addition, Mr. Holtz conducts comprehensive executive development courses designed to prepare law enforcement officials for the move up to sergeant, lieutenant, captain, inspector, deputy chief and chief.

For more information regarding specialized training, write to Holtz Learning Centers, Ltd., P.O. Box 265, Tuckahoe, New Jersey 08250, or contact the main office at 1-800-320-8653, or at **holtzlc@verizon.net**, or visit our website at **holtzlearningcenters.com**.

Dedicated
To the memory of the law enforcement officers
Who made the ultimate sacrifice while
Making our world a safer place.

———————————————

For Sue
My wife,
My best friend, and
My favorite police officer !

SUMMARY OF CONTENTS

PART I

ARREST, SEARCH AND SEIZURE

Summary of Contents

PART II

INTERVIEWS AND CONFESSIONS; EYEWITNESS IDENTIFICATION; AND THE SIXTH AMENDMENT RIGHTS TO COUNSEL AND CONFRONTATION

PART III

NARCOTIC DRUGS AND
OTHER DANGEROUS SUBSTANCES:
POSSESSION AND DISTRIBUTION

PART IV

LIABILITY

PART V

ADDENDA

DETAILED ANALYSIS
OF
CONTENTS

PART I

ARREST, SEARCH AND SEIZURE

Page

Detailed Analysis of Contents

Detailed Analysis of Contents

Detailed Analysis of Contents

Detailed Analysis of Contents

Detailed Analysis of Contents

Detailed Analysis of Contents

Detailed Analysis of Contents

PART II

INTERVIEWS AND CONFESSIONS; EYEWITNESS IDENTIFICATION; AND THE SIXTH AMENDMENT RIGHTS TO COUNSEL AND CONFRONTATION

Detailed Analysis of Contents

Detailed Analysis of Contents

Detailed Analysis of Contents

PART III

NARCOTIC DRUGS AND
OTHER DANGEROUS SUBSTANCES:
POSSESSION AND DISTRIBUTION

PART IV

LIABILITY

PART V

ADDENDA

[This page is intentionally blank.]

READING GUIDE

SAMPLE CASE

1{MIRANDA v. ARIZONA
Supreme Court of the United States
384 *U.S.* 436, 86 *S.Ct.* 1602 (1966) }3

2

QUESTION: Are self-incriminating statements elicited from an individual during incommunicado interrogation in a police-dominated atmosphere without full warnings of constitutional rights admissible in evidence? }4

ANSWER: NO. "[T]he prosecution may not use statements, whether exculpatory or inculpatory, stemming from custodial interrogation of the defendant unless it demonstrates the use of procedural safeguards effective to secure the privilege against self-incrimination." {*Id.* at 1612.}7 }5

RATIONALE: In this landmark decision, the United States Supreme Court clarifies its holding in *Escobedo v. Illinois*, 378 *U.S.* 478, 84 *S.Ct.* 1758 (1964), and provides "concrete constitutional guidelines for law enforcement agencies and courts to follow." {*Miranda* at 1611.}8

Initially, the Court defines "custodial interrogation" to "mean questioning initiated by law enforcement officers after a person has been taken into custody or otherwise deprived of his freedom of action in any significant way." *Id.* at 1612. As for the procedural safeguards to be employed, the Court requires that: }6

> Prior to any questioning, the person must be warned that he has the right to remain silent, that any statement he does make may be used as evidence against him, and that he has a right to the presence of an attorney, either retained or appointed. The *defendant may waive* effectuation of *these rights, provided the waiver is made voluntarily, knowingly, and intelligently.* If, however, he indicates in any manner and at any stage of the process that he wishes to consult with an attorney before speaking there can be no questioning. Likewise, if the individual is alone and indicates in any manner that he does not wish to be interrogated, the police may not question him.

*** }9

Id. [Emphasis added.] }10

READING GUIDE

EXPLANATION

1. *NAME OR TITLE OF CASE.*

2. *CASE CITATION:*

   Number on left = volume of book.
   Number on right = page number where case begins.
   If blank, (e.g., ___ U.S. ___) the case has not been published as of the printing date of the Handbook.

   MEANINGS OF ABBREVIATIONS BE-TWEEN NUMBERS:

   FEDERAL CASES:

   Texts which report cases from the U.S. Supreme Court:
   U.S. = United States Reports.
   S.Ct. = Supreme Court Reporter.
   L.Ed.2d = Lawyer's Edition of the U.S. Supreme Court Reports; Second Edition.
   U.S.L.W. = United States Law Week
   Texts which report cases from other (lower) federal courts:
   F.Supp. = Federal Supplement. (Cases generally from the Federal District Courts)
   F.2d = Federal Reporter; Second Edition. (Cases generally from the Federal Circuit Courts of Appeal)

   STATE CASES:

   A.2d = Atlantic Reporter; second edition (Cases from: CT, DE, DC, ME, MD, NH, NJ, PA, RI, VT)
   N.E.2d = North Eastern Reporter; second edition (Cases from: IL, IN, MA, NY, OH)
   N.W.2d = North Western Reporter; second edition (Cases from: IA, MI, MN, NE, ND, SD, WI)
   P.2d = Pacific Reporter; second edition (Cases from: AK, AZ, CA, CO, HI, ID, KS, MT, NV, NM, OK, OR, UT, WA, WY)
   So.2d = Southern Reporter; second edition (Cases from: AL, FL, LA, MS)
   S.E.2d = South Eastern Reporter; second edition (Cases from GA, NC, SC, VA, WV)
   S.W.2d = South Western Reporter; second edition (Cases from: AR, KY, MO, TN, TX)

3. *DATE CASE WAS DECIDED.*

4. *QUESTION OR ISSUE PRESENTED.*

5. *ANSWER TO THE QUESTION OR ISSUE PRESENTED* (Is normally the case "holding" or "rule of law.")

6. RATIONALE: The extended explanation for the rule of law.

7. *"SHORTHAND" CITATION FORMS:*

   "Id."— used to indicate a reference to a case or authority cited immediately preceding the present use.

   NOTE, MODIFICATION OF USE OF *Id.*: Unless otherwise specified, when the use of *Id.* refers the reader back to the CITATION immediately following the CASE TITLE, the reference shall *only* refer to the text cited immediately before the date. For example, "*Id.* at 1612" refers the reader to page 1612 of volume 86 of the Supreme Court Reporter. (*See* 1 and 2.)

8. OTHER "SHORTHAND" CITATION FORMS:

   "Miranda at 1611"— Periodically used instead of *Id.* for clarification. Either of these "shorthand" citation forms shall be used when the case speaks of, or refers to, more than one case or authority. The purpose is to clarify exactly which case or authority is being cited.
   "Supra"—Refers you back to a case or authority already cited in full. For example, "as was held in *Escobedo v. Illinois, supra,* ..."; or more simply, "as was held in *Escobedo, supra,* ...".
   "Infra"—Used in the same manner as *supra,* but instead of referring you "back," it refers you "ahead."

9. *OMITTED WORDS:*

   The ellipsis, " * * *, " is used to indicate that unnecessary words have been omitted.

10. *BRACKETED MATERIAL:*

   Consists of material added or changed by the Author. In this sample, the emphasis by italic type in the last paragraph has been added by the Author.

PART I

ARREST, SEARCH AND SEIZURE

CHAPTER 1

ARREST

§1.1. Introduction.

An **arrest** may be defined as a substantial physical interference with the liberty of a person, resulting in his apprehension and detention. It is generally effected for the purpose of preventing a person from committing a criminal offense, or calling upon a person to answer or account for an alleged completed crime.

An arrest may be effected "actually" or "constructively." An *actual* arrest occurs when a duly empowered law enforcement officer intentionally employs physical force (*e.g.*, a physical touching of the person), and delivers a formal communication of a present intention to arrest (*e.g.*, "You are under arrest!"). A *constructive* arrest occurs without an intentional use of physical force and without a formal statement indicating an intention to take the person into custody. Moreover, in constructive arrest situations, the power or authority of the arresting officer, along with his or her intention to effect the arrest, is implied by all the circumstances surrounding the encounter. In either case, to determine whether an arrest has occurred, a court will examine whether physical force has been applied—which may be accomplished by a mere touching of the suspect—or, where that is absent, whether there has been a *"submission* to the assertion of authority." *California v. Hodari D.*, 499 *U.S.* 621, 626, 111 *S.Ct.* 1547, 1551 (1991). [Court's emphasis.]

An arrest signifies the initial step toward a prospective prosecution and, as a governmental intrusion upon the "person," must be effectuated according to the dictates of the Fourth Amendment to the United States Constitution. The **Fourth Amendment** provides:

> The right of the people to be secure in their *persons*, houses, papers, and effects, against *unreasonable* searches and *seizures*,

shall not be violated, and no Warrants shall issue, but upon *probable cause*, supported by Oath or affirmation, and particularly describing the place to be searched, and the *persons* or things to be *seized*. [Emphasis added.]

Although the word "arrest" does not appear in the language of the Amendment, courts have consistently equated "arrest" with "seizure." In this respect, the United States Supreme Court has declared:

> [I]t is the command of the Fourth Amendment that no warrants either for searches or arrests shall issue except "upon probable cause[.]"

Henry v. United States, 361 *U.S.* 98, 100, 80 *S.Ct.* 168, 170 (1959). [Emphasis added.] Accordingly, "the Fourth Amendment speaks equally to both searches and seizures, and * * * an arrest, the taking hold of one's person, is quintessentially a seizure." *United States v. Watson*, 423 *U.S.* 411, 428, 96 *S.Ct.* 820, 830 (1976).

To determine whether an arrest has taken place, a court will apply an objective standard, focusing on the reasonable impression conveyed to the person subjected to the apprehension and detention. In this respect, the relative inquiry is whether, in view of all the circumstances surrounding the police-citizen encounter, "a reasonable person would have believed that he was not free to leave" at the conclusion of the officer's inquiry. *United States v. Mendenhall*, 446 *U.S.* 544, 554, 100 *S.Ct.* 1870, 1877 (1980). Thus, a law enforcement officer's subjective view that a suspect was not free to leave—so long as that view has not been conveyed to the person confronted—will not transform an objectively casual, voluntary encounter, or even a temporary investigative detention, into a full blown arrest. Significantly, the United States Supreme Court, almost without exception, has evaluated alleged violations of the law of arrest (as well as the law of search and seizure) by undertaking "an objective assessment of an officer's actions in light of the facts and circumstances then known to him." *Scott v. United States*, 436 *U.S.* 128, 137, 98 *S.Ct.* 1717, 1723 (1978). So long as the facts and circumstances, viewed objectively, justify an officer's course of action, such action will not be invalidated merely because the officer does not have the state of mind which technically parallels the constitutional rules which provide the legal justification for that course of action. *Scott* at 138, 98 *S.Ct.* at 1723. *See also Devenpeck v. Alford*, ___ *U.S.* ___, 125 *S.Ct.* 588, 593 (2005); *United States v. Robinson*, 414 *U.S.* 218, 236, 94 *S.Ct.* 467, 477 (1973).

The objective standard uniformly applied by the courts utilizes a "reasonable person" test to determine whether a particular police-citizen encounter requires a certain level of constitutional justification. The determination proceeds by reference to the "totality of the circumstances," *i.e.*, the whole picture. *Michigan v. Chesternut*, 486 *U.S.* 567, 108 *S.Ct.* 1975, 1979 (1989); *INS v. Delgado*, 466 *U.S.* 210, 215, 104 *S.Ct.* 1758, 1762 (1984); *United States v. Bugarin-Cases*, 484 *F.2d* 853, 854 n.1 (9th Cir. 1973), *cert. denied*, 414 *U.S.* 1136, 94 *S.Ct.* 881 (1974). Although the Court in *Chesternut* recognized that the reasonable person test may be "imprecise," for "what constitutes a restraint on liberty prompting a person to conclude that he is not free to 'leave' will vary, not only with the particular police conduct at issue, but also with the setting in which the conduct occurs[,]" it nonetheless concluded:

> The test's objective standard—looking to the reasonable man's interpretation of the conduct in question—allows police to determine in advance whether the conduct contemplated will implicate the Fourth Amendment. * * * This "reasonable person" standard also ensures that the scope of the Fourth Amendment protection does not vary with the state of mind of the particular individual being approached.

Id., 108 *S.Ct.* at 1979, 1980.

There are many police-citizen encounters which do not require any level of constitutional justification. "[L]aw enforcement officers do not violate the Fourth Amendment by merely approaching an individual on the street or in another public place, by asking him if he is willing to answer some questions, by putting questions to him if the person is willing to listen, or by offering in evidence in a criminal prosecution his voluntary answers to such questions." *Florida v. Royer*, 460 *U.S.* 491, 497, 103 *S.Ct.* 1319, 1324 (1983). These encounters, termed "mere inquiries," require no constitutional justification whatsoever. "Nor would the fact that the officer identifies himself as a police officer, without more, convert the encounter into a seizure requiring some level of objective justification." *Id.* at 497, 103 *S.Ct.* at 1324. Naturally, the person approached "need not answer any question put to him; indeed, he may decline to listen to the questions at all and may go on his way. * * * He may not be detained even momentarily without reasonable, objective grounds for doing so; and his refusal to listen or answer does not, without more, furnish those grounds. [Accordingly, i]f there is no detention—no seizure within the meaning of the Fourth Amendment— then no constitutional rights have been infringed." *Id.* at 498, 103 *S.Ct.* at 1324. *See also United States v. Smith*, 901 *F.*2d 1116, 1118 (D.C.Cir. 1990) (mere "encounter between a police officer and a citizen, involving no more than approach, questioning, and official identification, does not constitute a seizure and does not require probable cause, articulable suspicion, or any other 'kind of objective justification.' ") (quoting *United States v. Maragh*, 894 *F.*2d 415, 418 (D.C.Cir. 1990)).

Thus, to determine whether a police-citizen encounter has elevated into a Fourth Amendment arrest, courts will consider such factors as (1) whether the encounter was consensual; (2) the basis for the encounter (whether the officers had reasonable grounds to believe a criminal offense had occurred and the grounds for that belief); (3) the duration of the encounter; (4) the investigative methods used to confirm or dispel suspicions; (5) an officer's statement that the individual is the subject of an investigation; (6) an officer's statement that the individual is or is not free to leave; (7) whether the officer(s) blocked the individual's path or impeded his progress; (8) whether weapons were displayed, enforcement canines employed, or the use of force in any other way threatened; (9) the number of law enforcement officers present and their demeanor;

(10) the location of the encounter (public or private); (11) the extent to which the officer(s) restrained the individual; (12) whether the individual was transported to another location against his will (how far and why); and (13) whether the individual was free to choose between terminating or continuing the encounter with the officer(s). *See United States v. Mendenhall, supra,* 446 *U.S.* at 554-555, 100 *S.Ct.* at 1877-78; *Florida v. Royer, supra,* 460 *U.S.* at 499-503, 103 *S.Ct.* at 1324-1327; *United States v. Novak,* 870 *F.*2d 1345, 1351-52 (7th Cir. 1989); *United States v. Hammock,* 860 *F.*2d 390, 393 (11th Cir. 1988); *United States v. Johnson,* 626 *F.*2d 753 (1980); *Commonwealth v. Douglas,* 372 *Pa.Super.* 227, 539 *A.*2d 412 (1988).

Once it is determined that a police-citizen encounter has constitutional implications, that is, it has advanced beyond the point of a "mere inquiry," courts will examine, by reference to the totality of the circumstances, whether the official action was constitutionally justified. Significantly, the circumstances will be viewed from the vantage point of a prudent and reasonable law enforcement officer on the scene at the time of the encounter, who possesses a reasonable degree of training, experience and skill.

While the law, both on the state and federal levels, certainly prefers that an arrest be effected pursuant to a warrant, it is well settled that a law enforcement officer may effect a warrantless arrest when he or she has probable cause to believe that a crime has been or is being committed and that the person to be arrested has committed or is committing it. Moreover, when an officer must decide whether a warrantless arrest in a given set of circumstances is justified, he or she is not limited to consideration only of evidence admissible in a courtroom. Rather, the officer may consider all the facts and circumstances surrounding the prospective arrest, even that information coming from (preferably reliable) hearsay sources, when making the probable cause determination. Thus, "[t]he validity of the arrest does not depend on whether the suspect actually committed a crime[, and] the mere fact that the suspect is later acquitted of the offense for which he is arrested is irrelevant to the validity of the arrest." *Michigan v. De-Fillippo,* 443 *U.S.* 31, 36, 99 *S.Ct.* 2627, 2631 (1979).

The constitutional justification for an arrest, whether on the federal or state level, and whether effected with or without a warrant, is "probable cause." *See e.g., Michigan v. Summers,* 452 *U.S.* 692, 700, 101 *S.Ct.* 2587, 2593 (1981) (It is a "general rule that every arrest, and every seizure having the essential attributes of a formal arrest, is unreasonable unless it is supported by probable cause.").

An arrest based on probable cause serves several important interests that serve to justify the seizure. An arrest:

(1)   ensures that the suspect appears in court to answer charges;

(2)   prevents the suspect from continuing his offense;

(3)   safeguards evidence; and

(4)   enables officers to conduct a more thorough in-custody investigation.

See Virginia v. Moore, 553 *U.S.* ___, 128 *S.Ct.* 1598, 1605 (2008).

Probable cause is an elusive term which seems to carry varied meanings depending upon who is making the analysis. Virtually all courts and commentators tend to agree that it is generally more than "reasonable suspicion" but less than actual proof. In this respect, the United States Supreme Court has made it "clear that the kinds and degree of proof and the procedural requirements necessary for a conviction are not prerequisites to a valid arrest." *DeFillippo* at 36, 99 *S.Ct.* at 2631. The question, of course, then becomes *how much* more than suspicion and *how much* less than proof ?

Analysis of legal proof standards leads to the first-blush interposition of a preponderant standard between the two degrees. It would, however, be unduly restrictive to hold law enforcement to such a rigid "more-likely-than-not" standard. This would require officers to hold a greater degree of belief than what probable cause necessarily requires. Requiring the officer to have "preponderant cause" to arrest unnecessarily burdens law enforcement with an undue, rigid proof threshold to reach before official action may follow. In the end, society may be endangered, for certain criminal activity would realistically be permitted to advance or increase before law enforcement is permitted to act.

Therefore, probable cause must find its place somewhere above reasonable suspicion but below a preponderant level of proof. *See e.g., Gerstein v. Pugh,* 420 *U.S.* 103, 121, 95 *S.Ct.* 854, 867 (1975) (probable cause "does not require the fine resolution of conflicting evidence that a reasonable-doubt or even a preponderance standard demands"). It is established by building upon reasonable suspicion those additional facts necessary to indicate an objectively reasonable probability that an offense has been committed and the person in question is, in fact, a criminal participant. The officer builds his probable cause by a *step-by-step ascent* from his reasonable suspicion. [*See* Figure 1.1.] Depending upon the nature of the activity and the particular investigation, this ascent may take days, weeks, or months; then again, it might literally occur in seconds.

Naturally, before reaching the threshold, or *landing,* of "reasonable suspicion," there must be some sort of *stimulus* which evokes the attention of the officer. In this respect, an assortment of stimuli may be acquired through the officer's contact with persons, places, vehicles, or property, including any information received in such regard. The stimuli then mix with the officer's experience, training and education, and law enforcement intuition to build a reasonable basis for the activity which will follow. The officer now begins his ascent toward the "reasonable suspicion" threshold, or *landing*.

As the officer follows up or investigates each aspect of the "seasoned" stimuli, he either begins to corroborate and strengthen it, or he dispels it from his agenda. If the investigation proves fruitful, the officer now begins to enter the realm of "reasonable suspicion." He then must be able to collect all the steps of the ascent and articulate them in specific and objectively reasonable language. Once this is accomplished, the officer is safely on the *landing* of "reasonable suspicion."

The officer builds his "probable cause" by a *step-by-step ascent* from his reasonable suspicion. Its threshold is reached when the "specific and articulable facts," aided by the rational inferences drawn therefrom, not only support a reasonable basis for suspicion, *Terry v. Ohio*, 392 *U.S.* 1, 88 *S.Ct.* 1868 (1968), but magnify that suspicion to such an extent that a reasonable person, objectively viewing all the facts, would be excited to the belief that an offense did, in fact, occur, and the person in question is, in fact, a criminal participant.

Significantly, the degree or quantum of belief required before a court may conclude that probable cause exists is virtually the same for purposes of an arrest or a search. A court should not apply two standards when assessing the sufficiency of probable cause, that is, there should not be a dual determination of probable cause—one related to the probability level necessary for a search and seizure, and one related to a different probability level necessary for an arrest. Rather, the focus of the court's attention should always be on the quantum or sufficiency of those objective facts and circumstances surrounding the particular police procedure at the relevant time in order to determine whether the police possessed the requisite *degree* of belief prior to engaging in the challenged procedure. *See e.g., California v. Acevedo*, 500 *U.S.* 565, 111 *S.Ct.* 1982, 1989 (1991) ("the same probable cause to believe that a container holds drugs will allow the police to arrest the person transporting the container [in the passenger compartment of an automobile] and search it"); *Ybarra v. Illinois*, 444 *U.S.* 85, 105, 100 *S.Ct.* 338, 350 (1979) (Rehnquist, J., dissenting) ("Given probable cause to believe that a person possesses illegal drugs, the police need no warrant to conduct a full body search. They need only arrest that person and conduct the search incident to that arrest.").

Naturally, the application of the same degree or quantum of belief—the probable cause standard—will take on a different analysis when the probabilities must be assessed against the facts and circumstances justifying an arrest as opposed to the facts and circumstances justifying a search and seizure. In this respect, *probable cause to arrest* may be found to exist when the facts and circumstances within the officer's knowledge are sufficient to permit a prudent person, or one of reasonable caution, to conclude that there is a fair probability that a criminal offense is being or has been committed, and the suspect is or has been a criminal participant. *Probable cause to search* may be found to exist when the facts and circumstances within the officer's knowledge are sufficient to permit a prudent person, or one of reasonable caution, to conclude that there is a fair probability that particularly described property which is subject to official seizure may be presently found in a particular place.

Finally, it is important for the officer to realize that his or her probable cause determinations, many times made in the haste and hustle of dangerous investigations, will not be judged by after-the-fact, desk-side analyses made by legal scholars using strict standards and exacting calculations. Rather, probable cause will be assessed by everyday commonsensical probabilities upon which ordinary, reasonable people act.

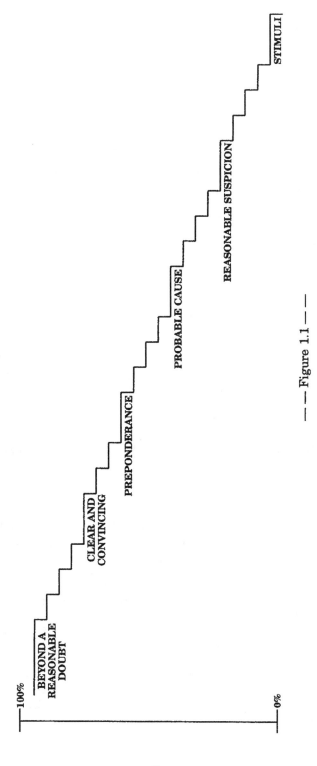

— — Figure 1.1 — —

UNITED STATES v. PARR
United States Court of Appeals
843 *F.*2d 1228 (9th Cir. 1988)

QUESTION: At what point in the below set of circumstances did the police-citizen encounter elevate into a Fourth Amendment arrest ?

CIRCUMSTANCES:

   POINTS:

   1. In the early morning hours of May 15, defendant was stopped by a Portland, Oregon police officer because the officer believed that defendant was driving with a suspended driver's license.

   2. As the officer was stopping defendant, he noticed defendant and a companion bend towards the floorboard and "make furtive movements."

   3. Defendant drove partially up on the sidewalk before stopping.

   4. After stopping the car, defendant was asked to step out of the car and was checked for, and found free of, weapons.

   5. Defendant was then placed in the patrol car.

   6. The officer returned to defendant's car and engaged in the same procedure with defendant's companion.

ANSWER: AT NO POINT. "[T]here is no *per se* rule that detention in a patrol car constitutes an arrest." *Id.* at 1230. Rather, " 'sitting in the patrol car for several minutes [i]s merely a normal part of traffic police procedure for identifying delinquent drivers' and d[oes] not constitute [a] custodial arrest." *Id.* (quoting *United States v. Rodriguez,* 831 *F.*2d 162, 166 (7th Cir. 1987)).

RATIONALE: The critical question in this case is whether defendant was subjected to treatment that rendered him "in custody." In addressing this question, however, there is "clearly no mechanical checklist to distinguish between [a temporary investigatory stop] and [a] formal arrest or the equivalent of [an] arrest." *Parr* at 1231. As the Court of Appeals for the 6th Circuit observed: There is "no bright-line for determining when an investigatory stop crosses the line and becomes an arrest." *United States v. Hatfield,* 815 *F.*2d 1068, 1070 (6th Cir. 1987).
   There is, however "no *per se* rule that detention in a patrol car constitutes an arrest. * * * '[S]itting in the patrol car for several minutes [is] merely a normal part of traffic procedure for identifying delinquent drivers' and d[oes] not constitute [a] custodial arrest." *Parr* at 1230 (quoting *Rodriguez, supra*). *See also United States v. Thompson,* 597 *F.*2d 187, 190 (9th Cir. 1979) (defendant's failure to produce valid driver's license justified the request that he get out of his car and sit in

the police car while a standard police identification process took place—held defendant not under arrest).

NOTE

1. The line between an investigatory stop and arrest has been drawn at the point of transporting the suspect to the police station. *Hayes v. Florida*, 470 *U.S.* 811, 816, 105 *S.Ct.* 1643, 1646 (1985). *See also Dunaway v. New York*, 442 *U.S.* 200, 216, 99 *S.Ct.* 2248, 2258 (1979) (arrest occurs when suspect is seized and transported to police headquarters for interrogation); *United States v. Hernandez*, 825 *F.*2d 846, 851 (5th Cir. 1987) (removal of suspect from scene of stop to police station usually marks the point at which an investigative stop becomes a *de facto* arrest).

2. In *United States v. Hill*, 91 *F.*3d 1064 (8th Cir. 1996), the court discussed the difference between an investigative stop and a constructive or "*de facto*" arrest. According to this court, a "*de facto* arrest" takes place when a law enforcement officer's conduct "is more intrusive than necessary for an investigative stop." *Id.* at 1070. To determine if a "*de facto*" arrest has occurred, a court will consider such factors as "the duration of a stop, whether the suspect was handcuffed or confined in a police car, whether the suspect was transported or isolated, and 'the degree of fear and humiliation that the police conduct engenders.'" *Id.* (quoting *United States v. Bloomfield*, 40 *F.*3d 910, 916-17 (8th Cir. 1994)).

UNITED STATES v. JOHNSON
United States Court of Appeals
626 *F.*2d 753 (9th Cir. 1980)

QUESTION: At which point in the below set of circumstances may defendant Johnson legally be considered under arrest ?

CIRCUMSTANCES:

POINTS:

1. On March 30, Lena Kearney received by mistake a letter addressed to E. Peterson, containing a United States Treasury check payable to Peterson in the amount of $4,681.00. Kearney decided to keep the check and called upon her sister-in-law, Wynona Powell, for help in cashing it.

2. The next day, Kearney, Powell, and three others met to discuss how to go about cashing the check. Among the group was defendant, Johnson, and an associate, Dodd. Johnson and Dodd took custody of the check and proceeded to make arrangements to have it cashed.

9

3. Special Agent Hemenway of the United States Secret Service began investigating the lost Treasury check. He questioned Kearney and was told that Johnson and Dodd were going to attempt to cash the check. Kearney identified Johnson for the agent from a photo array and then gave the agent Johnson's telephone number.

4. Agent Hemenway obtained an arrest warrant for Dodd, and then proceeded with Agent Pickering to Johnson's house on May 5, at approximately 6:00 p.m.

5. The agents took up a surveillance of Johnson's house, and within a short period of time observed Johnson drive up to the residence accompanied by the two other individuals.

6. The agents then approached the doorway of the residence, drew their weapons, pointed them downward and knocked, at first identifying themselves by fictitious names.

7. When Johnson opened the door, Hemenway introduced himself and Pickering as special agents and asked to talk with Johnson.

8. Johnson told the agents to come in.

9. Pickering then stood in the living room with Johnson, while Hemenway looked into the other rooms for other people who might be in the house and present a possible danger to the agents.

10. When everything seemed to be secure, Hemenway relayed that fact to Pickering and both agents returned their weapons to their holsters.

11. Hemenway then asked Johnson if he would step into the bedroom to talk with him, and Johnson agreed.

12. Before entering the bedroom, Hemenway informed Johnson of his constitutional rights.

13. Johnson responded that he wished to cooperate and then told Hemenway of his involvement in taking the Treasury check.

14. Officer Hemenway told Johnson that he was under arrest.

ANSWER: AT POINT 7. "From a review of all of the circumstances surrounding the encounter between Johnson and the special agents, [the court finds] that [Johnson's] arrest occurred as he stood within his home at the doorway of his home and was first confronted by the agents with their guns drawn. * * * It is extremely doubtful that Johnson would have believed that he was free to leave at any time or to request the officers to leave after the initial encounter. A reasonable person, under those circumstances, would have thought that he was under arrest." *Id.* at 755-756.

RATIONALE: "The two special agents testified that they had not intended to effect an arrest at the time they initially entered the residence of * * * Johnson. It was their belief that an arrest had not occurred until after the interview with Johnson. However, whether an arrest has occurred depends upon an objective, not subjective, evaluation of what a person innocent of a crime would have thought of the situation, given all of the factors involved." *Id.* at 755. According to the court, "[w]*hen* an arrest has occurred depends in each case upon an evaluation of all the surrounding circumstances. Primary among these is a determination of whether or not the defendant was free to choose between terminating or continuing the encounter with the law enforcement officers." *Id.* [Emphasis added.]

"From a review of all of the circumstances surrounding the encounter between Johnson and the special agents, [the court finds] that [Johnson's] arrest occurred as he stood within his home at the doorway of his home and was first confronted by the agents with their guns drawn. The agents then entered the home with their guns still drawn until the search of the home had been concluded. Johnson was held in the living room while the house was searched. One of the agents remained with Johnson at all times. It is extremely doubtful that Johnson would have believed that he was free to leave at any time or to request the officers to leave after the initial encounter. A reasonable person, under those circumstances, would have thought that he was under arrest." *Id.* at 755-756.

---

§1.2. Probable cause requirement.

UNITED STATES v. SANGINETO-MIRANDA
United States Court of Appeals
859 *F.*2d 1501 (6th Cir. 1988)

QUESTION: What will a court examine when determining whether probable cause exists for the arrest of a particular individual?

ANSWER: In determining whether probable cause exists, a court "must look at the 'totality of the circumstances,' * * * and view the facts 'as a whole and in a practical manner.' " *Id.* at 1508. [Citations omitted.]

RATIONALE: An arrest will be justified if, at the time of the arrest, "police officers have probable cause to believe that an offense has been, is being, or will be committed. * * * Probable cause exists where the 'facts and circumstances within the officer's knowledge * * * are sufficient to warrant a prudent person, or one of reasonable caution, in believing, in the circumstances shown, that the suspect has committed, is committing, or is about to commit an offense.' " *Id.* at 1508 (quoting *Michigan v. DeFillippo*, 443 *U.S.* 31, 37, 99 *S.Ct.* 2627, 2632 (1979)). Significantly, "[t]he probable cause requirement does 'not demand any showing that such a belief is correct or more likely true than false.' " *Id.* (quoting *Texas v. Brown*, 460 *U.S.* 730, 742, 103 *S.Ct.* 1535, 1543 (1983)).

Probable cause is 'a fluid concept—turning on the assessment of probabilities in particular factual contexts—not readily, or even usefully, reduced to a neat set of rules.' * * * [It] 'does not deal with hard certainties, but with probabilities. Long before the law of probabilities was articulated as such, practical people formulated certain common-sense conclusions about human behavior; jurors as factfinders are permitted to do the same—and so are law enforcement officers.' " *Id.* [Citations omitted.]

UNITED STATES v. DAVIS
United States Court of Appeals
458 *F.*2d 819 (D.C. Cir. 1972)

QUESTION: Was probable cause established to support the arrest of defendant in the below set of circumstances ?

CIRCUMSTANCES:

During the daylight hours, at approximately 6:40 p.m., Officers Gaston and Wingfield, wearing old armed forces jackets over their uniforms, traveling in an unmarked car, observed defendant among a group of five or six "shabbily dressed" men standing on the corner of a "high crime area." According to the officers, the individuals with defendant were "in a kind of daze," "in a sleepy mood," "twitchy and a little nervous." Officer Gaston testified that some of them exhibited traits symptomatic of drug addiction such as the "common nod." Based on Officer Gaston's training and experience, he concluded that the members of the group were under the influence of narcotics, demonstrating "the stereotype of what we call 'junkie.' "

Defendant then left the group, walked over to a well-dressed man, "furtively" looked about in a nervous and suspicious manner, and then "slid" an undetermined amount of paper currency to this man, receiving in exchange a small brown package.

Officer Gaston approached defendant, identified himself as a police officer, and requested that defendant accompany him to the unmarked car. Defendant took several steps in the opposite direction and appeared "as if he was just about to run." However, Officer Wingfield thereafter blocked defendant's path and effected his arrest. Defendant was found to be in possession of 73 heroin capsules.

ANSWER: YES. "Viewing the total circumstances, judged in light of the officers' experience, * * * there was a reasonable basis for their belief that a crime was being committed." *Id.* at 822. Therefore, "the arrest was founded upon probable cause." *Id.*

RATIONALE: "Probable cause exists when known facts and circumstances are sufficient to warrant a man of reasonable prudence in the belief that an offense has been or is being committed." *Id.* at 821 (citing *Beck v. Ohio*, 379 *U.S.* 89, 85 *S.Ct.* 223 (1964)). "Probable cause does not emanate from an antiseptic courtroom, [or a] sterile library[,] nor is it a * * * 'philosophical concept existing in a vacuum[.]' " *Id.* [Citation omitted.] Rather, "it requires a pragmatic analysis of 'everyday life on which reasonable and prudent men, not legal technicians, act.' " *Id.* (quoting *Brinegar v. United States*, 338 *U.S.* 160, 175, 69 *S.Ct.* 1302, 1310 (1949)). Moreover, probable cause is "to be viewed from the vantage point of a prudent, reasonable, cautious police officer on the scene at the time of the arrest guided by his experience and training." *Id.* The concept of probable cause depends upon the totality of the factors, that is, the facts and circumstances, of the particular case. "Viewed singly these factors may not be dispositive, yet when viewed in unison the puzzle may fit." *Davis* at 821.

In this case, the court concluded "that, although the factors viewed individually may not be dispositive of the probable cause issue, their sum total dictates [a probable cause finding]. The testifying officers, experienced and learned in their professions, related a number of highly suspicious circumstances surrounding the arrest to the court." *Id.* at 821-822. A police officer's training and experience reinforces the finding of probable cause and is a legitimate factor for consideration. Significantly, " 'conduct innocent in the eyes of the untrained may carry entirely different "messages" to the experienced or trained observer.' " *Id.* at 822. [Citation omitted.]

The officers testified that they observed defendant in the company of several "shabbily dressed" individuals who appeared to be under the influence of narcotics. According to the court, this fact alone does not end the inquiry, for a court would never authorize "arrest by association." *Id.*

The officers also testified that defendant nervously approached an equally nervous, well-dressed man, and stealthily "slid" money to him in exchange for a small package. "Surreptitious passing of a package has been recognized as a possible element in establishing the probable cause mix." *Id.* Additionally, there is some indication in the record that defendant was attempting to flee the scene of the crime. "Although flight has been a legitimate factor in a finding of probable cause, * * * it has not been considered a 'reliable indicator of guilt without other circumstances to make its import less ambiguous.' " [Citation omitted.]

"A final factor in [this probable cause assessment] is the geographical area of the crime. Although no presumption of guilt arises from the activities of inhabitants of an area in which the police know that narcotics offenses frequently occur, the syndrome of criminality in those areas cannot realistically go unnoticed[.] It too is a valid consideration when coupled with other reliable indicia or suspicious circumstances." *Id.*

Accordingly, in view of "the total circumstances, judged in light of the officers' experience, * * * there was a reasonable basis for their belief that a crime was being committed. * * * [Therefore,] the arrest was founded upon probable cause, thereby rendering the evidence admissible." *Id.*

NOTE

In *United States v. Harple*, 202 *F.*3d 194 (3rd Cir. 2000), Philadelphia Police Officers McCullough and Postowski, while working a plainclothes "burglary detail," were advised by their supervisor, Sergeant Neiman, to "be on the lookout for a blue over white vehicle with a third brake light." The vehicle reportedly was occupied by a group of five or more young white males, who were last seen leaving the area of a suspicious fire that occurred the night before in the vicinity of 2500 Butler Street.

At about 12:15 a.m., the officers received a radio transmission reporting another fire at 2500 Butler Street. The officers immediately responded and arrived at the fire scene within a minute of receiving the call. The officers surveyed the area and, within minutes, spotted a white Oldsmobile with a blue pinstripe and a third brake light, occupied by a group of white males. The vehicle was "less than three blocks away from the fire in an area that was not heavily traveled at that time of night." *Id.* at 195. The driver of the vehicle, according to Officer McCullough, was "excessively obeying traffic signal[s]." *Id.* In this respect, the officer explained that at one stop sign, the Oldsmobile "came to a complete stop, stayed there for approximately 15 to 30 seconds and then moved." *Id.* at 195 n.1.

Officers McCullough and Postowski enlisted the services of the police wagon and had the Oldsmobile stopped. There were five persons in the vehicle at the time. When the driver could not produce his license or the vehicle's registration, the officer directed him and the others out of the car.

"Officer McCullough then used his portable radio to inform other police officers that he had stopped the vehicle. At that point, he heard his radio transmission projected back at him from inside the Oldsmobile. When he stopped transmitting his message, he heard the fire department's radio frequency coming from inside the automobile. * * * Upon looking inside the automobile, Officer McCullough discovered a hand-held scanner that was tuned to the police and the fire departments' radio frequencies. Following the discovery of the hand-held scanner, the officers then proceeded to frisk the occupants and discovered lighters, matches, and rolled-up paper towels. The officers then searched the inside of the Oldsmobile and found a flashlight and a set of walkie-talkies." *Id.* at 196. [Citations omitted.]

In the appeal following the denial of his motion to suppress, Harple contended first that the police did not develop the required reasonable articulable suspicion for a motor vehicle stop, and second, that the circumstances did not support a finding of probable cause for an arrest and search. The Court of Appeals disagreed and affirmed.

14

Preliminarily, the court found that the officers clearly had a reasonable suspicion to perform an investigatory stop, given the temporal and geographic proximity of the Oldsmobile to the Butler Street fire, the fact that the Oldsmobile was driving in an otherwise desolate area, the fact that the Oldsmobile substantially matched the description which the officers had received from Sgt. [Neiman] (including the automobile having the brake light in the rear window area), the fact that the Oldsmobile started moving in an unusually careful manner, and the fact that, consistent with the briefing the officers had received that night, the Oldsmobile carried several white males who appeared young.

Id. at 196-97.

Regarding the issue of probable cause, the court said:

[T]he officers here did not rely solely upon Sergeant Neiman's description of the alleged arsonists as a young group of white males driving a blue on white automobile. Rather, there was other evidence linking Harple to the arson at 2500 Butler Street. * * * [T]he record here shows that the officers had knowledge of where the arson happened and that the officers stopped the car carrying Harple shortly after the arson occurred. Moreover, the officers spotted the white Oldsmobile moving in an abnormally cautious manner less than three blocks away from the fire. From that location, the occupants of the Oldsmobile could see the fire trucks that had arrived at the scene of the fire. After the stop, the officers discovered handheld scanners tuned to police and fire department frequencies, behavior that tended to show that the occupants of the Oldsmobile were monitoring police and fire department activity.

Id. at 197-98.

Accordingly, the court held that the officers had "probable cause to arrest the occupants of the Oldsmobile, including Harple, and to search the automobile." *Id.* at 198.

UNITED STATES v. ASHCROFT
United States Court of Appeals
607 *F.*2d 1167 (5th Cir. 1979)

QUESTION: Are the facts set forth below sufficient to establish probable cause to arrest defendant Ashcroft ?

FACTS: During the course of a narcotics investigation, DEA Agent DeGaglia met with William Panzica in late August and began negotiations for the purchase of five kilograms of cocaine. In the interim, DeGaglia made one purchase, acquiring four ounces of cocaine and paying $6,000.00 to Panzica. Negotiations for the five kilograms continued through August and into September. On September 15, Panzica telephoned Agent DeGaglia and offered him one pound of cocaine for $24,200.00. They arranged to meet at Panzica's apartment. Present at Panzica's apartment was defendant, Ashcroft. "Despite Ashcroft's presence in the room, he did not take part in the negotiations which eventually led to the purchase of one pound of cocaine for $23,900.00. Ashcroft sat on a sofa watching television about two feet away from Agent DeGaglia and the negotiating table where the cocaine was tested and examined. While Ashcroft did not talk, he could easily hear the entire conversation between Panzica and the DEA agent[]." *Id.* at 1169. On September 28, Agent DeGaglia received another call from Panzica indicating that he had another pound of cocaine for sale and that more was available. Another meeting was set up at Panzica's apartment. Ashcroft and Panzica's girlfriend were present at the apartment but departed the living room and remained in an adjoining bedroom with the door closed while the negotiations took place in the other room. "After examining the cocaine, Agent DeGaglia agreed to purchase the one pound of cocaine. Panzica and [another] DEA agent then went downstairs to purportedly get the money but instead Panzica was arrested." *Id.* A fan-out search resulted in the discovery of Ashcroft and Panzica's girlfriend in the bedroom.

ANSWER: YES. "Agent DeGaglia had probable cause to believe Ashcroft was involved in the conspiracy to distribute cocaine." *Id.* at 1171. "[P]robable cause ' is the sum total of layers of information and the synthesis of what the police have heard, what they know, and what they observe as trained officers. We weigh not individual layers but the "laminated" total.' " *Id.* [Citations omitted.]

RATIONALE: "The crucial issue is whether probable cause for the arrest [of Ashcroft] existed in light of the facts of this case. Probable cause for an arrest exists where the facts and circumstances within the knowledge of the arresting officer and of which he has reasonably trustworthy information are sufficient in themselves to warrant a man of reasonable caution in the belief that an offense has been or is being committed." *Id.* at 1170 (citing *Brinegar v. United States*, 338 *U.S.* 160, 69 *S.Ct.* 1302 (1949)). Moreover, "[a] showing of probable cause requires much less evidence than a finding sufficient to convict requires. * * * As the Supreme Court stated in *Brinegar*, when 'dealing with probable cause, however, as the very name implies, we deal with probabilities. These are not technical; they are the factual and practical considerations of everyday life on which reasonable and prudent men, not legal technicians, act.' " *Ashcroft* at 1171 (quoting *Brinegar* at 175, 69 *S.Ct.* at 1310).

"The facts and circumstances of this case justify the arrest of Ashcroft based on probable cause. Agent DeGaglia had seen Ashcroft at the prior drug sale on September 15[.] At that time Ashcroft was sitting only two feet away from the negotiations and heard all that transpired. * * * Both sales took place at the same apartment and Agent DeGaglia knew Ashcroft did not live there." *Id.* According to this court, probable cause existed on September 15. The probable cause "was merely intensified when Ashcroft was seen for a second time in an apartment that he did not live in where drug deals were consummated." *Id.* Consequently, "Agent DeGaglia had probable cause to believe Ashcroft was involved in the conspiracy to distribute cocaine." *Id.* As the District of Columbia Circuit has explained:

> Probable cause "is the sum total of layers of information and the synthesis of what the police have heard, what they know, and what they observe as trained officers. We weigh not individual layers but the 'laminated' total."

Id. (quoting *Smith v. United States*, 358 *F.*2d 833, 837 (D.C. Cir. 1966)).

The court also considered several other factors which tend to show the existence of probable cause.

> First, a drug sale involving large quantities of cocaine is a private transaction that does not usually occur in the open or in the presence of strangers. * * * This is the type of transaction shrouded in secrecy and closed to most people because of the nature of the activity. A reasonable person would think that someone present at two cocaine sales in the same apartment was somehow involved in the distribution of cocaine or a conspiracy to distribute cocaine, especially when he does not live in that apartment. Second, * * * the officers were aware of the practice followed by some drug dealers of hiding in another room until the deal is consummated in case there is an arrest so they can claim to be innocent bystanders. * * * It is also significant to note that there is apparently no other explanation given why Ashcroft and Panzica's girlfriend were waiting in the bedroom fully clothed and with the door closed[.]

Ashcroft at 1171. In light of these circumstances, the court concludes that "[a] reasonable person would think, after seeing Ashcroft for the second time at a cocaine sale that he was involved." *Id.*

Accordingly, "probable cause existed to arrest Ashcroft." *Id.*

NOTE

Probable cause based on an informant's tip. Draper v. United States, 358 *U.S.* 307, 79 *S.Ct.* 329 (1959), is a good example of a case in which the corroboration of an informant's tip provided probable cause for an arrest. In *Draper*, an F.B.I. informant named Hereford reported that Draper had taken up residence at a stated address in Denver and had been selling narcotics in that city. Several days later, Hereford reported that Draper had gone to Chicago the day before by train and that he was going to bring back three ounces of heroin. Hereford stated that Draper would be returning to Denver by train on the morning of one of two specified days. The informant gave a detailed physical description of Draper (describing him as a black male, light complexion, 27 years of age, 5 feet 8 inches tall, and weighing about 160 pounds), and predicted that he would be wearing a light colored raincoat, brown slacks and black shoes, that he would be carrying a tan zipper bag, and that he habitually "walked fast." *Id.* at 309, 79 *S.Ct.* at 331. From time to time, during the previous six months, Hereford had given information to the F.B.I. regarding violations of the narcotics laws, for which he was paid small sums of money. When a man believed to be Draper appeared at the Denver Union Station as predicted, alighting from an incoming Chicago train, having the exact physical attributes and wearing the precise clothing described by Hereford, and "walking fast" toward the exit carrying a tan zipper bag, an F.B.I. agent, accompanied by a police officer, immediately approached Draper, stopped and arrested him. The search incident to the arrest uncovered two envelopes containing heroin and a syringe.

Although Hereford did not state how he obtained his information, the United States Supreme Court nonetheless held that the tip was sufficiently detailed to establish probable cause when each aspect of it was verified by the police. As stated by the Court, the arresting officer "had personally verified every facet of the information given him by Hereford except whether [Draper] had accomplished his mission and had the three ounces of heroin on his person or in his bag. And surely, with every other bit of Hereford's information being thus personally verified, [the officer] had 'reasonable grounds' to believe that the remaining unverified bit of Hereford's information—that Draper would have the heroin with him—was likewise true." *Id.* at 313, 79 *S.Ct.* at 333.

UNITED STATES v. GREEN
United States Court of Appeals
670 *F*.2d 1148 (D.C. Cir. 1981)

QUESTION: At a motion to suppress hearing the below listed evidence was established. At what point was probable cause established for the arrest of defendant Green ?

POINTS:

1. Officer Allman, an experienced member of the Third District Drug Enforcement Unit of the District of Columbia, was stationed in an undisclosed observation point investigating narcotics activity at the intersection of 14th and V Streets, N.W.

2. This neighborhood is known as a high drug trafficking area.

3. At about 11:25 a.m., Officer Allman observed, with the aid of binoculars, three individuals: a man later identified as defendant, Gary Green; a woman later identified as Carol Turner; and an unidentified man on the southwest corner of the intersection.

4. Officer Allman saw the unidentified man approach Ms. Turner, converse briefly with her, and then hand her some paper currency.

5. Turner then walked several feet to Green and handed him the money.

6. Green took the money, stuffed it in his left trouser pocket, reached into a paper bag in his left jacket pocket, and appeared to hand a small object from the bag to Turner. Officer Allman was unable to see the exchanged object which was concealed in Green's cupped hand and then in Turner's.

7. Turner returned to the unidentified man and handed him the object. The unidentified man received the object and left the area.

8. Officer Allman then saw Green push the top of the brown paper bag back into his left jacket pocket, concealing it from view.

9. Believing that he had just observed a typical "two-party drug transaction," Officer Allman radioed descriptions of Green and Turner to officers awaiting his instructions in an unmarked patrol car two blocks away. Those officers drove to the intersection of 14th and V and Officer Willis spotted Green from Officer Allman's description.

10. Green seemed to recognize the unmarked patrol car or the officers as they approached. Green then walked quickly into

Willie's Carryout, looking back over his shoulder at Officer Willis, who had left the unmarked car to pursue Green on foot.

11.   Officer Willis saw Green open the carryout door with his left hand, move five or six feet inside the carryout, motion with his right hand, and then start to move back out the door.

12.   Officer Willis found a brown paper bag lying on the unoccupied counter inside the carryout, only three to five feet away from Green's position at the time of the confrontation with Officer Willis.

13.   The paper bag was within Green's reach and could have been placed on the counter by the movement of Green's right hand that Officer Willis had observed just before Green started out of the carryout.

14.   Officer Willis looked in the brown paper bag and discovered fourteen small packets of heroin.

15.   A search of Green resulted in the seizure of $242.00.

ANSWER: AT POINT 11. In this case, the "totality of the facts and circumstances" was sufficient to establish probable cause for Officer Willis' arrest of Green at the point where he walked quickly into the carryout store and made a motion as if to dispose of an object he was carrying. *Id.* at 1153.

RATIONALE: The United States Court of Appeals for the District of Columbia Circuit agreed with the District Court that three factors, "especially when observed by experienced police officers in an area noted for the regularity of narcotics trafficking, provided probable cause for the arrest." *Id.* at 1151. These included, "(1) the sequence of events between Green, Turner and the unidentified man, which was typical of a two-party narcotics transaction*; (2) the movement of the three persons' cupped hands and Green's subsequent stuffing of the protruding paper bag back into his coat pocket, suggesting an attempt to conceal the object of their transaction; and (3) the appearance of flight and evasion by Green when pursued by Officer Willis." *Id.*

In reaching this conclusion, the Court emphasized that no one of these factors alone would be adequate to establish probable cause. "First, a sequence of events which is typical of a common form of narcotics transaction may create a suspicion in a police officer's mind, but probable cause, of course, requires more than mere suspicion. * * *

---

* "The term 'two-party drug transaction' refers to a narcotics sale in which two individuals sell the narcotics. * * * [O]ne individual holds the drugs. A second individual—known as a 'runner'—receives the money from a customer, carries it to the individual holding the drugs, and returns the purchased drugs to the customer. This form of transaction provides the narcotics dealer some measure of protection from robbery." *Id.* at 1150-1151 n.1.

This court has never held that the observance of a suspicious transaction, without more, provides probable cause for arrest." *Id.*

"Second, the sole fact that individuals may seek to conceal the subject of their business from potentially prying eyes, even on a public sidewalk, does not grant the police the power to arrest them. While it is true that persons engaged in illegal transactions will desire to conceal those transactions, the desire for privacy in one's affairs is common among law-abiding persons as well. Thus, the police cannot conclude that merely because an object or transaction is not openly displayed, it is necessarily illegal." *Id.* at 1152.

"Third, * * * flight is not a 'reliable indicator of guilt without other circumstances to make its import less ambiguous.' * * * ' "Of course, when coupled with specific knowledge on the part of the officer relating the suspect to the evidence of crime," [flight or evasion] may properly be considered in assessing probable cause,' * * * but flight alone is insufficient to give the police probable cause to arrest." *Id.* [Citations omitted.]

Finally, "the presence of a person in a neighborhood notorious for the frequency of narcotic sales or other crimes does not create probable cause to arrest that person. [While] geographic area is a valid consideration in the probable cause calculus, * * * this fact without more does not even establish grounds for an investigatory stop, * * * let alone probable cause for an arrest." *Id.*

"Although none of these * * * factors is adequate by itself to establish probable cause, *it is their combination* in the particular circumstances confronting Officers Allman and Willis that is the proper subject of consideration." *Id.* [Emphasis added.]

> Probable cause is not determined by some single factor which this court has deemed relevant, or even by observing any certain number of them. Rather, *probable cause exists if the totality of the circumstances, as viewed by a reasonable and prudent police officer in light of his training and experience, would lead that police officer to believe that a criminal offense has been or is being committed.*

Id. at 1152 (citing *Beck v. Ohio*, 379 *U.S.* 89, 91, 85 *S.Ct.* 223, 225 (1964)). [Emphasis added.]

"In this case, the basis for that reasonable belief of criminal activity existed. When Officer Allman observed [Gary Green], Carol Turner, and the unidentified man engage in a pecuniary transaction of a type common to narcotics peddling, his suspicion was aroused. This was only natural given that Officer Allman is an experienced drug enforcement officer and that illegal drug activity is known to be common in that area. Watching the transaction closely, Officer Allman noticed that the parties to the transaction attempted to conceal the exchanged object. Then, when [Green] noticed Officer Willis approaching, he turned and walked rapidly into Willie's Carryout. Once inside, [Green] made a motion as if to dispose of an object he was carrying." *Id.* at 1152-1153.

"Given this set of events, and the order in which they occurred, Officers Allman and Willis concluded that [Green] had engaged in criminal activity. No plausible, innocent explanations for this sequence of behavior [has been suggested]." *Id*. at 1153. Accordingly, the court concludes "that when Green was arrested [by Officer Willis as he exited the carryout], there was a sufficient basis for Officers Willis and Allman reasonably to believe that [Green] had engaged in criminal activity." *Id*.

NOTE

1. *Field test not a mandatory prerequisite to development of probable cause. See United States v. Russell*, 655 F.2d 1261 (D.C.Cir. 1981), where the court rejected a defendant's contention that before an officer could effect an arrest for the possession of packets of white powder, a field test must be conducted. According to the court, probable cause merely "rests on a 'reasonable probability' that a crime has been committed, not on certainty that illegal activity is afoot." *Id*. at 1263-1264. Therefore, the court concluded that it would "unduly retard legitimate law enforcement methods if " it were to hold that prior to effecting an arrest for the possession of a controlled dangerous substance, officers were required to conduct a field test of the suspected substance. *Id*. at 1264.

2. *Nondisclosure of police surveillance location*. During the course of the suppression hearing in *Green, supra*, Officer Allman testified that he was in a "hidden observation post" near 14th and V Streets, N.W. Allman further testified that he was using a pair of 10 X 50 power binoculars to make his observations and the weather at the time was sunny and clear. Defense counsel, on cross-examination, attempted to ascertain the location of Officer Allman's hidden observation post. After Allman testified that he was 75 to 80 feet from the observed transaction and was about 40 feet above ground level, the Government objected to a question that might have identified the building in which Allman was located. The objection was sustained.

Agreeing with the District Court, the Circuit Court held that "the policy justifications analogous to those underlying the well-established informer's privilege[,]" *see McCray v. Illinois*, 386 U.S. 300, 87 S.Ct. 1056 (1967), support a *qualified privilege protecting police surveillance locations from disclosure*." *Green* at 1155. [Emphasis added.] "Like confidential informants, hidden observation posts may often prove to be useful law enforcement tools, so long as they remain secret. Just as the disclosure of an informer's identity may destroy his future usefulness in criminal investigations, the identification of a hidden observation post will likely destroy the future value of that location for police surveillance. The revelation of a surveillance location might also threaten the safety of police officers using the observation post, or lead to adversity for cooperative owners or occupants of the building. Finally, the assurance of nondisclosure of a surveillance location may be necessary to encourage property owners or occupants to allow the police to make such use of their property." *Id*. As a result, the court in *Green* was persuaded "to recognize what might be termed a 'surveillance location privilege.' " *Id*.

The court did, however, recognize that a criminal defendant has a strong interest in the effective cross-examination of an adverse witness at a suppression hearing. A defendant's competing interest in the location of the surveillance post may establish whether the observing officer's view was open or obstructed, whether the angle of the officer's view made the observations easy or difficult, and whether the distance from the criminal activity enhances or detracts from an officer's claimed observation of detail. *Id.* at 1156.

"Thus, because the location of the observation post may well be relevant to the defendant's interests, the trial court must attempt to balance the interests of the public and the police in nondisclosure and the interest of the defendant in accurate fact-finding." *Id.* The balancing of these competing interests should proceed on a case-by-case basis, the critical inquiry of which being whether the surveillance location is relevant and vital to the determination of probable cause. At all such hearings, however, the location of the surveillance post should not be disclosed to the defendant or the public. *See Hicks v. United States*, 431 *A.*2d 18 (D.C. 1981) (trial court may exercise its discretion to conduct *in camera* proceeding if the surveillance location is material and relevant to the determination of probable cause and if the evidence creates a substantial doubt about the credibility of the observer).

KARR v. SMITH
United States Court of Appeals
774 *F.*2d 1029 (10th Cir. 1985)

QUESTION: Is probable cause to be determined on the basis of the "collective" information known to the police involved in the arrest ?

ANSWER: YES. "Under the 'fellow officer' rule, 'probable cause is to be determined by the courts on the basis of the collective information of the police involved in the arrest, rather than exclusively on the extent of the knowledge of the particular officer who may actually make the arrest.'" *Id.* at 1031. [Citations omitted.]

RATIONALE: As a general rule, the validity of an arrest depends upon whether the arresting officer had probable cause. "Probable cause exists where the facts and circumstances within an officer's knowledge and of which he had reasonably trustworthy information are sufficient to warrant a prudent man in believing that an offense has been or is being committed." *Id.*

Rather than focusing exclusively on the extent of the knowledge of the particular officer who may actually have made the arrest, courts will determine the existence of probable cause "on the basis of the collective information" known to the police—all the officers involved in the arrest. This is known as the *fellow officer rule*. *Id.* (citing *United States v. Troutman*, 458 *F.*2d 217 (10th Cir. 1972)). Under this rule, " 'the collective information of * * * law enforcement officers involved in an arrest can form the basis for probable cause, even though that information is not within the knowledge of the arresting officer.' " *Karr* at 1031. [Citation omitted.]

NOTE

1. *See also Whiteley v. Warden*, 401 *U.S.* 560, 568, 91 *S.Ct.* 1031, 1037 (1971) ("Certainly, police officers called upon to aid other officers in executing arrest warrants are entitled to assume that the officers requesting aid offered the magistrate the information requisite to support an independent judicial assessment of probable cause.").

2. *The "collective knowledge" doctrine.*

(a) In *United States v. Rocha*, 916 *F.*2d 219 (5th Cir. 1990), the court emphasized that "[t]he arresting officer need not have personal knowledge of all the facts constituting probable cause but can rely upon the collective knowledge of the police when there is a communication among them." *Id.* at 238. *See also United States v. Bizier*, 111 *F.*3d 214, 217 (1st Cir. 1997) ("Probable cause is to be determined based on the 'collective knowledge and information of all the officers involved.' ") (citation omitted); *In re M.E.B.*, 638 *A.*2d 1123, 1129 (D.C.App. 1993) ("The 'collective knowledge' doctrine is firmly established in this jurisdiction in a line of cases going back at least thirty years."); *United States v. Wells*, 98 *F.*3d 808, 810 (4th Cir. 1996) ("[A]lthough the agent who actually seized the weapon pursuant to the supervising agent's instruction had no personal knowledge that Wells was a convicted felon, it is sufficient that the agents collectively had probable cause to believe the weapon was evidence at the time of the seizure."); *United States v. Lomas*, 706 *F.*2d 886, 892 (9th Cir. 1983) ("It is sufficient if the pool of objective data possessed by the group of agents acting in concert supplies the requisite probable cause."); *United States v. Nieto*, 510 *F.*2d 1118, 1120 (5th Cir. 1975) (probable cause can rest on the collective knowledge of police, rather than solely on the knowledge of the officer making the arrest, when there is some degree of communication between the two); *United States v. Gaither*, 527 *F.*2d 456, 458 (4th Cir. 1975) ("probable cause can rest upon the collective knowledge of the police, rather than solely on that of the officer who actually makes the arrest"); *Wood v. Crouse*, 436 *F.*2d 1077, 1078 (10th Cir. 1971) (*same*).

The court, in *Smith v. United States*, 123 *U.S.App.D.C.* 202, 358 *F.*2d 833 (1966), suggested the following standard for application of the fellow officer / collective knowledge rule:

> The correct test is whether a warrant if sought could have been obtained by law enforcement agency application which disclosed its corporate information, not whether any one particular officer could have obtained it on what information he individually possessed.

Id. at 204, 358 *F.*2d at 835.

(b) But see Rogers v. Powell, 120 *F*.3d 446 (3rd Cir. 1997), where the court cautioned that "statements by fellow officers conveying that there is probable cause for a person's arrest, *by themselves*, cannot provide the 'facts and circumstances' necessary to support a finding of probable cause." *Id.* at 453. [Emphasis added.] Rather, "[p]robable cause exists only if the statements made by fellow officers are supported by actual facts that satisfy the probable cause standard." *Id.* Thus, "[t]he legality of a seizure based solely on statements issued by fellow officers depends on whether the officers who *issued* the statements possessed the requisite basis to seize the suspect." *Id.* (citing *United States v. Hensley*, 469 *U.S.* 221, 231-32, 105 *S.Ct.* 675, 681-82 (1985)). [Emphasis in original.]

(c) In *United States v. Sawyer*, 224 *F*.3d 675 (7th Cir. 2000), the court further explained that "[w]hen law enforcement officers are in communication regarding a suspect, the knowledge of one officer can be imputed to the other officers under the collective knowledge doctrine." *Id.* at 680. For example,

> if officers from an Illinois police department have probable cause to arrest a suspect and they send a bulletin regarding the suspect to police departments in Wisconsin, a Wisconsin police officer may arrest the suspect without personal knowledge of the facts and circumstances supporting the probable cause possessed by the Illinois officers who sent the bulletin. * * * The same is true when the officers are all at the scene of an arrest.

Id.

3. *An officer's duty to investigate.* As the cases indicate, probable cause is to be determined from an analysis of the totality of the facts available to the officer at the time of the arrest. Moreover, an otherwise lawful arrest is not rendered illegal by the fact that it turns out that the arrestee is innocent, that the arrestee was mistaken for the actual perpetrator, or that other evidence exculpates the arrestee. *See United States v. Covelli*, 738 *F*.2d 847 (7th Cir. 1984) (counterfeiting arrest lawful notwithstanding fact that money proved to be legitimate); *Hill v. California*, 401 *U.S.* 797, 91 *S.Ct.* 1106 (1971) (arrest of Miller, found in Hill's apartment, upheld for "the police had probable cause to arrest Hill and * * * had a reasonable, good-faith belief that the arrestee Miller was in fact Hill"); *United States v. Bobo*, 992 *F*.2d 524 (8th Cir. 1993) (mistaken arrest of Marvin's brother Richard upheld as lawful where police had probable cause to arrest Marvin, Richard resembled Marvin, and was driving Marvin's car at the time of arrest); *Marx v. Gumbinner*, 905 *F*.2d 1503 (11th Cir. 1990) (blood test clearing arrestee did not impugn the lawfulness of his arrest for rape).

Courts have held, however, that "law enforcement officers have a duty to conduct a reasonably thorough investigation prior to arresting a suspect, at least in the absence of exigent circumstances and so long as 'law enforcement would not [be] unduly hampered.' " *See Kuehl v. Burtis*, 173 *F*.3d 646, 650 (8th Cir. 1999) (officer should have interviewed eyewitnesses to altercation prior to arrest, where such "would not have unduly hampered the process of law enforcement"); *Rankin v. Evans*, 133 *F*.3d 1425 (11th Cir. 1998) ("arresting officer is required to conduct a reasonable investigation to establish probable cause," particularly when information is readily obtainable). *See also Gardenshire v. Schubert*, 205 *F*.3d 303, 318 (6th Cir. 2000) (while "an officer does not have to investigate independently every claim of innocence, * * * this axiom does not suggest that an officer has no duty to investigate an alleged crime before making an arrest"); *BeVier v. Hucal*, 806 *F*.2d 123, 128 (7th Cir. 1986) (a police officer "may not close her or his eyes to facts that would help clarify the circumstances of an arrest").

The police are not required, however, to investigate unlikely alibis or otherwise "conduct a mini-trial" before arresting a criminal suspect. *See Brodnicki v. City of Omaha*, 75 *F*.3d 1261, 1264 (8th Cir. 1996). *See also Romero v. Fay*, 45 *F*.3d 1472, 1476-77 & n. 2 (10th Cir. 1995) (police need not interview alleged alibi witnesses but must "reasonably interview witnesses readily available at the scene, investigate basic evidence, or otherwise inquire if a crime has been committed at all before invoking the power of a warrantless arrest").

DEVENPECK v. ALFORD
Supreme Court of the United States
543 *U.S.* 146, 125 *S.Ct.* 588 (2004)

QUESTION: Is an arrest lawful under the Fourth Amendment when the criminal offense for which there is probable cause to arrest is not "closely related" to the offense cited by the arresting officer at the time of arrest ?

ANSWER: YES. An arrest is not rendered unlawful simply because an arresting officer's subjective reason for making an arrest is not the precise criminal offense as to which the known facts provide probable cause. Were the law otherwise, an arrest made by a knowledgeable, veteran officer would be valid, whereas an arrest made by a rookie in precisely the same circumstances might not.

RATIONALE: On the evening in question, a disabled automobile and its passengers were stranded on the shoulder of a divided highway in Pierce County, Washington. As he came upon the disabled vehicle, a "concerned citizen," later identified as Jerome Alford, pulled his car off the road behind the vehicle, activating his "wig-wag" (alternating) headlights. At about this time, Officer Joi Haner of the Washington State Patrol, passed the disabled car from the opposite direction. The officer turned around to check on the motorists. When he arrived, Alford, who had begun helping the motorists change a flat tire, hurried back to his car and drove away. The stranded motorists asked Officer Haner if Alford was a "cop," in light of his statements to them and his flashing headlights.

26

Based on this account, Officer Haner radioed his supervisor, Sergeant Devenpeck, and advised him that he was concerned that Alford was an "impersonator" or a "wannabe cop." *Id.* at 591. Thereafter, Officer Haner pursued Alford's vehicle and pulled it over. Through the passenger-side window, the officer noticed that Alford was listening to a police scanner. He also noticed a set of handcuffs in the car. These facts heightened Haner's suspicion that Alford was impersonating a police officer. "Haner thought, moreover, that [Alford] seemed untruthful and evasive: He told Haner that he had worked previously for the 'State Patrol,' but under further questioning, claimed instead to have worked in law enforcement in Texas and at a shipyard. He claimed that his flashing headlights were part of a recently installed car-alarm system, and acted as though he was unable to trigger the system; but during these feigned efforts Haner noticed that [Alford] avoided pushing a button near his knee, which Haner suspected (correctly) to be the switch for the lights." *Id.*

When Sergeant Devenpeck arrived on the scene, Officer Haner informed him of the basis for his belief that Alford had been impersonating a police officer. Devenpeck approached Alford's vehicle and inquired about the wig-wag headlights. Alford provided him with the same story he had given to Officer Haner. As the sergeant questioned Alford, he noticed a tape recorder on the passenger seat of Alford's car, with the play and record buttons depressed. The sergeant then ordered Officer Haner to remove Alford from the car. Devenpeck played the recorded tape, and found that Alford had been recording his conversations with the officers. At this time, Devenpeck informed Alford that he was under arrest for a violation of the Washington Privacy Act, Wash. Rev. Code 9.73.030 (1994). Alford immediately protested, saying that "a state court-of-appeals decision, a copy of which he claimed was in his glove compartment, permitted him to record roadside conversations with police officers." *Id.* at 592. Believing that Alford's act of recording the officers was, in fact, illegal, Devenpeck directed Officer Haner to take Alford to jail.

Shortly thereafter, Devenpeck reached by phone a deputy county prosecutor, to whom he recounted the events leading to Alford's arrest. "The two discussed a series of possible criminal offenses, including violation of the Privacy Act, impersonating a police officer, and making a false representation to an officer." *Id.* The prosecutor advised that there was "clearly probable cause," and suggested that Alford also be charged with "obstructing a public servant," based on the runaround he gave Devenpeck. The sergeant "rejected this suggestion, explaining that the State Patrol does not, as a matter of policy, 'stack charges' against an arrestee." *Id.*

Ultimately, the police charged Alford with violating the State Privacy Act, and issued a ticket to him for his unlawful flashing headlights. At court, the judge dismissed both charges.

Alford sued for false arrest and false imprisonment, arguing that the police arrested him without probable cause, and that, given the appellate case law on the subject, no reasonable officer in the same circumstances would have believed Alford's actions of taping the officers was unlawful.

On appeal, the Ninth Circuit determined that the officers could not have probable cause to arrest because they cited only the Privacy Act charge, and "[t]ape recording officers conducting a traffic stop is not a crime in Washington." *Id.* at 593. The Ninth Circuit also rejected the officers' claim that probable cause existed to arrest Alford for the offenses of impersonating a law enforcement officer and obstructing a law enforcement officer, because, it said, those offenses were not "closely related" to the offense invoked by Devenpeck as he took Alford into custody. According to the Ninth Circuit, the probable cause inquiry is "confined to the known facts bearing upon the offense actually invoked at the time of arrest, and that (in addition) the offense supported by these known facts must be 'closely related' to the offense that the officer invoked." *Id.*

Finding the Ninth Circuit's approach improper, the United States Supreme Court said:

> We find no basis in precedent or reason for this limitation. Our cases make clear that an arresting officer's state of mind (except for the facts that he knows) is irrelevant to the existence of probable cause. * * * That is to say, his subjective reason for making the arrest need not be the criminal offense as to which the known facts provide probable cause. As we have repeatedly explained, " 'the fact that the officer does not have the state of mind which is hypothecated by the reasons which provide the legal justification for the officer's action does not invalidate the action taken as long as the circumstances, viewed objectively, justify that action.' " * * * "[T]he Fourth Amendment's concern with 'reasonableness' allows certain actions to be taken in certain circumstances, *whatever* the subjective intent." * * *
>
> The rule that the offense establishing probable cause must be "closely related" to, and based on the same conduct as, the offense identified by the arresting officer at the time of arrest is inconsistent with this precedent. Such a rule makes the lawfulness of an arrest turn upon the motivation of the arresting officer— eliminating, as validating probable cause, facts that played no part in the officer's expressed subjective reason for making the arrest, and offenses that are not "closely related" to that subjective reason. * * * This means that the constitutionality of an arrest under a given set of known facts will "vary from place to place and from time to time," * * * depending on whether the arresting officer states the reason for the detention and, if so, whether he correctly identifies a general class of offense for which probable cause exists. An arrest made by a knowledgeable, veteran officer would be valid, whereas an arrest made by a rookie *in precisely the same circumstances* would not. We see no reason to ascribe to the Fourth Amendment such arbitrarily variable protection.

Id. at 593-94. [Citations omitted; Court's emphasis.]

The "closely related offense" rule has adverse consequences. The Court elaborated:

> While it is assuredly good police practice to inform a person of the reason for his arrest at the time he is taken into custody, we have never held that to be constitutionally required. Hence, the predictable consequence of a rule limiting the probable-cause inquiry to offenses closely related to (and supported by the same facts as) those identified by the arresting officer is not, as [Alford] contends, that officers will cease making sham arrests on the hope that such arrests will later be validated, but rather that officers will cease providing reasons for arrest. And even if this option were to be foreclosed by adoption of a statutory or constitutional requirement, officers would simply give every reason for which probable cause could conceivably exist.
>
> The facts of this case exemplify the arbitrary consequences of a "closely related offense" rule. Officer Haner's initial stop of [Alford] was motivated entirely by the suspicion that he was impersonating a police officer. Before pulling [him] over, Haner indicated by radio that this was his concern; during the stop, Haner asked [Alford] whether he was actively employed in law enforcement and why his car had wig-wag headlights; and when Sergeant Devenpeck arrived, Haner told him why he thought [Alford] was a "wannabe cop." In addition, in the course of interrogating [Alford], both officers became convinced that he was not answering their questions truthfully and, with respect to the wig-wag headlights, that he was affirmatively trying to mislead them. Only after these suspicions had developed did Devenpeck discover the taping, place [Alford] under arrest, and offer the Privacy Act as the reason. Because of the "closely related offense" rule, Devenpeck's actions render irrelevant both Haner's developed suspicions that [Alford] was impersonating a police officer and the officers' shared belief that [he] obstructed their investigation. If Haner, rather than Devenpeck, had made the arrest, on the stated basis of his suspicions; if Devenpeck had not abided the [] policy against "stacking" charges; or if either officer had made the arrest without stating the grounds; the outcome under the "closely related offense" rule might well have been different. We have consistently rejected a conception of the Fourth Amendment that would produce such haphazard results. * * *

Id. at 595.

_____

§1.3. Arrest with warrant.

An arrest warrant has the purpose of interposing a probable cause determination by a neutral and detached magistrate or judge between the law enforcement officer and the person to be arrested. Placing this "check-point between the Government and the citizen implicitly acknowledges that an officer engaged in the often competitive enterprise of ferreting out crime may lack sufficient objectivity to weigh correctly the strength of the evidence supporting the contemplated action against the individual's interests in protecting his own liberty and * * * privacy[.]" *Steagald v. United States*, 451 *U.S.* 204, 212, 101 *S.Ct.* 1642, 1648 (1981) (quoting *Johnson v. United States*, 333 *U.S.* 10, 14, 68 *S.Ct.* 367, 369 (1948)).

When an arrest warrant issues, it demonstrates that a detached and neutral magistrate or judge has determined that probable cause exists to believe that the subject of the warrant has committed an offense. As such, the warrant necessarily serves to protect individuals from unreasonable searches and seizures.

Once armed with an arrest warrant, a police officer has the right to execute the warrant by the arrest of the defendant not only in a public place but also at his or her home. *Payton v. New York*, 455 *U.S.* 573, 100 *S.Ct.* 1371 (1980).

MARYLAND v. BUIE
Supreme Court of the United States
494 *U.S.* 325, 110 *S.Ct.* 1093 (1990)

QUESTION: Does the Fourth Amendment permit a properly limited "protective sweep" in conjunction with an in-home arrest when the arresting officers have a reasonable and articulable suspicion that the area to be swept harbors a person who may pose a danger to the officers or others ?

ANSWER: YES. During the course of an in-home arrest, law enforcement officers may conduct a "protective sweep" of the premises so long as the officers possess specific and articulable facts which, taken together with the rational inferences from those facts, give rise to a reasonable suspicion "that the area to be swept harbors an individual posing a danger to those on the arrest scene." *Id.* at 1098. In addition, "as an incident to the arrest, the officers [may], as a precautionary matter and *without probable cause or reasonable suspicion*, look in closets and other spaces immediately adjoining the place of arrest from which an attack could be launched." *Id.* Such a protective sweep, however, is aimed only at protecting the arresting officers; it is *not* a full search of the premises, but only a "cursory inspection of those spaces where a person may be found." *Id.* at 1099. [Emphasis added.]

RATIONALE: "A 'protective sweep' is a quick and limited search of a premises, incident to an arrest and conducted to protect the safety of police officers or others. It is narrowly confined to a *cursory visual in-*

30

spection of those places in which a person might be hiding." *Id.* at 1094. [Emphasis added.] In this case, the United States Supreme Court sets forth the level of justification which "is required by the Fourth and Fourteenth Amendments before police officers, while effecting the arrest of a suspect in his home pursuant to an arrest warrant, may conduct a warrantless protective sweep of all or part of the premises." *Id.*

In early February, six or seven officers from the Prince George's County Police Department executed a warrant for the arrest of defendant, Jerome Buie, at his home. Defendant was wanted for the armed robbery of a restaurant in Prince George's County, Maryland. As soon as the officers entered defendant's home, they "fanned out through the first and second floors." One of the officers guarded the entry to the basement "so that no one could come up and surprise the officers." With his service revolver drawn, the officer twice shouted into the basement, ordering anyone down there to come up. When a voice answered, the officer announced three times: "this is the police, show me your hands." Shortly thereafter, a pair of hands appeared around the bottom of the stairwell and defendant Buie emerged from the basement. "He was arrested, searched, and handcuffed by [the officer]." After Buie's arrest, one of the detectives at the scene entered the basement just "in case there was someone else" down there. While in the basement, the detective discovered a "red running suit" lying in plain view on a stack of clothing. Recognizing that the running suit matched the description of the clothing worn by one of the armed robbers, the detective immediately seized it.

According to the Supreme Court, "until the point of Buie's arrest the police had the right, based on the authority of the arrest warrant, [and probable cause to believe Buie was in his home,] to search anywhere in the house that Buie might have been found, including the basement." *Id.* at 1096, 1097. "Once he was found, however, the search for him was over, and there was no longer that particular justification for entering any rooms that had not yet been searched." *Id.* at 1097. Because Buie retained an expectation of privacy in those remaining areas of his house, the detective's entry into one of those areas required an independent justification for purposes of the Fourth Amendment. If the detective possessed that additional justification (for his entry into the basement), "the seizure of the red running suit, which was in plain view and which the officer had probable cause to believe was evidence of a crime, [would be] lawful[.]" *Id.*

The Maryland court held that before the officer would have been justified in entering the basement, he would need "*probable cause* to believe that a serious and demonstrable potentiality for danger exist[ed]." *Id.* at 1096. [Emphasis added.] *The United States Supreme Court, however, disagreed,* finding that the standard of *reasonable suspicion* would provide the necessary constitutional justification.

Speaking for the Court, Justice White explained that "the Fourth Amendment would permit the protective sweep undertaken here if the searching officer 'possesse[d] a reasonable belief based on "specific and articulable facts which, taken together with the rational inferences from those facts, reasonably warrant[ed]" the officer in believing,' * * * that the area swept harbored an individual posing a danger to the officer or others." *Id.* at 1095. [Citations omitted.]

In *Terry v. Ohio*, 392 *U.S.* 1, 88 *S.Ct.* 1868 (1968) and *Michigan v. Long*, 463 *U.S.* 1032, 103 *S.Ct.* 3469 (1983), the Supreme Court "was concerned with the immediate interest of the police officers in taking steps to assure themselves that the persons with whom they were dealing were not armed with or able to gain immediate control of a weapon that could unexpectedly and fatally be used against them. In [this] case, there is an analogous interest of the officers in taking steps to assure themselves that the house in which a suspect is being or has just been arrested is not harboring other persons who are dangerous and who could unexpectedly launch an attack. The risk of danger in the context of an arrest in the home is as great as, if not greater than, it is in an on-the-street or roadside investigatory encounter. A *Terry* or *Long* frisk occurs before a police-citizen confrontation has escalated to the point of arrest. A protective sweep, in contrast, occurs as an adjunct to the serious step of taking a person into custody for the purpose of prosecuting him for a crime. Moreover, unlike an encounter on the street or along a highway, an in-home arrest puts the officer at a disadvantage of being on his adversary's 'turf.' An ambush in a confined setting of unknown configuration is more to be feared than it is in open, more familiar surroundings." *Buie* at 1097-1098.

Arresting officers, therefore, "are permitted in such circumstances to take reasonable steps to ensure their safety after, and while making the arrest." *Id.* at 1098. As a result, as a lawful incident to an in-home arrest, law enforcement "officers [may], as a precautionary matter and without probable cause or reasonable suspicion, look in closets and other spaces immediately adjoining the place of arrest from which an attack could be immediately launched. Beyond that, however, * * * there must be articulable facts which, taken together with the rational inferences from those facts, would warrant a reasonably prudent officer in believing that the area to be swept harbors an individual posing a danger to those on the arrest scene." *Id.*

NOTE

1. *Scope of the "protective sweep."* The Court in *Buie* emphasized that the protective sweep is "*not* a full search of the premises, but may extend only to a *cursory inspection* of those spaces where a person may be found." *Id.* at 1099. [Emphasis added.] According to the Court, the sweep is *not* a "top-to-bottom" search and it is *not* automatic. It "may be conducted only when justified by a reasonable, articulable suspicion that the house is harboring a person posing a danger to those on the arrest scene." *Id.* Moreover, the protective sweep is to last "no longer than is necessary to dispel the reasonable suspicion of danger and in any event no longer than it takes to complete the arrest and depart the premises." *Id.* Officers are reminded, however, that in the room where the arrest takes place, the sweep *is* automatic, and may be conducted in the *absence* of a reasonable suspicion. *Id.* at 1098.

2. *Buie on remand.* During the course of its opinion in *Buie*, the federal Supreme Court emphasized that "the Fourth Amendment would permit the protective sweep undertaken here if the searching officer [possessed a reasonable and articulable suspicion] that the area swept harbored an individual posing a danger to the officer or others." *Id.* at 1095. The Court did not, however, decide that issue; instead, it remanded the case to the Court of Appeals of Maryland for further proceedings.

On remand, the Maryland Court of Appeals, in *Buie v. State*, 580 A.2d 167 (1990), held that the "limited search" of the basement conducted by the arresting officer "was lawful." *Id.* at 170. According to the Maryland court:

> The police went into Buie's home to arrest him for the perpetration of a dangerous felony—armed robbery—which had been committed within the preceding 48 hours. The victim of the robbery had promptly identified the perpetrators, and warrants for Buie and Allen were obtained on the day of the offense. The police placed Buie's house under surveillance for two days, and it is a fair inference that they did not observe Buie or Allen during that time. * * * [In fact, the police] learned Buie was at home [only] through a pretext telephone call placed just prior to their entry. * * *
>
> [When Buie was ordered out of the basement, arrested, handcuffed and searched, n]o weapon was found. * * *
>
> Detective Frolich was present at the top of the stairs and observed the arrest of Buie. Frolich then descended the stairs, "in case there was someone else in the basement." * * * Detective Frolich was the original investigating officer in the armed robbery case. He reasonably believed that Buie and Allen had perpetrated the robbery. On the day of the offense, he had obtained warrants for the arrest of both of them. [Consequently, i]t was entirely reasonable, at that point, for Frolich to suspect that Allen might well have come to Buie's house with him after the robbery, and might well be in the basement. Moreover, Frolich knew that Buie had used a gun in the robbery, and the gun had not been found when Buie was arrested. * * *
>
> Keeping in mind that the test is one of reasonable suspicion, and not of proof beyond a reasonable doubt or even of probable cause, and adopting a practical and non-technical approach, it seems clear that a prudent officer in Frolich's position could reasonably suspect that the basement harbored an individual who posed a danger to those on the arrest scene, and thus he was justified in conducting a cursory sweep of that area to neutralize the danger.

Id. at 170-171 & n.2.

3. *Spaces immediately adjoining the place of arrest.* In *United States v. Ford*, 56 *F.*3d 265 (D.C.Cir. 1995), F.B.I. Special Agent Godfrey and five Washington Metropolitan police officers arrived at the home of Mark Ford's mother with an arrest warrant for Ford. The affidavit accompanying the arrest warrant alleged that Ford had shot

and killed a man after Ford and several accomplices robbed the man of cocaine. The officers also had knowledge that Ford's criminal history included a prior arrest for forcible robbery, drug possession and possession of a prohibited weapon. Upon entering the residence, Agent Godfrey saw Ford, having emerged from a back bedroom, walking down a short hallway toward the officers. The agent advised Ford that he was under arrest, after which he was handcuffed and confined by the other officers.

Godfrey walked into the bedroom from which Ford had emerged "to make sure there was no one there to harm [the arresting officers]." *Id.* at 267. The agent turned on the light in the bedroom and noticed a loaded .45 caliber magazine on the floor next to a set of box springs and mattresses. Except for the box springs and mattresses, a dresser, and several bags piled up in a corner, the room was devoid of furniture. As he looked around the room, Godfrey realized that there were no persons present. Nevertheless, he lifted one of the mattresses and discovered live ammunition, money, and crack cocaine. Upon lifting the window shades, he found a .45 caliber handgun on the window sill.

Ford moved to suppress the evidence seized. The District Court denied the motion, concluding that Agent Godfrey conducted a legitimate protective sweep and that the evidence discovered was admissible at trial. The Court of Appeals for the District of Columbia Circuit disagreed and reversed.

In *Maryland v. Buie*, the Court "identified two situations in which protective sweeps are justified, and two types of protective sweeps." *Ford* at 268. "The first involves '[l]ooking in closets and other spaces immediately adjoining the place of arrest from which an attack could be immediately launched.' The second goes 'beyond that,' but is nevertheless circumscribed—'such a protective sweep, aimed at protecting the arresting officers, if justified by the circumstances, is nevertheless not a full search of the premises, but may extend only to a cursory inspection of those spaces where a person may be found.' " *Id.* at 269. [Citation omitted.] While the first type of sweep requires no probable cause or reasonable suspicion, the second requires reasonable grounds to suspect that " 'the area to be swept harbors an individual posing a danger to those on the arrest scene.' " *Id.* [Citation omitted.]

"This case involves *Buie*'s first type of sweep. The law enforcement officers who arrested Ford lacked a reasonable belief based on specific and articulable facts that the area searched harbored a dangerous individual, which would justify *Buie*'s second type of sweep." *Ford* at 269.

The Government contended that, based on Ford's criminal history and the fact that the present warrant was for homicide, the officers had a reasonable suspicion that Ford might be armed and dangerous, thus justifying *Buie*'s second type of sweep. Rejecting this contention, the court pointed out that "when Godfrey began his sweep, [Ford] had already been arrested and placed in the custody of the officers." *Id.* An officer's awareness of a suspect's prior weapons conviction and that the suspect could be dangerous does not itself directly justify a protective sweep for the discovery of *other* armed and dangerous persons in the vicinity. *Id.*

The court also rejected the Government's second contention, that the affidavit accompanying the arrest warrant alleged that Ford had accomplices with him when he committed the crime for which he was being arrested. According to the court, this argument is also unpersuasive because the crime for which Ford was arrested "occurred almost seven months prior to his arrest, and the officers had absolutely no indication that the alleged accomplices were present in Ford's mother's apartment when the arrest occurred." *Id.*

"Under *Buie*'s first prong, however, as a precautionary matter and without probable cause or reasonable suspicion, Agent Godfrey was free to look in spaces immediately adjoining the place of Ford's arrest from which an attack could be immediately launched. Because the arrest took place in the hallway, Agent Godfrey could legitimately look in the bedroom for potential attackers. Upon seeing, in plain view, the gun clip, an object whose incriminating character is immediately apparent, Agent Godfrey was justified in seizing it." *Id.* at 270.

Godfrey was not permitted to search under the mattress or behind the window shades. The agent never suggested that a person could have been hiding under the mattress. "To the contrary, he testified that it would have been '[v]irtually impossible' for someone to do so." *Id.* Likewise, the agent's testimony regarding the gun on the window sill gave no indication that a person could have been hiding behind the shades.

Accordingly, the court held that the agent's

> search under the mattress and behind the window shades violated the Fourth Amendment because a search incident to an in-home arrest, under *Buie*'s first prong, permits only a "look in closets and other spaces immediately adjoining the place of arrest from which an attack could be immediately launched." ∗ ∗ ∗ There were no exigent circumstances in this case justifying a warrantless search beyond what was prescribed in *Buie*. Thus, the evidence seized from these spaces—under the mattress and behind the window shades—was improperly admitted at trial and Ford's conviction must be reversed.

Id. at 272.

In several closing comments, the court suggested that "the police could have telephoned a magistrate for a search warrant," pursuant to *Fed.R.Crim.P.* 41(c)(2)(A), or "they could have asked the owner of the apartment, [Ford's] mother, whether she would consent to a search of the apartment in lieu of waiting for a magistrate to issue a search warrant." *Id.* These alternatives, suggested the court, "would have avoided the infringement of Fourth Amendment rights, without in any way jeopardizing the safety of the officers." *Id.*

4. *When the arrest takes place outside the subject's residence.* The Court in *Maryland v. Buie* emphasized that the protective sweep should last "no longer than is necessary to dispel the reasonable suspicion of danger and in any event no longer than it takes to complete the arrest and depart the premises." *Id.*, 110 *S.Ct.* at 1093. What of an arrest that takes place immediately outside the open door of the sub-

ject's premises ? That was the situation in *United States v. Henry*, 48 *F*.3d 1282 (D.C.Cir. 1995).

In *Henry*, a team of U.S. Marshals and Washington Metropolitan police officers, armed with an arrest warrant, went to a Northeast Washington apartment building looking for Roland Henry, who was wanted for a parole violation. An informant had advised the officers that Henry was staying in Apartment 34, was armed, and might have confederates with him. The officers began a stakeout of the apartment at 9:30 a.m. At 1:30 p.m., Henry stepped from the apartment into the internal hallway of the building, leaving the door ajar behind him. Henry was immediately placed under arrest and handcuffed. At this point, one of the officers noticed Henry's codefendant, James Hamilton, outside the building peering into the hallway through a window, and heard Henry tell Hamilton that "they got me." Several officers then entered the apartment with Henry. The officers conducted a "security check" of the apartment's bedroom, bathroom, and kitchen to verify that there were no other armed individuals present who might pose a threat to the officers. In the bedroom, an officer found a gun sitting on top of a dresser and two bags of a white powdery substance in an open drawer, some of which was later determined to be heroin.

Finding the "protective sweep" of Henry's residence reasonable under the Fourth Amendment, the court explained:

> Although *Buie* concerned an arrest made in the home, the principles enunciated by the Supreme Court are fully applicable where, as here, the arrest takes place just outside the residence. * * * That the police arrested the defendant outside rather than inside his dwelling is relevant to the question of whether they could reasonably fear an attack by someone within it. The officers' exact location, however, does not change the nature of the appropriate inquiry: Did articulable facts exist that would lead a reasonably prudent officer to believe that a sweep was required to protect the safety of those on the arrest scene ? * * *

> [T]estimony at the suppression hearing [] established an objective basis for the officers to fear for their safety after the arrest. The informant had advised [the] officers that Henry would have weapons and that Henry's "boys" or "counterparts" (as alternatively described by the informant) might be with him.

> This information, coupled with the arrest just outside the open door, was sufficient to lead a reasonably prudent policeman to fear that he was vulnerable to attack. Moreover, the fact that the door was open could cause the officer to believe that anyone inside would be aware that Henry had been taken into custody, especially as Henry had been heard to tell Hamilton that "they got me." * * * While it is true that the officers could not be certain that a threat existed inside the apartment, this does not impugn the reasonableness of their taking protective action. It is enough that they

"have a reasonable basis for believing that their search will reduce the danger of harm." * * *

Id. at 1284. [Citations omitted.]

Other circuits have similarly held that a protective sweep of a home, as defined in *Buie*, would be permissible as incident to an arrest occurring just outside the home. *See United States v. Lawlor*, 406 *F.*3d 37, 41 (1st Cir. 2005) ("a protective sweep may be conducted following an arrest that takes place just outside the home, if sufficient facts exist that would warrant a reasonably prudent officer to fear that the area in question could harbor an individual posing a threat to those at the scene"); *United States v. Cavely*, 318 *F.*3d 987, 995-96 (10th Cir. 2003) (*same*); *United States v. Colbert*, 76 *F.*3d 773, 776-77 (6th Cir. 1996) ("in some circumstances, an arrest taking place just outside a home may pose an equally serious threat to the arresting officers"). *See also United States v. Kimmons*, 965 *F.*2d 1001, 1009-10 (11th Cir. 1992); *United States v. Oguns*, 921 *F.*2d 442, 446 (2d Cir. 1990); *United States v. Tisdale*, 921 *F.*2d 1095, 1097 (10th Cir. 1990). Those courts also agree that "a sweep incident to an arrest occurring just outside the home must be analyzed under the second prong of the *Buie* analysis requiring 'articulable facts which, taken together with the rational inferences from those facts, would warrant a reasonably prudent officer in believing that the area to be swept harbors an individual posing a danger to those on the arrest scene.' " *Sharrar v. Felsing*, 128 *F.*3d 810, 823-24 (3rd Cir. 1997) (quoting *Buie* at 334, 110 *S.Ct.* at 1098). As the court emphasized in *Sharrar*:

> Certainly, it would be imprudent to prohibit officers who are effecting an arrest or waiting until a warrant may be obtained from ensuring their safety and minimizing the risk of gunfire or other attack coming from inside the home if they have reason to believe that dangerous individuals are inside.

Id. at 824.

---

§1.4. Arrest without warrant.

While the law certainly prefers that an arrest be made pursuant to a warrant, a law enforcement officer is nonetheless permitted to effect a *warrantless* arrest when he or she has probable cause to believe that a crime has been or is being committed and that the person to be arrested is a criminal participant. In this context, the term, "crime," many times referred to as "felony," encompasses those offenses which carry a penalty of imprisonment for a year or more.

When an officer must decide whether a warrantless arrest in a given set of circumstances is justified, he or she is not confined to consideration only of evidence admissible in a courtroom. Rather, the officer may consider all the facts and circumstances surrounding the prospective arrest, even that information coming from (preferably reliable) hearsay sources, when making the probable cause determination.

Once probable cause exists for the arrest of an individual, the arrest may take place without a warrant when it is effected in a public place. The Fourth Amendment permits such warrantless (felony) arrests even though the law enforcement officer had sufficient time to obtain a warrant. *United States v. Watson*, 423 *U.S.* 411, 96 *S.Ct.* 820 (1976) (upholding a warrantless arrest, based upon probable cause, effected by a postal inspector at a public restaurant). In *Watson*, the United States Supreme Court refused to place a requirement of more than probable cause in a warrantless arrest situation. According to the Court, to require more than probable cause, *e.g.*, probable cause and exigent circumstances, would "encumber criminal prosecutions with endless litigation with respect to the existence of exigent circumstances, whether it was practicable to get a warrant, whether the suspect was about to flee, and the like." *Id.* at 423-424, 96 *S.Ct.* at 828. Accordingly, the two critical components for warrantless criminal arrests remain: (1) probable cause, and (2) an offense punishable by imprisonment for a year or more.

Respecting lower level offenses, *i.e.*, offenses punishable by imprisonment for less than one year, most jurisdictions require that the offense occur *in the presence* of the law enforcement officer. *"Presence,"* in this respect, means that the arresting officer has gained knowledge of the offense directly, and this may be accomplished by the use of any of his or her senses. Most commonly, the "in presence" requirement is satisfied by an officer directly viewing or seeing the offense occur, even if the officer uses a telescope or binoculars. The "in presence" requirement may also be satisfied if the officer witnesses the offense through his or her sense of hearing, smell or touch. *See e.g., Jakes v. State*, 398 *So.*2d 342 (Ala.Crim.App. 1981) ("it would not be essential that an officer actually see the commission of an offense if another of his physical senses, perhaps that of smell or hearing, could afford him a fair inference that the offense was indeed being perpetrated at that point in time"); *Clark v. State*, 117 *Tex.Crim.* 153, 35 *S.W.*2d 420 (1931) (An offense is deemed to have occurred within the presence or view of an officer when any of his senses afford an awareness of its occurrence."). An offense will also be deemed to have taken place in the officer's presence if the suspect admits to its commission in the officer's presence.

Courts consistently adhere to the "in presence" requirement for, "unless the officer himself knows of the offense and the offender, it is better, in light of the less serious nature of the alleged offense, to leave the determination of probable cause to an officer in the judicial branch." *State v. Morse*, 54 *N.J.* 32, 35, 252 *A.*2d 723 (1969). In this regard, it is not enough that an officer uses his or her senses *to learn that an offense has been committed*. The offense must be committed at the time the officer is on the scene. For example, an officer would not be authorized to make an in-presence arrest for a minor assault merely because he has been told by the victim that the perpetrator, who is still present at the scene, struck her prior to the arrival of the officer. This is so even if the victim's story is largely corroborated by the officer's observation of signs of injury on the victim's body. It has also been held that a minor theft offense did not occur in the officer's presence in a case where the officer viewed a grocery store's videotape of the offender engaging in the alleged shoplifting offense. *See Forgie-Buccioni v. Hannaford Bros., Inc.,* 413 *F.*3d 175, 180 (1st Cir. 2005) (a videotape alone does not provide a sufficient basis to satisfy the "in presence" requirement for warrantless arrests).

Naturally, since the "in presence" requirement is statutory in dimension, state legislatures are free to create exceptions. Common exceptions include probable-cause-based arrests for minor offenses committed in domestic violence settings, retail theft, and drunk driving.

ATWATER v. CITY OF LAGO VISTA
United States Supreme Court
532 *U.S.* 318, 121 *S.Ct.* 1536 (2001)

QUESTION: Does the Fourth Amendment prohibit a law enforcement officer from making a warrantless arrest for a minor offense not amounting to a breach of the peace, such as a motor vehicle seatbelt violation ?

ANSWER: NO. "The standard of probable cause applie[s] to all arrests," without the need to distinguish between serious offenses and minor offenses. "If an officer has probable cause to believe that an individual has committed even a very minor criminal offense in his presence, he may, without violating the Fourth Amendment, arrest the offender." *Id.* at 1557.

RATIONALE: In March, Gail Atwater was driving her pickup truck in Lago Vista, Texas, with her 3-year-old son and 5-year-old daughter in the front seat. No one was wearing a seatbelt. Lago Vista Police Officer Bart Turek noticed the seatbelt violations and stopped Atwater. Based on a prior contact with Atwater, the officer determined that an arrest was in order. Turek called for backup and asked to see Atwater's driving credentials. When Atwater told the officer that she did not have the papers because her purse had been stolen the day before, the officer placed her under arrest. A friend of Atwater's arrived at the scene and took charge of the children. Turek then handcuffed Atwater, placed her in his patrol car, and transported her to the station, where "booking officers had her remove her shoes, jewelry, and eyeglasses, and empty her pockets. Officers took Atwater's 'mug shot' and placed her, alone, in a jail cell for about one hour, after which she was taken before a magistrate and released on $310 bond." *Id.* at 1542.

"Atwater was charged with driving without her seatbelt fastened, failing to secure her children in seatbelts, driving without a license, and failing to provide proof of insurance. She ultimately pleaded no contest to the misdemeanor seatbelt offenses and paid a $50 fine; the other charges were dismissed." *Id.*

Under Texas law, a seatbelt violation is characterized as "a misdemeanor punishable by a fine not less than $25 or more than $50." *Tex.Tran. Code Ann.* §545.413(d). Texas law expressly authorizes officers to "arrest without warrant a person found committing a violation" of the seatbelt law, §543.001, although it permits police to issue citations in lieu of arrest, §§543.003-543.005. *Atwater* at 1541.

As a result of her arrest, Atwater filed suit under 42 *U.S.C.* §1983 against the City of Lago Vista, Officer Turek, and the city's chief of police, contending that Officer Turek violated Atwater's Fourth Amendment "right to be free from unreasonable seizure," *id.* at 1542, and seeking compensatory and punitive damages. At no time, however, during the course of the proceedings, did Atwater claim that Officer Turek did not have probable cause to arrest, or that the officer "conducted the arrest in an 'extraordinary manner, unusually harmful' to Atwater's privacy interests." *Id.* [Citation omitted.]

The main question addressed by the United States Supreme Court was whether the Fourth Amendment should be interpreted to limit a police officer's warrantless arrest authority for minor offenses. *The Court held that it should not be so interpreted.*

One of the primary contentions made by Atwater was that, historically and at common law, a police officer was not permitted to make a warrantless misdemeanor arrest unless the offense involved a "breach of the peace." The term "breach of the peace," however, has not been clearly defined over the years. It has been held that "every indictable offense [is] constructively a breach of the peace." *Id.* at 1543 n.2. When used "in reference to common-law arrest power," the term has been interpreted to require some "element of violence." *Id.* For purposes of this case, although the Court found it unnecessary to resolve the historical uncertainty surrounding the precise meaning of the term, it assumed that, "as used in the context of common-law arrest, the phrase 'breach of the peace' was understood narrowly, as entailing at least a threat of violence." *Id.* at 1543-44 n.2.

In addressing Atwater's contention, the Court conducted an extensive analysis of early statutory and common law, examining legislation, cases and commentary published as early as 1631. Although the common law was not necessarily consistent regarding this issue, the early English statutes leading up to the framing of our Constitution authorized warrantless arrests for "misdemeanor-level offenses not involving any breach of the peace." *Id.* at 1544.

Based on the available historical evidence, the Court simply could not conclude "that the Fourth Amendment, as originally understood, forbade peace officers to arrest without a warrant for misdemeanors not amounting to or involving breach of the peace." *Id.* at 1550. Moreover, since the framing of the Constitution, the development of the law has witnessed "two centuries of uninterrupted (and largely unchallenged) state and federal practice permitting warrantless arrests for misdemeanors not amounting to or involving breach of the peace."* *Id.* In this respect, the Court observed that

> both the legislative tradition of granting warrantless misdemeanor arrest authority and the judicial tradition of sustaining such statutes against constitutional attack are buttressed by legal commentary that, for more than a century now, has almost uniformly recognized the constitutionality of extending warrantless arrest power to misdemeanors without limitation to breaches of the peace. * * *

> Small wonder, then, that today statutes in all 50 States and the District of Columbia permit warrantless misdemeanor arrests by at least some (if not all) peace officers without requiring any breach of the peace, as do a host of congressional enactments. * * *

Id. at 1552.

Even though the historical evidence and treatment of this subject demonstrates a "majority view that the police need not obtain an arrest warrant merely because a misdemeanor stopped short of violence or a threat of it," *id.* at 1553, Atwater did not end her argument there. Instead, she asked the court "to mint a new rule of constitutional law," arguing for "a modern arrest rule, one not necessarily requiring violent breach of the peace, but nonetheless forbidding custodial arrest, even upon probable cause, when conviction could not ultimately carry any jail time and when the government shows no compelling need for immediate detention." *Id.*

While the Court was not prepared to adopt such a broad-based rule, it did pause to note that if it were to apply a rule specific for this case alone, "Atwater might well prevail." *Id.*

> She was a known and established resident of Lago Vista with no place to hide and no incentive to flee, and common sense says she would almost certainly have buckled up as a condition of driving off with a citation. In her case, the physical incidents of arrest were merely gratuitous humiliations imposed by a police officer who was (at best) exercising extremely poor judgment. Atwater's claim to live free of pointless indignity and confinement clearly outweighs anything the City can raise against it specific to her case.

Id.

---

* Although the Court has not had "much to say about warrantless misdemeanor arrest authority," what little it has said has focused primarily "on the circumstance that an offense was committed in an officer's presence, to the omission of any reference to a breach-of-the-peace limitation." *Id.* Clearly, there was no need in this case for the Court to "speculate whether the Fourth Amendment entails an 'in the presence' requirement for purposes of misdemeanor arrests." *Id.* at 1550 n.11 (citing *Welsh v. Wisconsin,* 466 *U.S.* 740, 756, 104 *S.Ct.* 2091, 2101 (1984) (White, J., dissenting) ("[T]he requirement that a misdemeanor must have occurred in the officer's presence to justify a warrantless arrest is not grounded in the Fourth Amendment * * * and we have never held that a warrant is constitutionally required to arrest for nonfelony offenses occurring out of the officer's presence.").

But the Court has "traditionally recognized that a responsible Fourth Amendment balance is not well served by standards requiring sensitive, case-by-case determinations of government need, lest every discretionary judgment in the field be converted into an occasion for constitutional review. * * * Often enough, the Fourth Amendment has to be applied on the spur (and in the heat) of the moment, and the object in implementing its command of reasonableness is to draw standards sufficiently clear and simple to be applied with a fair prospect of surviving judicial second-guessing months and years after an arrest or search is made. Courts attempting to strike a reasonable Fourth Amendment balance thus credit the government's side with an essential interest in readily administrable rules." *Id.* at 1553-54.

The Court rejected Atwater's argument that the Fourth Amendment should be interpreted to forbid warrantless arrests "for minor crimes not accompanied by violence or some demonstrable threat of it (whether 'minor crime' be defined as a fine-only traffic offense, a fine-only offense more generally, or a misdemeanor)." *Id.* at 1554. Regarding Atwater's contention that the Court could draw a line between "jailable" and "fine-only" offenses, between those for which conviction could result in commitment and those for which it could not, the Court said:

> The trouble with this distinction, of course, is that an officer on the street might not be able to tell. It is not merely that we cannot expect every police officer to know the details of frequently complex penalty schemes, * * * but that penalties for ostensibly identical conduct can vary on account of facts difficult (if not impossible) to know at the scene of an arrest. Is this the first offense or is the suspect a repeat offender? Is the weight of the marijuana a gram above or a gram below the fine-only line? Where conduct could implicate more than one criminal prohibition, which one will the district attorney ultimately decide to charge? And so on.

Id. at 1554-55. [Citations and footnotes omitted.]

Not only would Atwater's proposed rule be difficult to administer, but it would also "guarantee increased litigation over many of the arrests that would occur." *Id.* at 1555. The Court also would not adopt a rule for a "simple tie breaker for the police to follow in the field: if in doubt, do not arrest." *Id.* Such a tie breaker, the Court said,

> would boil down to something akin to a least-restrictive-alternative limitation, which is itself one of those "ifs, ands, and buts" rules, * * * generally thought inappropriate in working out Fourth Amendment protection. * * * Beyond that, whatever help the tie breaker might give would come at the price of a systematic disincentive to arrest in situations where even Atwater concedes that arresting would serve an important societal interest. An officer not quite sure that the drugs weighed enough to warrant jail time or not quite certain about a suspect's risk of flight would not arrest, even though it could perfectly well turn out that, in fact, the offense called for incarceration and the defendant was long gone on the day of trial. Multiplied many times over, the costs to society of such underen-

forcement could easily outweigh the costs to defendants of being needlessly arrested and booked, as Atwater herself acknowledges.

Id. at 1555-56.

Atwater is not, however, without protection. Under current law, a court will engage in an "individualized review" when a defendant makes "a colorable argument that an arrest, with or without a warrant, was 'conducted in an extraordinary manner, unusually harmful to [his] privacy or even physical interests.' " *Id.* at 1556. [Citations omitted.]

Contrary to Atwater's suggestions, the police are not routinely making, as in this case, "foolish, warrantless misdemeanor arrests." *Id.* "We are sure," said the Court, "that the country is not confronting anything like an epidemic of unnecessary minor-offense arrests. * * * That fact caps the reasons for rejecting Atwater's request for the development of a new and distinct body of constitutional law." *Id.*

Accordingly, the Court reaffirmed that "the standard of probable cause 'applie[s] to all arrests, without the need to "balance" the interests and circumstances involved in particular situations.' * * * If an officer has probable cause to believe that an individual has committed even a very minor criminal offense in his presence, he may, without violating the Fourth Amendment, arrest the offender." *Id.* at 1557.

In this case, the Court held that "Atwater's arrest satisfied constitutional requirements." *Id.* There was no dispute that Officer Turek had probable cause to believe that she had committed an offense in his presence. She admitted that neither she nor her children were wearing seat belts, as required by Texas law. "Turek was accordingly authorized (not required, but authorized) to make a custodial arrest without balancing costs and benefits or determining whether or not Atwater's arrest was in some sense necessary." *Id.*

Nor was there any evidence presented that this arrest was "made in an 'extraordinary manner, unusually harmful to [her] privacy or . . . physical interests.' * * * [T]he question whether a search or seizure is 'extraordinary' turns, above all else, on the manner in which the search or seizure is executed. * * * Atwater's arrest was surely 'humiliating,' * * * but it was no more 'harmful to . . . privacy or . . . physical interests' than [any other] normal custodial arrest. * * * The arrest and booking were inconvenient and embarrassing to Atwater, but not so extraordinary as to violate the Fourth Amendment." *Id.* at 1557-58.

Accordingly, the Court held that Atwater's arrest was constitutionally permissible.

NOTE

1. *Probable-cause based arrests which violate state law.* In *Virginia v. Moore,* 553 *U.S.* ___, 128 *S.Ct.* 1598 (2008), the United States Supreme Court held that the Fourth Amendment is not violated by an officer who makes an arrest that is based on probable cause but prohibited by state law.

The events of this case unfolded in mid-February, when two City of Portsmouth police officers stopped a car driven by defendant, David Lee Moore, based on a tip that he was driving with a suspended license. Once the officers confirmed that Moore's license was in fact suspended, they arrested him. A search incident to the arrest uncovered 16 grams of crack cocaine and $516 in cash.

Although the arrest was supported by probable cause, it violated Virginia statutory law, which required the issuance of a summons. Under Virginia law, however, that violation did not require the suppression of the evidence seized. Nonetheless, the Virginia Supreme Court held that since the arresting officers should have issued Moore a citation under state law, and the Fourth Amendment does not permit searches incident to citation (*Knowles v. Iowa,* 525 *U.S.* 113, 119 *S.Ct.* 484 (1998)), the officers' actions violated the Fourth Amendment. *The United States Supreme Court disagreed.*

The Fourth Amendment was never intended "to incorporate statutes." *Id.,* 128 *S.Ct.* at 1604. The law is settled that "when an officer has probable cause to believe a person committed even a minor crime in his presence, the * * * arrest is constitutionally reasonable." *Id.*

Naturally, a State may choose to protect privacy beyond the level that the Fourth Amendment requires. Such "additional protections," however, are treated "exclusively as matters of state law." *Id.* Thus, "whether or not a search is reasonable within the meaning of the Fourth Amendment," does not depend "on the law of the particular State in which the search occurs." *Id.* [Citation omitted.] State law does not alter the content of the Fourth Amendment, which is why it has never been held that violations of state arrest law are also violations of the Fourth Amendment.

An arrest based on probable cause serves several important interests that serve to justify the seizure. An arrest:

(1)   ensures that the suspect appears in court to answer charges;

(2)   prevents the suspect from continuing his offense;

(3)   safeguards evidence; and

(4)   enables officers to conduct a more thorough in-custody investigation.

Id. at 1605.

In *Atwater v. City of Lago Vista, supra,* it was expressly held that the Fourth Amendment allows an arrest "based on probable cause to believe a law has been broken in the presence of the arresting officer." *Moore* at 1606. The rule extends even to minor offenses "because of the need for a bright-line constitutional standard. If the constitutionality of arrest for minor offenses turned in part on inquiries as to risk of flight and danger of repetition, officers might be deterred from making legitimate arrests." *Id.*

Accordingly, the Court rejected the invitation to incorporate state-law arrest limitations into the federal Constitution. Clearly, "linking Fourth Amendment protections to state law would cause them to 'vary from place to place and from time to time.'" *Id.* at 1607. [Citation omitted.]

This case reaffirms that "warrantless arrests for crimes committed in the presence of an arresting officer are reasonable under the Constitution, and that while States are free to regulate such arrests however they desire, state restrictions do not alter the Fourth Amendment's protections." *Id.*

The Court also rejected the Virginia's Supreme Court's determination that *Knowles v. Iowa* required the suppression of the evidence seized from Moore. For further discussion of this issue, *see Section 3.2(a)* and the Note following *United States v. Robinson.*

2. *The reasonableness of a decision to arrest.* While a court may certainly inquiry into the reasonableness of *the manner* in which an arrest is conducted, it seems that "the most natural reading of *Atwater*" is that a court will not "inquire further into the reasonableness of *a decision to arrest* when it is supported by probable cause." *Hedgepeth v. Washington Metropolitan Area Transit Authority*, 386 *F.*3d 1148 (D.C. Cir. 2004). [Emphasis added.]

In *Hedgepeth*, 12-year-old Ansche Hedgepeth was arrested, searched and handcuffed for eating a single French fry in a transit authority Metrorail station. At the time of the arrest, the Washington Metropolitan Area Transit Authority had adopted a "zero tolerance" policy with respect to violations of certain ordinances, including one that makes it unlawful for any person to eat or drink in a Metrorail station. Adults who violate the ordinance typically receive a citation. District of Columbia law, however, does not provide for the issuance of citations for non-traffic offenses to those under eighteen years of age. The relevant statute merely provides that a minor violating the law "may be taken into custody." D.C. Code §16-2309(a)(2). While a plain reading of this statute allows an officer the discretion to simply give the juvenile a warning, the arrest provision becomes mandatory when paired with the Transit Authority's "zero tolerance enforcement policy." *Id.* at 1153 n.4.

On behalf of the minor, it was argued that *Atwater* "can only be understood in terms of the Court's concern to avoid interfering with the discretion of police officers called upon to decide, 'on the spur (and in the heat) of the moment,' * * * whether to arrest or to issue a citation." *Id.* at 1157. Because a rule allowing an "*ad hoc* reasonableness review of an arrest decision, even when there is probable cause, would hobble the officer's discretion," the *Atwater* Court "declined to engage in any inquiry beyond probable cause." *Id.* In Ansche's case, however, there was no exercise of discretion by the arresting officer, for he did not have the choice of issuing a citation. Thus, an inquiry into the reasonableness of the arrest would not intrude upon the officer's discretion.

Although the *Hedgepeth* court found this argument "creative," it was "ultimately unpersuaded," for it did not believe *Atwater* permitted an evaluation of the reasonableness of the police officer's decision to arrest, given the existence of probable cause." *Id.* at 1158. Said the court:

> It is certainly true that the Court in *Atwater* voiced concern that imposing Fourth Amendment reasonableness standards above and beyond probable cause would unduly intrude upon "discretionary judgment in the field" and interfere with "an officer on the street" called to act "on a moment's notice." * * * At the same time, however, law enforcement discretion is also exercised at more removed policy-making levels, as with the no-citation and zero-tolerance policies at issue here. There is no reason to suppose that the *Atwater* Court's conclusion—that the benefits from additional reasonableness standards beyond probable cause were not worth the burden on law enforcement discretion—was restricted to the burden on the officer in the field. * * *
>
> While we can inquire into the reasonableness of the manner in which an arrest is conducted, * * * the most natural reading of *Atwater* is that we cannot inquire further into the reasonableness of a decision to arrest when it is supported by probable cause. That is true whether the decision to arrest upon probable cause is made by the officer on the beat or at a more removed policy level.
>
> Moreover, insisting on the exercise of discretion by an arresting officer would be an unfamiliar imperative under the Fourth Amendment. * * * It is the high office of the Fourth Amendment to constrain law enforcement discretion; we see no basis for turning the usual Fourth Amendment approach on its head and finding a government practice unconstitutional solely because it lacks a sufficient role for discretionary judgment. * * * Given the undisputed existence of probable cause, *Atwater* precludes further inquiry into the reasonableness of Ansche's arrest under the Fourth Amendment. The judgment of the district court is affirmed.

Id. at 1158-59. [Citations omitted.]

UNITED STATES v. WHITE
United States Court of Appeals
607 *F*.2d 203 (7th Cir. 1979)

QUESTION: Must federal Drug Enforcement Administration (DEA) agents obtain an arrest warrant as soon as they develop probable cause ?

ANSWER: NO. 21 *U.S.C.* §878(a)(3) "allows a DEA agent to make a warrantless arrest for any felony cognizable under the laws of the United States, if he has probable cause to believe that the person to be arrested has committed or is committing a felony." *White* at 209. Even though the DEA agents in this case may have had defendant under surveillance for 24 hours preceding his arrest and had an opportunity to obtain a warrant, no arrest warrant was required since the agents had probable cause to effect the arrest and the arrest occurred in a public place. *Id.* at 209.

RATIONALE: During the course of a narcotics investigation, DEA agents developed probable cause to believe defendant, Howard White, orchestrated the shipment of one kilogram of cocaine from Lima, Peru to Houston, Texas. The shipment of cocaine arrived hidden inside a crated mirror. With the help of defendant's friend (turned Government informer), the agents began a surveillance which lasted approximately 24 hours. During the course of the surveillance, the agents had the time to procure an arrest warrant but no warrant was sought. Instead, the surveillance was maintained and White was subsequently arrested after he and an associate arrived and picked up the crated mirror. The arrest occurred during a motor vehicle stop in the terminal arrival area.

In this appeal, defendant argues, among other things, that an arrest warrant was required because the DEA agents had him under surveillance for 24 hours prior to the arrest. *The Court of Appeals for the Seventh Circuit disagreed.*

21 *U.S.C.* §878 provides in pertinent part:"(a) Any officer or employee of the Drug Enforcement Administration * * * may * * * (3) make arrests without warrant * * * (B) for any felony, cognizable under the laws of the United States, if he has probable cause to believe that the person to be arrested has committed or is committing a felony[.]" "At the time of White's arrest the DEA agent[s] had probable cause to believe White was committing a felony—importation of cocaine. Even though they may have had White under surveillance for the 24 hours preceding the arrest and had an opportunity to obtain a warrant, no arrest warrant was required to make th[is] arrest." *Id.* at 209 (citing *United States v. Watson*, 423 *U.S.* 411, 96 *S.Ct.* 820 (1976)).

NOTE

See also United States v. Schrenzel, 462 *F*.2d 765 (8th Cir. 1972), where the court rejected a drug dealer's contention that his arrest should have taken place well before the fourth sale of narcotics. Here, the court instructed that "[t]he reasonableness of police conduct in delaying an arrest in any particular case must be weighed against possible prejudice to the defendant." *Id.* at 775. Because Schrenzel was not prejudiced by reason of the manner in which the arrest was effected, and in light of the existence of ample probable cause for his arrest, the court found his contentions to be without merit. *Accord United States v. Sizer*, 292 F.2d 596 (4th Cir. 1961):

> Also without merit is [defendant's] contention that he should have been arrested immediately upon the first sale and not given the opportunity to make additional sales. The arrest was not unduly delayed, and it was not improper for the officers to see how far Sizer was prepared to go in his illegal conduct, and to discover, as they did, the source of his supply.

Id. at 599.

---

§1.5. Entry of a dwelling to effect an arrest.

PAYTON v. NEW YORK
Supreme Court of the United States
445 *U.S.* 573, 100 *S.Ct.* 1371 (1980)

QUESTION: May law enforcement officers make a warrantless, nonconsensual entry into a suspect's home in order to make a routine felony arrest ?

ANSWER: NO. Absent exigent circumstances, a law enforcement officer may not make a warrantless, nonconsensual entry into a suspect's home to arrest him even though probable cause exists to believe the suspect is, in fact, the perpetrator of a felony. *Id.* at 1374, 1375.

RATIONALE: A New York statute allowed police officers to conduct warrantless entries into suspects' homes with force, if necessary, to make routine felony arrests. The defendants challenged the constitutionality of this statute and their arrests by the New York police. In both cases (consolidated by the Supreme Court for review), the New York police conducted warrantless, nonconsensual entries into the defendants' homes in the absence of "exigent circumstances." [Exigent circumstances are real emergencies or dangerous situations which necessitate swift and immediate official action.]

The Court, speaking through Justice Stevens, holds that such entries are not permitted. "[T]he Fourth Amendment has drawn a firm line at the entrance to the house. Absent exigent circumstances, that threshold may not reasonably be crossed without a warrant." *Id.* at 1382. The intrusion into a person's home "is simply too substantial an invasion to allow without a warrant, at least in the absence of exigent circumstances, even when it is accomplished under statutory authority and when probable cause is clearly present." *Id.* at 1381 (quoting from *United States v. Reed*, 572 F.2d 412, 423 (2nd Cir. 1978)).

The thrust of the Fourth Amendment is that "[t]he right of the people to be secure in their * * * houses * * * shall not be violated." As a result, the Court construes this Amendment to bar warrantless, nonconsensual entries into suspects' homes absent exigent circumstances even when there is ample probable cause to believe the suspect is the perpetrator of a felony.

The arrest warrant will necessarily "suffice to interpose [a judge's] determination of probable cause between the zealous officer and the citizen." *Id.* at 1388. If the judge issues the warrant, "it is constitutionally reasonable to require [the suspect] to open his door to the officers of the law." *Id.* Therefore, "for Fourth Amendment purposes, an arrest warrant founded on probable cause implicitly carries with it the limited authority to enter a dwelling in which the suspect lives when there is reason to believe the suspect is within." *Id.*

NOTE

1. The New York statute addressed in *Payton, supra,* was found to be unconstitutional as violative of the Fourth Amendment.

2. The United States Supreme Court has observed that "physical entry of the home is the chief evil against which the wording of the Fourth Amendment is directed." *United States v. United States Dist. Court,* 407 *U.S.* 297, 313, 92 *S.Ct.* 2125, 2134 (1972). In the context of warrantless home entries, it should be emphasized that the doctrine of "exigent circumstances" will permit such an intrusion only where there is also probable cause to enter the home. *United States v. Sangineto-Miranda,* 859 *F.*2d 1501, 1511 n.6 (6th Cir. 1988); *United States v. Socey,* 846 *F.*2d 1439, 1444 n.5 (D.C. Cir. 1988); *United States v. Aquino,* 836 *F.*2d 1268, 1272 (10th Cir. 1988); *United States v. Howard,* 828 *F.*2d 552, 555 (9th Cir. 1987); *United States v. Cresta,* 825 *F.*2d 538, 553 (1st Cir. 1987). For a focused discussion of the exigent circumstances doctrine *see* §3.3, *infra.*

3. "Under *Payton,* officers executing an arrest warrant must have a '*reasonable belief* that the suspect resides at the place to be entered . . . and [have] reason to believe that the suspect is present' at the time the warrant is executed." *United States v. Risse,* 83 *F.*3d 212, 216 (8th Cir. 1996) (quoting *United States v. Lauter,* 57 *F.*3d 212, 215 (2nd Cir. 1995)). [Emphasis added.] *See also United States v. Magluta,* 44 *F.*3d 1530, 1535 (11th Cir. 1995); *Perez v. Simmons,* 998 *F.*2d 775, 776 (9th Cir. 1993). The officer's assessment need not in fact be correct; rather, the officer need only "reasonably believe" that the suspect resides at the dwelling to be entered and is present when the warrant is to be executed. *See Risse* at 216.

4. *The requirement of exigent circumstances in addition to probable cause.* In *Kirk v. Louisiana,* 536 *U.S.* 635, 122 *S.Ct.* 2458 (2002), police officers conducted a surveillance of defendant's home, based on an anonymous tip that drug sales were occurring there. After witnessing what appeared to be several drug purchases and allowing the buyers to leave the area, the officers stopped one of the buyers on the

street outside defendant's apartment. Immediately thereafter, the officers knocked on the door of the apartment, entered, and placed defendant under arrest. A search incident to the arrest uncovered a vial of cocaine found in defendant's underwear. In addition, while in the apartment, the officers observed other contraband in "plain view."

Finding the entry, arrest and search invalid under the rule set forth in *Payton*, the Court said:

> Here, the police had neither an arrest warrant for [defendant], nor a search warrant for [his] apartment, when they entered his home, arrested him, and searched him. The officers testified at the suppression hearing that the reason for their actions was a fear that evidence would be destroyed, but the Louisiana Court of Appeal did not determine that such exigent circumstances were present. * * * As *Payton* makes plain, police officers need either a warrant or probable cause plus exigent circumstances in order to make a lawful entry into a home.

Id., 122 *S.Ct.* at 2459.

5. *Assessing exigent circumstances.* In *United States v. Cattouse*, 846 *F.*2d 144 (2nd Cir. 1988), the Court of Appeals for the Second Circuit emphasized that the holding in *Payton v. New York* stands for the proposition that "[a] warrantless arrest of a person in his own home is 'presumptively unreasonable,' * * * and therefore prohibited by the fourth amendment, unless the government can show that 'exigent circumstances' required that the arrest be made before a warrant could be obtained." *Cattouse* at 146 (quoting *Payton* at 586, 100 *S.Ct.* at 1380). According to the court in *Cattouse*, there are several factors which may be considered when a determination must be made as to whether exigent circumstances existed at the time of the arrest to justify the warrantless entry of the prospective arrestee's home. These include, but are not limited to, "(1) the gravity or violent nature of the offense with which the suspect is to be charged; (2) whether the suspect 'is reasonably believed to be armed'; (3) 'a clear showing of probable cause * * * to believe the suspect committed the crime'; (4) 'strong reason to believe that the suspect is in the premises being entered'; (5) 'a likelihood that the suspect will escape if not swiftly apprehended'; and (6) the peaceful circumstances of the entry." *Id.* at 146 (quoting *United States v. Martinez-Gonzalez*, 686 *F.*2d 93, 100 (2nd Cir. 1982) and *United States v. Reed*, 572 *F.*2d 412, 424 (2nd Cir. 1978)). Moreover, as the court pointed out in *Cattouse*, this list is "illustrative, not exclusive," and "[t]he presence or absence of any one factor is not conclusive; rather, the essential question is whether there was 'urgent need' that 'justif[ied]' the warrantless entry." *Id.* at 146, 147. [Citation omitted.]

6. *Payton violations and the limits of the exclusionary rule.* Exactly how far will the exclusionary rule reach when a court determines that officers have violated the rule in *Payton* by effecting a warrantless nonconsensual entry into a suspect's home in order to make a routine felony arrest ? In *New York v. Harris*, 495 *U.S.* 14, 110 *S.Ct.* 1640 (1990),

the Court held that only that evidence which is obtained inside the home is the proper subject of suppression. So long as police have the requisite probable cause for the suspect's arrest (for a crime), any physical evidence or statements validly obtained after the arrest and outside the home will not be suppressed when neither is "the fruit of the fact that the arrest was made in the house rather than some place else." *Id.*, 110 *S.Ct.* at 1644. In this respect, the Court reasoned: "Even though we decline to suppress statements made *outside* the home following a *Payton* violation, the principal incentive to obey *Payton* still obtains: the police know that a warrantless entry will lead to the suppression of any evidence found or statements taken *inside* the home." *Harris* at 1644. [Emphasis added.] Further, the Court observed:

> Nothing in the reasoning of [the *Payton*] case suggests that an arrest in a home without a warrant but with probable cause somehow renders unlawful continued custody of the suspect once he is removed from the house. There could be no valid claim here that Harris is immune from prosecution because his person was the fruit of an illegal arrest. * * * Nor is there any claim that the warrantless arrest required the police to release Harris or that Harris could not be immediately rearrested if momentarily released. Because the officers had probable cause to arrest Harris for a crime, Harris was not unlawfully in custody when he was removed to the station house, given *Miranda* warnings and allowed to talk. * * *

Id. at 1643.

7. *Warrantless entry to monitor the movements of an arrestee.* In *Washington v. Chrisman*, 455 *U.S.* 1, 102 *S.Ct.* 812 (1982), the United States Supreme Court held that once an officer has effected a valid arrest of an individual, it is within that officer's authority to maintain custody and control over the arrestee and monitor his movements. Therefore, if the arrestee requests to go to his home to retrieve an item, such as his or her identification, the officer has a right to remain literally at the arrestee's elbow and seize any contraband discovered there in plain view. *Id.*, 102 *S.Ct.* at 816, 817.

In *Chrisman*, a campus police officer observed a student on school property carrying a half-gallon bottle of gin. Recognizing that such possession by an under-age student on campus is prohibited by law, the officer stopped the student and asked for identification. The student responded that the identification was back in his dorm room and that he would go get it. The officer followed the student (now under arrest) to his room. In the room, the officer observed marihuana seeds and a small smoking pipe lying on a desk in plain view.

According to the Court, "it is not unreasonable under the Fourth Amendment for a police officer, as a matter of routine, to monitor the movements of an arrested person, as his judgment dictates, following the arrest." *Id.* at 817. The safety of the officer plus the efficacy of the arrest necessitates such surveillance, which "is not an impermissible invasion of the privacy or personal liberty of an individual who has been arrested." *Id.* As stated by the Court, this "is a classic instance of incriminating evidence found in plain view when a police officer, for unrelated but entirely legitimate reasons, obtains lawful access to an individual's area of privacy." *Id.*

8. *The knock and announce rule.* 18 *U.S.C.* §3109 prohibits a federal officer from forcefully entering any dwelling for the purpose of executing a search warrant unless, "after notice of his authority and purpose" is given, "he is refused admittance." This requirement has also been applied in warrantless, in-home arrest contexts. *Ker v. California,* 374 *U.S.* 23, 39-40, 83 *S.Ct.* 1623, 1633 (1963). *See also United States v. Wylie,* 462 *F.2d* 1178, 1185 (D.C. Cir. 1972), where the court held that Section 3109 criteria govern entries "not only for warranted searches but also those contemplating warrantless arrests." Additionally, the court found that Section 3109 comes into play "even though the circumstances may be sufficiently exigent to dispense with the need for a warrant." *Id.* at 1185 (citing *Miller v. United States,* 357 *U.S.* 301, 78 *S.Ct.* 1190, (1958)). Judicial application of the knock and announce rule in warrantless, in-home arrest contexts demonstrates the interplay between the statutory commands of Section 3109 and the reasonableness requirement of the Fourth Amendment.

Exceptions to the knock and announce rule. The exceptions to the knock and announce rule which apply in the search warrant execution context apply with equal force in warrantless, in-home arrest situations. Thus, strict obedience to the rule is unnecessary when a victim or some other person is in peril, *Ker v. California, supra;* when the announcement would increase the risk of harm to the officers or others, *id.*; where there is a danger of flight, *id.*; where there is a danger of destruction of evidence, *id.*; or when the announcement would constitute a "useless gesture," either because it is clear to the officers that the occupant already knows the officers' purpose and authority, *Miller v. United States,* 357 *U.S.* 301, 78 *S.Ct.* 1190 (1958), or because the occupant is totally oblivious to the presence and the objective of the police officers seeking entry, *United States v. Wylie, supra,* 462 *F.2d* at 1187; *Bosley v. United States,* 426 *F.2d* 1257, 1262 (1970).

As the Court observed in *Ker, supra:*

"It must be borne in mind that the primary purpose of the constitutional guarantee is to prevent unreasonable invasions of the security of the people in their persons, houses, papers, and effects, and when an officer has reasonable cause to enter a dwelling to make an arrest and as an incident to that arrest is authorized to make a reasonable search, his entry and his search are not unreasonable. Suspects have no constitutional right to destroy or dispose of evidence, and no basic constitutional guarantees are violated because an officer succeeds in getting to a place where he is entitled to be more quickly than he would, had he complied with [the knock and announce rule. C]ompliance is not required if the officer's peril*

*would have been increased or the arrest frustrated had he de-
manded entrance and stated his purpose."*

Ker, supra at 39-40, 83 *S.Ct.* at 1633 (quoting *People v. Maddox*, 46
*Cal.*2d 301, 306, 294 *P.*2d 6, 9 (1956)). [Emphasis added.] For a further
discussion of the knock and announce rule, *see* §2.5(b), *infra*.

9. *Warrantless entry of a houseboat.* In *United States v. Hill*, 855
*F.*2d 664 (10th Cir. 1988), the court held that the principle of *Payton*,
requiring a warrant for an arrest in a suspect's home, does not apply
to a readily mobile houseboat: "We therefore hold that the houseboat
falls within the vehicle exception. * * * [B]ecause the houseboat could
have been searched without a warrant, the rule of *Payton* * * * is inapplicable." *Id.* at 668. [Emphasis added.] Interestingly, the *Hill* court
applied a search and seizure of property analysis to a set of circumstances involving a warrantless entry of a suspect's "dwelling" to effect
his arrest. *Payton* seems to lend support to such an analysis. *See id.* at
585-590, 100 *S.Ct.* at 1379-1382 (applying search and seizure principles in the arrest context). According to the court in *Hill*, "[i]f the police could have constitutionally boarded the houseboat to search it
without a warrant, then no warrant was necessary to board the boat
in order to arrest [the defendants]." *Hill* at 667.

10. *Probable cause to arrest developed during course of search warrant execution.* In *Payton v. New York*, the Court made clear that, absent exigent circumstances or a valid consent, an officer must obtain an
arrest warrant before entering a suspect's home to make an arrest. In
Mahlberg v. Mentzer, 968 *F.*2d 772 (8th Cir. 1992), police were in the
process of executing a search warrant for stolen property at Mahlberg's
home. Mahlberg returned home during the search and assisted the officers in locating the sought-after evidence. Immediately after the officers took custody of the stolen property, they arrested Mahlberg in his
home without a warrant. According to Mahlberg, his arrest was illegal
under *Payton* because the officers had neither an arrest warrant nor
exigent circumstances to justify arresting him in his home.

Rejecting Mahlberg's contention, the Court of Appeals for the
Eighth Circuit explained:

> Mahlberg reads *Payton* too broadly. "Physical entry of the home is
> the chief evil against which the wording of the Fourth Amendment
> is directed." * * * Therefore, "an entry to arrest and an entry to
> search for and to seize property implicate the same interest in pre-
> serving the privacy and sanctity of the home, and justify the same
> level of constitutional protection." * * * The officers were lawfully
> in Mahlberg's home to search. Mahlberg was present during the
> search, so his arrest did not extend the scope or duration of the
> search in any way. With the evidence this search produced, [the of-
> ficers] could have arrested Mahlberg without a warrant outside of
> his home. *We see no Fourth Amendment distinction between the au-
> thority to seize items in plain view incident to a lawful search and
> the authority to arrest a suspect in his home when the lawful search*

uncovers probable cause that the suspect has committed a crime. * * * Indeed the opposite conclusion would lead to absurd results. * * * The Fourth Amendment is concerned with reasonableness, not with meaningless formalities.

Id. at 775 (quoting *Payton* at 585, 588, 100 *S.Ct.* at 1379, 1381). [Emphasis added.]

11. *Presence of media during warrant execution violates the Fourth Amendment.* In *Wilson v. Layne*, 526 *U.S.* 603, 119 *S.Ct.* 1692 (1999), the United States Supreme Court held that "it is a violation of the Fourth Amendment for police to bring members of the media or other third parties into a home during the execution of a warrant when the presence of the third parties in the home was not in aid of the execution of the warrant." *Id.*, 119 *S.Ct.* at 1699. [For an extended discussion of this case, *see* §4.1.]

UNITED STATES v. SANTANA
Supreme Court of the United States
427 *U.S.* 38, 96 *S.Ct.* 2406 (1976)

QUESTION: May a suspect defeat a warrantless felony arrest, which is set in motion at the doorway of the suspect's home, by retreating into the home ?

ANSWER: NO. "[A] suspect may not defeat an arrest which has been set in motion in a public place * * * by the expedient of escaping to a private place." *Id.* at 2410.

RATIONALE: During the course of a narcotics investigation, members of the Philadelphia Narcotics Squad developed probable cause to believe that defendant, Dominga Santana, was involved in a narcotics distribution scheme and in possession of marked money used to make an earlier "controlled buy" of heroin. Based on this information, the officers went to Santana's home and saw her standing in the doorway of the house with a brown paper bag in her hand. The officers "pulled up within 15 feet of Santana and got out of their van, shouting 'police,' and displaying their identification. As the officers approached, Santana retreated into the vestibule of her house. The officers followed through the open door, catching her in the vestibule. As she tried to pull away, the bag tilted and 'two bundles of glazed paper packets with a white powder' fell to the floor. * * * When Santana was told to empty her pockets she produced $135, $70 of which could be identified as [the] marked money. The white powder in the bag was later determined to be heroin." *Id.* at 2408-2409.

According to the United States Supreme Court, the arrest of Santana and seizure of the evidence was entirely proper.

It is well settled that the Fourth Amendment permits the warrantless felony arrest of an individual in a public place upon probable cause. *United States v. Watson*, 423 *U.S.* 411, 96 *S.Ct.* 820 (1976). The first question, therefore, "is whether, when the police first sought to arrest Santana, she was in a public place." *Santana* at 2409. "While it may be true that under the common law of property the threshold of one's dwelling is 'private,' as is the yard surrounding the house, it is nonetheless clear that under the cases interpreting the Fourth Amendment *Santana was in a 'public' place*. She was not in an area where she had any expectation of privacy." *Id.* [Emphasis added.] As the Court stated in *Katz v. United States*, 389 *U.S.* 347, 351, 88 *S.Ct.* 507, 511 (1967): "What a person knowingly exposes to the public, even in his own house or office, is not a subject of Fourth Amendment protection."

At the doorway of her house, Santana "was not merely visible to the public but was as exposed to public view, speech, hearing, and touch as if she had been standing completely outside her house. * * * Thus, when the police, who concededly had probable cause to do so, sought to arrest her, they merely intended to perform a function which [this Court] approved in *Watson*." *Santana* at 2409.

"The only remaining question is whether her act of retreating into her house could thwart an otherwise proper arrest. [The Court holds] that it could not." *Id.* In *Warden v. Hayden* 387 *U.S.* 294, 87 *S.Ct.* 1642 (1967), the Court recognized the right of police, who had probable cause to believe that an armed robber had entered a house a few minutes before, to make a warrantless entry to arrest the robber. This right was based upon the "exigencies of the situation." *Warden* at 298, 87 *S.Ct.* at 1645.

The present case, "involving a true 'hot pursuit,' is clearly governed by *Warden*[.] * * * The fact that the pursuit here ended almost as soon as it began did not render it any the less a 'hot pursuit' sufficient to justify the warrantless entry into Santana's house." *Santana* at 2409-2410. Certainly, the term " 'hot pursuit' means some sort of chase, but it need not be an extended hue and cry 'in and about (the) public streets.' " *Id.* at 2410. Moreover, "[o]nce Santana saw the police there was likewise a realistic expectation that any delay would result in destruction of evidence." *Id.*

Accordingly, "a suspect may not defeat an arrest which has been set in motion in a public place, and is therefore proper under *Watson*, by the expedient of escaping to a private place." *Id.* The search, therefore, incident to Santana's valid arrest, "which produced the drugs and money was clearly justified." *Id.*

NOTE

1. *The doorway to one's home.*

(a) A number of jurisdictions have held, in general, that a warrantless arrest of an individual at the doorway of his or her home (or hotel or motel room) is lawful. *See e.g., United States v. Sewell*, 942 *F.*2d 1209 (7th Cir. 1991); *United States v. Carrion*, 809 *F.*2d 1120 (5th Cir. 1987); *United States v. Whitten*, 706 *F.*2d 1000 (9th Cir. 1983), *cert. denied*, 465 *U.S.* 1100, 104 *S.Ct.* 1593 (1984); *People v. Burns*, 200 *Colo.* 387, 615 *P.*2d 686 (1980); *Byrd v. State*, 481 *So.*2d 468 (Fla. 1985); *People* *v. Morgan,* 113 *Ill.App.*3d 543, 69 *Ill.Dec.* 590, 447 *N.E.*2d 1025 (1983); *Costillo v. Commissioner of Public Safety,* 416 *N.W.*2d 730 (Minn. 1987); *Edwards v. State,* 107 *Nev.* 150, 808 *P.*2d 528 (1991).

(b) A minority of jurisdictions have determined, however, that an individual does not surrender his or her reasonable expectation of privacy merely by opening his or her door in response to a knock by the police. Under these cases, it is arguably a violation of the Fourth Amendment for the police to arrest without a warrant an individual standing in the doorway to his or her home without the individual's acquiescence to the arrest. *See United States v. Berkowitz,* 927 *F.*2d 1376 (7th Cir. 1991); *United States v. McCraw,* 920 *F.*2d 224 (4th Cir. 1990); *Duncan v. Storie,* 869 *F.*2d 1100 (8th Cir.), *cert. denied,* 493 *U.S.* 852, 110 *S.Ct.* 152 (1989); *State v. Schlothauer,* 206 *Neb.* 670, 294 *N.W.*2d 382 (1980).

2. *Arresting a suspect after he comes out of his home pursuant to an order to exit.* A valid doorway arrest under *Santana* may be rendered unlawful under *Payton* if the defendant opens the door and exits his residence in response to coercive police activity outside the residence, such as flooding the residence with spotlights and calling to the defendant with bullhorns, or in response to deception, such as the police misrepresenting their identity when the defendant asked who was there before opening the door. *See e.g., United States v. Edmondson,* 791 *F.*2d 1512 (11th Cir. 1986); *United States v. Al-Azzawy,* 784 *F.*2d 890 (9th Cir. 1985); *United States v. Morgan,* 743 *F.*2d 1158 (6th Cir. 1984).

(a) In *United States v. Al-Azzawy, supra,* at about 9:00 a.m., police were summoned to investigate a disturbance at a trailer park. Upon their arrival, officers were met by Steven Williams, one of the park's residents. Williams told the officers that one of his neighbors, Al-Azzawy, had threatened to shoot him, to blow up the trailer park and to burn Williams' trailer. Williams also told the police that Al-Azzawy threatened him with a gun the day before.

The officers surrounded Al-Azzawy's trailer with their guns drawn, and ordered Al-Azzawy to come outside. When Al-Azzawy appeared, he was ordered to get on his knees and place his hands on his head, which he did. He was then frisked and questioned about the disturbance. Al-Azzawy admitted to having firearms in his trailer. Thereafter, during a consent-search of Al-Azzawy's trailer, police seized sawed-off weapons, an automatic pistol, three hand grenades, gunpowder, a gallon jug full of gasoline with matches glued to it, and other items.

The district court suppressed all evidence seized, holding that Al-Azzawy was arrested in his home without a warrant in violation of *Payton.* On appeal, the Ninth Circuit agreed with the district court that a warrantless arrest occurred as Al-Azzawy stood inside his residence. *Id.* at 893. The court reasoned:

[T]he police had completely surrounded [Al-Azzawy's] trailer with their weapons drawn and ordered him through a bullhorn to leave the trailer and drop to his knees. [He] was not free to leave, his freedom of movement was totally restricted, and the officers' show of force and authority was overwhelming. Any reasonable person would have believed he was under arrest in these circumstances. Moreover, since [Al-Azzawy] was in his trailer at the time he was surrounded by armed officers, and since he did not voluntarily expose himself to their view or control outside his trailer but only emerged under circumstances of extreme coercion, *the arrest occurred while he was still inside his trailer.*

Id. [Emphasis added.] *Cf. Elder v. Holloway,* 510 *U.S.* 510, 114 *S.Ct.* 1019, 1022 (1994) (*Al-Azzawy* explicitly "reaffirmed the rule that 'it is the location of the arrested person, and not the arresting agents, that determines whether an arrest occurs within a home.'") (citations omitted).

The court in *Al-Azzawy* ultimately ruled that exigent circumstances justified Al-Azzawy's warrantless arrest. *Id.* at 894.

(b) *See also United States v. Johnson,* 626 *F.*2d 753 (9th Cir. 1980), *aff'd on other grounds,* 457 *U.S.* 537, 102 *S.Ct.* 2579 (1982), where the court determined that the defendant was "arrested" as he stood inside his home and federal officers stood outside his home with guns drawn. Here, in *Johnson,* Treasury Agents converged on defendant Johnson's house, armed with information that Johnson was involved in a scheme to unlawfully cash a United States Treasury check written in the amount of $4,681.00. As the agents approached defendant's doorway, they drew their weapons, pointed them downward and knocked, at first identifying themselves by fictitious names. When defendant opened the door, the agents identified themselves and asked to talk with defendant. Defendant told the agents to come in. It was at this point that the court found defendant to be "under arrest." *Id.* at 755.

Finding the arrest unlawful, the court distinguished the facts in *Santana,* and noted that the defendant in *Johnson* "opened the door of his dwelling after the agents misrepresented their identities; thus, Johnson's initial exposure to the view and physical control of the agents was not consensual on his part. * * * Moreover, Johnson's invitation to the agents to enter after the door was opened was hardly voluntary in light of the coercive effect of the weapons brandished by the agents." *Id.* at 757.

This is not the typical case where the arrest occurs after the officers make entry. "In this case," the court said, "we are confronted with the situation where the suspect was arrested as he stood inside his home and the officers stood outside his home with drawn weapons. *In these circumstances, it is the location of the arrested person, and not the arresting agents, that determines whether an arrest occurs within a home.* Otherwise, arresting officers could avoid illegal 'entry' into a home simply by remaining outside the doorway and controlling the movements of suspects within through the use of weapons that greatly extend the 'reach' of the arresting officers." *Id.* [Emphasis added.] According to the court, "it cannot be said that Johnson voluntarily exposed himself to warrantless arrest by opening his door to agents who misrepresented their identities." *Id.* Because Johnson's arrest did not occur in a "public" place, but instead, as he stood within the "zone of privacy" of his home, it violated the Fourth Amendment. *Id.*

WELSH v. WISCONSIN
Supreme Court of the United States
466 *U.S.* 740, 104 *S.Ct.* 2091 (1984)

QUESTION: May law enforcement officers conduct a warrantless entry into a suspect's home to arrest him for a nonjailable traffic offense, when they have probable cause to believe the suspect is, in fact, the perpetrator of the offense ?

ANSWER: NO. The Fourth Amendment bars the warrantless entry into a suspect's home to affect his arrest when the underlying offense is a "nonjailable traffic offense," and the circumstances do not amount to an exigency. *Id.* at 2093.

RATIONALE: Officers gained entry into the defendant's home and arrested him for driving while intoxicated. They acted on information received from a witness who observed the defendant driving erratically, veering from roadside to roadside, and finally swerving off the road. The defendant abandoned his vehicle in the presence of the witness and walked home. Within minutes the police arrived on the scene. The witness relayed the events "specifically noting that the driver was very inebriated or very sick." *Id.* at 2094. The officers checked the registration of the vehicle for ownership, discovered that the defendant lived nearby, and responded to his home to effect his arrest.

The defendant contends that the warrantless arrest was invalid. *The United States Supreme Court agreed.*

The Court, speaking through Justice Brennan, cautions law enforcement personnel with the reminder that "as a basic principle of Fourth Amendment law[,] * * * searches and seizures inside a home without a warrant are presumptively unreasonable." *Id.* at 2097 (quoting *Payton v. New York*, 445 *U.S.* 573, 586, 100 *S.Ct.* 1371, 1380 (1980)). The police must not only have probable cause, but they must display the presence of "exigent circumstances." *Welsh* at 2097. The *Payton* decision, while allowing warrantless home arrests upon a showing of probable cause AND exigent circumstances, was expressly limited to felony arrests." *Welsh* at 2097 n.11.

The arrest here was for a nonjailable traffic offense. "When the government's interest is only to arrest for a minor offense, that presumption of unreasonableness is difficult to rebut[.]" *Id.* at 2098. Minor offenses will generally *not* give rise to the requisite exigent circumstances. The exigent circumstances exception to the warrant requirement is strictly limited, and, when applied, will be closely scrutinized for real, rather than imagined or contrived emergencies.

As a result, "an important factor to be considered when determining whether any exigency exists is the gravity of the underlying offense for which the arrest is being made." *Id.* at 2099. If the underlying offense is a serious crime, probable cause alone will not create the exigency. More is required. [Such examples might include hot pursuit of a fleeing felon, destruction of evidence, a working fire, etc.] It is even more difficult to establish the requisite exigent circumstances "when there is probable cause to believe that only a minor offense * * * has been committed." *Id.*

Thus, the "exigent circumstances exception in the context of a home entry should rarely be [permitted when the arrest is based on] probable cause to believe that only a minor offense * * * has been committed." *Id.*

IN RE SEALED CASE No. 96-3167
United States Court of Appeals
153 *F.*3d 759 (D.C.Cir. 1998)

QUESTION: In the below set of circumstances, was the warrantless entry justified by probable cause and "exigent circumstances"?

CIRCUMSTANCES: In the early evening, Officers Riddle and Wilber were driving in an unmarked patrol car through a residential neighborhood in northeast Washington, D.C. While on patrol, they observed defendant running or "walking quickly" down the street. *Id.* at 762. Neither officer knew defendant or knew where he lived. The officers followed him until he came to a house. "Neither officer knew who lived in the house. They watched as the defendant ran up a path leading to the front door, opened the outer screen door, and 'struck the wooden door * * * with his shoulder in such a force that * * * it appeared * * * he was forcing the door open.' " *Id.* The officers decided to approach and investigate.

As Officer Wilber went to the back door, Officer Riddle walked to the front, where he noticed that the wood around the door lock was broken, leading him "to believe that the house was being burglarized." *Id.* There were no lights on in the downstairs area of the house and it was dark inside. "Riddle loudly and repeatedly announced that he was a police officer, but received no response. After again announcing his presence, Riddle tried to push on the front door. Someone immediately pushed back from the other side without saying anything. This pushing back and forth lasted approximately five to ten seconds, after which the pushing on the other side stopped and Riddle could hear footsteps away from the door. Based on what he had seen, Officer Riddle 'believed that someone was burglarizing the house with the intent to either steal an item or injure someone within the house.' " *Id.*

Riddle then entered the house, saw defendant running up a flight of steps, and chased after him. Ultimately, the officers placed defendant in custody. In the large bedroom where defendant was apprehended, Officer Riddle discovered " 'laying in a chair, a plastic bag, which appeared to have busted open, or come open in some manner, and several large white rocks,' later identified as crack cocaine. On the floor beside the chair was a semiautomatic handgun." *Id.* at 763.

ANSWER: YES. "[P]robable cause to believe a burglary is in progress constitutes exigent circumstances sufficient to permit [a] warrantless entry." *Id.* at 766.

RATIONALE: " 'It is axiomatic that the physical entry of the home is the chief evil against which the wording of the Fourth Amendment is directed.' " *Id.* at 764 (quoting *Welsh v. Wisconsin*, 466 *U.S.* 740, 748, 104 *S.Ct.* 2091, 2097 (1984)). As a result, searches and seizures conducted in a person's home without a warrant are presumptively unreasonable unless the police can demonstrate the presence of "exigent circumstances." Similarly, "warrantless felony arrests in the home are prohibited by the Fourth Amendment, absent probable cause and exigent circumstances." *Id.*

In this case, the police did not have a warrant. Therefore, in order for the entry of defendant's house to be lawful, "the government must meet two distinct burdens: it must demonstrate that the police had probable cause to believe a crime was being committed, and that there were exigent circumstances justifying the police's failure to procure a warrant." *Id.*

Preliminarily, the court held that the officers had probable cause to believe a burglary was in progress. In this respect, the court observed:

> The police observed someone appear to break open the door to an unlit house and enter it without turning on the lights. When the police approached the door to investigate, they discovered that the lock was indeed broken. When Riddle identified himself as a police officer, the person who had entered the house did not respond in any way. And, when Riddle again identified himself as a police officer and tested the door, the person inside pushed back for several seconds. The officer then heard steps going away from the door. The totality of these circumstances gave the officer probable cause to believe a burglary was in progress.

Id.

In burglary cases, a "forced door or window" is a commonly recognized element. The same may be said of "the absence of lights," and of "silence in response to an officer's calls." *Id.* at 764-65. Defendant's "apparent flight away from the door also added to the probable cause." *Id.* at 765. Moreover, when Officer Riddle pushed against the door and "defendant pushed back without any explanation, without requesting identification from the officer, and without identifying himself as the homeowner," the officer had "further grounds to believe he had discovered a burglary." *Id.*

The court also determined that it was "irrelevant to the probable cause inquiry that the officers later learned the defendant had entered his own house, and that he later offered evidence that the door had been broken for several years prior to this incident. The officers did not know these things at the time they entered the home." *Id.* What mattered, held the court, was "their reasonable belief that unlawful activity was in progress at the time of the entry and arrest." *Id.*

"Probable cause alone does not justify the warrantless entry of a home. There must also be some exception to the warrant requirement." *Id.* Although the court based its decision on the theory of "exigent circumstances," instead of "hot pursuit," it did pause to observe:

> "Hot pursuit" is, of course, just one form of "exigent circumstance." * * * The Supreme Court also has recognized that "[t]he need to protect or preserve life or avoid serious injury is justification for what would be otherwise illegal absent an exigency or emergency." [*See also*] *Minnesota v. Olson*, 495 *U.S.* 91, 100, 110 *S.Ct.* 1684 (1990) (recognizing that warrantless entry may be justified by "the risk of danger to the police or to other persons inside or outside the dwelling") * * *.

Id. at 766.

While the United States Supreme Court has not provided a catalog of all possible exigencies, this Circuit has recognized that "[t]he test for exigent circumstances is whether police had an 'urgent need' or 'an immediate major crisis in the performance of duty afford[ing] neither time nor opportunity to apply to a magistrate.' " *Id.* (quoting *United States v. (James) Johnson*, 802 *F.*2d 1459, 1461 (D.C.Cir. 1986). *See also United States v. MacDonald*, 916 *F.*2d 766, 769 (2d Cir. 1990) (en banc) ("The essential question in determining whether exigent circumstances justified a warrantless entry is whether law enforcement agents were confronted by an 'urgent need' to render aid or take action.").

As a general matter, the government shoulders the "heavy burden" of establishing "urgent need." Similar to the assessment of probable cause, "the question of whether there were 'exigent circumstances' is judged according to the totality of the circumstances. * * * And like the standard for probable cause, the standard for exigent circumstances is an objective one, focusing 'on what a reasonable, experienced police officer would believe.' " *Id.* [Citations omitted.]

In this case, the officers' belief that defendant "was engaged in an ongoing burglary attempt that could have endangered the occupants of the house if the police had paused to obtain a warrant" was "objectively reasonable." *Id.* Indeed, "[n]umerous other circuits have found that probable cause to believe a burglary is in progress constitutes exigent circumstances sufficient to permit warrantless entry." *Id.*

Burglarizing a dwelling " 'creates a substantial risk of confrontation between the perpetrator and an occupant. * * * And where such a confrontation occurs, there is a substantial risk that serious injury * * * will occur.' " *Id.* [Citation omitted.] Thus, "*[t]he need to prevent such a confrontation, by intercepting the burglar before he potentially confronts (or is confronted by) an occupant, is surely an exigent circumstance.*" *Id.* at 767. [Emphasis added.] Indeed, the police "did not have to wait until they heard shots fired or an occupant scream. By that time, the purpose of permitting immediate entry—preventing such shots and screams—would have been lost. 'Speed here was essential,' * * * and that is the essence of an exigent circumstance." *Id.*

Accordingly, the officers' entry "to prevent what appeared to be a burglary in progress" was constitutional, and for the same reason, "the warrantless apprehension of the defendant for that suspected burglary was lawful." *Id.*

STEAGALD v. UNITED STATES
Supreme Court of the United States
451 *U.S.* 204, 101 *S.Ct.* 1642 (1981)

QUESTION: May law enforcement officers legally search for the subject of an arrest warrant in the home of a third party without first obtaining a search warrant ?

ANSWER: NO. Absent consent or exigent circumstances, law enforcement officers may not legally "search for the subject of an arrest warrant in the home of a third party without first obtaining a search warrant." *Id.* at 1644.

RATIONALE: Federal agents received information that a particular fugitive could be found at the home of another party in Atlanta, Georgia. The agents, armed with an arrest warrant for the fugitive, forcibly entered the home of the defendant and searched for the fugitive. The search of the defendant's home did not produce the fugitive, but it did produce 43 pounds of cocaine.

The defendant moved to suppress the cocaine on the ground that the federal agents illegally obtained it by failing to secure a search warrant for the fugitive before entering his home.

The Supreme Court of the United States agreed. Although the federal agents had an arrest warrant for the fugitive, the Fourth Amendment claim is not raised by that fugitive. Rather, the "challenge to the search is asserted by a person not named in the warrant who was convicted on the basis of evidence uncovered during a search of his residence for [a fugitive from justice]." *Id.* at 1647.

The question boils down to "whether an arrest warrant—as opposed to a search warrant—is adequate to protect the Fourth Amendment interests of persons not named in the warrant, when their homes are searched without their consent and in the absence of exigent circumstances." *Id.* at 1648.

The Court holds that it is not and reasons that a search warrant is necessary to protect the Fourth Amendment interests of persons not named in the arrest warrant. While the warrant here demonstrated a judicial finding that there was probable cause to believe the fugitive had committed a felony, it only authorized the seizure of that fugitive. It did not authorize the invasion of the defendant's home to search for the fugitive.

The Government asserts that this unduly hampers law enforcement given the ready mobility of persons. The Court rejects this assertion and explains that "the subject of an arrest can be readily seized before entering or after leaving the home of a third party." *Id.* at 1652. Any additional burden placed on law enforcement by a search warrant requirement is outweighed by the right of "innocent people to be secure in their homes from unjustified, forcible intrusions by the Government[.]" *Id.* at 1653.

NOTE

1. *The interests at stake.* The Fourth Amendment claim in *Steagald* was asserted by a person not named in the warrant who was convicted on the basis of evidence uncovered during a search of his residence for a fugitive. The "narrow issue" addressed by the Court, therefore, was "whether an arrest warrant—as opposed to a search warrant—is adequate to protect the Fourth Amendment interests of *persons not named in the warrant*, when their homes are searched without their consent and in the absence of exigent circumstances." *Id.* at 212, 101 *S.Ct.* at 1648. [Emphasis added.] Stated another way, the issue was "not whether the subject of an arrest warrant can object to the absence of a search warrant when he is apprehended in another's home, but rather whether the residents of that home can complain of the search." Significantly, the Court in *Steagald* did not decide whether the person named in the warrant could successfully challenge his arrest and the fruits thereof on the grounds that his arrest occurred in the home of a third party in the absence of a search warrant.

2. *Overnight guests.* In *Minnesota v. Olson,* 495 *U.S.* 91, 110 *S.Ct.* 1684 (1990), the Supreme Court rejected the State's contention that defendant's status as an "overnight guest" (at a duplex) precludes a finding of a Fourth Amendment violation by the government's warrantless, non-consensual entry to effect his arrest because defendant could not claim to have the reasonable expectation of privacy normally enjoyed by a householder. According to the Court, defendant's "status as an overnight guest is *alone* enough to show that he had an expectation of privacy in the home that society is prepared to recognize as reasonable." *Id.,* 110 *S.Ct.* at 1688. [Emphasis added.] This decision reaffirms the established principle that " 'a person can have a legally sufficient interest in a place other than his own home so that the Fourth Amendment protects him from unreasonable governmental intrusion into that place.' " *Id.* (quoting *Rakas v. Illinois,* 439 *U.S.* 128, 141-142, 99 *S.Ct.* 421, 429-430 (1978)).

Since the decision in *Katz v. United States,* 389 *U.S.* 347, 88 *S.Ct.* 507 (1967), it has been well settled that "the Fourth Amendment protects people, not places," *id.* at 351, 88 *S.Ct.* at 511, and the "capacity to claim the protection of the Fourth Amendment depends * * * upon whether the person who claims the protection of the Amendment has a legitimate expectation of privacy in the invaded place." *Rakas, supra* at 143, 99 *S.Ct.* at 430. The decision here in *Olson,* therefore—that an overnight guest has a legitimate expectation of privacy in his host's home—"merely recognizes the everyday expectations of privacy that we all share." *Olson* at 1689.

Speaking for the Court, Justice White observed:

> Staying overnight in another's home is a longstanding social custom that serves functions recognized as valuable by society. We stay in others' homes when we travel to a strange city for business or pleasure, when we visit our parents, children, or more distant relatives out of town, when we are in between jobs or homes, or when we house-sit for a friend. We will all be hosts and we will all be guests many times in our lives. From either perspective, we think that society recognizes that a houseguest has a legitimate expectation of privacy in his host's home.
>
> From the overnight guest's perspective, he seeks shelter in another's home precisely because it provides him with privacy, a place where he and his possessions will not be disturbed by anyone but his host and those his host allows inside. * * * Society expects at least as much privacy in those places as in a telephone booth— "a temporary private place whose momentary occupants' expectations of freedom from intrusion are recognized as reasonable," *Katz*, 389 *U.S.* at 361, 88 *S.Ct.* at 517 (Harlan, J., concurring).

Olson at 1689.

Moreover, the fact that defendant did not have the ultimate legal authority to determine who may or may not enter the household does not alter the outcome of this case. "If the untrammeled power to admit and exclude were essential to Fourth Amendment protection, an adult daughter temporarily living in the home of her parents would have no legitimate expectation of privacy because her right to admit or exclude would be subject to her parent's veto." *Id.* at 1689-1690. This is certainly not the law.

3. If the person to be arrested is "just a guest of the third party, then the police must obtain a search warrant for the third party's dwelling in order to use evidence found against the third party." *United States v. Litteral*, 910 *F.*2d 547, 553 (9th Cir. 1990). *See also United States v. Risse*, 83 *F.*3d 212, 216 (8th Cir. 1996). If, however, "the suspect is a co-resident of the third party, then *Steagald* does not apply, and *Payton* allows both arrest of the subject of the arrest warrant and use of evidence found against the third party." *Id. See also Washington v. Simpson*, 806 *F.*2d 192, 196 (8th Cir. 1986) (officers may enter residence of a third party without a search warrant when the subject of the arrest warrant co-resides with the third party).

4. *Guests staying for a brief, "business-related" visit.* In *Minnesota v. Carter*, 525 *U.S.* 83, 119 *S.Ct.* 469 (1998), Officer James Thielen, of the Eagan, Minnesota, Police Department, went to an apartment, later identified as being leased by Kimberly Thompson, to investigate a tip from a confidential informant. "The informant said that he had walked by the window of a ground-floor apartment and had seen people putting a white powder into bags. The officer looked in the same window through a gap in the closed blind and observed the bagging operation for several minutes. He then notified headquarters, which

began preparing affidavits for a search warrant while he returned to the apartment building." *Id.* at 471. Shortly thereafter, defendants Carter and Johns left the apartment, driving off in a Cadillac, which was subsequently stopped by the police. As the officers "opened the door of the car to let Johns out, they observed a black zippered pouch and a handgun, later determined to be loaded, on the vehicle's floor. Carter and Johns were arrested, and a later police search of the vehicle the next day discovered pagers, a scale, and 47 grams of cocaine in plastic sandwich bags." *Id.*

A search of the apartment under the authority of the warrant uncovered cocaine residue and drug paraphernalia. Officer Thielen identified Carter, Johns, and Thompson as the three people he had observed bagging the cocaine. He later learned that "while Thompson was the lessee of the apartment, Carter and Johns lived in Chicago and had come to the apartment for the sole purpose of packaging the cocaine. Carter and Johns had never been to the apartment before and were only in the apartment for approximately 2 hours. In return for the use of the apartment, Carter and Johns had given Thompson one-eighth of an ounce of the cocaine." *Id.* at 471-72.

Carter and Johns moved to suppress all evidence obtained from the apartment and the Cadillac, as well as their post-arrest incriminating statements, arguing that Officer Thielen's "initial observation of their drug packaging activities was an unreasonable search in violation of the Fourth Amendment and that all evidence obtained as a result of this unreasonable search was inadmissible as fruit of the poisonous tree." *Id.* at 472. The Minnesota Supreme Court held that the defendants had "standing" to claim the protection of the Fourth Amendment because they had "a legitimate expectation of privacy in the invaded place." *Id.* (quoting *Rakas v. Illinois*, 439 *U.S.* 128, 143, 99 *S.Ct.* 421, 429 (1978)). As a result, the Minnesota court went on to rule that Thielen's observation constituted a search of the apartment and that search was unreasonable. The United States Supreme Court disagreed.

In *Rakas*, the Court expressly rejected the notion that a person's legitimate expectation of privacy is to be examined under the "standing" doctrine. The *Rakas* Court held that "automobile passengers could not assert the protection of the Fourth Amendment against the seizure of incriminating evidence from a vehicle where they owned neither the vehicle nor the evidence." *Carter* at 472. Central to the Court's analysis "was the idea that in determining whether a defendant is able to show the violation of his (and not someone else's) Fourth Amendment rights, the 'definition of those rights is more properly placed within the purview of substantive Fourth Amendment law than within that of standing.' " *Id.* [Citation omitted.] Thus, the Court held that "in order to claim the protection of the Fourth Amendment, a defendant must demonstrate that he personally has an expectation of privacy in the place searched, and that his expectation is reasonable; *i.e.*, one which has 'a source outside of the Fourth Amendment, either by reference to concepts of real or personal property law or to understandings that are recognized and permitted by society.' " *Id.* (quoting *Rakas* at 143-44 & n.12, 99 *S.Ct.* 421, 429 & n.12).

The Fourth Amendment protects persons against unreasonable searches of "their persons [and] houses," and thus it "is a personal right that must be invoked by an individual." *Id.* "But the extent to which the Fourth Amendment protects people may depend upon where those people are * * * [and] 'upon whether the person who claims the protection of the Amendment has a legitimate expectation of privacy in the invaded place.' " *Id.* at 473. [Citations omitted.]

While the language of the Fourth Amendment suggests that its protections extend only to people in "their" houses, the Court has held that in some instances, a person may have a legitimate expectation of privacy in the house of someone else. Thus, in *Minnesota v. Olson, supra*, the Court held that an overnight guest in a house had a reasonable expectation of privacy.

Here, in *Carter*, the Court ruled that while "an overnight guest in a home may claim the protection of the Fourth Amendment," a person "who is merely present with the consent of the householder may not." *Id.* at 474. *See also id.* at 477 ("whereas it is plausible to regard a person's overnight lodging as at least his 'temporary' residence, it is entirely impossible to give that characterization to an apartment that he uses to package cocaine") (Scalia, J., concurring); *id.* at 479 (These defendants "have established nothing more than a fleeting and insubstantial connection with Thompson's home. * * * [They] used Thompson's house simply as a convenient processing station, their purpose involving nothing more than the mechanical act of chopping and packing a substance for distribution.") (Kennedy, J., concurring).

The defendants in this case "were obviously not overnight guests, but were essentially present for a business transaction and were only in the home a matter of hours. There is no suggestion that they had a previous relationship with Thompson, or that there was any other purpose to their visit. Nor was there anything similar to the overnight guest relationship in *Olson* to suggest a degree of acceptance into the household. While the apartment was a dwelling place for Thompson, it was for these [defendants] simply a place to do business." *Id.* at 473-74.

If the overnight guest in *Minnesota v. Olson* may be regarded as an example of one who may "claim the protection of the Fourth Amendment in the home of another, and one merely 'legitimately on the premises' as typifying those who may not do so, the present case is obviously somewhere in between. But the purely commercial nature of the transaction engaged in here, the relatively short period of time on the premises, and the lack of any previous connection between [defendants] and the householder," all prompted the Court to conclude that defendants' position "is closer to that of one simply permitted on the premises." *Id.* at 474. *See also New York v. Burger*, 482 U.S. 691, 700, 107 *S.Ct.* 2636, 2642 (1987) ("An expectation of privacy in commercial premises, however, is different from, and indeed less than, a similar expectation in an individual's home.").

Consequently, the Court held that "any search which may have occurred did not violate their Fourth Amendment rights." Because the Court concluded that the defendants "had no legitimate expectation of privacy in the apartment," it did not decide whether Officer Thielen's observation constituted a "search."

[Although not a part of the majority's ruling, Justice Breyer would have ruled that Officer Thielen's observation into Thompson's apartment would not have constituted a search even if Thompson herself brought the motion to suppress. The officer observed the apartment's interior from a "public vantage point." In this respect, Justice Breyer observed: "One who lives in a basement apartment that fronts a publicly traveled street, or similar space, ordinarily understands the need for care lest a member of the public simply direct his gaze downward." *Id.* at 480-81(Breyer, J., concurring).]

---

§1.6. Use of force to effect arrest.

TENNESSEE v. GARNER
Supreme Court of the United States
471 *U.S.* 1, 105 *S.Ct.* 1694 (1985)

QUESTION: May a law enforcement officer use deadly force to prevent the escape of an unarmed, nondangerous felon ?

ANSWER: NO.   "Deadly force may not be used unless it is necessary to prevent the escape [of the felon] *and* the officer has probable cause to believe that the suspect poses a significant threat of death or serious physical injury to the officer or others." *Id.* at 1697. [Emphasis added.]

RATIONALE: At approximately 10:45 p.m., in early October, two Memphis police officers were dispatched to answer a "prowler inside call." When the officers arrived on location, "they saw a woman gesturing toward the adjacent house. She told them she had heard glass breaking and that 'they' or 'someone' was breaking in next door." *Id.* at 1697. While one officer radioed the dispatcher to say that they were on the scene, the other officer went behind the house. "He heard a door slam and saw someone run across the backyard. The fleeing suspect, * * * Edward Garner, stopped at a 6-foot-high chain link fence at the edge of the yard. With the aid of a flashlight, [the officer] was able to see Garner's face and hands. He saw no sign of a weapon, and, though not certain, was 'reasonably sure' and 'figured' that Garner was unarmed. * * * He thought Garner was 17 or 18 years old and about 5'5" or 5'7" tall. [Actually, Garner, an eighth grader, was 15.] While Garner was crouched at the base of the fence, [the officer] called out 'police, halt' and took a few steps toward him. Convinced that if Garner made it over the fence he would elude capture, [the officer] shot him. The bullet hit Garner in the back of the head. Garner was taken by ambulance to a hospital, where he died on the operating table. Ten dollars and a purse taken from the house were found on his body." *Id.*

In this appeal, the United States Supreme Court set forth the standard to be applied in the context of a law enforcement officer's use of deadly force, and additionally determined "the constitutionality of the use of deadly force to prevent the escape of an apparently unarmed suspected felon." *Id.*

Preliminarily, the Court noted that "[w]henever an officer restrains the freedom of a person to walk away, he has seized that person. * * * While it is not always clear just when minimal police interference becomes a seizure, * * * *apprehension by the use of deadly force is a seizure subject to the reasonableness requirement of the Fourth Amendment.*" *Id.* at 1699. [Emphasis added.]

When a court analyzes the constitutionality of a seizure effected by the use of deadly force, it will balance the nature and necessity of such an intrusion on the individual's Fourth Amendment rights against the importance of the government's interests in effective law enforcement particularly alleged to justify the intrusion. Since one of the determining factors is the extent of the intrusion, it is plain that its reasonableness will depend not only on when a seizure is made, but also the manner in which it is carried out. The test to be used is whether the "totality of the circumstances" justifies the particular seizure utilized in the situation at issue. *Id.* at 1700.

Therefore, "the use of deadly force to prevent the escape of all felony suspects, whatever the circumstances, is constitutionally unreasonable." *Id.* at 1701. Without an imminent threat of death or serious bodily injury directed toward the officer or another, "the harm resulting from failing to apprehend [the suspect] does not justify the use of deadly force to do so." *Id.*

While clearly acknowledging the difficulty of a law enforcement officer's decision in this regard, the Court heavily emphasized the nature of the fundamental rights at stake. Justice White observed:

> It is no doubt unfortunate when a suspect who is in sight escapes, but the fact that the police arrive a little late or are a little slow afoot does not always justify killing a suspect. A police officer may not seize an unarmed, nondangerous suspect by shooting him dead.

Id. Where, however, "the officer has probable cause to believe that the suspect poses a threat of serious physical harm, either to the officer or to others, it is not constitutionally unreasonable to prevent escape by using deadly force. Thus, *if the suspect threatens the officer with a weapon or there is probable cause to believe that he has committed a crime involving the infliction or threatened infliction of serious personal harm, deadly force may be used if necessary to prevent escape, and if, where feasible, some warning has been given.*" *Id.* [Emphasis added.]

NOTE

The United States Supreme Court, in *Brower v. County of Inyo*, 489 *U.S.* 593, 109 *S.Ct.* 1378 (1989), held that a Fourth Amendment "seizure" occurred when, during the course of a motor vehicle pursuit of a fleeing suspect, police officials (1) placed an unilluminated 18-wheel tractor-trailer across both lanes of a two-lane highway, (2) "effectively concealed" the truck behind a curve in the road in order to,

(3) block the path of the fleeing suspect, while at the same time, (4) positioning a police car with its headlights on, between the suspect's oncoming vehicle and the truck, so that the suspect would be "blinded" on his approach, which (5) subsequently resulted in the suspect's death when he crashed into the police roadblock.

The posture of the case arose from a 42 *U.S.C.* §1983 suit by heirs of William Caldwell (Brower). Brower was killed when the stolen car he was driving at high speeds for approximately 20 miles in an effort to elude pursuing police crashed into a police roadblock.

In this appeal, Brower's heirs allege that the law enforcement officials involved "used 'brutal, excessive, unreasonable and unnecessary force' in establishing the roadblock, and thus effected an unreasonable seizure of Brower, in violation of the Fourth Amendment." *Id.* , 109 *S.Ct.* at 1380.

Analogizing the "stop" of Brower to the "stop" which occurred in *Tennessee v. Garner, supra*, the Court determined that the intentional police conduct involved here in *Brower* did, in fact, constitute a *seizure* within the meaning of the Fourth Amendment. In *Garner*, the Court concluded that a "police officer's fatal shooting of a fleeing suspect constituted a Fourth Amendment 'seizure.' " *Brower* at 1380. Similar to *Garner*, "Brower's independent decision to continue the chase can no more eliminate the [officers'] responsibility for the termination of his movement effected by the roadblock than Garner's independent decision to flee eliminated the Memphis police officer's responsibility for the termination of his movement effected by the bullet." *Id.*

According to the Court, "a roadblock is not just a significant show of authority to induce a voluntary stop, but is designed to produce a stop by physical impact if voluntary compliance does not occur." *Id.* at 1382. Nor does the Court think it possible, "in determining whether there has been a seizure in a case such as this, to distinguish between a roadblock that is designed to give the oncoming driver the option of a voluntary stop (*e.g.*, one at the end of a long straightway), and a roadblock that is designed to produce a collision (*e.g.*, one located just around a bend). * * * [It is] enough for a seizure that a person be stopped by the very instrumentality set in motion or put in place in order to achieve that result. It was enough here, therefore, that * * * Brower was meant to be stopped by the physical obstacle of the roadblock—and that he was so stopped." *Id.* "That is enough to constitute a 'seizure' within [the] meaning of the Fourth Amendment." *Id.* at 1383.

Of course, in this 42 *U.S.C.* §1983 action, "seizure" alone is not enough for liability; the seizure must be unreasonable. Brower's heirs may only recover for Brower's death if, upon remand, they can establish that the officers precisely set "up the roadblock in such a manner as to be likely to kill him." *Id.*

ROBINETTE v. BARNES
United States Court of Appeals
854 *F*.2d 909 (6th Cir. 1988)

QUESTION: When a properly trained police dog is used in an appropriate manner to apprehend a felony suspect, does such use of the dog constitute deadly force ?

ANSWER: NO. "[T]he use of a properly trained police dog to apprehend a felony suspect does not carry with it a 'substantial risk of causing death or serious bodily harm.' * * * [Therefore,] when a properly trained police dog is used in an appropriate manner to apprehend a felony suspect, the use of the dog does not constitute deadly force." *Id.* at 912-13. In certain cases, however, an officer's "intent in using a police dog, or the use of an improperly trained dog, could transform the use of the dog into deadly force[.]" *Id.* at 913.

RATIONALE: Since 1972, the Metropolitan Government of Nashville and Davidson County (Metro) has maintained within its police department a "K-9" division comprising of teams of officers and police canines. "Each officer-dog team is trained according to guidelines established by the United States Police Canine Association (USPCA), a national organization. Building searches are among the law enforcement tasks the 'K-9' teams are trained to perform." *Id.* at 910.

Defendant, "police officer Ronnie Barnes, and his police dog, Casey, completed an initial training program in June 1981. Since at least January 1984, they have participated in a retraining program which requires that the proficiency of each 'K-9' team be re-evaluated every three weeks. Building search procedure is among the skills re-evaluated." *Id.*

"According to the head of Metro's 'K-9' division, Lieutenant Charles Spain, the dogs are trained to track and apprehend suspects when they hear the voice command, 'Find him.' Spain emphasized that the dog is trained to apprehend a person by seizing an arm. However, he also stated that if a suspect's arm is not available, the dog will 'get the first thing that [is] offered to him.' " *Id.* at 910-11.

On the night in question, the "K-9" team of Barnes and Casey was summoned shortly after midnight to the Superb Motors car dealership in Nashville, Tennessee. "A burglar alarm inside the building had been activated. * * * [B]y the time Barnes arrived at the dealership, '[o]fficers already on the scene had located a point of entry, a broken glass door, and had seen a suspect inside the building looking out at them.' " *Id.* at 911.

"Barnes and Casey entered the building and stood in a small entry room. Barnes shouted a warning that he had a police dog and that anyone inside the building should come out or he would turn the dog loose. Approximately thirty seconds later, Barnes repeated the warning. After another thirty seconds passed, Barnes released Casey. The dog ran to a closed door at one end of the room. Barnes opened the door for the dog." *Id.* At that point, " '[t]he dog took a few steps [] and [Barnes] shouted again, "You'd better come out." Then the dog turned around and [returned to Barnes].' " *Id.*

"As soon as Casey returned, Barnes gave the command, 'Find him.' Barnes and the dog then began to search the building. The dog ran ahead of Barnes while the officer checked some closed doors that Casey bypassed. Eventually, Barnes followed Casey into a darkened bay area of the car dealership. His flashlight revealed that Casey had the suspect's neck in his mouth. The man was lying face down on the floor with half of his body underneath a car. He did not move. A substantial amount of blood had collected around him and more was oozing from his neck." *Id.*

"Barnes ordered Casey to come to him, leashed the dog and then called for an ambulance. The suspect, Daniel Briggs, was pronounced dead on arrival." *Id.*

On behalf of Briggs' estate, Dorothy Robinette sued Barnes, Metro and the Chief of Metro's police department, contending that the officer's use of a police dog to apprehend Briggs constituted the unlawful and "unnecessary use of deadly force which deprived him of his fourth and fourteenth amendment rights." *The United States Court of Appeals for the Sixth Circuit disagreed.*

In *Tennessee v. Garner*, 471 *U.S.* 1, 105 *S.Ct.* 1694 (1985), the United States Supreme Court held that the apprehension of a criminal suspect "by the use of deadly force is a seizure subject to the reasonableness requirement of the Fourth Amendment." *Id.* at 7, 105 *S.Ct.* at 1699. "Although the Court elaborated on the factors relevant for an assessment of a seizure's reasonableness, the Court did not expressly define what constitutes deadly force." *Barnes* at 911.

"In *Garner*, a police officer seized an unarmed, fleeing burglary suspect when he shot and killed him. Thus, the deadly force in issue in that case was the kind which undoubtedly comes to mind first, a firearm. However, many law enforcement tools possess the potential for being deadly force, including a * * * nightstick * * * and a police officer's vehicle. * * * Indeed, as any faithful reader of mystery novels can attest, an instrument of death need not be something as obviously lethal as a gun or knife. [A] 'blunt object' kills just as effectively." *Id.* at 912.

"Thus, whether deadly force has been used to seize a criminal suspect must be determined in the context of each case." *Id.* In this respect, *two factors may be considered "most relevant to the determination of whether the use of a particular law enforcement tool constitutes deadly force: the intent of the officer to inflict death or serious bodily harm, and the probability, known to the officer but regardless of the officer's intent, that the law enforcement tool, when employed to facilitate an arrest, creates a 'substantial risk of causing death or serious bodily harm.'" Id.* (citing Model Penal Code §3.11(2)). [Emphasis added.]

Application of the factors set forth above to the facts of this case led the court to conclude that "Barnes did not employ deadly force to apprehend Daniel Briggs * * * when [Barnes] commanded his police dog, Casey, to search for Briggs in the Superb Motors building." *Id.* According to the court, there was "no indication from the evidence that Barnes intended Briggs to die or suffer serious bodily harm, or that Barnes in any way deviated from proper procedures for conducting a building search with a police dog." *Id.*

Accordingly, the court held that *the use of a properly trained police dog to apprehend a felony suspect does not carry with it a "substantial risk of causing death or serious bodily harm." Id.* [Emphasis added.] Although the court could not ignore the fact that, in this case, the use of a police dog did result in a person's death, it also could not

> ignore the evidence in the record which indicates that this tragic event was an extreme aberration from the outcome intended or expected. Lieutenant Spain's deposition testimony was unequivocal on the fact that the dogs are trained to seize suspects by the arm and then wait for an officer to secure the arrestee. While it is impossible to know for certain what happened when Casey found Briggs in the bay of the car dealership, the conclusion compelled by the evidence is that when the dog found the suspect, he was hidden underneath a car, his arms were not within the dog's reach and, unfortunately, his neck was. Since the dog had been trained to seize whatever part of anatomy was nearest if an arm was unavailable, the dog acted consistent with its training by seizing Briggs' exposed neck. *Given the remote chance that this particular scenario would occur, we cannot conclude that Barnes released the dog with the knowledge that by doing so, he was creating "a substantial risk" that the dog might kill Briggs.*

> Lieutenant Spain stated that to his knowledge, no trained police dog has ever killed an individual before these events occurred. Corroborating this statement is Barnes' deposition testimony that the records of the USPCA, which have been maintained for over 20 years, also indicate that this is the first time a person has died as a result of being apprehended by a police dog. These statements, along with the fact that our own research has failed to reveal any reported case involving similar circumstances, lead us to conclude that *when a properly trained police dog is used in an appropriate manner to apprehend a felony suspect, the use of the dog does not constitute deadly force.* While an officer's intent in using a police dog, or the use of an improperly trained dog, could transform the use of the dog into deadly force, we find no such intent or improper training present in this case. * * *

> Indeed, [the use of] these dogs often can help prevent officers from having to resort to, or be subjected to, such force. Any attempt to apprehend a criminal suspect presents the officer with [a] difficult and frightening situation, but certainly an attempt to arrest a suspect hidden inside an unfamiliar building during the nighttime presents a particularly confusing one. The use of dogs can make it more likely that the officers can apprehend suspects without the risks attendant to the use of firearms in the darkness, thus, frequently enhancing the safety of the officers, bystanders and the suspect.

> [Moreover], we are not persuaded by the evidence presented that the remote possibility that the use of a police dog to apprehend a

felon might, under extraordinary circumstances, cause death, out-weighs the dogs' proven benefits for effective law enforcement. * * *

We do not dispute the fact that trained police dogs can appear to be dangerous, threatening animals. The dogs' ability to aid law enforcement would be minimal if they did not possess this trait. However, the mere recognition that a law enforcement tool is dangerous does not suffice as proof that the tool is an instrument of deadly force. As we have already stated, the totality of the factors present in a particular case determine whether deadly force was used to apprehend a suspect. Accordingly, we affirm the district court's conclusion that, although in this particular case the use of a police dog to apprehend a suspected felon resulted in that felon's death, deadly force was not used to seize the felon. * * *

Id. at 912-13, 914. [Emphasis added.]

NOTE

1. *Motor vehicle stops & flight.* In *Matthews v. Jones*, 35 *F*.3d 1046 (6th Cir. 1994), in the early morning hours in Jefferson County, Kentucky, Scott Matthews was observed by the police driving his automobile recklessly and at an excessive speed. As the police began to pursue, Matthews fled. Eventually, he pulled his car off the road and ran into nearby woods. Within a minute, Officer Watkins, a K-9 officer, and his Rottweiler partner, Roscoe, arrived at the scene. A helicopter also arrived but could not locate Matthews because he had fled into a heavy wooded area with thick undergrowth. "At this point, the officers did not know the extent of the crimes Matthews might have committed, whether he was armed, or why he fled his vehicle." *Id.* at 1048.

As soon as the officers arrived on the scene, they called out to Matthews and ordered him to surrender. Matthews did not respond. "Officer Watkins and Roscoe then began to track Matthews. Roscoe was on a leash during the entire tracking period. Eventually Roscoe stopped at the edge of a swampy, heavily wooded area and reacted as if the suspect were nearby. Officer Watkins ordered Matthews to surrender and warned that the dog would be released if he did not. Matthews did not respond. Watkins warned Matthews again, and again there was no response." *Id.*

"Watkins then released Roscoe from his leash and Roscoe ran approximately fifty feet into the woods, stopped and alerted. Watkins shined his flashlight in the immediate area near Roscoe and discovered Matthews lying on his stomach in the weeds, his hands underneath his body. Watkins ordered Matthews not to move and informed him that if he remained still the dog would be recalled. Instead of complying with Officer Watkins's order, Matthews quickly rose to his knees; Roscoe reacted to the sudden movement by biting Matthews on the arm and holding him there. Matthews struggled with the dog, causing Roscoe to reposition his bite. At that point, Watkins ordered Roscoe to release Matthews and took Matthews into custody." *Id.* Matthews was charged with driving while under the influence of alcohol, reckless driving, attempting to elude, resisting arrest, and operating on a suspended license.

In this appeal, Matthews argued, among other things, that the use of a police dog, which resulted in extensive injuries, constituted the use of deadly force, or at least excessive force, in violation of the Fourth and Fourteenth Amendments. The Sixth Circuit Court of Appeals disagreed. The court stated:

> In the case at hand, it is not disputed that the officers on the scene did not know the extent of the crimes that Matthews might have committed nor did they know whether he was armed. Neither is it disputed, however, that the police officer pursuing Matthews had legally sufficient grounds to stop him, and that before the officer could do so, Matthews fled from his car into a densely wooded area in the dark of night. Matthews was obviously fleeing in an attempt to evade the police; the area into which he fled in the darkness provided a strategic advantage to Matthews in that he could easily ambush the officers; and Matthews's extreme behavior provided cause for the officers to believe that he was involved in activity considerably more nefarious than mere traffic violations.

Id. at 1051. Accordingly, the court held that "a reasonable police officer under these circumstances would have believed that Matthews posed a threat to the officers' safety as well as the safety of others, and that this case cannot be distinguished from *Robinette* on the basis of the officer's lack of specific cause to believe Matthews was a felon." *Id.*

The court also determined that the record in this case contained no evidence of inadequate or improper training of Roscoe; nor was there any evidence of an intent on the part of Officer Watkins to create a substantial risk of death or serious bodily harm. "To the contrary, it is clear from the record that Officer Watkins gave Matthews every chance to avoid any contact with Roscoe." *Id.*

The court ruled, therefore, that Roscoe was used in an "appropriate manner." *Id.* "Officer Watkins not only warned Matthews several times before releasing Roscoe to apprehend him, but when he found Matthews lying in the weeds, his hands concealed beneath his body, Watkins explicitly ordered him not to move, advising that if Matthews remained still, Roscoe would be recalled. Matthews chose to move, and Roscoe enforced the order." *Id.* This was not the use of deadly force, nor was it the use of excessive force. The use of the police dog to apprehend Matthews was, therefore, "objectively reasonable." *Id.* at 1052.

2. *Compare Chew v. Gates*, 27 F.3d 1432, 1447 (9th Cir. 1994), where a plurality of the Ninth Circuit declared: "We are certain that *Robinette* is not consistent with the law of this circuit today, * * * and seriously doubt whether we would ever have reached a similar result."

Chew was stopped by an officer of the Los Angeles Police Department at about 2:00 p.m. for a traffic violation. Chew subsequently fled from the officer on foot and hid in a nearby scrapyard. Upon discovering that there were three outstanding warrants for Chew's arrest, the officer radioed for assistance. A police perimeter was set up around the scrapyard, and a helicopter and canine units were summoned to search for Chew.

Officer Bunch and his canine partner, Volker, arrived at the search site. Bunch unleashed Volker and, about two hours after Chew had fled to the yard, Volker found him crouching between two metal bins. "According to Chew, as soon as he became aware of Volker's presence, he attempted to surrender and yelled to the police to call off the dog." *Id.* at 1436. The officer did not immediately call off the dog. Volker bit Chew several times and then seized him, causing severe lacerations to Chew's left side and left forearm.

Chew sued in federal district court, alleging violations of his Fourth and Fourteenth Amendment rights, and alleging that his injuries resulted from the city's policy regarding the use of canine force. In a plurality opinion, the Ninth Circuit ruled that the issue whether the officer's decision to release the dog was reasonable could not be decided as a matter of law. Rather, that issue must be remanded to the district court for a trial on whether Officer Bunch's release of Volker constituted the use of unreasonable force. *Id.* at 1440.

To determine the reasonableness of an officer's use of force, several factors must be taken into consideration. In balancing the nature and quality of the intrusion on a person's Fourth Amendment interests against the governmental interests at stake, the factfinder must "evaluate the type and amount of force inflicted." *Id.* Moreover, *Graham v. Connor* instructs that the following should be taken into account: "(1) the severity of the crime at issue, (2) whether the suspect poses an immediate threat to the safety of the officers or others, and (3) whether he is actively resisting arrest or attempting to evade arrest by flight." *Chew* at 1440.

In applying the above criteria, the court determined that

> [b]y all accounts, the force used to arrest Chew was severe. Chew was apprehended by a German Shepherd taught to seize suspects by biting hard and holding. According to the defendants, Volker had to bite the suspect three times before he could achieve an effective hold. Chew adds that, gripping his left side and then his left arm with his jaws, the dog dragged him between four and ten feet from his hiding place. Chew asserts that his arm was nearly severed.
>
> Bunch had good reason to expect that Chew might sustain exactly this type of mauling when he released Volker. All of the K-9 officers testified that the police dogs were trained to bite suspects unless a countermanding order was given by the handler. Here, because Volker was sent to locate a *concealed* suspect, the dog would almost necessarily be out of sight of its handler, and hence beyond the reach of a countermanding order, if and when he came upon Chew. Further, [one of the sergeants responsible for canine training indicated] that if a suspect attempted to elude the dog's bite instead of passively allowing the animal to maintain its hold, the dog would repeatedly bite the suspect in an effort to obtain a sustained grip with its jaws.

Id. at 1441. [Court's emphasis.]

The court also noted that the facts of the case do not

> reveal an articulable basis for believing that Chew was armed or that he posed an immediate threat to anyone's safety. * * * Chew was initially stopped for a traffic violation. Before he fled, he was asked for his driver's license, and he produced it. * * * It appears from the record that after fleeing Chew hid in the scrapyard for an hour and a half before Bunch released Volker in an effort to capture him. The defendants do not suggest that Chew engaged in any threatening behavior during this time, or that he did anything other than hide quietly. In light of these facts, a rational jury could easily find that Chew posed no *immediate* safety threat to anyone.

Id. at 1442-43. [Court's emphasis.]

> The other two specified *Graham* factors cut in favor of the defendants, but not by much. With respect to whether Chew was "actively resisting arrest," it is undisputed that he fled and then hid from the police. He did not, however, resist arrest to the point of offering any physical resistance to the arresting officers, nor, at the time the officers released the dogs, did they have any particular reason to believe that he would do so. * * *

> Turning to the severity of the crime for which Chew was arrested, although he was initially stopped for a traffic violation, the traffic officer later discovered the existence of three outstanding felony warrants for his arrest. * * * However, in view of the fact that the record does not reveal the *type* of felony for which Chew was wanted, the existence of the warrants is of limited significance * * * [and] is thus not strong justification for the use of dangerous force. The significance of the warrants is further diminished by the facts that Chew was completely surrounded by the police, and that the prospects for his imminent capture were far greater than are those of the many fleeing suspects who are fleeter than the police officers chasing them.

Id. at 1442-43. [Court's emphasis.]

Accordingly, the court concluded that the record did "not render reasonable *as a matter of law* the considered judgment to unleash a German Shepherd trained to seize suspects by 'biting hard and holding,' by mauling and sometimes seriously injuring them." *Id.* at 1443.

The court also observed that it could be concluded that Chew's injury was caused by a city policy. In fact, the city conceded that its canine policy "authorized seizure of *all* concealed suspects—resistant or nonresistant, armed or unarmed, violent or nonviolent—by dogs trained to bite hard and hold." *Id.* at 1444. The evidence presented established that "the dogs bit suspects in over 40% of the instances in which they were used." *Id.* at 1445. This, according to the court, underscores the proposition that:

Where the city equips its police officers with potentially dangerous animals, and evidence is adduced that those animals inflict injury in a significant percentage of the cases in which they are used, a failure to adopt a departmental policy governing their use, or to implement rules or regulations regarding the constitutional limits of that use, evidences a "deliberate indifference" to constitutional rights. Under such circumstances, a jury could, and should, find that Chew's injury was caused by the city's failure to engage in any oversight whatsoever of an important departmental practice involving the use of force.

Id.

GRAHAM v. CONNOR
Supreme Court of the United States
490 *U.S.* 386, 109 *S.Ct.* 1865 (1989)

QUESTION: When an excessive force claim arises in the context of an arrest or investigatory stop of a free citizen, what constitutional standard governs ?

ANSWER: "[A]ll claims that law enforcement officers have used excessive force—deadly or not—in the course of an arrest, investigatory stop, or other 'seizure' of a free citizen should be analyzed under the Fourth Amendment and its 'reasonableness' standard, rather than under a 'substantive due process' approach." *Id.* at 1871. In this context, "[a] 'seizure' triggering the Fourth Amendment's protections occurs only when government actors have, 'by means of physical force or show of authority, . . . in some way restrained the liberty of a citizen[.]' " *Id.* at 1871 n.10.

RATIONALE: Plaintiff Graham brings a 42 *U.S.C.* §1983 action against the City of Charlotte, North Carolina and the police officers who were involved in the alleged use of excessive force during the course of an investigative stop. Plaintiff seeks money damages for the injuries he sustained.
  "On November 12, 1984, Graham, a diabetic, felt the onset of an insulin reaction. He asked a friend, William Berry, to drive him to a nearby convenience store so he could purchase some orange juice to counteract the reaction." *Id.* at 1867-1868. When Graham arrived at the store, he rapidly exited the car and ran inside. When he saw four or five persons at the counter, he decided not to wait. He then ran out of the store, re-entered Berry's car, and told Berry to take him to a friend's house where he could obtain the orange juice he needed.
  This entire episode was witnessed by defendant, Officer Connor, who was parked in his patrol car outside the convenience store. As Berry drove away from the store, Officer Connor followed. "About one-half mile from the store, he made an investigative stop. Although

Berry told Connor that Graham was simply suffering from a 'sugar reaction,' the officer ordered Berry and Graham to wait while he found out what, if anything, had happened at the convenience store. When Officer Connor returned to his patrol car to call for backup assistance, Graham got out of the car, ran around it twice, and finally sat down on the curb, where he passed out briefly." *Id.* at 1868.

When Officer Connor's backup arrived, "[o]ne of the officers rolled Graham over on the sidewalk and cuffed his hands tightly behind his back, ignoring Berry's pleas to get him some sugar. * * * Several officers then lifted Graham up from behind, carried him over to Berry's car, and placed him face down on the hood. Regaining consciousness, Graham asked the officers to check his wallet for a diabetic decal that he carried. In response, one of the officers told him to 'shut up' and shoved his face down against the hood of the car. Four officers grabbed Graham and threw him head-first into the police car. A friend of Graham's brought some orange juice to the car, but the officers refused to let him have it. Finally, Officer Connor received a report that Graham had done nothing wrong at the convenience store, and the officers drove him home and released him." *Id.*

In this Section 1983 action, plaintiff Graham seeks damages for the injuries he sustained, including a broken foot, cuts on his wrists, a bruised forehead, and an injured shoulder. Graham contends that the officers' actions during the investigative stop constituted "excessive force," in violation of his constitutional rights.

In analyzing Connor's claim, the lower courts used a "substantive due process" standard which required consideration of four factors to determine whether the excessive use of force gives rise to a cause of action under Section 1983. These included: "(1) the need for the application of force; (2) the relationship between that need and the amount of force that was used; (3) the extent of the injury inflicted; and (4) '(w)hether the force was applied in a good faith effort to maintain and restore discipline or maliciously and sadistically for the very purpose of causing harm.'" *Id.* [Citation omitted.]

The United States Supreme Court granted *certiorari*, reversed the lower court's ruling, and held "that *all* claims that law enforcement officers have used excessive force—deadly or not—in the course of an arrest, investigatory stop, or other 'seizure' of a free* citizen should be analyzed under the Fourth Amendment and its 'reasonableness' standard rather than under a 'substantive due process' approach." *Id.* at 1871.

"In addressing an excessive force claim brought under §1983, analysis begins by identifying the specific constitutional right allegedly infringed by the challenged application of force. * * * Where, as here, the excessive force claim arises in the context of an arrest or investigatory stop of a free citizen, it is most properly characterized as one invoking the protections of the Fourth Amendment, which guarantees citizens the right 'to be secure in their persons . . . against unreasonable . . . seizures' of the person." *Id.* at 1870-1871. This was made clear in *Tennessee v.*

---

* After conviction, the Eighth Amendment 'serves as the primary source of substantive protection . . . in cases . . . where the deliberate use of force is challenged as excessive and unjustified.'" *Id.* at 1871 n.10. [Citation omitted.]

Garner, 471 *U.S.* 1, 105 *S.Ct.* 1694 (1985), where the Court "addressed a claim that the use of deadly force to apprehend a fleeing suspect who did not appear to be armed or otherwise dangerous violated the suspect's constitutional rights, notwithstanding the existence of probable cause to arrest. Though the complaint alleged violations of both the Fourth Amendment and the Due Process Clause, [the Court] analyzed the constitutionality of the challenged application of force solely by reference to the Fourth Amendment's prohibition against unreasonable seizures of the person, holding that the 'reasonableness' of a particular seizure depends not only on *when* it is made, but also on *how* it is carried out." *Connor* at 1871 (citing *Garner* at 7-8, 105 *S.Ct.* at 1699-1700.

"Determining whether the force used to effect a particular seizure is 'reasonable' under the Fourth Amendment requires a careful balancing of 'the nature and quality of the intrusion on the individual's Fourth Amendment interests' against the countervailing governmental interests at stake." *Connor* at 1871. [Citations omitted.] Significantly, it has long been recognized "that the right to make an arrest or investigatory stop necessarily carries with it the right to use some degree of physical coercion or threat thereof to effect it." *Id*. The proper application of force in the context of an arrest or investigatory stop does, however, require "careful attention to the facts and circumstances of each particular case, including *the severity of the crime at issue, whether the suspect poses an immediate threat to the safety of the officers or others, and whether he is actively resisting arrest or attempting to evade arrest by flight.*" *Id*. at 1871-1872. [Emphasis added.] As stated in *Garner, supra*, the question is "whether the totality of the circumstances justifie[s] a particular sort of * * * seizure[.]" *Garner* at 8-9, 105 *S.Ct.* at 1699-1700.

Additionally, the Court emphasizes that "[t]he 'reasonableness' of a particular use of force must be judged from the perspective of a reasonable officer on the scene, rather than with the 20/20 vision of hindsight." Connor at 1872. [Emphasis added.] " 'Not every push or shove, even if it may later seem unnecessary in the peace of a judge's chambers,' * * * violates the Fourth Amendment. The calculus of reasonableness must embody allowance for the fact that police officers are often forced to make split-second judgments—in circumstances that are tense, uncertain, and rapidly evolving—about the amount of force that is necessary in a particular situation." Id. [Citation omitted.]

As a result, "the 'reasonableness' inquiry in an excessive force case is an objective one: the question is whether the officers' actions are 'objectively reasonable' in light of the facts and circumstances confronting them, without regard to their underlying intent or motivation. * * * An officer's evil intentions will not make a Fourth Amendment violation out of an objectively reasonable use of force; nor will an officer's good intentions make an objectively unreasonable use of force constitutional." *Id*.

Because the lower court in this case used the wrong standard governing this issue, "its judgment must be vacated and the case remanded to that court for reconsideration of that issue under the proper Fourth Amendment standard." *Id*. at 1873.

NOTE

1. In *Pittman v. Nelms*, 87 *F*.2d 116 (4th Cir. 1996), Marinda Pittman was injured by a bullet fired by Wicomico County, Maryland, Deputy Sheriff Robert Nelms. The injury occurred when Nelms and his partner, Chris Banks, attempted to stop a vehicle driven by Tim Hudson, a suspected drug dealer. "Banks approached the vehicle from the driver's side, and Nelms from the front and passenger side. Banks leaned into the open window to speak to Hudson, but Hudson started to drive away. Banks' arm became caught inside the window of the car, which carried him for twenty-five to thirty feet before it swerved to the right and released his arm. Nelms then fired at the car and the bullet struck Pittman, who was seated in the back seat." *Id.* at 118.

According to Pittman, Nelms and Banks had a long-standing and on-going feud with Hudson. When Deputy Banks attempted to stop Hudson, his arm became entangled in the vehicle, "most likely when he tried to grab the keys, and he was thrown aside when the vehicle made a turn to the right." *Id.* at 120. At this time, "Banks got back on his feet, ran towards the vehicle and fired at it as it was speeding away towards the street. Meanwhile, Nelms, whose bullet actually pierced the vehicle and injured [Pittman], fired at the vehicle at the same time that Banks' shot was fired, when Nelms had a clear and unobstructed view of Banks, [and] could see that Banks had not been run over and killed. Nelms' shot was fired," stated Pittman, "when the vehicle was approximately twenty-five [] feet away from him, driving *away* from him * * *." *Id.* [Court's emphasis.]

On appeal, accepting as true Pittman's version of the facts, the Fourth Circuit determined that the force used by Nelms was not excessive. The court explained:

> Force is not excessive if it is " 'objectively reasonable' in light of the facts and circumstances confronting [the officer], without regard to [his] underlying intent or motivation." * * *

> Pittman does not dispute that the entire series of events took only a few short seconds, and that during that period Banks was in serious danger. In the terminology of the Supreme Court's decision in *Graham*, the situation was "tense, uncertain, and rapidly evolving." * * * In light of *Graham* * * *, we cannot conclude that the force Nelms used was excessive under clearly established law. Under these circumstances, an objectively reasonable officer certainly could have believed that his decision to fire was legally justified.

Id. at 120. [Citations omitted.]

See also Drewitt v. Pratt, 999 *F*.2d 774 (4th Cir. 1993), where the court upheld Officer Pratt's qualified immunity against an excessive force claim where the officer, after observing Drewitt driving recklessly, ran toward the car with his gun drawn and ordered him to stop. When Drewitt sped up, Pratt was caught on the hood of the car. Pratt fired at Drewitt. This use of force was, according to the court, "objectively reasonable." *Id.* at 780.

2. *Pressure-point, pain-compliance techniques.* In *Brownell v. Figel*, 950 *F.*2d 1285 (7th Cir. 1991), the court addressed the reasonableness of police use of pressure-point, pain-compliance techniques.

At about 2:45 a.m., Donald Brownell lost control of his car while traveling on Route 24 in Allen County, Indiana. While out of control, he crossed the median and struck a guardrail on the opposite side of the highway. Shortly after the accident, police and emergency medical technicians discovered Brownell, apparently unconscious, lying across the passenger seat of his 1980 El Camino. They also noticed a strong smell of alcohol emanating from Brownell, and several beer cans in the car. When the E.M.T.s attempted to examine Brownell for injuries, Brownell opened his eyes, stated that he was not injured, and told the officers not to touch him and to leave him alone. Brownell then became combative, pushed one of the E.M.T.s away, and cursed at him. The E.M.T.s removed Brownell from the car, placed him on a backboard and transported him to the Parkview Hospital emergency room. During this process, Brownell fought against the backboard restraints and attempted to remove the straps. The E.M.T.'s report indicated that Brownell exhibited no obvious signs of injury.

Brownell remained combative at the hospital, being described by one doctor as "the most abusive person he had encountered in his five years" at the hospital. The doctor found no sign of injury, concluded that Brownell was "simply intoxicated," and released him to the police. Brownell would not, however, voluntarily enter the patrol car for the trip to the police station. With the help of two security guards, one of the officers—Officer Roth—lifted Brownell into the front passenger seat of his patrol car.

At the police station, Officer Roth asked Brownell to get out of the car. When Brownell again failed to move, Roth lifted him out of the cruiser and placed him on the ground. A second police officer, Joseph Bickel, and a civilian jailer, Thomas Bird, were summoned to help out. "The officers continued talking to Brownell in an attempt to get him to respond. When asked to cooperate in the administration of the Breathalyzer test, Brownell responded, 'I can't. My arms and legs don't move.' [] The only movement Brownell made during this time was batting motions with his hands, apparently in an effort to make the officers leave him alone." *Id.* at 1288.

"In an attempt to arouse Brownell from his stupor, Bickel applied a 'pen hold,' a technique designed to put pressure on the knuckles to evoke a pain response. Brownell did not respond. Bickel then tried a 'mandibular angle pressure point' on Brownell, which involves applying pressure to a nerve behind the jaw bone and pushing straight forward toward the chin. The second time Bickel applied this technique, Brownell winced. Concluding [that] Brownell would not stand up of his own volition, the officers tried, unsuccessfully, to stand him on his feet." *Id.*

The officers arrested Brownell for drunk driving, and carried him over to the processing counter. Brownell continued to verbally abuse the officers and flail his arms about in a sluggish manner. The officers then placed Brownell on the floor of a cell to "sleep it off." Believing that Brownell was feigning his inability to move, "and in a final attempt to arouse him, Bird sprayed some 'CS gas' (a repellent similar to mace) on Brownell's stomach. Brownell did not react." *Id.*

By 11:30 a.m., Brownell still had not moved. He was returned to the Parkview Hospital, where doctors diagnosed a "fractured, displaced vertebra, and permanent quadriplegia." *Id.* at 1289. At that time, nearly 12 hours after the accident, Brownell had a blood-alcohol concentration of .14%.

In this appeal, Brownell contended that the officers violated his constitutional rights by employing unreasonable and excessive force against him. Rejecting Brownell's contention, the court preliminarily noted that

> [a]ll claims that law enforcement officers have used excessive force in the course of an arrest are analyzed under the fourth amendment and its reasonableness standard * * *. Under the fourth amendment, the question is whether the officers' actions were "objectively reasonable" in light of the facts and circumstances confronting them, without regard to their underlying intent or motivation. * * * Reasonableness in this context is judged from the perspective of a reasonable officer on the scene, rather than with the "20/20 vision of hindsight."

Id. at 1292 (quoting *Graham v. Connor* at 395-97, 109 *S.Ct.* at 1871-72).

In view of the standard set forth above, the court found Brownell's excessive force claim to be "speculative" at best, particularly in light of "the absence of specific wrongdoing" on the part of the police. *Id.* at 1293. The court elaborated:

> Brownell's only evidence of excessive force is the [officers'] use of two pain techniques on him. In particular he notes that the mandibular angle pressure hold could easily have supplied the force necessary to *aggravate* his spinal injury. (No suggestion is made that this technique alone could have supplied the force necessary to actually fracture his spine.) * * * *But the question is not whether, as a matter of fact, these techniques may have aggravated Brownell's (undiscovered) spinal injury, but whether the use of these techniques was objectively reasonable under the circumstances.* Faced with an apparently intoxicated driver, the officers had a duty to determine Brownell's blood-alcohol content. Perceiving uncooperative behavior in administering a Breathalyzer test, the [officers], acting with knowledge of the doctor's diagnosis, attempted to rouse Brownell from his apparent stupor. * * * [T]he pain techniques involved little force. And, upon discovering they were ineffective, the officers did not resort to a higher degree of force but merely attempted to process Brownell as best they could under the circumstances. * * * Brownell's injury is unfortunate and regrettable; however, absent any evidence it was caused by the unreasonable conduct of these state actors, rather than his automobile accident, no constitutional deprivation occurred.

Id. at 1293. [Court's emphasis.]

3. *The failure to provide officers with mace.* In *Roy v. Inhabitants of the City of Lewiston*, 42 *F.*3d 691 (1st Cir. 1994), two officers responded to a domestic dispute at the home of Michael and Edith Roy. Upon their arrival, the officers learned that Michael Roy ("Roy") was armed with two knives and had threatened to use them against any police officer who approached him. The officers entered the residence and found Roy, apparently very drunk, lying on the floor. The officers then learned that a third officer was on his way to the residence to serve Roy with a summons for assaulting another woman earlier that day. When the third officer arrived, Roy refused to accept the summons. As a result, the officer pushed it into Roy's pocket. Roy then became extremely upset, stated, " 'I'll show you,' entered his home, and then—following out Edith Roy who was screaming—returned carrying a steak knife in each hand." *Id.* at 693.

At this point, the officers drew their firearms and ordered Roy to drop the knives. Roy refused; instead, he advanced on the officers, flailing his arms while continuing to hold the knives. "The officers retreated back to a sharp downward incline. After some maneuvering in which the officers repeated their warnings and made some effort to distract and disarm Roy, Roy made a kicking-lunging motion toward [the officers]." *Id.* Roy was shot twice, arrested and hospitalized. Ultimately, Roy recovered and sued the officers.

In this appeal, among the issues presented was the question whether the officers should have been equipped with "pepper mace." According to one expert, because this spray was not made available to Lewiston police officers, they were required to place undue emphasis on their firearms. Rejecting this contention, the court said:

> As for the police chief and the town, nothing in the expert's affidavit would make anyone think that the failure to provide mace was so unusual or patently improper as to reflect "deliberate indifference" under the circumstances.

Id. at 696. *See also McKinney v. DeKalb County, Georgia*, 997 *F.*2d 1440 (11th Cir. 1993).

4. *The events leading up to the use of deadly force.* Does the Fourth Amendment prohibit creating a foreseeably dangerous situation in which to arrest a suspect ? In *Carter v. Buscher*, 973 *F.*2d 1328 (7th Cir. 1992), the court said no. According to the Seventh Circuit Court of Appeals, *Tennessee v. Garner* and *Brower v. County of Inyo* "do not suggest that the Fourth Amendment prohibits creating unreasonably dangerous circumstances in which to effect a legal arrest of a suspect. The Fourth Amendment prohibits unreasonable *seizures* not unreasonable, unjustified or outrageous conduct." *Carter* at 1332. "Therefore, pre-seizure conduct is not subject to Fourth Amendment scrutiny," ruled the court. *Id.*

In *Carter*, the Illinois State Police developed probable cause to arrest Raymond Ruhl for solicitation to murder his wife, Lisa Ruhl Carter. Based on reliable information, the state police knew that Ruhl ran a gun shop out of his home and bragged that he was always armed—even while working inside a prison as a correctional officer for the Illinois Department of Corrections (DOC), in violation of DOC regulations. "To minimize Ruhl's access to weapons and thereby reduce the risk of injury to state police officers and bystanders, the state police officers concocted a scheme to arrest Ruhl on U.S. 51, just south of the Oconee, Illinois, intersection." *Id.* at 1330.

To set the plan in motion, several officers enlisted the help of an assistant DOC warden. One of the officers telephoned Ruhl at the correctional institution, and asked him to assist his niece, who was supposedly having car trouble on Route 51. Three officers, dressed in street clothes, took part in the scheme. One officer played the part of Ruhl's niece; two others acted as friends of the niece who had been riding along with her. The scheme did not go as planned. When Ruhl arrived, instead of exiting his car to assist, he remained in his car with the motor on and the car in gear approximately 20 to 25 feet behind the "stranded car." One of the officers approached Ruhl and attempted to persuade him to look at her car's engine. A second officer, becoming impatient with the first officer's progress, approached Ruhl, shined his flashlight into Ruhl's eyes, and announced, "state police." Ruhl responded by drawing a semi-automatic weapon and opening fire on the officers. The one-minute shootout resulted in the death of Ruhl and one of the state police officers; a second officer was injured.

Ironically, Carter, the intended victim of Ruhl's murder plot, brought suit, contending that "by reason of their ill conceived plan in the attempt to arrest [Ruhl] along a darkened highway instead of inside the correctional institution where he worked, the [officers] provoked a situation whereby unreasonable deadly force was used in an attempt to seize his person[.]" *Id.*

Finding no Fourth Amendment violation, the court explained that, up until the shooting, no seizure occurred: the officers did not physically restrain Ruhl, nor did he submit or yield to the authority of the officers. Quite the contrary—"when [Officer] Bensyl announced 'state police,' Ruhl did not submit to Bensyl; he shot him." *Id.* at 1333. The court continued:

> Was shooting Ruhl "reasonable" under the Fourth Amendment? We need not linger long on this question. Ruhl's shooting rampage threatened the lives of all the officers at the scene. Therefore, the rule in *Garner* unquestionably justified the use of deadly force to seize Ruhl.
>
> Even if the [officers] concocted a dubious scheme to bring about Ruhl's arrest, it is the arrest itself and not the scheme that must be scrutinized for reasonableness under the Fourth Amendment.

Id.

5. *Use of force after arrest.* The Supreme Court has "not resolved the question whether the Fourth Amendment continues to provide individuals with protection against the deliberate use of excessive force beyond the point at which arrest ends and pretrial detention begins[.]"

Graham at 395 n.10, 109 *S.Ct.* at 1871 n.10. As a result, lower courts have addressed the issue by reference to a "custodial continuum," running from an individual's initial seizure and arrest, to his or her post-arrest but pre-hearing custody, to pretrial detention, and through the individual's post-conviction incarceration. *See e.g., Austin v. Hamilton,* 945 *F.*2d 1155, 1158 (10th Cir. 1991). The objectionable use of force is examined by reference to the point along the continuum at which it occurred, and a determination is then made as to "what constitutional protection controls at which particular juncture." *Id.* at 1158. *See also Titran v. Ackman,* 893 *F.*2d 145, 147 (7th Cir. 1990) (recognizing different points along the custodial continuum to which variable constitutional standards may attach).

A number of courts have resolved the Fourth Amendment issue by holding that Fourth Amendment principles should be applied after arrest to protect detainees from their arresting officer's use of excessive force, at least up until arraignment or formal charge. *See e.g., Austin v. Hamilton, supra* at 1160 ("We conclude that just as the fourth amendment strictures continue in effect to set the applicable constitutional limitations regarding both duration (reasonable period under the circumstances of arrest) and legal justification (judicial determination of probable cause), its protections also persist to impose restrictions on the treatment of the arrestee detained without a warrant."); *Powell v. Gardner,* 891 *F.*2d 1039, 1044 (2nd Cir. 1989) ("We think the Fourth Amendment standard probably should be applied at least to the period prior to the time when the person arrested [pursuant to a warrant] is arraigned or formally charged, and remains in the custody * * * of the arresting officers."). See also *Hammer v. Gross,* 884 *F.*2d 1200, 1204 (9th Cir. 1989) (Fourth Amendment principles govern the analysis of claims seeking redress for post-arrest use of excessive force in connection with searches incident to arrest), *vacated en banc on other grounds,* 932 *F.*2d 842, 845 n.1, 850-51 (2nd Cir. 1991) (vacating panel opinion but noting agreement regarding application of Fourth Amendment standards).

6. *Use of force after conviction and incarceration.* As the Court noted in *Graham,* "[a]fter conviction, the Eighth Amendment 'serves as the primary source of substantive protection * * * in cases * * * where the deliberate use of force is challenged as excessive and unjustified.'" *Id.* at 1871 n.10. [Citation omitted.] In *Hudson v. McMillian,* 503 *U.S.* 1, 112 *S.Ct.* 995 (1992), the Court emphasized that "whenever prison officials stand accused of using excessive force in violation of the Cruel and Unusual Punishments Clause, the core judicial inquiry is * * * whether force was applied in a good-faith effort to maintain or restore discipline, or maliciously and sadistically to cause harm." *Id.,* 112 *S.Ct.* at 999. In the Eighth Amendment setting, the determination whether the use of force was "wanton and unnecessary" will include an evaluation of "the need for application of force, the relationship between that need and the amount of force used, the threat 'reasonably perceived by the responsible officials,' and 'any efforts made to temper the severity of a forceful response.'" *Id.* (quoting *Whitley v. Albers,* 475 *U.S.* 312, 321, 106 *S.Ct.* 1078, 1085 (1986)). Additionally, while the absence or

presence of serious injury is "relevant to the Eighth Amendment inquiry," *id.*, the fact that a prisoner does not suffer serious injury will not be dispositive of the question whether the use of excessive physical force against the inmate constitutes cruel and unusual punishment. *Id.* at 997. In this respect, the Court observed, "[w]hen prison officials maliciously and sadistically use force to cause harm, contemporary standards of decency always are violated. * * * This is true whether or not significant injury is evident." *Id.* at 1000.

ESTATE OF LARSEN v. MURR
United States Court of Appeals
511 *F.*3d 1255 (10th Cir. 2008)

QUESTION: In the below circumstances, was the officer's use of deadly force reasonable?

CIRCUMSTANCES: In the middle of April, just after midnight, the Denver police received a 911 call from Lyle Larsen threatening to "kill someone or himself." *Id.* at 1258. "Officers Randy Murr and David Brase were dispatched to Larsen's residence and arrived in separate vehicles. They parked on the street near the home and approached by foot from different directions. * * * As the officers approached the house, Larsen stood alone on the front porch. In his hands, he held a large knife with a blade over one foot long. Because of its size, Murr initially thought the knife was a pipe. Officer Brase, who at first had a better angle, described the knife as looking like 'a small sword.' As they neared Larsen, Brase warned Murr that Larsen was armed, and both men drew their service pistols. Brase told Larsen in a loud voice: 'I'm Corporal Brase, the Denver police. I need you to put that knife down right now.' Larsen appeared to bend over, as if intending to place the knife on the ground, but then straightened up with the weapon still in his hand. * * * Murr believed Larsen was within 7 to 12 feet. Larsen's eyes became 'the size of quarters.' Appearing agitated, he raised the knife above his shoulder with the blade pointed outward and turned towards Officer Murr." *Id.* Murr ordered Larsen to "Drop the knife, drop the knife, * * * [d]rop the knife or I'll shoot. Larsen turned and took a step towards Murr, who was on the sidewalk below. Fearing for his life, Murr fired twice, hitting Larsen in the chest and killing him." *Id.* at 1258-59.

ANSWER: YES. "[T]he use of deadly force in these circumstances was objectively reasonable. The undisputed evidence paints a picture that Officers Murr and Brase were faced with an armed suspect in an agitated condition, who ignored repeated warnings to drop his weapon, and appeared willing and able to attack." *Id.* at 1263.

RATIONALE: In this case, Larsen's next of kin brought a 42 *U.S.C.* § 1983 lawsuit, arguing that Officer Murr used excessive force during the encounter in violation of the Fourth Amendment. *The Tenth Circuit Court of Appeals disagreed.*

The plaintiff's claim of excessive force centered on "whether Larsen posed an immediate threat to the officers or the safety of others." *Id.* at 1260. Deadly force is justified under the Fourth Amendment if a reasonable officer in Officer Murr's position "would have had 'probable cause to believe that there was a *threat of serious physical harm to [himself]* or to others.' " *Id.* [Court's emphasis; citation omitted.] "A reasonable officer need not await the 'glint of steel' before taking self-protective action; by then, it is 'often . . . too late to take safety precautions.' " *Id.* [Citation omitted.]

In assessing the degree of threat facing officers, courts will consider a number of non-exclusive factors. These include:

(1)   whether the officers ordered the suspect to drop his weapon, and the suspect's compliance with police commands;

(2)   whether any hostile motions were made with the weapon towards the officers;

(3)   the distance separating the officers and the suspect; and

(4)   the manifest intentions of the suspect.

Id. In the end, "the inquiry is always whether, from the perspective of a reasonable officer on the scene, the totality of the circumstances justified the use of force." *Id.* In this case, the court found:

> (1) Larsen had already threatened violence against himself and others; (2) the officers responded to an emergency call late at night; (3) when the officers arrived, they encountered a man armed with a knife; (4) both officers repeatedly told Larsen to put down the knife; (5) the knife was a large weapon with a blade over a foot in length rather than a mere pocket knife or razor blade; (6) Larsen refused to cooperate with the officers' repeated orders to drop his weapon; (7) Larsen held the high ground visa-vis the officers; (8) Larsen raised the knife blade above his shoulder and pointed the tip towards the officers; (9) Officer Brase was also prepared to use force and was moving into position to be able to do so; (10) Larsen turned and took a step toward Officer Murr; (11) the distance between Murr and Larsen at the time of the shooting, though disputed, was somewhere between 7 and 20 feet.

> Examining the totality of the circumstances and the undisputed facts, we agree with the district court that the officer's use of deadly force was objectively reasonable. This is a prototypical case where police officers were "forced to make split-second judgments," and even if Officer Murr's assessment of the threat was mistaken, it was not objectively unreasonable.

Id. at 1260-61.

During the course of its opinion, the court noted that in *Walker v. City of Orem*, 451 *F*.3d 1139, 1160 (10th Cir. 2006), it had held that "where an officer had reason to believe that a suspect was only holding a knife, not a gun, and the suspect was not charging the officer and had made no slicing or stabbing motions toward him, that it was unreasonable for the officer to use deadly force against the suspect."

Unlike *Walker,* in this case "Larsen did make hostile actions toward Murr. The undisputed facts here show that Larsen ignored at least four police commands to drop his weapon and then turned and stepped toward the officer with a large knife raised in a provocative motion. Under these circumstances, Murr reasonably concluded Larsen posed an immediate threat to his safety." *Id.* at 1263.

Accordingly, the court concluded that "the use of deadly force in these circumstances was objectively reasonable." *Id.*

---

§1.7. Substantive and procedural due process of law.

The Due Process Clause of the Fifth Amendment provides, "No person shall * * * be deprived of life, liberty, or property, without due process of law[.]" The safeguards flowing from this particular Fifth Amendment provision are not directed to the states; rather, they are addressed solely to the federal government. *Palko v. Connecticut*, 302 *U.S.* 319, 58 *S.Ct.* 149 (1937). On the state level, the Due Process Clause of the Fourteenth Amendment affords analogous protection, commanding, "nor shall any State deprive any person of life, liberty, or property, without due process of law[.]" In the broadest sense, due process of law requires the states and the federal government, in their legislative enactments and criminal prosecutions, to "respect certain decencies of civilized conduct" by avoiding "methods that offend 'a sense of justice.'" *Rochin v. California*, 342 *U.S.* 165, 172, 72 *S.Ct.* 205, 209 (1952).

The Due Process clauses have been interpreted by the United States Supreme Court as protecting individuals against two types of government action. First, they provide "substantive" protection by preventing government agents from engaging in conduct, and the Congress or state legislatures from enacting any law, which tramples upon a citizen's fundamental or vested rights, or unnecessarily restricts a citizen's liberty. Thus, the guarantee of "substantive" due process of law prohibits law enforcement agents from engaging in conduct that "shocks the conscience," *Rochin* at 172, 72 *S.Ct.* at 209, or unjustifiably interferes with fundamental rights held to be "implicit in the concept of ordered liberty." *Palko* at 325-326, 58 *S.Ct.* at 152. Moreover, substantive due process requires that criminal legislation be written in reasonably definite and understandable terms, that it not be retroactive or arbitrary in its classification, and that it have a cognizable relationship to a legitimate end of government, *e.g.*, protecting the public health, safety or welfare; and when legislation touches upon or limits the exercise of fundamental constitutional rights, it will receive the strictest form of review by the courts.

Once a court determines that a particular government action affecting a person's life, liberty, or property is justified, or that a particular criminal statute is fairly and clearly limited in the manner and extent to which it defines what is unlawful, the government action or legislation survives the "substantive" due process inquiry. The next step requires an inquiry into whether the action or legislation has been implemented in a fair, just and reasonable manner. *Mathews v. Eldridge*, 424 *U.S.* 319, 335, 96 *S.Ct.* 893, 903 (1976). This second layer of protection has traditionally been referred to as "procedural" due process of law.

---

§1.7(a). Substantive due process.

KOLENDER v. LAWSON
Supreme Court of the United States
461 *U.S.* 352, 103 *S.Ct.* 1855 (1983)

QUESTION: Will a state criminal statute violate the Due Process clause of the Fourteenth Amendment when it makes it an offense for a person to loiter or wander upon the streets or from place to place without apparent reason or business and who fails to identify himself and to account for his presence upon request of a law enforcement officer, who has a reasonable suspicion that criminal activity may be afoot ?

ANSWER: YES. Such a statute is unconstitutionally vague within the meaning of the Fourteenth Amendment. "A person who is stopped on less than probable cause cannot be punished for failing to identify himself." *Id.* at 1857. "[W]hile police have a right to request citizens to answer voluntarily questions concerning unsolved crimes, they have no right to compel them to answer." *Id.* at 1860 n.9.

RATIONALE: The defendant challenged a California statute on the grounds of it being unconstitutionally vague within the meaning of the Due Process clause of the Fourteenth Amendment. The statute made it an offense for a person to loiter or wander:

> upon the streets or from place to place without apparent reason or business and who refuses to identify himself and to account for his presence when requested by any peace officer so to do, if the surrounding circumstances are such to indicate to a reasonable man that the public safety demands such identification. Calif. Penal Code Ann. §647(e) (West 1970).

Id. at 1856 n.1. The California courts interpreted this statute to require a person stopped on reasonable suspicion to provide a "credible and reliable" identification and to "account for his presence." *Id.* at 1857, 1858.

The Supreme Court of the United States held, however, that this statute, as construed by the California courts, was "unconstitutionally vague within the meaning of the Fourteenth Amendment by failing to clarify what is contemplated by the requirement that a suspect provide a 'credible and reliable' identification." *Id.* at 1856.

Justice O'Connor explained that the "void-for-vagueness doctrine requires that a penal statute define the criminal offense with sufficient definiteness that ordinary people can understand what conduct is prohibited and in a manner that does not encourage arbitrary and discriminatory enforcement." *Id.* at 1858.

The Court demonstrated much distaste for statutes which give police complete and uncontrolled discretion. Although it recognized that there is an important need for "strengthened law enforcement tools to combat the epidemic of crime that plagues our Nation," *id.* at 1860, such need cannot justify indefinite and unclear criminal statutes. "Merely to facilitate the general law enforcement objectives of investigating and preventing unspecified crimes, States may not authorize the arrest and criminal prosecution of an individual for failing to produce identification or further information on demand by a police officer." *Id.* at 1861 (Brennan, J., concurring).

As a result, the statute, as construed by the California courts, is repugnant to the Constitution because its vague language "encourages arbitrary enforcement by failing to describe with sufficient particularity what a suspect must do in order to satisfy [its terms]." *Id.* at 1860.

NOTE

1. As a general principle, a statute or ordinance which fails to give sufficient notice of its scope and adequate guidance for proper application cannot withstand the constitutional prohibition against "vague" laws. Clarity in the terms of a criminal law is a fundamental due process requirement seated in notions of fair play. *Colten v. Kentucky*, 407 *U.S.* 104, 110, 92 *S.Ct.* 1953, 1957 (1972); *Lanzetta v. New Jersey*, 306 *U.S.* 451, 455, 59 *S.Ct.* 618-620 (1939). The underlying principle is that "no man shall be held criminally responsible for conduct which he could not reasonably understand" to be illegal. *Colten, supra.* As the Court explained in *Grayned v. City of Rockford*:

> Vague laws offend several important values. First, because we assume that man is free to steer between lawful and unlawful conduct, we insist that laws give a person of ordinary intelligence a reasonable opportunity to know what is prohibited, so that he may act accordingly. Vague laws may trap the innocent by not providing fair warning. Second, if arbitrary and discriminatory enforcement is to be prevented, laws must provide explicit standards for those who apply them. A vague law impermissibly delegates basic policy matters to police[officers], judges, and juries for resolution on an ad hoc and subjective basis, with the attendant dangers of arbitrary and discriminatory application.

408 *U.S.* 104, 108-09, 92 *S.Ct.* 2294, 2298-99 (1972). Thus, a law will be unconstitutional if it is phrased in terms that are "so vague" that persons of "common intelligence must necessarily guess at its meaning and differ as to its application." *See Coates v. Cincinnati*, 402 *U.S.* 611, 614, 91 *S.Ct.* 1686 (1971) (statute prohibiting groups of three or more persons to gather on the sidewalk and "annoy" passers-by deemed "void for vagueness"). To survive the constitutional prohibition against vagueness, the language of the penal statute or ordinance must be clear; it must identify the "forbidden conduct with particularity," and the terms used must enable persons of "common intelligence, in light of ordinary experience" to know what the law commands or forbids; and to understand whether their contemplated conduct will fall within the law's scope. *United States v. Lanier*, 520 *U.S.* 259, 117 *S.Ct.* 1219, 1224 (1997). *See also Bouie v. City of Columbia*, 378 *U.S.* 347, 351, 84 *S.Ct.* 1697, 1701 (1964) (" 'The principle is that no man shall be held criminally responsible for conduct which he could not reasonably understand to be proscribed.' ") (quoting *United States v. Harris*, 347 *U.S.* 612, 617, 74 *S.Ct.* 808, 811-12 (1954)). In the words of Justice Holmes, a person must be provided with "fair warning," in "language that the common world will understand, of what the law intends to do if a certain line is passed. To make the warning fair, so far as possible the line should be clear." *McBoyle v. United States*, 283 *U.S.* 25, 27, 51 *S.Ct.* 340, 341 (1931).

2. A criminal statute or ordinance may be challenged in two ways: (1) "facially" and (2) "as applied" to a particular set of facts. A law challenged "facially" may be found unconstitutional by a court only if it is "impermissibly vague in all its application," meaning that there is absolutely no conduct that the law prohibits with sufficient certainty. *Village of Hoffman Estates v. Flipside, Hoffman Estates*, 455 *U.S.* 489, 495, 102 *S.Ct.* 1186, 1192 (1982). If, however, the challenge to a particular criminal law focuses on the way it is "applied" to a particular defendant in a particular set of circumstances, the challenge may be successful if the law does not, in a sufficiently clear manner, prohibit the conduct against which it is sought to be enforced. *See Palmer v. City of Euclid*, 402 *U.S.* 544, 91 *S.Ct.* 1563 (1971). Moreover, a defendant may "test a law for vagueness as applied only with respect to his or her particular conduct; if a statute is vague as applied to that conduct, it will not be enforced even though the law might be validly imposed against others not similarly situated. * * * Conversely, if a statute is not vague as applied to a particular party, it may be enforced even though it might be too vague as applied to others." *State v. Cameron*, 100 *N.J.* 586, 593 (1985).

3. Vagrancy ordinances. In *Papachristou v. City of Jacksonville*, 405 *U.S.* 156, 92 *S.Ct.* 839 (1972), the Court struck down a Jacksonville, Florida, municipal vagrancy ordinance which classified vagrancy as an offense punishable by 90 days' imprisonment, a $500 fine, or both. At the time, the ordinance included the following types of people within its definition of "vagrant":

Rogues and vagabonds, or dissolute persons who go about begging, common gamblers, persons who use juggling or unlawful games or plays, common drunkards, common night walkers, thieves, pilferers or pickpockets, traders in stolen property, lewd, wanton and lascivious persons, keepers of gambling places, common railers and brawlers, persons wandering or strolling around from place to place without lawful purpose or object, habitual loafers, disorderly persons, persons neglecting all lawful business and habitually spending their time by frequenting houses of ill fame, gaming houses, or places where alcoholic beverages are sold or served, persons able to work but habitually living upon the earnings of their wives or minor children[.]

According to the Court, "[t]his ordinance is void for vagueness, both in the sense that it 'fails to give a person of ordinary intelligence fair notice that his contemplated conduct is forbidden by the statute,' * * * and because it encourages arbitrary and erratic arrests and convictions." *Id.*, 92 *S.Ct.* at 843. [Citations omitted.]

"Living under a rule of law entails various suppositions, one of which is that '[all persons] are entitled to be informed as to what the State commands or forbids.' " *Id.* [Citation omitted.] Due process of law mandates that a law provide "fair notice of the offending conduct."

The Jacksonville ordinance makes criminal activities which by modern standards are normally innocent. "Nightwalking" is one. * * * We know, however, from experience that sleepless people often walk at night, perhaps hopeful that sleep-inducing relaxation will result.

Luis Munoz-Marin, former Governor of Puerto Rico, commented once that "loafing" was a national virtue in his Commonwealth and that it should be encouraged. It is, however, a crime in Jacksonville.

"[P]ersons able to work but habitually living upon the earnings of their wives or minor children"—like habitually living "without visible means of support"—might implicate unemployed pillars of the community who have married rich wives. * * * [This classification] may also embrace unemployed people out of the labor market, by reason of a recession or disemployed by reason of technological or so-called structural displacements.

Persons "wandering or strolling" from place to place have been extolled by Walt Whitman and Vachel Lindsay. The qualification "without any lawful purpose or object" may be a trap for innocent acts. Persons "neglecting all lawful business and habitually spending their time by frequenting . . . places where alcoholic beverages are sold or served" would literally embrace many members of golf clubs and city clubs. * * *

The difficulty is that these activities are historically part of the amenities of life as we have known them. They are not mentioned in the Constitution or in the Bill of Rights. These unwritten amenities have been in part responsible for giving our people the feeling of independence and self-confidence, the feeling of creativity. These amenities have dignified the right of dissent and have honored the right to be nonconformists and the right to defy submissiveness. They have encouraged lives of high spirits rather than hushed, suffocating silence.

Id. at 844. [Citations and footnotes omitted.]

"It would certainly be dangerous," states the Court, if a state legislature " 'could set a net large enough to catch all possible offenders, and leave it to the courts to step inside and say who should be set [free].' " *Id.* at 845. [Citation omitted.] Here, however, the cast of the net is large, "not to give the courts the power to pick and choose but to increase the arsenal of the police." *Id.* The "unfettered discretion" that the ordinance places in the hands of the Jacksonville police is "not compatible with our Constitution." *Id.* at 846-47.

> Those generally implicated by the imprecise terms of the ordinance—poor people, nonconformists, dissenters, idlers—may be required to comport themselves according to the life style deemed appropriate by the Jacksonville police and the courts. Where, as here, there are no standards governing the exercise of the discretion granted by the ordinance, the scheme permits and encourages an arbitrary and discriminatory enforcement of the law. It furnishes a convenient tool for "harsh and discriminatory enforcement by local prosecuting officials, against particular groups deemed to merit their displeasure." * * * It results in a regime in which the poor and the unpopular are permitted to "stand on a public sidewalk . . . only at the whim of any police officer." * * *
>
> Of course, vagrancy statutes are useful to the police. * * * But the rule of law implies equality and justice in its application. Vagrancy laws of the Jacksonville type teach that the scales of justice are so tipped that even-handed administration of the law is not possible. The rule of law, evenly applied to minorities as well as majorities, to the poor as well as the rich, is the great mucilage that holds society together.
>
> The Jacksonville ordinance cannot be squared with our constitutional standards and is plainly unconstitutional.

Id. at 847-48. [Citations omitted.]

4. *"Stop and Identify" laws upheld.* In *Hiibel v. Sixth Judicial Dist. Court of Nevada, Humboldt Co.*, 542 *U.S.* 177, 124 *S.Ct.* 2451 (2004), the United States Supreme Court upheld Nevada's "stop and identify" law.

In *Hiibel*, during the afternoon, the Humboldt County Sheriff's Department received a phone call regarding a man assaulting a woman in a red and silver GMC truck on Grass Valley Road. "Deputy Sheriff Lee Dove was dispatched to investigate. When the officer arrived at the scene, he found the truck parked on the side of the road. A man was standing by the truck, and a young woman was sitting inside it. The officer observed skid marks in the gravel behind the vehicle, leading him to believe it had come to a sudden stop." *Id.*, 124 *S.Ct.* at 2455.

"The officer approached the man and explained that he was investigating a report of a fight. The man appeared to be intoxicated. The officer asked him if he had 'any identification' on him. The man refused to identify himself and asked why the officer wanted to see identification. The officer responded that he was conducting an investigation and needed to see some identification. The unidentified man became agitated and insisted he had done nothing wrong. The officer explained that he wanted to find out who the man was and what he was doing there. After continued refusals to comply with the officer's request for identification, the man began to taunt the officer by placing his hands behind his back and telling the officer to arrest him and take him to jail. This routine kept up for several minutes: the officer asked for identification 11 times and was refused each time. After warning the man that he would be arrested if he continued to refuse to comply, the officer placed him under arrest." *Id.*

Ultimately, the man was identified as Larry Hiibel. He was charged with willfully obstructing "a public officer in discharging or attempting to discharge any legal duty of his office," in violation of Nev. Rev. Stat. (*N.R.S*) 199.280. The obstruction charge was based on Section 171.123, a Nevada statute that defines the legal rights and duties of a police officer in the context of an investigative stop:

> 1. Any peace officer may detain any person whom the officer encounters under circumstances which reasonably indicate that the person has committed, is committing or is about to commit a crime. * * *

> 3. The officer may detain the person pursuant to this section only to ascertain his identity and the suspicious circumstances surrounding his presence abroad. Any person so detained shall identify himself, but may not be compelled to answer any other inquiry of any peace officer.

Hiibel was convicted and fined $250.

N.R.S. 171.123(3) is an enactment sometimes referred to as a "stop and identify" statute. To date, approximately 20 states have such laws: Ala., Ark., Colo., Del., Fla., Ga., Ill., Kan., La., Mo., Mont., Neb., N. H., N.M., N.Y., N.D., R. I., Utah, Vt., and Wis.

As explained by the Court, "[s]top and identify statutes often combine elements of traditional vagrancy laws with provisions intended to regulate police behavior in the course of investigatory stops. The statutes vary from State to State, but all permit an officer to ask or require a suspect to disclose his identity. These statutes have their roots in early English vagrancy laws that required suspected vagrants to face arrest unless they gave 'a good account of themselves.' " *Id.* at 2456. [Citation omitted.] In recent years, however, the Court has found these traditional vagrancy laws to be unconstitutional.

In this case, however, there was no question that the initial stop was based on reasonable suspicion, satisfying Fourth Amendment requirements. Moreover, the Nevada statute is narrow and precise, and has been interpreted by the Nevada Supreme Court as to require only that a suspect "disclose his name." *Id.* at 2457. The suspect is " 'not required to provide private details about his background, but merely to state his name to an officer when reasonable suspicion exists.' " *Id.* [Citation omitted.]

Thus, the Nevada "stop and identify" statute "does not require a suspect to give the officer a driver's license or any other document. Provided that the suspect either states his name or communicates it to the officer by other means—a choice * * * that the suspect may make—the statute is satisfied and no violation occurs." *Id.*

In discussing the police need for a suspect's identity, the Court observed:

> Asking questions is an essential part of police investigations. In the ordinary course, a police officer is free to ask a person for identification without implicating the Fourth Amendment. "[I]nterrogation relating to one's identity or a request for identification by the police does not, by itself, constitute a Fourth Amendment seizure." * * * Beginning with *Terry v. Ohio*, * * * the Court has recognized that a law enforcement officer's reasonable suspicion that a person may be involved in criminal activity permits the officer to stop the person for a brief time and take additional steps to investigate further. * * * To ensure that the resulting seizure is constitutionally reasonable, a *Terry* stop must be limited. The officer's action must be "justified at its inception, and . . . reasonably related in scope to the circumstances which justified the interference in the first place." * * * For example, the seizure cannot continue for an excessive period of time, * * * or resemble a traditional arrest[.]

> [Our] decisions make clear that questions concerning a suspect's identity are a routine and accepted part of many *Terry* stops. * * * Obtaining a suspect's name in the course of a *Terry* stop serves important government interests. Knowledge of identity may inform an officer that a suspect is wanted for another offense, or has a record of violence or mental disorder. On the other hand, knowing identity may help clear a suspect and allow the police to concentrate their efforts elsewhere. Identity may prove particularly important in cases such as this, where the police are investigating what appears to be a domestic assault. Officers called to investigate domestic disputes need to know whom they are dealing with in order to assess the situation, the threat to their own safety, and possible danger to the potential victim.

Id. at 2458.

Although it has been well established that an officer may ask a suspect to identify himself during the course of a *Terry* stop, the question remains whether the police can arrest and prosecute a suspect's refusal to answer. Earlier case law has suggested that a person detained in an investigative stop can be questioned but is "not obliged to answer, answers may not be compelled, and refusal to answer furnishes no basis for an arrest." *Id.* at 2459. Contrary to Hiibel's contention, this language does not establish a "right to refuse to answer questions during a *Terry* stop." *Id.* Indeed, the Fourth Amendment "does not impose obligations on the citizen but instead provides rights against the government. As a result, the Fourth Amendment itself cannot require a suspect to answer questions." *Id.*

This case presents a different issue. Here, the source of the legal obligation arises from state law, not the Fourth Amendment. Further, the statutory obligation does not go beyond answering an officer's request to disclose a name; and, according to the Court, the "principles of *Terry* permit a State to require a suspect to disclose his name in the course of a *Terry* stop. The reasonableness of a seizure under the Fourth Amendment is determined 'by balancing its intrusion on the individual's Fourth Amendment interests against its promotion of legitimate government interests.' * * * The Nevada statute satisfies that standard. The request for identity has an immediate relation to the purpose, rationale, and practical demands of a *Terry* stop. The threat of criminal sanction helps ensure that the request for identity does not become a legal nullity. On the other hand, the Nevada statute does not alter the nature of the stop itself: it does not change its duration, * * * or its location. A state law requiring a suspect to disclose his name in the course of a valid *Terry* stop is consistent with Fourth Amendment prohibitions against unreasonable searches and seizures." *Id.*

Finally, the Court also rejected Hiibel's argument that his conviction violated the Fifth Amendment's prohibition on compelled self-incrimination. According to the Court:

> To qualify for the Fifth Amendment privilege, a communication must be testimonial, incriminating, and compelled. * * * "[T]o be testimonial, an accused's communication must itself, explicitly or implicitly, relate a factual assertion or disclose information." Stating one's name may qualify as an assertion of fact relating to identity. Production of identity documents might meet the definition as well. * * * Even if these required actions are testimonial, however, [Hiibel's] challenge must fail because in this case disclosure of his name presented no reasonable danger of incrimination. * * * As best [as the Court could tell, Hiibel] refused to identify himself only because he thought his name was none of the officer's business.

Id. at 2460-61.

"The narrow scope of the disclosure requirement is also important. One's identity is, by definition, unique; yet it is, in another sense, a universal characteristic. Answering a request to disclose a name is likely to be so insignificant in the scheme of things as to be incriminating only in unusual circumstances. * * * In every criminal case, it is known and must be known who has been arrested and who is being tried. * * * Even witnesses who plan to invoke the Fifth Amendment privilege answer when their names are called to take the stand." *Id.* at 2461.

Accordingly, in this case, the stop, the request, and the State's requirement of a response did not violate the Fourth Amendment.

---

§1.7(b). Procedural due process.

The "procedural" guarantee of due process of law prohibits the states and federal government from implementing the law in an unfair, unreasonable or arbitrary manner. It guarantees that government will employ a fair and reasonable decision-making process before engaging in any action which might impair an individual's life, liberty, or property. As the term reflects, this aspect of due process refers only to matters of procedure, that is, only to the fairness of the process, with the ultimate inquiry being, "What is the nature of the process that is due ? "

In the area of criminal law and procedure, it is clear that a defendant's life, liberty, or property is at stake. Consequently, the government owes him or her a fair procedure and a reasonable decision-making process before embarking upon a course of action designed in some way to adversely affect the individual's life, liberty, or property.

Whenever a criminal defendant is to be deprived of his or her liberty for a substantial period of time, procedural "due process" safeguards, as well as Fourth Amendment "probable cause" requirements, come into play. In this respect, before a warrant may issue for a person's arrest, an independent inquiry must be made by a neutral and detached judge or authorized judicial officer as to whether probable cause exists to believe that (1) an offense has occurred, and (2) the accused is or was a criminal participant. *Giordenello v. United States*, 357 *U.S.* 480, 486, 78 *S.Ct.* 1245, 1250 (1958). In order to properly make an independent judgment that probable cause exists for the issuance of the arrest warrant, the judicial officer must be supplied with sufficient information.

When drafting the complaint/affidavit in support of the issuance of an arrest warrant, the police officer/affiant must do more than merely insert the accused's name on a form which sets forth the relevant crime in general terms. The complaint/affidavit must indicate how the officer/affiant knows, or why he or she believes, that the accused committed the crime. *Overton v. Ohio*, 534 *U.S.* 982, 122 *S.Ct.* 389 (2001) (Statement of Justices Breyer, Stevens, O'Connor and Souter respecting denial of *certiorari*). Thus, in *Giordenello, supra*, the Court found that the complaint failed to meet the "probable cause" requirement because it contained "no affirmative allegation that the affiant spoke with personal knowledge of the matters contained therein," failed to "indicate any sources for the complainant's belief," and neglected to "set forth any other sufficient basis upon which a finding of probable cause could be made." *Id.* at 487, 78 *S.Ct.* at 1245. For those reasons, the Magistrate could not "assess independently the probability" that the accused "committed the crime charged." *Id. See also Whiteley v. Warden, Wyo. State Penitentiary*, 401 *U.S.* 560, 564-65, 91 *S.Ct.* 1031 (1971) (complaint in support of warrant did not permit a finding of probable cause, for it consisted of "nothing more than the complainant's conclusion that the individuals named therein perpetrated the offense described").

While there are, of course, many circumstances in which a law enforcement officer may effect an arrest without a warrant, if the arrestee is to be detained for any significant period of time, the Fourth

Amendment requires a "prompt," independent judicial determination of probable cause as a prerequisite to the extended pretrial detention. *Gerstein v. Pugh*, 420 *U.S.* 103, 113-114, 125, 95 *S.Ct.* 854, 862-863, 868-869 (1975). Significantly, *Gerstein* does not require an independent probable cause determination immediately upon taking a suspect into custody and completing booking procedures. Rather, the Court left it up to the individual States to integrate prompt, independent probable cause determinations into their differing systems of pretrial procedures. *Id.* at 123-124, 95 *S.Ct.* at 867-868. "[A] jurisdiction that provides judicial determinations of probable cause *within 48 hours of arrest* will, as a general matter, comply with the promptness requirement of *Gerstein*." *County of Riverside v. McLaughlin*, 500 *U.S.* 44, 111 *S.Ct.* 1661, 1670 (1991). [Emphasis added.] Where an arrested individual does not receive an independent probable cause determination within 48 hours of the arrest, "the burden shifts to the government to demonstrate the existence of a bona fide emergency or other extraordinary circumstance." *Id.*, 111 *S.Ct.* at 1670. (Intervening holidays or weekends do not qualify as an "extraordinary circumstance.").

Recent developments in the area of "issuance of process," demonstrate a preference for release on summons rather than incarceration pursuant to an arrest warrant. In fact, virtually all states have set forth procedural rules or other provisions which mandate an accused's release on a summons when certain factors—including the severity of the offense alleged—taken as a whole, indicate that such release is appropriate. *See also Fed.R.Crim.P.* 4 (Arrest warrant or summons on a complaint).

Certainly, an accused who is to be released on a summons will be detained for that period of time necessary to prepare and serve that summons. This detention, however, is normally not prolonged and therefore the restraint on the accused's liberty and freedom is not nearly as significant as the restraint occasioned by detention pursuant to a warrant. Moreover, when an accused is merely mailed his summons, there is no arrest, detention or *any* restraint on his liberty other than the requirement that he subsequently appear for a court hearing.

Fed.R.Crim.Pro. 4(a) authorizes the issuance of a summons instead of an arrest warrant "[u]pon the request of the attorney for the government[.]" As in the case of an arrest warrant, this rule permits the issuance of more than one summons on the same complaint. If, however, the defendant fails to appear in response to the summons, a warrant shall be issued for his arrest. *Id.* The appearance or form of the summons is virtually the same as a warrant, with the exception that instead of commanding that the defendant be arrested, it merely directs "the defendant to appear before a magistrate judge at a stated time and place." *R.* 4(c)(2). The summons may be served anywhere in the United States, *R.* 4(d)(2), by any person authorized to serve a summons in a civil action. *R.* 4(d)(1). Further, *R.* 4(d)(3) requires that the summons "be served upon a defendant by delivering a copy to the defendant personally, or by leaving it at the defendant's dwelling house or usual place of abode with some person of suitable age and discretion then residing therein *and* by mailing a copy of the summons to the defendant's last known address." [Emphasis added.]

Even when the risk of a significant detention is absent, the accused's interests in liberty and freedom from unreasonable restraint and prosecution remain paramount; but the law enforcement procedures required to protect those interests need not be as fixed, rigid or extreme because the threat to those interests is not as substantial.

Accordingly, in order to determine "what process is due," it is necessary to balance the relevant interests involved. The analysis takes into account not only the magnitude of the threat to the liberty of an accused but also the added burden the process may place on effective law enforcement. This analysis was highlighted in *Delaware v. Prouse*, 440 *U.S.* 648, 99 *S.Ct.* 1391 (1979), where the federal Supreme Court determined that "the permissibility of a particular law enforcement practice is judged by balancing its intrusion on the individual's Fourth Amendment interests against its promotion of legitimate governmental interests." *Id.* at 654, 99 *S.Ct.* at 1996. Moreover, the focus of this balancing analysis should always be on the intrusiveness of the process procedure and not on the seriousness of the consequences that would result should a conviction ensue. *See Gerstein* at 118-119, 95 *S.Ct.* at 865-866. Ultimately, the key inquiry will be whether there was, in fact, a "significant restraint" on the liberty of the accused.

When an accused is issued a summons, he is not necessarily subject to such a significant restraint on his personal liberty that it would trigger a constitutional requirement that a neutral and detached court official determine probable cause. *See Gerstein, supra*, 420 *U.S.* at 119, 125 n.26, 95 *S.Ct.* at 865, 869 n.26 (declaring that a probable cause determination is not required in a prosecution by information, but "is required only for those suspects who suffer restraints on liberty other than the condition that they appear for trial."); *United States v. Birkenstock*, 823 *F.*2d 1026 (7th Cir. 1987). *See also United States v. Bohrer*, 807 *F.*2d 159 (10th Cir. 1986) (holding that the federal Constitution does not mandate an independent probable cause determination when a summons instead of a warrant issues on an information charging a violation of the Internal Revenue Code). Where, however, an accused demands that he receive an independent probable cause determination, the proper procedure may be to afford him the hearing if the crime charged so warrants. *See United States v. Millican*, 600 *F.*2d 723, 725 (5th Cir. 1979) ("as a matter of practice * * * defendant should have been afforded a probable cause hearing" where he had repeatedly asked for one), *cert.* den., 455 *U.S.* 915, 100 *S.Ct.* 1274 (1980).

Another constitutional dimension in this inquiry into what process is due is the requirement of proper "notice." In this regard, Justice Jackson, speaking for the Court in *Mullane v. Central Hanover Bank & Trust Co.*, 339 *U.S.* 306, 70 *S.Ct.* 652 (1950), declared:

An elementary and fundamental requirement of due process in any proceeding which is to be accorded finality is *notice reasonably calculated, under all the circumstances, to apprise interested parties of the pendency of the action and afford them an opportunity to present their objection.*

Id. at 314, 70 *S.Ct.* at 657. Beyond that, an accused should be apprised, with reasonable certainty, of the factual nature of the accusation against him. *See e.g., Russell v. United States,* 369 *U.S.* 749, 82 *S.Ct.* 1038 (1962). *See also R.* 3 (requiring that the complaint contain "a written statement of the essential facts constituting the offense charged").

CHAPTER 2

SEARCH WARRANTS

§2.1. Introduction: The written warrant requirement.

The Fourth Amendment to the Constitution safeguards the "right of the people to be secure in their persons, houses, papers, and effects, against unreasonable searches and seizures[.]" Additionally, the Amendment commands that "no Warrants shall issue, but upon probable cause, supported by Oath or affirmation, and particularly describing the place to be searched, and the persons or things to be seized."

Generally, the United States Supreme Court has viewed a search and seizure as *"per se* unreasonable within the meaning of the Fourth Amendment unless it is accomplished pursuant to a judicial warrant issued upon probable cause and particularly describing the [places to be searched and] the items to be seized." *United States v. Place*, 462 *U.S.* 696, 701, 103 *S.Ct.* 2637, 2641 (1983). As a fundamental principle of constitutional criminal procedure, search warrants are strongly favored under both the federal constitution and all state constitutions. The judicial preference which underscores the written warrant requirement is predicated upon the proposition that the necessity, validity and reasonableness of a prospective search or seizure can best be determined by a "neutral and detached magistrate" instead of a law enforcement officer. As the Supreme Court has stated, the warrant procedure serves primarily "to advise the citizen that the intrusion is authorized by law and [is] limited in its permissible scope[,] and to interpose a neutral magistrate between the citizen and the law enforcement officer 'engaged in the often competitive enterprise of ferreting out crime.'" *National Treasury Employees Union v. Von Raab*, 489 *U.S.* 656, 109 *S.Ct.* 1384, 1391 (1989) (quoting *Johnson v. United States*, 333 *U.S.* 10, 14, 68 *S.Ct.* 367, 369 (1948)).

The warrant procedure is not a mere formality. As the Court put it in *McDonald v. United States*, 335 *U.S.* 451, 455-456, 69 *S.Ct.* 191 (1978):

> The presence of a search warrant serves a high function. Absent some grave emergency, the Fourth Amendment has interposed a magistrate between the citizen and the police. This was done not to shield criminals nor to make the home a safe haven for illegal activities. It was done so that an objective mind might weigh the need to invade that privacy in order to enforce the law. The right of privacy was deemed too precious to entrust to the discretion of those whose job is the detection of crime and the arrest of criminals. . . . And so the Constitution requires a magistrate to pass on the desires of the police before they violate the privacy of the home. We cannot be true to that constitutional requirement and excuse the absence of a search warrant without a showing by those who seek exemption from the constitutional mandate that the exigencies of the situation made that course imperative.

The driving force behind the Fourth Amendment, along with the history of its application, demonstrates that the Amendment's purpose and design is the protection of the "people" against arbitrary action by their own Government. "People," for purposes of the Fourth Amendment means "people of the United States," *United States v. Verdugo-Urquidez*, 494 *U.S.* 259, 110 *S.Ct.* 1056, 1061 (1990), referring to "a class of persons who are part of a national community or who have otherwise developed sufficient connections with this country to be considered part of that community." *Id.*, 110 *S.Ct.* at 1061. Thus, it has been held that the Fourth Amendment has no application to an unlawful search and seizure conducted by federal agents outside the United States of premises owned by an alien, even though that alien (a Mexican citizen) is physically (and involuntarily) present in the United States for purposes of criminal prosecution. *Id.* at 1064. Significantly, aliens receive constitutional protection only "when they have come within the territory of the United States and developed substantial connections with this country." *Id.* Consequently, " 'once an alien lawfully enters and resides in this country he becomes invested with the rights guaranteed by the Constitution to all people within our borders.' " *Id.* [Citations omitted.]

While the principal object of the Fourth Amendment is the protection of *people* against unreasonable invasions of *privacy*, in certain cases the constitutional protection may extend directly to a person's property, even though privacy or liberty interests may not be immediately implicated. For example, in *Soldal v. Cook County, Ill.*, 506 *U.S.* 56, 113 *S.Ct.* 538 (1992), deputy sheriffs assisted the owners of a mobile home park in evicting the Soldal family. As the deputies stood and watched, the park owners wrenched the sewer and water connections off the side of the Soldal trailer, disconnected the telephone, tore the trailer's canopy and skirting, pulled it free from its moorings and towed it away. Finding the Fourth Amendment clearly applicable, the Court held:

As a result of the state action in this case, the Soldals' domicile was not only seized, it literally was carried away, giving a new meaning to the term "mobile home." We fail to see how being unceremoniously dispossessed of one's home in the manner alleged to have occurred here can be viewed as anything but a seizure invoking the protection of the Fourth Amendment. * * * The Amendment protects the people from unreasonable searches and seizures of "their persons, houses, papers, and effects." * * * [A]nd our cases unmistakably hold that the Amendment protects property as well as privacy. * * * We thus are unconvinced that * * * the Fourth Amendment protects against unreasonable seizures of property only where privacy or liberty is also implicated. * * *

What matters is the intrusion on the people's security from governmental interference. Therefore, the right against unreasonable seizures would be no less transgressed if the seizure of the house was undertaken to collect evidence, verify compliance with a housing regulation, effect an eviction by the police, or on a whim, for no reason at all.

Id., 113 *S.Ct.* at 543-545, 548.

The Exclusionary Rule and the Fourth Amendment

Although the Fourth Amendment contains no provision which specifically prohibits the use of evidence seized in violation of its terms, the Supreme Court has created a tool which is designed ultimately to safeguard Fourth Amendment rights. The tool is called the *Exclusionary Rule,* and since 1961 it has been disallowing the use of evidence obtained in violation of the Fourth Amendment in state as well as federal prosecutions. *See Mapp v. Ohio,* 367 *U.S.* 643, 81 *S.Ct.* 1684 (1961) ("all evidence obtained by searches and seizures in violation of the Constitution is, by that same authority, inadmissible in a state court"). Rather than a personal constitutional right belonging to the victim of an illegal search or seizure, the exclusionary rule operates as a judicially-created remedy which protects Fourth Amendment rights generally by deterring wrongful police conduct. *United States v. Leon,* 468 *U.S.* 897, 104 *S.Ct.* 3405 (1984). "Deterrence," then, is the linchpin of the exclusionary rule. *See United States v. Janis,* 428 *U.S.* 433, 96 *S.Ct.* 3021 (1976) ("the 'prime purpose' of the [exclusionary] rule, if not the sole one, 'is to deter future unlawful police conduct' "); *United States v. Calandra,* 414 *U.S.* 338, 94 *S.Ct.* 613 (1974) (the exclusionary rule is not "a personal constitutional right of the party aggrieved").

Thus, simply stated, *the exclusionary rule is a judicially-created device which is employed by the courts to prohibit the use of evidence at a criminal trial when that evidence has been seized by law enforcement officials in violation of the Constitution.*

The remedy of exclusion applies generally to criminal prosecutions, prohibiting the use of evidence obtained in violation of federal or state constitutional rights. *James v. Illinois,* 493 *U.S.* 307, 311, 110 *S.Ct.* 648, 651 (1990). The exclusionary rule has never been interpreted, however, to prohibit the use of illegally seized evidence "in all proceedings or against all persons. As with any remedial device, the application of the rule has been restricted to those areas where its remedial objectives" are thought to be best served. *United States v. Calandra, supra,* 94 *S.Ct.* at 620. If application of the exclusionary rule in a particular situation "does not result in appreciable deterrence," its use may be "unwarranted." *See, e.g., United States v. Janis, supra,* 96 *S.Ct.* at 3034 (illegally seized evidence may be used in a federal civil tax proceeding); *United States v. Calandra, supra* at 621-22 (illegally seized evidence may be used in grand jury proceedings); *United States v. Havens,* 446 *U.S.* 620, 627, 100 *S.Ct.* 1912, 1916-17 (1980) (illegally seized evidence may be used to impeach a defendant who takes the stand and testifies); *I.N.S. v. Lopez-Mendoza,* 468 *U.S.* 1032, 104 *S.Ct.* 3479 (1984) (exclusionary rule not applicable to a civil deportation proceeding).

Moreover, the exclusionary rule applies only to unlawful actions by government officials. It has no application to searches and seizures by private individuals. Thus, illegally obtained evidence, which would be subject to suppression if secured by a government official, need not be suppressed when obtained by a private citizen acting on his or her own behalf. *See United States v. Jacobsen,* 466 *U.S.* 109, 113-14, 104 *S.Ct.* 1652, 1656 (1984) (exclusionary rule is "wholly inapplicable 'to a search or seizure, even an unreasonable one, effected by a private individual not acting as an agent of the Government or with the participation or knowledge of any governmental official' ") (citation omitted). This issue is further explored in Chapter 5.

When confronted with an unreasonable search and seizure, a state court is free, and indeed encouraged, to rely on its own constitution to provide greater protection to the privacy interests of its citizens than that afforded under parallel provisions of the federal Constitution. As a well-established principle of our federalist system, state constitutions may be the source of "individual liberties more expansive than those conferred by the federal Constitution." *Pruneyard Shopping Center v. Robins,* 447 *U.S.* 74, 81, 100 *S.Ct.* 2035, 2040 (1980). This means that a state court is free as a matter of its own law to impose greater restrictions on police activity than those the United States Supreme Court holds to be necessary under federal constitutional standards. The federal Constitution, then, represents the base-line, floor of protection, and of course, a state may not drop below the federal floor; it may, however, rely on its own state constitution to heighten that floor of protection.

State law enforcement officers are cautioned, therefore, that their state may establish, as a matter of its own law, a ceiling of protection for its citizens which may have the effect of placing additional restrictions upon, or requiring the exercise of additional precautions by, its officers. Consequently, throughout the material which follows, state officers will be continually alerted as to those areas where state law may depart from the federal search and seizure standards. A review of local rules in those areas is strongly recommended.

§2.2. Judicial requirements.

The Fourth Amendment to the federal Constitution and virtually all state counterparts have been interpreted to require the issuance of a search warrant by a magistrate or judge who must, after receiving an "oath or affirmation" from the warrant applicant, make an independent, "neutral and detached" determination whether probable cause exists to believe that (1) particularly described property, (2) which is subject to official seizure, (3) may be presently found, (4) at a particular place.

Generally, it is the law enforcement officer's responsibility to present the facts and circumstances comprising his or her probable cause to the appropriate issuing authority (federal magistrate judge or state judge) by way of application. This document is normally called the search warrant "affidavit" and the officer who swears to the facts and circumstances contained in the affidavit is normally called the "affiant." Significantly, most states have procedures in place which require officers to first present their search warrant and supporting affidavit(s) to a deputy attorney general or to the appropriate county prosecutor or district attorney, or his designee, for review and approval before submission to a judge for authorization.

There are times when relevant facts arise or come to the officer's attention after the officer has completed his or her warrant application. In these circumstances, it is critical that this "additional" information be presented to the issuing authority and sworn to by the affiant. It then becomes the general responsibility of the issuing authority to either record the affiant's oral testimony and have the tape transcribed, or create a contemporaneous (or nearly so) written summary of the officer's sworn testimony. Such a procedure ensures reliable corroboration of what went on before the issuing authority in a form that will give a reviewing court some real assurance as to what information upon which the issuing judicial officer actually relied. *See e.g., State v. Fariello*, 71 *N.J.* 552, 560 (1976) (failure to record contemporaneously the oral representations of the affiant precludes the later use of oral reconstruction of that nontranscribed testimony at a motion to suppress evidence); *Glodowski v. State*, 196 *Wis.* 265 (1928) ("validity of judicial action cannot be made to depend upon the facts recalled by a fallible human memory at a time somewhat removed from that when the judicial determination was made"); *Fed.R.Crim.P.* 41(d)(2)(B) (The judge may wholly or partially dispense with a written affidavit and base a warrant on sworn testimony if doing so is reasonable under the circumstances); *Fed.R.Crim.P.* 41(d)(2)(C) ("Testimony taken in support of a warrant must be recorded by a court reporter or by a suitable recording device, and the judge must file the transcript or recording with the clerk, along with any affidavit.").

Rule 41(b) of the *Federal Rules of Criminal Procedure* authorizes the issuance of a (federal) search warrant, at "the request of a federal law enforcement officer or an attorney for the government." The term "federal law enforcement officer" is defined as "a government agent (other than an attorney for the government) who is engaged in enforcing the criminal laws and is within any category of officers authorized by the Attorney General to request a search warrant. *Rule* 41(a)(2)(C). In accordance with *Rule* 41(b), when a search warrant request is made,

(1) a magistrate judge with authority in the district—or if none is reasonably available, a judge of a state court of record in the district—has authority to issue a warrant to search for and seize a person or property located within the district;

(2) a magistrate judge with authority in the district has authority to issue a warrant for a person or property outside the district if the person or property is located within the district when the warrant is issued but might move or be moved outside the district before the warrant is executed; and

(3) a magistrate judge—in an investigation of domestic terrorism or international terrorism (as defined in 18 *U.S.C.* §2331)—having authority in any district in which activities related to the terrorism may have occurred, may issue a warrant for a person or property within or outside that district.

Id.

Under *Rule* 41(b)(2), above, the federal magistrate judge is authorized to issue a search warrant for property located within the district, when that property is moving or may move outside the district. This implicitly recognizes that "when property is in motion, there may be good reason to delay execution until the property comes to rest." (*Advisory Committee's Note*). This aspect of the rule provides a practical tool for federal law enforcement officers that avoids the necessity of their either seeking several warrants in different districts for the same property or relying on an exception to the warrant requirement for the search of property (or a person) that has (or who has) moved outside a district. For example, federal law enforcement officers are now authorized to conduct a "search of luggage moving aboard a plane." *Id.*

Federal search warrants may issue authorizing the search and/or seizure of "(1) evidence of a crime; (2) contraband, fruits of crime, or other items illegally possessed; (3) property designed for use, intended for use, or used in committing a crime; or (4) a person to be arrested or a person who is unlawfully restrained." *Rule* 41(c). "Property" is defined generally to include "documents, books, papers, any other tangible objects, and information."

Under the procedures governing the "traditional" search warrant, the affiant will personally appear before the appropriate issuing authority and present his or her supporting affidavit(s) establishing the grounds for the issuance of the warrant. *See Rule* 41(d)(2). Once the judge is satisfied that probable cause to search for and/or seize a person or property exists, the judge must issue the warrant, *Rule* 41(d)(1), identifying "the person or property to be searched," any "person or property to be seized," along with designating the magistrate judge to whom it must be returned. *Rule* 41(e)(2).

When all of the necessary procedures are correctly followed and a search warrant issues, a reviewing court will accord substantial deference to the issuing authority's discretionary determination resulting in the issuance of the warrant. This is because the law places a premium on searches conducted under the authority of a warrant. Given this judicial preference for warranted searches, a reviewing court may, in "doubtful or marginal" cases, uphold the validity of a search conducted under a warrant where that same search would not be sustainable without a warrant. *See United States v. Ventresca*, 308 *U.S.* 102, 106, 109, 85 *S.Ct.* 741, 744, 746 (1965) ("Although in a particular case it may not be easy to determine when an affidavit demonstrates probable cause, the resolution of doubtful or marginal cases in this area should be largely determined by the preference to be accorded to warrants.") (citing *Jones v. United States*, 362 *U.S.* 257, 270, 80 *S.Ct.* 725, 735 (1960)). *See also Aguilar v. Texas*, 378 *U.S.* 108, 110-111, 84 *S.Ct.* 1509, 1512 (1964) ("An evaluation of the constitutionality of a search warrant should begin with the rule that 'the informed and deliberate determinations of [judges] empowered to issue warrants * * * are to be preferred over the hurried action of officers * * *'") (citation omitted); *United States v. Zayas-Diaz*, 95 *F.*3d 105, 111 (1st Cir. 1996) ("Reviewing courts, including both the district court and the court of appeals, must accord 'considerable deference' to the 'probable cause' determination made by the issuing magistrate.").

Thus, where the police do what the Constitution requires, that is, they obtain a warrant from a detached and neutral judicial officer "upon probable cause, supported by Oath or affirmation," and that warrant "particularly describ[es] the place to be searched, and the persons or things to be seized," their actions "should be sustained under a system of justice responsive to both the needs of individual liberty and to the rights of the community." *United States v. Ventresca*, *supra* at 112, 85 *S.Ct.* at 748.

The admissibility of evidence obtained under a search warrant is generally determined according to the law of the jurisdiction of the court in which the evidence is sought to be admitted. Thus, "evidence obtained in accordance with federal law is admissible in federal court—even though it [may have been] obtained by state officers in violation of state law." *United States v. Rickus* 737 *F.*2d 360, 363-64 (3rd Cir. 1984). *See also United States v. Stiver*, 9 *F.*3d 298, 300 (3rd Cir. 1993) ("'the additional deterrent effect to be gained from excluding this evidence in federal trials for federal offenses is small, and is far outweighed by the costs to society of excluding the evidence'") (quoting *Rickus* at 364).

Naturally, different procedures apply when an officer seeks a telephonic search warrant. *See generally* Section 2.6.

---

§2.2(a). The neutral and detached magistrate.

The United States Supreme Court has explained that "[t]he point of the Fourth Amendment * * * is not that it denies law enforcement the support of the usual inferences which reasonable men draw from evidence. Its protection consists in requiring that those inferences be drawn by a *neutral and detached magistrate* instead of being judged by the officer engaged in the often competitive enterprise of ferreting out crime." *Johnson v. United States*, 333 *U.S.* 10, 13-14, 68 *S.Ct.* 367, 369 (1947). [Emphasis added.] A law enforcement officer's right to invade the privacy and sanctity of a person's home is "a grave concern, not only to the individual but to a society which chooses to dwell in reasonable security and freedom from surveillance. *When* the right of privacy must reasonably yield to the right of search is, as a rule, to be decided by a judicial officer, not by a police [officer] or Government enforcement agent." *Id.* at 14, 68 *S.Ct.* at 369. [Emphasis added.]

COOLIDGE v. NEW HAMPSHIRE
Supreme Court of the United States
403 *U.S.* 443, 91 *S.Ct.* 2022 (1971)

QUESTION: What is the effect of a search warrant which is signed and issued by the State Attorney General who had taken charge of the investigation and was later to serve as chief prosecutor at the trial, but who acted as a justice of the peace to issue the warrant?

ANSWER: The warrant is invalid because it is not issued by a "neutral and detached magistrate." *Id.* at 2029, 2031.

RATIONALE: During the course of a murder investigation, Manchester, New Hampshire, police officers developed reason to believe that defendant, Edward Coolidge, was responsible for the death of Pamela Mason. "[T]he results of the investigation were presented at a meeting between the police officers working on the case and the State Attorney General, who had personally taken charge of all police activities relating to the murder, and was later to serve as chief prosecutor at the trial. At this meeting, it was decided that there was enough evidence to justify the arrest of Coolidge on the murder charge and a search of his house and two cars. At the conclusion of the meeting, the Manchester police chief made formal application, under oath, for the arrest and search warrants. * * * The warrants were then signed and issued by the Attorney General himself, acting as a justice of the peace. Under New Hampshire law in force at that time, all justices of the peace were authorized to issue search warrants." *Id.* at 2028.

In this appeal, defendant argues, among other things, that the search warrant was invalid because it was "not issued by a 'neutral and detached magistrate.'" *Id.* at 2029. *The United States Supreme Court agreed.*

"In this case, the determination of probable cause was made by the chief 'government enforcement agent' of the State—the Attorney General—who was actively in charge of the investigation and later was to be chief prosecutor at trial." *Id.* This was patently improper. "Without disrespect to the state law enforcement agent here involved, the whole point of the basic rule [requiring a neutral and detached magistrate] is that prosecutors and police [officers] simply cannot be asked to maintain the requisite neutrality with regard to their own investigations—the 'competitive enterprise' that must rightly engage their single-minded attention." *Id.* at 2029-2030.

With respect to the New Hampshire method of issuing warrants, the Court stated:

> But it is too plain for extensive discussion that this now abandoned New Hampshire method of issuing "search warrants" violated a fundamental premise of both the Fourth and Fourteenth Amendments[.]

Id. at 2031.

Accordingly, the search and seizure conducted was invalid for it "cannot constitutionally rest upon the warrant issued by the state official who was the chief investigator and prosecutor in the case. Since he was not the neutral and detached magistrate required by the Constitution, the search stands on no firmer ground than if there had been no warrant at all." *Id.*

NOTE

1. *Judge's compensation directly dependent on how many warrants issued.* In *Connally v. Georgia,* 429 *U.S.* 245, 97 *S.Ct.* 546 (1977), the Supreme Court held that Georgia's system for the issuance of search warrants by unsalaried justices of the peace who received a statutory fee for the *issuance* of the search warrant but no fee for the denial of the warrant violated the Fourth and Fourteenth Amendments to the United States Constitution. *Id.* at 251, 97 *S.Ct.* at 549. Under the then-applicable statute, a justice of the peace received a $5 fee each time he or she issued a search warrant. If the requested warrant was refused, the justice collects no fee for reviewing and denying the application. Moreover, the justice of the peace was not salaried.

According to the Court, the justice's "financial welfare," is "enhanced by positive action and is not enhanced by negative action." *Id.* at 250, 97 *S.Ct.* at 548. Such a situation offers " 'a possible temptation to the average man as a judge . . . or which might lead him not to hold the balance nice, clear and true between the State and the accused.' It is, in other words, (a) situation where the defendant is subjected to what surely is judicial action by an officer of a court who has 'a direct, personal, substantial, pecuniary interest' in his conclusion to issue or deny the warrant." *Id.* [Citation omitted.] Certainly, not the "neutral and detached" judicial officer contemplated by the Constitution.

2. *Judge's participation in the search or application process.* In *Lo-Ji Sales, Inc. v. New York*, 442 *U.S.* 319, 99 *S.Ct.* 2319 (1979), an investigator for the New York State Police applied to a Town Justice for a warrant to search defendant's "adult" book store. The investigator's affidavit asserted that at the store, defendant offered for sale films which violated the state obscenity laws. The affidavit also requested that the Town Justice accompany the investigator to defendant's store to supervise execution of the warrant and to "determine independently if any other items at the store were possessed in violation of the law and subject to seizure. The Town Justice agreed." *Id.* at 321, 99 *S.Ct.* at 2322. At the time the Town Justice signed the warrant, however, the warrant failed to list or describe specifically the items to be seized.

Thereafter, the Town Justice, four state police officers, several detectives, and three members of the local prosecutor's office—11 in all—entered the bookstore and engaged in a search which lasted almost six hours. During the search, the Town Justice viewed 23 films (which were adjusted for "free" viewing), determined that there was probable cause to believe they were obscene, and then ordered the officers to seize the films and projectors.

The Town Justice then had the officers remove the clear cellophane wrappers from the magazines in the store and began to inspect them for violations of the obscenity laws. In all, 397 magazines were taken. Miscellaneous other items were also seized, including additional reels of film from the display case and numerous business records.

According to the United States Supreme Court: "This search warrant and what followed the entry of [defendant's] premises are reminiscent of the general warrant or writ of assistance of the 18th century against which the Fourth Amendment was intended to protect." *Id.* at 325, 99 *S.Ct.* at 2323. Not only did the warrant fail to particularly describe the items to be seized, it constituted an unlawful "open-ended" warrant, which was to be completed while the search was being conducted and items seized, or after the seizure had been carried out. This contravenes the letter and spirit of the Fourth Amendment.

Moreover, "[t]he Town Justice did not manifest the neutrality and detachment of a judicial officer when presented with a warrant application for a search and seizure." *Id.* at 326, 99 *S.Ct.* at 2324. Although his intentions were good, "the objective facts of record manifest an erosion of whatever neutral and detached posture existed at the outset. He allowed himself to become a member, if not the leader, of the search party which was essentially a police operation. Once in the store, he conducted a generalized search under authority of an invalid warrant; he was not acting as a judicial officer but as an adjunct law enforcement officer." *Id.* at 327, 99 *S.Ct.* at 2324-2325. As the Court points out, it was "difficult to discern when he was acting as a 'neutral and detached' judicial officer and when he was one with the police and prosecutors in the executive seizure[.]" *Id.* at 328, 99 *S.Ct.* at 2325.

Compare United States v. Whitehorn, 829 *F.*2d 1225 (2nd Cir. 1987), where a United States magistrate spent his Saturday afternoon—almost six hours—at F.B.I. headquarters while F.B.I. agents prepared a 38-page search warrant affidavit for his review and signature. As he waited, the magistrate overheard several radio transmissions reporting the progress of the official investigation which was the subject of the prospective search warrant. At about 7:15 p.m., the magistrate issued the warrant.

In the appeal which followed the denial of defendant's motion to suppress, defendant argued that this federal magistrate abandoned his "neutral and detached" role in issuing the warrant. The Court of Appeals for the Second Circuit disagreed.

According to the court, the magistrate "did not assist in the drafting of the warrant or in any aspect of the F.B.I.'s investigation. Nor is there anything that suggests that he was in F.B.I. headquarters for any reason other than to facilitate the issuance of the warrant on a Saturday." *Id.* at 1232. The conduct of this magistrate, therefore, "hardly rises to the level of the excessive magisterial zeal found unacceptable by the Supreme Court in *Lo-Ji*." *Id.* Significantly, the *Lo-Ji* Court "specifically contrasted th[e] town judge with a magistrate who leaves his regular office 'in order to make himself readily available to law enforcement officers who may wish to seek the issuance of warrants by him'; the latter, the Court made clear, does not thereby lose his 'neutral and detached' character." *Whitehorn* at 1232-1233 (quoting *Lo-Ji* at 328 n.6, 99 *S.Ct.* at 2325 n.6). According to the court, the magistrate here in *Whitehorn* "did little more than save valuable time by waiting in F.B.I. headquarters until the F.B.I.'s search warrant application was ready." *Id.* at 1233.

---

§2.2(b). The Oath or affirmation.

One of the express requirements of the Fourth Amendment is that "no Warrants shall issue," unless "supported by Oath or affirmation * * *." The "Oath or affirmation" has been described as "a formal assertion of, or attestation to, the truth of what has been, or is to be, said. It is designed to ensure that the truth will be told by insuring that the witness or affiant will be impressed with the solemnity and importance of his words. The theory is that those who have been impressed with the moral, religious or legal significance of formally undertaking to tell the truth are more likely to do so then those who have not made such an undertaking or been so impressed." *United States v. Turner*, 558 *F.*2d 46, 50 (2nd Cir. 1977). *See also Frazier v. Roberts*, 441 *F.*2d 1224, 1228 (8th Cir. 1971).

---

§2.3. The probable cause requirement.

§2.3(a). Sources of information.

One of the most valuable assets in the law-enforcement battle against crime is the police informant. In fact, over the course of time, the proper utilization of information imparted by informants has led the courts to "consistently accept[] the use of informants in the discovery of evidence of a crime as a legitimate investigatory procedure consistent with the Constitution." *Arizona v. Fulminante*, 499 *U.S.* 279, 111 *S.Ct.* 1246, 1262-63 (1991) (Opinion of Rehnquist, C.J., dissenting in part).

Generally, informants are classified into three distinct types: criminal informants, citizen informants, and anonymous tips. The "type" of informant becomes important when a determination must be made as to whether the information imparted provides a sufficient constitutional justification for a particular police action. Moreover, knowledge of the type of informant the police are dealing with becomes critical when a determination must be made as to how much independent police investigation must be employed to verify or corroborate the information reported.

1. *Criminal informants.* In the totality-of-the-circumstances analysis, the reliability of a criminal informant's hearsay information, along with the informant's credibility, remains a relevant inquiry. In fact, the hallmark of the competent criminal investigator is the ability to clearly and thoroughly document in an affidavit not only the credibility of his or her confidential informant but the reliability of the information relayed and the informant's basis of knowledge. These items are "closely intertwined issues" which make up the "commonsense, practical question whether there is 'probable cause' to believe that contraband or evidence is located in a particular place." *Illinois v. Gates*, 462 *U.S.* 213, 103 *S.Ct.* 2317, 2328 (1983).

Perhaps the most common way reliability is established is by documenting the past use of the particular informant and the number of times the information imparted by that informant proved not only to be true and correct but also led to the arrest and successful prosecution of the subject of the information. A mere bare bones statement in an affidavit that an informant is reliable and has proved to be reliable in the past is not enough. Officers should strive to include (1) how often the informant has been used; (2) the nature or character of the investigations in which the informant has previously supplied information (*e.g.*, narcotics, burglary, stolen property, arson, etc.); (3) how many times the information proved to be true and correct; (4) whether the information led to the arrest of the subject of the information; and (5) whether the subsequent prosecution led to conviction. Naturally, if any of the aforementioned indicators of reliability is absent or unknown, the affidavit would merely be silent in that regard.

Reliability may also be adequately established if, during the course of supplying information, the informant supplies his own name to the police and includes a "statement against his penal interest," *United States v. Harris* 403 *U.S.* 573, 583, 91 *S.Ct.* 2075, 2081-82 (1971), for example, the case where the informant admits to buying narcotics on several occasions from a named individual. In such a case—where the informant admits to criminal conduct during the course of supplying information to the police—"[c]ommon sense in the important daily affairs of life would induce a prudent and disinterested observer to credit these statements. People do not lightly admit a crime and place critical evidence in the hands of the police in the form of their own admissions." *Id.* at 583, 91 *S.Ct.* 2082. As the court pointed out in *United States v. Clark*, 24 *F*.3d 299, 303 (D.C.Cir. 1994), "officers could reasonably believe that precisely because [the informant] was actively engaged in drug trafficking, he would know—and thus be able to identify—the source of his trading goods; furthermore, because he was seeking leniency at the hands of the law, [the informant] would have little reason to prove himself an unreliable informant."

Reliability may be further enhanced if the informant provides the police with such information with the hope of changing his or her criminal ways. In this respect, it has been stated: "We are in a time when cocaine addiction is on the verge of epidemic proportion, and the public is extensively aware of the devastation created by it. Consequently, when a cocaine user voluntarily turns in his supplier to the police in the hope of shaking his reliance on the drug, and in doing so admits to his own criminal conduct, *such evidence sharply increases the degree of reliability* needed for the issuance of a search warrant." *State v. Goldberg*, 214 *N.J.Super.* 401 (App. Div. 1986). [Emphasis added.]

The informant's basis of knowledge may be established by documenting, in as much detail as possible, the informant's personal observations. This establishes how (and when) the informant came by his or her information, and demonstrates what precisely the informant personally saw, heard, smelled, tasted or touched. Persuasive in this regard would be details of the physical appearance of the target residence, exactly where in the residence the subject keeps or conceals the evidence or contraband, what the evidence or contraband looked like, how it was packaged, the name and detailed physical description of the subject and others who may also live at or occasion the target premises, and so on. *See e.g., United States v. Hill*, 91 *F*.3d 1064, 1069 (8th Cir. 1996) (confidential informant's report was based on *direct observations* of the subject, entitling " 'his tip to greater weight than might otherwise be the case' ") (quoting *Illinois v. Gates*, 462 *U.S.* 213, 234, 103 *S.Ct.* 2317, 2330 (1983)). This type and degree of detail not only fortifies the reliability of the information supplied but constitutes a material consideration in the totality-of-the-circumstances analysis. Indeed, even if the informant's statements and the events the informant describes "diverge in minor ways, the magistrate may reasonably choose to credit the statements and disregard petty inconsistencies." *See United States v. Schaefer*, 87 *F*.2d 562, 567 (1st Cir. 1996); *United States v. Zayas-Diaz*, 95 *F*.3d 105, 112 (1st Cir. 1996).

The final ingredient in the totality-of-the-circumstances approach calls for the independent corroboration of as many of the facts relayed by the informant as possible. If time permits, all the information relayed should be confirmed by independent investigation. In this respect, a deficiency in any of the foregoing elements may be counterbalanced by the officer's independent investigation—the touchstone of the totality-of-the-circumstances approach. *See e.g., United States v. Burke*, 999 *F.*2d 596, 598 (1st Cir. 1993) ("It [] is significant that the source's information was based on personal observation.").

2. *Citizen informants.* In marked contrast to the criminal informant, an ordinary citizen presumably has no ties or connections with the criminal world. In this respect, courts will impart an assumption grounded in common experience that such a person, regarded as a law-abiding and cooperative member of the general public, is motivated by factors that are consistent with law enforcement goals. Consequently, an individual of this kind may be regarded as trustworthy and the information imparted by him or her to a law enforcement officer concerning a criminal episode would not especially entail further exploration or verification of the citizen's personal credibility or reliability before suitable action may be taken. As the court explained in *State v. Lakomy*:

> A different rationale exists for establishing the reliability of named "citizen-informers" as opposed to the traditional idea of unnamed police contacts or informers who usually themselves are criminals. Information supplied to officers by the traditional police informer is not given in the spirit of a concerned citizen, but often is given in exchange for some concession, payment, or simply out of revenge against the subject. The nature of these persons and the information which they supply convey a certain impression of unreliability, and it is proper to demand that some evidence of their credibility and reliability be shown. One practical way of making such a showing is to point to accurate information which they have supplied in the past.
>
> However, an ordinary citizen who reports a crime which has been committed in his presence, or that a crime is being or will be committed, stands on much different ground than a police informer. He is a witness to criminal activity who acts with an intent to aid the police in law enforcement because of his concern for society or for his own safety. He does not expect any gain or concession in exchange for his information. An informer of this type usually would not have more than one opportunity to supply information to the police[.]

126 *N.J.Super.* 430, 435, 315 *A.*2d 46 (App.Div. 1974).

Credibility and reliability in this respect may be further enhanced if the particular citizen is "more than the ordinary citizen," for example, fire fighters, first aid or ambulance squad members, security personnel and the like. These individuals, while not sworn law enforcement officers, are more involved and presumably more public spirited than the average citizen, and in and of themselves may be considered credible sources of information.

Finally, the information imparted by a citizen-informer who is himself or herself a victim or complainant, should be taken at face value. *See e.g., Easton v. City of Boulder*, 776 *F.*2d 1441, 1449 (10th

Cir. 1985) ("[T]he skepticism and careful scrutiny usually found in cases involving informants, sometimes anonymous, from the criminal milieu, is appropriately relaxed if the informant is an identified victim."). *See also Sharrar v. Felsing*, 128 *F*.3d 810, 818 (3rd Cir. 1997) ("When a police officer has received a reliable identification by a victim of his or her attacker, the police have probable cause to arrest.").

3. *Anonymous tips.* Of all the types of information acted upon by law enforcement, the anonymous tip requires the most independent verification. By its very nature, the anonymous tip carries with it none of the traditional indicators of reliability which may attach to information imparted by citizen informants or even criminal informants. Thus, to develop the reliability of information imparted by the anonymous tip, officers must engage in two critical procedures: (1) comprehensive detail development, and (2) independent verification.

First, the individual who takes the call or receives the information must elicit as much detail as possible from the informer. Comprehensive detail development is crucial; it demonstrates the anonymous informant's "basis of knowledge," and provides substance and meaning to the second procedure in the development of reliability. Naturally, the call-taker should not initially attempt to ascertain the caller's identity. It is all too often that the question, "What is your name ?", is followed by the sound of a dial tone. Rather, the call-taker should try to ascertain as much detail as possible as to what exactly the caller has observed (or is presently observing), the physical description of the subject of the caller's observations, how far away the subject was (or is presently) from the caller, whether the caller is presently watching the subject and if not, how long ago the observations were made, the exact location of the subject, whether there were or presently are any other people or vehicles in the area, and whether the caller would stay on the line while officers are dispatched. Once the call-taker has elicited as much detail as possible from the caller, the call-taker may then consider asking more "dangerous" questions, such as, "Are you a resident of the neighborhood ?" "Do you live next to where these things are taking place ?" "Where do you live ?" "What is your name ?"

The second step requires independent investigation directed at confirming or verifying each of the facts related in the anonymous tip. It is this independent corroboration which provides a foundation for a reviewing court to conclude that a substantial basis exists for crediting the hearsay information imparted by the anonymous tip. Significantly, as the officer proceeds to corroborate each of the details of the tip, it becomes increasingly evident that " '[b]ecause [the] informant is right about some things, he is more probably right about other facts[.]' " *Illinois v. Gates, supra*, 103 *S.Ct.* at 2335 (quoting *Spinelli v. United States*, 393 *U.S.* 410, 427, 89 *S.Ct.* 584, 594 (1969) (White, J., concurring)). Once an officer has personally verified every possible facet of the information contained in the tip, reasonable grounds may then exist to believe that the remaining unverified bit of information—that a criminal offense is occurring, or has occurred—is likewise true. *Draper v. United States*, 358 *U.S.* 307, 79 *S.Ct.* 329 (1959). As the United States Supreme Court has stated, "such tips, particularly when supplemented by independent police investigation, frequently contribute to the solution of otherwise 'perfect crimes.'" *Gates* at 2332.

4. *The "fellow officer" rule.* During the course of various types of investigations, police must rely on facts and information imparted by fellow officers. As a general rule, courts will consider information stemming from the observations and discoveries of fellow officers inherently trustworthy, and consequently, further exploration or verification of a fellow officer's personal credibility or reliability is not required. In this respect, the Supreme Court has determined that "[o]bservations of fellow officers of the Government engaged in a common investigation are plainly a reliable basis for a warrant applied for by one of their number." *United States v. Ventresca*, 380 *U.S.* 102, 111, 85 *S.Ct.* 741, 747 (1965). *See also United States v. Griffin*, 827 *F.*2d 1108, 1112 (7th Cir. 1987) (the "'affiant's fellow agents'" may "'plainly [] be regarded as a reliable source by the magistrate'") (quoting *United States v. Pritchard*, 745 *F.*2d 1112, 1120 (7th Cir. 1984)). *Accord United States v. Cooper*, 949 *F.*2d 737, 745 (5th Cir. 1991) (if the combined knowledge of police from two different jurisdictions was such that they collectively had probable cause to believe criminal evidence was located in a robbery suspect's car, officers from either jurisdiction could lawfully have conducted a warrantless search).

DISCLOSURE OF AN INFORMANT'S IDENTITY: THE "INFORMER'S PRIVILEGE"

"What is usually referred to as the informer's privilege is in reality the Government's privilege to withhold from disclosure the identity of persons who furnish information of violations of law to officers charged with enforcement of that law. * * * The purpose of the privilege is the furtherance and protection of the public interest in effective law enforcement. The privilege recognizes the obligation of citizens to communicate their knowledge of the commission of crimes to law-enforcement officials and, by preserving their anonymity, encourages them to perform that obligation." *Roviaro v. United States*, 353 *U.S.* 53, 59, 77 *S.Ct.* 623, 627 (1957).

"The scope of the privilege is limited by its underlying purpose. Thus, where the disclosure of the contents of a communication will not tend to reveal the identity of an informer, the contents are not privileged." *Id.* at 60, 77 *S.Ct.* at 627. *See also Grodjesk v. Faghani*, 104 *N.J.* 89, 96 (1986) ("contents of informer's communications with a law enforcement official are not privileged unless disclosure of the communications would probably reveal the identity of the informer"). "Likewise, once the identity of the informer has been disclosed to those who would have cause to resent the communication, the privilege is no longer applicable. A further limitation on the applicability of the privilege arises from the fundamental requirements of fairness. Where the disclosure of an informer's identity, or of the contents of his communication, is relevant and helpful to the defense of an accused, or is essen-

116

tial to a fair determination of a cause, the privilege must give way. In these situations the trial court may require disclosure and, if the Government withholds the information, dismiss the action." *Roviaro* at 60-61, 77 *S.Ct.* at 627-628.

There is, however, no fixed rule respecting disclosure. "The problem is one that calls for balancing the public interest in protecting the flow of information against the individual's right to prepare his defense." *Id.* at 62, 77 *S.Ct.* at 628-629. Consequently, a court's decision to compel the disclosure of an informant's identity will depend on "the particular circumstances of each case, taking into consideration the crime charged, the possible defenses, the possible significance of the informer's testimony, and other relevant factors." *Id.* at 62, 77 *S.Ct.* at 629.

---

§2.3(b). The totality-of-the-circumstances test.

ILLINOIS v. GATES
Supreme Court of the United States
462 *U.S.* 23, 103 *S.Ct.* 2317 (1983)

QUESTION: May probable cause be established for the issuance of a search warrant on the basis of a detailed anonymous tip, in the absence of information demonstrating that the anonymous informant was honest or the information reliable, or that the informant had a basis for the information imparted, when a substantial part of the tip is corroborated by the affiant's independent investigation?

ANSWER: YES. An officer's independent investigation, which uncovers facts that substantially corroborate a detailed anonymous tip, may, together with the tip, provide probable cause for the issuance of a search warrant.

In this landmark case, the United States Supreme Court redefined over fifteen years of law governing the issuance of search warrants based upon information received from police informants. The Court abandoned the rigid "two-pronged test" originally established in *Aguilar v. Texas* and *Spinelli v. United States*, and determined that in its place, the "totality of the circumstances" analysis should be used to test the sufficiency of probable cause.

RATIONALE: On May 3, 1978, the Bloomingdale Police Department received in the mail an anonymous handwritten letter which read as follows:

> "This letter is to inform you that you have a couple in your town who strictly make their living on selling drugs. They are Sue and Lance Gates, they live on Greenway, off Bloomingdale Rd. in the condominiums. Most of their buys are done in Florida. Sue, his wife, drives their car to Florida, where she leaves it to be loaded up with drugs, then Lance flys down and drives it back. Sue flys back after she drops the car off in Florida. May 3

she is driving down there again and Lance will be flying down in a few days to drive it back. At the time Lance drives the car back he has the trunk loaded with over $100,000.00 in drugs. Presently they have over $100,000.00 worth of drugs in their basement.

"They brag about the fact they never have to work, and make their entire living on pushers.

"I guarantee if you watch them carefully you will make a big catch. They are friends with some big drugs dealers, who visit their house often.

> Lance and Susan Gates
> Greenway
> in Condominiums"

Id. at 2325.

Following up on the tip, Detective Mader discovered that a driver's license had been issued to Lance Gates. The detective also ascertained Gates' address and learned from an officer assigned to the O'Hare Airport that "L. Gates" had made a reservation on Eastern Airlines flight 245 to West Palm Beach, Florida, scheduled to depart from Chicago on May 5 at 4:15 p.m.

Detective Mader then made arrangements with an agent of the Drug Enforcement Administration (DEA) for surveillance of the May 5th Eastern Airlines flight. "The agent later reported to Mader that Gates had boarded the flight, and that federal agents in Florida had observed him arrive in West Palm Beach and take a taxi to the nearby Holiday Inn. They also reported that Gates went to a room registered to one Susan Gates and that, at 7:00 a.m. the next morning, Gates and an unidentified woman left the motel in a Mercury bearing Illinois license plates and drove northbound on an interstate frequently used by travelers to the Chicago area. In addition, the DEA agent informed Mader that the license plate number on the Mercury registered to a Hornet station wagon owned by Gates. The agent also advised Mader that the driving time between West Palm Beach and Bloomingdale was approximately 22 to 24 hours." *Id.* at 2325-26.

Detective Mader incorporated the foregoing facts into an affidavit and submitted it, together with a copy of the anonymous letter, to a judge of the Circuit Court of DuPage County. The judge issued the warrant, authorizing a search of the Gates' residence and their automobile.

At 5:15 a.m. on May 7th, "only 36 hours after he had flown out of Chicago, Lance Gates, and his wife, returned to their home in Bloomingdale, driving the car in which they had left West Palm Beach some 22 hours earlier. The Bloomingdale police were awaiting them, searched the trunk of the Mercury, and uncovered approximately 350 pounds of marijuana. A search of Gates' home revealed marijuana, weapons, and other contraband." *Id.* at 2326.

The Illinois courts ruled that the evidence obtained must be suppressed because the anonymous letter, standing alone, would not provide the basis for a judge's determination that there was probable cause to believe contraband would be found in the Gates' home and car. The Illinois Supreme Court concluded that the letter provided "virtually nothing from which one might conclude that its author is either honest or his information reliable; likewise, the letter g[ave] absolutely no indication of the basis for the writer's predictions regarding the Gates' criminal activities." *Id.* The Illinois Supreme Court also determined that the affidavit did not contain sufficient additional information to sustain a determination of probable cause. *The United States Supreme Court disagreed and reversed.*

In finding the affidavit insufficient to establish probable cause, the Illinois courts applied the "two-pronged test" derived from the United States Supreme Court's decisions in *Aguilar v. Texas*, 378 *U.S.* 108, 84 *S.Ct.* 1509 (1964), and *Spinelli v. United States*, 393 *U.S.* 410, 89 *S.Ct.* 584 (1969). The two-pronged *Aguilar-Spinelli* test provides a method for evaluating the existence of probable cause when a search warrant affidavit is based upon information supplied to the police by an informant. Under this test, the issuing judge must be informed of (1) some of the underlying circumstances relied upon by the informant in concluding that the facts are as he or she claims they are, and (2) some of the underlying circumstances from which the officer concluded that (a) the informant was "credible," or (b) the information imparted was "reliable." *Gates* at 2326-27 n.3. Under *Aguilar* and *Spinelli*, then,

> the letter, as supplemented by Mader's affidavit, first had to adequately reveal the "basis of knowledge" of the letter writer—the particular means by which he came by the information given in his report. Second, it had to provide facts sufficiently establishing either the "veracity" of the affiant's informant, or, alternatively, the "reliability" of the informant's report in this particular case.

Gates at 2337.

Rather than continue to adhere to the rigid, two-pronged test of *Aguilar* and *Spinelli*, the Court held that *the information contained in the affidavit should be analyzed by reference to the totality of the circumstances presented therein.* Speaking for the Court, Justice Rehnquist elaborated:

> [A]n informant's "veracity," "reliability" and "basis of knowledge" are all highly relevant in determining the value of his report. We do not agree, however, that these elements should be understood as entirely separate and independent requirements to be rigidly exacted in every case[.] * * * Rather, * * * they should be understood simply as closely intertwined issues that may usefully illuminate the commonsense, practical question whether there is "probable cause" to believe that contraband or evidence is located in a particular place.

> This totality of the circumstances approach is far more consistent with our prior treatment of probable cause than is any rigid demand that specific "tests" be satisfied by every informant's tip. Perhaps the central teaching of our decisions bearing on the probable cause standard is that it is a "practical, nontechnical conception."

[P]robable cause is a fluid concept—turning on the assessment of probabilities in particular factual contexts—not readily, or even usefully reduced to a neat set of legal rules. Informants' tips doubtless come in many shapes and sizes from many different types of persons. * * * Rigid legal rules are ill-suited to an area of such diversity.

Id. at 2337-39. [Citation omitted.]

The Court further explained that the informant's "veracity," or "reliability" and his "basis of knowledge" are "better understood as *relevant considerations in the totality of the circumstances analysis* that traditionally has guided probable cause determinations: *a deficiency in one may be compensated for, in determining the overall reliability of a tip, by a strong showing as to the other, or by some other indicia of reliability.*" *Id.* at 2339. [Emphasis added.]

"If, for example, a particular informant is known for the unusual reliability of his predictions of certain types of criminal activities in a locality, his failure, in a particular case, to thoroughly set forth the basis of his knowledge surely should not serve as an absolute bar to a finding of probable cause based on his tip. * * * Likewise, if an unquestionably honest citizen comes forward with a report of criminal activity—which if fabricated would subject him to criminal liability—we have found rigorous scrutiny of the basis of his knowledge unnecessary. * * * Conversely, even if we entertain some doubt as to an informant's motives, his explicit and detailed description of alleged wrongdoing, along with a statement that the event was observed first-hand, entitles his tip to greater weight than might otherwise be the case." *Id.* at 2329-30.

Unlike a totality of circumstances analysis, which permits a balanced assessment of the relative weights of all the various indicia of reliability (and unreliability) attending an informant's tip, the "two-pronged test" has encouraged an excessively technical dissection of informants' tips, with undue attention being focused on isolated issues that cannot sensibly be divorced from the other facts presented to the magistrate. * * *

[A]ffidavits "are normally drafted by nonlawyers in the midst and haste of a criminal investigation. Technical requirements of elaborate specificity * * * have no proper place in this area. * * * "

The strictures that inevitably accompany the "two-pronged test" cannot avoid seriously impeding the task of law enforcement[.] * * * If, as the Illinois Supreme Court apparently thought, that test must be rigorously applied in every case, anonymous tips seldom would be of value in police work. * * * Likewise, as the Illinois Supreme Court observed in this case, the veracity of persons supplying anonymous tips is by hypothesis largely unknown, and unknowable. As a result, anonymous tips seldom could survive a rigorous application of either of the [] prongs. Yet, such tips, particularly when supplemented by independent police investigation, frequently contribute to the solution of otherwise "perfect crimes." While a conscientious assessment of the basis for crediting such tips is required by the Fourth Amendment, a standard that leaves virtually no place for anonymous citizen informants is not.

Id. at 2330-32.

Accordingly, by its decision in this case, the Court "abandon[ed] the 'two-pronged test' established by * * * *Aguilar* and *Spinelli*," and in its place reaffirmed "the totality of the circumstances analysis that traditionally has informed probable cause determinations." *Id.* at 2332.

> The task of the issuing magistrate is simply to make a practical, common-sense decision whether, given all the circumstances set forth in the affidavit before him, including the "veracity" and "basis of knowledge" of persons supplying hearsay information, there is a fair probability that contraband or evidence of a crime will be found in a particular place. And the duty of a reviewing court is simply to ensure that the magistrate had a "substantial basis for . . . conclud[ing]" that probable cause existed.

Id. [Citation omitted.]

Applying the "totality of the circumstances" analysis to the facts of this case, the Court concluded that the information set forth in the affidavit established probable cause for the warrant that issued. First, the Court noted that the facts obtained through the independent investigation of Detective Mader and the DEA at least suggested that the Gates were involved in drug trafficking; for example, the fact that Florida is a well-known source of narcotics and other illegal drugs, Lance Gates' flight to Palm Beach, his brief, overnight stay in a motel, and his immediate return north to Chicago in the family car conveniently waiting for him, "is as suggestive of a pre-arranged drug run, as it is of an ordinary vacation trip." *Id.* at 2334.

In addition, the anonymous letter "had been corroborated in major part" by Mader's efforts. "The corroboration of the letter's predictions that the Gates' car would be in Florida, that Lance Gates would fly to Florida in the next day or so, and that he would drive the car north toward Bloomingdale all indicated, albeit not with certainty, that the informant's other assertions also were true. 'Because an informant is right about some things, he is more probably right about other facts[.]' " *Id.* at 2334-35. [Citation omitted.]

"Finally, the anonymous letter contained a range of details relating not just to easily obtained facts and conditions existing at the time of the tip, but to future actions of third parties ordinarily not easily predicted. The letter writer's accurate information as to the travel plans of each of the Gates was of a character likely obtained only from the Gates themselves, or from someone familiar with their not entirely ordinary travel plans. If the informant had access to accurate information of this type, a magistrate could properly conclude that it was not unlikely that he also had access to reliable information of the Gates' alleged illegal activities." *Id.* at 2335.

Consequently, there was "a fair probability that the writer of the anonymous letter had obtained his entire story either from the Gates or someone they trusted. And corroboration of major portions of the letter's predictions provide[d] just this probability." *Id.* It is apparent, therefore, that the warrant authorizing the search of the Gates' home and car was supported by probable cause. *Id.* at 2336.

NOTE

1. *Warrants supported by hearsay.* It is well settled that "hearsay may be the basis for issuance of [a search] warrant 'so long as there * * * [is] a substantial basis for crediting the hearsay.' " *United States v. Ventresca,* 308 *U.S.* 102, 108, 85 *S.Ct.* 741, 745 (1965) (quoting *Jones v. United States,* 362 *U.S.* 257, 80 *S.Ct.* 725, 736 (1960)). In fact, an affidavit based on hearsay information " 'need not reflect the direct personal observations of the affiant,' " so long as the judge is " 'informed of some of the underlying circumstances' supporting the affiant's conclusions and his belief that any informant involved 'whose identity need not be disclosed * * * was "credible" or his information "reliable." ' " *Id.* at 108, 85 *S.Ct.* at 745-746. [Citation omitted.]

Probable cause will not, however, be established by an affidavit which is "purely conclusory," setting forth only the affiant's or an informant's belief—that certain evidentiary items may be presently found in a particular place—"without detailing any of the 'underlying circumstances' upon which that belief is based." *Id.* at 108-109, 85 *S.Ct.* at 746. In this respect, it is essential that the affidavit set forth the underlying facts and circumstances which support the probable cause conclusion if the issuing judge "is to perform his detached function and not serve merely as a rubber stamp for the police." *Id.* at 109, 85 *S.Ct.* at 746. Naturally, should any of the credibility or reliability aspects of an informant's hearsay information be deficient in some respect, the deficiency may be offset by independent police investigation directed at corroborating the information relayed—the hallmark of *Illinois v. Gates* and the totality-of-the-circumstances approach.

2. *The constitutionality of the information relied upon: Trash pulls.* In *United States v. Deaner,* 1 *F.*3d 192 (3rd Cir. 1993), federal agents searched defendant's home pursuant to a warrant and seized a variety of marijuana plants, equipment and other items used in growing marijuana, as well as pre-packaged harvested marijuana. In this appeal, defendant argued, among other things, that the magistrate improperly relied on the search warrant's affidavit because it did not demonstrate that an earlier search of his garbage was constitutionally performed. According to defendant, while *California v. Greenwood,* 486 *U.S.* 35, 108 *S.Ct.* 1625 (1988), permits a warrantless search and seizure of garbage left for collection outside the curtilage of one's home, the agents still had to demonstrate that the garbage they inspected was "readily accessible to the public." *Deaner* at 196.

Rejecting defendant's contention, the court stated:

> While the better practice might have been to include in the affidavit a statement on the location of the garbage at the time it was seized, the absence of an express specification of this location is not fatal. The natural implication of defendant's argument is that every

piece of evidence relied upon by an affiant must be shown to have been acquired constitutionally. This would constitute a substantial burden on affiants, as imaginative defense counsel will often successfully be able to argue that the failure to disprove some hypothetical set of facts left it ambiguous as to whether the facts contained within the four corners of the affidavit established that the evidence was seized in a constitutional manner.

More importantly, accepting the defendant's argument that the facts recited in an affidavit must establish that the particular evidence was seized in a constitutional manner would subject probable cause determinations to a hyper-technical analysis insupportable under governing case law. As explained by the Supreme Court in *Illinois v. Gates*: "Technical requirements of elaborate specificity * * * have no proper place in this area."

Deaner at 196-97. [Citations & internal quotes omitted.]

MASSACHUSETTS v. UPTON
Supreme Court of the United States
466 *U.S.* 727, 104 *S.Ct.* 2085 (1984)

QUESTION: Rather than using a fixed and rigid formula, should the Fourth Amendment's probable cause requirement for the issuance of a warrant be applied in light of the "totality of the circumstances" made known to the magistrate or judge ?

ANSWER: YES. The "totality-of-the-circumstances" analysis, *i.e.,* examining the "whole picture," is "more in keeping with the practical, common-sense decision demanded of the magistrate." *Id.* at 2088.

RATIONALE: The Court reaffirms its holding in *Illinois v. Gates*, 462 *U.S.* 213, 103 *S.Ct.* 2317 (1983), and reiterates that the *Gates* decision did not merely refine or qualify the rigid "two pronged test" of *Aguilar v. Texas*, 378 *U.S.* 108, 84 *S.Ct.* 1509 (1964), and *Spinelli v. United States*, 393 *U.S.* 410, 89 *S.Ct.* 584 (1969), previously used for determinations of whether "an affidavit [properly supports] the issuance of a search warrant [when police rely] on an informant's tip." *Upton* at 2087. In fact, the Court expressly rejected the two pronged test as "hypertechnical and divorced from the factual and practical considerations of everyday life on which reasonable and prudent men, not legal technicians, act." *Id.* (quoting from *Brinegar v. United States*, 338 *U.S.* 160, 69 *S.Ct.* 1302 (1949)).

Prior to the Court's decision in *Gates*, an informant's tip was dissected and analyzed with two separate inquiries. First, is the informant's basis of information, *i.e.,* the particular means by which he learned of the information, reliable ? Second, is the informant, himself, reliable ? These two inquiries represented the two prongs of the *Aguilar* and *Spinelli* doctrine.

Here, the Court notes that such "technical dissection" of informants' tips tends to focus undue attention "on isolated issues that cannot sensibly be divorced from other facts presented to the magistrate." *Upton* at 2088.

Instead, the judge should consider the "totality of the circumstances," *i.e.*, the "whole picture," when assessing applications for warrants. Affidavits should be viewed in their entirety, and, significance should be given "to each relevant piece of information," while according a proper balance of "the relative weights of all the various indicia of reliability (and unreliability) attending the [informant's] tip." *Id.*

NOTE

1. *The nexus between the place to be searched and the things to be seized.* In *United States v. Anderson*, 851 *F*.2d 727 (4th Cir. 1988), the court addressed the issue whether the nexus between the place to be searched and the items to be seized may be established by the nature of the item and the normal inferences of where one would likely keep such evidence. The search warrant which issued described the items to be seized as a .45 caliber pistol and a silencer attachment. The affidavit in support of the warrant presented evidence that defendant had offered to sell the pistol and silencer to three informers. The affidavit also relayed the fact that defendant told the informers that "the gun for sale was used to kill somebody." In the search which followed, Investigators for the Commonwealth of Virginia located the gun and silencer in defendant's residence. Nowhere in the affidavit, however, was there any information which directly indicated that the gun and silencer could be found at defendant's residence. In this appeal, therefore, defendant contends "that there was no probable cause to believe that the pistol and the silencer would be found in the residence." *Id.* at 729. The United States Court of Appeals for the Fourth Circuit disagreed.

According to the court, "[t]he primary question confronting us is whether the magistrate acted properly in issuing a warrant for the search of [defendant's] home." *Id.* at 728. In this respect, the United States Supreme Court has instructed:

> The task of the issuing magistrate is simply to make a practical, common sense decision whether, given all the circumstances set forth in the affidavit before him, including the "veracity" and "basis of knowledge" of persons supplying hearsay information, there is a fair probability that contraband or evidence of a crime will be found in a particular place. And the duty of a reviewing court is simply to ensure that the magistrate had a "substantial basis for . . . conclud[ing]" that probable cause existed.

Illinois v. Gates, 462 *U.S.* 213, 238-239, 103 *S.Ct.* 2317, 2332 (1983). [Citation omitted.] On the basis of this instruction, the court agrees with the Government's argument that it was reasonable to assume that individuals keep weapons in their homes, particularly in the case of this defendant. Accordingly, the court concludes that "the nexus between the place to be searched and the items to be seized may be established by the nature of the item and the normal inferences of where one would likely keep such evidence." *Anderson* at 729.

See also United States v. Johnson, 726 *F*.2d 1018, 1021-1022 (4th Cir. 1984) (it was reasonable to conclude, given the distances involved, that evidence of defendant's possession of explosive devices would be found in his automobile); *United States v. Jacobs*, 715 *F*.2d 1343, 1346 (9th Cir. 1983) (magistrate's conclusion that articles of clothing would remain at the residence was reasonable); *United States v. Steeves*, 525 *F*.2d 33, 38 (8th Cir. 1975) (people who own pistols generally keep them at home or on their persons); *United States v. Rahn*, 511 *F*.2d 290, 293 (10th Cir. 1975), *cert. denied*, 423 *U.S.* 825, 96 *S.Ct.* 41 (1975) (it was reasonable to assume that persons keep weapons in their homes); *Bastida v. Henderson*, 487 *F*.2d 860, 863 (5th Cir. 1973) (a very likely place to find the guns would be either on the persons of the assailants or about the premises where they lived).

But see United States v. Lockett, 674 *F*.2d 843, 846 (11th Cir. 1982) (there must be a "substantial basis" to conclude that the instrumentalities of the crime will be discovered on the searched premises); *United States v. Charest*, 602 *F*.2d 1015, 1017 (1st Cir. 1979) (affidavit contains no information from which a factual finding could be made that the gun used in the shooting was located at defendant's premises).

In *Anderson, supra,* the court did pause to note that "sloppily prepared or executed warrants directly affront the Fourth Amendment to the United States Constitution * * * [and] judicial officers and police [officers] should exercise care to see their warrants and supporting affidavits are correct * * *." *Id.* at 730 n.1.

The prudent officer would include the necessary information in his or her affidavit which provides the nexus or connection between the items sought and the place to be searched.

2. State officers are reminded that state courts are free, and indeed encouraged, to rely on their own constitutions to provide greater protection to the privacy interests of their citizens than that afforded under parallel provisions of the United States Constitution. Naturally, when a state goes beyond the federal "floor of protection," and provides more expansive individual liberties on the basis of its state constitution, law enforcement in that state is thereby counteractively restricted. With this principle in mind, state officers should be aware that the "totality-of-the-circumstances" test adopted in *Illinois v. Gates*, and reaffirmed in *Massachusetts v. Upton*, has been receiving mixed treatment at the state level.

For example, in New Jersey, a state which relies heavily on its own constitution to provide its citizens enhanced individual liberties, the less restrictive "totality-of-the-circumstances" test has nonetheless been adopted "to test the validity of search warrants under the probable cause standard set forth in [A]rticle I, paragraph 7 of the New Jersey Constitution." *State v. Novembrino*, 105 *N.J.* 95, 122 (1987). *See also Commonwealth v. Gray*, 509 *Pa.* 476 (1985), and *Commonwealth v. Silverman*, 373 *Pa.Super.* 274 (1988) (Pennsylvania endorses the "totality-of-the-circumstances" test); *State v. Barton*, 219 *Conn.*

529, 594 *A*.2d 917, 926 (1991) (abandoning the rigid, compartmental-ized *Aguilar-Spinelli* test and adopting the *Gates* totality-of-the-circumstances test as a matter of state constitutional law.)

In New York, however, the *Gates* totality-of-the-circumstances test has been rejected. *See People v. Johnson*, 66 *N.Y*.2d 398, 497 *N.Y.S*.2d 618, 488 *N.E*.2d 439 (1985) (holding that in a warrantless arrest or search situation, the *Gates* totality-of-the-circumstances test was in-applicable as a matter of state constitutional law.)

UNITED STATES v. JORDAN
United States Court of Appeals
999 *F*.2d 11 (1st Cir. 1993)

QUESTION: May probable cause be established for the issuance of a search warrant when neither the investigating officer nor his infor-mant had direct contact with the defendant or directly observed the controlled buy of narcotics ?

ANSWER: YES. Under the totality of the circumstances test, probable cause to believe a defendant's home contains contraband may be established even though neither the investigating officer nor his informant had direct contact with the defendant or directly observed the controlled buy of narcotics at the defendant's home.

RATIONALE: Agent McGill of the Maine Bureau of Intergovernmen-tal Drug Enforcement drafted an affidavit for a warrant to search de-fendant's residence for marijuana. The affidavit was based on two con-trolled marijuana "buys," within the preceding ten days, from one Don-ald Moyse, a convicted drug offender, by a confidential informant acting under the direct control and surveillance of Agent McGill. "McGill at-tested that the confidential informant previously had provided reliable tips and had cooperated with local authorities in other controlled mari-juana 'buys.'" *Id.* at 12. "The affidavit related that Donald Moyse told the confidential informant that the marijuana involved in both con-trolled 'buys' had come from [defendant] Jordan's residence, and that both 'buys' had been conducted in essentially the same manner: the con-fidential informant would meet with one Cary LaFrance at a local rest stop area and turn over the agreed purchase price (supplied by Agent McGill). LaFrance would drive to Donald Moyse's residence, and the two would proceed to the Jordan residence where the marijuana was kept. Moyse and LaFrance would then meet with the informant at a local school and deliver the marijuana." *Id.* at 12-13.

Immediately before each controlled buy (and before he provided the purchase money), McGill searched the informant for contraband; and prior to the second controlled buy, McGill searched the infor-mant's car as well. "McGill then surveilled the unfolding transaction, observing as the informant delivered the 'buy' money to LaFrance, fol-lowing LaFrance to Moyse's house, and watching LaFrance and Moyse as they proceeded to Jordan's residence, then to the local school." *Id.*

at 13. In each instance, McGill's affidavit indicated that "the informant told McGill that the marijuana had been turned over to him by Moyse and LaFrance at the school and that it had been obtained, according to Moyse, at Jordan's residence. Following the second 'buy,' the informant told McGill that Moyse had stated that there was a 'large quantity' of marijuana at the Jordan residence. Finally, the affidavit represented that [a] urinalysis conducted while Moyse was on probation occasionally revealed positive results for marijuana use." *Id.*

The warrant issued and, during the course of the search of Jordan's home, Maine law enforcement officials seized more than a kilogram of marijuana, a triple beam scale, $5,880 in cash, six firearms, and nearly 1000 rounds of assault-rifle ammunition.

In this appeal, following the denial of his motion to suppress, defendant contended that "the warrant was issued without probable cause." *Id. The United States Court of Appeals for the First Circuit disagreed.*

Defendant's attack on the McGill affidavit may be summarized as follows:

> [N]either McGill nor the informant had any direct contact with Jordan, nor directly observed any drug buy or transfer at the Jordan residence; Moyse's representations that the marijuana came from Jordan's home are "double hearsay"; Moyse, a marijuana user and convicted drug offender, was not a reliable hearsay declarant and, finally, the affidavit did not demonstrate a "fair probability" that marijuana or related contraband would be found at the Jordan residence since the marijuana Moyse sold to the informant could have come from LaFrance, Moyse, the school, or Jordan's residence.

Id.

The court agreed that "nothing in the McGill affidavit excluded the possibility that the marijuana may have come from some place other than the Jordan residence. Nevertheless, viewing the totality of the circumstances related in the affidavit, rather than judging 'bits and pieces of information in isolation,' " the court determined that "the affidavit was sufficient to support the issuing judge's 'common-sense' determination of probable cause." *Id.* The court elaborated:

> Hearsay statements, like those of Moyse and the informant, often are the stuff of search warrant affidavits. * * * Their reliability may be corroborated by various means, including direct surveillance or circumstantial evidence, or vouchsafed by the affiant—in this case a highly experienced law enforcement officer. * * * McGill attested that the confidential informant had provided reliable information and investigative assistance to the police in the past, which may have been sufficient in itself to establish the reliability of the informant's hearsay statements. * * * Moreover, McGill also attested that (i) Moyse was an unwitting participant in the controlled "buy," and (ii) unbeknownst to Moyse, McGill observed Moyse's entrance to Jordan's residence on both occasions, thereby

establishing that Moyse was in a position to know whether Jordan kept marijuana at his residence. * * *

Finally, McGill contemporaneously surveilled all conspicuous steps taken in the course of both controlled "buys," which proceeded exactly as foretold by the confidential informant, and included stops at Jordan's home, the site of the search. Thus, independent corroboration lent further credence to the confidential informant's statements (*i.e.*, the location of the marijuana). * * *

[Defendant] nevertheless correctly observes that these factors in combination do not exclude the possibility that Moyse might have obtained the marijuana at some place along the drug "buy" route other than Jordan's residence. But given the experience and training of the affiant, the confidential informant's proven reliability, and the corroboration of the informant's and Moyse's hearsay reports by means of direct police surveillance, the issuing judge was not required to credit the speculative possibility that the marijuana might have been obtained elsewhere along the drug route than Jordan's residence. Nor may we do so.

Id. at 13-14.

Accordingly, the totality of the circumstances "related in the supporting affidavit, together with reasonable inferences therefrom, provided a 'substantial basis' for the issuing judge's common-sense determination that there was a fair probability that Jordan's home contained contraband or evidence of a crime." *Id.* at 14.

NOTE

A "controlled buy" that corroborates an informant's tip. In *United States v. Warren*, 42 *F.*3d 647 (D.C.Cir. 1994), United States Park Police officers, along with a S.W.A.T. team, arrived at a residence on Galveston Place, S.W., in the District of Columbia, to execute a search warrant. "A federal magistrate had issued the search warrant the previous day based upon an affidavit prepared by Park Police Officer [] Holman. In the affidavit, Officer Holman stated that a 'confidential reliable source' had advised Park Police within the previous seven days that crack cocaine was being stored and sold at 76 Galveston Place, S.W., apartment number one. * * * Holman stated that his informant had 'proven reliable in the past,' having provided information that 'resulted in the seizure of large quantities of cocaine, about 8 guns and about 52 defendants.' [] The informant 'had never been proven unreliable,' Holman said, noting that every search warrant issued pursuant to information provided by the informant yielded illegal drugs or firearms." *Id.* at 649-50.

"In the affidavit, Officer Holman also described a controlled drug buy conducted within the previous 72 hours in which the informant entered the apartment building with Park Police funds and emerged a short time later with a rock of crack cocaine. According to the affida-

vit, '[t]he source stated he had purchased the substance from apt #1.' "
Id. at 650.

The search conducted under the authority of the warrant uncovered, among other items, a total of 36.12 grams of crack, a loaded .38 caliber revolver, and $1,309 in cash.

In upholding the warrant, the court declared: "We hold that a reliable informant's tip, combined with a controlled drug buy, established probable cause for the search in this case." *Id.* at 649. Rejecting defendant's argument that "no substantial basis for a finding of probable cause existed in this case," *id.* at 652, the court stated:

> Officer Holman's affidavit informed the magistrate that a confidential informant of proven reliability had stated that 76 Galveston Place, apartment number one, was being used for the storing and selling of crack cocaine, and that the informant's account had been corroborated by a controlled drug buy. Our cases consistently have recognized that *police establish probable cause for a search where they corroborate a reliable informant's tip about drug activity at a residence by conducting a single controlled buy of illegal narcotics.*

Id. at 652. [Emphasis added.]

UNITED STATES v. WILLIAMS
United States Court of Appeals
3 *F.*3d 69 (3rd Cir. 1993)

QUESTION: Does the following affidavit establish probable cause for the issuance of a search warrant ?

AFFIDAVIT: "On October 5, 1989, these Affiants received information from a housekeeper at the [Greentree Holiday Inn], that the occupants of rooms 331 and 333 are engaged in illicit drug dealing.

"The anonymous informant, which the Affiants believe to be reliable, advised that two black males, one from California, had rented two adjoining rooms, paying cash for the rooms, in addition to other hotel services. The informant saw one of the two display a large roll of paper currency, the majority of which were 100 dollar bills. They were also observed leaving room 331 or 333 individually, and upon returning, knocking on the room door in a distinctive 'coded' manner, that being two knocks, a pause, followed by three more knocks. This manner of leaving and reentering the room continued throughout the day.

"The informant also observed one of the room occupants meet on several occasions in the hotel parking lot with unidentified persons who remained in their vehicle throughout the meeting. When they returned to their room, they entered with the before mentioned 'coded' knock.

"It was also learned that the housekeeper, when attempting to clean rooms 331 and 333, observed small plastic baggies, in addition to cigarette rolling papers. She described the plastic baggies as similar to those she recognized while watching a news segment about drug sales, that are commonly used by drug dealers. These items were observed only after the housekeeper was refused admittance to clean the room until a box of unknown content was removed by the occupants from the room to be cleaned, into the adjoining room. These Affiants' investigation reveals that rooms 331 and 333 were rented to Darin Birts, B/M, D.O.B. 12/4/64, California operator's license number C2064168, 5625 Blackwedger St., Los Angeles, CA 90019. A criminal history check of this individual revealed several aliases, along with at least two convictions on felony drug offenses on 9/7/86, and 10/14/86, both of which resulted in prison sentences.

"These Affiants request a search warrant to be issued on the abovementioned information from an anonymous informant which these affiants recognize as fitting the profile of individuals involved in drug transactions. In addition to fitting the profile of drug dealers, is the fact that Darin Birts' criminal history includes felony drug convictions." [*Id.* at 70-71.]

ANSWER: YES. The information supplied by the housekeeper, along with the information discovered in the ensuing investigation, provided probable cause to believe contraband or evidence of a crime would be found in the motel rooms. *Id.* at 73.

RATIONALE: As the Court explained in *Illinois v. Gates*, 462 *U.S.* 213, 103 *S.Ct.* 2317 (1983):

> The task of the issuing magistrate is simply to make a practical commonsense decision whether, given all the circumstances set forth in the affidavit before him[,] * * * there is a fair probability that contraband or evidence of a crime will be found in a particular place. And the duty of a reviewing court is simply to ensure that the magistrate had a "substantial basis for * * * conclud[ing]" that probable cause existed.

Williams at 72 (quoting *Gates* at 238-39, 103 *S.Ct.* at 2332).

"[T]he most reasonable reading of the affidavit is that 'the anonymous informant' referred to in the second sentence is the Holiday Inn 'housekeeper' referred to in the immediately preceding sentence. This is strongly suggested by the proximity of the two references and the use of a 'the' rather than an 'an' before the second reference. It seems confirmed by the facts reflected on the face of the affidavit, that (1) the housekeeper was a police informant in this matter whose name was not reported; (2) a housekeeper would be in a position to observe what the 'informant' observed and reported; (3) it would be highly unlikely that anyone other than a housekeeper or a member of the party occupying Rooms 331 and 333 could have observed all that the informant reported; and (4) a member of the Birts party undoubtedly would have reported more information than the 'informant' reported and would not have reported it from the outsider perspective employed by the 'informant.' While it is conceivable to us that the informant was someone other than the housekeeper as the district court speculated, [this court does] not think such a conclusion flows from a common sense reading of the affidavit." *Id.*

"Once the anonymous informant is understood to be the house-keeper, [this court believes] the affidavit offers substantial evidence supporting the reliability of the information received by the Greentree Police." *Id.* While it is true that "the bare assertion by the police affiants that they believed the housekeeper to be reliable does not alone suffice, that assertion does indicate that the police had no information which caused them to doubt the housekeeper's reliability. More importantly, the affidavit offers affirmative evidence that the source of the affiants' information was akin to the proverbial 'disinterested witness' whose reliability has been celebrated through the years * * *." *Id.*

As the Court in *Illinois v. Gates* made clear, a history of providing reliable tips should not be understood to be the only way that the reliability of an anonymous source can be established. Indeed, evidence that the anonymous informant "is unlikely to have an ulterior motive in th[is] case provides greater assurance of reliability than does evidence indicating the informant has been reliable in other matters." *Id.* at 73.

> We know from the affidavit in this case that the informant was a motel employee and that the information supplied concerned observations which a housekeeper might well make in the course of her work. The magistrate was entitled to take judicial notice that guests in a Holiday Inn are likely to be temporary visitors who reside elsewhere. In this instance, it appears likely from the affidavit that the guests came from as far away as California. Based on these facts, the magistrate was entitled to infer that the housekeeper and the guests, more likely than not, had no relationship other than that of motel housekeeper and motel guest and, accordingly, that the housekeeper, more likely than not, had no motive to supply the police with fabricated information about the guests.
>
> In assessing the housekeeper's reliability, the magistrate also was entitled to rely on the fact that the housekeeper's report of drug activity was corroborated to some degree by the independent investigation of the police which uncovered Birts' drug record. Based on this corroboration, the apparent disinterestedness of the informant, and the absence of any information suggesting unreliability, [this court believes] the magistrate was entitled to credit the housekeeper's information.

Id.

The remaining question is "whether the information supplied by the housekeeper and the information discovered in the ensuing investigation provided a substantial basis for the magistrate to believe that contraband or evidence of a crime probably would be found in the motel rooms." *Id.* Concluding that it did, the court reasoned:

> The affidavit stated that the occupants of Rooms 331 and 333 (1) regulated entries to the rooms through a coded knock; (2) excluded the housekeeper from one of the rooms until a box could be removed from the room to be cleaned; (3) had in their possession items (*i.e.*, small plastic bags and cigarette rolling papers) which frequently are used in the marketing and consumption of drugs; (4)

engaged in repeated contacts in the hotel parking lot with persons who remained in their vehicles; (5) possessed large amounts of cash and used only cash to pay for the rooms and hotel services; and (6) included a person who utilized several aliases and only three years earlier had been convicted of drug felonies which resulted in the imposition of prison sentences. We agree with the district court that innocuous explanations could exist for each of these phenomena in isolation. Moreover, we acknowledge that even taken in combination, they do not prove beyond doubt that the occupants were guilty of a crime. The magistrate was entitled to infer, however, that the occupants *probably were engaged in illegal activity, that the illegal activity probably involved drug trafficking*, and that, more likely than not, a search of the rooms would reveal drugs, drug paraphernalia, illegally generated cash, and/or weapons.

Id. [Emphasis added.]

---

§2.3(c). Staleness.

In the context of a search and seizure, the probable cause requirement focuses on the facts and circumstances presently confronting the police, that is, a "current" or "fresh" situation. Therefore, the facts and circumstances making up an officer's probable cause must permit a neutral and detached magistrate or judge to conclude that there is a reasonable probability that contraband or other evidence subject to official seizure may *presently* be found in a particular place. Such proof "must be of facts so closely related to the time of the issue of the warrant as to justify a finding of probable cause at that time. Whether the proof meets this test must be determined by the circumstances of each case." *Sgro v. United States*, 287 *U.S.* 206, 210-211, 53 *S.Ct.* 138, 140 (1932).

In order to guard against the execution of a search warrant at a time when the probable cause has become "stale," a majority of jurisdictions have adopted the "10-day rule." See, e.g., Fed.R.Crim.P. 41(e)(2)(A) (officer must "execute the warrant within a specified time no longer than 10 days"). Execution of the search warrant beyond the 10-day requirement "makes [the] warrant void." Sgro at 211, 53 S.Ct. at 140.

Accordingly, because the "time" when the events (relied upon by the officer-affiant) occurred is so vital to the probable cause assessment, the officer must document in the affidavit "when" the material events took place and his or her reasons for believing that a "present" search will produce the described items. Nonetheless, problems do arise when a court must determine whether an officer's information—which at one point in time may have established probable cause to believe an item may be found at a particular location—has become "stale."

1. *Relevant factors for staleness determinations.* "Age of the information supporting a warrant application is a factor in determin-

ing probable cause. If too old, the information is stale, and probable cause may no longer exist. Age alone, however, does not determine staleness. 'The determination of probable cause is not merely an exercise in counting the days or even months between the facts relied on and the issuance of the warrant.' Rather, we must also examine the nature of the crime and the type of evidence." *United States v. Harvey,* 2 *F.*3d 1318 (3rd Cir. 1993). [Citation omitted.] *See also United States v. Stiver,* 9 *F.*3d 298, 300-01 (3rd Cir. 1993).

There are, therefore, a number of factors that a court may consider when determining whether the information supporting the issuance of a warrant has grown stale. These factors include: (1) the nature and quality of the seized evidence (whether perishable and easily transferable or of enduring utility to its holder), (2) the ease with which the evidence may be disposed of, (3) the character of the place to be searched (whether one of incidental use for mere convenience or a secure base of operations), (4) the lapse of time between the information and the warrant, (5) the character of the criminal (whether isolated and fleeting or entrenched), and (6) the character of the crime (whether chance encounter or continuing illegal scheme). *See United States v. Holliday,* 474 *F.*2d 320 (10th Cir. 1973); *United States v. Johnson,* 461 *F.*2d 285, 287 (10th Cir. 1972); *Commonwealth v. Alewine,* 384 *Pa.Super.* 283, 558 *A.*2d 542, 543 (1989).

2. *Continuing illegal schemes.* The continuity of the illegal scheme may be established by the inherent nature of the criminal activity itself or through evidence that the activity has extended over a period of time. In either respect, "[i]f past circumstances would have justified the search, there must be reason to believe that those circumstances still exist at the time of the search." *United States v. Dennis,* 625 *F.*2d 782 (8th Cir. 1980). The length of the delay, therefore, must be "considered with the nature of the unlawful activity * * * [a]nd they are considered in the light of common sense." *Id.* at 792.

Thus, in *United States v. Johnson, supra,* a three-week delay did not diminish the probable cause where the illegal distilling was an on going business, rather than a mere isolated violation. In *United States v. Dennis, supra,* probable cause was not vitiated by the passage of three months where the affidavit clearly indicated the continuing nature of defendant's loansharking operation. And in *Andresen v. Maryland,* 427 *U.S.* 463, 478, 96 *S.Ct.* 2737, 2747 (1976), a three month delay did not undermine the probable cause because the warrants were for business records which were likely to be maintained for a long time.

See also Commonwealth v. Karns, 389 *Pa.Super.* 58, 566 *A.*2d 615 (1989), where the court rejected a defendant's claim that the affidavit failed to establish the "freshness" of the information relied upon, finding that the information provided by two informants relating the ongoing enterprise of marijuana cultivation over the course of two years, with the additional information that defendant would be harvesting the crop within the next month, satisfied the probable cause requirement. *Id.,* 566 *A.*2d at 617-618.

Similarly, in *United States v. McNeese*, 901 *F.*2d 585 (7th Cir. 1990), the court held that a seven-month delay between the informant's last drug pick-up from the target's residence and the issuance of the search warrant did not serve to render the warrant defective on staleness grounds. According to the court, while the age of the information supporting the application for a search warrant is one factor to consider in determining whether probable cause exists to believe that the evidence sought may *presently* be found in the place to be searched, it is not the only factor.

> If the information is too old, it is considered stale and probable cause no longer exists. * * * Nevertheless, the warrant can be issued if other factors indicate that the information is reliable and that the object of the search will still be on the premises. * * * Courts have found that search warrants were not stale when based on information nine months old[, *see United States v.*] *Batchelder*, 824 *F.*2d [563,] 564 [7th Cir. 1987)]; six months old[, *see*] *United States v. Williams*, 603 *F.*2d 1168, 1172 (5th Cir. 1979)[;] or five months old[, *see*] *United States v. Grandstaff*, 813 *F.*2d 1353, 1357 (9th Cir. [1987]). Moreover, *when a conspiracy to distribute drugs has been ongoing for years, and is clearly an activity of a protracted and continuous nature, the passage of time between the last described act and the application for the warrant diminishes in significance.*
>
> In this case, the cocaine distribution conspiracy had been ongoing for more than two years.

Id. at 596-97. [Emphasis added.]

3. *"Staleness" analytically different from "ripeness."* In *Sgro v. United States*, 287 *U.S.* 206, 53 *S.Ct.* 138 (1932), the federal Supreme Court emphasized that the proof necessary to establish probable cause

> must be of facts so closely related to the time of the issue of the warrant as to justify a finding of probable cause at that time. Whether the proof meets this test must be determined by the circumstances of each case. [P]robable cause must properly appear when the warrant issues[, and t]he proof supplied must * * * speak as of th[at] time[.] * * *

Id. at 210-11, 53 *S.Ct.* at 140.

> The supporting affidavit must relate to facts which tend to show an unlawful situation actually or probably *existing at the moment.*

Id. at 215-16, 53 *S.Ct.* at 142 (McReynolds, J. concurring). [Emphasis added.]

It is critical that the affiant's belief—that a fair probability exists that evidence will be found in a particular place—be a *present* belief; a belief existing *at the time the warrant issues.* A search warrant's supporting affidavit must, therefore, set forth an "informational time frame" from which a judge may reasonably ascertain *when* the affiant gained his information from his informants, *when* the informants themselves obtained the information they conveyed to the affiant, and if probable cause *presently* exists to believe that at the very moment the warrant issues, the evidence sought will be at a particular place. *See Commonwealth v. Conner*, 452 *Pa.* 333, 339-40, 305 *A.2d* 341, 345 (1973). *See also Commonwealth v. Flaherty*, 400 *Pa.Super.* 397, 583 *A.2d* 1175, 1178 (1990) (ripeness of probable cause questioned where the only information tending to implicate the defendant's automobile was the statement made by him to an informant that defendant "will deliver the [drugs] to special customers using his car"; informant did not indicate that he had seen drugs in defendant's car, "nor had he any reason to believe that drugs were present in the car at the time of his statement to police").

When the issuing authority is presented with an affidavit which sets forth a reasonable time frame, a fair determination may then be made that a *present* search will yield the desired evidence—that (1) probable cause had been satisfactorily established at some point in the past, and (2) probable cause still exists.

It is thus clear that the issue of "staleness" is analytically different from the issue of "ripeness." "Staleness," presupposes that at some earlier point in time probable cause existed, that is, the information was once "fresh." *See Flaherty*, 583 *A.2d* at 1179. On the other hand, a "ripeness" problem focuses on the informational time frame and the fact that there has been no *initial* showing of probable cause to believe that particularly described items had *ever been* (or *ever would be*) at a particular place at *any* time.

The problem of ripeness may, of course, be rectified by the affiant's express inquiry into the time frame of the information received; and if that is not yet available, the affiant should allow the investigation to progress or ripen to a point when it is.

---

§2.3(d). Anticipatory search warrants.

An "anticipatory" search warrant is a warrant that is signed and issued by a judge based on an affidavit demonstrating probable cause to believe that, within a reasonable time in the future (but not at the time the affidavit is presented), contraband or criminal evidence will arrive at a particular place. When properly drafted and used, anticipatory warrants have been held to be constitutional and a valuable law enforcement tool. *United States v. Grubbs*, 547 *U.S.* 90, 126 *S.Ct.* 1494, 1499 (2006); *See also United States v. Loy*, 191 *F.*3d 360, 364 (3rd Cir. 1999); *State v. Ulrich*, 265 *N.J.Super.* 569, 576, 628 *A.2d* 368 (App.Div. 1993). Such warrants are typically used when law enforcement officials have arranged or will be monitoring a controlled delivery of contraband.

The anticipatory search warrant and the affidavit in support thereof must demonstrate several things not normally found in the traditional search warrant. First, the affidavit must set forth facts demonstrating a *strong probability* that the sought-after evidence will be at the target premises when the warrant is executed. *See State v. Mier*, 147 *N.J.Super.* 17, 21, 370 *A.*2d 515 (App.Div. 1977). In *Mier*, the court held that the use of an anticipatory warrant was appropriate where there was a reasonably strong probability that "the contraband will reach its destination before execution of the warrant because of the controlled delivery by the authorities." *Id.* at 21. Thus, a judge must be able to conclude from the affidavit that "there is a strong probability that the continuation of the process already initiated by the shipment of contraband will in the natural course of events result in the consummation of the crime at the time and place anticipated[.]" *Id.* at 21-22. *See also People v. Glen, supra*, 30 *N.Y.*2d at 259 (it is only the strong probability that the seizable property will be on the premises when searched that distinguishes the anticipatory warrant from the "hated general writs of assistance of pre-Revolutionary times").

The required showing of a strong probability that the contraband will be at the target premises when the warrant is to be executed has been held to be easily met when the facts set forth in the affidavit indicate that "the contraband is in the custody of the authorities who can control the time and method of its delivery." *Ulrich* at 575. Even where the contraband is not in the custody of the authorities, courts have not hesitated to conclude that it is "both permissible and desirable to obtain anticipatory warrants when time permits." *See State v. Bell*, 195 *N.J.Super.* 49, 55, 477 *A.*2d 1272 (App.Div. 1984). In this latter category of cases, the facts and circumstances recited in the affidavit should demonstrate in even greater detail a clear showing of probable cause to believe the contraband or criminal evidence will be at the target location at the time specified.

In all cases, however, the facts set forth in the affidavit should show in detail how the affiant knows that the contraband or criminal evidence will at some future time be located at the place indicated, and how reliable his or her sources are. *United States v. Garcia*, 882 *F.*2d 699, 703-04 (2nd Cir.), *cert. denied*, 493 *U.S.* 943, 110 *S.Ct.* 348 (1989); *United States ex rel. Beal v. Skaff*, 418 *F.*2d 430, 433 (7th Cir. 1969). In designating the future time, the affiant should be reasonably specific; for example, "the morning of," or "the afternoon of" a certain day should suffice. If police officials will play a part in the delivery, the affidavit should clearly indicate that, and set forth the anticipated amount of official involvement.

When drafting the affidavit and preparing the search warrant form, the affiant should not use (or should delete any existing) language which indicates that the described items are "now located" or "presently located" at the target premises. In place of such language, the affidavit should indicate that the described items will arrive at the place to be searched promptly following the issuance of the warrant.

It is critical that the affidavit contain language which expressly declares that the search warrant will not be executed until the happening of a specific event. This portion of the affidavit should contain specific and objective criteria which adequately assure the judge that the warrant will not be executed prematurely.

Finally, the affiant should examine the search warrant form to insure that there is no form language which states that the warrant is to be executed "immediately" or "forthwith." Such language should be replaced with language indicating that the warrant shall "be executed only upon the occurrence of" one or more specified events. *Ulrich* at 576 n.2. Like the affidavit, those events must be detailed. In the warrant, those events become "conditions" governing its execution; and those conditions must be "explicit, clear and narrowly drawn so as to avoid misunderstanding or manipulation[.]" *United States v. Garcia, supra*, 882 *F*.2d at 703-04. This provides the issuing judge a measure of control over the process and permits him or her to guard against premature execution of the warrant.

If the anticipated event upon which the warrant is based never occurs, the warrant may not be executed. Because the warrant's validity is contingent on the happening of a stated event at a particular time, once the critical time passes without the event's occurrence, the warrant becomes void.

UNITED STATES v. GRUBBS
Supreme Court of the United States
547 *U.S.* 90, 126 *S.Ct.* 1494 (2006)

QUESTION: Does the Fourth Amendment require that an anticipatory search warrant specifically set forth the triggering condition that must occur prior to the warrant's execution?

ANSWER: NO. "[T]he Fourth Amendment does not require that the triggering condition for an anticipatory search warrant be set forth in the warrant itself." *Id.* at 1501. Officers executing such a warrant, however, have the responsibility to examine the affidavit to ensure that the triggering condition has been satisfied before undertaking the search.

RATIONALE: Defendant Jeffrey Grubbs purchased a videotape containing child pornography from a Web site operated by an undercover postal inspector. Thereafter, several postal inspectors arranged a controlled delivery of a package containing the videotape to Grubbs' residence. One of the inspectors sought to obtain a search warrant based on an affidavit describing the proposed operation in detail. In pertinent part, the affidavit provided:

> Execution of this search warrant will not occur unless and until the parcel has been received by a person(s) and has been physically taken into the residence[.] At that time, and not before, this search warrant will be executed by me and other United States Postal inspectors, with appropriate assistance from other law enforcement officers in accordance with this warrant's command.

Id. at 1497.

"In addition to describing this triggering condition, the affidavit referred to two attachments, which described Grubbs' residence and the items officers would seize. These attachments, but not the body of the affidavit, were incorporated into the requested warrant." *Id.*

Two days after the warrant issued, an undercover postal inspector delivered the package. "Grubbs' wife signed for it and took the unopened package inside. The inspectors detained Grubbs as he left his home a few minutes later, then entered the house and commenced the search. Roughly 30 minutes into the search, Grubbs was provided with a copy of the warrant, which included both attachments but not the supporting affidavit that explained when the warrant would be executed." *Id.* at 1498. During questioning, Grubbs admitted ordering the videotape. He was placed under arrest, and subsequently indicted for possession of child pornography.

In this appeal, Grubbs contended first that, as a general matter, anticipatory search warrants are unconstitutional, and second, that the anticipatory warrant was invalid because it did not specifically set forth the triggering condition. *The United States Supreme Court rejected both contentions.*

"An anticipatory warrant is 'a warrant based upon an affidavit showing probable cause that at some future time (but not presently) certain evidence of crime will be located at a specified place.' * * * Most anticipatory warrants subject their execution to some condition precedent other than the mere passage of time—a so-called 'triggering condition.' The affidavit at issue here, for instance, explained that '[e]xecution of th[e] search warrant will not occur unless and until the parcel [containing child pornography] has been received by a person(s) and has been physically taken into the residence.' If the government were to execute an anticipatory warrant before the triggering condition occurred, there would be no reason to believe the item described in the warrant could be found at the searched location; by definition, the triggering condition which establishes probable cause has not yet been satisfied when the warrant is issued." *Id.* at 1498-99. [Citation omitted.]

Ruling that anticipatory search warrants are constitutional, the Court explained:

> Probable cause exists when "there is a fair probability that contraband or evidence of a crime will be found in a particular place." * * * Because the probable-cause requirement looks to whether evidence will be found *when the search is conducted,* all warrants are, in a sense, "anticipatory." In the typical case where the police seek permission to search a house for an item they believe is already located there, the [judge's] determination that there is probable cause for the search amounts to a prediction that the item will still be there when the warrant is executed.

Id. at 1499. [Court's emphasis; citations omitted.]

"Thus, when an anticipatory warrant is issued, 'the fact that the contraband is not presently located at the place described in the warrant is immaterial, so long as there is probable cause to believe that it will be there when the search warrant is executed.' " *Id.* [Citations omitted.]

"Anticipatory warrants are, therefore, no different in principle from ordinary warrants. They require the [judge] to determine (1) that it is *now probable* that (2) contraband, evidence of a crime, or a fugitive *will be* on the described premises (3) when the warrant is executed. It should be noted, however, that where the anticipatory warrant places a condition (other than the mere passage of time) upon its execution, the first of these determinations goes not merely to what will probably be found *if* the condition is met. (If that were the extent of the probability determination, an anticipatory warrant could be issued for every house in the country, authorizing search and seizure *if* contraband should be delivered—though for any single location there is no likelihood that contraband will be delivered.) Rather, the probability determination for a conditioned anticipatory warrant looks also to the likelihood that the condition will occur, and thus that a proper object of seizure will be on the described premises. In other words, for a conditioned anticipatory warrant to comply with the Fourth Amendment's requirement of probable cause, two prerequisites of probability must be satisfied. It must be true not only that *if* the triggering condition occurs 'there is a fair probability that contraband or evidence of a crime will be found in a particular place,' * * * but also that there is probable cause to believe the triggering condition *will occur*. The supporting affidavit must provide the [judge] with sufficient information to evaluate both aspects of the probable-cause determination." *Id.* at 1500. [Court's emphasis; citations omitted.]

"In this case, the occurrence of the triggering condition—successful delivery of the videotape to Grubbs' residence—would plainly establish probable cause for the search. In addition, the affidavit established probable cause to believe the triggering condition would be satisfied. Although it is possible that Grubbs could have refused delivery of the videotape he had ordered, that was unlikely." *Id.*

The Court went on to hold that an anticipatory search warrant's triggering condition(s) need not be set forth on the face of the warrant. First, the Fourth Amendment's particularity requirement specifies only two matters that must be particularly described in the warrant: "the place to be searched" and "the persons or things to be seized." The particularity requirement "does not include the conditions precedent to execution of the warrant." *Id.* at 1501.

Second, the Fourth Amendment does not require that the warrant set forth the judge's "basis for finding probable cause * * *. Much less does it require description of a triggering condition." *Id.*

Moreover, setting forth the triggering condition in the warrant is not necessary to " 'assur[e] the individual whose property is searched or seized of the lawful authority of the executing officer, his need to search, and the limits of his power to search.' " *Id.* [Citation omitted.] In this regard, there is no constitutional requirement that the executing officer present the property owner with a copy of the warrant *before* conducting his search.

Accordingly, "the Fourth Amendment does not require that the triggering condition for an anticipatory search warrant be set forth in the warrant itself[.]" *Id.*

---

§2.3(e). Attacking the sufficiency or integrity of the affidavit.

FRANKS v. DELAWARE
Supreme Court of the United States
438 U.S. 154, 98 S.Ct. 2674 (1978)

QUESTION:　Does a criminal defendant ever have the right, under the Fourth and Fourteenth Amendments, after the issuance of a search warrant, to challenge the truthfulness of factual statements made in the affidavit supporting the warrant ?

ANSWER: YES.　"[W]here a defendant makes a substantial pre-liminary showing that a false statement knowingly and intentionally, or with reckless disregard for the truth, was included by the affiant in the warrant affidavit, and if the allegedly false statement is necessary to the finding of probable cause, the Fourth Amendment requires that a hearing be held at the defendant's request. In the event that at that hearing the allegation of perjury or reckless disregard is established by the defendant by a preponderance of the evidence, and, with the affida-vit's false material set to one side, the affidavit's remaining content is insufficient to establish probable cause, the search warrant must be voided and the fruits of the search excluded to the same extent as if probable cause was lacking on the face of the affidavit." *Id.* at 2676.

RATIONALE:　By deciding that, in certain circumstances, a defen-dant may be permitted to attack the veracity of a search warrant affi-davit after the warrant has been issued and executed, the Court relies on the "language of the Warrant Clause itself, which surely takes the affiant's good faith as its premise: '[N]o Warrants shall issue, but upon probable cause, supported by Oath or affirmation . . . ' " *Id.* at 2681. In this respect, " 'when the Fourth Amendment demands a factual show-ing sufficient to comprise "probable cause," the obvious assumption is that there will be a *truthful* showing.' " *Id.* [Citation omitted; emphasis in original.]

This does not mean "truthful" in the sense that every fact re-cited in the warrant affidavit is necessarily correct, for probable cause may be founded upon hearsay and upon information received from informants, as well as upon information within the affiant's own knowledge that sometimes must be garnered hastily. But surely it is to be "truthful" in the sense that the information put forth is believed or appropriately accepted by the affiant as true.

Id. at 2681.

As a general rule, "a warrant affidavit must set forth particular facts and circumstances underlying the existence of probable cause, so as to allow the magistrate to make an independent evaluation of the matter. If an informant's tip is the source of information, the affidavit must recite 'some of the underlying circumstances from which the informant concluded' that relevant evidence might be discovered, and 'some of the underlying circumstances from which the officer concluded that the informant, whose identity need not be disclosed, * * * was "credible" or his information "reliable." ' " *Id.* [Citation omitted.] "Because it is the magistrate who must determine independently whether there is probable cause * * *, it would be an unthinkable imposition upon his authority if a warrant affidavit, revealed after the fact to contain a deliberately or reckless false statement, were to stand beyond impeachment." *Id.*

The rule announced in this case is, however, "limited [in] scope, both in regard to when exclusion of the seized evidence is mandated, and when a hearing on allegations of misstatements must be accorded." *Id.* 2682. At the outset, there is "a presumption of validity with respect to the affidavit supporting the search warrant. To mandate an evidentiary hearing, the challenger's attack must be more than conclusory and must be supported by more than a mere desire to cross-examine." *Id.* at 2684. An evidentiary hearing on the sufficiency or integrity of the affidavit will only be permitted when:

   1. The defendant presents "allegations of deliberate falsehood or of reckless disregard for the truth,"

   2. Those allegations are "accompanied by an offer of proof[,]"

   3. The allegations "point out specifically the portion of the warrant affidavit that is claimed to be false[,]" and

   4. The allegations are "accompanied by a statement of supporting reasons. Affidavits or sworn or otherwise reliable statements of witnesses should be furnished, or their absence satisfactorily explained."

Id. at 2684. Significantly, mere "[a]llegations of negligence or innocent mistake are insufficient. The deliberate falsity or reckless disregard whose impeachment is permitted [by this case] is only that of the affiant, not of any nongovernmental informant." *Id.*

Accordingly, if the above "requirements are met, and if, when material that is the subject of the alleged falsity or reckless disregard is set to one side, there remains sufficient content in the warrant affidavit to support a finding of probable cause, no hearing is required. On the other hand, if the remaining content is insufficient, the defendant is entitled, under the Fourth and Fourteenth Amendment, to his hearing. Whether he will prevail at that hearing is, of course, another issue." *Id.* at 2684-2685.

NOTE

1. In *United States v. Figueroa*, 750 *F*.2d 232 (2nd Cir. 1984), the court emphasized that a *Franks* "hearing is required only when a defendant makes a 'substantial preliminary showing' that the affiant knowingly, intentionally or with reckless disregard for the truth made false statements and that those statements were necessary to support the finding of probable cause." *Id.* at 237. According to this court:

> The Supreme Court in *Franks*, which established the right to this type of hearing, was concerned that frivolous challenges could lead to unnecessary pretrial delays. Consequently, it adopted the substantial preliminary showing requirement and stressed the need for a "sensible threshold" before a hearing would be required.

Id. (quoting *Franks* at 170, 98 *S.Ct.* at 2683).

2. *A report writing error could give the appearance of an untruthful statement.* In *United States v. Vanness*, 85 *F*.3d 661 (D.C.Cir. 1996), the court addressed the sufficiency of a detective's search warrant affidavit. "The three-page, single spaced, typed affidavit reported that during the preceding months, three independent informants told the police that an individual was selling crack cocaine from a" particular basement apartment located in the District of Columbia. *Id.* at 662. At one point in the affidavit, the detective reported that, on a particular day, undercover agents, accompanied by the third informant, approached the target's (Vanness's) apartment to make a controlled buy. As they neared the apartment, the informant identified Vanness as he was driving away. Police stopped the car and asked Vanness to step out. At this point, Vanness threw two pouches containing 31 packets of a rock-like substance out of the passenger window. The substance later field tested positive for cocaine.

When the detective incorporated this information into the affidavit, it was unclear as to who actually witnessed Vanness throw the pouches from the vehicle. In pertinent part, the affidavit provided:

> * * * The target was approached and asked to step from the vehicle. The target was observed to throw out of the passenger compartment two pouches. * * *

Id.

In the appeal following his conviction for possessing with intent to distribute more than 50 grams of cocaine base, and possessing with intent to distribute cocaine base within 1000 feet of a school, Vanness argued that the sentence in the affidavit—"The target was observed to throw out of the passenger compartment two pouches."—constituted a *material misrepresentation* requiring, under *Franks v. Delaware*, suppression of the cocaine. Although the court would not agree to suppression of evidence as a remedy in this case, it did pause to observe the following:

Read in isolation, the sentence was strictly true: someone—the passenger, it turns out—did observe Vanness throwing drugs out of the car. Yet we have no doubt the judge issuing the warrant had the misimpression that the someone was a police officer. The affidavit's immediately preceding sentence stated: "The target was approached and asked to step from the vehicle." And so, when the next sentence reported what someone observed during the stop, one would naturally assume the observer was also a police officer. No other candidates appear. The affidavit does not even mention that Vanness had a passenger.

Id.

The court determined that the evidence did not need to be suppressed, however, because it was not convinced that the detective phrased the sentence in order to mislead or in some way hide the truth. *Id.* at 662-63. "And there was no reason to suppose the detective omitted the detail about the passenger in reckless disregard of the truth." *Id.* at 663. Finally, the presence of probable cause in this case "did not turn on whether the police or a passenger saw Vanness toss the drugs. The remaining information in the warrant still would have established probable cause to search Vanness's apartment." *Id.*

UNITED STATES v. McDONALD
United States Court of Appeals
723 *F.*2d 1288 (7th Cir. 1983)

QUESTION: At a Motion to Suppress hearing, the facts set forth below were established. Did defendant make out the required "substantial preliminary showing" so as to entitle him to a *Franks* hearing?

FACTS: On the morning of June 5, a confidential, reliable informant notified Detective Richard Smith of the Chicago Police Department Narcotics Unit that he had been offered cocaine by a person known as "James" in the "front room" of "James'" apartment at 2701 S. Indiana, Apartment 1907, Chicago, Illinois. The informant stated that he used the cocaine and experienced the same "high" as he had on previous occasions when using the drug. The informant also told Detective Smith that upon leaving "James'" apartment, he had seen an additional quantity of cocaine in a plastic bag in the "front room" of the apartment.

Based upon this information and the informant's past reliability, Detective Smith applied for, and received a warrant to search:

'James,' [a] Male/Negro, Approx. 45 yrs. 5'10" 175 lbs. Blk. hair and 2701 S. Indiana Apartment #1907 Chicago, Cook, Ill. and seize Cocaine: to wit a Narcotic Drug & Proof of Residency.

Id. at 1290.

Detective Smith and four other officers executed the warrant, seizing quantities of marijuana and cocaine, two handguns, and several pieces of stolen mail. Defendant, James McDonald, was given a copy of the search warrant.

At the suppression hearing, defendant alleged that the warrant which the officers presented to him contained no physical description of himself, no apartment number, and no judge's signature. Defendant testified that he left the warrant on the dining room table just before he was taken to the police department. Defendant then testified that after posting bail, he returned to his apartment and found a second warrant on the dining table but that this warrant now contained a physical description of himself, the apartment number, and a judge's signature.

Defendant additionally asserted that, contrary to what Detective Smith asserts in his affidavit, he did not offer cocaine to anyone on the morning of June 5; that he was on his boat at the time in the Triplex Boat Marina. Defendant then offered the testimony of a Mr. Ronald Nash. Nash stated that he arrived on defendant's boat at 11:00 p.m. on June 4, and left sometime during the early morning hours on June 5, while it was still dark and defendant was still asleep.

ANSWER: NO. The facts established at the suppression hearing "reveal[] that [defendant] failed to make a 'substantial preliminary showing' that the affiant, Detective Smith, knowingly and intentionally, or with reckless disregard for the truth, included a false statement in his affidavit." *Id.* at 1293.

RATIONALE: "A *Franks* hearing affords a defendant the opportunity to show, by a preponderance of the evidence, that the warrant affidavit contained perjury or a reckless disregard for the truth. If the defendant meets this burden, the court will set aside the 'false material' contained in the warrant affidavit, and if probable cause cannot be established from the valid and truthful portion of the affidavit, the entire search warrant is deemed to be invalid and the ensuing search is void." *Id.* at 1292.

In order "[t]o qualify for a *Franks* hearing, the defendant must make a 'substantial preliminary showing that a false statement knowingly and intentionally, or with reckless disregard for the truth, was included by the affiant in the warrant affidavit, and (that) the allegedly false statement (was) necessary to the finding of probable cause[.]' " *Id.* (quoting *Franks v. Delaware*, 438 *U.S.* 154, 155-156, 98 *S.Ct.* 2674, 2676 (1978)). If a defendant does make out this " 'substantial preliminary showing,' then 'the Fourth Amendment requires that a hearing be held at the defendant's request.' " *Id.* at 1293 (quoting *Franks* at 156, 98 *S.Ct.* at 2676). Significantly, " '(t)he deliberate falsity or reckless disregard whose impeachment is permitted . . . is only that of the affiant, not of any nongovernmental informant.' " *Id.* (quoting *Franks* at 171, 98 *S.Ct.* at 2684).

Defendant asserts "that he qualifies for a *Franks* hearing because he made a 'substantial preliminary showing' that Detective Smith intentionally falsified the warrant affidavit and that the false statement was necessary for the finding of probable cause." *McDonald* at 1292. *The United States Court of Appeals for the Seventh Circuit rejected defendant's contentions.*

According to the court, the evidence presented at the suppression hearing demonstrated that McDonald "failed to make a 'substantial preliminary showing' that the affiant, Detective Smith, knowingly and intentionally, or with reckless disregard for the truth, included a false statement in his affidavit. [McDonald relied] solely upon his own self-serving testimony and that of Ronald Nash to establish that he (McDonald) was not at his apartment during the morning hours of June 5, * * * and, therefore, could not have offered cocaine to an informant during those hours. This testimony, as presented, attacks the truth of the informant's statements, not the statements of the affiant, Detective Smith." *Id.* at 1293. As the Supreme Court brought out in *Franks*, "this attack upon the informant's truthfulness does not satisfy the 'substantial preliminary showing' of affiant falsity required for a *Franks* hearing. '[A]llegations that . . . an informant, whose story was recited by an affiant, was lying are insufficient to require a *Franks* hearing since the falsity or recklessness alleged is not that of the affiant, but that of the third party.'" *McDonald* at 1293. [Citations omitted.]

"Even a broad interpretation of the evidence presented by McDonald at the Motion to Suppress hearing, namely that no informant existed and Detective Smith intentionally falsified the entire affidavit, failed to mandate a *Franks* hearing. The Court in *Franks* stated:

> There is, of course, a presumption of validity with respect to the affidavit supporting the search warrant. To mandate an evidentiary hearing, the challenger's attack must be more than conclusory and must be supported by more than a mere desire to cross-examine. There must be allegations of deliberate falsehood or of reckless disregard for the truth, and those allegations must be accompanied by an offer of proof. They should point out specifically the portion of the warrant affidavit that is claimed to be false; and they should be accompanied by a statement of supporting reasons. Affidavits or sworn or otherwise reliable statements of witnesses should be furnished, or their absence satisfactorily explained."

McDonald at 1293-1294 (quoting *Franks* at 171, 98 *S.Ct.* at 2684).

At the suppression hearing, defendant's offer of proof consisted of Ronald Nash testifying that he arrived at defendant's boat at 11:00 p.m. on June 4, fell asleep, and woke up in the early morning. Noting that McDonald was still sleeping, Nash left the boat while it was still dark, on the morning of June 5th. Significantly, Nash was unable to testify as to McDonald's whereabouts on June 5th, between the time he left the boat and 10:52 a.m., when the search warrant issued. "Because McDonald is the only one who testified as to his whereabouts during this time, the issue becomes one of McDonald's word against Detective Smith's word," *id.* at 1294, and the court below "found this self-serving testimony to be unbelievable[.]" *Id.*

Accordingly, the court holds that, "in this instance, where the district court did not believe [defendant's] self-serving statement, to support his conclusion that no informant existed, [defendant] failed to make a substantial preliminary showing that Detective Smith, knowingly and intentionally or with reckless disregard, falsified the affidavit and, therefore, [defendant] was not entitled to a *Franks* hearing." *Id.*

NOTE

An informant's false statements. Generally, an attack upon a nongovernmental informant's truthfulness does not satisfy the "substantial preliminary showing" of affiant falsity required for a *Franks* hearing. Thus, if an informant knowingly or recklessly makes a false statement to an affiant, that does not present grounds to challenge the search warrant so long as the affiant believes that the statements are true and, in good faith, accurately represents what the informant told him, and so long as the informant is a private individual. "However, when the informant is himself a government official, a deliberate or reckless [statement or] omission by the informant can still serve as grounds for a *Franks* suppression." *United States v. Wapnick,* 60 *F.*3d 948, 956 (2nd Cir. 1995). *See also United States v. DeLeon,* 979 *F.*2d 761, 764 (9th Cir. 1992). "Otherwise, the government would be able to shield itself from *Franks* suppression hearings by deliberately insulating affiants from information material to the determination of probable cause." *Wapnick* at 956.

---

§2.4. The particularity requirement.
The Warrant Clause of the Fourth Amendment declares:

> * * * no Warrants shall issue, but upon probable cause, supported by Oath or affirmation, and *particularly describing* the place to be searched, and the persons and things to be seized. (emphasis added).

The "particularity" requirement flows directly from this constitutional provision, and it "prevents the issue of warrants on loose, vague or doubtful bases of fact." *Go-Bart Importing Co. v. United States,* 282 *U.S.* 344, 357, 51 *S.Ct.* 153, 158 (1931). "The manifest purpose" of the requirement "was to prevent *general searches.*" *Maryland v. Garrison,* 480 *U.S.* 79, 107 *S.Ct.* 1013, 1017 (1987). [Emphasis added.] Even before our Government came into existence, such general searches had been "deemed obnoxious to fundamental principles of liberty[, and are presently] denounced in the constitutions or statutes of every State in the Union." *Id.* at 357, 51 *S.Ct.* at 158. As the Supreme Court explained in *Coolidge v. New Hampshire,* 403 *U.S.* 443, 467, 91 *S.Ct.* 2022, 2038 (1971), "the problem [posed by the general warrant] is not that of intrusion *per se,* but of a general exploratory rummaging in a person's belongings." The problem is addressed by the Fourth Amendment's "particularity" requirement. *Id.* at 467, 91 *S.Ct.* at 2038. "By limiting the authorization to search to the specific areas and things for which there is probable cause to search, the requirement ensures that the search will be carefully tailored to its justifications, and will not take on the character of the wide-ranging exploratory searches the Framers [of our Constitution] intended to prohibit." *Garrison*, 107 *S.Ct.* at 1017.

Accordingly, the specific "requirement that warrants shall particularly describe the *things to be seized* makes general searches under them impossible and prevents the seizure of one thing under a warrant describing another. As to what is to be taken, nothing is left to the discretion of the officer executing the warrant." *Marron v. United States*, 275 *U.S.* 192, 196, 48 *S.Ct.* 74, 76 (1927). [Emphasis added.] The companion requirement, that warrants shall particularly describe the *place to be searched*, is satisfied where "the description is such that the officer with a search warrant can with reasonable effort ascertain and identify the place intended." *Steele v. United States*, 267 *U.S.* 498, 503, 45 *S.Ct.* 414, 416 (1925).

---

§2.4(a). The places to be searched.

MARYLAND v. GARRISON*
Supreme Court of the United States
480 *U.S.* 79, 107 *S.Ct.* 1013 (1987)

QUESTION: After a search warrant is issued and executed, it is learned that the description of the place to be searched is overly broad, being based on the mistaken belief that there was only one apartment on the third floor of the target premises; will that factual mistake retroactively invalidate the warrant when, with the benefit of hindsight, the defendant demonstrates to the reviewing court that the third floor consisted of two separate dwelling units ?

ANSWER: NO. The constitutionality of police conduct must be judged "in light of the information available to them at the time they acted." *Id.* at 1017. In this respect, the validity of the search warrant will "be assessed on the basis of the information that the officers disclosed, or had a duty to discover and disclose, to the issuing magistrate." *Id.* at 1018. "Those items of evidence that emerge after the warrant is issued have no bearing on whether or not a warrant was validly issued. Just as the discovery of contraband cannot validate a warrant invalid when issued, so is it equally clear that the discovery of facts demonstrating that a valid warrant was unnecessarily broad does not retroactively invalidate the warrant." *Id.* at 1017-1018.

RATIONALE: "Baltimore police officers obtained and executed a warrant to search the person of Lawrence McWebb and 'the premises known as 2036 Park Avenue third floor apartment' for 'Marihuana, related paraphernalia, monies, books, papers, and photographs pertaining to the illegal distribution of Marihuana. . . .'" *Id.* at 1015, 1015 n.1. At the time the officers "applied for the warrant and when they

---

* *See* §2.5(c) for other question raised and answered by this case.

conducted the search pursuant to the warrant, they reasonably believed that there was only one apartment on the premises described in the warrant." *Id.* at 1015. Significantly, the trial court found that "after making a reasonable investigation, including a verification of information obtained from a reliable informant, an exterior examination of the three-story building at 2036 Park Avenue, and an inquiry of the utility company, the officer who obtained the warrant reasonably concluded that there was only one apartment on the third floor and that it was occupied by McWebb." *Id.* at 1015.

"In fact, the third floor was divided into two apartments, one occupied by McWebb and one by [defendant]. Before the officers executing the warrant became aware that they were in a separate apartment occupied by [defendant], they had discovered the contraband that provided the basis for [defendant's] conviction for violating Maryland's Controlled Substances Act." *Id.* Defendant now appeals, challenging the seizure of that contraband.

"The Warrant Clause of the Fourth Amendment categorically prohibits the issuance of any warrant except one 'particularly describing the place to be searched and the persons or things to be seized.' *The manifest purpose of this particularity requirement was to prevent general searches.* By limiting the authorization to search to the specific areas and things for which there is probable cause to search, the requirement ensures that the search will be carefully tailored to its justifications, and will not take on the character of the wide-ranging exploratory searches the Framers intended to prohibit. Thus, the scope of a lawful search is 'defined by the object of the search and the places in which there is probable cause to believe that it may be found.' " *Id.* at 1017. [Emphasis added; citation omitted.]

Defendant does not claim that the warrant inadequately described the "persons or things to be seized," nor does he assert "that there was no probable cause to believe that those things might be found in the 'place to be searched' as it was described in the warrant." *Id.* Rather, defendant contends, with the benefit of hindsight, that the description of the place to be searched "was broader than appropriate because it was based on the mistaken belief that there was only one apartment on the third floor of the building at 2036 Park Avenue." *Id.* Thus, according to the Court, "[t]he question is whether that factual mistake invalidated a warrant that undoubtedly would have been valid if it had reflected a completely accurate understanding of the building's floor plan." *Id.*

Naturally, "if the officers had known, or even if they should have known, that there were two separate dwelling units on the third floor of 2036 Park Avenue, they would have been obligated to exclude [defendant's] apartment from the scope of the requested warrant." *Id.* Nonetheless, the constitutionality of their conduct must be judged "in light of the information available to them at the time they acted. Those items of evidence that emerge after the warrant is issued have no bearing on whether or not a warrant was validly issued. Just as the discovery of contraband cannot validate a warrant invalid when issued, so it is equally clear that the discovery of facts demonstrating that a valid warrant was unnecessarily broad does not retroactively invalidate the warrant. The validity of the warrant must be assessed on the basis of the information that the officers disclosed, or had a duty to discover and disclose, to the issuing magistrate." *Id.* at 1017-1018.

In this case, the officer "made specific inquiries to determine the identity of the occupants of the third floor premises. The officer went to 2036 Park Avenue and found that it matched the description given by the informant: a three-story brick dwelling with the numerals 2 - 0 - 3 - 6 affixed to the front of the premises. The officer 'made a check with the Baltimore Gas and Electric Company and discovered that the premises of 2036 Park Ave. third floor was in the name of Lawrence McWebb[; and that the] third floor was only listed to Lawrence McWebb.'" *Id.* at 1018 n.10.

Accordingly, the Court concludes, on the basis of the information known and available to the police at the time they presented the affidavit and warrant to the issuing magistrate, "that the warrant * * * was valid when it issued." *Id.* at 1018.

NOTE

The Supreme Court in *Garrison, supra,* was extremely firm in its admonishment to the law enforcement community when it stated:

> We expressly distinguish the facts of this case from a situation in which the police know there are two apartments on a certain floor of a building, and have probable cause to believe that drugs are being sold out of that floor, but do not know in which of the two apartments the illegal transactions are taking place. A search pursuant to a warrant authorizing a search of the entire floor under those circumstances would present quite different issues from the ones before us in this case.

Id. at 1019 n.13.

UNITED STATES v. PROUT
United States Court of Appeals
526 *F.*2d 380 (5th Cir. 1976)

QUESTION: Will a minor error in the description of premises to be searched always invalidate the search warrant and the ensuing search ?

ANSWER: NO. "An error in description is not automatically fatal to the validity of a search warrant. * * * '[T]he determining factor as to whether a search warrant describes the premises to be searched with sufficient particularity is not whether the description given is technically accurate in every detail but rather whether the description is sufficient to enable the executing officer to locate and identify the premises with reasonable effort, and whether there is any reasonable probability that another premises might be mistakenly searched which is not the one intended to be searched under the search warrant.' " Id. at 387-388. [Citations omitted.]

RATIONALE: In this appeal, defendant argued that his motion to suppress the evidence seized from his apartment should have been granted because the search warrant named the premises to be searched only as "Quick Sales Real Estate Office, 1001 Nunez St., New Orleans, La." According to defendant, the warrant description of the premises to be searched authorized only a search of the realty office and did not authorize a search of his upstairs apartment. *Id.* at 386.

The real estate office "is in a one-story building attached to a slightly taller two-story building, formerly a garage, in which the apartment is located. The municipal address of Quick Sales Realty is 1001 Nunez Street. The municipal address of the apartment is 441 Newton Street. However, the entrance on Nunez Street, which is unmarked, opens into a common foyer between the realty office and the downstairs kitchen of the apartment, each of which has an interior door opening into the foyer. Neither interior door bears any number or marking to identify the rooms beyond as separate premises. Within the apartment there is a stairway from the kitchen to the rooms upstairs, where [defendant] was arrested and the evidence in question seized." *Id.* Later examination of the premises revealed that the office and apartment have separate utility meters, visible only from Newton Street. "Neither the affidavit nor the warrant mentions the existence of the apartment or the 441 Newton Street address." *Id.*

Defendant contended that through their surveillance of the premises, the government agents knew or should have known of the separate character of the apartment, and through reasonable diligence should have discovered the separate utility meters and different municipal addresses.

On the other hand, the government maintained that "the warrant sufficiently described the premises to authorize [a] search of the apartment as well as the office. The apartment was directly above the realty office. The Nunez Street door to the common foyer bears no municipal number; nor are the interior doors marked. The separate utility meters are not visible from Nunez Street." *Id.* at 387. Additionally, the government argued, and the court below found, that "the doorway fronting on Nunez Street gave access both to the premises bearing the municipal number 1001 Nunez Street and to the kitchen of the premises bearing the municipal number 441 Newton Street. On each occasion when [he was] observed by surveillance agents, [defendant] used the 1001 Nunez entrance to the apartment." *Id.*

The Court of Appeals for the Fifth Circuit agreed with the government's arguments, and held that the description of the premises to be searched satisfied the particularity requirement of the Fourth Amendment. *Id.* at 388.

"The test for whether a sufficient description of the premises to be searched is given in a search warrant" has been stated:

> It is enough if the description is such that the officer with a search warrant can, with reasonable effort, ascertain and identify the place intended.

Steele v. United States, 267 *U.S.* 498, 503, 45 *S.Ct.* 414, 416 (1925) (upholding the search of 609 West 46th Street under a warrant describing the premises as 611 West 46th Street, where the building was a large warehouse having both numbers and being only partly partitioned). *Prout* at 387.

"An error in description is not automatically fatal to the validity of a search warrant." *Id.* As recognized in *United States v. Darensbourg*, 520 *F.*2d 985, 987 (5th Cir. 1975), and *United States v. Melancon*, 462 *F.*2d 82, 94 (5th Cir. 1972), "the determining factor as to whether a search warrant describes the premises to be searched with sufficient particularity is not whether the description given is technically accurate in every detail but rather whether the description is sufficient to enable the executing officer to locate and identify the premises with reasonable effort, and whether there is any reasonable probability that another premises might be mistakenly searched which is not the one intended to be searched under the search warrant." *Prout* at 387-388.

In light of these principles, the court held that "the description of the premises to be searched was sufficient to validate the search of the apartment. The warrant authorized search of 'the premises known as Quick Sales Real Estate Office, 1001 Nunez Street.' The Nunez Street entrance gave access to both the realty office and the apartment. Neither the exterior entrance to the building nor the interior doors to the apartment and office bore any municipal numbers or other identifying marks to indicate the existence of two separate premises, so the executing officers could reasonably search the apartment as part of the premises described." *Id.* at 388. Moreover, "[g]iven the physical layout of the premises and their use by [defendant], as observed by the surveillance officers, a warrant describing the premises as '1001 Nunez Street' was sufficient so that 'there was little likelihood that the wrong premises would be searched—as indeed they were not.'" *Id.* [Citation omitted.]

NOTE

1. *Retail establishment occupying more than one address.* In *United States v. Lemmons*, 527 *F.*2d 662 (6th Cir. 1976), a warrant for the search of a building occupied by a retail clothing business described the place to be searched as "Imported Fashions of Tomorrow" located at 9300 Woodward Avenue, Detroit, Michigan. The warrant authorized a search of the first floor and basement area of the store which was "designated by the number 9300 above the doorway." *Id.* at 663. During the search, one of the officers discovered 16 packets of heroin in a file cabinet in an office area located at the rear of the store. It was later learned that the store actually occupied two addresses, 9300 Woodward Avenue and 9304 Woodward Avenue, and the drugs were found in an area of the store located at 9304 Woodward. The record indicated that there originally were separate businesses in 9300 and 9304, and they were separated by a wall. At the time of the search, however, there was only one public entrance to the store located at 9300 Woodward, and an archway had been opened between the two addresses, with the clothing store using both portions of the building for the business. According to the court, "the warrant in this case was sufficiently definite to authorize a search of the entire store." *Id.* at 666.

2. In *United States v. Jordan*, 349 *F.*2d 107 (6th Cir. 1965), the court upheld the search of the second floor of a two-story house over defendant's objection that the second floor was a separate living unit over which he had no control. Here, the court found that defendant was the sole lessee listed on the rental agreement, that the utilities for both floors were contracted for in defendant's name, that he acknowledged the premises to be "his residence," and that there was no external indication that the house might be divided into more than one living unit before the search was undertaken. According to the court, "the Fourth Amendment 'safeguard is designed to require a description which particularly points to a definitely ascertainable place so as to exclude all others.' " *Id.* [Citation omitted.]

3. *Sufficient physical description of premises and executing officer's knowledge of exact apartment to be searched saves warrant.* In *United States v. Burke*, 784 *F.*2d 1090 (11th Cir. 1986), a search warrant issued authorizing a search of apartment 840 at the premises located at "38 Throop Street, being a two-story red brick building, trimmed in a reddish-brown paint with a shingled roof and three adjacent apartments, with apartment 840 being the far left apartment at that address looking at it from the front." In fact, the true address was "Carver Homes Housing Project, 48 Troup Street, apartment 840."

Prior to executing the warrant, the search team met in front of the Carver Homes Housing Project, and one of the officers, having prior knowledge of the exact location of the target premises, pointed out the specific apartment to be searched. The search team executed the warrant at 48 Troup Street, apartment 840, and incriminating evidence was seized.

In this appeal, the United States Court of Appeals for the Eleventh Circuit held that the warrant "satisfied the particularity requirements of the Fourth Amendment." *Id.* at 1093. According to the court:

> A warrant's description of the place to be searched is not required to meet technical requirements or have the specificity sought by conveyancers. The warrant need only describe the place to be searched with sufficient particularity to direct the searcher, to confine his examination to the place described, and to advise those being searched of his authority. *The Fourth Amendment requires only that the search warrant describe the premises in such a way that the searching officer may "'with reasonable effort ascertain and identify the place intended.'"* United States v. Weinstein, 762 F.2d 1522, 1532 (11th Cir. 1985) (citations omitted).

Burke at 1092. [Emphasis added.]

"Although the search warrant named 'Throop Street,' there is no such street in Atlanta, and the only street in Atlanta with a name closely resembling that name is Troup Street. On Troup Street, although there was no residence numbered '38,' the buildings in the close vicinity of the one in which [defendant] resided were numbered '36,' '42,' '48,' and '52.' [Moreover, t]he search warrant contained a detailed physical description of the building, minimizing the possibility that an apartment in any building other than the correct one would be searched. * * * In addition, the warrant correctly named the apartment number, and there was only one apartment with the number '840' in the Carver Homes Housing Project in which [defendant] resided." *Id.*

The court also found significant that prior to the execution of the warrant, an officer with knowledge of the exact location of the target premises pointed out that location to the executing officers. In this respect, the court stated: "In evaluating the effect of a wrong address on the sufficiency of a warrant, this Court has also taken into account the knowledge of the officer executing the warrant, even where such knowledge was not reflected in the warrant or in the affidavit supporting the warrant." *Id.* at 1092-1093. Where, as here, it is shown that the executing officers knew precisely which premises were to be searched, there is further assurance that there was no possibility that the wrong premises would be searched.

Consequently, the court held that, "under these circumstances, the search warrant described the premises to be searched with sufficient particularity to direct the officers to the correct apartment, to confine the officers' examination to that apartment, and to place the occupants on sufficient notice of the officers' authority to search the premises. The warrant therefore satisfied the particularity requirements of the Fourth Amendment." *Id.* at 1093.

See also United States v. Alva, 885 F.2d 250, 252 (5th Cir. 1989) (description in search warrant will be sufficient so long as the searching officers "can, with reasonable effort ascertain and identify the place intended"); *United States v. Rome,* 809 F.2d 665, 670 (10th Cir.

1987) (a description of the place to be searched will meet the requirements of the Fourth Amendment "if the description is sufficient to enable the officers to ascertain the place to be searched"); *United States v. Alberts*, 721 *F.*2d 636, 639 (8th Cir. 1983) (the particularity requirement demands sufficient specificity "in order to avoid any reasonable probability that another place might mistakenly be searched"); *United States v. Heldt*, 668 *F.*2d 1238, 1262 (D.C.Cir. 1981) (the "authority to search granted by any warrant is limited to the specific places described in it and does not extend to additional or different places"), *cert. denied*, 456 *U.S.* 926, 102 *S.Ct.* 1971 (1982); *United States v. Johnson*, 541 *F.*2d 1311, 1313 (8th Cir. 1976) (per curiam) ("The underlying measure of adequacy in the description is whether, given the specificity in the warrant, a violation of personal rights is likely[;] the standard * * * is one of practical accuracy rather than technical nicety.").

4. *Attaching photograph of premises to be searched.* In *United States v. Mabry*, 809 *F.*2d 671 (10th Cir. 1987), the court endorsed the procedure of attaching a photograph of the place to be searched to the search warrant itself. The warrant in *Mabry* described the place to be searched as "SC P.O. Box 30, Tijeras, New Mexico, a single family dwelling, frame and brown stucco." Because the canyon area where defendants' home was located made it "difficult to verbally identify particular homes," *id.* at 681, a photograph of the home was attached to enable the executing officers to locate and identify it with reasonable effort. According to the court, when the description of the premises is viewed in connection with the attached photograph, the Fourth Amendment's particularity requirement has been satisfied. *Id.*

5. *Vehicles found on the premises.* When law enforcement officials intend to search vehicles normally located at the target premises, the safest, and perhaps the best, procedure is to include a description of each vehicle in the affidavit and search warrant. Nonetheless, it has been held that such a practice is not necessarily mandated in every instance by the Fourth Amendment. *See e.g. United States v. Gottschalk*, 915 *F.*2d 1459, 1461 (10th Cir. 1990) (warrant authorizing a general search of a premises for methamphetamine, laboratory equipment and related paraphernalia, while failing to specifically list any vehicles to be searched, nonetheless includes an implicit authorization to search "any vehicles located within the curtilage if the objects of the search might be located within," when the vehicles are either "actually owned or under the control and dominion of the premises owner or, alternatively, [when] those vehicles [] appear, based on objectively reasonable indicia present at the time of the search, to be so controlled"); *United States v. Percival*, 756 *F.*2d 600, 612 (7th Cir. 1985) (search warrant authorizing a search of particularly described premises permits the search of a vehicle found on the premises so long as the vehicle is owned or controlled by the owner of the premises); *United States v. Bulgatz*, 693 *F.*2d 728, 730 n.3 (8th Cir. 1982) (warrant for search of house justifies search of car parked in garage attached to the house), *cert. denied*, 459 *U.S.* 1210, 103 *S.Ct.* 1203 (1983); *United States v. Freeman*, 685 *F.*2d 942, 955 (5th Cir. 1982) (warrant for search of

premises justifies search of jeep parked on premises); *United States v. Napoli*, 530 *F*.2d 1198, 1200 (5th Cir. 1976) (warrant authorizing the search of "the premises known as 3027 Napoleon Avenue" encompassed a vehicle parked in the driveway on those premises).

But see United States v. Stanley, 597 *F*.2d 866, 870 (4th Cir. 1979) (warrant to search mobile home does not justify a search of a car parked nearby when car is in a common tenant parking lot not annexed to the home or within a general enclosure surrounding the home).

6. *Vehicles arriving at the premises during warrant execution.* In *United States v. Alva*, 885 *F*.2d 250, 252 (5th Cir. 1989), officers of the San Antonio, Texas, Police Department obtained and executed a search warrant for cocaine at the premises located at 223 Burcham. The description of the premises in the warrant provided for a search of the house, all structures located on the lot, and "any and all motor vehicles found parked on the premises of 223 Burcham." During the course of the search, defendant Alva, the owner and lessor of the premises, arrived in his pickup truck, parked it within fifteen feet of the home and entered the home without knocking. Alva was immediately detained and his truck was searched. The search uncovered a .25 caliber semi-automatic pistol.

Finding that the search of Alva's truck fell within the scope of the warrant's language, the court held that police officials may search "vehicles voluntarily driven onto the premises by persons named in a warrant during the course of a valid search." *Id.* at 252. According to the court, "[i]n such circumstances, officers are only limited in their search of the vehicle to areas that they reasonably believe could contain the items described in the warrant." *Id.* Further, the court noted:

> Alva's reading of the language, that it prohibits police from searching vehicles arriving after the search begins, unnaturally cramps the warrant's temporal authority. Searches do not take place in an instant; they occur over a period of time, sometimes many hours. Thus, vehicles arriving during the course of a search are vehicles "found parked" on the premises if they reasonably could contain the items for which law enforcement officials are searching. Alva's pickup truck was such a vehicle.

Id.

See also United States v. Cole, 628 *F*.2d 897, 899 (5th Cir. 1980) (upholding the search of defendant's pickup truck by the police after they had arrived simultaneously with the defendant at the premises described in the warrant). *But see United States v. Gentry*, 839 *F*.2d 1065, 1069 (5th Cir. 1988) (holding that police may not search vehicles arriving at the perimeter fence of a large premises during a search, and that police may not forcibly lead a vehicle onto the premises to effect a search).

§2.4(b). The things to be seized.

STANFORD v. STATE OF TEXAS
Supreme Court of the United States
379 *U.S.* 476, 85 *S.Ct.* 506 (1965)

Mr. Justice STEWART delivered the opinion of the Court.

* * * * *

"The [defendant] has attacked the constitutional validity of this search and seizure upon several grounds. We rest our decision upon just one, without pausing to assess the substantiality of the others. For we think it is clear that this warrant was of a kind which it was the purpose of the Fourth Amendment to forbid—a general warrant." *Id.* at 509.

"The Fourth Amendment provides that 'no Warrants shall issue, but upon probable cause, supported by Oath or affirmation, and *particularly describing* the place to be searched, and the persons or *things to be seized.*' (Emphasis supplied.)" *Id.*

"These words are precise and clear. They reflect the determination of those who wrote the Bill of Rights that the people of this new Nation should forever 'be secure in their persons, houses, papers, and effects' from intrusion and seizure by officers acting under the unbridled authority of a general warrant. Vivid in the memory of the newly independent Americans were those general warrants known as writs of assistance under which officers of the Crown had so bedeviled the colonists. The hated writs of assistance had given customs officials blanket authority to search where they pleased for goods imported in violation of the British tax laws. They were denounced by James Otis as 'the worst instrument of arbitrary power, the most destructive of English liberty, and the fundamental principles of law, that ever was found in an English law book,' because they placed 'the liberty of every man in the hands of every petty officer.' The historic occasion of that denunciation, in 1761 at Boston, has been characterized as 'perhaps the most prominent event which inaugurated the resistance of the colonies to the oppression of the mother country.' 'Then and there,' said John Adams, * * * 'was the first scene of the first act of opposition to the arbitrary claims of Great Britain. Then and there the child Independence was born.'" *Id.* at 509-10.

"But while the Fourth Amendment was most immediately the product of contemporary revulsion against a regime of writs of assistance, its roots go far deeper. Its adoption in the Constitution of this new Nation reflected the culmination in England a few years earlier of a struggle against oppression which had endured for centuries. [That was the struggle against] the use of general warrants as instruments of oppression from the time of the Tudors, through the Star Chamber, the Long Parliament, the Restoration, and beyond." *Id.* at 510.

"What is significant to note is that this history is largely a history of conflict between the Crown and the press. It was in enforcing the laws licensing the publication of literature and, later, in prosecutions for seditious libel that general warrants were systematically used in the sixteenth, seventeenth, and eighteenth centuries. In Tudor England officers of the Crown were given roving commissions to search where they pleased in order to suppress and destroy the literature of dissent. In later years warrants were sometimes more specific in content, but they typically authorized the arrest and search of the premises of all persons connected with the publication of a particular libel, or the arrest and seizure of all the papers of a named person thought to be connected with libel." *Id.*

"It was in the context of the latter kinds of general warrants that the battle for individual liberty and privacy was finally won[.]" *Id.*

"In short, what this history indispensably teaches is that *the constitutional requirement that warrants must particularly describe the 'things to be seized' is to be accorded the most scrupulous exactitude when the 'things to be seized' are books, and the basis for their seizure is the ideas which they contain.* * * * No less a standard could be faithful to First Amendment freedoms." Id. at 511-12. [Emphasis added.]

" 'The requirement that warrants shall particularly describe the things to be seized makes general searches under them impossible and prevents the seizure of one thing under a warrant describing another. As to what is to be taken, nothing is left to the discretion of the officer executing the warrant.' " *Id.* at 512. [Citation omitted.]

"We need not decide in this case whether the description of the things to be seized would have been too generalized to pass constitutional muster, had the things been weapons [or] narcotics[.] * * * The point is that it was not any contraband of that kind which was ordered to be seized, but literary material—'books, records, pamphlets, cards, receipts, lists, memoranda, pictures, recordings and other written instruments concerning the Communist Party of Texas, and the operations of the Communist Party in Texas.' The indiscriminate sweep of that language is constitutionally intolerable. To hold otherwise would be false to the terms of the Fourth Amendment, false to its meaning, and false to its history." *Id.*

NOTE

1. *Items which establish ownership, control or occupancy.* In *United States v. Whitten*, 706 *F.*2d 1000 (9th Cir. 1983), the court rejected the defendant's contention that the search warrant authorizing in part the seizure of "telephone books, diaries, photographs, utility bills, telephone bills, and any other papers indicating the ownership or occupancy of said residence" was impermissibly broad. According to the court, "warrants authorizing the seizure of items which establish the identity of persons in control of premises" have been consistently upheld. *Id.* at 1009. Particularly where, as here, "multiple defendants were suspected to have utilized the premises as a laboratory and headquarters for a large-scale illegal drug operation, it was reasonable to authorize the arresting agents to search for evidence showing who occupied and controlled the premises." *Id.* Naturally, while a warrant authorizing the seizure of any papers, photographs or diaries might be impermissibly overbroad, "here the scope of those words was qualified by the accompanying language 'indicating the ownership or occupancy of said residence.' " *Id.*

See also United States v. Marques, 600 *F*.2d 742, 751 n.5 (9th Cir. 1979), *cert.* den. 444 *U.S.* 1019, 100 *S.Ct.* 674 (1980) (warrant authorizing the seizure of "articles of personal property tending to establish the identity of persons and control of premises" upheld); *United States v. Rettig*, 589 *F*.2d 418, 421 (9th Cir. 1978) (warrant authorizing the seizure of items constituting "indicia of the identity of the residents of said house including, but not limited to, canceled mail, keys, rent receipts, utility bills, deeds, leases and photographs" upheld); *United States v. Reed*, 726 *F*.2d 339 (7th Cir. 1984) (warrant authorizing the seizure of "proof of residency" upheld because such proof "is easily recognizable, quickly found, and does not authorize a general search of personal papers").

2. *Warrants authorizing the seizure of documents.* Additional care should be exercised in setting forth the description of items to be seized when those items encompass personal papers or documents. Such items will generally be the subject of intense scrutiny under the particularity requirement. In this respect, the United States Supreme Court has noted: "We recognize that there are grave dangers inherent in executing a warrant authorizing a search and seizure of a person's papers that are not necessarily present in executing a warrant to search for physical objects whose relevance is more easily ascertainable. In searches for papers, it is certain that some innocuous documents will be examined, at least cursorily, in order to determine whether they are, in fact, among those papers authorized to be seized. * * * [In such a search,] responsible officials, including judicial officials, must take care to assure that they are conducted in a manner that minimizes unwarranted intrusions upon privacy." *Andresen v. Maryland*, 427 *U.S.* 463, 482 n.11, 96 *S.Ct.* 2737, 2749 n.11 (1976).

But see United States v. Dennis, 625 *F*.2d 782 (8th Cir. 1980), where the court permitted a lesser degree of particularity for evidence of a loansharking operation, the exact identity of which evidence was unknown at the time the warrant issued. In this situation, held the court, "certain books and records relating to the 'extortionate credit transaction business' was a permissible generic class and set reasonable parameters for the search." *Id.* at 792. "'Where the precise identity of goods cannot be ascertained at the time the warrant is issued, naming only the generic class of items will suffice because less particularity can be reasonably expected than for goods (such as those stolen) whose exact identity is already known at the time of issuance.'" *Id.* (quoting *United States v. Johnson*, 541 *F*.2d 1311, 1314 (8th Cir. 1976)).

3. *Use of a generic description.* A search warrant's description of the things to be seized must be sufficiently specific to enable "the searcher to reasonably ascertain and identify" the items authorized to be seized. *United States v. Wolfenbarger*, 696 *F*.2d 750, 752 (10th Cir. 1982). Nonetheless, "even a 'warrant that describes items to be seized in broad and generic terms may be valid if the description is as specific as [the] circumstances and nature of the activity under investigation permits.'" *United States v. Robertson*, 21 *F*.3d 1030, 1033 (10th Cir. 1994) (quoting *United States v. Harris*, 903 *F*.2d 770, 775 (10th Cir. 1990)).

In *Robertson*, federal agents obtained a warrant to search Robertson's apartment for evidence related to a recent carjacking. The warrant described the property to be seized as "a Braun Aromatic box, a red and white plastic ice chest, a green rubberized bag with clothes in it, yellow jumper cables," and "other instrumentalities and fruits of the crime of armed carjacking." *Id.* at 1032. The federal agents tried to get a more detailed description of the stolen items from the victim of the carjacking before seeking the warrant. However, the victim was distraught and could not specifically describe more than a few items. Indeed, most of the things taken during the carjacking were so commonplace that the victim "never could have given the agents any distinguishing details about them." *Id.* at 1033.

Finding the warrant's description of the things to be seized to be specific enough to pass constitutional muster, the court stated:

> Because the officers therefore could not give "an exact description of the fruits and instrumentalities" of the crime, they could "only be expected to describe the generic class of items" they sought. * * *

> Even if generic descriptions are necessary, however, "the fourth amendment requires that the government describe the items to be seized with as much specificity as the government's knowledge and circumstances allow, and 'warrants are conclusively invalidated by their substantial failure to specify as nearly as possible the distinguishing characteristics of the goods to be seized.'" * * * The warrant could have been a little more specific by listing men's clothing of an approximate size, various categories of household goods, and a pistol, rather than just listing "instrumentalities and fruits" of the crime. Although this would seem more specific, it would not better identify the "distinguishing characteristics of the goods to be seized" or better enable the agents to identify the things to be seized. Since Robertson had his own clothes and household goods in the apartment, the only truly distinguishing characteristic was ownership, not the general type of item. The warrant therefore could not have given the agents any more guidance in determining what they could seize.

> The warrant in this case differs from those authorizing seizure of any evidence relating to violations of broad statutes. * * * Rather than permitting search and seizure of almost anything, the "fruits" of the crime were limited by the context to things that [the victim] might have had in his car when it was stolen. Likewise, the "instrumentalities" of the crime could mean little else than a gun of some sort, since carjacking requires the use of a firearm. *See* 18 *U.S.C.* §2119. * * * [I]n this case, the "fruits and instrumentalities" were limited to the "crime of carjacking." Rather than authorizing the agents to seize anything at their own discretion, the warrant only authorized them to seize items that they could somehow determine were [the victim's] and thus were "fruits" of the crime, or that had been used to commit the carjacking.

Id. at 1033-34. [Citations omitted.]

4. *Contraband goods.* Generally, a lesser standard or degree of particularity is required in a search warrant for contraband goods such as illicit drugs, automatic weapons, explosives and the like. *United States v. Rome,* 809 *F.*2d 665, 670 (10th Cir. 1987). *See also United States v. Caves,* 890 *F.*2d 87, 93 (8th Cir. 1989) (the degree of specificity required in a search warrant varies; less specificity is required when the object of the search constitutes controlled substances); *United States v. DeLuna,* 763 *F.*2d 897 (8th Cir. 1985) (permitting a generic description of contraband when the precise identity may not be known at the time); *United States v. Grimaldi,* 606 *F.*2d 332 (1st Cir. 1979) (finding the phrase, "other paraphernalia used in the manufacture of counterfeit federal reserve notes" to be a sufficient description of items of contraband in a search warrant).

GROH v. RAMIREZ
Supreme Court of the United States
540 *U.S.* 551, 124 *S.Ct.* 1284 (2004)

QUESTION: May the fact that a search warrant *application* adequately describes the "things to be seized" be used to save the constitutionality of the *warrant,* which does not?

ANSWER: NO. The fact that a search warrant *application* adequately describes the "things to be seized" may not be used to "save the *warrant* from its facial invalidity. The Fourth Amendment by its terms requires particularity in the warrant, not in the supporting documents." *Id.* at 1289. [Court's emphasis.]

RATIONALE: Acting on a tip from a concerned citizen, Special Agent Groh of the Bureau of Alcohol, Tobacco and Firearms (ATF) prepared and signed an application for a warrant to search the Montana ranch of Joseph Ramirez. The citizen had reported that during several visits to the Ramirez ranch, he had seen "a large stock of weaponry, including an automatic rifle, grenades, a grenade launcher, and a rocket launcher." *Id.* at 1288. The search warrant application stated that the search was for "any automatic firearms or parts to automatic weapons, destructive devices to include but not limited to grenades, grenade launchers, rocket launchers, and any and all receipts pertaining to the purchase or manufacture of automatic weapons or explosive devices or launchers." *Id.* Agent Groh supported the application with a detailed affidavit, which he also prepared and executed, that set forth the basis for his belief that the listed items were concealed on the ranch. Groh then presented these documents to a Magistrate, along with a warrant form. The Magistrate signed the warrant form.

Although the application particularly described the place to be searched and the things to be seized, "the warrant itself was less specific; it failed to identify any of the items that [Agent Groh] intended to seize. In the portion of the form that called for a description of the 'person or property' to be seized, [the agent] typed a description of [Ramirez's] two-story blue house rather than the alleged stockpile of firearms." *Id.* Moreover, the warrant "did not incorporate by reference the itemized list contained in the application." *Id.*

On the day after the warrant issued, Agent Groh led a team of law enforcement officers, including both federal agents and members of the local sheriff's department, in the search. The search uncovered no illegal weapons or explosives. When the officer left the premises, they gave Mrs. Ramirez a copy of the search warrant, but not a copy of the application, which had been sealed. Ultimately, no charges were filed against Ramirez.

Finding the search warrant to be "plainly invalid," *id.* at 1289, the United States Supreme Court observed:

> The Fourth Amendment states unambiguously that "no Warrants shall issue, but upon probable cause, supported by Oath or affirmation, and *particularly describing* the place to be searched, and *the persons or things to be seized.*" The warrant in this case complied with the first three of these requirements: It was based on probable cause and supported by a sworn affidavit, and it described particularly the place of the search. On the fourth requirement, however, the warrant failed altogether * * *. [I]t was deficient in particularity because it provided no description of the type of evidence.

Id. at 1289. [Court's emphasis.]

"The fact that the *application* adequately described the "things to be seized" does not save the *warrant* from its facial invalidity. The Fourth Amendment by its terms requires particularity in the warrant, not in the supporting documents." Thus, "a warrant that fails to conform to the particularity requirement of the Fourth Amendment is unconstitutional." *Id.* [Citations omitted.] The Court elaborated:

> "The presence of a search warrant serves a high function," * * * and that high function is not necessarily vindicated when some other document, somewhere, says something about the objects of the search, but the contents of that document are neither known to the person whose home is being searched nor available for her inspection. We do not say that the Fourth Amendment forbids a warrant from cross-referencing other documents. Indeed, most Courts of Appeals have held that a court may construe a warrant with reference to a supporting application or affidavit if the warrant uses appropriate words of incorporation, and if the supporting document accompanies the warrant. * * * But in this case the warrant did not incorporate other documents by reference, nor did either the affidavit or the application (which had been placed under seal) accompany the warrant.

Id. at 1289-90. [Citation omitted.]

In this case, the warrant "did not simply omit a few items from a list of many to be seized, or misdescribe a few of several items. Nor did it make what fairly could be characterized as a mere technical mistake or typographical error. Rather, in the space set aside for a description of the items to be seized, the warrant stated that the items consisted of a 'single dwelling residence . . . blue in color.' In other words, the warrant did not describe the items to be seized at all. In this respect the warrant was so obviously deficient that we must regard the search as 'warrantless' within the meaning of our case law." *Id.* at 1290.

As a general rule of law, "a search conducted pursuant to a warrant that fails to conform to the particularity requirement of the Fourth Amendment is unconstitutional." *Id.* at 1291. "[U]nless the particular items described in the affidavit are also set forth in the warrant itself (or at least incorporated by reference, and the affidavit present at the search), there can be no written assurance that the Magistrate actually found probable cause to search for, and to seize, every item mentioned in the affidavit." *Id.*

"It is incumbent on the officer executing a search warrant to ensure the search is lawfully authorized and lawfully conducted. Because [the agent] did not have in his possession a warrant particularly describing the things he intended to seize, proceeding with the search was clearly 'unreasonable' under the Fourth Amendment," and the resultant "search was unconstitutional." *Id.* at 1293.

NOTE

The posture of *Groh v. Ramirez* is a civil lawsuit by Ramirez against Agent Groh for damages. Since the Court concluded that constitutional violation occurred, it went on to address the question whether Agent Groh was entitled to qualified immunity despite that violation. "The answer," stated the Court,

> depends on whether the right that was transgressed was "clearly established"—that is, "whether it would be clear to a reasonable officer that his conduct was unlawful in the situation he confronted." * * * Given that the particularity requirement is set forth in the text of the Constitution, no reasonable officer could believe that a warrant that plainly did not comply with that requirement was valid.

Id. at 1293. As stated in *Harlow v. Fitzgerald*, 457 *U.S.* 800, 818-819, 102 *S.Ct.* 2727 (1982), if the "law was clearly established, the immunity defense ordinarily should fail, since a reasonably competent public official should know the law governing his conduct."

According to the Court, even a "cursory reading of the warrant in this case—perhaps just a simple glance"—"would have revealed a glaring deficiency that any reasonable police officer would have known was constitutionally fatal." *Groh* at 1294.

UNITED STATES v. HUMPHREY
United States Court of Appeals
104 *F.*3d 65 (5th Cir. 1997)

QUESTION: In the proper case, may a search warrant that authorizes the search of a residence for evidence of a fraudulent brokerage service including "all records" connected thereto be upheld as constitutionally valid?

ANSWER: YES. An "all records" warrant for the search of a residence "is valid in the specific circumstances of this case where the residence was the primary place of business for the defendants, where the fraud was pervasive, where there was a significant overlap in the business and personal lives of the defendants, where the defendants maintained no known bank accounts, and where the warrant was limited to financial records." *Id.* at 67.

RATIONALE: Defendants Bruce and Fay Humphrey were convicted of mail fraud and three counts of wire fraud for their operation of a "scam" loan brokerage service. The primary issue on appeal was whether the search warrant that authorized a search of the defendants' home and "all records" was valid.

"The warrant authorizing the search of the Humphreys' residence included a list of four generic categories of property, all related to financial records to be seized." *Id.* at 68. The warrant authorized the seizure of:

1. Books, records, receipts, notes, ledgers and other documents relating to financial transactions and relationships with financial institutions.

2. Ledger paper, column paper, check registers, checks, U.S. currency, deposit slips, receipts, bank statements, cashier's checks, association checks, check order forms, new account information forms, wire transfers and receipts, signature cards, correspondence, and all other documents relating to banking, banking transactions, and transactions at savings and loan institutions, and in particular all documents relating to the purchasing, cashing, transferring and depositing of cashier's checks.

3. Credit cards, debit cards, and all statements, receipts, applications, letters, notices, and other documents which relate to the use of credit cards or debit cards.

4. Computer storage devices containing records, documents, and other information described in paragraphs 1 thru 3, and related equipment and materials for adequately retrieving and reviewing the information, including central processing units, printers, monitors, floppy discs and instruction manuals which could be used to store information regarding customer files and banking information.

Id. at 68-69 n.1.

The search warrant was supported by an F.B.I. agent's three-page affidavit, which set forth the extensive nature of the Humphreys' scam brokerage business, and the extent to which their home doubled as their "business office."

In upholding the validity of the warrant, the court pointed out that in *Williams v. Kunze*, 806 *F.*2d 594 (5th Cir. 1986), it had upheld an "all records" warrant that authorized a search of a *business* where probable cause existed to believe that the "entire business was merely a scheme to defraud," or that all the records of the business were "likely to constitute evidence." *Kunze* at 598. It is clear, therefore, that the warrant here in *Humphrey*

> would be valid had it authorized a search of a business rather than a home, because, undoubtedly, the affidavit supports the conclusion that the entire business operated by the Humphreys was merely a scheme to defraud. The warrant, however, authorized a search of the Humphreys' home, and [this court] must decide whether, and when, the reasoning of *Kunze* should be extended to cover searches of private residences.

Id. at 69.

In a similar case, the First Circuit, in *United States v. Falon*, 959 *F.*2d 1143 (1st Cir. 1992), instructed that an "all records" warrant must be examined with caution "when an allegedly fraudulent business [i]s operated out of a residence." *Id.* at 1148. The *Falon* court observed that "it would require extraordinary proof to demonstrate that an individual's entire life is consumed by fraud and that all records found in the home were subject to seizure," and that absent such a showing, the "broad categories of items that may be seized pursuant to an 'all records' search of a home must be sufficiently linked to the alleged criminal activity so as to distinguish them from innocent personal materials." *Id.* at 1148.

Here, in *Humphrey*, the Fifth Circuit agreed that "the Fourth Amendment requires much closer scrutiny of an all records search of a residence." *Id.* at 69. And the court went on to hold that in this case, "the search warrant was valid in the light of the pervasive nature of the fraud, the considerable overlap of the Humphreys' business and personal lives, and the limitation of the warrant to records pertaining to financial transactions." *Id.* Therefore, the evidence gained through the search was properly admitted at trial.

In several concluding remarks, however, the court cautioned that its holding

> should not be read as a broad authorization for the issuance of all records searches of homes. We caution law enforcement to draft warrants carefully to ensure the mandates of the Fourth Amendment are satisfied and note that it is only in extreme cases, such as the one before us today, that we will uphold warrants of this type.

Id. at 69 n.2.

---

§2.5. Warrant execution.

When a neutral and detached judicial officer determines that an affiant's search warrant application contains probable cause to believe that a present search of a particularly described premises will yield specific items subject to official seizure, the judicial officer will generally issue the search warrant by attaching his or her signature thereto. Thereafter, certain rules will come into play by which the warrant must be executed. Because the rules of warrant execution may vary from state to state, state law enforcement officials are encouraged to consult their individual state rules of criminal practice or procedure in this respect.

On the federal level, Title 18 of the United States Code and the Federal Rules of Criminal Procedure dictate the method by which a search warrant is to be executed. For example, *Rule* 41(e)(1) requires that when a magistrate (or state) judge issues a search warrant, it must be issued "to an officer authorized to execute it." Also, 18 *U.S.C.* §3105 provides that "[a] search warrant may in all cases be served by any of the officers mentioned in its direction or by an officer authorized by law to serve such warrant, but by no other person, except in aid of the officer on his requiring it, he being present and acting in its execution." *See also* 18 *U.S.C.* §3107 (giving express authority to the Director, Associate Director, Assistant Directors, agents and inspectors of the Federal Bureau of Investigation to execute warrants for violation of the laws of the United States).

Rule 41(f)(1) requires the officer executing the warrant to "enter on its face the exact date and time it is executed." In addition, the rule provides that an officer (any officer) "present during the execution of the warrant must prepare and verify an inventory of any property seized. The officer must do so in the presence of another officer and the person from whom, or from whose premises, the property was taken. If either one is not present, the officer must prepare and verify the inventory in the presence of at least one other credible person." *Rule* 41(f)(2). Moreover, the officer executing the warrant must: "give a copy of the warrant and a receipt for the property taken to the person from whom, or from whose premises, the property was taken; or [] leave a copy of the warrant and receipt at the place where the officer took the property." *Rule* 41(f)(3).

Finally, the officer executing the warrant "must promptly return it—together with a copy of the inventory—to the magistrate judge designated on the warrant." *Rule* 41(f)(4). *See* Section 2.5(d) for a discussion of search warrant return procedures.

---

§2.5(a). Time.

Fed.R.Crim.P. 41(e)(2) requires the search warrant to specify the period of time in which the search may take place. *In no event, however, may the warrant be executed beyond 10 days of its issuance.* Moreover, the rule requires that the warrant be executed "during the daytime, unless the judge for good cause expressly authorizes execution at another time[.]" *Rule* 41(e)(2)(B). "Daytime" means "the hours between 6:00 a.m. and 10:00 p.m. according to local time." *Rule* 41(a)(2)(B).

At the state level, the time in which a warrant may be executed varies with local rule. Consequently, state officers should consult their local rules of criminal practice. *See e.g., R.* 2005(d) of the Pennsylvania Rules of Criminal Procedure, requiring warrant execution to take place no later than *two* days from the time of issuance.

---

§2.5(b). Entry.

Prior to entering a dwelling to execute a search warrant, police must knock and announce their presence, authority and purpose, and demand entry. This common law "knock and announce" principle "forms a part of the reasonableness inquiry under the Fourth Amendment." *Wilson v. Arkansas,* 514 *U.S.* 927, 115 *S.Ct.* 1914 (1995). "Given the longstanding common-law endorsement of the practice of announcement," the Court in *Wilson* had "little doubt that the Framers of the Fourth Amendment thought that the method of an officer's entry into a dwelling was among the factors to be considered in assessing the reasonableness of a search or seizure." *Id.,* 115 *S.Ct.* at 1918. The common-law rule was based in part on the belief that an announcement would avoid " 'the destruction or breaking of any house * * * by which great damage and inconvenience might ensue.' " *Id.* [Citation omitted.]

The "knock and announce" rule is codified at 18 *U.S.C.* §3109, which provides: "The officer may break open any outer or inner door or window of a house, or any part of a house, or anything therein, to execute a search warrant, *if, after notice of his authority and purpose, he is refused admittance or when necessary to liberate himself or a person aiding him in the execution of the warrant.*" [Emphasis added.] The rule requires "notice in the form of an express announcement by the officers of their [authority and] purpose for demanding admission." *Miller v. United States,* 357 *U.S.* 301, 309, 78 *S.Ct.* 1190, 1196 (1958). As the Court explained in *Miller,*

> [t]he requirement of prior notice and purpose before forcing entry into a home is deeply rooted in our heritage and should not be given grudging application. Congress, codifying a tradition embedded in Anglo-American law, had declared in §3109 the reverence of the law for the individual's right of privacy in his house. Every householder, the good and the bad, the guilty and the innocent, is entitled to the protection designed to secure the common interest against unlawful invasion of the house.

Id. at 313, 78 *S.Ct.* at 1198. Compliance with the rule "is also a safeguard for the police themselves who might be mistaken for prowlers and be shot down by a fearful householder." *Id.* at 313 n.12, 78 *S.Ct.* at 1198 n.12.

Accordingly, the "knock and announce" rule has three underlying purposes: (1) to reduce the risk of violence that inheres in an unannounced, forced entry; (2) to protect privacy by reducing the risk of entering the wrong premises; and (3) to prevent unnecessary physical damage to the property.

Officers are required to adhere to the "knock and announce" rule even if the entry could be made without the use of force, *i.e.*, by merely opening a closed but unlocked door, *Sabbath v. United States*, 391 *U.S.* 585, 88 *S.Ct.* 1755 (1968), or by the use of a passkey. *Munoz v. United States*, 325 *F.2d* 23 (9th Cir. 1963). As the Court stated in *Sabbath*: "An unannounced intrusion into a dwelling—what §3109 basically proscribes—is no less an unannounced intrusion whether officers break down a door, force open a chain lock on a partially open door, open a locked door by use of a passkey, or, as here, open a closed but unlocked door." *Id.* at 590, 88 *S.Ct.* at 1758.

Over the course of time, however, courts have recognized that "not every entry must be preceded by an announcement. * * * [L]aw enforcement interests may also establish the reasonableness of an unannounced entry." *Wilson v. Arkansas, supra*, 115 *S.Ct.* at 1918-19. Exceptions to the "knock and announce" rule which have been recognized to date include a reasonable suspicion that knocking and announcing would:

(1) present a threat of physical violence, *e.g.*, where the officers' peril would be increased if knocking preceded entry;

(2) be futile or a "useless gesture";

   (a) For example, where a prisoner escapes from the police and retreats to his dwelling, knocking and announcing would be considered a "useless gesture" or a "senseless ceremony" prior to entering the premises to regain custody of the escaping offender.

   (b) Also, where no one is home at the target premises, knocking and announcing would be futile or a "useless gesture" when there is no one home to hear the police knocking.

(3) cause the arrest to be frustrated, when entry of a premises is necessary to execute an "arrest" warrant or effect a warrantless arrest with exigent circumstances; or

(4) result in the loss or destruction of evidence, and immediate action is required to preserve the evidence.

See Wilson v. Arkansas, supra at 1919. *See also United States v. Banks*, 540 *U.S.* 31, 124 *S.Ct.* 521, 525 (2003).

Naturally, if at the time of search warrant procurement, the affiant possesses a reasonable suspicion that one or more of the foregoing factors are present, a judge would be "acting within the Constitution to authorize a 'no knock' entry." *See Banks, supra*, 124 *S.Ct.* at 525.

Under the Fourth Amendment, a violation of the "knock and announce" requirement will not necessarily lead to the suppression of evidence. In this regard, the Court, in *Hudson v. Michigan*, 547 *U.S.* 586, 126 *S.Ct.* 2159 (2006), determined that

> the social costs of applying the exclusionary rule to knock-and-announce violations are considerable; the incentive to such violations is minimal to begin with, and the extant deterrences against them are substantial[.] Resort to the massive remedy of suppressing evidence of guilt is unjustified.

Id., 126 *S.Ct.* at 2168, 2170.

UNITED STATES v. REMIGIO
United States Court of Appeals
767 *F.*2d 730 (10th Cir. 1985)

QUESTION: Must government officials comply with the "knock and announce" rule when, armed with a search warrant, they approach the target premises and observe that the door is open and a defendant is standing in the doorway?

ANSWER: NO. "Government officials, armed with a warrant, entering a house through an open door and in the presence of a defendant, need not comply with the provisions of 18 *U.S.C.* §3109." *Id.* at 733.

RATIONALE: Over the course of a five-month investigation, federal and state law enforcement officers developed probable cause to believe that defendant Remigio and co-defendant Johnson were engaged in the manufacture of methamphetamine. The agents obtained a federal search warrant and shortly before midnight, the agents split into two teams, with half the agents proceeding to the front door of Johnson's residence, and the other half to the back door. "As the lead agent for the back-door team was about to reach the rear door of the residence, the co-defendant Johnson opened the screened back door and peered out. The first agent immediately entered through the open door and subdued Johnson on the landing. Simultaneously, the other agents entered through the open door and proceeded through another open door into the kitchen, shouting 'Police' and 'FBI.' The officers and agents did not announce their identity or purpose prior to entering the residence." *Id.* at 732. They did, however, take the defendants into custody and seize various chemicals, formulas, and chemical equipment.

In this appeal, defendant Remigio argues, among other things, that the evidence seized should have been suppressed because the officers, in the execution of the search warrant, failed to knock and announce prior to entering the residence, as is required by 18 *U.S.C.* §3109. *The United States Court of Appeals for the Tenth Circuit disagreed.*

Given the fact that the back door was open at the time the co-defendant was looking outside, "the issue becomes whether the officials' entry into the house was unlawful because of their failure to announce their authority and purpose." *Id.* Section 3109 provides:

> The officer may break open any outer or inner door or window of a house, or any part of a house, or anything therein, to execute a search warrant, if, after notice of his authority and purpose, he is refused admittance or when necessary to liberate himself or a person aiding him in the execution of the warrant.

"The purpose of 18 *U.S.C.* §3109 is to restrict the authority of the government to intrude upon the privacy of its citizens, and to protect law enforcement officers who might be mistaken as unlawful intruders if they were to enter a residence unannounced. * * * The statute requires law enforcement officials to announce their authority and purpose, and to be denied admittance, before they break down the door of a house." *Id.*

In *Sabbath v. United States,* 391 *U.S.* 585, 88 *S.Ct.* 1755 (1968), the Supreme Court "found that the use of force was not an essential element of the statute, and ruled that unlatching a closed, unlocked door was an 'unannounced intrusion' in violation of the statute." *Remigio* at 732. The issue in this case, however, is whether "entry through an open door is an 'unannounced intrusion.'" *Id.* [Emphasis added.] Significantly, the facts of this case establish that a defendant was present at the open door at the time the officials approached the residence. Thus, a "defendant observed the officials before they entered the house." *Id.* at 733.

Other circuits have addressed the issue of whether officials must comply with the knock and announce statute prior to entering through an open door, and the majority rule is that entry through an open door is not a "breaking" within the meaning of the federal knock and announce statute. *United States v. Lopez,* 475 *F.*2d 537, 541 (7th Cir.), *cert. denied,* 414 *U.S.* 839, 94 *S.Ct.* 89 (1973); *United States v. Johns,* 466 *F.*2d 1364, 1365 (5th Cir. 1972); *United States v. Conti,* 361 *F.*2d 153, 157 (2d Cir. 1966), *vacated on other grounds,* 390 *U.S.* 204, 88 *S.Ct.* 899 (1968); *Ng Pui Yu v. United States,* 352 *F.*2d 626, 632 (9th Cir. 1965); *United States v. Williams,* 351 *F.*2d 475, 477 (6th Cir. 1965), *cert. denied,* 383 *U.S.* 917, 86 *S.Ct.* 910 (1966); *Contra Hair v. United States,* 289 *F.*2d 894, 895-896 (D.C.Cir. 1961).

Accordingly, this court is "persuaded by the majority rule," and holds "that government officials, armed with a warrant, entering a house through an open door and in the presence of a defendant, need not comply with the provisions of 18 *U.S.C.* §3109. [Consequently,] the entry in this case was lawful, and the motion to suppress was properly denied." *Remigio* at 733.

NOTE

1. *Closed doors within a residence.* In *Remigio, supra,* defendant disputed the fact, as found by the District Court, that the interior kitchen door was open. His contention was that the "interior door to the kitchen was closed," *id.* at 732, and the knock and announce rule was violated at that threshold also. Rejecting defendant's contention, the court noted that even if true, this fact was nondispositive. According to the court: "Once law enforcement officials lawfully enter a house, they need not always comply with the knock and announce statute before entering every other closed door within the residence." *Id.* at 732 n.2. *See also United States v. Crawford,* 657 *F.*2d 1041, 1045 (9th Cir. 1981).

2. *Noncompliance with the knock and announce rule.* In *Sabbath v. United States,* 391 *U.S.* 585, 591 & n.8, 88 *S.Ct.* 1755, 1759 & n.8 (1968), the Supreme Court recognized that exceptions to the knock and announce rule of section 3109 may apply in exigent circumstances. *See also United States v. Manfredi,* 722 *F.*2d 519 (9th Cir. 1983), where the court observed that "a police officer's 'reasonable belief that announcement might place him or his associates in physical peril * * * justifies non-compliance with the announcement provisions of the statute.'" *Id.* at 524 (quoting *United States v. Kane,* 637 *F.*2d 974, 978 (3rd Cir. 1981)). *And see United States v. Turner,* 926 *F.*2d 883, 886-887 (9th Cir. 1981) ("exigent circumstances" excuse noncompliance with the knock and announce rule).

Failure to state purpose. In *United States v. James,* 764 *F.*2d 885 (D.C.Cir. 1985), the defendant argued that because the officers announced only "police" when knocking at the door and did not state in addition that the officers were there to execute a search warrant, the forced entry was gained in violation of the knock and announce rule and therefore all evidence gathered as a result of the search should be suppressed. Rejecting defendant's contention, the court reasoned:

> In the ordinary case an officer is required to state both his authority *and his purpose.* * * * In this case, however, the police, after knocking and announcing their authority repeatedly, but without eliciting a response, heard someone running down the back stairs. A reasonable interpretation of such sounds is that the inhabitants are well aware of the purpose of the police visit and are moving to destroy evidence. This is especially true where, as here, the police knew they had reliable information that cocaine was being sold at that location. Faced with the probable imminent destruction of evidence, the police acted properly by entering the premises at once. *To require the police in these circumstances to announce that they are there to execute a search warrant would be to require a futile act.* * * * Compliance with section 3109 is unnecessary in such circumstances.

Id. at 888. [Emphasis added.]

3. *Blanket exception for felony drug investigations rejected; "reasonable suspicion" is the standard.* In *Richards v. Wisconsin*, 520 *U.S.* 385, 117 *S.Ct.* 1416 (1997), the United States Supreme Court rejected the Wisconsin Supreme Court's rule that "police officers are never required to knock and announce their presence when executing a search warrant in a felony drug investigation." *Id.* at 1418. In *Richards*, Madison, Wisconsin police officers obtained a warrant to search Steiney Richards' hotel room for drugs and related paraphernalia based on probable cause to believe that Richards and several other persons were dealing drugs from that location. The officers requested a "no-knock search warrant," but the magistrate would not authorize a no-knock entry, and explicitly deleted that portion from the warrant.

The officers arrived at Richards' hotel room at 3:40 a.m. to execute the warrant. "Officer Pharo, dressed as a maintenance man, led the team. With him were several plainclothes officers and at least one man in uniform." *Id.* at 1419. Pharo knocked on the door, advising that he was the maintenance man. Richards cracked the door open, noticed the uniformed police officer, and then slammed the door closed. Within two or three seconds, the officers forced their way into Richards' room and caught him as he was attempting to escape through a window. A search of the room uncovered a quantity of cash and cocaine hidden in plastic bags above the bathroom ceiling tiles.

In the appeal following his unsuccessful motion to suppress, Richards argued that the evidence should have been suppressed because the officers failed to knock and announce their presence prior to forcing entry into the room.

Preliminarily, the Court recognized that in *Wilson v. Arkansas*, it had determined that

> the "knock and announce" requirement could give way "under circumstances presenting a threat of physical violence," or "where police officers have reason to believe that evidence would likely be destroyed if advance notice were given."

Id. at 1420 (quoting *Wilson v. Arkansas*, 514 *U.S.* 927, 936, 115 *S.Ct.* 1914, 1919 (1995)). "It is indisputable," stated the *Richards* Court, "that felony drug investigations may frequently involve both of these circumstances." *Id.* The Court would not, however, adopt a "blanket exception" for felony drug investigations. Rather, the Court ruled:

> *In order to justify a "no-knock" entry, the police must have a reasonable suspicion that knocking and announcing their presence, under the particular circumstances, would be dangerous or futile, or that it would inhibit the effective investigation of the crime by, for example, allowing the destruction of evidence.* This standard—as opposed to a probable cause requirement—strikes the appropriate balance between the legitimate law enforcement concerns at issue in the execution of search warrants and the individual privacy interests affected by no-knock entries. * * * This showing is not high, but the police should be required to make it whenever the reasonableness of a no-knock entry is challenged.

Id. at 1421-22. [Emphasis added.]

Although the Court would not adopt a blanket exception to the "knock and announce" requirement for felony drug investigations, it nonetheless found the officers' "no-knock entry" into Richards' hotel room lawful under the Fourth Amendment, for it was based on "a reasonable suspicion that Richards might destroy evidence if given further opportunity to do so." *Id.* at 1422.

> [I]t was reasonable for the officers executing the warrant to believe that Richards knew, after opening the door to his hotel room the first time, that the men seeking entry to his room were the police. [] Once the officers reasonably believed that Richards knew who they were, * * * it was reasonable for them to force entry immediately given the disposable nature of the drugs.

Id.

The Court also paused to note that the lawfulness of the no-knock entry in this case is not altered by the fact that the magistrate who signed the search warrant deleted that portion of the warrant that would have authorized a "no-knock entry." In this respect, the Court emphasized that the magistrate's initial decision *"did not alter the reasonableness of the officers' decision, which must be evaluated as of the time they entered the hotel room." Id.* [Emphasis added.] The Court elaborated:

> At the time the officers obtained the warrant, they did not have evidence sufficient, in the judgment of the magistrate, to justify a no-knock warrant. Of course, the magistrate could not have anticipated in every particular the circumstances that would confront the officers when they arrived at Richards' hotel room. These actual circumstances—[Richards'] apparent recognition of the officers combined with the easily disposable nature of the drugs—justified the officers' ultimate decision to enter without first announcing their presence and authority.

Id.

See also Hudson v. Michigan, 547 *U.S.* 586, 126 *S.Ct.* 2159 (2006), where the United States Supreme Court reaffirmed that, to avoid the "knock and announce" requirement, the police are only required to demonstrate a "reasonable suspicion" that knocking and announcing would present a "threat of physical violence," result in the likelihood that evidence would be destroyed, or be "futile." *Id.,* 126 *S.Ct.* at 2162-63. "This showing," acknowledged the Court, "is not high." *Id.* at 2163.

4. *When the "no knock" entry results in property destruction.* Does the Fourth Amendment hold officers to a "higher standard" than that set forth in *Richards v. Wisconsin* when a "no knock" entry might result in the destruction of property? In *United States v. Ramirez,* 523 *U.S.* 65, 118 *S.Ct.* 992 (1998), the Court held that it does not.

Ramirez involved an attempt to regain custody of Alan Shelby, a prisoner who had escaped custody while being transported to court by deputy sheriffs. To accomplish his escape, Shelby slipped out of his handcuffs and knocked over one of the deputies. This was not Shelby's first escape attempt. "In 1991 he struck an officer, kicked out a jail door, assaulted a woman, stole her vehicle, and used it to ram a police vehicle. Another time he attempted escape by using a rope made from torn bedsheets. He was reported to have made threats to kill witnesses and police officers, to have tortured people with a hammer, and to have said that he would 'not do federal time.'" *Id.* at 995. The police also had information that Shelby had access to large supplies of weapons.

Subsequently, the authorities received information from a reliable confidential informant that he had seen a person he believed to be Shelby at Hernan Ramirez's home in Boring, Oregon. An investigator and the informant then drove to an area near the Ramirez home and observed a man working outside who resembled Shelby.

In light of this information, the officials obtained a "no-knock" warrant granting permission to enter and search Ramirez's home. The confidential informant also advised the authorities that Ramirez may have a stash of guns and drugs hidden in his garage. As a result, approximately 45 officers gathered to execute the warrant. "The officers set up a portable loud speaker system and began announcing that they had a search warrant. Simultaneously, they broke a single window in the garage and pointed a gun through the opening, hoping thereby to dissuade any of the occupants from rushing to the weapons the officers believed might be in the garage." *Id.*

Ramirez and his family were asleep inside the house at the time. Awakened by the noise, Ramirez thought that he was being burglarized. "He ran to his utility closet, grabbed a pistol, and fired it into the ceiling of his garage. The officers fired back and shouted 'police.'" *Id.* Ramirez then realized that it was law enforcement officials who were trying to enter his home. "He ran to the living room, threw his pistol away, and threw himself onto the floor. Shortly thereafter, he, his wife, and their child left the house and were taken into police custody." *Id.* Shelby was not found.

The main question in this appeal was whether the law enforcement officials had violated both the Fourth Amendment and 18 *U.S.C.* §3109 due to "insufficient exigent circumstances" to justify the police officer's destruction of property in their execution of the warrant. The Court of Appeals for the Ninth Circuit held that the police must demonstrate "more specific inferences of exigency" to justify any property destruction upon making a no-knock entry. *The United States Supreme Court disagreed and reversed.*

According to the Court, under *Richards v. Wisconsin*, "a no-knock entry is justified if police have a 'reasonable suspicion' that knocking and announcing would be dangerous, futile, or destructive to the purposes of the investigation. *Whether such a 'reasonable suspicion' exists depends in no way on whether police must destroy property in order to enter.*" *Id.* at 996. [Emphasis added.]

The Court was quick to add, however, that this should not be interpreted to mean that "the Fourth Amendment speaks not at all to the manner of executing a search warrant. The general touchstone of reasonableness which governs Fourth Amendment analysis * * * gov-

173

erns the method of execution of the warrant." *Id.* In this respect, the Court emphasized:

> *Excessive or unnecessary destruction of property in the course of a search may violate the Fourth Amendment, even though the entry itself is lawful and the fruits of the search not subject to suppression.*

Id. [Emphasis added.]

Based on the principles set forth above, the Court concluded that no constitutional violation occurred. "A reliable confidential informant had notified the police that Alan Shelby might be inside [Ramirez's] home, and an officer had confirmed this possibility. Shelby was a prison escapee with a violent past who reportedly had access to a large supply of weapons. He had vowed that he would 'not do federal time.' The police certainly had a 'reasonable suspicion' that knocking and announcing their presence might be dangerous to themselves or to others." *Id.* at 996-97.

Regarding the manner of entry, the officers here broke a single garage window. "They did so because they wished to discourage Shelby, or any other occupant of the house, from rushing to the weapons that the informant had told them [might be present] there. Their conduct was," the Court concluded, "clearly reasonable." *Id.* at 997.

The Court also ruled that the officers in this case did not violate 18 *U.S.C.* §3109. Section 3109 provides:

> The officer may break open any outer or inner door or window of a house, or any part of a house, or anything therein, to execute a search warrant, if, after notice of his authority and purpose, he is refused admittance or when necessary to liberate himself or a person aiding him in the execution of the warrant.

By its terms, section 3109 "prohibits nothing." Rather, it "merely authorizes officers to damage property in certain instances." Here, in *Ramirez*, the Court declared:

> We remove whatever doubt may remain on the subject and hold that §3109 codifies the exceptions to the common-law announcement requirement. If §3109 codifies the common law in this area, and the common law in turn informs the Fourth Amendment, our decisions in *Wilson* and *Richards* serve as guideposts in construing the statute. In *Wilson* * * *, we concluded that the common-law principle of announcement is "an element of the reasonableness inquiry under the Fourth Amendment," but noted that the principle "was never stated as an inflexible rule requiring announcement under all circumstances." [] In *Richards* * * *, we articulated the test used to determine whether exigent circumstances justify a particular no-knock entry. * * * *We therefore hold that §3109 includes an exigent circumstances exception* and that the exception's applicability in a given instance is measured by the same standard we articulated in *Richards*. The police met that standard here and §3109 was therefore not violated.

Id. at 997-98. [Emphasis added.]

5. *"No knock" warrantless entries.* The "knock and announce" rule which applies in the context of search warrant execution also applies in the context of warrantless entries. This was made clear in 1963 by the United States Supreme Court in *Ker v. State of California*, 374 *U.S.* 23, 83 *S.Ct.* 1623 (1963). Quoting California Justice Traynor, the Court explained:

> It must be borne in mind that the primary purpose of the con-stitutional guarantee is to prevent unreasonable invasions of the security of the people in their persons, houses, papers, and effects, and when an officer has reasonable cause to enter a dwelling to make an arrest and as an incident to that arrest is authorized to make a reasonable search, his entry and his search are not unrea-sonable. Suspects have no constitutional right to destroy or dispose of evidence, and no basic constitutional guarantees are violated be-cause an officer succeeds in getting to a place where he is entitled to be more quickly than he would, had he complied with [the knock and announce rule]. *[C]ompliance is not required if the officer's peril would have been increased or the arrest frustrated had he de-manded entrance and stated his purpose.*

Id. at 39-40, 83 *S.Ct.* at 1633 (quoting *People v. Maddox*, 46 *Cal.*2d 301, 306, 294 *P.*2d 6, 9 (1956)). [Emphasis added.]

6. *The time between announcement and entry.*

(a) Officers may not knock and announce their presence, au-thority, and purpose and immediately enter the target premises. Al-though there is no set time for every case, to pass constitutional mus-ter, the time lapse between the police announcement and any forced entry must be reasonable under the circumstances, but not necessarily extensive in length.

(b) *A 15- to 20-second wait before a forcible entry.* In *United States v. Banks*, 540 *U.S.* 31, 124 *S.Ct.* 521 (2003), the Court held that, under the "totality of the circumstances" presented, a 15- to 20-second wait between an officer's knock and announcement of authority and the forcible entry satisfied the Fourth Amendment.

In *Banks*, based on information that Banks was selling cocaine at his home, police officers and FBI agents obtained a warrant to search his two-bedroom apartment. "As soon as they arrived there, about 2 o'clock on a Wednesday afternoon, officers posted in front called out 'police search warrant' and rapped hard enough on the door to be heard by officers at the back door. There was no indication whether anyone was home, and after waiting for 15 to 20 seconds with no an-swer, the officers broke open the front door with a battering ram." *Id.*, 124 *S.Ct.* at 523. Banks was in the shower at the time. The search un-covered weapons, crack cocaine, and other evidence of drug dealing.

In this case, the United States Supreme Court analyzed the "standard of reasonableness" in connection with "the length of time police with a warrant must wait before entering without permission after knocking and announcing their intent in a felony case." *Id.* at 524. According to the Court, the police must wait "a reasonable time under all the circumstances." *Id.* at 528. The Court explained:

> Since most people keep their doors locked, entering without knocking will normally do some damage, a circumstance too common to require a heightened justification when a reasonable suspicion of exigency already justifies an unwarned entry. We have accordingly held that police in exigent circumstances may damage premises so far as necessary for a no-knock entrance without demonstrating the suspected risk in any more detail than the law demands for an unannounced intrusion simply by lifting the latch. *United States v. Ramirez,* 523 *U.S.* 65, 70-71, 118 *S.Ct.* 992 (1998). Either way, it is enough that the officers had a reasonable suspicion of exigent circumstances.

> Like *Ramirez*, this case turns on the significance of exigency revealed by circumstances known to the officers, for the only substantive difference between the two situations goes to the time at which the officers reasonably anticipated some danger calling for action without delay. * * *

> [T]he issue comes down to whether it was reasonable to suspect imminent loss of evidence after the 15 to 20 seconds the officers waited prior to forcing their way. Though we agree * * * that this call is a close one, * * * we think that after 15 or 20 seconds without a response, police could fairly suspect that cocaine would be gone if they were reticent any longer. * * *

Id. at 525-26.

In this appeal, Banks argued that 15 to 20 seconds was just "too brief." In rejecting this argument, the Court pointed out that each of Banks's

> reasons for saying that 15 to 20 seconds was too brief rests on a mistake about the relevant inquiry: the fact that he was actually in the shower and did not hear the officers is not to the point, and the same is true of the claim that it might have taken him longer than 20 seconds if he had heard the knock and headed straight for the door. As for the shower, it is enough to say that the facts known to the police are what count in judging reasonable waiting time, * * * and there is no indication that the police knew that Banks was in the shower and thus unaware of an impending search that he would otherwise have tried to frustrate.

> And the argument that 15 to 20 seconds was too short for Banks to have come to the door ignores the very risk that justified prompt

entry. * * * In this case[,] the police claim exigent need to enter, and the crucial fact in examining their actions is not time to reach the door but the particular exigency claimed. On the record here, what matters is the opportunity to get rid of cocaine, which a prudent dealer will keep near a commode or kitchen sink. The significant circumstances include the arrival of the police during the day, when anyone inside would probably have been up and around, and the sufficiency of 15 to 20 seconds for getting to the bathroom or the kitchen to start flushing cocaine down the drain. That is, when circumstances are exigent because a pusher may be near the point of putting his drugs beyond reach, it is imminent disposal, not travel time to the entrance, that governs when the police may reasonably enter; since the bathroom and kitchen are usually in the interior of a dwelling, not the front hall, there is no reason generally to peg the travel time to the location of the door, and no reliable basis for giving the proprietor of a mansion a longer wait than the resident of a bungalow, or an apartment like Banks's. And 15 to 20 seconds does not seem an unrealistic guess about the time someone would need to get in a position to rid his quarters of cocaine.

Once the exigency had matured, of course, the officers were not bound to learn anything more or wait any longer before going in, even though their entry entailed some harm to the building. *Ramirez* held that the exigent need of law enforcement trumps a resident's interest in avoiding all property damage, * * * and there is no reason to treat a post-knock exigency differently from the no-knock counterpart in *Ramirez* itself. Our emphasis [is] on totality analysis[.] * * *

One point in making an officer knock and announce, then, is to give a person inside the chance to save his door. That is why, in the case with no reason to suspect an immediate risk of frustration or futility in waiting at all, the reasonable wait time may well be longer when police make a forced entry, since they ought to be more certain the occupant has had time to answer the door. It is hard to be more definite than that, without turning the notion of a reasonable time under all the circumstances into a set of sub-rules * * *. Suffice it to say that the need to damage property in the course of getting in is a good reason to require more patience than it would be reasonable to expect if the door were open. Police seeking a stolen piano may be able to spend more time to make sure they really need the battering ram. * * * [Indeed, a]ttention to cocaine rocks and pianos tells a lot about the chances of their respective disposal and its bearing on reasonable time. * * *

Absent exigency, the police must knock and receive an actual refusal or wait out the time necessary to infer one. But in a case like this, where the officers knocked and announced their presence, and forcibly entered after a reasonable suspicion of exigency had ripened, their entry satisfied * * * the Fourth Amendment, even without refusal of admittance.

Id. at 527-29. [Citations omitted.]

7. *Violations of the "knock and announce" rule under the Fourth Amendment.* In *Hudson v. Michigan,* 547 *U.S.* 586, 126 *S.Ct.* 2159 (2006), the United States Supreme Court held, for the first time, that, under the Fourth Amendment, a violation of the "knock-and-announce" rule does not require suppression of evidence found in a search.

In 1995, in *Wilson v. Arkansas,* 115 *S.Ct.* 1914, the Court determined that the "knock and announce" rule was not only a creature of statute but was also a command of the Fourth Amendment. Yet, the *Wilson* Court also noted the many situations in which it is not necessary to knock and announce. For example, it is not necessary when "circumstances present a threat of physical violence," or if there is "reason to believe that evidence would likely be destroyed if advance notice were given," or if knocking and announcing would be "futile." *Hudson,* 126 *S.Ct.* at 2163. [Citations omitted.] Moreover, the law only requires that the police have a "reasonable suspicion" under the particular circumstances that one of these grounds for failing to knock and announce exists.

The *Wilson* Court did not decide, however, what the appropriate "remedy" would be for a violation of the knock-and-announce requirement. *Wilson* specifically declined to decide whether the exclusionary rule is appropriate for a violation.

In addressing the appropriate remedy, the Court, here in *Hudson,* preliminarily noted that "suppression of evidence"

> has always been our last resort, not our first impulse. The exclusionary rule generates "substantial social costs," which sometimes include setting the guilty free and the dangerous at large. We have therefore been "cautio[us] against expanding" it[,]* * * and have held it to be applicable only * * * "where its deterrence benefits outweigh its substantial social costs."

Id. at 2163.

In this case, "the constitutional violation of an illegal *manner* of entry was *not* a but-for cause of obtaining the evidence. Whether that preliminary misstep had occurred *or not,* the police would have executed the warrant they had obtained, and would have discovered the gun and drugs inside the house." *Id.* at 2164. [Court's emphasis.]

Up until the point at which a valid warrant issues, "citizens are entitled to shield 'their persons, houses, papers, and effects' * * * from the government's scrutiny." *Id.* at 2165. "Exclusion of the evidence obtained by a warrantless search vindicates that entitlement. The interests protected by the knock-and-announce requirement are quite different—and do not include the shielding of potential evidence from the government's eyes." *Id.*

The knock-and-announce rule protects privacy and dignity that can be destroyed by a sudden entrance. It gives residents the opportunity to prepare themselves for the entry of the police. "The brief interlude between announcement and entry with a warrant may be the opportunity that an individual has to pull on clothes or get out of bed." *Id.* In other words, "it assures the opportunity to collect oneself before answering the door." *Id.*

"What the knock-and-announce rule has never protected," emphasized the Court, "is one's interest in preventing the government from seeing or taking evidence described in a warrant. Since the interests that *were* violated in this case have nothing to do with the seizure of the evidence," the Court held that *"the exclusionary rule is inapplicable." Id.* [Emphasis added.]

The prospect of civil liability should be enough of a deterrent. Today, citizens and lawyers "are much more willing to seek relief in the courts for police misconduct." *Id.* at 2167. According to the Court, "civil liability is an effective deterrent here," as it has been in other contexts. *Id.* at 2167-68.

"Another development over the past half-century that deters civil-rights violations is the increasing professionalism of police forces, including a new emphasis on internal police discipline." *Id.* at 2168. Today, there is "increasing evidence that police forces across the United States take the constitutional rights of citizens seriously. There have been 'wide-ranging reforms in the education, training, and supervision of police officers.'" *Id.* [Citation omitted.] Indeed, "[f]ailure to teach and enforce constitutional requirements exposes municipalities to financial liability. * * * Moreover, modern police forces are staffed with professionals; it is not credible to assert that internal discipline, which can limit successful careers, will not have a deterrent effect. There is also evidence that the increasing use of various forms of citizen review can enhance police accountability." *Id.*

In sum, "the social costs of applying the exclusionary rule to knock-and-announce violations are considerable," while "the incentive to such violations is minimal[.]" *Id.* Accordingly, the Court held that, under the Fourth Amendment, "[r]esort to the massive remedy of suppressing evidence of guilt is unjustified." *Id.*

UNITED STATES v. VILLEGAS
United States Court of Appeals
899 *F*.3d 1324 (2nd Cir. 1990)

QUESTION:　Is the Fourth Amendment violated by the use of a warrant that authorizes a search without a seizure of tangible property, and a covert entry without contemporaneous notice ?

ANSWER:　NO.　The Fourth Amendment is not violated by the use of a "covert entry" ("sneak and peek") search warrant that authorizes the seizure of only "intangible" evidence through the use of photography. *Id.* at 1335.

RATIONALE:　During the course of an extensive investigation into the manufacture and distribution of cocaine, in and about the Northern District of New York, agents of the United States Drug Enforcement Administration ("DEA") developed probable cause to believe that defendant, Ricardo Villegas, had set up an operational cocaine factory at his 377-acre dairy farm on Johnnycake Road in Herkimer County.

On May 12th, the agents applied for a warrant to search defendant's farm premises. The affidavit submitted in support of the warrant stated that "covert physical surveillance of the premises was difficult by reason of the farm's remote location," and that "there was no informant who could infiltrate the operation, and that numerous coconspirators remained to be identified." *Id.* at 1330. The affidavit stated that the DEA agents did not wish to immediately "seize the evidence believed to be on the premises; rather, the agents requested authorization to conduct a search, at any time in the day or night, in order 'to take photographs but not physically to seize any tangible items of evidence at this time.' The agents also requested permission to postpone giving Villegas notice of the search for seven days, or for a longer period if the period were extended by the court." *Id.*

The warrant was executed on May 13th, late at night when no one was present. The agents seized nothing, but observed and photographed various parts of the house, the garage and their contents, noting particularly the presence of numerous items used in the manufacture and processing of cocaine. The agents did not leave a copy of the warrant at the house, "and thereafter repeatedly sought extensions, eight in all, to allow them to continue the investigation without alerting the targets." *Id.* at 1331. The extensions were granted.

On July 14th, the agents applied for and obtained another search warrant based on the affidavit submitted in support of the May 12th warrant, the observations made in the May 13th search, and the information gathered thereafter. "The July 14 warrant directed that the premises be searched and that any cocaine, cocaine base, and other indicia of the manufacture and processing of cocaine be seized." *Id.* That evening, the warrant was executed by seven DEA agents and about a dozen state police officers. During the search, the agents seized, among other things, large quantities of packaged cocaine, 17 drums containing cocaine in varying stages of crystallization, a hydraulic press, and glass containers of hydrochloric acid. Eleven defendants were arrested.

In this appeal, the court rejected Villegas's contention that the May 12th "covert entry" search warrant violated the Fourth Amendment and Rule 41 of the Federal Rules of Criminal Procedure.

Preliminarily, the court noted that

> Rule 41 does not define the extent of the court's power to issue a search warrant. Obviously, the Fourth Amendment long antedated the Federal Rules of Criminal Procedure, which were first adopted in 1944. Given the Fourth Amendment's warrant requirements, and assuming no statutory prohibition, the courts must be deemed to have inherent power to issue a warrant when the requirements of that Amendment are met. * * *

Id. at 1334.

Fed.R.Crim.P. 41 provides in pertinent part:

> **(b) Property . . . Which May Be Seized With a Warrant.** A warrant may be issued under this rule to search for and seize any (1) property that constitutes evidence of the commission of a criminal offense; or (2) contraband, the fruits of crime, or things otherwise criminally possessed; (3) property designed or intended for use or which is or has been used as the means of committing a criminal offense. . . .

> **(d) Execution and Return With Inventory.** The officer taking property under the warrant shall give to the person from whom or from whose premises the property was taken a copy of the warrant and a receipt for the property taken or shall leave the copy and receipt at the place from which the property was taken. The return shall be made promptly and shall be accomplished by a written inventory of any property taken.

> **(h) Scope and Definition.** . . . The term "property" is used in this rule to include documents, books, papers and any other tangible objects.

While the rule expressly mentions only "documents, books, papers and any other tangible objects," it is "clear that both the Rule and the Fourth Amendment extend to searches for and seizures of intangibles as well." *Villegas* at 1334. For example, in *United States v. New York Telephone Co.*, 434 *U.S.* 159, 164, 168, 98 *S.Ct.* 364, 368, 370 (1977), the Court noted that a search warrant may validly authorize the use of a pen register, noting that what is seized in such a procedure is "information." *Villegas* at 1335. *See also Silverman v. United States*, 365 *U.S.* 505, 511, 81 *S.Ct.* 679, 682 (1961) (conversations overheard by means of a microphone touching a heating duct); *Berger v. New York*, 388 *U.S.* 41, 54-60, 87 *S.Ct.* 1873, 1881-84 (1967) (conversations intercepted by wiretap); *United States v. Knotts*, 460 *U.S.* 276, 285, 103 *S.Ct.* 1081, 1087 (1983) (upholding the interception of information gained through the placement of location-monitoring beepers in movable property).

The court rejected, therefore, Villegas's contention that "the district court was without authority to issue a search warrant pursuant to which only intangible evidence would be seized." *Accord United States v. Freitas*, 800 *F.*2d 1451, 1455 (9th Cir. 1986) (ruling that search-without-seizure warrant was authorized, but was not validly issued in light of its failure to make any provision for notice and its failure to particularly describe the intangible property to be seized). *See also United States v. Freitas*, 856 *F.*2d 1425, 1433 (9th Cir. 1988).

Moreover, the court determined that Villegas's contention that

> any authorization for seizure of only intangible property breaches the particularity requirement of the Fourth Amendment is wide of the mark. The particularity requirement means that the warrant must, while indicating the crime under investigation, specify " 'the place to be searched,' " and " 'the persons or things to be seized.' " *Berger v. New York*, * * *. This requirement was plainly met in the present case. The May 12 warrant authorized a search of

>> a farmhouse, a barn, two outbuildings and surrounding land on [Johnnycake] Road, near Little Falls, Herkimer County, New York, owned by B & V Village Farms, Inc., c/o Silk & Slonim, 275 Madison Avenue, New York, New York.

> The warrant authorized search for the following specific items: "cocaine, cocaine base, ether, acetone, filter paper, drying racks, [screens, and] records of telephone numbers." Since the warrant went on to forbid a seizure of "tangible property," it obviously authorized the seizure only of visual images of the items for which the search was authorized.

Id. at 1335.

The court concluded, therefore, that the items listed above sufficiently indicated that the crime to which the sought-after evidence was to relate was "manufacture of cocaine, and that the warrant was sufficiently particular in its description of the place to be searched and the visual images to be seized." *Id.* at 1336.

Finally, the court also rejected Villegas's contention that "the July 14 warrant should have been suppressed because the May 13 search was initiated by means of a covert entry into the farm or because notice of the entry and search was not given to him until after his arrest on July 14." *Id.* While the court believed that "certain safeguards" are required where an entry is to be covert and only intangible evidence is to be seized, it nonetheless concluded that "appropriate conditions were imposed in this case." *Id.* The court said:

> Certain types of searches or surveillances depend for their success on the absence of premature disclosure. The use of a wiretap, or a "bug," or a pen register, or a video camera would likely produce little evidence of wrongdoing if the wrongdoers knew in advance that their conversations or actions would be monitored. When nondisclosure of the authorized search is essential to its success, neither Rule 41 nor the Fourth Amendment prohibits covert entry.

Id. (citing *Dalia v. United States*, 441 *U.S.* 238, 248, 99 *S.Ct.* 1682, 1689 (1979) ("[T]he Fourth Amendment does not prohibit *per se* a covert entry performed for the purpose of installing otherwise legal electronic bugging equipment.") (footnote omitted)).

Accordingly, "when the authorized entry is to be covert and no tangible property is to be seized, there must be some safeguard to minimize the possibility that the officers will exceed the bounds of propriety without detection. In order to balance the individual's privacy and property interests against appropriate law enforcement interests," *id.* at 1336, *the following "two limitations on the issuance of warrants for covert-entry searches" are to be followed*:

> First, the court should not allow the officers to dispense with advance or contemporaneous notice of the search unless they have made a showing of reasonable necessity for the delay. * * * [In this respect,] the officers must at least satisfy the issuing authority that there is good reason for delay.

> Second, if a delay in notice is to be allowed, the court should nonetheless require the officers to give the appropriate person notice of the search within a reasonable time after the covert entry. *See United States v. Freitas*, 800 *F.*2d at 1456. What constitutes a reasonable time will depend on the circumstances of each individual case. We would, however, agree with the *Freitas* court that *as an initial matter, the issuing court should not authorize a notice delay of longer than seven days*. For good cause, the issuing court may thereafter extend the period of delay. Such extensions should not be granted solely on the basis of the grounds presented for the first delay; rather, the applicant should be required to make a fresh showing of the need for further delay.

> If these limitations on the withholding of notice are followed, and the court places the usual time limits on the execution of the warrant and the making of the return to the court, we believe the interests of both the individual and the government will be adequately served.

Id. at 1337-38. [Emphasis added.]

Based on the procedures set forth above, the "covert entry" search warrant utilized in this case satisfied the Fourth Amendment and *Fed.R.Crim.P.* 41.

NOTE

In *United States v. Pangburn*, 983 *F.*2d 449 (2nd Cir. 1993), the court re-emphasized that a "covert entry" search warrant for intangibles " 'is less intrusive than a conventional search with physical seizure because the latter deprives the owner not only of privacy but also of the use of his property. It is less intrusive than a wiretap or video camera surveillance because the physical search is of relatively short duration, focuses the search specifically on the items listed in the warrant, and produces information as of a given moment.' " *Id.* at 454-55 (quoting *Villegas* at 1337).

The *Pangburn* court further instructed that the seven-day notice requirement is rooted in Rule 41, not in the Fourth Amendment. The court said:

> The Fourth Amendment does not deal with notice of any kind, but Rule 41 does. It is from the Rule's requirements for service of a copy of the warrant and for provision of an inventory that we derive the requirement of notice in cases where a search warrant authorizes covert entry to search and to seize intangibles.

Id. at 455.

---

§2.5(c). Scope of the search.

As a general rule, the "scope" of a lawful search is "defined by the object of the search and the places in which there is probable cause to believe that it may be found." *United States v. Ross*, 456 *U.S.* 798, 824, 102 *S.Ct.* 2157, 2172 (1982). Whenever a search is made pursuant to the authority of a valid search warrant, it may naturally extend to the entire area covered by the warrant's description. Therefore, "if the place to be searched is identified by street number, the search is not limited to the dwelling house, but may also extend to the garage and other structures deemed to be within the curtilage and the yard within the curtilage." W. Lafave, 2 *Search and Seizure: A Treatise on the Fourth Amendment* §4.10(a) (3rd ed. 1996), at 654.

When a law enforcement officer executes a warrant authorizing the search of only a portion of a particular structure, only that portion may be searched. Thus, if the warrant specifically authorized a search of the third floor of a building, the officer may not lawfully search any other floor. And when the probable cause delineated in the warrant describes stolen property believed to be in the garage, that information would not support a search for that item in an upstairs bedroom. *See Ross* at 824, 102 *S.Ct.* at 2172.

Individual rooms, places or objects within the described premises do not require any additional showing of probable cause when their access requires an additional act of entry. As the United States Supreme Court explained in *Ross, supra*:

> A lawful search of fixed premises generally extends to the entire area in which the object of the search may be found and is not limited by the possibility that separate acts of entry or opening may be required to complete the search. Thus, a warrant that authorizes an officer to search a home for illegal weapons also provides authority to open closets, chests, drawers, and containers in which the weapon might be found. A warrant to open a footlocker to search for marijuana would also authorize the opening of packages found

inside. A warrant to search a vehicle would support a search of every part of the vehicle that might contain the object of the search.

Id. at 821, 102 *S.Ct.* at 2170-71. Accordingly, when law enforcement officers are engaged in a legitimate search pursuant to a warrant whose "purpose and limits have been precisely defined, nice distinctions between glove compartments, upholstered seats, trunks, and wrapped packages, in the case of a vehicle, must give way to the interest in the prompt and efficient completion of the task at hand." *Id.* at 821, 102 *S.Ct.* at 2127.

A critical distinction, however, must be drawn between the premises to be searched and vehicles at the premises. In this respect, " 'a warrant to search a building does not include authority to search vehicles at the premises, [and, the a]uthority to search a vehicle does not include authority to enter private premises to effect a search of a vehicle within those premises.' " *Lafave* at §4.10(a), p. 315. [Citation omitted.]

MICHIGAN v. SUMMERS
Supreme Court of the United States
452 *U.S.* 692, 101 *S.Ct.* 2587 (1981)

QUESTION: Does a valid warrant to search for contraband carry with it the implicit authority to detain the occupants of the premises while the search is conducted ?

ANSWER: YES.   "If the evidence that a citizen's residence is harboring contraband is sufficient to persuade a judicial officer that an invasion of the citizen's privacy is justified, it is constitutionally reasonable to require that citizen to remain while officers of the law execute a valid warrant to search his home." *Id.* at 2595. Therefore, for Fourth Amendment purposes, "a warrant to search for contraband founded upon probable cause implicitly carries with it the limited authority to detain the occupants of the premises while a proper search is conducted." *Id.*

RATIONALE: "As Detroit police officers were about to execute a warrant to search a house for narcotics, they encountered [defendant] descending the front steps. They requested his assistance in gaining entry and detained him while they searched the premises." *Id.* at 2589. Inside, the officers discovered eight additional occupants, all of whom were detained during the search. When the officers found narcotics in the basement, they thereafter ascertained that defendant owned the house. Defendant was placed under arrest, a search of his person was conducted, and in his coat pocket the officers discovered an envelope containing 8.5 grams of heroin.

Defendant moved to suppress the heroin found on his person, arguing that because it was unlawful for the officers to detain him during the execution of the search warrant, the subsequent seizure of the heroin from his person violated the Fourth Amendment. The Michigan Courts agreed.

The United States Supreme Court, however, found no constitutional violation. According to the Court, the critical "question in this case is whether the initial detention of [defendant] violated his constitutional right to be secure against an unreasonable seizure of his person." *Id.* at 2590.

In *Terry v. Ohio,* 392 *U.S.* 1, 88 *S.Ct.* 1868 (1968), and the cases which have thereafter followed, it has been recognized that "some seizures admittedly covered by the Fourth Amendment constitute such limited intrusions on the personal security of those detained and are justified by such substantial law enforcement interests that they may be made on less than probable cause, so long as police have an articulable basis for suspecting criminal activity." *Id.* at 2592-93. Moreover, this exception for limited intrusions which is "justified by special law enforcement interests is not confined to the momentary on-the-street detention[.]" *Id.* at 2593.

In order to determine whether the officers were justified in forcibly detaining defendant while they executed the search warrant, "it is necessary to examine both the character of the official intrusion and its justification." *Id.* at 2593. First, the police had obtained a warrant to search defendant's home. Certainly, "[t]he detention of the residents while the premises were searched, although admittedly a significant restraint on [their] liberty, was * * * less intrusive than the search itself. Indeed, we may safely assume that most citizens—unless they intend flight to avoid arrest—would elect to remain in order to observe the search of their possessions." *Id.* Additionally, such a temporary detention "is not likely to be exploited by the officer or unduly prolonged in order to gain more information, because the information the officers seek normally will be obtained through the search not through the detention." *Id.* at 2594.

"In assessing the justification for the detention of an occupant of premises being searched for contraband pursuant to a valid warrant, both the law enforcement interest and the nature of the 'articulable facts' supporting the detention are relevant. Most obvious is the legitimate law enforcement interest in preventing flight in the event that incriminating evidence is found. Less obvious, but sometimes of greater importance, is the interest in minimizing the risk of harm to the officers." *Id.* Significantly, "the execution of a warrant to search for narcotics is the kind of transaction that may give rise to sudden violence or frantic efforts to conceal or destroy evidence." *Id.* Consequently, "[t]he risk of harm to both the police and the occupants is minimized if the officers routinely exercise unquestioned command of the situation." *Id.* A final factor to consider is that "the orderly completion of the search may be facilitated if the occupants of the premises are present. Their self-interest may induce them to open locked doors or locked containers to avoid the use of force that is not only damaging to property but may also delay the completion of the task at hand." *Id.*

The next consideration is "the nature of the articulable and individualized suspicion on which the police base the detention of the occupant of a home subject to a search warrant[.]" *Id.* In this context, the mere existence of the warrant "provides an objective justification for the detention. A judicial officer has determined that police have probable cause to believe that someone in the home is committing a crime." *Id.* Therefore, "[t]he connection of an occupant to that home gives the police an easily identifiable and certain basis for determining that suspicion of criminal activity justifies a detention of that occupant." *Id.* at 2594-95.

Accordingly, "[i]f the evidence that a citizen's residence is harboring contraband is sufficient to persuade a judicial officer that an invasion of the citizen's privacy is justified, it is constitutionally reasonable to require that citizen to remain while officers of the law execute a valid warrant to search his home. Thus, for Fourth Amendment purposes, * * * a warrant to search for contraband founded on probable cause implicitly carries with it the limited authority to detain the occupants of the premises while a proper search is conducted." *Id.* at 2595.

"Because it was lawful to require [defendant] to re-enter and to remain in the house until evidence establishing probable cause to arrest him was found, his arrest and the search incident thereto were constitutionally permissible." *Id.* at 2596.

NOTE

1. *Detaining people coming from or going to the target premises.* *See Baker v. Monroe Tp.*, 50 *F.*3d 1186, 1192 (3rd Cir. 1995), where the court held that "[a]lthough *Summers* itself only pertains to a resident of the house under warrant, it follows that the police may stop people coming to or going from the house if police need to ascertain whether they live there."

2. *Presence of media during warrant execution violates the Fourth Amendment.* In *Wilson v. Layne*, 526 *U.S.* 603, 119 *S.Ct.* 1692, 1699 (1999), and *Hanlon v. Berger*, 526 *U.S.* 808, 119 *S.Ct.* 1706 (1999), the United States Supreme Court held that "it is a violation of the Fourth Amendment for police to bring members of the media or other third parties into a home during the execution of a warrant when the presence of the third parties in the home was not in aid of the execution of the warrant." [For an extended discussion of this issue, *see* §4.1.]

3. *Protective sweeps made in conjunction with a search warrant exception.* In *United States v. Daoust*, 916 *F.*2d 757 (1st Cir. 1990), Maine police officials entered defendant's home under the authority of a search warrant and immediately found the object of their search—a semi-automatic handgun hanging from the ceiling over the kitchen sink. Thereafter, the officers conducted a quick "protective sweep" of several rooms inside the home and discovered and seized additional weapons. Finding the sweep lawful, the court reasoned:

The Supreme Court has recently held that the Constitution permits police officers, entering a house with an arrest warrant, to conduct a protective sweep of the house provided that the officers possess "a reasonable belief based on specific and articulable facts that the area to be swept harbors an individual posing a danger to those on the arrest scene." *Maryland v. Buie*, 494 *U.S.* 325, 110 *S.Ct.* 1093, 1100 [] (1990). In doing so, the Court applied to arrests in the home the same "reasonable suspicion" test that it had previously applied when police, on the street, make an on-the-spot stop and frisk for weapons. *See Terry v. Ohio* * * *.

We assume * * * that this same standard applies to a "protective sweep" made in conjunction with a search warrant, a proper conclusion given that the search was for an instrument of violence unlawfully possessed by the home's occupant. * * *

The officers searched the house at 7:00 a.m., a time when Daoust might have been at home sleeping, they knew that Daoust had a prior criminal history of violent behavior, they knew he owned a handgun, which he kept in a rather unusual place in the kitchen, and they knew he lived in an isolated place, far from the nearest neighbor. * * * It seems to us that "individualized suspicion" was present.

Id. at 759.

4. *Resident's request to use the toilet.* In *Hunter v. Namanny*, 219 *F.*3d 825 (8th Cir. 2000), narcotics officers executed a drug search warrant at Hunter's home at approximately 2:00 a.m. The officers knocked and announced their presence, and upon receiving no response, used a battering ram to gain entry. "Upon entering, the officers drew their weapons and identified themselves as Des Moines narcotics officers. Hunter had been asleep on the couch in her underclothes, and asked to be allowed to put on some more clothing. The officers initially refused, but then permitted Hunter to dress herself. Hunter also asked to be allowed to use the toilet, explaining that she was disabled and taking medication that caused her to urinate frequently. The officers refused Hunter's repeated requests until she urinated and defecated on herself." *Id.* at 828.

Finding the officers' actions reasonable in this regard, the court held that a person lawfully detained pursuant to the execution of a search warrant has no right "to use a toilet upon demand." *Id.* at 831. The court said:

Although Hunter's dignity was certainly compromised by what transpired as the search was conducted, we are unable to conclude that the Constitution requires that police engaged in a search for drugs allow a resident of the subject property access to a ready means of disposal of such contraband. * * *

Id.

MUEHLER v. MENA
Supreme Court of the United States
544 *U.S.* 93, 125 *S.Ct.* 1465 (2005)

QUESTION: In the circumstances below, did the officers' use of handcuffs to detain Mena during the execution of the search warrant violate the Fourth Amendment?

CIRCUMSTANCES: During an investigation into a gang-related, driveby shooting, Officers Muehler and Brill learned that at least one member of a gang—the West Side Locos—lived at 1363 Patricia Avenue. Suspecting that the individual was armed and dangerous, the officers obtained a search warrant that authorized "a broad search of the house and premises for, among other things, deadly weapons and evidence of gang membership." *Id.* at 1468. Given the high degree of risk involved, a Special Weapons and Tactics (SWAT) team was used to secure the residence and grounds before the search.

On the day in question, at 7:00 a.m., the officers executed the warrant. Iris Mena was asleep in her bed when the SWAT team entered her bedroom and placed her in handcuffs at gunpoint. The SWAT team also handcuffed three other individuals found on the property. The officers then took those individuals and Mena into a converted garage, which contained several beds and some other bedroom furniture. "While the search proceeded, one or two officers guarded the four detainees, who were allowed to move around the garage but remained in handcuffs" for the duration of the search, which took two to three hours. *Id.*

"Aware that the West Side Locos gang was composed primarily of illegal immigrants, the officers had notified the Immigration and Naturalization Service (INS) that they would be conducting the search, and an INS officer accompanied the officers executing the warrant. During their detention in the garage, an officer asked for each detainee's name, date of birth, place of birth, and immigration status. The INS officer later asked the detainees for their immigration documentation. Mena's status as a permanent resident was confirmed by her papers." *Id.*

"The search of the premises yielded a .22 caliber handgun with .22 caliber ammunition, a box of .25 caliber ammunition, several baseball bats with gang writing, various additional gang paraphernalia, and a bag of marijuana. Before the officers left the area, Mena was released." *Id.* at 1469.

ANSWER: NO. "[T]he officers' detention of Mena in handcuffs during the execution of the search warrant was reasonable and did not violate the Fourth Amendment." *Id.* at 1472. In addition, "the officers' questioning during that detention did not violate her Fourth Amendment rights." *Id.* at 1468.

RATIONALE: In her §1983 suit against the officers, Mena alleged that "she was detained 'for an unreasonable time and in an unreasonable manner' in violation of the Fourth Amendment." *Id.* at 1469. She also alleged that the officers' questioning during that detention constituted a separate Fourth Amendment violation.

In *Michigan v. Summers*, 452 *U.S.* 692, 101 *S.Ct.* 2587 (1981), the Court held that "officers executing a search warrant for contraband have the authority 'to detain the occupants of the premises while a proper search is conducted.' " *Muehler* at 1469. [Citation omitted.] Such detentions are appropriate, "because the character of the additional intrusion caused by detention is slight and because the justifications for detention are substantial." *Id.*

There are "three legitimate law enforcement interests that provide substantial justification for detaining an occupant: 'preventing flight in the event that incriminating evidence is found'; 'minimizing the risk of harm to the officers'; and facilitating 'the orderly completion of the search,' as detainees' 'self-interest may induce them to open locked doors or locked containers to avoid the use of force.' " *Id.* [Citation omitted.]

In this case, the Court determined that Mena's detention was, under *Summers*, "plainly permissible. An officer's authority to detain incident to a search is categorical; it does not depend on the 'quantum of proof justifying detention or the extent of the intrusion to be imposed by the seizure.' " *Id.* at 1470. [Citation omitted.] "Thus, Mena's detention for the duration of the search was reasonable under *Summers* because a warrant existed to search 1363 Patricia Avenue and she was an occupant of that address at the time of the search." *Id.*

"Inherent in *Summers*' authorization to detain an occupant of the place to be searched is the authority to use reasonable force to effectuate the detention." In this case, the "officers' use of force in the form of handcuffs to effectuate Mena's detention in the garage, as well as the detention of the three other occupants, was reasonable because the governmental interests outweigh the marginal intrusion." *Id.*

"The imposition of correctly applied handcuffs on Mena, who was already being lawfully detained during a search of the house, was undoubtedly a separate intrusion in addition to detention in the converted garage. The detention was thus more intrusive than that which [was] upheld in *Summers*. * * * But this was no ordinary search. The governmental interests in not only detaining, but using handcuffs, are at their maximum when, as here, a warrant authorizes a search for weapons and a wanted gang member resides on the premises. In such inherently dangerous situations, the use of handcuffs minimizes the risk of harm to both officers and occupants. * * * Though this safety risk inherent in executing a search warrant for weapons was sufficient to justify the use of handcuffs, the need to detain multiple occupants made the use of handcuffs all the more reasonable." *Id.* at 1470-71.

During the course of this appeal, Mena also argued that, even if the use of handcuffs to detain her in the garage was reasonable as an initial matter, "the duration of the use of handcuffs made the detention unreasonable." *Id.* at 1471. The Court disagreed.

Naturally, the duration of a detention can affect the lawfulness of the detention. "However, the 2- to 3-hour detention in handcuffs in this case [did] not outweigh the government's continuing safety interests. * * * [T]his case involved the detention of four detainees by two officers during a search of a gang house for dangerous weapons." *Id.*

Accordingly, "the detention of Mena in handcuffs during the search was reasonable." *Id.*

Finally, the Court also determined that the officers did not violate Mena's Fourth Amendment rights by questioning her about her immigration status during the detention. In this regard, "mere police questioning does not constitute a seizure." *Id.* Since the detention was not prolonged by the questioning, "there was no additional seizure within the meaning of the Fourth Amendment. Hence, the officers did not need reasonable suspicion to ask Mena for her name, date and place of birth, or immigration status." *Id.*

Accordingly, "the officers' detention of Mena in handcuffs during the execution of the search warrant was reasonable and did not violate the Fourth Amendment. Additionally, the officers' questioning of Mena did not constitute an independent Fourth Amendment violation." *Id.* at 1472.

NOTE

In *Los Angeles County, California v. Rettele*, ___ U.S. ___, 127 *S.Ct.* 1989 (2007), during the course of a fraud and identity-theft investigation, officers obtained a valid warrant to search a house where they believed the suspects were staying. The officers were unaware, however, that the suspects being sought had moved out three months earlier, when the house had been sold to Max Rettele. After purchasing the house, Rettele moved into it with his girlfriend, Judy Sadler, and Sadler's 17-year-old son, Chase, all of whom were Caucasian.

On the morning of the search, the officers were informed that they would be looking for three African-American suspects, one of whom owned a registered handgun. At approximately 7:15 a.m., seven deputies knocked on the door of the residence and announced their presence. Chase answered the door. After ordering Chase to lie face down on the ground, the deputies entered the house and then the bedroom where Rettele and Sadler had been sleeping. With guns drawn, the deputies ordered the two to "get out of their bed and to show their hands. They protested that they were not wearing clothes. Rettele stood up and attempted to put on a pair of sweatpants, but deputies told him not to move. Sadler also stood up and attempted, without success, to cover herself with a sheet. Rettele and Sadler were held at gunpoint for one to two minutes before Rettele was allowed to retrieve a robe for Sadler. He was then permitted to dress. Rettele and Sadler left the bedroom within three to four minutes to sit on the couch in the living room." *Id.* at 1991.

"By that time the deputies realized they had made a mistake. They apologized to Rettele and Sadler, thanked them for not becoming upset, and left within five minutes." *Id.* Later that morning, the actual suspects were located, arrested and ultimately convicted.

Rettele and the other residents sued the deputies under 42 *U.S.C.* § 1983, accusing them of violating the Fourth Amendment right to be free from unreasonable searches and seizures. Although the District Court granted summary judgment to all named defendants, the Ninth Circuit Court of Appeals reversed, concluding both that the deputies violated the Fourth Amendment and that they were not entitled to qualified immunity "because a reasonable deputy would have stopped the search upon discovering that [the residents] were of a different race than the suspects and because a reasonable deputy would not have ordered [Rettele and Sadler] from their bed." *Id.* at 1990. *The United States Supreme Court disagreed.*

Said the Court:

> When the deputies ordered [Rettele and Sadler] from their bed, they had no way of knowing whether the African-American suspects were elsewhere in the house. The presence of some Caucasians in the residence did not eliminate the possibility that the suspects lived there as well. As the deputies stated in their affidavits, it is not uncommon in our society for people of different races to live together. Just as people of different races live and work together, so too might they engage in joint criminal activity. The deputies, who were searching a house where they believed a suspect might be armed, possessed authority to secure the premises before deciding whether to continue with the search.

Id. at 1992.

In *Michigan v. Summers,* 452 *U.S.* 692, 101 *S.Ct.* 2587 (1981), the Court held that officers executing a search warrant for contraband may take reasonable actions to detain the occupants of the premises while a proper search is conducted. This prevents flight in the event that incriminating evidence is found; it minimizes the risk of harm to the officers; and facilitates the orderly completion of the search. *See also Muehler v. Mena,* 544 *U.S.* 93, 125 *S.Ct.* 1465 (2005).

"The orders by the police to the occupants, in the context of this lawful search, were permissible, and perhaps necessary, to protect the safety of the deputies. Blankets and bedding can conceal a weapon, and one of the suspects was known to own a firearm, factors which underscore this point. The Constitution does not require an officer to ignore the possibility that an armed suspect may sleep with a weapon within reach." *Id.* at 1993.

"The deputies needed a moment to secure the room and ensure that other persons were not close by or did not present a danger. Deputies were not required to turn their backs to allow Rettele and Sadler to retrieve clothing or to cover themselves with the sheets. Rather, '[t]he risk of harm to both the police and the occupants is minimized if the officers routinely exercise unquestioned command of the situation.' " *Id.*

"This is not to say, of course, that the deputies were free to force Rettele and Sadler to remain motionless and standing for any longer than necessary. [This Court has] recognized 'special circumstances, or possibly a prolonged detention' might render a search unreasonable. * * * There is no accusation that the detention here was prolonged. The deputies left the home less than 15 minutes after arriving. The detention was shorter and less restrictive than the 2-to 3-hour handcuff detention upheld in *Mena.* * * * And there is no allegation that the deputies prevented Sadler and Rettele from dressing longer than necessary to protect their safety. Sadler was unclothed for no more than two minutes, and Rettele for only slightly more time than that. Sadler testified that once the police were satisfied that no immediate threat was presented, 'they wanted us to get dressed and they were pressing us really fast to hurry up and get some clothes on.' " *Id.*

In several concluding remarks, the Court noted that the

> Fourth Amendment allows warrants to issue on probable cause, a standard well short of absolute certainty. Valid warrants will issue to search the innocent, and people like Rettele and Sadler unfortunately bear the cost. Officers executing search warrants on occasion enter a house when residents are engaged in private activity; and the resulting frustration, embarrassment, and humiliation may be real, as was true here. When officers execute a valid warrant and act in a reasonable manner to protect themselves from harm, however, the Fourth Amendment is not violated. * * *

Id. at 1993-94.

YBARRA v. ILLINOIS
Supreme Court of the United States
444 *U.S.* 85, 100 *S.Ct.* 338 (1979)

QUESTION: Does a valid warrant to search for narcotics at a particular tavern also provide the officers with the authority to automatically search or frisk any person who happens to be on the premises during the execution of that warrant ?

ANSWER: NO. A person's mere presence at the target premises, standing in close proximity "to others independently suspected of criminal activity does not, without more, give rise to probable cause to search that person. * * * This requirement cannot be undercut or avoided by simply pointing to the fact that coincidentally there exists probable cause to search or seize another or to search the premises where the person may happen to be." *Id.* at 342. Additionally, the " 'narrow scope' of the *Terry* [rule] does not permit a frisk for weapons on less than reasonable belief or suspicion directed at the person to be frisked, even though that person happens to be on the premises where an authorized narcotics search is taking place." *Id.*

RATIONALE: Officers from the Illinois Bureau of Investigation arrived at the Aurora Tap Tavern in the late afternoon to execute a search warrant. The warrant authorized a search of "the Aurora Tap Tavern," and the person of "Greg," the bartender, a 25-year-old white male with blonde hair, for evidence of narcotics possession, that being " '[h]eroin, contraband, other controlled substances, money, instrumentalities and narcotics paraphernalia used in the manufacture, processing and distribution of controlled substances.'" *Id.* at 340-341.

Upon entering the tavern, "the officers announced their purpose and advised all those present that they were going to conduct a 'cursory search for weapons.' One of the officers then proceeded to pat down each of the 9 to 13 customers present in the tavern while the remaining officers engaged in an extensive search of the premises." *Id.* at 341. During the patdown of defendant, Ventura Ybarra, the officer felt what he described as "a cigarette pack with objects in it." The officer did not, however, remove this pack immediately. Instead, he proceeded to pat down the remaining customers. The officer then returned to Ybarra, relocated and retrieved the cigarette pack from Ybarra's pants pocket, and found it to contain six tinfoil packets of a brown substance which later proved to be heroin.

Although the Illinois courts found the search of Ybarra constitutional, relying on the strength of an Illinois statute (authorizing officers to detain and search any person found on premises being searched pursuant to a search warrant), *the United States Supreme Court found that procedure violative of the Fourth and Fourteenth Amendments.*

According to the Court:

> There is no reason to suppose that, when the search warrant was issued * * * the authorities had probable cause to believe that any person found on the premises of the Aurora Tap Tavern, aside from "Greg," would be violating the law. The search warrant complaint did not allege that the bar was frequented by persons illegally purchasing drugs. It did not state that the informant had ever seen a patron of the tavern purchase drugs from "Greg" or from any other person. Nowhere, in fact, did the complaint even mention the patrons of the Aurora Tap Tavern.

Id. at 341-342. Significantly, probable cause to search Ybarra was not only absent at the time the warrant issued but it was still missing during warrant execution. "Upon entering the tavern, the police did not recognize Ybarra and had no reason to believe that he had committed, was committing, or was about to commit any offense under state or federal law. Ybarra made no gestures indicative of criminal conduct, made no movements that might suggest an attempt to conceal contraband, and said nothing of a suspicious nature to the police officers. In short, the agents knew nothing in particular about Ybarra, except that he was present, along with several other customers in a public tavern, at a time when police had reason to believe that the bartender would have heroin for sale." *Id.* at 342.

While it is true that the officers here possessed a warrant based on probable cause to search the tavern in which Ybarra happened to be at the time the warrant was executed, this fact—a person merely being in close proximity to others independently suspected of criminal activity—"does not, without more, give rise to probable cause to search that person." *Id.* "Where the standard is probable cause, a search or seizure of a person must be supported by probable cause particularized with respect to that person. This requirement cannot be undercut or avoided by simply pointing to the fact that coincidentally there exists probable cause to search or seize another or to search the premises where the person may happen to be." *Id.*

Consequently, the search warrant which gave the officers the authority to search the Aurora Tap Tavern and "Greg," provided "no authority whatever to invade the constitutional protections possessed individually by the tavern's customers." *Id.* It follows, therefore, "that a warrant to search a place cannot normally be construed to authorize a search of each individual in that place." *Id.* at 342-343 n.4.

Notwithstanding the absence of probable cause to search Ybarra, the State argues that the patdown search "constituted a reasonable frisk for weapons under the doctrine of *Terry*[.]" *Id.* at 343. Rejecting this argument, the Court stated:

> We are unable to take even the first step required by this argument. The initial frisk of Ybarra was simply not supported by a reasonable belief that he was armed and presently dangerous, a belief which this Court has invariably held must form the predicate to a patdown of a person for weapons.

Id. When the officers entered the tavern, "the lighting was sufficient for them to observe the customers. Upon seeing Ybarra, they neither recognized him as a person with a criminal history nor had any particular reason to believe that he might be inclined to assault them." *Id.* Additionally, there was testimony that Ybarra gave no indication of possessing a weapon; his hands were empty, he made no gestures or other actions indicative of an intent to commit an assault, nor did he act in a manner which could be interpreted as threatening. "In short, the State is unable to articulate any specific fact that would have justified a police officer at the scene in even suspecting that Ybarra was armed and dangerous. * * * The 'narrow scope' of the *Terry* exception *does not permit a frisk for weapons on less than reasonable belief or suspicion directed at the person to be frisked*, even though that person happens to be on premises where an authorized narcotics search is taking place." *Id.* [Emphasis added.]

Accordingly, the State's request that this Court "permit evidence searches of persons who, at the commencement of the search, are on 'compact' premises subject to a search warrant, at least where the police have a 'reasonable belief' that such persons 'are connected with' drug trafficking and 'may be concealing or carrying away the contraband[,]' " is hereby rejected. *Id.* at 344. *See also United States v. Di Re,* 332 *U.S.* 581, 583-587, 68 *S.Ct.* 222, 223-225 (1948) (Government concession and Court recognition that officers could not search all the persons in a house being searched pursuant to a search warrant).

NOTE

The close confines of an automobile. During the course of its opinion in *Ybarra*, the Court observed:

Where the standard is probable cause, a search or seizure of a person must be supported by probable cause particularized with respect to that person. This requirement cannot be undercut or avoided by simply pointing to the fact that coincidentally there exists probable cause to search or seize another or to search the premises where the person may happen to be.

Id. at 91, 100 *S.Ct.* at 342.

In *Maryland v. Pringle*, 540 *U.S.* 366, 124 *S.Ct.* 795 (2003), at 3:16 a.m., an officer stopped a Nissan Maxima for speeding. There were three occupants in the car: Donte Partlow, the driver and owner, defendant Joseph Pringle, the front-seat passenger, and Otis Smith, the back-seat passenger. "The officer asked Partlow for his license and registration. When Partlow opened the glove compartment to retrieve the vehicle registration, the officer observed a large amount of rolled-up money in the glove compartment. The officer returned to his patrol car with Partlow's license and registration to check the computer system for outstanding violations. The computer check did not reveal any violations. The officer returned to the stopped car, had Partlow get out, and issued him an oral warning." *Id.* at 798.

After a second patrol car arrived, Partlow consented to a search of the vehicle. "The search yielded $763 from the glove compartment and five plastic glassine baggies containing cocaine from behind the back-seat armrest. When the officer began the search, the armrest was in the upright position flat against the rear seat. The officer pulled down the armrest and found the drugs, which had been placed between the armrest and the back seat of the car." *Id.*

"The officer questioned all three men about the ownership of the drugs and money, and told them that if no one admitted to ownership of the drugs he was going to arrest them all. The men offered no information regarding the ownership of the drugs or money. All three were placed under arrest and transported to the police station." *Id.*

Finding the arrest based on probable cause, the Court said:

This case is quite different from *Ybarra*. Pringle and his two companions were in a relatively small automobile, not a public tavern. * * * '[A] car passenger—unlike the unwitting tavern patron in *Ybarra*—will often be engaged in a common enterprise with the driver, and have the same interest in concealing the fruits or the evidence of their wrongdoing.' * * * Here we think it was reasonable for the officer to infer a common enterprise among the three men. The quantity of drugs and cash in the car indicated the likelihood of drug dealing, an enterprise to which a dealer would be unlikely to admit an innocent person with the potential to furnish evidence against him.

Pringle at 801. [Citation omitted.]

UNITED STATES v. MICHELI
United States Court of Appeals
487 *F*.2d 429 (1st Cir. 1973)

QUESTION: What may a court examine to determine whether a personal effect, such as a briefcase, falls within the scope of a warrant to search premises which fails to name the particular effect as one of the things to be seized ?

ANSWER: "In determining to what extent a recognizable personal effect not currently worn, but apparently temporarily put down, such as a briefcase, falls [within] the scope of a warrant to search the premises, * * * the relationship between the person and the place" may be examined. *Id.* at 431.

RATIONALE: After weeks of investigation by the United States Secret Service, a search warrant issued for the office of the Hillside Press, authorizing a search of "those rooms of the second floor of those premises known as 81 Canal Street, Boston, being used as the place of business of the Hillside Press[.]" *Id.* at 430. "At the same time an arrest warrant was issued for [defendant's] brother who, with [defendant], was co-owner of the Press. That evening government agents surrounded the premises, and observed [defendant] enter the building, carrying a brown leather briefcase. Approximately one half hour later, at 6:20 p.m., the agents entered the building, arrested [defendant's] brother, and proceeded to search the premises. * * * In their search of the front room, the agents discovered what they knew to be [defendant's] briefcase on the floor under a desk. Inside the briefcase they found what proved to be forty-three counterfeit five dollar Federal Reserve notes, and papers identifying [defendant] as the owner of the briefcase." *Id.*

In the appeal which followed the denial of defendant's motion to suppress the evidence seized, defendant argued that the agents knew the briefcase was his personal property "and therefore its search did not come within the scope of the warrant to search the premises of the Press." *Id. The Court of Appeals for the First Circuit disagreed.*

As a general rule, "a warrant to search premises does not permit a personal search of one who merely happens to be present at the time." *Id.* at 431 (citing *United States v. Di Re*, 332 *U.S.* 581, 68 *S.Ct.* 222 (1948)). In this case, however, "the question is: [W]hat is a personal search ? A search of clothing currently worn is plainly within the ambit of a personal search and outside the scope of a warrant to search the premises. But a personal effect such as a briefcase, carried on to the premises and then tucked under a desk, does not clearly fall either within the realm of a personal search or a search of the premises." *Id.*

To determine, therefore, "to what extent a recognizable personal effect not currently worn, but apparently temporarily put down, such as a briefcase, falls outside the scope of a warrant to search the premises, [the appropriate course is] to examine the relationship between the person and the place." *Id.* In this respect, "[t]he purpose of a search warrant is to assure that any governmental intrusion is justified by a careful prior determination of probable cause and necessity. Furthermore, any searches which are deemed necessary should be as limited as possible. * * * This further objective is achieved by requiring that the warrant contain a particular description of the things to be seized and give a clear idea of the scope of things to be searched. It should not be assumed that whatever is found on the premises described in the warrant necessarily falls within the proper scope of the search; rather, it is necessary to examine why a person's belongings happen to be on the premises. '[T]he Fourth Amendment protects people, not places,' * * * and the protective boundary established by requiring a search warrant should encompass those extensions of a person which he reasonably seeks to preserve as private, regardless of where he may be." *Id.* at 431-432. [Citation omitted.]

Thus, while a warrant to search a private home or office for specific objects might reasonably include within its scope household items, containers, and personal accessories belonging to the owner of the premises, those same objects "might not fall within the reasonable scope of a warrant to search a more public place, such as a meeting hall, a restaurant, or a barbershop * * * where the individual who owns the objects is a transient visitor or customer." *Id.* at 432. Yet, a visitor in a private home or office stands in a different position from the patron of a business establishment. It is therefore "more consistent with the Fourth Amendment that searches of the personal effects of visitors to premises be appraised by reference to the reasonable expectations of privacy which visitors bring to premises[.]" *Id.*

In light of the foregoing, the court holds that defendant's briefcase fell within the scope of the warrant to search the premises of the Press. The rationale, however, does not rest upon the fact that at the time of the search his brief case was out of his physical possession. Rather, the court bases its "decision on the fact that, as a co-owner of the Hillside Press, [defendant] was not in the position of a mere visitor or passerby who suddenly found his belongings vulnerable to a search of the premises. He had a special relation to the place, which meant that it could reasonably be expected that some of his personal belongings would be there. Thus, the showing of probable cause and necessity which was required prior to the initial intrusion into his office reasonably comprehended within its scope those personal articles, such as his briefcase, which might be lying about the office. The search of the briefcase, under these circumstances, was properly carried out within the scope of the warrant." *Id.*

NOTE

The court in *Micheli, supra,* cautioned that its opinion should not be read to suggest that anything found on private premises would necessarily fall within the scope of a warrant to search the premises. In addition, the court emphasized that it did not mean to

> imply that the result would be different if, when the officers entered, [defendant] was physically holding the briefcase. To allow our decision to be interpreted as giving carte blanche to seize any

objects [located] within premises covered by a warrant would be a disservice to law enforcement officials, individuals who may find their personal privacy invaded by a premises search warrant, and courts which must rule on suppression motions. * * * Had [defendant] been a doctor on call at the Press and had the agents reason to know that the briefcase belonged to him, we would not reach the result we do here.

Id. at 430-431.

In a concurring opinion, Judge Campbell emphasized that he would not limit the authority of the police to search by reference to the relationship between the person and the premises. According to Judge Campbell:

A search of such objects is neither more nor less intrusive than would be the search of similar objects whose owner, having deposited them, had left the premises before the police arrived. Any search is an invasion of privacy; but I think the cause for issuance of the original warrant allows a search of relevant personal effects not in the possession of their owner as well as of all other relevant objects on the premises. The contraband or incriminating evidence covered by the warrant is as likely to be within the briefcases or bags just brought on the premises as within other objects on the premises. It is true that if the officer knows the owner of the briefcase has no "relationship" to the premises, he might have less reason to search. But in many cases the police would have no way of knowing, in advance, what is the individual's actual connection with the premises. When the stranger in the betting parlor solemnly announces that he is the family doctor, I am less sure than is the court that I would require police to believe him—or inquire further before searching his bag.

Id. at 433 (Campbell, J., concurring).

MARYLAND v. GARRISON*
Supreme Court of the United States
480 *U.S.* 79, 107 *S.Ct.* 1013 (1987)

QUESTION: When, during the course of the execution of a search warrant, the executing officers did not, and could not reasonably know that the warrant's description of the place to be searched was overly broad—being based on the mistaken belief that there was only one apartment on the third floor of the target premises—will that factual mistake retroactively invalidate the warrant when, with the benefit of hindsight, the defendant demonstrates to the reviewing court that the third floor actually consisted of two separate dwelling units ?

ANSWER: NO. The constitutionality of police conduct must be judged "in light of the information available to them at the time they acted." *Id.* at 1017. A search warrant will not be automatically invalidated due "to an officer's reasonable failure to appreciate that a valid warrant describes too broadly the premises to be searched." *Id.* at 1019. The validity of the search of defendant's third-floor "apartment pursuant to a warrant authorizing the search of the entire third floor depends on whether the officers' failure to realize the overbreadth of the warrant was objectively understandable and reasonable. Here, it unquestionably was. The objective facts available to the officers at the time suggested no distinction between [the target] apartment and the third-floor premises." *Id.*

RATIONALE: "Baltimore police officers obtained and executed a warrant to search the person of Lawrence McWebb and 'the premises known as 2036 Park Avenue third floor apartment' for 'Marihuana, related paraphernalia, monies, books, papers, and photographs pertaining to the illegal distribution of Marihuana . . . .' " *Id.* at 1015, 1015 n.1. At the time the officers "applied for the warrant and when they conducted the search pursuant to the warrant, they reasonably believed that there was only one apartment on the premises described in the warrant." *Id.* at 1015. Significantly, the trial court found that "after making a reasonable investigation, including a verification of information obtained from a reliable informant, an exterior examination of the three-story building at 2036 Park Avenue, and an inquiry of the utility company, the officer who obtained the warrant reasonably concluded that there was only one apartment on the third floor and that it was occupied by McWebb." *Id.* at 1015.

Six Baltimore police officers executed the search warrant. When they arrived at 2036 Park Avenue, they encountered McWebb standing in front of the building. The officers used McWebb's "key to gain admittance to the first floor hallway and to the locked door at the top of the stairs to the third floor. As they entered the vestibule on the third floor, they encountered [defendant, Harold Garrison], who was standing in the hallway area. The police could see into the interior of

---

* *See* §2.4(a) for other question raised and answered by this case.

both McWebb's apartment to the left and [Garrison's] to the right, for the doors to both were open. Only after [Garrison's] apartment had been entered and heroin, cash, and drug paraphernalia had been found did any of the officers realize that the third floor contained two apartments." *Id.* Up until that time, all of the officers "reasonably believed that they were searching McWebb's apartment." *Id.* Neither Garrison nor McWebb indicated to the officers during the search that there were two apartments. Moreover, while the search was in progress, one of the officers in Garrison's apartment answered the telephone. "The caller asked for 'Red Cross'; that was the name by which McWebb was known to the confidential informant." *Id.* at 1015 n.2. As soon as the officers became aware of the fact that the third floor consisted of two separate apartments, the search was discontinued. The evidence seized, however, "provided the basis for [Garrison's] conviction for violating Maryland's Controlled Substance Act." *Id.* Defendant now appeals, challenging the seizure of that contraband.

"With the benefit of hindsight, * * * we now know that the description of [the place to be searched] was broader than appropriate because it was based on the mistaken belief that there was only one apartment on the third floor of 2036 Park Avenue." *Id.* at 1017. The question is whether the execution of this search warrant, by officers relying on that description, "violated [Garrison's] right to be secure in his home[.]" *Id.* at 1018.

The Court has "no difficulty concluding that the officers' entry into the third-floor common area was legal; they carried a warrant for those premises, and they were accompanied by McWebb, who provided the key that they used to open the door giving access to the third-floor common area. If the officers had known, or should have known, that the third floor contained two apartments before they entered the living quarters on the third floor, and thus had been aware of the error in the warrant, they would have been obligated to limit their search to McWebb's apartment. Moreover, as the officers recognized, they were required to discontinue the search of [Garrison's] apartment as soon as they discovered that there were two separate units on the third floor and therefore were put on notice of the risk that they might be in a unit erroneously included within the terms of the warrant." *Id.* Consequently, it appears that "[t]he officers' conduct and the limits of the search were based on the information available as the search proceeded." *Id*

"While the purposes justifying a police search strictly limit the permissible extent of the search, the Court has also recognized the need to allow some latitude for honest mistakes that are made by officers in the dangerous and difficult process of making arrests and executing search warrants. * * * In this respect, an officer's reasonable failure to appreciate that a valid warrant describes too broadly the premises to be searched [does not automatically invalidate that warrant]." *Id.* at 1018-1019. Consequently, the validity of the search of Garrison's apartment, which was conducted "pursuant to a warrant authorizing the search of the entire third floor[,] depends on whether the officers' failure to realize the overbreadth of the warrant was objectively understandable and reasonable. Here it unquestionably was. The objective facts available to the officers at the time suggested no distinction between McWebb's apartment and the third-floor premises." *Id.* at 1019.

For these reasons, states the Court, "the officers properly responded to the command contained in a valid warrant even if the warrant is interpreted as authorizing a search limited to McWebb's apartment rather than the entire third floor. Prior to the officers' discovery of the factual mistake, they perceived McWebb's apartment and the third-floor premises as one and the same; therefore their execution of the warrant reasonably included the entire third floor. Under either interpretation of the warrant, the officers' conduct was consistent with a reasonable effort to ascertain and identify the place intended to be searched within the meaning of the Fourth Amendment." *Id.*

UNITED STATES v. CLARK
United States Court of Appeals
531 *F.*2d 928 (8th Cir. 1976)

QUESTION: In the below set of circumstances, did the search of defendant's residence and repair shop exceed the scope of the search warrant ?

CIRCUMSTANCES: On December 19, at approximately 11:00 a.m., criminal investigators from South Dakota executed a search warrant at the residence and repair shop of defendant, James E. Clark. The warrant was designed for, and limited to, the seizure of "controlled dangerous substances." "Clark owned a motorcycle repair shop which was attached to his home, located in a rural area adjacent to the south side of North Sioux City, South Dakota. In conjunction with the search, the investigators executed an arrest warrant for James E. Clark based on unauthorized distribution of controlled substances." *Id.* at 930.

When the officers arrived at defendant's repair shop, they immediately placed him under arrest and began the search. The officers searched the repair shop, the basement and the residence, but no controlled substances were found. The officers then "examined hand-tools, cycle motors and other property located in the shop area of the premises. Serial numbers taken from the inspected property were recorded on clipboards carried by the agents." *Id.*

The officers then conducted a further search of defendant's residence. As serial numbers of his stereo equipment were recorded, defendant was asked whether he had any firearms. He responded "that there were three or four shoulder-type rifles hanging in the living room and a 9-mm. Browning semiautomatic handgun in the nightstand drawer." *Id.* Without defendant's knowledge, one of the officers recorded the serial number of the pistol in the bedroom.

Further investigation into the origin of the handgun revealed possible violations of federal firearms statutes that prohibit the illegal interstate transportation of a firearm and false statements made in connection with the purchase of a firearm. Based on this information, a second search warrant was obtained and the 9-mm. Browning semi-automatic handgun was seized.

ANSWER: YES. "The search of [defendant's] premises * * * went beyond the scope of the search warrant. The search warrant was issued as authorization for a search for controlled substances only," *id.* at 931, and according to the court, the search and seizure conducted pursuant to that warrant "was unreasonable." *Id.* at 930.

RATIONALE: "The Fourth Amendment requires that search warrants particularly describe objects to be seized. This specificity of description requirement furthers the Fourth Amendment's goal of privacy by ensuring that even searches deemed necessary and supported by a magistrate's determination of probable cause should be as limited as possible." *Id.* at 931. Adherence to the requirement that the items to be seized be specifically described guards against any unauthorized " 'general, exploratory rummaging in a person's belongings.' " *Id.* [Citations omitted.]

In this case, the first search of defendant's premises "went beyond the scope of the search warrant. The search warrant was issued as authorization for a search for controlled substances only. Despite this limited authorization, * * * the investigating officers proceeded to inventory a significant quantity of Clark's personal and business property. Serial numbers were methodically taken from motorcycles, tools, and other shop equipment. The agents also recorded serial numbers from Clark's television, stereo equipment, and other personal effects. Moreover, the inspection of [Clark's] personal and business property and the concomitant recordation of serial numbers taken from that property were accomplished without [his] consent. In fact, the recordation of the serial number on the pistol was done without Clark's knowledge." *Id.*

According to the court, "[i]t is beyond dispute that the random recordation of serial numbers from items of personal and business property could not have furthered the officers' ostensible and otherwise legitimate search for controlled substances." *Id.* at 931-932. Consequently, the court concludes that the search conducted pursuant to the first search warrant "was an exploratory search violative of the [defendant's] Fourth Amendment right of privacy." *Id.* at 932.

NOTE

1. The court in *Clark, supra,* rejected the Government's plain view argument, finding that the third requirement of the plain view doctrine had not been met. According to the court, there was nothing in the record to "reveal a sufficient factual basis which would have given the officers reasonable cause to believe the pistol was contraband" or in any way connected with the unauthorized distribution of a controlled substance. *Id.* at 932. Moreover, before the incriminating nature of the handgun became known, it was necessary to turn the serial number over to the Bureau of Alcohol, Tobacco and Firearms for investigation. For a full discussion of the plain view doctrine, *see generally* §4.3, *infra.*

2. *Answering the telephone during warrant execution.* In *United States v. Stiver*, 9 *F*.3d 298 (3rd Cir. 1993), the court rejected the defendant's contention that the police exceeded their authority under the search warrant by answering his telephone, speaking with some of his heroin customers and taking orders from them. The court stated:

> As the Seventh Circuit recently observed, officers executing a search warrant are "required to interpret it," and they are "not obliged to interpret it narrowly." *Hessel v. O'Hearn*, 977 *F*.2d 299, 302 (7th Cir. 1992). Here, * * * the warrant authorized the officers to search for and seize, among other things, "all drug paraphernalia." In ordinary usage, the term "paraphernalia" is defined to mean "equipment [and] apparatus . . . used in or necessary for a particular activity." * * * In light of the fact that the officers had ample cause to believe that the defendant had been using the apartment to make heroin sales, including sales to individuals who wanted the drug for personal use, the officers had an entirely reasonable basis for concluding that the defendant's telephone was a piece of "equipment" or "apparatus" that was "used in or necessary for [the defendant's] particular activity," namely, selling drugs to users and others from his residence. The officers therefore acted properly in "searching" the telephone, *i.e.*, answering it.
>
> We also believe that the officers' conduct was authorized by the portion of the warrant permitting them to search for "[a]ny items to prove residency." Telephone calls for the defendant at the premises would provide evidence that he resided there. Thus, the officers were justified in answering the telephone to obtain evidence regarding the defendant's residence.

Id. at 303. [Citations and footnotes omitted.] *See also United States v. Passarella*, 788 *F*.2d 377, 380-81 (6th Cir. 1986); *United States v. Ordonez*, 737 *F*.2d 793, 810 (9th Cir. 1984); *United States v. Vadino*, 680 *F*.2d 1329, 1335 (11th Cir. 1982), *cert. denied*, 460 *U.S.* 1082, 103 *S.Ct.* 1771 (1983).

UNITED STATES v. FERRERAS
United States Court of Appeals
192 *F*.3d 5 (1st Cir. 1999)

QUESTION: In the below set of circumstances, did the officers' search of defendant's attic exceed the scope of the search warrant ?

CIRCUMSTANCES: On February 19th, at 4:30 p.m., Providence police detectives executed a search warrant at 30 Pekin Street, Providence, Rhode Island. The warrant's supporting affidavit provided that the police had information from a "reliable informant" that Damian Ferreras was "storing and selling cocaine from his apartment located at 30 Pekin Street, 2nd floor apt., and also storing cocaine in the basement." *Id*. at 8. The affidavit described the premises, a three-story tenement house, as a "2 story dwelling and being grey with white trim in color." *Id*. On the face of the warrant, the place and person to be searched were described as: "30 Pekin Street, 2nd floor apartment and basement"; "Damian Ferreras, John Doe, dob-2-21-75." *Id*.

At the house, the detectives stopped Ferreras as he was leaving, seized an electronic pager from him and brought him back to the house. Using a key from Ferreras's key ring, a detective opened the side door of the building, and entered along with the rest of the search warrant team. Just inside the entrance, the detectives found a door, "leading to the cellar and a flight of stairs up to the second floor. At the top of the stairs was a door with a lock. The door opened into a small hallway on the second floor, and was closed but not locked." *Id*. at 8. To the right of the stairway door "was a locked door which the police opened with a key from Ferreras's key ring. Through this door, the police entered living quarters on the second floor * * *. About eight feet across the vestibule from the door to the second floor living quarters another set of steps led to the attic. There was no door at the bottom, or at the top of the steps from the second floor hallway to the attic." *Id*.

"In the attic the police saw a hall with three rooms in a row on the left-hand side. These rooms appeared to have been recently constructed and not part of the original building. The first room's door was closed and locked and a detective opened it with another key from Ferreras's key ring. Inside was a box-spring and mattress and a closet full of a man's clothes," *id*., including a pair of high leather boots. The detective reached inside one of the boots and discovered a clear plastic bag containing over 100 grams of crack and $1,750 in cash. The room also had a television set with a cable leading through a hole in the floor to the second story. "Searching the room further, the detective found, in a frame for a stereo speaker, an electronic digital scale of a type commonly used to weigh narcotics. On top of the frame the detective found several pieces of personal paperwork bearing the name of Damian Ferreras, including recent court documents." *Id*. at 7.

"The second room also had a bed and appeared to have been lived in. The third one had only a mattress. The right-hand side of the hallway was divided into two unfinished rooms which were still under construction and revealed plaster, sheetrock, tools, dirty floors, and in one room a metal can of urine. There was no sink, shower, bathtub, kitchen, refrigerator, stove, or pantry, and no running water anywhere in the attic. There was a space heater in one of the attic rooms. The only access to the attic was via the set of steps from the small hallway on the second floor. A detective examined the electric meters on the exterior of the building and found that one was for the first floor apartment, and the other for the second floor. There was none for the attic." *Id.* at 8-9.

Based on their discoveries, the detectives placed Ferreras under arrest.

ANSWER: NO. "Given that: (1) the attic was open to the second floor, but not to the street or the first floor apartment; (2) the third floor was not equipped for independent living; and (3) the occupant of the third floor had access to the second floor kitchen and bathroom," the detectives reasonably concluded that the two floors within the premises were "all one apartment," and that the search warrant for the second floor apartment included "the half story above it." *Id.* at 11.

RATIONALE: As a general matter, "[t]he authority to search granted by any warrant is limited to the specific places described in it, and does not extend to additional or different places." *Id.* The court held, however, that the attic at 30 Pekin Street was not an "additional or different place." The court said:

> * * * the search of the attic at 30 Pekin Street must be reasonably considered part of the area intended to be searched.
>
> When one reached the second floor apartment at 30 Pekin Street, there was a door with a lock (although at the time of the search, the door was closed but not locked). The door opened into a small hallway on the second floor. In this hallway, about eight feet across the vestibule from the door to the second floor living quarters, another set of steps led to the attic. There was no door at either the bottom or the top of the steps securing access to the attic.
>
> It is clear from the evidence that the attic was not independent from the second floor living quarters. Cable television was supplied to the attic by a cable through a hole in the floor to the second story. While three of the rooms in the attic had either a mattress or a bed, two rooms in the attic were unfinished and contained sheetrock, tools, dirty floors, and a metal can of urine. There was no sink, shower, bathtub, kitchen, refrigerator, stove, food, or running water in the attic. While there was an electric meter for the first floor, and one for the second floor, there was none for the attic.

Id. at 10-11.

"Given that: (1) the attic was open to the second floor, but not to the street or the first floor apartment; (2) the third floor was not equipped for independent living; and (3) the occupant of the third floor had access to the second floor kitchen and bathroom," the court concluded that "the two floors were all one apartment," and the search warrant for the second floor apartment included the half story above it[.]" *Id.* at 11.

---

§2.5(d). Search warrant return.

To fully "execute" a search warrant, there are a number of procedures that must be followed after completion of the search. First, *Fed.R.Crim.P.* 41(f)(1) requires the officer executing the warrant to "enter on its face the exact date and time it is executed." Next, the officer executing the warrant must "give a copy of the warrant and a receipt for the property taken to the person from whom, or from whose premises, the property was taken." *Rule* 41(f)(3). If no one is present at the time, the officer should leave a copy of the warrant and receipt for any property seized in a conspicuous location within the premises. *Id.*

If property is seized by the officers executing the search warrant, an inventory of that property must be made. The inventory serves the purpose of assuring that all items seized are within the contemplated scope of the warrant and are accounted for in the return to the issuing authority. For efficiency, the written receipt, which is made for the personal records of the property owner or custodian, should be sufficiently detailed so that its contents may also serve as the formal written inventory.

Rule 41(f)(2) requires that an officer (any officer) "present during the execution of the warrant must prepare and verify an inventory of any property seized. The officer must do so in the presence of another officer and the person from whom, or from whose premises, the property was taken. If either one is not present, the officer must prepare and verify the inventory in the presence of at least one other credible person." *Rule* 41(f)(2). Ideally, the officer should have the property owner, or other person who is present at the time of the search, sign the receipt/inventory acknowledging the removal of the property from the premises. If the person refuses to sign the receipt/inventory form, that fact should be noted on the form and in the officer's formal report.

Next, *Rule* 41(f)(4) mandates that the officer executing the warrant "must promptly return it—together with a copy of the inventory—to the magistrate judge designated on the warrant." In effect, this means that the officer who executed the warrant must, immediately after the search, return to the federal magistrate judge who issued the warrant and file with that judge the original search warrant, the original receipt/inventory, and the search warrant return form. This step should be followed even if no property is seized. Thereafter, upon request, the issuing judge will "give a copy of the inventory to the person from whom, or from whose premises, the property was taken and to the applicant for the warrant." *Id.*

The final step in the process requires the federal magistrate judge, "to whom the warrant is returned," to "attach to the warrant a copy of the return, of the inventory, and of all other related papers and [] deliver them to the clerk in the district where the property was seized." *Rule* 41(i).

Any person "aggrieved by an unlawful search and seizure of property or by the deprivation of property may move for the property's return. The motion must be filed in the district where the property was seized." *Rule* 41(g).

NOTE

Police need not inform owner of the procedures for property return. When law enforcement officers seize property under the authority of a search warrant, "due process requires them to take reasonable steps to give notice that the property has been taken so that the owner can pursue available remedies for its return." *City of West Covina v. Perkins*, 525 *U.S.* 234, 119 *S.Ct.* 678, 681 (1999). Moreover, when the owner of the property is not present at the time of the search, such individualized notice that law enforcement officials have taken property is necessary "because the property owner would have no other reasonable means of ascertaining who was responsible for his loss." *Id.*, 119 *S.Ct.* at 681. There is no requirement, however, that officers inform the property owner of the procedures for seeking return of the seized property. As emphasized by the United States Supreme Court in *Perkins*, the Due Process Clause does not require law enforcement officials "to give detailed and specific instructions or advice to owners who seek return of property lawfully seized but no longer needed for police investigation or criminal prosecution." *Id.* at 679. Once the property owner is informed that his property has been seized, he or she can turn to published statutes, court rules, or case law to learn about the remedial procedures available for property return. *Id.* at 681-82. *See e.g., Rule* 41(e)(e) (Motion for Return of Property).

---

§2.6. Telephonic search warrants.

UNITED STATES v. TURNER
United States Court of Appeals
558 *F*.2d 46 (2nd Cir. 1977)

QUESTION: Does the "long-distance" swearing which takes place during the acquisition of a telephonic search warrant violate the Fourth Amendment's requirement that the warrant be "supported by Oath or affirmation"?

ANSWER: NO. "In the one hundred years since Alexander Graham Bell invented the telephone, Long Distance has truly become, in the words of the advertisement, 'the next best thing to being there.' The Fourth Amendment is sufficiently flexible to account for such technological advances." *Id.* at 50.

RATIONALE: "In a ritualistic sense, it may be that an oath taken over the telephone appears less formal or less solemn than one taken in the physical presence of the oath taker. The constitutionality of oaths does not depend, however, on such purely ritualistic considerations." *Id.* at 50. Consequently, defendant's argument—"that for constitutional purposes an oath or affirmation is invalid merely because it is taken over the telephone"—must be rejected. *Id.* "The moral, religious and legal significance of the undertaking remains the same whether the oath taker and the witness communicate face-to-face or over the telephone." *Id.*

Significantly, the court finds "no suggestion in this case that the use of the telephone was designed to hide the identity of the affiants, * * * or that the Fourth Amendment 'Oath or affirmation' requirement was 'cavalierly brushed aside as an empty formality[.]' " *Id.* at 50-51 (quoting *Dow v. Baird*, 389 *F*.2d 882, 884 (10th Cir. 1968)).

Accordingly, this court holds "that search warrant application procedures can constitutionally be brought into line with twentieth century technology." *Id.* at 50.

NOTE

1. Most states have provisions in place for law enforcement officers to resort when faced with circumstances of exigency sufficient to forego the traditional written warrant. Whether by rule or statute, these provisions delineate specific procedures for the acquisition of a search warrant over the telephone.

2. At the federal level, *Rules* 41(d)(3) and 41(e)(3) are illustrative:

Rule 41(d)(3). Requesting a Warrant by Telephonic or Other Means.

(A) In General. A magistrate judge may issue a warrant based on information communicated by telephone or other appropriate means, including facsimile transmission.

(B) Recording Testimony. Upon learning that an applicant is requesting a warrant, a magistrate judge must:

>   **(i)** place under oath the applicant and any person on whose testimony the application is based; and

>   **(ii)** make a verbatim record of the conversation with a suitable recording device, if available, or by a court reporter, or in writing.

(C) Certifying Testimony. The magistrate judge must have any recording or court reporter's notes transcribed, certify the transcription's accuracy, and file a copy of the record and the transcription with the clerk. Any written verbatim record must be signed by the magistrate judge and filed with the clerk.

(D) Suppression Limited. Absent a finding of bad faith, evidence obtained from a warrant issued under Rule 41(d)(3)(A) is not subject to suppression on the ground that issuing the warrant in that manner was unreasonable under the circumstances.

* * * *

Rule 41(e)(3). Warrant by Telephonic or Other Means. If a magistrate judge decides to proceed under Rule 41(d)(3)(A), the following additional procedures apply:

(A) Preparing a Proposed Duplicate Original Warrant. The applicant must prepare a "proposed duplicate original warrant" and must read or otherwise transmit the contents of that document verbatim to the magistrate judge.

(B) Preparing an Original Warrant. The magistrate judge must enter the contents of the proposed duplicate original warrant into an original warrant.

(C) Modifications. The magistrate judge may direct the applicant to modify the proposed duplicate original warrant. In that case, the judge must also modify the original warrant.

(D) Signing the Original Warrant and the Duplicate Original Warrant. Upon determining to issue the warrant, the magistrate judge must immediately sign the original warrant, enter on its face the exact time it is issued, and direct the applicant to sign the judge's name on the duplicate original warrant.

As with the procedures attached to the traditional search warrant, the officer executing the telephonic warrant must "enter on its face the exact date and time it is executed." *Rule* 41(f)(1).

---

a. Congressional intent.

(1) In *United States v. Cuaron*, 700 *F*.2d 582, 588 (10th Cir. 1983), the court pointed out that the legislative history of Rule 41(c)(2) "demonstrates that Congress intended to encourage police to procure telephone warrants where 'the existence of exigent circumstances is a close question and the police might otherwise conduct a warrantless search.'" [Citations omitted.]

(2) In 1993, *Rule* 41(c)(2)(A) [now 41(d)(3)(A), as a result of the 2002 rule amendments] was amended in recognition of the "value of, and the public's increased dependence on facsimile machines to transmit written information efficiently and accurately. As amended, the Rule should thus encourage law enforcement officers to seek a warrant, especially when it is necessary, or desirable, to supplement oral telephonic communications by written materials which may now be transmitted electronically as well." *1993 Advisory Committee Note.* The Committee rejected, however, amendments to the Rule which "would have permitted other means of electronic transmission, such as the use of computer modems. In its view, facsimile transmissions provide some method of assuring the authenticity of the writing transmitted by the affiant." *Id.*

b. Time required to obtain telephonic warrant.

(1) In *United States v. Cattouse*, 846 *F*.2d 144 (2nd Cir. 1988), the defendant argued that the DEA agents should have secured a telephonic search warrant prior to effecting their warrantless, nonconsensual entry into his home, pointing out that the twenty minutes which had elapsed between the time the agents developed their probable cause and the time of his arrest was ample time in which to secure a telephonic warrant. Rejecting defendant's contentions, the court explained that

> even under the procedure for issuance of a warrant by telephone, "a reasonable period of time, surely most often longer than twenty minutes, must be allowed for reaching a magistrate," *United States v. Gallo-Roman*, 816 *F*.2d 76, 81 (2nd Cir. 1987), as well as time to prepare the duplicate original warrant and read the information to the magistrate, and time for the magistrate carefully to consider the application. [Consequently,] "twenty minutes is

hardly a sufficient period of time in which to effectuate the procedures contemplated by Rule 41." 816 *F*.2d at 81.

Cattouse at 147-148.

See also United States v. Lindsey, 877 *F*.2d 777 (9th Cir. 1989),
where the court held that the warrantless entry into defendant's home
after the police delayed one hour for the purpose of waiting for
backup—in the face of the possibility that "guns and bombs" were in
the target premises—was constitutionally valid. Here, this court also
observed that "obtaining a telephonic warrant is not a simple procedure." *Id*. at 782 (citing *United States v. Good*, 780 *F*.2d 773, 775 (9th
Cir.), *cert. denied*, 475 *U.S.* 1111, 106 *S.Ct.* 1523 (1986)). " 'A telephonic warrant may not be obtained simply by calling a magistrate.
Among other things, a "duplicate original warrant" must be prepared
in writing and read to the magistrate verbatim.' " *Id*. (quoting *United
States v. Manfredi*, 722 *F*.2d 519, 523 (9th Cir. 1983)).

*(2) Contacting an Assistant United States Attorney before seek-
ing a telephonic warrant.* In *United States v. Ogbuh*, 928 *F*.2d 1000
(6th Cir. 1993), government agents conducted a warrantless search of
the defendant's hotel room, based on probable cause and the belief that
there was no time to secure a telephonic warrant. According to one of
the agents, it would have taken from forty-five minutes to an hour to
obtain the telephonic warrant, particularly with the requirement in this
jurisdiction that an Assistant United States Attorney be contacted prior
to calling a magistrate for such a warrant.

Finding error in the failure to secure a telephonic warrant, the
court stated:

> As has frequently been pointed out in the cases on exigent cir-
> cumstances, * * * the government may not erect a system of proce-
> dural delay and then use it as an excuse for not obtaining a war-
> rant. That is what happened in th[is] case * * *. First, it is not
> clear that an hour would have been required to obtain the warrant
> by telephone had reasonable procedures been used. Delay due to any
> difficulty in locating an Assistant U.S. Attorney to approve the war-
> rant request does not excuse abrogation of the requirements of the
> Fourth Amendment. [*Fed.R.Crim.Pro.* 41] does not require any
> such conversation with an Assistant U.S. Attorney. U.S. Attorneys
> should set up a system for fast action if this step is required. While
> such a policy may be desirable to help ensure that only worthy
> cases are brought to the attention of magistrates, the added costs
> of the policy in terms of delay may not be used as a justification for
> sidestepping entirely the warrant requirement under the rubric of
> "exigent circumstances."
>
> * * * The question is one of motivation and incentive. If police have
> little incentive to obtain a warrant, they will not do so. The law
> must provide that incentive; otherwise, the warrant requirement
> of the Fourth Amendment will become a dead letter.

Id. at 1004.

c. Application & the duplicate original warrant. In *United States v. Shorter*, 600 *F.*2d 585 (6th Cir. 1979), Judge Merritt discussed the *Fed.R.Crim.P.* 41(c)(2)(B) requirement that an officer who requests a telephonic search warrant "shall prepare a document to be known as a *duplicate original warrant* and shall read such duplicate original warrant, verbatim, to the federal magistrate." According to Judge Merritt:

> The rule requires the federal magistrate on the other end of the line to have before him from the beginning the "original warrant" and to "enter, verbatim, what is so read to such magistrate on a document to be known as the original warrant."
>
> After the officer on one end of the line gives the information from the warrant to the magistrate on the other end, the magistrate must then decide whether the oral information given is sufficient to permit the search, now precisely described on the "original warrant." If the magistrate decides to issue the warrant, the procedure is for him to direct "the person requesting the warrant to sign the federal magistrate's name on the duplicate original warrant" and for the federal magistrate then to "immediately sign the original warrant and enter on the face of the original warrant the exact time when the warrant was ordered to be issued." * * *
>
> The correct handling of the "duplicate original warrant" and the "original warrant" is * * * crucial * * *. The "duplicate original warrant" process is important because it requires the officer to write down, and therefore deliberate and consider in advance, the precise nature of the search to be undertaken. *He may not simply pick up the telephone and call the magistrate. He must first get out a pencil and paper, consider his actions, and write down the scope of the search with sufficient particularity for the magistrate to know what he is authorizing.* * * * The purpose of such a requirement is to slow down the process and to require actors to deliberate before they act. * * *

Id. at 589-590 (Merritt, J., concurring). [Emphasis added.]

d. Unrecorded preliminary conversations with the magistrate. In *United States v. Rome*, 809 *F.*2d 665 (10th Cir. 1987), two F.B.I. agents discussed some of the facts of a prospective search in several unrecorded telephone calls with a federal magistrate. The last call culminated in recorded testimony which formed the basis of a telephonic search warrant for defendant's residence. Significantly, when the federal magistrate recorded the conversation that formed the basis for the warrant, some of the information which had been discussed in earlier calls had not been reiterated. Moreover, at the time of the recorded telephone call, the agent did not have access to a duplicate original warrant form. He therefore read a "rough draft" of his affidavit to the magistrate, which the agent later reorganized but did not change substantively. Later review indicated several variations between the contents of the affidavit and the contents of the original and duplicate original search warrants. Thus, the requirements that the affidavit (duplicate original warrant) be read, verbatim, to the magistrate, and that the information contained in the original warrant be the same as the information contained in the affidavit, were also not met.

The issue before the court, therefore, was whether those "violations of *R.* 41(c)(2) [we]re of a magnitude sufficient to invalidate the search conducted pursuant to the rule." *Rome* at 667. Listing the above and additional violations, the court pointed out that the federal magistrate:

> (1) participat[ed] in one or more unrecorded telephone conversations in which this search was discussed; (2) authoriz[ed] a search when he knew or should have known that [the agent] was not reading, *verbatim*, from a duplicate original search warrant as required[;] * * * (4) fail[ed] to record, verbatim, what [the agent] read to him by way of affidavit onto the original warrant; and (5) fail[ed] to "immediately" sign the original warrant.

Id. at 668. [Emphasis in original.] According to the court, the above-listed "violations of Rule 41(c)(2) stem from the fact that neither [the m]agistrate nor [the F.B.I. agent] were familiar with all the requirements of the rule and neither of them had a copy of it in his possession." *Id.*

Nonetheless, none of the violations, concluded the court, "suggest[s] an absence of good faith" on the part of either the federal magistrate or the federal agent. *Id.* at 558.

> Although we believe that F.B.I. agents should be prepared for exigencies of this type when they are in the field, such lack of preparation does not constitute bad faith. With respect to [the magistrate's] conduct, we hold he was not abandoning his detached and neutral function[.]
>
> [While we] conclude that in [this] case, the violations of Rule 41(c)(2) were harmless[,] * * * [w]e do not condone careless police work and lack of preparation, nor do we hold that the failure to understand the rules governing their conduct will excuse law enforcement officers from compliance therewith. We simply hold that in this case * * * [e]xclusion of the evidence obtained in the search of Rome's residence would not best serve the "remedial objectives" of the exclusionary rule[.] * * * [I]n this case the violations of Rule 41(c)(2) were not egregious enough to warrant the extreme sanction of exclusion.

Id. at 668, 670-671.

   e. The requirement of the "immediate" oath. In *United States v. Stefanson,* 648 *F.*2d 1231 (9th Cir. 1981), the defendant argued that the process by which the telephonic search warrant was secured violated *R.* 41(c)(2) because the federal magistrate failed to place the A.T.F. agent under oath *before* accepting testimony from him. Rejecting defendant's "technical reading of th[e] rule," the court held that the procedure in this case—placing the agent under oath *after* the receipt of his testimony—constituted neither a "deliberate nor prejudicial" violation of *R.* 41(c)(2). Since the violation was "only technical" in nature, and "since the warrant was supported by an oath of the affiant," the court concluded that "the Fourth Amendment warrant requirement was substantially satisfied." *Id.* at 1235.

See also United States v. Turner, 926 *F*.2d 883 (9th Cir. 1991), where the court upheld the validity of an oath given after the officer provided the state judge with the supporting facts. Adopting the approach set forth in *United States v. Stefanson, supra*, the court held that noncompliance with subparagraph (D) of *R.* 41(c)(2) "results in suppression only when (1) the noncompliance clearly violates the federal constitution, (2) 'there was "prejudice" in the sense that the search might not have occurred or would not have been so abrasive if the rule had been followed,' " or "(3) 'there is evidence of intentional and deliberate disregard of a provision in the Rule.' " *Id.* at 886 (quoting *Stefanson* at 1235). According to the *Turner* court, "[m]erely failing to place the affiant under oath until after she had recited the supporting facts did not invalidate the warrant." *Id.*

Cf. Campbell v. Minnesota, 553 *F*.2d 40 (7th Cir. 1977), where the court upheld the validity of an oath given at the conclusion of an officer's testimony which was used to supplement a written application for a search warrant. In *Campbell*, the judge administered the oath after the officer had given the additional oral information, but before the warrant was signed, and the officer understood that the oath pertained to both the oral statements and written affidavit in support of the search warrant. According to the court, the "oral statements would be considered sworn testimony since the officer[] understood the oath to relate back to them." *Id.* at 42. *See also Frazier v. Roberts*, 441 *F*.2d 1224, 1228 (8th Cir. 1971).

But see United States v. Shorter, 600 *F*.2d 585 (6th Cir. 1979), where the court determined that "Congress clearly intended the oath to be administered *in advance* of the testimony given where face-to-face confrontation between witness and magistrate was impossible." *Id.* at 588. According to the *Shorter* court, "[t]he congressional purpose was doubtless to impress on the telephone caller the solemnity of the proceeding in spite of the lack of formal appearance before a court." *Id.* The court concluded, therefore, that "the command of *Fed.R.Crim.P.* 41(c)(2)(D) speaks more of substance than procedure and must be obeyed." *Shorter* at 589.

f. Suppression of evidence. Senate Report No. 95-354 provides that "subparagraph (c)(2)(G) makes it clear that, absent a finding of bad faith by the government, the magistrate's judgment that the circumstances made it reasonable to dispense with a written affidavit—a decision that does not go to the core question of whether there was probable cause to issue a warrant—is not a ground for granting a motion to suppress evidence." S.Rep.No. 95-354, 95th Cong., 1st Sess. 1, 11, reprinted in [1977] *U.S.Code Cong. & Admin.News*, pp. 527, 535.

Respecting the suppression of evidence for *R.* 41 violations generally, *see United States v. Stefanson*, 648 *F*.2d 1231 (9th Cir. 1981), where the court declared:

[U]nless a clear constitutional violation occurs, noncompliance with Rule 41 requires suppression of evidence only where, "(1) there was 'prejudice' in the sense that the search might not have occurred or would not have been so abrasive if the rule had been followed, or (2) there is evidence of intentional and deliberate disregard of a provision in the Rule."

Id. at 1235 (quoting *United States v. Radlick*, 581 *F.*2d 225, 228 (9th Cir. 1978). *Accord United States v. Rome*, 809 *F.*2d 665, 669 (10th Cir. 1987); *United States v. Comstock*, 805 *F.*2d 1194, 1206 (5th Cir. 1986); *United States v. Loyd*, 721 *F.*2d 331, 333 (11th Cir. 1983); *United States v. Mendel*, 578 *F.*2d 668, 673-674 (7th Cir.), *cert. denied*, 439 *U.S.* 964, 99 *S.Ct.*, 450 (1978); *United States v. Gitcho*, 601 *F.*2d 369, 372 (8th Cir.), *cert. denied*, 444 *U.S.* 871, 100 *S.Ct.* 148 (1978). Thus, in the absence of either bad-faith conduct, or a deliberate or prejudicial violation of *R.* 41, mere "technical" violations should not lead to suppression of evidence so long as the core requirements of the Fourth Amendment have been satisfied.

CHAPTER 3

EXCEPTIONS TO THE WRITTEN WARRANT REQUIREMENT

§3.1. Introduction.

As an established principle of contemporary criminal procedure, searches and seizures conducted without a written warrant are *"per se* unreasonable within the meaning of the Fourth Amendment," *United States v. Place*, 462 *U.S.* 696, 701, 103 *S.Ct.* 2637, 2641 (1983), unless they fall within one of the recognized exceptions to the Fourth Amendment's written warrant requirement. *See e.g., Thompson v. Louisiana*, 469 *U.S.* 17, 105 *S.Ct.* 409, 411 (1984); *Mincey v. Arizona*, 437 *U.S.* 385, 98 *S.Ct.* 2408, 2412 (1978); *United States v. Edwards*, 415 *U.S.* 800, 802, 94 *S.Ct.* 1234, 1236 (1974). There is a strong judicial preference for the acquisition of a search warrant by a law enforcement officer prior to intruding into an individual's realm of privacy, and this requirement is not to be dispensed with lightly. Significantly, once a search or seizure is conducted without a warrant, the burden is upon the Government, as the party seeking to validate the warrantless search, to bring it clearly within one of the recognized exceptions created by the United States Supreme Court.

The rule demonstrates the desirability of placing a judge's probable cause determination, and assessment of whether the circumstances are exigent (where applicable), between the law enforcement officer and the victim of the search or seizure, to provide the necessary security against unreasonable intrusions into an individual's right to privacy.

The Constitution does not, however, prohibit all warrantless searches or seizures; the Constitution only " 'forbids * * * unreasonable searches and seizures.' " *Terry v. Ohio*, 392 *U.S.* 1, 9, 88 *S.Ct.* 1868, 1873 (1968) (quoting *Elkins v. United States*, 364 *U.S.* 206, 222, 80 *S.Ct.* 1437, 1446 (1960)). Thus, over the course of time, the United States Supreme Court has carved out of the Fourth Amendment several carefully tailored exceptions to its warrant requirement. Those formally recognized include: (1) searches conducted as an incident to a lawful arrest; (2) probable-cause based searches conducted in the face of exigent circumstances; (3) searches of motor vehicles based on probable cause; (4) searches conducted for the purpose of cataloging a person's property through established inventory procedures; (5) searches conducted pursuant to a valid consent; and those law enforcement activities which are not considered "searches" within the meaning of the Constitution, either because the property in question is situated in the (6) open fields, or has been (7) abandoned, or the areas of concern are within (8) plain view.

The following materials discuss each of the judicially recognized exceptions to the written warrant requirement and explore the impact each has on law enforcement.

---

§3.2. Search incident to a lawful arrest.

§3.2(a). The person of the arrestee and the area within his immediate control.

When a law enforcement officer effects a lawful custodial arrest based on probable cause, he or she is permitted to conduct a contemporaneous search of the person of the arrestee. Such a search safeguards the arresting officer and others nearby from harm while ensuring that the arrestee will not discard or destroy evidence.

Before a search incident to an arrest may be deemed valid, however, the arrest itself must be lawful. An officer may not justify an arrest by the search and at the same time justify the search by the arrest. *Johnson v. United States*, 333 *U.S.* 10, 16-17, 68 *S.Ct.* 367, 370 (1948). In this respect, if an officer makes an unlawful arrest, any evidence seized during the search incident to that arrest will be inadmissible in court. Thus, the propriety of the incident search depends upon the validity of the arrest.

An incident search of an individual's person may not, therefore, be undertaken for the purpose of gathering evidential justification for that individual's arrest. Even if the desired evidence is found on the individual's person, an arrest thereafter will not be valid in the absence of probable cause for the arrest based on information separate and distinct from that which the search of the person disclosed. As the Supreme Court stated in *Sibron v. New York*, 392 *U.S.* 40, 63, 88 *S.Ct.* 1889, 1902 (1968): "It is axiomatic that an incident search may not precede an arrest and serve as part of its justification." *See also Smith v. Ohio*, 494 *U.S.* 541, 110 *S.Ct.* 1288, 1290 (1990) (The exception for searches incident to arrest "does not permit the police to search any citizen without a warrant or probable cause so long as an arrest immediately follows.").

It has been held, however, that so long as probable cause for an arrest exists prior to the undertaking of any search of the prospective arrestee's person, it does not matter whether the search immediately precedes the formal arrest. As the United States Supreme Court explained in *Rawlings v. Kentucky*, 448 *U.S.* 89, 111, 100 *S.Ct.* 2556, 2564-65 (1980), "where the formal arrest followed quickly on the heels of the challenged search of [an individual's] person, we do not believe it particularly important that the search preceded the arrest rather than vice versa," so long as what the search disclosed was "not necessary to support probable cause to arrest." In these circumstances, if the arrest is lawful—apart from the search or what the search disclosed—and if the arrest and the search occurred as continuous steps in a single, integrated transaction, then the evidence disclosed by the search should not be lost merely because, in the precise sequence of events, the search preceded the arrest.

There is no requirement that the probable cause justifying the lawful custodial arrest, and therefore a search incident to that arrest, be "for the charge eventually prosecuted." *United States v. Bizier*, 111 *F.*3d 214, 218 (1st Cir. 1997). "Probable cause need only exist as to any offense that *could be charged* under the circumstances." *Barna v. City of Perth Amboy*, 42 *F.*3d 809, 819 (3rd Cir. 1994). [Emphasis added.] This means that an officer with probable cause to believe a person has committed *any offense justifying a full custodial arrest* has the authority to conduct a search incident to that arrest.

Once an individual has been lawfully arrested, not only may the police conduct a full search of the individual's person but they may also conduct a search of the area within that person's immediate control. This rule was pronounced by the United States Supreme Court in *Chimel v. California*, 395 *U.S.* 752, 89 *S.Ct.* 2034 (1969), where it was held that a valid custodial arrest creates the circumstance which justifies the contemporaneous warrantless search of the person arrested and of the immediately surrounding area. According to the Court, such searches have long been considered valid because of the law enforcement need "to remove any weapons that [the arrestee] might seek to use in order to resist arrest or effect his escape" and the need to prevent the destruction or concealment of evidence. *Id.* at 763, 89 *S.Ct.* at 2040. These underlying reasons need not, however, be litigated in every case. *See New York v. Belton*, 453 *U.S.* 454, 460-61, 101 *S.Ct.* 2860, 2864 (1981); *United States v. Robinson*, 414 *U.S.* 218, 235, 94 *S.Ct.* 467, 476 (1973).

CHIMEL v. CALIFORNIA
Supreme Court of the United States
395 *U.S.* 752, 89 *S.Ct.* 2034 (1969)

QUESTION: Under the Fourth Amendment, what is the permissible scope of a search incident to a lawful arrest ?

ANSWER: "When an arrest is made, it is reasonable for the arresting officer to search the person arrested in order to remove any weapons that the [arrestee] might seek to use in order to resist arrest or effect his escape. Otherwise, the officer's safety might well be endangered, and the arrest itself frustrated. In addition, it is entirely reasonable for the arresting officer to search for and seize any evidence on the arrestee's person in order to prevent its concealment or destruction. And the area into which an arrestee might reach in order to grab a weapon or evidentiary items must, of course, be governed by a like rule. A gun on a table or in a drawer in front of one who is arrested can be as dangerous to the arresting officer as one concealed in the clothing of the person arrested. There is ample justification, therefore, for a search of the arrestee's person and the area 'within his immediate control'—construing that phrase to mean the area from within which he might gain possession of a weapon or destructible evidence." *Id.* at 2040.

RATIONALE: In the middle of September, late one afternoon, three police officers arrived at defendant's Santa Ana, California, home with a warrant authorizing his arrest for the burglary of a coin shop. "The officers knocked on the door, identified themselves to [defendant's] wife, and asked if they might come inside. She ushered them into the house, where they waited 10 or 15 minutes until [defendant] returned home from work. When [defendant] entered the house, one of the officers handed him the arrest warrant and asked for permission to 'look around.' [Defendant] objected, but was advised that 'on the basis of the lawful arrest,' the officers would nonetheless conduct a search." *Id.* at 2035.

Accompanied by defendant's wife, "the officers then looked through the entire three-bedroom house, including the attic, the garage, and a small workshop. In some rooms the search was relatively cursory. In the master bedroom and sewing room, however, the officers directed [defendant's] wife to open drawers and 'to physically move contents of the drawers from side to side so that [they] might view any items that would have come from [the] burglary.' After completing the search, they seized numerous items—primarily coins, but also several medals, tokens, and a few other objects. The entire search took between 45 minutes and an hour." *Id.*

The critical question in this appeal was whether the warrantless search of defendant's entire house was constitutionally justified as an incident to his arrest. *The Court held that it was not.*

The right of the police to conduct a warrantless search incident to a lawful arrest was first articulated by the Court in 1914 in *Weeks v. United States*, 232 *U.S.* 383, 34 *S.Ct.* 341, in which the Court stated:

What then is the present case? Before answering that inquiry specifically, it may be well by a process of exclusion to state what it is not. It is not an assertion of the right on the part of the Government, always recognized under English and American law, to search the person of the accused when legally arrested to discover and seize the fruits or evidences of crime.

Id. at 2036 (quoting *Weeks* at 392, 34 *S.Ct.* at 344).

Here, in *Chimel,* the Court determined that, as a permissible incident of a lawful arrest, the police may not only search the person of the arrestee, but also the area within the arrestee's immediate control, meaning, the area within his reach. Writing for the Court, Justice Stewart held:

> When an arrest is made, it is reasonable for the arresting officer to search the person arrested in order to remove any weapons that the [arrestee] might seek to use in order to resist arrest or effect his escape. Otherwise, the officer's safety might well be endangered, and the arrest itself frustrated. In addition, it is entirely reasonable for the arresting officer to search for and seize any evidence on the arrestee's person in order to prevent its concealment or destruction. And the area into which an arrestee might reach in order to grab a weapon or evidentiary items must, of course, be governed by a like rule. A gun on a table or in a drawer in front of one who is arrested can be as dangerous to the arresting officer as one concealed in the clothing of the person arrested. *There is ample justification, therefore, for a search of the arrestee's person and the area "within his immediate control"—construing that phrase to mean the area from within which he might gain possession of a weapon or destructible evidence.*

* * * *

There is no comparable justification, however, for routinely searching any room other than that in which an arrest occurs—or, for that matter, for searching through all the desk drawers or other closed or concealed areas in that room itself. Such searches, in the absence of well-recognized exceptions, may be made only under the authority of a search warrant. The "adherence to judicial processes" mandated by the Fourth Amendment requires no less.

This is the principle that underlay our decision in *Preston v. United States,* 376 *U.S.* 364. In that case three men had been arrested in a parked car, which had later been towed to a garage and searched by police. We held the search to have been unlawful under the Fourth Amendment, despite the contention that it had been incidental to a valid arrest. Our reasoning was straightforward:

> The rule allowing contemporaneous searches is justified, for example, by the need to seize weapons and other things

which might be used to assault an officer or effect an escape, as well as by the need to prevent the destruction of evidence of the crime—things which might easily happen where the weapon or evidence is on the accused's person or under his immediate control. But these justifications are absent where a search is remote in time or place from the arrest.

Id. at 2040-41. (quoting *Preston* at 367). [Emphasis added.]

Applying the principles set forth above to the facts of this case, the Court determined that the search here went far beyond the defendant's "person and the area from within which he might have obtained either a weapon or something that could have been used as evidence against him. There was no constitutional justification, in the absence of a search warrant, for extending the search beyond that area. The scope of the search was, therefore, 'unreasonable' under the Fourth and Fourteenth Amendments[.]" *Id.* at 2042.

NOTE

1. In *Vale v. Louisiana*, 399 *U.S.* 30, 90 *S.Ct.* 1969 (1970), the Court re-emphasized that "[a] search may be incident to an arrest 'only if it is substantially contemporaneous with the arrest and is confined to the *immediate* vicinity of the arrest.'" *Id.* at 1971. [Citations omitted; emphasis added.] Donald Vale was arrested on the steps leading to his home. Incident to the arrest, a search was conducted inside Vale's home, and a quantity of narcotics was found in the rear bedroom. Finding the search unlawful, the Court stated: "If a search of a house is to be upheld as incident to an arrest, that arrest must take place *inside the house*, * * * not somewhere outside—whether two blocks away, * * * twenty feet away, * * * or on the sidewalk near the front steps." *Id.* [Citations omitted; emphasis added.] Naturally, even if the arrest does take place inside the house, the search incident to the arrest must be confined to the area within the arrestee's "immediate control." *See Chimel, supra.*

2. In *United States v. Abdul-Saboor*, 85 *F.*3d 664 (D.C.Cir. 1996), two deputy U.S. Marshals went to Abdul-Saboor's (defendant's) apartment to arrest him on a bench warrant. Defendant, who opened the door wearing a bathrobe, asked and was permitted to get dressed before leaving the apartment. As he entered his bedroom, which was dark except for the glow of a television set, defendant stealthily picked up a loaded .45 caliber handgun from the television table and tried to hide it in front of his body. Deputy Parker saw the maneuver, drew his weapon and ordered defendant to drop the gun—which defendant did not do until the officer threatened to shoot him. At this point, Deputy Skillman handcuffed defendant and seated him in a chair located about four feet outside the bedroom doorway.

When Deputy Parker returned to the bedroom to pick up defendant's handgun, he noticed a loaded semi-automatic MAC-11 pistol and a magazine with ammunition lying on the television table. He took the weapons and the magazine to the kitchen, and then watched defendant as Skillman went to the car to request assistance. Upon

Skillman's return, Parker re-entered the bedroom and opened the blinds for light. As he did so, he saw on top of the television set, "partially obstructed by a framed picture, several small bags of what looked like crack." *Id.* at 666. "Parker then searched the apartment for additional weapons. He discovered a sawed-off shotgun under a mattress and another shotgun wrapped in a white plastic trash bag lying on the floor, protruding from the doorway of an open closet. Back in the kitchen, Parker found a stun gun on top of the refrigerator. He also noticed boxes of ammunition on open shelves in the dining room." *Id.* at 666-67.

"The next day Parker obtained and executed a search warrant for evidence that Abdul-Saboor lived in the apartment. He and other officers thoroughly searched the entire apartment, finding ample documentary and physical evidence that the defendant lived there." *Id.* at 667.

In this appeal, defendant argued that the district court should have suppressed the drugs and shotguns that Deputy Parker seized when he "re-entered" the bedroom. According to the Government, however, the search was valid as a search incident to defendant's lawful arrest. And in this respect, defendant urged that the area searched was "not accessible to him at the time of the search." *Id. The Court of Appeals for the District of Columbia Circuit agreed with the Government.*

"A warrantless search or seizure inside a home is presumptively unreasonable within the meaning of the Fourth Amendment. * * * There are certain exceptions, though, one of which is for the search, incident to a lawful arrest, of the area within the arrestee's 'immediate control.'" *Id.* (citing *Chimel v. California*, 395 *U.S.* 752, 763, 89 *S.Ct.* 2034, 2040 (1969) (authorizing, as an incident to arrest, "a search of the arrestee's person and the area 'within his immediate control'—construing that phrase to mean the area from within which he might gain possession of a weapon or destructible evidence"), and *New York v. Belton*, 453 *U.S.* 454, 460 & n.4, 101 *S.Ct.* 2860, 2864 & n.4 (1981) (applying *Chimel* and determining that a search incident to a lawful arrest extended to the areas within the arrested persons' immediate control at the time they were arrested). "This exception reflects the 'potential dangers lurking in all custodial arrests.' * * * Accordingly, even though the reasons for conducting a search incident to arrest, namely 'to disarm and to discover evidence,' may be stronger in some situations than in others, the Government is not obliged to justify each such search in the particular context in which it occurs." *Abdul-Saboor* at 667.

The critical issue in this case was whether defendant's bedroom was an "area within his immediate control at the relevant time." *Id.* The Government asserted that the question whether the shotguns and drugs were within defendant's area of immediate control should be answered by reference to the time at which the arrest occurred, not the time at which the search occurred. The court agreed:

> [A] search is conducted incident to an arrest so long as it is an "integral part of a lawful custodial arrest process." [] Indeed, [the focus should not be] upon "whether the suspect held the item in his grasp or could have reached for it at the moment of the arrest." The

relevant distinction turns not upon the moment of the arrest versus the moment of the search but upon whether the arrest and search are so separated in time or by intervening events that the latter cannot fairly be said to have been incident to the former. * * *

Indeed, if the courts were to focus exclusively upon the moment of the search, we might create a perverse incentive for an arresting officer to prolong the period during which the arrestee is kept in an area where he could pose a danger to the officer. That danger is not necessarily terminated by the arrest.

Id. at 668-69. [Citations omitted.]

Defendant argued that the drugs and shotguns were not within his immediate control either at the time of his arrest or the time of the search because he was arrested at his apartment door when he first answered the marshals' knock and all of the relevant contraband was in the bedroom. "Deputy Parker testified that at the time of the disputed (second) search of the bedroom, Abdul-Saboor was handcuffed and seated in a chair in the entrance area that also served as the dining room, about four feet from the bedroom door." *Id.* at 669. Rejecting defendant's contention, the court stated:

In our view, Abdul-Saboor artificially segments his arrest and the search; they were, as a practical matter, one continuous event. The defendant was unclothed when the marshals announced their purpose to arrest him. At his request the marshals permitted him to go to the bedroom, where he armed himself with a pistol and might well have thereby gained control over the other weapons and the drugs but for one of the arresting officers having seen him grab the gun. By arming himself after the process of arrest had begun, Abdul-Saboor turned the routine execution of a bench warrant into a life-threatening process—which began at the door of the apartment, continued into the bedroom, and was not over until Abdul-Saboor was handcuffed and seated some four feet outside the bedroom.

Id.

In *Chimel*, the United States Supreme Court held that a search of any "area within which [the arrestee] might gain possession of a weapon or destructible evidence" is constitutionally permissible. And in this case, the court determined that "the room that was searched was within the area where the arrest occurred; moreover, it was not only an area from which the defendant in theory 'might gain possession of a weapon' but the area from which he had in fact obtained a weapon." *Abdul-Saboor* at 669.

Accordingly, the Government "satisfactorily demonstrated both that the area in question was within Abdul-Saboor's 'immediate control' at the time of his arrest—as required by the Supreme Court in *Chimel* and *Belton*—and that the area was 'conceivably accessible' to Abdul-Saboor at the time of the search—as required by the [precedent in this Circuit]." *Id.* at 671.

UNITED STATES v. ROBINSON
Supreme Court of the United States
414 *U.S.* 218, 94 *S.Ct.* 467 (1973)

QUESTION: When a law enforcement officer has effected a full custodial arrest of a motorist for driving with a revoked license, may that
officer thereafter conduct a full search of the person of that motorist as
a contemporaneous incident of that lawful arrest ?

ANSWER: YES. The general authority to search incident to a lawful custodial arrest should not be qualified or limited on "an assumption that persons arrested for the offense of driving while their licenses have been revoked are less likely to possess dangerous weapons
than are those arrested for other crimes. * * * A custodial arrest of a
suspect based upon probable cause is a reasonable intrusion under the
Fourth Amendment; that intrusion being lawful, a search incident to
the arrest requires no additional justification." Id. at 476-477.

RATIONALE: At approximately 11 p.m., Officer Richard Jenks of
the District of Columbia Metropolitan Police Department observed defendant driving a 1965 Cadillac. The officer had reason to believe that
defendant was operating his vehicle during a period when his driving
privileges had been revoked. This information was developed as a result of an investigation conducted four days earlier when the officer
learned that defendant's operator's permit had been revoked. "This is
an offense defined by statute in the District of Columbia which carries
a mandatory minimum jail term, a mandatory minimum fine, or both."
Id. at 470.

Officer Jenks conducted a motor vehicle stop and informed defendant that he was under arrest for "operating after revocation and
obtaining a permit by misrepresentation." *Id.* Thereafter, Jenks conducted a full search of defendant's person. In defendant's left breast
pocket of the heavy coat he was wearing, Jenks felt an object. He
"couldn't tell what it was," and "couldn't actually tell the size of it."
Id. at 471. "Jenks then reached into the pocket and pulled out the
object, which turned out to be a 'crumpled up cigarette package.'
Jenks testified that at this point he still did not know what was in
the package: 'As I felt the package I could feel objects in the package
but I couldn't tell what they were .... I knew they weren't cigarettes.' The officer then opened the cigarette pack and found 14 gelatin capsules of white powder which he thought to be, and which later
analysis proved to be, heroin." *Id.*

The United States Supreme Court concluded that the search conducted by Officer Jenks, as an incident to the arrest of defendant, "did
not offend the limits imposed by the Fourth Amendment." *Id.*

"It is well settled that a search incident to a lawful arrest is a traditional exception to the warrant requirement of the Fourth Amendment. This general exception has historically been formulated into two
distinct propositions. The first is that a search may be made of the
person of the arrestee by virtue of the lawful arrest. The second is that

a search may be made of the area within the control of the arrestee." *Id.* As far back as 1925, this Court has given recognition to the validity of a search incident to a lawful arrest:

> The right without a search warrant contemporaneously to search persons lawfully arrested while committing crime and to search the place where the arrest is made in order to find and seize things connected with the crime as its fruits or as the means by which it was committed, as well as weapons and other things to effect an escape from custody is not to be doubted.

Id. at 472 (quoting *Agnello v. United States*, 269 *U.S.* 20, 30, 46 *S.Ct.* 4, 5 (1925)). Thereafter, in 1969, the propriety of the search incident to a lawful arrest was reaffirmed:

> When an arrest is made, it is reasonable for the arresting officer to search the person arrested in order to remove any weapons that the latter might seek to use in order to resist arrest or effect his escape. Otherwise, the officer's safety might well be endangered, and the arrest itself frustrated. In addition, it is entirely reasonable for the arresting officer to search for and seize any evidence on the arrestee's person in order to prevent its concealment or destruction.

Robinson at 472 (quoting *Chimel v. California*, 395 *U.S.* 752, 762-763, 89 *S.Ct.* 2034, 2040 (1969)).

While it is true that "[t]he justification or reason for the authority to search incident to a lawful arrest rests quite as much on the need to disarm the suspect in order to take him into custody as it does on the need to preserve evidence on his person for later use at trial[,]" *Robinson* at 476, these reasons supporting the authority for such a search need not "be litigated in each case." *Id.* at 477. Nor should the general authority to search incident to a lawful custodial arrest be limited based "on an assumption that persons arrested for the offense of driving while their licenses are revoked are less likely to possess dangerous weapons than are those arrested for other crimes." *Id.* at 476. "The danger to the police officer flows from the fact of the arrest, and its attendant proximity, stress, and uncertainty, and not from the grounds for arrest." *Id.* at 476 n.5. Thus, all custodial arrests should be treated alike "for purposes of search justification." *Id.* at 476. In this respect, the Court explained:

> A police officer's determination as to how and where to search the person of a suspect whom he has arrested is necessarily a quick *ad hoc* judgment which the Fourth Amendment does not require to be broken down in each instance into an analysis of each step in the search. The authority to search the person incident to a lawful custodial arrest, while based upon the need to disarm and to discover evidence, does not depend on what a court may later decide was the

probability in a particular arrest situation that weapons or evidence would in fact be found upon the person of the suspect.

Id. at 477. Based upon this rationale, the Court declares: "*A custodial arrest of a suspect based on probable cause is a reasonable intrusion under the Fourth Amendment; that intrusion being lawful, a search incident to the arrest requires no additional justification. It is the fact of the lawful arrest which establishes the authority to search*[.]" *Id.* [Emphasis added.] Accordingly, "in the case of a lawful custodial arrest a full search of the person is not only an exception to the warrant requirement of the Fourth Amendment, but is also a 'reasonable' search under that Amendment." *Id.*

The search of defendant's "person conducted by Officer Jenks in this case and the seizure from him of the heroin, were permissible under established Fourth Amendment law. * * * Since it is the fact of the custodial arrest which gives rise to the authority to search, it is of no moment that Jenks did not indicate any subjective fear of the [defendant] or that he did not himself suspect that [defendant] was armed. Having in the course of a lawful search come upon the crumpled package of cigarettes, he was entitled to inspect it; and when his inspection revealed the heroin capsules, he was entitled to seize them as 'fruits, instrumentalities, or contraband' probative of criminal conduct." *Id.*

NOTE

1. *Arrests for minor motor vehicle violations.* In *Gustafson v. Florida*, 414 *U.S.* 260, 94 *S.Ct.* 488 (1973), the Court emphasized that " 'it is the fact of the lawful arrest which establishes the authority to search, and * * * in the case of a lawful custodial arrest a full search of the person is not only an exception to the warrant requirement of the Fourth Amendment, but is also a "reasonable" search under that Amendment.' " *Id.*, 94 *S.Ct.* at 491 (quoting *Robinson* at 235, 94 *S.Ct.* at 477).

At about 2:00 a.m., an Eau Gallie, Florida, police officer stopped Gustafson for a minor motor vehicle violation. Gustafson was driving a white Cadillac, bearing New York license plates. When Gustafson could not produce a driver's license, the officer placed him under arrest. A search of Gustafson's person incident to the arrest yielded a small quantity of marijuana.

At the Supreme Court, Gustafson argued that there was "no evidentiary purpose for the search conducted" by the officer; the offense for which he was arrested was "benign or trivial in nature," carrying with it no mandatory minimum sentence, and, unlike *Robinson*, there were no police regulations in effect which required the officer to take him into custody. Gustafson also points to the fact that here, as in *Robinson*, the officer expressed no fear for his own safety or for that of others. As a result, Gustafson contends that the search was unreasonable under the Fourth and Fourteenth Amendments. The United States Supreme Court disagreed.

Speaking for the Court, Justice Rehnquist explained:

Though the officer here was not required to take [Gustafson] into custody by police regulations as he was in *Robinson*, and there did not exist a departmental policy establishing the conditions under which a full-scale body search should be conducted, we do not find these differences determinative of the constitutional issue. * * * It is sufficient that the officer had probable cause to arrest [Gustafson] and that he lawfully effected the arrest, and placed [Gustafson] in custody. In addition, as our decision in *Robinson* makes clear, the arguable absence of "evidentiary" purpose for a search incident to a lawful arrest is not controlling. * * * "The authority to search the person incident to a lawful custodial arrest, while based upon the need to disarm and to discover evidence, does not depend on what a court may later decide was the probability in a particular arrest situation that weapons or evidence would be found upon the person of the suspect."

Id. at 491-492 (quoting *Robinson* at 235, 94 *S.Ct.* at 477).

Consequently, "upon arresting [Gustafson] for the offense of driving his automobile without possession of a valid operator's license, and taking him into custody, [the officer] was entitled to make a full search of [Gustafson's] person incident to that lawful arrest. Since it is the fact of custodial arrest which gives rise to the authority to search, it is of no moment that [the officer] did not indicate a subjective fear of [Gustafson] or that he did not himself suspect that [Gustafson] was armed. Having in the course of his lawful search come upon the box of cigarettes, [the officer] was entitled to inspect it; and when his inspection revealed the homemade cigarettes which he believed to contain an unlawful substance, he was entitled to seize them as 'fruits, instrumentalities or contraband' probative of criminal conduct." *Id.* at 492.

2. *Search incident to citation rejected.* In *Knowles v. Iowa,* 525 *U.S.* 113, 119 *S.Ct.* 484 (1998), the Supreme Court rejected the contention that the "search incident to arrest" exception to the written warrant requirement includes searches "incident to citation."

Knowles was stopped in Newton, Iowa, for traveling 43 miles per hour in a 25-mile-per-hour zone. Although the officer could have arrested Knowles under Iowa law, he issued him a citation instead. Thereafter, the officer conducted a full search incident to arrest. Under the driver's seat, the officer found a bag of marijuana and a "pot pipe." The officer then placed Knowles under arrest and charged him with the drug offenses.

Finding this "search incident to citation" unlawful, the Court preliminarily instructed that in *United States v. Robinson, supra,* it had identified two "historical rationales" for the "search incident to arrest" exception: "(1) the need to disarm the suspect in order to take him into custody, and (2) the need to preserve evidence for later use at trial." *Knowles,* 119 *S.Ct.* at 487. The Court concluded, however, that "neither of these underlying rationales for the search incident to arrest exception is sufficient to justify the search in the present case." *Id.*

While the first rationale—that of officer safety—is both "legitimate and weighty," the actual "threat to officer safety" arising from the issuing of a traffic citation is, according to the Court, a "good deal less than in the case of a custodial arrest." *Id.* A custodial arrest involves a danger to the law enforcement officer because of " 'the extended exposure which follows the taking of a suspect into custody and transporting him to the police station.' * * * 'The danger to the police officer flows from the fact of the arrest, and its attendant proximity, stress, and uncertainty, and not from the grounds for arrest.' " *Id.* at 488. [Citations omitted.] "A routine traffic stop, on the other hand, is a relatively brief encounter and 'is more analogous to a so-called *"Terry* stop" . . . than to a formal arrest.' " *Id.* [Citations omitted.] Although there certainly is concern for officer safety in the case of a traffic stop, such concern does not, held the Court, "by itself justify the often considerably greater intrusion attending a full field-type search." *Id.*

In addition, there has been no showing in this case that the second justification for the authority to search incident to arrest—"the need to discover and preserve evidence"—has been satisfied. "Once Knowles was stopped for speeding and issued a citation, all the evidence necessary to prosecute that offense had been obtained. No further evidence of excessive speed was going to be found either on the person of the offender or in the passenger compartment of the car." *Id.* On this basis, the Court also expressly rejected the Iowa Supreme Court's reasoning that, "so long as the arresting officer had probable cause to make a custodial arrest, there need not in fact have been a custodial arrest." *Id.*

In *Robinson,* the Court held that "the authority to conduct a full field search as incident to an arrest was a 'bright-line rule,' which was based on the concern for officer safety and destruction or loss of evidence, but which did not depend in every case upon the existence of either concern." *Knowles* at 488. In this case, the Court refused to extend that "bright-line rule" to "a situation where the concern for officer safety is not present to the same extent and the concern for destruction or loss of evidence is not present at all." *Id.*

3. *The "lawful" arrest.* In *Virginia v. Moore,* 553 U.S. ___, 128 S.Ct. 1598 (2008), two officers stopped the car Moore was driving based on a tip that he was driving with a suspended license. Once the officers confirmed that Moore's license was in fact suspended, they arrested him. A search incident to the arrest uncovered 16 grams of crack cocaine and $516 in cash.

Although the arrest was supported by probable cause, it violated Virginia statutory law, which required the issuance of a summons. Under Virginia law, however, that violation did not require the suppression of the evidence seized. Nonetheless, the Virginia Supreme Court held that since the arresting officers should have issued Moore a citation under state law, and the Fourth Amendment does not permit searches incident to citation, *see Knowles v. Iowa, supra,* the officers' conduct violated the Fourth Amendment. *The United States Supreme Court disagreed.*

It is well established that "officers may perform searches incident to constitutionally permissible arrests in order to ensure their safety and safeguard evidence." This rule covers any "lawful arrest," which the Court equates with "an arrest based on probable cause." *Id.*, 128 *S.Ct.* at 1607.

It is true that many state-court decisions have defined the lawfulness of arrest in terms of compliance with state law. But the term "lawful," as used in the *Robinson* case, should be construed as a shorthand expression for "compliance with constitutional constraints." *Moore* at 1607.

The interests justifying a search are present whenever an officer makes an arrest. "A search enables officers to safeguard evidence, and, most critically, to ensure their safety during 'the extended exposure which follows the taking of a suspect into custody and transporting him to the police station.' * * * Officers issuing citations do not face the same danger," and in *Knowles v. Iowa,* it was held that "they do not have the same authority to search." *Moore* at 1707-08.

Knowles does not, however, control the outcome of this case. "The state officers arrested Moore, and therefore faced the risks that are 'an adequate basis for treating all custodial arrests alike for purposes of search justification.' " *Id.* at 1608. [Citation omitted.]

"The Virginia Supreme Court may have concluded that *Knowles* required the exclusion of evidence seized from Moore because, under state law, the officers who arrested Moore should have issued him a citation instead. * * * But the arrest rules that the officers violated were those of state law alone, and * * * it is not the province of the Fourth Amendment to enforce state law. That Amendment does not require the exclusion of evidence obtained from a constitutionally permissible arrest." *Id.*

Accordingly, "[w]hen officers have probable cause to believe that a person has committed a crime in their presence, the Fourth Amendment permits them to make an arrest, and to search the suspect in order to safeguard evidence and ensure their own safety." *Id.*

4. *When the search precedes the arrest.* As a matter of procedure, the search incident to arrest is generally conducted *after* the lawful arrest. There may be times, however, when the circumstances of the encounter prompt the officer to conduct the search *before* the arrest. If an officer does reverse the procedure, *conducting the search before the arrest*, that fact alone should not render the search illegal so long as probable cause for the arrest existed at the time of the search. As the Court explained in *Rawlings v. Kentucky*, 448 *U.S.* 89, 111, 100 *S.Ct.* 2556, 2564-65 (1980), "where the formal arrest followed quickly on the heels of the challenged search of [defendant's] person, we do not believe it particularly important that the search preceded the arrest rather than vice versa," so long as what the search disclosed was "not necessary to support probable cause to arrest." *See also United States v. Turpin*, 920 *F.*2d 1377, 1386 (8th Cir. 1990) (substantially contemporaneous search may precede arrest so long as probable cause to arrest existed before the search).

5. *Delayed searches incident to arrest.* May the police ever conduct a search incident to an arrest in the room from which an arrestee has been removed ? The Ninth Circuit said yes in *United States v.*

Turner, 926 *F*.2d 883 (9th Cir. 1991). In *Turner*, defendant was arrested in the bedroom of his apartment under the authority of a warrant charging cocaine distribution offenses and a firearms offense. As defendant was placed under arrest, police discovered a .45 caliber revolver lying beside him beneath the sheets. The officers handcuffed him and took him into another room. They then returned to the bedroom and a search of the bed uncovered baggies of cocaine from underneath his pillow and jacket (which was on the bed).

Generally, a search incident to an arrest "must be conducted at 'about the same time as the arrest.'" *Id*. at 887. [Citation omitted.] In this case, before the search, the officers handcuffed Turner and took him to another room. They then returned to the place of arrest to conduct the incident search. To decide whether this procedure was lawful, the court adopted the two-part analysis set forth in *United States v. Fleming*, 677 *F*.2d 602, 607 (7th Cir. 1982), where the Seventh Circuit held that a search incident to an arrest was valid even though it was conducted five minutes after the arrest, while the arrestee was handcuffed. *Turner* at 887.

The first part of the analysis questions whether the searched object "was within the arrestee's immediate control *when he was arrested*." *Id*. [Emphasis in original.] If so, the analysis next requires an inquiry into "whether events occurring after the arrest but before the search made the search unreasonable." *Id*. In *Fleming*, the court "determined that the officers acted reasonably and out of a concern for their safety when they delayed the search five minutes and first handcuffed the arrestee. The court reasoned that 'it does not make sense to prescribe a constitutional test that is entirely at odds with safe and sensible police procedures.'" *Turner* at 887-888 (quoting *Fleming* at 607).

Here, in *Turner*, the court first found that the baggies of cocaine were within Turner's immediate control when he was arrested. At the time of the arrest, he was on the bed with the baggies. *Id*. at 88. Next, the court determined that the events subsequent to the search did not make the search unreasonable. The officers placed Turner in handcuffs and removed him from the bedroom out of a concern for their safety. Significantly, they had already discovered a concealed weapon beneath the bedding. "They did not take him far away or delay for long before conducting the search." *Id*. Accordingly, the court concluded that "[t]he baggies were validly seized during a search incident to arrest." *Id*.

6. *Unlocked, hand-carried suitcases*. In *United States v. Garcia*, 605 *F*.2d 349 (7th Cir. 1979), *cert. denied*, 446 *U.S*. 984, 100 *S.Ct*. 2966 (1980), the court held "that a warrantless search of the contents of hand-carried luggage, seized incident to and inspected contemporaneous with a lawful custodial arrest does not" violate the Fourth Amendment. *Id*. at 350. Defendant Garcia and her associate, Valentin, were arrested at the baggage area of Chicago's O'Hare Airport. The arrest was based upon probable cause to believe that Garcia and Valentin both violated several federal narcotics laws. Immediately prior to Garcia's arrest, she was observed picking up two suitcases at the baggage claim area. As Garcia exited the terminal, she was carrying one plaid suitcase in one hand, and a vinyl suitcase as well as her coat and

shoulder bag in the other. When she stepped through the doorway, she was approached by one of the investigating officers and placed under arrest. The two suitcases, which were zippered shut but not secured by a lock, were then seized and searched. One of the suitcases contained nine plastic bags of heroin.

In upholding the search and seizure in this case, the court preliminarily noted that "a warrantless search conducted incident to a lawful arrest is a traditional exception to the warrant requirement of the Fourth Amendment. * * * Such searches have been held to be reasonable * * * when effected for the purpose of disarming the arrestee or to preserve evidence probative of criminal conduct." *Id.* at 352-353. Next, the court pointed out that the search incident to a valid arrest "may be undertaken pursuant to a valid arrest if it is substantially contemporaneous with the arrest and is confined to the person and immediate vicinity of the arrestee." *Id.* at 353 (citing *Vale v. Louisiana*, 399 *U.S.* 30, 90 *S.Ct.* 1969 (1970) and *Shipley v. California*, 395 *U.S.* 818, 89 *S.Ct.* 2053 (1969)). Thus, such a search is reasonable when it is "conducted substantially contemporaneous with the arrest and [is] spatially limited to the person of the arrestee, the possessions immediately associated with the person of the arrestee, and the area within the arrestee's immediate control."

Here, "[t]he objects seized consisted of two hand-carried, portable suitcases which were quite capable of being opened quickly by the defendant in order to gain access to a weapon or evidence, or removed by a waiting accomplice of the defendant. * * * [T]he search * * * was undertaken immediately upon the defendant's arrest. The officers approached the defendant as soon as she exited the baggage terminal building, placed her under arrest, seized the luggage she carried, and undertook a search of its contents in the defendant's presence and within fifteen seconds of the announcement of the arrest. Accordingly, the search was neither remote in time or place from the arrest, and since the police had probable cause to effect the arrest and exigent circumstances were present, the warrantless search of the contents of the luggage was justified as a search incident to arrest." *Garcia* at 354.

The court in *Garcia* distinguished *United States v. Chadwick* 433 *U.S.* 1, 97 *S.Ct.* 2476 (1977), where "the object seized was a cumbersome, two hundred pound, double-locked footlocker, which obviously could be neither opened nor rapidly removed by the defendants or an accomplice at the time of arrest." *Garcia* at 323. Significantly, the search in *Chadwick* "was not undertaken in close proximity to the time and place of the arrest and seizure. Rather, the footlocker was opened more than one hour following the arrest, and then only after it had been removed along with the defendants to the police station. Moreover, since the defendants were incarcerated, the only persons present at the time of the search were police officers. Under the [*Chadwick*] circumstances, ample justification existed to delay the search until a warrant could be obtained." *Garcia* at 353. Consequently, the *Garcia* court found the following language in *Chadwick* to be inapposit: "[W]arrantless searches of luggage or other property seized at the time of an arrest cannot be justified as incident to that arrest either if the 'search is remote in time or place from the arrest,'

* * * or no exigency exists. Once law enforcement officers have reduced luggage or other personal property not immediately associated with the person of the arrestee to their exclusive control, and there is no longer any danger that the arrestee might gain access to the property to seize a weapon or destroy evidence, a search of that property is no longer an incident of the arrest." *Chadwick* at 15, 97 *S.Ct.* at 2485. [Footnote and citation omitted.]

7. *Paper bags.* In *United States v. Fleming*, 677 *F.*2d 602 (7th Cir. 1982), the court upheld the seizure and search of two closed paper bags which were in the possession of the individuals arrested. The search of defendant Fleming's bag occurred immediately upon his arrest. The search of defendant Rolenc's bag occurred approximately five minutes after his arrest, when additional backup officers arrived on the scene. Fleming's bag contained $10,000.00 in cash and Rolenc's bag contained a quantity of cocaine. In the appeal which followed their conviction, the defendants argued that the searches of the bags, after the bags had been recovered from them and were securely in police custody, were illegal in the absence of a warrant, consent, or exigent circumstances. The court, however, refused "to impose on police a requirement that the search be absolutely contemporaneous with the arrest, no matter what the peril to themselves or to bystanders." *Id.* at 607. In this respect, the court stated: "It is surely possible for a *Chimel* search to be undertaken too long after the arrest and too far from the arrestee's person. That is the lesson of *Chadwick*. But we do not consider that the presence of more officers than suspects invalidated the immediate search of Fleming's bag. Nor do we think that a five-minute delay between seizing Rolenc's bag and opening it, occasioned by [the officer's] handcuffing Rolenc and moving with him to the street, defeated [the officer's] right to search under *Chimel* principles." *Fleming* at 607-608. Significantly, at the point when the police first seized the bags, "the bags were within Fleming's and Rolenc's grabbing area." *Id.* at 607. Moreover, "[a] valid search incident to arrest has as a corollary that any container 'may, of course, be searched, whether it is open or closed, since the justification for the search is not that the arrestee has no privacy in the container, but that the lawful custodial arrest justifies the infringement of any privacy interest the arrestee may have.'" *Id.* at 608. [Citation omitted.]

See also United States v. Litman, 739 *F.*2d 137 (4th Cir. 1984), where the court upheld the seizure and search of the shoulder bag defendant was carrying at the time of his narcotics arrest, and expressly rejected the argument that an article seized by an officer incident to an arrest cannot be subjected to a warrantless search because that article has been brought within the officer's exclusive control. Quoting *New York v. Belton*, 453 *U.S.* 454, 461 n.5, 101 *S.Ct.* 2860, 2865 n.5 (1981), the court noted that " 'under this fallacious theory no search or seizure incident to a lawful custodial arrest would ever be valid; by seizing an article even on the arrestee's person, an officer may be said to have reduced that article to his "exclusive control." ' " *Litman* at 139.

UNITED STATES v. EDWARDS
Supreme Court of the United States
415 *U.S.* 800, 94 *S.Ct.* 1234 (1974)

QUESTION: Once an accused has been lawfully arrested and is incarcerated, may the effects in his possession at the place of detention that were subject to search and seizure at the time and place of arrest be lawfully searched and seized without a warrant even after a substantial time has elapsed (here, 10 hours) between the arrest and subsequent seizure ?

ANSWER: YES. "[O]nce the accused is lawfully arrested and is in custody, the effects in his possession at the place of detention that were subject to search at the time and place of his arrest may lawfully be searched and seized without a warrant even though a substantial period of time has elapsed between the arrest and subsequent administrative processing, on the one hand, and the taking of the property for use as evidence, on the other." *Id.* at 1239.

RATIONALE: After defendant's arrest for attempting to break into the Lebanon City Post Office, he was taken to the local jail and placed in a cell. "Contemporaneously or shortly thereafter, investigation at the scene revealed that the attempted entry had been made through a wooden window which apparently had been pried up with a pry bar, leaving paint chips on the window sill and wire mesh screen." *Id.* at 1236. The next morning, approximately ten hours after the arrest, the authorities purchased defendant a replacement set of clothing, and seized the clothing he was wearing (and had been wearing at the time of his arrest) as evidence. Laboratory analysis indicated that defendant's clothing contained paint chips matching the samples taken from the scene of the attempted burglary.

In this appeal, defendant argues that the warrantless seizure of his clothing, ten hours after his arrest, and the results of the laboratory examination should have been suppressed as violative of the Fourth Amendment. *The United States Supreme Court disagreed.*

One of the recognized exceptions to the Fourth Amendment's written warrant requirement is that which embraces the search of the person and the items in his possession as an incident to a lawful custodial arrest. *United States v. Robinson*, 414 *U.S.* 218, 94 *S.Ct.* 467 (1973). The exception "has traditionally been justified by the reasonableness of searching for weapons, instruments of escape, and evidence of crime when a person is taken into official custody and lawfully detained." *Edwards* at 1237. As the Court explained in *Robinson:*

> A custodial arrest of a suspect based on probable cause is a reasonable intrusion under the Fourth Amendment; that intrusion being lawful, a search incident to the arrest requires no additional justification. It is the fact of the lawful arrest which establishes the authority to search, and we hold that in the case of a lawful custodial arrest a full search of the person is not only an exception

to the warrant requirement of the Fourth Amendment, but is also a "reasonable" search under that Amendment.

Id., 414 *U.S.*, at 235, 94 *S.Ct.*, at 477.

It is also well established "that searches and seizures that could be made on the spot at the time of arrest may legally be conducted later when the accused arrives at the place of detention." *Edwards* at 1237. "[B]oth the person and the property in his immediate possession may be searched at the station house after the arrest has occurred at another place and if evidence of crime is discovered, it may be seized and admitted in evidence. Nor is there any doubt that clothing or other belongings may be seized upon arrival of the accused at the place of detention and later subjected to laboratory analysis or that the test results are admissible at trial." *Id.*

At the moment of defendant's incarceration, the authorities were entitled, with or without probable cause "not only to search [defendant's] clothing but also to take it from him and keep it in official custody. * * * The police were also entitled to take from [defendant] any evidence of the crime in his immediate possession, including his clothing." *Id.* at 1237-1238. Significantly, the police in this case had probable cause, developed contemporaneously with or shortly after the time defendant went to his cell, to believe that the clothing he wore constituted material evidence of the crime for which he had been arrested. "But it was late at night; no substitute clothing was then available for [defendant] to wear, and it would certainly have been unreasonable for the police to have stripped [him] of his clothing and left him exposed in his cell throughout the night. When the substitutes were purchased the next morning, the clothing he had been wearing at the time of arrest was taken from him and subjected to laboratory analysis. This was no more than taking from [defendant] the effects in his immediate possession that constituted evidence of crime." *Id.* at 1238. According to the Court, this procedure

> was and is a normal incident of a custodial arrest, and reasonable delay in effectuating it does not change the fact that Edwards was no more imposed upon than he could have been at the time and place of the arrest or immediately upon his arrival at the place of detention. The police did no more [the morning after] than they were entitled to do incident to the usual custodial arrest and incarceration.

Id.

As a result, "once [an] accused is lawfully arrested and is in custody, the effects in his possession at the place of detention that were subject to search at the time and place of his arrest may lawfully be searched and seized without a warrant even though a substantial period of time has elapsed between the arrest and subsequent administrative processing, on the one hand, and the taking of the property for use as evidence, on the other. This is true where the clothing or effects are immediately seized upon arrival at the jail, held under the defendant's name in the 'property room' or the jail, and at a later time searched and taken for use at the subsequent criminal trial. The result is the same where the property is not physically taken from the defendant until sometime after his incarceration." *Id.* at 1239.

TINETTI v. WITTKE
United States District Court
479 *F.Supp.* 486 (E.D.Wis. 1979)*

QUESTION: May law enforcement officers routinely strip search persons arrested for non-misdemeanor traffic offenses ?

ANSWER: NO. Non-misdemeanor traffic violators who are arrested and then incarcerated solely due to their inability to post bail, may not be routinely strip searched as an incident to that arrest in the absence of probable cause to believe they are concealing weapons or contraband on their body. 479 *F.Supp.* at 491.

RATIONALE: Plaintiff, Jill Tinetti, brings this civil action against the Sheriff of Racine County, Wisconsin and a matron of the Racine County Jail, seeking to restrain the defendants from strip searching persons arrested for non-misdemeanor traffic violations absent probable cause to believe the offender is concealing weapons or contraband on his body.

Tinetti, a resident of Colorado, was stopped for speeding in Racine County, Wisconsin. Because she was not a resident of Wisconsin, she was placed under arrest and advised that she would have to post a $40.00 cash bond. When Tinetti advised the officer that she did not have the $40.00, she was brought to the Racine County Jail, booked, photographed, and then strip searched by the jail matron. Upon completion of the strip search procedure, Tinetti was incarcerated in a cell for about two hours until her uncle arrived and posted the $40.00 cash bail.

The matron's strip search of Tinetti was performed according to a written policy of the Racine County Sheriff's Department which required all persons detained in the Racine County Jail to be strip searched regardless of the offense.

In this action, the court agrees with Tinetti and holds that, "as a matter of law, the strip searching of [Tinetti], a non-misdemeanor traffic violator who was incarcerated due to the inability to post cash bail, was an unconstitutional denial of the personal liberty guaranteed by the United States Constitution." *Id.* at 490. While it is true that a search incident to a lawful arrest is a recognized exception to the written warrant requirement, "[t]he mere fact that a person is arrested, however, does not mean that he may be subject to any search which the arresting officer feels is necessary. * * * Such searches have traditionally been justified by the reasonableness of the discovery of, (1) weapons or instruments of escape; or (2) evidence which could be otherwise concealed or destroyed. * * * Neither of these justifications [exist in

---

* *aff'd o.b.*, 620 *F.*2d 160 (7th Cir. 1980).

this] case. Plaintiff was not searched by the arresting officer, who apparently felt that there was no reason to believe plaintiff carried any weapons on her person or in her motor vehicle. Plaintiff's offense itself, a non-misdemeanor traffic violation, generally does not involve the use of a weapon." *Id.*

"Furthermore, the discovery of evidence was not a sufficient justification for the search of plaintiff, given the type of offense she committed. The only materially probative pieces of evidence as to plaintiff's exceeding of the speed limit were the reading on the speedometer of the plaintiff's automobile, as remembered by plaintiff or her passengers, and the reading on the officer's speed measuring device. As such, plaintiff had no reason to conceal, and the officer had no reason to suspect, the existence of any evidence which could be discovered through a strip search of plaintiff." *Id.*

When a court must evaluate whether a particular search and seizure is unreasonable within the meaning of the Fourth Amendment:

> [T]he permissibility of a particular law enforcement practice is judged by balancing its intrusion on the individual's Fourth Amendment interests against its promotion of legitimate government interests . . . the reasonableness standard usually requires, at a minimum, that the facts upon which an intrusion is based be capable of measurement against an "objective standard," whether this be probable cause or a less stringent test.

Delaware v. Prouse, 440 *U.S.* 648, 654, 99 *S.Ct.* 1391, 1396 (1979). "The undisputed facts show that plaintiff was strip searched as a part of a routine, long-standing policy of defendants, without consideration as to whether probable cause existed to believe that she was concealing weapons or contraband. While law enforcement personnel do have a legitimate interest in discovering weapons or contraband, that interest cannot be indiscriminately satisfied by the strip searching of non-misdemeanor traffic violators where there is no reason to believe that the violators have concealed any such articles. The intrusion on one's personal dignity occasioned by such searches requires that some justifiable basis exist." *Tinetti* at 490.

"[T]here is little reason to suspect that traffic violators will conceal contraband or weapons, particularly when they are incarcerated solely due to their inability to post cash bail. Defendants' blanket strip search policy cannot be maintained when to do so intrudes into the personal dignity of traffic violators without any relation to the likelihood of [their] concealment of weapons or contraband. [Such a policy], as a matter of law, violates the Fourth, Fifth [denial of liberty without due process of law], and Fourteenth Amendments of the United States Constitution." *Id.* at 491.

"Accordingly, for the reasons given, this Court declares that the defendants' subjection of plaintiff, a non-misdemeanor traffic violator incarcerated only due to the inability to post cash bond, to a strip search without probable cause to believe that she was concealing weapons or contraband on her body was a violation of the plaintiff's rights under the Fourth, Fifth, and Fourteenth Amendments of the United States Constitution." *Id.*

NOTE

1. In *Bell v. Wolfish*, 441 *U.S.* 520, 559, 99 *S.Ct.* 1861, 1884 (1979), the Supreme Court instructed: "Strip searches of detainees are constitutionally constrained by due process requirements of reasonableness under the circumstances. In each case it requires the balancing of the need for the particular search against the invasion of personal rights that the search entails. Courts must consider the scope of the particular intrusion, the manner in which it is conducted, the justification for initiating it, and the place in which it is conducted."

See also Masters v. Crouch, 872 *F.*2d 1248 (6th Cir. 1989) (strip search of person arrested on a warrant for the failure to appear in court for traffic offenses held unlawful in the absence of an individualized reasonable suspicion); *Jones v. Edwards*, 770 *F.*2d 739 (8th Cir. 1985) (person arrested for refusing to sign a leash law summons may not be strip searched); *Giles v. Ackerman*, 746 *F.*2d 614 (9th Cir. 1984) (persons arrested for minor offenses may not be strip searched in the absence of a reasonable suspicion that they are concealing weapons or contraband or suffering from a communicable disease); *Logan v. Shealy*, 660 *F.*2d 1007 (4th Cir. 1981) (strip search of drunk-driving offender who was to be detained for four hours while the effects of the alcohol wore off held unlawful).

2. In *Kennedy v. Los Angeles Police Dept.*, 887 *F.*2d 920 (9th Cir. 1989), the Ninth Circuit had occasion to address the constitutionality of a blanket strip search policy instituted by the City of Los Angeles Police Department (LAPD). In pertinent part, the policy provided:

> Arrestees booked into Department facilities on all felony offenses, and misdemeanor offenses related to the use of narcotics, shall be given a skin search. Skin searches of arrestees booked on other misdemeanor charges shall be made when there is probable cause to believe that an arrestee is concealing contraband or weapons.
>
> When there is probable cause to believe that an arrestee is concealing contraband or weapons inside a body cavity, a visual body-cavity search shall be conducted.

While the policy facially appears to acknowledge the difference between a skin (strip) search and a body-cavity search (requiring probable cause for the latter), in practice, the LAPD had eliminated this distinction in its construction and implementation of the policy. In fact, at trial, a LAPD officer "testified that the body-cavity search was part of a skin or strip search, and so the skin search, strip search, and visual body-cavity search were really 'one and the same.' " *Id.* at 928.

In this Section 1983 civil rights action, plaintiff, Karen Kennedy, was arrested for the theft of some of her roommate's property. The value of the property—two wicker chairs and a television set—made the theft a felony. At the jail, Kennedy was forced to submit to a body-cavity search. "Kennedy first was forced to strip off all her clothing. After exposing her naked body to two policewomen, Kennedy then was required to insert her fingers into her vagina and anus so that the policewomen could check whether she had any concealed drugs or contraband in these body cavities. * * * After the [fruitless] search, Kennedy was placed in a cell until, hours later, bond was posted." *Id.* at 929.

At the conclusion of trial, the jury found that the LAPD policy and the procedures employed in this case violated Kennedy's rights, and as a result, awarded Kennedy $25,000.00 in actual damages against the City of Los Angeles. Additionally, the district court issued an opinion holding that "the LAPD's policy of conducting a visual body-cavity search of *all* felony arrest detainees, regardless of reasonable suspicion, violate[d] the [F]ourth [A]mendment." *Id.* at 928. [Emphasis in original.] The Ninth Circuit agreed and affirmed.

According to the court, "[t]he intrusiveness of a body-cavity search cannot be overstated. Strip searches involving the visual exploration of body cavities are dehumanizing and humiliating." *Id.* at 928-929. Nonetheless, as a search, the procedure complained of here requires analysis under the Fourth Amendment's reasonableness standard.

> In each case it requires a balancing of the need for the particular search against the invasion of personal rights that the search entails. Courts must consider the scope of the particular intrusion, the manner in which it is conducted, the justification for initiating it, and the place in which it is conducted.

Id. at 930 (quoting *Bell v. Wolfish*, 441 *U.S.* 520, 559, 99 *S.Ct.* 1861, 1884 (1979)).

Here, it does not appear that Kennedy's search was performed abrasively or in an inappropriate place. Rather, "[t]he critical inquiry is whether the LAPD ha[d] sufficient justification for imposing its blanket search policy. [The defendants argue that concerns] 'for safety, security, and the proper administration of the jail system provided the foundation for such a policy' and that '[p]rison officials have a legitimate penological interest in preventing drugs, contraband weapons or other unlawful objects from entering penal facilities.' " *Id.*

While the court recognized that those concerns and that interest are no doubt "weighty," it nevertheless emphasized that "the enacted policy, if it is to be constitutional, must be 'reasonably related' to the penal institution's interest in maintaining security." *Id.* at 930, 931. [Citations omitted.] In this case, "the LAPD fail[ed] to offer a serious justification for subjecting all felony arrestees to a body-cavity search as a matter of course, whereas only those misdemeanor arrestees charged with offenses relating to narcotics or suspected of concealing contraband or weapons are forced to undergo such a search." *Id.* at 931.

> The principle that courts must provide wide latitude to prison policies needed to maintain institutional order and security * * * necessarily presupposes that the administrators have crafted those policies with careful deliberation. The LAPD's justification is devoid of any trace of such care; instead, it rests on "assum[ptions]" and "societal judgment[s]." A glaring omission from LAPD's justification is any documentation (or even assertion) that felony arrestees have

attempted to smuggle contraband into the jail in greater frequency than misdemeanor arrestees. * * *

Indeed, * * * this case itself underscores the inherent failings of a search policy predicated solely on a felony / misdemeanor classification.

Id. at 931. Significantly, had the arresting officer determined that the two wicker chairs and the television set had a value of $399 and not $400 (the minimum required for a felony theft), Kennedy would not have been subjected to the search at issue. *Id.* at 931-932. "Kennedy's arrest involved an ordinary squabble between two roommates. Unfortunately for Kennedy, the arresting officers, making 'an educated guess at best,' * * * valued the missing items in excess of $399, and trans[formed] this domestic squabble into an arrest for grand theft, a felony under California law necessitating a body-cavity search." *Id.* at 932. "In short, the LAPD's felony / misdemeanor classification alone indicates little about the likelihood of the arrestee's concealing drugs, weapons, or contraband, the basis for subjecting an arrestee to a visual body-cavity search." *Id.*

Accordingly, the court concluded: "On balance, the LAPD's policy cannot withstand the constitutional review articulated in *Wolfish*." *Kennedy* at 932.

The court's conclusion that the LAPD's strip search policy was unconstitutional did not, however, end the inquiry. "[A] search, although not supportable under an institutional standard, is not *per se* unconstitutional." *Id.* at 933. In addition, an examination of the particular circumstances surrounding the arrest is required to determine whether there was a reasonable and articulable suspicion to conduct a visual body-cavity search. *See e.g., Giles v. Ackerman*, 746 *F.*2d 614, 617 (9th Cir. 1984) ("arrestees charged with minor offenses may be subjected to a strip search only if jail officials possess a reasonable suspicion that the individual arrestee is carrying or concealing contraband"); *Weber v. Dell*, 804 *F.*2d 796, 802 (2d Cir. 1986) (requiring a particularized, reasonable suspicion).

In this respect, the court observed:

That this case involves a felony arrest does not alter the level of cause required to justify a visual body-cavity search. Logically, the classification of the offense in some cases might inform the *presence* of suspicion, but it does not inform the *level* of suspicion. Indeed, the reasonable suspicion standard * * * prudently invites the consideration of the nature of the crime charged in determining the constitutionality of an individual search. * * * "Reasonable suspicion may be based on such factors as the nature of the offense, the arrestee's appearance and conduct, and the prior arrest record." * * *

Grand theft, a felony, thus properly could be considered in deciding whether to search Kennedy. And in some cases, the charge itself may give rise to reasonable suspicion. *See e.g., Dufrin v. Spreen*, 712 *F.*2d 1084, 1089 (6th Cir. 1983) [] ("Reasonableness under the [F]ourth [A]mendment must afford police the right to strip search arrestees whose offenses posed the very threat of violence by weapons or contraband drugs that they must curtail in prisons."). This is certainly not such a case. The grand theft charge here centered around an ordinary disagreement between two roommates. No weapons, no drugs, no contraband, no violent acts of any kind were involved. Nor were there any other circumstances that provided reasonable suspicion to believe that Kennedy concealed contraband.

Id. at 933-934 (footnote omitted).

---

§3.2(b). Motor vehicle searches incident to arrest.

NEW YORK v. BELTON
Supreme Court of the United States
453 *U.S.* 454, 101 *S.Ct.* 2860 (1981)

QUESTION: When a law enforcement officer has made a lawful custodial arrest of an occupant of an automobile, may he or she then conduct a search of the vehicle's passenger compartment as an incident to that arrest ?

ANSWER: YES. When an officer has effected a lawful custodial arrest of an occupant of an automobile, he or she "may, as a contemporaneous incident of that arrest, search the passenger compartment of that automobile." *Id.* at 2864. In addition, the officer "may also examine the contents of any containers found within the passenger compartment," regardless of whether such containers are open or closed. *Id.*

RATIONALE: Defendant, Roger Belton, was one of four occupants of an automobile which was stopped by a state trooper on the New York Thruway for speeding. The trooper asked to see the driver's license and registration, and learned that none of the vehicle's occupants owned the car or was related to the owner. During this time, the trooper also detected the odor of burnt marijuana emanating from the vehicle's interior, and had seen on the floor of the car an envelope marked "Supergold" that he associated with marijuana. He therefore directed the occupants to step out of the car, and placed them under arrest for the unlawful possession of marijuana. The trooper then picked up the envelope marked "Supergold" and discovered that it contained marijuana. A further search of the passenger compartment revealed, on the back seat, a black leather jacket belonging to Belton. The trooper unzipped one of the pockets of the jacket and discovered a quantity of cocaine. Subsequently, Belton was indicted for the unlawful possession of a controlled substance.

In the appeal which followed the denial of Belton's motion to suppress, the New York Court of Appeals held that the search of Belton's jacket violated the Fourth Amendment because " '[a] warrantless search of the zippered pockets of an [i]naccessible jacket may not be upheld as a search incident to a lawful arrest where there is no longer any danger that the arrestee or a confederate might gain access to the article.' " *Id.* at 2862. [Citation omitted.] *The United States Supreme Court disagreed and reversed.*

In *Chimel v. California*, 395 *U.S.* 752, 89 *S.Ct.* 2034 (1960), the Court held that "a lawful custodial arrest creates the situation which justifies the contemporaneous search without a warrant of the person arrested and of the immediately surrounding area." *Belton* at 2862. "Such searches have long been considered valid because of the need 'to remove any weapons that [the arrestee] might seek to use in order to resist arrest or effect his escape' and the need to prevent the conceal-ment or destruction of evidence." *Id.* (quoting *Chimel* at 763, 89 *S.Ct.* at 2040). These reasons—supporting the authority for the search inci-dent to a lawful arrest—need not, however, " 'be litigated in each case.' " *Id.* at 2863 (quoting *United States v. Robinson*, 414 *U.S.* 218, 235, 94 *S.Ct.* 467, 477 (1973)).

Although the *Chimel* principle may be stated clearly enough—that a "search incident to an arrest may not stray beyond the area within the immediate control of the arrestee"—many "courts have found no workable definition of 'the area within the immediate control of the arrestee' when that area arguably includes the interior of an automo-bile and the arrestee is its recent occupant." *Belton* at 2864. Thus, rather than setting forth " '[a] highly sophisticated set of rules, quali-fied by all sorts of ifs, ands, and buts and requiring the drawing of subtle nuances and hairline distinctions,' " the Court here in *Belton* determined that " '[a] single, familiar standard * * * to guide police officers' " in the performance of their day-to-day responsibilities must be adopted regarding "the proper scope of a search of the interior of an automobile incident to a lawful custodial arrest of its occupants" after the arrestees are no longer in it. *Id.* at 2863. [Citations omitted.]

The Court therefore concluded that

> articles inside the relatively narrow compass of the passenger compartment of an automobile are in fact generally, even if not in-evitably, within "the area into which an arrestee might reach in order to grab a weapon or evidentiary ite[m]."

Id. at 2864. Accordingly, when a police officer "has made a lawful cus-todial arrest of the occupant of an automobile, he may, as a contempo-raneous incident of that arrest, search the passenger compartment of that automobile." *Id.* [Footnote omitted.]

"It follows from this conclusion that the police may also examine the contents of any containers found within the passenger compart-ment, for if the passenger compartment is within reach of the ar-restee, so also will containers in it be within his reach. * * * 'Con-tainer' here denotes any object capable of holding another object. It thus includes closed or open glove compartments, consoles, or other receptacles located anywhere within the passenger compartment, as well as luggage, boxes, bags, clothing and the like." *Id.* at 2864 & n.4. Moreover, "[s]uch a container may, of course, be searched whether it is open or closed since the justification for the search is not that the arrestee has no privacy interest in the container, but that the lawful custodial arrest justifies the infringement of any privacy interest the arrestee may have." *Id.* at 2864. Significantly, this "holding encompasses only the interior of the passenger compartment of an automobile and does not encompass the trunk." *Id.* at 2864 n.4.

Applying the principles set forth above to the facts of this case, it is beyond question that defendant Belton was the subject of a lawful custodial arrest on the charge of possessing marijuana. The search of his jacket followed immediately upon that arrest. "The jacket was located inside the passenger compartment of the car in which [Belton] had been a passenger just before he was arrested." *Id.* at 2865. Consequently, the jacket was "within the arrestee's immediate control" as defined by *Chimel,* and "[t]he search of the jacket, therefore, was a search incident to a lawful custodial arrest, and it did not violate the Fourth and Fourteenth Amendments." *Id.*

NOTE

1. During the course of its opinion in *Belton,* the Court recognized that there may be times that some containers found inside the passenger compartment will "be such that they could hold neither a weapon nor evidence of the criminal conduct for which the suspect was arrested." *Id.* at 2864. Nonetheless, a search incident to the arrest of the occupant of an automobile would include all such containers. In this respect, the Court emphasized that in *United States v. Robinson, supra,* it had already

> rejected the argument that such a container—there a "crumpled up cigarette package"—located during a search of Robinson incident to his arrest could not be searched: "The authority to search the person incident to a lawful custodial arrest, while based on the need to disarm and to discover evidence, does not depend on what a court may later decide was the probability in a particular arrest situation that weapons or evidence would in fact be found upon the person of the suspect. *A custodial arrest of a suspect based on probable cause is a reasonable intrusion under the Fourth Amendment; that intrusion being lawful, a search incident to the arrest requires no additional justification."*

Belton at 2864 (quoting *Robinson* at 235, 94 *S.Ct.* at 476). [Emphasis added.]

2. *The permissible scope of a Belton search.* In *Belton,* the Court expressly held that a vehicle search incident to arrest extends to the entire passenger compartment and "any containers found within the passenger compartment." *Id.,* 101 *S.Ct.* at 2864. "Courts have interpreted the 'passenger compartment' requirement broadly in order to effectuate its purpose of protecting police officers and citizens from

defendants reaching for a weapon or destroying evidence." *United States v. Veras*, 51 *F.*3d 1365, 1371 (7th Cir. 1995). *See also United States v. Thompson*, 906 *F.*2d 1292, 1298 (8th Cir. 1990) ("passenger compartment is interpreted broadly by most courts and generally includes whatever area is within a passenger's reach").

(a) Removable stereo casing. In *United States v. Willis*, 37 *F.*3d 313, 316 (7th Cir. 1994), the court held that the officer's search of the inside of a removable stereo casing was proper as a search incident to arrest. In this respect, the removable stereo was held to be a "container" under *Belton* because it was an object capable of holding another object. *Id.* at 317.

(b) Secret compartments. In *United States v. Veras, supra,* the court held that the search of a secret compartment located in the back seat of defendant's car was part of the "passenger compartment," and therefore a permissible area for the officers to search.

(c) Trucks. See United States v. Chapman, 954 *F.*2d 1352, 1358 (7th Cir. 1992) (holding that the rear area of a truck and duffle bag found therein functioned as a passenger compartment of the vehicle).

(d) Station wagons. See United States v. Pino, 855 *F.*2d 357, 364 (6th Cir. 1988) (rear section of a mid-sized station wagon qualified as a passenger compartment).

(e) Hatchbacks and sport utility vehicles. In order to determine whether a search of a vehicle is permissible in scope, courts will examine whether the area searched is generally "reachable without exiting the vehicle, without regard to the likelihood in the particular case that such a reaching was possible." *United States v. Allen*, 469 *F.*3d 11, 15 (1st Cir. 2006). Thus, in *United States v. Doward*, 41 *F.*3d 789, 794 (1st Cir. 1994), the court applied the *Belton* rationale to a search of the hatchback area of a two-door Ford Mustang, finding the area searched to have been "generally reachable without exiting the vehicle." *See also United States v. Mayo*, 394 *F.*3d 1271, 1276 (9th Cir. 2005) (search of hatchback of Honda civic valid under *Belton*); *United States v. Russell*, 670 *F.*2d 323, 327 (D.C.Cir. 1982) (hatchback area qualified as a passenger compartment).

This bright-line rule also extends to sport utility vehicles. *See United States v. Allen, supra* at 15 (the *Belton* rule applies to an Isuzu Rodeo, a medium-size sport utility vehicle equipped with a rear storage area that "is clearly reachable without exiting the vehicle"); *United States v. Olguin-Rivera*, 168 *F.*3d 1203, 1205 (10th Cir. 1999) (covered cargo area of an SUV); *United States v. Henning*, 906 *F.*2d 1392, 1396 (10th Cir 1991) (Where "the vehicle contains no trunk, the entire inside of the vehicle constitutes the passenger compartment and may be lawfully searched.").

Accordingly, where the scope of the search is limited to areas accessible from within the passenger compartment, including areas that are "hatches," or rear storage areas, it will be permissible.

(f) Locked containers. In holding that a vehicle incident search extends to the entire passenger compartment and "any containers" found therein, the *Belton* Court determined that "[s]uch a container may, of course be searched whether it is open or closed, since the justification for the search is not that the arrestee has no privacy interest in the container, but that the lawful custodial arrest justifies the infringement of any privacy interest the arrestee may have." *Belton,* 101 *S.Ct.* at 2864. The Court defined "container" as "any object capable of holding another object. It thus includes closed or open glove compartments, consoles, or other receptacles located anywhere within the passenger compartment, as well as luggage, boxes, bags, clothing, and the like." *Id.* at 2864 n.4.

What is not entirely clear by the majority's opinion in *Belton* is whether the Court's reference to "any containers" also covers "locked" containers. In this respect, Justices Brennan and Marshall, in their dissent, read the majority's holding as including locked containers, reasoning that the result would "presumably be the same" even if the search "had extended to locked luggage." Justice White, joined by Justice Marshall, interpreted the majority opinion as permitting the vehicle incident search of "any containers found therein, whether locked or not."

Subsequent treatment of this issue by various circuit courts has resulted in the finding that the *Belton* vehicle incident search covers locked containers. *See e.g., United States v. Gonzalez,* 71 *F.*3d 819 (11th Cir. 1996) (search of glove compartment "whether locked or unlocked" permissible under *Belton*); *United States v. Woody,* 55 *F.*3d 1257 (7th Cir. 1995) (*Belton* vehicle incident search lawfully extended to "the locked glove compartment"); *United States v. Thomas,* 11 *F.*3d 620 (6th Cir. 1993) (search of locked firebox permissible under *Belton*); *United States v. McCrady,* 774 *F.*2d 868 (8th Cir. 1985) (search of locked glove compartment permissible under *Belton*); *Staten v. United States,* 562 *A.*2d 90 (D.C.App. 1989) (search of locked glove box permissible under *Belton*).

3. *A search that is a "contemporaneous incident" of an arrest.* In *United States v. Doward,* 41 *F.*3d 789 (1st Cir. 1994), Manchester police stopped the Ford Mustang that Doward was driving after it made an illegal turn. A routine license check disclosed that Doward was wanted in Ohio on an outstanding arrest warrant. He was therefore ordered out of the car, arrested, handcuffed, and then placed in the patrol car. Immediately thereafter, the police instructed Doward's front seat passenger to step out of the car and stand on the sidewalk as the front and back seat areas of the car were searched. Although the hatch area was accessible from the rear seat, one of the officers decided to gain access by unlocking the hatch from outside the vehicle. The hatch area contained two partially zipped suitcases. In one, the

officer found a gun cleaning kit and ammunition. As the officer continued to search, the police van arrived and transported defendant to the station. Thereafter, a search of the second suitcase uncovered a loaded .38 caliber handgun. The search occurred approximately three minutes after Doward's arrest, and concluded approximately thirty seconds after he was transported from the scene.

Finding the search lawful under *Belton*, the court rejected Doward's contention that the search that yielded the handgun was not "sufficiently contemporaneous with his arrest because the handgun was seized *after* he had been removed from the scene, at a time when there was no conceivable risk that he could have reached it." *Doward* at 791. [Court's emphasis.] The court explained:

> * * * *Belton* upheld a warrantless search of the entire "passenger compartment" against a claim that all its occupants were *outside* the vehicle at the time of the search—thus, as a practical matter, no longer within "reach" of any weapons, evidence or contraband located within the passenger compartment. * * *

> [The *Belton* Court's] circumspect use of the discrete phrase "contemporaneous *incident* of that arrest," rather than the less expansive phrase "contemporaneous *with* that arrest"—as Doward would have us read it—plainly implies greater temporal leeway between the custodial arrest and the search than Doward [suggests]. Moreover, the temporal limitation urged by Doward would undermine *Belton*'s bright-line rule by requiring courts to second-guess the security assessments made by law enforcement officers at the scene.

> * * * Nothing in [*Belton*] even remotely implies that law enforcement officers must *discontinue* a passenger compartment search— properly initiated as a contemporaneous *incident* of an occupant's arrest—the instant the arrestee is transported from the scene. As must be the usual case in automobile-related arrests, Belton and the three passengers were no longer in the vehicle when the automobile search began. Although their location outside the vehicle virtually eliminated any chance that they could "reach" into the passenger compartment for any purpose, the Court conspicuously passed up the opportunity to limit its bright-line rule by requiring that the warrantless search cease once all occupants were removed from the passenger compartment.

Id. at 792, 793. [Court's emphasis.]

4. *Making contact with the person arrested after he has already left the vehicle.* In *New York v. Belton*, the Court held that when a police officer has made a lawful custodial arrest of an occupant of an automobile, the officer may conduct a search of the passenger compartment of that vehicle as a contemporaneous incident of the arrest. In *Thornton v. United States,* 541 *U.S.* 615, 124 *S.Ct.* 2127 (2004), the Court held that *Belton*'s rule is not limited to situations where the officer makes contact

with the occupant while the occupant is inside the vehicle. According to the Court, "*Belton* governs even when an officer does not make contact until the person arrested has left the vehicle." *Id.*, 124 *S.Ct.* at 2129.

In *Thornton*, while on patrol, Officer Nichols noticed the Lincoln Town Car that defendant Marcus Thornton was driving slow down so as to avoid driving next to him. At the time, Nichols was in uniform but was driving an unmarked police car. Nichols suspected that Thornton knew he was a police officer and for some reason did not want to pull next to him. Nichols pulled off onto a side street and allowed Thornton to pass him. The officer then ran a check on Thornton's vehicle registration, which revealed that the license plates had been issued to a 1982 Chevy two-door and not to a Lincoln Town Car. Before Officer Nichols had an opportunity to pull him over, however, Thornton drove into a parking lot, parked, and got out of the vehicle. Nichols immediately pulled in behind him, parked the patrol car, approached Thornton and asked him for his driver's license. Nichols also told Thornton his license tags did not match the vehicle that he was driving.

At the time, Thornton "appeared nervous. He began rambling and licking his lips; he was sweating." *Id.* Concerned for his safety, Nichols asked Thornton if he had any narcotics or weapons on him or in his vehicle. Thornton said no. Nichols then asked Thornton if he could pat him down; Thornton agreed. During the patdown, Nichols felt a bulge in Thornton's left front pocket and again asked him if he had "any illegal narcotics on him." *Id.* This time, Thornton stated that he did, "and he reached into his pocket and pulled out two individual bags, one containing three bags of marijuana and the other containing a large amount of crack cocaine." *Id.* Officer Nichols handcuffed Thornton, informed him that he was under arrest, and placed him in the back seat of the patrol car. He then searched the Lincoln Town Car and found a 9-millimeter handgun under the driver's seat.

In this appeal, defendant argued that the search of his vehicle's passenger compartment incident to his arrest exceeded the scope of the *Belton* rule, contending that *Belton* should be limited to situations where the officer initiates contact with an arrestee while the arrestee is still an occupant of the car. *The United States Supreme Court disagreed.*

In *New York v. Belton*, the Court set forth a "bright line" rule governing motor-vehicle related searches incident to arrest. The *Belton* rule did not turn on the fact that "the officer in *Belton* ordered the occupants out of the vehicle, or initiated contact with them while they remained within it." *Thornton* at 2131. Nor did the Court here in *Thornton* find "such a factor persuasive in distinguishing the current situation[.]" The Court reasoned:

> There is simply no basis to conclude that the span of the area generally within the arrestee's immediate control is determined by whether the arrestee exited the vehicle at the officer's direction, or whether the officer initiated contact with him while he remained in the car. * * *

In all relevant aspects, the arrest of a suspect who is next to a vehicle presents identical concerns regarding officer safety and the destruction of evidence as the arrest of one who is inside the vehicle. An officer may search a suspect's vehicle under *Belton* only if the suspect is arrested. A custodial arrest is fluid and "[t]he danger to the police officer flows from *the fact of the arrest*, and its attendant proximity, stress, and uncertainty. " * * * The stress is no less merely because the arrestee exited his car before the officer initiated contact, nor is an arrestee less likely to attempt to lunge for a weapon or to destroy evidence if he is outside of, but still in control of, the vehicle. In either case, the officer faces a highly volatile situation. It would make little sense to apply two different rules to what is, at bottom, the same situation.

Id. at 2131. [Emphasis in original.]

During the course of its opinion, the Court observed that in some circumstances, "it may be safer and more effective for officers to conceal their presence from a suspect until he has left his vehicle. Certainly that is a judgment officers should be free to make." *Id.*

"*Belton* allows police to search the passenger compartment of a vehicle incident to a lawful custodial arrest of both 'occupants' and 'recent occupants.' Indeed, the [defendant] in *Belton* was not inside the car at the time of the arrest and search; he was standing on the highway. In any event, while an arrestee's status as a 'recent occupant' may turn on his temporal or spatial relationship to the car at the time of the arrest and search, it certainly does not turn on whether he was inside or outside the car at the moment that the officer first initiated contact with him." *Id.*

"To be sure, not all contraband in the passenger compartment is likely to be readily accessible to a 'recent occupant.' It is unlikely in this case that [Thornton] could have reached under the driver's seat for his gun once he was outside of his automobile. But the firearm and the passenger compartment in general were no more inaccessible than were the contraband and the passenger compartment in *Belton*. The need for a clear rule, readily understood by police officers and not depending on differing estimates of what items were or were not within reach of an arrestee at any particular moment, justifies the sort of generalization which *Belton* enunciated. Once an officer determines that there is probable cause to make an arrest, it is reasonable to allow officers to ensure their safety and to preserve evidence by searching the entire passenger compartment." *Id.* at 2132.

Accordingly, so long as an arrestee is the sort of "recent occupant" of a vehicle such as Thornton was here, "officers may search that vehicle incident to the arrest." *Id.*

5. *New Federalism and the Belton "bright line" rule.* The United States Supreme Court's interpretations of the Fourth Amendment establish not the ceiling but only the base-line floor of minimum constitutional protection. Thus, many state courts have not hesitated to afford state citizens greater protection against unreasonable searches

and seizures under parallel state constitutional provisions than would be the case under the Fourth Amendment. As noted in other sections, it is well settled that, as an established principle of our federalist system, state constitutions may be a source of "individual liberties more expansive than those conferred by the Federal Constitution." *Prune-Yard Shopping Center v. Robins,* 447 *U.S.* 74, 81, 100 *S.Ct.* 2035, 2040 (1980). *See also Oregon v. Hass,* 420 *U.S.* 714, 718, 95 *S.Ct.* 1215, 1218-19 (1975); "Symposium: The Emergence of State Constitutional Law," 63 *Tex. L.Rev.* 959 (1985); Pollock, "State Constitutions as Separate Sources of Fundamental Rights," 35 *Rutgers L.Rev.* 707 (1983); Brennan, "State Constitutions and the Protection of Individual Rights," 90 *Harv. L.Rev.* 489 (1977).

For example, in flatly rejecting *Belton*'s "bright line" rule, the New Jersey Supreme Court, in *State v. Eckel,* 185 *N.J.* 523, 888 *A.*2d 1266 (2006), addressed the issue whether the police may conduct a warrantless search of an automobile as incident to an arrest after the occupants have been arrested, removed from the vehicle, and secured in police custody. Said the Court:

> Because the search incident to arrest exception to the warrant requirement was limned for two specific purposes—the protection of the police and the preservation of evidence—and because neither purpose can be advanced by searching the vehicle of a person who effectively is incapacitated, we hold that such a search is incompatible with Article I, Paragraph 7 of the New Jersey Constitution. To the extent *New York v. Belton* * * * has concluded otherwise in interpreting the Federal Constitution, we respectfully part company with the United States Supreme Court.

Id., 185 *N.J.* at 524.

See also State v. Gant, 216 *Ariz.* 1, 162 *P.*3d 640 (2007) (the "search incident to arrest" exception does not permit a search of an arrestee's car when the scene is secure and the arrestee is handcuffed, seated in the back of a patrol car, and under the supervision of a police officer"); *Commonwealth v. Toole,* 389 *Mass.* 159, 448 *N.E.*2d 1264, 1267 (1983) (incident search of truck's passenger compartment is unlawful under Massachusetts law where defendant had been arrested, handcuffed, and placed in the custody of two officers while the search was conducted"); *Camacho v. State,* 119 *Nev.* 395, 75 *P.*3d 370, 374 (2003) (Nevada has rejected *Belton*'s reasoning, choosing instead to follow *Chimel v. California*); *State v. Arredondo,* 123 *N.M.* 628, 944 *P.*2d 276, 284-85 (Ct.App. 1997), *overruled on other grounds by State v. Steinzig,* 127 *N.M.* 752, 987 *P.*2d 409 (1999) ("New Mexico Constitution requires a fact-specific inquiry" rather than *Belton*'s "bright-line rule"); *People v. Blasich,* 73 *N.Y.*2d 673, 543 *N.Y.S.*2d 40, 541 *N.E.*2d 40, 43 (1989) (refusing to adopt *Belton*'s "bright-line approach to automobile searches incident to arrest as a matter of State constitutional law"); *State v. Kirsch,* 69 *Or.App.* 418, 686 *P.*2d 446 (1984) ("*Belton* is not the law of Oregon"); *Commonwealth v. White,* 543 *Pa.* 45, 669 *A.*2d 896, 902 (1995) (rejecting *Belton,* holding that a warrantless incident search of an automobile is limited to a "search of the person and the immediate area which the person occupies during his custody"); *Vasquez v. State*, 990 *P*.2d 476, 489 (Wyo. 1999) (the Wyoming Constitution "requires a search be reasonable under all circumstances," resulting in "a narrower application than *Belton*").

UNITED STATES v. PATTERSON
United States Court of Appeals
65 *F*.3d 68 (7th Cir. 1995)

QUESTION: May the interior of a motor vehicle be exposed to a narcotics detection dog as part of a search incident to an occupant's lawful arrest ?

ANSWER: YES. As a valid incident of a motor vehicle occupant's lawful arrest, the interior of the motor vehicle may be searched, and this search may include the exposing of the interior of the vehicle to the trained sniff of a narcotics detection dog. *Id*. at 71.

RATIONALE: In the third week of April, Trooper Brown, while patrolling I-94 in Dunn County, Wisconsin, observed a black GMC Jimmy pulled over to the side of the road. At the time, two people were standing beside it. Brown stopped to investigate, first speaking to an individual identified as Elzie Johnson. Johnson told the trooper that they were having transmission trouble and that the car belonged to the second individual, (defendant) Michael Patterson, who was working under the hood of the car. Trooper Brown then spoke to Patterson, who stated that he was the owner of the car, and that he was adding transmission fluid and did not need a tow. Brown noticed a crack in the vehicle's windshield, and told Patterson that he was going to issue him a warning. "Brown observed that Patterson appeared to be nervous and ill at ease, would not make eye contact, and was sweating profusely, even though the temperature was in the upper sixties. Standing by the passenger window, Trooper Brown also noticed a very strong smell of air freshener and saw a cellular phone amidst a debris of fast-food wrappers and soda cans, all of which raised Brown's suspicions as to whether Patterson might be a drug courier in transit. Brown returned to his patrol vehicle to check out the status of Patterson's driver's license and his criminal history. A check of his driving record revealed that Patterson's license was suspended and that he had prior drug convictions. At this time, Brown requested the assistance of a drug-sniffing dog at the scene." *Id*. at 69.

Brown arrested Patterson on the driving-while-suspended charge and, as Patterson sat in the rear of the patrol car, Brown questioned Johnson. Johnson told Brown that "he had taken a bus to Chicago from Minneapolis and was getting a ride home to Minneapolis with Patterson. Trooper Brown then questioned Patterson, who contradicted Johnson and said that the two of them had driven from Minneapolis to Chicago and were returning. Shortly after this conversation, sheriff's deputies arrived with a drug-sniffing Labrador Retriever named Gabby." *Id.*

"Deputy Frawley approached the GMC Jimmy from the rear, downwind, and brought Gabby up to the passenger side of the vehicle. Gabby reacted strongly to the seam of the passenger door and 'sniffed it hard.' Deputy Frawley then cracked open the passenger door" and Gabby gave an even stronger alert. *Id.* at 70. Frawley then permitted Gabby to enter the vehicle and search inside of it. She could not, however, identify the specific location of the drugs.

"At that point, Trooper Brown, believing that he had probable cause to search the vehicle, folded down the tailgate. He noticed that all the screws were missing from the factory-installed cover on the tailgate's interior. Lifting off the cover, Trooper Brown found two plastic bags containing large chunks of an off-white substance, which was later determined to be 474.51 grams of cocaine base." *Id.*

In this appeal, Patterson argued that the narcotics detection dog should not have been allowed to enter the vehicle. *The court of appeals for the Seventh Circuit disagreed.*

Trooper Brown had placed Patterson "under full custodial arrest for driving with a suspended license," after Patterson had failed to post the required bond, and there was no contention in this case that this arrest was improper. The trooper was, therefore, "permitted to search the GMC Jimmy pursuant to the search incident to arrest doctrine." *Id.* at 70-71.

This case is very similar to *United States v. Fiala*, 929 *F*.2d 285 (7th Cir. 1991), where an Illinois state trooper noticed a heavily loaded vehicle driving on the highway. After the vehicle veered from its lane, the trooper pulled it over and issued a warning for improper lane usage. A radio check revealed that the driver had a suspended license; the trooper called for a drug-sniffing dog. The dog alerted the trooper to the possible presence of drugs in the trunk and in a box on the backseat, and the trooper found quantities of marijuana in both locations. Although the defendants challenged the action, this court held that, "under *Belton*, it was a permissible search of the vehicle." *Patterson* at 71 (citing *Fiala* at 288).

As in *Fiala*, "Patterson's behavior and the condition of his vehicle led Trooper Brown to suspect that he was a drug courier." *Id.* Following *Fiala*, the court held that "exposing the vehicle to Gabby's drug-sniffing alert was a permissible search incident to Patterson's arrest. Although Patterson argue[d] that Gabby should not have been let inside the car, the law is clear that pursuant to a custodial arrest, a police officer may 'search the passenger compartment [as well as] the contents of any containers found within the passenger compartment.'" *Patterson* at 71 (quoting *Belton* at 460, 101 *S.Ct.* at 2864).

Trooper Brown could not, however, under the "search incident to arrest" exception, *dismantle* a portion of the interior of the vehicle and search that area. "In order to take apart the tailgate of Patterson's GMC Jimmy, the officers needed probable cause to believe that drugs were inside the vehicle." *Id. See Carroll v. United States*, 267 *U.S.* 132, 153-56, 45 *S.Ct.* 280, 285-86 (1925) (under the "automobile exception" all parts of a vehicle may be searched without a warrant *if there is probable cause to believe* the car contains contraband or evidence of a crime).

251

In this case, the court held that "probable cause existed to search behind the tailgate panel. First, Trooper Brown suspected that drugs were in the car given a number of factors that in his experience indicated the existence of a drug courier: the heavy odor of air freshener, the cellular phone, Patterson's nervous disposition, and fast-food wrappers strewn around the car." *Id.* at 71. "Trooper Brown's suspicions were further aroused when Patterson and Johnson gave inconsistent stories regarding their previous travel arrangements. Finally, probable cause existed to search when Gabby alerted to the odor of drugs and the troopers noticed screws missing from the tailgate interior." *Id.*

Accordingly, the court held that the search of Patterson's car was lawful, and the evidence admissible.

---

§3.3. Exigent circumstances.

MINCEY v. ARIZONA
Supreme Court of the United States
437 U.S. 385, 98 S.Ct. 2408 (1978)

QUESTION: Will the exigent circumstances surrounding the investigation of a serious crime permit the creation of a "crime scene exception" to the written warrant requirement ?

ANSWER: NO. The seriousness of the offense under investigation does not itself create "exigent circumstances of the kind that under the Fourth Amendment justify a warrantless search." *Id.* at 2414. Therefore, "the murder scene exception created by the Arizona Supreme Court is inconsistent with the Fourth and Fourteenth Amendments[. Consequently,] the warrantless search of Mincey's apartment was not constitutionally permissible simply because a homicide had recently occurred there." *Id.* at 2415.

RATIONALE: During the course of a narcotics arrest inside defendant's apartment, defendant shot and killed a Tucson, Arizona narcotics officer. After the shooting, other narcotics officers, "thinking that other persons in the apartment might have been injured, looked about quickly for other victims. They found a young woman wounded in the bedroom closet and [defendant] Mincey apparently unconscious in the bedroom, as well as Mincey's three acquaintances * * * in the living room." *Id.* at 2411.

Homicide detectives arrived on the scene within ten minutes and took charge of the investigation. They supervised the removal of all of the apartment's occupants, and then proceeded to gather evidence. "Their search lasted four days, during which period the entire apartment was searched, photographed, and diagrammed. The officers opened drawers, closets, and cupboards, and inspected their contents; they emptied clothing pockets; they dug bullet fragments out of the walls and floors; they pulled up sections of the carpet and removed them for examination." *Id.* Anywhere from 200 to 300 objects were seized. No warrant was ever obtained.

The Arizona Supreme Court affirmed the trial court's denial of defendant's motion to suppress the evidence seized, holding that "the warrantless search of the scene of a homicide is constitutionally permissible." *Id.* at 2412.

The United States Supreme Court, per Justice Stewart, disagreed.

As a general rule, the Fourth Amendment prohibits "*unreasonable* searches and seizures, and it is a cardinal principle that 'searches conducted outside the judicial process, without prior approval by judge or magistrate, are *per se* unreasonable under the Fourth Amendment—subject only to a few specifically established and well-defined exceptions.' " *Id.* [Emphasis added; citations omitted.] In this case, "[t]he Arizona Supreme Court did not hold that the search of [Mincey's] apartment fell within any of the exceptions to the warrant requirement * * * but rather that the search of a homicide scene should be recognized as an additional exception." *Id.* The United States Supreme Court, however, would not adopt such a "generic exception." *Id.*

While the Court does recognize "the vital public interest" in the prompt investigation of very serious crimes, it nonetheless concludes that "the mere fact that law enforcement may be made more efficient can never by itself justify disregard of the Fourth Amendment." *Id.* at 2414. "The investigation of crime would always be simplified if warrants were unnecessary. But the Fourth Amendment reflects the view of those who wrote the Bill of Rights that the privacy of a person's home and property may not be totally sacrificed in the name of maximum simplicity in enforcement of the criminal law." *Id.* This is the reason "warrants are generally required to search a person's home or his person unless 'the exigencies of the situation' make the needs of law enforcement so compelling that the warrantless search is objectively reasonable under the Fourth Amendment." *Id.*

"Except for the fact that the offense under investigation was a homicide, there were no exigent circumstances in this case[.] * * * There was no indication that evidence would be lost, destroyed or removed during the time required to obtain a search warrant. * * * And there is no suggestion that a search warrant could not easily and conveniently have been obtained." *Id.*

As a result, the Court "decline[s] to hold that the seriousness of the offense under investigation itself creates exigent circumstances of the kind that under the Fourth Amendment justify a warrantless search." *Id.* Accordingly, "the 'murder scene exception' created by the Arizona Supreme Court is inconsistent with the Fourth and Fourteenth Amendments[;] the warrantless search of Mincey's apartment was not constitutionally permissible simply because a homicide had recently occurred there." *Id.* at 2415.

NOTE

1. *Protective, victim/suspect fan-out searches.* In one portion of the Court's opinion in *Mincey, supra,* the Court addressed the State's contention that "a possible homicide presents an emergency situation de-

manding immediate action." *Id.* at 2413. Although the Court declined to hold that the seriousness of the offense under investigation itself creates exigent circumstances of the kind that justify a warrantless search, it nonetheless did recognize "the right of the police to respond to emergency situations [and to make] warrantless entries and searches when they reasonably believe that a *person* within is in need of immediate aid." *Id.* [Emphasis added.] Additionally, "when the police come upon a scene of a homicide they may make a prompt warrantless search of the area to see if other victims or if a killer is still on the premises." *Id.* In this respect, "*[t]he need to protect or preserve life or avoid serious injury is justification* for what would be otherwise illegal absent an exigency or emergency." *Id.* [Emphasis added.] Naturally, during the course of this protective, victim/suspect fan-out search, "police may seize any evidence that is in plain view[.]" *Id.*

2. *There is no "murder scene exception" to the warrant requirement.*

(a) In *Thompson v. Louisiana*, 469 *U.S.* 17, 105 *S.Ct.* 409 (1984), the United States Supreme Court revisited the question whether the Fourth Amendment would tolerate a "murder scene exception" to the written warrant requirement. In *Thompson*, defendant's daughter summoned several deputies of the Parish Sheriff's Department in reference to a possible homicide. Upon arrival, the deputies were admitted to the house by defendant's daughter. They then conducted an immediate protective, victim/suspect fan-out search and discovered defendant's husband in a bedroom dead from a gunshot wound. In another bedroom, the deputies discovered defendant lying unconscious due to an apparent drug overdose. After defendant was transported to a hospital, the deputies secured the scene. Thirty-five minutes later homicide investigators arrived, "entered the residence and commenced what they described at the motion to suppress hearing as a 'general exploratory search for evidence of a crime.' During the search, which lasted approximately two hours, the detectives examined each room of the house." *Id.* at 410. The search produced a pistol found inside a chest of drawers in the same room as the deceased's body, a torn-up note found in a wastepaper basket in an adjoining bathroom, and another letter (alleged to be a suicide note) found folded up inside an envelope containing a Christmas card on the top of a chest of drawers.

Preliminarily, the Court pointed out that "[a]lthough the homicide investigators in this case may well have had probable cause to search the premises, it is undisputed that *they did not obtain a warrant.* Therefore, for the search to be valid, it must fall within one of the narrow and specifically drawn exceptions to the warrant requirement." *Id.* at 411. [Emphasis added.] The Court then emphasized that in *Mincey v. Arizona, supra*, it "unanimously rejected the contention that one of the exceptions to the Warrant Clause is a 'murder scene exception.'" *Id.* [Citation omitted.]

While it is true that *Mincey* involved a 4-day search of the premises, and the search here in *Thompson* took only two hours and was conducted on the same day as the murder, "[a] 2-hour general search remains a significant intrusion on [a person's] privacy and therefore may only be conducted subject to the constraints—including the warrant requirement—of the Fourth Amendment." *Id.*

Significantly, the Court here in *Thompson* again underscored the right of the police to make warrantless entries and conduct protective, victim/suspect fan-out searches when they have reasonable grounds to believe that a person within the premises is in immediate need of assistance. Moreover, the Court again emphasized that if, during the course of such a victim/suspect search, the police discover evidence in plain view, they are permitted to seize that evidence without a warrant. *Thompson* at 412.

(b) In *Flippo v. West Virginia*, 528 *U.S.* 11, 120 *S.Ct.* 7 (1999), the United States Supreme Court once again held that there is no "murder scene exception" to the Fourth Amendment's written warrant requirement. The Court had made this clear in the earlier cases of *Mincey v. Arizona* and *Thompson v. Louisiana.*

In *Flippo*, the Court unanimously rejected the holding of the West Virginia court, which had denied James Flippo's motion to suppress the evidence seized in a warrantless search of a "homicide crime scene" on the ground that "the police were entitled to make a thorough search of any crime scene and the objects found there." *Id.* at 7.

On the day in question, Flippo and his wife were vacationing at a cabin in a state park. Some time during the evening, Flippo called 911 to report that he and his wife had been attacked. When the police arrived on the scene, Flippo met them outside the cabin, showing injuries to his head and legs. The police questioned him and then entered the cabin and found the body of Flippo's wife with fatal head wounds. The officers immediately sealed off the area and had Flippo taken to the hospital. They then searched the exterior and interior of the cabin for footprints or signs of forced entry. Thereafter, at about 5:30 a.m. when a police photographer arrived, the officers reentered the cabin and started processing the crime scene. "For over 16 hours, they took photographs, collected evidence, and searched through the contents of the cabin." *Id.* Among the things found at the scene was a briefcase, which the officers, "in the ordinary course of investigating a homicide," opened. *Id.* In the briefcase, the officers found and seized various photographs and negatives.

Flippo was subsequently indicted for the murder of his wife. At his motion to suppress evidence, the trial court concluded that the police officers, " 'having secured, for investigative purposes, the homicide crime scene, were clearly within the law to conduct a thorough investigation and examination of anything and everything found within the crime scene area.' " *Id.* at 8. *The United States Supreme Court disagreed and reversed.*

As a general rule of criminal procedure, "[a] warrantless search by the police is invalid unless it falls within one of the narrow and well-delineated exceptions to the warrant requirement[.]" *Id.* In 1978, the Court, in *Mincey v. Arizona*, rejected the prospect of a "murder scene exception" to the Fourth Amendment's written warrant requirement. While the police certainly may make "warrantless entries onto premises if they reasonably believe a person is in need of immediate aid and may make prompt warrantless searches of a homicide scene for possible other victims or a killer on the premises," *id.*, they may not conduct full-blown, probing searches of murder scenes without a warrant, valid consent or other *recognized* exception to the written warrant requirement.

As in *Mincey*, there was no indication here in *Flippo* that the evidence would have been lost, destroyed or removed during the time required to obtain a search warrant. Accordingly, once investigating officers have safely secured a murder or other serious crime scene, a warrant (or a properly obtained consent to search) is required in order to conduct a full search of the premises for evidence of the offense.

3. *The need to protect or preserve life.* In *Wayne v. United States*, 318 *F*.2d 205 (D.C.Cir. 1963), the District of Columbia Circuit recognized that "[t]he appraisal of exigent circumstances surrounding * * * forcible entries without a search warrant presents difficult and delicate problems." *Id.* at 211. Moreover, "[t]hese cases do not arise in the calm of the courtroom or library. They are rarely if ever seen by courts except in cases where criminal activity has been uncovered by the challenged police actions." *Id.*

The police in *Wayne* responded to a radio broadcast that there was "an unconscious person in apartment 614 of the Rhode Island Avenue Plaza." The officers were ultimately led to apartment 618, the actual location of the emergency. The officers knocked and identified themselves, but received no answer. After approximately ten minutes of knocking, the police broke down the door and inside found a woman dead from an apparent illegal abortion attempt. While inside, the officers seized several items of evidence found in plain view.

Finding the entry and seizure of the evidence lawful, the court stated: "No one seeking entry 'knew' as a fact that she was dead and no one had a right to assume it was a 'body,' rather than a dying or unconscious person, as the police thought." *Id.* at 212. Additionally, "[b]reaking into a home by force is not illegal if it is reasonable in the circumstances. * * * [A] warrant is not required to break down a door to enter a burning home to extinguish a fire, to prevent a shooting or to bring emergency aid to an injured person. The need to protect or preserve life or avoid serious injury is justification for what would otherwise be illegal absent an exigency or emergency. * * * [T]he business of police[] and fire [officials] is *to act*, not to speculate or meditate on whether the report is correct. People could well die in emergencies if police tried to act with calm deliberation associated with the judicial process. Even the apparently dead are often saved by swift police response." *Id.* Consequently, this court rejects "the idea that society can be frustrated and denied reasonable protection by mechanical adherence to formalism. Police should not be required to lay siege to an apartment to await a search warrant while a life may be at stake. * * * Human life is more important than th[at]." *Id.* at 214.

Accordingly, when police officers or fire fighters "are confronted with evidence which would lead a prudent and reasonable official to see a need to act to protect life or property, they are authorized to act on that information even if ultimately found erroneous." *Id.* at 212.

4. *Police delay and the evaporation of the exigency.* The fact that exigent circumstances may exist at some point during the investigation of a crime will not necessarily justify a warrantless entry "if there is a period of unnecessary delay during which the exigency evaporates or the police might have obtained a warrant." *United States v. Harris,* 629 A.2d 481 (D.C.App. 1993). Where a substantial period of time has elapsed between the commission of the crime and the warrantless entry, a number of questions concerning the timing of the entry are raised. For example:

(1) At what time did the police decide they had sufficient cause to pursue the suspect ?

(2) Did the police act reasonably in waiting that long to do so ?

(3) By the time the police were ready to move against the suspect, were the circumstances still exigent to justify the warrantless entry ?

(4) If so, did the police enter the premises without unreasonable delay ?

Harris at 488. *See also United States v. Minick,* 455 A.2d 874, 876 (D.C.App. 1983) (*en banc*).

BRIGHAM CITY, UTAH v. STUART
Supreme Court of the United States
547 *U.S.* 398, 126 *S.Ct.* 1943 (2006)

QUESTION: May the police enter a home without a warrant when they have an objectively reasonable basis for believing that an occupant is seriously injured or imminently threatened with such injury?

ANSWER: YES. Law enforcement officers "may enter a home without a warrant to render emergency assistance to an injured occupant or to protect an occupant from imminent injury." *Id.* at 1947.

RATIONALE: In late July, at about 3 a.m., "four police officers responded to a call regarding a loud party at a residence. Upon arriving at the house, they heard shouting from inside, and proceeded down the driveway to investigate. There, they observed two juveniles drinking beer in the backyard. They entered the backyard, and saw—through a screen door and windows—an altercation taking place in the kitchen of the home." *Id.* at 1946. At the time, "four adults were attempting, with some difficulty, to restrain a juvenile. The juvenile eventually broke free, swung a fist and struck one of the adults in the face." *Id.* The victim of the blow was then observed spitting blood into a nearby sink. "The other adults continued to try to restrain the juvenile, pressing him up against a refrigerator with such force that the refrigerator began moving across the floor. At this point, an officer opened the screen door and announced the officers' presence. Amid the tumult, nobody noticed. The officer entered the kitchen and again cried out, and as the occupants slowly became aware that the police were on the scene, the altercation ceased." *Id.* The officers subsequently arrested the adults, charging them with various offenses.

In this appeal, the defendants argued that the warrantless entry violated the Fourth Amendment. *The United States Supreme Court disagreed.*

As a basic principle of Fourth Amendment law, warrantless searches and seizures inside a home are "presumptively unreasonable." *Id.* at 1947. "Nevertheless, because the ultimate touchstone of the Fourth Amendment is 'reasonableness,' the warrant requirement is subject to certain exceptions." *Id.* For example, law enforcement officers may make a warrantless entry onto private property to fight a fire and investigate its cause, *Michigan v. Tyler*, 436 *U.S.* 499, 98 *S.Ct.* 1942 (1978), to prevent the imminent destruction of evidence, *Ker v. California*, 374 *U.S.* 23, 83 *S.Ct.* 1623 (1963), or to engage in "hot pursuit" of a fleeing suspect, *United States v. Santana*, 427 *U.S.* 38, 96 *S.Ct.* 2406 (1976). Thus, the "exigencies of the situation" may make the needs of law enforcement "so compelling that [a] warrantless search is objectively reasonable under the Fourth Amendment." *Stuart* at 1947.

"One exigency obviating the requirement of a warrant is the need to assist persons who are seriously injured or threatened with such injury. The need to protect or preserve life or avoid serious injury is justification for what would be otherwise illegal absent an exigency or emergency.'" *Id.* [Citations omitted.] "Accordingly, law enforcement officers may enter a home without a warrant to render emergency assistance to an injured occupant or to protect an occupant from imminent injury." *Id.*

During the course of this appeal, defendants contended that the officers' entry was unreasonable because they were more interested in making arrests than quelling violence. In rejecting this contention, the Court emphasized that an officer's action is "reasonable" under the Fourth Amendment, "regardless of the individual officer's state of mind, 'as long as the circumstances, viewed *objectively,* justify [the] action.' * * * The officer's subjective motivation is irrelevant." *Id.* at 1948. [Citations omitted; Court's emphasis.] "It therefore does not matter * * * whether the officers entered the kitchen to arrest [defendants] and gather evidence against them or to assist the injured and prevent further violence." *Id.*

The defendants also argued that their conduct was not serious enough to justify the officers' intrusion into the home. The Court disagreed.

> Here, the officers were confronted with *ongoing* violence occurring *within* the home. * * * We think the officers' entry here was plainly reasonable under the circumstances. The officers were responding, at 3 o'clock in the morning, to complaints about a loud party. As they approached the house, they could hear from within

"an altercation occurring, some kind of a fight." * * * The officers heard "thumping and crashing" and people yelling "stop, stop" and "get off me." * * * The noise seemed to be coming from the back of the house; after looking in the front window and seeing nothing, the officers proceeded around back to investigate further. They found two juveniles drinking beer in the backyard. From there, they could see that a fracas was taking place inside the kitchen. A juvenile, fists clenched, was being held back by several adults. As the officers watch, he breaks free and strikes one of the adults in the face, sending the adult to the sink spitting blood.

Id. at 1949. [Court's emphasis.]

In light of these circumstances, the Court held that "the officers had an objectively reasonable basis for believing both that the injured adult might need help and that the violence in the kitchen was just beginning. Nothing in the Fourth Amendment required them to wait until another blow rendered someone 'unconscious' or 'semi-conscious' or worse before entering. The role of a peace officer includes preventing violence and restoring order, not simply rendering first aid to casualties; an officer is not like a boxing (or hockey) referee, poised to stop a bout only if it becomes too one-sided." *Id.*

"The manner of the officers' entry was also reasonable. After witnessing the punch, one of the officers opened the screen door and 'yelled in police.' * * * When nobody heard him, he stepped into the kitchen and announced himself again. Only then did the tumult subside. The officer's announcement of his presence was at least equivalent to a knock on the screen door. Indeed, it was probably the only option that had even a chance of rising above the din. Under these circumstances, there was no violation of the Fourth Amendment's knock-and-announce rule. Furthermore, once the announcement was made, the officers were free to enter; it would serve no purpose to require them to stand dumbly at the door awaiting a response while those within brawled on, oblivious to their presence." *Id.*

Accordingly, all of the officers' actions in this case were lawful.

MURDOCK v. STOUT
United States Court of Appeals
54 *F*.3d 1437 (9th Cir. 1995)

QUESTION: Will probable cause to believe a burglary is in progress, or has just occurred and that someone within the premises might be in need of assistance, provide sufficient exigent circumstances to justify an immediate warrantless entry ?

ANSWER: YES. When a law enforcement officer has probable cause to believe that a burglary or other crime is in progress, or has just occurred and that someone within the premises might be in need of assistance, sufficient exigent circumstances arise to justify an immediate warrantless entry of the premises. *Id.* at 1442, 1443.

RATIONALE: On March 23rd, Fontana police responded to a call of a "possible burglary" or other crime taking place at a particular residence. The caller identified himself, indicated that he lived in the neighborhood, and informed the dispatcher that a passerby had told him that he saw a young person run from the residence across the street, enter an automobile and drive away.

Officers Jacobson, Walby and Robins arrived at the house to investigate shortly before 8:30 p.m. The officers noted that, although the house was secure in the front, a sliding door, located in the rear of the house, was open about 8 to 10 inches. "Inside, a television was on 'at a low setting' and the lights were 'dim.' Officer Jacobson twice announced his presence by shouting, 'Fontana Police, anybody home?' The announcement was sufficiently loud for Officer Walby to hear it across the street. No one responded. The telephone then rang several times. No one answered, and an answering machine was activated." *Id.* at 1439.

Officers Jacobson and Robins entered the house and, using their flashlights, and with their guns drawn, searched the living room and kitchen. When they entered the bedroom, they discovered a man, later identified as Clyde Murdock, lying on the bed, partially covered by a blanket. "Officer Jacobson announced that he was a police officer. Because the man's hands were hidden under the blanket, Officer Jacobson eventually removed the blanket, discovering that Murdock was fully clothed and was wearing shoes." *Id.*

"Officer Robins then let Officer Walby in the house. As Murdock had yet to be identified, Walby and Robins continued to search the house for 'possible suspects.' They found nothing. While this additional search was being performed, Murdock refused to answer Officer Jacobson's questions regarding his name and address." *Id.* at 1439-40. Murdock was frisked, and then finally identified by his driver's license. "He continued to act belligerently toward the officers and demanded their badge numbers." *Id.* at 1440. The officers gave Murdock their badge numbers and left, stopping at the complainant's house to inform him that no burglary or other crime had occurred.

Murdock filed a civil lawsuit seeking 20 million dollars in damages. *The Court of Appeals for the Ninth Circuit rejected Murdock's claim.*

"Police entry into a house without a warrant is not [] always unreasonable." *Id.* Rather, a number of "well delineated" exceptions to the written warrant requirement permit law enforcement officers to conduct constitutionally reasonable searches and seizures without a warrant. This case involves the "exigent circumstances" exception to the search warrant requirement.

The hallmark of the "exigent circumstances" exception "is the need for quick action in an emergency situation." *Id.* It has been defined to include

> "those circumstances that would cause a reasonable person to believe that entry . . . was necessary to prevent physical harm to the officers or other persons, the destruction of relevant evidence, the

escape of the suspect, or some other consequence improperly frustrating legitimate law enforcement efforts."

Id. at 1441. [Citations omitted.] The reasonableness of a warrantless entry will be evaluated by reference to "the totality of the circumstances from the perspective of the police officers at the time of the entry." *Id.*

"Although *exigent circumstances* relieve the police officer of the obligation of obtaining a warrant, they *do not relieve an officer of the need to have probable cause to enter the house.*" *Id.* [Emphasis added.] "Probable cause requires only a fair probability or substantial chance of criminal activity, not an actual showing that such activity occurred." *Id.* In examining whether the officers in this case had probable cause to enter Murdock's home, the court observed:

> When three Fontana police officers arrived at the house, they knew that there had been a report of suspicious activity indicating a possible burglary or other crime had been or was being committed. Upon moving to the rear of the house, the officers discovered an open door. Based on these facts, we doubt that there would be sufficient probable cause to support entry. We have upheld, as have other courts, exigent circumstance searches based on officers finding physical evidence of a burglary, such as a broken window or forced lock. *See [United States v.] Valles-Valencia,* 811 *F.*2d [1232,] 1236 [(9th Cir.), *amended,* 823 *F.*2d 381 (1987)] (officers observed signs that front window was pried open); *United States v. Johnson,* 9 *F.*3d 506, 509-510 (6th Cir. 1993) (officers discovered broken window and people inside house who had no identification or keys) * * *; *United States v. Dart,* 747 *F.*2d 263, 267 (4th Cir. 1984) (officers observed locks sawed off and door forced open) * * *. *In our judgment, the open door at Murdock's house was itself not sufficient to satisfy the standards in these cases where physical signs of burglary were evident.*
>
> The police officers did not, however, enter the house based only on the open door and the neighbor's report. They observed several indications that a resident was or should have been at the residence. The lights were on and a television was on, in addition to the door being open. The officers prudently attempted to make contact with the resident, no doubt to make sure the resident was safe in light of the officers' concern that a burglary or other crime might have occurred. Officer Jacobson shouted twice, but received no answer, nor did any resident answer the telephone. These additional pieces of information, indicating that a resident should have been home, but was not responding, combined with the earlier report of suspicious activity and the presence of the open door tip the scales to supply the officers with probable cause to believe that some criminal activity had occurred or was occurring or that a resident in the house might have been in danger or injured.

Id. at 1441-42. [Citations omitted; emphasis added.]

Because the court was convinced that probable cause was clearly present, it had "little difficulty in concluding that exigent circumstances justified the immediate warrantless entry." *Id.* at 1442. The court said:

> [W]hen police are responding to a possible crime, police judgments should be afforded an "extra degree of deference." * * *

> * * * The facts known to the police officers indicated that a resident was not responding when the circumstances inside the house strongly suggested that a resident should have been present. This gave the officers reason to enter immediately without a warrant. Indeed, we are convinced that citizens in the community would have understandably viewed the officers' actions as poor police work if they had left the scene or failed to investigate further at once.

> Once the officers were inside the house they conducted a brief search of the house in order to locate any occupant. After they found Murdock, fully-clothed, wearing shoes, lying on a bed with his hands covered by a blanket, they tried to ascertain his identity. Murdock was uncooperative. The officers acted reasonably in briefly seizing Murdock and conducting a patdown search to look for weapons. * * * After Murdock was identified, the officers immediately left the premises.

Id. [Citations omitted.]

Accordingly, the court held that the officers' behavior was reasonable under all the circumstances—their actions were based on probable cause and "their conduct never exceeded the scope of the exigency." *Id.* at 1442, 1444. Moreover, the fact that the officers' suspicions turned out to be wrong did not alter the court's view that "the circumstances known to them outside the house justified all of their actions." *Id.* at 1444.

NOTE

"Burglaries-in-progress" and patrol dogs cross-trained for narcotics detection. In *United States v. Reed*, 141 *F.*3d 644 (6th Cir. 1998), at 7:30 p.m., four police officers responded to a call of a "burglary in progress" at Joseph Reed's apartment. Within ten minutes of the officers' arrival, Reed arrived and advised the officers that he lived in the bottom unit, where the burglar alarm had sounded. One of the officers explained to Reed that they were going to send in a police K-9 to check the apartment for intruders. Reed agreed that using the dog was a good idea and gave the officers the key to the front door to allow the dog to enter. Once inside, the K-9, "Cheddy," and his handler, Officer Sweat, began a search for intruders. At the time, Reed was unaware that Cheddy was also trained to search for drugs, albeit in response to a different command, and in conjunction with a substantially different "leashing" procedure designed to protect the dog from ingesting drugs. During the search process, Cheddy was not directed to search for

drugs. Nonetheless, he alerted for drugs in several areas during the search. "According to Sweat, an award-winning police canine handler, judge, and certifier, this was a first for the award-winning Cheddy." *Id.* at 647. "Cheddy's conditioned response to an intruder is to bark. In contrast, the dog is trained, when alerting on drugs, to scratch, dig, or bite at the object containing the drugs until Sweat pulls him off. Cheddy first scratched at the livingroom couch indicating drugs, but Sweat called him off thinking the alert was to human scent coming from the basement through a nearby heating duct. Thus, Sweat again ordered Cheddy to 'find them.' In due course, Cheddy entered the master bedroom, and alerted on a dresser by scratching at the right-hand dresser drawers. Sweat, upon hearing the commotion, entered the master bedroom. Although it is unknown whether the dresser drawers were open before Cheddy entered the room, apparently the dog had knocked the top drawer off its runners and into the second drawer, which was also open. To protect Cheddy, whose head was in the top drawer, Sweat pulled the dog away, and noticed a bag of cocaine plainly visible in his bright mag-light beam." *Id.* Sweat and Cheddy continued the intruder search and ultimately gave an "all-clear-of-suspects" announcement. Officer Sweat and the dog had been inside Reed's apartment for about five minutes.

A second officer took Reed inside the apartment to determine whether anything had been stolen by the suspected intruder. Reed proceeded directly to examine the dresser in the master bedroom. During the inspection of the apartment, the officer observed a box for a triple-beam Ohaus scale in the spare bedroom, and cigarette rolling papers on a table near the couch. Reed was informed about the drugs that were found and was placed under arrest. A later search conducted under the authority of a search warrant resulted in the seizure of 23.47 grams of crack, previously seen in the top right-hand dresser drawer, over 53 grams of crack and a quantity of marijuana from the top left dresser drawer, along with drug paraphernalia and a handgun and ammunition found in other areas of the apartment.

Finding the police entry and search entirely proper, the court preliminarily explained that, absent the existence of some recognized exception to the written warrant requirement, police may not conduct a warrantless search of an individual's home. "*One exception,*" observed the court, "*allows police to enter a residence without a warrant if there is probable cause to believe that there is a burglary in progress.*" *Id.* at 649. [Emphasis added.] Under such circumstances, the "initial intrusion" that brings the police "within plain view" of an incriminating article is supported, "not by a warrant, but by one of the recognized exceptions to the warrant requirement." *Horton v. California*, 496 *U.S.* 128, 135, 110 *S.Ct.* 2301, 2307 (1990). "Thus, an officer (1) who is lawfully at a vantage point; (2) who observes obviously incriminating evidence in plain view; and (3) who has lawful access to the contraband, may seize the evidence without offending the Fourth Amendment." *Reed* at 649. "Such a plain viewing and seizure, even if accomplished with the aid of a flashlight, * * * does not exceed the scope of a search * * *." *Id.*

In discussing the use of the K-9, the court observed that it is well settled that a "sniff" by a trained narcotics detection dog "does not unreasonably intrude upon a person's reasonable expectation of privacy." *Id.* The " 'sniff discloses only the presence or absence of narcotics, a contraband item.' * * * Therefore, the limited and discriminating nature of a sniff does 'not constitute a "search" within the meaning of the Fourth Amendment.' " *Id.* (quoting *United States v. Place*, 462 *U.S.* 696, 706-07, 103 *S.Ct.* 2637, 2644-45 (1983)). The court elaborated:

> Just as the sniffing of contraband by trained canines does not constitute an unlawful search, neither does the viewing by humans of contraband in plain sight amount to an unlawful search. As long as the observing person or the sniffing canine are legally present at their vantage when their respective senses are aroused by obviously incriminating evidence, a search within the meaning of the Fourth Amendment has not occurred. In addition, just as contraband in plain view may be seized if legally accessed and may also provide probable cause to obtain a search warrant, so, too, "[a] positive reaction by a properly trained narcotics dog can establish probable cause for the presence of controlled substances."

Id. at 649. [Citation omitted.]

In this appeal, Reed argued that if, during the course of Cheddy's search, the dog moved the drawers, the result is that Officer Sweat's discovery was outside the plain-view doctrine. The court disagreed.

We now take the opportunity to clarify that a canine sniff is not a search within the meaning of the Fourth Amendment. Of course, the canine team must lawfully be present at the location where the sniff occurs. * * * Here, the canine team was lawfully present in Reed's flat, either due to the pursuit of a burglar, or Reed's consent. Any contraband seen by Sweat, or sniffed by Cheddy, therefore, fell within the "plain-view" doctrine or the "canine-sniff" rule. Thus, there was no illegal search in this instance, even assuming that Cheddy moved the drawers * * *. This is so because the movement of the drawers, if any, would have been occasioned by Cheddy's instinctive reactions to the nature of the contraband. Indeed, at least two circuits have found that, absent police misconduct, the instinctive acts of trained canines, such as trying to open a container containing narcotics, do not violate the Fourth Amendment. *See United States v. Lyons*, 957 *F.*2d 615, 617 (8th Cir. 1992); *United States v. Stone*, 866 *F.*2d 359, 364 (10th Cir. 1989). Moreover, the alert itself provided sufficient probable cause for the warrant to issue, such that Sweat's observation was not critical in any event. In fact, the initial alert on the couch, which involved no opening of closed containers, provided probable cause once Sweat realized that no human scent was coming from the locked basement.

Here, Cheddy's alert on the couch, and his alert on the dresser, occurred without any interference with Reed's possessory interest in the contraband, both because no movement was necessary, and because there is no possessory interest in contraband. In addition, Sweat concededly did not move anything when he observed the immediately incriminating appearance of the baggie, and if Cheddy instinctively aided Sweat's observation, there was no violation of the Fourth Amendment.

Id. at 650.

UNITED STATES v. RICHARDSON
United States Court of Appeals
208 *F.*3d 626 (7th Cir. 2000)

QUESTION: May law enforcement officers rely on a "911 call," made by an identified person, to support a warrantless entry and search of a residence reported to be the scene of a murder ?

ANSWER: YES. "911 calls reporting an emergency can be enough to support warrantless searches under the exigent circumstances exception, particularly where, as here, the caller identified himself." *Id.* at 630. "A 911 call is one of the most common—and universally recognized—means through which police and other emergency personnel learn that there is someone in a dangerous situation who urgently needs help. This fits neatly with a central purpose of the exigent circumstances (or emergency) exception to the warrant requirement, namely, to ensure that the police or other government agents are able to assist persons in danger or otherwise in need of assistance." *Id.*

RATIONALE: In the first week of May, "Milwaukee police received a 911 call reporting that a 19-year-old African-American man named 'Lucky' had raped and murdered a female. The caller said that the victim could be found in the basement at 1704 N. 37th Street, a residence the caller described as 'a drug house.' The caller identified himself to the 911 operator as 'Anthony Carter' and explained that he lived at the same address." *Id.* at 627-28. One week prior to this call, the police had received a 911 call reporting a murder at the same address, a call which turned out to be a "false alarm." *Id.* at 628.

Officers responded to 1704 N. 37th Street, a duplex with upper and lower units. "Standing in front of the building was an African-American male holding a dog on a chain. The man identified himself to the police as Clarence Richardson and said he resided at 1704 N. 37th Street. The police officers explained to Richardson that they had received a 911 call reporting a murder," *id.*, and instructed him to secure his dog. "Before the officers entered the duplex, they directed anyone else inside to come out. That call prompted Shannon Purnell, another African-American male, to come outside. The officers then entered the lower unit of the duplex and conducted a search of the entire house." *Id.*

"In the first floor unit the officers observed drugs (marijuana and crack cocaine) and drug-packaging materials on the dining room table. In the southern part of the basement, they saw more marijuana, two scales of the type commonly used to weigh drugs, and over 200 baggies. One officer spotted a Mossberg pistol grip shotgun on the bed in the front bedroom. Also on the bed were envelopes addressed to Clarence Richardson and prescription medications with his name and the 1704 N. 37th Street address on the labels. The officers did not find a female murder victim." *Id.*

Finding the officers' warrantless entry lawful, the court first instructed that " 'the Fourth Amendment does not bar police officers from making warrantless entries and searches when they reasonably believe a person within is in need of immediate aid.' " *Id.* [Citation omitted.] Exigent circumstances have been found to exist "where the police reasonably feared for the safety of someone inside the premises." *Id.* at 629. "However, a police officer's subjective belief that exigent circumstances exist is insufficient to make a warrantless search. Instead, as is normally the case for Fourth Amendment inquiries, the test is objective: 'the government must establish that the circumstances as they appeared at the moment of entry would lead a reasonable, experienced law enforcement officer to believe that someone inside the house, apartment, or hotel room required immediate assistance.' " *Id.* [Citation omitted.]

In this case, the officers' claim of exigent circumstances "was based entirely on the 911 call, and the 911 operators had received a bogus call with almost exactly the same report only a week earlier." *Id.* In this regard, given the risk of fraud or the report of unreliable information, Richardson contended that "a 911 call cannot by itself justify a warrantless search or furnish a reasonable basis for an officer to believe that someone inside the residence needs assistance. *Id.* at 629-30. Rejecting this contention, the court said:

> This line of argument goes too far * * *; it invites us to adopt a presumption under which a 911 call could never support a finding of exigent circumstances. Many 911 calls are inspired by true emergencies that require an immediate response. Those factors have led both this court and others to conclude that 911 calls reporting an emergency can be enough to support warrantless searches under the exigent circumstances exception, particularly where, as here, the caller identified himself. * * * A 911 call is one of the most common—and universally recognized—means through which police and other emergency personnel learn that there is someone in a dangerous situation who urgently needs help. This fits neatly with a central purpose of the exigent circumstances (or emergency) exception to the warrant requirement, namely, to ensure that the police or other government agents are able to assist persons in danger or otherwise in need of assistance. * * * The efficient and effective use of the emergency response networks requires that the police (and

other rescue agents) be able to respond to such calls quickly and without unnecessary second-guessing. * * *

Id. at 630.

The court also rejected Richardson's argument that, on the facts of this case, the police search of the house was "objectively unreasonable" because the "911 caller did not indicate that a rape or murder was in progress; the caller said instead that the crime was complete." *Id.* at 631. The court said:

> [T]he police officers testified that in their experience, laypersons without medical knowledge are not in a position to determine whether a person is dead or alive. Someone who appeared to be dead might revive with immediate medical treatment. The officers stated, therefore, that they assume that anyone reported dead might be alive unless the report comes from qualified personnel such as a paramedic unit. It was on the basis of this assumption that they entered the house. Last, the officers testified that they did not personally know about the earlier bogus report.

Id.

Accordingly, the court held that "it was objectively reasonable for the officers to conclude that the situation presented exigent circumstances on these particular facts." *Id.*

> This is not a case where the report indicated that the body had been languishing in the house for several days. Nor is it a case where other evidence might have made it clear that the victim was indeed dead, and not hovering on the verge of death. A *modus operandi* that is designed to save potential fatalities, where it is objectively reasonable to think that this is possible, is permissible.

Id.

Last, Richardson asserted that "to find exigent circumstances on these facts would lead to abuse of the 911 system: people with a grudge would have an incentive to make phony calls about their neighbors in order to allow the police to enter and search their neighbors' property without a warrant. Or perhaps competing drug dealers would report murders on one another's property so the premises would be searched and the competitor put out of business." *Id.* In rejecting this assertion, the court observed:

> While we do not exclude the possibility of a case in which it would be objectively unreasonable for a police officer to rely on a 911 call, because of additional information available to the officer, this is not that case. It may even be possible, in those rare cases where a false emergency call is made, that the "victim" (that is, the person whose house is searched) might have a remedy against the caller. Whether or not this is true, we have no evidence indicating that the 911 system is abused so often that it is objectively

unreasonable for the police to rely on a call like the one Carter made here.

Id.

Accordingly, the court held that the warrantless search in this case "fell within the exigent circumstances exception to the warrant requirement." *Id.*

EXIGENT CIRCUMSTANCES AND
TELEPHONIC WARRANTS

UNITED STATES v. BERICK
United States Court of Appeals
710 *F.*2d 1035 (5th Cir. 1983)

QUESTION: When assessing the nature of the exigent circumstances facing an officer, will a court consider the time which would have been needed to obtain a telephonic warrant ?

ANSWER: YES. "In assessing the exigencies of circumstances, * * * courts should consider the time needed to obtain a telephonic warrant." *Id.* at 1038.

RATIONALE: Federal magistrates are authorized under *Rule* 41(c)(2), of the Federal Rules of Criminal Procedure, to issue warrants based on telephonic communications. The *Rule* provides that "[i]f the circumstances make it reasonable to dispense with a written affidavit, a Federal Magistrate may issue a warrant based upon sworn oral testimony communicated by telephone or other appropriate means." As the court notes, the "[l]egislative history reflects that an important purpose for the rule was to encourage law enforcement personnel to obtain warrants."* *Id.* at 1038.

"Because the government has the burden of establishing the exigency of the circumstances in order to excuse a warrantless search, the government must ordinarily introduce evidence of the time required to obtain a telephonic warrant and the availability of that warrant." *Id.* By the same token, "in assessing the exigencies of circum-

---

* "Use of search warrants can best be encouraged by making it administratively feasible to obtain a warrant when one is needed. One reason for the nonuse of the warrant has been the administrative difficulties involved in getting a warrant, particularly at times of the day when a judicial officer is ordinarily unavailable. * * *. Federal law enforcement officers are not infrequently confronted with situations in which the circumstances are not sufficiently 'exigent' to justify the serious step of conducting a warrantless search of private premises, but yet there exists a significant possibility that critical evidence would be lost in the time it would take to obtain a search warrant by traditional means." *Fed.R.Crim.P.* 41(c)(2), Notes of Advisory Committee on Rules, 1977 Amendment, reprinted in [1977] U.S.Code Cong. & Ad. News 527, 534.

stances, * * * [a] trial court[] should consider the time needed to obtain a telephonic warrant" and its availability. *Id.* at 1038, 1039-40.

NOTE

1. It is now well settled that the government bears the burden of establishing circumstances of sufficient exigency in order to justify a warrantless search. Moreover, it is similarly becoming well settled that part of that burden requires the demonstration that a search warrant could not have been obtained in time, even by telephone under the procedure authorized by *Fed.R.Crim.P.* 41(c)(2). *United States v. Manfredi*, 722 *F.*2d 519 (9th Cir. 1983); *United States v. Cuaron*, 700 *F.*2d 582 (10th Cir. 1983); *United States v. Jones*, 696 *F.*2d 479 (7th Cir. 1982); *United States v. McEachin*, 670 *F.*2d 1139 (D.C.Cir. 1981); *United States v. Hackett*, 638 *F.*2d 1179 (9th Cir. 1980).

2. *Not just another telephone call.* In *United States v. Manfredi*, 722 *F.*2d 519 (9th Cir. 1983), the court recognized that telephonic search warrants are not instantaneously obtained by the placing of a quick telephone call. In this respect, the court stated: "a telephonic warrant may not be obtained simply by calling a magistrate. Among other things, a 'duplicate original warrant' must be prepared in writing and read to the magistrate verbatim." *Id.* at 523; *Fed.R.Crim.P.* 41(c)(2)(B). Consequently, the time necessary to create the "duplicate original warrant" must be taken into account *unless*, as the court pointed out in *United States v. McEachin, supra*, "it is clear that the exigency in a particular case was so great that it precluded recourse to any warrant procedure, however brief." *McEachin* at 1147.

---

§3.3(a). Easily lost or destroyed evidence.

VALE v. LOUISIANA
Supreme Court of the United States
399 *U.S.* 30, 90 *S.Ct.* 1969 (1970)

QUESTION: Will a narcotics arrest which takes place on the steps outside the arrestee's home provide its own "exigent circumstance" so as to justify a warrantless search of the home ?

ANSWER: NO. A narcotics arrest, in and of itself, which takes place on the steps outside the arrestee's home, will not "provide its own 'exigent circumstance' so as to justify a warrantless search of the * * * house." *Id.* at 1972.

RATIONALE: In late April, officers approached defendant Vale's residence armed with two arrest warrants. They approached in unmarked cars, and upon arrival set up a surveillance of the house. After about fifteen minutes, the officers observed a green Chevrolet drive up, sound the horn, back into a parking space, and then blow the horn again. At this point, defendant Vale, who was well known to one of the officers, was seen coming out of the house. Vale approached the passenger side of the Chevrolet where he had a brief, close conversation with the driver; and after looking up and down the street, returned inside his house. After a few minutes, Vale reappeared on the porch, looked cautiously up and down the street, and then proceeded to the passenger side of the Chevrolet, leaning through the window. Convinced that a narcotics sale had taken place, the officers approached Vale. As the officers neared, Vale looked up and, obviously recognizing the officers, turned around, walking quickly toward the house. "At the same time the driver of the Chevrolet started to make his get away when the car was blocked by the police vehicle." *Id.* at 1971. Several officers quickly alighted from the car and called to Vale to stop as he reached the front steps of the house, telling him he was under arrest. As Vale was placed under arrest, another officer approached the driver of the Chevrolet and, from past dealings, recognized him to be a known narcotics addict. As the officer neared, the driver quickly placed some object in his mouth; he was placed immediately under arrest.

"Because of the transaction they had just observed, [the officers] informed [defendant] Vale they were going to search the house, and thereupon advised him of his constitutional rights. After they all entered the front room * * * a cursory inspection of the house [disclosed that no one else was present.] * * * The search of a rear bedroom revealed a quantity of narcotics." *Id.*

"The Louisiana Supreme Court thought the search independently supportable because it involved narcotics, which are easily removed, hidden, or destroyed." *Id.* at 1972. According to the Louisiana court, it would be unreasonable " 'to require the officers under the facts of the case to first secure a search warrant before searching the premises, as time is of the essence inasmuch as the officers never know whether there is anyone on the premises to be searched who could very easily destroy the evidence.' " *Id.* [Citation omitted.] *The United States Supreme Court disagreed.*

The reasoning of the Louisiana Supreme Court "could not apply to the present case, since by their own account the arresting officers satisfied themselves that no one else was in the house when they first entered the premises. But entirely apart from that point, our past decisions make clear that only in 'a few specifically established and well-delineated' situations, * * * may a warrantless search of a dwelling withstand constitutional scrutiny, even though the authorities have probable cause to conduct it. The burden rests on the State to show the existence of such an exceptional situation. * * * And the record [in this case] discloses none." *Id.* [Citations omitted.]

"The officers were not responding to an emergency. * * * They were not in hot pursuit of a fleeing felon. * * * The goods ultimately seized were not in the process of destruction. * * * Nor were they about to be removed from the jurisdiction." *Id.* [Citations omitted.]

"The officers were able to procure two warrants for Vale's arrest. They also had information that he was residing at the address where they found him. There is thus no reason * * * to suppose that it was impracticable for them to obtain a search warrant as well." *Id.* The Court, therefore, declines "to hold that an arrest on the street can provide its own 'exigent circumstance' so as to justify a warrantless search of the arrestee's house." *Id.*

"The Louisiana courts committed constitutional error in admitting into evidence the fruits of the illegal search. * * * Accordingly, the judgment is reversed"; the evidence must be suppressed. *Id.* at 1972-1973.

NOTE

In *United States v. Sangineto-Miranda*, 859 *F.*2d 1501 (6th Cir. 1988), the court emphasized that when officers seek to rely on exigent circumstances to justify a warrantless entry, "they must show an objectively reasonable basis for concluding that the loss or destruction of evidence is imminent." *Id.* at 1512. As the Supreme Court held in *Vale v. Louisiana, supra,* "an arrest outside the arrestee's home does not automatically justify a warrantless entry into the home on the assumption that evidence is likely to be destroyed. * * * Before exigent circumstances are present, * * * the police must have a reasonable basis for believing there is someone in the house who would likely destroy evidence." *Sangineto-Miranda* at 1512. Accordingly, the Sixth Circuit concludes that "a police officer can show an objectively reasonable belief that contraband is being, or will be destroyed within a residence if he can demonstrate: 1) a reasonable belief that third parties are inside the dwelling; and 2) a reasonable belief that these third parties may soon become aware the police are on their trail, so that the destruction of evidence would be in order." *Id.*

ILLINOIS v. McARTHUR
Supreme Court of the United States
31 *U.S.* 326, 121 *S.Ct.* 946 (2001)

QUESTION 1: May police officers, with probable cause to believe a person has hidden contraband or criminal evidence within his home, prevent that person from entering his home while officers obtain a search warrant ?

ANSWER: YES. "[T]he police officers in this case had probable cause to believe that a home contained contraband, which was evidence of a crime. They reasonably believed that the home's resident, if left free of any restraint, would destroy that evidence." *Id.* at 953. It was reasonable, therefore, for the officers to restrict the resident from entering the home pending the acquisition of a search warrant. The period of restraint—two hours—was "no longer than reasonably necessary for the police, acting with diligence, to obtain the warrant." *Id.* at 951.

QUESTION 2:   Pending the arrival of a search warrant, if a person detained outside of his home asks to enter the home, may the police enter with him to ensure that evidence is not destroyed ?

ANSWER: YES. The need to "preserve evidence" of this "jailable" drug offense "was sufficiently urgent or pressing to justify" the restriction that entry would be permitted only in the company of an officer. *Id.* at 953. "In this case, the police had good reason to fear that, unless restrained, McArthur would destroy the drugs before they could return with a warrant. The reasonable restraint imposed by the police merely prevented McArthur from entering his home "unaccompanied." *Id.* In this respect, the Court said, "the reasonableness of the greater restriction (preventing reentry) implies the reasonableness of the lesser (permitting reentry conditioned on observation)." *Id.* at 952.

RATIONALE: In early April, Tera McArthur approached two police officers and asked them to accompany her to the trailer where she lived with her husband, Charles, "so that they could keep the peace while she removed her belongings." *Id.* at 948. At about 3:15 p.m., the officers arrived at the trailer with Tera, who entered to collect her belongings. Charles was present at the time.

Upon exiting the trailer, Tera spoke to one of the officers, who was standing on the porch, and advised him that he should "check the trailer" because "Chuck had dope in there." *Id.* at 949. According to Tera, Chuck "slid some dope underneath the couch." *Id.*

The officer knocked on the trailer door, told Charles what Tera had said, and asked for permission to search the trailer. When Charles refused to consent to a search, one of the officers departed to apply for a search warrant. The officer remaining at the scene told Charles, who by this time was also on the porch, that he "could not reenter the trailer unless a police officer accompanied him." *Id.* Nonetheless, Charles "reentered the trailer two or three times (to get cigarettes and to make phone calls)," and each time the officer "stood just inside the door to observe what Charles did." *Id.*

The search warrant was obtained by about 5:00 p.m. A search of the trailer uncovered, from underneath the sofa, a marijuana pipe, a box for marijuana (a "one-hitter" box), and a small quantity of marijuana. The officers then placed Charles under arrest, and subsequently charged him with the unlawful possession of marijuana (under 2.5 grams) and drug paraphernalia, both misdemeanors.

Finding the officers' actions reasonable under the Fourth Amendment, Justice Breyer, writing for the Court, held that the lower court erred in granting McArthur's motion to suppress the evidence seized. In so ruling, the Court rejected McArthur's argument that the pipe, box, and marijuana were the fruits of an "unlawful police seizure," *id.*, (the refusal to let him reenter the trailer unaccompanied).

Preliminarily, the Court pointed out that the "central requirement" of the Fourth Amendment "is one of reasonableness." *Id.* In "the 'ordinary case,' " the seizure of property is " 'unreasonable within the meaning of the Fourth Amendment,' " unless that seizure is " 'accomplished pursuant to a judicial warrant,' " issued by a neutral and detached judge after finding probable cause. *Id.* [Citation omitted.]

There are, however, a number of recognized exceptions to the warrant requirement. In this case, the Court could not say that the warrantless seizure was *per se* unreasonable, for it involved "a plausible claim of specially pressing or urgent law enforcement need, *i.e.,* 'exigent circumstances.' " *Id.* at 950 (citing *United States v. Place* 462 *U.S.* 696, 701, 103 *S.Ct.* 2637, 2641 (1983) ("the exigencies of the circumstances" may permit the temporary seizure of property without a warrant)). Beyond that, the restraint at issue here in *McArthur* "was tailored to that need, being limited in time and scope * * * and avoiding significant intrusion into the home itself[.]" *Id.*

In deciding this case, the Court, "rather than employing a *per se* rule of unreasonableness," instead balanced "the privacy-related and law enforcement-related concerns to determine if the intrusion was reasonable." *Id.* In this respect, the Court determined that the officers' actions were reasonable, and hence lawful, in light of the following circumstances.

> First, the police had probable cause to believe that McArthur's trailer home contained evidence of a crime and contraband, namely, unlawful drugs. The police had had an opportunity to speak with Tera McArthur and make at least a very rough assessment of her reliability. They knew she had had a firsthand opportunity to observe her husband's behavior, in particular with respect to the drugs at issue. * * *

> Second, the police had good reason to fear that, unless restrained, McArthur would destroy the drugs before they could return with a warrant. They reasonably might have thought that McArthur realized that his wife knew about his marijuana stash; observed that she was angry or frightened enough to ask the police to accompany her; saw that after leaving the trailer she had spoken with the police; and noticed that she had walked off with one policeman while leaving the other outside to observe the trailer. They reasonably could have concluded that McArthur, consequently suspecting an imminent search, would, if given the chance, get rid of the drugs fast.

> Third, the police made reasonable efforts to reconcile their law enforcement needs with the demands of personal privacy. They neither searched the trailer nor arrested McArthur before obtaining a warrant. Rather, they imposed a significantly less restrictive restraint, preventing McArthur only from entering the trailer unaccompanied. They left his home and his belongings intact—until a neutral Magistrate, finding probable cause, issued a warrant.

> Fourth, the police imposed the restraint for a limited period of time, namely, two hours. * * * [T]his time period was no longer than reasonably necessary for the police, acting with diligence, to

obtain the warrant. * * * Given the nature of the intrusion and the law enforcement interest at stake, this brief seizure of the premises was permissible.

Id. at 950-51.

The Court's conclusion is consistent with prior law. For example, in *Segura v. United States*, 468 *U.S.* 796, 104 *S.Ct.* 3380 (1984), the Court addressed the issue concerning the admissibility of drugs which the police had found in "a lawful, warrant-based search of an apartment, but only after unlawfully entering the apartment and occupying it for 19 hours." The Court there held that the drugs "were admissible because, had the police acted lawfully throughout, they could have discovered and seized the drugs pursuant to the validly issued warrant." *McArthur* at 951.

The United States Supreme Court has never held unlawful a "temporary seizure that was supported by probable cause and was designed to prevent the loss of evidence while the police diligently obtained a warrant in a reasonable period of time." *Id.* at 951-52.

During the course of the lower court proceedings, the Illinois Appellate Court concluded that the officers could not order McArthur to stay outside his home because the porch, where he stood at the time, was part of his home; hence the order amounted to a "constructive eviction," of McArthur from his residence. In rejecting this conclusion, Justice Breyer, speaking for the Court, pointed out that "a person standing in the doorway of a house is in a 'public' place, and hence subject to arrest without a warrant * * *." *Id.* at 952. Nonetheless, the Court did not believe that the difference—porch versus, *e.g.*, front walk—"could make a significant difference here as to the reasonableness of the police restraint; and that, from the Fourth Amendment's perspective, is what matters." *Id.*

Furthermore, under the circumstances, the Court found it reasonable that the officer remaining at the scene, with McArthur's consent, stepped inside the trailer's doorway to observe McArthur when he reentered the trailer on two or three occasions. This officer's actions were in response to McArthur's reentry of his home "simply for his own convenience, to make phone calls and to obtain cigarettes." *Id.* In this respect, the Court said, "the reasonableness of the greater restriction (preventing reentry) implies the reasonableness of the lesser (permitting reentry conditioned on observation)." *Id.*

The Court also rejected McArthur's argument that *Welsh v. Wisconsin*, 466 *U.S.* 740, 104 *S.Ct.* 2091 (1984), requires suppression of the evidence obtained in this case. *Welsh* held that police could not make a warrantless entry of a home to prevent the loss of evidence of drunk driving (namely, the defendant's blood alcohol level) because the offense was a "nonjailable traffic offense." *McArthur* at 952. The evidence seized from McArthur's home was of crimes that were "jailable," not "nonjailable." *Id.* Under Illinois law, the possession of less than 2.5 grams of marijuana is punishable by up to 30 days in jail; the possession of drug paraphernalia is punishable by up to one year in jail.

The restriction here was even less serious. "Temporarily keeping a person from entering his home, a consequence whenever police stop a person on the street, is considerably less intrusive than police entry into the home itself in order to make a warrantless arrest or conduct a search." *Id.* at 953. The Court thus found it clear that "the need to preserve evidence of a 'jailable' offense was sufficiently urgent or pressing to justify the restriction upon entry that the police imposed." *Id.* The Court did not decide, however, whether the circumstances would have justified a greater restriction for this type of offense or the same restriction were only a "nonjailable" offense at issue.

"In sum, the police officers in this case had probable cause to believe that a home contained contraband, which was evidence of a crime. They reasonably believed that the home's resident, if left free of any restraint, would destroy that evidence. And they imposed a restraint that was both limited and tailored reasonably to secure law enforcement needs while protecting privacy interests." *Id.* This restraint, held the Court, met the Fourth Amendment's reasonableness requirement.

UNITED STATES v. RUBIN
United States Court of Appeals
474 *F.*2d 262 (3rd Cir. 1973)

QUESTION: Before exigent circumstances may be found to justify a warrantless search of a residence, must the police have direct knowledge that evidence was *actually* being destroyed or removed ?

ANSWER: NO. This court finds "no requirement that officers must know of the [actual] removal or destruction [of evidence] in order to make the search. * * * When Government agents * * * have probable cause to believe contraband is present and, in addition, based on the surrounding circumstances or the information at hand, they reasonably conclude that the evidence will be destroyed or removed before they can secure a search warrant, a warrantless search is justified." *Id.* at 268.

RATIONALE: During the month of July, customs agents received reliable information that a bronze statue containing a large shipment of illegal drugs would be shipped from Europe to a hospital in the Philadelphia area. "As a result of this information, agents or 'look-outs' were posted at the Philadelphia International Airport and the waterfront." *Id.* at 264. On July 26, a crate, fitting the description given to the agents by the informant, arrived at the airport. The customs agents inspected the crate and statue, and removed a small sample of the contents for chemical analysis. The analysis indicated that the substance was hashish; the statue contained approximately ninety pounds of it. Thereafter, the agents resealed the crate and continued their surveillance. Also during this time, it was learned that Louis Agnes was a possible suspect in this operation. As a result, his house, located at 1819 S. 9th Street in Philadelphia, was placed under continued surveillance.

As expected, on July 28, at approximately 4:00 p.m., the crate was picked up. The pickup was made by two men, one of whom was identified as Louis Agnes. Agnes placed the crate in his car and drove it to 1819 S. 9th Street, where it was unloaded at about 5:00 p.m. "Shortly thereafter, a customs agent was dispatched at approximately 5:10 p.m. * * * to prepare and procure a search warrant. Subsequently, defendant Agnes left the South Ninth Street address at about 6:00 p.m., without the crate, but in his car. He was, of course, placed under surveillance. During this surveillance, [one of the agents] testified that 'it appeared to us that the vehicle (Agnes' car) was becoming evasive and aware we were behind it, and we stopped it and took the operator in custody.' The actual arrest occurred at a gasoline station (some six blocks from Agnes' home), between 6:20 and 6:30 p.m." *Id.*

As defendant Agnes was being taken into custody, he "yelled to the gas station attendants and spectators, 'Call my brother.' The agents testified that at this point they reasonably believed that there existed the 'threat of destruction' to the 'hashish,' which had been de-livered to defendant Agnes' home. Thus, the agents proceeded to en-ter defendant's home in order to preserve the evidence contained therein. Once inside, the officers found the co-defendants, Earl Melvin Agran, Paul Gary Rubin, and Jan Massaar, in the process of packing the 'hashish' for possible distribution; all were arrested and the 'hash-ish' seized." *Id.* This search was made without a search warrant, and upon the arrest of Agnes, the efforts set in motion to obtain a search warrant were abandoned.

At the suppression hearing, the district court rejected the Gov-ernment's argument that the warrantless search of 1819 S. 9th Street was permissible on the basis of exigent circumstances. Because the district court believed that Government officials must have knowledge that evidence is *actually* being removed or destroyed, found lacking in this case, it ordered the suppression of the evidence seized. *The United States Court of Appeals for the Third Circuit disagreed,* finding more persuasive the Government's argument that "the evidence should be admissible because the agents had a reasonable belief that the hash-ish they knew was in the residence was about to be destroyed or re-moved." *Id.* at 264-265.

"Despite the clear preference of the law for searches authorized by warrants, the Supreme Court has recognized several 'exceptional cir-cumstances in which, on balancing the need for effective law enforce-ment against the right of privacy, it may be contended that a magis-trate's warrant for search may be dispensed with.'" *Id.* at 265 (quoting *Johnson v. United States,* 333 *U.S.* 10, 14-15, 68 *S.Ct.* 367, 369 (1948)). In *Johnson,* the Court noted that, in the proper case, it might consider as an exigent circumstance the threatened removal or destruction of evidence or contraband. Later cases have demonstrated the need, how-ever, for circumstances indicating to police officers that evidence was "likely to be destroyed," *McDonald v. United States,* 335 *U.S.* 451, 455, 69 *S.Ct.* 191 (1948), or faced "imminent destruction, removal, or con-cealment." *United States v. Jeffers,* 342 *U.S.* 48, 52, 72 *S.Ct.* 93 (1951).

Significantly, in *Schmerber v. California,* 384 *U.S.* 757, 86 *S.Ct.* 1826 (1966), the Court approved a warrantless blood test performed on a motorist who had been in an accident and was suspected of drinking. A warrant was not required because the officer "might reasonably have believed he was confronted with an emergency, in which the delay necessary to obtain a warrant, under the circumstances, threatened 'the destruction of evidence[.]' " *Id.* at 770, 86 *S.Ct.* at 1835. "Although, if scientific knowledge were imputed to the officer in *Schmerber*, it could be said he had knowledge that evidence was actually being destroyed, the court spoke of 'threatened' destruction. It would seem unwise to put undue emphasis on the use of the word 'threatened' in *Schmerber*. At the same time, however, it cannot be said that the Court was requiring the officer [to] have knowledge [that] evidence was in the process of destruction before any warrantless search could be approved." *Rubin* at 266.

Chimel v. California, 395 *U.S.* 752, 89 *S.Ct.* 2034 (1969), *Vale v. Louisiana*, 399 *U.S.* 30, 90 *S.Ct.* 1969 (1970), and *Coolidge v. New Hampshire*, 403 *U.S.* 443, 91 *S.Ct.* 2022 (1971), represent the three cases relied upon by the district court to suggest "that actual knowledge that evidence was being destroyed or removed was required under the emergency exception." *Rubin* at 266. Although the court here in *Rubin* recognizes that each of these cases speaks of the high standards of exigency which must be present to justify warrantless searches, the court "cannot agree with the district court that these cases allow 'emergency' justification only when the searching officers have knowledge that evidence is actually being removed or destroyed." *Id.*

"In *Chimel*, the police had had time to obtain an arrest warrant. There was no showing that it would have been 'unduly burdensome' for police to have also obtained a search warrant. * * * No emergency had occurred during the arrest to indicate to the officers that removal or destruction of evidence was imminent or threatened." *Rubin* at 266-267. In *Coolidge*, it was held that "when there is not even a reasonable threat that evidence could be destroyed, a warrantless search cannot be justified." *Rubin* at 267. Nowhere in *Coolidge*, however, is there a "requirement that officers have knowledge of destruction taking place to justify a warrantless search." *Rubin* at 267. Finally, in *Vale*, the Supreme Court rejected the contention that exigent circumstances existed, stating: "[B]y their own account the arresting officers satisfied themselves that no one else was in the house when they first entered the premises." 399 *U.S.* at 34, 90 *S.Ct.* at 1972. "The facts did not support a belief by the arresting officers that there was even a 'threatened' destruction or removal of the narcotics. * * * Further supporting the suppression of the evidence in *Vale* was the lack of any evidence suggesting that 'it was impracticable for [the officers] to obtain a search warrant[.]' " *Rubin* at 267-268. [Citation omitted.]

In light of the foregoing, this court finds "no requirement that officers must know of the [actual] removal or destruction in order to make the search." *Id.* at 268. There are standards, however, by which warrantless searches under emergency circumstances should be judged. "Probable cause to believe contraband is present is necessary to justify a warrantless search, but it alone is not sufficient. Probable cause must exist to support *any* search[; however, m]ere probable cause does not provide the exigent circumstances necessary to justify a search without a warrant." *Id.*

"When Government agents * * * have probable cause to believe contraband is present and, in addition, based on the surrounding circumstances or the information at hand, they reasonably conclude that the evidence will be destroyed or removed before they can secure a search warrant, a warrantless search is justified. The emergency circumstances will vary from case to case, and the inherent necessities of the situation at the time must be scrutinized." *Id.*

In the present case, the facts surrounding the entry into 1819 S. 9th Street demonstrate to this court that "the customs agents 'might reasonably have believed that [they were] confronted with an emergency, in which the delay necessary to obtain a warrant, under the circumstances, threatened the destruction of evidence.' " *Id.* at 269. [Citation omitted.] "The agents possessed more than enough information to establish probable cause that hashish was on the premises. * * * The agents also possessed information that the statue had been broken open by the time of the search, as 'kief,' a form of hashish, was found all over Agnes' clothes when he was arrested. They therefore could reasonably conclude that distribution of the hashish was in progress. * * * [T]he agents were aware that men were in the Agnes household at the time the decision to search was made. At least one of them had been seen with Agnes at the time he backed his automobile into his garage with the crated statue in the trunk. The agents therefore could reasonably conclude that at least this person was involved in the narcotics operation." *Id.*

Just prior to Agnes' arrest, he "intentionally pulled into a gasoline station a half dozen blocks from the searched premises, where it appeared to the agents he was known to some of the persons present. When arrested, he yelled, 'Call my brother.' It was not unreasonable for agents to believe that this might be a signal to alert persons still at 1819 South 9th Street of Agnes' arrest and of imminent police intervention into their activities * * *. The nature of the narcotics business necessitates rapid distribution of goods in order to prevent apprehension. Hashish is easily destroyed. Agnes was apprehended in the neighborhood of his home and apparently in the presence of people whom he knew. * * * Although the agents had been watching both doors of the Agnes home, they could not be certain of how quickly the contraband could be destroyed or what surreptitious means might be available for its removal." *Id.*

Based on these facts, the court finds that "[t]he agents had reasonable grounds to conclude that in light of the emergency, it was necessary to enter the premises without awaiting the search warrant. * * * [T]he agents could reasonably have concluded that even a short wait might have been too long." *Id.* at 269-270.

In concluding, the court pauses to note:

> We do not minimize the historic and essential importance of the fourth amendment's protection in shielding the citizen from unwarranted intrusions into his privacy. The strong preference of the Constitution for searches pursuant to warrants is clear. Only the emergency circumstances here justified the entry into Agnes'

house. These circumstances were sufficiently compelling in tipping the delicate balance in favor of protecting societal interests. Our vigilance in protecting the privacy of the individual in his home must not absolutely preclude officers of the law, when they are confronted with exigent circumstances, from effective criminal investigation and law enforcement in curbing illegal narcotics traffic.

Id. at 270.

NOTE

1. The concept of "exigent circumstances" is approached on a case by case basis. As a result, certain factors have emerged which courts consistently find relevant in their determination whether the circumstances confronting an officer in a particular situation were in fact exigent. Such factors include: (1) the degree of urgency involved and the amount of time necessary to obtain a warrant, *United States v. Aquino*, 836 *F*.2d 1268 (10th Cir. 1988); *United States v. Pino*, 431 *F*.2d 1043 (2d Cir. 1970); *Niro v. United States*, 388 *F*.2d 535 (1st Cir. 1968); (2) the reasonable belief that evidence or contraband is about to be removed, *United States v. Davis*, 461 *F*.2d 1026 (3rd Cir. 1972); *Hailes v. United States*, 267 A.2d 363 (D.C.C.A. 1970); (3) information giving rise to an objectively reasonable belief that the destruction of evidence was imminent, *United States v. Socey*, 846 *F*.2d 144 (2d Cir. 1988); (4) the possibility of danger to the police officers guarding the site while a search warrant is sought, *United States v. Chavez*, 812 *F*.2d 1295 (10th Cir. 1987); *United States v. Pino, supra* at 1045; (5) information indicating the possessors of the contraband are aware that the police are on their trail, *United States v. Cattouse*, 846 *F*.2d 144 (2d Cir. 1988); *United States v. Doyle*, 456 *F*.2d 1246 (5th Cir. 1972); and (6) the ready destructibility of the contraband and the knowledge "that efforts to dispose of narcotics and to escape are characteristic behavior of persons engaged in the narcotics traffic," *United States v. Manning*, 448 *F*.2d 992, 998-999 (2d Cir. 1971); *United States v. Davis, supra* at 1031-1032.

See also United States v. Mabry, 809 *F*.2d 671 (10th Cir. 1987) (warrantless entry into and "protective sweep" of defendant's home justified where "experience had taught that if the [drug] sellers did not return to the residence of the source within a short period of time, the supplier would either proceed to destroy the cocaine on the premises and secret the cash or depart the premises with the cocaine and cash"); *United States v. Palumbo*, 735 *F*.2d 1095 (8th Cir. 1984) (warrantless entry and arrest justified where officers feared defendant would become suspicious when party cooperating with police failed to return at expected time and that he would destroy or remove the cocaine before they could obtain a warrant); *United States v. Cuaron*, 700 *F*.2d 582 (10th Cir. 1983) (warrantless search upheld where agents had "reasonable grounds to believe [defendant] might become alarmed and either destroy" cocaine or leave with the drugs and money if co-conspirator cooperating with agents failed to return as expected).

2. *Police-created exigent circumstances.* While the exigent circumstances in *Rubin, supra,* were "police created" in the sense that the customs agents' arrest of defendant at the gas station precipitated the concern that the drugs in his residence might be destroyed, the court apparently did not perceive that the conduct of the agents should affect its conclusion that the warrantless entry was justified. Significantly, it may be said that the agents' conduct in *Rubin* did not rise to the level of an impermissible creation of exigent circumstances, but rather constituted legitimate law enforcement exigencies which arise naturally in the course of appropriate police investigation.

Law enforcement officers may not, however, deliberately create emergency circumstances in order to circumvent the Fourth Amendment's warrant requirement. Several courts have indicated that police-created exigent circumstances, particularly where the officers' conduct was unreasonable or unnecessary, would not justify a warrantless entry. As the court pointed out in *United States v. Aquino,* 836 *F.*2d 1268, 1272 (10th Cir. 1988), "[a]n exception to the warrant requirement that allows police fearing the destruction of evidence to enter the home of an unknown suspect should be * * * supported by clearly defined indicators of exigency that are not subject to police manipulation or abuse." *See also United States v. Munoz-Guerra,* 788 *F.*2d 295, 298 (5th Cir. 1986) ("the government [can]not justify a warrantless search on the basis of exigent circumstances of its own making"); *United States v. Webster,* 750 *F.*2d 307, 327 (5th Cir. 1984), *cert. denied,* 471 *U.S.* 1106, 105 *S.Ct.* 2340 (1985) ("agents, of course, cannot deliberately create exigent circumstances in order to subvert the warrant requirement of the Fourth Amendment"); *United States v. Rosselli,* 506 *F.*2d 627 (7th Cir. 1974) (agents' knocking at apartment door and identifying themselves as police officers unnecessarily created emergency circumstances, especially since there was "no attempt to obtain a warrant" and "no consideration * * * given to placing the defendant's apartment under surveillance while an attempt to secure a warrant was being made."); *United States v. Curran,* 498 *F.*2d 30, 34 (9th Cir. 1974) ("If exigency arises because of unreasonable and deliberate delay by officers, it is not an exigent circumstance capable of dispensing with the requirement of a warrant.").

It appears, therefore, that the appropriate course is to distinguish between police-created exigent circumstances which are designed to subvert the warrant requirement and law enforcement exigencies which arise naturally in the course of legitimate police practices. Illustrative in this respect is *United States v. Webster, supra,* where the defendants brought a motion to suppress the evidence seized during the course of a warrantless search of their hotel room, contending that DEA agents deliberately delayed procuring a search warrant and deliberately refrained from apprehending defendants until they entered the room, whereupon the agents made an immediate warrantless entry and search. The court rejected defendants' contentions and upheld the warrantless entry and search. During the course of its decision, the Fifth Circuit explained:

Agents, of course, cannot deliberately create exigent circumstances in order to subvert the warrant requirement of the fourth amendment. Our first concern in analyzing a claim of manufactured exigency is whether agents could have obtained a search warrant prior to the development of the exigent circumstances upon which they relied. * * *

Moreover, an officer's failure to avail himself of an early opportunity to obtain a warrant will not automatically preclude him from relying on exigent circumstances that may arise thereafter. ("The exigency may arise at any time, and the fact that the police might have obtained a warrant earlier does not negate the possibility of a current situation's necessitating prompt police action.") That the exigency was foreseeable at the time the decision was made to forego or postpone obtaining a warrant does not, by itself, control the legality of a subsequent warrantless search triggered by that exigency. * * *

Warrantless searches based on exigent circumstances must, of course, be reasonable, and "the opportunity to obtain a warrant is one of the factors to be weighed." * * * [T]he reasonableness inquiry should also be informed by the nature of the investigation of which the warrantless activity is a part: *a delay in obtaining a warrant is more likely to be reasonable when part of an "immediate, ongoing investigation" rather than a "planned" or "routine" search or arrest.* * * * "Indeed, in the case of the immediate ongoing investigation, new suspects and evidence of crimes committed bec[ome] known only later in the investigation. Thus, unlike the case of the 'routine' felony arrest, where a given individual and a distinct crime is involved, the fluidity of an ongoing investigation of the distribution of narcotics makes the obtaining of an adequate search warrant more difficult to time in the flow of events. While the possibility of discovering additional participants or evidence of crimes does not negate the warrant requirement, we find that it is one factor to weigh in determining the reasonableness of the government's arrest."

* * * [W]e treat cases differently where agents do more than delay attempts to obtain a warrant and then act upon exigent circumstances that naturally arise. Where agents create the exigency themselves, warrantless activity is *per se* unreasonable and we require suppression of any evidence obtained thereby.

Webster at 327-28. [Citation omitted.]

See also United States v. Hultgren, 713 *F.*2d 79, 87-88 (5th Cir. 1983) (exigent circumstances arose naturally when the transmitter worn by a confidential informant participating in a drug buy suddenly failed; concern for the informant's safety justified the warrantless entry).

SCHMERBER v. CALIFORNIA
Supreme Court of the United States
384 U.S. 757, 86 S.Ct. 1826 (1966)

QUESTION: When, after a motor vehicle accident involving injuries, the driver of the involved car is lawfully placed under arrest for driving while intoxicated, may the police compel that driver to submit to a blood test ?

ANSWER: YES. The Fourth Amendment is not violated by "compelled intrusions into the body for blood to be analyzed for alcohol content" so long as (1) the intrusion is "justified in the circumstances"—that there is a "clear indication" that evidence of intoxication will be found, (2) the test utilized is a reasonable one, and (3) the test is "performed in a reasonable manner"—in a medical environment according to accepted medical practices. *Id.* at 1835, 1836.

RATIONALE: Defendant was arrested for drunk driving. The arrest occurred at a hospital while defendant was receiving treatment for injuries suffered in an accident involving the automobile that he had been driving. At the direction of a police officer, and over the objection of defendant, a blood sample was taken by a physician. "The chemical analysis of this sample revealed a percent by weight of alcohol in his blood at the time of the offense which indicated intoxication, and the report of this analysis was admitted in evidence at the trial." *Id.* at 1829.

According to the Supreme Court, "the questions we must decide in this case are whether the police were justified in requiring [defendant] to submit to the blood test, and whether the means and procedures employed in taking his blood respected relevant Fourth Amendment standards of reasonableness." *Id.* at 1834. In this respect, it is clear that "[s]uch testing procedures plainly constitute searches of 'persons,' and depend antecedently upon seizures of 'persons,' within the meaning of that Amendment." *Id.* In this case, we are dealing with an intrusion into the human body for blood to be analyzed for alcohol content, and "the Fourth Amendment's proper function is to constrain, not against all intrusions as such, but against intrusions which are not justified in the circumstances, or which are made in an improper manner." *Id.*

Here, defendant's warrantless arrest was based clearly on probable cause to believe he had been driving an automobile while under the influence of intoxicating liquor. "The officer who arrived at the scene shortly after the accident smelled liquor on [defendant's] breath, and testified that [defendant's] eyes were 'bloodshot, watery, sort of glassy appearance.' The officer saw defendant again at the hospital, within two hours of the accident. There he noticed symptoms of drunkenness." *Id.* at 1834-1835. At that point, defendant was placed under arrest. This is not, however, the typical case in which a search incident to a valid arrest is generally permissible. The search incident to arrest cases "have little application with respect to searches involving intrusions beyond the body's surface. The interests in human dignity and privacy which the Fourth Amendment protects forbids any such intrusions on the mere chance that desired evidence might be found. *In the absence of a clear indication that in fact such evidence will be found,* these fundamental human interests require law enforcement officers to suffer the risk that such evidence may disappear unless there is an immediate search." *Id.* at 1835. [Emphasis added.]

The facts which established probable cause to arrest in this case, however, "also suggested the required relevance and likely success of a test of [defendant's] blood for alcohol[.] * * * [Additionally, t]he officer * * * might reasonably have believed that he was confronted with an emergency, in which the delay necessary to obtain a warrant, under the circumstances, threatened 'the destruction of evidence'[—] * * * the percentage of alcohol in the blood begins to diminish shortly after drinking stops, as the body functions to eliminate it from the system." *Id.* [Citation omitted.] "Particularly in a case such as this, where time had to be taken to bring the accused to a hospital and to investigate the scene of the accident, there was no time to seek out a magistrate and secure a warrant. Given these special facts, [the Court concludes] that the attempt to secure evidence of blood-alcohol content in this case was an appropriate incident to [defendant's] arrest." *Id.* at 1836.

"Similarly, [the Court is] satisfied that the test chosen to measure [defendant's] blood-alcohol level was a reasonable one. Extraction of blood samples for testing is a highly effective means of determining the degree to which a person is under the influence of alcohol. * * * Such tests are commonplace in these days of periodic physical examinations and experience with them teaches that the quantity of blood extracted is minimal, and that for most people the procedure involves virtually no risk, trauma, or pain." *Id.*

"Finally, the record shows that the test was performed in a reasonable manner. [Defendant's] blood was taken by a physician in a hospital environment according to accepted medical practices." *Id.*

Accordingly, this case presents "no violation of [defendant's] right under the Fourth and Fourteenth Amendments to be free of unreasonable searches and seizures." *Id.* The Court cautions, however, "that we reach this judgment only on the facts of [this case]. The integrity of an individual's person is a cherished value of our society. That we hold that the Constitution does not forbid the State's minor intrusions into an individual's body under stringently limited conditions in no way indicates that it permits more substantial intrusions, or intrusions under other conditions." *Id.*

NOTE

1. *Extraction contemplates chemical testing.* In *United States v. Snyder,* 852 *F.*2d 471 (9th Cir. 1988), the court held that "so long as blood is extracted incident to a valid arrest based on probable cause to believe that the suspect was driving under the influence of alcohol, the subsequent performance of a blood-alcohol test has no independent significance for fourth amendment purposes, regardless of how promptly the test is conducted." *Id.* at 474. Snyder was arrested after the automobile he was driving struck and injured a military police officer. Detecting a strong odor of an alcoholic beverage on Snyder's

breath, the arresting officers took him to a hospital where a blood sample was drawn without his consent. *Two days later*, a blood test performed on the sample revealed a blood-alcohol concentration of .17%. In this appeal, Snyder challenges the warrantless analysis of the sample, calling it an unreasonable search under the Fourth Amendment. "Because the analysis was not conducted until two days after the initial extraction, any exigency had dissipated, he argues, and the government was required to obtain a warrant." *Id.* at 473.

According to the court, "[t]he flaw in Snyder's argument is his attempt to divide his arrest, and the subsequent extraction and testing of his blood, into too many separate incidents, each to be given independent significance for fourth amendment purposes. He would have [this court] hold that his person was seized when he was arrested, his blood was seized again upon extraction at the hospital, and finally his blood was searched two days later when the blood test was conducted. It seems clear, however, that *Schmerber* viewed the seizure and separate search of the blood as a single event for fourth amendment purposes. The only justification for the seizure of defendant's blood was the need to obtain evidence of alcohol content. [Consequently,] the right to seize the blood * * * encompasses the right to conduct a blood-alcohol test at some later time." *Id.* at 473-474.

2. *Formal arrest held not critical to nonconsensual seizure of blood.* In *United States v. Berry*, 866 *F*.2d 887 (6th Cir. 1989), defendant was taken to the hospital after a one-car collision. During the entire time he was treated, he remained unconscious or semiconscious. Also during this time, the medical personnel and the investigating officer detected an odor of alcohol on defendant's breath. At the request of the officer, a nurse took a blood sample for purposes of blood-alcohol testing. When the laboratory results returned, indicating a .15% blood-alcohol concentration, defendant was charged with driving while intoxicated.

Contrary to defendant's contentions, the Sixth Circuit held that the officer's failure to arrest defendant before ordering the blood test was "not determinative." *Id.* at 891. The court interprets *Schmerber* as involving "an application of the exigent circumstances exception to the warrant requirement. * * * Because evidence of intoxication begins to dissipate promptly, it is evident in this case that there were exigent circumstances indicating the need to take such action." *Berry* at 891. In this respect, the court finds "no constitutional violation in police direction of qualified medical personnel at a medical institution or facility without a warrant to administer a blood test when the police have probable cause to suspect that the results of the blood test would be positive." *Id.*

See also United States v. Harvey, 701 *F*.2d 800, 805-806 (9th Cir. 1983) (involuntary taking of unconscious defendant's blood who was not under arrest at the time held not a violation of the Fourth Amendment).

3. *Compelled surgical intrusions into a person's body for evidence.* The Court in *Schmerber* cautioned:

That we today hold that the Constitution does not forbid the State's minor intrusions into an individual's body under stringently limited conditions in no way indicates that it permits more substantial intrusions, or intrusions under other conditions.

Schmerber at 772, 86 *S.Ct.* at 1836.

In *Winston v. Lee*, 470 *U.S.* 753, 105 *S.Ct.* 1611 (1985), the prosecution sought to compel defendant, Rudolph Lee, to undergo a surgical procedure under a general anesthetic for removal of a bullet lodged in his chest. Lee had been shot by a shopkeeper during an unsuccessful armed-robbery attempt. The government contended that the bullet would provide evidence of Lee's guilt or innocence.

Applying the *Schmerber* balancing test, the Court in *Lee* preliminarily noted that "[a] compelled surgical intrusion into an individual's body for evidence [ ] implicates expectations of privacy and security of such magnitude that the intrusion may be 'unreasonable' even if likely to produce evidence. * * * The reasonableness of surgical intrusions beneath the skin depends on a case-by-case approach, in which the individual's interests in privacy and security are weighed against society's interests in conducting the procedure. In a given case, the question whether the community's need for evidence outweighs the substantial privacy interests at stake is a delicate one[.]" *Id.*, 105 *S.Ct.* at 1617. On the one hand, a court must consider "the extent to which the procedure may threaten the safety or health of the individual." *Id.* "Another factor is the extent of intrusion upon the individual's dignitary interests in personal privacy and bodily integrity." *Id.* On the other hand is society's "interest in fairly and accurately determining guilt or innocence." *Id.* at 1618.

Based on this analysis, the Court concluded that the procedure sought by the government represents an example of the "more substantial intrusion" cautioned against in *Schmerber*, and "to permit the procedure would violate [Lee's] right to be secure in his person guaranteed by the Fourth Amendment." *Lee* at 1614. While probable cause plainly existed to support the search, the threats to the health or safety of Lee posed by the surgery are in dispute. The government "proposes to take control of [Lee's] body, to 'drug this citizen—not yet convicted of a criminal offense—with narcotics and barbiturates into a state of unconsciousness,' * * * and then to search beneath his skin for evidence of a crime. This kind of surgery involves a virtually total divestment of [this defendant's] ordinary control over surgical probing beneath his skin." *Id.* at 1619.

"The other part of the balance concerns the [government's] need to intrude into [Lee's] body to retrieve the bullet." *Id.* In this respect, the record indicates that the prosecution "has available substantial additional evidence" of the origin of the bullet. "[A]lthough the bullet may turn out useful to the [government's case, it] has failed to demonstrate a compelling need for it. [Consequently, under the circumstances of this case, the prosecution] has failed to demonstrate that it would be 'reasonable' under the terms of the Fourth Amendment to search for evidence of this crime by means of the contemplated surgery." *Id.* at 1620.

4. *Stomach pumping.* In *Rochin v. California,* 342 *U.S.* 165, 72 *S.Ct.* 205 (1952), having "some information" that Rochin was selling narcotics, three officers forced open the door to his room and found him sitting on his bed, partially dressed. As the officers noticed two capsules on a night stand beside the bed, Rochin grabbed the pills and put them in his mouth. A struggle ensued, with the officers grabbing Rochin and unsuccessfully trying to retrieve the pills from his mouth. Rochin was taken to a nearby hospital where, at the direction of one of the officers, a doctor pumped his stomach. This procedure produced vomiting, and in the vomited matter, the police found two capsules which proved to contain morphine.

In holding that the police action violated Due Process, the Court declared:

> This is conduct that shocks the conscience. Illegally breaking into the privacy of [Rochin], the struggle to open his mouth and remove what was there, the forcible extraction of his stomach's contents— this course of proceeding by agents of the government to obtain evidence is bound to offend even hardened sensibilities. They are methods too close to the rack and screw to permit constitutional differentiation.

Id. at 172, 72 *S.Ct.* at 209-10.

5. *Swallowing contraband.* In *State v. Hodson,* 907 *P.*2d 1155 (Utah 1995), a police informant participated in a controlled buy of heroin with defendant Hodson. After completing the purchase, the informant gave a prearranged signal to drug enforcement agents Garcia and Smith. The agents then activated their overhead emergency lights and drove to Hodson's automobile. As they neared his vehicle, "Hodson apparently saw their lights and 'threw something in his mouth.' " *Id.* at 1156. Smith alerted Garcia of Hodson's actions, and both agents exited their vehicle.

"While Hodson was still sitting in the driver's seat of his vehicle, Garcia ran up to him, grabbed him by the cheeks, held a gun to the side of his face, and ordered him to 'spit it out.' When he did not comply with the order, Garcia placed his gun on top of the vehicle, and as Smith opened the door, Garcia pulled him out of the vehicle and onto the ground. Garcia placed his arm around Hodson's neck and again ordered him to spit out the contents of his mouth. Hodson spat out some plastic-wrapped chips, and Garcia retrieved additional chips by inserting his fingers in Hodson's mouth. A total of eight heroin chips were recovered from his mouth." *Id.*

In this appeal, Hodson argued that the seizure of the heroin was constitutionally unreasonable. The Supreme Court of Utah agreed. Relying on *Winston v. Lee, supra,* the court set forth the test for determining the reasonableness of a particular search procedure. In this respect, the reasonableness of the use of force in a given search-and-seizure context must be measured against:

(1) the extent to which the procedure used may threaten the safety or health of the individual,

(2) the extent of the intrusion upon the individual's dignitary interests in personal privacy and bodily integrity, and

(3) the community's interest in fairly and accurately determining guilt or innocence.

Id. at 1157 (citing *Winston* at 761-62, 105 *S.Ct.* at 1617-18).

Preliminarily, the court determined that a police officer's act of holding a loaded gun to the head of a person, with the implicit statement that failure to comply will result in the use of the gun, is not "a legitimate means to extract either information or physical evidence[.]" *Id.* According to this court, "in the absence of any resistance, violence, or opposition to them, police officers cannot reasonably threaten to hurt people they are searching." *Id.* The court elaborated:

> Immediately after being threatened with a firearm, this defendant was dragged from his vehicle, thrown to the ground, and ordered to spit out what was in his mouth by an officer whose arm was around his neck. * * * [W]hether or not this defendant's airflow or blood supply was actually impaired, the level of violence and force used by the officer was unreasonable because of the enormous *risk* of such results. It is not plausible to us that in a struggle of this nature, there would not be a very high risk of choking and a very low likelihood of a careful "placing" of hands on the suspect's neck to prevent swallowing without choking. In the totality of the circumstances, there was a considerable risk to defendant's safety and health under the first part of the *Winston* test.

> The dangers presented by constricting the throat make such force anything but reasonable. "The application of force to a person's throat is a dangerous and sensitive activity. It is the type of force that, more than any other, is likely to result in violent resistance by the arrestee." *People v. Trevino*, 72 *Cal.App.*3d 686, 140 *Cal.Rptr.* 243, 246 (1977); *accord People v. Jones*, 209 *Cal.App.*3d 725, 257 *Cal.Rptr.* 500, 503 (1989). [Indeed, in some cases,] death has resulted when officers have constricted a suspect's throat. *See e.g., Williams v. Kelly*, 624 *F.*2d 695, 696-97 (5th Cir. 1980); *McQurter v. City of Atlanta*, 572 *F.Supp.* 1401, 1407-08 (N.D.Ga. 1983). In the refined atmosphere of an appellate court, we can discuss the possibility of a specialty grip that prevents swallowing without choking. However, in the arrest situation, the necessity of immediately constricting the throat and the suspect's predictable lack of cooperation preclude carefully selecting points on the throat prior to applying force. *See People v. Cappellia*, 208 *Cal.App.*3d 1331, 256 *Cal.Rptr.* 695, 701 (1989) [.] The officer will be compelled to prevent swallowing by using whatever brute force is available.

The second part of the *Winston* test assesses intrusions on bodily integrity and dignitary interests, and the level of intrusion here was likewise very high. Defendant was assaulted with a loaded weapon, dragged to the ground, had some degree of force applied to his throat, and had fingers inserted in his mouth without his consent or cooperation. Thus, the weight of the risk and the intrusion under the first two parts of the *Winston* test was considerable, and the critical determination is whether the third factor—the need to preserve evidence of criminal behavior—can shift the balance.

The justification for the force used in this case is the need to preserve evidence and protect defendant from harm. However, we do not know, and cannot ascertain from the record, any of the necessary facts which might have supported a reasonable fear by the officers that swallowing the plastic-wrapped chips would render their contents nondiscoverable or harmful to defendant. * * *

In the absence of an urgent need to preserve evidence, there cannot be a justification for the significant risks to health and safety posed by using the kind of force in this case to get a suspect to spit out what is believed to be a mouthful of drugs. It is true that the suspect has no right to refuse an order to disgorge, but refusal does not lift all limits on what is reasonable police behavior.

Hodson at 1158-59.

The court concluded, therefore, that in this case, the totality of the circumstances demonstrated "an unreasonable search and seizure. The level of force exerted by the searching officer—taking into account the threatening use of the gun, the manhandling of defendant, and the pressure of an arm around defendant's throat to force him to disgorge the contents of his mouth—was excessive and not shown to be required by the need to preserve the evidence or protect defendant." *Id.* at 1159. The court thus declined to adopt a rule which would permit "the placing of officers' hands on the throats of arrestees absent evidence showing that such practices can be safely carried out in the majority of arrest situations." *Id.*

During the course of its decision, the Utah Supreme Court recognized that a majority of courts that have considered the issue have permitted some degree of touching of a suspect's throat to prevent swallowing, so long as no impairment of breathing or blood flow results. The court would not, however, adopt a generalized rule permitting such a procedure "in the absence of expert testimony to the effect that safe methods exist (and can be predictably applied) for placing hands upon arrestees' throats to prevent swallowing without risk to breathing or circulation." *Id.*

6. *Medical emergencies.*

(a) In *State v. Castro*, 238 *N.J.Super.* 482, 570 A.2d 40 (App.Div. 1990), police responded to a vice-principal's call reporting that 18-year-old Phillip Castro stuffed a packet of cocaine in his mouth after being caught in the boy's restroom holding cellophane paper inches from the face of another student who was inhaling the substance. When Officer Monteiro arrived at the school, he was informed that Vice-Principal Belz personally witnessed Phillip stuff the packet of white powder into his mouth. Monteiro also learned from the other participating student that the substance Phillip was using was cocaine, and that "Phil has been doing cocaine in the gym all morning." *Id.*, 238 *N.J.Super.* at 484. According to the vice-principal, when he caught Phillip in the act, Phillip immediately fled from the school.

Officer Monteiro decided to check Phillip's home which was only two or three blocks from the school. James Castro, Phillip's 19-year-old cousin, answered Officer Monteiro's knock and informed Monteiro that Phillip was not home. According to Monteiro, he was invited to step into the foyer of the house due to the extremely cold weather. "As Monteiro stood facing the foot of the stairs, he saw and heard movements behind a first floor door. James was at the top of the stairs, and Monteiro asked, 'Are you sure there's no one home with you?' When he answered, 'no,' the officer went to the doorway where the movements occurred and he saw Phillip. * * * Phillip's left hand was clenched. He then dropped and kicked what appeared to be a white plastic or cellophane ball under the baseboard heater." *Id.* at 485. At this point, Monteiro grabbed Phillip, conducted a pat-down, and then retrieved a small, cellophane ball object, containing white powder, from under the heater.

At the motion to suppress, Monteiro testified that he "believed Phillip was in some danger from ingesting whatever white powder was in that packet Mr. Belz saw." *Id.* On cross-examination, Monteiro stated that he was definitely concerned for Phillip's health, and, " '[a]t that time I was under the impression he had swallowed a packet of unknown size' and that it could have been a very little or a lot." *Id.* Monteiro further testified that his purpose in going to the house was to "contact an ambulance and get him assistance." *Id.* Significantly, "Officer Monteiro immediately summoned an ambulance which arrived within minutes after Phillip was discovered." *Id.*

According to the court, "[t]he sole legal question * * * is whether there was sufficient exigency created by the information imparted at the school to justify immediate action by Monteiro, as distinct from retreating and initiating the warrant procedures." *Id.* at 487.

Finding these circumstances to constitute a "genuine exigency," that is, " '[t]he need to preserve life or avoid serious injury,' " *id.* at 488, the court held that "there was a reasonable basis to believe that this 18-year-old student had been using cocaine at school, and that he had probably swallowed an unknown amount of cocaine before fleeing from school." *Id.* at 487-488. [Citation omitted.] "There was a visual observation by Belz, substantially confirmed by the second participating student whom he observed." *Id.* at 488. Moreover, "there was nothing to dispute Officer Monteiro's testimony that his prime concern was not to arrest a suspected drug possessor, but to insure the physical safety of an 18-year-old who was thought to have ingested a package containing an unknown quantity of cocaine." *Id.*

The court explained:

> A police officer with drug arrest experience does not need a physician to be aware that the probability of ingestion of an unknown quantity of cocaine by mouth poses an *immediate medical danger of unknown severity*, which varies depending upon the substance, its purity and quantity, and the susceptibility of the person involved. Anyone who reads newspapers or watches television has to be aware of this kind of danger, not to mention a police officer who has received 40 hours of narcotics instruction and participated in 50 to 100 narcotics arrests.

Id. [Emphasis added.]

Contrary to the trial court's holding that "an officer's reasonable belief of medical emergency requires a showing that imminent death is probable, and there is near certainty as to the presence of the person at risk in the premises," *id.* at 488-89, the Appellate Division here holds that "[t]he exigency test may also be met by a prudent and reasonably based belief that there is a *potential medical emergency of unknown dimension*." *Id.* at 489. [Emphasis added.] Further, the court stated: "It is far easier to turn away from trouble than to steer into it. We can think of nothing more likely to chill diligent police efforts to preserve life than to here require proof of actual danger of death and certainty of location to justify the limited and focused incursion made in the present case. Monteiro acted only after the human noises coupled with James' statement that no one else was in the house made it likely that someone was hiding or being concealed in the stairwell. In the circumstances, considering the officer's reasonable belief that he was at Phillip's place of residence, the flight and the proximity to the school, it was reasonable to believe that the someone was Phillip." *Id.*

(b) The need to protect or preserve life. The court in Castro relied heavily on the reasoning of former Chief Justice (then judge) Burger in *Wayne v. United States*, 318 *F.*2d 205 (D.C.Cir. 1963), *cert. den.*, 375 *U.S.* 860, 84 *S.Ct.* 125 (1963), where it was observed:

> When policemen, firemen or other public officers are confronted with evidence which would lead a prudent and reasonable official to see a need to act to protect life or property, they are authorized to act on that information, even if ultimately found erroneous. [What gives rise to genuine exigent circumstances is t]he need to protect or preserve life or avoid serious injury.

Id. at 212.

> Fires or dead bodies are reported to the police by cranks where no fires or bodies are to be found. * * * But the business of policemen and firemen is *to act*, not to speculate or meditate on whether the

report is correct. People could well die in emergencies if police tried to act with the calm deliberation associated with the judicial process.

Id. [Emphasis in original.]

---

§3.3(b). Dangerous weapons or instrumentalities.

UNITED STATES v. McEACHIN
United States Court of Appeals
670 *F.*2d 1139 (D.C. Cir. 1981)

QUESTION: In the context of a warrantless search and seizure conducted in the presence of probable cause and exigent circumstances, will the degree of exigency be heightened when the evidence which is about to be removed is a deadly weapon ?

ANSWER: YES.   In this case, the search of defendant's apartment was "justified in order to prevent imminent removal of contraband and evidence of a crime. [Moreover, t]he exigency was heightened by the fact that the evidence about to be removed was a deadly weapon." *Id.* at 1144.

RATIONALE: During the course of an armed-robbery investigation, Officer Oldham of the Metropolitan Police Department developed probable cause to believe that defendant not only played an active role in the robbery but carried a sawed-off shotgun during the crime. After defendant's associate had been arrested for his role in the robbery, Officer Oldham learned from a confidential source that defendant still had possession of the sawed-off shotgun and that defendant was nervous because the first suspect in the robbery had been arrested. Additionally, the source stated that defendant was "going to move" or "get rid of" the shotgun. The source further stated that defendant keeps the shotgun in his room where he lives. According to Officer Oldham, the source's basis of information was from "first hand knowledge." This information corroborated information received earlier from a different informant who had not only provided Officer Oldham with defendant's address but further advised that defendant kept the sawed-off shotgun in his room in a wardrobe closet.

   After speaking with his confidential source for approximately forty-five minutes, Officer Oldham went to defendant's apartment, explained the purpose for his visit, and requested permission to search the premises. Defendant stated that the room was not his and that he could not give the police permission to search it. Officer Oldham nevertheless entered the room with defendant, walked directly to the wardrobe closet, and searched it. Inside he found the sawed-off shotgun wrapped in paper.

In this appeal, defendant argues, among other things, that Officer Oldham lacked the necessary "exigent circumstances" to engage in the warrantless search of his apartment. *The Court of Appeals for the District of Columbia Circuit disagreed.*

"Even if supported by probable cause, warrantless searches are '*per se* unreasonable under the Fourth Amendment—subject only to a few specifically established and well-delineated exceptions.' * * * One recognized exception is the presence of exigent circumstances necessitating an immediate search—for example, when contraband or evidence of a crime is threatened with imminent removal or destruction." *Id.* at 1144. [Citations omitted.]

The facts of this case causes the court to "conclude that Officer Oldham was faced with exigent circumstances as soon as he learned from [his confidential source that defendant] was going to dispose of the shotgun in his apartment. At that point in time an immediate search of [defendant's] apartment would have been justified in order to prevent imminent removal of contraband and evidence of a crime." *Id.* Moreover, *"[t]he exigency was heightened by the fact that the evidence about to be removed was a deadly weapon." Id.* [Emphasis added.] The court also concluded that the time constraints facing Officer Oldham excused his failure to seek either a traditional or a telephonic search warrant. *Id.* at 1148.

Accordingly, the warrantless search of defendant's apartment was supported by probable cause and justified by exigent circumstances. The evidence seized therefore was properly admitted at his trial. *Id*

NOTE

1. *See also United States v. Saadeh*, 61 *F*.3d 510 (7th Cir. 1995), where the court emphasized that the existence of exigent circumstances will be analyzed "from the perspective of the officers at the scene," and, in doing so, courts will "ask not what the police *could* have done, but whether they had, at the time, a reasonable belief that there was a compelling need to act and no time to obtain a warrant." *Id.* at 516. [Court's emphasis.]

2. In *Llaguno v. Mingey*, 763 *F*.2d 1560 (7th Cir. 1985), Chicago police were pursuing two men who had committed two armed robberies, killed four people and wounded three others (including a police officer), and abducted a young girl. When the getaway car crashed, officers were able to shoot and capture one of the killers and recover the young girl unharmed; the other killer escaped on foot. The officers ran a check of the license plate number and then immediately proceeded to the address of the vehicle's registered owner. The officers gained entry to the house, rushed in with guns drawn, and searched the premises for the other killer. He was not there.

In the appeal which followed a civil rights action brought under 42 *U.S.C.* §1983, the court held that "exigent circumstances existed to justify the warrantless entry into the plaintiffs' home." *Id.* at 1573.

According to the court, "'an important factor to be considered when determining whether any exigency exists is *the gravity of the underlying offense for which the arrest is being made.' " Id.* at 1572. [Citations omitted; emphasis added.] Here, "[t]he situation was an emergency in about as vivid a sense as can be imagined. A man had (with his partner) just shot seven people. There was no reason to think he had finished shooting; there was every reason to think he would put up a violent resistance. If the police delayed for a warrant, the killer might barricade the house, take hostages, or flee and kill again before they could catch up with him." *Id.* at 1564.

"The greater the danger to the public safety if the police delay entering premises in search of a criminal suspect, the more reason they have for not waiting[.] * * * [I]n determining whether police are reasonable in entering a house without a warrant [a consideration should be made of] not only how great the risk of delay was—that is, the probability of injury, escape, or destruction of evidence—* * * but also how great the harm would have been had the risk materialized. The greater that harm would be, the less need be the probability that it would actually have occurred to justify the police in invading the interest (great though it is) in the privacy of the home. The potential harm from waiting for a search warrant in this case was very great even though it was far from certain that an immediate search would be productive." *Id.*

See also United States v. Echegoyen, 799 *F.*2d 1271 (9th Cir. 1986), where the court held that the existence of an explosive fire hazard and the likely presence of illegal drug manufacturing activities were exigent circumstances that justified the warrantless entry of defendant's home. According to the court, the officers' testimony as to chemical smell, the activity in the home, the early morning hour, the remoteness of the area along with the fact that the officers were approximately forty to forty-five minutes from their station, and the limited availability of firefighting resources all justified the initial warrantless entry. *Id.* at 1278-1279, 1280.

UNITED STATES v. GOOD
United States Court of Appeals
780 *F.*2d 773 (9th Cir. 1986)

QUESTION: In the following set of facts, did "exigent circumstances" justify the warrantless entry into defendant's home ?

FACTS: During a get-together at the home of Susan Wallace, a drunken altercation erupted between Wallace, John Snyder, Sharon Bullock, and defendant, Larry Good, as a result of Snyder's improper sexual advances towards Bullock. "After Good retrieved a revolver from his truck, he and Snyder engaged in a fight during which Good pistol-whipped Snyder, and in which both Snyder and Bullock were stabbed." After Good left Wallace's home with Bullock, the police were called.

"When the police arrived, they found that Snyder had been stabbed and saw two pools of blood on the floor. Both Snyder and Wallace were intoxicated, but made it clear that Good's female companion also had been stabbed, that not all of the blood on the floor was Snyder's, and that Bullock had left with Good. Snyder said that he believed that Bullock was in danger. They also gave the police a description of Good and his truck."

Good's truck was located approximately four hours later parked in front of his home. Immediately thereafter, the officers entered Good's house without a warrant, placed him under arrest, and seized a rifle as Good was reaching for it.

ANSWER: YES. "[T]he facts in this case gave rise to exigent circumstances. The officers thought that a woman had been stabbed, they had seen the blood on the floor and knew a drunken, violent confrontation had taken place. They were told that the female victim had left with Good and that she was in danger. * * * [Thus, t]he officers reasonably could conclude that someone with Good had been seriously injured and that entry was necessary to assist the injured person." *Id.* at 774-775.

RATIONALE: In this appeal, Good argues that "he was unlawfully arrested and the rifle improperly seized because the officers lacked exigent circumstances when they entered his home without a warrant." *Id.* at 774. *The Court of Appeals for the Ninth Circuit disagreed.*

The facts of this case "clearly establish that the officers reasonably thought that a woman in Good's company had been stabbed and had lost blood, but were unaware of the extent of her injuries." *Id.* The concept of exigent circumstances has been defined as "circumstances involving 'a substantial risk of harm to the persons involved,' * * * in which 'a reasonable person (would) believe that entry * * * was necessary to prevent physical harm to the officers or other persons.' " *Id.* [Citations omitted.]

The facts of this case certainly gave rise to the requisite exigency. "The officers thought that a woman had been stabbed, they had seen the blood on the floor and knew a drunken, violent confrontation had taken place. They were told that the female victim left with Good and that she was in danger. * * * [Thus, t]he officers reasonably could conclude that someone with Good had been seriously injured and that entry was necessary to assist the injured person." *Id.* at 775.

"Exigent circumstances alone, however, are insufficient as the government must also show that a warrant could not have been obtained in time. * * * The record reveals that a warrant could not have been obtained for several hours because a magistrate was unavailable. The government, however, must also show that a telephonic warrant was unavailable or impracticable." *Id.*

The grounds for issuance of a warrant—whether traditional or telephonic—did not arise in this case until the officers located Good's house and truck. Thus, contrary to Good's contentions, there was not ample time to secure even a telephonic warrant.

According to the court, "[o]btaining a telephonic warrant is not a simple procedure; '[a]mong other things, a "duplicate original warrant" must be prepared in writing and read to the magistrate verbatim.'

* * * The only step that is saved is the trip to the magistrate's office. Since a warrant could not have been prepared until Good's house was identified, [the court concludes] that under the circumstances, the government has satisfied its burden of showing that the delay associated with obtaining a telephonic warrant would have unduly increased the risk to the stabbing victim that the officers reasonably believed to be in Good's home and in need of assistance." *Id.* [Citations omitted.]

UNITED STATES v. LINDSEY
United States Court of Appeals
877 *F.*2d 777 (9th Cir. 1989)

QUESTION: Prior to, and after, an undercover buy of narcotics and arrest of the seller, the seller tells the police that the home at which he obtained the narcotics has "a bunch of crazy bikers with guns and bombs" living there. Did the seller's statement provide the police with sufficient *exigent circumstances* to enter the bikers' home without a warrant?

ANSWER: YES.   "[T]he facts known to the officers in this case gave rise to exigent circumstances justifying the warrantless entry into [defendant's] house[, particularly in light of the fact that] dangerous explosives [may have been] involved." *Id.* at 781.

RATIONALE: In the middle of August, a narcotics informant arranged for Detective Cook of the Buena Park Police Department to buy methamphetamine from a local drug dealer named Ogata. Ogata was to obtain the drug from a nearby house, bring it back for Cook's inspection, and, as far as Ogata believed, complete the sale. When Ogata returned to the parking lot where Cook was waiting, he handed Cook an envelope containing the methamphetamine, stating that he had just obtained the drugs from "a bunch of crazy bikers with guns and bombs." *Id.* at 779. Ogata was then placed under arrest. Thereafter, he refused to cooperate in the arrest of his drug source and repeated his comment about the "guns and bombs."

Cook believed that Ogata's source "fronted" him the drugs and would be waiting his return with the payment. As a result, Cook phoned the Orange Police Department to request uniformed backup officers. The additional officers arrived about one hour later. "During that hour, Cook did not attempt to obtain a warrant to search the [target residence] or place the house under surveillance." *Id.*

"When four backup officers arrived, the police proceeded to the house. They approached the door with weapons drawn[, and upon spotting defendant] through a window[,] ordered him to put his hands in the air." *Id.* at 779-780. Once inside the house, the officers handcuffed defendant, placed him under arrest, and then received an oral and written consent to search his home. "The search uncovered a sawed-off shotgun, automatic weapons, methamphetamine, thousands of rounds of ammunition, and plastic explosives." *Id.* at 780.

In this appeal, defendant contends, among other things, that the evidence seized should have been suppressed because the circumstances were not sufficiently exigent to validate the officers' warrantless entry of his home. *The United States Court of Appeals for the Ninth Circuit disagreed.*

"Exigent circumstances are defined as 'those circumstances that would cause a reasonable person to believe that entry * * * was necessary to prevent physical harm to the officers or other persons, the destruction of relevant evidence, the escape of the suspect, or some other consequence improperly frustrating legitimate law enforcement efforts.' " *Id.* at 780-781 (quoting *United States v. McConney*, 728 *F.*2d 1195, 1199 (9th Cir.), *cert. denied*, 469 *U.S.* 824, 105 *S.Ct.* 101 (1984)). " 'The exigencies must be viewed from the totality of the circumstances known to the officers at the time of the warrantless intrusion.' * * * Moreover, because exigent circumstances necessarily imply insufficient time to obtain a warrant, the government must also show that a warrant could not have been obtained in time." *Id.* at 781. [Citations omitted.]

Here in *Lindsey*, the court concludes that the facts known to the officers "gave rise to exigent circumstances justifying the warrantless entry into [defendant's] house. Exigent circumstances[, in this context,] are frequently found when dangerous explosives are involved." *Id.* "The police reasonably believed that Ogata's source at [defendant's house] possessed guns and bombs." *Id.* "Prior to learning Cook's real identity, Ogata told the detective that his source possessed guns and bombs. Ogata repeated this comment after arrest. He refused to cooperate in the arrest of his source and appeared genuinely afraid of his source. Ogata himself carried a loaded gun. Furthermore, the police knew from their own experience that methamphetamine dealers were often armed. Under the totality of the circumstances, the police could reasonably believe that Ogata's source possessed guns and bombs." *Id.*

Detective Cook and the other officers involved "were justifiably concerned about the presence of bombs in a densely populated residential neighborhood. Moreover, this concern was heightened by a reasonable belief that Ogata's source would learn of police intervention and use the guns and bombs to resist arrest. * * * [Further, logic and precedent dictate] that the apprehension of a drug courier can itself create an exigency if the drug supplier is likely to become suspicious when the courier fails to return." *Id.* (citing *United States v. Perdomo*, 800 *F.*2d 916, 919 (9th Cir. 1986), and *United States v. Kunkler*, 679 *F.*2d 187, 192 (9th Cir. 1982)). "The police believed that Ogata's source had 'fronted' him the drugs and would be waiting for Ogata to return with the payment. Cook formed this belief based on his two years of experience as a narcotics officer and his participation in 50 to 75 methamphetamine transactions." *Id.* Thus, Cook's conclusion that Ogata's source would suspect police intervention due to Ogata's failure to return was clearly reasonable.

Defendant argues that the one-hour delay mandates a finding that the circumstances were not truly exigent. This argument asks the court to "evaluate exigent circumstances from the circumstances known to the police *after* the warrantless entry. Exigent circumstances, however, must be viewed from the circumstances known to the police *prior* to the warrantless action. * * * Immediately after Ogata's arrest, the officers requested reinforcements from the local police department. The officers did not realize that there would be a delay. As each minute passed, the officers reasonably expected the reinforcements to arrive momentarily. When the additional officers arrived, the police moved quickly to secure [defendant's] house. Under these circumstances, [this court] cannot find that the delay evidenced a lack of real exigency." *Id.* at 781-782. [Emphasis in original.]

[Having concluded that the warrantless entry and arrest were lawful, and that defendant validly consented to the search of his home, the court affirmed the judgment of the district which denied defendant's motion to suppress the evidence seized.]

NOTE

1. For a discussion of the one-hour delay and the time it takes to obtain a telephonic search warrant, *see* §2.6.

2. In *Washington v. United States*, 585 A.2d 167 (D.C.App. 1991), four officers of the Metropolitan Police Department responded, at about 1:45 p.m., to a Clifton Street, N.W. apartment, after receiving a call of "a woman with a gun." Upon arrival at the apartment, a young woman answered the door and advised the officers that, "my sister has a gun, and I want it out of the house." Three of the officers forced their way into defendant's locked bedroom and discovered defendant sitting on the bed with her three-year-old son. One of the officer's asked her, "Where is the gun ?" Defendant replied, "I have no gun." A search of the bedroom clothes closet uncovered a loaded, semi-automatic machine gun.

On appeal from a denial of defendant's motion to suppress, the District of Columbia Court of Appeals concluded that the warrantless, forcible entry and search of defendant's bedroom violated the Fourth Amendment. According to the court:

> * * * [T]he officers, at the time of entry, lacked probable cause to believe that any criminal activity had occurred, let alone the commission of a grave offense. Although the officers had information that [defendant] possessed a gun, they did not know what kind of gun she possessed, whether the gun was registered, whether [defendant] was licensed to, or did in fact, carry it, or whether she had used it. The mere possession of a gun in a dwelling place, without more, is not a criminal offense. For all they knew, at the time they entered [defendant's] bedroom, the officers were intervening to recover a lawfully owned, registered gun. Prior to the forcible entry and discovery of the gun, therefore, there was no probable cause to believe that [defendant] had committed *any* crime.

Id. at 169. [Emphasis in original; footnote omitted.]

Accordingly, the court held that exigent circumstances are not created "by the presence of a gun in a residence where there is no probable cause to believe, as here, that the gun is a dangerous or illegal one used in the commission of a crime, or indeed, no probable cause [] to believe that a crime has been committed." *Id.* at 169-170.

§3.3(c). Emergency aid and community caretaking functions.

There are many situations in which the police are required to enter premises without a warrant and without probable cause to believe a crime has occurred. Police officers perform various complex and multiple tasks in addition to conducting criminal investigations and identifying and apprehending criminal suspects. Beyond the "crime fighting" function, the police are also expected to: (1) "reduce the opportunities for the commission of some crimes through preventative patrol and other measures," (2) "aid individuals who are in danger of physical harm," (3) "assist those who cannot care for themselves," (4) "resolve conflict," (5) "create and maintain a feeling of security in the community," and (6) "provide other services on an emergency basis." *ABA Standards for Criminal Justice* §1-1.1 (2nd ed. 1980).

As observed by the former Chief Justice (then Judge) Burger in *Wayne v. United States*, 318 *F.*2d 205, 212 (D.C.Cir. 1963), in such situations there must be a "balancing of interests and needs." "When policemen, firemen or other public officers are confronted with evidence which would lead a prudent and reasonable official to see a need to act to protect life or property, they are authorized to act on that information, even if ultimately found erroneous." *Id.*

Thus, when an emergency arises—for example, a medical emergency—the police should not be required to hold a belief that the imminent death of a person is probable, or that there is a near certainty as to the presence of a person at risk in a premises. Rather, the test should be whether the police have "a prudent and reasonably based belief" that, at the premises, there is a potential medical or other emergency of unknown dimension. As stated in *Wayne*:

> [A] warrant is not required to break down a door to enter a burning home to rescue occupants or extinguish a fire, to prevent a shooting or to bring emergency aid to an injured person. The need to protect or preserve life or avoid serious injury is justification for what would be otherwise illegal absent an exigency or emergency. Fires or dead bodies are reported to the police by cranks where no fires or bodies are to be found. * * * But the business of policemen and firemen is *to act*, not to speculate or meditate on whether the report is correct. People could well die in emergencies if police tried to act with the calm deliberation associated with the judicial process. Even the apparently dead often are saved by swift police response.

Id. at 212. [Emphasis in original.] What gives rise to the genuine exigency is the police need to protect or preserve life or prevent serious injury.

The "emergency aid" doctrine has been treated by most courts as a recognized exception to the written warrant requirement. *See* 3 Wayne R. LaFave, *Search and Seizure, A Treatise on the Fourth Amendment* §6.6(a) (4th ed 2004), at 451-452. A close examination of it, however, reveals that it is nothing more than a specific application of the exigent circumstances exception.

To justify a warrantless entry or search under the emergency aid doctrine, the following three elements must be met:

(1) There must be a reasonable and objective basis to believe that a *real* emergency exists and *immediate action* is required to protect or preserve life or to prevent serious injury;

(2) Any entry or search conducted must not be primarily motivated by the desire to find evidence; and

(3) There must be a connection or nexus between the emergency and the area entered or searched.

LaFave at 392-93. *See also Commonwealth v. Norris*, 498 *Pa.* 308, 313, 446 *A.2d* 246, 248 (1982) (warrantless entry permitted when the police have a "good faith" belief that someone within is in peril of bodily harm); *Commonwealth v. Silo*, 509 *Pa.* 406, 410, 502 *A.2d*173, 176 (1985) (police officers are not prohibited from making warrantless entries and searches of houses "when they reasonably believe a person within is in need of immediate aid").

In upholding warrantless entries based on the emergency aid doctrine, many courts have observed that the officers would have been derelict in their duty had they not acted. In the final analysis, the State is not required to prove than an actual emergency existed at the time of the officers' warrantless entry. Rather, the State need only show that the facts and circumstances surrounding the entry and search were such that the officers reasonably believed that an emergency existed which made obtaining a search warrant impracticable.

Traveling hand in hand with the emergency aid doctrine is the "community caretaking" function of the police. In a similar vein, it is now well recognized that, in addition to investigating crimes, the police also engage in "community caretaking" functions, which are "totally divorced from the detection, investigation, or acquisition of evidence relating to the violation of a criminal statute." *Cady v. Dombrowski*, 413 *U.S.* 433, 441, 93 *S.Ct.* 2523, 2528 (1973). As with the emergency aid doctrine, the performance of community caretaking responsibilities may provide the necessary authority for warrantless police activity as part and parcel of an officer's duty to serve and protect.

The "community caretaking" function may also be implicated where something abnormal is observed concerning the operation of a motor vehicle. The circumstances surrounding the vehicle's operation should be unusual enough for the time and place to warrant a reasonable belief that the driver or an occupant is in need of immediate assistance.

Regarding warrantless entries under the "community caretaking" function or "emergency aid" doctrine, the key factor in such cases is the officer's *objectively reasonable belief* that, given the totality of the circumstances, a person *is in need of assistance*. In deciding whether an officer's belief was reasonable, courts may consider such factors as:

(1) the nature and level of the distress exhibited by the individual;

(2) the location of the individual;

(3) whether or not the individual was alone and/or had access to assistance other than that offered by the officer; and

(4) to what extent the individual, if not assisted, presented a danger to himself or others.

Thus, whether termed an action under the emergency aid doctrine, or an action in furtherance of the community caretaking function of the police, warrantless entries have been upheld where immediate police action was necessary to:

(1) rescue people from a burning building;

(2) seek an occupant reliably reported to be missing;

(3) seek a person known to be suffering from a gunshot or knife wound;

(4) locate a dead body;

(5) check on an odor of rotting flesh;

(6) check on the well-being of unattended children;

(7) ensure that a weapon within the premises does not remain accessible to children there;

(8) assist a person reported to be ill or injured;

(9) retrieve an object which had obstructed the breathing passage of a child, where the child's doctor needed to examine the object to provide proper medical treatment;

(10) locate a high school student who, a short time earlier, swallowed an undetermined amount of cocaine and ran home;

(11) attempt to discover what substance might have been eaten by several children who were critically ill;

(12) stop an apparent suicide attempt;

(13) ensure the prompt involuntary commitment of a person who is apparently mentally ill and dangerous;

(14) respond to a fight within the premises;

(15) locate an occupant who made an hysterical telephone call to the police; and

(16) determine the well-being of the occupants of a residence where screams were recently heard by neighbors who were unable to get anyone to answer the phone at the residence.

See LaFave, *supra* §6.6(a), at 396-400; 2003 Pocket Part, §6.6, at 97; and the cases listed therein.

Once inside the premises, an officer's conduct "must be carefully limited to achieving the objective which justified the entry— the officer may do no more than is reasonably necessary to ascertain whether someone is in need of assistance and to provide that assistance." *Id.* at 401. If the officer determines that his or her assistance is, in fact, not needed, the officer must immediately depart the premises, rather than exploring further. If, however, the officer's "community caretaking/emergency assistance" entry results in the "plain view" discovery of evidence of a crime or contraband, that evidence may be admissible under "plain view" principles.

---

§3.4. Impounded vehicles and inventory searches.

Since 1976, it has been well recognized that police may conduct an inventory of the contents of lawfully impounded vehicles as a routine, administrative community caretaking function, in order to protect the vehicle and the property in it, to safeguard the police and others from potential danger, and to insure against claims of lost, stolen, or vandalized property. *South Dakota v. Opperman*, 428 *U.S.* 364, 369, 96 *S.Ct.* 3092, 3097 (1976).

In *Opperman*, the defendant's illegally parked car was towed to the city impound lot where an officer of the Vermillion Police Department observed several articles of personal property within the vehicle. As the officer proceeded to inventory the contents of the car, he discovered a plastic bag containing marijuana in the unlocked glove compartment.

Finding the initial impoundment lawful, the Supreme Court determined that the automobile impoundment was sanctioned by the " 'community caretaking functions' " incumbent upon law enforcement officials in situations wherein the public safety and efficient movement of vehicular traffic are in jeopardy. *Id.* at 368, 96 *S.Ct.* at 3096 (quoting *Cady v. Dombrowski*, 413 *U.S.* 433, 441, 93 *S.Ct.* 2523, 2528 (1973)). Respecting the inventory, the Court ruled that such intrusions into automobiles legally "impounded or otherwise in lawful police custody" have been widely sustained as reasonable under the Fourth Amendment "where the process is aimed at securing or protecting the car and its contents." *Id.* at 373, 96 *S.Ct.* at 3099.

As a result, the Court declared that the officer in *Opperman* was "indisputably engaged in a caretaking search of a lawfully impounded automobile. * * * The inventory was conducted only after the car had been impounded for multiple parking violations. The owner, having left his car illegally parked for an extended period, and thus subject to impoundment, was not present to make other arrangements for the safekeeping of his belongings. The inventory itself was prompted by the presence in plain view of a number of valuables inside the car. * * * [T]here is no suggestion whatever that this standard procedure, essentially like that followed throughout the country, was a pretext concealing an investigatory police motive. [Accordingly,] in following standard police procedures, prevailing throughout the country and approved by the overwhelming majority of courts, the conduct of [this officer] was not 'unreasonable' under the Fourth Amendment." *Id.* at 375-376, 96 *S.Ct.* at 3100.

COLORADO v. BERTINE
Supreme Court of the United States
479 *U.S.* 367, 107 *S.Ct.* 738 (1987)

QUESTION: May law enforcement officers, consistent with the Fourth Amendment, open closed containers found inside an impounded vehicle when conducting a routine inventory search?

ANSWER: YES. Law enforcement officers may, consistent with the Fourth Amendment, open closed containers while conducting a routine inventory search of an impounded vehicle. "[R]easonable police regulations relating to inventory procedures administered in good faith satisfy the Fourth Amendment[.]" *Id.* at 742.

RATIONALE: Defendant, Bertine, was arrested in Boulder, Colorado, for driving while intoxicated. While the police officers waited for the arrival of a tow truck to take defendant's van to an impound lot, they inventoried the contents of the van. During the inventory, one of the officers opened a closed backpack which was found directly behind the front seat, and discovered cocaine, methaqualone tablets, drug paraphernalia, and over $700.00 in cash.

Defendant, subsequently charged with driving under the influence of alcohol and the unlawful possession of the controlled substances, moved to suppress the evidence found during the inventory search. He contended that the search of the closed backpack and containers found within exceeded the permissible scope of such a search under the Fourth Amendment.

The United States Supreme Court, per Chief Justice Rehnquist, disagreed.

Inventory searches, "now a well-defined exception to the warrant requirement, * * * serve to protect an owner's property while it is in the custody of the police, to insure against claims of lost, stolen, or vandalized property, and to guard the police from danger." *Id.* at 741. In this case, there is "no showing that the police, who were following standardized procedures, acted in bad faith or for the sole purpose of investigation. * * * [T]he police were potentially responsible for the property taken into their custody. By securing the property, the police protected the property from unauthorized interference. Knowledge of the precise nature of the property helped to guard against claims of theft, vandalism, or negligence. Such knowledge also helped to avert any danger to police or others that may have been posed by the property." *Id.* at 742. Additionally, "the trial court found that the police department's procedures mandated the opening of closed containers and the listing of their contents." *Id.* at 742 n.6. This finding was critical "to the requirement that inventories be conducted according to standardized criteria." *Id.*

Accordingly, "reasonable police regulations relating to inventory procedures administered in good faith satisfy the Fourth Amendment[.]" *Id.* at 742.

JUSTICE BLACKMUN, with whom JUSTICE POWELL and JUSTICE O'CONNOR join, concurring.

"The Court today holds that police officers may open closed containers while conducting a routine inventory search of an impounded vehicle. I join the Court's opinion, but write separately to underscore the importance of having such inventories conducted only pursuant to standardized police procedures. The underlying rationale for allowing an inventory exception to the Fourth Amendment warrant rule is that police officers are not vested with discretion to determine the scope of the inventory search. * * * This absence of discretion ensures that inventory searches will not be used as a purposeful and general means of discovering evidence of crime. Thus, it is permissible for police officers to open closed containers in an inventory search only if they are following standard police procedures that mandate the opening of such containers in every impounded vehicle." *Id.* at 744.

NOTE

1. *Requirement of a pre-existing policy.* In *Florida v. Wells*, 495 *U.S.* 1, 110 *S.Ct.* 1632 (1990), the Supreme Court re-emphasized the importance of "standardized criteria" in the area of impounded motor vehicle inventory searches, and delivered a strong message to law enforcement agencies that a pre-existing *department policy* or written *general order* covering the subject of impounded motor vehicle inventories is required before the procedure will receive judicial approval. *Id.*, 110 *S.Ct.* at 1635.

2. *Oral versus written policies.* In *United States v. Mancera-Londono*, 912 *F.*2d 373 (9th Cir. 1990), the court determined that while a "written" impound/inventory procedure may be more indicative of a "standardized" procedure, it is not a prerequisite to a valid inventory search. In this respect, the court held:

> We reject [defendant]'s suggestion that inventory procedures need be written to be standardized. "[I]n order to ensure that the inventory search is 'limited in scope to the extent necessary to carry out the caretaking function,' it must be carried out in accordance with the standard procedures" of the law enforcement agency. * * * *Such procedures need not be written, however.*

Id. at 375. [Emphasis added.] *See also United States v. Feldman*, 788 *F.*2d 544, 550-53 (9th Cir. 1986) (upholding an inventory search conducted pursuant to the oral procedures of the Orange County Police Department), *cert. denied*, 479 *U.S.* 1067, 107 *S.Ct.* 955 (1987).

3. *Scope of the inventory.*

(a) In *Florida v. Wells, supra*, after his arrest for driving while under the influence of alcohol, defendant Wells gave an officer of the Florida Highway Patrol permission to open the trunk of his impounded vehicle. "[A]n inventory search of the car turned up two marijuana cigarette butts in an ashtray and a locked suitcase in the trunk. Under the trooper's direction, employees of the [impound] facility forced open the suitcase and discovered a garbage bag containing a considerable amount of marijuana." *Id.* at 1633. *The Florida Highway Patrol did not, however, have any policy whatsoever covering the opening of closed containers found during inventory searches.* Subsequently, Wells was charged with the possession of the marijuana.

According to the Court, in the absence of a standardized policy covering the subject of impounded vehicle inventory searches, and the opening of closed containers encountered during such procedures, the trooper's search of the trunk in this case "was not sufficiently regulated to satisfy the Fourth Amendment and[, as a result,] the marijuana which was found in the suitcase * * * was properly suppressed[.]" *Id.* at 1635.

In the Court's view, "standardized criteria," or "established routine" ["policy"] must govern "the opening of containers found during inventory searches[.]" *Id.* This requirement "is based on the principle that an inventory search must not be a ruse for a general rummaging in order to discover incriminating evidence. The policy or practice governing inventory searches should be designed to produce an inventory. The individual police officer must not be allowed so much latitude that inventory searches are turned into 'a purposeful and general means of discovering evidence of crime[.]'" *Id.* (quoting *Bertine, supra*, 479 *U.S.* at 376, 107 *S.Ct.* at 744 (Blackman, J., concurring)).

Yet, the Court points out that in creating a "policy" or general order in this area, police departments need not adopt an "all or nothing" philosophy. Rather, "[a] police officer may be allowed sufficient latitude to determine whether a particular container should or should not be opened in light of the nature of the search and characteristics of the container itself. Thus, while policies of opening all containers or of opening no containers are unquestionably permissible, it would be equally permissible, for example, to allow the opening of closed containers whose contents officers determine they are unable to ascertain from examining the containers' exteriors. The allowance of the exercise of judgment based on concerns related to the purposes of an inventory search does not violate the Fourth Amendment." *Id.*

(b) *Searching behind door panels.* In *United States v. Best*, 135 *F.*3d 1223 (8th Cir. 1998), the court held that the officer's act of looking inside an automobile's door panel exceeded the permissible scope of an inventory search.

At about 12:30 a.m., Trooper Byrd, of the Arkansas State Police, stopped Best's automobile for weaving. Best was driving a Ford Taurus rented from Budget Car Rental. As Trooper Byrd issued a warning for the improper lane usage, he also checked on the status of Best's driver's license. The computer check indicated that Best was a suspended driver. As a result, the trooper issued him a ticket for driving with a suspended license and informed Best that his vehicle had to be towed. Trooper Byrd then performed an inventory search of the car, looking "particularly for damage to protect the government and the wrecker service from false claims against them." *Id.* at 1224.

"While checking the automobile, Trooper Byrd discovered the right front window would only roll down part of the way and the back windows would not roll down at all." *Id.* He shined his flashlight into the right front window to see if there was an obstruction, and as he did so he saw what appeared to be a bundle of marijuana. Trooper Byrd then pulled the inside door panel away from the right front door and retrieved the bundle of marijuana. Best was placed under arrest and his vehicle was towed to headquarters, where the police completed the search. A total of nineteen bundles of marijuana was seized from the automobile.

In the appeal following his unsuccessful motion to suppress evidence, Best argued that the "search performed by Trooper Byrd exceeded the permissible scope of a warrantless inventory search." *Id.* The Court of Appeals for the Eighth Circuit agreed.

In *South Dakota v. Opperman*, 428 *U.S.* 364, 96 *S.Ct.* 3092 (1976), the United States Supreme Court set forth "the following three justifications for an inventory search: (1) protection of the owner's property while in police custody; (2) protection of the police from claims of lost, stolen or damaged property; and (3) protection of the police from potential danger." *Best* at 1225 (citing *Opperman* at 369, 96 *S.Ct.* at 3097). These justifications do not, however, "justify an unlimited search of the automobile." *Id.*

To meet the standard of Fourth Amendment reasonableness, an inventory search must be performed pursuant to "standard police procedures" and for the purpose of "protecting the car and its contents." *Id.* In a similar case decided by the Tenth Circuit, the court determined that

> [a]lthough the permissible scope of an inventory search has not been well-defined, searching behind the door panel of a vehicle does not qualify as "standard police procedure," and does not serve the purpose of "protecting the car and its contents" under any normal construction of those terms * * *.

United States v. Lugo, 978 *F.*2d 631, 637 (10th Cir. 1992).

With similar reasoning, the court here concluded "that Trooper Byrd's search of Best's automobile did not fall within the permissible scope of an inventory search." *Best* at 1225. At the suppression hearing, Trooper Byrd testified that "the Arkansas State Police inventory policy includes inventory of the contents of the automobile including the opening of any opaque containers but does not specifically allow looking inside door panels. More importantly, Trooper Byrd's use of a flashlight to look inside the window and his opening [of] Best's door panel did not serve the purpose of 'protecting the car and its contents.' Best would not have a legitimate claim for protection of property hidden in the door panel and therefore Trooper Byrd did not have a legitimate interest in seeking such property." *Id.* According to the court, the trooper "could have simply indicated that the power windows did not work properly." *Id.*

The court ruled, therefore, that the continued search of Best's car exceeded "the permissible scope of an inventory search" and constituted "an unreasonable search under the Fourth Amendment." *Id.*

(c) Opening notebooks. In *United States v. Andrews*, 22 F.2d 1328 (5th Cir. 1994), the court held that the page-by-page inspection of a notebook, to determine whether it contained any valuables between its pages, was a procedure consistent with the aims of an inventory search designed to protect the city and the law enforcement agency from claims of lost or stolen property. *Id.* at 1335. According to the court, "[c]ash, credit cards, negotiable instruments, and any number of other items could be hidden between the pages of a notebook, and could give rise to a claim against the city if lost." *Id. See also United States v. Khoury*, 901 F.2d 948, 959 (11th Cir.) (agent's "initial inspection of the notebook was necessary and proper to ensure that there was nothing of value hidden between the pages of the notebook"), *modified on other grounds*, 910 F.2d 713 (11th Cir. 1990); *United States v. Pace*, 989 F.2d 1218, 1243 (7th Cir. 1990) (police were permitted to leaf through the pages of record books "to determine whether any items, such as credit cards, might be stuck between the pages").

4. *Federal agents and local police policies.* The Fifth Circuit, in *United States v. Hahn*, 922 F.2d 243 (5th Cir. 1991), invalidated an inventory search conducted, by Internal Revenue Service (IRS) agents, of a vehicle located in a private impound lot within the jurisdiction of the Midland, Texas, Police Department, notwithstanding the fact that the agents followed, albeit unknowingly, a lawful Midland police inventory policy. According to the court, "one of the most important factors making inventory searches reasonable is adherence to standard police procedures." *Id.* at 246. While it is true that "the search conducted by the IRS agents *in fact* complied with Midland police department procedures, and would have been constitutional if conducted by the Midland police pursuant to those procedures[,]" the IRS itself, however, "had no procedures for inventory searches," the IRS agents were, at the time of the inventory, unaware of the Midland police inventory policy, no Midland officer was present during the search, and the Midland inventory policy did not cover inventory searches by federal officers in circumstances such as those presented here. *Id.* at 246-47. As a result, the court concluded that the warrantless inventory search conducted by the federal agents in this case, "having been conducted in the absence of standardized procedures, may not be validated as an inventory search." *Id.* at 247.

ILLINOIS v. LAFAYETTE
Supreme Court of the United States
462 *U.S.* 640, 103 *S.Ct.* 2605 (1983)

QUESTION: Is it consistent with the Fourth Amendment for police, as part of a routine procedure incident to incarcerating an arrestee, to search any container or article in his possession, in accordance with established inventory procedures?

ANSWER: YES. It is reasonable under the Fourth Amendment "for police to search the personal effects of a person under lawful arrest as part of the administrative procedure at a police station house incident to booking and jailing the suspect." *Id.* at 2608, 2611.

RATIONALE: Defendant was arrested at the Town Cinema in Kankakee, Illinois for disturbing the peace. He was handcuffed and transported to the police station, during which time he was carrying a purse-type shoulder bag. At the police station defendant was taken to the booking room where he was instructed to empty his pockets and place the contents on the counter. The officer then emptied the contents of the shoulder bag and discovered 10 amphetamine pills inside.

Defendant was subsequently charged with possession of a controlled dangerous substance. The Illinois trial court, however, suppressed the pills and the Illinois appellate court affirmed, finding that the warrantless search of defendant's shoulder bag was not a valid inventory of his belongings, and thus violated the Fourth Amendment.

The United States Supreme Court, per Chief Justice Burger, disagreed and reversed.

As a well-defined exception to the warrant requirement, the inventory search constitutes "an incidental administrative step following arrest and preceding incarceration." *Id.* at 2608. Its justification "does not rest on probable cause, and hence the absence of a warrant is immaterial to the reasonableness of the search." *Id.*

In order to determine whether the search of defendant's shoulder bag was reasonable, the Court balances the intrusion on the person's Fourth Amendment interests against the promotion of legitimate governmental interests. "At the station house, it is entirely proper for police to remove and list or inventory property found on the person or in the possession of an arrested person who is to be jailed." *Id.* at 2609. Such a standardized procedure not only deters false claims, but also guards against theft or careless handling of property taken from the arrestee. Moreover, the Court observes that:

> Arrested persons have also been known to injure themselves—or others—with belts, knives, drugs, or other items on their person while being detained. Dangerous instrumentalities—such as razor blades, bombs, or weapons—can be concealed in innocent-looking articles taken from the arrestee's possession.

Id. Additionally, this procedure assists "the police in ascertaining or verifying the arrestee's identity." *Id.* at 2610. These considerations therefore suggest that "a stationhouse search of every item carried on or by a person who has lawfully been taken into custody by the police will amply serve the important and legitimate governmental interests involved." *Id.*

As a result, the Court concludes that "every consideration of orderly police administration benefiting both police and the public points toward the appropriateness of the examination of [defendant's] shoulder bag prior to his incarceration." *Id.*

"Even if less intrusive means existed of protecting some particular types of property, it would be unreasonable to expect police officers in the everyday course of business to make fine and subtle distinctions in deciding which containers or items may be searched and which may be sealed as a unit." *Id.*

Accordingly, it is reasonable "for police, as part of the routine procedure incident to incarcerating an arrested person, to search any container or article in his possession, in accordance with established inventory procedures." *Id.* at 2611.

---

§3.5. Motor vehicles: The "automobile exception."

In 1925, in the landmark case of *Carroll v. United States*, 267 *U.S.* 132, 45 *S.Ct.* 280, the United States Supreme Court established the "automobile exception" to the written warrant requirement. Speaking for the Court, Chief Justice Taft declared:

> On reason and authority the true rule is that if the search and seizure without a warrant are made upon probable cause, that is, upon a belief, reasonably arising out of the circumstances known to the seizing officer, that an automobile or other vehicle contains that which by law is subject to seizure * * *, the search and seizure are valid. * * *

> [T]he guaranty of freedom from unreasonable searches and seizures by the Fourth Amendment has been construed, practically since the beginning of the government, as recognizing a necessary difference between a search of a store, dwelling house or other structure in respect of which a proper official warrant readily may be obtained and a search of a ship, motor boat, wagon, or automobile for contraband goods, where it is not practicable to secure a warrant, because the vehicle can be quickly moved out of the locality or jurisdiction in which the warrant must be sought. * * *

> [We] thus establish[] that contraband goods concealed and illegally transported in an automobile or other vehicle may be searched for without a warrant * * * [when] there is known to a competent official, authorized to search, probable cause for believing that the[] vehicle[is] carrying contraband or illegal merchandise. * * *

Id. at 149, 153-54, 45 *S.Ct.* at 283-84, 285.

UNITED STATES v. ROSS
Supreme Court of the United States
456 *U.S.* 798, 102 *S.Ct.* 2157 (1982)

QUESTION: When an officer has probable cause to believe a lawfully stopped motor vehicle contains contraband concealed somewhere within it, may the officer conduct a probing search of the entire vehicle, including closed compartments, packages and containers within the vehicle whose contents are not in plain view ?

ANSWER: YES. The scope of a warrantless search of a lawfully stopped vehicle based on probable cause "is no narrower—and no broader—than the scope of a search" that could be authorized by a search warrant. *Id.* at 2172. "If probable cause justifies the search of a lawfully stopped vehicle, it justifies the search of every part of the vehicle and its contents that may conceal the object of the search." *Id.* at 2173. This rule applies equally to all compartments, containers and packages found within the vehicle "in which the object of the search may be found." *Id.* at 2160, 2172, 2173.

RATIONALE: Since 1925, it has been well settled that "a warrantless search of an automobile stopped by police officers who had probable cause to believe the vehicle contained contraband was not unreasonable within the meaning of the Fourth Amendment." *Id.* at 2160 (citing *Carroll v. United States*, 267 *U.S.* 132, 45 *S.Ct.* 280 (1925)). The Court in *Carroll* did not, however, specifically address the scope of the search that is authorized under this so-called "automobile exception." Here in *Ross*, the Court addressed the "extent to which police officers—who have legitimately stopped an automobile and who have probable cause to believe that contraband is concealed somewhere within it—may conduct a probing search of compartments and containers within the vehicle whose contents are not in plain view." *Id.* at 2160.

In late November, a reliable, confidential informant advised Detective Marcum of the District of Columbia Police Department that an individual known as "Bandit" was selling narcotics out of the trunk of his "purplish maroon" Chevrolet Malibu. According to the informant, the car had D.C. license plates and at the time was parked at 439 Ridge Street. The informant provided a detailed description of Bandit, and further stated that he had just observed Bandit complete a sale and that Bandit had told him that additional narcotics were in the trunk. Detective Marcum, along with several other officers, immediately responded to the area and located the Malibu parked in front of 439 Ridge Street. A computer check revealed that the vehicle was registered to defendant, Albert Ross, and that Ross fit the description provided by the informant and used the alias of "Bandit."

To avoid detection, the officers left the area. Within five minutes they returned for a "drive by" and observed the maroon Malibu turning off of Ridge Street. The officers caught up to the car, pulled alongside and noticed that the driver of the car matched the description given by the informant. The vehicle was stopped and a search of the passenger compartment uncovered a bullet on the car's front seat and a pistol in the glove compartment. Based on this discovery, Ross was placed under arrest and handcuffed. Immediately thereafter, a search of the trunk disclosed a paper bag containing a number of glassine baggies of heroin. A more thorough search conducted at the police station uncovered a zippered red leather pouch containing $3,200 in cash, which was found in the vehicle's trunk.

Finding the search and seizure constitutionally valid, the United States Supreme Court held that once police have probable cause to believe a lawfully stopped vehicle contains contraband, "they may conduct a search of the vehicle *that is as thorough as a magistrate could authorize in a [search] warrant[.]" Id.* at 2160. [Emphasis added.]

In *Carroll,* the Court defined the nature of the "automobile exception" and "emphasized the importance of the requirement that officers have probable cause to believe that the vehicle contains contraband * * * 'or illegal merchandise.'" *Ross* at 2164 (quoting *Carroll* at 153-154, 45 *S.Ct.* at 285).

> [T]he probable-cause determination must be based on objective facts that could justify the issuance of a warrant by a magistrate and not merely on the subjective good faith of the police officers. * * * [S]earches of vehicles that are supported by probable cause * * * [are] not unreasonable if based on facts that would justify the issuance of a warrant, even though a warrant has not actually been obtained.

Id.

In this case, the police had probable cause to search defendant's "entire vehicle." *Id.* at 2169. The permissible scope of such a search includes the entire vehicle and any containers or packages found therein. *Id.* at 2170. In this respect, the Court observed:

> Contraband goods rarely are strewn across the trunk or floor of a car; since by their very nature such goods must be withheld from public view, they rarely can be placed in an automobile unless they are enclosed within some form of container. The Court in *Carroll* held that "contraband goods *concealed* and illegally transported in an automobile or other vehicle may be searched for without a warrant." * * * [This holding] "merely relaxed the requirements for a warrant on grounds of practicability." It neither broadened nor limited the scope of a lawful search based on probable cause.

Ross at 2170 (emphasis in original). [Citation omitted.]

"[A] warrant that authorizes an officer to search a home for illegal [merchandise] also provides authority to open closets, chests, drawers, and containers in which the [merchandise] might be found. * * * A warrant to search a vehicle would support a search of every part of the vehicle that might contain the object of the search. When a legitimate search is under way, and when its purpose and its limits have been precisely defined, nice distinctions between closets, drawers, and containers, in the case of a home, or between glove compartments, upholstered seats, trunks, and wrapped packages, in the case of a vehicle, must give way to the interest in the prompt and efficient completion of the task at hand." *Id.* at 2171.

The scope of a warrantless search of a lawfully stopped vehicle "based on probable cause is no narrower—and no broader—than the scope of a search authorized by a warrant supported by probable cause. Only the prior approval of the magistrate is waived; the search otherwise is as the magistrate could authorize." *Id.* at 2172. Moreover, "[t]he practical considerations that justify a warrantless search of an automobile continue to apply until the entire search of the automobile and its contents has been completed." *Id.* at 2171 n.28.

The scope of the search contemplated by the automobile exception "is not defined by the nature of the container in which the contraband is secreted. Rather, it is defined by the object of the search and the places in which there is probable cause to believe that it may be found. Just as probable cause to believe that a stolen lawnmower may be found in a garage will not support a warrant to search an upstairs bedroom, probable cause to believe that undocumented aliens are being transported in a van will not justify a warrant-less search of a suitcase. Probable cause to believe that a container placed in the trunk of a taxi contains contraband does not justify a search of the entire cab." *Id.* at 2172.

Accordingly, when "probable cause justifies the search of a lawfully stopped vehicle, it justifies the search of every part of the vehicle and its contents that may conceal the object of the search." *Id.* at 2173.

NOTE

1. *A "readily mobile" motor vehicle and the impracticability of securing a warrant.*

(a) The "automobile exception" has two primary elements: a "readily mobile" motor vehicle and probable cause to believe the vehicle contains contraband or criminal evidence. In its landmark "automobile exception" case, the United States Supreme Court, in *Carroll v. United States*, 267 *U.S.* 132, 45 *S.Ct.* 280 (1925), was presented with an automobile that had been stopped on the open highway. During the course of its opinion, the Court observed:

> [T]he guaranty of freedom from unreasonable searches and seizures by the Fourth Amendment has been construed, practically since the beginning of the government, as recognizing a difference between a search of a store, dwelling house, or other structure in respect of which a proper official warrant readily may be obtained and a search of a ship, motor boat, wagon, or automobile for contraband goods, *where it is not practicable to secure a warrant, because the vehicle can be quickly moved out of the locality or jurisdiction* in which the warrant must be sought.

Id. at 153, 45 *S.Ct.* 285. [Emphasis added.] The impracticability of securing a warrant stems from the recognition that " 'exigent circumstances' justify the warrantless search of 'an automobile *stopped on the* *highway,'* where there is probable cause, because the car is 'movable, the occupants are alerted, and the car's contents may never be found again if a warrant must be obtained.' '[T]he opportunity to search is fleeting. * * * ' " *Coolidge v. New Hampshire,* 403 *U.S.* 443, 460, 91 *S.Ct.* 2022, 2035 (1971) (Court's emphasis) (quoting *Chambers v. Maroney,* 399 *U.S.* 42, 51, 90 *S.Ct.* 1975, 1981 (1979)).

As the Court emphasized in *Chambers,* however, neither *Carroll* nor other cases decided by the Court suggest that "in every conceivable circumstance" the search of a motor vehicle may be made without a search warrant. *Id.* at 50, 90 *S.Ct.* at 1980. "The word 'automobile' is not a talisman in whose presence the Fourth Amendment fades away and disappears." *Coolidge* at 461, 91 *S.Ct.* at 2035.

(b) In *State v. Colvin,* 123 *N.J.* 428, 587 *A.2d* 1278 (1991), the court addressed the question whether a warrant must be obtained prior to a search of a "parked" car. Within fifteen minutes of defendant Colvin's arrest for the possession of cocaine, a confidential informant advised the arresting officers that "drugs had been stashed in defendant's car, which was parked within a block of the arrest site, and that other people knew about the arrest and would attempt to remove the drugs from the car." *Id.,* 123 *N.J.* at 430. The informant described the car as a "white four-door Cadillac" which "would be unlocked [and] could be started without a key." *Id.* at 435. Immediately thereafter, the officers proceeded to the area indicated by the informant and found a car that matched the informant's description. As soon as the officers confirmed that the Cadillac belonged to defendant, they "entered the unlocked car, searched it, and found tinfoil packets of cocaine underneath the dashboard." *Id.* at 430.

The trial court suppressed the evidence seized, concluding that although the officers did have probable cause to believe the car contained contraband, they should have guarded the vehicle until they obtained a warrant to search it. The New Jersey Supreme Court disagreed, however, and reversed.

As a general principle, the "automobile exception"

"permits police to stop and search a moving or readily movable vehicle when there is probable cause to believe the vehicle contains criminally related objects. The rationale for this exception is grounded in the exigent circumstances created by the inherent mobility of vehicles and the somewhat lessened expectation of privacy in one's vehicle."

Id. at 429. [Citation omitted.] The specific question addressed in this case is "whether the exigency ordinarily created by the mobility of the automobile is dissipated when the vehicle containing the contraband is found parked on a public street." *Id.*

Preliminarily, the Court noted that "[n]o case has established the proposition that law-enforcement officers in 'every conceivable circumstance' may dispense with the warrant requirement in the context of an automobile search." *Id.* at 431. Instead, the expression "automobile exception" is merely "a shorthand way of stating the circumstances under which law-enforcement officers may conduct a warrantless search of a car." *Id.*

In *Coolidge v. New Hampshire*, 403 *U.S.* 443, 91 *S.Ct.* 2022 (1971), the federal Supreme Court suppressed evidence obtained from an automobile found parked in the residence driveway of one who had been arrested because there were no circumstances in the case

> "to invoke the meaning and purpose of [the] *Carroll* [automobile exception]—no alerted criminal bent on flight, no fleeting opportunity on an open highway after a hazardous chase, no contraband or stolen goods or weapons, no confederates waiting to move the evidence, not even the inconvenience of a special police detail to guard the immobilized automobile. In short, by no possible stretch of the legal imagination can this be made into a case where 'it is not practicable to secure a warrant[.]' "

Colvin at 432 (quoting *Coolidge* at 462, 91 *S.Ct.* at 2036 (Stewart, J.) (quoting *Carroll v. United States*, 267 *U.S.* 132, 153, 45 *S.Ct.* 280, 285 (1925)).

Under federal law, however, there is no *per se* rule requiring a warrant to search a parked vehicle. In fact, even while dissenting in *United States v. Ross*, 456 *U.S.* 798, 102 *S.Ct.* 2157 (1982), Justice Marshall emphasized that the federal Supreme Court

> "has refused to require a warrant in situations where the process of obtaining such a warrant would be more intrusive than the actual search itself. * * * Therefore, even where police *can* bring both the defendant and the automobile to the station safely and can house the car while they seek a warrant, the police are permitted to decide whether instead to conduct an immediate search of the car. In effect, the warrantless search is permissible because a warrant requirement would not provide significant protection of the defendant's Fourth Amendment interests."

Colvin at 434 (quoting *Ross* at 831, 102 *S.Ct.* at 2176) (Marshall, J., dissenting) (emphasis in original). Consequently, "if the police have probable cause sufficient to seize the vehicle in order to prevent the loss of the evidence, they have justification to conduct the search at the scene." *Id.*

Similarly, in this State, "the automobile exception does not stand or fall on the fact that a moving car was stopped and then searched." *Id.* at 433. *See e.g. State v. Esteves*, 93 *N.J.* 498, 505 (1983) (warrantless search of vehicle found parked in a parking lot upheld); *State v. Alston*, 88 *N.J.* 211, 234 (1981) ("exigent circumstances do not dissipate simply because the particular occupants of the vehicle may have been removed from the car, arrested, or otherwise restricted in their freedom of movement").

In cases involving a "parked" car, therefore, the core question is whether there are any circumstances which make it *impracticable to secure a warrant*. Here, "nearly all of the factors missing in *Coolidge* were present. Any element of surprise had been lost; the vehicle contained [] 'contraband' drugs; there were 'confederates waiting to move the evidence'; [and] the police would need 'a special police detail to guard the immobilized automobile.'" *Id.* at 434-435. [Citation omitted.] "In such circumstances, 'it would often be unduly burdensome and unreasonably restrictive to require the police to post a guard and repair to the courthouse for a warrant once they have probable cause to search' the car." *Id.* at 435. [Citation omitted.]

Accordingly, "[t]he justification to conduct a warrantless automobile search does not turn on whether the vehicle is parked or moving. The justification turns on the circumstances that make it impracticable to obtain a warrant when the police have probable cause to search the car. When, as here, the police have no advance knowledge of the events to unfold, no warrant is required to search a parked car if the police have probable cause to believe that the car contains criminal contraband *and have articulable reasons to search the vehicle immediately to prevent the loss or destruction of the evidence.*" *Id.* at 437. [Emphasis added.]

(c) Inoperable vehicles. In *United States v. Hatley*, 999 F.2d 393 (9th Cir. 1993), the police conducted a warrantless search of defendant's Corvair based on probable cause to believe it contained a quantity of cocaine. The Corvair was parked in the driveway of defendant's residence. At some point in time after the search, the police learned that at the time of the search, the Corvair was inoperable and had been so for four months.

In the appeal following the denial of his motion to suppress, defendant argued that the automobile exception did not apply because the Corvair was inoperable and on his property at the time of the search. Rejecting defendant's contentions, the court suggested several factors to consider in deciding whether or not a vehicle comes within the automobile exception:

"its location, whether the vehicle is readily mobile or instead, for instance, elevated on blocks, whether the vehicle is licensed, whether it is connected to utilities, and whether it has convenient access to a public road."

Id. at 395. [Citation omitted.] According to the court, with the exception of "whether the vehicle is readily mobile," the factors set forth above indicate that the search of the Corvair came within automobile exception. "The car was not connected to utilities, and '[b]ecause it was located in a residential driveway, it had easy access to a public road.'" *Id.* [Citation omitted.]

Though the Corvair was not *actually* mobile, it was *apparently* mobile. There was nothing apparent to the officers to suggest the car was immobile. It was not up on blocks, and there was no information in the record to indicate the tires were flat or that wheels of the car were missing. In matters of search and seizure, we apply an objective test of reasonableness: would the facts available to the officer at the moment warrant a person of reasonable caution to believe that the car was operable ? * * *

It would be unduly burdensome to require the police to establish that every car that appeared to be mobile was indeed mobile before making the search. We therefore hold * * * that *the Fourth Amendment does not require that officers ascertain the actual functional capacity of a vehicle in order to satisfy the exigency requirement.* * * * In this case, the Fourth Amendment's reasonableness requirement was met because the officers reasonably believed the car was mobile.

Id. [Emphasis added.]

See also United States v. Hepperle, 810 *F.*2d 836, 840 (8th Cir.), *cert. denied,* 483 *U.S.* 1025, 107 *S.Ct.* 3274 (1987).

2. *Exigent circumstances not required.* In *Pennsylvania v. Labron,* 518 *U.S.* 938, 116 *S.Ct.* 2485 (1996), the United States Supreme Court reversed two consolidated cases* decided by the Pennsylvania Supreme Court on the basis of an incorrect interpretation of the automobile exception to the Fourth Amendment's warrant requirement.

In *Labron,* police observed Labron and others engaging in a series of drug transactions on a street in Philadelphia. "The police arrested the suspects, searched the trunk of a car from which the drugs had been produced, and found bags containing cocaine." *Id.,* 116 *S.Ct.* at 2486.

In *Kilgore,* an undercover informant agreed to buy drugs from Randy Lee Kilgore's accomplice, Kelly Jo Kilgore. "To obtain the drugs, Kelly Jo drove from the parking lot where the deal was made to a farmhouse where she met with Randy Kilgore and obtained the drugs. After the drugs were delivered and the Kilgores were arrested, police searched the farmhouse with the consent of its owner and also searched Randy Kilgore's pickup truck; they had also seen the Kilgores walking to and from the truck, which was parked in the driveway of the farmhouse." *Id.* The search of the truck, which was determined to be based on probable cause, turned up a quantity of cocaine.

The Pennsylvania Supreme Court found that the searches in *Labron* and *Kilgore* violated the Fourth Amendment because, in its view, the automobile exception requires the existence of exigent circumstances in addition to probable cause. The United States Supreme Court disagreed and summarily reversed. The Court said:

Our first cases establishing the automobile exception to the Fourth Amendment's warrant requirement were based on the automobile's "ready mobility," an exigency sufficient to excuse failure to obtain a search warrant once probable cause to conduct the search is clear. * * * More recent cases provide a further justification: the individual's reduced expectation of privacy in an automobile, owing to its

---

* *Commonwealth v. Labron,* 543 *Pa.* 86, 669 *A.*2d 917 (1995); *Commonwealth v. Kilgore,* 544 *Pa.* 439, 677 *A.*2d 311 (1995).

pervasive regulation. * * * *If a car is readily mobile and probable cause exists to believe it contains contraband, the Fourth Amendment thus permits police to search the vehicle without more.* As the state courts found, there was probable cause in both of these cases: Police had seen [] Labron put drugs in the trunk of the car they searched, and had seen [] Kilgore act in ways that suggested he had drugs in his truck. We conclude the searches of the automobiles in these cases did not violate the Fourth Amendment.

Id. at 2487. [Emphasis added.]

3. During the course of its opinion in *Ross*, the Court pointed out that, unlike *United States v. Chadwick*, 433 *U.S.* 1, 97 *S.Ct.* 2476 (1977), and *Arkansas v. Sanders*, 442 *U.S.* 753, 99 *S.Ct.* 2586 (1979), "in this case the police officers had probable cause to search [defendant's] entire car." *Ross* at 2168-69. In *Chadwick*, federal agents had probable cause to believe a 200-pound footlocker contained contraband. The officers waited for Chadwick to place the footlocker in the trunk of his car before they searched it. The search uncovered a large quantity of marijuana. In holding that the warrantless search of the footlocker violated the Fourth Amendment, the *Chadwick* Court emphasized that closed packages and containers may not be searched without a warrant. In *Sanders*, police had probable cause to believe defendant's green suitcase contained marijuana. The officers watched as Sanders gave his suitcase to a companion, who placed it in the trunk of a taxi. Sanders and his companion rode off in the taxi and within minutes were stopped by the police. The officers immediately opened the trunk of the cab, searched the green suitcase and discovered a quantity of marijuana. Finding the search of the suitcase violative of the Fourth Amendment, the *Sanders* Court emphasized that the defendant's act of placing the suitcase in the trunk of the taxi did not automatically make the *Carroll* automobile exception applicable. The officers had probable cause to believe the suitcase contained marijuana; they had no probable cause related to the taxi itself. According to the *Ross* Court, "in neither *Chadwick* nor *Sanders* did the police have probable cause to search the vehicle or anything within it except the footlocker in the former and the green suitcase in the latter." *Ross* at 2167.

The law respecting motor vehicle searches and related container searches has thus branched off in two different directions: The *Carroll-Ross* line of cases involving searches of lawfully stopped vehicles—based on probable cause to believe that contraband or other seizable evidence may be found somewhere within the vehicle—which uncover a package; and the *Chadwick-Sanders* line of cases for searches of such vehicles based on probable cause to believe that a particular package placed inside the vehicle contains contraband or other seizable evidence. Under the *Carroll-Ross* pure automobile exception, a warrantless search of the package would be constitutionally reasonable. Under the *Chadwick-Sanders* set of circumstances, however, officers could seize the package, but could not conduct a search of its contents without a warrant.

CALIFORNIA v. ACEVEDO
Supreme Court of the United States
500 *U.S.* 565, 111 *S.Ct.* 1982 (1991)

QUESTION: Does the Fourth Amendment require the police to obtain a warrant to open a closed package located in a motor vehicle when their probable cause relates only to the package and not the entire vehicle ?

ANSWER: NO. "The line between probable cause to search a vehicle and probable cause to search a package in that vehicle is not always clear, and separate rules that govern the two objects to be searched" are no longer appropriate. *Id.* at 1988. "The *Chadwick-Sanders* rule not only has failed to protect privacy but it has also confused courts and police officers and impeded effective law enforcement." *Id.* at 1989. It is better, therefore, "to adopt one clear-cut rule to govern" vehicle searches: The *Sanders* warrant requirement for closed containers is eliminated; "[t]he police may search an automobile and the containers within it where they have probable cause to believe contraband or evidence is contained." *Id.* Consequently, "[t]he interpretation of the *Carroll* doctrine set forth in *Ross* now applies to all searches of containers found in an automobile." *Id.* at 1991.

RATIONALE: In late October, at about 12:30 p.m., Officer Coleman of the Santa Ana, California, Police Department observed defendant, Charles Acevedo, leaving an apartment carrying a brown paper bag. At the time, Coleman had probable cause to believe the bag contained marijuana. Acevedo walked to a silver Honda in the parking lot, placed the bag in the trunk of the car, and started to drive away. "Fearing the loss of evidence, officers in a marked police car stopped him. They opened the trunk and the bag, and found the marijuana." *Id.* at 1985.

The California Court of Appeal held that the marijuana found in the paper bag in the car's trunk was unlawfully seized because, even though the officers had probable cause to believe the paper bag contained contraband, they lacked probable cause to believe Acevedo's car, itself, otherwise contained contraband. According to the California Court, because the officers' probable cause was directed specifically at the bag, the case was controlled by *United States v. Chadwick*, 433 *U.S.* 1, 97 *S.Ct.* 2476 (1977), rather than *United States v. Ross*, 456 *U.S.* 798, 102 *S.Ct.* 2157 (1982). The California court therefore concluded that while the officers were permitted to "seize" the paper bag, under *Chadwick* they could not open the bag without first obtaining a search warrant. *The United States Supreme Court disagreed and reversed.*

Speaking for the Court, Justice Blackmun first noted that in the area of motor vehicle searches and related container searches, an anomaly exists in the dichotomy between the rule in *Chadwick* and the rule in *Ross*. "That dichotomy dictates that if there is probable cause to search a car, then the entire car—including any closed container found therein—may be searched without a warrant [*Ross*], but if there is probable cause only as to a container in the car, the container may be held but not searched until a warrant is obtained [*Chadwick*]." *Acevedo* at 1985. Thus, the *Acevedo* Court undertook a reexamination of the law applicable to closed containers located in motor vehicles; a subject, the Court observed, "that has troubled courts and law enforcement officers since it was first considered in *Chadwick*." *Id.* at 1985.

In *Carroll v. United States*, 267 *U.S.* 132, 45 *S.Ct.* 280 (1925), the Court established an exception to the written warrant requirement for moving vehicles, recognizing:

> a necessary difference between a search of a store, dwelling house or other structure in respect of which a proper official warrant may be obtained, and a search of a ship, motor boat, wagon or automobile, for contraband goods, where it is not practicable to secure a warrant because the vehicle can be quickly moved out of the locality or jurisdiction in which the warrant must be sought.

Id. at 153, 45 *S.Ct.* at 285. The *Carroll* Court held, therefore, that a probable-cause based, warrantless search of a motor vehicle was reasonable within the meaning of the Fourth Amendment.

In *United States v. Ross*, the Court held "that a warrantless search of an automobile under the *Carroll* doctrine could include a search of a container or package found inside the car when such a search was supported by probable cause." *Acevedo* at 1986. *Ross* "clarified the scope of the *Carroll* doctrine as properly including a 'probing search' of compartments and containers within the automobile so long as the search is supported by probable cause." *Acevedo* at 1986 (quoting *Ross* at 800, 102 *S.Ct.* at 2160).

"In addition to this clarification, *Ross* distinguished the *Carroll* doctrine from the separate rule that governed the search of * * * luggage and other closed packages, bags, and containers, [as set forth] in *United States v. Chadwick*[.]" *Acevedo* at 1986.

> In *Chadwick*, federal narcotics agents had probable cause to believe a 200-pound double-locked footlocker contained marijuana. The agents tracked the locker as the defendants removed it from a train and carried it through the station to a waiting car. As soon as the defendants lifted the locker into the trunk of the car, the agents arrested him, seized the locker, and searched it. [At the Supreme Court, the government] did not contend that the locker's brief contact with the automobile's trunk sufficed to make the *Carroll* doctrine applicable. Rather, the United States urged that the search of movable luggage could be considered analogous to the search of an automobile.

Acevedo at 1986. Rejecting the Government's contention, the *Chadwick* Court concluded that "a person expects more privacy in his luggage and personal effects than he does in his automobile." *Acevedo* at 1986.

The *Chadwick* rule was extended in *Arkansas v. Sanders*, 442 *U.S.* 753, 99 *S.Ct.* 2586 (1979), to apply to a suitcase actually being transported in the trunk of a car.

In *Sanders*, the police had probable cause to believe a suitcase contained marijuana. They watched as the defendant placed the suitcase in the trunk of a taxi and was driven away. The police pursued the taxi for several blocks, stopped it, found the suitcase in the trunk, and searched it.

Acevedo at 1987. According to the *Sanders* Court, the *Carroll-Ross* automobile exception did not apply to the warrantless search of personal luggage "merely because it was located in an automobile lawfully stopped by the police." *Sanders* at 765, 99 *S.Ct.* at 2594. "Again, the *Sanders* [Court] stressed the heightened privacy expectation in personal luggage and concluded that the presence of luggage in an automobile did not diminish the owner's expectation of privacy in his personal items." *Acevedo* at 1987.

Thus, we have the dichotomy—the *Carroll-Ross* line of cases which covers searches of automobiles when the police have probable cause to search the *entire* vehicle, and the *Chadwick-Sanders* line of cases which governs searches of luggage and other closed packages when officers have probable cause to search only a container within the vehicle. In the *Carroll-Ross* set of circumstances, "the police could conduct a reasonable search under the Fourth Amendment without obtaining a warrant, whereas in a [*Chadwick-*]*Sanders* situation, the police [would have] to obtain a warrant before they searched." *Acevedo* at 1987. Interestingly, the Court in *Ross* "rejected *Chadwick's* distinction between containers and cars. It concluded that the expectation of privacy in one's vehicle is equal to one's expectation of privacy in the container, and noted that 'the privacy interests in a car's trunk or glove compartment may be no less than those in a movable container.' * * * It also recognized that it was arguable that the same exigent circumstances that permit a warrant-less search of an automobile would justify the warrantless search of a movable container." *Acevedo* at 1987-88 (quoting *Ross* at 823, 102 *S.Ct.* at 2172).

The *Ross* Court did not, however, seek to reconcile the anomalous dichotomy between the *Carroll* line of cases and the *Chadwick-Sanders* line of cases. Here, in *Acevedo*, the Court directly addressed "the question deferred in *Ross*: whether the Fourth Amendment requires the police to obtain a warrant to open [a closed container] in a movable vehicle simply because they lack probable cause to search the entire car." *Acevedo* at 1988.

Holding that no warrant is required, the Court concluded that there is "no principled distinction in terms of either the privacy expectation or the exigent circumstances between the paper bag found by the police in *Ross* and the paper bag found by the police here. Furthermore, by attempting to distinguish between a container for which the police are specifically searching and a container which they come across in a car, [the prior cases have] provided only minimal protection for privacy and have impeded effective law enforcement." *Id.* In this respect, Justice Blackmun explained that "[t]he line between probable cause to search a vehicle and probable cause to search a package in that vehicle is not always clear, and separate rules that govern the two objects to be searched" are no longer appropriate. *Id.* at 1988. As observed in *Ross*: " 'prohibiting police from opening immediately a container in which the object of the search is most likely to be found and instead forcing them first to comb the entire vehicle would actually exacerbate the intrusion on privacy interests.' * * * If the police know that they may open a bag only if they are actually searching the entire car, they may search more extensively than they otherwise would in order to establish the general probable cause required by *Ross*." *Acevedo* at 1988. [Citation omitted.]

"To the extent that the *Chadwick-Sanders* rule protects privacy, its protection is minimal. Law enforcement officers may seize a container and hold it until they obtain a search warrant[, and] * * * 'we can assume that a warrant will be routinely forthcoming in the overwhelming majority of cases.' " *Acevedo* at 1989. [Citation omitted.] In light of this minimal safeguard to privacy, the Court held "that the Fourth Amendment does not compel separate treatment for an automobile search that extends only to a container within the vehicle." *Id.*

"The *Chadwick-Sanders* rule not only has failed to protect privacy but it has also confused courts and police officers and impeded effective law enforcement." *Id.* at 1989. In so many cases, the Court has "noted the virtue of providing 'clear and unequivocal' guidelines to the law enforcement profession." *Id.* at 1990. [Citation omitted.] The guidelines set forth in the *Chadwick-Sanders* line of cases are anything but "clear and unequivocal." *Id.*

The existence of two separate rules for automobile searches that uncover containers has proved to be confusing, and accordingly, the Court declared "that *it is better to adopt one clear-cut rule to govern automobile searches and eliminate the warrant requirement for closed containers set forth in Sanders.*" *Acevedo* at 1991. [Emphasis added.] "The interpretation of the *Carroll* doctrine set forth in *Ross* now applies to all searches of containers found in an automobile. In other words, the police may search without a warrant if their search is supported by probable cause. The Court in Ross put it this way:

> The scope of a warrantless search of an automobile . . . is not defined by the nature of the container in which the contraband is secreted. Rather, it is defined by the object of the search and the places in which there is probable cause to believe that it may be found."

Acevedo at 1991 (quoting *Ross* at 824, 102 *S.Ct.* at 2172). Significantly, the *Ross* Court went on to emphasize that, " '[p]robable cause to believe that a container placed in the trunk of a taxi contains contraband or evidence does not justify a search of the entire cab.' " *Id.* Here, in *Acevedo*, the Court "reaffirm[ed] that principle." *Id.* In this case, the police had probable cause to believe that the paper bag in the vehicle's trunk contained marijuana. "That probable cause now allows a warrantless search of the paper bag." *Id.* The police did not, however, have "probable cause to believe that contraband was hidden in any other part of the automobile and a search of the entire vehicle would have been without probable cause and unreasonable under the Fourth Amendment." *Id.*

In several concluding remarks, Justice Blackmun observed:

> Until today, this Court has drawn a curious line between the search of an automobile that coincidentally turns up a container and the search of a container that coincidentally turns up in an automobile. The protections of the Fourth Amendment must not turn on such coincidences. *We therefore interpret Carroll as providing one rule to govern all automobile searches. The police may search an automobile and the containers within it where they have probable cause to believe contraband or evidence is contained.*

Id. at 1991. [Emphasis added.]

NOTE

1. *Probable cause to search versus probable cause to arrest.* During the course of its opinion, the Court in *Acevedo* observed that, "the same probable cause to believe that a container holds drugs will allow the police to arrest the person transporting the container and search it." *Id.* at 1989. In this respect, the Court pointed out an interesting alternative: Under *New York v. Belton*, 453 *U.S.* 454, 101 *S.Ct.* 2860 (1981), once an officer has effected " 'a lawful custodial arrest of the occupant of an automobile, he may, as a contemporaneous incident of that arrest, search the passenger compartment of that automobile[, including] the contents of any containers found within the passenger compartment.' " *Acevedo* at 1989 (quoting *Belton* at 460, 101 *S.Ct.* at 2864 (footnote omitted)). The validity of such a search turns, not so much on the existence of probable cause to believe that a package within the automobile contains contraband or other illegal items, but upon the lawful custodial arrest which, ironically, is based upon probable cause to believe that the occupant is committing a crime in the officer's presence, that being the unlawful possession of such contraband or illegal merchandise. Had Acevedo placed his package of marijuana in the passenger compartment of his automobile, an arrest could have been justified under *United States v. Watson*, 423 *U.S.* 411, 418-421, 96 *S.Ct.* 820, 825-826 (1976), and the search of the package, as an incident to the arrest, authorized by *New York v. Belton, supra.*

In his concurring opinion, Justice Scalia observed:

> And there are more anomalies still. Under our precedents (as at common law), a person may be arrested outside his home on the basis of probable cause, without an arrest warrant. *United States v. Watson* * * *. Upon arrest, the person, as well as the area within his grasp, may be searched for evidence related to the crime. *Chimel v. California*, 395 *U.S.* 752, 762-763, 89 *S.Ct.* 2034, 2039-2040 [] (1969) * * *. Under these principles, if a known drug dealer is carrying a briefcase reasonably believed to contain marijuana (the unauthorized possession of which is a crime), the police may arrest him and search his person on the basis of probable cause alone. And, under our precedents, upon arrival at the station house, the police may inventory his possessions, including the

briefcase, even if there is no reason to suspect that they contain contraband. *Illinois v. Lafayette*, 462 *U.S.* 640, 103 *S.Ct.* 2605 [] (1983). According to our current law, however, the police may not take the less intrusive step of stopping the individual on the street and demanding to see the contents of his briefcase. That makes no sense * * *.

Id. at 1993-94 (Scalia, J., concurring).

See also Ybarra v. Illinois, 444 *U.S.* 85, 105, 100 *S.Ct.* 338, 350 (1979), where, in a strongly worded dissent, Justice Rehnquist declared: "Given probable cause to believe that a person possesses illegal drugs, the police need no warrant to conduct a full body search. They need only arrest that person and conduct the search incident to that arrest."

2. *The scope of the search and the personal belongings of passengers.* When police have probable cause to believe an automobile contains contraband or evidence of a crime, may they search the entire car, including the contents of a *passenger's* personal belongings that may be capable of holding the object of the search? In *Wyoming v. Houghton*, 526 *U.S.* 295, 119 *S.Ct.* 1297 (1999), the United States Supreme Court said *yes*.

In *Houghton*, in the early morning hours, a patrol officer stopped an automobile for speeding and having a faulty brake light. In the front seat, there were three passengers: the driver, David Young, his girlfriend, and defendant Sandra Houghton. As he spoke to Young, the officer noticed a hypodermic syringe in Young's shirt pocket. With the assistance of two backup officers, the patrol officer instructed Young to step out of the car and place the syringe on the hood. When the officer asked Young why he had a syringe, "with refreshing candor, Young replied that he used it to take drugs." *Id.*, 119 *S.Ct.* at 1299.

At this point, the backup officers told the two female passengers to step out of the car and asked them to produce identification. Defendant falsely identified herself as "Sandra James" and stated that she did not have any identification. Meanwhile, the officer searched the passenger compartment of the car for contraband. On the back seat, he found a purse, which defendant claimed as hers. The officer removed from the purse a wallet containing her driver's license, identifying her properly as Sandra K. Houghton. She told the officer that she lied about her name, "[i]n case things went bad." *Id.*

A further search of the purse uncovered drug paraphernalia and two syringes, each containing a quantity of methamphetamine. The officer also found fresh needle-track marks on defendant's arms. Accordingly, he placed her under arrest.

Based on these circumstances, the Wyoming Supreme Court determined that the search of Houghton's purse violated the Fourth and Fourteenth Amendments because the officer "knew or should have known that the purse did not belong to the driver, but to one of the passengers," and because "there was no probable cause to search the passengers' personal effects and no reason to believe that contraband had been placed [or hidden] within the purse." *Id.* at 1300. The United

States Supreme Court disagreed and reversed. In this case, it was "uncontested" that the police "had probable cause to believe there were illegal drugs in the car. In such circumstances, the "automobile exception" to the written warrant requirement, as refined by the Court in *United States v. Ross*, 456 *U.S.* 798, 102 *S.Ct.* 2157 (1982), applies. *Ross* held:

> "If probable cause justifies the search of a lawfully stopped vehicle, it justifies the search of *every part of the vehicle and its contents* that may conceal the object of the search."

Houghton at 1301 (Court's emphasis) (quoting *Ross* at 825, 102 *S.Ct.* 2157).

Later cases interpreting *Ross* have characterized the rule "as applying broadly to *all* containers within a car, without qualification as to ownership." *Id.* [Court's emphasis.] Moreover, *Ross* itself "concluded from the historical evidence that the permissible scope of a warrantless car search 'is defined by the object of the search and the places in which there is probable cause to believe that it may be found.'" *Houghton* at 1301. [Citation omitted.] Thus, it appears that none of the earlier automobile-search cases identified any sort of distinction among packages or containers based on ownership.

Clearly the better rule, observed the Court, provides that "[w]hen there is probable cause to search for contraband in a car, it is reasonable for police officers * * * to examine packages and containers without a showing of individualized probable cause for each one. A passenger's personal belongings, just like the driver's belongings or containers attached to the car, like a glove compartment, are 'in' the car, and the officer has probable cause to search for contraband *in* the car." *Id.* [Court's emphasis.] Moreover,

> [e]ffective law enforcement would be appreciably impaired without the ability to search a passenger's personal belongings when there is reason to believe contraband or evidence of criminal wrongdoing is hidden in the car. As in all car-search cases, the "ready mobility" of an automobile creates the risk that the evidence or contraband will be permanently lost while a warrant is obtained.

Id. at 1302.

During the course of its opinion, the Court appropriately observed that to require law enforcement officers to

> have positive reason to believe that the passenger and driver were engaged in a common enterprise, or positive reason to believe that the driver had time and occasion to conceal the item in the passenger's belongings, surreptitiously or with friendly permission, is to impose requirements so seldom met that a "passenger's property" rule would dramatically reduce the ability to find and seize contraband and evidence of crime. * * * But once a "passenger's property" exception became widely known, one would expect passenger confederates to claim everything as their own. And one would anticipate a bog of litigation—in the form of both civil lawsuits and

motions to suppress in criminal trials—involving such questions as whether the officer should have believed a passenger's claim of ownership, whether he should have inferred ownership from various objective factors, whether he had probable cause to believe that the passenger was a confederate, or to believe that the driver might have introduced the contraband into the package with or without the passenger's knowledge. When balancing the competing interests, our determinations of "reasonableness" under the Fourth Amendment must take account of these practical realities. We think they militate in favor of the needs of law enforcement * * *.

Id. at 1303.

Accordingly, the Court held that "police officers with probable cause to search a car may inspect passengers' belongings found in the car that are capable of concealing the object of the search." Moreover, such property may be searched, "whether or not its owner is present as a passenger or otherwise, because it may contain the contraband that the officer has reason to believe is in the car." *Id.* at 1304.

3. *The inferences drawn by police officers.* In *Ornelas v. United States*, 517 *U.S.* 690, 116 *S.Ct.* 1657 (1996), the United States Supreme Court emphasized that, while "determinations of reasonable suspicion and probable cause should be reviewed *de novo* on appeal," courts should nonetheless give "due weight" to inferences drawn by police officers based on their "own experience in deciding whether probable cause exists." *Id.*, 116 *S.Ct.* at 1663.

In *Ornelas*, sheriff's officers stopped the defendants' automobile on the basis of a reasonable suspicion that the defendants were involved in drug trafficking. During a consent search of the vehicle (stipulated as not including any secret compartments), K-9 Officer Luedke, "who over the past nine years had searched approximately 2,000 cars for narcotics," noticed that "a panel above the right rear passenger arm rest felt somewhat loose." Suspecting that the area behind the panel may have been used to store contraband, Luedke examined the area more closely. He noticed that a screw in the door jamb adjacent to the loose panel was rusty, suggesting that the screw had been removed at some time. Luedke dismantled and removed the panel. Behind it, he discovered two kilograms of cocaine. *Id.*, 116 *S.Ct.* at 1660. In discussing the appropriate form of appellate court review, the Court observed:

To a layman, the sort of loose panel below the back seat arm rest in the automobile involved in this case may suggest only wear and tear, but to Officer Luedke, who had searched roughly 2,000 cars for narcotics, it suggested that drugs may be secreted inside the panel. An appeals court should give due weight to a trial court's finding that the officer was credible and the inference was reasonable.

Id. at 1663.

UNITED STATES v. RICKUS
United States Court of Appeals
737 *F*.2d 360 (3rd Cir. 1984)

QUESTION: At what point in the below set of facts did the officers develop probable cause for the search of defendant's automobile ?

FACTS:

POINTS:

1. At approximately 3:00 a.m., Officer Halpin was sitting in his patrol car in a parking lot in the business district of Richboro, Pennsylvania, when he observed a black and gold Buick traveling up the highway and then, thirty minutes later, observed the same car traveling back again.

2. At the time of the second sighting, the car was moving very slowly past the closed stores of the commercial district.

3. Halpin followed the vehicle as it drove through the commercial district and into a nearby residential area. Aware that the residential area recently had been victimized by as many as twelve unsolved nighttime burglaries, although none had been reported that night, Halpin called for assistance.

4. When Sergeant Quaste and Officer Berwind responded to the call (in an unmarked vehicle), both police cars followed the Buick through the residential area for several minutes. During this entire time, the Buick continued to travel slowly, and at one point it stopped momentarily in front of a residence.

5. Finally, when the car made a legal U-turn, Halpin pulled in front of the car and stopped it. Quaste and Berwind continued on in their car.

6. The driver, Dennis Nazarok, exited the vehicle as Halpin approached. When Halpin asked Nazarok for identification, Nazarok responded that he did not have his driver's license or any other identification with him.

7. When Halpin then asked the passenger, Robert Rickus, for identification, Rickus did not acknowledge the request and remained motionless. Halpin asked again and Rickus replied that he had none.

8. Nazarok eventually produced from the car's glove compartment an insurance card bearing the name of Bernadette Nazarok. While Nazarok was looking for the insurance card, Halpin illuminated the car's interior with his flashlight. He then noticed a screwdriver and pliers on the floor behind the passenger area, and roadmaps and a flashlight on the front seat.

9. At this point, Halpin asked Nazarok and Rickus where they had been. They stated that they had been drinking at a few bars, but could not remember the name or location of any of them. Additionally, Halpin could not detect any odor of alcohol on their breath. Throughout the encounter, both Nazarok and Rickus repeatedly exchanged furtive glances and generally acted in a nervous manner.

10. Sergeant Quaste and Officer Berwind returned to the scene and, as Halpin was talking to Nazarok, Quaste noticed Rickus slowly backing away from the car. Quaste told Rickus to return. Within a few minutes, Rickus again started to back away from the car and again was told by Quaste to return.

11. While Halpin spoke to Nazarok and Rickus, he noticed a bulge in the left pocket of Nazarok's jacket and the top of a bullet proof vest sticking out above the jacket.

12. After Halpin had asked Nazarok (several times) to remove his jacket, Nazarok finally complied—revealing a full upperbody bullet-proof vest.

13. At this point, both men was asked to face the Buick and place their hands on it while they were patted down. Halpin handed Nazarok's jacket to Sergeant Quaste.

14. In the jacket, the sergeant found two pairs of surgical gloves.

15. In the passenger compartment of the Buick, the sergeant found the screwdriver, pliers, flashlight and maps, along with a hunting knife and a pair of brown work gloves.

16. When asked why he and Rickus were wearing bullet-proof vests, Nazarok stated that they were going to "hit" a drug dealer, but the deal "had gone sour."

17. Sergeant Quaste then removed the keys from the ignition, opened the trunk, and there found a loaded .22 caliber semi-automatic pistol, and a mask.

[Nazarok and Rickus were then placed under arrest and each was subsequently charged with possession of a firearm by a convicted felon.]

ANSWER: AT POINT 12. The officers' discovery that each defendant was wearing a full, upper-body bullet-proof vest, taken in light of all the circumstances up to this point, provided them with "probable cause to search the car under the automobile exception to the warrant requirement[.]" *Id.* at 367.

RATIONALE: Preliminarily, the court concluded that the motor vehicle stop effected in this case was lawful. "Defendants were traveling

through a closed business district at 3:00 in the morning at a speed
15-20 miles per hour below the posted speed limit when first they
aroused Officer Halpin's suspicions. They then turned into a residential area that Halpin knew had recently been victimized by a spate of
burglaries, and continued their slow and apparently aimless course for
several minutes before being stopped. [Under these circumstances,
t]he reputation of an area for criminal activity is an articulable fact
upon which a police officer may legitimately rely. * * * Considering the
rash of burglaries in this location, [the court] believe[d] that Halpin's
observations were sufficient to raise a reasonable suspicion in the
mind of an experienced police officer that the car or its occupants were
involved, or about to become involved in criminal activity." *Id.* at 365.

The next question, according to the court, is whether the search of
the entire vehicle was valid. "Although such a search cannot be justified by the mere 'reasonable suspicion' that validates an investigatory
stop, in this case the information available to the police after stopping
the car quickly matured from the initial 'reasonable suspicion' into the
requisite 'probable cause' to believe that the automobile contained contraband. In the course of the valid investigatory stop, Halpin learned
that neither defendant could produce any identification or indicia of
ownership of the automobile. In plain view from the outside of the car,
Halpin saw a screwdriver and pliers on the rear floor and maps and a
flashlight on the front seat of the car[,]" *id.* at 366, and "[c]ontrary to
defendant Rickus' suggestion, the use of the flashlight to aid the officer's vision did not transform the observations justified under the
'plain view doctrine' into an illegal search." *Id.* at 366 n.3. "Recognizing that these instruments could be used in a burglary, Halpin asked
the defendants what they were doing—only to receive patently unsat-
isfactory answers. The continual furtive glances between the defendants, their stilted speech patterns, and the apparent attempts of
Rickus to leave the scene further aroused the officers' suspicions. Finally, after sighting the bulge in Nazarok's jacket pocket and a portion
of a bullet-proof vest protruding above the jacket, the officers discovered that both defendants were wearing full upper-body bullet-proof
vests." *Id.* at 366-367. *It was at this point that the officers had developed "probable cause to search the car under the automobile exception
to the warrant requirement[.]" Id.* at 367. [Emphasis added.]

The information gathered by the officers, considered in light of the
totality of the circumstances facing them, "supplied probable cause for
the officers to conclude that a burglary had been or was about to be
committed and that a search of the car would reveal evidence of the
crime. No more was required. Probable cause deals with probabilities,
not certainties. The facts known to the officers must be judged in accordance with 'the factual and practical considerations of everyday life
on which reasonable and prudent men, not legal technicians, act.'" *Id.*
(quoting *Brinegar v. United States*, 338 *U.S.* 160, 175, 69 *S.Ct.* 1302,
1310 (1949)). Moreover, the process of determining the existence of
probable cause should proceed as " 'a practical, common sense decision
whether, given all the circumstances * * *, there is a fair probability
that contraband or evidence of a crime will be found in a particular
place[,' * * * and t]he objective facts in this case certainly justified the

officers in concluding that there was a fair probability that evidence of a burglary would be found in the car." *Id.* [Citation omitted.]

Finally, contrary to the district court's opinion, federal law does not require the government to demonstrate the existence of independent probable cause to believe that the trunk of an automobile contains contraband before a "trunk search" will be permitted. As the United States Supreme Court held in *United States v. Ross*, 456 *U.S.* 798, 102 *S.Ct.* 2157 (1982):

> If probable cause justifies the search of a lawfully stopped vehicle, it justifies the search *of every part of the vehicle* and its contents that may conceal the object of the search.

Rickus at 367 (emphasis added) (quoting *Ross* at 825, 102 *S.Ct.* at 2172). Thus, law enforcement officers need have no more cause "to search a trunk than [is] required to search the passenger compartment under the automobile exception, nor need they have independent reason to believe that the contraband for which they are searching is located specifically in the trunk. * * * In this case, * * * the police were presented with ample evidence to give them probable cause to [believe] that the automobile contained evidence of a crime. That being the case, and the trunk clearly being a 'part of the vehicle' capable of concealing 'the object of the search,' * * * they were justified in searching the [entire automobile]." *Id.* [Citation omitted.]

UNITED STATES v. JOHNS
Supreme Court of the United States
469 *U.S.* 478, 105 *S.Ct.* 881 (1985)

QUESTION: May a law enforcement officer conduct a warrantless search of packages several days after those packages were removed from a lawfully stopped vehicle that the officer had probable cause to believe contained contraband ?

ANSWER: YES. When police have probable cause to believe a lawfully stopped vehicle contains contraband, they are entitled to conduct a warrantless "search of every part of the vehicle and its contents that may conceal the object of the search." *Id.* at 885. Moreover, the warrantless search of packages taken from that vehicle will not be deemed unreasonable merely because it occurs several days after the packages were unloaded from the vehicle. According to the Court, where officers are entitled to seize a package "and continue to have probable cause to believe that it contains contraband, * * * delay in the execution of the warrantless search is [not] necessarily unreasonable." *Id.* at 886-887.

RATIONALE: In *United States v. Ross*, 456 *U.S.* 798, 102 *S.Ct.* 2157 (1982), the United States Supreme Court ruled that "if police officers have probable cause to search a lawfully stopped vehicle, they may conduct a warrantless search of any containers found inside that may conceal the object of the search." *Johns* at 883. The issue here in *Johns* is "whether *Ross* authorizes a warrantless search of packages several days after they were removed from vehicles that police officers had probable cause to believe contained contraband." *Johns* at 883.

During the course of an investigation into a drug smuggling operation, United States Customs officers developed reasonable grounds to suspect that two pickup trucks were being used to transport illegal drugs. The trucks were previously observed traveling to a remote private airstrip near Bowie, Arizona, approximately 50 miles from the Mexican Border. While at the airstrip, the officers observed two small airplanes land and rendezvous with the trucks. Two Customs officers approached to investigate and one of the officers observed an individual at the rear of one of the trucks covering the contents with a blanket. The officer then ordered everyone out from behind the trucks and to lie down on the ground. "As he and the other officer walked towards the trucks, they smelled the odor of marihuana. They saw in the back of the trucks packages wrapped in dark green plastic and sealed with tape. Based on their prior experience, the officers knew that smuggled marihuana is commonly packaged in this manner." *Id.*

"The Customs officers did not search the pickup trucks at the desert airstrip. Instead, after arresting the [defendants] who were at the scene, the Customs officers took the trucks back to Drug Enforcement Administration (DEA) headquarters in Tucson. The packages were removed from the trucks and placed in a DEA warehouse. Without obtaining a search warrant, DEA agents opened some of the packages and took samples that later proved to be marihuana." *Id.* Three days later, the agents conducted a full and complete search of the packages seized from the pickup trucks.

In this appeal, defendants argue that the lower courts' order of suppression was correct because the Customs officers never had probable cause to conduct a vehicle search. Additionally, it is contended that the subsequent search was unreasonable because it occurred three days after the packages were unloaded from the pickup trucks. *The United States Supreme Court disagreed and reversed the order of suppression.*

Initially, the Court states that defendants' contention that the officers did not have probable cause to believe the pickup trucks contained contraband is "not persuasive." *Id.* at 884. According to the Court, "[t]he events surrounding the rendezvous of the aircraft and the pickup trucks at the isolated desert airstrip indicated that the vehicles were involved in smuggling activity. * * * After the officers came closer and detected the distinct odor of marihuana, they had probable cause to believe that the vehicles contained contraband. * * * Given their experience with drug smuggling cases, the officers no doubt suspected that the scent was emanating from the packages that they observed in the back of the pickup trucks. The officers, however, were unaware of the packages until they approached the trucks, and contraband might well have been hidden elsewhere in the vehicles." *Id.* The Customs officers, therefore, "had probable cause to believe that not only the packages but also the vehicles themselves contained contraband." *Id.*

The main issue presented by this case is "whether the subsequent warrantless search was unreasonable merely because it occurred three days after the packages were unloaded from the pickup trucks." *Id.* at 885. As recognized in *United States v. Ross*, the automobile exception to the written warrant requirement "allows a search of the same scope as could be authorized by a [search warrant issued by a judge]." *Johns* at 885. In this respect, " '[a] warrant to search a vehicle would support a search of every part of the vehicle that might contain the object of the search.' " *Id.* [Citation omitted.] "Consequently, '[i]f probable cause justifies the search of a lawfully stopped vehicle, it justifies the search of every part of the vehicle and its contents that may conceal the object of the search.' " *Id.* [Citation omitted.]

Under *Ross*, the Customs officers could have lawfully searched the packages when they were first discovered inside the trucks at the desert airstrip. Additionally, "the officers acted permissibly by waiting until they returned to DEA headquarters before they searched the vehicles and removed their contents. * * * *There is no requirement that the warrantless search of a vehicle[, based on probable cause,] occur contemporaneously with its lawful seizure.*" *Johns* at 885. [Emphasis added.] According to the Court, " 'the justification to conduct such a warrantless search does not vanish once the [vehicle] has been immobilized.' * * * A vehicle lawfully in police custody may be searched on the basis of probable cause to believe that it contains contraband, and there is no requirement of exigent circumstances to justify such a warrantless search." *Id.* [Citations omitted.]

Accordingly, "[t]he warrantless search of the packages was not unreasonable merely because the Customs officers returned to Tucson and placed the packages in a DEA warehouse rather than immediately opening them. * * * The practical effect of the opposite conclusion would only be to direct police officers to search immediately all containers that they discover in the course of a vehicle search." *Id.* at 886. This result, according to the Court, would be of little benefit to the person whose property is searched and to the police. "[W]here police officers are entitled to seize the container and continue to have probable cause to believe that it contains contraband, [the Court does] not think that delay in the execution of the warrantless search is necessarily unreasonable." *Id.* at 886-887. "Inasmuch as the Government was entitled to seize the packages and could have searched them immediately without a warrant, * * * the warrantless search three days after the packages were placed in the DEA warehouse was reasonable and consistent with [Fourth Amendment principles]." *Id.* at 887.

NOTE

1. The decision in *Johns* should not be read to "suggest that police officers may indefinitely retain possession of a vehicle and its contents before they complete a vehicle search." *Id.* at 887. The Court did not "foreclose the possibility that the owner of a vehicle or its contents might attempt to prove that delay in the completion of a vehicle search

was unreasonable because it adversely affected a privacy or possessory interest." *Id.* The defendants in *Johns* did not, however, even allege, much less prove, that the delay in the search of the packages adversely affected any legitimate interests protected by the Fourth Amendment.

2. *Delayed searches.*

(a) In *Chambers v. Maroney*, 399 *U.S.* 42, 90 *S.Ct.* 1975 (1970), a pre-*Ross* case, suspects in an armed robbery were stopped by police on a public street in a station wagon one hour after the crime occurred. The occupants of the car were immediately placed under arrest, and the station wagon was driven to police headquarters where an immediate search uncovered two revolvers and other items associated with the armed robbery. Despite the fact that the car was in police custody and there was no danger that the suspects or the vehicle would leave the jurisdiction, the Supreme Court declared: "For constitutional purposes we see no difference between on the one hand seizing and holding a car before presenting the probable cause issue to a magistrate and on the other hand carrying out an immediate search without a warrant. *Given probable cause to search, either course is reasonable under the Fourth Amendment.*" *Id.* at 51-52, 90 *S.Ct.* at 1980-1981. [Emphasis added.]

(b) The *Chambers* principle was affirmed in *Texas v. White*, 423 *U.S.* 67, 68, 96 *S.Ct.* 304, 305 (1975) ("the probable cause factor that developed on the scene still obtained at the station house"), and then reaffirmed in *Michigan v. Thomas*, 458 *U.S.* 259, 102 *S.Ct.* 3079 (1982), where the Court emphasized that "when police officers have probable cause to believe there is contraband inside an automobile that has been stopped on the road, the officers may conduct a warrantless search of the vehicle, *even after it has been impounded and is in police custody.*" *Thomas* at 261, 102 *S.Ct.* at 3080. [Emphasis added.] Thus, it is "clear that the justification to conduct such a warrantless search does not vanish once the car has been immobilized; nor does it depend upon a reviewing court's assessment of the likelihood in each particular case that the car would have been driven away, or that its contents would have been tampered with, during the period required for the police to obtain a warrant." *Id.* at 3080-3081. *See also United States v. Shepherd*, 714 *F.2d* 316, 320-321 (4th Cir. 1983); *United States v. Mitchell*, 538 *F.2d* 1230, 1232 (5th Cir. 1976) (en banc), *cert. denied*, 430 *U.S.* 945, 97 *S.Ct.* 1578 (1977).

3. *Privacy interests and the odor of marijuana.*

(a) *Odors emanating from the vehicle.* During the course of its opinion in *Johns*, the Court found "debatable" whether the defendants "ever had a privacy interest in the packages reeking of marijuana." *Id.* at 886. Speaking for the Court, Justice O'Connor observed that "certain containers may not support a reasonable expectation of privacy because their contents can be inferred from their outward appearance, *Arkansas v. Sanders*, 442 *U.S.* 753, 764-765 n.13, 99 *S.Ct.* 2586, 2593 n.13 [] (1979), and based on this rationale the Fourth Circuit has held that 'plain odor' may justify a warrantless search of a container. *See United States v. Haley*, 669 *F*.2d 201, 203-204, & n.3 (4th Cir. 1982), *cert. denied*, 457 *U.S.* 1117, 102 *S.Ct.* 2928 [] (1982)." *Johns* at 886.

For an additional analysis of this subject, *see* §4.3, *Minnesota v. Dickerson*, and the Notes that follow.

(b) Odors emanating from the driver. In *United States v. Caves*, 890 *F*.2d 87 (8th Cir. 1989), defendant was stopped by a Minnesota state trooper for driving at an excessive rate of speed. Defendant's vehicle bore Oklahoma license plates and had been traveling northbound on Interstate 35, approximately four miles north of Owatonna, Minnesota. As the trooper approached on foot, defendant got out of his car and met him before the officer reached defendant's vehicle. During a credentials check, the trooper detected "an intense odor of burnt marijuana" on defendant's breath and person. Finding that under the totality of the circumstances the trooper "had probable cause to believe that unused marijuana was still present in [defendant's] automobile[,]" *id.* at 91, the court reasoned:

> Although the odor of burnt marijuana on the driver alone is undoubtedly less probative of the existence of unused marijuana in the automobile than would be the odor of unburnt marijuana emanating from both the driver and the vehicle, we are unable to conclude that the odor of burnt marijuana on Caves' breath and person, when considered in the context of the circumstances confronting the trooper, was insufficient to establish probable cause for the search of the automobile. * * * [T]he trooper was qualified to detect the odor of marijuana and [] he in fact smelled a strong odor of burnt marijuana on Caves' breath and person. When the trooper detected the marijuana odor, he was aware that Caves had just emerged from a vehicle driven from another state several hundred miles away. It was reasonable for the [officer] to conclude from the lateness of the hour (approximately 10:50 p.m.) and the location of the stop (Interstate 35 north) that Caves and [his passenger] had spent many hours riding in the automobile from Oklahoma, and that consequently the vehicle was the probable location where Caves had smoked marijuana or at least had been in the presence of the drug while it was being smoked. By exiting the automobile and meeting the trooper behind the vehicle instead of waiting in the vehicle and rolling down his window when the trooper arrived, Caves may have been trying to prevent the [officer] from plainly observing, or detecting the odor of, marijuana in the interior of the automobile.

Id.

(c) The odor of burnt marijuana and trunk searches. Will a police officer's detection of an odor of burnt marijuana provide probable cause to search the trunk of a car, when there is no corroborating evidence that the motorist had recently smoked marijuana and the officer's search of the vehicle's passenger compartment uncovered no

marijuana? The court, in *United States v. Nielsen*, 9 *F*.3d 1487 (10th Cir. 1993), said no.

Nielsen was stopped for speeding at approximately 4:30 p.m. As the officer spoke to Nielsen, he immediately detected the smell of burnt marijuana coming from the open window of Nielsen's car. The officer asked Nielsen about the marijuana, and Nielsen said that he had none. The officer then asked if he could search the passenger compartment of the vehicle, and Nielsen consented. When the search uncovered no contraband, the officer ran a computer check on Nielsen and learned that he had been arrested for a misdemeanor marijuana offense in 1977. Thereafter, the officer told Nielsen that he believed that there was marijuana in the car and that he was going to search the trunk. He took the keys from the car's ignition, opened the trunk, and found a set of scales and approximately two kilograms of cocaine.

Finding the search of the trunk unlawful, the court stated:

> The officer here said he smelled *burnt* marijuana, and we need only decide whether that provides probable cause to search a trunk, after a consented-to search of the passenger compartment produced no evidence to support the officer's suspicions. * * *

> The smell of burnt marijuana would lead a person of ordinary caution to believe the passenger compartment might contain marijuana. In [this case, the officer's] consensual search of the passenger compartment revealed no marijuana or related contraband. We do not believe under the circumstances that there was a fair probability that the *trunk* contained marijuana, or that a disinterested magistrate would so hold if asked to issue a warrant. * * * Defendant's nervousness and fifteen year old misdemeanor drug conviction do not persuade us otherwise. * * * We hold that under all of the circumstances there was no probable cause to search the trunk.

Id. at 1491. [Court's emphasis.]

UNITED STATES v. McBEE
United States Court of Appeals
659 *F*.2d 1302 (5th Cir. 1981)

QUESTION: Where police seek a particularly-described automobile wanted in connection with a freshly-committed bank robbery, and promptly find that vehicle unoccupied and parked within a few miles of the scene of the crime, and by examining the vehicle develop probable cause to believe the vehicle was an instrumentality used in the robbery, may they then seize the vehicle, remove it to police headquarters, and there conduct a warrantless search of it?

ANSWER: YES. Where police actively seek a certain automobile believed to be an instrumentality used in a freshly-committed crime, and they promptly discover the vehicle unoccupied and parked reasonably near the scene of the crime, they may lawfully seize that vehicle and remove it to the station house where a warrantless search on the basis of probable cause may be conducted. *Id.* at 1305-1306.

RATIONALE: Several days before Christmas, between 9:00 and 9:15 a.m., a Decatur, Georgia, branch of the Citizens & Southern National Bank was robbed by, according to the bank tellers' description, a lone black male wearing a blue hooded sweatshirt. Immediately after the robbery, a private citizen informed the police that he had observed a black male wearing a blue hooded sweatshirt park his car near the bank, walk into the bank, return to his car, and drive away. "As the man exited the bank, the witness heard the bank's alarm. The witness described the man's car as a 1980 maroon-colored Buick Regal bearing a D.L. Claborn dealer tag. Between 9:15 and 9:30 police issued a lookout over the radio for the vehicle and the black male that had been described to them." *Id.* 1304.

"Within two minutes of the radio alert, a police [officer] located an unoccupied automobile exactly matching the broadcast description. The car was parked on a street between two and three miles from the scene of the bank robbery. The [officer] observed that the car appeared to be locked, but he saw a blue hooded sweatshirt in the vehicle. He felt warm air coming from the car's front grill, indicating that the car had been parked there for a short period of time." *Id.*

The Buick was photographed and impounded, and between 10:00 and 10:30 a.m., it was searched. During the search, police recovered the blue hooded sweatshirt, two leather gloves, several items of paper and documents bearing the name "William Keith McBee." Subsequent investigation led to the arrest and ultimate conviction of McBee for the robbery of several banks in the Atlanta area.

In this appeal, McBee challenges the denial of his motion to suppress evidence, contending that the warrantless search of his Buick Regal was in violation of the Fourth Amendment. *The United States Court of Appeals for the Fifth Circuit rejected McBee's contention*, holding that "the search in this case falls squarely within the 'automobile exception' to the warrant requirement." *Id.*

"An automobile may be searched without a warrant where there are both exigent circumstances and probable cause to believe that the car contains articles that law enforcement officers are entitled to seize. * * * In this case, there were several facts giving rise to probable cause sufficient for the police to seize and search the Buick. First, the vehicle exactly matched the description of the car driven away from the bank by the black male who had left the scene as the bank's alarm sounded. Second, the blue hooded sweatshirt—in plain view in the car— connected this car not only to the witness' description of the male who was seen leaving the bank, but also to the bank tellers' description of the robber. Finally, the location of the car and the warmth of its engine strongly supported the connection." *Id.*

"Given the existence of probable cause, the exigencies of the situation would have justified a search of the automobile when it was found parked on the street. The fleeing bank robber had not been apprehended or even identified, and any evidence that could have informed the police of the identity and possible location of the robber would have been subject to easy removal. This was clearly a case where an immediate warrantless search would have been proper, a case where it was 'not practicable to secure a warrant because the vehicle [could have been] quickly moved out of the locality or jurisdiction in which the warrant [would have been] sought.'" *Id.* at 1304-1305 (quoting *Carroll v. United States*, 267 *U.S.* 132, 153, 45 *S.Ct.* 280, 285 (1925)).

Defendant contends, however, that exigent circumstances no longer existed after police impounded the vehicle. This contention has no merit. In *United States v. Mitchell*, 538 *F.*2d 1230 (5th Cir. 1976) (en banc), *cert. denied*, 430 *U.S.* 945, 97 *S.Ct.* 1578 (1977), this court disposed of a similar argument:

> [The] contention, that by the time of the search [the vehicle] had been immobilized, exigence had passed, and a warrant could have been obtained at leisure, is foreclosed by *Chambers v. Maroney* and *Cardwell v. Lewis* [, 417 *U.S.* 583, 94 *S.Ct.* 2464 (1974)]. Both of these authorities recognize that *exigence is to be determined as of the time of the seizure of an automobile, not as of the time of the search*; the fact that in these cases sufficient time to obtain a warrant had passed between each seizure and the corresponding search did not invalidate either.

McBee at 1305 (quoting *Mitchell* at 1232). As a result, "the exigencies at the time of the seizure of McBee's car legitimated the warrantless search which took place after the car had been impounded." *Id.*

"Although obtaining a warrant before an intrusion into an automobile may be preferable, the Constitution does not mandate that procedure in all circumstances. '[L]ess rigorous warrant requirements govern [automobile searches] because the expectation of privacy with respect to one's automobile is significantly less than that relating to one's home or office.'" *Id.* (quoting *South Dakota v. Opperman*, 428 *U.S.* 364, 367, 96 *S.Ct.* 3092, 3096 (1976)). "'The ultimate standard set forth in the Fourth Amendment is reasonableness.'" *Id.* (quoting *Cady v. Dombrowski*, 413 *U.S.* 433, 439, 93 *S.Ct.* 2523, 2527 (1973)).

As noted above, the police had probable cause to search McBee's vehicle. "Instead of utilizing a special detail of officers to secure the automobile during a search on the street, which would have been both inconvenient and inefficient, the police determined that the search could best be conducted at police headquarters. Law enforcement agents seized the vehicle and had it under their control, but there may still have been danger that the vehicle or its contents may have been moved before a valid search warrant could be obtained." *Id.* at 1306.

Accordingly, the officers in this case were "justified in carrying out the warrantless search. The procedure was reasonable and the [F]ourth [A]mendment was satisfied; the automobile exception to the warrant requirement still obtained after the seizure since the mobility problem, though slight, continued to exist." *Id.*

NOTE

1. In *United States v. Cooper*, 949 *F.*2d 737 (5th Cir. 1991), the court reaffirmed that the "seizure of a car as evidence of crime is consistent with the [] 'automobile exception' to the Fourth Amendment's warrant requirement." *Id.* at 746. According to the court, probable cause

> suffices to justify seizing a vehicle on a public street as evidence or instrument of crime. As a warrant is not required when the police have probable cause to believe that the car *contains* evidence of crime, there is little sense in requiring a warrant before seizing a car when the police have probable cause to believe the car itself *is* such evidence or is an instrument of crime.

Id. at 747. [Court's emphasis; footnotes omitted.]

Accordingly, the court held that "the police may seize a car from a public place without a warrant when they have probable cause to believe that the car itself is an instrument or evidence of crime." *Id.* The court emphasized, however, that "absent probable cause to believe the car contains contraband or evidence of crime, a warrantless seizure must be based on probable cause to believe the car itself is an instrument or evidence of crime, not merely that the car's owner committed a crime." *Id.* at 748.

2. *Seizure of automobile for forfeiture purposes.* Many forfeiture statutes authorize the seizure and potential forfeiture of certain forms of contraband and criminally-related evidence, including automobiles. In *Florida v. White*, 526 *U.S.* 559, 119 *S.Ct.* 1555 (1999), the United States Supreme Court held that the Fourth Amendment does not require the police to obtain a warrant before seizing an automobile from a public place when they have probable cause to believe that it is "forfeitable contraband." *Id.*, 119 *S.Ct.* at 1557.

In *White*, on three occasions, the police observed defendant White using his car to deliver cocaine, and thereby developed probable cause to believe that his car was subject to forfeiture under the Florida Contraband Forfeiture Act. Several months later, defendant was arrested at his place of employment on unrelated charges. At the same time, the arresting officers seized defendant's automobile without first obtaining a warrant. The officers took possession of defendant's vehicle solely because they believed it was subject to the provisions of their state's forfeiture statute. Later, during an inventory search of defendant's car, the police found a small quantity of crack cocaine in the ashtray.

At the Supreme Court, Justice Thomas, writing for the majority, rejected defendant's contention that the cocaine seized by the police constituted the "fruit of the poisonous tree" because the warrantless seizure of his automobile violated the Fourth Amendment. *Id.* at 1558.

In *Carroll v. United States*, 267 *U.S.* 132, 45 *S.Ct.* 280 (1925), the Court originally held that when "officers have probable cause to believe that an automobile contains contraband, the Fourth Amendment does not require them to obtain a warrant prior to searching the car for and seizing the contraband." *White* at 1558. Although the police in this case lacked probable cause to believe that defendant's car contained contraband, "they certainly had probable cause to believe that the vehicle *itself* was contraband under Florida law." *Id.* at 1559. [Court's emphasis.] In this respect, the "[r]ecognition of the need to seize readily movable contraband before it is spirited away," observed the Court, "undoubtedly underlies" the law upon which *Carroll* was based. *Id.* "This need is equally weighty when the *automobile*, as opposed to its contents, is the contraband that the police seek to secure." *Id.* [Court's emphasis.]

Moreover, under the Fourth Amendment, the Court has "consistently accorded law enforcement officials greater latitude in exercising their duties in public places." *Id.* Thus,

> although a warrant presumptively is required for a felony arrest in a suspect's home, the Fourth Amendment permits warrantless arrests in public places where an officer has probable cause to believe that a felony has occurred. * * * In explaining this rule, [the Court has] drawn upon the established "distinction between a warrantless seizure in an open area and such a seizure on private premises."

Id. [Citation omitted.]

For example, in *G.M. Leasing Corp. v. United States*, 429 *U.S.* 338, 97 *S.Ct.* 619 (1977), the Court held that federal agents did not violate the Fourth Amendment by failing to secure a warrant prior to seizing automobiles in partial satisfaction of income tax assessments. The Court reasoned that the seizures of the automobiles in the *G.M. Leasing* case " 'took place on public streets, parking lots, or other open places, and did not involve any invasion of privacy.' " *White* at 1560. [Citation omitted.] Here, in *White*, because the police seized defendant's automobile from a public area—his employer's parking lot—the warrantless seizure also did not involve any invasion of defendant's privacy.

Accordingly, the Fourth Amendment did not require the officers to secure a warrant prior to seizing defendant's automobile under the circumstances presented.

3. *The "getaway" car.* In *United States v. Robinson*, 533 *F.*2d 578 (D.C.Cir. 1976) (en banc), the court upheld the warrantless search of

an unoccupied, parked and locked "getaway" car which was located within one hour of a completed armed bank robbery. According to the court, "this getaway car case entails exigent circumstances that justify a warrantless search of the car for clues as to identity or location of suspects." *Id.* at 583. The court reasoned: "There was need to proceed as quickly as possible to apprehend the robbers who had used this as the getaway car in an armed bank robbery consummated about an hour prior to the search. * * * Bank robbers known to have been armed were at large, posing current dangers to the police and other citizens. An immediate search of the car could well produce the information needed to speedily apprehend the culprits. Delay to obtain a warrant would have impeded a promising police investigation and conceivably provided the added time needed by the bank robbers to avoid capture altogether." *Id.* Moreover,

> [t]he lesser expectation of privacy for an automobile, as contrasted with a person or building interior, is of particular significance to a getaway car whose very function is to use the public highway in the course of completing a crime. Mandatory licensing and registration and distinctive aspects of appearance and size in general combine to create a likelihood that a getaway car will be discovered early in a criminal investigation when the police are still "hot" on the trail. The getaway car may still contain fruits and instrumentalities of the crime, as was the case here, and in any event is likely to be a repository of clues as to the identity and location of the criminals. In sum, the prompt search of a getaway car may well be crucial in apprehending the criminals, recovering the fruits of the crime, and preventing other crimes.
>
> Separately, none of these factors is conclusive, but taken together they identify exigent circumstances amply justifying the police in conducting an immediate warrantless search of the getaway car.

Id. at 584. *See also United States v. Shye*, 473 *F.*2d 1061 (6th Cir. 1973).

UNITED STATES v. REYES
United States Court of Appeals
792 *F.*2d 536 (5th Cir. 1986)

QUESTION: May probable cause for the search of an automobile be established on the basis of information supplied by a "first-time" informant ?

ANSWER: YES. Under the Fourth Amendment, information supplied by a "first-time" informant may be used to establish probable cause to search a motor vehicle if the credibility of the informant and his basis of knowledge is sufficiently corroborated by the "totality of the circumstances." *Id.* at 539, 540.

RATIONALE: In the first week of October, United States Customs Investigator Gordon Ridings received a phone call from a confidential informant whom he had known for two years. Though the informant had never supplied investigative information to Ridings in the past, on this particular occasion he told Ridings that a Mexican named Daniel, who had been staying in Room 414 of the Holiday Inn on Highway 80 between Odessa and Midland, Texas, for the past ten days, was in possession of a large quantity of cocaine. In addition, the informant stated that Daniel, whom he described as heavily armed and dangerous, drove a black and silver 1985 Chevrolet Blazer with a temporary California license tag located in the back window. The informant further indicated that he had personally seen cocaine in Daniel's vehicle and motel room within the previous twenty-four hours. This information was subsequently related to Sergeant Dixon of the Odessa Sheriff's Department Narcotics Division.

Later that same morning, Sergeant Dixon and Officer Clark traveled to the Holiday Inn in an attempt to corroborate the informant's story before seeking a search warrant. Upon arrival, they immediately observed a Mexican male loading suitcases and gun cases into a vehicle fitting the description given by the informant. "The Blazer was parked in front of Room 414. Dixon entered the motel and requested the records for Room 414 from the motel manager. The manager provided records from September 29 to October 7, ✳ ✳ ✳ and informed Dixon that the occupant's name was Daniel Reyes. The records indicated approximately $600 worth of long distance telephone calls made in that period of time. Before leaving the motel, Dixon noticed that the Mexican male he had observed earlier was standing at the front desk. Dixon overheard him say that his name was Daniel Reyes and that he would like to check out of room 414. Dixon and Clark then left the motel area, radioed for assistance, and parked where they could observe the Blazer." *Id.* at 538.

Reyes departed from the motel in the Blazer and within ten minutes Dixon and Clark, along with two local police officers who had joined them, stopped him, removed him from the Blazer, and placed him in handcuffs. "The four law enforcement officers then proceeded to search the Blazer, including the suitcases which contained $12,000 in cash, a gun, a shoulder holster, and a smaller locked nylon bag. Dixon then took the keys out of the ignition and opened this bag. Inside were one and one-half pounds of eighty-three percent pure cocaine, diazepam, and some pills. They also found four handguns, one of which was loaded, a rifle, and a shotgun." *Id.*

In this appeal of the denial of his motion to suppress evidence, defendant argues that "the search of his vehicle and the articles therein was unlawful because it was not based on probable cause. He contends that probable cause was lacking because the police relied on information provided by an untested informant and failed to corroborate any significant facts which could reasonably lead the police to believe that he possessed narcotics." *Id. The Court of Appeals for the Fifth Circuit could not agree.*

Preliminarily, the court emphasizes that " '[a] citizen does not surrender all the protections of the Fourth Amendment by entering an automobile.' * * * The automobile exception to the [F]ourth [A]mendment's warrant requirement protects only searches supported by probable cause. Only the prior approval of the magistrate is waived; the search otherwise must be such as the magistrate could authorize." *Id.* [Citations omitted.]

"[T]he automobile exception applies where there are both exigent circumstances and probable cause to believe that the vehicle in question contains property that the government may properly seize[, and in this case,] probable cause is based upon an informant's tip." *Id.* at 538. Thus, the applicable standard of review requires that a "totality of the circumstances" test be applied to determine whether the informant's tip provided probable cause. As the United States Supreme Court observed in *Illinois v. Gates*, 462 *U.S.* 213, 103 *S.Ct.* 2317 (1983), "the search for probable cause involves 'a practical, common-sense decision whether, given all the circumstances * * *, including the "veracity" and "basis of knowledge" of persons supplying hearsay information, there is a fair probability that contraband will be found in a particular place.' " *Reyes* at 539 (quoting *Gates* at 238, 103 *S.Ct.* at 2332). "Although an informant's veracity, reliability, and basis of knowledge still should be considered, 'a deficiency in one may be compensated for, in determining the overall reliability of a tip, by a strong showing as to the other, or by some other indicia of reliability.' " *Id.* (quoting *Gates* at 233, 103 *S.Ct.* at 2329).

"Although the usual method of proving an informant's reliability is to point to information provided in the past that turned out to be truthful, this is not the only method. An informant's tip can be confirmed by independent police work which corroborates the information received. * * * Additionally, the credibility of an informant's tip is strengthened if it is made in great detail, thus evincing a strong basis for the informant's knowledge. * * * [Moreover, t]he surrounding facts and information are not to be viewed in isolation but must be viewed in light of their having been evaluated by trained law enforcement officials. What appears quite innocent to the untrained eye may be significant to the trained law enforcement official. * * * Finally, an informant's tip is buttressed by the fact that it is based on his own personal observation rather than on hearsay." *Id.*

In this case, the court finds that under the totality of the circumstances, "there was probable cause to believe Reyes' automobile contained narcotics." *Id.* First, "Ridings had known the informant for more than two years and considered him to be reliable even though he had never supplied Ridings with information leading to an arrest or conviction. The informant had gained Ridings' trust because on several occasions Ridings had questioned him concerning his whereabouts at particular times which were already known by Ridings. Each time the informant answered truthfully." *Id.*

"Just as important, numerous detailed facts were supplied by the informant. Specifically, he informed Ridings of (i) the suspect's first name, (ii) where he was staying, (iii) how long he had been there, (iv) the make, year, and color of his vehicle, (v) the type of contraband, and (vi) the fact the suspect was armed. [Significantly], all this information was based on the informant's personal knowledge, which is evinced by his statement to Ridings that he had seen the cocaine in the Blazer and Room 414 within the past twenty-four hours." *Id.*

"Additionally, much of the information supplied by the informant was corroborated by Dixon during his visit to the Holiday Inn. His observation of a Mexican male loading suitcases and gun cases into a black and silver Blazer outside of Room 414 corroborated the tip. Further corroboration was provided by Dixon's discovery that the occupant at Room 414 had been there for the past ten days and was named Daniel. A finding of probable cause was also strengthened by Dixon's own independent observations while at the Holiday Inn. He observed records that showed that Reyes had placed $600 worth of phone calls during his ten-day stay, which were paid for in cash. In fact, Dixon learned that Reyes paid his entire motel bill, about $1,000, in cash." *Id.* at 540.

"Since Dixon was able to corroborate the informant's tip, the government was justified in believing the statement that cocaine was in the Blazer. Moreover, since Dixon personally observed Reyes check out of the motel and pack his belongings into the Blazer, the government could reasonably infer that the cocaine supposedly located in the motel room was transferred into the Blazer. Therefore, when all the information gathered from the informant and Dixon's personal observations is considered in the light of Dixon's extensive narcotic investigation experience, [it is clear] that the authorities had probable cause to believe contraband was inside the Blazer when Reyes exited the Holiday Inn parking lot." *Id.*

Finally, "[t]he exigent circumstances surrounding the investigation were also sufficient to justify a warrantless search of the Blazer. Since the officers were at the motel attempting to corroborate the informant's tip to justify obtaining a search warrant, they cannot be faulted for failing to have one in their possession at that time. More important, the suspicion that Reyes would soon depart was clearly warranted by the fact that immediately after loading the Blazer, he checked out of his room and left the motel in the Blazer. [Consequently,] the circumstances were sufficiently exigent to justify the search and seizure." *Id.*

NOTE

The moment that probable cause is established. In *United States v. Arzaga,* 9 *F.*3d 91 (10th Cir. 1993), the court rejected the defendant's invitation to adopt a rule requiring the police to procure a search warrant, and conduct a search, "at the very moment that mere suspicion ripens into probable cause." *Id.* at 94. The court stated:

> This we are unwilling, and unable, to do. There are all kinds of perfectly legal reasons why police might choose to wait on a search warrant: previously unknown co-conspirators could enter an apartment, larger quantities of drugs might be brought inside, or the environment might be too threatening to the officers' safety. All such possibilities counsel against our adopting such a restrictive interpretation of the Fourth Amendment's warrant requirement.
>
> In any event, our decision in *United States v. Crabb,* 952 *F.*2d 1245 (10th Cir. 1991) (citing cases), where we held that once law enforcement agents have probable cause to believe that a vehicle contains contraband, their "time and opportunity to obtain a warrant are irrelevant, as constitutional analysis ends with finding probable cause," *id.* at 1246, is dispositive. In that case, federal agents waited with the defendant in his motel room for three hours before executing a warrantless search of his automobile based solely on the officers' estimation that they had probable cause to believe the vehicle contained contraband.
>
> Here, * * * the Oklahoma City Police had probable cause to believe that Arzaga was engaging in illicit drug transactions—based on the information received from the FBI—and that Arzaga's automobile was the most likely location of the contraband. Arzaga does not dispute that determination. Possessing probable cause, the police were under no obligation to obtain a warrant before searching Arzaga's automobile.

Arzaga at 94.

———————————

CALIFORNIA v. CARNEY
Supreme Court of the United States
471 *U.S.* 386, 105 *S.Ct.* 2066 (1985)

QUESTION: Does a fully mobile motor home, which is located in a public parking lot, fall within the "automobile exception" to the Fourth Amendment warrant requirement ?

ANSWER: YES. The warrantless search of a fully mobile motor home, based upon probable cause, is proper under the "automobile exception" to the Fourth Amendment warrant requirement. *Id*. at 2070.

RATIONALE: In late May, DEA Agent Robert Williams watched defendant Carney approach a youth in downtown San Diego. "The youth accompanied Carney to a Dodge Mini Motor Home parked in a nearby lot. Carney and the youth closed the window shades in the motor home, including one across the front window. Agent Williams had previously received uncorroborated information that the same motor home was used by another person who was exchanging marijuana for sex. Williams, with assistance from other agents, kept the motor home under surveillance for the entire one and one-quarter hours that Carney and the youth remained inside. When the youth left the motor home, the agents followed and stopped him. The youth told the agents that he had received marijuana in return for allowing Carney sexual contacts." *Id*. at 2067.

"At the agents' request, the youth returned to the motor home and knocked on the door; Carney stepped out. The agents identified themselves as law enforcement officers. Without a warrant or consent, one agent entered the motor home and observed marijuana, plastic bags, and a scale of the kind used in weighing drugs on a table. Agent Williams took Carney into custody and took possession of the motor home. A subsequent search of the motor home at the police station revealed additional marijuana in the cupboards and refrigerator." *Id*. Carney was arrested and charged with the possession of marijuana for sale.

At the Supreme Court, the main question was whether the "automobile exception" to the warrant requirement should apply. While it is true that the vehicle involved here possessed some, if not many of the attributes of a home, the Court nonetheless found it "equally clear that" Carney's motor home fell within the scope of the "automobile exception" established in *Carroll v. United States*, 267 *U.S.* 132, 45 *S.Ct.* 280 (1925). *Carney* at 2070.

A motor vehicle's capacity to be "quickly moved" was "clearly the basis of the holding in *Carroll*," and later cases have "consistently recognized ready mobility as one of the principal bases of the automobile exception." *Id*. at 2069. Ready mobility is not, however, the only basis for the exception. " 'Besides the element of mobility, less rigorous warrant requirements govern because the expectation of privacy with respect to one's automobile is significantly less than that relating to one's home or office.' " *Id*. [Citation omitted.] Reduced expectations of privacy result not from the fact that the area to be searched is in plain view, "but from the pervasive regulation of vehicles capable of traveling on the public highways." *Id*.

> Automobiles, unlike homes, are subject to pervasive and continuing governmental regulation and controls, including periodic inspection and licensing requirements. As an everyday occurrence, police stop and examine vehicles when license plates or inspection stickers have expired, or if other violations, such as exhaust fumes or excessive noise, are noted, or if headlights or other safety equipment are not in proper working order.

Id. at 2069-70. Citizens are, therefore, fully aware that they are accorded less privacy in their automobiles "because of this compelling governmental need for regulation." *Id.* at 2070.

"When a vehicle is being used on the highways, or if it is readily capable of such use and is found stationary in a place not regularly used for residential purposes—temporary or otherwise—the two justifications for the vehicle exception come into play. First, the vehicle is obviously readily mobile by the turn of an ignition key, if not actually moving. Second, there is a reduced expectation of privacy stemming from its use as a licensed motor vehicle subject to a range of police regulation inapplicable to a fixed dwelling. At least in these circumstances, the overriding societal interests in effective law enforcement justify an immediate search before the vehicle and its occupants become unavailable." *Id.*

In this case, the Court determined that Carney's vehicle came within the scope of the automobile exception. His "motor home was readily mobile. Absent the prompt search and seizure, it could readily have been moved beyond the reach of the police. Furthermore, the vehicle was licensed to 'operate on public streets; [was] serviced in public places; * * * and [was] subject to extensive regulation and inspection.' * * * And the vehicle was so situated that an objective observer would conclude that it was being used not as a residence, but as a vehicle." *Id.* [Citation omitted.]

The Court rejected Carney's contention that his vehicle should be distinguished because it was "capable of functioning as a home." In this respect, the Court observed:

> In our increasingly mobile society, many vehicles used for transportation can be and are being used not only for transportation but for shelter, *i.e.*, as a home or residence. To distinguish between [defendant's] motor home and an ordinary sedan for purposes of the vehicle exception would require that we apply the exception depending upon the size of the vehicle and quality of its appointments. Moreover, to fail to apply the exception to vehicles such as a motor home ignores the fact that a motor home lends itself easily to use as an instrument of illicit drug traffic and other illegal activity. * * * We decline today to distinguish between "worthy" and "unworthy" vehicles which are either on the public roads and highways, or situated such that it is reasonable to conclude that the vehicle is not being used as a residence.

Id.

Accordingly, the Court concluded that the search in this case was clearly reasonable. "The DEA agents had fresh, direct, uncontradicted evidence that [Carney] was distributing a controlled substance from the vehicle, apart from evidence of other possible offenses. The agents thus had abundant probable cause to enter and search the vehicle for evidence of a crime notwithstanding its possible use as a dwelling place." *Id.* at 2071.

NOTE

The vehicle exception will not apply if the motor home is situated in such "a way or place that objectively indicates that it is being used as a residence." *Id.* at 2071 n.3. Each of the following factors should be considered in determining whether the vehicle is being used as a residence and, therefore, whether a warrant must be obtained before its search:

a. the vehicle's location;

b. whether the vehicle is readily mobile or, instead, elevated on blocks or connected to utilities;

c. whether the vehicle is licensed; and

d. whether the vehicle has convenient access to a public road.

Id.

UNITED STATES v. HILL
United States Court of Appeals
855 *F.*2d 664 (10th Cir. 1988)

QUESTION: Does a fully mobile houseboat, which is observed traveling up and down a large lake, fall within the "automobile exception" to the Fourth Amendment warrant requirement?

ANSWER: YES. The warrantless search of the fully mobile houseboat in this case, based upon probable cause, was proper, and fell within the "automobile exception" to the Fourth Amendment warrant requirement. *Id.* at 668.

RATIONALE: In January of 1987, DEA agents developed probable cause to believe that defendants, Rocky Hill and Lewis Pemberton, were manufacturing methamphetamine on board a houseboat which had been seen traveling up and down Lake Texoma, Oklahoma. After keeping the houseboat under surveillance for two days, the agents decided to board the boat when they learned that "storm warnings had been issued for the lake." They obtained a lake patrol boat for this purpose.

When the agents approached the houseboat, they announced themselves and, after receiving no response, boarded the houseboat. Once aboard, they arrested Hill and Pemberton, and then made a cursory search for other occupants. During the cursory search, the agents discovered an "operating amphetamine laboratory." In light of "the volatility of the chemicals used, the officers turned off the electricity to the boat and ventilated it. They then took the boat to shore and secured it. Later they obtained a search warrant and searched the boat. They found drugs and equipment used to manufacture drugs." *Id.* at 666.

In this appeal, defendants argue, among other things, that the officers needed an arrest warrant to board the houseboat, and the failure to obtain the warrant effectively made their arrests "illegal." *Id. The United States Court of Appeals for the Tenth Circuit disagreed.*

"In addition to having probable cause, police must obtain a warrant before making a 'nonconsensual entry into a suspect's home in order to make a routine felony arrest.' " *Id.* at 667 (quoting *Payton v. New York*, 445 *U.S.* 573, 576, 100 *S.Ct.* 1371, 1375 (1980)). "A warrant would therefore be required in this case if the houseboat constitutes a home for the purposes of *Payton*." *Hill* at 667. Relevant in this regard are the cases dealing with searches of motor vehicles. "If the police could have constitutionally boarded the houseboat to search it without a warrant, then no warrant was necessary to board the boat in order to arrest Hill and Pemberton." *Id.*

The Supreme Court, in *California v. Carney*, 471 *U.S.* 386, 105 *S.Ct.* 2066 (1985), "held that police did not need a warrant in order to enter a mobile home parked in a public place. The motor home was capable of functioning as a home; it was stationary; and the shades were drawn, including one across the front window. Indeed, the Court observed that the motor home 'possessed some, if not many of the attributes of a home.' " *Hill* at 667 (quoting *Carney* at 393, 105 *S.Ct.* at 2070). Notwithstanding the home-oriented attributes, the Court held that it is "clear that the vehicle falls [squarely] within the scope" of the vehicle exception to the warrant requirement. *Carney* at 393, 105 *S.Ct.* at 2070. In reaching this conclusion, the Court in *Carney* focused on "the ready mobility of the vehicle," and its "presence in a setting that objectively indicates that the vehicle is being used for transportation." *Id.*

Although *Carney* involved a motor home and this case deals with a houseboat, the court here in *Hill* concludes that "the two vehicles are similar. Both are of the 'hybrid character' that place them 'at the crossroads between the privacy interests that generally forbid warrantless invasions of the home and the law enforcement interests that support the exception for warrantless searches of automobiles based on probable cause.' " *Hill* at 668. [Citation omitted.] "Both a houseboat and a motor home are readily capable of functioning as both vehicle and home[,]" *id*, and the principles of *Carney*, therefore, control.

"The houseboat here was obviously readily mobile and therefore satisfies the first *Carney* requirement. Indeed, the officers had observed it traveling up and down the lake during much of the night. Furthermore, Lake Texoma is a large lake, and the boat's occupants could have easily eluded the officers. The second *Carney* requirement is also satisfied. Given the Supreme Court's determination in *Carney*, [this court] cannot say that the boat in this case was present in a set-ting that objectively indicated it was being used as a residence. [This court is] persuaded that an objective observer would conclude that a moving boat navigating the waters of a large lake on a cold winter night was not being used as a residence." *Hill* at 668.

Accordingly, "the houseboat falls within the vehicle exception. [B]ecause the houseboat could have been searched without a warrant, the rule of *Payton* requiring a warrant for an arrest in a suspect's home is inapplicable here. Since no warrant was required, [defen-dants'] arrest based on probable cause was valid[.]" *Id.*

NEW YORK v. CLASS
Supreme Court of the United States
475 *U.S.* 106, 106 *S.Ct.* 960 (1986)

QUESTION: In order to observe a Vehicle Identification Number (VIN) generally visible from outside an automobile, may a law en-forcement officer reach into the passenger compartment of a vehicle to move papers obscuring the VIN after its driver has been lawfully stopped for traffic violations and has exited the vehicle ?

ANSWER: YES. In light of the "pervasive governmental regula-tion of the automobile and the efforts by the Federal Government to ensure that the VIN is placed in plain view, [there is] no reasonable expectation of privacy in the VIN[, and the] * * * viewing of the for-merly obscured VIN was not * * * a violation of the Fourth Amend-ment." *Id.* at 966.

RATIONALE: Two New York City police officers observed defen-dant, Class, driving above the speed limit in an automobile with a cracked windshield. When the officers stopped defendant's vehicle, de-fendant exited and approached one of the officers. The other officer approached defendant's vehicle to inspect the Vehicle Identification Number (VIN). The officer first checked the left door jamb in which pre-1969 automobiles had the VIN located. When the VIN was not found there, the officer reached into the interior of the vehicle to move some papers obscuring the area of the dashboard where the VIN is located in all post-1969 automobiles. "In doing so, [the officer] saw the handle of a gun protruding about one inch from underneath the driver's seat." *Id.* at 963. The officer immediately seized the gun and arrested defendant.

It was "undisputed that the police officers had no reason to sus-pect that [defendant's] car was stolen, that it contained contraband, or that [defendant] had committed an offense other than the traffic violations." *Id.*

The New York Court of Appeals [New York's highest court] sup-pressed the gun, finding no reason for the officers to suspect criminal activity (other than the traffic violations), or to act to protect their own safety, and, no justification for the entry of the defendant's auto.

The United States Supreme Court disagreed and reversed.

The Court, speaking through Justice O'Connor, reasoned that an automobile's VIN "is roughly analogous to a serial number, but it can be deciphered to reveal not only the place of the automobile in the manufacturer's production run, but the make, model, engine type, and place of manufacture of the vehicle." *Id.* at 964. In addition to allowing for vehicle identification and other governmental functions, federal law requires that the VIN be placed in plain view of someone *outside* the automobile:

> The VIN for passenger cars (manufactured after 1969) shall be located inside the passenger compartment. It shall be readable, without moving any part of the vehicle, through the vehicle glazing under daylight lighting conditions by an observer having 20/20 vision whose eye point is located *outside the vehicle* adjacent to the left windshield pillar. Each character in the VIN subject to this paragraph shall have the minimum height of 4 mm. 49 CFR §571.115 (S. 4.6) (1984) (Emphasis added.)

Id. at 964-65.

The Court has continually recognized that a person's expectation of privacy is significantly diminished in the area of automobile ownership and use. In addition, "automobiles are justifiably the subject of pervasive regulation by the State. Every operator of a motor vehicle must expect that the State, in enforcing its regulations, will intrude to some extent upon that operator's privacy[.]" *Id.* at 965.

Amidst this pervasive governmental regulation, the VIN plays an integral part. "[I]t is unreasonable to have an expectation of privacy in an object required by law to be located in a place ordinarily in plain view from the exterior of the automobile." *Id.* at 966. Analogous to the exterior of the automobile, the VIN "is thrust into the public eye, and thus to examine it [from the outside of the auto] does not constitute a search [within the meaning of the Fourth Amendment]." *Id.*

It made no difference that the papers in the defendant's automobile obscured the VIN from the sight of the officer. Persons may not create a reasonable expectation of privacy where none would otherwise exist. *Oliver v. United States*, 466 *U.S.* 170, 104 *S.Ct.* 1735 (1984). "Here, where the object at issue is an identification number behind the transparent windshield of an automobile driven upon the public roads[, the Court believes that] the placement of the obscuring papers was insufficient to create a privacy interest in the VIN. The mere viewing of the formerly obscured VIN was not, therefore, a violation of the Fourth Amendment." *Class* at 966.

In upholding the admissibility of the gun observed in plain view by the officer during his VIN inspection, the Court conducts a balancing analysis between the governmental need to search or seize and the particular intrusion occasioned by the particular search or seizure. Here, "[t]he search was focused in its objective and no more intrusive than necessary to fulfill that objective [the examination of the VIN]." *Id.* at 968.

The officer checked the two locations that a VIN might reasonably be found, and only those two locations. "He did not reach into any compartments or open any containers. He did not even intrude into the interior at all until after he had checked the door jamb for the VIN." *Id.* When the officer did enter the vehicle's interior, it was for the limited purpose of moving the obscuring papers to examine the VIN on the dashboard.

As a result, "this search was sufficiently unintrusive to be constitutionally permissible in light of the lack of a reasonable expectation of privacy in the VIN and the fact that the officers observed [defendant] commit two traffic violations." *Id.*

Since the motor vehicle stop was lawful, and the officer was lawfully in the area in which he inadvertently observed the firearm, his seizure of it was proper, and its admission in evidence should have been allowed.

The judgment of the New York Court of Appeals is reversed.

NOTE

Officers should not conclude from this case that they are always permitted to enter a vehicle to view a dashboard-mounted VIN from the inside of the vehicle's passenger compartment. Where the VIN is visible from the outside of the vehicle, there is no justification for the officer to intrude into the passenger compartment to examine it.

---

§3.6. Consent.

§3.6(a). Introduction.

As a recognized exception to the written warrant requirement, consensual searches continue to provide the law enforcement community with access to those areas in which an officer, desirous of searching, has less than the requisite probable cause to conduct a constitutional search or to secure a warrant. When a search is conducted pursuant to a valid consent, it may be conducted without a warrant and without probable cause. *United States v. Matlock*, 415 *U.S.* 164, 165, 94 *S.Ct.* 988, 990 (1974); *Schneckloth v. Bustamonte*, 412 *U.S.* 218, 222, 93 *S.Ct.* 2041, 2045 (1973).

When a person consents to a search of his property, he relinquishes his or her constitutional right to be free from unreasonable searches and seizures. Therefore, in order to be valid, the consent must be "voluntarily" given. *Bumper v. North Carolina*, 391 *U.S.* 543, 548, 88 *S.Ct.* 1788 (1968). To be voluntary, the consent must be unequivocal and specific. In this respect, mere "acquiescence cannot substitute for free consent." *United States v. Gonzales*, 842 *F.*2d 748, 754 (5th Cir. 1988). The consent must also be freely and intelligently given, " 'uncontaminated by any duress or coercion, actual or implied.' " *United States v. Morrow*, 731 *F.*2d 233 (4th Cir. 1984) (quoting *United States v. Vickers*, 387 *F.*2d 703, 706 (4th Cir. 1967) and *Channel v. United States*, 285 *F.*2d 217, 219 (9th Cir. 1960)). In all cases, "the question whether a consent to a search was in fact 'voluntary' or was the product of duress or coercion, express or implied, is a question of fact to be determined from the totality of the circumstances." *Schneckloth* at 227, 93 *S.Ct.* at 2047-2048. Moreover, the burden of proof is on the Government to establish that the consent was so given. *Id.*

There are several factors that a court will examine to determine whether a consent was in fact voluntarily given, or coerced. Factors which may suggest that consent was coerced include: (1) the presence of abusive, overbearing, or dictatorial police procedures; (2) police use of psychological ploys, or subtle psychological pressure or language, or a tone of voice which indicates that compliance with the request might be compelled; (3) statements or acts on the part of the police which convey to the consenting party that he is not free to refuse the search or to walk away from the officer; (4) that the consent was given by a person already in custody or placed under arrest; (5) that consent was obtained despite the consenting party's denial of guilt; (6) that consent was obtained only after the consenting party had refused initial requests for consent to search; (7) that consent was given after the police blocked or otherwise impaired the consenting party's progress, or in some other way physically restrained the individual, for example, by the use of handcuffs, by surrounding the individual with uniformed officers, by physically maneuvering the individual in a particular direction, by coercing the individual to move from a public area to a private area or office, or by the intimidating use of enforcement canines; (8) that consent was obtained only after the investigating officer retained possession of the consenting party's identification or plane, train or bus ticket; or (9) that consent was obtained only after an officer informed the consenting party that if he were innocent, he would cooperate with the police.

Among the factors suggesting that the consent was voluntarily given are: (1) that the consenting party was not under arrest or in custody at the time the consent was given; (2) that (if in custody) the consenting party's custodial status was voluntary; (3) that consent was given where the consenting party had reason to believe that the police would find no contraband; (4) that the consenting party was aware of his right to refuse consent; (5) that the consenting party was informed by the police prior to the request for consent of what exactly they were looking for; (6) that the consenting party signed a "consent-to-search" form prior to the search; (7) that the consenting party admitted his guilt before giving consent; (8) that the consenting party affirmatively assisted the police in conducting the search; (9) that the consenting party used his own key to provide the police with access to the area to be searched; (10) that the consenting party demonstrated a cooperative posture throughout the encounter; (11) that the consenting party was not in any way restrained by the police; (12) that the consenting party knew the officers conducting the search; (13) that the consenting party was educated or intelligent; and (14) that the consenting party was no stranger to the criminal justice system. *United States v. Mendenhall*, 446 *U.S.* 544, 555-557, 100 *S.Ct.* 1870, 1877-1878 (1980); *United States v. Watson*, 423 *U.S.* 411, 424, 96 *S.Ct.* 820, 828 (1976); *United States v. Carter*, 854 *F.*2d 1102, 1106 (8th Cir. 1988); *United States v. Galberth*,

846 *F.*2d 983 (5th Cir. 1988); *United States v. Chenault*, 844 *F.*2d 1124, 1128-29 (5th Cir. 1988); *United States v. Chemaly*, 741 *F.*2d 1346, 1353 (11th Cir. 1984), *vacated*, 741 *F.*2d 1363, *reinstated on reh'g*, 764 *F.*2d 747 (11th Cir. 1985) (en banc); *United States v. Morrow, supra*, 731 *F.*2d at 236; *United States v. Ruigomez*, 702 *F.*2d 61, 65 (5th Cir. 1983); *United States v. Robinson*, 690 *F.*2d 869, 875 (11th Cir. 1982); *United States v. Berry*, 670 *F.*2d 583, 597, 604 (5th Cir. Unit B 1982) (en banc); *United States v. Setzer*, 654 *F.*2d 354, 357-58 (5th Cir. Unit B 1981), *cert. denied*, 459 *U.S.* 1041, 103 *S.Ct.* 457 (1982).

A consent sufficient to avoid the necessity of a warrant may be express or implied from the circumstances surrounding the police-citizen encounter. In fact, an *implied* consent has been held to be as effective as any express consent to search. A consent may be "implied" when it is found to exist merely because of the person's particular responses to police inquiry or the person's conduct in engaging in a certain activity. *See e.g., United States v. Price*, 599 *F.*2d 494 (2nd Cir. 1979) (valid search where defendant told police he did not care if they searched bag because it was not his and he had picked it up by mistake); *State v. Fredette*, 411 *A.*2d 65, 70 (Me. 1979) (defendant initiated police presence through urgent calls to police; invited them into his home; and continually cooperated with police as they searched his home); *cf. North Carolina v. Butler*, 441 *U.S.* 369, 375-376, 99 *S.Ct.* 1755, 1758-1759 (1979) (an express waiver is not invariably necessary to support a finding that the defendant waived his rights). Thus, an implied voluntary consent may be found where the defendant has initiated police contact and has adopted a "cooperative posture in the mistaken belief that he could thereby divert or prevent police suspicion of him." W. LaFave, *Search & Seizure: A Treatise on the Fourth Amendment*, §8.2(g), at 204 (2d ed. 1987). *See also Steigler v. State*, 277 *A.*2d 662, 667 (Del. 1971) (actions of fully cooperative defendant amounted to implied consent to search and seizure: "One can hardly expect the police to get a search warrant for a house or building when the owner is obviously cooperative and gives every appearance of being the victim, rather than the perpetrator, of a crime").

A valid consent may also be obtained from one other than the accused, *i.e.*, from a third party, so long as the consenting third party has the authority to bind the accused. In these circumstances, the inquiry whether a third-party consent is constitutionally valid focuses on whether the consenting third party possesses *common authority* over or other sufficient relationship to the premises or effects sought to be inspected. *Matlock v. United States*, 415 *U.S.* 164, 169-172, 94 *S.Ct.* 988, 993 (1974). The concept of third-party consent rests not upon the law of property, however, but upon the "mutual use of the property by persons generally having joint access or control for most purposes, so that it is reasonable to recognize that any of the cohabitants has the right to permit the inspection in his own right and that others have assumed the risk that one of their number might permit the common area to be searched." *Id*. at 171-172, 94 *S.Ct.* at 993. Naturally, the Government must also demonstrate that the third-party consent was given freely and voluntarily.

§3.6(b). Voluntariness.

SCHNECKLOTH v. BUSTAMONTE
Supreme Court of the United States
412 *U.S.* 218, 93 *S.Ct.* 2041 (1973)

QUESTION: In order to establish a "voluntary" consent under the Fourth and Fourteenth Amendments, must the Government always demonstrate that, in addition to the absence of duress or coercion, the consenting party knew that he had a right to refuse the consent?

ANSWER: NO. "[W]hen the subject of a search is not in custody and the [prosecution] attempts to justify a search on the basis of his consent, the Fourth and Fourteenth Amendments require that it demonstrate that the consent was in fact voluntarily given, and not the result of duress or coercion, express or implied. Voluntariness is a question of fact to be determined from all the circumstances, and while the subject's knowledge of a right to refuse is a factor to be taken into account, the prosecution is not required to demonstrate such knowledge as a prerequisite to establishing a voluntary consent." *Id.* at 2059.

RATIONALE: Defendant was one of six occupants of a motor vehicle which was stopped by police because of a defective headlight and license plate light. When the driver could not produce an operator's license, the officer asked if any of the other five had any evidence of identification. One of the front seat passengers, Joe Alcala, produced a driver's license and explained that the car was his brother's. At this point, the officer asked Alcala if he could search the car. Alcala replied, "Sure, go ahead." "Prior to the search, no one was threatened with arrest and, according to [the officer's] uncontradicted testimony, it 'was all very congenial at this time.'" *Id.* at 2044. In fact, one of the other occupants testified "that Alcala actually helped in the search of the car, by opening the trunk and glove compartment." *Id.* The search yielded three stolen checks found "[w]added up under the left rear seat." *Id.*

In the appeal which followed the denial of defendant Bustamonte's motion to suppress evidence, the courts focused on the question whether the Fourth and Fourteenth Amendments required the Government to establish, as an indispensable prerequisite to a voluntary consent, "that Alcala had *known* that his consent could have been withheld and that he could have refused to have his vehicle searched[.]" *Id.* at 2045. [Emphasis added.] At the Supreme Court, Justice Stewart rephrased the issue, stating that "[t]he precise question in this case * * * is what must the prosecution prove to demonstrate that a consent was 'voluntarily' given." *Id.*

Preliminarily, the Court emphasized that it is "well settled that one of the specifically established exceptions to the requirements of both a warrant and probable cause is a search that is conducted pursuant to consent." *Id.* at 2043-2044 (citing *Davis v. United States*, 328 *U.S.* 582, 593-594, 66 *S.Ct.* 1256, 1261-1262 (1946), and *Vale v. Louisiana*, 399

U.S. 30, 35, 90 *S.Ct.* 1969, 1972 (1970)). When the prosecution " 'seeks to rely upon consent to justify the lawfulness of a search, [it] has the burden of proving that the consent was, in fact, freely and voluntarily given.' " *Id.* at 2045 (quoting *Bumper v. North Carolina*, 391 *U.S.* 543, 548, 88 *S.Ct.* 1788, 1792 (1968)).

The courts below found that Alcala's consent had been "freely given without coercion or submission to authority." In addition to the police officer, the driver of the car "testified that Alcala's assent to the search of his brother's automobile was freely, even casually given[,]" and that "Alcala even attempted to aid in the search." *Id.* at 2044.

The question, therefore, in light of this seemingly noncoercive government procurement of an individual's consent, is whether the absence of a showing that the consenting party knew of his right to refuse consent, in itself, requires a finding of involuntariness. Holding that it does not, the Court ruled "that the question whether a consent to a search was in fact 'voluntary' or was the product of duress or coercion, express or implied, is a question of fact to be determined from the totality of all the circumstances." *Id.* at 2047-2048. Moreover, "[w]hile knowledge of the right to refuse is one factor to be taken into account, the government need not establish such knowledge as [an indispensable prerequisite] of an effective consent. As with police questioning, two competing concerns must be accommodated in determining the meaning of a 'voluntary' consent—the legitimate need for such searches and the equally important requirement of assuring the absence of coercion." *Id.* at 2048.

Respecting the legitimacy of the consent procedure itself, the Court observed that "[c]onsent searches are part of the standard investigatory techniques of law enforcement agencies. They normally occur on the highway, or in a person's home or office, and under informal and unstructured conditions. The circumstances that prompt the initial request to search may develop quickly or be a logical extension of investigative police questioning." *Id.* at 2050. Additionally, the Court pointed out:

> In situations where the police have some evidence of illicit activity, but lack probable cause to arrest or search, a search authorized by a valid consent may be the only means of obtaining important and reliable evidence. * * * And in those cases where there is probable cause to arrest or search, but where the police lack a warrant, a consent search may still be valuable. If the search is conducted and proves fruitless, that in itself may convince the police that an arrest with its possible stigma and embarrassment is unnecessary, or that a far more extensive search pursuant to a warrant is not justified. In short, a search pursuant to consent may result in considerably less inconvenience for the subject of the search, and, properly conducted, is a constitutionally permissible and wholly legitimate aspect of effective police activity.

Id.

The Constitution requires, however, "that a consent not be coerced, by explicit or implicit means, by implied threat or covert force." *Id.* Therefore, "[i]n examining all the surrounding circumstances to determine if in fact the consent to search was coerced, account must be taken of subtly coercive police questions, as well as the possibly vulnerable subjective state of the person who consents." *Id.* at 2049. But, traditional notions of "voluntariness" do not require that the prosecution "affirmatively prove that the subject of the search knew that he had a right to refuse consent[.]" *Id.* Moreover, requiring police to advise the subject of such a search that he has the right to refuse consent would impose a "thoroughly impractical" burden by adding to the normal consent search procedure "the detailed requirements of an effective warning[,]" and "the strict standard of waiver" which, in a Fourth Amendment setting, is wholly inappropriate. *Id.* at 2049-2050, 2055. In the latter respect, Justice Stewart stresses that "it would be next to impossible to apply to a consent search the ["waiver"] standard of 'an intentional relinquishment or abandonment of a known right or privilege.'" *Id.* at 2056.

Consequently, "proof of knowledge of the right to refuse consent is [not] a necessary prerequisite to demonstrating a 'voluntary' consent. Rather, it is only by analyzing all the circumstances of an individual consent that it can be ascertained whether in fact it was voluntary or coerced." *Id.*

NOTE

1. *Voluntariness.*

(a) *Requesting consent and advising of the existence of a search warrant.* Whenever an officer asks an individual for consent to search a particular area and at the same time advises that he possesses, or will shortly possess, a search warrant, courts have held that the consent which thereafter follows is implicitly coerced. In this respect, the Supreme Court has stated that "[w]hen a law enforcement officer claims authority to search a home under a warrant, he announces in effect that the occupant has no right to resist the search. The situation is instinct with coercion—albeit colorably lawful coercion[; and w]here there is coercion there cannot be consent." *Bumper v. North Carolina*, 391 *U.S.* 543, 550, 88 *S.Ct.* 1788, 1792 (1967). *See also United States v. Alberts*, 721 *F.*2d 636, 640 (8th Cir. 1983) (holding invalid a consent given after officers advised the subject that they had a search warrant for the property sought to be inspected, where warrant ultimately was found to be defective); *United States v. Allison*, 619 *F.*2d 1254, 1264 (8th Cir. 1980) (reading *Bumper* as prohibiting searches on the basis of consent "when consent has been given after an official has asserted that he or she possesses a warrant * * *").

Different considerations may attach, however, when an officer couples his or her request for consent with an affirmative valid statement that in the absence of consent a search warrant *will be* pursued. So long as the officer has the requisite probable cause for the acquisition of a search warrant at the time the statement is made, the power to detain or guard the target item or premises may be more intrusive than the affirmative statement of the lawful alternative is coercive. Moreover, the individual is always free, under these circumstances, to exercise his or her right to refuse consent and demand that the police pursue the alternative of a search warrant. Consequently, a finding of involuntariness in this regard would be improper.

See e.g., United States v. Dennis, 625 *F*.2d 782 (8th Cir. 1980), where the defendant argued that his consent was coerced because he was in custody and the FBI agents told him, after an initial refusal of consent, that they "would get" or "would attempt to get" a warrant to search his car. Finding the consent valid, the court initially emphasized that "[t]he test in reviewing a consent search is whether, in the totality of the circumstances, the consent is given voluntarily and without coercion." *Id.* at 793. In this respect, "custody alone does not make the consent involuntary and coerced." *Id.* (citing *United States v. Watson*, 423 *U.S.* 411, 424, 96 *S.Ct.* 820, 828 (1976). "Further, 'where law enforcement officers indicate only that they will attempt to obtain or are getting a warrant such a statement cannot serve to vitiate an otherwise consensual search.' " *Id.* (quoting *United States v. Culp*, 472 *F*.2d 459, 461 n.1 (8th Cir.), *cert. denied*, 411 *U.S.* 970, 93 *S.Ct.* 2161 (1973)).

Similarly, in *United States v. Tompkins*, 130 *F*.3d 117, 122 (5th Cir. 1997), the court observed that an officer's statement to a suspect concerning the prospect of securing a search warrant "is but one factor to be considered among the totality of the circumstances in evaluating the voluntariness of [the suspect's] consent." During the course of the appeal, Tompkins argued that his consent was coerced in light of the investigating officer's failure, when informing Tompkins of the consequences of his refusal to consent, to distinguish between *procuring* a search warrant and *attempting to procure* a search warrant. According to Tompkins, because he was told by the officer that a warrant *would be obtained*, rather than merely *sought* or *applied for*, he was given the impression that a search was inevitable.

Rejecting Tompkins' contentions and finding his consent voluntary under all the circumstances, the court said:

> [T]he distinction between a suspect's being told by an officer that he "would obtain" a warrant rather than that he "would apply for" a warrant, is largely semantic and that, under the circumstances of this case, the distinction weighs only slightly in favor of a coercion finding.

> Considering all the relevant factors, Officer Brown's choice of words is not sufficiently significant * * *. Tompkins was not taken into custody and thus was apparently free to leave; other coercive police procedures were absent, *i.e.*, Tompkins was not handcuffed * * *, no threats or violence were used, and there was no overt display of authority; when Tompkins initially refused to allow the officers to enter his room, he was told that he did not have to consent to a search; Tompkins cooperated to the extent of providing his

identification and ultimately permitting the search; [and] Tompkins was found by the [district] court to be a man of average intelligence who, with charges pending against him in California, was not unfamiliar with the criminal justice system * * *.

Id. at 122.

(b) Requesting consent of a person in handcuffs. While the process of asking an arrestee for consent to search while the arrestee is in handcuffs is certainly indicative of a coercive atmosphere, it is not conclusive of the question whether the arrestee's provision of consent is "voluntary." For example, in *United States v. Kozinski*, 16 *F.*3d 795 (7th Cir. 1994), four federal and state law enforcement agents, acting pursuant to a valid arrest warrant, arrested a co-defendant (Havelka) at his residence. According to the agents' testimony, they entered Havelka's apartment, arrested and handcuffed him, placed him on the couch, and read him his *Miranda* rights. One of the agents held a gun to Havelka's head during the first few minutes of the arrest and then holstered it after he was handcuffed. While Havelka was handcuffed and seated on the couch, the agents asked for his consent to search the apartment. Havelka told the agents that he had nothing to hide. After being advised of his right to refuse consent, Havelka gave his permission for the search and signed a written consent form.

Finding that Havelka voluntarily consented to the requested search, the court said:

> When determining the voluntariness of the consent, [a] court must look to the "totality of all the circumstances," * * * and may consider factors such as: age, education, and intelligence of the defendant; advisement of his rights; how long he was detained prior to the consent; repeated requests for consent; physical coercion; and whether he was in custody. * * *

> In this case, Havelka, who owned his own business, did not lack any mental capacity to form consent. Although Havelka was handcuffed, no agent physically or mentally coerced him. He was only detained for "a few minutes" prior to being asked for his consent so there is no concern that he was worn out and consenting from sheer exhaustion. He was nervous initially, but he had calmed down by the time he consented. He was advised not only of his *Miranda* rights, but also of the right to refuse to consent. The agents did not ask for his consent repeatedly or harass him in any fashion. Furthermore, Havelka stated to the agents that he had nothing to hide. Based on this evidence, the district court's ruling of voluntariness was not clearly erroneous.

Id. at 810.

2. *Knowledge of the right to refuse.*

(a) State officers should be aware that the subject of searches and seizures conducted under the authority of an individual's consent presents yet another area in which state courts are free to rely on their own constitutions to provide enhanced protection to the privacy interests of their citizens. *See e.g., State v. Johnson,* 68 *N.J.* 349, 346 *A.*2d 66 (1975) (Where the State seeks to justify a search on the basis of consent, it has the burden of showing that the suspect was made aware of his right to refuse.).

(b) Working the buses and advice of the right to refuse. In *Florida v. Bostick,* 501 *U.S.* 429, 111 *S.Ct.* 2382 (1991), the United States Supreme Court held that police officers do not violate the Fourth Amendment by approaching bus passengers at random, asking questions, and requesting their consent to search, provided a reasonable person would understand that he or she is free to decline the officers' requests or otherwise terminate the encounter. In light of all the facts presented, the Court in *Bostick* noted the significance of the fact that the officer who asked for consent also advised the passenger that he had the right to refuse.

Since the United States Supreme Court's decision in *Bostick,* various lower courts have ruled that evidence obtained during suspicionless drug interdiction efforts aboard buses must be suppressed unless the officers have advised passengers of their right not to cooperate and to refuse consent to a search.

In *United States v. Drayton,* 536 *U.S.* 194, 122 *S.Ct.* 2105 (2002), the Court directly addressed this issue and held that the police are not required to specifically advise bus passengers during these encounters of their right not to cooperate.

In *Drayton,* three police officers conducted a "routine drug and weapons interdiction effort" on board a Greyhound bus during a scheduled stop in Tallahassee, Florida. *Id.* at 2109. During the operation, Officer Hoover knelt on the driver's seat and faced the rear of the bus, as Officers Land and Blackburn went to the rear of the bus. "Blackburn remained stationed there, facing forward. Lang worked his way toward the front of the bus, speaking with individual passengers as he went. He asked the passengers about their travel plans and sought to match passengers with luggage in the overhead racks. To avoid blocking the aisle, Lang stood next to or just behind each passenger with whom he spoke." *Id.* Any passenger who declined to cooperate with him or who chose to exit the bus would have been allowed to do so without interference.

The defendants, Christopher Drayton and Clifton Brown, Jr., were seated next to each other on the bus. Drayton sat in the aisle seat, and Brown was seated next to the window. Lang approached the two from the rear and leaned over Drayton's shoulder. Lang held up his badge long enough for Drayton and Brown to identify him as a police officer. With his face 12-to-18 inches away from Drayton's, Lang stated in a polite, quiet voice, "I'm Investigator Lang with the Tallahassee Police

Department. We're conducting [a] bus interdiction, attempting to deter drugs and illegal weapons being transported on the bus. Do you have any bags on the bus?" *Id.*

Both defendants pointed to a single green bag in the overhead luggage rack. Lang asked, "Do you mind if I check it?" Brown replied, "Go ahead." *Id.* The bag contained no contraband.

Officer Lang noticed that both Drayton and Brown were wearing heavy jackets and baggy pants despite the warm weather. "In Lang's experience, drug traffickers often use baggy clothing to conceal weapons or narcotics. The officer thus asked Brown if he had any weapons or drugs in his possession. And he asked Brown: 'Do you mind if I check your person?' Brown answered, 'Sure,' and cooperated by leaning up in his seat, pulling a cell phone out of his pocket, and opening up his jacket." *Id.* Officer Lang "reached across Drayton and patted down Brown's jacket and pockets, including his waist area, sides, and upper thighs. In both thigh areas, Lang detected hard objects similar to drug packages detected on other occasions. Lang arrested and handcuffed Brown. Officer Hoover escorted Brown from the bus." *Id.*

"Lang then asked Drayton, 'Mind if I check you?' Drayton responded by lifting his hands about eight inches from his legs. Lang conducted a pat-down of Drayton's thighs and detected hard objects similar to those found on Brown. He arrested Drayton and escorted him from the bus. A further search revealed that [defendants] had duct-taped plastic bundles of powder cocaine between several pairs of their boxer shorts. Brown possessed three bundles containing 483 grams of cocaine. Drayton possessed two bundles containing 295 grams of cocaine." *Id.* at 2109-10.

Finding the officers' actions entirely proper, the United States Supreme Court held that the defendants' consent to search was "voluntary." *Id.* at 2110.

In earlier cases, the Court has rejected the suggestion that police officers must "always inform citizens of their right to refuse when seeking permission to conduct a warrantless consent search. * * * 'While knowledge of the right to refuse consent is one factor to be taken into account, the government need not establish such knowledge as the *sine qua non* of an effective consent.' " *Id.* at 2113 (quoting *Schneckloth v. Bustamonte,* 412 *U.S.* 218, 227, 93 *S.Ct.* 2041, 2049 (1973)). The procedure does not become invalid simply because "a citizen consented without explicit notification that he or she was free to refuse to cooperate. Instead, the Court has repeated that the totality of the circumstances must control, without giving extra weight to the absence of this type of warning. * * * Although Officer Lang did not inform [the defendants] of their right to refuse the search, he did request permission to search, and the totality of the circumstances indicate[d] that their consent was voluntary, so the searches were reasonable." *Id.* at 2113-14.

"In a society based on law, the concept of agreement and consent should be given a weight and dignity of its own. Police officers act in full accord with the law when they ask citizens for consent. It reinforces the rule of law for the citizen to advise the police of his or her wishes and for the police to act in reliance on that understanding. When this exchange takes place, it dispels inferences of coercion." *Id.* at 2114.

During the course of its opinion, the Court paused to observe:

> We need not ask the alternative question whether, after the arrest of Brown, there were grounds for a *Terry* stop and frisk of Drayton, though this may have been the case. It was evident that Drayton and Brown were traveling together. Officer Lang observed the pair reboarding the bus together; they were each dressed in heavy, baggy clothes that were ill-suited for the day's warm temperatures; they were seated together on the bus; and they each claimed responsibility for the single piece of green carry-on luggage. Once Lang had identified Brown as carrying what he believed to be narcotics, he may have had reasonable suspicion to conduct a *Terry* stop and frisk on Drayton as well. That question, however, has not been presented to us. *The fact the officers may have had reasonable suspicion does not prevent them from relying on a citizen's consent to the search. It would be a paradox, and one most puzzling to law enforcement officials and courts alike, were we to say, after holding that Brown's consent was voluntary, that Drayton's consent was ineffectual simply because the police at that point had more compelling grounds to detain him.* After taking Brown into custody, the officers were entitled to continue to proceed on the basis of consent and to ask for Drayton's cooperation.

Id. at 2114. [Emphasis added.]

Accordingly, the Court held that the defendants' "consent to the search of their luggage and their persons was voluntary. Nothing Officer Lang said indicated a command to consent to the search. Rather, when [defendants] informed Lang that they had a bag on the bus, he asked for their permission to check it. And when Lang requested to search Brown and Drayton's persons, he asked first if they objected, thus indicating to a reasonable person that he or she was free to refuse. Even after arresting Brown, Lang provided Drayton with no indication that he was required to consent to a search. To the contrary, Lang asked for Drayton's permission to search him ('Mind if I check you?'), and Drayton agreed." *Id.* at 2113.

[For an extended discussion of the "mere inquiry" versus "seizure" issue, *see* Section 8.2(a).]

3. *The consent must be "unequivocal and specific."* In *United States v. Worley*, 193 *F.*3d 380 (6th Cir. 1999), the court held that the defendant's comment, "You've got the badge, I guess you can," to the officers who requested consent to search, was insufficient to convey a valid consent. In this respect, the court reminded that to establish that a "valid and voluntary consent was rendered," the content of the consenting party's statement must be examined "to ensure that it 'unequivocally, specifically, and intelligently' indicates" that the party voluntarily consented. *Id.* at 386. The court ruled that the defendant's comment

in this case was not "an unequivocal statement of free and voluntary consent," but "merely a response conveying an expression of futility in resistence to authority or acquiescing in the officers' request." *Id.*

OHIO v. ROBINETTE
Supreme Court of the United States
519 *U.S.* 33, 117 *S.Ct.* 417 (1996)

QUESTION: Does the Fourth Amendment require the police to advise a lawfully detained person that he or she is "free to go" before the person's consent to search will be recognized as voluntary?

ANSWER: NO. There is no requirement under the Fourth Amendment that police, during the course of a motor vehicle stop or other investigative detention, advise the person detained that he or she is "free to go" before a consent to search may be lawfully obtained. *Id.* at 419.

RATIONALE: Deputy Sheriff's Officer Roger Newsome stopped defendant, Robert Robinette, after the officer clocked Robinette's vehicle traveling 69 miles per hour in a construction zone having a posted speed limit of 45 miles per hour. During the stop, Officer Newsome asked for and obtained Robinette's driver's license, and ran a computer check which indicated that Robinette had no previous violations. Newsome then asked Robinette to step out of his vehicle; the officer turned on his patrol vehicle's mounted video camera, and proceeded to issue a verbal warning to Robinette, whereupon the officer returned Robinette's license.

At this point, Officer Newsome asked, "One question before you get gone: [A]re you carrying any illegal contraband in your car? Any weapons of any kind, drugs, anything like that?" When Robinette replied no, Officer Newsome asked if he could search the car. Robinette consented to the search. In the car, Newsome found a small amount of marijuana and, in a film container, a pill which was later determined to be a form of methamphetamine. Robinette was then arrested and charged with the possessory drug offenses.

In the appeal following his unsuccessful motion to suppress evidence,* the Ohio Supreme Court adopted what it believed to be a "bright-line prerequisite" which would require a detaining officer to clearly advise any citizen stopped for a traffic offense that the citizen is free to leave once the valid detention has ended. According to the Ohio Supreme Court, " 'any attempt at consensual interrogation must be preceded by the phrase, "At this time you legally are free to go," or words of similar import.' " *Id.* at 420 (quoting *State v. Robinette,* 653 *N.E.2d* 695,

---

* At the hearing on the motion to suppress evidence, the sheriff's deputy testified that at the time he stopped Robinette, he "was on drug interdiction patrol." The officer testified that he routinely requested permission to search automobiles he stopped for traffic violations. In the year that Robinette's stop took place, the deputy indicated that he had requested consent to search in 786 traffic stops. Id. at 422 (Ginsburg, J. concurring).

696 (Ohio 1995)). In addition, the Ohio Supreme Court held that " '[w]hen the motivation behind a police officer's continued detention of a person stopped for a traffic violation is not related to the purpose of the original, constitutional stop, and when that continued detention is not based on articulable facts giving rise to a suspicion of some separate illegal activity justifying an extension of this detention, the continued detention constitutes an illegal seizure.' " *Id.* [Citation omitted.]

*The United States Supreme Court rejected the Ohio Supreme Court's so-called per se "first-tell-then-ask" rule.** Under the circumstances, held the Court, a *per se* rule is inappropriate. Rather, "[t]he Fourth Amendment test for a valid consent search is that the consent be voluntary, and '[v]oluntariness is a question of fact to be determined from all the circumstances[.]' " *Id.* at 421 (quoting *Schneckloth v. Bustamonte*, 412 *U.S.* 218, 248-49, 93 *S.Ct.* 2041, 2059 (1973)).

Accordingly, during the course of a motor vehicle stop, the Court ruled, "it would be unrealistic to require police officers to always inform detainees that they are free to go before a consent to search may be deemed voluntary." *Id.*

NOTE

1. *Robinette on remand.* In *Ohio v. Robinette (Robinette I)*, the United States Supreme Court rejected the Ohio Supreme Court's "bright-line rule" mandating that, in the absence of reasonable suspicion of criminal activity separate and apart from what prompted the initial motor vehicle stop, once the stop has been concluded, the officer must inform the motorist that he or she is now "free to go," before the officer may ask questions unrelated to the stop and before seeking consent to search. In a concurring opinion, Justice Ginsburg emphasized that the Court's ruling did "not pass judgment on the wisdom" of Ohio's "first-tell-then-ask rule." *Id.*, 117 *S.Ct.* at 422 (Ginsburg, J., concurring). Instead, the Court's ruling simply clarified that the Ohio court's instruction to Ohio police officers is not "the command of the Federal Constitution." *Id.* Justice Ginsburg further observed that the federal Supreme Court's ruling does not in any way prevent state courts from interpreting their own state constitutions so as to provide greater protection of individual rights than that mandated by the United States Constitution. *Id.*

The federal Supreme Court concluded in *Robinette I* that the test for a voluntary consent obtained during the course of a motor vehicle stop is "a question of fact to be determined from all the circumstances." *Id.* at 421. The Court therefore remanded the case to the Ohio Supreme Court for further proceedings.

On remand, the Ohio Supreme Court determined that Robinette's encounter with Deputy Newsome could not be viewed as a single continuous lawful detention. Rather, the court found that Robinette had

---

* The Court also rejected the second aspect of the Ohio Supreme Court's ruling. In this regard, the Court said: "We think that under our recent decision in *Whren v. United States*, 517 *U.S.* 806[, 116 *S.Ct.* 1769] (1996) (decided after the Supreme Court of Ohio decided the present case), the subjective intentions of the officer did not make the continued detention of [defendant] illegal under the Fourth Amendment." *Id.* at 420.

been subjected to two separate, successive encounters, the second of which constituted an *unlawful* detention. *State v. Robinette*, 80 *Ohio St.*3d 234, 685 *N.E.*2d 762, 771 (1997) (*Robinette II*).

In *Robinette II*, the Ohio Supreme Court preliminarily recognized the recent trend of state courts relying on their own state constitutions to provide broader protection for individual rights, independent of protections afforded by the United States Constitution. "This movement toward enforcing state constitutions independently has been called 'New Federalism.'" *Robinette II*, 685 *N.E.*2d at 770. Yet, despite this wave of New Federalism, the Ohio Supreme Court found that Article I, Section 14 of "the Ohio Constitution affords protections that are coextensive with those provided by the Fourth Amendment." *Id.* at 770-71. On remand, therefore, the court now ruled that an Ohio police officer is not required "to inform an individual, stopped for a traffic violation, that he or she is free to go before the officer may attempt to engage in a consensual interrogation." *Id.*

Under the totality of the circumstances, however, the Ohio Supreme Court concluded that Newsome was not justified in the continued detention of Robinette because he did not have a reasonable articulable suspicion to support it. In addition, the court held that Robinette's consent was not "an independent act of free will," because, under the circumstances, a reasonable person would have believed that he was not free to go until he answered Newsome's additional questions. The court found that the transition between the lawful motor vehicle stop and the attempt at a "consensual exchange" was so "seamless" that the untrained eye could not notice when it has occurred. *Id.* at 771. Finding Robinette's consent involuntary, the Ohio Supreme Court concluded that evidence seized must be suppressed.

---

§3.6(c). Third parties: Common and apparent authority.

UNITED STATES v. MATLOCK
Supreme Court of the United States
415 *U.S.* 164, 94 *S.Ct.* 988 (1974)

QUESTION: Is a warrantless search valid when based on the consent of a third party who possesses common authority over or other sufficient relationship to the property sought to be searched?

ANSWER: YES. A warrantless search is valid when based on the consent of a third party who possesses "common authority over or other sufficient relationship to the premises or effects sought to be inspected." *Id.*, 415 *U.S.* at 171. "Common authority," in this respect, does not rest on the third party's "property interest." *Id.* Instead, "common authority" rests "on mutual use of the property by persons generally having joint access or control for most purposes[.]" *Id.* at 171 n.7.

RATIONALE: At the time of the search at issue, Matlock lived in a house in Pardeeville, Wisconsin, along with a Mrs. Marshall, several of her children, including her daughter, Gayle Graff, and Graff's three-year-old son. Police responded to the residence to arrest Matlock for bank robbery. Upon their arrival, they located Matlock and arrested him in the yard in front of the residence. "Although the officers were aware at the time of the arrest that [Matlock] lived in the house, they did not ask him which room he occupied or whether he would consent to a search. Three of the arresting officers went to the door of the house and were admitted by Mrs. Graff, who was dressed in a robe and was holding her son in her arms. The officers told her they were looking for money and a gun, and asked if they could search the house." *Id.* at 166.

Mrs. Graff voluntarily consented to a search of the house, "including the east bedroom on the second floor which she said was jointly occupied by Matlock and herself." *Id.* She led the officers to the bedroom, and advised them that she and Matlock shared the one dresser in the room and that the woman's clothing in the room was hers. The bedroom was searched, and robbery proceeds—$4,995 in cash—was found in a diaper bag in the closet. At the time, Mrs. Graff and Matlock had been sleeping together in the east bedroom regularly. During the search of the bedroom, the officers discovered two pillows on the double bed, which had been slept in, men's and women's clothes in the closet, and men's and women's clothes in separate drawers of the dresser.

Finding the consent valid, the Court said:

> It appears to us, * * * that the Government sustained its burden of proving by the preponderance of the evidence that Mrs. Graff's voluntary consent to search the east bedroom was legally sufficient to warrant admitting into evidence the $4,995 found in the diaper bag.

Id. at 177.

Earlier cases have already established that "the consent of one who possesses common authority over premises or effects is valid as against the absent, nonconsenting person with whom that authority is shared." *Id.* at 171. *See e.g., Frazier v. Cupp,* 394 *U.S.* 731, 740, 89 *S.Ct.* 1420 (1969) (consent of defendant's cousin to the search of a duffel bag, used jointly by both men, found valid; by allowing the cousin the use of the bag, Frazier assumed the risk that his cousin would allow someone else to look inside); *United States v. Sferas,* 210 *F.*2d 69, 74 (7th Cir. 1954) (where two persons have equal rights to the use or occupation of premises, either may give consent to a search).

Accordingly, a warrantless search is valid when based on the consent of a third party who possesses "common authority over or other sufficient relationship to the premises or effects sought to be inspected." *Id.* at 171. In this respect, "common authority" is

> not to be implied from the mere property interest a third party has in the property. The authority which justifies the third-party consent does not rest upon the law of property, with its attendant historical

and legal refinements, *see Chapman v. United States*, 365 *U.S.* 610, 81 *S.Ct.* 776 (1961) (landlord could not validly consent to the search of a house he had rented to another), *Stoner v. California*, 376 *U.S.* 483, 84 *S.Ct.* 889 (1964) (night hotel clerk could not validly consent to search of customer's room), but rests rather on mutual use of the property by persons generally having joint access or control for most purposes, so that it is reasonable to recognize that any of the co-inhabitants has the right to permit the inspection in his own right, and that the others have assumed the risk that one of their number might permit the common area to be searched.

Id. at 171 n.7.

UNITED STATES v. WARNER
United States Court of Appeals
843 *F.*2d 401 (9th Cir. 1988)

QUESTION: Do landlords have the authority to consent to a search of premises inhabited by a tenant who is not at home at the time of the police request?

ANSWER: NO. Landlords "do not have authority to waive the [F]ourth [A]mendment's warrant requirement by consenting to a search of premises inhabited by a tenant who is not at home at the time of a police call. The security of tenants' residences is not dependent solely upon the discretion of landlords." *Id.* at 403.

RATIONALE: The landlord and tenant (defendant) in this case had an agreement which permitted the landlord to enter the leased premises from time to time to make certain repairs and to mow the lawn. In the middle of June, the landlord entered the garage defendant leased in order to utilize the power source therein for his electrical drill to make several repairs. While inside, the landlord observed numerous boxes of chemicals. He compiled a list and ultimately called the police and informed them of what he had discovered.

When an officer arrived at the premises, the landlord provided access to the leased garage. Defendant was not home at the time. When they entered the garage, they observed boxes of chemicals partially covered by tarps. The officer recognized that such chemicals are often used in the manufacture of illicit drugs. All of the chemicals were immediately seized.

In this appeal, the Government argues, among other things, that the landlord had provided the requisite consent for the warrantless search of the leased garage. *The Court of Appeals for the Ninth Circuit could not agree.*

There are three factors that a court will consider when determining when a third party may effectively consent to a search of another's property. "These factors are: (1) whether the third party has an equal right of access to the premises searched; (2) whether the suspect is present at the time the third party consent is obtained; and (3) if so, whether the suspect actively opposes the search." *Id.* at 403. In this case, factors (2) and (3) are not implicated because of defendant's absence. "Thus, the issue of consent turns upon whether the landlord had an equal right of access to the premises." *Id.*

"The landlord in this case did not have any right of access for most purposes. As noted by the district court, 'at best, the landlord had permission to enter the property for the limited purpose of making specified repairs and occasionally mowing the lawn.' Here, * * * the landlord 'had reserved only [a] limited right to enter the garage, * * * the agreement * * * was oral [and could not be interpreted] as conveying an unlimited right of access.' " *Id.*

The officer testified that he did not obtain a warrant because he believed that no warrant was necessary if the landlord consented to the entry. Landlords do not, however, "have authority to waive the fourth amendment's warrant requirement by consenting to a search of premises inhabited by a tenant who is not at home at the time of a police call. The security of tenants' residences is not dependent solely upon the discretion of landlords." *Id.*

Accordingly, the landlord in this case could not give effective consent for the search of defendant's leased garage.

NOTE

Consent provided by a third party. The constitutional validity of third-party consent searches was settled by the United States Supreme Court in *Matlock v. United States*, 415 *U.S.* 164, 94 *S.Ct.* 988 (1974). *Matlock* set forth the principle that the consent of one who possesses common authority over premises sought to be inspected is valid as against the absent, nonconsenting person with whom that authority is shared. The issue to be resolved, therefore, in any third-party consent case, is whether the consenting party possessed a *sufficient relationship* to the searched premises to validate the search. In this respect, courts will examine whether the consenting party enjoyed a mutual use of the property, had joint access to the property or exercised joint control over the property. *Id.* at 171 & n.7, 94 *S.Ct.* at 993 & n.7.

(a) Consent provided by hotel/motel personnel. Once a hotel or motel room's rental period has expired, the guest's right of occupancy is thereby terminated and management has the right to reenter the room and ready it for the next paying guest. Consequently, after check-out time, the room's former occupant may not claim a reasonable expectation of privacy in the room itself or items left behind in plain view or in areas uncoverable in the normal or routine course of room preparation for subsequent occupancy. In this respect, a warrantless police search of the room based on consent provided by hotel or motel personnel is permissible, for such a procedure does not implicate the Fourth Amendment. *See e.g., United States v. Rahme*, 813 *F.*2d 31, 34-35 (2d Cir. 1987); *United States v. Lee*, 700 *F.*2d 424, 426 (10th Cir. 1983); *United States v. Akin*, 562 *F.*2d 459, 464 (7th Cir. 1977); *United States v. Parizo*, 514 *F.*2d 52, 54-55 (2d Cir. 1975); *United States v. Croft*, 429 *F.*2d 884, 887 (10th Cir. 1970).

A different result may obtain, however, with respect to the contents of closed personal luggage or other closed containers left behind by the former guest. For example, in *Commonwealth v. Brundidge*, 404 *Pa.Super.* 106, 590 *A.*2d 302 (1991), the court rejected the contention that hotel or motel personnel had the authority to consent to a police search of concealed personal effects left in a room one-half hour after check-out time. The court reasoned:

> We know of no theory which would give motel management dominion over the contents of discrete and personal items of luggage and the like of their motel guests. Third party consent search theory is grounded on the premise that the third party possessed common authority over the premises or effects to be searched so as to permit the conclusion that the person asserting the right assumed the risk that the third party would allow the search. * * * However, no such conclusion can be reached with respect to enclosed personal effects such as luggage found in a motel room shortly after check-out time which clearly have not been either abandoned or left open for public access. In such cases, "manifestations of retained privacy by the absent person could [not] be stronger, [n]or the indications of assumed risks of third person permission to inspect, lower." *United States v. Block*, 590 *F.*2d 535, 541 (4th Cir. 1978) (mother's authority to consent to search of son's room did not extend to a search of a locked foot-locker in room); *see also United States v. Padron*, 657 *F.Supp.* 840 (D.Del. 1987), *aff'd without op. sub nom.*, *United States v. Rubio*, 857 *F.*2d 1466 (3d Cir. 1988), *cert. denied*, 488 *U.S.* 974, 109 *S.Ct.* 512 [] (1988) (authority of driver to consent to search of car does not extend to passenger's luggage).

Brundidge, 590 *A.*2d at 309.

The court also noted that the *Brundidge* facts and circumstances provided "no reasonable basis for the police to believe that motel management had authority to consent to the search of [the defendant's] enclosed personal effects." *Id.* at 309 n.9. "Under the circumstances," the court concluded that "the police were not entitled to assume that the manager's authority over the premises extended to the guest's concealed, personal effects." *Id.*

(b) Spousal consent. While it is clear that a husband or wife may provide the authorities with permission to search the marital home, or at least those areas of the home over which both retain "common authority," questions arise as to the validity of an estranged spouse's consent. In circumstances where consent is sought from a spouse who has left the marital home, the question will still focus on whether the estranged spouse retains a "sufficient relationship" to the premises sought to be inspected by the police. *See United States v. Trazaska*, 859 *F.*2d 1118, 1120 (2nd Cir. 1988) (consent of defendant's estranged wife held valid notwithstanding fact that she and the children moved out of the apartment two weeks earlier, where wife had the key to the apartment and, during the course of the search, retrieved several of her personal belongings); *United States v. Crouthers*, 669

*F.*2d 635, 642-643 (10th Cir. 1982) (consent of defendant's wife held valid even though she had moved out of their apartment two weeks earlier and was living with her parents, because she had not abandoned the marriage or apartment completely and still retained the key to the apartment); *United States v. Long,* 524 *F.*2d 660, 661 (9th Cir. 1975) (wife who was joint owner of house had right to give consent notwithstanding fact that husband had changed the locks, where wife left house out of fear of husband and where she collected personal belongings during the search).

(c) *Shared apartments.* When an apartment is shared, "one ordinarily assumes the risk that a co-tenant might consent to a search, at least to all common areas and those areas to which the other has access." *United States v. Ladell,* 127 *F.*3d 622, 624 (7th Cir. 1997). The authority to consent does not, however, automatically extend to a search of a co-tenant's private bedroom. *See e.g., United States v. Duran,* 957 *F.*2d 499, 505 (7th Cir. 1992) ("Two friends inhabiting a two-bedroom apartment might reasonably expect to maintain exclusive access to their respective bedrooms without explicitly making this expectation clear to one another."). Rather, one co-tenant's authority to consent to the search of another's room will depend on the extent of the consenting tenant's mutual use of, joint access to, or control over the other's room. Thus, in *United States v.* Aghedo, 159 *F.*3d 308 (7th Cir. 1998), the court found that the defendant assumed the risk that Dairo, the co-tenant of the two-bedroom apartment where defendant stayed, could lawfully consent to a search of his room, where the apartment lease was solely in Dairo's name, where she had free access to his room, which was never locked, and where she periodically entered his room to clean it and store her clothing there.

(d) *Third-party consents and rented vehicles.* In *United States v. Dunkley,* 911 *F.*2d 522 (11th Cir. 1990), a Georgia state trooper stopped an automobile driven by Joseph Brown for a minor traffic violation. Defendant Coval Baker occupied the front passenger seat and defendant Audley Dunkley was seated in the rear. During a credentials check, the trooper learned that the car was a rental vehicle, which Brown advised was rented to his "old lady." Brown could not, however, produce the rental agreement. The trooper requested and received consent from Brown to search the car. With the help of a narcotics detection dog, the trooper discovered a quantity of crack cocaine located inside a stuffed rabbit which was lying on the back seat of the vehicle. Additionally, the trooper found a loaded handgun inside the unlocked glove box and some rolling papers in the center console between the two front seats. Later, it was learned that the vehicle was actually rented by Baker's wife; that she had given Baker permission to use the car; and that Baker, in turn, gave Brown permission to drive the car.

In upholding the validity of the consent, the Eleventh Circuit relied heavily on the Supreme Court's decision in *Matlock v. United States, supra,* which held that "the voluntary consent of any joint occupant of a residence to search the premises is valid against the co-occupant, permitting evidence discovered in the search to be used against the co-occupant at a criminal trial." *Dunkley* at 525. In such cases, the authority to provide consent arises from

> "mutual use of the property by persons generally having joint access or control for most purposes, so that it is reasonable to recognize that any of the co-inhabitants has the right to permit the inspection in his own right and that the others have assumed the risk that one of their number might permit the common area to be searched."

Id. (quoting *Matlock* at 172 n.7, 94 *S.Ct.* at 993 n.7).

Finding "no reason not to apply *Matlock's* 'joint access or control' test for [a] valid third-party consent to the search of a vehicle[,]" the *Dunkley* court reasoned:

> Under the rationale of *Matlock*, a third party in sole possession and control of a vehicle clearly has the authority to consent to its search. * * * By relinquishing possession to another, the owner or lessee of the vehicle evidences an abandonment of his or her privacy interest in the vehicle; thus, it is reasonable to conclude that the third party to whom possession was surrendered was also given authority to consent to a search of all areas of the vehicle. *See [United States v. Morales*, 861 *F.*2d 396, 399 n.8 (3rd Cir. 1988).]
>
> It is a somewhat different question whether an owner/lessee of a vehicle who is a passenger in the vehicle completely abandons his or her property interests to the driver, to the extent that the third-party driver may rightfully consent to a full search of the entire vehicle. [] It is clear, however, that even if the owner/lessee is present as a passenger, the driver of a vehicle has some amount of joint access to the vehicle, and, in fact, the driver has immediate control over the vehicle.
>
> In this case, defendant Brown, as [the] driver, * * * had joint access to and control at least over the front and back seats of the vehicle. Brown consented to the search within the presence and hearing of defendant Baker, the defendant with the superior interest in the car. Thus, Brown's act of giving consent and the scope of consent given were apparent to Baker; his failure to object confirms that Brown indeed had the requisite authority to consent to the search of the vehicle.
>
> [Moreover], Brown told [the trooper] that his "old lady" had rented the car, and it was Brown who took the lead in dealing with the [trooper] and who consented to the search. All of this occurred within the hearing of Baker, and yet he made no objection. [Accordingly,] Brown was authorized to consent to the search of the vehicle.

Dunkley at 526.

(e) *Rental vehicles and standing.* In *United States v. Riazco*, 91 *F.*3d 752 (5th Cir. 1996), Investigator Gary Gresham, a Texas narcotics task force officer, stopped a motor vehicle driven by Harold Riazco for minor traffic and equipment violations. Gresham asked Riazco to step out of the car and produce his driver's license. A passenger in the vehicle, Margarita Gonzalez-Morin, told the officer that Riazco did not speak English. The officer then tried to obtain information from Riazco in "poor, halting Spanish." *Id.* at 753. Riazco produced identification showing that his name was Raul Serrano Lugo, and told the officer that he and Margarita were on their way to Dallas for two days.

Investigator Gresham approached Margarita, "determined that the car was rented, and asked her to produce the rental agreement. She complied, and Gresham noted that neither she nor Riazco was listed as an authorized driver on the rental agreement. The agreement specified that the vehicle was not to be used for illegal activity, and it was five days overdue for return to the rental company." *Id.*

"Gresham issued Riazco a citation (in English) for failing to maintain one lane. Riazco signed it without reading it. Gresham then asked him to sign a consent-to-search form (also in English). Riazco signed that as well, again without reading it." *Id.* [At the suppression hearing, Riazco testified that he believed both forms related to the traffic violation. *Id.* at 753 n.2.] The search of the vehicle uncovered two bricks of cocaine hidden in the speaker cavities. At this point, both Riazco and his passenger were arrested.

In this appeal, the Government argued that neither Riazco nor his passenger had "standing to challenge the search on the ground that neither (1) had rented the car, (2) was listed in the rental agreement as an authorized additional driver, or (3) had been given permission by the renter or the rental company" to use the car. *Id.* at 754. The Fifth Circuit agreed.

The Supreme Court has established "a two-pronged test for determining whether a defendant has standing to bring a Fourth Amendment challenge to an allegedly illegal search: 'Such a determination depends on 1) whether the defendant is able to establish an actual, subjective expectation of privacy with respect to the place being searched or items being seized, and 2) whether that expectation of privacy is one which society would recognize as [objectively] reasonable.' " *Id.* [Citation omitted.] "Under this analysis," ruled the Fifth Circuit, "Riazco lacked standing to challenge the validity of the search." *Id.* In this respect, the court observed:

> Riazco, the driver of the car, did not assert a property or possessory interest in the vehicle. He neither owned nor rented it. The rental vehicle specifically stated that the car was to be driven only by persons authorized by the car rental company, and Riazco was not so authorized. In fact, he admitted at the suppression hearing that he did not even have the renter's permission to drive it.

> Even if we assume that Riazco actually, subjectively expected privacy with respect to the ordinarily inaccessible recesses of the car—*e.g.*, the speaker cavities—such an expectation of privacy was not objectively reasonable. We have already held that, '[t]ypically, a passenger without a possessory interest in an automobile lacks standing to complain of its search because his privacy expectation is not infringed.' * * * There is no logical reason

to adopt a different rule for a driver simply because he happens to be behind the wheel when the car is stopped.

Id. at 754-55.

During the course of its opinion, the court pointed out that other circuit courts have ruled that persons driving rental cars without the authorization of the rental company have no standing to challenge the validity of the search because they do not have a legitimate expectation of privacy in such circumstances. *See e.g., United States v. Wellons,* 32 *F.*3d 117, 119 & n.4 (4th Cir. 1994); *United States v. Roper,* 918 *F.*2d 885, 887-88 (10th Cir. 1990). And the Eighth Circuit has held that, at the very least, the driver must have obtained permission from the lawful renter in order to establish a legitimate expectation of privacy. *See United States v. Muhammad,* 58 *F.*3d 353, 355 (8th Cir. 1995).

Accordingly, the court concluded that it was not objectively reasonable for Riazco or his passenger to expect privacy with respect to the car's speaker cavities. Because the objective reasonableness prong of the standing test was not met, these two individuals failed to establish an expectation of privacy that society would be prepared to recognize as reasonable.

COMMONWEALTH v. MAXWELL
Supreme Court of Pennsylvania
505 *Pa.* 152, 477 *A.*2d 1309 (1984)

QUESTION: Does an underage child, who lives in her parent's home, have the capacity to give the police consent to search a common area of the home ?

ANSWER: YES. "Although age is one element to acknowledge in ascertaining whether consent was given willingly, minority status alone does not prevent one from giving consent." *Id.,* 505 *Pa.* at 162.

RATIONALE: In June of 1979, defendant summoned an Encyclopedia Britannica salesman to his home for the purpose of robbing, and if necessary, killing him. While the salesman was sitting in defendant's dining room, defendant shot him twice in the head at close range. The victim's body was stuffed in trash bags and carried down to defendant's basement. The next day, defendant's daughters discovered the victim's body in the basement and informed the police of what they had seen. The police requested permission to enter the house and defendant's sixteen-year-old daughter, Yolanda, granted it.

Among the arguments raised in this appeal, defendant contends that his Fourth Amendment right to privacy was infringed by the warrantless search of his home, and that the salesman's body should have been suppressed. Defendant argues that the police intimidated his daughter, Yolanda, thus negating her consent. Moreover, argues defendant, Yolanda was incapable of giving consent because she was only sixteen years of age. *The Pennsylvania Supreme Court disagreed.*

While it is true that a "mere acquiescence to a claim of lawful authority does not discharge the burden that consent must be freely and voluntarily given," *id.* at 162, the evidence in this case demonstrates that it was defendant's daughter, Yolanda, "who approached the police officers * * * and requested them to come inside the house because she wanted to show them what was in the trash bag in the basement. The police neither forced themselves upon Yolanda nor used their authority as a pretext to gain entry into [defendant's] house. The police officers' actions in searching the house were in direct response to Yolanda's directives. There was nothing intimidating in this scenario." *Id.*

Nor is the fact that Yolanda was only sixteen years old at the time she gave the officers consent to search defendant's home fatal to the validity of such consent. "Although age is one element to acknowledge in ascertaining whether consent was given willingly, minority status alone does not prevent one from giving consent." *Id.* Moreover, there is no evidence in this record to "indicate that Yolanda's age itself prevented her from giving a valid consent. Nor is there evidence of any emotional immaturity or mental instability. On the contrary the record reveals that Yolanda made a very rational decision when she left her house after discovering the body. The evidence establishes that consent existed irrespective of Yolanda's age." *Id.* at 163.

ILLINOIS v. RODRIGUEZ
Supreme Court of the United States
497 *U.S.* 177, 110 *S.Ct.* 2793 (1990)

QUESTION: May a warrantless entry into a suspect's residence be upheld as constitutional when it is based upon the consent of a third party whom the police, at the time of the entry, reasonably believe to possess common authority over the premises, but who in fact has no such authority ?

ANSWER: YES. The Constitution is not violated "when officers enter without a warrant because they reasonably (though erroneously) believe that the person who has consented to their entry is a resident of the premises," or has common authority over the premises. *Id.* at 2800. "[T]o satisfy the 'reasonableness' requirement of the Fourth Amendment, what is generally demanded of the many factual determinations that must regularly be made by agents of the government * * * is not that they always be correct, but that they always be reasonable." *Id.*

"As with other factual determinations bearing upon search and seizure, determination of consent * * * must 'be judged against an objective standard: would the facts available to the officer at the moment . . . "warrant a man of reasonable caution in the belief " ' that the consenting party had authority over the premises ? * * * If not, then warrantless entry is unlawful unless authority actually exists. But if so, the search is valid." *Id.* at 2801.

RATIONALE: Since the Court's decision in *United States v. Matlock*, 415 *U.S.* 164, 94 *S.Ct.* 988 (1974), it has been well recognized that "a warrantless entry and search by law enforcement officers does not violate the Fourth Amendment's [prohibition against] 'unreasonable searches and seizures' if the officers have obtained the consent of a third party who possesses common authority over the premises." *Rodriguez* at 2797. " 'Common authority' rests 'on mutual use of the property by persons generally having joint access or control for most purposes[' and t]he burden of establishing that common authority rests upon the State." *Id.* at 2797 (quoting *Matlock* at 171 n.7, 94 *S.Ct.* at 993 n.7). Thus, when an individual does in fact possess common authority over the place to be searched, the law is clear. This case presents the problem of a warrantless entry based upon the consent of a third party who does not actually possess common authority over the premises, but who may have reasonably appeared to have had such authority at the time the police obtained her consent.

In late July, police were informed by Gail Fischer that she had been assaulted by defendant, Edward Rodriguez, earlier that day in a Chicago apartment. At the time of the report, Fischer exhibited signs of a severe beating. "Fischer stated that Rodriguez was then asleep in the apartment, and she consented to travel there with the police in order to unlock the door with her key so that the officers could enter and arrest him. During this conversation, Fischer several times referred to the apartment * * * as 'our' apartment, and said that she had clothes and furniture there. It is unclear whether she indicated that she currently lived at the apartment, or only that she used to live there." *Id.*

The police officers drove to the apartment accompanied by Fischer. "They did not obtain an arrest warrant for Rodriguez, nor did they seek a search warrant for the apartment. At the apartment, Fischer unlocked the door with her key and gave the officers permission to enter. They moved through the door into the living room, where they observed in plain view drug paraphernalia and containers filled with white powder that they believed (correctly, as later analysis showed) to be cocaine. They proceeded to the bedroom, where they found Rodriguez asleep and discovered additional containers of white powder in two open attache cases. The officers arrested Rodriguez and seized the drugs and related paraphernalia." *Id.*

"Rodriguez was charged with possession of a controlled substance with intent to deliver. He moved to suppress all evidence seized at the time of his arrest, claiming that Fischer had vacated the apartment several weeks earlier and had no authority to consent to the entry." *Id.* The Illinois county circuit court granted defendant's motion, ruling that, "at the time she consented to the entry, Fischer did not have common authority over the apartment." *Id.* The Illinois court concluded that Fischer was not a "usual resident" but rather an "infrequent visitor" at the apartment. In addition, the circuit court rejected the State's contention that "even if Fischer did not possess common authority over the premises, there was no Fourth Amendment violation if the police *reasonably believed* at the time of their entry that Fischer possessed the authority to consent." *Id.* [Emphasis in original.]

Preliminarily, the United States Supreme Court agreed that on the basis of this record, the State failed to meet its burden of establishing

Fischer's common authority over the apartment, that is, her mutual use of the property for most purposes. "The evidence showed that although Fischer, with her two small children, had lived with Rodriguez beginning in December 1984, she had moved out on July 1, 1985, almost a month before the search at issue here, and had gone to live with her mother. She took her and her children's clothing with her, though leaving behind some furniture and household effects. During the period after July 1, she sometimes spent the night at Rodriguez's apartment, but never invited her friends there, and never went there herself when he was not home. Her name was not on the lease nor did she contribute to the rent. She had a key to the apartment, which she said at trial she had taken without Rodriguez's knowledge[.]" *Id.* at 2797-98. "On these facts," states the Court, "the State has not established that, with respect to [Rodriguez's] apartment, Fischer had 'joint access or control for most purposes.'" *Id.* at 2798. To the contrary, Fischer had no common authority over the apartment. *Id.*

The State contends, however, that "even if Fischer did not in fact have authority to give consent, it suffices to validate the entry that the law enforcement officers reasonably believed she did." *Id. The Supreme Court agreed.*

"The fundamental objective that alone validates all unconsented government searches is, of course, the seizure of persons who have committed or are about to commit crimes, or of evidence related to crimes. But 'reasonableness,' with respect to this necessary element, does not demand that the government be factually correct in its assessment that that is what a search will produce." *Id.* at 2799. For example, "[w]arrants need only be supported by 'probable cause,' which demands no more than a proper 'assessment of probabilities in particular factual contexts[.] * * * ' If a magistrate, based upon seemingly reliable but factually incorrect information, issues a warrant for the search of a house in which the sought after felon is not present, has never been present, and was never likely to have been present, the owner of that house suffers one of the inconveniences we all expose ourselves to as the cost of living in a safe society; he does not suffer a violation of the Fourth Amendment." *Id.*

The Court has never held "that the Fourth Amendment requires factual accuracy." *Id.* Thus, in *Hill v. California*, 401 *U.S.* 797, 91 *S.Ct.* 1106 (1971), the Court upheld a search incident to an arrest, even though the arrest was made of the wrong person. The Court there reasoned:

> "The upshot was that the officers in good faith believed Miller was Hill and arrested him. They were quite wrong as it turned out, and subjective good-faith belief would not in itself justify either the arrest or the subsequent search. But sufficient probability, not certainty, is the touchstone of reasonableness under the Fourth Amendment and on the record before us the officers' mistake was understandable and the arrest a reasonable response to the situation facing them at the time."

Rodriguez at 2800 (quoting *Hill* at 803-804, 91 *S.Ct.* at 1110-11).

"It is apparent that in order to satisfy the 'reasonableness' requirement of the Fourth Amendment, what is generally demanded of the many factual determinations that must regularly be made by agents of the government—whether the magistrate issuing a warrant, the police officer executing a warrant, or the police officer conducting a search or seizure under one of the exceptions to the warrant requirement—*is not that they always be correct, but that they always be reasonable." Id.* [Emphasis added.] As stated in *Brinegar v. United States,* 338 *U.S.* 160, 69 *S.Ct.* 1302 (1949):

> "Because many situations which confront officers in the course of executing their duties are more or less ambiguous, room must be allowed for some mistakes on their part. But the mistakes must be those of reasonable men, acting on facts leading sensibly to their conclusions of probability."

Rodriguez at 2800 (quoting *Brinegar* at 176, 69 *S.Ct.* at 1311).

Accordingly, the Court holds that the same principles apply to "facts bearing upon the authority to consent to a search. Whether the basis for such authority exists is the sort of recurring factual question to which law enforcement officers must be expected to apply their judgment; and all the Fourth Amendment requires is that they answer it reasonably. The Constitution is no more violated when officers enter without a warrant because they reasonably (though erroneously) believe that the person who has consented to their entry is a resident of the premises, than it is violated when they enter without a warrant because they reasonably (though erroneously) believe they are in pursuit of a violent felon who is about to escape." *Id.*

The case is reversed and remanded to the Illinois court for a determination whether the officers reasonably believed that Fischer had the authority to consent.

NOTE

1. *Third-party consents to be judged against an "objective standard."* During the course of the Court's opinion in Rodriguez, it cautioned:

> [W]hat we hold today does not suggest that law enforcement officers may always accept a person's invitation to enter premises. Even when the invitation is accompanied by an explicit assertion that the person lives there, the surrounding circumstances could conceivably be such that a reasonable person would doubt its truth and not act upon it without further inquiry. As with other factual determinations bearing upon search and seizure, determination of consent * * * must "be judged against an objective standard: would the facts available to the officer at the moment . . . 'warrant a man of reasonable caution in the belief' " that the consenting party had authority over the premises ? * * * If not, then warrantless entry is unlawful unless authority actually exists. But if so, the search is valid.

Id. at 2801. [Citations omitted.]

2. To assess whether apparent authority exists, officers should "look for indicia of actual authority." *United States v. Saadeh*, 61 *F*.3d 510, 517 (7th Cir. 1995). " 'The question is not who comes to the door so much as it is whether whoever appears there projects an aura of authority upon which one can reasonably rely.' " *Id.* (quoting *United States v. Rosario*, 962 *F*.2d 733, 738 (7th Cir. 1992)).

3. *Live-in caretakers.* In *United States v. Dearing*, 9 *F*.3d 1428 (9th Cir. 1993), defendant, a single, custodial parent of two teenaged children, hired Don Blevins to assist him in caring for his daughter Michele, who has cerebral palsy. Blevins also helped with the housekeeping. In exchange for his services, Blevins received a room and salary.

Six months after he was hired, while defendant was out of town with Michele, Blevins called an agent of the Bureau of Alcohol, Tobacco and Firearms. He told her that he lived in the house to help with defendant's daughter, and had seen in defendant's bedroom what he thought was a machine gun. Blevins also provided the agent with the serial numbers from the gun.

Several days later, the ATF agent met Blevins at defendant's home and secured his consent for a search. Blevins told the agent that he had access to the entire house, and then signed a written consent-to-search form. Blevins also stated that he was planning to move out of the house soon. The search uncovered a fully automatic machine gun, found in defendant's bedroom.

Granting defendant's motion to suppress, the district court ruled that Blevins had neither actual nor apparent authority to consent. The Ninth Circuit agreed.

"A consensual search is reasonable when the consent-giver has authority over the area searched. * * * A third party has *actual authority* when he has 'mutual use of the property [and also has] joint access or control for most purposes.' * * * When the facts do not support a finding of actual authority, a search is reasonable if the consent-giver *apparently* has actual authority." *Id.* at 1429. [Court's emphasis; citations omitted.]

"The existence of apparent authority entails a three-part analysis. First, did the searching officer believe some untrue fact that was then used to assess the extent of the consent-giver's use of and access to or control over the area searched ? * * * Second, was it under the circumstances objectively reasonable to believe that the fact was true ? * * * Finally, assuming the truth of the reasonably believed but untrue fact, would the consent-giver have had actual authority ?" *Id.* at 1429-30.

Preliminarily, the court agreed with the district judge that Blevins did not have actual authority over defendant's bedroom. According to the district judge, "[n]ot only did [Blevins] lack joint access or control for most purposes, he lacked it for *any purpose.*" *Id.* at 1430. [Court's emphasis.]

Therefore, the critical question was whether the agent's mistaken belief that Blevins had authority over the bedroom was objectively reasonable. Holding that it was not, the court stated:

At the time of the search, [the agent] knew that Blevins lived in the house as caretaker and occasional housekeeper. Her belief that he had authority over the common areas of the house was clearly reasonable. But she also believed that Blevins had use of and access to or control over [defendant's] bedroom. The district judge found that this belief was not objectively reasonable. We agree.

[The ATF agent] knew only that Blevins had been in the bedroom on prior occasions. The mere fact of access, without more, does not indicate that the access was authorized. The bedroom door was closed at the time of the search. Blevins said and did nothing to indicate that [defendant] knew of, or authorized, his excursions into the bedroom. And [the agent] knew that Blevins' relationship with [defendant] was nearing an end. But she never inquired into the extent of Blevins' currently authorized access to the bedroom, or the extent to which [defendant] kept his bedroom off-limits. Under these circumstances, the district judge held that a reasonable agent would have inquired further, and we agree. * * * Here, the lack of knowledge about the extent of Blevins' permission to enter [defendant's] bedroom is precisely what made [the agent's] reliance on Blevins' assertions unreasonable.

Id.

4. *Personal property found within an automobile.* In *United States v. Welch*, 4 *F.*3d 761 (9th Cir. 1993), Welch and her co-defendant, McGee, were detained at the Circus Circus Hotel in Las Vegas on suspicion of passing counterfeit twenty-dollar bills. McGee consented to a general search of the rental car that he and Welch had driven to Las Vegas. During the search, officers located a woman's purse in the trunk. They opened the purse and discovered Welch's driver's license inside, along with $500 in counterfeit twenty-dollar bills.

Holding that McGee had no authority to consent to a search of Welch's purse, the court explained:

The government has the burden of establishing the effectiveness of a third party consent. * * * It can do so in three ways. First, the government can come forward with persuasive evidence of both shared use *and* joint access to or control over a searched area, which would demonstrate actual authority to consent. * * * Second, it can show that the owner of the property to be searched has expressly authorized a third party to give consent to the search. Finally, it may establish consent by means of the "apparent authority doctrine." * * *

First,—as to actual authority—McGee could lawfully give consent to a search of the rental car because he and Welch had joint access to and mutual use of it. * * * By sharing access to and use of the car with McGee, Welch relinquished, in part, her expectation of privacy in the vehicle. * * * [But,] Welch's purse is another matter entirely. The fact that she had a limited expectation of privacy in the car by virtue of her sharing arrangement with McGee does not mean that she had similarly limited privacy expectations in items within the car which are independently the subject of such expectations. The shared control of "host" property does not serve to forfeit the expectation of privacy in containers within that property. * * *

Here, there is no question that Welch had a reasonable expectation of privacy in the contents of her purse. Indeed, a purse is a type of container in which a person possesses the highest expectations of privacy. * * * Therefore, the government must show shared control with respect to the purse as well as with respect to the vehicle if it is to prevail on a mutual use and joint control theory. In this case it cannot do so; there is simply nothing in the record demonstrating that McGee had use of, let alone joint access to or shared control over, Welch's purse. * * * Thus, the first theory is of no avail.

Little need be said with regard to the second means by which effective third-party consent could be established—express authorization. There is simply nothing in the record which indicates that Welch expressly authorized McGee to give consent to a search of her purse. The remaining question, therefore, is whether consent can be deemed effective as an exercise of apparent authority.

Under the apparent authority doctrine, a search is valid if the government proves that the officers who conducted it reasonably believed that the person from whom they obtained consent had the actual authority to grant that consent. However, the doctrine is applicable only if the facts believed by the officers to be true would justify the search as a matter of law. * * * A mistaken belief as to the law, no matter how reasonable, is not sufficient. * * *

When the [] officers decided to search Welch's purse, they knew that 1) she was McGee's girlfriend, 2) she had traveled with him to Las Vegas in the rental car, and 3) the handbag in the trunk of the car belonged to a woman. There is nothing about these facts that would have led a reasonable officer to believe that Welch had expressly given McGee authority to consent to the search of the purse. Nor would any of these facts have caused a reasonable officer to believe that McGee shared the use of and had joint access to or control over Welch's purse and that the search was justified for that reason. Moreover, any such belief would have necessarily rested on the erroneous legal assumption that the mere presence of the handbag in the trunk gave McGee control over it or access to its contents, or, to put it differently, that Welch's leaving the purse in the car gave McGee the right to open it without her consent. Such an assumption would have been erroneous and would have reflected a mistaken belief as to the law. * * * Therefore the facts available to the officers at the time of the search do not support application of the apparent authority doctrine.

* * * Because the government failed to carry its burden of demonstrating that the consent to search Welch's purse was valid, we must hold the search unlawful.

Id. at 764-65. [Citations omitted; court's emphasis.]

GEORGIA v. RANDOLPH
Supreme Court of the United States
547 *U.S.* 103, 126 *S.Ct.* 1515 (2006)

QUESTION: Can the police search the common areas of a home based on the consent of one occupant, when the other co-occupant is present and objects to the search?

ANSWER: NO. The police are not permitted to conduct a search of a premises based on the consent of one occupant, when a co-occupant is physically present and objects to the search.

RATIONALE: In early July, as a result of a domestic dispute, Janet Randolph contacted the police to report that her husband, defendant Scott Randolph, took their son away. When officers arrived at the residence, Janet told them that her husband was "a cocaine user whose habit had caused financial troubles. She mentioned the marital problems and said that she and their son had only recently returned after a stay of several weeks with her parents." *Id.* at 1519. Minutes later, Scott Randolph returned and explained that he had taken the child to a neighbor's home. Upon questioning, he told the police that he did not use cocaine, and countered that it was, in fact, his wife who abused drugs and alcohol.

"One of the officers, Sergeant Murray, went with Janet Randolph to reclaim the child, and when they returned she not only renewed her complaints about her husband's drug use, but also volunteered that there were 'items of drug evidence' in the house. Sergeant Murray asked Scott Randolph for permission to search the house, which he unequivocally refused." *Id.*

The sergeant then asked Janet for consent to search, which she readily gave. Janet escorted Sergeant Murray upstairs to Scott's bedroom, where he discovered a quantity of suspected cocaine. Subsequently, Scott Randolph was indicted for possession of cocaine.

In this appeal, the United States Supreme Court addressed the issue of whether one occupant may give law enforcement effective consent to search shared premises, when a co-occupant is physically present and objects to the search.

As a general matter, the Fourth Amendment permits the police to make a warrantless entry and search of premises based on the voluntary consent of a third party—generally an occupant—who shares "common authority" over the premises or effects sought to be inspected. "Common authority," in this respect, does not rest on the third party's "property interest." Rather, "common authority" rests on "mutual use of the property by persons generally having joint access or control for most purposes." *United States v. Matlock,* 415 *U.S.* 164, 171 n.7, 94 *S.Ct.* 988, 993 n.7 (1974).

In *Illinois v. Rodriguez,* 497 *U.S.* 177, 110 *S.Ct.* 2793 (1990), the Court extended the rule of *Matlock* to cover a warrantless search based on the consent of a person whom the police reasonably, albeit mistakenly, believed had common authority over the premises. Thus, the warrantless entry and search of a home is lawful when the police obtain the voluntary consent of an occupant who shares, *or is reasonably believed to share,* authority over the area in common with a co-occupant who may later object to the use of any evidence so obtained.

Significantly, in *Matlock,* the defendant was not present with the opportunity to object to the co-occupant's consent; defendant was in a squad car not far away. Also, in *Rodriguez,* the defendant was actually asleep in the apartment, but was not at the door when the apparent co-occupant consented to the police entry.

Here, in *Randolph,* the Court addressed the missing component of the earlier cases, namely, the situation where the police have obtained a voluntary consent to search from the occupant of a home when a co-occupant is physically present at the scene and expressly objects to the proposed search.

The Court held that *"a physically present co-occupant's stated refusal to permit entry prevails,* rendering the warrantless search unreasonable and invalid as to him." *Id.* at 1519. [Emphasis added.] Said the Court:

> Unless the people living together fall within some recognized hierarchy, like a household of parent and child or barracks housing military personnel of different grades, there is no societal understanding of superior and inferior * * *. The law does not ask who has the better side of the conflict * * *.

> Since the co-tenant wishing to open the door to a third party has no recognized authority in law or social practice to prevail over a present and objecting co-tenant, his disputed invitation, without more, gives a police officer no better claim to reasonableness in entering than the officer would have in the absence of any consent at all.

* * * *

> Yes, we recognize the consenting tenant's interest as a citizen in bringing criminal activity to light * * *. And we understand a co-tenant's legitimate self-interest in siding with the police to deflect suspicion raised by sharing quarters with a criminal * * *. But society can often have the benefit of these interests without relying on a theory of consent that ignores an inhabitant's refusal to allow a warrantless search. The co-tenant acting on his own initiative may be able to deliver evidence to the police[,] and can tell the po-

lice what he knows, for use before a [judge] in getting a warrant.
* * *

Id. at 1523-24.

During the course of its opinion, the Court rejected the dissent's contention that such a rule would potentially shield spousal abusers and other violent co-tenants who will refuse to allow the police to enter a dwelling when their victims call for help. This case, noted the Court, has no adverse effect on the ability of the police to protect victims of domestic abuse. Naturally, the police have the authority to enter a dwelling to protect a resident from domestic violence or from the threat of violence, so long as they have good reason to believe such a threat exists. "Thus, the question whether the police might lawfully enter over objection in order to provide any protection that might be reasonable is easily answered yes." *Id.* at 1525. In cases where the defendant has victimized a third party, " 'the emergency nature of the situation is such that the third-party consent should validate a warrantless search despite a defendant's objections.' " *Id.* at 1526. [Citations omitted.]

Accordingly, "a warrantless search of a shared dwelling for evidence over the express refusal of consent by a physically present resident cannot be justified as reasonable as to him on the basis of consent given to the police by another resident." *Id.*

The Court's ruling sets forth a fine-line distinction between the facts of this case and those of *United States v. Matlock* and *Illinois v. Rodriguez*:

> [I]f a potential defendant with self-interest in objecting is in fact at the door and objects, the co-tenant's permission does not suffice for a reasonable search, whereas the potential objector, nearby but not invited to take part in the threshold colloquy, loses out.

> This is the line we draw, and we think the formalism is justified. So long as there is no evidence that the police have removed the potentially objecting tenant from the entrance for the sake of avoiding a possible objection, there is practical value in the simple clarity of complementary rules, one recognizing the co-tenant's permission when there is no fellow occupant on hand, the other according dispositive weight to the fellow occupant's contrary indication when he expresses it. * * * [It would simply be unreasonable to require] the police to take affirmative steps to find a potentially objecting co-tenant before acting on the permission they had already received. * * *

Randolph at 1527.

In applying the rule set forth above to the facts of this case, the Court found it clear that defendant Scott Randolph—a cohabitant who was physically present—expressly objected to the police search. This objection was dispositive as to him, regardless of the consent of his wife. Moreover, there were no facts in this case to justify the search on grounds independent of Janet Randolph's consent. There was no indication that she was in need of police protection inside the home. Moreover, there were no facts to justify "the entry and search under the rubric of exigent circumstances, owing to some apprehension by the police officers that Scott Randolph would destroy evidence of drug use before any warrant could be obtained." *Id.* at 1528.

Consequently, the police entry and search in this case violated the Fourth Amendment.

NOTE

1. During the course of its opinion in *Randolph*, the Court noted that there may be times when a co-tenant, acting on her own initiative, may be able to deliver evidence to the police, *see e.g., Coolidge v. New Hampshire*, 403 *U.S.* 443, 91 *S.Ct.* 2022 (1971) (suspect's wife retrieved his guns from the couple's house and turned them over to the police), or may tell the police what she knows, for use in obtaining a warrant. "Sometimes, of course, the very exchange of information like this in front of the objecting inhabitant may render consent irrelevant by creating an exigency that justifies immediate action on the police's part[.]" *Randolph* at 1524 n.6.

2. *Timing a request for consent to search when officers know the target would be out of town.* In *Commonwealth v. Yancoskie*, 915 A.2d 111 (Pa.Super. 2006), during an investigation, narcotics agents learned from defendant's wife, Deborah Yancoskie, that she intended to leave her husband, and that she wanted to notify law enforcement authorities of defendant's illegal marijuana manufacturing operation. On April 12th, Deborah advised the agents that defendant was scheduled to be out of town on a fishing trip the following week. Thereafter, on April 20th, the agents entered defendant's home and obtained Deborah's written consent for a search of the house. The search uncovered, among other things, marijuana, drug paraphernalia, a pistol, and more than $90,000.

In this appeal, defendant argued that his wife's consent was invalid under *Randolph, supra,* because the agents purposely waited until he was out of town to go to his residence. *The Superior Court disagreed.*

In *Georgia v. Randolph, supra,* the Court held that "a warrantless search of a shared dwelling for evidence *over the express refusal of consent by a physically present resident* cannot be justified as reasonable as to him on the basis of consent given to the police by another resident." *Id.,* 126 *S.Ct.* at 1526. [Emphasis added.] The Court noted, however, that its holding may not benefit a co-occupant who has a self-interest in objecting to a search, but, because they may be a short distance away, are not invited to take part in the process.

Acknowledging that it was "drawing a fine line," the Court in *Randolph* explained:

"This is the line we draw, and we think the formalism is justified. *So long as there is no evidence that the police have removed the potentially objecting tenant from the entrance for the sake of avoiding a possible objection*, there is practical value in the simple clarity of complementary rules, one recognizing the cotenant's permission when there is no fellow occupant on hand, the other according dispositive weight to the fellow occupant's contrary indication when he expresses it."

Yancoskie at 114 (quoting *Randolph* at 1527). [Emphasis added.]

Relying on the above-italicized language, defendant contended that the agents' search of his residence was unreasonable, because, "by purposely timing their search to coincide with [his] out-of-town fishing trip, the police removed [him] 'from the entrance for the sake of avoiding a possible objection.'" *Id.* at 115. [Citation omitted.] The court rejected this contention.

The Supreme Court's analysis in *Randolph* made it clear that the police are not required to take affirmative steps to find a potentially objecting co-tenant before acting on the permission they had already received. Although the record in this case supports defendant's assertion that the agents timed their request for his wife's consent to search the house with a time when they knew defendant would be out of town, the court could not conclude that such a strategy amounted "to a police removal of [defendant] from the entrance to his home under *Randolph*. Indeed, there is no evidence that [defendant's] fishing trip was anything other than of his own volition." *Id.*

Accordingly, the court held that "by voluntarily absenting himself from the house he shared with [his wife], the contents of which he obviously was aware, [defendant] assumed the risk that [she] would allow someone else, namely, the agents, to conduct a search." *Id.*

---

§3.6(d). Scope of consent.

FLORIDA v. JIMENO
Supreme Court of the United States
500 U.S. 248, 111 S.Ct. 1801 (1991)

QUESTION: Will a motorist's consent to a general search of his automobile extend to closed containers found inside the vehicle when, under the circumstances, it is objectively reasonable for the searching officer to believe that the scope of the consent permitted the opening of closed containers located within the vehicle ?

ANSWER. YES. When, after a motorist gives a police officer permission to search his automobile, the officer opens a closed container found within the car that might reasonably hold the object of the search, the Fourth Amendment will be satisfied so long as, "under the circumstances, it is objectively reasonable for the [searching] officer to believe that the scope of the suspect's consent permitted him to open a particular container within the automobile." *Id.* at 1803.

RATIONALE: During the course of a motor vehicle stop for a minor traffic violation, Dade County Police Officer Frank Trujillo asked the driver, defendant Jimeno, for permission to search the car. At the time of the request, the officer had grounds to suspect that Jimeno was transporting narcotics in his car, and in fact advised Jimeno of his suspicions. Officer Trujillo additionally advised Jimeno that he did not have to consent to the search. Jimeno stated that he "had nothing to hide," and gave the officer permission to search the car. Trujillo walked over "to the passenger side, opened the door, and saw a folded, brown paper bag on the floorboard. The officer picked up the bag, opened it, and found a kilogram of cocaine inside." *Id.* at 1803.

At his suppression hearing, defendant argued that "his consent to search the car did not extend to the closed paper bag inside the car." *Id.* The trial court granted his motion and the Florida District Court of Appeal affirmed, concluding that a "consent to a general search for narcotics does not extend to 'sealed containers within the general area agreed to by the defendant.'" *Id.* [Citation omitted.] *The United States Supreme Court disagreed and reversed.*

"The touchstone of the Fourth Amendment is reasonableness. * * * The Fourth Amendment does not proscribe all state-initiated searches and seizures; it merely proscribes those which are unreasonable. * * * Thus, [this Court has] long approved consensual searches because it is no doubt reasonable for the police to conduct a search once they have been permitted to do so." *Id.* [Citations omitted.] "The standard for measuring the scope of a suspect's consent under the Fourth Amendment is that of 'objective reasonableness'—what would the typical reasonable person have understood by the exchange between the officer and the suspect?" *Id.* at 1803-04.

The critical question in this case, then, "is whether it is reasonable for an officer to consider a suspect's general consent to a search of his car to include consent to examine a paper bag lying on the floor of the car." *Id.* at 1804. According to the Court, it is reasonable. *Id.*

"The scope of a search is generally defined by its expressed object. * * * In this case, the terms of the search's authorization were simple. [Jimeno] granted Officer Trujillo permission to search his car, and did not place any explicit limitation on the scope of the search. Trujillo had informed [Jimeno] that he believed [Jimeno] was carrying narcotics, and that he would be looking for narcotics in the car." *Id.* It was, therefore, "objectively reasonable for the police to conclude that the general consent to search [Jimeno's] car included consent to search containers within that car which might bear drugs. A reasonable person may be expected to know that narcotics are generally carried in some form of container. 'Contraband goods rarely are strewn across the trunk or floor of a car.'" *Id.* [Citation omitted.] Accordingly, "the authorization to search in this case * * * extended beyond the surfaces of the car's interior to the paper bag lying on the car's floor." *Id.*

NOTE

1. *Locked containers and compartments.*

(a) The Court in *Jimeno* emphasized that a search of a motor vehicle conducted under the authority of a general consent could not extend to the forcible entry of a locked briefcase located inside the vehicle. In this respect, the Court stated, "[i]t is very likely unreasonable to think that a suspect, by consenting to the search of his trunk, has agreed to the breaking open of a locked briefcase within the trunk, but it is otherwise with respect to a closed paper bag." *Id.* at 1804.

At the Supreme Court, Jimeno also argued that "if police wish to search closed containers within a car they must separately request permission to search each container." *Id.* Rejecting this contention, the Court emphasized:

> [W]e see no basis for adding this sort of superstructure to the Fourth Amendment's basic test of objective reasonableness. * * * A suspect may of course delimit as he chooses the scope of the search to which he consents. But if his consent would reasonably be understood to extend to a particular container, the Fourth Amendment provides no grounds for requiring a more explicit authorization.

Id.

(b) Compare United States v. Martinez, 949 *F.*2d 1117 (11th Cir. 1992), where the court held that a general consent to search a locked "mini-storage unit" for drugs included permission to pry open and search the locked trunk of an automobile stored inside. The court reasoned:

> In this case, Martinez consented to a search of the mini-storage unit leased in her name. Neither the document she signed nor her oral statements to the police placed any limitations on the agents' authority to search the mini-warehouse. The question thus becomes whether Martinez's general consent included permission to search the locked trunk of the 1949 Dodge located therein. * * *
>
> As this court has noted, "When an individual gives a general statement of consent without express limitations, the scope of a permissible search is not limitless. Rather, it is constrained by the bounds of reasonableness: what a police officer could reasonably interpret the consent to encompass." * * * In conducting the reasonableness inquiry, the court must consider what the parties knew at the time to be the object of the search. * * * *Permission to search a specific area for narcotics, for example, may be construed as permission to search any compartment or container within the specified area where narcotics may be found.* * * * On the other hand, general permission to search does not include permission to inflict intentional damage to the places or things to be searched.

In this case, Martinez understood that the officers wanted to search the mini-warehouse unit for narcotics. Under the reasonableness inquiry, her permission to search the mini-warehouse could be construed as permission to search any compartment or container therein that might reasonably contain narcotics, including the 1949 Dodge.

Id. at 1119-20. [Citations omitted; emphasis added.]

The difficulty in this case, however, is that the trunk of the car was locked and the police had to pry it open. According to Martinez, the police exceeded the scope of her consent by "breaking the trunk lock." The court disagreed.

Analogizing the scope of a general consent to search with that of a search warrant, the court held that "a general consent to search a specific area for specific things includes consent to open locked containers that may contain the objects of the search, in the same manner that such locked containers would be subject to search pursuant to a valid warrant." *Id.* at 1120. In this respect,

the limits of a consensual search are defined by the terms of the consent in the same way that the scope of a warrant search is defined by the specifications of the warrant. * * * Where a warrant has been issued, "a lawful search of fixed premises generally extends to the entire area in which the object of the search may be found and is not limited by the possibility that separate acts of entry or opening may be required to complete the search."

* * * In this case, the locked trunk was within the scope of Martinez's consent because it was within the area authorized to be searched, and it was reasonably capable of containing the object of the search * * *

As to prying open the trunk, the record does not show, and Martinez does not allege, that it involved [any sort of] "mutilation" [of the automobile]. Indeed, * * * forcing open locked compartments or containers has been held to be within the scope of general warrant searches and consent searches. * * *

Id. at 1120-21. [Citations omitted.]

2. *Failure to state the purpose of a consent search.* In *United States v. Snow,* 44 *F.*3d 133 (2nd Cir. 1995), defendant was a passenger in an automobile stopped by the police on Route 490 in Monroe County, New York. The vehicle, which was stopped for a number of traffic violations, was owned by defendant. During the course of the stop, the officer asked for and obtained defendant's consent to search the car. At no time did the officer advise defendant of the reason for, or object of, the search. In the back seat, the officer discovered a duffel bag, which he opened. Inside he found parts for an automatic pistol. The officer also found marijuana inside a closed bag jammed under the back seat of the car.

In this appeal, the court rejected defendant's contention that the police officer's failure to inform him of the reason for, or object of, the consent search rendered the search of the two bags outside the scope of his consent, and therefore unlawful. The court stated:

> * * * Snow was not informed of the purpose of the search, and now argues that this missing factor from the *Jimeno* equation requires a different result. We disagree.
>
> The inquiry under *Jimeno* is the same: "whether it is reasonable for an officer to consider a suspect's general consent to a search of his car to include consent to examine a paper bag lying on the floor of the car." * * * What meaning would a reasonable person attach to the word "search" ?
>
> The word "search" carries a common meaning to the average person. Dictionary definitions furnish some guide: "to go over or look through for the purpose of finding something; explore; rummage; examine," "to examine closely and carefully; test and try; probe," "to find out or uncover by investigation." *Webster's New World Dictionary* 1210 (3d ed. 1988). The Oxford English Dictionary (2d ed. 1989) is not much different: "examination or scrutiny for the purpose of finding a person or thing," "look though, examine internally (a building, an apartment, a receptacle of any kind) in quest of some object concealed or lost." *Id.* at 804, 805.
>
> Thus, under either the King's or the Colonist's English, the term "search" implies something more than a superficial, external examination. It entails "looking through," "rummaging," "probing," "scrutiny," and "examining internally."

Id. at 135. [Citation omitted.]

Accordingly, the court held that "[b]ased on the plain meaning of the word 'search,' an individual who consents to a search of his car should reasonably expect that readily-opened, [closed] containers discovered inside the car will be opened and examined." *Id.* at 136.

3. *An officer's request to "have a look in" a motorist's automobile.* In *United States v. Rich*, 992 F.2d 502, 503 (5th Cir. 1993), the court held that an individual's affirmative response to a police officer's request to "have a look in" the individual's automobile was the functional equivalent of a general consent to search the automobile and its contents, including the individual's luggage. Rich was stopped at 11:35 p.m. by a Texas Department of Public Safety trooper for driving a pickup truck with a burned-out license plate light. During the course of the motor vehicle stop, the trooper developed grounds to suspect that Rich may have been transporting narcotics. As a result, the trooper asked Rich whether he had any narcotics or weapons in the vehicle. Rich stated that he did not. The trooper then asked, "Can I have a look in your truck ?" Rich did not respond right away. However, after several more requests, Rich said yes, and the trooper instructed

him to go stand back near the patrol car. The officer entered Rich's pickup truck, pulled out a suitcase that was resting behind the passenger seat and opened it. The suitcase contained marijuana packed in fabric softener tissues.

Finding the consent and subsequent search valid under the Fourth Amendment, the court preliminarily observed:

> "The standard for measuring the scope of a suspect's consent under the Fourth Amendment is that of 'objective' reasonableness[.]" * * * The key inquiry focuses on what the "typical reasonable person [would] have understood by the exchange between the officer and the suspect."

Id. at 505. [Citation omitted.]

In this appeal, Rich contended that the trooper's request to "have a look in" the truck—under the "objective reasonableness" standard— was "only a request to 'see inside' the vehicle." *Id.* at 506. In a similar vein, the lower court rested its decision to suppress the evidence in part on the failure of the trooper to use the more precise term "search" in his request. Rejecting Rich's contention and reversing the court below, the Fifth Circuit Court of Appeals stated:

> We decline the defendant's invitation to establish a list of specific terms from which an officer must select the most appropriate for each individual situation and/or defendant. To so hamper law enforcement officials in their everyday duties would be an unjustified extension of the Fourth Amendment's requirement that searches be reasonable. Several other circuits have held that a request to "look in" or "look through" a vehicle is the equivalent of a request to "search" the vehicle. We take this opportunity to establish a similar rule for our own circuit: it is not necessary for an officer specifically to use the term "search" when he requests consent from an individual to search a vehicle. We hold that any words, when viewed in context, that objectively communicate to a reasonable individual that the officer is requesting permission to examine the vehicle and its contents constitute a valid search request for Fourth Amendment purposes.

Id.

The court held, therefore, that the trooper's request to "have a look in" Rich's pickup truck effectively communicated to Rich that the officer was asking for his consent to search the vehicle. The court further determined that the consent contemplated a search of the luggage.

> When the conversation between [the trooper] and Rich is considered *in toto*, it is indisputable that Rich knew that the object of [the officer's] search was illegal weapons or narcotics. * * * [I]f, as a result of the verbal exchange, an objectively reasonable individual would understand the object of the officer's search, then the object of the search has been sufficiently delineated for purposes of

the Fourth Amendment. We are convinced that such delineation took place in this case.

Id. at 506-07.

Finally, the court addressed Rich's contention that, because he was told to stand away from the truck, he did not have the opportunity to object to the search or limit its scope. And, continued Rich, even if he could have seen what the trooper was doing, the search took place so quickly that he did not have time to object. In this respect, the court said:

> Even if Rich was unable to see what was going on, however, we are unwilling to read [*Florida v.*] *Jimeno* to hold, as Rich suggests, that enforcement officials must conduct all searches in plain view of the suspect, and in a manner slowly enough that he may withdraw or delimit his consent at any time during the search. When the [*Jimeno* C]ourt stated that "[a] suspect may of course delimit as he chooses the scope of the search to which he consents," it meant that Rich, knowing the contents of the vehicle and its various containers at the time he gave his consent, had the responsibility to limit the scope of the consent if he deemed it necessary to do so. Rich knew what containers were in the truck when he gave his consent to search; he had the ability at that time to impose any restrictions he saw fit on the scope of that consent. The fact that the search was not conducted in a manner that made it conducive or even possible for Rich to later withdraw or limit his consent does not automatically make that search violative of the Fourth Amendment. Under the facts of this case, we find that the scope of Rich's consent was not violated by this lack of opportunity to limit or withdraw his consent.

Id. at 507.

The Supreme Court in *Jimeno* made clear that, if a suspect's consent "would reasonably be understood to extend to a particular container, the Fourth Amendment provides no grounds for requiring a more explicit authorization." *Jimeno*, 111 *S.Ct.* at 1804. Here, in *Rich*, the Fifth Circuit similarly determined that it was "objectively reasonable" for the trooper "to conclude that Rich's consent to search the vehicle included his consent to search containers found within the vehicle that could hold illegal narcotics or weapons, the expressed object of [the trooper's] search." *Rich* at 508.

4. *Vehicles containing more than one occupant.* In *United States v. Infante-Ruiz*, 13 *F*.3d 498 (1st Cir. 1994), police stopped the vehicle defendant was occupying for the purpose of arresting him on an outstanding warrant for a federal narcotics charge. After defendant was placed under arrest, one of the officers asked the driver of the car, Felipe de la Paz, for consent to search the vehicle. De la Paz verbally gave consent and the officer searched the passenger compartment. The officer then asked de la Paz for the key to the car's trunk. De la Paz

handed over the key and stood without objection as the trunk was searched. Inside the trunk were two briefcases, one black and one brown. When asked, de la Paz said that he owned the brown briefcase. The officer opened the briefcase and searched it without objection from de la Paz. The officer then asked who owned the black briefcase. De la Paz said that it belonged to the defendant, Infante. Without specifically asking defendant or de la Paz for permission to search the black briefcase, the officer unlocked and opened it. Inside, he discovered various documents belonging to defendant, as well as items belonging to de la Paz, and a loaded .22 caliber Derringer pistol.

Finding the consent provided by de la Paz to be invalid as to the black briefcase, the court held that it was not reasonable for the police officers to have believed that de la Paz gave his consent, or had the authority to consent, to a search of Infante's briefcase. *Id.* at 504. The court elaborated:

> What leads us to hold that the scope of de la Paz's consent did *not* include defendant's briefcase, is that de la Paz's general permission to search the car and its trunk was qualified by de la Paz's further statement to the officer, before the latter opened and searched the briefcase, that the briefcase belonged to Infante. Even though Infante was nearby, handcuffed in the squad car, the police officers never sought his permission to search his briefcase. We do not think that it was "objectively reasonable," in these circumstances, for the officer to believe that de la Paz's prior consent to search the vehicle and its trunk encompassed opening that particular briefcase, later clearly identified by de la Paz as belonging solely to another nearby passenger. De la Paz's identification of the briefcase as belonging to another nearby passenger suggested precisely the contrary. * * * At the very least, the scope of de la Paz's consent was ambiguous—an ambiguity that could have been but was not clarified by further inquiry of de la Paz, Infante or both.

Id. at 505. [Court's emphasis.]

5. *General consent to search home includes authorization to forcibly remove boards blocking entrance to the home's attic.* In *United States v. Ibarra*, 948 F.2d 903 (5th Cir. 1991), Houston police obtained defendant's general consent to search his house and garage for evidence of money laundering and drug trafficking. On their first time through the house, the officers uncovered evidence of money laundering. On the second time through, one of the officers noted the presence of an attic, but found that its entrance, located in the bedroom closet, was boarded up. The officer used the handle of a sledgehammer to knock out the boards. Upon entering the attic, the police found nearly $1,000,000 in cash, ledgers, and a money counting machine.

Finding the entry of the attic and seizure of evidence within the scope of defendant's consent, the court observed:

Nothing in the record suggests that the police disturbed the structural integrity of the * * * house. * * * [T]he house was built with an attic space and [] a passageway to this space was located in the bedroom closet. Though the entrance was covered with boards, one officer testified that through them he could see what appeared to be a bag. The police did not alter the frame of the house; they merely removed a barrier blocking a visible, pre-existing passageway.

The removal of such a barrier does not constitute the type of brutal conduct that implicates the Due Process Clause. * * *

Nor does the entrance to the attic constitute a Fourth Amendment violation. * * *

Whether [defendant] agreed to a search of the attic is a question of objective reasonableness: would "the typical reasonable person" understand the consent to extend to the attic? [Defendant] consented to a general search of the premises for evidence of drug trafficking and money laundering. He did not limit the search in any way, at any time, though he was present throughout its duration. We find that an objective onlooker could understand this consent to extend to all integral parts of the house—closets, attic, and basement included.

Id. at 906-907. [Citations omitted.]

6. *Consent to search an individual's person.*

(a) Does a general request to conduct a body search for drugs reasonably contemplate a "traditional frisk search" of the crotch area? In *United States v. Rodney*, 956 *F.*2d 295 (D.C. Cir. 1992), the court said it does.

Rodney had stepped off a bus that had arrived in Washington, D.C., from New York City. As Rodney left the station, Detective Beard, dressed in plain clothes, approached him from behind, displayed his police identification and asked if Rodney would speak to him. A second officer stood nearby. Rodney told Detective Beard that he lived in Florida, but had come to Washington to try to find his wife. Rodney stated that she lived somewhere on Georgia Avenue, but was unable to say exactly where. The detective asked Rodney if he was carrying drugs in his travel bag. When Rodney said no, Beard obtained permission to search the bag. During the search, the second officer advanced to within about five feet of Rodney. The search disclosed no contraband. Detective Beard then asked Rodney whether he was carrying drugs on his person. When Rodney replied no, the detective requested permission to conduct a "body search." Rodney said "sure" and raised his hands above his head. "Beard placed his hands on Rodney's ankles and, in one sweeping motion, ran them up the inside of Rodney's legs. As he passed over the crotch area, Beard felt small, rock-like objects. Rodney exclaimed: 'That's me!' Detecting otherwise, Beard placed Rodney under arrest." *Id.* at 296. At the police station, Detective Beard unzipped

Rodney's pants and retrieved a plastic bag containing a rock-like substance that appeared to be, and later proved to be, a cocaine base.

In the appeal following the denial of his motion to suppress evidence, Rodney argued that his general consent to a body search did not include authorization to search his "crotch area." The United States Court of Appeals for the District of Columbia Circuit disagreed and affirmed. According to the court, "a reasonable person would have understood that consent to encompass the search undertaken here." *Id.* at 297.

As a general rule, "[a] consensual search cannot exceed the scope of the consent. The scope of the consent is measured by a test of 'objective reasonableness': it depends on how broadly a reasonable observer would have interpreted the consent under the circumstances." *Id.* [Citation omitted.]

Florida v. Jimeno makes clear that "[t]he scope of a search is generally defined by its expressed object." *Rodney* at 297. [Citation omitted.] In this case, Rodney authorized a search for drugs; and, according to the court, "[d]ealers frequently hide drugs near their genitals." *Rodney* at 297. *See also United States v. Broxton*, 926 *F.*2d 1180, 1181 (D.C.Cir. 1991) (*per curiam*); *United States v. Wright*, 924 *F.*2d 545, 546 (4th Cir. 1991); *United States v. Winfrey*, 915 *F.*2d 212, 215-16 (6th Cir. 1990). "Indeed, Beard testified that his colleagues make up to 75 percent of their drug recoveries from around the crotch area." *Rodney* at 297-98.

The court concluded, therefore, that "a request to conduct a body search for drugs reasonably includes a request to conduct some search of [the crotch] area." *Id.* at 298.

> We hold only that Rodney's generalized consent authorized the kind of "traditional frisk search" undertaken here * * *.

Id.

> The court cautioned, however, that at some point a body search may

> become so intrusive that we would not infer consent to it from a generalized consent, regardless of the stated object of the search. For example, although drugs can be hidden virtually anywhere on or in one's person, a generalized consent to a body search for drugs surely does not validate everything up to and including a search of body cavities.

Id. at 298.

Nonetheless, the search undertaken in this case, held the court, "was not so unusually intrusive, at least relative to body searches generally[,] * * * as to require a separate consent above and beyond the consent to a body search that Rodney had given voluntarily." *Id.* The body search initially involved only "a continuous sweeping motion over Rodney's outer garments, including the trousers covering his crotch area. In this respect, the search was no more invasive than the typical pat-down frisk for weapons described by the Supreme Court [in *Terry v. Ohio*]." *Rodney* at 298.

Concluding that Detective Beard's hands were lawfully *on the touching area*, the court did not hesitate to further hold that Detective Beard had probable cause to arrest Rodney after feeling the small, rock-like objects near his groin. The court observed:

> Beard, a police officer for more than twenty years, arrested Rodney after witnessing several curious events. First, Rodney gave Beard the improbable story that he had come to Washington to find his wife, who lived at an address unknown to him. * * * Then, Beard felt small rock-like objects hidden near Rodney's crotch, which, Beard detected, were not part of Rodney's body. Finally, when Rodney falsely declared that they were, Beard logically concluded that Rodney was likely carrying drugs. * * * As a result of th[e] frisk, * * * Beard had probable cause to arrest Rodney.

Id. at 299.

[For a more extensive discussion of the "plain touch" corollary to the plain view doctrine, *see* §4.3, *Minnesota v. Dickerson* and the Note which immediately follows.]

(b) *Compare United States v. Blake*, 888 F.2d 795 (11th Cir. 1989), where the court held that several Broward County sheriff's deputies, while working the South Terminal in the Fort Lauderdale/Hollywood International Airport, exceeded the scope of both defendant Blake's and defendant Eason's consent to a search of their "persons," when, upon receiving consent, the officers immediately reached into each defendant's crotch area and felt their genitals. According to the court:

> It has long been recognized that police officers, possessing neither reasonable suspicion nor probable cause, may nonetheless search an individual without a warrant so long as they first obtain the voluntary consent of the individual in question. * * * In conducting a search pursuant to a properly obtained, voluntary consent, however, the extent of the search must be confined to the terms of its authorization. * * * "A suspect's consent can impose limits on the scope of a search in the same way as do the specifications of a warrant," and those limits serve to restrain the permissible boundaries of the search. * * *
>
> [W]hether there were any limitations placed on the consent given and whether the search conformed to those limitations is to be determined by the totality of the circumstances. * * *
>
> [T]he district court * * * held that the consent given by the defendants allowing the officers to search their "persons" could not, under the circumstances, be construed as authorization for the officers to touch their genitals in the middle of a public area in the Fort Lauderdale Airport. In making this determination the court

reasoned that the search conducted constituted such a serious intrusion into the defendants' privacy that, under the circumstances, it could not be said that [they] had knowingly and voluntarily consented to the search in question.

Looking at all the evidence and surrounding circumstances, we cannot say that this conclusion is clearly erroneous. * * * [A] general understanding of a request to search one's "person" under the circumstances of this case simply did not lend itself to an interpretation that the officers were requesting to conduct a search as intrusive as the ones conducted here. [The officer's] request to search [defendants'] "persons," without more explanation, need not have been reasonably construed as a request for permission to touch [their] genitals. * * *

[T]he request for the search took place in a public airport terminal[; g]iven this public location, it cannot be said that a reasonable individual would understand that a search of one's person would entail an officer touching his or her genitals. * * * [Consequently,] the district court was not clearly erroneous in concluding that the consent given in this case, under all the circumstances, did not extend to touching the genitals. * * *

Our conclusion, of course, does not imply that such an intrusive search may never be consensual; it merely requires that an officer obtain proper consent.

Id. at 800-801. [Citations omitted.]

CHAPTER 4

PRIVACY EXPECTATIONS:
THE LIMITS OF CONSTITUTIONAL PROTECTION

§4.1. Privacy expectations.

At the federal level, in order to determine whether a particular area or object warrants Fourth Amendment protection, courts will engage in a two-part inquiry. The first part of the inquiry questions whether an individual has exhibited "an actual (or subjective) expectation of privacy" in the area or item in question. *Katz v. United States*, 389 *U.S.* 347, 361, 88 *S.Ct.* 507, 516 (1967) (Harlan, J., concurring). Next, it must be determined whether the expectation is "one that society is prepared to recognize as 'reasonable.' " *Id.* Taken as a whole, the *Katz* "twofold requirement" stands for the proposition that "wherever an individual may harbor a reasonable 'expectation of privacy,' * * * he is entitled to be free from unreasonable governmental intrusion." *Terry v. Ohio*, 392 *U.S.* 1, 9, 88 *S.Ct.* 1868, 1873 (1968).

Thus, "[t]he touchstone of Fourth Amendment analysis is whether a person has a 'constitutionally protected reasonable expectation of privacy.' " *California v. Ciraolo*, 476 *U.S.* 207, 211, 106 *S.Ct.* 1809, 1811 (1986) (quoting *Katz* at 361, 88 *S.Ct.* at 516 (Harlan, J., concurring)). In this respect, police conduct will implicate the Fourth Amendment only if it intrudes into an area (or significantly interferes with the possession of an item) in which an individual has "manifested a subjective expectation of privacy * * * that society accepts as objectively reasonable." *California v. Greenwood*, 486 *U.S.* 35, 39, 108 *S.Ct.* 1625, 1628 (1988).

In certain cases, however, the constitutional protection may extend directly to a person's property, even though privacy or liberty interests may not be immediately implicated. For example, in *Soldal v. Cook County, Ill.*, 506 *U.S.* 56, 113 *S.Ct.* 538 (1992), deputy sheriffs assisted the owners of a mobile home park in evicting the Soldal family. As the deputies stood and watched, the park owners wrenched the sewer and water connections off the side of the Soldal trailer, disconnected the telephone, tore the trailer's canopy and skirting, pulled it free from its moorings and towed it away. Finding the Fourth Amendment clearly applicable, the Court held:

> As a result of the state action in this case, the Soldals' domicile was not only seized, it literally was carried away, giving a new meaning to the term "mobile home." We fail to see how being unceremoniously dispossessed of one's home in the manner alleged to

have occurred here can be viewed as anything but a seizure invoking the protection of the Fourth Amendment. * * * The Amendment protects the people from unreasonable searches and seizures of "their persons, houses, papers, and effects." * * * [A]nd our cases unmistakably hold that the Amendment protects property as well as privacy. * * * We thus are unconvinced that * * * the Fourth Amendment protects against unreasonable seizures of property only where privacy or liberty is also implicated.

Id., 113 *S.Ct.* at 543, 544, 545.

KATZ v. UNITED STATES
Supreme Court of the United States
389 *U.S.* 347, 88 *S.Ct.* 507 (1967)

QUESTION: Do law enforcement officials violate the Fourth Amendment by electronically listening to and recording a person's words spoken into a telephone receiver in a public telephone booth without prior judicial authorization ?

ANSWER: YES. "[T]he Fourth Amendment governs not only the seizure of tangible items, but extends as well to the recording of oral statements overheard without any 'technical [physical intrusion].'" *Id.* at 512. Thus, the FBI agents' conduct "in electronically listening to and recording the [defendant's] words violated the privacy upon which he justifiably relied while using the telephone booth and thus constituted a 'search and seizure' within the meaning of the Fourth Amendment. The fact that the electronic device employed to achieve that end did not happen to penetrate the wall of the booth can have no constitutional significance." *Id.*

RATIONALE: Defendant, Charles Katz, was convicted in federal court of transmitting wagering information by telephone from Los Angeles to Miami and Boston, a violation of 18 *U.S.C.* §1084. At trial, the Government introduced evidence of defendant's end of telephone conversations, overheard by FBI agents who had attached an electronic listening and recording device to the outside of the public telephone booth from which he had placed his calls. The Court of Appeals, in affirming defendant's conviction, held that the actions of the FBI agents did not constitute a violation of the Fourth Amendment, because "[t]here was no physical entrance into the area occupied by [the defendant]." *Id.* at 509. *The United States Supreme Court disagreed and reversed.*
Preliminarily, the Court pointed out that

the Fourth Amendment cannot be translated into a general constitutional "right to privacy." That Amendment protects individual privacy against certain kinds of governmental intrusion, but its protections go further, and often have nothing to do with privacy at all.ᵃ Other provisions of the Constitution protect personal privacy from other forms of governmental invasion.ᵇ But the protection of a person's *general* right to privacy—his right to be left alone by other people—is, like the protection of his property and of his very life, left largely to the law of the individual States.

Id. at 510-11. [Court's emphasis.]

Both the Government and the defendant have "attached great significance to the characterization of the telephone booth from which the [defendant] placed his calls." *Id.* at 511. The defendant maintains that it is a "constitutionally protected area." The Government urges that it was not. According to the Court, "this effort to decide whether or not a given 'area,' viewed in the abstract, is 'constitutionally protected' deflects attention from the problem presented by this case." *Id.*

*For the Fourth Amendment protects people, not places. What a person knowingly exposes to the public, even in his own home or office, is not a subject of Fourth Amendment protection. * * * But what he seeks to preserve as private, even in an area accessible to the public, may be constitutionally protected.*

Id. [Emphasis added.]

The fact that the telephone booth is constructed partly of glass and that defendant was visible after he entered it is not dispositive.

[W]hat he sought to exclude when he entered the booth was not the intruding eye—it was the uninvited ear. He did not shed his right to do so simply because he made his calls from a place where he might be seen. No less than an individual in a business office, in a friend's apartment, or in a taxicab, a person in a telephone booth may rely on the protection of the Fourth Amendment. One who occupies it, shuts the door behind him, and pays the toll that permits him to place a call is surely entitled to assume that the words he utters into the mouthpiece will not be broadcast to the world. To read the Constitution more narrowly is to ignore the vital role that the public telephone has come to play in private communication.

Id. at 511-12.

ᵃ " 'The average man would very likely not have his feelings soothed any more by having his property seized openly than by having it seized privately and by stealth. * * * And a person can be just as much, if not more, irritated, annoyed and injured by an unceremonious public arrest by a policeman as he is by a seizure in the privacy of his office or home.' " *Id.* at 510 n.4. [Citation omitted.]

ᵇ "The First Amendment, for example, imposes limitations upon governmental abridgment of 'freedom to associate and privacy in one's associations.' * * * The Third Amendment's prohibition against the unconsented peacetime quartering of soldiers protects another aspect of privacy from governmental intrusion. To some extent, the Fifth Amendment too 'reflects the Constitution's concern for * * * "the right of each individual to a private enclave where he may lead a private life." ' * * * Virtually every governmental action interferes with personal privacy to some degree. The question in each case is whether that interference violates a command of the United States Constitution." *Id.* at 510-11 n.5.

The Court also rejected the Government's contention that the activities of the FBI agents in this case "should not be tested by Fourth Amendment requirements, for the surveillance technique they employed involved no physical penetration of the telephone booth[.]" *Id.* at 512. "Physical" penetration is not the key to the constitutional inquiry; for "the Fourth Amendment governs not only the seizure of tangible items, but extends as well to the recording of oral statements overheard without any 'technical [physical intrusion].'" *Id.*

> Once this much is acknowledged, and once it is recognized that the Fourth Amendment protects people—and not simply "areas"—against unreasonable searches and seizures, it becomes clear that the reach of that Amendment cannot turn upon the presence or absence of a physical intrusion into any given enclosure.

Id.

Accordingly, the FBI agents' conduct "in electronically listening to and recording the [defendant's] words violated the privacy upon which he justifiably relied while using the telephone booth and thus constituted a 'search and seizure' within the meaning of the Fourth Amendment. The fact that the electronic device employed to achieve that end did not happen to penetrate the wall of the booth can have no constitutional significance." *Id.* Prior to beginning the electronic surveillance in this case, the FBI agents developed a "strong probability" that defendant was using the telephone in question to transmit gambling information to persons in other States, in violation of federal law. This information should have been presented to a duly authorized magistrate. Indeed, "a federal court may empower government agents to employ a concealed electronic device 'for the narrow and particularized purpose of ascertaining the truth of the * * * allegations' of a 'detailed factual affidavit alleging the commission of a specific criminal offense.'" *Id.* at 513. [Citation omitted.] Such a court order would afford protections similar to those "of conventional warrants authorizing the seizure of tangible evidence." *Id.* In this case, a "judicial order could have accommodated 'the legitimate needs of law enforcement' by authorizing the carefully limited use of electronic surveillance." *Id.* at 514.

Finally, in response to the Government's suggestion that the Court should retroactively validate the conduct of the FBI agents in this case because they did no more than they might properly have done with a court order, the Court stated:

> That we cannot do. It is apparent that the agents in this case acted with restraint. Yet, the inescapable fact is that this restraint was imposed by the agents themselves, not by a judicial officer. * * * Searches conducted without warrants have been held unlawful "notwithstanding facts unquestionably showing probable cause," * * * for the Constitution requires "that the deliberate, impartial judgment of a judicial officer * * * be interposed between the citizen and the police." * * * "Over and again this Court has emphasized that the mandate of the [Fourth] Amendment requires adherence

to judicial processes," * * * and that searches conducted outside the judicial process, without prior approval by judge or magistrate, are *per se* unreasonable under the Fourth Amendment—subject only to a few specifically established and well-delineated exceptions.[c]

* * * These considerations do not vanish when the search in question is transferred from the setting of a home, an office, or a hotel room to that of a telephone booth. Wherever a man may be, he is entitled to know that he will remain free from unreasonable searches and seizures.

Id. at 515. [Citations omitted.]

The Court concluded, therefore, that the FBI agents in this case failed to adhere to a central requirement of the Fourth Amendment—they failed to obtain prior judicial approval for the electronic surveillance. Prior judicial authorization is a procedure, held the Court, that is "a constitutional precondition of the kind of electronic surveillance involved in this case." *Id.* "Because the surveillance here failed to meet that condition, and because it led to the [defendant's] conviction, the judgment must be reversed." *Id.*

Mr. Justice HARLAN, concurring.

"I join the opinion of the Court, which I read to hold only (a) that an enclosed telephone booth is an area where, like a home, * * * and unlike a field, * * * a person has a constitutionally protected reasonable expectation of privacy; (b) that electronic as well as physical intrusion into a place that is in this sense private may constitute a violation of the Fourth Amendment; and (c) that the invasion of a constitutionally protected area by federal authorities is, as the Court has long held, presumptively unreasonable in the absence of a search warrant.

"As the Court's opinion states, 'the Fourth Amendment protects people, not places.' The question, however, is what protection it affords to those people. Generally, as here, the answer to that question requires reference to a 'place.' My understanding of the rule that has emerged from prior decisions is that there is a twofold requirement, first that a person have exhibited an actual (subjective) expectation of privacy and, second, that the expectation be one that society is prepared to recognize as 'reasonable.' Thus, a man's home is, for most purposes, a place where he expects privacy, but objects, activities, or statements that he exposes to the 'plain view' of outsiders are not 'protected' because no intention to keep them to himself has been exhibited. On the

---

[c] The Court found it "difficult to imagine" how any of the recognized exceptions to the written warrant requirement could ever apply to the sort of search and seizure involved in this case. An electronic surveillance, even if conducted "substantially contemporaneous" with an individual's arrest, "could hardly be deemed an 'incident' of that arrest." *Id.* at 514. In this respect, the Court stated, "the concept of an 'incidental' search cannot readily be extended to include surreptitious surveillance of an individual either immediately before, or immediately after, his arrest." *Id.* at 514-15 n.20. "Nor could the use of electronic surveillance without prior authorization be justified on grounds of 'hot pursuit.' And, of course, the very nature of electronic surveillance precludes its use pursuant to the suspect's consent." *Id.* at 515.

other hand, conversations in the open would not be protected against being overheard, for the expectation of privacy under the circumstances would be unreasonable.

"The critical fact in this case * * * is not that the [telephone] booth is 'accessible to the public' at other times, * * * but that it is a temporarily private place whose momentary occupants' expectations of freedom from intrusion are recognized as reasonable." *Id.* at 516-17.

NOTE

Presence of media during warrant execution violates the Fourth Amendment. In *Wilson v. Layne*, 526 *U.S.* 603, 119 *S.Ct.* 1692 (1999), the United States Supreme Court held that "it is a violation of the Fourth Amendment for police to bring members of the media or other third parties into a home during the execution of a warrant when the presence of the third parties in the home was not in aid of the execution of the warrant." *Id.*, 119 *S.Ct.* at 1699.

In *Layne*, as officers executed an arrest warrant in a private home, invited members of the media accompanied them. The officers were looking for a fugitive, Dominic Wilson, who had violated his probation on previous charges of robbery, theft, and assault. The computer report contained certain "caution indicators" that Wilson was "likely to be armed, to resist arrest, and to assaul[t] police." *Id.* at 1695. Three arrest warrants issued for Wilson, one for each of the probation violations. Each warrant was addressed to "any duly authorized peace officer," and commanded the officer to arrest the subject and bring him "immediately" before the court. The warrants contained no reference to the presence or assistance of the media.

In the middle of April, in the early morning hours, a team of Montgomery County police officers and Deputy United States Marshals assembled near the Wilson home to execute the arrest warrants. Along with the team were a reporter and a photographer from the Washington Post, "who had been invited by the Marshals to accompany them on their mission as part of a Marshal's Service ride-along policy." *Id.* at 1695-96. The officers entered the home at about 6:45 a.m., with the media representatives close behind. After entering the home and physically restraining at least one of the residents, the officers learned that Dominic Wilson was not in the house. While the officers were in the home, the Washington Post photographer took various pictures. In the living room, the reporter watched as the police restrained Dominic Wilson's father, Charles.

Holding that such a "media ride-along" violates the Fourth Amendment, the Court's analysis began with the famous *Semayne's Case* of 1603, where the English Court observed that "the house of every one is to him as his castle and fortress, as well for his defence against injury and violence, as for his repose." 5 *Co.Rep.* 91a, 91b, 77 *Eng.Rep.* 194, 195 (K.B. 1603). This "centuries-old principle of the respect for the privacy of the home," is embodied in the Fourth Amendment. *Wilson* at 1697.

Although the officers in this case were entitled to enter the Wilson home in order to execute the arrest warrant for Dominic Wilson, they were not, emphasized the Court, necessarily entitled "to bring a newspaper reporter and a photographer with them." *Id.*

As a matter of law, the scope of a search may not exceed that permitted by the terms of a validly issued warrant, or the parameters of a recognized exception to the warrant requirement. "While this does not mean that every police action while inside a home must be explicitly authorized by the text of the warrant, * * * the Fourth Amendment does require that police actions in execution of a warrant be related to the objectives of the authorized intrusion[.]" *Id.* at 1697-98. In this respect, the Court observed:

> Certainly the presence of reporters inside the home was not related to the objectives of the authorized intrusion. * * * [T]he reporters did not engage in the execution of the warrant, and did not assist the police in their task. The reporters therefore were not present for any reason related to the justification for police entry into the home—the apprehension of Dominic Wilson.

> This is not a case in which the presence of the third parties directly aided in the execution of the warrant. Where the police enter a home under the authority of a warrant to search for stolen property, the presence of third parties for the purpose of identifying the stolen property has long been approved by this Court and our common-law tradition. * * *

Id. at 1698.

During the course of the case, the Court was presented with several arguments of how the presence of members of the news media in the Wilsons' home "served a number of legitimate law enforcement purposes." The Court found, however, that those purposes were outweighed by the important "right of residential privacy at the core of the Fourth Amendment." *Id.*

The court did acknowledge the officers' argument that the presence of the media could serve the law enforcement purpose of "publicizing the government's efforts to combat crime, and facilitate accurate reporting on law enforcement activities." *Id.* The Court ruled, however, that "the possibility of good public relations for the police is simply not enough, standing alone, to justify the ride-along intrusion into a private home." *Id.*

In response to the argument that "the presence of third parties could serve in some situations to minimize police abuses and protect suspects, and also to protect the safety of the officers," *id.* at 1699, the Court said:

> While it might be reasonable for police officers to themselves videotape home entries as part of a "quality control" effort to ensure that the rights of homeowners are being respected, or even to preserve evidence * * *, such a situation is significantly different from the media presence in this case. The Washington Post reporters in the Wilsons' home were working on a story for their own purposes. They were not present for the purpose of protecting the officers, much less the Wilsons. A private photographer was acting for private purposes, as evidenced in part by the fact that the newspaper

and not the police retained the photographs. Thus, although the presence of third parties during the execution of a warrant may in some circumstances be constitutionally permissible, [] the presence of these third parties was not.

Id.

Accordingly, the "media ride-along," employed in this case violated the Fourth Amendment.

In a related case, decided the same day as *Wilson v. Layne*, the Court in *Hanlon v. Berger*, 526 *U.S.* 808, 119 *S.Ct.* 1706 (1999), reached the same result in a situation involving the execution of a search warrant and the invited presence of a crew of photographers and reporters from the Cable News Network, Inc. (CNN).

KYLLO v. UNITED STATES
Supreme Court of the United States
33 *U.S.* 27, 121 *S.Ct.* 2038 (2001)

QUESTION: Does the use of a thermal-imaging device, aimed at a private home to detect relative amounts of heat within the home, constitute a Fourth Amendment "search" ?

ANSWER: YES. Where law enforcement officers use "a device that is not in general public use, to explore details of the home that would previously have been unknowable without physical intrusion, the surveillance is a 'search' and is presumptively unreasonable without a warrant." *Id.* at 2046.

RATIONALE: During the course of a drug investigation, Agent Elliott came to suspect that defendant, Danny Kyllo, was growing marijuana in his home, which was part of a triplex in Florence, Oregon. Recognizing that indoor marijuana growth typically requires high-intensity lamps, Agent Elliott decided to scan the triplex, at 3:20 a.m. on January 16th, to determine whether an amount of heat was emanating from Kyllo's home consistent with the use of such lamps. Elliott used an Agema Thermovision 210 thermal imager. "Thermal imagers detect infrared radiation, which virtually all objects emit but which is not visible to the naked eye. The imager converts radiation into images based on relative warmth— black is cool, white is hot, shades of gray connote relative differences; in that respect, it operates somewhat like a video camera showing heat images." *Id.* at 2041.

"The scan of Kyllo's home took only a few minutes and was performed from the passenger seat of Agent Elliott's vehicle across the street from the front of the house and also from the street in back of the house." *Id.* The scan revealed that the roof over the garage and a side wall of the home were relatively hot compared to the rest of the home and substantially warmer than neighboring homes in the triplex. Agent Elliott thus believed that Kyllo was using high-intensity lights to grow marijuana in his house. A search warrant was obtained based on the thermal imaging, along with tips from informants and utility bills. The search uncovered an indoor growing operation involving more than 100 plants.

In the lower court proceedings, the District Court found the Agema 210 to be "a non-intrusive device which emits no rays or beams and shows a crude visual image of the heat being radiated from the outside of the house"; it "did not show any people or activity within the walls of the structure." *Id.* The Court of Appeals determined that since Kyllo had made no attempt to conceal the heat escaping from his home, he had shown "no subjective expectation of privacy," and, even if he had, "there was no objectively reasonable expectation of privacy because the imager "did not expose any intimate details of Kyllo's life," only "amorphous 'hot spots' on the roof and exterior wall." *Id. The United States Supreme Court disagreed and reversed.*

With very few exceptions, the warrantless search of a home is generally deemed to be unlawful. The more difficult question, however, is whether or not a Fourth Amendment "search" has occurred. "When the Fourth Amendment was adopted, as now, to 'search' meant '[t]o look over or through for the purpose of finding something; to explore; to examine by inspection * * *.' " *Id.* at 2042 n.1. [Citation omitted.]

A Fourth Amendment search does not occur, however, "even when the explicitly protected location of a house is concerned," unless " 'the individual manifested a subjective expectation of privacy in the object of the challenged search,' and 'society [is] willing to recognize that expectation as reasonable.' " *Id.* at 2042-43 (quoting *California v. Ciraolo,* 476 *U.S.* 207, 211, 106 *S.Ct.* 1809, 1811 (1986)).

In *Ciraolo,* the Court upheld the lawfulness of the warrantless aerial surveillance of a private home, noting that the "Fourth Amendment protection of the home has never been extended to require law enforcement officers to shield their eyes when passing by a home on public thoroughfares." *Ciraolo* at 213, 106 *S.Ct.* at 1812. *See also Florida v. Riley,* 488 *U.S.* 445, 109 *S.Ct.* 693 (1989). Thus, the Court determined that the aerial surveillance of a private home and its surrounding area does not constitute a search.

"The present case involves officers on a public street engaged in more than naked-eye surveillance of a home." *Kyllo* at 2043. In prior cases, the Court had "reserved judgment as to how much technological enhancement of ordinary perception from such a vantage point, if any, is too much." *Id.* Here, in *Kyllo,* the Court pointed out:

> It would be foolish to contend that the degree of privacy secured to citizens by the Fourth Amendment has been entirely unaffected by the advance of technology. For example, * * * the technology enabling human flight has exposed to public view (and hence, we have said, to official observation) uncovered portions of the house and its curtilage that once were private. * * * The question we confront today is what limits there are upon this power of technology to shrink the realm of guaranteed privacy.

Id.

In this case, the Court was not prepared to allow the Fourth Amendment protection of privacy, which clearly attaches to the interior of one's home, to be eroded by "police technology." The Court ruled:

> We think that *obtaining by sense-enhancing technology any information regarding the interior of the home that could not otherwise have been obtained without physical 'intrusion into a constitutionally protected area'* * * * *constitutes a search—at least where (as here) the technology in question is not in general public use.* This assures preservation of that degree of privacy against government that existed when the Fourth Amendment was adopted.

Id. [Emphasis added.]

Consequently, the Court held that "the information obtained by the thermal imager in this case was the product of a search." *Id.*

During the course of the appeal, the Government argued that the thermal imaging process should be upheld because it detects "only heat radiating from the external surface of the house." *Id.* at 2044. The dissenting Justices found this persuasive, pointing out that there is a "fundamental difference" between "off-the-wall" observations and "through-the-wall surveillance." *Id.* Speaking for the Court's majority, Justice Scalia found that this approach missed the mark.

> [J]ust as a thermal imager captures only heat emanating from a house, so also a powerful directional microphone picks up only sound emanating from a house, and a satellite capable of scanning from many miles away would pick up only visible light emanating from a house. [Such a] mechanical interpretation of the Fourth Amendment * * * would leave the homeowner at the mercy of advancing technology—including imaging technology—that could discern all human activity in the home. While the technology used in the present case was relatively crude, the rule we adopt must take account of more sophisticated systems that are already in use or in development.

Id.

The Government also contended that the use of thermal imaging should be found constitutional because it does not "detect private activities occurring in private areas." *Id.* at 2045. Rejecting this contention as well, the Court emphasized that the "Fourth Amendment's protection of the home has never been tied to measurement of the quality or quantity of information obtained." *Id.* Prior cases have made clear that "any physical invasion of the structure of the home, 'by even a fraction of an inch,' was too much. * * * In the home, * * * all details are intimate details, because the entire area is held safe from prying government eyes." *Id.* [Citation omitted.] Thus, the detail of how warm—or even how relatively warm—Kyllo was heating his home should be considered an "intimate detail," precisely because it may be considered a detail of the home; and the use of hi-tech measurement to detect the emanations from his home must be considered a Fourth Amendment search.

The Agema Thermovision 210 might disclose, for example, at what hour each night the lady of the house takes her daily sauna and bath—a detail that many would consider "intimate"; and a much more sophisticated system might detect nothing more intimate than the fact that someone left a closet light on.

Id.

The Court has stressed that the Fourth Amendment draws "a firm line at the entrance to the house." *Id.* at 2046. That line, held the Court, "must be not only firm but also bright—which requires clear specification of those methods of surveillance that require a warrant." *Id.*

Accordingly, "[w]here, as here, the Government uses a device that is not in general public use, to explore details of the home that would previously have been unknowable without physical intrusion, the surveillance is a 'search' and is presumptively unreasonable without a warrant." *Id.* The Thermovision imaging employed in this case was, therefore, "an unlawful search." *Id.* The Court remanded the matter to the District Court to determine whether, without the thermal-imaging evidence, the search warrant that issued in this case was supported by probable cause—and if not, whether there is any other basis for supporting admission of the evidence that the search pursuant to the warrant produced.

UNITED STATES v. CLARK
United States Court of Appeals
22 *F.*3d 799 (8th Cir. 1994)

QUESTION: Does a suspect or an arrestee have a reasonable expectation of privacy in statements made to a companion while seated in the rear of a police car ?

ANSWER: NO. "[A] person does not have a reasonable or legitimate expectation of privacy in statements made to a companion while seated in a police car." *Id.* at 802. "A police car is not the kind of public place, like a phone booth, * * * where a person should be able to reasonably expect that his conversation will not be monitored." *Id.*

RATIONALE: Defendant, Samuel Clark, was a passenger in a car driven by Jerome Mozee. An Iowa state trooper stopped them because the vehicle's windows were excessively tinted, in violation of Iowa law. During the course of the motor vehicle stop, the trooper developed grounds to suspect that Clark and Mozee were involved in drug trafficking. He therefore requested and obtained consent to search Mozee's vehicle. Clark asked the trooper if he could sit in the patrol car with Mozee during the search rather than stand by the roadside. The trooper agreed.

Unbeknownst to Clark and Mozee, the trooper had activated a tape recorder and left it sitting on the dash of the patrol car. The two men had a discussion, during which Clark indicated that "it" was not in the car, but inside his pants. After finding nothing of evidentiary value in Mozee's car, the trooper reached in and took the tape recorder off the dash. He listened to the tape, and then obtained Clark's consent to a search of his person—including his underwear. In Clark's underwear, the trooper found a plastic bag containing crack cocaine. Thereafter, both Clark and Mozee were arrested.

In the appeal following defendants' successful motion to suppress, the government argued that "a person cannot have a reasonable expectation of privacy while seated in a patrol car." *Id.* at 801. *The United States Court of Appeals for the Eighth Circuit agreed and reversed.*

Under either the Fourth Amendment or the Wiretap Act, 18 U.S.C. §2110 *et seq.*, the proper inquiry in a case such as this is "1) whether defendant manifested a subjective expectation of privacy, and 2) if so, whether society is prepared to recognize that expectation as reasonable." *Id.*

Preliminarily, the court accepted that the defendant had a "subjective" expectation of privacy. Thus, the main question was whether such an expectation is one that society is prepared to recognize as reasonable. The inquiry into "reasonableness" asks

> "whether, if the particular form of surveillance practiced by the police is permitted to go unregulated by constitutional restraints, the amount of privacy and freedom remaining to citizens would be diminished to a compass inconsistent with the aims of a free society."

Id. [Citation omitted.] The court concluded that "defendants' expectation of privacy while seated in the police car was not reasonable." *Id.*

In *United States v. McKinnon*, 985 *F.2d* 525 (11th Cir. 1993), the Eleventh Circuit was faced with a similar set of circumstances.

> While police searched a vehicle in which he was a passenger, Mr. McKinnon voluntarily waited in a patrol car with his cohort. Both before and after his arrest, McKinnon made incriminating statements during discussions with his companion. The district court, and the Eleventh Circuit Court of Appeals, held squarely that "a person seated in a police car does not have a reasonable expectation of privacy under [the Wiretap Act or] the Fourth Amendment to the Constitution." * * * The [c]ourt refused to recognize a distinction between pre- and post-arrest statements, for purposes of analyzing the reasonableness of a defendant's expectation of privacy.

Clark at 801 (quoting *McKinnon* at 526).

Agreeing with the rationale of the Eleventh Circuit, the court here in *Clark* further observed:

> A marked police car is owned and operated by the state for the express purpose of ferreting out crime. It is essentially the trooper's office, and is frequently used as a temporary jail for housing and transporting arrestees and suspects. The general public has no reason to frequent the back seat of a patrol car, or to believe that it

is a sanctuary for private discussions. A police car is not the kind of public place, like a phone booth (*e.g., Katz v. United States*, 389 *U.S.* 347, 88 *S.Ct.* 507 [] (1967)), where a person should be able to reasonably expect that his conversation will not be monitored. In other words, allowing police to record statements made by individuals seated inside a patrol car does not intrude upon privacy and freedom to such an extent that it could be regarded as inconsistent with the aims of a free and open society.

Id. at 801-02.

Accordingly, "a person does not have a reasonable or legitimate expectation of privacy in statements made to a companion while seated in a police car." *Id.* at 802. Both the statements made by Clark and the cocaine seized as a result of those statements are admissible in this case.

UNITED STATES v. SMITH
United States Court of Appeals
978 *F.*2d 181 (5th Cir. 1992)

QUESTION: Are cordless telephone conversations protected by the Fourth Amendment?

ANSWER: It depends on the cordless telephone. Any determination as to the reasonableness of an individual's expectation of privacy in conversations conducted over a cordless telephone "will depend largely upon the specific technology used," and "upon the specific telephone at issue." *Id.* at 180.

RATIONALE: Acting at the direction of the Port Arthur, Texas, police, Michael Varing tape-recorded several of David Smith's cordless telephone conversations. Varing, a neighbor of Smith, had been intercepting Smith's conversations over a Bearcat scanner.[a] The intercepted calls and the tape recordings eventually led to Smith's arrest on drug-trafficking charges. Subsequently, Smith was convicted of one count of conspiracy to distribute cocaine, one count of using or carrying a firearm during or in relation to a drug trafficking offense, and three counts of using a telephone to cause or facilitate a drug felony.

In the appeal following his convictions, Smith argued that the interception of his cordless telephone conversations violated both Title III of the Omnibus Crime Control and Safe Streets Act, 18 *U.S.C.*

---

[a] "A Bearcat scanner is a type of radio receiver which allows the user to monitor a number of radio frequencies. The scanner sequentially monitors all programmed frequencies. When a conversation on one of these frequencies is picked up, the scanner locks in on that frequency to allow the user to listen in. Bearcat scanners, along with similar scanners made by competitors, are commercially available at most radio and electronics stores." *Id.* at 173 n.1.

§§2510-2521, and the Fourth Amendment. *The United States Court of Appeals for the Fifth Circuit disagreed and affirmed.*

Title III

Preliminarily, the court rejected Smith's contention that Title III applies to cordless telephone communications. Title III prohibits the nonconsensual interception of "wire," "oral,"[b] and "electronic" communication without prior judicial approval. *See* 18 *U.S.C.* §§2516-2518. While Smith conceded that Title III expressly excludes cordless telephone transmissions from the definitions of "wire" and "electronic" communication, he contended that "his conversations are nonetheless entitled to Title III protection because they fit within the definition of 'oral communications.'" *Id.* at 175. The court found Smith's contention to be "out of step with both the plain language of Title III and with its legislative history."

> By its own terms, Title III limits the definition of oral communications to "any oral communication uttered by a person." 18 *U.S.C.* §2510(2). In this case, it was not Smith's actual utterances that were overheard and recorded by the Varings; it was a radio signal produced by Smith's cordless phone that was intercepted, and it was a reconstruction[c] of the conversation produced by the Bearcat scanner that was tape recorded. Thus, by the plain terms of the statute, Smith's cordless telephone conversations do not fit within the terms of "oral communication." * * *

> It is also important to note that the 1986 amendments [to Title III] expressly excluded cordless telephone conversations from the definitions of "wire" and "electronic" communications because Congress felt that it was "inappropriate to make the interception of such a communication a criminal offense" since some types of cordless communications can be so easily intercepted.

Id. at 175-176. [Citations omitted.]

Expectations of Privacy under the Fourth Amendment

Concluding that Smith's cordless telephone conversations were not protected by Title III did not end the court's inquiry. The question remains whether the Fourth Amendment protects such conversations. "The key inquiry," according to the court, "is whether the interception of Smith's phone calls constituted a search within the meaning of the Fourth Amendment." *Id.* at 176.

---

[b] "Oral communications" is defined as "any oral communication uttered by a person exhibiting an expectation that such communication is not subject to interception under circumstances justifying such expectation." 18 *U.S.C.* §2510(2).

[c] According to the court, "[t]he Bearcat scanner did not actually intercept the sound of Smith's voice. Instead, the cordless phone reduced the sound of Smith's voice to radio waves. These radio waves were picked up by the scanner. The scanner then reconstructed the sound waves of the conversation." *Id.* at 175 n.5.

Generally, "a search occurs when the government infringes an expectation of privacy that society is prepared to consider reasonable." *Id.* at 177.

> While it is true that the right to privacy in a personal conversation is generally a reasonable expectation, the actions of the parties to the conversation may reduce this expectation to the point that it is no longer "reasonable." * * * "What a person knowingly exposes to the public, even in his own home or office, is not a subject of Fourth Amendment protection." *Katz v. United States*, 389 *U.S.* 347, 351, 88 *S.Ct.* 507, 511 [] (1967).

> * * * In any consideration of the "societal understanding" about the privacy expectations of cordless phone users, it is perhaps instructive to note the important role that all forms of telecommunication, including various cordless systems, play in today's society. As early as 1967, the Supreme Court recognized the "vital role" that the telephone plays in modern communication. *Katz*, 389 *U.S.* at 352, 88 *S.Ct.* at 512. No one would dispute that the importance of telecommunications today has outstripped anything imagined twenty five years ago. In recent years, one of the fastest growing areas in the field of telecommunications has been "wireless" technology. * * * Cordless phones, in particular, are threatening to outstrip sales of traditional land line telephones. Today, nearly half of the 95 million U.S. households use cordless telephones, and more than 16 million new cordless phones are expected to be sold this year. * * * If, as some experts predict, we are moving inexorably toward a completely cordless telephone system, the decision as to whether cordless telephone conversations are protected by the Fourth Amendment may ultimately determine whether *any* telephone conversation is protected by the Fourth Amendment.

Id. at 177. [Citations omitted; court's emphasis.]

"From a Fourth Amendment standpoint," observed the court, "the problem with cordless phones is figuring out how to characterize them. Are they more like traditional telephones or more like radio transmitters. This difference is important because the Fourth Amendment clearly protects communications carried by land-based telephone lines." *Id.* "On the other hand, pure radio communications are afforded no such protection because '[b]roadcasting communications into the air by radio waves is more analogous to carrying on an oral communication in a loud voice or with a megaphone than it is to the privacy afforded by a wire.' " *Id.* [Citations omitted.]

"Cordless phones are difficult to characterize because they do not fit neatly into either category. In one sense, the cordless telephone is just what the name implies, a telephone. It looks and sounds like a normal land line telephone. * * * In actual operation, however, the cordless phone actually uses a radio signal. The typical cordless phone consists of a base unit, attached to the land-based telephone line, and a mobile unit which transmits and receives the radio signals that carry the actual conversation to and from the base unit." *Id.* at 178. [Citations omitted.]

Prior cases that have addressed the issue whether a user of a cordless phone has a reasonable expectation of privacy have determined that, "based upon the particular characteristics of the cordless phone in question, there could have been no reasonable expectation of privacy in the cordless phone transmissions due to the ease with which they could be monitored." *Id.* at 179. *See Tyler v. Berodt*, 877 *F.*2d 705 (8th Cir. 1989); *State v. Howard*, 235 *Kan.* 236, 679 *P.*2d 197 (1984); *State v. Delaurier*, 488 *A.*2d 688 (R.I. 1985); *State v. Smith*, 149 *Wis.*2d 89, 438 *N.W.*2d 571 (1989). "[A]lthough the individual communication at issue would normally be subject to Fourth Amendment protection, the defendants [in the cited cases] had 'knowingly exposed' the communication to the public by using a technology that could be so easily intercepted." *Smith*, 978 *F.*2d at 179.

Since those cases were decided, cordless technology has continued to evolve. Today's cordless telephones are very different from the models at issue in *Howard* and *Delaurier*.

> The effective range of cordless phones varies greatly from model to model; many are limited to a range of about sixty feet, barely beyond the average house or yard. Obviously it is more reasonable to expect privacy from a broadcast that cannot be heard outside your own property than it is to expect privacy for a broadcast that covers a whole neighborhood. Cordless phones are also no longer "preset" to one frequency. Instead, most cordless phones sold today can monitor all available frequencies and automatically select one that is unused. This greatly reduces the chance that a cordless phone will pick up conversations from other cordless phones. Today's cordless phones broadcast on radio frequencies not utilized by commercial radio so that conventional radios can no longer pick up cordless phone communications. Although radio *scanners*—like the one used by Mr. Varing—can still monitor most cordless phones, only a small percentage of people own such scanners. * * * Finally, cordless phones now appearing on the market actually scramble the radio signal so that even radio scanners cannot intercept the communication.

Smith at 179. [Court's emphasis]

The issue is not, therefore, "whether it is *conceivable* that someone could eavesdrop on conversation but whether it is *reasonable* to expect privacy. * * * No matter how technologically advanced cordless communication becomes, some people will always find a way to eavesdrop on their neighbors." *Id.* [Court's emphasis.]

Although the court here in *Smith* would not express an opinion "as to what features or circumstances would be necessary to give rise to a reasonable expectation of privacy," it nonetheless opined that "it should be obvious that as technological advances make cordless communications more private, at some point such communication will be entitled to Fourth Amendment protection." *Id.* at 180. It would thus be improper for a court to determine that interception of a conversation does not implicate the Fourth Amendment simply because it is carried on by a "cordless" phone. "Application of the Fourth Amendment in a given case will depend largely upon the specific technology used[.]" *Id.*

During the course of this appeal, Smith argued that "the interception of his cordless telephone conversations violated his Fourth Amendment rights * * * [because he] did not know that his conversations would not be private." *Id.* He did not, however, introduce any evidence to support his argument. In this respect, the court emphasized that

> subjective expectations of privacy are not enough to give rise to Fourth Amendment protection. The real question is whether Smith's subjective expectation of privacy is one that society is prepared to recognize as reasonable. As discussed earlier, the reasonableness of any expectation of privacy for a cordless phone will depend, in large part, upon the specific telephone at issue. * * * Smith introduced absolutely no evidence—such as the phone's frequency or range—that would tend to show that his subjective expectation of privacy was reasonable. * * * [His] motion to suppress was properly denied.

Id. at 180-81.

NEW YORK v. CLASS
Supreme Court of the United States
475 *U.S.* 106, 106 *S.Ct.* 960 (1986)

QUESTION: May a motorist claim a reasonable expectation of privacy in the vehicle identification number (VIN) attached to his or her automobile ?

ANSWER: NO. There is "no reasonable expectation of privacy in the VIN." *Id.* at 966.

RATIONALE: "[T]he State's intrusion into a particular area, whether in an automobile or elsewhere, cannot result in a Fourth Amendment violation unless the area is one in which there is a 'constitutionally protected reasonable expectation of privacy.' " *Id.* at 965. According to the Court, the VIN of an automobile, roughly analogous to a serial number, plays an important part in "the pervasive regulation by the government" of motor vehicles.

> A motorist must surely expect that such regulation will on occasion require the State to determine the VIN of his or her vehicle, and the individual's reasonable expectation of privacy in the VIN is thereby diminished. This is especially true in the case of a driver who has committed a traffic violation. * * *

In addition, it is unreasonable to have an expectation of privacy in an object required by law to be located in a place ordinarily in plain view from the exterior of the automobile. The VIN's mandated visibility makes it more similar to the exterior of the car than to the trunk or glove compartment. The exterior of a car, of course, is thrust into the public eye, and thus to examine it does not constitute a "search." *See Cardwell v. Lewis*, [417 *U.S.* 583, 588-89, 94 *S.Ct.* 2464, 2468 (1974)].

Class at 965-66.

Consequently, the Court concluded that, "because of the important role played by the VIN in the pervasive governmental regulation of the automobile and the efforts by the Federal Government to ensure that the VIN is placed in plain view," there is "no reasonable expectation of privacy in the VIN." *Id.* at 966. [*See* §3.5 where *New York v. Class* is discussed in greater detail.]

NOTE

1. *License plates.* In *State v. Harding*, 670 *P.*2d 383 (Ariz. 1983), the court rejected the defendant's claim that the police had no right to randomly run a computer check on the license plate of the automobile he was driving. The court said:

> The defendant cites no authority for the proposition that a police[officer] may not conduct a check on a license plate at will even without reasonable suspicion, and we have found none. We believe that there is no expectation of privacy in the license plate affixed to the exterior of one's motor vehicle driven in public meriting constitutional protection. Also, there was no search or seizure of the vehicle at the time the license check was made. Neither was there a detention of the defendant.

Id. at 392. *See also State v. Donis*, 157 *N.J.* 44, 54-55, 723 *A.*2d 35 (1998) (applying the *Class* rationale to a vehicle's license plate, which is displayed on the exterior of the car in plain view).

2. *Reasonable expectations of privacy and a person's physical appearance.*

(a) *Facial characteristics.* In *United States v. Dionisio*, 410 *U.S.* 1, 14, 93 *S.Ct.* 764, 771 (1973), the Court announced that no person has a reasonable expectation of privacy in his or her "facial characteristics" for "one cannot reasonably expect that his face will be a mystery to the world." *See also Doe v. Poritz*, 142 *N.J.* 1, 80, 662 *A.*2d 367 (1995), where the court held that "[b]ecause a person's physical appearance is necessarily and constantly exposed to public view, no person can have a reasonable expectation of privacy in his appearance." *See also id.*, 142 *N.J.* at 81 (requiring a Megan's Law registrant to submit to photographing "does not implicate any privacy interest").

(b) Fingerprints. Similarly, no person can have a reasonable expectation of privacy in his or her fingerprints. *See Cupp v. Murphy,* 412 *U.S.* 291, 295, 93 *S.Ct.* 2000, 2003 (1973) (no reasonable expectation of privacy attaches to one's fingerprints, which are mere "physical characteristics" that are "constantly exposed to the public").

(c) The physical characteristics of a person's voice. In *United States v. Dionisio,* 410 *U.S.* 1, 93 *S.Ct.* 764 (1973), the Court held that "[t]he physical characteristics of a person's voice, its tone and manner, as opposed to the content of a specific conversation, are constantly exposed to the public," so that "[n]o person can have a reasonable expectation of privacy that others will not know the sound of his voice[.]" *Id.* at 14, 93 *S.Ct.* at 771. "Like a man's facial characteristics, or handwriting, his voice is repeatedly produced for others to hear." *Id.*

(d) Handwriting. In a companion case to *United States v. Dionisio,* the Court reached the same result as to a person's handwriting. *See United States v. Mara,* 410 *U.S.* 19, 93 *S.Ct.* 774 (1973) ("Handwriting, like speech, is repeatedly shown to the public, and there is no more expectation of privacy in the physical characteristics of a person's script than there is in the tone of his voice."). *See also United States v. Euge,* 444 *U.S.* 707, 100 *S.Ct.* 874 (1980) ("compulsion of handwriting exemplars is neither a search nor a seizure subject to Fourth Amendment protections").

(e) Soles of a person's shoes. The visual inspection of the soles of a detainee's shoes has been held not to constitute a "search" within the meaning of the Fourth Amendment. *See e.g., State v. Holloman,* 197 *Neb.* 139, 145, 248 *N.W.*2d 15, 19 (1976) (police officer's action in lifting and turning over shoes that were in plain view was not unreasonable); *People v. Eddington,* 387 *Mich.* 551, 198 *N.W.*2d 297 (1972); *State v. Bruzzese,* 94 *N.J.* 210, 239, 463 *A.*2d 320 (1983).

3. *Arrest records. See Paul P. v. Verniero,* 170 *F.*3d 396 (3rd Cir. 1999), where, in upholding sex offender registration and community notification laws, the court determined "that arrest records and related information are not protected by a right to privacy."

4. *The space between the floor and the door of a public restroom stall.* In *United States v. Billings,* 858 *F.*2d 617 (10th Cir. 1988), two Denver narcotics officers, while on duty at the Stapleton International Airport, observed defendant disembark a plane which had just arrived from Miami, Florida, wearing a distinctive turquoise jumpsuit. They watched as defendant walked toward the main terminal. He then stopped suddenly, turned around, looked over his shoulder, and entered a nearby restroom. "The officers' suspicions aroused, one of them entered the restroom * * *. While standing a few feet away at a place where any member of the public would normally stand, the officer saw the unusual turquoise pant legs, that he had just observed on the defendant, between the bottom of the stall and the floor. Al-

though the door to the stall remained closed, the pant legs were visible in the approximate one-foot opening above the floor." *Id.* at 617. As the officer watched in silence, defendant pulled up the pant of his left leg and, when he tugged on his sock, a clear bag with a white powdery substance was openly displayed, taped to the inside of his left ankle. When defendant left the restroom, the officers approached him, identified themselves as police officers, and asked for identification. Defendant could produce no identification, but verbally identified himself and agreed to permit the officers to search the bag he was carrying. The moment the officers discovered two plastic bags of white powder in the bag, defendant fled but was quickly apprehended. A search incident to the arrest disclosed two more packages of cocaine taped to defendant's ankles.

In the appeal which followed the denial of his motion to suppress evidence, defendant argued that the investigative detention, the request for identification, and the subsequent search were invalid because they flowed from the officer's sighting of cocaine on defendant's pant leg in the bathroom stall. According to defendant, when the officer looked at the bottom of the stall "he violated defendant's reasonable expectation of privacy; therefore, any later evidence which flowed from the initial observation was fatally tainted." *Id.* at 618. The United States Court of Appeals for the Tenth Circuit could not agree.

According to the court, under *Katz v. United States*, 389 *U.S.* 347, 88 *S.Ct.* 507 (1967), "the defendant could have no reasonable objective expectation of privacy despite what he might have subjectively believed." *Billings* at 618. ["What a person knowingly exposes to the public, even in his own home or office, is not a subject of Fourth Amendment protection." *Katz* at 351-352, 88 *S.Ct.* at 511.] Here, "once the officer was in the public restroom, at a place where patrons are normally found, he was plainly able to see the contraband which defendant had taped to his leg, in the one-foot open area between the stall and the floor. [Thus,] the trial court properly denied defendant's motion to suppress the police officer's observations of the defendant's feet and legs, plainly visible, in the gap between the restroom stall and the floor, because the defendant had no reasonable expectation of privacy in that open area of the stall where any patron of this public restroom could easily see." *Billings* at 618.

5. *The passenger area of a commercial bus.* In *United States v. Ramos*, 960 *F.*2d 1065 (D.C. Cir. 1992), defendant hid a clear plastic bag containing drug paraphernalia between the seats of a commercial bus when, during a scheduled stop, the bus was boarded by police officers. One of the officers recovered the bag, placed defendant under arrest and discovered another plastic bag on defendant's person, this one containing cocaine base.

In the appeal following the denial of his motion to suppress, defendant argued that when he hid "the bag containing empty vials in the crevice between the seats, he clearly possessed a reasonable expectation of privacy in that bag[,]" just as he would were he instead traveling with "a valise or a suitcase." *Id.* at 1067. Additionally, defendant argued that the crevice between the seats should be treated as "the constitutional equivalent of an opaque container," with the seats constituting "an area in which an occupant may reasonably expect fourth amendment protection." *Id.* The United States Court of Appeals for the District of Columbia disagreed.

Preliminarily, the court noted that the plastic bag defendant hid between the seats was transparent. Therefore, "he could have no expectation of privacy in the bag itself," for the Fourth Amendment "provides protection to the owner of only a 'container that conceals its contents from plain view.'" *Id.* [Citation omitted.]

In addition, the court determined that the area in which defendant secreted the plastic bag is not one in which he could reasonably expect any degree of privacy.

> "Legitimation of expectations of privacy by law * * * must have a source outside of the Fourth Amendment, either by reference to concepts of real or personal property law or to understandings that are recognized and permitted by society." * * * *A passenger on a commercial bus certainly has no property interest in the crevice between the seats or for that matter in the rack above the seats, the area beneath the seats, or anywhere else that personal effects may be stowed. Nor are we aware of any socially recognized expectation of privacy in the interior of a bus.* * * *

> [Defendant] could not reasonably expect privacy in a clear plastic bag merely because he put it out of sight in a recess in the interior of a public bus.

Id. at 1067-68 (quoting *Rakas v. Illinois,* 439 *U.S.* 128, 143 n.12, 99 *S.Ct.* 421, 430 n.12 (1978)). [Emphasis added.]

6. *Parking lots. See United States v. Ludwig,* 10 *F.*3d 1523 (10th Cir. 1993) (defendant could claim no reasonable expectation of privacy in a motel parking lot that was open, unfenced, and visible from the public roads bordering it); *United States v. Dunkel,* 900 *F.*2d 105, 107 (7th Cir. 1990) (defendant had no legitimate expectation of privacy in the parking lot of a private office; lot was open to invitees of eight tenants and was not fenced), *vacated on other grounds,* 498 *U.S.* 1043, 111 *S.Ct.* 747 (1991); *United States v. Reed,* 733 *F.*2d 492, 501 (8th Cir. 1984) (officer's initial entry into business lot was not a search where lot was bound on three sides by public streets and visible from streets on two sides, and its fenced gate was completely open to a public street); *United States v. Edmonds,* 611 *F.*2d 1386, 1388 (5th Cir. 1980) (no legitimate expectation of privacy found in a business loading dock and parking lot).

ALVAREZ v. MONTGOMERY COUNTY
United States Court of Appeals
147 *F*.3d 354 (4th Cir. 1998)

QUESTION: In order to comply with the Fourth Amendment when responding to a call for service at a particular home, must law enforcement officers always knock at the front door before attempting to contact the occupant elsewhere on the premises ?

ANSWER: NO. "[O]fficers who seek to talk to the occupant of a home do not necessarily violate the Fourth Amendment by entering the backyard of a dwelling although they have failed to knock at the front door." *Id.* at 358.

RATIONALE: During the evening hours, Montgomery County, Maryland, police officers received a 911 telephone complaint related to an underage drinking party in the neighborhood. Officer Romack and several other officers drove toward Sunrise Drive, the area of the complaint. As the officers neared the Alvarez home, they noticed multiple alcohol containers in front of the home, as well as a number of cars parked there in an "odd" fashion. Believing that he had found the underage drinking party, Officer Romack approached the front door while the other officers waited by the driveway. When Romack reached the front stoop, another officer noticed a sign affixed to a lamppost in the front driveway which read: "Party In Back." An arrow on the sign pointed toward the backyard. "Without knocking, Officer Romack walked away from the front door, read the sign, then entered the backyard with the other officers." *Id.* at 357.

"Once in the backyard, the officers saw several guests, and Officer Romack asked to speak with the party's host or the homeowner." *Id.* While waiting, the officers observed what appeared to be the underage consumption of an alcoholic beverage.

Finding the officers' actions entirely lawful, the court preliminarily observed:

> Not every police encounter with a person or approach to a building implicates the Fourth Amendment. * * * [P]olice may approach a building, including the front entranceway to a residential dwelling, without committing a search where a person lacked a reasonable expectation of privacy in the area.

Id. at 357.

In this case, the Alvarezes proposed a rule requiring law enforcement officers "under all circumstances to knock at the front door before attempting to contact the occupant elsewhere on the premises." *Id.* at 358. The court would not, however, adopt such an "inflexible approach," which directly conflicts with the "reasonableness" standard of the Fourth Amendment. *Id.*

"In line with this reasonableness approach, this circuit has permitted law enforcement officers to enter a person's backyard without a warrant

when they have a legitimate law enforcement purpose for doing so." *Id.*
See e.g., United States v. Bradshaw, 490 *F.*2d 1097, 1100 (4th Cir. 1974)
(federal agents were "clearly entitled" to go onto defendant's premises in
order to talk to him, and when they were unable to get an answer at the
front door, an agent was permitted to walk around to the back door).

Similarly, other circuits have found that the "Fourth Amendment
does not invariably forbid an officer's warrantless entry into the area
surrounding a residential dwelling even when the officer has not first
knocked at the front door." *Alvarez* at 358. In *United States v. Daoust,*
916 *F.*2d 757 (1st Cir. 1990), for example,

> the First Circuit held that police officers, who found the front door
> of the defendant's house inaccessible, did not violate the Fourth
> Amendment when they went around to the back. ✳✳✳ The court
> reasoned that "[a] policeman may lawfully go to a person's home to
> interview him" and if the front door is inaccessible "there is nothing
> unlawful or unreasonable about going to the back of the house to
> look for another door, all as part of a legitimate attempt to inter-
> view the person." *Id.* [at 758.] *Daoust* thus supports the view that
> officers who seek to talk to the occupant of a home do not necessar-
> ily violate the Fourth Amendment by entering the backyard of a
> dwelling although they have failed to knock at the front door. Sev-
> eral other circuits similarly have held that an officer's warrantless
> entry of areas other than a residence's front entranceway does not
> always violate the Fourth Amendment. [*See e.*]g., *United States v.
> Garcia,* 997 *F.*2d 1273, 1279-80 (9th Cir. 1993) (entering back porch
> of apartment); *United States v. Anderson,* 552 *F.*2d 1296, 1299-1300
> (8th Cir. 1977) (entering back porch of home).

Alvarez at 358.

Based on the principles set forth above, the court concluded that
the officers in this case did not violate the Fourth Amendment. The
court said:

> The officers' entry into the backyard satisfied the Fourth Amend-
> ment's reasonableness requirement. They were responding to a 911
> call about an underage drinking party and, based on the alcohol
> containers and the awkwardly parked cars, believed they had found
> the party. They entered the Alvarezes' property simply to notify the
> homeowner or the party's host about the complaint ✳✳✳. Thus,
> ✳✳✳ the officers in this case had a "legitimate reason" for entering
> the Alvarezes' property "unconnected with a search of such prem-
> ises[.]" ✳✳✳ In furtherance of this purpose, they obviously could
> approach the front door in an attempt to contact the Alvarezes.
> ✳✳✳ And in light of the sign reading "Party In Back" with an arrow
> pointing toward the backyard, it surely was reasonable for the offi-
> cers to proceed there directly as part of their efforts to speak with
> the party's host.
>
> Nor did the officers' conduct after they had entered the backyard
> violate the Fourth Amendment. The intrusion was minimal. ✳✳✳

Id. at 358-59.

Accordingly, while "the curtilage of the home 'typically is afforded the most stringent Fourth Amendment protection,'" it was not unreasonable in this case "for officers responding to a 911 call to enter the backyard when circumstances indicated that they might find the homeowner there." *Id.* at 359. [Citations and internal quotes omitted.]

NOTE

1. *Use of a flashlight.* As a general principle, an individual's subjective expectation of privacy as to that which is located in an area of common access or view will be deemed unreasonable; and as a result, visual observation of evidence located in open view in an unprotected area does not constitute a search within the meaning of the Fourth Amendment. Thus, it has been held that no "search" takes place when police use artificial means, such as a flashlight, to illuminate a darkened area. *See e.g., United States v. Dunn,* 480 *U.S.* 294, 107 *S.Ct.* 1134, 1141 (1987) ("officers' use of the beam of a flashlight, directed through the essentially open front of [defendant's] barn, did not transform their observations into an unreasonable search within the meaning of the Fourth Amendment"); *Texas v. Brown,* 460 *U.S.* 730, 739-740, 103 *S.Ct.* 1535, 1542 (1983) (officer's "action in shining his flashlight to illuminate the interior of [defendant's] car trenched upon no right secured to the latter by the Fourth Amendment"); *United States v. Lee,* 274 *U.S.* 559, 563, 47 *S.Ct.* 746, 748 (1927) ("[The] use of a search light is comparable to the use of a marine glass or a field glass. It is not prohibited by the Constitution"). *See also United States v. Rickus,* 737 *F.*2d 360, 366 n.3 (3rd Cir. 1984) ("use of a flashlight to aid the officer's vision did not transform the observations justified under the 'plain view doctrine' into an illegal search"); *United States v. Chesher,* 678 *F.*2d 1353, 1356-1357 n.2 (9th Cir. 1982); *United States v. Ocampo,* 650 *F.*2d 421, 427 (2d Cir. 1981); *United States v. Pugh,* 566 *F.*2d 626, 627 n.2 (8th Cir. 1977); *People v. Waits,* 580 *P.*2d 391 (Colo. 1978); *Redd v. State,* 243 *S.E.*2d 16 (Ga. 1978); *State v. Chattley,* 390 *A.*2d 472 (Me. 1978); *State v. Vohnoutka,* 292 *N.W.*2d 756 (Minn. 1980); *Commonwealth v. Chiesa,* 478 *A.*2d 850 (*Pa.Super.* 1984).

2. *Drug field test not a search. See United States v. Jacobsen,* 466 *U.S.* 109, 104 *S.Ct.* 1652 (1984), where the Court held that a chemical field test "that merely discloses whether or not a particular substance is cocaine does not compromise any legitimate interest in privacy." *Id.,* 104 *S.Ct.* at 1662. Here the Court explained that a field test discloses "only one fact previously unknown to [an officer]— whether or not a suspicious [substance is an illegal drug]." *Id.* at 1661. "It is probably safe," stated the Court, "to assume that virtually all of the tests conducted under the circumstances [of this case] would result in a positive finding; in such cases, no legitimate interest has been compromised. But even if the results are negative—merely disclosing that the substance is something other than [a particular illegal drug]—such a result reveals nothing of special interest." *Id.* at 1662. As in the case of the "sniff test" conducted by a trained narcotics detection dog, the like-

lihood that a chemical field test of suspected narcotics will actually compromise any legitimate interest in privacy "seems too remote to characterize the testing as a search subject to the Fourth Amendment." *Id.* Moreover, the permanent interference with the defendant's possessory interest by the destruction of a minuscule portion of the powder during the test was sufficiently counter-balanced by the significant law enforcement interests at stake. "[B]ecause only a trace amount of material was involved, * * * the 'seizure' could, at most, have only a *de minimis* impact on any protected property interest." *Id.* at 1663.

3. *Chemical analysis of an arrestee's clothing.* In *State v. Joyce,* 229 *Conn.* 10, 639 *A.*2d 1007 (1994), the Connecticut Supreme Court addressed the question whether its state constitution required the police, while lawfully in possession of a suspect's clothing, to obtain a warrant before subjecting the clothing to a chemical analysis. The defendant, Wallace Joyce, was severely burned in a fire which violently erupted at a residence in East Haven, Connecticut. At the scene, in order to facilitate treatment, paramedics cut off all of defendant's clothing. Thereafter, a police detective took custody of the clothing and, within a day of the fire, when Joyce became a suspect, turned the clothing over to the fire marshal. The fire marshal took the clothing to the state forensic laboratory for analysis. At the laboratory, a gas chromatography analysis revealed the presence of gasoline. At no time was a warrant secured for the seizure of the clothing or for the subsequent analysis.

Preliminarily, the Connecticut High Court presumed that the police had probable cause at the time of the chemical test to believe that defendant started the fire. The court also accepted the trial court's conclusion that the police had lawfully taken custody of defendant's clothing "pursuant to their community caretaking function." *Id.,* 639 *A.*2d at 1010. The court went on to hold, however, that the chemical analysis of defendant's clothing was an illegal search under article first, §7, of the Connecticut Constitution.

To determine whether the results of such chemical testing should have been suppressed under the state exclusionary rule as the product of a "search," an initial inquiry must be made as to "(1) whether there was a reasonable expectation of privacy in the clothing; (2) whether the testing of the clothing at the state laboratory constituted a search; and (3) if so, whether the circumstances of this case fall within a recognized exception to the warrant requirement." *Id.* at 1013.

The court first determined that "defendant's expectation of privacy was a reasonable one under article first, §7, of the state constitution." *Id.* at 1015. He "adequately exhibited his subjective expectation of privacy, as he 'merely left his property behind him, more or less of necessity, making no attempt, however, to discard it or disassociate it from himself.'" *Id.* at 1014. In addition, the court held defendant's expectation of privacy to be one that society would be prepared to recognize as reasonable. "Although the items of clothing tested at the state laboratory were unusable as clothing and reduced to rags, they were still the defendant's rags," the court said. *Id.*

In light of the court's holding that defendant had "a reasonable expectation of privacy in the invisible and odorless chemicals present in his clothing," it found it "obvious" that the laboratory testing of the clothing—testing which was "capable of determining a multitude of private facts about an individual"—constituted "a search under article first, §7, of the state constitution." *Id.* at 1015.

Finally, the court determined that there was no recognized exception to the warrant requirement under the state constitution that would encompass the warrantless search of the defendant's clothing. It therefore concluded that the results of the chemical analysis of defendant's clothing "should have been suppressed." *Id.* at 1017.

4. *Beepers.* In *United States v. Diaz-Lizaraza*, 981 *F.*2d 1216 (11th Cir. 1993), the court rejected defendant's contention that the police exceeded the scope of a search incident to arrest by reinserting the batteries in his beeper and verifying that a previously-obtained number, when called, activated the beeper. According to the court, the law enforcement agents

> acted reasonably in inserting batteries into the beeper and calling it to see if it would ring when [the suspected] beeper number was dialed. The agents had probable cause to believe that the beeper was connected to criminal activity. It is commonly known that drug dealers often use beepers to conduct their business. * * * [T]he agents knew that * * * Diaz had been wearing the beeper, fully assembled moments before it appeared on the floor of the truck, dysfunctional for lack of batteries. Although no one saw how the beeper got from Diaz's belt to the floor of his truck, this was suspicious enough to warrant reactivating and testing the beeper. * * *

> By inserting batteries into the disassembled beeper, the agents conducted a nonintrusive field test to determine whether this was the beeper of "George," the person who arranged the transaction with Agent Jordan. Because it could not respond to a call without batteries, the agents had to reactivate the beeper in order to gain this information from it. This procedure was similar to the accepted law enforcement practice of conducting simple chemical field tests to determine the identity of a substance * * *. This nonintrusive field test of the beeper was reasonable in light of the agents' probable cause to believe that the beeper was connected to criminal activity.

> Moreover, actually calling a beeper does not violate the Fourth Amendment under any circumstances. There simply is no reasonable expectation of privacy in not having a beeper called. * * * In this case, Diaz could not have had a subjective expectation of privacy in his beeper number because he had given it to Agent Jordan. * * * However, even if Diaz had had a subjective expectation of privacy, it would not have been reasonable. The only reason to obtain a beeper is to allow other people to call it. Beepers are ob-

tained with the expectation, even the purpose, of letting other people call them. Therefore, there is no reasonable expectation of privacy in not having a beeper called, and calling a beeper does not implicate Fourth Amendment concerns.

Id. at 1223.

The court also summarily rejected Diaz's argument that the Electronic Communications Privacy Act, 18 *U.S.C.* §2510, *et seq.*, requires suppression of evidence of the beeper's sounding because the agents illegally "intercepted the transmission" from the phone to the beeper. The Act, ruled the court, "simply does not apply to parties to the transmission. * * * In this case, the agents lawfully possessed the beeper and essentially called themselves. The agents were not merely a party to the transmission; they were the only party to the transmission. Therefore, the agents did not intercept a transmission." *Id.* at 1220 n.1.

5. *Electronic tracking devices.* Electronic tracking devices, sometimes called transponders, beacons or "beepers," are battery-operated devices that emit periodic signals which can be picked up on radio frequency. The signals help law enforcement agents establish the approximate location of the object to which the device is attached. In determining whether the use of such a device constitutes a search or seizure within the meaning of the Fourth Amendment, courts tend to focus on two issues: (1) the initial attachment of the device to an object; and (2) the subsequent monitoring of the movement of the device in order to determine the location or treatment of the object to which it was attached.

(a) In *United States v. Knotts*, 460 *U.S.* 276, 103 *S.Ct.* 1081 (1983), the United States Supreme Court held that the warrantless tracking of the movements of an automobile containing a drum of chloroform, by monitoring a beeper attached to the drum, was not an illegal surveillance prohibited by the Fourth Amendment. In this case, a beeper was placed in a five-gallon drum containing chloroform purchased by one of defendant's associates. Chloroform is one of the so-called "precursor" chemicals used to manufacture illicit drugs. *Id.* at 277. The installation of the beeper took place with the consent of the seller prior to the sale. The delivery of the drum was made by another of defendant's associates, Petschen. By monitoring the progress of the car carrying the chloroform, Minnesota law enforcement agents were able to trace the drum of chloroform from its place of purchase in Minneapolis to defendant's secluded cabin near Shell Lake, Wisconsin.

Information obtained through the use of the beeper, along with additional information obtained during three days of visual surveillance of defendant's cabin, provided grounds for a search warrant. "During execution of the warrant, officers discovered a fully operable, clandestine drug laboratory in the cabin. In the laboratory area, officers found formulas for amphetamine and methamphetamine, over $10,000 worth of laboratory equipment, and chemicals in quantities sufficient to produce 14 pounds of pure amphetamine. Under a barrel outside the cabin, officers located the five-gallon container of chloroform." *Id.* at 279.

Finding the warrantless monitoring of defendant's vehicle constitutional, the Court explained:

> The governmental surveillance conducted by means of the beeper in this case amounted principally to the following of an automobile on public streets and highways. * * * A car has little capacity for escaping public scrutiny. * * * A person traveling in an automobile on public thoroughfares has no reasonable expectation of privacy in his movements from one place to another. When Petschen traveled over the public streets he voluntarily conveyed to anyone who wanted to look the fact that he was traveling over particular roads in a particular direction, the fact of whatever stops he made, and the fact of his final destination when he exited from public roads onto private property. [Defendant] Knotts, as the owner of the cabin and surrounding premises to which Petschen drove, undoubtedly had the traditional expectation of privacy within a dwelling place insofar as the cabin was concerned[.] * * *
>
> But no such expectation of privacy extended to the visual observation of Petschen's automobile arriving on his premises after leaving a public highway, nor to movements of objects such as the drum of chloroform outside the cabin in the "open fields." * * * Visual surveillance from public places along Petschen's route or adjoining Knotts' premises would have sufficed to reveal all of these facts to the police. The fact that the officers in this case relied not only on visual surveillance, but also on the use of the beeper to signal the presence of Petschen's automobile to the police receiver, does not alter the situation. Nothing in the Fourth Amendment prohibited the police from augmenting the sensory faculties bestowed upon them at birth with such enhancement as science and technology afforded them in this case.

Id. at 281-82.

During the course of its opinion, the Court emphasized that the information obtained from the beeper stopped at the doorstep of defendant's cabin. The Court said:

> [N]othing in this record indicates that the beeper signal was received or relied upon after it had indicated that the drum containing the chloroform had ended its automotive journey at rest on [defendant's] premises in rural Wisconsin. Admittedly, because of the failure of the visual surveillance, the beeper enabled the law enforcement officials in this case to ascertain the ultimate resting place of the chloroform when they would not have been able to do so had they relied solely on their naked eyes. But scientific enhancement of this sort raises no constitutional issues which visual surveillance would not also raise. A police car following Petschen at a distance throughout his journey could have observed him leaving the public highway and arriving at the cabin owned by [defen-

dant], with the drum of chloroform still in the car. This fact, along with others, was used by the government in obtaining a search warrant which led to the discovery of the clandestine drug laboratory. But there is no indication that the beeper was used in any way to reveal information as to the movement of the drum within the cabin, or in any way that would not have been visible to the naked eye from outside the cabin.

Id. at 284-85.

Accordingly, the Court held that the warrantless monitoring of the beeper signals did not invade any legitimate expectation of privacy. Therefore, this action did not constitute either a "search" or a "seizure" within the contemplation of the Fourth Amendment. *Id.* at 285.

(b) In *United States v. Karo*, 468 *U.S.* 705, 104 *S.Ct.* 3296 (1984), the Court similarly held that the warrantless installation of a beeper in a drum of ether for the purpose of tracking the drum's movement did not violate the Fourth Amendment, for the installation of the beeper was made in a drum originally belonging to the DEA. Under the circumstances, the defendants had no legitimate, reasonable expectation of privacy in the drum. Even with the substitution of the DEA's drum for one of the drums in the shipment sold to the defendants, the Court held that the consent of the owner in possession of the drum was sufficient to validate installation of the beeper. *See id.* at 711, 104 *S.Ct.* at 3301.

In addition, the Court held that the transfer of the drum thereafter was not a "search," because at the time of the transfer, the beeper was not monitored, and therefore did not give any information infringing upon defendants' reasonable expectation of privacy. Similarly, the transfer did not constitute a "seizure," because it was not a "meaningful" interference with defendants' possessory interests. *Id.* at 712, 104 *S.Ct.* at 3302.

The Court went on to hold, however, that the monitoring of a beeper to determine the location of the drum *in a private residence* required a search warrant. The Court reasoned that any information obtained through the beeper from a private residence, but unavailable through visual surveillance, violated the Fourth Amendment. Law enforcement agents may not, therefore, surreptitiously use a beeper to obtain information that they could not have obtained from outside the curtilage of a home. *Id.* at 714, 104 *S.Ct.* at 3303.

(c) In both *Knotts* and *Karo*, the beepers were secreted in containers (a drum of chloroform in *Knotts*, and a drum of ether in *Karo*) of which government agents had full control, dominion, and possessory interests prior to installation, and before the defendants obtained possession of the drums through a purchase. A different result would obtain, however, if a defendant had a legitimate and reasonable privacy and possessory expectation in an item of property prior to the installation of a beeper by government agents. *See, e.g., State v. Kelly*, 68 *Haw.* 213, 708 *P.*2d 820 (1985) (warrantless, ten-day seizure from postal authorities of a photo album addressed to defendant, for the purpose of

installing an electronic beeper in the back cover of the album, violated the Fourth Amendment).

(d) While the attachment of a beeper to the outside of a motor vehicle located on a public street may not implicate Fourth Amendment concerns, *see, e.g., United States v. McIver,* 186 *F.*3d 1119 (9th Cir. 1999), the entry of a private garage or similar place in order to gain access to the vehicle to attach a beeper is a Fourth Amendment search. *See United States v. Hufford,* 539 *F.*2d 32 (9th Cir. 1976) (entry of garage to place a beeper on defendant's truck required a search warrant).

(e) Many tracking cases involve the police placing a beeper inside an item of property before it comes into the possession of a criminal suspect. *See, e.g., United States v. Most,* 789 *F.*2d 1411 (9th Cir. 1986) (electronic tracking device placed inside packages opened by customs agents and found to contain narcotics); *United States v. Emery,* 541 *F.*2d 887 (1st Cir. 1976) (*same*); *United States v. Bishop,* 530 *F.*2d 1156 (5th Cir. 1976) (a bank teller acting as a police agent placing a beeper into a money bag taken by a bank robber); *United States v. Bailey,* 628 *F.*2d 938 (6th Cir. 1980) (beeper placed in packages of chemicals prior to their purchase for use in manufacturing illicit substances); *United States v. Perez,* 526 *F.*2d 859 (5th Cir. 1976) (beeper placed in personal effects undercover officers traded for drugs).

(f) On December 1, 2006, the Federal Rules of Criminal Procedure were amended to specifically address the use of "tracking devices." While such searches are recognized both by statute, *see* 18 *U.S.C.* § 3117(a), and by case law, *see e.g., United States v. Karo, supra,* and *United States v. Knotts, supra,* warrants may be required to monitor tracking devices when they are used to monitor persons or property in areas where there is a reasonable expectation of privacy.

The amendment to Rule 41(b) provides that "a magistrate judge with authority in the district has authority to issue a warrant to install within the district a tracking device; the warrant may authorize use of the device to track the movement of a person or property located within the district, outside the district, or both. *Rule* 41(b)(4). The judge's authority under this rule includes the authority to permit entry into an area where there is a reasonable expectation of privacy, installation of the tracking device, and maintenance and removal of the device.

In accordance with *Rule* 41(e)(2)(B), the "tracking-device warrant must identify the person or property to be tracked, designate the magistrate judge to whom it must be returned, and specify a reasonable length of time that the device may be used. The time must not exceed 45 days from the date the warrant was issued."

Thus, if officers intend to install or use the device in a constitutionally protected area, they must obtain judicial approval to do so. If, on the other hand, the officers intend to install and use the device without implicating any reasonable expectation of privacy under the Fourth Amendment, there is no need to obtain the warrant.

§4.2. Open fields.

The "open fields" doctrine, originally set forth in *Hester v. United States*, 265 *U.S.* 57, 44 *S.Ct.* 445 (1924), authorizes law enforcement officers to enter and search an "open" field without a warrant. In *Hester*, Justice Holmes explained that the special and unique safeguards provided by the Fourth Amendment to the people in their "persons, houses, papers, and effects," is not extended to open fields. Open fields are not "houses" nor may they be considered "effects."

The final analysis always boils down to the question of whether a person has a "constitutionally protected reasonable expectation of privacy" in the particular area in question. *Katz v. United States*, 389 *U.S.* 347, 360, 88 *S.Ct.* 507, 516 (1967) (Harlan, J., concurring). However, the Amendment will only protect "those expectations that society is prepared to recognize as 'reasonable.' " *Id.* at 361, 88 *S.Ct.* at 516.

The home, of course, since the inception of this Nation, has been one of these areas which commands the sanctity and privacy recognized by our society. Privacy has also been extended to the "land immediately surrounding and associated with the home." *Oliver v. United States*, 466 *U.S.* 170, 180, 104 *S.Ct.* 1735, 1742 (1984). However, this "curtilage," as a part of the "home," is not only separate, but distinguished from neighboring open fields. "[O]pen fields do not provide the setting for those intimate activities that the [Fourth] Amendment is intended to shelter from government interference or surveillance." *Id.* at 179, 104 *S.Ct.* at 1741. Not only is there no societal interest in protecting the privacy of crop cultivation or field irrigation, "as a practical matter, these lands usually are accessible to the public and the police in ways that a home, an office, or commercial structure would not be." *Id.* A typical example would be the common viewing of such fields by airplane or helicopter.

OLIVER v. UNITED STATES
Supreme Court of the United States
466 *U.S.* 170, 104 *S.Ct.* 1735 (1984)

QUESTION: Do law enforcement officers need a search warrant or probable cause to search a field which is not only in a secluded area, but fenced in with locked gates and "No Trespassing" signs posted at regular intervals ?

ANSWER: NO. Fencing in a secluded field and placing locked gates and "No Trespassing" signs does not create a constitutionally protected area.

RATIONALE: The Supreme Court of the United States here reaffirms its holding in *Hester v. United States*, 265 *U.S.* 57, 44 *S.Ct.* 445 (1924). The rule states that "an individual may not legitimately demand privacy for activities conducted out of doors in fields, except in the area immediately surrounding the home." *Oliver*, at 1741.

The High Court actually decided two cases; one from Maine, the other from Kentucky. Both cases had very similar fact patterns. The Maine and Kentucky defendants were both growing marijuana patches in fields located a distance from their homes. The Kentucky defendant fenced in his field, erected a locked gate, and posted "No Trespassing" signs. The Maine defendant used chicken wire for his fence and also posted "No Trespassing" signs.

The Court then proceeded to decide both cases with but one rationale—the "open fields" doctrine. Justice Powell, while reaffirming *Hester*, explained that "no expectation of privacy legitimately attaches to open fields." *Id.* at 1742. Both defendants attempted to conceal their criminal activities by planting marijuana upon secluded land with fencing and "No Trespassing" signs. It seems as if they were trying to protect or create an expectation of privacy. However, the test of whether a person may have a legitimate expectation of privacy is "not whether the individual chooses to conceal assertedly 'private' activity. Rather, the correct inquiry is whether the government's intrusion infringes upon the personal and societal values protected by the Fourth Amendment." *Id.* at 1743.

Since the government's intrusion upon an open field is not a "search" within the meaning of the Fourth Amendment, the contraband subsequently seized may be properly admitted in court.

UNITED STATES v. DUNN
Supreme Court of the United States
480 *U.S.* 294, 107 *S.Ct.* 1134 (1987)

QUESTION: Is the area near a barn, located approximately 50 yards from a fence surrounding a ranch house, within the curtilage of the house for Fourth Amendment purposes ?

ANSWER: NO. "[T]he barn and the area around it lay outside the curtilage of the [ranch] house." *Id.* at 1137.

RATIONALE: DEA agents, accompanied by an officer from the Houston Police Department, made a warrantless entry onto defendant's ranch property, crossing over the perimeter fence and one interior fence. The ranch comprised approximately 198 acres and was completely encircled by the perimeter fence. An interior fence encircled the ranch house and a nearby small greenhouse. Two barns were located approximately 50 yards from this fence, with the front of the larger barn enclosed by a wooden fence. This barn had an open overhang, but locked, waist-high gates barred entry into the barn proper, and netting material stretched from the ceiling to the top of the wooden gates.

As the officers stood approximately midway between the residence and the barns, the DEA agent detected an odor of what he believed to be phenylacetic acid coming from the direction of the barns. As the officers approached the larger barn, they crossed a barbed wire fence as well as the wooden fence that enclosed the front portion of the barn. They then "walked under the barn's overhang to the locked wooden gates and, shining a flashlight through the netting on top of the gates, peered into the barn. They observed what the DEA agent thought to be a phenylacetone laboratory." At this point, the officers departed from the ranch property and subsequently obtained a search warrant. Upon execution of the warrant, the officers seized chemicals and equipment from the alleged phenylacetone laboratory, as well as bags of amphetamines discovered in a closet in the ranch house.

The District Court denied defendant's motion to suppress the evidence seized, and, defendant was convicted by jury of conspiring to manufacture phenylacetone and amphetamine, and to possess amphetamine with the intent to distribute, contrary to federal law.

The United States Supreme Court agreed that the evidence was properly admitted, finding "that the barn and the area around it lay outside the curtilage of the house[.]" *Id.* at 1137.

In *Oliver v. United States*, 466 *U.S.* 170, 104 *S.Ct.* 1735 (1984), the Court recognized that "the Fourth Amendment protects the curtilage of a house and that the extent of the curtilage is determined by factors that bear upon whether an individual reasonably may expect that the area in question should be treated as the home itself." *Dunn* at 1139 (citing *Oliver* at 180, 104 *S.Ct.* at 1742). The "central component" of the curtilage inquiry is "whether the area harbors the 'intimate activity associated with the sanctity of a man's home and the privacies of life.'" *Dunn* at 1139. [Citations omitted.]

Thus, "curtilage questions should be resolved with particular reference to four factors:

[1]   the proximity of the area claimed to be curtilage to the home,

[2]   whether the area is included within an enclosure surrounding the home,

[3]   the nature of the uses to which the area is put, and

[4]   the steps taken by the resident to protect the area from observation by people passing by."

Id. While not a finely-tuned mechanical formula, these factors nonetheless are "useful analytical tools" which may be used to determine "whether the area in question is so intimately tied to the home itself that it should be placed under the home's 'umbrella' of Fourth Amendment protection." *Id.*

The Court then applied each of the four factors delineated above to defendant's barn and to the area immediately surrounding it and concluded that "this area lay outside the curtilage of the ranch house." *Id.* at 1140.

The final portion of the Court's opinion quickly dispelled defendant's contention "that he possessed an expectation of privacy, independent from his home's curtilage, in the barn and its contents." *Id.*

Here, the Court reasoned that "the term 'open fields' may include any unoccupied or underdeveloped area outside of the curtilage. An open field need be neither 'open' nor a 'field' as those terms are used in common speech" *Id.* at 1141 (quoting *Oliver* at 180, 104 *S.Ct.* at 1742). "It follows that no constitutional violation occurred here when the officers crossed over [the defendant's] ranch-style perimeter fence, and over several similarly constructed interior fences, prior to stopping at the locked front gate of the barn. * * * [T]he officers never entered the barn, nor did they enter any structure on [defendant's] premises. Once at their vantage point, they merely stood, outside the curtilage of the house and in the open fields upon which the barn was constructed, and peered into the barn's open front. And, standing as they were in the open fields, the Constitution did not forbid them to observe the phenylacetone laboratory located in [defendant's] barn. * * * Under *Oliver* and *Hester*, there is no constitutional difference between police observations conducted while in a public place and while standing in the open fields." *Dunn* at 1141.

Additionally, "the officers' use of the beam of a flashlight, directed through the essentially open front of [defendant's] barn, did not transform their observations into an unreasonable search within the meaning of the Fourth Amendment." *Id.*

Accordingly, the officers "lawfully viewed the interior of [defendant's] barn, and their observations were properly considered by the magistrate in issuing a search warrant for [defendant's] premises." *Id.*

NOTE

1. *Curtilage questions and multiple-unit buildings.* In *United States v. Acosta*, 965 *F.*2d 1248 (3rd Cir. 1992), the court addressed the question whether the first-floor tenants of the three-story, multi-unit apartment building, located at the corner of West Venango and Randolph Streets in Philadelphia, maintained a reasonable expectation of privacy in the fenced-in backyard adjacent to the first-floor apartment. Finding the absence of any reasonable expectation of privacy, the court first determined that the four factors of the curtilage inquiry set forth in *United States v. Dunn, supra,* could not be mechanically applied to an apartment building in an urban setting. Rather, in such a setting,

> [t]he more fundamental question is whether the backyard constitutes curtilage * * * at all.

> [A]lthough the *Dunn* factors also apply to determine extent-of-curtilage questions in urban areas, certain factors may be less determinative in a city setting because of the physical differences in the properties. * * * We believe that the weight of the factors is diminished further as applied to apartment dwellings. * * * It seems clear, for example, that "the configuration of the streets and houses in many parts of the city may make it impossible, or at least highly impracticable to screen one's home and yard from

view." * * * In addition, * * * tenants generally have neither the authority nor the investment incentive to take steps to protect a yard from view by doing such things as erecting a solid fence or planting trees and shrubbery. Instead, the tenant generally takes the property as he finds it, with or without fencing or other types of obstructions in place. In this context, the *Dunn* factors are not as useful analytically as in other settings.

Acosta at 1256. [Citations omitted.]

Thus, whether the defendants in this case can demonstrate an invasion of their own Fourth Amendment privacy interests depends upon "whether the person who claims the protection of the amendment has a *legitimate expectation of privacy* in the invaded place." *Id.* [Court's emphasis; citation omitted.] According to the court, one part of this inquiry looks to whether the particular tenant enjoys any "property interest" in the area claimed to be curtilage; for example, whether the tenant's lease gives him a legal interest in the backyard area, or a "right to use" the area. *Id.*

Here, the lease did not grant the defendants the right to use the backyard of the first-floor apartment. *Id.* at 1257. Although they had permission to use it, they hardly did. Moreover, "the landlord used the backyard freely, as did his employees. Indeed, the landlord stored his boat in the backyard." *Id.* Accordingly, the court held that

the fact that defendants had permission to use the yard did not create any legitimate expectation of privacy in it. * * * Defendants' insubstantial privacy interest arising from their authorized but limited use of the yard renders the four *Dunn* factors of insignificant value on this record in deciding the curtilage issue. * * *

[T]he district court made a mistake in finding that the backyard was a curtilage of defendants' apartment. It follows that defendants had no expectation that entitled them to Fourth Amendment privacy in the backyard. Thus, the [officer's] observ[ations] from his vantage point in the yard [were constitutionally permissible].

Id.

2. Under the federal Constitution, it is clear that an expectation of privacy in an "open field" will not be deemed reasonable. For Fourth Amendment purposes, "an individual may not legitimately demand privacy for activities conducted out of doors in fields, except in the area immediately surrounding the home." *Oliver v. United States, supra,* 466 *U.S.* at 178, 104 *S.Ct.* at 1741. Federal constitutional law does not, however, end the inquiry. A state court is certainly free to address the doctrine of "open fields" as a matter of its own law, and conclude that the federal precedents in this subject fail to adequately protect the individual rights of that state's citizens. Thus, in *State v. Kirchoff,* 587 *A.2d* 988 (Vt. 1991), the Supreme Court of Vermont, relying on Chapter I, Article 11, of the Vermont Constitution, determined

that some activities taking place in the open fields may be sufficiently private to warrant constitutional protection. According to this court:

> While generally there is not an expectation of privacy in unoccupied lands, such is not the case where the landowner has taken steps, such as fencing or posting, to indicate that privacy is exactly what is sought. The *Oliver* Court informs us that an individual's expectations of privacy in land—regardless of steps taken to establish that expectation—can never be legitimate. [*Oliver*] at 182, 104 *S.Ct.* at 1743. This per se approach cannot be squared with Article 11 * * *.

> [T]here is no empirical evidence on whether society is willing to recognize an expectation of privacy in "open fields" as reasonable or unreasonable. Certainly, it was a bold and unsupported pronouncement in *Oliver* that society is not prepared under any circumstances to recognize as reasonable an expectation of privacy in all lands outside the curtilage. Indeed, the fact that society may adjudge one who trespasses on such lands a criminal belies the claim. * * *

> We do not believe * * * that the difficulty of determining the degree of privacy to afford a particular "open field" is any greater than the difficulty in deciding, case by case, whether a search has invaded the curtilage * * *. [H]owever easy the bright-line test of *Oliver* is to apply, the test simply fails to do justice to the values underlying Article 11.

> We recently stated that Article 11 protects people of the state "from unreasonable, warrantless governmental intrusion into affairs which they choose to keep private." * * * *Oliver's* per se rule, that a person may never legitimately demand privacy under the Fourth Amendment in his or her land beyond the borders of the curtilage, fails to guarantee that right. *We now hold that a lawful possessor may claim privacy in "open fields" under Article 11 of the Vermont Constitution where indicia would lead a reasonable person to conclude that the area is private.* On the other hand, Article 11 does not afford protection against searches of lands where steps have not been taken to exclude the public. By this standard, we seek to protect the constitutional rights of those who have sought privacy in their lands, while not preventing police from using evidence of affairs that were not kept private—that were, in *Katz's* terms, "knowingly expose[d] to the public."

Kirchoff at 993-994. [Citations omitted; emphasis added.]

Thus, under the Vermont Constitution, "[w]here indicia, such as fences, barriers or 'no trespassing' signs reasonably indicate that strangers are not welcome on the land, the owner or occupant may reasonably expect privacy. * * * The inquiry is objective—whether a reasonable person should know that the occupant has sought to exclude the public. Whether the steps taken are adequate for this purpose will depend on the specific facts of each case." *Id.* at 994. Moreover, the burden is on the State "to prove that a warrantless search of open fields is not prohibited under the[se] principles[.]" *Id.* at 996.

See also State v. Dixon-Digby, 307 *Or.* 195, 211-212, 766 *P.*2d 1015, 1024 (1988) (rejecting a *per se* "open fields" doctrine under the Oregon Constitution and holding that "[a] person who wishes to preserve a constitutionally protected privacy interest in land outside the curtilage must manifest an intention to exclude the public by erecting barriers to entry, such as fences, or by posting signs").

---

§4.3. Plain View.

The "plain view" doctrine, as originally set forth in *Coolidge v. New Hampshire*, 403 *U.S.* 443, 91 *S.Ct.* 2022 (1971), and later modified by *Texas v. Brown*, 460 *U.S.* 730, 103 *S.Ct.* 1535 (1983), authorizes law enforcement officers to seize evidence of a crime, contraband, or other items subject to official seizure without first obtaining a search warrant. So long as an officer has a prior constitutional justification for an intrusion into an individual's realm of privacy, and in the course thereof discovers a piece of incriminating evidence, a warrantless seizure of that evidence may be immediately effected.

Although the plain view doctrine is often characterized as one of the exceptions to the written warrant requirement, the Supreme Court has indicated that "[i]f an article is already in plain view, neither its observation nor its seizure would involve any invasion of privacy." *Horton v. California*, 496 *U.S.* 128, 110 *S.Ct.* 2301, 2306 (1990). Thus, it may be said that the plain view doctrine simply "provides the grounds for seizure of an item when an officer's access to an object has some prior justification under the Fourth Amendment." *Brown* at 738, 103 *S.Ct.* at 1541. In this respect, rather than being viewed as an independent exception to the warrant requirement, the doctrine merely " 'serves to supplement the prior justification—whether it be a warrant for another object, hot pursuit, search incident to lawful arrest, or some other legitimate reason for being present' " in the viewing area. *Horton*, 110 *S.Ct.* at 2307 (quoting *Coolidge* at 466, 91 *S.Ct.* at 2038). The constitutional requirements which follow, therefore, must attach, not to the government's *observation* of an item lawfully discovered in plain view, but to its *seizure* of that item. In these circumstances, it is the seizure by the government of a citizen's property which clearly invades the owner's possessory interest, and as a result, the dispossession must be constitutionally justified. *Horton* at 2306. *See also United States v. Jacobsen*, 466 *U.S.* 109, 113, 104 *S.Ct.* 1652, 1656 (1984); *United States v. Jackson*, 131 *F.*3d 1105, 1108 (4th Cir. 1997) ("The 'plain view' doctrine provides an exception to the warrant requirement for the *seizure* of property, but it does not provide an exception for a search.") (emphasis in original).

Historically, the United States Supreme Court required three conditions to be satisfied before the plain view doctrine could be invoked. First, the law enforcement officer must have been lawfully in the viewing area. This required the initial intrusion to be constitutionally reasonable, *i.e.*, officers may not violate the Constitution in arriving at the place from which the evidence could be plainly viewed. Second, an officer's discovery of the incriminating evidence must have been inadvertent. The officer could not have known in advance where the items were located nor intend to seize them beforehand. This requirement traditionally guarded against the transformation of an initially valid (and therefore limited) search into a "general" one. Finally, the incriminating character of the evidence must have been "immediately apparent," and since 1987, this has meant that the officer must have "probable cause" to believe the evidence is associated with criminal activity. *Arizona v. Hicks*, 480 *U.S.* 321, 327, 107 *S.Ct.* 1149, 1153 (1987).

In 1990, the United States Supreme Court re-examined the plain view doctrine and eliminated the "inadvertence" requirement. In *Horton v. California, supra*, the Court reasoned that "evenhanded law enforcement is best achieved by the application of objective standards of conduct, rather than standards that depend upon the subjective state of mind of the officer." *Id.* at 2309. Thus, even though an officer may be interested in an item of evidence and fully expects to find it in the course of a search, that subjective fact "should not invalidate its seizure if the search is confined in area and duration by the terms of a warrant or a valid exception to the warrant requirement." *Id.*

Accordingly, in order to validly invoke the plain view doctrine, two requirements must be met:

> 1. The officer must be lawfully in the viewing area; that is, officers may not violate the Constitution in arriving at the place from which the evidence could be plainly viewed; and

> 2. The officer must have probable cause to believe the evidence is somehow associated with criminal activity.

If both prongs of the doctrine are satisfied, the evidence may then be immediately seized without a search warrant. Significantly, it has been held that this procedure "involves no invasion of privacy and is presumptively reasonable[.]" *Horton*, 110 *S.Ct.* at 2310; *Brown* at 741-742, 103 *S.Ct.* at 1543. *See also Payton v. New York*, 445 *U.S.* 573, 587, 100 *S.Ct.* 1371, 1380 (1980).

TEXAS v. BROWN
Supreme Court of the United States
460 *U.S.* 730, 103 *S.Ct.* 1535 (1983)

QUESTION: Before law enforcement officers may seize incriminating evidence found in "plain view," must it be "immediately apparent" to the officers that the items they observe are evidence of a crime, contraband, or otherwise subject to official seizure ?

ANSWER: NO. The "immediately apparent" prong of the plain view criteria is modified so as only to require the officers to have probable cause to associate the items with criminal activity. *Id.* at 1542.

RATIONALE: Shortly before midnight, Officer Maples of the Fort Worth, Texas, Police Department stopped an automobile driven by defendant, Clifford Brown. As the officer stood alongside the driver's window of Brown's car, he asked Brown for his driving credentials. "At roughly the same time, Maples shined his flashlight into the car and saw Brown withdraw his right hand from his right pants pocket. Caught between the two middle fingers of the hand was an opaque, green party balloon, knotted about one-half inch from the tip. Brown let the balloon fall to the seat beside his leg, and then reached across the passenger seat and opened the glove compartment." Based on the officer's prior experience in making drug arrests, he was aware that narcotics were frequently packaged in party balloons.

As Brown rummaged through the glove compartment looking (unsuccessfully) for his driver's license, Officer Maples noticed that it contained "several plastic vials, quantities of loose white powder, and an open bag of party balloons." The officer "then instructed him to get out of the car and stand at its rear. Brown complied, and, before following him to the rear of the car, Maples reached into the car and picked up the green balloon[,]" which appeared to contain "a sort of powdery substance within the tied-off portion." Based on this discovery, Maples placed Brown under arrest. Subsequent laboratory analysis confirmed that the white powder was heroin.

The Texas Court of Criminal Appeals ruled that the evidence seized by Officer Maples must be suppressed because the officer did not "know" for a fact that "incriminatory evidence was before him" when he seized the balloon. According to the Texas court, because it was not "immediately apparent" to the officer that the balloon contained contraband, its seizure could not be justified under the "plain view" doctrine.

Because of the uncertainty surrounding this particular aspect of the "plain view" doctrine, the United States Supreme Court granted *certiorari*, and reversed the Texas ruling.

As originally stated, the "plain view" doctrine allowed the police to make warrantless seizures of evidence when three conditions were met:

(1) The officer must "lawfully make the initial intrusion" or "lawfully be in the viewing area";

(2) The officer must discover the incriminating evidence "inadvertently," *i.e.*, he may not know in advance that the evidence is in a particular location nor intend to seize it beforehand; and

(3) It must be "immediately apparent" to the officer that the items observed may be evidence of a crime, contraband, or otherwise subject to official seizure.

Id. at 1540 (citing *Coolidge v. New Hampshire*, 403 *U.S.* 443, 91 *S.Ct.* 2022 (1971)).

This doctrine has led to the general rule "that if, while lawfully engaged in an activity in a particular place, police officers perceive a suspicious object, they may seize it immediately." *Brown* at 1541. However, holding law enforcement officers to the "immediately apparent" condition implies "an unduly high degree of certainty as to the incriminating character of the evidence." *Id.* at 1542.

Since the seizure of evidence in plain view involves no invasion of privacy and is presumptively reasonable within the meaning of the Fourth Amendment, it should be sufficient to merely require the officers to have probable cause to associate the items with criminal activity. *Id.*

Justice Rehnquist explained that "probable cause is a flexible, common sense standard." *Id.* at 1543.

It merely requires that the facts available to the officer would warrant a man of reasonable caution in the belief that certain items may be contraband or stolen property or useful as evidence of a crime; it does not demand any showing that such a belief be correct or more likely true than false. A practical, nontechnical probability that incriminating evidence is involved is all that is required. [Justice Rehnquist's citations omitted.]

Id.

As a result, it is clear that the officer here "possessed probable cause to believe that the balloon in the defendant's hand contained an illicit substance." *Id.* Additionally, the officer was lawfully in the viewing area, for his motor vehicle stop of the defendant was entirely proper. Finally, the officer's discovery of the heroin was inadvertent. Nowhere in the evidence did it appear that the officer knew in advance that the defendant would be in possession of heroin.

The evidence seized should not have been suppressed. *Id.* at 1544.

NOTE

"Worthy" versus "unworthy" containers. In *United States v. Ross*, 456 *U.S.* 798, 102 *S.Ct.* 2157 (1982), the Court concluded that even though a distinction between "worthy" and "unworthy" containers

perhaps could evolve in a series of cases in which paper bags, locked trunks, lunch buckets, and orange crates were placed on one side of the line or the other, the central purpose of the Fourth Amendment forecloses such a distinction. For just as the most frail

cottage in the kingdom is absolutely entitled to the same guarantees of privacy as the most majestic mansion, so also may a traveler who carries a toothbrush and a few articles of clothing in a
paper bag or knotted scarf claim an equal right to conceal his possessions from official inspection as the sophisticated executive with
the locked attache case.

Id. at 822, 102 *S.Ct.* at 2171. Additionally, the Court noted that if the
"worthy" versus "unworthy" container distinction

is based on the proposition that the Fourth Amendment protects
only those containers that objectively manifest an individual's reasonable expectation of privacy, however, the propriety of a warrantless search necessarily would turn on much more than the fabric of the container. A paper bag stapled shut and marked "private"
might be found to manifest a reasonable expectation of privacy, as
could a cardboard box stacked on top of two pieces of heavy luggage. The propriety of the warrantless search seemingly would turn
on an objective appraisal of all the surrounding circumstances.

Id. at 822 n.30, 102 *S.Ct.* at 2171 n.30.

In *Texas v. Brown, supra,* the "unworthy" container at issue was a
green, opaque party balloon, observed with the help of a flashlight
shone from an officer's vantage point outside Brown's lawfully stopped
automobile. The balloon came into the officer's plain view when Brown
withdrew his hand from his pants pocket; the balloon was caught between the two middle fingers of Brown's hand. In upholding the seizure and search of the balloon, the Court declared that the officer

possessed probable cause to believe that the balloon in Brown's
hand contained an illicit substance. [The officer] testified that he
was aware, both from his participation in previous narcotics arrests and from discussions with other officers, that balloons tied in
the manner of the one possessed by Brown were frequently used to
carry narcotics. * * * *The fact that [the officer] could not see
through the opaque fabric of the balloon is all but irrelevant; the
distinctive character of the balloon itself spoke volumes as to its
contents—particularly to the trained eye of the officer.*

Brown at 742-43, 103 *S.Ct.* at 1543-44. [Emphasis added.] Thus, there
may exist a group of containers—*e.g.,* filled opaque balloons—"which
may be less worthy than others." *See* Holtz, *The "Plain Touch" Corollary: A Natural and Foreseeable Consequence of the Plain View Doctrine,* 95 Dickinson L.Rev. 521, 539 (1991). It is significant to note,
however, that in addition to the opaque, green party balloon, the officer in Brown also observed "several small plastic vials, quantities of
loose white powder, and an open bag of party balloons in the interior
of the open glove compartment." These additional observations, according to the Court, "revealed further suggestions" that the party balloon contained an illicit substance. *Id.* at 743, 103 *S.Ct.* at 1543-44.

Film canisters. During the course of a pat-down frisk of Albert Harris, Officer Von Canon of the Henrico County, Virginia, Police Department, felt a bulge in Harris' pocket. Von Canon removed a film canister from Harris' pocket and asked him what was in it. Harris replied, "Film." The officer opened the canister and discovered that it contained a quantity of white powder which he believed (correctly as later analysis showed) to be cocaine. Von Canon placed Harris under arrest, searched him, and discovered another film canister and a small plastic bag, both of which contained white powder later identified as cocaine.

In the appeal following the denial of his motion to suppress evidence, the Commonwealth sought to sustain the validity of the first search by contending that Von Canon had probable cause to believe the container contained drugs. The Virginia Supreme Court, in *Harris v. Commonwealth*, 400 *S.E.*2d 191 (Va. 1991), disagreed.

According to the court, the scope of a *Terry* frisk is limited solely to a protective pat down " 'of the outer clothing of the suspect for concealed objects which might be used as instruments of assault.' " *Id.* at 194. [Citations omitted.]

> However, Von Canon's seizure and search of the film canister during the weapon search was not permissible because the canister was not a weapon and he did not search the canister for a weapon. Rather, he had a "hunch" that the canister contained illegal drugs and therefore conducted a generalized search.

Id.

At the suppression hearing, Von Canon testified as follows:

> *Question*: [W]hen you patted [Harris] down for weapons you indicated that you felt a film canister.
> *Answer*: Yes sir.
> *Question*: You knew that was not a weapon, didn't you ?
> *Answer*: That's correct.
> *Question*: And what did you think that was ?
> *Answer*: I thought it was probably drugs.
> *Question*: When you felt that film canister, that meant something to you ?
> *Answer*: My first reaction was, "this is drugs, it's not film, it's drugs."

Id. at 194-95. Respecting this aspect of the case, the court concluded that Von Canon's search of Harris should have been cut off once the officer "assured himself that Harris possessed no weapons." *Id.* at 195.

The Court also held that Officer Von Canon's plain touch did not provide him with probable cause to associate the film canister with criminal activity.

> [T]he record in this case does not indicate that Von Canon had probable cause to believe that Harris' film canister contained contraband. The evidence contained in this [case] falls far short of the

quantum of proof established in *Brown*. It is true that Von Canon knew from his personal experience of working "plain clothes assignments" and "making arrests" that certain people keep their narcotics and drugs in film canisters and "things of that nature." However, law-abiding citizens, on a daily basis, also use film canisters to store film, which is a legitimate use. At best, Von Canon had a "hunch[.]"

Id. at 196.

A similar result was reached by the New Jersey Supreme Court in *State v. Demeter*, 124 *N.J.* 374, 590 *A.*2d 1179 (1991). In *Demeter*, defendant's van was stopped by the police because of a defective license plate light. While standing by the driver's side door, the officer observed a black, opaque 35-millimeter film canister lying in the storage area of the van's front console. When the officer noticed the absence of a camera in the van, he asked defendant to hand over the canister. As he did so, defendant advised the officer that the film container was used to store bridge tokens. The officer removed the film canister's lid, detected an odor of marijuana and noticed some marijuana residue inside.

At the suppression hearing, the officer testified that in his seven years of experience as a law enforcement officer, "he had investigated at least forty narcotics incidents with 'at least half of them' involving the use of 35-millimeter film containers to hold drugs." The officer further testified that he asked defendant to hand him the film canister "for no reason other than that *his* past experience showed that a high percentage of such film containers, when found without cameras, contained narcotics."

According to the New Jersey High Court, "[w]hether viewed under the automobile exception or plain view doctrine," *id.* at 380, the facts of the case failed to establish probable cause to believe the film canister contained contraband. *Id.*, 124 *N.J.* at 386. The court reasoned that a police officer's search and seizure will

> be considered reasonable only if it conform[s] to "an *objective* standard of reasonableness." * * * Thus, the subjective beliefs of the officer, even if justified by his personal circumstances, are not dispositive. Rather, what is dispositive are the objective factors that would lead any officer with similar training and experience reasonably to conclude that drugs were in the canister. The experience that the officer detailed at the suppression hearing [was] not sufficient to warrant that conclusion with any objective probability.
>
> In contrast, the officer in *Texas v. Brown*, detailed his experience with similar narcotics containers and explained how the surrounding circumstances, including his observation of plastic vials, loose white powder, and other party balloons, led him to form a belief based on probable cause that the balloon contained drugs. * * *
>
> Although the officer here said that half of his drug encounters involved the use of similar containers to hold narcotics, [he did not indicate] the number of times he examined film canisters without result. Nor did the officer convey what other special expertise and

training allowed him to conclude that there was a "fair probability" that narcotics would be found within the container. * * * Had there been such proof here, it would justify the risk that an innocent owner might be subject to such a limited search—a risk all of us bear no matter what the justification for the search inasmuch as probable cause, not certainty, is the standard. * * *

Had there been proof here, as in *Texas v. Brown* [] of *regularized police experience* that objects such as the film canister are the probable containers of drugs, we would have a different case. *But here the evidence was the experience of only one officer and even that evidence supplied no information about what percentage of observed containers held drugs.*

[We emphasize that] a finding of probable cause in the sense of "a fair probability" must be shown to be warranted by the objective factors that would permit a comparably well-trained police officer to reach such a conclusion. That showing has not been made here.

Id. at 383-386. [Citations omitted; emphasis added.]

WASHINGTON v. CHRISMAN
Supreme Court of the United States
455 *U.S.* 1, 102 *S.Ct.* 812 (1982)

QUESTION: May a law enforcement officer, consistent with the Fourth Amendment, accompany an arrested person into his residence and seize contraband discovered there in plain view ?

ANSWER: YES. Once an officer has effected a valid arrest of an individual, it is within that officer's authority to maintain custody and control over the arrestee and monitor his movements. Therefore, if the arrestee requests to go to his home to retrieve identification, the officer has a right to remain literally at the arrestee's elbow, and seize any contraband discovered there in plain view. *Id.* at 816, 817.

RATIONALE: "The 'plain view' exception to the Fourth Amendment warrant requirement permits a law enforcement officer to seize what clearly is incriminating evidence or contraband when it is discovered in a place where the officer has a right to be." *Id.* at 816.

Here, a Washington State University police officer observed a student on campus carrying a half-gallon bottle of gin. Such possession by an under-age student on campus is prohibited by state law. The officer stopped the student and asked for identification. The student responded that the identification was back in his dorm room and that he would go get it. The officer followed the student (now under arrest) to his room. In the room, the officer observed marihuana seeds and a small smoking pipe lying on a desk in plain view. The student's roommate was present in the room. The officer read both students their rights as per *Miranda*, and received a written consent-to-search for the entire dorm room. The search yielded additional marihuana and LSD.

The Supreme Court of Washington held that the officer had no right to enter the dorm room under the Fourth Amendment.

The United States Supreme Court disagreed.

Once a law enforcement officer has validly placed a person under arrest, that officer must retain custody and control of that arrestee. "[I]t is not unreasonable under the Fourth Amendment for a police officer, as a matter of routine, to monitor the movements of an arrested person, as his judgment dictates, following the arrest." *Id.* at 817. The safety of the officer plus the efficacy of the arrest necessitates such surveillance, and as such, "is not an impermissible invasion of the privacy or personal liberty of an individual who has been arrested." *Id.*

As a result, the Court held that the University police officer's conduct was entirely proper. Chief Justice Burger noted that "[t]his is a classic instance of incriminating evidence found in plain view when a police officer, for unrelated but entirely legitimate reasons, obtains lawful access to an individual's area of privacy." *Id.* Because the plain view seizure of the marihuana was lawful, the Court found the subsequent seizure pursuant to both roommates' consent to search lawful. *Miranda* was read and a voluntary and intelligent waiver was received in writing. Therefore, the "seizure of the drugs * * * did not violate the Fourth Amendment." *Id.* at 818.

NOTE

Directing the arrestee into or about his or her residence.

(a) In *United States v. Butler*, 980 *F.*2d 619 (10th Cir. 1992), several U.S. Marshals and county sheriff's officers arrested Butler outside his rural trailer home near Nashoba, Oklahoma, under the authority of a warrant. The grounds immediately surrounding Butler's home "were strewn with litter, including broken glass, several hundred beer cans, and [] parts from various motor vehicles[.]" *Id.* at 620. As one of the marshals handcuffed Butler, the marshal noticed that Butler had no shoes, and also noticed the broken glass on the ground near Butler's feet. "Given the state of the ground, there was no route by which Butler might have been conveyed safely to the officers' vehicles." *Id.* When asked if he had any shoes, Butler stated that he did, but that they were in the trailer. The marshal told Butler, "Well, let's go on in and get them." The marshal helped Butler inside the trailer and followed him into a bedroom, where the marshal discovered and seized a loaded shotgun. The shotgun subsequently formed the basis of a one-count indictment charging Butler with the unlawful possession of a firearm by a convicted felon.

In the appeal following the denial of his motion to suppress, Butler argued that the seizure of the firearm represented a violation of his rights under the Fourth Amendment because, unlike the defendant in *Chrisman*, Butler did not invite the officer into his residence. The United States Court of Appeals for the Tenth Circuit disagreed. According to the court, the distinction drawn by Butler is not persuasive. The evidence is uncontradicted that there was broken glass on the ground in the area where Butler was arrested. And * * * there was no evidence that the concern for Butler's welfare, as manifested by the police instruction for him to put on some shoes, was a pretext by which the police sought to enter the mobile home. That is, there is no evidence that the police action was done in bad faith. * * *

Id. at 621.

Agreeing with those courts that have addressed the issue, this court held that the "police may conduct a limited entry into an area for the purpose of protecting the health or safety of an arrestee." *Id.* The court emphasized, however, that its decision

> in no way creates a blank check for intrusion upon the privacy of the sloppily dressed. * * * [E]ntry into the defendant's residence cannot be effected, in the absence of consent or exigent circumstances, solely upon the desire of law enforcement officers to complete the arrestee's wardrobe.

Id. at 621-22. In the present case, there was a "legitimate and significant threat to the health and safety of the arrestee. There was no evidence * * * that the concern for the arrestee's health and safety was pretextual. To the contrary, the record is clear that taking Butler to the officers' vehicle would have posed a serious risk to his health." *Id.* at 622.

(b) In *United States v. Titus*, 445 *F*.2d 577 (2nd Cir.), *cert. denied*, 404 *U.S.* 957, 92 *S.Ct.* 323 (1971), Titus was naked when he was arrested in his home by several FBI agents. As the agents looked for clothing for him, they discovered evidence connecting Titus to a recent bank robbery. Upholding the discovery of evidence under the plain view doctrine, the Second Circuit found that the agents' search for clothing for their arrestee was proper since the agents "were bound to find some clothing for Titus rather than take him nude to FBI headquarters on a December night[.]" *Id.* at 579.

(c) In *United States v. DiStefano*, 555 *F*.2d 1094 (2nd Cir. 1977), defendant was wearing only a nightgown and bathrobe when she was arrested outside her home. The arresting officers requested that defendant get dressed, and she was accompanied into her house by a female officer. Once inside, the officer observed evidence which connected defendant to a bank robbery. Upholding the warrantless, plain view seizure, the court stated, "[t]he officers had a duty to find clothing for [defendant] to wear[.]" *Id.* at 1101.

(d) *But see United States v. Anthon*, 648 *F*.2d 669 (10th Cir. 1981), *cert. denied*, 454 *U.S.* 1164, 102 *S.Ct.* 1039 (1982), where defendant had been arrested in a hotel hallway after he had left his room clad only in his swimming trunks. After being read his rights, defendant was directed back into his hotel room where he was allowed to change clothes and gather his personal effects. He was then questioned by the police in the hotel room for 30 to 40 minutes. Inside the room, the officers discovered a vial of cocaine and a marijuana cigarette. Finding the warrantless entry into defendant's hotel room violative of the Fourth Amendment, the Tenth Circuit emphasized that the defendant never consented to the entry of the police into his hotel room, nor did he ask to be allowed to retrieve his clothes. *Id.* at 675. Moreover, the court determined that the arrest in the hallway did not provide exigent circumstances for the warrantless entry; the officers were not responding to an emergency call, they were not in pursuit of a fleeing felon, and they were not acting to prevent the loss or destruction of evidence. *Id.*

ARIZONA v. HICKS
Supreme Court of the United States
480 *U.S.* 321, 107 *S.Ct.* 1149 (1987)

QUESTION: May law enforcement officers seize incriminating evidence found in "plain view," when they have a "reasonable suspicion" that the item may be evidence of a crime, contraband, or otherwise subject to official seizure ?

ANSWER: NO. The "plain view" doctrine may only be invoked when the law enforcement officer has *"probable cause"* to believe that the item in question is evidence of a crime, contraband, or otherwise subject to official seizure. *Id.* at 1153.

RATIONALE: Law enforcement officers were lawfully inside defendant's apartment investigating a fresh shooting incident. While inside, one of the officers noticed two sets of expensive stereo components, which seemed out of place in defendant's "squalid and otherwise ill-appointed four-room apartment." Suspecting that the stereo equipment was stolen, one officer slightly moved the components to read and record their serial numbers which he reported by phone to his headquarters. When he was informed that one component was stolen in an armed robbery, he seized it immediately. When it was subsequently determined that some of the other serial numbers matched those on other stereo equipment taken in the same robbery, a warrant was obtained and executed, and that equipment was seized as well.

The trial court suppressed all the evidence and the State appealed. The Arizona Court of Appeals affirmed and the Arizona Supreme Court denied review. The State then petitioned the United States Supreme Court and *certiorari* was granted "to decide whether [the] 'plain view' doctrine may be invoked when police have less than probable cause to believe that the item in question is evidence of a crime or contraband." *Id.* at 1151.

As an initial matter, the Court found that "the mere recording of the serial numbers did not constitute a seizure." *Id.* at 1152. While it was the "first step in the process by which defendant was ultimately deprived of the stereo equipment, it did not, however, in and of itself, 'meaningfully interfere' with [defendant's] possessory interest in either the serial numbers or the equipment, and therefore did not amount to a seizure." *Id.* [Citation omitted.]

The officer's "moving of the equipment, however, did constitute a 'search' separate and apart from the search for the shooter, victims, and weapons that was the lawful objective of his entry into the apartment. Merely inspecting those parts of the [stereo components] that came into view during the latter search would not have constituted an independent search, because it would have produced no additional invasion of [defendant's] privacy. * * * But taking action, unrelated to the objectives of the authorized intrusion, which exposed to view concealed portions of the apartment or its contents, did produce a new invasion of [defendant's] privacy unjustified by the exigent circumstances that validated the entry." *Id.* For Fourth Amendment purposes, "the 'distinction between looking at a suspicious object in plain view and moving it even a few inches' is much more than trivial. It matters not that the search uncovered nothing of any great personal value to the [defendant]—serial numbers rather than (what might conceivably have been hidden behind or under the equipment) letters or photographs. A search is a search, even if it happens to disclose nothing but the bottom of a turntable." *Id.* at 1152-1153.

The question then is whether the search was "reasonable" under the Fourth Amendment. Such a search would be valid if the "plain view" doctrine would have permitted the seizure of the equipment. In the present set of circumstances, there is "no doubt" that it would have done so if the officer "had probable cause to believe that the equipment was stolen. The State has conceded, however, that he had only a 'reasonable suspicion,' by which it means something less than probable cause." *Id.* at 1153. This degree of belief was not enough.

"We now hold that probable cause is required. To say otherwise would be to cut the 'plain view' doctrine loose from its theoretical and practical moorings. The theory of that doctrine consists of extending to nonpublic places such as the home, where searches and seizures are presumptively unreasonable, the police's longstanding authority to make warrantless seizures in public places of such objects as weapons and contraband. * * * And the practical justification for that extension is the desirability of sparing police, whose viewing of the object in the course of a lawful search is as legitimate as it would have been in a public place, the inconvenience and the risk—to themselves or to preservation of the evidence—of going to obtain a warrant. * * * Dispensing with the need for a warrant is worlds apart from permitting a lesser standard of *cause* for the seizure than a warrant would require, *i.e.*, the standard of probable cause." *Id.* at 1153-1154 (emphasis supplied).

Accordingly, before the doctrine of "plain view" may be legitimately invoked, officers must have probable cause to believe the item or items are evidence of a crime, contraband, or otherwise subject to official seizure. *Id.* at 1154.

HORTON v. CALIFORNIA
Supreme Court of the United States
496 *U.S.* 128, 110 *S.Ct.* 2301 (1990)

QUESTION: Is the warrantless seizure of incriminating evidence found in plain view prohibited by the Fourth Amendment if the discovery of the evidence was not *inadvertent* ?

ANSWER: NO. "[E]ven though inadvertence is a characteristic of most legitimate 'plain view' seizures, it is not a necessary condition." *Id.* at 2304. Once an officer has a lawful right of access to an object and possesses probable cause to associate the object with criminal activity, "no additional Fourth Amendment interest is furthered by requiring that the discovery of evidence be inadvertent." *Id.* at 2309-2310.

RATIONALE: During the course of an armed robbery investigation, Sergeant LaRault developed probable cause to believe defendant's home contained proceeds of the robbery and weapons used by the robbers. "His affidavit for a search warrant referred to police reports that described the weapons as well as the proceeds, but the warrant issued by the Magistrate only authorized a search for the proceeds, including three specifically described rings." *Id.* at 2304.

Under the authority of the warrant, Sergeant LaRault searched defendant's home, but he did not find the stolen property. He did find, however, the weapons in plain view and seized them. Among the items seized were an Uzi machine gun, a .38 caliber revolver, two stun guns, and a handcuff key.

In the appeal which followed the denial of his motion to suppress evidence, the California court rejected defendant's contention that because the government failed to satisfy the "inadvertence" requirement of the plain view doctrine, the Fourth Amendment required suppression of all evidence seized which had not been listed in the search warrant. *Id.* at 2305. After the California Supreme Court denied defendant's request for review, the United States Supreme Court granted *certiorari* to address "the unresolved issue" whether "the warrantless seizure of evidence of crime in plain view is prohibited by the Fourth Amendment if the discovery of the evidence was not inadvertent." *Id.* at 2304, 2305.

In a seven-to-two opinion delivered by Justice Stevens, the Court concluded "that even though inadvertence is a characteristic of most legitimate 'plain view' seizures, it is not a necessary condition." *Id.* at 2304.

The criteria that generally guide 'plain view' seizures were set forth in *Coolidge v. New Hampshire*, 403 *U.S.* 443, 91 *S.Ct.* 2022 (1971), and later refined by *Texas v. Brown*, 460 *U.S.* 730, 103 *S.Ct.* 1535 (1983), and *Arizona v. Hicks*, 480 *U.S.* 321, 107 *S.Ct.* 1149 (1987). These cases stand for the proposition that under certain circumstances the police may seize evidence in plain view without a search warrant. In *Coolidge*, Justice Stewart instructed that one " 'example of the applicability of the "plain view" doctrine is the situation in which the police have a warrant to search a given area for specified objects, and in the course of the search come across some other article of incriminating character. * * * [Another example involves the situation w]here the initial intrusion that brings the police within plain view of such an article is supported, not by a warrant, but by one of the recognized exceptions to the warrant requirement, [and here] the seizure is also legitimate. Thus, the police may inadvertently come across evidence while in "hot pursuit" of a fleeing suspect. * * * And an object that comes into view during a search incident to arrest that is appropriately limited in scope under existing law may be seized without a warrant. * * * Finally, the "plain view" doctrine has been applied where a police officer is not searching for evidence against the accused, but nonetheless inadvertently comes across an incriminating object.'" *Horton* at 2307 (quoting *Coolidge* at 465-466, 91 *S.Ct.* at 2037-2038). [Citations omitted.]

" 'What the "plain view" cases have in common is that the police officer in each of them had a prior justification for an intrusion in the course of which he came inadvertently across a piece of evidence incriminating the accused. The doctrine serves to supplement the prior justification—whether it be a warrant for another object, hot pursuit, search incident to lawful arrest, or some other legitimate reason for being present unconnected with a search directed against the accused—and permits the warrantless seizure.'" *Horton* at 2307 (quoting *Coolidge* at 466, 91 *S.Ct.* at 2038). Thus, the first prong of the plain view doctrine requires the officer to be lawfully in the viewing area and have "a lawful right of access to the object itself." *Id.* at 2038. In this respect, it is essential that "the officer did not violate the Fourth Amendment in arriving at the place from which the evidence could be plainly viewed." *Id.*

Once an item is lawfully discovered and is in plain view, the second prong of the doctrine requires that its incriminating character be "immediately apparent," which is to say, the officer's perception of the item must provide him or her with "probable cause to believe the item is associated with criminal activity." *Texas v. Brown, supra* at 741-742, 103 *S.Ct.* at 2038; *Arizona v. Hicks, supra* at 327-328, 107 *S.Ct.* at 1153-1154. *Horton* at 2308.

Finally, the Court in *Coolidge* required, as the third prong of the plain view doctrine, that the discovery of the incriminating item be "inadvertent," that is, the officer could not know in advance that the particular item of evidence would be where it was ultimately found and intend to seize it beforehand. The requirement of "inadvertence" was considered "necessary to avoid a violation of the express constitutional requirement that a valid warrant must particularly describe the things to be seized." *Horton* at 2308. In *Coolidge*, Justice Stewart reasoned that a plain-view seizure must:

> "* * * not turn an initially valid (and therefore limited) search into a 'general' one * * *. [W]here the discovery is anticipated, where the police know in advance the location of the evidence and intend to seize it, the situation is altogether different. The requirement of a warrant to seize imposes no inconvenience whatever, or at least none which is constitutionally cognizable in a legal

system that regards warrantless searches as 'per se unreasonable' in the absence of 'exigent circumstances.'

If the initial intrusion is bottomed upon a warrant that fails to mention a particular object, though the police know its location and intend to seize it, then there is a violation of the express constitutional requirement of 'Warrants ... particularly describing ... [the] things to be seized.' "

Horton at 2308 (quoting *Coolidge* at 469-471, 91 *S.Ct.* at 2040-2041).

Finding two flaws in this reasoning, the Court here in *Horton* declared: "*First, evenhanded law enforcement is best achieved by the application of objective standards of conduct, rather than standards that might depend upon the subjective state of mind of the officer.* The fact that an officer is interested in an item of evidence and fully expects to find it in the course of a search should not invalidate its seizure if the search is confined in area and duration by the terms of a warrant or a valid exception to the warrant requirement. If the officer has knowledge approaching certainty that the item will be found, we see no reason why he or she would deliberately omit a particular description of the item to be seized from the application for a search warrant. Specification of the additional item could only permit the officer to expand the scope of the search." *Id*. at 2308-2309. [Emphasis added.]

"Second, the suggestion that the inadvertence requirement is necessary to prevent the police from conducting general searches, or from converting specific warrants into general warrants, is not persuasive because that interest is already served by the requirements that no warrant issue unless it 'particularly describ[es] the place to be searched and the persons or things to be seized,' * * * and that a warrantless search be circumscribed by the exigencies which justify its initiation. * * * *Scrupulous adherence to these requirements serves the interests in limiting the area and duration of the search that the inadvertence requirement inadequately protects.* Once those commands have been satisfied and the officer has a lawful right of access, however, *no additional Fourth Amendment interest is furthered by requiring that the discovery of evidence be inadvertent.*" *Id*. at 2309-10. [Emphasis added; citations omitted.] If the scope of the search exceeds that permitted by the terms of a validly issued warrant or the character of the relevant exception from the warrant requirement, "the subsequent seizure is unconstitutional without more." *Id*. at 2310.

"In this case, the scope of the search was not enlarged in the slightest by the omission of any reference to the weapons in the warrant. Indeed, if the three rings and other items named in the warrant had been found at the outset—or if [defendant] had them in his possession and had responded to the warrant by producing them immediately—no search for weapons could have taken place." *Id*. at 2310.

Accordingly, "the items seized from [defendant's] home were discovered during a lawful search authorized by a valid warrant. When they were discovered, it was immediately apparent to the officer that they constituted incriminating evidence. He had probable cause, not only to obtain a warrant to search for stolen property, but also to believe that the weapons and handguns had been used in the crime he was investigating. The search was authorized by the warrant, the seizure was authorized by the 'plain view' doctrine." *Id.* at 2310-11.

NOTE

1. *Lawfully in the viewing area.* When an officer is lawfully in the viewing area, and discovers an object that has been left exposed to view in that area, the officer's observation of that item will not be considered a search within the meaning of the Fourth Amendment.

(a) Photographs and recordings. When objects or persons are in "plain view," an officer does not violate the Fourth Amendment by "recording" his observation by camera or videotape. *See e.g., United States v. Holland,* 438 *F.*2d 887 (6th Cir. 1971) (lawful to photograph person who voluntarily came to the police station); *United States v. McMillon,* 350 *F.Supp.* 593 (D.D.C. 1972) (pictures and videotape of marijuana growing in defendant's back yard, obtained without a warrant, admissible because the plants were in plain view); *People v. Green,* 298 *Ill.App.*3d 1054, 233 *Ill.Dec.* 389, 700 *N.E.*2d 1087 (1998) (taking photos of a lawfully stopped suspect not a search where the officer "took the photographs * * * in a public place where it was lawful for him to be"). *See also United States v. McIver,* 186 *F.*3d 1119 (9th Cir. 1999) (use of unmanned still and video cameras in national forest not a search when defendant's activities were captured by the cameras which were triggered by his motion).

(b) In *United States v. Daoust,* 916 *F.*2d 757 (1st Cir. 1990), defendant argued that the police had no right to be in the rear of his home and, as a result, their observation through a rear window of a semi-automatic hand gun "hanging from the ceiling over the kitchen sink" did not amount to a lawful "plain view." The record under review indicated that during the course of a narcotics investigation, Maine police officials learned that defendant might have some useful information. Several officers went to his home, "an isolated log house dug into the side of a hill, apparently without electricity or telephone," and found the front door inaccessible. The door was about five feet above the ground and had no steps. The officers knocked on a glass cellar door, but received no answer, and left. They returned approximately two weeks later and again knocked on the glass cellar door. When no one answered their knock, the officers walked to the rear of the home. While they were at the back, one of the officers looked up through a kitchen window and saw the gun hanging above the sink.

Finding no constitutional violation, the court held:

> A police [officer] may lawfully go to a person's home to interview him. * * * In doing so, he obviously can go up to the door * * * and, * * * if that door is inaccessible there is nothing unlawful or unreasonable about going to the back of the house to look for another door, all as part of a legitimate attempt to interview a person. * * *

On the basis of this record the district court found that the police went to the back "looking for an accessible main floor entrance" not to see if unlawful activity was taking place, but as part of their efforts to interview Daoust. It further found that they looked up through the window simply to see if someone was at home. The record adequately supports these findings. ∗ ∗ ∗ And, that being so, the conduct of the police was lawful.

Id. at 758.

See also United States v. Jackson, 131 *F*.3d 1105, 1110 (4th Cir. 1997) (officer's shift in position by a few steps for a few seconds to obtain a better look at what was already in plain view "did not meaningfully intrude on any privacy interest beyond the intrusion" already authorized by the resident's consent to search for a fugitive); *United States v. Taylor*, 90 *F*.3d 903, 908-09 (4th Cir. 1996) (officer lawfully at the front door of a house did not violate the Fourth Amendment when he walked three steps down the porch in order to look through a front window and, while there, observed incriminating evidence); *United States v. Anderson*, 552 *F*.2d 1296, 1300 (8th Cir. 1977) (finding it reasonable for police to proceed to rear of home to look for a back entrance); *United States v. Hersh*, 464 *F*.2d 228, 230 (9th Cir.) (finding it reasonable for police to look through a window while standing at the front door trying to locate and interview defendant), *cert. denied*, 409 *U.S.* 1008, 93 *S.Ct.* 442 (1972). *But see Texas v. Gonzales*, 388 *F*.2d 145, 147 (5th Cir. 1968) (police have no right to look through a window simply to see if drug activity is taking place inside).

2. *Probable cause to associate the item with criminal activity.* "Some opaque containers induce assumptions about their contents. Refrigerators contain food. Under the hoods of automobiles are engines. These are predictions, based on experience." *United States v. Prandy-Binett*, 995 *F*.2d 1069 (D.C.Cir. 1993). In *Prandy-Binett*, the court addressed the question whether a narcotics officer's observation of a small rectangular block wrapped in silver duct tape, in the possession of the defendant, Prandy-Binett, gave the detective probable cause for an arrest.

Detective Centrella and another narcotics officer were on duty at Union Station in Washington, D.C., meeting trains arriving from New York City, a "source city" for drugs. "As they watched departing passengers, their attention was drawn to an individual walking through the station faster than the others and trying to get around them. When the individual—Prandy-Binett—made eye contact with the detectives, who were in plain clothes, he moved even more quickly toward the exit. The detectives approached him and identified themselves. After telling the officers he had come from New Jersey, Prandy-Binett produced a one-way train ticket, purchased with cash, showing that his trip originated at Penn Station, New York City. After saying he lived in Washington, D.C., he handed the officers a driver's license showing Hyattsville, Maryland, as his residence." *Id.* at 1069. The detectives' suspicions were heightened by the cloth "tote" or "gym" bag Prandy-Binett carried on his shoulder. He told the detectives that he spent a week working in New Jersey. Yet, his only luggage was the small gym bag. Detective Centrella requested permission to search the bag. "Prandy-Binett replied that he did not have to consent and that the bag contained only clothing. He took the bag from his shoulder, placed it on the ground, knelt down (as did the detective next to him), unzipped the bag and began pulling out a pair of blue jeans." *Id.* at 1070. "As Prandy-Binett continued to manipulate the blue jeans, a portion of a rectangular block, wrapped in silver duct tape, slid out of [a] perfume bag. Unprompted, Prandy-Binett said, in evident reference to the perfume bag, 'this is a gift.' Believing the block to contain illegal drugs, Detective Centrella handcuffed Prandy-Binett, examined the wrapped object further, and seized it and the gym bag. A later field test on the contents of the wrapped block revealed cocaine." *Id.*

In its discussion of whether, under the circumstances presented, the detectives' observation of the rectangular block wrapped in silver duct tape provided them with probable cause for an arrest, the court stated:

> Somewhere between "less than evidence which would justify [a] conviction" and "more than bare suspicion," probable cause is satisfied. * * * The precise point is indeterminate. We are concerned not simply with probabilities, but with conditional probabilities: if one event occurs, how likely is it that another event will occur ? This is why the detectives' observations up to the time the block slipped out of the perfume bag cannot be disregarded. It is why in similar cases we ask, although sometimes tacitly, what is the probability that a train passenger arriving at Union Station from New York City will be carrying cocaine ? Quite low, we trust, despite New York's status as a source city for narcotics. Is the probability increased if the passenger moves quickly through the station after leaving the train ? Greater if the passenger also gives apparently deceptive answers when the police question him ? Greater still if the passenger opens his bag and refers to a package wrapped in duct tape inside a fancy perfume bag as a "gift ?" Neither courts nor law enforcement officers, nor anyone else for that matter, can quantify any of this. A mathematician could not perform the calculations because there is no way of assigning probabilities to the individual events. The information is simply unavailable, as will doubtless be true in every Fourth Amendment case. Still, we are convinced that, up to the sighting of the duct tape package, the conditional probability was low, much too low to have satisfied the Fourth Amendment in light of the interests it protects.

Id. at 1070-71.

Thus, the critical question in this case was whether the detectives' "inference of narcotics from the appearance of the wrapped block," enhanced the probability of Prandy-Binett's possessing drugs. *Id.* at 1071. In this respect, the court observed:

> Upon seeing the kilo-sized rectangular package wrapped in duct tape sticking out of the perfume bag, Detective Centrella and his partner immediately concluded that it held narcotics. Detective Centrella testified: "As soon as I saw that, in my mind, that's drugs." The record firmly supports the detective's inference.

There was first the block's bulk. The weight of consumer goods in this country is usually described in pounds and ounces. Perhaps because of foreign influence, the weight of illicit narcotics is usually measured—in statutes and on the street—in terms of the metric system. The evidence showed that in the drug trade, a kilogram of cocaine or heroin is a standardized unit of exchange, commonly referred to as a "kilo brick" or simply a "kilo." (A kilogram equals 2.2046 pounds.) Detective Centrella was quite familiar with the bulk package containing one kilogram of cocaine. During his 20 years of service, he personally had seized 100 such kilos and had seen many more. Both Detective Centrella, and his partner, an experienced narcotics officer who had undergone training at the Drug Enforcement Administration, thus had good reason for believing that the wrapped block in Prandy-Binett's gym bag was about the size of a package containing one kilogram of cocaine.

The second consideration was the rectangular shape of the object. The portion protruding from the perfume bag was consistent with what the detectives knew to be the standard configuration, the typical "kilo brick." The bag itself, roughly four inches wide and between six and ten inches deep, was the right size for holding a kilo of narcotics so packaged. The brick-like shape of the object thus further alerted the detectives, in light of their training and experience, to the possible presence of narcotics.

The third factor was [the] wrapping—silver duct tape (over plastic). Duct tape is attractive to traffickers because fingerprints are difficult to lift from its surface and because some criminals believe— erroneously—that it masks the odor of the drugs from police dogs. Detective Centrella testified that he had seen "several hundred" packages wrapped in silver duct tape similar in appearance to the one in Prandy-Binett's bag. Every one contained contraband. He also reported that approximately 95 percent of the kilogram-sized quantities of cocaine he had seized in his career were so packaged. * * * Detective Centrella's experience replicates that of narcotics agents in New York City. The agent in *United States v. Barrios-Moriera*, 872 *F*.2d 12, 17 (2nd Cir. [1989)], "had participated in the seizure of three or four hundred separate kilos of cocaine," which were typically "wrapped in some variety of tape." The Second Circuit therefore held that "the rectangular package, measuring a certain size, wrapped in duct tape" proclaimed its illicit contents, so much so that the agent legally seized it without a warrant as contraband in plain view.

To Detective Centrella the wrapped block thus conveyed the message "one kilo of narcotics" just as surely as if the words were written on the tape. * * * The record shows that the detective had a solid foundation from which to evaluate relative frequency, to judge the percentage of times such packages hold narcotics. * * * Of the hundreds of packages of this type Detective Centrella had seen in his 20 years as a narcotics officer, every one contained drugs. Not once, in all his years as a narcotics officer, had he encountered a duct-taped package containing something other than drugs. * * *

Id. at 1071-72.

Accordingly, the court concluded that, under the circumstances of this case, the detectives' observation of Prandy-Binett's possession of the rectangular package wrapped in duct tape provided probable cause for his arrest.

MINNESOTA v. DICKERSON
Supreme Court of the United States
508 *U.S.* 366, 113 *S.Ct.* 2130 (1993)

QUESTION: Does the plain view doctrine embody a "plain touch" corollary ?

ANSWER: YES. The plain view doctrine "has an obvious application by analogy to cases in which an officer discovers contraband through the sense of touch during an otherwise lawful search." *Id.* at 2137. For example, if a police officer conducts a lawful protective frisk of "a suspect's outer clothing and feels an object whose contour or mass makes its identity immediately apparent, there has been no invasion of the suspect's privacy beyond that already authorized by the officer's search for weapons; if the object is contraband, its warrantless seizure would be justified by the same practical considerations that [exist] in the plain view context." *Id.* "[W]hether the officer detects the contraband by sight or by touch, however, the Fourth Amendment[] require[s] that the officer have probable cause to believe the item is contraband before seizing it[.]" *Id.*

RATIONALE: In this case, the Court considered "whether the Fourth Amendment permits the seizure of contraband detected through a police officer's sense of touch during a protective patdown search." *Id.* at 2133.

On November 9, 1989, two Minneapolis police officers were patrolling the north side of the city in a marked squad car. At about 8:15 p.m., the officers observed a man leaving a multi-unit apartment building. The male, later identified as defendant, Timothy Dickerson, aroused suspicion because the building he had just left had been the recent target of several search warrants, and was the subject of numerous complaints of drug sales taking place in the building's hallways. According to the officers, the apartment building was known as a notorious "crack house."

As Dickerson left the building, he began walking toward the officers but, "upon spotting the squad car and making eye contact with one of the officers, abruptly halted and began walking in the opposite direction. His suspicion aroused, this officer watched as [Dickerson] turned and entered an alley on the other side of the apartment building." *Id.*

Deciding to stop Dickerson and investigate further, the officers pulled their squad car into the alley and ordered Dickerson to stop and submit to a protective frisk. The patdown revealed no weapons, but the officer conducting the frisk did detect a small lump in Dickerson's nylon jacket. According to the officer:*

> "[A]s I pat-searched the front of his body, I felt a lump, a small lump, in the front pocket. I examined it with my fingers and it slid and it felt to be a lump of crack cocaine in cellophane."

Id. [Citation omitted.]

The officer then reached into Dickerson's pocket and retrieved a small plastic bag containing one fifth of one gram of crack cocaine which, according to the Minnesota Supreme Court, was *about the size of a pea or a marble.* Dickerson was arrested and charged with possession of a controlled substance.

The Minnesota Supreme Court held that both the stop and frisk of Dickerson were valid under *Terry v. Ohio,* but found the seizure of cocaine to be unconstitutional. That court "expressly refused 'to extend the plain view doctrine to the sense of touch' on the grounds that 'the sense of touch is inherently less immediate and less reliable than the sense of sight' and that 'the sense of touch is far more intrusive[.]' " *Dickerson* at 2134. [Citation omitted.]

Rejecting the Minnesota court's categorical ban on "plain touch" seizures, the United States Supreme Court herein adopted what "[m]ost state and federal courts have recognized [as] a 'plain feel' or 'plain touch' corollary to the plain-view doctrine." *Id.* at 2134 n.1.

Analysis of the question "whether contraband detected through the sense of touch during a patdown search may be admitted into evidence," *id.* at 2134, requires an examination of the law underlying the right of a police officer to stop and detain an individual suspected of criminal activity and to conduct a protective frisk upon reason to believe that individual is armed and dangerous. In this respect, *Terry v. Ohio* held that

> "where a police officer observes unusual conduct which leads him reasonably to conclude in light of his experience that criminal activity may be afoot" the officer may briefly stop the suspicious person and make "reasonable inquiries" aimed at confirming or dispelling his suspicions. * * * *Terry* further held that "[w]hen an officer is justified in believing that the individual whose suspicious behavior he is investigating at close range is armed and presently dangerous to the officer or to others," the officer may conduct a patdown search "to determine whether the person is in fact carrying a weapon."

---

* In the lower courts, it had been determined that at the time the officer discovered the contraband, he had been a 14-year veteran of the Minneapolis Police Department, with over 11 of those years spent on the north side. He had extensive experience working on cases involving narcotics and weapons, and testified that he had felt crack cocaine in clothing on approximately 50 to 75 prior occasions. *See State v. Dickerson,* 481 *N.W.*2d 840 (Minn. 1992).

Dickerson at 2135-36. [Citations omitted.] The purpose of the *"Terry frisk,"* of course, " 'is not to discover evidence of crime, but to allow the officer to pursue his investigation without fear of violence[,]' * * * [and it] must be strictly 'limited to that which is necessary for the discovery of weapons which might be used to harm the officer or others nearby.' " *Id.* at 2136. [Citations omitted.]

The critical question in this case "is whether police officers may seize non-threatening contraband detected during a protective pat-down search of the sort permitted by *Terry.*" *Id.* According to the Court, "the answer is clearly that they may, so long as the officer's search stays within the bounds marked by *Terry.*" *Id.*

The Supreme Court has already held that in certain situations police officers may seize contraband detected during a lawful *Terry* search. For example, in *Michigan v. Long*, the Court held that where police have a reasonable, articulable suspicion that a motorist may be armed and dangerous, they may conduct a *Terry*-type protective search for weapons not only of the person of the motorist but also of the passenger compartment of the automobile. The protective inspection of the passenger compartment must, however, be limited to those areas in which a weapon may be placed or hidden. The Court in *Long* went on to hold that " '[i]f, while conducting a legitimate *Terry* search of the interior of the automobile, the officer should, as here, discover contraband other than weapons, he clearly cannot be required to ignore the contraband, and the Fourth Amendment does not require its suppression in such circumstances.' " *Dickerson* at 2136. [Citations omitted.]

The basis of the second part of the holding in *Long* was the plain view doctrine. "Under that doctrine, if police are lawfully in a position from which they view an object, if its incriminating character is immediately apparent, and if the officers have a lawful right of access to the object, they may seize it without a warrant. * * * If, however, the police lack probable cause to believe that an object in plain view is contraband without conducting some further search of the object—*i.e.*, if 'its incriminating character [is not] "immediately apparent," ' * * * the plain-view doctrine cannot justify its seizure." *Dickerson* at 2136-37. [Citations omitted.]

The plain view doctrine, held the Court, "has an obvious application by analogy to cases in which an officer discovers contraband through the sense of touch during an otherwise lawful search." Id. at 2137. [Emphasis added.] The Court elaborated:

> The rationale of the plain view doctrine is that if contraband is left in open view and is observed by a police officer from a lawful vantage point, there has been no invasion of a legitimate expectation of privacy and thus no "search" within the meaning of the Fourth Amendment—or at least no search independent of the initial intrusion that gave the officers their vantage point. * * * The warrantless seizure of contraband that presents itself in this manner is deemed justified by the realization that resort to a neutral magistrate under such circumstances would often be impracticable and would do little to promote the objectives of the Fourth Amendment. * * *

The same can be said of tactile discoveries of contraband. If a police officer lawfully pats down a suspect's outer clothing and feels an object whose contour or mass makes its identity immediately apparent, there has been no invasion of the suspect's privacy beyond that already authorized by the officer's search for weapons; if the object is contraband, its warrantless seizure would be justified by the same practical considerations that [exist] in the plain view context.

Id. at 2137. [Emphasis added.]

Addressing the concerns that the sense of touch is inherently less reliable than the sense of sight, and that touch is more intrusive into privacy than is sight, the Court pointed out first that "*Terry* itself demonstrates that the sense of touch is capable of revealing the nature of an object with sufficient reliability to support a seizure." *Id.*

The very premise of *Terry*, after all, is that officers will be able to detect the presence of weapons through the sense of touch and *Terry* upheld precisely such a seizure. Even if it were true that the sense of touch is generally less reliable than the sense of sight, that only suggests that officers will less often be able to justify seizures of unseen contraband. Regardless of whether the officer detects the contraband by sight or touch, however, the Fourth Amendment's requirement that the officer have probable cause to believe that the item is contraband before seizing it ensures against excessively speculative seizures.

Id.

Regarding the second concern—that touch is more intrusive than sight—the Court found it "inapposite in light of the fact that the intrusion * * * has already been authorized by the lawful search for weapons. The seizure of an item whose identity is already known," emphasized the Court, "occasions no further invasion of privacy." *Id.* at 2138.

Accordingly, the Court held that the plain view doctrine does indeed contemplate a "plain touch" corollary.

Applying the principles set forth above to the case before it, the Court determined that the officer was not "acting within the bounds marked by *Terry* at the time he gained probable cause to believe that the lump in [Dickerson's] jacket was contraband." *Id.* "[T]he officer determined that the lump was contraband only after 'squeezing, sliding and otherwise manipulating the contents of [Dickerson's] pocket'—a pocket which the officer already knew contained no weapon." *Id.* [Citation omitted.] Thus, the officer's continued exploration of the pocket "was unrelated to '[t]he sole justification of the search [under *Terry*:] . . . the protection of the police officer and others nearby.' * * * It therefore amounted to the sort of evidentiary search that *Terry* expressly refused to authorize[.]" *Id.* at 2138-39.

Although the officer was lawfully in a position to feel the lump in [Dickerson's] pocket, because *Terry* entitled him to place his hands upon [Dickerson's] jacket, * * * the incriminating character of the object was not immediately apparent to him. Rather, the officer determined that the item was contraband only after conducting a further search, one not authorized by *Terry* or by any other exception to the warrant requirement. Because this further search of [Dickerson's] pocket was constitutionally invalid, the seizure of the cocaine that followed [was] likewise unconstitutional.

Id. at 2139.

NOTE

1. *"Plain touch" as a corollary to the plain view doctrine.* The "plain touch" corollary to the plain view doctrine should not be characterized as a "new exception" to the written warrant requirement, for it is not. As its name implies, it is merely a corollary to a doctrine which over the years has become an appropriate, familiar and useful tool in the law enforcement trade. Once a court determines that the plain touch corollary should be applied to a particular set of circumstances, its application should proceed with a formulation which merely continues the familiar standards while furnishing a bright-line rule of law enforcement procedure. The decision should be predicated on the proposition that probable cause *is* probable cause, and it matters not whether its development flows from an officer's sense of sight, touch or some other sense. In this respect, any attempt to differentiate or prioritize the Fourth Amendment's probable cause standard by reference to the human senses from which it flows could only lead to confusing and absurd results.

Thus, before a law enforcement officer may validly invoke the "plain touch" corollary to the plain view doctrine, the government bears the burden of establishing three requirements. First, the officer must be lawfully in the *touching* area; and similar to the first prong of the plain view doctrine, the officer may not violate the Fourth Amendment by arriving at the place from which the evidence could be tactilely perceived. Second, the officer must have some independent constitutional justification for placing his or her hands on the property or person in question. This requirement—though not unrelated to the mandate that the officer be lawfully in the perceiving area—should receive separate scrutiny which probes the independent and distinct constitutional justification for the touching of the person or evidentiary item. In this regard, the second prong of the plain touch formulation requires the officer's hands to be lawfully *on* the touching area. Finally, upon touching the area in question, the officer must, through the process of tactile recognition, garner probable cause to believe the object which he or she is touching constitutes evidence of crime, contraband, or is otherwise subject to official seizure. Additionally, the development of probable cause should be reasonably contemporaneous with the initial touching to avoid the danger of an inoffensive touching graduating into a governmental massage which, "by virtue of its intolerable intensity and scope," may violate the Fourth Amendment. In this respect, "[t]he scope of the [touching] must be 'strictly tied to and justified by' the circumstances which rendered its initiation permissible." *See Terry v. Ohio*, 392 *U.S.* 1, 18, 19, 88 *S.Ct.* 1868, 1878 (1968).

If each of the three prongs of the plain touch corollary is satisfied, the warrantless seizure of the item in question is constitutionally warranted. *See Minnesota v. Dickerson, supra,* 113 *S.Ct.* at 2137; *United States v. Coleman,* 969 *F.*2d 126, 132 (5th Cir. 1992); *United States v. Salazar,* 945 *F.*2d 47, 51 (2nd Cir. 1991); *United States v. Buchannon,* 878 *F.*2d 1065, 1067 (8th Cir. 1989). *And see United States v. Most,* 876 *F.*2d 191, 194-95 (D.C.Cir 1989) (re-affirming that plain touch represents "a corollary to the well-established principle that inspection of materials in plain view does not constitute a search governed by the fourth amendment"); *United States v. Norman,* 701 *F.*2d 295, 296 (4th Cir. 1983) (plain view doctrine contemplates the use of all an officer's senses); *United States v. Russell,* 655 *F.*2d 1261, 1264 (1981), *modified on other grounds,* 670 *F.*2d 323 (D.C.Cir. 1982) (search warrant not required to "uncover[] what [the officer's] sense of touch revealed"); *United States v. Ocampo,* 650 *F.*2d 421, 429 (2d Cir. 1981) ("[w]here the contents of a container are easily discernible by frisking the exterior of a package * * * [the] contents [may] be examined under what amounts to a 'plain feel' version of the 'plain view' doctrine"); *United States v. Portillo,* 633 *F.*2d 1313, 1320 (9th Cir. 1980) (tactile recognition of weapon through paper bag justified its warrantless seizure where officer's initial touching was lawful); *United States v. Ceballos,* 719 *F.Supp.* 119, 127 (E.D. N.Y. 1989) (recognizing "the 'plain feel' version of the 'plain view' doctrine if the 'feel' was proper"); *United States v. Pace,* 709 *F.Supp.* 948 (C.D.Cal. 1989) (adopting the plain touch corollary); *People v. Chavers,* 33 *Cal.*3d 462, 189 *Cal.Rptr.* 169 (1983) (sense of touch is as "meaningful and accurate as if the container had been transparent"); *People v. Lee,* 194 *Cal.App.*3d 975, 240 *Cal.Rptr.* 32 (Cal. App. 1 Dist. 1987) (plain touch of heroin-filled balloons recognized during the course of a lawful pat down held to constitute probable cause for their seizure where officer identified the objects as contraband "simultaneously with the elimination of the possibility of a weapon," and where the officer testified that he had recognized the object from "his experience on at least 100 prior occasions involving similar balloons filled with heroin"); *State v. Trine,* 236 *Conn.* 216, 234, 673 *A.*2d 1098 (1996) (adopting the "plain feel" doctrine); *Jordan v. State,* 531 *A.*2d 1028 (Md. App. 1987) (recognizing the existence of a plain touch concept); *People v. Champion,* 452 *Mich.* 92, 105, 549 *N.W.*2d 849, 856 (1996) (adopting the plain feel exception, determining that "an object felt during an authorized patdown search may be seized without a warrant if the item's incriminating character is immediately apparent, *i.e.,* if the officer develops probable cause to believe that the item felt is contraband"); *State v. Alamont,* 577 *A.*2d 665 (R.I. 1990) (tactile recognition of a "one-inch cylindrical plastic vial" which the detective recognized to be "crack cocaine" by its "distinctive size and shape," and from handling similar vials on "hundreds" of prior occasions, coupled with the discovery of similar vials containing crack only moments earlier, provided the detective with "probable cause to subject the defendant to a more extensive search"). *See also* 2 W. LaFave, *Search and Seizure* §7.2(d) at 67 (2nd Ed. 1987) ("assuming lawful physical contact with the container, this 'plain touch' may reveal the contents so unquestionably that * * * no warrant requirement exists merely because there is a container between the officer and the seizable object").

For a comprehensive discussion of the "plain touch" corollary, *see* Holtz, *The "Plain Touch" Corollary: A Natural and Foreseeable Consequence of the Plain View Doctrine*, 95 Dickinson L.Rev. 521 (1991).

2. Recognizing the item as contraband or evidence. "Since *Dickerson*, many courts have focused on exactly how 'immediately' an officer must know that something felt during a *Terry* search is contraband or precisely how much a clothed object can be manipulated before a search becomes illegal." *United States v. Yamba*, 506 F.3d 251 (3rd Cir. 2007). In *Yamba*, during the course of a valid *Terry* frisk for weapons, Officer Livingstone felt a plastic bag in Yamba's right jacket pocket. The officer testified as follows:

> As I was conducting the pat-down, along the right side, right coat pocket, I could feel a plastic bag. I noted through training and experience [that] narcotics are stored and transported in plastic baggies. After a brief second of just feeling it, I could tell that there was a soft spongy-like substance that is consistent with marijuana inside. I then recovered the bag from his pocket and found it contained suspected marijuana.

Id. at 254.

In upholding the lawfulness of the seizure of the marijuana, the court explained:

> We reject a narrow focus on how quickly and certainly the nature of an object felt during a *Terry* search is known and on how much manipulation of a person's clothing is acceptable. In *Terry*, the Supreme Court authorized police officers to perform a routine pat-down search for weapons. Such searches necessarily involve a certain amount of "squeezing, sliding and otherwise manipulating" of a suspect's outer clothing * * * in an attempt to discern whether weapons are hidden underneath. [T]he problem with the officer's actions in *Dickerson* [is that] he "already knew [the pocket] contained no weapon." * * * [T]he officer's continued exploration of [Dickerson's] pocket *after having concluded that it contained no weapon* was unrelated to the sole justification of the search under *Terry*: the protection of the police officer and others nearby. It therefore amounted to the sort of evidentiary search that *Terry* expressly refused to authorize and that we have condemned in subsequent cases. * * *

The proper question under *Dickerson*, therefore, is not the immediacy and certainty with which an officer knows an object to be contraband or the amount of manipulation required to acquire that knowledge, but rather what the officer believes the object is by the time he concludes that it is not a weapon. That is, a *Terry* search cannot purposely be used to discover contraband, but it is permissible that contraband be confiscated if spontaneously discovered during a properly executed *Terry* search. Moreover, when determining whether the scope of a particular *Terry* search was proper, the areas of focus should be whether the officer had probable cause to believe an object was contraband before he knew it not to be a weapon and whether he acquired that knowledge in a manner consistent with a routine frisk.

Assuming that an officer is authorized to conduct a *Terry* search at all, he is authorized to assure himself that a suspect has no weapons. He is allowed to slide or manipulate an object in a suspect's pocket, consistent with a routine frisk, until the officer is able reasonably to eliminate the possibility that the object is a weapon. If, before that point, the officer develops probable cause to believe, given his training and experience, that an object is contraband, he may lawfully perform a more intrusive search. If, indeed, he discovers contraband, the officer may seize it, and it will be admissible against the suspect. If, however, the officer "goes beyond what is necessary to determine if the suspect is armed, it is no longer valid under *Terry* and its fruits will be suppressed."

Yamba at 258-59. [Court's emphasis; citations omitted.]

Here, Officer Livingstone "felt around" or otherwise "manipulated" the contents of Yamba's pocket "in the process of checking for weapons when he came across what in his experience could be contraband. It is not key whether Livingstone was certain that the object in Yamba's pocket was contraband by the time he knew it not to be a weapon; what is key is whether Livingstone had probable cause to believe that it was and this occurred at the same moment or before he determined that Yamba had no gun on his person. The record demonstrates that probable cause indeed existed before Livingstone's search went beyond the bounds of *Terry*." *Id.* at 259-60.

See also United States v. Mattarolo, 209 *F.*3d 1153, 1158 (9th Cir. 2000) ("Had the officer continued to manipulate the object beyond what was necessary to ascertain that it posed no threat, he would have run afoul of the Supreme Court's holding in *Minnesota v. Dickerson.*"); *United States v. Proctor,* 148 *F.*3d 39 (1st Cir. 1998) (During a lawful patdown, the officer touched the bulge in defendant's jacket pocket and felt a soft, leafy substance in a glassine bag which he immediately and reasonably recognized as a bag containing marijuana); *United States v. Rogers,* 129 *F.*3d 76, 79 (2nd Cir.1997) (During a lawful patdown, Sergeant Mason "felt the heavy object in Rogers' coat pocket. He manipulated the object for 'a few seconds' to determine what it was, and felt 'a hard object and then a softer object.' At that point, Mason was not yet able to exclude the possibility that there was a weapon in the pocket, so that the search was still within the bounds of *Terry,* and Mason had become 'fairly certain' the pocket contained drugs. That belief, combined with Rogers' evasive and suspicious conduct, gave the officers probable cause to search Rogers' pocket for contraband.").

   3. *Perception: the sense of sight versus the sense of touch.*

   (a) See United States v. Pace, 709 *F.Supp.* 948, 955 (C.D.Cal. 1989), where the court held, contrary to defendant's assertions, "that the tactile sense is [not] inherently less reliable than the sense of sight." *Id.* at 955. According to the *Pace* court, "[w]hen objects have a distinctive and consistent feel and shape that an officer has been trained to detect and has previous experience in detecting, then touching these objects provides the officer with the same recognition his sight would have produced." *Id. See also United States v. Proctor,* 148 *F.*3d 39 (1st Cir. 1998) (finding credible the officer's testimony that he "was consistently able to determine the feel of marijuana from conducting numerous pat-downs of suspects," in the context of a pat-down which occurred at a residence where five pounds of marijuana had just been delivered); *Henderson v. State,* 535 *So.*2d 659, 660-61 (Fla.App. 3 Dist. 1988) (finding no constitutional difference between the sense of touch and other senses); *People v. Lee,* 194 *Cal.App.*3d 975, 985, 240 *Cal.Rptr.* 32, 38 (Cal. Ct. App. 1987) *(same).*

   (b) In *State v. Washington,* 396 *S.W.*2d 156 (Wis. 1986), the officer tactilely recognized three watches (which he had probable cause to believe were recently stolen in a jewelry store burglary) in Washington's pocket during the course of a valid *Terry* frisk. The court held that because the officer's lawful plain touch provided him with "probable cause to believe that there [was] a connection between the evidence and criminal activity," the warrantless seizure of the watches was constitutionally reasonable. *Id.* at 161. In this respect, the court observed: "Though a pat-down provides no justification to search for evidence of a crime, it does not mean that the police must ignore evidence of a crime which is inadvertently discovered." *Id.*

   4. *Plain view and other senses.* Plain view principles have also been extended to encompass: (1) **Plain smell,** *see e.g., Johnson v. United States,* 333 *U.S.* 10, 13, 68 *S.Ct.* 367, 369 (1947) (strong odor of burning opium provided officers with probable cause and "might very well be found to be evidence of the most persuasive character"); *United States v. Lueck,* 678 *F.*2d 895, 903 (11th Cir. 1982) (contents of packages were "inferable" within the meaning of the *Sanders* footnote where * * * the "packages reeked of marijuana"); *United States v. Haley,* 669 *F.*2d 201, 203 (4th Cir. 1982) (A "characteristic which brings the contents into plain view is the odor given off by those contents."); *United States v. Haynie,* 637 *F.*2d 227, 233 (4th Cir. 1980) (odor of marijuana emanating from the back of defendant's car "established probable cause for the search of the trunk as well as placing the search within the plain view doctrine"); *United States v. Pagan,* 395 *F.Supp.* 1052, 1061 (D.P.R. 1975), *aff'd* 537 *F.*2d 554 (1st Cir. 1976) (plain view "doctrine has been extended to cover that evidence that can be per-

ceived by the sense of smell"); and (2) **Plain hearing**, *see e.g., United States v. Jackson*, 588 *F*.2d 1046 (5th Cir. 1979) (statements overheard without the benefit of listening devices by police officers stationed at a lawful vantage point are admissible for proper purposes at trial); *United States v. Fisch*, 474 *F*.2d 1071 (9th Cir. 1973) (*same*).

BOND v. UNITED STATES
Supreme Court of the United States
529 *U.S.* 334, 120 *S.Ct.* 1462 (2000)

QUESTION: In the absence of reasonable suspicion or probable cause, will an officer's physical manipulation of a bus passenger's carry-on luggage violate the Fourth Amendment?

ANSWER: YES. It is a "[p]hysically invasive inspection" for an officer to conduct "a probing tactile examination" of a bus passenger's carry-on luggage. *Id.* at 1464. Bus passengers maintain a reasonable expectation of privacy in carry-on luggage placed in overhead compartments. *Id.* at 1465. Thus, in the absence of probable cause to believe the bag contains evidence of a crime or contraband, or at least a reasonable suspicion that the bag contains a weapon, an officer's physical manipulation of a bus passenger's carry-on luggage is a search that violates the Fourth Amendment. *Id.*

RATIONALE: Defendant Bond was a passenger on a Greyhound bus when the bus stopped, "as it was required to do, at the permanent Border Patrol checkpoint in Sierra Blanca, Texas." *Id.* at 1463. During the stop, a Border Patrol agent walked onto the bus to "check the immigration status of its passengers." *Id.* The agent worked his way to the back of the bus, completed his check, and concluded that the passengers were lawfully in the United States. Then, as he walked toward the front of the bus, the agent systematically "squeezed the soft luggage which passengers had placed in the overhead storage space above the seats." *Id.*

Bond was seated four to five rows from the back of the bus. As the agent examined the carry-on luggage in the compartment above Bond's seat, "he squeezed a green canvas bag and noticed that it contained a 'brick-like' object." *Id.* Bond admitted that the bag belonged to him. Upon opening the bag, the agent found a "brick" of methamphetamine. "The brick had been wrapped in duct tape until it was oval-shaped and then rolled in a pair of pants." *Id.* at 1464.

Bond was placed under arrest and charged with various drug offenses. At his motion to suppress, he argued that the Border Patrol agent conducted an illegal search of his bag. Although Bond agreed that other passengers had access to his carry-on luggage, in this appeal he urged that the agent "manipulated the bag in a way that other passengers would not," and, as a result, violated his right to privacy under the Fourth Amendment. *The United States Supreme Court agreed.*

Preliminarily, the Court instructed that a traveler's "personal luggage is clearly an 'effect' protected by the [Fourth] Amendment." *Id.* Under that Amendment, Bond possessed a privacy interest in his bag.

This is not a case where the defendant had exposed his property to "visual" observation. Instead, this case deals with "tactile" observation, and, in this respect, the Court explained:

> Physically invasive inspection is simply more intrusive than purely visual inspection. For example, in *Terry v. Ohio* * * * we stated that a "careful [tactile] exploration of the outer surfaces of a person's clothing all over his or her body" is a "serious intrusion upon the sanctity of the person, which may inflict great indignity and arouse strong resentment, and is not to be undertaken lightly."

Id. [Citation omitted.]

Although the agent in this case did not "frisk" Bond's person, he did in fact conduct "a probing tactile examination" of Bond's carry-on bag—a repository that is normally used to transport "personal items." *Id.*

The Court concluded that Bond maintained a reasonable expectation of privacy in his "opaque" carry-on bag, which he placed directly above his seat. As a matter of common experience, when a bus passenger places carry-on luggage "in an overhead bin, he expects that other passengers or bus employees may move it for one reason or another. Thus, a bus passenger clearly expects that his bag may be handled. He does not expect that other passengers or bus employees will, as a matter of course, feel the bag in an exploratory manner. But this is exactly what the agent did here." *Id.* at 1465.

Accordingly, the Court concluded that the Border Patrol agent's physical manipulation of Bond's bag violated the Fourth Amendment.

NOTE

The officer's hands must be lawfully on the touching area. Strikingly absent from the Court's opinion in *Bond* was any discussion or mention of *Minnesota v. Dickerson.* In order to have a constitutional "plain touch" seizure under *Dickerson, each* of the three requirements must be met:

(1) The officer must be lawfully **in** the touching area;

(2) The officer's hands must be lawfully **on** the touching area; the officer must have some independent constitutional justification for placing his or her hands on the property or person in question.

(3) Upon touching the area, it must be immediately apparent to the officer that the object he or she is touching constitutes evidence of a crime or contraband.

In *Bond,* the Border Patrol agent failed to meet the second requirement of the "plain touch" formulation. He had no independent constitutional justification for placing his hands on Bond's carry-on luggage. Consequently, under a "plain touch" analysis, his seizure of evidence was unconstitutional.

CALIFORNIA v. CIRAOLO
Supreme Court of the United States
476 *U.S.* 207, 106 *S.Ct.* 1809 (1986)

QUESTION: Is the Fourth Amendment violated by the warrantless naked-eye aerial observation, at an altitude of 1,000 feet, of marijuana plants growing in a person's fenced-in backyard, within the curtilage of his home ?

ANSWER: NO. "In an age where private and commercial flight in the public airways is routine, it is unreasonable for [a person] to expect that his marijuana plants [growing in his fenced-in backyard curtilage] were constitutionally protected from being observed with the naked eye from an altitude of 1,000 feet." *Id.* at 1813.

RATIONALE: Officers of the Santa Clara, California, police department received an anonymous telephone tip that defendant Ciraolo was growing marijuana in his backyard. Surrounding defendant's yard was a six-foot outer fence and a ten-foot inner fence which made it impossible for the officers to observe the contents of the yard at ground level.

That same day, the officers secured a private plane and flew over defendant's home at an altitude of 1,000 feet (within navigable airspace). From that height, the officers, trained in marijuana identification, "readily identified marijuana plants 8 feet to 10 feet in height growing in a 15- by 25-foot plot in [defendant's] backyard; they photographed the area with a standard 35mm camera." *Id.* at 1811.

A search warrant was obtained and executed, yielding the seizure of 73 marijuana plants. Defendant was convicted of marijuana cultivation.

In upholding the conviction, the United States Supreme Court, per Chief Justice Burger, found that the officers' "observations * * * took place within navigable airspace * * * in a physically nonintrusive manner," allowing them to readily detect the marijuana plants. *Id.* at 1813.

"Such an observation is precisely what a judicial officer needs to provide a basis for a warrant. Any member of the public flying in this airspace who glanced down could have seen everything that these officers observed." *Id.*

The Court arrives at this conclusion by reasoning that the keynote of "Fourth Amendment analysis is whether a person has a 'constitutionally protected reasonable expectation of privacy.' " *Id.* at 1811 (citing *Katz v. United States*, 389 *U.S.* 347, 88 *S.Ct.* 507 (1967)). The analysis contains a two-pronged inquiry: "first, has the individual manifested a subjective expectation of privacy in the object of the challenged search ? Second, is society willing to recognize that expectation as reasonable ?" *Id.*

While defendant appears to have met the first prong, that of a subjective expectation of privacy, the Court finds that the second prong was not met—that the government's intrusion did not infringe " 'upon the personal and societal values protected by the Fourth Amendment.' " *Id*. at 1812. [Citation omitted.]

The Court acknowledges that defendant's backyard and marijuana crop did fall within the curtilage to his home, but emphasizes that the area "within the curtilage does not itself bar all police observation. The Fourth Amendment protection of the home (and curtilage) has never been extended to require law enforcement officers to shield their eyes when passing by a home on public thoroughfares." *Id*. Although a person takes some measures to restrict some views of his affairs, "[w]hat a person knowingly exposes to the public, even in his own home or office, is not a subject of Fourth Amendment protection." *Id*. at 1813. [Citation omitted.]

As a result, "[i]n an age where private and commercial flight in the public airways is routine, it is unreasonable for [a person] to expect that his marijuana plants [growing in his fenced-in backyard curtilage] were constitutionally protected from being observed with the naked eye from an altitude of 1,000 feet. The Fourth Amendment simply does not require the police traveling the public airways at this altitude to obtain a warrant to observe what is visible to the naked eye." *Id*. at 1813-14.

FLORIDA v. RILEY
Supreme Court of the United States
488 *U.S.* 445, 109 *S.Ct.* 693 (1989)

QUESTION: Does the surveillance of the interior of a partially covered greenhouse in a residential backyard from the vantage point of a helicopter located 400 feet above the greenhouse constitute a "search" for which a warrant is required under the Fourth Amendment?

ANSWER: NO. In accordance with the holding in *California v. Ciraolo, supra*, the surveillance of the interior of a partially covered greenhouse in a residential backyard from the vantage point of a helicopter located 400 feet above the greenhouse does not constitute a "search" for which a warrant is required, and as a result, does not violate the Fourth Amendment. *Id*. at 697.

RATIONALE: Acting on an anonymous tip that defendant Riley was growing marijuana in a greenhouse located on his property, an officer from the Sheriff's Department of Pasco County, Florida, traveled to defendant's residence to investigate. Upon arrival, the officer discovered that he could not see the contents of the greenhouse from the road. Defendant "lived in a mobile home located on five acres of rural property. A greenhouse was located 10 to 20 feet behind the mobile home. Two sides of the greenhouse were enclosed. The other two sides were not enclosed but the contents of the greenhouse were obscured from view from surrounding property by trees, shrubs and the mobile home. The greenhouse was covered by corrugated roofing panels, some translucent and some opaque." *Id.* at 695. Additionally, "two of the panels, amounting to approximately 10% of the roof area, were missing. A wire fence surrounded the mobile home and the greenhouse, and the property was posted with a 'DO NOT ENTER' sign." *Id.*

After assessing the situation, the officer secured a helicopter and circled twice over defendant's property at a height of 400 feet. "With his naked eye, he was able to see through the openings in the roof and one or more of the open sides of the greenhouse and to identify what he thought was marijuana growing in the structure. A warrant was obtained based on these observations, and the ensuing search revealed marijuana growing in the greenhouse." *Id.* Defendant was arrested and charged with its possession.

Relying on *California v. Ciraolo, supra,* the Court reiterated that "[w]hat a person knowingly exposes to the public, even in his own home or office, is not a subject of Fourth Amendment protection. * * * As a general proposition, the police may see what may be seen from a public vantage point where they have a right to be." *Riley* at 696. [Citations omitted.]

Similar to *Ciraolo,* the property surveyed in this case was within the curtilage of defendant's home. "Riley no doubt intended and expected that his greenhouse would not be open to public inspection, and the precautions he took protected against ground-level observation. Because the sides and roof of his greenhouse were left partially open, however, what was growing in the greenhouse was subject to viewing from the air. Under the holding in *Ciraolo,* Riley could not reasonably have expected the contents of his greenhouse to be immune from examination by an officer seated in a fixed-wing aircraft flying in navigable airspace at an altitude of 1,000 feet[.]" *Id.* Although the inspection in this case was made from a helicopter, helicopter air travel, similar to travel by fixed-wing planes, is "routine in this country." *Id.* "Riley could not reasonably have expected that his greenhouse was protected from public or official observation from a helicopter had it been flying within the navigable airspace for fixed-wing aircraft." *Id.*

In reaching this decision, the Court found that it made no "difference for Fourth Amendment purposes that the helicopter was flying at 400 feet when the officer saw what was growing in the greenhouse through the partially open roof and sides of the structure. We would have a different case if flying at that altitude had been contrary to law or regulation. But helicopters are not bound by the lower limits of the navigable airspace allowed to aircraft. * * * This is not to say that an inspection of the curtilage of a house from an aircraft will always pass muster under the Fourth Amendment simply because the plane is within the navigable airspace specified by law. But it is of obvious importance that the helicopter in this case was not violating the law, and there is nothing [here] to suggest that helicopters flying at 400 feet are sufficiently rare in this country to lend substance to [Riley's] claim that he reasonably anticipated that his greenhouse would not be subject to observation from that altitude." *Id.* at 696-697.

Accordingly these circumstances present "no violation of the Fourth Amendment." *Id.* at 697.

NOTE

Florida v. Riley, supra, was a plurality opinion. Justice White delivered the opinion for the Court in which Chief Justice Rehnquist, Justice Scalia, and Justice Kennedy joined. It should be noted that in her concurring opinion, Justice O'Connor agreed that "the police observation of the greenhouse in Riley's curtilage from a helicopter passing at an altitude of 400 feet did not violate an expectation of privacy that society is prepared to recognize as reasonable." *Id.* at 697. She wrote separately, however, to emphasize her belief that "the plurality's approach rests the scope of Fourth Amendment protection too heavily on compliance with FAA regulations whose purpose is to promote air safety not to protect '(t)he right of the people to be secure in their persons, houses, papers, and effects, against unreasonable searches and seizures.' " *Id.* [Citation omitted.] Justice O'Connor would judge an expectation of privacy reasonable not because the aircraft was operating where it had a "right to be," but because the particular type of air travel involved in the case is "a sufficiently routine part of modern life that it is unreasonable for persons on the ground to expect that their curtilage will not be observed from the air at that altitude." *Id.* at 698. Justice O'Connor reasons: "To require individuals to completely cover and enclose their curtilage is to demand more than the 'precautions customarily taken by those seeking privacy.' " *Id.* [Citation omitted.] Thus, the relevant inquiry is "whether the helicopter was in the public airways at an altitude at which members of the public travel with sufficient regularity that Riley's expectation of privacy from aerial observation was not 'one that society is prepared to recognize as reasonable.' " *Id.* [Citation omitted.]

---

§4.4. Abandonment.

The relevance of abandoned property in the realm of constitutional criminal procedure lies in the notion that the safeguards of the Fourth Amendment simply do not extend to it. "[W]here one abandons property, he is said to bring his right of privacy therein to an end, and may not later complain about its subsequent seizure and use in evidence against him. In short, the theory of abandonment is that no issue of search is presented in such a situation, and the property so abandoned may be seized without probable cause." Mascolo, *The Role of Abandonment in the Law of Search and Seizure: An Application of Misdirected Emphasis*, 20 Buff.L.Rev. 399, 400-401 (1971).

The keynote to the concept of abandonment is the actor's intention to relinquish all claim to the property—either personal or real—with the concomitant intention of not reclaiming or resuming ownership, possession, or control over it. Once this situation exists, it may then be said that the actor's relinquishment took place under circumstances which demonstrate that he retained no reasonable expectation of privacy in the property so discarded. For example, in *Abel v. United States,* 362 *U.S.* 217, 80 *S.Ct.* 683 (1960), an FBI agent undertook a warrantless search of defendant's hotel room immediately after defendant had paid his bill and vacated the room. During the search, the entire contents of the room's wastepaper basket were seized and found to contain evidence which was subsequently used against defendant in his espionage prosecution. Finding the search and seizure entirely lawful, the Court explained:

> * * * at the time of the search, [defendant] had vacated the room. The hotel then had the exclusive right to its possession, and the hotel management freely gave its consent that the search be made. Nor was it unlawful to seize the entire contents of the wastepaper basket, even though some of its contents had no connection with crime. * * * *[Defendant] had abandoned these articles.* He had thrown them away. So far as he was concerned, they were bona vacantia.* There can be nothing unlawful in the Government's appropriation of such abandoned property.

Id. at 241. [Emphasis added.]

As a result, for criminal procedure purposes, the relevant inquiry is whether the actor, by dispossessing himself of his property, has so relinquished his reasonable expectation of privacy in that property that a subsequent government inspection and appropriation of that property cannot be said to constitute a "search and seizure" within the meaning of the Fourth Amendment. As the United States Supreme Court noted, there can be "no seizure in the sense of the law when * * * [law enforcement] officers examine[] * * * the contents of [personal property] after it ha[s] been abandoned." *Hester v. United States,* 265 *U.S.* 57, 58, 44 *S.Ct.* 445 (1924).

---

* "Vacant, unclaimed, or stray goods." The Court's use of "bona vacantia" is a property law reference to those "things in which nobody claims a property [interest], and which belonged, under the common law, to the finder." Black's Law Dictionary 160 (5th Ed. 1979). The property law concept of abandonment, however, should be distinguished from abandonment in the criminal procedure sense. As one court appropriately explained: "In the law of property, the question * * * is whether the owner has voluntarily, intentionally, and unconditionally relinquished his interest in the property so that another, having acquired possession, may successfully assert his superior interest. * * * In the law of search and seizure, however, the question is whether the defendant has, in discarding the property, relinquished his reasonable expectation of privacy so that its seizure and search is reasonable within the limits of the Fourth Amendment. * * * In essence, what is abandoned is not necessarily the defendant's property, but his reasonable expectation of privacy therein." *City of St. Paul v. Vaughn,* 306 *Minn.* 337, 237 *N.W.2d* 365 (1975).

CALIFORNIA v. GREENWOOD
Supreme Court of the United States
486 *U.S.* 35, 108 *S.Ct.* 1625 (1988)

QUESTION: Does the Fourth Amendment prohibit the warrantless search and seizure of garbage left for collection outside the curtilage of a home ?

ANSWER: NO. When garbage is left for collection outside the curtilage of one's home, it is sufficiently exposed to the public so that any search or seizure thereof falls outside the parameters of the Fourth Amendment. *Id.* at 1628.

RATIONALE: Acting on information that defendant, Greenwood, might be engaged in narcotics trafficking, Investigator Jenny Stracner of the Laguna Beach Police Department began a surveillance of defendant's home. When she was satisfied that the vehicular and pedestrian traffic in and out of defendant's home matched the profile of one dealing in drugs, she made arrangements with the neighborhood trash collector for the pick-up of defendant's plastic garbage bags that he left on the curb in front of his house and to turn the bags over to her without mixing their contents with garbage from other houses. "The trash collector cleaned his bin of other refuse, collected the garbage bags from the street in front of defendant's home, and turned the bags over to Stracner. The officer searched through the rubbish and found items indicative of narcotics use." *Id.* at 1627.

Stracner then incorporated the factual information heretofore developed into an affidavit in support of a warrant to search defendant's home. The search of defendant's home, conducted pursuant to the warrant, yielded quantities of cocaine and hashish, and accordingly, defendant was arrested on felony narcotics charges.

After defendant posted bail, the Laguna Police Department again received reports of many late-night visitors to the Greenwood home. This time, Investigator Rahaeuser conducted the seizure of defendant's garbage bags left at the curb, and again the search revealed evidence of narcotics use. "Rahaeuser secured another search warrant for Greenwood's home based on the information from the second trash search. The police found more narcotics and evidence of narcotics trafficking when they executed the warrant. Greenwood was again arrested." *Id.* at 1627-1628.

In this appeal, defendant contends that the seizure of the opaque plastic garbage bags was in violation of the Fourth Amendment; that he exhibited an expectation of privacy with respect to the trash by placing it in opaque plastic. Moreover, asserts defendant, "[t]he trash was only temporarily on the street, and there was little likelihood that it would be inspected by anyone." *Id.* at 1628.

The United States Supreme Court, per Justice White, disagreed. "The warrantless search and seizure of the garbage bags left at the curb outside the Greenwood house would violate the Fourth Amendment only if [defendant] manifested a subjective expectation of privacy in [his] garbage that society accepts as objectively reasonable. * * * It may well be that [Greenwood] did not expect that the content's of [his] garbage bags would become known to the police or other members of the public." *Id.* This subjective privacy expectation does not, however, end the inquiry. "An expectation of privacy does not give rise to Fourth Amendment protection, * * * unless society is prepared to accept that expectation as objectively reasonable." *Id.*

In this case, it must be concluded that defendant "exposed [his] garbage to the public sufficiently to defeat [his] claim to Fourth Amendment protection. It is common knowledge that plastic garbage bags left on or at the side of a public street are readily accessible to animals, children, scavengers,* snoops, and other members of the public." *Id.* at 1628-1629. Additionally, defendant placed his garbage "at the curb for the express purpose of conveying it to a third party, the trash collector, who might himself have sorted through [defendant's] trash or permitted others, such as the police, to do so." *Id.* at 1629.

"Accordingly, having deposited [his] garbage 'in an area particularly suited for public inspection and, in a manner of speaking, public consumption, for the express purpose of having strangers take it,' [defendant] could have had no reasonable expectation of privacy in the inculpatory items that [he] discarded." *Id.* [Citation omitted.] Consequently, the Court concludes "that society would not accept as reasonable [defendant's] claim to an expectation of privacy in trash left for collection in an area accessible to the public[.]" *Id.*

NOTE

1. In a strongly worded dissent, Justice Brennan declared: "Scrutiny of another's trash is contrary to commonly accepted notions of civilized behavior. I suspect, therefore, that members of our society will be shocked to learn that the Court, the ultimate guarantor of liberty, deems unreasonable our expectation that the aspects of our private lives that are concealed safely in a trash bag will not become public." *Id.*, 108 *S.Ct.* at 1632.

A single bag of trash testifies eloquently to the eating, reading, and recreational habits of the person who produced it. A search of trash, like a search of the bedroom, can relate intimate details about sexual practices, health, and personal hygiene. Like rifling through desk drawers or intercepting phone calls, rummaging through trash can divulge the target's financial and professional status, political affiliations and inclinations, private thoughts, personal relationships, and romantic interests. It cannot be doubted that a sealed trash bag harbors telling evidence of the "ultimate activity associ-

---

* "It is not only the homeless of the Nation's cities who make use of others' refuse. For example, a nationally syndicated consumer columnist has suggested that apartment dwellers obtain cents-off coupons by 'mak(ing) friends with the fellow who handles the trash' in their buildings, and has recounted the tale of 'the Rich lady' from Westmont who once a week puts on rubber gloves and hip boots and wades into the town garbage dump looking for labels and other proofs of purchase needed to obtain manufacturer's refunds." *Id.* at 1629 n.3 (quoting M. Sloan, "The Supermarket Shopper's" 1980 Guide to Coupons and Refunds 74, 161 (1980)).

ated with the 'sanctity of a man's home and the privacies of life,' "
which the Fourth Amendment is designed to protect.

Id. at 1634 (Brennan, J., dissenting).

2. The principles set forth in *California v. Greenwood* have been
receiving mixed treatment in several states. For example, in a pre-
Greenwood case, the Hawaii Supreme Court determined that:

> People reasonably believe that police will not indiscriminately
> rummage through their trash bags to discover their personal ef-
> fects. Business records, bills, correspondence, magazines, tax re-
> cords, and other telltale refuse can reveal much about a person's
> activities, associations and beliefs.

State v. Tanaka, 67 *Haw.* 658, 662, 701 *P.*2d 1274, 1276-77 (1985). As
a result, the court ruled, on independent state constitutional grounds,
that its citizens maintain a reasonable expectation of privacy in the
contents of their garbage, and that the Hawaii Constitution prohibits
warrantless garbage searches.

See also People v. Krivda, 5 *Cal.*3d 357, 367, 486 *P.*2d 1262, 96
Cal.Rptr. 62 (1971) (garbage left outside curtilage is constitutionally
protected; "defendants had a reasonable expectation that their trash
would not be rummaged through and picked over by police officers acting without a search warrant"), *vacated*, 409 *U.S.* 33, 93 *S.Ct.* 32 (1972)
(remanded for a determination whether the court's ruling was based on
state or federal constitution), *on remand*, 8 *Cal.*3d 623, 504 *P.*2d 457,
105 *Cal.Rptr.* 521 (original holding reincorporated on independent state
constitutional grounds), *cert. denied*, 412 *U.S.* 919, 93 *S.Ct.* 2734 (1973);
State v. Hempele, 120 *N.J.* 182, 223, 576 *A.*2d 793 (1990) (while the police need "no cause" to seize a citizen's curbside garbage, a warrant
based on probable cause must be secured in order to search it); *State v.
Boland*, 115 *Wash.*2d 571, 581, 800 *P.*2d 1112, 1117 (1990) (leaving
one's garbage at the curb for collection does not extinguish one's expectation of privacy in its contents; warrantless seizure and search, therefore, held unreasonable under state constitution).
    Cf. State v. Smith, 510 *P.*2d 793, 798 (Alaska) (reasoning that "al-
most every human activity ultimately manifests itself in waste products and * * * any individual may understandably wish to maintain
the confidentiality of his refuse"; but upholding the warrantless search
of a dumpster), *cert. denied*, 414 *U.S.* 1086, 94 *S.Ct.* 603 (1973).

Compare *State v. DeFusco*, 224 *Conn.* 627, 639, 620 *A.*2d 746, 753
(1993) (Connecticut citizens harbor no reasonable expectation of privacy in the contents of garbage left at the curb for collection; consequently, the warrantless search and seizure of such does not violate
article first, §7 of the Connecticut constitution).

3. *Shredded documents and curbside garbage.* In *United States v. Scott*, 975 *F.*2d 927 (1st Cir. 1992), the court addressed the question whether the Fourth Amendment prohibited the warrantless seizure and reconstruction of shredded documents found in trash bags located outside the curtilage of defendant's home. Stated another way, the question is whether the shredding of private documents gives rise to a constitutionally recognizable expectation of privacy "which follows the shredded remnants, individually and collectively, even after they become public garbage." *Id.* at 928.

Defendant "was suspected by the Internal Revenue Service (IRS) of involvement in a scheme to defraud the United States through the filing of false income tax returns. IRS agents systematically combed through garbage bags left for collection in front of [defendant's] house. Their search revealed numerous shredded documents reduced to 5/32-inch strips, which when painstakingly pieced together produced incriminating evidence. The agents then used this evidence as the basis for establishing probable cause to request various search warrants." *Id.* The search warrants were issued and executed, and additional incriminating evidence was found.

Rejecting defendant's contention that by shredding the documents he manifested an objectively reasonable expectation of privacy in the shredded remnants, the court stated:

> We start out with the obvious proposition that what we are dealing with here *is* trash. More important is the fact that at the time the challenged evidence came into the hands of the authorities, it was *public* trash. That is, irrespective of whether [defendant] intended to keep secret the contents of the documents in question by shredding them, there can be no doubt that [defendant] also intended to dispossess himself of those documents once they were shredded, and to place their fractured remnants in a public area accessible to unknown third parties. * * * Thus, it is appropriate to call the evidence at issue "public" trash because it was trash left for collection in a public place and over which its producer had relinquished possession. * * *

> In our view, a person who places trash at a curb to be disposed of or destroyed by a third person abandons it[.] * * * The fact that the abandoned property was partially destroyed by shredding, although constituting evidence of [defendant's] subjective desire or hope that the contents be unintelligible to third parties, does not change the fact that it is as a result of [defendant's] own actions that the shredded evidence was placed in the public domain.

> What we have here is a failed attempt at secrecy by reason of underestimation of police resourcefulness, not invasion of constitutionally protected privacy. There is no constitutional protection from police scrutiny as to information received from a failed attempt at secrecy.

> [Defendant] here thought that reducing the documents to 5/32-inch pieces made them undecipherable. It turned out he was wrong. He is in no better position than the citizen who merely tears up a document by hand and discards the pieces [o]nto the sidewalk. * * * Should the mere use of more sophisticated "higher" technology in attempting destruction of the pieces of paper grant higher constitutional protection to this failed attempt at secrecy? We think not. There is no constitutional requirement that police techniques in the detection of crime must remain stagnant while those intent on keeping their nefarious activities secret have the benefit of new knowledge.

> In our view, shredding garbage and placing it in the public domain subjects it to the same risks regarding privacy, as engaging in a private conversation in public where it is subject to the possibility that it may be overheard by other persons. Both are failed attempts at maintaining privacy whose failure can only be attributed to the conscious acceptance by the actor of obvious risk factors. * * * In both situations the expectation of privacy has been practically eliminated by the citizen's own actions.

> The mere fact that [defendant] shredded his garbage before he placed it outside of his home does not create a reasonable heightened expectation of privacy under the Fourth Amendment. [Defendant] still discarded this garbage in an area particularly suited for public inspection and consumption. * * * The Fourth Amendment, however, does not protect [defendant] when a third party expends the effort and expense to solve the jigsaw puzzle created by shredding.

Id. at 928-30. [Court's emphasis; footnote omitted.]

4. *Denying ownership.*

(a) In *United States v. Colbert*, 474 F.2d 174 (5th Cir. 1973) (*en banc*), officers approached two men who were walking along a street in Birmingham, Alabama. According to the officers, one of the two men fit the description of a wanted felon. Upon seeing the police, the two men set the briefcases which they had been carrying on the sidewalk. In response to questions posed by one of the officers, the two claimed that they were "book salesmen." Yet, they denied ownership of the briefcases they were carrying. After being frisked by the officers, the two men began walking away, leaving their briefcases behind. A warrantless search of the briefcases uncovered illegal firearms. According to the Fifth Circuit:

> The facts of this case show conclusively that [the defendants] abandoned their briefcases before the searches took place. In response to police questions they both disclaimed any interest in the briefcases and began to walk away from them. The police officers in no way compelled these actions. Under these circumstances[,

470

defendants] could entertain no reasonable expectation of privacy in them. * * *

Id. at 177. The court concluded that "[t]he legal effect of the abandonment is * * * to deprive [defendants] of standing to challenge the subsequent searches." *Id.*

A number of circuits have similarly held that an abandonment occurs where, in response to police questioning, a suspect denies ownership of the property in question. *See United States v. Carrasquillo*, 877 F.2d 73 (D.C.Cir. 1989) (abandonment found where train passenger denied ownership of garment bag under his feet and no other person claimed it); *United States v. McBean*, 861 F.2d 1570 (11th Cir. 1988) (defendant abandoned any reasonable expectation of privacy in the contents of luggage in the trunk of his car when he told police that it was not his luggage and that he knew nothing of its contents); *United States v. Roman*, 849 F.2d 920 (5th Cir. 1988) (abandonment found where defendant checked his suitcases at an airport and then told agents that he had not checked any luggage and had no baggage other than his carry-on bag). *See also United States v. Clark*, 891 F.2d 501 (4th Cir. 1989); *United States v. Moskowitz*, 883 F.2d 1142 (2nd Cir. 1989); *United States v. Nordling*, 804 F.2d 1466 (9th Cir. 1986); *United States v. Lucci*, 758 F.2d 153 (6th Cir. 1985), *cert. denied*, 474 U.S. 843, 106 S.Ct. 129 (1985).

(b) *Silence in response to a police inquiry about ownership.* An abandonment of property would not be found solely from a person's silence or failure to respond to a police officer's questions regarding ownership of an item. As one commentator reasoned, " 'To equate a passive failure to claim potentially incriminating evidence with an affirmative abandonment of property would be to twist both logic and experience in a most uncomfortable knot.' " 1 LaFave, *Search and Seizure*, §2.6(b), at p. 469 n.54 (2d ed. 1987). [Citation omitted.]

5. *Throwing or placing property on the hood or trunk of a car.* In *Smith v. Ohio*, 494 U.S. 541, 110 S.Ct. 1288, 1290 (1990), the United States Supreme Court accepted the conclusion that "a citizen who attempts to protect his private property from inspection, after throwing it on [the hood of his] car to respond to a police officer's inquiry, clearly has not abandoned that property." For a further discussion of this case, *see* §8.4 and the Notes following *United States v. Place*.

See also Commonwealth v. Sanders, 407 Pa.Super. 270, 595 A.2d 635, 637 (1991), where the court held that a drug suspect's act of placing a black pouch on the trunk of a car he was standing near, just prior to the approach of a police officer, did not reflect "a clear intent to relinquish his interest in the property." According to the court, because the defendant "did not walk away from the car or otherwise attempt to disassociate himself further from the pouch," his equivocal act of " 'placing' the pouch on the hood cannot be equated with acts in other cases where the defendant made clear an intent to abandon by discarding the evidence." *Id.*, 595 A.2d at 637. Significantly, the sparse facts presented at the suppression hearing made it impossible for the court to determine whether the defendant's act was an attempt to discard the evidence in reaction to the lawful approach of a police officer. In this respect, the court elaborated:

> Indeed, the record is silent concerning whether [defendant] was even *aware* of [the officer's] presence: there is no record evidence that [the officer] was in uniform or in a marked police car, or that [defendant] looked in her direction as she approached or otherwise indicated an awareness of her presence. Thus, this case is unlike "the typical case in which abandonment has been found because the defendant attempted to disassociate himself from incriminating evidence by throwing it away upon the lawful approach of the police."

Id. at 637. [Citations omitted; emphasis in original.]

6. *Abandoned houses.*

(a) Discarding keys. In *Commonwealth v. Rodriguez*, 385 *Pa.Super.* 1, 559 A.2d 947 (1989), the Commonwealth argued that "the storing of narcotics in a vacant property without permission of the owner or anyone else authorized to allow entry does not establish a constitutionally protected right to privacy of possessions placed therein[.]" 559 A.2d at 948.

In *Rodriguez*, defendant was observed selling cocaine by two undercover Philadelphia police officers in the 600 block of West Shiller Street. The officers approached and indicated their desire to purchase twenty dollars worth. They handed defendant's associate a prerecorded $20 bill and she gave it to defendant who thereafter entered 645 West Shiller Street, unlocking the door with a key. Defendant then quickly reappeared with a bag of cocaine. As they drove off, the officers field-tested the substance, confirming the fact that it was cocaine. The officers were then joined by several uniformed officers, all of whom returned to the place of sale in a marked police car. When defendant saw the officers approaching, she dropped the keys to the house. As she was placed under arrest, two officers went to the house and inspected the premises through the windows. The officers concluded the house was abandoned "because no curtains, window shades, or furniture could be seen. They entered with the keys [defendant] had dropped and discovered 93 bags of cocaine sealed with white tape, weighing a total of two pounds. The prerecorded $20 bill was also retrieved inside the house." *Id.* at 947.

Finding that defendant abandoned the property seized as a matter of law, the Superior Court held that this defendant had "no standing to challenge the police search of the house and consequent seizure of the narcotics." *Id.* at 948. In this respect, the court found defendant's reliance upon the "automatic standing" rule of *Commonwealth v. Sell*, "misplaced." *Rodriguez* at 948.

" 'The test for abandonment is whether the complaining party could retain a reasonable expectation of privacy in the property allegedly abandoned.' " *Id.* [Citation omitted.] As the Supreme Court stated in *Sell*, " 'personal possessions remain constitutionally protected ... until their owner meaningfully abdicates his control, ownership or possessory interest therein.' " *Rodriguez* at 949 (quoting *Sell* at 67).

Therefore, the relevant question becomes whether defendant's "throwing away of the keys to the abandoned house constitutes such a relinquishment of interest in the contents of the house so that [defendant] may no longer assert a reasonable expectation of privacy in its contents." *Id.* This court held that it did. Defendant "had no ownership rights to the abandoned house other than her set of keys which allowed her access to the premises. By abandoning the keys when the officers approached, [defendant] effectively relinquished all rights she had in the premises and the items stored in the house were no longer protected by any expectation of privacy on [defendant's] part." *Id.*

Accordingly, this defendant "lacked standing as a matter of law to challenge the seizure of narcotics and the prerecorded $20 bill." *Id.*

(b) *Mere structures.* In *Commonwealth v. Cameron*, 385 *Pa.Super.* 492, 561 A.2d 783 (1989), the court held that "under the Pennsylvania Constitution, as well as under the Constitution of the United States, it is unreasonable to expect that one has a privacy interest in an abandoned structure which is not one's dwelling place." 561 A.2d at 786-787. According to the court: "Although the home has always been as sacrosanct in search and seizure jurisprudence in this Commonwealth as under the fourth amendment, the same considerations which create those privacy concerns are not necessarily present when one is discussing not a home, but a mere structure." *Id.* at 787.

In this case, Philadelphia police conducted a warrantless search of an abandoned rowhouse on Ruby Street in West Philadelphia which, according to the Commonwealth, had been used by defendant to facilitate an illegal narcotics operation. At the suppression hearing, Sergeant Perrone testified that in the rowhouse, "there were no bathroom facilities, or cooking appliances * * * no running water or electricity." *Id.* at 784. The second floor "was littered with human waste and trash and other debris. The window[, which] at one time had glass in it, was plywooded over[.]" *Id.* The sergeant further testified that he knew no one lived in the house, and that upon defendant's arrest, defendant gave his address as 535 North Roger Street. At the time of defendant's arrest, the room in which he was arrested "contained a couch, a table, and a television set, which was * * * on at the time[.]" *Id.* Perrone stated that he also observed an "aluminum type foil platter" on the table with food on it.

The court found it clear that defendant manifested a "subjective" expectation of privacy in the abandoned rowhouse. "However, it cannot be said that his expectation of privacy is one that society is prepared to accept as reasonable." *Id.* at 785. Privacy expectations must not be examined in a vacuum.

"Legitimate expectations of privacy by law must have a source outside the Fourth Amendment, either by reference to concepts of real or personal property law or to understandings that are recognized and permitted by society. One of the main rights attaching to property is the right to exclude others ... and one who owns or lawfully possesses or controls property will in all likelihood have a legitimate expectation of privacy by virtue of this right to exclude."

Id. at 785-786 (quoting *Rakas v. Illinois*, 439 *U.S.* 128, 143 n.12, 99 *S.Ct.* 421, 430 n.12 (1978)).

"Although the property interest involved need not amount to an ownership interest, there must be some legal or *de facto* right to control the area in question." *Id.* at 786. In this case, there is no evidence demonstrating that defendant had any legal or *de facto* right to control the house. "The testimony of Sergeant Perrone indicated that the house was abandoned, and, although there was some evidence to show that [defendant] was 'squatting' there, the record contains no facts which would lead [this court] to believe that he had any rights against the owner, or as against any other person who attempted to enter the house. He therefore could not expect to exclude any other person who attempted to enter." *Id.* Defendant therefore had no reasonable expectation of privacy in the abandoned house.

Moreover, the court found that under Article I, Section 8, of the Pennsylvania Constitution, the rationale and result are the same—"it is unreasonable to expect that one has a privacy interest in an abandoned structure which is not one's dwelling place." *Id.* at 786-787. While the court did "not decide whether in other circumstances a vacant structure *might be considered* to be a 'dwelling place' within the purview of [A]rticle I, Section 8[, it merely found] that under the facts of this case, a television, a couch, and a platter of food are insufficient attributes of a home, and so failed to call the protection against unreasonable searches and seizures into play." *Id.* at 787-788. [Emphasis added.]

7. *Hotel & motel rooms.*

(a) Expired rental periods. In *Commonwealth v. Brundidge*, 404 *Pa.Super.* 106, 590 *A.2d* 302 (1991), defendant registered at the Greencastle Travelodge Motel for one night. Based on motel policy, the desk clerk informed him, as she did all guests, that check-out time was at twelve noon. In addition, there was a sign displayed at the front desk informing motel guests of the twelve noon check-out time. Defendant left the motel at approximately twelve midnight and did not return that night. He did, however, leave his car at the motel.

The following day, at approximately twelve noon, a housekeeper called defendant's room to see if he wished to retain the room for a second night. When she received no answer, she entered the room and found that the beds had not been disturbed. On one of the beds she discovered a diagram of the motel floor plan labeled "front desk," and on a table she found several one-inch square plastic bags. Fearing a possible robbery, the housekeeper reported what she found to the hotel manager. At the time, a state trooper was in the manager's office investigating an unrelated matter. The manager and trooper went to the room, and at approximately 12:20 p.m., the trooper entered the room. In plain view, he observed the diagram and small plastic bags. Immediately thereafter, he searched the closet and discovered a jacket with a protective plastic bag over it. He inspected the jacket, and in a pocket found a plastic bag filled with white powder, which was later determined to be 206.6 grams of cocaine. At 12:45 p.m., defendant returned to the motel and registered for a second night.

In the appeal following defendant's judgment of sentence, the Commonwealth argued, among other things, that the items left in defendant's motel room were "abandoned" and therefore "outside the protection of the Fourth Amendment." *Id.*, 590 A.2d at 308 n.7. Rejecting this contention, the court held that "under the circumstances of this case, where only a relatively short period of time had elapsed since check-out time, [defendant's] car remained parked at the motel, the room remained locked, and [defendant] returned shortly thereafter to register for a second night, it cannot be said that [he] manifested an intent to discard or relinquish his interest in the property left in his room." *Id.* (citing *Commonwealth v. Shoatz, supra* at 553, 366 A.2d at 1219-20). The court stressed, however, that its holding should not be interpreted to

> mean that a court can never find that a motel guest has relinquished privacy interests in both the motel room *and* in belongings left therein. In another case, additional facts may lead a court reasonably to conclude that a motel guest has relinquished all legitimate expectations of privacy in both the room and articles left in it. Today, we hold simply that a citizen's privacy interest in enclosed personal possessions inside a motel room do[es] not terminate automatically at check-out time.

Id. at 308 n.8. [Emphasis in original.]

Significantly, the court's holding was limited to a guest's "closed or secured" personal effects left in his or her room after check-out time. Such a guest will, however, be deemed to have abandoned his or her expectation of privacy "in the room" or in any item left "in plain view to anyone readying the room for the next occupant" after check-out time. *Id.* at 306-07.

See also United States v. Ramirez, 810 F.2d 1338, 1341 (5th Cir.) (no reasonable expectation of privacy in hotel room after rental period expired), *cert. denied*, 484 U.S. 844, 108 S.Ct. 136 (1987); *United States v. Larson*, 760 F.2d 852, 854-55 (8th Cir.) (no legitimate expectation of privacy at time of search when rental period elapsed and defendant did not sufficiently communicate with motel personnel his intention to renew term), *cert. denied*, 474 U.S. 849, 106 S.Ct. 143 (1985). Interestingly, in *United States v. Croft*, 429 F.2d 884 (10th Cir. 1970), defendant argued that the "expiration of the rental period should not control * * * because his arrest prior to check-out time prevented him from returning to the motel and perhaps extending the rental period." Rejecting this argument, the Tenth Circuit held that "it was defendant's own conduct[, *i.e.*, his illegal activity,] that prevented his return to the motel." *Id.* at 887.

(b) *Abandonment prior to checkout.*

(*i*) While a guest in a motel or hotel retains a constitutionally protected expectation of privacy in his or her room during the period of time for which it is rented, "[t]his is not to say that intentional abandonment, and therefore a relinquishment of privacy interests, of rented premises can never be found even if the rental period has *not* expired." *Brundidge* at 306 n.5. [Emphasis added.]

(*ii*) In *State v. Oken*, 569 A.2d 1218 (Me. 1990), the Supreme Judicial Court of Maine found that the defendant abandoned his Coachman motel room when, within six hours after paying in advance for one night's stay by credit card, he left the motel, drove to Freeport and checked into the Freeport Inn, and only left behind a bloody jersey, a half bottle of vodka and some orange juice. Although defendant had not "officially" checked out of his room at the Coachman, the motel manager listed his room as "unoccupied" by 8:00 a.m., and permitted the police to search it at 8:30 a.m., two and one-half hours before the normal check-out time. The court found, however, that the circumstances of this case supported the conclusion that defendant "did not intend to return to the Coachman," and in all respects, abandoned his constitutional interest in the room's contents. *Id.* at 1221.

In Maine, therefore, " '[a]bandonment is primarily a question of intent, and intent may be inferred from words spoken, acts done, and other objective facts. All relevant circumstances existing at the time of the alleged abandonment should be considered. *United States v. Colbert*, 474 *F*.2d 174, 176 (5th Cir. 1973). Abandonment in the constitutional sense, *i.e.*, in the law of search and seizure, exists only if the defendant has voluntarily discarded the property, left it behind, or otherwise relinquished his interest therein under circumstances indicative of his forgoing any further reasonable expectation of privacy with regard to it at the time of the search.' " *Oken* at 1220 (quoting *State v. Philbrick*, 436 A.2d 844, 859 (Me. 1981)).

See also City of St. Paul v. Vaughn, 237 *N.W.*2d 365, 370-371 (Minn. 1975) (recognizing that property voluntarily abandoned is "exempted" from Fourth Amendment protection).

8. *Storage lockers. See United States v. Reyes*, 908 *F*.2d 281 (8th Cir. 1990), where the court, relying heavily on *United States v. Croft*, *supra*, held that "a defendant has no standing to contest a warrantless search of a rented locker which took place after the rental period had expired even when he was prevented from renewing the rental period or removing the locker's contents because of his lawful arrest." *Id.* at 286. According to the court, Reyes could claim no reasonable expecta-

tion of privacy in the contents of his Greyhound bus station storage locker when the challenged search occurred on December 12, the locker's rental period expired on December 1, and the locker displayed a warning that if he did not renew his rental period or remove his property, it would be removed and possibly sold by Greyhound personnel. *Id.* at 284-85.

CHAPTER 5

NON-GOVERNMENTAL SEARCHES

Section
5.1   Cases and materials

§5.1. Cases and materials.

The Fourth Amendment to the federal Constitution begins by commanding that the "right of the people to be secure in their persons, houses, papers, and effects, against unreasonable searches and seizures, shall not be violated * * *." A *search* compromises an individual's interest in privacy, and takes place "when an expectation of privacy that society is prepared to recognize as reasonable is infringed." *United States v. Jacobsen*, 466 *U.S.* 109, 113, 104 *S.Ct.* 1652, 1656 (1984). *See also Horton v. California*, 496 *U.S.* 128, 110 *S.Ct.* 2301, 2306 (1990). A *seizure* "deprives the individual of dominion over his or her * * * property," *Horton*, 110 *S.Ct.* at 2306, and constitutes a "meaningful interference" with the owner's possessory interests in that property. *Maryland v. Macon*, 472 *U.S.* 463, 469, 105 *S.Ct.* 2778, 2782 (1985); *Jacobsen* at 113, 104 *S.Ct.* at 1656.

These principles do not, however, apply to private action. In fact, over the course of time, they have been consistently interpreted as prohibiting only unreasonable *government* action; they are "wholly inapplicable 'to a search or seizure, even an unreasonable one, effected by a private individual not acting as an agent of the Government or with the participation or knowledge of any governmental official.'" *Jacobsen* at 113-114, 104 *S.Ct.* at 1656 (quoting *Walter v. United States*, 447 *U.S.* 649, 662, 100 *S.Ct.* 2395, 2404 (1980) (Blackmun, J. dissenting)). *See also Burdeau v. McDowell*, 256 *U.S.* 465, 41 *S.Ct.* 574 (1921). Therefore, evidence obtained by private citizens in pursuit of personal goals will not implicate the commands of the Fourth Amendment, and may thereafter be turned over to the government, so long as no government official played a part in the search or in the acquisition of the evidence. In this respect, the United States Supreme Court has explained:

> Although the Fourth Amendment does not apply to a search or seizure, even an arbitrary one, effected by a private party on his own initiative, the Amendment protects against such intrusions if the private party acted as an instrument or agent of the government.

Skinner v. Railway Labor Executives Ass'n., 489 *U.S.* 602, 109 *S.Ct.* 1402, 1411 (1989). "Whether a private party should be deemed an agent or instrument of the Government for [constitutional] purposes necessarily turns on the degree of the Government's participation in the private party's activities, * * * a question that can only be resolved 'in light of all the circumstances.'" *Id.* at 1411 (quoting *Coolidge v. New Hampshire*,

403 *U.S.* 443, 91 *S.Ct.* 2022, 2026 (1971)). *See also Hoagburg v. Harrah's Marina Hotel Casino*, 585 *F.Supp.* 1167, 1171, 1174 (D. N.J. 1984).

Accordingly, the target of the exclusionary rule is "official," not "private," misconduct. For purposes of the discussion which follows, the pivotal factor will be whether the private individual, in light of all the circumstances, must be regarded as having acted as an "instrument" or "agent" of the police.

A person will act as a "police agent" if:

1. The police instigate, encourage, or foster the search;

2. There is joint participation between private citizens and police officers;

3. The police have significantly involved themselves in the search; or

4. The police have preknowledge of the private individual's expressed intent to conduct a search or seizure, and acquiesce in its effectuation.

If an unlawful private search or seizure is effected with any of the aforementioned relationships existing between the police and the private person(s) effecting the search or seizure, the Fourth Amendment's Exclusionary Rule will bar the admissibility of any evidence obtained. On the other hand, if it is found that the police had no significant connection with the private search or seizure, or any knowledge of it until after the fact, the evidence delivered to them may be admitted. *See Coolidge v. New Hampshire*, 403 *U.S.* 443, 487-488, 91 *S.Ct.* 2022, 2048-2049 (1971). *But see Flagg Bros. v. Brooks*, 436 *U.S.* 149, 98 *S.Ct.* 1729 (1978) (where the Court intimated that where state involvement in private action constitutes *no more* than mere acquiescence or tacit approval, the private action is not automatically transformed into state action).

UNITED STATES v. JACOBSEN
Supreme Court of the United States
466 *U.S.* 109, 104 *S.Ct.* 1652 (1984)

QUESTION: Does the following set of circumstances give rise to a "governmental" search within the meaning of the Fourth Amendment to the Constitution ?

CIRCUMSTANCES: Federal Express employees opened a damaged cardboard box and, pursuant to written company policy regarding insurance claims, examined the contents. Within the box they found five to six pieces of crumbled newspaper covering a tube about 10 inches long. The tube was made of silver duct tape. The employees then cut into the tube and found a series of four ziplock plastic bags, the outermost enclosing the other three, and the innermost containing about six ounces of a suspicious-looking white powder.

The employees then notified the DEA. Before the DEA agent arrived, the Federal Express employees put everything back into the cardboard box. When the DEA agent arrived, he opened the box, opened the duct tape tube, opened the plastic baggies, and conducted a field test of the white powder. The powder tested positive for cocaine. The DEA agent seized the cocaine.

ANSWER: NO. The DEA agent's inspection of the contents of the package did not constitute a "search" within the meaning of the Constitution.

RATIONALE: The Fourth Amendment's protection against unreasonable searches and seizures applies only to governmental action. *Id.* at 1656. It does not apply to a search or seizure, or even an unreasonable search or seizure, effected by a private individual who does not act as an agent of the Government. *Id.*

Although the wrapped parcel delivered to the private freight carrier was "questionably an 'effect' within the meaning of the Fourth Amendment," *id.*, at 1657, the initial invasions of the owner's package "were occasioned by private action." *Id.* "[T]he fact that agents of the private carrier opened the package and made an examination that might have been impermissible for a government agent cannot render the otherwise reasonable official conduct unreasonable." *Id.* As a result, the initial invasions did not violate the Fourth Amendment because they were private in character.

The question now becomes whether the action of the DEA agent exceeded the scope of the private search. As a rule, the Government may not exceed the scope of the private search already conducted "unless it has the right to make an independent search." *Walter v. United States,* 447 *U.S.* 649, 657, 100 *S.Ct.* 2395, 2401 (1980) (Opinion of Stevens, J., joined by Stewart, J.). "[T]he legality of the government search will be tested by the scope of the antecedent private search." *Jacobsen* at 1658. Therefore, the Fourth Amendment will not bar the governmental inspection of what has been previously and independently examined by private parties and turned over to the government agent.

Here, the owner of the package "could have no privacy interest in the contents of the package, since it remained unsealed and since the Federal Express employees had just examined the package and had, on their own accord, invited the federal agent to their offices for the express purpose of viewing its contents." *Id.* at 1659, 1660.

As a result, the DEA agent's inspection "of what a private party had freely made available for his inspection did not violate the Fourth Amendment." *Id.* at 1660. Additionally, the agent's "assertion of dominion and control" over the contents of the package did not constitute an unreasonable "seizure" within the meaning of the Fourth Amendment. *Id.* To the trained eye of the officer, it was readily "apparent that the tube and plastic bags contained contraband and little else." *Id.* at 1661. Therefore, it was constitutionally reasonable for the officer to seize the contents. "[I]t is well settled that it is constitutionally reasonable for law enforcement officials to seize 'effects' that cannot support a justifiable expectation of privacy without a warrant, based upon probable cause to believe they contain contraband." *Id.*

Finally, the additional intrusion of the "field test," which had not been conducted by the Federal Express employees, seems to have exceeded the scope of the initial private search. However, "[a] chemical test that merely discloses whether or not a particular substance is cocaine does not compromise any legitimate interest in privacy." *Id.* at 1662. The procedure may be likened to the "sniff test" conducted by the narcotics detection dog in *United States v. Place*, 462 *U.S.* 696, 103 *S.Ct.* 2637 (1983). [*See infra* at §8.4.] "Here, as in *Place*, the likelihood that official conduct of [this kind] will actually compromise any legitimate interest in privacy seems much too remote to characterize the testing as a search subject to the Fourth Amendment." *Jacobsen* at 1662. The destruction of a minuscule portion of the powder during the test was sufficiently countermanded by the law enforcement interests justifying the procedure. Thus, "[t]o the extent that a protected possessory interest was infringed, the infringement was *de minimus* [very small or trifling] and constitutionally reasonable." *Id.* at 1663.

NOTE

Police inspection must not exceed the scope of the initial private search. United States v. Jacobsen is an example of the typical "third-party intervention" case. Because the initial violation of Jacobsen's privacy was the result of private action, the Court determined that the Fourth Amendment was not violated when the DEA agents re-examined the package. Where the police expand the scope of the initial private search, however, the third-party intervention exception may no longer apply to the fruits of the expanded search.

(a) In *State v. Saez*, 268 *N.J.Super.* 250, 633 *A.2d* 551 (App.Div. 1993), *rev'd on dissent*, 139 *N.J.* 279, 653 *A.2d* 1130 (1995), county investigators met with a citizen informant who, at the time, was living at 111A Fifth Avenue in Asbury Park. The informant told the investigators that she had observed drug-related activity several times over the past month, occurring in the basement of the adjoining residence, 111B Fifth Avenue. The building containing 111A and 111B is a one-story, ranch-type house with two separate entrances. The basement of the building is divided by a wooden wall constructed in a somewhat slipshod way, in that "certain types of wood are used in one part, other types used in the area in question, vertical slats in one part, horizontal slats in another." *Id.*, 268 *N.J.Super.* at 257. The informant reported that she was able to see the activity through holes or gaps in the wood partition. She identified the occupant of the adjacent premises as defendant, Eddie Saez, and then invited the investigators to observe the activity.

The investigators decided to initiate an investigation of the property. One of the investigators went into the informant's basement and, while there, was able to observe activity next door almost immediately. He observed Eddie and Luis Saez, and a third individual, Orlando Navarro, in the process of "rerocking" cocaine. The investigator was able to make these observations through little holes and through horizontal cracks in the wooden wall. He also used a piece of broken mirror that he had found in the basement, and, while holding it over his head, he could see the activity in the adjoining basement through a gap in the wall located above a furnace. None of this activity could have been seen through any of the basement windows of 111B, because they had been painted over and covered with cloth. After about thirty minutes of observation, the investigator noticed another male enter the basement and assist in the rerocking process.

Shortly thereafter, Luis Saez and Navarro left the premises, and were subsequently arrested. Based on the information at hand, the officers applied for, and obtained, a warrant to search 111B Fifth Avenue. The search uncovered evidence of narcotic activity, and, at that time, the officers arrested Eddie Saez.

In this appeal, the defendants argued that the investigators' observations through the common wall of the basement constituted an unlawful search and seizure. The New Jersey Supreme Court agreed. According to the Court, "the extended and continuous police surveillance" was an improper "expansion of the informer's prior observation of the activities conducted in the adjacent basement." *Id.*, 139 *N.J.* at 281. The investigators' observations must, therefore, be characterized as a separate search, unsupported by any constitutional justification.

> In the present case, the police were not invited to view specific, [unchangeable] objects that the tenant-informant had reduced to possession. The police were invited to participate in the surveillance of a basement and any activities which might occur in that basement during the police surveillance. Because no one could predict with certainty what the police would see, unlike the *Jacobsen* line of cases, each moment of surveillance was a new invasion of privacy. * * *

> * * * [D]efendant had gone to unusual lengths to protect the privacy of his activities. He conducted those activities in his basement, by definition a place affording only limited opportunities for scrutiny by unauthorized persons. Defendant enhanced the base-

ment's inherent privacy by shielding its windows. Unknown to defendant, however, there were chinks in his wall of privacy which permitted a neighbor to place defendant's basement under surveillance. The neighbor's surveillance did not violate the Fourth Amendment because it was private action.

The police surveillance was government action, thereby implicating constitutional guarantees against unreasonable searches.

Id., 268 *N.J.Super.* at 272, 276.

Because the officers' observations went beyond the scope of the private party's inspection, their search was unreasonable. Accordingly, the evidence obtained as a result of that search should have been suppressed. *Id.* at 279.

(b) In *Walter v. United States,* 447 *U.S.* 649, 100 *S.Ct.* 2395 (1980), a shipping company erroneously delivered twelve cartons to "L'Eggs Products, Inc." instead of to "Leggs, Inc." When the L'Eggs Products employees opened the cartons, they discovered film canisters inside, with labels that indicated that they contained scenes of homosexual activity. The employees did not screen the films or otherwise view their content. They did, however, call the FBI, whose agents picked up the cartons and viewed the films utilizing a projector.

The Court held that the FBI agents' viewing of the films was a warrantless search which violated the Fourth Amendment. According to the Court, the FBI's viewing of the films was a separate search that had expanded the scope of the private search.

The projection of the films was a significant expansion of the search that had been conducted previously by a private party and therefore must be characterized as a separate search. That separate search was not supported by any exigency, or by a warrant even though one could have been obtained.

* * * *

The fact that the cartons were unexpectedly opened by a third party before the shipment was delivered to its intended [recipient] does not alter [that party's] legitimate expectation of privacy. The private search merely frustrated that expectation in part. It did not simply strip the remaining unfrustrated portion of that expectation of all Fourth Amendment protection. Since the additional search conducted by the FBI—the screening of the films—was not supported by any justification, it violated that Amendment.

Id. at 657-59, 100 *S.Ct.* at 2402-03.

UNITED STATES v. SHAHID
United States Court of Appeals
117 *F*.3d 322 (7th Cir. 1997)

QUESTION: Are searches and seizures conducted by private shopping mall security officers "government action" within the meaning of the Fourth Amendment?

ANSWER: NO. "[T]he security officers' primary role is to provide safety and security for all persons on mall property. Part of that role * * * is to assist retailers in stopping shoplifters * * * and holding them until the arrival of law enforcement officers." *Id.* at 326. Such conduct does not transform the private security officer into a government actor for purposes of the Fourth Amendment.

RATIONALE: "A search and seizure by a private party does not implicate the Fourth Amendment. * * * However, the Fourth Amendment does apply to a search or seizure by a party (even if otherwise a private party) who is acting as an 'instrument or agent' of the government." *Id.* at 325.

Generally, there are two critical factors in the "instrument or agent" analysis. The first is whether the government knew of and acquiesced in the private action. The second is whether the private party's purpose in conducting the search or seizure was to assist law enforcement officers or to further its own ends. "Other useful criteria are whether the private actor acted at the request of government and whether the government offered the private actor a reward." *Id.* The analysis proceeds on a case-by-case basis and it is the defendant who "bears the burden of proving that the private party was acting as an instrument or agent of the government." *Id. See also United States v. McAllister*, 18 *F*.3d 1412, 1417 (7th Cir. 1994).

In this case, it was not shown that the private shopping mall security officers' actions in stopping, detaining and searching defendant constituted "government action." The court explained:

> A private party cannot be deemed a government agent unless it was induced to act by some government action. [] "Private parties may, of their own accord, pursue the same objectives they have set for their elected officials without acquiring the legal status of government agent." [] A private citizen might decide to aid in the control and prevention of criminal activity out of his or her own moral conviction, concern for his or her employer's public image or profitability, or even desire to incarcerate criminals, but even if such private purpose should happen to coincide with the purposes of government, "this happy coincidence does not make a private actor an arm of the government."

Shahid at 325-26. [Citations omitted.]

The primary role of the private security officers at the Castleton Square Mall "is to provide safety and security for all persons on mall property. Part of that role * * * is to assist retailers in stopping shop-lifters (and, apparently, attempted shoplifters) and holding them until the arrival of law enforcement officers." *Id.* at 326. "However, that a private party 'might also have intended to assist law enforcement does not transform him into a government agent so long as the private party has had a legitimate independent motivation for engaging in the challenged conduct.' " *Id.* [Citations and internal quotes omitted.]

Here, the court had no doubt that the mall security officers "acted to ensure the safety and security of the mall in order to further private purposes, such as satisfying their employer and the mall's retailers." *Id.* The court did point out, however, that "even if the sole or para-mount intent of the security officers had been 'to assist law enforce-ment'—which the evidence does not suggest in this case—such an in-tent would not transform a private action into a public action without the government's knowledge of the action (or of the policy or practice of performing such actions), combined with 'some exercise of govern-mental power over the private entity,' *i.e.,* 'some manifestation of con-sent and the ability to control.' " *Id.* [Citations omitted.]

Accordingly, because the court could find no evidence in this case to suggest that the local law enforcement agency was able to control or induce decisions of mall security officers to stop and search persons on mall property, it concluded that the security officers were not "instru-ments or agents" of the police. *Id.* at 327-28. Presumably, the security officers would try to stop and detain someone if so requested by a local law enforcement officer, but that was not the situation in this case.

UNITED STATES v. LAMBERT
United States Court of Appeals
771 *F.*2d 83 (6th Cir. 1985)

QUESTION: At which point in the below set of facts did the police informant become a "police agent" ?

FACTS:

POINTS:
1. In December, defendant Lambert hired Diana Hall to be his housekeeper, and during the course of her employment Hall observed Lambert and his friends openly use illegal drugs in the house.

2. The following May, Hall approached the FBI and provided in-formation about Lambert's drug activities. The FBI paid Hall some of her "expense money," but her decision to go to the FBI was not moti-vated by the money. According to Hall, she acted because of her con-cerns about the negative effects of drug use, particularly on young people, and her worry about Lambert's health.

3. Over the course of the year, Hall contacted the FBI approximately 25 times concerning Lambert's activities. At no time, however, did the FBI ask Hall to retrieve any items from Lambert's house or even suggest that this would be helpful to them.

4. During several of her meetings with the FBI, Hall brought items which she had taken from the Lambert house. Those included test tubes, pills, and other drug paraphernalia, as well as check stubs and phone bills which Hall thought might be related to Lambert's drug transactions. She insisted that these items had been discarded or abandoned by Lambert and that she had picked them up while performing her housekeeping duties.

5. At one of her meetings with the FBI, Hall expressed her desire to search Lambert's closed safe and his garage, but the agents specifically told her not to do so.

6. Hall's final encounter with the FBI was prompted by a meeting which took place at Lambert's house, in his basement, between Lambert, defendant Block, and several other persons. As the meeting progressed, Hall, who was working upstairs, smelled chemical odors coming from the basement. She believed that the odors were caused by cocaine being cut or purified. The next day, as she was cleaning the basement, Hall went into a closet and discovered a small football-sized object. Next to it was a thermos which contained white powder. Suspecting cocaine, Hall brought a sample from the thermos to the FBI.

7. The FBI analyzed the powder in its crime lab and determined that it was indeed cocaine.

8. Based upon the information and evidence supplied by Hall, along with information developed through the later use of several wire taps and the FBI's own investigation, a warrant was obtained for the search of Lambert's home. The evidence seized formed the basis of defendants' indictment for conspiracy to distribute cocaine, methaqualone and marijuana; distribution of cocaine; and distribution of illegal drugs to a minor.

ANSWER: AT NO POINT. "[T]he FBI never instructed or encouraged Hall to take items from Lambert's home. In fact, [on at least one occasion] she was told * * * that she should not take items from the house. Under these circumstances, Hall's search must be deemed to be a private search and, therefore, not within the purview of the Fourth Amendment." *Id.* at 89.

RATIONALE: As a general rule, "the Fourth Amendment proscribes only governmental action and does not apply to a search or seizure, even an unreasonable one, conducted by a private individual not acting as an agent of the government or with the participation or knowledge of any governmental official." *Id.* at 89. The question in this case, therefore, is whether Diana Hall was acting as an agent for the government when she took the incriminating evidence from the Lambert residence.

"A person will not be acting as a police agent merely because there was some antecedent contact between that person and the police. * * * Rather, two facts must be shown. First, the police must have instigated, encouraged or participated in the search. [] Second, the individual must have engaged in the search with the intent of assisting the police in their investigative efforts." *Id.* (citing *United States v. Howard*, 752 F.2d 220, 227 (6th Cir. 1985)). "While it is clear that Diana Hall acted with the requisite agent intent, the record fails to show that the FBI instigated, encouraged or participated in her searches. Both Hall and [the] FBI [a]gent * * * expressly testified that the FBI never instructed or encouraged Hall to take items from Lambert's home. In fact, the record shows that she was told on several occasions that she should not take items from the house. Under these circumstances, Hall's search must be deemed to be a private search and, therefore, not within the purview of the Fourth Amendment." *Id.*

Moreover, "Hall's search and seizure is not brought within the scope of the Fourth Amendment simply because she brought the seized items to the FBI. As this court has previously held, 'there is no seizure within the meaning of the Fourth Amendment when an object discovered in a private search is voluntarily relinquished to the government.' " *Id.* (quoting *United States v. Coleman*, 628 F.2d 961, 966 (6th Cir. 1980)).

NOTE

1. *Going beyond the controlled buy.* In *Commonwealth v. Borecky*, 277 Pa.Super. 244 (1980), a Pennsylvania state trooper utilized an informant to develop sufficient information to seek and obtain a warrant to search defendant's home. Rather than merely using the informant to engage in a controlled buy, however, the informant was permitted— with the prior knowledge and concurrence of the state trooper—to surreptitiously enter defendant's home, gain access to defendant's attic, and secure a sample of drying marijuana.

Finding the informant's warrantless search and seizure imputable to the police, the court concluded that "since the sample contraband unlawfully seized by the informant obviously supplied the foundation upon which the subsequent warrant was obtained, all of the evidence seized pursuant to the warrant must be suppressed as a 'fruit of the poisonous tree.' " *Id.* at 251.

As a general rule, "evidence gathered through a search by a private individual must come to the state upon a 'silver platter' and not as a result of any instigation by state authorities or participation by them in the illegal activities." *Id.* at 249. "The critical factor * * * 'is whether (the private individual) in light of all the circumstances of the case, must be regarded as an "instrument" or agent of the state[.]' " *Id.* [Citation omitted.] Moreover, a private party will be deemed an "instrument" of the state when state authorities "ratify" the individual's actions. *Id.* at 250.

Here, in *Borecky*, notwithstanding the fact that "the police neither initiated the search nor instructed the informant to conduct the search, the state trooper's admitted *prior knowledge* of the warrantless search, *and acquiescence therein,* was *sufficient to constitute ratification of the informant's illegal activity* on behalf of the Commonwealth." *Id.* at 251. [Emphasis added.]

2. *Repossessions by private creditors.* In *United States v. Coleman,* 628 *F.*2d 961 (6th Cir. 1980), the court held that a "private creditor who alone repossesses secured collateral does not act under color of state law," and reaffirmed the principle that self-help repossession "does not constitute state action." *Id.* at 963. Thus, here in *Coleman,* the acceptance by police of defendant Coleman's briefcase containing a shotgun which was discovered in defendant's pickup truck by Clarke, an employee of the Midwest Auto Recovery Company, who was repossessing the truck under Michigan's "self-help" statute, was held not to constitute a search or seizure within the meaning of the Fourth Amendment. According to the court, "[t]he police neither encouraged nor directed Clarke to repossess the truck in a particular manner. Their presence at the scene was not an indispensable prerequisite for repossession of the truck. Their benign attendance was not designed to assist Clarke in repossession of the truck; rather, it was in furtherance of their official duties. The position assumed by the police was devised to anticipate and prevent any violent confrontation between debtor and creditor which repossession of collateral can entail. Under the facts of this case, mere acquiescence by the police to 'stand by in case of trouble' was insufficient to convert the repossession of the truck into state action." *Id.* at 964. Consequently, the repossession of Coleman's pick-up truck was held to be "a wholly legitimate seizure of collateral by a private party." *Id.*
"Authority to seize the truck did not, however, encompass dominion over the personal belongings inside the truck. Since Clarke had no legal right or title to Coleman's personal effects, he planned to deposit them at the police station so that Coleman might conveniently retrieve them. In an exercise of their community caretaking functions, the police agreed to keep the personal effects until Coleman claimed them." *Id.* These actions were " 'totally divorced from the detection, investigation, or acquisition of evidence relating to the violation of a criminal statute.' * * * Since the police did not instigate, encourage, or participate in the search of the truck, the search by Clarke was outside the scope of the Fourth Amendment." *Id.* at 965. Additionally, there was "no seizure within the meaning of [that Amendment] when [the briefcase and shotgun] discovered in [the] private search [were] voluntarily relinquished to the government." *Id.* at 966.

3. *Bank security officers.* In *United States v. Garlock,* 19 *F.*3d 441 (8th Cir. 1994), the court rejected the defendant's contention that bank security officials were required to administer *Miranda* warnings prior to questioning her about missing bank funds. The court explained that the bank investigators were not subject to the Fifth Amendment simply because they were "engaged in the 'public function' of law enforcement." *Id.* at 443.

The courts have consistently held that the mere fact that an individual's job involves the investigation of crime does not transform him into a government actor. * * * This is true even when the government requires that certain security measures be taken.

Id. at 443-44 (referring to 12 *C.F.R.* §21 (requiring banks to designate a security officer whose duties include developing a program to help identify persons committing crimes within the bank), and §21.11 (encouraging the reporting of most crimes to law enforcement officials)).

CHAPTER 6

REGULATORY AND ADMINISTRATIVE SEARCHES; BORDER SEARCHES

§6.1. Regulatory and administrative searches.

Whether a search or seizure is reasonable under the Fourth Amendment depends on an analysis of the totality of the circumstances and the nature of the search or seizure itself. In most typical cases involving law enforcement practice and procedure, there is a constitutional preference for a judicial determination of probable cause and the issuance of a written warrant. Yet, there are recognized exceptions to the warrant requirement, and in the area of regulatory and administrative searches, the courts will apply two types of analyses: "balancing of interests" and "special needs."

The "balancing of interests" analysis. In some circumstances, courts will apply a general Fourth Amendment "balancing test," examining the totality of the circumstances to assess, on the one side, the degree to which a search or seizure intrudes upon a person's reasonable expectation of privacy, and, on the other side, the degree to which it is needed for the promotion of legitimate governmental interests. *Brown v. Texas,* 443 *U.S.* 47, 99 *S.Ct.* 2637 (1979); *Samson v. California,* 547 *U.S.* 843, 126 *S.Ct.* 2193, 2197 (2006).

For example, in *Michigan Dept. of State Police v. Sitz,* 496 *U.S.* 444, 110 *S.Ct.* 2481 (1990), the Court utilized a "balancing of interests" analysis in upholding the constitutionality of highway sobriety checkpoints. According to the Court, this test involved balancing the state's substantial interest in preventing harm caused by drunk drivers, the degree to which sobriety checkpoints advance that public interest, and the minimal level of intrusion upon individual motorists who are briefly stopped. *See also United States v. Martinez-Fuerte,* 428 *U.S.* 543, 96 *S.Ct.* 3074 (1976) (applying the "balancing of interests" approach to approve highway checkpoints for detecting illegal aliens).

Similarly, the Court, in *Illinois v. Lidster,* 540 *U.S.* 419, 427-28, 124 *S.Ct.* 885, 890-91 (2004), upheld the brief stop of motorists at a roadside checkpoint, where police sought information about a recent hit-and-run fatal accident. Utilizing the *Brown v. Texas* "balancing of interests" approach, the Court looked to the gravity of the public concerns served by such a seizure, the degree to which the seizure advanced the public interest, and the severity of the interference with individual liberty.

While the "balancing of interests" approach is an easier test for the prosecution to satisfy, the "special needs" approach involves a more stringent analysis. In this regard, if a "special need" does exist, courts may then make an exception to the probable cause and warrant requirements only after balancing the nature and quality of the intrusion on the individual's constitutional rights against "the importance of the governmental interests alleged to justify the intrusion." *See United States v. Place*, 462 *U.S.* 696, 703, 103 *S.Ct.* 2637, 2642 (1983).

The "special needs" analysis. There are some areas of law enforcement and criminal procedure, where "special needs," beyond the normal need for law enforcement, authorize government action without the standard constitutional justifications which typically apply. In this regard, the United States Supreme Court has utilized a "special needs" analysis to carve out an exception to the familiar probable cause and judicial warrant requirements normally associated with the Fourth Amendment.

The first use of the "special needs" analysis may be found in Justice Blackmun's concurrence in *New Jersey v. T.L.O.*, 469 *U.S.* 325, 351, 105 *S.Ct.* 733, 747-48 (1985), where it was determined that a school official's search of a student's belongings based on individualized suspicion was reasonable. In this regard, Justice Blackmun explained that probable cause and a warrant were not required where "special needs, beyond the normal need for law enforcement, make the warrant and probable-cause requirements impracticable." *Id.* at 351, 105 *S.Ct.* at 748 (Blackmun, J., concurring).

When confronted with a special government or law enforcement need for greater flexibility, the Court has not hesitated to apply this analysis. Thus, it has been held that in certain circumstances, government investigators conducting searches or inspections of "closely regulated" businesses need not adhere to the usual warrant or probable-cause requirements as long as their searches meet reasonable legislative or administrative standards. *See e.g., New York v. Burger*, 482 *U.S.* 691, 702-03, 107 *S.Ct.* 2636, 2643 (1987) (warrantless inspections of automobile junkyard businesses come within exception for closely regulated industries); *Donovan v. Dewey*, 452 *U.S.* 594, 605, 101 *S.Ct.* 2534, 2541 (1981) (warrantless inspections under the Federal Mine Safety and Health Act); *United States v. Biswell*, 406 *U.S.* 311, 92 *S.Ct.* 1593 (1972) (warrantless inspection of pawnshops licensed to sell weapons); *Colonnade Corp. v. United States*, 397 *U.S.* 72, 77, 90 *S.Ct.* 774, 777 (1970) (warrantless inspection of businesses in the liquor industry).

Thereafter, in *O'Connor v. Ortega*, 480 *U.S.* 709, 107 *S.Ct.* 1492 (1987), the Court held that the "special needs" of government workplaces permit government employers and supervisors to conduct warrantless, work-related searches of employees' desks, file cabinets and offices without a warrant or probable cause.

Similarly, in *Griffin v. Wisconsin*, 483 *U.S.* 868, 873-74, 107 *S.Ct.* 3164, 3168 (1987), the Court held that "a State's operation of a probation system, like its operation of a school, government office or prison, or its supervision of a regulated industry, likewise presents 'special needs' beyond normal law enforcement that may justify departures from the usual warrant and probable-cause requirements." According to the Court, "supervision" in the probation system is the "special need" of the State "permitting a degree of impingement upon privacy that would not be constitutional if applied to the public at large." *Id.* at 875, 107 *S.Ct.* at 3169. *See also Bd. of Educ. of Indep. Sch. Dist. No. 92 v. Earls,* 536 *U.S.* 822, 829-30, 122 *S.Ct.* 2559, 2564 (2002) (applying "special needs" principles to validate school's drug testing of all students participating in extracurricular activities); *Vernonia Sch. Dist. 47J v. Acton,* 515 *U.S.* 646, 653, 115 *S.Ct.* 2386, 2391 (1995) (applying a "special needs" analysis to sustain drug-testing programs for student athletes).

In upholding mandatory, suspicionless drug testing of United States Customs Service employees seeking promotion to drug-interdiction positions, the Court, in *National Treasury Employees Union v. Von Raab,* 489 *U.S.* 656, 109 *S.Ct.* 1384 (1989), instructed:

> [W]here a Fourth Amendment intrusion serves special governmental needs, beyond the normal need for law enforcement, it is necessary to balance the individual's privacy expectations against the Government's interests to determine whether it is impractical to require a warrant or some level of individualized suspicion in the particular context.

Id. at 665, 109 *S.Ct.* at 1390.

NEW JERSEY v. T.L.O.
Supreme Court of the United States
469 *U.S.* 325, 105 *S.Ct.* 733 (1985)

QUESTION: Does the Fourth Amendment's prohibition on unreasonable searches and seizures apply to searches conducted by public school officials ?

ANSWER: YES. "In carrying out searches and other disciplinary functions pursuant to [publicly mandated educational and disciplinary] policies, [public] school officials act as representatives of the State, not merely as surrogates for the parents, and they cannot claim the parents' immunity from the strictures of the Fourth Amendment." *Id.* at 741.

RATIONALE: On March 7, 1980, a teacher at the Piscataway High School in Middlesex County, New Jersey, discovered two girls smoking in the girl's bathroom, a prohibited smoking area. One of the two girls was T.L.O, a 14-year-old high school freshman. Because smoking in the bathroom was a violation of a school rule, the teacher took the two girls to the Principal's office, where they met with Assistant Vice Principal Theodore Choplick. In response to questioning by Mr. Choplick, T.L.O.'s companion admitted that she had been smoking. Mr. Choplick assigned her to a three-day smoking clinic. T.L.O., however, denied that she had been smoking in the girl's lavatory, and claimed that she did not smoke at all.

Mr. Choplick asked T.L.O. to come into his private office. He closed the door and demanded that she turn over her purse. At this time, they were both seated at a desk, he behind and she in front. When Mr. Choplick opened the purse on the desk, he saw a pack of Marlboros. He picked up the cigarettes, removed them from the purse and said, "You lied to me." As he removed the cigarettes from the purse, Mr. Choplick noticed a package of cigarette rolling papers in plain view. In his experience, possession of rolling papers by high school students was closely associated with the use of marijuana. Suspecting that a closer examination of the purse might yield further evidence of drug use, Mr. Choplick proceeded to search the purse more thoroughly. The search revealed a metal pipe of the kind used for smoking marijuana, a number of empty plastic bags, and one plastic bag containing a small amount of marijuana. His search also uncovered $40 in currency, most of it in one-dollar bills, and an index card reading "People who owe me money," followed by a list of names and amounts of $1.50 and $1.00. In addition, there were two letters in the purse, one from T.L.O. to another student, and a return letter, both containing language clearly implicating T.L.O. in drug dealing.

Mr. Choplick notified T.L.O.'s mother and the police, and turned the evidence of drug dealing over to the police. At the request of the police, T.L.O.'s mother took her daughter to police headquarters, where T.L.O. confessed that she had been selling marijuana at the high school. On the basis of the confession and the evidence seized by Mr. Choplick, the State brought delinquency charges against T.L.O. in Juvenile Court.

Contending that the vice principal's search violated the Fourth Amendment, T.L.O. moved to suppress the evidence found in her purse, as well as her confession, which, she argued, was tainted by the allegedly unlawful search.

The New Jersey courts found that the action of the school officials was "State action" for Fourth Amendment purposes, but held that the search conducted was unreasonable and, therefore, suppressed the evidence found in T.L.O.'s purse.

The United States Supreme Court agreed with the New Jersey courts—that the action of the public school officials was "State action" for Fourth Amendment purposes—but disagreed on the reasonableness issue.

In a plurality opinion,* the Court, per Justice White, held that the principal's search was reasonable in light of a new standard for searches and seizures conducted by public school officials in public school settings.

---

* *See* Glossary.

First, the Court instructed that the Fourth Amendment was not intended to regulate only searches and seizures carried out by law enforcement officers. *Id.* at 740. Rather, the Amendment's prohibitions on unreasonable searches and seizures are restraints on "governmental action" referring to the activities of "sovereign authority." *Id.* For example, it applies to building inspectors, OSHA inspectors, "and even firemen entering privately owned premises to battle a fire." *Id.* "[T]he basic purpose of this Amendment * * * is to safeguard the privacy and security of individuals against arbitrary intrusions by governmental officials [not limited to law enforcement officials]." *Id.* (quoting from *Camara v. Municipal Court*, 387 *U.S.* 523, 528, 87 *S.Ct.* 1727, 1730 (1967)).

The public school officials in today's public school arena "do not merely exercise authority voluntarily conferred on them by individual parents; rather, they act in furtherance of publicly mandated educational and disciplinary policies." *Id.* at 741. As the officials conduct "searches and other disciplinary functions pursuant to such policies, [they] act as representatives of the State, not merely as surrogates for the parents, and they cannot claim the parents' immunity from the strictures of the Fourth Amendment." *Id.*

In this case, the Court established new standards for searches conducted by public school officials in the public school environment. In doing so, it balanced the student's legitimate expectation of privacy and personal security against such public school needs as maintaining discipline and order in the classrooms and on school grounds, and preservation of the educational atmosphere. *Id.* at 741, 742. In striking such a balance, the Court adopted a flexible standard.

First, public school officials are not subject to the warrant requirement. *Id.* at 743. Requiring a warrant would "unduly interfere with the maintenance of the swift and informal disciplinary procedures needed in schools." *Id.* Second, the level of suspicion applicable to public school officials has been reduced from probable cause to a standard which turns "simply on the reasonableness, under all of the circumstances, of the search." *Id.* at 744, 745. Reasonableness will be assessed by a two-fold inquiry: "first, one must consider whether the action was justified at its inception[;] second, one must determine whether the search as actually conducted was reasonably related in scope to the circumstances which justified the interference in the first place." *Id.* at 744. [Citations omitted.]

In applying these rules to the facts before it, the Court held that the principal's actions were entirely reasonable in light of the surrounding circumstances. T.L.O. had been caught smoking in the bathroom, but she denied it and also denied that she smoked at all. Thus, the principal had a reasonable suspicion that T.L.O. had cigarettes in her purse, and, his search for the cigarettes was reasonable. When he found the cigarette pack he also observed a pack of rolling papers. This "gave rise to a reasonable suspicion that T.L.O. was carrying marihuana as well as cigarettes," *id.* at 747, and justified the more extensive search of the purse. *Id.* Therefore, the discovery of the remaining evidence was properly grounded in the principal's reasonable suspicion which continued to shade up from the initial inspection for the pack of cigarettes.

As a result, because the search was reasonable, the evidence obtained from the search should have been admitted in evidence, along with the fruits thereof, *i.e.*, the subsequent confession.

NOTE

1. *Courthouse security procedures.* Under the "administrative search" exception, "a limited warrantless search of a person seeking to enter sensitive facilities is lawful if 'conducted as part of a general regulatory scheme in furtherance of an administrative purpose, rather than as part of a criminal investigation to secure evidence of crime.'" *Klarfeld v. United States*, 944 *F.*2d 583, 586 (9th Cir. 1991) (quoting *United States v. Davis*, 482 *F.*2d 893, 908 (9th Cir. 1973)). To pass constitutional muster, however, the administrative search "must meet the Fourth Amendment's standard of reasonableness." *Davis* at 910.

Thus, in *McMorris v. Alioto*, 567 *F.*2d 897, 900-01 (9th Cir. 1978), the court held that courthouse security procedures in the San Francisco Hall of Justice, including the use of a magnetometer, fell into the category of permissible administrative searches. The court, taking judicial notice of the threats of violence directed at courthouses that had given rise to an urgent need for protective measures, concluded that security measures that included a pat-down search as a secondary search procedure were reasonable under the Fourth Amendment. *Id.* at 900.

2. *Drug testing of student athletes.* Vernonia School District 47J operates one high school and three grade schools in Vernonia, Oregon. In the fall of 1989, the school district implemented a Student Athlete Drug Policy, the expressed purpose of which was "to prevent student athletes from using drugs, to protect their health and safety, and to provide drug users with assistance programs." *Vernonia School District 47J v. Acton*, 515 *U.S.* 646, 115 *S.Ct.* 2386, 2389 (1995). The policy applied to all students participating in interscholastic athletics. Students wishing to play sports were required to sign a form consenting to the testing, along with obtaining the written consent of their parents. Athletes were tested at the beginning of the season for their sport, and, once each week of the season, the names of athletes were placed in a "pool" from which a student, with the supervision of two adults, blindly selected the names of 10% of the athletes for random testing. "Those selected are notified and tested that same day if possible." *Id.* at 2389.

The United States Supreme Court held that the school district's drug-testing policy passed constitutional muster. Preliminarily, the Court observed that "state-compelled collection and testing of urine, such as that required by the Student Athlete Drug Policy, constitutes a 'search' subject to the demands of the Fourth Amendment." *Id.* at 2390.

As the text of the Fourth Amendment indicates, the ultimate measure of the constitutionality of a governmental search is "reasonableness." * * * [W]hether a particular search meets the reasonableness standard " 'is judged by balancing its intrusion on the individual's Fourth Amendment interests against its promotion of legitimate governmental interests.' "

Id. [Citations omitted.]

A search and seizure may be reasonable even in the absence of a warrant or probable cause " 'when special needs, beyond the normal need for law enforcement, make the warrant and probable-cause requirement impracticable.' " *Id.* at 2391. [Citation omitted.] Such "special needs" have been found to exist in the "public school" context, where the warrant requirement "would 'unduly interfere with the maintenance of the swift and informal disciplinary procedures [that are] needed,' and 'strict adherence to the requirement that searches be based on probable cause' would undercut 'the substantial need of teachers and administrators for freedom to maintain order in the schools.' " *Id.* (quoting *T.L.O.* at 340, 341, 105 *S.Ct.* at 742).

In balancing "the decreased expectation of privacy" of student athletes, "the relative unobtrusiveness of the search, and the severity of the need met by the search," the Court concluded that "Vernonia's Policy is reasonable and hence constitutional." *Id.* at 2396. The Court paused to caution, however, that this case should not lead to "the assumption that suspicionless drug testing will readily pass constitutional muster in other contexts. The most significant element in this case is * * * that the Policy was undertaken in furtherance of the government's responsibilities, under a public school system, as guardian and tutor of children entrusted to its care." *Id.*

3. *Candidates for public office.* In *Chandler v. Miller*, 520 *U.S.* 305, 117 *S.Ct.* 1295 (1997), the Court addressed a Georgia statute that requires candidates for designated state offices to present a certification from a state-approved laboratory that they have taken a drug test within 30 days prior to qualifying for nomination or election and that the results were negative. The Court determined that the statute violated the Fourth Amendment for it did "not fit within the closely guarded category of constitutionally permissible suspicionless searches." *Id.*, 117 *S.Ct.* at 1298. Georgia's "ballot-access, drug testing statute," observed the Court, does not satisfy the "special needs" analysis: "Georgia asserts no evidence of a drug problem among the State's elected officials, those officials typically do not perform high-risk, safety-sensitive tasks, and the required certification immediately aids no interdiction effort. The need revealed, in short, is symbolic, not 'special' as that term draws meaning from our case law." *Id.* at 1305.

4. *Drug testing of students who participate in competitive extracurricular activities.* In *Bd. of Ed. of Independent School Dist. v. Earls*, 536 *U.S.* 822, 122 *S.Ct.* 2559 (2002),the Supreme Court extended the holding in *Vernonia*, and upheld a drug-testing policy which applied "to competitive extracurricular activities" such as the "Academic Team, Future Farmers of America, Future Homemakers of America, band, choir, pom-pom, cheerleading, and athletics." *Id.* at 826, 122 *S.Ct.* at 2562-63. The policy required all students to submit to an initial drug test before beginning an extracurricular activity, to submit to random drug testing during the period of participation, and to "agree to be tested at any time upon reasonable suspicion." *Id.* at 826, 122 *S.Ct.* at 2563.

In applying essentially the same balancing test set forth in *Vernonia*, the *Earls* Court first looked to "the nature of the privacy interests allegedly compromised by the drug testing." *Earls* at 830, 122 *S.Ct.* at 2565. It reaffirmed that "the context of the public school environment serves as the backdrop for the analysis of the privacy interest at stake and the reasonableness of the drug testing policy in general." *Id.* at 830, 122 *S.Ct.* at 2565. The Court also emphasized that in upholding the drug-testing program in *Vernonia*, it considered "the school context central and the most significant element." *Id.* at 831 n.3, 122 *S.Ct.* at 2565 n.3. [Citation and internal quotes omitted.]

As in *Vernonia*, the *Earls* Court determined that the privacy interests of students are limited "in a public school environment where the State is responsible for maintaining discipline, health, and safety." *Id.* at 830, 122 *S.Ct.* at 2565. It rejected the notion that "because children participating in non-athletic extracurricular activities are not subject to regular physicals and communal undress, they have a stronger expectation of privacy than the athletes tested in *Vernonia*." *Id.* at 831, 122 *S.Ct.* at 2565. Rather, the Court found that, like athletes, students who engage in non-athletic extracurricular activities "voluntarily subject themselves to many of the same intrusions on their privacy[.]" *Id.* at 831, 122 *S.Ct.* at 2566. Such intrusions involve "occasional off-campus travel," "communal undress," and special "rules and requirements for participating students that do not apply to the student body as a whole." *Id.* at 832, 122 *S.Ct.* at 2566.

As it did in *Vernonia*, the Court in *Earls* concluded that the process of collecting urine was "minimally intrusive," noting also that the students' test results were kept confidential and were not forwarded to law enforcement authorities. *Id.* at 833, 122 *S.Ct.* at 2566. It further noted that positive test results did not "lead to the imposition of discipline or have any academic consequences," except to "limit the student's privilege of participating in extracurricular activities." *Id.* at 833, 122 *S.Ct.* at 2566-67.

Concerning the immediacy and nature of the government's interests, the Court considered "the nationwide drug epidemic," as well as "the need to prevent and deter the substantial harm of childhood drug use[.]" *Id.* at 836, 122 *S.Ct.* at 2568. The Court refused, therefore, to require the school district to demonstrate "some identifiable drug abuse problem among a sufficient number of those subject to the testing[.]" *Id.* The Court reasoned that "it would make little sense to require a school district to wait for a substantial portion of its students to begin using drugs before it was allowed to institute a drug testing program designed to deter drug use." *Id.*

Accordingly, the Court concluded that the drug-testing policy and program was constitutional, and "a reasonable means of furthering the School District's important interest in preventing and deterring drug use among its schoolchildren." *Id.* at 838, 122 *S.Ct.* at 2569.

O'CONNOR v. ORTEGA
Supreme Court of the United States
480 *U.S.* 709, 107 *S.Ct.* 1492 (1987)

QUESTION: Does a government employer need a search warrant or probable cause to conduct reasonable work-related searches of employees' offices, desks, or file cabinets ?

ANSWER: NO. A government employer needs neither a search warrant nor probable cause to conduct reasonable work-related searches of their employees' offices, desks, or file cabinets. *Id.* at 1500-1501, 1502-1503.

RATIONALE: The posture of this case arose from a 42 *U.S.C.* §1983 civil rights suit by Dr. Ortega, a physician and psychiatrist, alleging that his employer, Napa State Hospital, conducted a search of his office in violation of the Fourth and Fourteenth Amendments. The search was conducted by Napa State Hospital officials for the purpose of investigating work-related misconduct on the part of their employee, Dr. Ortega.

In a plurality opinion, the United States Supreme Court held that "[s]earches and seizures by government employers or supervisors of private property of their employees * * * are subject to the restraints of the Fourth Amendment, but neither a search warrant nor probable cause is necessary to constitutionally search their employees' workplace." "Workplace," in this context, "includes those areas and items that are related to work and are generally within the employer's control. At a hospital, for example, the hallways, cafeteria, offices, desks, and file cabinets, among other areas, are all part of the workplace. These areas remain part of the workplace context even if the employee has placed personal items in them[.] * * * [This, however,] does not necessarily apply to a piece of closed luggage, a handbag or a briefcase that happens to be within the employer's business address." *Id.* at 1497.

While the Court recognized that "employees may have a reasonable expectation of privacy against intrusions by police[,] * * * [t]he operational realities of the workplace, however, may make *some* employees' expectation of privacy unreasonable when an intrusion is by a supervisor rather than a law enforcement official. Public employees' expectations of privacy in their offices, desks, and file cabinets like similar expectations of employees in the private sector, may be reduced by virtue of actual office practices and procedures, or by legitimate regulation." *Id.* at 1498. [Emphasis in original.] In fact, "some government offices may be so open to fellow employees or the public that no expectation of privacy is reasonable." *Id.*

In this case, the Court concludes that Dr. Ortega had an expectation of privacy in his office, but, as "stated in *T.L.O.*, '[t]o hold that the Fourth Amendment applies to searches conducted by (public employers) is only to begin the inquiry into the standards governing such searches. . . . [W]hat is reasonable depends on the context within which a search takes place.' " *Id.* at 1499 (quoting *T.L.O.* at 337). "A determination of the standard of reasonableness applicable to a particular class of searches requires 'balanc[ing] the nature and quality of the intrusion on the individual's Fourth Amendment interests against the importance of the governmental interests alleged to justify the intrusion.' " *Id.* (quoting *United States v. Place,* 462 *U.S.* 696, 703, 103 *S.Ct.* 2637, 2642 (1983)). In circumstances involving searches and seizures conducted by a public employer, a court must "balance the invasion of the employee's legitimate expectations of privacy against the government's need for supervision, control and the efficient operation of the workplace." *Ortega* at 1499.

"The legitimate privacy interests of public employees in the private objects they bring to the workplace may be substantial. Against these privacy interests, however, must be balanced the realities of the workplace, which strongly suggest that a warrant requirement would be unworkable. * * * [R]equiring an employer [or supervisor] to obtain a warrant whenever the employer wished to enter an employee's office, desk, or file cabinets for a work related purpose would seriously disrupt the routine conduct of business and would be unduly burdensome." *Id.* at 1500. Accordingly, in such circumstances a warrant is not required; "imposition of a warrant requirement would conflict with 'the common-sense realization that government offices could not function if every employment decision became a constitutional matter.' " *Id.* at 1501. [Citation omitted.]

Whether probable cause is required for public employer searches of their employees' offices, desks, or file cabinets presents a more complex inquiry. As explained in *T.L.O.,* "[t]he fundamental command of the Fourth Amendment is that searches and seizures be reasonable, and although 'both the concept of probable cause and the requirement of a warrant bear on the reasonableness of a search, . . . in certain limited circumstances neither is required.' " *T.L.O.* at 340. [Citation omitted.] As a result, " '[w]here a careful balancing of governmental and private interests suggests that the public interest is best served by a Fourth Amendment standard of reasonableness that stops short of probable cause, [the Court has] not hesitated to adopt such a standard.' " *Ortega* at 1501 (quoting *T.L.O.* at 341). Therefore, to facilitate public employer searches of either a "noninvestigatory work-related" type or "an investigatory search for evidence of suspected work-related employee misfeasance," *id.* at 1501, probable cause is not necessary. "[A] probable cause requirement for searches of the type at issue here would impose intolerable burdens on public employers. The delay in correcting the employee misconduct caused by the need for probable cause rather than reasonable suspicion will be translated into tangible and often irreparable damage to the agency's work, and ultimately to the public interest." *Id.* at 1502. Rather, "a reasonableness standard will permit regulation of the employer's conduct 'according to the dictates of reason and common sense.' " *Id.* [Citations omitted.] Such a reasonableness standard "will neither unduly burden the efforts of government employers to ensure the efficient and proper operation of the workplace, nor authorize arbitrary intrusions upon the privacy of public employees." *Id.*

Accordingly, it is held "that public employer intrusions on the constitutionally protected privacy interests of government employees for noninvestigatory, work-related purposes, as well as for investigations of work-related misconduct, should be judged by the standard of reasonableness under all the circumstances. Under this reasonableness standard, both the inception and the scope of the intrusion must be reasonable[.]" *Id.* at 1502-1503.

"Ordinarily, a search of an employee's office by a supervisor will be 'justified at its inception' when there are reasonable grounds for suspecting that the search will turn up evidence that the employee is guilty of work-related misconduct, or that the search is necessary for a noninvestigatory work-related purpose such as to retrieve a needed file. * * * The search will be permissible in scope when 'the measures adopted are reasonably related to the objectives of the search and not excessively intrusive in light of . . . the nature of the (misconduct).' " *Id.* at 1503 (quoting *T.L.O.* at 341, 342).

Accordingly, the case is remanded. The "District Court must determine the justification for the search and seizure, and evaluate the reasonableness of both the inception of the search and its scope." *Id.* at 1504.

GRIFFIN v. WISCONSIN
Supreme Court of the United States
483 U.S. 868, 107 S.Ct. 3164 (1987)

QUESTION: May a probation officer conduct a search of a probationer's home, pursuant to State regulation, without a warrant and without probable cause ?

ANSWER: YES. "A State's operation of a probation system, like its operation of a school, government office or prison, or its supervision of a regulated industry, likewise presents 'special needs' beyond normal law enforcement that may justify departures from the usual warrant and probable cause requirements." *Id* at 3168.

RATIONALE: "Wisconsin law puts probationers in the legal custody of the State Department of Health and Social Services and renders them 'subject . . . to . . . conditions set by the court and rules and regulations established by the department.' " *Id.* at 3166. One such regulation "permits any probation officer to search a probationer's home without a warrant as long as his supervisor approves and as long as there are 'reasonable grounds' to believe the presence of contraband—including any item that the probationer cannot possess under probation conditions." *Id.*

Probationer Griffin's residence was searched by Wisconsin probation department personnel. The officers were acting on a tip from a detective of the Beloit Police Department that there might be guns in Griffin's apartment. During the subsequent warrantless search, the probation officials found a handgun.

Griffin moved to suppress the handgun, arguing that the search, conducted without a warrant and without probable cause, violated the Fourth Amendment.

The United States Supreme Court, per Justice Scalia, disagreed.

"A probationer's home, like anyone else's, is protected by the Fourth Amendment's requirement that searches be 'reasonable.'" *Id.* at 3167. However, the Court has permitted exceptions to the warrant and probable cause requirements "when 'special needs,' beyond the normal need for law enforcement, make the warrant and probable cause requirements impracticable." *Id.*

"A State's operation of a probation system, like its operation of a school, government office or prison, or its supervision of a regulated industry, likewise presents 'special needs' beyond normal law enforcement that may justify departures from the usual warrant and probable cause requirements. Probation, like incarceration, is 'a form of criminal sanction imposed by a court upon an offender after verdict, finding, or plea of guilty.' * * * [It] is simply one point (or, more accurately, one set of points) on a continuum of possible punishments ranging from solitary confinement in a maximum security facility to a few hours of mandatory community service." *Id.* at 3168. Thus, "probationers * * * do not enjoy 'the absolute liberty to which every citizen is entitled, but only . . . conditional liberty properly dependent on observance of special (probation) restrictions.'" *Id.* [Citation omitted.] "These restrictions are meant to assure that the probation serves as a period of genuine rehabilitation and that the community is not harmed by the probationer's being at large. * * * These same goals require and justify the exercise of supervision to assure that the restrictions are in fact observed. * * * Supervision, then, is a 'special need' of the State permitting a degree of impingement upon privacy that would not be constitutional if applied to the public at large." *Id.*

As a result, "the special needs of Wisconsin's probation system make the warrant requirement impracticable and justify replacement of the standard of probable cause by 'reasonable grounds,'" *id.* at 3169, defined by the Wisconsin Supreme Court to include, as here, a tip from a law enforcement official who had no reason to supply inaccurate information, and who had specifically identified the probationer. *Id.* at 3167.

Accordingly, "[t]he search of Griffin's residence was 'reasonable' within the meaning of the Fourth Amendment because it was conducted pursuant to a valid regulation governing probationers." *Id.* at 3171.

NOTE

1. *See also Wyman v. Jones*, 400 *U.S.* 309, 91 *S.Ct.* 381 (1971) (social worker's warrantless visitation to welfare recipient's home did not implicate the Fourth Amendment); *United States v. Cardona*, 903 *F.*2d 60 (1st Cir. 1990) (extending *Griffin* to parole officers' warrantless searches of parolees' residences).

2. *Searches of probationers' homes and the "reasonable suspicion" standard.* In *United States v. Knights,* 534 *U.S.* 112, 122 *S.Ct.* 587 (2001), the Court held that the warrantless search of a probationer's home, supported by a reasonable suspicion and authorized by his probation, was reasonable under the Fourth Amendment. Knights was sentenced to probation for a drug offense. The probation order included the condition that Knights would:

> Submit his . . . person, property, place of residence, vehicle, personal effects, to search at anytime, with or without a search warrant, warrant of arrest or reasonable cause by any probation officer or law enforcement officer.

Knights signed the probation order and agreed to abide by its terms. Thereafter, investigation by the Napa County Sheriff's Department led to a reasonable suspicion that Knights had committed numerous acts of vandalism, including an act of arson, against the Pacific Gas & Electric (PG&E) Company.

Based on this suspicion, a Sheriff's Department detective decided to conduct a search of Knights' apartment. The detective was aware of the search condition in Knights' probation order and thus believed that a warrant was not necessary. The search uncovered a detonation cord, ammunition, liquid chemicals, instruction manuals on chemistry and electrical circuitry, bolt cutters, telephone pole-climbing spurs, drug paraphernalia, and a brass padlock stamped "PG&E."

Knights was arrested, and subsequently indicted for conspiracy to commit arson, possession of an unregistered destructive device, and being a felon in possession of ammunition.

Speaking for a unanimous Supreme Court, Chief Justice Rehnquist preliminarily observed that the "search condition" contained in the probation order provided that Knights will submit to a search "by any probation officer or law enforcement officer." *Id.,* 122 *S.Ct.* at 590. Significantly, it did not contain any limiting purpose. *The question then is whether the Fourth Amendment limits searches pursuant to this probation condition to those with a "probationary" purpose.*

In *Griffin v. Wisconsin, supra,* the Court "upheld a search of a probationer conducted pursuant to a Wisconsin regulation permitting 'any probation officer to search a probationer's home without a warrant as long as his supervisor approves and as long as there are "reasonable grounds" to believe the presence of contraband.'" *Knights* at 590. [Citation omitted.] The regulation applied to all probationers, "with no need for a judge to make an individualized determination that the probationer's conviction justified the need for warrantless searches." *Id. Griffin* thus held that "a State's operation of its probation system presented a 'special need' for the 'exercise of supervision to assure that [probation] restrictions are in fact observed.'" *Knights* at 590. That "special need" for supervision "justified the Wisconsin regulation and the search pursuant to the regulation was thus reasonable." *Id.*

In this appeal, Knights argues that "a warrantless search of a probationer satisfies the Fourth Amendment only if it is just like the search at issue in *Griffin—i.e.,* a 'special needs' search conducted by a probation officer monitoring whether the probationer is complying with probation restrictions." *Id.* The United States Supreme Court disagreed.

According to the Court, "the search of Knights was reasonable under [the] general Fourth Amendment approach of 'examining the totality of the circumstances,' with the probation search condition being a salient circumstance." *Id.* at 591.

"The touchstone of the Fourth Amendment is reasonableness, and the reasonableness of a search is determined 'by assessing, on the one hand, the degree to which it intrudes upon an individual's privacy and, on the other, the degree to which it is needed for the promotion of legitimate governmental interests.' " *Id.* In this respect, the Court elaborated:

> Knights's status as a probationer subject to a search condition informs both sides of that balance. "Probation, like incarceration, is 'a form of criminal sanction imposed by a court upon an offender after verdict, finding, or plea of guilty.' " Probation is "one point . . . on a continuum of possible punishments ranging from solitary confinement in a maximum-security facility to a few hours of mandatory community service." * * * Inherent in the very nature of probation is that probationers "do not enjoy 'the absolute liberty to which every citizen is entitled.' " Just as other punishments for criminal convictions curtail an offender's freedoms, a court granting probation may impose reasonable conditions that deprive the offender of some freedoms enjoyed by law-abiding citizens.

Id. [Citations omitted.]

The probation order issued in this case was conditioned on Knights's acceptance of the search provision. "It was reasonable to conclude that the search condition would further the two primary goals of probation—rehabilitation and protecting society from future criminal violations. The probation order clearly expressed the search condition and Knights was unambiguously informed of it. The probation condition thus significantly diminished Knights's reasonable expectation of privacy." *Id.* at 591-92.

> In assessing the governmental interest side of the balance, it must be remembered that "the very assumption of the institution of probation" is that the probationer "is more likely than the ordinary citizen to violate the law." * * * And probationers have even more of an incentive to conceal their criminal activities and quickly dispose of incriminating evidence than the ordinary criminal because probationers are aware that they may be subject to supervision and face revocation of probation, and possible incarceration, in proceedings in which the trial rights of a jury and proof beyond a reasonable doubt, among other things, do not apply.

Id. at 592. [Citations omitted.]

Accordingly, the Court held that, on balance, the Constitution "requires no more than reasonable suspicion to conduct a search of this probationer's house. The degree of individualized suspicion required of a search is a determination of when there is a sufficiently high probability that criminal conduct is occurring to make the intrusion on the individual's privacy interest reasonable. Although the Fourth Amendment ordinarily requires the degree of probability embodied in the term 'probable cause,' a lesser degree satisfies the Constitution when the balance of governmental and private interests makes such a standard reasonable. Those interests warrant a lesser than probable-cause standard here. When an officer has reasonable suspicion that a probationer subject to a search condition is engaged in criminal activity, there is enough likelihood that criminal conduct is occurring that an intrusion on the probationer's significantly diminished privacy interests is reasonable." *Id.*

The Court concluded that "the warrantless search of Knights, supported by reasonable suspicion and authorized by a condition of probation, was reasonable within the meaning of the Fourth Amendment."

3. *Suspicionless searches based on a condition of release.* In *United States v. Knights, supra,* the search at issue was based on both the probation search condition and reasonable suspicion. Therefore, the Court did not reach the question whether the search would have been reasonable under the Fourth Amendment had it been solely based upon the condition of probation. In *Samson v. California,* 547 *U.S.* 843, 126 *S.Ct.* 2193 (2006), the Court addressed the question left open in *Knights,* and held that a state condition of release "can so diminish or eliminate a released prisoner's reasonable expectation of privacy that a suspicionless search by a law enforcement officer would not offend the Fourth Amendment." *Samson* at 2196.

Similar to probation searches, searches of parolees are necessary to the promotion of legitimate governmental interests. Parolees are on the "continuum" of state-imposed punishments. "On this continuum, parolees have fewer expectations of privacy than probationers, because parole is more akin to imprisonment than probation is to imprisonment." *Id.* at 2198. The "essence of parole is release from prison, before the completion of sentence, on the condition that the prisoner abides by certain rules during the balance of the sentence." *Id.*

In this case, Donald Samson was released on parole in California upon the stated condition that he "shall agree in writing 'to be subject to search or seizure by a parole officer or another peace officer at any time of the day or night, with or without a search warrant and with or without cause.' " *Id.* at 2196. [Citation omitted.] On the day in question, a police officer noticed Samson walking down the street with a woman and a child. Based on a prior contact with him, the officer was aware that Samson was on parole. After checking for wants and warrants, the officer decided to search Samson based solely on his status as a parolee. During the search, the officer found a cigarette box in Samson's left breast pocket. Inside the box, the officer found a plastic baggie containing methamphetamine.

Finding the search lawful, the Court said:

> [T]he parole search condition under California law—requiring inmates who opt for parole to submit to suspicionless searches by a parole officer or other peace officer "at any time"— * * * was "clearly expressed" to [Samson]. He signed an order submitting to the condition and thus was "unambiguously" aware of it. [ ] In *Knights,* we found that acceptance of a clear and unambiguous search condition "significantly diminished Knights' reasonable expectation of privacy." * * * Examining the totality of the circumstances pertaining to [Samson's] status as a parolee, "an established variation on imprisonment," * * * including the plain terms of the parole search condition, we conclude that [Samson] did not have an expectation of privacy that society would recognize as legitimate.
>
> The State's interests, by contrast, are substantial. This Court has repeatedly acknowledged that a State has an "overwhelming interest" in supervising parolees because "parolees . . . are more likely to commit future criminal offenses." * * * Similarly, this Court has repeatedly acknowledged that a State's interests in reducing recidivism and thereby promoting reintegration and positive citizenship among probationers and parolees warrant privacy intrusions that would not otherwise be tolerated under the Fourth Amendment.

Id. at 2199-2200.

In light of the foregoing, the Court determined that imposing a reasonable suspicion requirement, as urged by Samson, "would give parolees greater opportunity to anticipate searches and conceal criminality." *Id.* at 2201.

Accordingly, "the Fourth Amendment does not prohibit a police officer from conducting a suspicionless search of a parolee." *Id.* at 2202.

4. *Warrantless forcible entries to enforce an involuntary civil commitment order.* In *McCabe v. Life-Line Ambulance Service,* 77 F.3d 540 (1st Cir. 1996), the court determined that an officer's warrantless residential entry and search to effect an involuntary civil commitment order issued by a doctor "falls squarely within a recognized class of *systematic* 'special need' searches which are conducted without warrants in furtherance of important administrative purposes." *Id.* at 546. [Court's emphasis.] "On balance," found the court, the "City policy permitting forcible, warrantless entries by police officers in possession of a pink paper [physician's emergency involuntary commitment order] properly issued pursuant to Mass.Gen.Laws ch. 123 §12(a), is reasonable under the Fourth Amendment." *Id.* at 547. The court reasoned:

> The legitimacy of the State's *parens patriae* and "police power" interests in ensuring that "dangerous" mentally ill persons not harm themselves or others is beyond dispute. * * * The potential consequences attending a delayed commitment both to the men-

tally ill subject and others may be extremely serious, sometimes including death or bodily injury. * * *

Id.

In addition, the court found that "[c]ompliance with the warrant requirement in the context of these temporary, involuntary commitments for medical-psychiatric examination would entail critical delays in safeguarding the mentally ill person, and others, without affording commensurate privacy protections to the subject." *Id.* at 549. This ruling was, however, limited to home entries and searches by law enforcement officers in possession of "a pink paper," duly issued under the Massachusetts emergency involuntary commitment statute. *Id.* at 554. *See* M.G.L. c. 123, §12(a).

PENNSYLVANIA BD. OF PROBATION v. SCOTT
Supreme Court of the United States
524 *U.S.* 357, 118 *S.Ct.* 2014 (1998)

QUESTION: Does the exclusionary rule, which generally prohibits the use at a criminal trial of evidence obtained in violation of the Fourth Amendment, apply in parole revocation hearings ?

ANSWER: NO. The exclusionary rule, which generally prohibits the use at criminal trials of evidence obtained in violation of the Fourth Amendment, does not apply in parole revocation hearings. *Id.* at 2018. Therefore, "parole boards are not required by federal law to exclude evidence obtained in violation of the Fourth Amendment." *Id.* at 2022.

RATIONALE: Generally, "the State's use of evidence obtained in violation of the Fourth Amendment does not itself violate the Constitution. * * * Rather, a Fourth Amendment violation is 'fully accomplished' by the illegal search or seizure, and no exclusion of evidence from a judicial or administrative proceeding can 'cure the invasion of the defendant's rights which he has already suffered.' " *Id.* at 2019. [Citations and internal quotes omitted.] Instead, *the exclusionary rule is "a judicially created means of deterring illegal searches and seizures." Id.* [Emphasis added.] As such, the rule does not prohibit the introduction of illegally seized evidence in all proceedings or against all persons, but applies only where its "remedial objectives" are thought to be best served. *Id.*

In this case, the parolee, Keith Scott, was released from prison after serving about 10 years for the commission of a third-degree murder. One of the express conditions of his parole was that he must refrain from "owning or possessing any firearms or other weapons." *Id.* at 2018. In addition, Scott signed the following parole agreement:

I expressly consent to the search of my person, property and residence, without a warrant by agents of the Pennsylvania Board of

Probation and Parole. Any items, [] the possession of which constitutes a violation of parole/reparole shall be subject to seizure, and may be used as evidence in the parole revocation process.

Id.

Approximately five months later, Scott was arrested for several violations of his parole and taken into custody. Prior to being transferred to a correctional facility, Scott gave the parole officers the keys to his residence. At the residence, Scott's mother directed the officers to Scott's bedroom, but the search uncovered no evidence. The officers then searched an adjacent sitting room where they found five firearms, a compound bow, and three arrows.

At his parole revocation hearing, Scott objected to the introduction of the evidence obtained during the search of his home, arguing that the search violated his rights under the Fourth Amendment. Upon appeal, the Pennsylvania Supreme Court determined that the federal exclusionary rule applied to this case because the officers who conducted the search were aware of Scott's parole status, and, if the rule were not applied, "illegal searches would be undeterred where officers know that the subjects of their searches are parolees and that illegally obtained evidence can be introduced at parole hearings." *Id.* at 2018. *The United States Supreme Court disagreed and reversed.*

There are a number of proceedings, outside the criminal trial context, in which the United States Supreme Court has determined that the exclusionary rule does not apply. For example, the exclusionary rule does not apply to grand jury proceedings. *United States v. Calandra*, 414 *U.S.* 338, 343-46, 349-50, 94 *S.Ct.* 613, 620-21 (1974). The exclusionary rule does not prevent the introduction of unlawfully seized evidence in a civil tax proceeding, for the costs of excluding such relevant and reliable evidence outweighs the marginal benefits. *United States v. Janis*, 428 *U.S.* 433, 448, 454, 96 *S.Ct.* 3021, 3029, 3032 (1976). The exclusionary rule has not been extended to civil deportation proceedings. *See INS v. Lopez-Mendoza*, 468 *U.S.* 1032, 1050, 104 *S.Ct.* 3479, 3489 (1984). And it has been held that the exclusionary rule does not apply when the illegally seized evidence is used to impeach a defendant's testimony. *United States v. Havens*, 446 *U.S.* 620, 627-28, 100 *S.Ct.* 1912, 1916-17 (1980).

Here, in *Scott*, the Court again declined to extend the exclusionary rule "beyond the criminal trial context." *Id.* at 2020.

Application of the exclusionary rule would both hinder the functioning of state parole systems and alter the traditionally flexible, administrative nature of parole revocation proceedings. The rule would provide only minimal deterrence benefits in this context, because application of the rule in the criminal trial context already provides significant deterrence of unconstitutional searches.

Id.

The Court held, therefore, "that the federal exclusionary rule does not bar the introduction at parole revocation hearings of evidence seized in violation of parolees' Fourth Amendment rights." *Id.* In so ruling, the Court observed:

> Parole agents, in contrast to police officers, are not "engaged in the often competitive enterprise of ferreting out crime," * * *; instead, their primary concern is whether their parolees should remain free on parole. Thus, their relationship with parolees is more supervisory than adversarial.

Id. at 2022. [Citation omitted.]

SKINNER v. RAILWAY LABOR EXECUTIVES ASS'N.
Supreme Court of the United States
489 U.S. 602, 109 S.Ct. 1402 (1989)

QUESTION 1: Does the collection and chemical testing of an individual's breath and urine constitute a "search" and seizure within the meaning of the Fourth Amendment ?

ANSWER: YES. "Because it is clear that the collection and testing of urine intrudes upon expectations of privacy that society has long recognized as reasonable, * * * these intrusions must be deemed searches under the Fourth Amendment." *Id.* at 1413. The same is true of the breath-testing procedures. *Id.* at 1412.

QUESTION 2: May railroad employees in "safety sensitive" positions be compelled by their (government) employer to submit to breath and urine testing after certain railroad accidents when their employer does not have a search warrant, probable cause or reasonable suspicion ?

ANSWER: YES. The compelling government interests served by the Federal Railroad Administration's regulations would be significantly hindered if railroads were required to either secure a search warrant, have probable cause, or point to specific facts giving rise to a reasonable suspicion of impairment before testing a given employee's breath or urine. *Id.* at 1416, 1419, 1421. The employees who are "subject to the tests discharge duties fraught with such risks of injury to others that even a momentary lapse of attention can have disastrous consequences." *Id.* at 1419.

RATIONALE: "Finding that alcohol and drug abuse by railroad employees poses a serious threat to safety, the Federal Railroad Administration (FRA) has promulgated regulations that mandate blood and urine tests of employees who are involved in certain train accidents. The FRA also has adopted regulations that do not require, but do authorize, railroads to administer breath and urine tests to employees who violate certain safety rules." *Id.* at 1407. The United States Supreme Court granted *certiorari* to determine whether these regulations, which authorize the taking of breath and urine tests by a government employer,* violate the Fourth Amendment.

As a general rule of criminal procedure, "where, as here, the Government seeks to obtain physical evidence from a person, the Fourth Amendment may be relevant at several levels. * * * The initial detention necessary to procure the evidence may be a seizure of the person * * * if the detention amounts to a meaningful interference with his freedom of movement. * * * Obtaining and examining the evidence may also be a search * * * if doing so infringes an expectation of privacy that society is prepared to recognize as reasonable." *Id.* at 1412. [Citations omitted.]

Significantly, the Court has "long recognized that a 'compelled intrusio(n) into the body for blood to be analyzed for alcohol content' must be deemed a Fourth Amendment search." *Id.* (citing *Schmerber v. California,* 384 *U.S.* 757, 767-768, 86 *S.Ct.* 1826, 1833-1834 (1966)). Moreover, "it is obvious that this physical intrusion, penetrating beneath the skin, infringes an expectation of privacy that society is prepared to recognize as reasonable. [Additionally, t]he ensuing chemical analysis of the sample to obtain physiological data is a further invasion of the tested employee's privacy interest." *Skinner* at 1412.

"Unlike the blood-testing procedure at issue in *Schmerber,* the procedures prescribed by the FRA regulations for collecting and testing urine samples do not entail a surgical intrusion into the body. It is not disputed, however, that chemical analysis of urine, like that of blood, can reveal a host of private facts about an employee, including whether she is epileptic, pregnant, or diabetic. Nor can it be disputed that the process of collecting the sample to be tested, which may in some cases involve visual or aural monitoring of the act of urination, itself implicates privacy interests." *Id.* at 1413. Consequently, "[b]ecause it is clear that the collection and testing of urine intrudes upon expectations of privacy that society has long recognized as reasonable, * * * these intrusions must be deemed searches under the Fourth Amendment." *Id.* at 1413.

"To hold that the Fourth Amendment is applicable to the drug and alcohol testing prescribed by the FRA regulations is only to begin the inquiry into the standards governing such [an] intrusion. * * * For the Fourth Amendment does not proscribe all searches and seizures, but only those that are unreasonable." *Id.* at 1413-1414. Naturally, what is reasonable " 'depends on all the circumstances surrounding the search or seizure and the nature of the search or seizure itself.' " *Id.* at 1414. [Citation omitted.] Moreover, whether a particular practice is reasonable will be " 'judged by balancing its intrusion on the individual's Fourth Amendment interests against its promotion of legitimate

---

* The Court concluded that the "specific features of the regulations combine to" make these "private" railroads "government instruments." *Id.* at 1411-1412. According to the Court: "The Government has removed all legal barriers to the testing authorized * * * and indeed has made plain not only its strong preference for testing, but also its desire to share the fruits of such intrusions. * * * These are clear indices of the Government's encouragement, endorsement, and participation, and suffice to implicate the Fourth Amendment." *Id.* at 1412.

governmental interests.' " *Id.* (quoting *Delaware v. Prouse,* 440 *U.S.* 648, 654, 99 *S.Ct.* 1391, 1396 (1979)).

Generally, a search or seizure is not reasonable unless it is accomplished pursuant to a warrant issued upon probable cause. The Court has, however, recognized exceptions to this rule "when 'special needs, beyond the normal need for law enforcement, make the warrant and probable-cause requirement impracticable.' " *Skinner* at 1414 (quoting *Griffin v. Wisconsin,* 483 *U.S.* 868, 107 *S.Ct.* 3164, 3167 (1987)). Those "special needs" are implicated by this case.

"The Government's interest in regulating the conduct of railroad employees to ensure safety, like its supervision of probationers, or regulated industries, or its operation of a government office, school, or prison, 'likewise presents "special needs" beyond normal law enforcement that may justify departures from the usual warrant and probable cause requirements.' * * * The FRA has prescribed toxicological tests, not to assist in the prosecution of employees, but rather 'to prevent accidents and casualties in railroad operations that result from impairment of employees by alcohol or drugs.' " *Skinner* at 1414-1415. [Citations omitted.] Because the "governmental interest in ensuring the safety of the traveling public and of the employees themselves plainly justifies prohibiting covered employees from using alcohol or drugs, on duty, or while subject to being called for duty[,]" *id.* at 1415, neither a warrant nor probable cause is necessary or "essential to render the intrusions here at issue reasonable under the Fourth Amendment." *Id.* at 1416.

Further, "the government interest in testing without a showing of individualized suspicion is compelling. Employees subject to the tests discharge duties fraught with such risks of injury to others that even a momentary lapse of attention can have disastrous consequences." *Id.* 1419. Although there is no procedure which "can identify all impaired employees with ease and perfect accuracy, the FRA regulations supply an effective means of deterring employees engaged in safety-sensitive tasks from using controlled substances or alcohol in the first place. * * * By ensuring that employees in safety-sensitive positions know they will be tested upon the occurrence of a triggering event, the timing of which no employee can predict with certainty, the regulations significantly increase the deterrent effect of the administrative penalties associated with the prohibited conduct, [while at the same time] increasing the likelihood that employees will forgo using drugs or alcohol while subject to being called for duty." *Id.* at 1419-1420.

Based on the foregoing analysis, the Court finds that "the compelling government interests served by the FRA's regulations would be significantly hindered if railroads were required to point to specific facts giving rise to a reasonable suspicion of impairment before testing a given employee." *Id.* at 1421. Since the Court finds that "the toxicological testing contemplated by the regulations is not an undue infringement on the justifiable expectations of privacy of covered employees," *id.*, it concludes that "the Government's compelling interests" here demonstrated outweigh those privacy concerns. *Id.* In this respect, the Court emphasizes:

The possession of unlawful drugs is a criminal offense that the Government may punish, but it is a separate and far more dangerous wrong to perform certain sensitive tasks while under the influence of those substances. Performing those tasks while impaired by alcohol is, or course, equally dangerous, although consumption of alcohol is legal in most other contexts. The Government may take all necessary and reasonable regulatory steps to prevent or deter that hazardous conduct, and since the gravamen of the evil is performing certain functions while concealing the substance in the body, it may be necessary, as in this case before us, to examine the body or its fluids to accomplish the regulatory purpose. The necessity to perform that regulatory function with respect to railroad employees engaged in safety-sensitive tasks, and the reasonableness of the system for doing so, have been established in this case.

Id. at 1421-1422.

Accordingly, "[i]n light of the limited discretion exercised by the railroad employers under the regulations, the surpassing safety interests served by toxicological tests in this context, and the diminished expectation of privacy that attaches to information pertaining to the fitness of covered employees, [the Court holds] that it is reasonable to conduct such tests in the absence of a warrant[, probable cause,] or reasonable suspicion that any particular employee may be impaired." *Id.* at 1422.

NOTE

The Court in *Skinner* focused its attention upon two subsections of the Federal Railroad Administration's (FRA) regulations which apply to employees assigned to perform service subject to the Hours of Service Act, 45 *U.S.C.* §61 *et seq.* Such service includes persons engaged in handling orders concerning train movement, operating crews, and those engaged in the maintenance and repair of signal systems. According to the Court, "these and other covered employees are engaged in safety-sensitive tasks." *Id.* at 1414. With respect to employee testing, Subpart C of the regulations, entitled "Post Accident Toxicological Testing," is mandatory. Subpart D, entitled "Authorization to Test for Cause," is permissive. *Id.* at 1408, 1409.

Subpart C requires blood and urine samples taken for toxicological testing upon the occurrence of certain specified events. "[T]esting is required following 'a major train accident,' which is defined as any train accident that involves (i) a fatality, (ii) the release of hazardous material accompanied by an evacuation or a reportable injury, or (iii) damage to railroad property over $500,000." *Id.* at 1408. Covered employees must also submit to blood and urine testing after an "impact accident," (a collision resulting in a reportable injury, or in damage to railroad property of $50,000 or more), and after any train accident involving a fatality to any on-duty railroad employee. *Id.* at 1409.

Subpart D of the regulations authorizes railroads to require covered employees to submit to breath or urine tests in certain circumstances not covered by Subpart C. "Breath or urine tests, or both, may be ordered (1) after a reportable accident or incident, where a supervisor has a 'reasonable suspicion' that an employee's acts or omissions contributed to the occurrence or severity of the accident or incident, * * * or (2) in the event of certain specific rule violations, including noncompliance with a signal and excessive speeding." *Id.* Covered employees may also be required to submit to breath tests "where a supervisor has a 'reasonable suspicion' that an employee is under the influence of alcohol, based upon specific, personal observations concerning the appearance, behavior, speech, or body odors of the employee." *Id.* Additionally, "where impairment is suspected, [an employee may be required to submit to] urine tests, but only if two supervisors make the appropriate determination, * * * and, where the supervisors suspect impairment due to a substance other than alcohol, at least one of those supervisors must have received specialized training in detecting the signs of drug intoxication." *Id.* at 1409-1410. Finally, if the employer intends to use the results of either the breath or urine tests for a disciplinary proceeding, "the employee must be given the opportunity to provide a blood sample for analysis at an independent medical facility." *Id.* at 1410.

Playing a significant part in the Court's decision that a warrant was not necessary, was the fact that "[b]oth the circumstances justifying toxicological testing and the permissible limits of such intrusions are defined narrowly and specifically in the regulations that authorize them, and [the fact that the regulations] are well known to covered employees. * * * Indeed, in light of the standardized nature of the tests and the minimal discretion vested in those charged with administering the program, there are virtually no facts for a neutral magistrate to evaluate." *Id.* at 1415-1416.

As a result, the Court found that the (1) blood tests, (2) breath tests, and (3) urine tests which are mandated by Subparts C and D of the FRA's regulations meet the Fourth Amendment's reasonableness requirement. *Id.* at 1422.

NATIONAL TREASURY EMPLOYEES UNION v. VON RAAB
Supreme Court of the United States
489 *U.S.* 656, 109 *S.Ct.* 1384 (1989)

QUESTION: Does the Government's requirement of mandatory drug testing of any U.S. Customs Service employee who seeks transfer or promotion to (1) a position involving direct participation in drug interdiction (detection and control) or enforcement of related laws, or (2) a position in which the employee is required to carry a firearm violate the Fourth Amendment?

ANSWER: NO. "[T]he suspicionless testing of employees who apply for promotion to positions directly involving the interdiction of illegal drugs, or to positions which require the incumbent to carry a firearm, is reasonable. The Government's compelling interests in preventing the promotion of drug users to positions where they might endanger the integrity of our Nation's borders or the life of the citizenry outweigh the privacy interests of those who seek promotion to these positions, who enjoy a diminished expectation of privacy by virtue of the special, and obvious, physical and ethical demands of the positions." *Id.* at 1397-98.

RATIONALE: Within the Department of the Treasury, the United States Customs Service is responsible for processing persons, carriers, cargo, and mail into the United States, collecting revenue from imports, and enforcing customs and related laws. An important responsibility of the Service is the interdiction and seizure of contraband, including illegal drugs. In this regard, many Customs agents carry and use firearms in connection with their official duties. *Id.* at 1387.

While it is clear that urine tests are "searches" within the meaning of the Fourth Amendment, when the government intrusion serves "special governmental needs, beyond the normal need for law enforcement, it is necessary to balance the individual's privacy expectations against the Government's interests to determine whether it is impracticable to require a warrant or some level of individualized suspicion in the particular context." *Id.* at 1390.

"It is clear that the Customs Service's drug testing program is not designed to serve the ordinary needs of law enforcement. * * * The purposes of the program are to deter drug use among those eligible for promotion to sensitive positions within the Service and to prevent the promotion of drug users to those positions. These substantial interests present a special need that may justify departure from the ordinary warrant and probable cause requirements." *Id.* at 1390-91.

Furthermore, every employee under the Customs program "who seeks a transfer to a covered position knows that he must take a drug test, and is likewise aware of the procedures the Service must follow in administering the test. A covered employee is simply not subject 'to the discretion of the official in the field.'" *Id.* at 1391. [Citation omitted.]

Beyond the warrant and probable cause issue, the Court found that the Government's need to conduct "suspicionless" searches "outweigh[ed] the privacy interests of the employees engaged directly in drug interdiction, and of those who otherwise are required to carry firearms. It is readily apparent that the Government has a compelling interest in ensuring that front-line interdiction personnel are physically fit, and have unimpeachable integrity and judgment. The national interest in self protection could be irreparably damaged if those charged with safeguarding it were, because of their own drug use, unsympathetic to their mission of interdicting narcotics. The public interest demands effective measures to bar drug users from positions directly involving the interdiction of illegal drugs." *Id.* at 1392, 1393.

"The public interest likewise demands effective measures to prevent the promotion of drug users to positions that require the incumbent to carry a firearm, even if the incumbent is not engaged directly in the interdiction of drugs. Customs employees who may use deadly weapons plainly 'discharge duties fraught with such risks of injury to others that even a momentary lapse of attention can have disastrous consequences.'" *Id.* at 1393. [Citation omitted.] "[T]he public should not bear the risk that employees who may suffer from impaired perception and judgment will be promoted to positions where they may need to employ deadly force." *Id.*

"Against these valid public interests we must weigh the interferences with individual liberty that results from requiring these classes of employees to undergo a urine test." *Id.* According to the Court, "Customs employees who are directly involved in the interdiction of illegal drugs or who are required to carry firearms in the line of duty have a diminished expectation of privacy in respect to the intrusions occasioned by a urine test. Unlike most private citizens or government employees in general, employees involved in drug interdiction reasonably should expect effective inquiry into their fitness[, honesty and integrity]. Much the same is true of employees who are required to carry firearms. Because successful performance of their duties depends uniquely on their judgment and dexterity, these employees cannot reasonably expect to keep from the Service personal information that bears directly on their fitness. While reasonable tests designed to elicit this information [certainly] infringe some privacy expectations, [the Court does] not believe these expectations outweigh the Government's compelling interests in safety and in the integrity of our borders." *Id.* at 1394.

Significantly, "the almost unique mission of the Service gives the Government a compelling interest in ensuring that many of these covered employees do not use drugs even off-duty, for such use creates risks of bribery and blackmail against which the Government is entitled to guard. In light of the extraordinary safety and national security hazards that would attend the promotion of drug users to positions that require the carrying of firearms or the interdiction of controlled substances, the Service's policy of deterring drug users from seeking such promotions cannot be deemed unreasonable." *Id.* at 1395.

Accordingly, "the suspicionless testing of employees who apply for promotion to positions directly involving the interdiction of illegal drugs, or to positions which require the incumbent to carry a firearm, is reasonable. The Government's compelling interest in preventing the promotion of drug users to positions where they might endanger the integrity of our Nation's borders or the life of the citizenry outweigh the privacy interests of those who seek promotion to these positions, who enjoy a diminished expectation of privacy by virtue of the special, and obvious, physical and ethical demands of those positions." *Id.* at 1397-98.

As a general principle, the Fourth Amendment's prohibition against unreasonable searches and seizures is applicable to commercial businesses as well as private dwellings. *New York v. Burger*, 482 *U.S.* 691, 107 *S.Ct.* 2636 (1987); *See v. City of Seattle*, 387 *U.S.* 541, 543, 546, 87 *S.Ct.* 1737, 1739, 1741 (1967). While an owner or operator of a commercial establishment may have a lesser expectation of privacy in the establishment's premises than that enjoyed by a homeowner in his dwelling place, the owner or operator nonetheless maintains a legitimate expectation of privacy in the commercial establishment. *Donovan v. Dewey*, 452 *U.S.* 594, 101 *S.Ct.* 2534 (1981). This expectation of privacy exists with respect to administrative inspections designed to enforce regulatory schemes as well as to traditional searches conducted by police for the gathering of evidence of a crime. *See Burger, supra*, 482 *U.S.* at 699, 107 *S.Ct.* at 2642). *See also Marshall v. Barlow's Inc.*, 436 *U.S.* 307, 312-13, 98 *S.Ct.* 1816, 1820 (1978).

Normally, prior to conducting a regulatory search, officers are required to obtain an administrative search warrant. In "closely regulated industries," however, "an exception to the warrant requirement has been carved out for searches of premises pursuant to an administrative inspection scheme." *Shoemaker v. Handel*, 795 *F.*2d 1136, 1142 (3rd Cir. 1986). As the court stated in *Lovgren v. Byrne*, 787 *F.*2d 857 (3rd Cir. 1986):

> [O]ne who is engaged in an industry, that is pervasively regulated by the government or that has been historically subject to such close supervision, is ordinarily held to be on notice that periodic inspections will occur and, accordingly, has [a significantly reduced] expectation of privacy in the areas where he knows those inspections will occur.

Id. at 865. *See also United States v. Biswell*, 406 *U.S.* 311, 316-17, 92 *S.Ct.* 1593, 1596-97 (1972) (sale of guns); *Colonnade Catering Corp. v. United States*, 397 *U.S.* 72, 76-77, 90 *S.Ct.* 774, 777 (1970) (liquor industry); *Shoemaker v. Handel, supra*, 795 *F.*2d at 1142 (horse racing).

In order to be constitutionally valid, a warrantless, administrative inspection of a closely regulated commercial establishment must satisfy three requirements:

> (1) There must be a substantial government interest in the regulatory scheme under which the warrantless, administrative inspection is conducted;

(2) The warrantless, administrative inspection must be necessary to further the regulatory scheme; and

(3) The warrantless inspection, by reason of the certainty of its terms and regularity of its application, must provide a constitutionally sufficient substitute for a search warrant. In this respect, similar to a search warrant, the regulatory scheme under which the inspection is conducted must advise the property owner that:

(a) the administrative inspection is being conducted under legal authority;

(b) by reason of that authority, the scope of the inspection is clearly defined; and

(c) the discretion of the inspecting officer is appropriately limited.

New York v. Burger, supra at 702, 713, 107 *S.Ct.* at 2644, 2649.

When each of the three requirements is satisfied, the warrantless, administrative inspection is constitutionally reasonable and the discovery of evidence of crimes in the course of an otherwise proper administrative inspection should not render the search illegal or the administrative scheme suspect. *See Burger* at 716, 107 *S.Ct.* at 2651.

UNITED STATES v. MALDONADO
United States Court of Appeals
56 *F.*3d 130 (1st Cir. 2004)

QUESTION: Is "interstate commercial trucking" a "pervasively regulated industry" for purposes of the administrative / regulatory search exception to the Fourth Amendment's warrant requirement?

ANSWER: YES. "Interstate commercial trucking is a pervasively regulated industry," and, as a result, comes within the purview of the administrative / regulatory search exception to the Fourth Amendment's warrant requirement. *Id.* at 132.

RATIONALE: The circumstances in *Maldonado* unfolded in the first week of August when Trooper Flint of the Maine State Police stopped an "Allied Van Lines" truck that was traveling northbound on the Maine Turnpike at an excessive rate of speed. Investigation at the scene of the stop revealed that the driver, defendant Maldonado, had violated several federal trucking regulations. For example, he had failed to keep his log book current, 49 *C.F.R.* §395.8; failed to wear a seat belt; and operated the truck without a valid license. For that reason, Flint summoned Trooper Nichols, a member of the state police who specializes in enforcing commercial trucking regulations. Flint also summoned a tow truck "because he realized that Maldonado would not be allowed to drive with a suspended license." *Id.* at 132.

Initially, Trooper Nichols asked Maldonado for "the truck's operating authority (a document that cedes the right to operate a commercial vehicle in Maine). Maldonado did not have any such paperwork. Nichols then requested Maldonado's fuel and toll receipts. Maldonado had no receipts for fuel and only three toll receipts (from Massachusetts, New Hampshire, and Maine, respectively). Nichols viewed this as suspicious because, in his experience, commercial truckers undertaking long cross-country hauls typically have 'a pile' of such receipts and he expected to see, at a bare minimum, additional toll receipts from New Jersey and New York." *Id.* at 133.

"Nichols next requested Maldonado's shipping papers (he testified that most moving vans carrying household goods take along what amounts to an inventory of the cargo). Maldonado had no papers; he claimed to have left them in his motel room. On further inquiry, however, he could not name the motel, pinpoint its location, or produce a room key." *Id.*

"Having grown increasingly suspicious, Nichols asked Maldonado to step out of the vehicle. He searched the cab area, knowing that the truck was destined to be towed. He was surprised to find neither luggage nor extra clothing (he did, however, find a machete)." *Id.* At this point, Nichols called in a canine drug search unit. While this unit was en route, Flint departed. Nichols proceeded to run the license plate. This check revealed that the truck's registration was expired.

"Nichols then asked Maldonado to unlock the trailer. Maldonado opened the doors of the unlocked storage compartments but did not have keys to unlock the sealed units. He asked Nichols for bolt cutters but Nichols had none. By that time, the tow truck had arrived, and the driver proffered his bolt cutters. Maldonado cut the padlocks. When the doors to the van were opened, Nichols noticed an upside-down couch and a pile of boxes." *Id.* at 133. Inside, near the front of the trailer, the trooper discovered a box containing what appeared to be marijuana. By then, the canine unit had arrived and the drug dog responded positively to the opened box.

At this point, Trooper Nichols placed Maldonado under arrest, and the truck was towed to a holding facility. A subsequent search of the truck, conducted pursuant to a warrant, revealed no additional contraband.

Finding the trooper's actions valid under the "administrative search exception to the warrant requirement," *id.* at 134, the court observed:

> Commerce, by its very nature, often results in a heightened governmental interest in regulation. This increased interest necessarily results in a diminution of the privacy interests of those who operate commercial premises. *See New York v. Burger*, 482 *U.S.* 691, 700, 107 *S.Ct.* 2636 (1987). That trend crests when an industry operates under pervasive regulation. In such circumstances, warrantless inspections of commercial sites may be constitutionally permissible.

Under the *Burger* doctrine, such inspections must satisfy three criteria in order to pass Fourth Amendment muster. First, there must be a "substantial government interest that informs the regulatory scheme pursuant to which the inspection is made." Second, inspections must be necessary to advance the regulatory agenda. Finally, the inspection program must provide constitutionally adequate safeguards to ensure both the certainty and regularity of its application. This last criterion looks to notice as to the scope of the search as well as limitations on the discretion afforded to inspecting officers.

Maldonado at 134-35. [Citations omitted.]

For purposes of the *Burger* doctrine, the court could see "no meaningful distinction between commercial premises and commercial vehicles." *Id.* at 135. Consequently, the court held that "interstate commercial trucking is regulated to the extent necessary to give rise to the administrative search exception." *Id.* This holding is in line with the holdings of a number of other circuit courts of appeal. *See, e.g., United States v. Vasquez-Castillo*, 258 *F*.3d 1207, 1210 (10th Cir. 2001); *United States v. Fort*, 248 *F*.3d 475, 480 (5th Cir. 2001); *United States v. Dominguez-Prieto*, 923 *F*.2d 464, 468 (6th Cir. 1991). *See also United States v. V-1 Oil Co.*, 63 *F*.3d 909, 911 (9th Cir. 1995) (finding regulation under the Hazardous Materials Transportation Act pervasive).

The court went on to rule that the regulatory scheme surrounding the interstate commercial trucking industry satisfies the tripartite *Burger* standard. The court reasoned:

As to the first criterion, * * * the government has a significant interest in regulating the interstate trucking industry (*e.g.*, to ensure traveler safety, hold costs in check, and restrict what commodities may be transported interstate). * * * [T]hese justifications comprise a set of legitimate and substantial interests. As to the second criterion, we think it self-evident that warrantless inspections of commercial trucks are necessary to further the regulatory scheme. Because the industry is so mobile, surprise is an important component of an efficacious inspection regime. * * * Fairly measured, the interests justifying warrantless searches in the interstate trucking industry are even greater than those present in *Burger* (which involved the regulation of junkyards) because of the speed with which commercial vehicles move from place to place. * * * And, finally, because violations of the regulatory scheme often are not apparent to a patrolling officer, inspections are sometimes the only way in which violations can be discovered. We conclude, therefore, that effective enforcement of the regulatory regime would be impossible in the absence of impromptu inspections.

The regulatory scheme applicable to the interstate commercial trucking industry also satisfies the final *Burger* criterion. The carefully delineated scope of the federal regulations suitably cabins the discretion of the enforcing officer. Moreover, the regulations themselves give ample notice to interstate truckers that inspections will be made on a regular basis[; and] commercial drivers are required by law to be familiar with the applicable regulations, *see* 49 *C.F.R.* § 390.3(e)(2)[. Indeed], Maldonado concedes that he was aware that his vehicle could be searched "at the discretion of an inspecting officer."

Since all three of the *Burger* criteria are satisfied, it follows [] that an administrative search of a commercial truck is constitutionally permissible.

Id. at 135-36.

Accordingly, "the warrantless inspection" of Maldonado's moving van was "consistent with the Fourth Amendment[.]" *Id.* at 137.

---

§6.2. Border searches.

From before the adoption of the Fourth Amendment, to today, border searches "have been considered to be 'reasonable' by the single fact that the person or item in question had entered into our country from outside. There has never been any additional requirement that the reasonableness of a border search depended on the existence of probable cause. This longstanding recognition that searches at our borders without probable cause and without a warrant are nonetheless 'reasonable' has a history as old as the Fourth Amendment itself." *United States v. Ramsey*, 431 *U.S.* 606, 619, 97 *S.Ct.* 1972, 1980 (1977).

UNITED STATES v. ORIAKHI
United States Court of Appeals
57 *F.*3d 1290 (4th Cir. 1995)

QUESTION: Does the border search exception apply only to persons and objects *entering* into our country from outside ?

ANSWER: NO. The border search exception "extends to all routine searches at the nation's borders, irrespective of whether persons or effects are entering or exiting from the country." *Id.* at 1297.

RATIONALE: In this appeal, defendant Oriakhi acknowledged that the New Jersey port search of his freight container and the New York airport search of his luggage were searches that "occurred 'at the border'[a] and that routine searches of persons and effects *entering* the country may be conducted at the border without a warrant, probable cause, or any level of individualized suspicion." *Id.* at 1295. [Court's emphasis.]

---

[a] Oriakhi did not dispute that the Port Elizabeth and J.F.K. Airport searches were conducted at the "functional equivalent" of the border. *See Almeida-Sanchez v. United States,* 413 *U.S.* 266, 272-73, 93 *S.Ct.* 2535, 2539 (1973).

Defendant argued, however, that the border search exception to the Fourth Amendment "does not apply to persons and their effects *leaving* the country," and that the principle case setting forth the border search exception—*United States v. Ramsey*—"is ambiguous as to whether the exception applies to exit searches." *Oriakhi* at 1295. [Court's emphasis.]

The issue of whether the border search exception to the Fourth Amendment extends to exit searches "is one of first impression in this circuit. While this circuit has yet to rule on this issue, every other circuit addressing the issue has held that the exception applies regardless of whether the person or items searched are entering or exiting the United States." *Id.* at 1296.[b]

"The rationale for exempting border searches from the Fourth Amendment's probable cause and warrant requirements rests on fundamental principles of national sovereignty, which apply equally to exit and entry searches. Even though Oriakhi places great emphasis on language in *Ramsey* that '[t]he border search exception is grounded in the recognized right of the sovereign to control . . . who and what may *enter* the country,' " the Court "also emphasized that the right to control who and what enters the country is derived from a broader and more basic principle, the 'long-standing right of the sovereign to protect itself.' " *Id.* at 1296 (court's emphasis) (quoting *Ramsey* at 620, 616, 97 *S.Ct.* at 1980, 1978).

"National sovereignty is the undivided power of a people and their government within a territory, and a nation draws on that power when it acts in relationship to other nations. * * * [I]nherent in national sovereignty are the overarching rights of a nation to defend itself from outside threats, to act in relation to other nations, and to secure its territory and assets." *Id.* As the Court pointed out in *United States v. Curtiss-Wright Export Corp.*, 299 *U.S.* 304, 315-18, 57 *S.Ct.* 216, 218-20 (1936), the power of the United States to act as a sovereign nation is defined "not in the provisions of the Constitution, but in the law of nations."

"From the sovereign's power to protect itself is derived its power to exclude harmful influences, including undesirable aliens, from the sovereign's territory, * * * as well as its power to prohibit the export of its currency, national treasures, and other assets. * * * In the exercise of the sovereign's right to protect itself, it has been long recognized that the sovereign must be able to conduct routine searches of persons and their effects at its borders. As the Court noted in *Ramsey*, a routine border search has for this reason always been excepted from the requirements of the Fourth Amendment. For the same reason, a border search that goes beyond the routine is nevertheless justified merely by reasonable suspicion, a lesser standard than required for analogous non-border searches." *Oriakhi* at 1297.

---

[b] *See e.g., United States v. Ezeiruaku*, 936 *F.*2d 136, 143 (3rd Cir. 1991); *United States v. Hernandez-Salazar*, 813 *F.*2d 1126, 1137 (11th Cir. 1987); *United States v. Des Jardins*, 747 *F.*2d 499, 504 (9th Cir. 1984); *United States v. Udofot*, 711 *F.*2d 831, 839-40 (8th Cir. 1983); *United States v. Ajlouny*, 629 *F.*2d 830, 834 (2nd Cir. 1980). *See also Julian v. United States*, 463 *U.S.* 1308, 103 *S.Ct.* 3522 (1983) (Rehnquist, Circuit Justice) (a chambers opinion applying the border search exception articulated in *Ramsey* to a person and his effects as he attempted to *depart* the country on a flight destined for Peru).

"While it is undoubtedly true that border searches are more often conducted in furtherance of the sovereign's interest in excluding undesirable outside influences, such as entrants with communicable diseases, narcotics, or explosives, * * * that interest in *exclusion* is not the only function of the border search. As important is the sovereign's interest in regulating foreign commerce and, in particular, in regulating and controlling its currency. The economic lifeblood of a nation is drawn from its monetary supply, and the protection of the nation's currency is crucial to its economic survival." *Id.* [Court's emphasis.] As one court noted, " '[t]he governmental interest in stemming the flow of unreported currency out of the United States is substantial.' " *Id.* [Citation omitted.]

"While the sovereign's ability to regulate its currency is important in itself, it is even more significant in light of the overwhelming flow of illegal narcotics into the United States. Regulating the export of currency provides a mechanism for controlling the import of narcotics since there must be an accompanying outflow of cash to pay for the import of billions of dollars worth of illegal drugs. It is therefore also recognized that the 'dictates of public policy [against drug trafficking] reinforce the necessity of identifying, if not monitoring or controlling, a cash outflow from the country as well as an influx of narcotics into the country.' " *Id.* [Citation omitted.]

Accordingly, "even though in *Ramsey* the border search under consideration involved opening mail used to *import* heroin into the United States, the principles articulated in that case also apply to the sovereign interest of protecting and monitoring exports from the country, including, importantly, its currency." *Id.* [Emphasis added.] This court, therefore, joins "the several other circuit courts which have held that the *Ramsey* border search exception extends to all routine searches at the nation's borders, irrespective of whether persons or effects are entering or exiting from the country." *Id.*

NOTE

Is the removal or dismantling of a motorist's fuel tank a "routine" border search for which no suspicion whatsoever is required? In *United States v. Flores-Montano*, 541 *U.S.* 149, 124 *S.Ct.* 1582 (2004), at the international border in southern California, customs officials seized 37 kilograms—a little more than 81 pounds—of marijuana from defendant Manuel Flores-Montano's gas tank. Chief Justice Rehnquist, speaking for a unanimous Court, held that the routine border search in question did not require reasonable suspicion.

According to the Court,

The Government's interest in preventing the entry of unwanted persons and effects is at its zenith at the international border. Time and again, we have stated that "searches made at the border, pursuant to the longstanding right of the sovereign to protect itself by stopping and examining persons and property crossing into this country, are reasonable simply by virtue of the fact that they occur at the border." * * *

That interest in protecting the borders is illustrated in this case by the evidence that smugglers frequently attempt to penetrate our borders with contraband secreted in their automobiles' fuel tank. Over the past 51/2 fiscal years, there have been 18,788 vehicle drug seizures at the southern California ports of entry. Of those 18,788, gas tank drug seizures have accounted for 4,619 of the vehicle drug seizures, or approximately 25%. In addition, instances of persons smuggled in and around gas tank compartments are discovered at the ports of entry of San Ysidro and Otay Mesa at a rate averaging 1 approximately every 10 days.

Id. at 1585-86. [Citations omitted.]

In this case, the Court rejected defendant's contention that he had "a privacy interest in his fuel tank, and that the suspicionless disassembly of his tank [was] an invasion of his privacy." *Id.* at 1586. The Court said:

[T]he expectation of privacy is less at the border than it is in the interior. * * * We have long recognized that automobiles seeking entry into this country may be searched. * * * It is difficult to imagine how the search of a gas tank, which should be solely a repository for fuel, could be more of an invasion of privacy than the search of the automobile's passenger compartment.

Id.

The Court also rejected defendant's argument that "the disassembly and reassembly of his gas tank" was "a significant deprivation of his *property* interest because it may damage the vehicle." *Id.* [Emphasis added.] In this respect, the Court observed that defendant did not, and could not, truly contend that:

the procedure of removal, disassembly, and reassembly of the fuel tank in this case or any other has resulted in serious damage to, or destruction of, the property. According to the Government, for example, in fiscal year 2003, 348 gas tank searches conducted along the southern border were negative (*i.e.*, no contraband was found), the gas tanks were reassembled, and the vehicles continued their entry into the United States without incident.

[Defendant] cites not a single accident involving the vehicle or motorist in the many thousands of gas tank disassemblies that have occurred at the border. A gas tank search involves a brief procedure that can be reversed without damaging the safety or operation of the vehicle. * * * While the interference with a motorist's possessory interest is not insignificant when the Government removes, disassembles, and reassembles his gas tank, it nevertheless is justified by the Government's paramount interest in protecting the border.

Id. at 1586-87.

Accordingly, the Court held that "the Government's authority to conduct suspicionless inspections at the border includes the authority to remove, disassemble, and reassemble a vehicle's fuel tank. While it may be true that some searches of property are so destructive as to require a different result, this was not one of them." *Id.* at 1587.

CHAPTER 7

FIRE SCENES

Section
7.1   The warrant requirement and fire-scene entries
7.2   Warrantless entries at the scene of a fire

As a general rule, an individual's reasonable expectation of privacy and his Fourth Amendment protections are not diminished simply because the official conducting the search at a fire scene wears the uniform of a firefighter rather than a police officer, or because his purpose is to determine the cause of a fire rather than to look for evidence of a crime, or because the fire might have been started deliberately. Firefighters, like police officers, are government officials, and as such, are subject to the constraints of the federal and state constitutions.

§7.1. The warrant requirement and fire-scene entries.

INTRODUCTION

As a general matter, whenever a fire official wishes to re-enter a "cold" fire scene in the absence of consent, exigent (emergency) circumstances, or complete devastation or destruction, a warrant is required. A "cold" fire scene may be defined as an area containing property which has been freshly fire-damaged, existing at a time when the fire has been completely extinguished and all fire and police officials have departed. Any entries during this "cold" period will be considered by the courts as being *beyond* the "reasonable time to investigate the cause of a blaze after it has been extinguished," in the absence of consent, exigent circumstances, or total devastation. *Michigan v. Tyler*, 436 *U.S.* 499, 510, 98 *S.Ct.* 1942, 1950 (1978). Cold-scene entries and searches require a warrant.

There are two types of warrants available to the investigating fire official, and, the "object of the search determines the type of warrant required." *Michigan v. Clifford*, 464 *U.S.* 287, 294, 104 *S.Ct.* 641, 647 (1984). If the fire official's prime objective is to determine the *cause* and *origin* of a recent fire, an "administrative warrant" must be obtained. "Probable cause to issue an administrative warrant exists if reasonable legislative, administrative, or judicially prescribed standards for conducting an inspection are satisfied with respect to a particular dwelling." *Id.* at 294 n.5, 104 *S.Ct.* at 647 n.5. *See also Camara v. Municipal Court*, 387 *U.S.* 523, 538, 87 *S.Ct.* 1727, 1735-1736 (1967). This procedural requirement is accomplished by the official personally appearing before a judge, who will examine the official's affidavit and/or take his or her sworn testimony. At this meeting, the official must show that (1) a "fire of undetermined origin has occurred on the premises," (2) the "scope of the proposed search is reasonable[,]" (3) the "search will not intrude unnecessarily on the fire victim's privacy," and (4) the "search will be executed at a reasonable and convenient time." *Clifford* at 294, 104 *S.Ct.* at 647. (Naturally, "convenience" here refers to that time convenient to the fire victim, not the fire official).

If, however, the fire official's prime objective is to gather evidence of criminal activity, *e.g.*, arson, a "criminal search warrant" must be secured. This is accomplished only upon a showing (before a judge) of "probable cause to believe that relevant evidence will be found in the place to be searched." *Id.* Probable cause will be found to exist "where the facts and circumstances within a person's knowledge and of which he has reasonably trustworthy information are sufficient in themselves to warrant a man of reasonable caution and prudence in the belief that an offense has been or is being committed." *Draper v. United States*, 358 *U.S.* 307, 313, 79 *S.Ct.* 329, 333 (1959).

Naturally, if, during the course of a valid administrative search, evidence of arson is discovered, the official may lawfully seize that evidence under the "plain view" doctrine. [*See* §2.3(f)(2).] "This evidence may then be used to establish probable cause to obtain a criminal search warrant." *Clifford* at 294, 104 *S.Ct.* at 647. The *Clifford* Court warns, however, that, "[f]ire officials may not * * * rely on this evidence to increase the scope of their administrative search without first making a successful showing of probable cause to an independent judicial officer." *Id.* Additionally, the keynote to an administrative warrant is the "specific limitation" in the scope of the official inspection. Therefore, "[a]n administrative search into the cause of a recent fire does not give fire officials license to roam freely through the fire victim's private residence." *Id.* at 298, 104 *S.Ct.* at 649.

Because there is no bright line separating the firefighter's investigation into the cause of a fire from an investigatory search for evidence of arson, questions naturally arise as to when the administrative search becomes "excessive in scope," and, whether the scope of such a search should necessarily expand or constrict in relation to the nature of the particular structure involved.

MICHIGAN v. TYLER
Supreme Court of the United States
436 *U.S.* 499, 98 *S.Ct.* 1942 (1978)

QUESTION: In order to secure an administrative warrant to investigate the cause of a fire, must a fire investigator show more than the bare fact that a fire has occurred ?

ANSWER: YES. "To secure a warrant to investigate the cause of a fire, an official must show more than the bare fact that a fire has occurred." *Id.* at 1949. The investigator must provide the judge with sufficient information to assure him "that the proposed search will be reasonable, a determination that requires inquiry into the need for the intrusion on the one hand, and the threat of disruption to the occupant on the other." *Id.*

RATIONALE: When a judge is requested to sign an administrative warrant for building inspections, a reasonable balance between competing concerns, such as the governmental need for the search weighed against the individual's privacy interests, is "usually achieved by broad legislative or administrative guidelines specifying the purpose, frequency, scope, and manner of conducting the inspections." *Id.*

"In the context of investigatory fire searches, which are not programmatic but are responsive to individual events, a more particularized inquiry may be necessary." *Id.* Before a judge will authorize the issuance of an administrative warrant to conduct an investigation into the cause of a fire, he or she will want to know:

1. The "number of prior entries,"

2. The "scope of the search,"

3. The "time of day when it is proposed to be made,"

4. The "lapse of time since the fire,"

5. The "continued use of the building," and

6. The "owner's efforts to secure it against intruders[.]"

Id. While it is true that "a fire victim's privacy must normally yield to the vital social objective of ascertaining the cause of the fire, the [judge can nonetheless] perform the important function of preventing harassment by keeping that invasion to a minimum." *Id.*

As a result, a general rule arises which requires "official entries to investigate the cause of a fire [to] adhere to the warrant procedures of the Fourth Amendment." *Id.* In this regard, the United States Supreme Court agreed with the Michigan high court, ruling:

"Where the cause (of a fire) is undetermined, and *the purpose of the investigation is to determine the cause* and to prevent such fires from occurring or recurring, a . . . *search may be conducted pursuant to a warrant issued in accordance with* reasonable legislative or administrative standards or, absent their promulgation, *judicially prescribed standards;* if evidence of wrongdoing is discovered, it may, of course, be used to establish probable cause for the issuance of a criminal investigative search warrant or in prosecution. [But i]f the authorities are seeking evidence to be used in a criminal prosecution, the usual standard (of probable cause) will apply."

Id. [Citation omitted; emphasis added.]

MICHIGAN v. CLIFFORD
Supreme Court of the United States
464 U.S. 287, 104 S.Ct. 641 (1984)

QUESTION 1: In the below set of circumstances, at what point did the search undertaken by the arson investigators become unlawful under the Fourth (and Fourteenth) Amendments ?

CIRCUMSTANCES:
The Detroit Fire Department responded to an early morning blaze at the home of Raymond and Emma Jean Clifford.

POINTS:

1. Firefighters arrived on the scene at about 5:40 a.m. on October 18th.

2. The fire was extinguished and all fire officials and police left the premises at 7:04 a.m.

3. At 8:00 a.m., Lieutenant Beyer, a fire investigator with the arson section of the Detroit Fire Department, was instructed to investigate the Clifford fire, and was informed that the Fire Department suspected arson.

4. After completing his other assignments, Lt. Beyer and his partner finally arrived at the scene at approximately 1:00 p.m.

5. Upon arrival, Lt. Beyer and his partner observed a work crew on the scene boarding up the house and pumping out the water from the basement. A neighbor told the investigators that he had called Mr. Clifford who instructed him to request the Cliffords' insurance company to send a boarding crew out to secure the house. The neighbor also informed Beyer that the Cliffords would not be returning that day.

6. While waiting for the water to be removed, the investigators discovered in the driveway a Coleman fuel can which they

seized and marked as evidence. [The can had been found by the firefighters who had fought the blaze earlier that morning. The firefighters had removed the can and put it by the side door where Lt. Beyer discovered it.]

7. At 1:00 p.m., upon the completion of the water removal, Lt. Beyer and his partner entered the Clifford residence, without obtaining consent or an administrative warrant, and began their investigation into the cause of the fire.

8. Their search began in the basement and they quickly confirmed that the fire had originated there beneath the basement stairway.

9. They detected a strong odor of fuel throughout the basement and found two more Coleman fuel cans beneath the stairway.

10. As they dug through the debris, the investigators also found a crock pot with attached wires leading to an electrical timer that was plugged into an outlet a few feet away. It was set to turn on at 3:45 a.m. and to turn back off at 9:00 a.m. It had stopped somewhere between 4:00 and 4:30 a.m.

11. All of this evidence was seized and marked.

12. After determining that the fire had originated in the basement, the investigators conducted an extensive and thorough warrantless search of the remainder of the house.

13. The investigators called in a photographer to take pictures throughout the house.

14. They searched through drawers and closets and found them full of "old" clothes.

15. They inspected the rooms and noted that there were nails on the walls but no pictures.

16. They found wiring and cassettes for a video tape machine but no machine.

ANSWER: The investigators' actions became unlawful and violative of the Fourth and Fourteenth Amendments **AT POINT SEVEN**. "[The] discovery of two of the fuel cans, the crock pot, the timer and cord—as well as the investigators' related testimony—were the product of [an] unconstitutional post-fire search of the Cliffords' residence." *Id.* at 649. Additionally, in the absence of "exigent circumstances justifying the upstairs search, and [because] it was undertaken without a prior showing of probable cause before an independent judicial officer," this search was also "unreasonable under the Fourth and Fourteenth Amendments[.]" *Id.* Thus, all the evidence discovered within the home is inadmissible at trial. The Coleman fuel can discovered in plain view in the Cliffords' driveway, however, is admissible—whether seized by the firefighters while engaged in the actual fighting of the fire, or in the driveway by the arson investigators. *Id.* at 649-650.

QUESTION 2: Will privacy expectations ever vary with the type of property, the amount of fire damage, the prior and continued use of the premises, or the owner's efforts to secure it against intruders ?

ANSWER: YES. "Privacy expectations will vary with the type of property, the amount of fire damage, the prior and continued use of the premises, and in some cases the owner's efforts to secure it against intruders." *Id.* at 646.

RATIONALE: The United States Supreme Court in *Michigan v. Tyler*, 436 *U.S.* 499, 504-508, 98 *S.Ct.* 1942, 1947-1948 (1978), set forth the rule that administrative searches generally require warrants. The Court, here in *Clifford*, "reaffirms that view." *Clifford* at 646. As a matter of constitutional law, "the nonconsensual entry and search of property are governed by the warrant requirement of the Fourth and Fourteenth Amendments. The constitutionality of warrantless and nonconsensual entries onto fire-damaged premises, therefore, normally turns on several factors:

> [1] whether there are legitimate privacy interests in the fire-damaged property that are protected by the Fourth Amendment;

> [2] whether exigent circumstances justify the government intrusion regardless of any reasonable expectations of privacy; and,

> [3] whether the object of the search is to determine the cause of the fire or to gather evidence of criminal activity."

Id.

[1] *PRIVACY INTERESTS*

It should be recognized that although a particular property may have been damaged by fire, reasonable privacy expectations may still remain. "People may go on living in their homes or working in their offices after a fire. Even when that is impossible, private effects often remain in the fire-damaged premises." *Tyler* at 505, 98 *S.Ct.* at 1948.

Privacy expectations, however, can vary. "Some fires may be so devastating that no reasonable privacy interests remain in the ash and ruins, regardless of the owner's subjective expectations. The test essentially is an objective one: whether 'the expectation (is) one that society is prepared to recognize as *reasonable.*' " *Clifford* at 646 (quoting *Katz v. United States*, 389 *U.S.* 347, 361, 88 *S.Ct.* 507, 516 (1967) (Harlan, J. concurring)). [Emphasis added.] "If reasonable privacy interests remain in the fire-damaged property, the warrant requirement applies, and any official entry must be made pursuant to a warrant in the absence of consent or exigent circumstances." *Clifford* at 646.

[2] *EXIGENT CIRCUMSTANCES*

Naturally, a burning building creates the exigency (or emergency set of circumstances) that will justify "a warrantless entry by fire officials to fight the blaze." *Id.* Additionally, as the *Tyler* Court held, "once in the building, officials need no warrant to *remain* for 'a reasonable time to investigate the cause of a blaze after it has been extinguished.'" *Tyler* at 510, 98 *S.Ct.* at 1950. [Emphasis added.] Significantly, however, firefighters, during the course of fighting a fire, do not normally "remain" within the involved building. Circumstances vary and many times the actual entry may be put off—as being too dangerous—until the fire has been completely extinguished, and even then the imminent danger of falling ceilings and collapsing walls may exist. "Thus, the effort to ascertain the cause of a fire may extend over a period of time with entry and reentry. The critical inquiry is whether reasonable expectations of privacy exist in the fire-damaged premises at a particular time, and if so, whether exigencies justify the reentries." *Clifford* at 646 n.3. Where such reasonable expectations of privacy do remain, however, "in the fire-damaged property, additional investigations begun after the fire has been extinguished and fire and police officials have left the scene, generally must be made pursuant to a warrant or the identification of some new exigency." *Id.* at 647.

"The aftermath of a fire often presents exigencies that will not tolerate the delay necessary to obtain a warrant or to secure the owner's consent to inspect the fire-damaged premises. For example, an immediate threat that the blaze might rekindle presents an exigency that would justify a warrantless and nonconsensual post-fire investigation. 'Immediate investigation may also be necessary to preserve evidence from intentional or accidental destruction.'" *Id.* at 647, 647 n.4. [Citation omitted.]

In these cases, the warrant requirement does not apply "[b]ecause determining the cause and origin of a fire serves a compelling public interest." *Id.* at 647.

[3] *THE OBJECT OF THE SEARCH*

[*See generally*, Introduction to §7.1 for an extended explanation of the "Object of the Search" inquiry for determining whether an administrative or criminal search warrant should be obtained.]

Note, however, that "[t]he object of the search is important even if exigent circumstances exist. Circumstances that justify a warrantless search for the cause of a fire may not justify a search to gather evidence of criminal activity once that cause has been determined." *Id.* at 647. For example, when "the administrative search is justified by the immediate need to ensure against rekindling, the scope of the search may be no broader than reasonably necessary to achieve its end." *Id.* As a result, a fire official may not "search to gather evidence of criminal activity [which is] not in plain view [without] a criminal warrant upon a traditional showing of probable cause." *Id.*

In the present case, the searches conducted at the home of the Cliffords can be broken down into two separate intrusions: (1) the delayed search of the basement area, and (2) the extensive search of the residential portion of the house. While it is true that the Clifford home was uninhabitable when Lt. Beyer and his partner arrived, the home nonetheless contained the Cliffords' personal belongings, and, they had arranged to have the house secured against intrusion in their absence. "Under these circumstances, and in light of the strong expectations of privacy associated with a home," the Court holds "that the Cliffords retained *reasonable privacy interests* in their fire-damaged residence and that the post-fire investigations were subject to the warrant requirement. Thus, the warrantless and nonconsensual searches of both the basement and the upstairs of the house would have been valid only if exigent circumstances had justified the object and scope of each." *Id.* at 648. [Emphasis added.] Exigent circumstances, in this case, were absent.

VARYING PRIVACY EXPECTATIONS

The *Clifford* Court distinguishes the *Clifford* set of circumstances from those found in *Tyler* (*see* §2.6(b), *infra*). In *Tyler*, the Court upheld a warrantless post-fire search of a furniture store, even with the absence of exigent circumstances, "on the ground that it was a continuation of a valid search begun immediately after the fire." *Clifford* at 648. The *Tyler* investigation began as the final part of the fire was being extinguished, but could not be completed or continued due to the darkness, smoke and heat. There, "the search was resumed promptly after the smoke cleared and daylight dawned. Because the post-fire search was interrupted for reasons that were evident, [the *Tyler* Court] held that the early morning search was 'no more than an actual continuation of the first, and that the lack of a warrant thus did not invalidate the resulting seizure of evidence.'" *Clifford* at 648. [Citation omitted.]

In the *Clifford* set of circumstances, "the challenged search was not a continuation of an earlier search." *Id.*

Between the time the firefighters had extinguished the blaze and left the scene and the arson investigators first arrived about 1 p.m. to begin their investigation, the Cliffords had taken steps to secure the privacy interests that remained in their residence against further intrusion.

Id. According to the Court, "[t]hese efforts separate the entry made to extinguish the blaze from that made later by different officers to investigate its origin." *Id.* Moreover, *"the privacy interests in the residence—particularly after the Cliffords had acted—were significantly greater than those in the fire-damaged [Tyler] furniture store,* making the delay between the fire and the midday search unreasonable absent a warrant, consent, or exigent circumstances." *Id.* [Emphasis added.] Here, the Court emphasizes that *"privacy interests are especially strong in a private residence." Id.* [Emphasis added.]

The Court also notes that "[r]easonable expectations of privacy in fire-damaged premises will vary depending particularly on the type and use of the building involved. Expectations of privacy[, while] particularly strong in private residences and offices[,]" may nonetheless be diminished "in commercial premises." *Id.* at 648 n.7. As a result, "[t]hese facts—the interim efforts to secure the burned-out premises and the heightened privacy interests in the home—distinguish [the *Clifford*] case from *Tyler*." *Clifford* at 648.

Accordingly, the Court rules that "[a]t least where the homeowner has made a reasonable effort to secure his fire-damaged home after the blaze has been extinguished and the fire and police units have left the scene, * * * a subsequent post-fire search must be conducted pursuant to a warrant, consent, or the identification of some new exigency. So long as the primary purpose is to ascertain the cause of the fire, an administrative warrant will suffice." *Id.* at 648-649. Here in *Clifford*, "[b]ecause the cause of the fire was then known, the search of the upper portion of the house * * * could only have been a search to gather evidence of the crime of arson. Absent exigent circumstances, such a search requires a criminal warrant." *Id.* at 649.

---

§7.2. Warrantless entries at the scene of a fire.

INTRODUCTION

Court decisions have generally recognized that warrantless entries into dwellings, business establishments, or other structures by criminal law enforcement officers "may be legal when there is compelling need for official action and no time to secure a warrant." *Michigan v. Tyler*, 436 *U.S.* 499, 509, 98 *S.Ct.* 1942, 1949 (1978). One example often cited is *Warden v. Hayden*, 387 *U.S.* 294, 87 *S.Ct.* 1642 (1967), where the United States Supreme Court upheld the warrantless entry of a home by police officers who were in "hot pursuit" of an armed robbery suspect. Another example is *Ker v. California*, 374 *U.S.* 23, 83 *S.Ct.* 1623 (1963), where the Court upheld a warrantless and unannounced entry by police to prevent the imminent destruction of evidence.

In the regulatory field, court decisions have recognized the importance of "prompt inspections, even without a warrant . . . in emergency situations." *Camara v. Municipal Court*, 387 *U.S.* 523, 539, 87 *S.Ct.* 1727, 1736 (1967). Naturally, a burning building presents such an emergency. As Justice Stewart explained:

> A burning building clearly presents an exigency of sufficient proportions to render a warrantless entry "reasonable." Indeed, it would defy reason to suppose that firemen must secure a warrant or consent before entering a burning structure to put out the blaze.

Tyler at 509, 98 *S.Ct.* at 1950. If a firefighter—once inside the building and during the course of fighting the blaze—discovers evidence of arson that is in "plain view," he may lawfully seize that evidence. Accordingly, "an entry to fight a fire requires no warrant," and, once inside the building, if evidence of arson is discovered, it is seizable and "admissible at trial[.]" *Id.* at 512, 98 *S.Ct.* at 1951. If, however, investigating fire officials during this time period "find probable cause to believe that arson has occurred and require further access to gather evidence for a possible prosecution, they [must] obtain a warrant * * * upon a traditional showing of probable cause applicable to searches for evidence of crime." *Id.* at 511, 98 *S.Ct.* at 1951.

These decisions indicate that fire officials do not need a "warrant to remain in a building *for a reasonable amount of time* to investigate the cause of a blaze after it has been extinguished." *Id.* [Emphasis added.] Reasonableness determinations are made by reference to the Fourth Amendment which requires that:

> The right of the people to be secure in their persons, houses, papers, and effects, against *unreasonable* searches and seizures, shall not be violated, and no Warrants shall issue, but upon probable cause, supported by Oath or affirmation, and particularly describing the place to be searched, and the persons or things to be seized. [Emphasis added.]

The hallmark of the Fourth Amendment is the protection of "the privacy and security of individuals against arbitrary invasions by governmental officials." *Camara* at 528, 87 *S.Ct.* at 1730, and naturally, these government officials may be health officials, firefighters, arson investigators, building inspectors, and so forth.

Problems do arise, however, when a determination must be made as to what constitutes a "reasonable time" to investigate. Courts will generally address this issue by giving appropriate recognition "to the exigencies that confront officials serving under these conditions, as well as to individuals' reasonable expectations of privacy." *Tyler* at 510 n.6, 98 *S.Ct.* at 1950 n.6.

MICHIGAN v. TYLER
Supreme Court of the United States
436 *U.S.* 499, 98 *S.Ct.* 1942 (1978)

QUESTION 1: In the following set of circumstances, were the Fire Chief's re-entries of the fire scene and seizure of the two plastic containers of flammable liquid, pieces of carpet, and sections of the taped stairway reasonable within the meaning of the Fourth (and Fourteenth) Amendments ?

CIRCUMSTANCES: The fire department responded to a fire which broke out shortly before midnight at Tyler's Auction, a furniture store in Oakland County, Michigan. At about 2:00 a.m., when the firefighters were watering down the smoldering embers, Fire Chief See arrived on the scene. His responsibility was to determine the cause of the fire and to make out the reports. Upon Chief See's arrival, he was informed that two plastic containers of flammable liquid had been found in the building. Thereafter, Chief See, using a portable light, entered the building to examine the containers. Suspecting arson, Chief See called Police Detective Webb, who arrived at approximately 3:30 a.m. Webb took several photos of the containers and of the interior of the store, but had to abandon his efforts due to the darkness, smoke and steam. By 4:00 a.m., the fire had been extinguished, the firefighters departed, and Chief See seized the two containers which he turned over to Detective Webb for safekeeping. The officials had neither consent nor a warrant for the entries into the building, nor for the removal of the containers.

Four hours later, Chief See returned with Assistant Chief Somerville, whose job was to determine the "origin of all fires that occur within the township." A cursory examination was made of the interior of the building and they then departed. At 9:00 a.m., Somerville returned with Detective Webb. With the light of day and the absence of the smoke, steam and heat, the officials discovered suspicious burn marks in the carpet, and pieces of tape with burn marks, on the stairway. They removed portions of the carpet and sections of the stairs to be retained as evidence suggestive of a "fuse trail." Again, there was neither consent nor a warrant for these entries and seizures.

ANSWER: YES. "[A]n entry to fight a fire requires no warrant, and once in the building, officials may remain there for a reasonable time to investigate the cause of the blaze." *Id.* at 1951. The early morning entries conducted by Chief See and/or his assistants "were no more than an actual continuation of the first, and the lack of a warrant thus did not invalidate the resulting seizure of evidence." *Id.*

RATIONALE: "Fire officials are charged not only with extinguishing fires, but with finding their causes. Prompt determination of the fire's origin may be necessary to prevent its recurrence, as through the detection of continuing dangers such as faulty wiring or a defective furnace." *Id.* at 1950. Moreover, a prompt or "[i]mmediate investigation may also be necessary to preserve evidence from intentional or

535

accidental destruction. And, of course, the sooner the officials complete their duties, the less will be their subsequent interference with the privacy and recovery efforts of the victims." *Id.*

As a result, fire officials do not need a warrant "to remain in a building for *a reasonable amount of time* to investigate the cause of a blaze after it has been extinguished. And if the warrantless entry to put out the fire and determine its cause is constitutional, the warrantless seizure of evidence while inspecting the premises for these purposes also is constitutional." *Id.* [Emphasis added.]

In this set of circumstances, Chief See and his assistants began their investigation as the fire was being extinguished, "but visibility was severely hampered by darkness, steam, and smoke. Thus, they departed at 4 a.m. and returned shortly after daylight to continue their investigation." *Id.* at 1951. As the Court points out, "[l]ittle purpose would have been served by their remaining in the building, except to remove any doubt about the legality of the warrantless search and seizure later that morning." *Id.*

Accordingly, under the circumstances of this case, the morning entries which occurred at approximately 8:00 a.m. and 9:00 a.m. "were no more than an actual continuation of the first, and the lack of a warrant thus did not invalidate the resulting seizure" of either the two plastic containers of flammable liquid or the portions of carpet or taped sections of stairway. *Id.*

QUESTION 2: Does the following continuation of the earlier set of circumstances also display a "continuation of the first entry" described above ?

CIRCUMSTANCES CONTINUED: Twenty five days later, Sergeant Hoffman of the Michigan State Police Arson Section returned to the Tyler's furniture store to take photographs. While inside the store, he supervised the inspection of circuit breakers, the furnace, and the remains of several television sets found in the ashes. Hoffman also found a piece of fuse. The evidence collected by Hoffman, and the opinions he formed, played a substantial role at trial in establishing arson as the cause of the fire. Hoffman's entries were without consent or warrant.

ANSWER: NO.   These entries "were clearly detached from the initial exigency and warrantless entry. Since * * * these searches were conducted without valid warrants and without consent, they were invalid under the Fourth and Fourteenth Amendments, and any evidence obtained as a result of those entries must, therefore, be excluded at the [defendant's] retrial." *Id.* at 1951.

CHAPTER 8

INVESTIGATIVE DETENTIONS; STOP AND FRISK

§8.1. Introduction.

Courts have consistently distinguished investigatory "stops" from arrests, and "frisks" of outer clothing for weapons from full searches for evidence of a crime. "An arrest is a wholly different kind of intrusion upon individual freedom from a [temporary stop and] limited search for weapons, and the interests each is designed to serve are likewise quite different. An arrest is the initial stage of a criminal prosecution. It is intended to vindicate society's interest in having its laws obeyed, and it is inevitably accompanied by future interference with the individual's freedom of movement, whether or not trial or conviction ultimately follows. The [temporary stop and] protective search for weapons, on the other hand, constitutes a brief, though far from inconsiderable, intrusion upon the sanctity of the person." *Terry v. Ohio*, 392 *U.S.* 1, 26, 88 *S.Ct.* 1868, 1882 (1968).

Notwithstanding the Supreme Court's separate and independent treatment of the investigative "stop and frisk," many texts have nonetheless treated this particular law enforcement procedure as an exception to the written warrant requirement. The topic, however, realistically necessitates independent and distinct treatment. Investigative detentions, or temporary stops for interview, maintain a substantially unique and vitally important position in law enforcement activity, and, therefore, the topic shall occupy a chapter in and of itself. Additionally, the "frisk," which so often follows such stops, has also been placed with the investigative detention material to round out the presentation. The frisk is also "essential to the officer's investigative duties, for without it, the answer to the police officer['s inquiries] may be a bullet[.]" *Terry* at 8, 88 *S.Ct.* at 1873.

The Fourth Amendment governs the area of investigative detentions and frisks. It is here that it may be noted that the Amendment does not forbid all government searches and seizures; only unreasonable ones. *Id.* at 9, 88 *S.Ct.* at 1873. Therefore, the relevant inquiry of this chapter will be whether, in the totality of the circumstances surrounding these types of police-citizen encounters, the citizen's right to personal security and liberty was violated by unreasonable official action.

In *Terry*, the United States Supreme Court addressed the circumstances in which a law enforcement officer may stop and question a suspect, without his consent, in the absence of probable cause for arrest. The analysis required the balancing of significant governmental interests. On one side of the scale rests the societal interest in prohibiting unreasonable and unjustified governmental intrusions upon private citizens; on the other, the law enforcement interest not only in the prompt and efficient investigation of crime but "the more immediate interest of the police officer in taking steps to assure himself that the person with whom he is dealing is not armed with a weapon that could unexpectedly and fatally be used against him." 392 *U.S.* at 23, 88 *S.Ct.* at 1881.

Thus, we have the *Terry* rule:

> [W]here a police officer observes unusual conduct which leads him reasonably to conclude in light of his experience that criminal activity may be afoot and that the persons with whom he is dealing may be armed and presently dangerous, where in the course of investigating this behavior he identifies himself as a police [officer] and makes reasonable inquiries, and where nothing in the initial stages of the encounter serves to dispel his reasonable fear for his own or others' safety, he is entitled for the protection of himself and others in the area to conduct a carefully limited search of the outer clothing of such persons in an attempt to discover weapons which might be used to assault him.

Id. at 30-31, 88 *S.Ct.* 1884-1885.

This rule has three distinct components. The first component concerns the level of "reasonable suspicion" that must exist before an "investigatory stop" may be conducted. This standard involves a level of belief which is something less than the probable cause standard needed to support an arrest. *See* §1.1, Figure 1.1. To justify such an intrusion, a law enforcement officer *"must be able to point to specific and articulable facts which, taken together with rational inferences from those facts," collectively provide " 'a particularized and objective basis' for suspecting the person stopped of criminal activity." Terry* at 21, 88 *S.Ct.* at 1880; *Ornelas v. United States*, 517 *U.S.* 690, 116 *S.Ct.* 1657, 1661 (1996) (quoting *United States v. Cortez*, 499 *U.S.* 411, 417-18, 101 *S.Ct.* 690, 694-95 (1981)). [Emphasis added.] *See also United States v. Arvizu*, 534 *U.S.* 266, 122 *S.Ct.* 744 (2002) ("the Fourth Amendment is satisfied if the officer's action is supported by reasonable suspicion to believe that criminal activity 'may be afoot' ").

The question whether an officer had a reasonable suspicion to support a particular investigative detention will be addressed by the courts by reference to an "objective" standard: Would the facts available to the officer at the moment of the stop or frisk warrant an officer "of reasonable caution in the belief that the action taken was appropriate." *Terry* at 22, 88 *S.Ct.* at 1880. To determine if the standard has been met in a particular case, a court will give due weight, not to an officer's "unparticularized" suspicions or hunches, but to the "specific reasonable inferences" which the officer is entitled to draw from the facts in light of his or her experience. *Id.* at 27, 88 *S.Ct.* at 1883. *See also Ornelas, supra,* 116 *S.Ct.* at 1663 (due deference should be given to the inferences drawn by an officer who necessarily "views the facts through the lens of his police experience and expertise").

Thus, more is required than mere generalizations and subjective impressions. The officer must be able to articulate specific facts gleaned from the "totality of the circumstances"—the whole picture— from which he or she reasonably inferred that the person confronted was involved in criminal activity.

In *United States v. Arvizu,* 534 *U.S.* 266, 122 *S.Ct.* 744 (2002), the Court further explained that the "totality of the circumstances" approach for determining whether a detaining officer has a "particularized and objective basis" for suspecting legal wrongdoing "allows officers to draw on their own experience and specialized training to make inferences from and deductions about the cumulative information available to them that 'might well elude an untrained person.'" *Id.,* 122 *S.Ct.* at 750-51. [Citation omitted.] In this analysis, the officer is not required to rule out "the possibility of innocent conduct." *Id.* at 753. Many times, facts and circumstances susceptible to innocent explanation when considered in isolation will, when viewed together, as a whole, suffice to form a reasonable and articulable suspicion of criminal activity. In this respect, the *Arvizu* Court said:

> Although an officer's reliance on a mere "hunch" is insufficient to justify a stop, * * * the likelihood of criminal activity need not rise to the level required for probable cause, and it falls considerably short of satisfying a preponderance of the evidence standard[.]

> Our cases have recognized that the concept of reasonable suspicion is somewhat abstract. * * * But we have deliberately avoided reducing it to "a neat set of legal rules[.]" * * *

> We think that the approach taken by the [lower court in this case was incorrect]. The court's evaluation [of the facts] in isolation from each other does not take into account the "totality of the circumstances," as our cases have understood that phrase. The court appeared to believe that each observation by [the police officer] that was by itself readily susceptible to an innocent explanation was entitled to "no weight." * * * *Terry,* however, precludes this sort of divide-and-conquer analysis. * * *

Id. at 751.

The second component of the *Terry* rule involves an inquiry separate from whether the initial stop and detention was permissible. This component questions whether there was sufficient cause for an officer to conduct a protective "frisk" of the person being detained. It permits an officer to protect himself and others by conducting a limited search for weapons where he has reason to believe that he is dealing with an armed and dangerous individual, regardless of whether he has probable cause to arrest the individual for a crime. The officer need not be absolutely certain that the individual is armed. The issue is whether a reasonably prudent [officer] in the circumstances would be warranted in the belief that his safety or that of others was in danger.

Id. at 27, 88 *S.Ct.* at 1883.

The third component concerns the permissible scope of the protective frisk. Once a sufficient basis has been established for the investigatory detention and the limited pat-down frisk, the final inquiry is whether the search was narrowly restricted to the purposes such an intrusion is supposed to serve. Because "[t]he sole justification of the search * * * is the protection of the police officer and others nearby * * * it must * * * be confined in scope to an intrusion reasonably designed to discover guns, knives, clubs, or other hidden instruments for the assault of the police officer." *Id.* at 29, 88 *S.Ct.* at 1884. As the Supreme Court explained in *Adams v. Williams*, 407 *U.S.* 143, 146, 92 *S.Ct.* 1921, 1923 (1972):

> The purpose of this limited search is not to discover evidence of crime, but to allow the officer to pursue his investigation without fear of violence.

Accordingly, investigative stops or detentions may only be conducted when an officer has an objective reasonable suspicion that criminal activity may be afoot. The protective frisk of a suspect's outer clothing may be conducted only when the officer is in possession of additional specific and articulable facts from which he can reasonably infer that the individual he is confronting is armed and presently dangerous. Moreover, the frisk must be strictly limited in scope; designed solely to uncover hidden weapons. The facts must be objectively realistic and not be grounded in speculation, subjective feelings or intuition. To allow "[a]nything less would invite intrusions upon constitutionally guaranteed rights based on nothing more substantial than inarticulate hunches, a result which [courts will not allow]." *Terry* at 22, 88 *S.Ct.* at 1880.

---

§8.2. Investigative detentions of persons.

§8.2(a). The point at which a "seizure" occurs.

Whenever a law enforcement officer significantly interferes with the life, liberty, or property of a citizen, that interference registers on the constitutional scale as a seizure. The seizure will be lawful only when it is supported by a justification sufficient to balance the constitutional scale. For example, if the interference with a citizen's liberty is an "investigative detention," that detention registers on the constitutional scale as a "seizure," albeit a minimally intrusive one. Such a seizure will be lawful when counterbalanced with the constitutional justification of a "reasonable articulable suspicion." If the police-citizen encounter becomes more intrusive than an investigative detention, a higher level of constitutional justification is required. Thus, if the significant interference with a citizen's liberty is an "arrest," the encounter similarly registers on the constitutional scale as a "seizure," but this seizure will be lawful only when counterbalanced with the constitutional justification of "probable cause."

There are some police-citizen encounters which do not require any level of constitutional justification because the interaction does not involve a "significant interference" with an individual's life, liberty, or property. "[L]aw enforcement officers do not violate the Fourth Amendment by merely approaching an individual on the street or in another public place, by asking him if he is willing to answer some questions, by putting questions to him if the person is willing to listen, or by offering in evidence in a criminal prosecution his voluntary answers to such questions." *Florida v. Royer*, 460 *U.S.* 491, 497, 103 *S.Ct.* 1319, 1324 (1983). "Even when law enforcement officers have no basis for suspecting a particular individual, they may pose questions, ask for identification, and request consent to search luggage provided they do not induce cooperation by coercive means. * * * If a reasonable person would feel free to terminate the encounter, then he or she has not been seized." *United States v. Drayton*, 536 *U.S.* 194, 122 *S.Ct.* 2105, 2110 (2002). These consensual encounters, called "mere inquiries" or "field inquiries," require no constitutional justification because the interaction does not register on the constitutional scale; the encounter is not a "seizure" within the meaning of the Fourth Amendment.

In the setting of a "mere inquiry," the person is free to ignore the officer and walk away. If the person chooses not to cooperate, the officer must allow him or her to leave. The person "may not be detained even momentarily without reasonable, objective grounds for doing so; and his [or her] refusal to listen or answer does not, without more, furnish those grounds. [Thus,] if there is no detention—no seizure within the meaning of the Fourth Amendment—then no constitutional rights have been infringed." *Royer* at 498, 103 *S.Ct.* at 1324. *See also Illinois v. Wardlow*, 528 *U.S.* 119, 125, 120 *S.Ct.* 673, 676 (2000) (Since a mere field inquiry may be conducted without reasonable suspicion, the individual approached "has a right to ignore the police and go about his business.").

"Nor would the fact that the officer identifies himself as a police officer, without more, convert the encounter into a seizure requiring some level of objective justification." *Royer* at 497, 103 *S.Ct.* at 1324. *See also United States v. Drayton, supra*, 122 *S.Ct.* at 2112 (the action of a "plain clothes" officer showing a person his or her badge does not convert a mere inquiry into a seizure). Similarly, a simple police request for identification, *without more*, should not convert a mere inquiry into a seizure.

The determination whether a police-citizen encounter has elevated to one requiring a constitutional justification is measured from the "citizen's perspective." A police officer's belief that the citizen was "free to leave" is not probative. Rather, the correct inquiry is whether the citizen, under all of the attendant circumstances, reasonably believed he could walk away without answering any of the officer's questions. Therefore, officers who wish to maintain a police-citizen encounter as a mere inquiry would be well advised to (1) pose their questions in a conversational manner; (2) avoid making demands or issuing orders; and (3) ensure that the questions they ask are not overbearing or harassing in nature.

Once it is determined that a police-citizen encounter has constitutional implications, that is, it has advanced beyond the point of a "mere inquiry" and now registers on the constitutional scale as a seizure, courts will examine the totality of the circumstances to determine whether this seizure was justified by the required level of constitutional justification.

MICHIGAN v. CHESTERNUT
Supreme Court of the United States
486 U.S. 567, 108 S.Ct. 1975 (1988)

QUESTION: Will any "investigative pursuit" of a person undertaken by the police necessarily constitute a "seizure" within the meaning of the Fourth Amendment?

ANSWER: NO. A person is "seized" within the meaning of the Fourth Amendment " 'only if, in view of all the circumstances surrounding the incident, a reasonable person would have believed that he was not free to leave.' " *Id.* at 1979. [Citation omitted.] Under this standard, "the police conduct in this case did not amount to a seizure, for it would not have communicated to a reasonable person that he was not at liberty to ignore the police presence and go about his business." *Id.* at 1977.

RATIONALE: In the early afternoon, four Detroit police officers were engaged in uniformed patrol in a marked police cruiser in metropolitan Detroit. Upon reaching an intersection, one of the officers observed a car pull over to the curb, a man exit and walk over to defendant Chesternut, who was standing alone on the corner. When defendant saw the police car approaching, he turned and began to run. According to one officer's testimony, the patrol car followed defendant around the corner "to see where he was going." *Id.* at 1977. "The cruiser quickly caught up with [defendant] and drove alongside him for a short distance. As they drove beside him, the officers observed [him] discard a number of packets he pulled from his right-hand pocket." One of the officers retrieved the packets, discovered that they contained narcotics, and, catching up with defendant (who had run only a few paces farther), placed him under arrest. A search conducted at the stationhouse revealed another packet of pills in defendant's hatband, along with a package of heroin and a hypodermic needle.

At defendant's preliminary hearing, the magistrate dismissed all charges, finding that defendant had been unlawfully seized during the police pursuit preceding his disposal of the packets. The magistrate ruled that a police "chase," like the one herein involved, "implicated Fourth Amendment protections and could not be justified by the mere fact that the suspect ran at the sight of the police." *Id.* at 1978.

The United States Supreme Court disagreed. Preliminarily, the Court noted that "any assessment as to whether police conduct amounts to a seizure implicating the Fourth Amendment must take into account 'all the circumstances surrounding the incident' in each individual case." *Id.* at 1979. [Citations omitted.]

The Court in *Terry v. Ohio*, 392 *U.S.* 1, 88 *S.Ct.* 1868 (1968), specifically noted:

> Obviously, not all personal intercourse between policemen and citizens involves "seizures" of persons. Only when the officer, by means of physical force or show of authority, has in some way restrained the liberty of a citizen may we conclude that a "seizure" has occurred.

Id. at 19 n.16, 88 *S.Ct.* at 1879 n.16. Later, in *United States v. Mendenhall*, 446 *U.S.* 544, 100 *S.Ct.* 1870 (1980), this analysis was transposed into a test to be applied in determining whether a "person has been 'seized' within the meaning of the Fourth Amendment." *Id.* at 554, 100 *S.Ct.* at 1877. "This test provides that *the police can be said to have seized an individual 'only if, in view of all of the circumstances surrounding the incident, a reasonable person would have believed that he was not free to leave.'"* *Chesternut* at 1979 (quoting *Mendenhall* at 554, 100 *S.Ct.* at 1877). [Emphasis added.]

The Court does recognize, however, that this "test is necessarily imprecise, because it is designed to assess the coercive effect of police conduct, taken as a whole, rather than to focus on particular details of that conduct in isolation. Moreover, what constitutes a restraint on liberty prompting a person to conclude that he is not free to 'leave' will vary, not only with the particular police conduct at issue, but also with the setting in which the conduct occurs." *Chesternut* at 1979.

Nonetheless, "the test is flexible enough to be applied to the whole range of police conduct in an equally broad range of settings, [and must be consistently applied] from one police encounter to the next, regardless of the particular individual's response to the actions of the police. The test's objective standard—looking to the reasonable man's interpretation of the conduct in question—allows the police to determine in advance whether the conduct contemplated will implicate the Fourth Amendment." *Id.* at 1979-1980. Additionally, "[t]his 'reasonable person' standard also ensures that the scope of the Fourth Amendment protection does not vary with the state of mind of the particular individual being approached." *Id.*

Applying this test to the facts of this case, the Court concludes that defendant "was not seized by the police before he discarded the packets containing the controlled substance." *Id.* at 1980. Although the magistrate who originally dismissed the complaint characterized the police conduct as a "chase," that "characterization is not enough, standing alone, to implicate Fourth Amendment protections. Contrary to [defendant's] assertion that a chase necessarily communicates that detention is intended and imminent, * * * the police conduct involved here would not have communicated to the reasonable person an attempt to capture or otherwise intrude upon [defendant's] freedom of movement." *Id.* As one of the officers testified, "the goal of the 'chase' was not to capture [defendant], but 'to see where he was going.' "* *Id.* "The record does not reflect that the police activated a siren or flashers; or that they commanded [defendant] to halt, or displayed any weapons; or that they operated the car in an aggressive manner to block [defendant's] course or otherwise control the direction or speed of his movement." *Id.*

"While the very presence of a police car driving parallel to a running pedestrian could be somewhat intimidating, this kind of police presence does not, standing alone, constitute a seizure. * * * Without more, the police conduct here—a brief acceleration to catch up with [defendant], followed by a short drive alongside him—was not 'so intimidating' that [defendant] could reasonably have believed that he was not free to disregard the police presence and go about his business. * * * The police therefore were not required to have 'a particularized and objective basis for suspecting [defendant] of criminal activity,' in order to pursue him." *Id.* at 1980-1981. [Citations omitted.]

Accordingly, because defendant "was not unlawfully seized during the initial police pursuit," the Court concludes that the "charges against him were improperly dismissed." *Id.* at 1981.

CALIFORNIA v. HODARI D.
Supreme Court of the United States
499 *U.S.* 621, 111 *S.Ct.* 1547 (1991)

QUESTION: At what point in the below set of circumstances was Hodari "seized" within the meaning of the Fourth Amendment ?

CIRCUMSTANCES:

1. Officers McColgin and Pertoso were patrolling a high-crime area in Oakland, California, in an unmarked car. The officers were dressed in street clothes but were wearing jackets with "Police" embossed on both front and back.

2. As they turned onto 63rd Avenue, "they saw four or five youths huddled around a small red car parked at the curb."

3. When the youths saw the officers' car approaching, they panicked and took flight.

---

* "Of course, the subjective intent of officers is relevant to an assessment of the Fourth Amendment implications of police conduct only to the extent that the intent has been conveyed to the person confronted." *Chesternut* at 1980 n.7.

4. Hodari and a second youth ran west through an alley; the others fled south. The red car also headed south, at a high rate of speed.

5. The officers gave chase. McColgin remained in the car and continued south on 63rd Avenue; Pertoso left the car and pursued Hodari. Hodari circled the block in one direction and ultimately emerged on 62nd Avenue running north. Officer Pertoso circled in the other direction and emerged on 62nd Avenue running south.

6. Looking behind him as he ran, Hodari did not turn and see Pertoso until the officer was almost upon him, whereupon he tossed away what appeared to be a small rock.

7. A moment later, Pertoso tackled Hodari.

8. Pertoso then handcuffed Hodari and radioed for assistance. Hodari was found to be carrying $130 in cash and a pager; the rock he had discarded was later determined to be crack cocaine.

ANSWER: AT POINT 7. Assuming that Officer Pertoso's pursuit constituted a "show of authority" directing Hodari to halt, since Hodari did not comply with that direction, "he was not seized until he was tackled." *Id.* at 1552. Therefore, "[t]he cocaine abandoned while he was running was * * * not [a poisonous] fruit of [an unlawful] seizure." *Id.* The term "seizure" in this respect, "does not remotely apply [] to the prospect of a police [officer] yelling 'Stop, in the name of the law!' at a fleeing form that continues to flee. That is no seizure." *Id.* at 1550. *A seizure does not occur when the subject "does not yield." Id.* [Emphasis added.]

RATIONALE: The critical issue in this case "is whether, at the time he dropped the drugs, Hodari had been 'seized' within the meaning of the Fourth Amendment." *Id.* at 1549. If so, Hodari argued that the drugs were the fruit of that illegal seizure[a] and the evidence concerning them could not be used against him. "If not, the drugs were abandoned by Hodari and lawfully recovered[b] by the police[.]" *Id.*

The Fourth Amendment's protection against "unreasonable seizures" includes "seizure of the person." *Id.* "Seizure" has always meant a "taking possession," and "for most purposes at common law," the

---

[a] In the lower courts, the prosecution conceded that Officer Pertoso did not possess the required reasonable and articulable suspicion to perform an investigative detention under *Terry v. Ohio*. For purposes of its decision, the Court did not decide that point but merely relied on the prosecution's concession. Nonetheless, Justice Scalia, speaking for the seven-member majority, noted: "That it would be unreasonable to stop, for brief inquiry, young men who scatter in panic upon the mere sighting of the police is not self-evident, and arguably contradicts proverbial common sense. *See* Proverbs 28:1 ('The wicked flee when no man pursueth')." *Id.* at 1549 n.1.

[b] Here, the Court points out that Pertoso's observation of the rock of cocaine, "at least if he recognized it as such," would have provided him with a "reasonable suspicion for the unquestioned seizure that occurred when he tackled Hodari." *Id.* at 1549.

word included "not merely grasping, or applying physical force to, the animate or inanimate object in question, but *actually bringing it within physical control." Id.* at 1549-50. [Citations omitted; emphasis added.] "To constitute an arrest, however—the quintessential 'seizure of the person' under [the] Fourth Amendment[]—the mere grasping or application of physical force with lawful authority, whether or not it succeeded in subduing the arrestee, was sufficient." *Id.*

Hodari urged that Officer Pertoso's "uncomplied-with show of authority was a common-law arrest," and asserted the proposition that "all common-law arrests are seizures." *Id.* at 1551. *The Court, however, could not agree.*

"To say that an arrest is effected by the slightest application of physical force, despite the arrestee's escape, is not to say that for Fourth Amendment purposes there is a *continuing* arrest during the period of [flight]. If, for example, Pertoso had laid his hands upon Hodari to arrest him, but Hodari had broken away and had *then* cast away the cocaine, it would hardly be realistic to say that the disclosure had been made during the course of an arrest. * * * The present case, however, is even one step further removed. It does not involve the application of any physical force; Hodari was untouched by Officer Pertoso at the time he discarded the cocaine." *Id.* at 1550. [Emphasis in original.]

According to the Court, "an arrest requires *either* physical force * * * *or*, where that is absent, *submission* to the assertion of authority." *Id.* at 1551. [Emphasis in original.]

> "Mere words will not constitute an arrest, while, on the other hand, no actual, physical touching is essential. The apparent inconsistency in the two parts of this statement is explained by the fact that an assertion of authority and purpose to arrest followed by submission of the arrestee constitutes an arrest. *There can be no arrest without either touching or submission."* * * *
>
> We do not think it desirable, even as a policy matter, to stretch the Fourth Amendment beyond its words and beyond the meaning of arrest, as [Hodari] urges.

Id. (quoting Perkins, *The Law of Arrest,* 25 Iowa L.Rev. 201, 206 (1940)). [Emphasis added.]

Hodari further argued that "a seizure occurs 'when [an] officer, by means of physical force *or show of authority,* has in some way restrained the liberty of a citizen.' " *Id.* [Court's emphasis; citation omitted.] The Court accepted (for purposes of this decision) that "Officer Pertoso's pursuit qualified as a 'show of authority' calling upon Hodari to halt[,]" *id.,* but held that "with respect to a show of authority as with respect to application of physical force," *a seizure does not occur when the subject "does not yield." Id.* [Emphasis added.]

"The word 'seizure' readily bears the meaning of a laying on of hands or application of physical force to restrain movement, even when it is ultimately unsuccessful. * * * It does not remotely apply, however, to the prospect of a police [officer] yelling "Stop, in the name of the law!" at a fleeing form that continues to flee. That is no seizure."

Id. Moreover, for constitutional purposes, an *attempted* seizure is not a seizure. *Id.* at 1550 & n.2.

Finally, Hodari contended that the test set forth in *United States v. Mendenhall*, 446 *U.S.* 544, 100 *S.Ct.* 1870 (1980), and reaffirmed in *Michigan v. Chesternut*, 486 *U.S.* 567, 108 *S.Ct.* 1975 (1988), supports his position. Under the *Mendenhall* test: " 'A person has been "seized" within the meaning of the Fourth Amendment *only if*, in view of all the circumstances surrounding the incident, a reasonable person would have believed that he was not free to leave.' " *Hodari* at 1551 (quoting *Mendenhall* at 554, 100 *S.Ct.* at 1877). [Emphasis added.] According to the Court, Hodari fails to read this formulation carefully. "It says that a person has been seized 'only if,' not that he has been seized 'whenever'; it states a *necessary*, but not a *sufficient* condition for seizure—or, more precisely, for seizure effected through a 'show of authority.' *Mendenhall* establishes that the test for existence of a 'show of authority' is an objective one: not whether the citizen perceived that he was being ordered to restrict his movement, but whether the officer's words and actions would have conveyed that to a reasonable person." *Hodari* at 1551. [Emphasis in original.] Application of this objective test formed the basis of the Court's decision in *Chesternut, supra*, where it concluded that the patrol car's slow following of the defendant did not convey the message that he was not free to disregard the police and go about his business. *Chesternut* did not decide, however, the question whether, "if the *Mendenhall* test was met—if the message that the defendant was not free to leave had been conveyed—a Fourth Amendment seizure would have occurred." *Hodari* at 1552. [Citation omitted.]

Perhaps more on point is the decision reached in *Brower v. Inyo County*, 489 *U.S.* 593, 109 *S.Ct.* 1378 (1989). In *Brower*, "police cars with flashing lights had chased the decedent for 20 miles—surely an adequate 'show of authority'—but he did not stop until his fatal crash into a police-erected blockade. The issue was whether his death could be held to be the consequence of an unreasonable seizure in violation of the Fourth Amendment." *Hodari* at 1552. The possibility that a seizure could have occurred during the course of the chase was not even a consideration because "that 'show of authority' did not produce his stop. * * * The same is true here." *Id.*

"In sum, assuming that Pertoso's pursuit in the present case constituted a 'show of authority' [directing] Hodari to halt, since Hodari did not comply with that [direction] he was not seized until he was tackled. The cocaine abandoned while he was running was in this case not the fruit of a seizure, and his motion to exclude evidence of it was properly denied." *Id.*

NOTE

1. During the course of its opinion in *Hodari D.*, the Court observed:

> Street pursuits always place the public at some risk, and compliance with police orders to stop should therefore be encouraged. Only a few of those orders, we must presume, will be without adequate

basis, and since the addressee has no ready means of identifying the deficient ones it almost invariably is the responsible course to comply. Unlawful orders will not be deterred, moreover, by sanctioning through the exclusionary rule those of them that are *not* obeyed. Since police [officers] do not command "Stop !" expecting to be ignored, or give chase hoping to be outrun, it fully suffices to apply the deterrent to their genuine, successful seizures.

Id. at 1551. [Emphasis in original.]

See also Hester v. United States, 265 *U.S.* 57, 44 *S.Ct.* 445 (1924), where revenue agents picked up containers dropped by moonshiners whom they were pursuing without adequate warrant. As explained by the Court in *Hodari D.*, the *Hester* moonshine was "not excluded as the product of an unlawful seizure because '[t]he defendant's own acts, and those of his associates, disclosed the jug, the jar and the bottle— and there was no seizure in the sense of the law when the officers examined the contents of each after they had been abandoned.' " *Hodari D.* at 1552 (quoting *Hester* at 58, 44 *S.Ct.* at 446).

2. *Submission to a show of authority. Hodari D.* makes clear that a "seizure" of a person will occur not only when the person is subject to a full-blown arrest, and a *"Terry v. Ohio"* investigative detention, but also during the course of any other police-citizen encounter where the person is detained against his will. Thus, a person will be "seized" within the meaning of the Constitution when an officer, by means of physical force or show of authority, has in some way restrained the liberty of a citizen. In the absence of physical force, the seizure requires that the citizen submit to the assertion of the officer's show of authority.

(a) In *Albright v. Oliver*, 510 *U.S.* 266, 114 *S.Ct.* 807 (1994) (plurality opinion), upon learning of the existence of an outstanding warrant for his arrest, Albright appeared at the police station and turned himself in. According to the Court, Albright's "surrender to the State's authority constituted a seizure for purposes of the Fourth Amendment." *Id.* at 272, 114 *S.Ct.* 812.

(b) In *Mettler v. Whitledge*, 165 *F.*3d 1197 (8th Cir. 1999), the court held that an officer's act of sending in a police dog to locate a person in a garage was not a "seizure," in the absence of evidence of physical contact or acquiescence to the assertion of police authority).

(c) In *United States v. Wood*, 981 *F.*2d 536 (D.C. Cir. 1992), in the middle of July, Officer Webb was assigned to patrol the area of 17th and Q Streets, Southeast, in the District of Columbia. At about 9:00 p.m., Webb, in full uniform, saw defendant Wood walking away from a group of nine or ten men towards an apartment building at 1606 17th Street. The officer was about twelve feet away when he noticed that Wood was "cradling his arms" across his mid-section. Webb could not, however, see anything bulging from Wood's jacket. As Wood walked away, he looked back at another officer, Brevard, who was following Wood to his right side.

Wood entered the apartment building at 1606 17th Street, with Officer Webb following closely behind him. As Wood attempted to enter one of the apartments, Webb ordered him to "halt right there," "stop." *Id.* at 537. Wood "froze in his tracks; a dark heavy object then fell from the area of Wood's waist and dropped between his feet. While drawing his gun, Webb grabbed Wood by the front of his neck and held him up against the wall." *Id.* When Officer Brevard entered the building, Webb released Wood, handcuffed him, and then recovered a TEC-9 semi-automatic pistol that had fallen between Wood's legs. Wood told the officers, "that's not mine; I was just carrying it." *Id.*

In the appeal following the denial of defendant's motion to suppress, the Government conceded that, until Wood dropped his gun, "Officer Webb had no reasonable articulable suspicion to justify a *Terry* stop." *Id.* at 538. Therefore, the primary issues before the court were "(1) whether Wood was seized before he dropped the gun; and (2) assuming Wood was seized, whether dropping the gun was an independent act that somehow dissipated the taint of the seizure." *Id.*

Employing the rationale of *Hodari D.*, the court first addressed the question whether defendant was subjected to a "show of authority."

> [T]he test for whether a "show of authority" was made is objective, and looks to the totality of the circumstances. * * * Specific factors [may] include whether the suspect was physically intimidated or touched, whether the officer displayed a weapon, wore a uniform, or restricted the defendant's movements, the time and place of the encounter, and whether the officer's "use of language or tone of voice indicat[ed] that compliance with the officer's request might be compelled."

Id. at 539. [Citations omitted.]

Applying the test set forth above, the court found that, "there can be little doubt over the fact that Wood was subjected to a 'show of authority.'" *Wood* at 540.

> Officers Webb and Brevard, armed and in full uniform, followed Wood, at night, into a dark apartment building. Webb, positioning himself directly behind Wood, ordered him to "halt right there," "stop." When Officer Webb told Wood to stop, he was not extending a greeting or positing a question; rather, he was giving an order in "language * * * indicating that compliance * * * might be compelled." * * * As Justice Scalia said in *Hodari D.*, "policemen do not command 'Stop!' expecting to be ignored." * * *

> Moreover, Officer Webb's positioning at the moment he gave the order significantly restricted [] Wood's movements. Webb was so close to Wood when he told him to stop that * * * Wood had "nowhere to go." * * * A reasonable person could not possibly feel free to ignore a direct order to stop given by a police officer, in uniform and armed, standing directly behind him.

[Accordingly], Webb made a clear show of authority when he told Wood to "halt right there," "stop[.]"

Id. at 540.

The court also found it clear that Wood's actions constituted a "submission to the assertion of authority." *Id.*

> Unlike the defendant in *Hodari D.*, Wood did not flee from the police officers. Webb first confronted Wood as [he] attempted to enter a doorway in the apartment building. Upon Webb's order to stop, Wood froze in his tracks and immediately dropped the weapon between his feet. We cannot imagine a more submissive response to a police officer's order to "halt right there." Wood did not try to escape into the nearby apartment, or struggle past the officer, or otherwise ignore the officer's order, or turn the weapon on the officer—rather, he rendered himself helpless in the face of a show of authority.

Id.

Finally, the court ruled that Wood's discarding the gun was not an act wholly independent from the police seizure of his person.

> "Unless an intervening event or other attenuating circumstance purges the taint of the initial illegality, evidence discovered during an illegal seizure must be suppressed." * * * Once an illegal seizure is established, the Government has the burden of proving that the causal chain was sufficiently attenuated by an independent act to dissipate the taint of the illegality. * * *

> In this case, the Government failed entirely to meet its burden of proving that Wood's act was independent of the illegal seizure. Immediately after Officer Webb told Wood to stop, [Wood] dropped the gun between his feet. * * * Wood did not attempt to hide the gun on his person [or throw it away]. [T]he Government presented no evidence which showed that "an intervening event or other attenuating circumstance purge[d] the taint of the initial illegality." * * * No time elapsed and no intervening events occurred between the commencement of the seizure and the dropping of the gun. Therefore, we find a direct nexus between the illegal seizure and the recovery of the weapon. * * *

> The District Court erred in denying [defendant's] motion to suppress.

Id. at 541. [Citations omitted.]

3. *New Federalism.* Refusing to follow the United States Supreme Court's lead in *California v. Hodari D.*, the Connecticut Supreme Court held, in *State v. Oquendo*, 223 *Conn.* 635, 613 *A.*2d 1300 (1992), that under article first, §§7 and 9 of the Connecticut Constitution, a person

is "seized" when " 'by means of physical force or a show of authority, his freedom of movement is restrained.' " *Id.* at 647, 613 *A*.2d at 1307 (quoting *State v. Ostroski,* 186 *Conn.* 287, 291, 440 *A*.2d 984 (1982) and *United States v. Mendenhall,* 446 *U.S.* 544, 553-54, 100 *S.Ct.* 1870, 1876-77 (1980)). In determining whether a seizure has occurred under the state constitution, a Connecticut court will consider whether " 'in view of all the circumstances surrounding the incident, a reasonable person would have believed that he was not free to leave.' " *Id.* at 647, 613 *A*.2d at 1307-1308. [Citations omitted.] The *Oquendo* court thus

> decline[d] to adopt the restrictive definition of a seizure employed by the United States Supreme Court in *Hodari D.* and adhere[d] to [its] precedents in determining what constitutes a seizure under the state constitution.

Id. at 652, 613 *A*.2d at 1310.

FLORIDA v. BOSTICK
Supreme Court of the United States
501 *U.S.* 429, 111 *S.Ct.* 2382 (1991)

QUESTION: Does a Fourth Amendment "seizure" occur when police board a public bus, approach a passenger at random, ask a few questions, ask to see the passenger's identification, and then request consent to search his or her bags ?

ANSWER: NO. "[N]o seizure occurs when police ask questions of an individual, ask to examine the individual's identification, and request consent to search his or her luggage—so long as the officers do not convey a message that compliance with their request is required." *Id.* at 2388. "[I]n order to determine whether a particular encounter constitutes a seizure, a court [will] consider all the circumstances surrounding the encounter to determine whether the police conduct would have communicated to a reasonable person that the person was not free to decline the officers' requests or otherwise terminate the encounter. That rule applies to encounters that take place on a city street, [on a train,] or in an airport lobby, and it applies equally to encounters on a bus." *Id.* at 2388, 2389.

RATIONALE: It is well settled that the police do not violate the Fourth Amendment by approaching "individuals at random in airport lobbies and other public places to ask them questions and to request consent to search their luggage, so long as a reasonable person would understand that he or she could refuse to cooperate." *Id.* at 2384. This case examines whether the same rule applies to police-citizen encounters that take place on a bus.

"Drug interdiction efforts have led to the use of police surveillance at airports, train stations, and bus depots. Law enforcement officers stationed at such locations routinely approach individuals, either randomly or because they suspect in some vague way that the individuals may be engaged in criminal activity, and ask them potentially incriminating questions. Broward County has adopted such a program. County Sheriff's Department officers routinely board buses at scheduled stops and ask passengers for permission to search their luggage." *Id.*

In this case,

> "[t]wo officers, complete with badges, insignia and one of them holding a recognizable zipper pouch, containing a pistol, boarded a bus bound from Miami to Atlanta during a stopover in Fort Lauderdale. Eyeing the passengers, the officers admittedly without articulable suspicion, picked out the defendant passenger and asked to inspect his ticket and identification. [These items were immediately returned to defendant] as unremarkable. However, the two police officers persisted and explained their presence as narcotics agents on the lookout for illegal drugs. In pursuit of that aim, they then requested the defendant's consent to search his luggage[, and specifically advised defendant that he had the right to refuse consent]."

Id. at 2384-85. [Citation omitted.] The search uncovered a quantity of cocaine discovered in one of defendant's suitcases. Significantly, the record under review indicated that the officer who carried the zipper pouch containing a pistol—the equivalent of carrying a gun in a holster—at no time removed the gun from its pouch, pointed it at defendant, or otherwise used it in a threatening manner. *Id.* at 2385.

Defendant was arrested and charged with "trafficking in cocaine." In this appeal, he argued that the cocaine seized must be suppressed as a "tainted fruit" because the officers lacked the reasonable suspicion required to justify a seizure, and that this encounter, taking place "in the cramped confines of a bus," constituted a seizure because "a reasonable bus passenger would not have felt free to leave under the circumstances * * * because there is nowhere to go on a bus[,] * * * the bus was about to depart[,] * * * [and had he] disembarked, he would have risked being stranded and losing whatever baggage he had locked away in the luggage compartment." *Id.* at 2386-87. *The Supreme Court, however, could not agree.*

The cases in this area "make it clear that a seizure does not occur simply because a police officer approaches an individual and asks a few questions. So long as a reasonable person would feel free 'to disregard the police and go about his business,' * * * the encounter is consensual and no reasonable suspicion is required. The encounter will not trigger Fourth Amendment scrutiny unless it loses its consensual nature." *Id.* at 2386. [Citations omitted.]

Here, "[t]here is no doubt that if this same encounter had taken place before Bostick boarded the bus or in the lobby of the bus terminal, it would not rise to the level of a seizure." *Id.* In this respect, the Court observed that in prior cases

> [w]e have stated that even when officers have no basis for suspecting a particular individual, they may generally ask questions of

that individual, * * * ask to examine the individual's identification, * * * and request consent to search his or her luggage, * * * as long as the police do not convey the message that compliance with their request is required.

Id. [Citations omitted.]

According to the Court, Bostick's argument that "a reasonable bus passenger would not have felt free to leave under the circumstances" missed the mark. "When police attempt to question a person who is walking down the street or through an airport lobby, it makes sense to inquire whether a reasonable person would feel free to continue walking. But when the person is seated on a bus and has no desire to leave, the degree to which a reasonable person would feel free that he or she could leave is not an accurate measure of the coercive effect of the encounter." *Id.* at 2387.

"[T]he mere fact that Bostick did not feel free to leave the bus does not mean that the police seized him. Bostick was a passenger on a bus that was scheduled to depart. He would not have felt free to leave the bus even if the police had not been present. Bostick's movements were 'confined' in a sense, but this was the natural result of his decision to take the bus; it says nothing about whether or not the police conduct at issue was coercive." *Id.*

Thus, "Bostick's freedom of movement was restricted by a factor independent of police conduct—*i.e.*, by his being a passenger on a bus. Accordingly, the 'free to leave' analysis on which Bostick relie[d] is inapplicable. In such a situation, the appropriate inquiry is *whether a reasonable person would feel free to decline the officers' requests or otherwise terminate the encounter.* * * * [T]he crucial test is whether, taking into account all of the circumstances surrounding the encounter, the police conduct would 'have communicated to a reasonable person that he was not at liberty to ignore the police presence and go about his business.' * * * Where the encounter takes place is one factor, but it is not the only one." Id.* [Emphasis added.]

Accordingly, no seizure occurs when police approach an individual in a public place, "ask questions of [the individual], ask to examine [his or her] identification, and request consent to search his or her luggage—so long as the officers do not convey a message that compliance with their request is required." *Id.* at 2388. The Fourth Amendment inquiry here—"whether a reasonable person would have felt free to decline the officers' requests or otherwise terminate the encounter—applies equally to police encounters that take place on trains, planes, [or on] city streets[,] * * * and it applies equally to encounters on a bus." *Id.* at 2388, 2389.

NOTE

1. Although the facts in *Bostick* left the Court with some doubt as to whether or not Bostick was "seized" within the meaning of the Fourth Amendment, it nonetheless refrained from deciding that issue, and instead, remanded the case to the Florida Supreme Court so that it could evaluate the facts under "the correct legal standard." *Id.* at 2388.

The Court did, however, expressly reject Bostick's argument "that he must have been seized because no reasonable person would freely consent to a search of luggage that he or she knows contains drugs." *Id.* According to the Court, "[t]his argument cannot prevail because the 'reasonable person' test presupposes an *innocent* person." *Id.* (citing *Florida v. Royer*, 460 *U.S.* 491, 519 n.4, 103 *S.Ct.* 1319, 1335 n.4 (1983) (Blackmun, J., dissenting) ("The fact that [defendant] knew the search was likely to turn up contraband is of course irrelevant; the potential intrusiveness of the officers' conduct must be judged from the viewpoint of an innocent person in [his] position"). [Emphasis in original.]

Significantly, the Court did pause to observe that "[t]he Fourth Amendment proscribes unreasonable searches and seizures; it does not proscribe voluntary cooperation." *Id.* at 2389.

> Clearly, a bus passenger's decision to cooperate with law enforcement officers authorizes the police to conduct a search without first obtaining a warrant *only* if the cooperation is voluntary. "Consent" that is the product of official intimidation or harassment is not consent at all. Citizens do not forfeit their constitutional rights when they are coerced to comply with a request that they would prefer to refuse. The question to be decided by the Florida courts on remand is whether Bostick chose to permit the search of his luggage.

Id. at 2388. [Emphasis in original.]

2. *Working the buses.—Revisited.* In *United States v. Drayton*, 536 *U.S.* 194, 122 *S.Ct.* 2105 (2002), in early February, three Tallahassee police officers boarded a Greyhound bus during a scheduled stop in Tallahassee, Florida. The bus driver allowed the officers to board the bus as part of the police department's "routine drug and weapons interdiction effort." *Id.* at 2109. At the time, the officers were dressed in plain clothes and carried concealed weapons and visible badges.

Once on board the bus, "Officer Hoover knelt on the driver's seat and faced the rear of the bus. He could observe the passengers and ensure the safety of the two other officers without blocking the aisle or otherwise obstructing the bus exit. Officers Lang and Blackburn went to the rear of the bus. Blackburn remained stationed there, facing forward. Lang worked his way toward the front of the bus, speaking with individual passengers as he went. He asked the passengers about their travel plans and sought to match passengers with luggage in the overhead racks. To avoid blocking the aisle, Lang stood next to or just behind each passenger with whom he spoke." *Id.* Any passenger who declined to cooperate with him or who chose to exit the bus would have been allowed to do so without interference.

The defendants, Christopher Drayton and Clifton Brown, Jr., were seated next to each other on the bus. Drayton sat in the aisle seat, and Brown was seated next to the window. Lang approached the two from the rear and leaned over Drayton's shoulder. Lang held up his badge long enough for Drayton and Brown to identify him as a police officer. With his face 12 to 18 inches away from Drayton's, Lang stated in a polite, quiet voice: "I'm Investigator Lang with the Tallahassee Police Department. We're conducting [a] bus interdiction, attempting to deter drugs and illegal weapons being transported on the bus. Do you have any bags on the bus?" *Id.*

Both defendants pointed to a single green bag in the overhead luggage rack. Lang asked, "Do you mind if I check it?" Brown replied, "Go ahead." *Id.* The bag contained no contraband.

Officer Lang noticed that both Drayton and Brown were wearing heavy jackets and baggy pants despite the warm weather. "In Lang's experience drug traffickers often use baggy clothing to conceal weapons or narcotics. The officer thus asked Brown if he had any weapons or drugs in his possession. And he asked Brown: 'Do you mind if I check your person?' Brown answered, 'Sure,' and cooperated by leaning up in his seat, pulling a cell phone out of his pocket, and opening up his jacket." *Id.* Officer Lang "reached across Drayton and patted down Brown's jacket and pockets, including his waist area, sides, and upper thighs. In both thigh areas, Lang detected hard objects similar to drug packages detected on other occasions. Lang arrested and handcuffed Brown. Officer Hoover escorted Brown from the bus." *Id.*

"Lang then asked Drayton, 'Mind if I check you?' Drayton responded by lifting his hands about eight inches from his legs. Lang conducted a pat-down of Drayton's thighs and detected hard objects similar to those found on Brown. He arrested Drayton and escorted him from the bus. A further search revealed that [defendants] had duct-taped plastic bundles of powder cocaine between several pairs of their boxer shorts. Brown possessed three bundles containing 483 grams of cocaine. Drayton possessed two bundles containing 295 grams of cocaine." *Id.* at 2109-10.

Finding the officers' actions entirely proper, the United States Supreme Court held that "the police did not seize the [defendants] when they boarded the bus and began questioning passengers." *Id.* at 2112.

In *Florida v. Bostick*, 501 *U.S.* 429, 111 *S.Ct.* 2382 (1991), the landmark case on this subject, the Court held that "[t]he Fourth Amendment permits police officers to approach bus passengers at random to ask questions and to request their consent to searches, provided a reasonable person would understand that he or she is free to refuse." *Drayton* at 2109.

Here, in *Drayton*, the Court reaffirmed that "the traditional rule, which states that a seizure does not occur so long as a reasonable person would feel free 'to disregard the police and go about his business,' * * * is not an accurate measure of the coercive effect of a bus encounter." *Id.* at 2111. [Citations omitted.] In this respect, "[a] passenger may not want to get off a bus if there is a risk it will depart before the opportunity to reboard. * * * A bus rider's movements are confined in this sense, but this is the natural result of choosing to take the bus; it says nothing about whether the police conduct is coercive." *Id.* Thus, the "proper inquiry 'is whether a reasonable person would feel free to decline the officers' requests or otherwise terminate the encounter.' " *Id.* [Citation omitted.]

Here, in *Drayton*, the Court concluded that the police did not seize the defendants

> when they boarded the bus and began questioning passengers. The officers gave the passengers no reason to believe that they were required to answer the officers' questions. When Officer Lang approached [defendants], he did not brandish a weapon or make any intimidating movements. He left the aisle free so that [defendants] could exit. He spoke to passengers one by one and in a polite, quiet voice. Nothing he said would suggest to a reasonable person that he or she was barred from leaving the bus or otherwise terminating the encounter.

Id. at 2112.

The Court concluded that in this case, the encounter between Officer Lang and the defendants "was cooperative." *Id.* There was "nothing 'coercive [or] confrontational' about the encounter." *Id.* [Citation omitted.] "There was no application of force, no intimidating movement, no overwhelming show of force, no brandishing of weapons, no blocking of exits, no threat, no command, not even an authoritative tone of voice. It is beyond question that had this encounter occurred on the street, it would be constitutional. The fact that an encounter takes place on a bus does not on its own transform standard police questioning of citizens into an illegal seizure." *Id.* "Indeed, because many fellow passengers are present to witness officers' conduct, a reasonable person may feel even more secure in his or her decision not to cooperate with police on a bus than in other circumstances." *Id.*

Moreover, the fact that Officer Lang displayed his badge does not change the result. A seizure does not occur merely because a police officer identifies himself or herself as a law enforcement officer or shows a person his or her badge. In this case, while neither Lang nor his colleagues were in uniform or visibly armed, the Court determined that

> those factors should have little weight in the analysis. Officers are often required to wear uniforms and in many circumstances this is cause for assurance, not discomfort. Much the same can be said for wearing sidearms. That most law enforcement officers are armed is a fact well known to the public. The presence of a holstered firearm thus is unlikely to contribute to the coerciveness of the encounter absent active brandishing of the weapon.

> Officer Hoover's position at the front of the bus also does not tip the scale in [defendants'] favor. Hoover did nothing to intimidate passengers, and he said nothing to suggest that people could not exit and indeed he left the aisle clear. * * *

Id. at 2112.

At the Supreme Court, Drayton argued that "even if Brown's cooperation with the officers was consensual, Drayton was seized because no reasonable person would feel free to terminate the encounter with the officers after Brown had been arrested." *Id.* at 2113. Rejecting this argument, the Court said:

> The arrest of one person does not mean that everyone around him has been seized by police. If anything, Brown's arrest should have put Drayton on notice of the consequences of continuing the encounter by answering the officers' questions. Even after arresting Brown, Lang addressed Drayton in a polite manner and provided him with no indication that he was required to answer Lang's questions.

Turning now from the question whether defendants were seized to whether they were subjected to an unreasonable search, *i.e.,* whether their consent to the suspicionless search was involuntary, the Court observed:

> In circumstances such as these, where the question of voluntariness pervades both the search and seizure inquiries, the respective analyses turn on very similar facts. And, as the facts above suggest, [defendants'] consent to the search of their luggage and their persons was voluntary. Nothing Officer Lang said indicated a command to consent to the search. Rather, when [defendants] informed Lang that they had a bag on the bus, he asked for their permission to check it. And when Lang requested to search Brown and Drayton's persons, he asked first if they objected, thus indicating to a reasonable person that he or she was free to refuse. Even after arresting Brown, Lang provided Drayton with no indication that he was required to consent to a search. To the contrary, Lang asked for Drayton's permission to search him ("Mind if I check you?"), and Drayton agreed.

Id. at 2113.

3. *Physical manipulation of a bus passenger's carry-on luggage.* In *Bond v. United States,* 529 *U.S.* 334, 120 *S.Ct.* 1462 (2000), the Court held that a law enforcement officer's physical manipulation of a bus passenger's carry-on luggage constituted an unreasonable search and seizure under the Fourth Amendment. [For a full discussion of this case, turn to Section 4.3 and the materials covering "plain touch."]

4. Consider *INS v. Delgado,* 466 *U.S.* 210, 104 *S.Ct.* 1758 (1984), where the issue focused on the INS' practice of visiting factories at random and questioning employees to determine whether any were illegal aliens. Several INS agents would wait near the building's exits, while other agents walked through the factory questioning workers. According to the Court, while the workers may not have been free to leave their worksite, that was not the result of police activity: "Ordinarily, when people are at work their freedom to move about has been meaningfully restricted, not by the actions of law enforcement officials, but by the workers' voluntary obligations to their employers." *Id.* at 218, 104 *S.Ct.* at 1763. Thus, the Court concluded that no seizure

occurred because, even though the workers were not free to leave the building without being questioned, the conduct of the INS agents should have given the employees "no reason to believe that they would be detained if they gave truthful answers to the questions put to them or if they simply refused to answer." *Id.*

5. For an application of *Bostick* to a "consensual encounter" at the doorway of an Amtrak train passenger's roomette, *see United States v. Kim*, 27 *F.*3d 947 (3rd Cir. 1994).

UNITED STATES v. GALBERTH
United States Court of Appeals
846 *F.*2d 983 (5th Cir. 1988)

QUESTION: At what point in the below set of facts did the police-citizen encounter turn into a Fourth Amendment "seizure"?

FACTS:

1. In late June, Drug Enforcement Administration (DEA) Agent Kirk Griffith observed defendant Galberth disembark from American Airlines Flight 6, arriving at the Dallas/Fort Worth International Airport from Miami, Florida.

2. Agent Griffith also observed an "extremely nervous" male passenger deplane just before defendant, and noticed that defendant and the male passenger appear to look at one another.

3. Defendant also appeared to be nervous, and kept looking ahead at the male, but remained about 20 to 30 feet behind him as they walked through the concourse.

4. When defendant entered the unsecured area of the terminal, Agent Griffith approached her, identified himself as a narcotics officer, and asked if he might speak with her. Defendant was "startled and rather nervous," but did not object.

5. Griffith then asked to see defendant's airline ticket, which she took from her purse and handed to him. "It was a one-way cash fare from Miami, Florida, to Lawton, Oklahoma, via Dallas/Fort Worth International Airport, issued that day in the name of 'Betty Davis.'"

6. Griffith returned her airline ticket and asked to see defendant's identification.

7. As defendant handed Griffith a hospital card with her real name on it, Griffith noticed that her hands were shaking. Moreover, throughout their entire conversation, defendant's voice quivered.

8. Griffith questioned defendant about the discrepancy in the names but did not receive a clarifying response. He therefore again identified himself as a DEA agent and asked permission to look in her purse and carry-on bag. Again, defendant consented.

9. As Griffith examined the bags, another officer approached and stood about ten feet away.

10. During this period, Agent Griffith noticed an unnatural bulge on defendant's lower abdomen under her clothing. "When asked if she was carrying anything under her clothing, [defendant] 'became visibly more nervous' and appeared 'scared'; she was shaking, the artery in her neck began to throb, and her voice was quivering, but she replied that she was not carrying anything under her clothes."

11. Griffith then asked defendant to press her hands against her stomach in three different places, and after the third time could clearly see that the bulge was not part of her body.

12. Agent Griffith next asked defendant "if she would mind if a female officer patted her down for possible narcotics." Defendant replied, "Okay."

13. Griffith instructed the other agent to arrange for a female customs inspector to perform the search. During the ten minutes that it took for the female officer to arrive, Griffith and defendant waited in the lounge area of the airport and engaged in "small talk."

14. As soon as the female customs inspector arrived, she took defendant into the women's public restroom, conducted a pat-down, and immediately felt a bulge in defendant's midriff section.

15. The inspector asked defendant whether the bulge was a part of her body and defendant stated that it was not. The inspector then removed the "bulge" from between defendant's panty hose and underwear, and discovered a "pound-and-a-quarter bundle of white powder," subsequently determined to be 447 grams of 91% pure cocaine.

ANSWER: AT POINT 13. While the stop of defendant at this point "transformed itself into a 'seizure' for [F]ourth [A]mendment purposes, the 'seizure' was supported by the requisite reasonable suspicion." *Id.* at 994.

RATIONALE: Initially, the court notes that "not all police-citizen contact invokes the [F]ourth [A]mendment." *Id.* at 988. Rather, "there are three levels of police-citizen encounters:

[1] communication between police and citizens involving no coercion or detention and therefore without the compass of the Fourth Amendment[; 2] so-called *Terry* stops or brief "seizures" that must

be supported by reasonable suspicion[; and 3] full-scale arrests that must be supported by probable cause."

Id. (quoting *United States v. Berry*, 670 *F*.2d 583, 591 (5th Cir. 1982)).

"At the first level, there is no element of detention or coercion, and the [F]ourth [A]mendment is not implicated. The second level involves brief detentions or investigatory stops and requires 'reasonable suspicion' on the part of the detaining officer, based upon 'specific and articulable facts which, taken together with the rational inferences from these facts, reasonably warrant an intrusion.' The third level, arrest, obviously requires the existence of probable cause." *Id.* at 988-989 (quoting *Terry v. Ohio*, 392 *U.S.* 1, 19, 88 *S.Ct.* 1868, 1878-79 (1968)).

In this case, "[t]he facts establish that Officer Griffith initially approached Galberth and made inquiries that constituted the mere communication level of contact. * * * No coercion was shown by the officer's words or conduct, nor did he intimate that an innocent individual would certainly cooperate with police." *Id.* at 989. The court therefore concludes that Griffith's requests to speak with Galberth, and her subsequent consent for him to look at her airline ticket and then inspect her purse and carry-on bag, "fall within the first level of police-citizen contact. The stop was extremely restricted in scope and was conducted in a completely non-coercive manner. After requesting to see Galberth's ticket and identification, Officer Griffith immediately returned them to her. Galberth was free to leave at any time, and in view of all the circumstances surrounding the incident, a reasonable person would have believed that she was free to leave at any time." *Id.*

"Although the officer's request for Galberth to allow him to examine her purse and bag for narcotics may be argued to have elevated the discussion to a '*Terry*-type' detention, * * * she voluntarily consented to the examination. The interview was conducted in a public area of the airport terminal, not * * * in one of the private offices. There was no coercion or trickery on the part of the officer, and the interview was not prolonged or repetitious. The officer did nothing to lead her to believe that she had to consent to the search or that she was not free to leave." *Id.* at 990. Thus, up until the point where the encounter was prolonged for the purpose of arranging for a female officer to conduct a search of Galberth's person, the encounter constituted a "mere inquiry," or as this court has termed it, a "mere communication level of contact." *Id.* at 989.

"Galberth testified at trial that from the moment Griffith confronted her with the fact that he was a narcotics officer, she felt that she had to do everything he 'requested' or that she would go to jail." *Id.* at 990. But as the United States Supreme Court held in *Michigan v. Chesternut*, 486 *U.S.* 567, 108 *S.Ct.* 1975 (1988), under the "reasonable person" standard, " 'Fourth Amendment protection does not vary with the state of mind of the particular individual being approached.' " *Galberth* at 990 (quoting *Chesternut*, 108 *S.Ct.* at 1980). *See also United States v. Bengivenga*, 845 *F*.2d 593, 597 (5th Cir. 1988) (en banc) ("subjective belief of suspect [is] irrelevant to the custody determination"). Galberth's knowledge (or ignorance) that the other officer with Griffith was also a law enforcement officer "is similarly irrelevant beyond her presently-argued subjective apprehension that they were not going to let her go." *Galberth* at 990. Nor is the subjective intent of the law enforcement officer to detain or, assumedly, not detain relevant, "'except insofar as that [intention] may have been conveyed to the [suspect].'" *Id.* at 991 (quoting *United States v. Mendenhall,* 446 *U.S.* 544, 554 n.6, 100 *S.Ct.* 1870, 1877 n.6 (1980)).

While it may be said that Galberth was still providing her voluntary consent for the extended encounter pending the arrival of the female customs inspector, a reasonable interpretation of the circumstances leads to the inescapable conclusion that at that point (#13), "the stop of Galberth transformed itself into a 'seizure' for [F]ourth [A]mendment purposes[.]" *Id.* at 994. That seizure, however, "was supported by the requisite reasonable suspicion[,]" *id.*, and could have proceeded "even if Galberth had refused consent." *Id.* at 990.

"[P]rior to the search request, the officer's inquiries established that Galberth was attempting to hide her true identity by lying to the officer[] about her name. This action, coupled with her obvious anxiousness and the additional facts observed by the officer[] up to that point, constituted articulable facts that would reasonably warrant further inquiry by the officer * * *. Furthermore, she was returning from a known source city for illegal narcotics, her airline ticket was a cash one-way ticket from Florida to Oklahoma, and she admitted to having been in Miami for only twenty-four hours." *Id.* at 989. Added to these facts, Officer Griffith observed, during the course of the voluntary encounter, an "unnatural bulge" protruding from Galberth's abdomen which she could not or would not satisfactorily explain.

Consequently, the initial voluntary encounter, along with the subsequent investigative detention, violated no concerns implicated by the Fourth Amendment.

---

§8.2(b). The *"Terry* stop."

UNITED STATES v. SOKOLOW
Supreme Court of the United States
490 *U.S.* 1, 109 *S.Ct.* 1581 (1989)

QUESTION: Before an officer is permitted to stop and briefly detain a person for investigative purposes, must that officer—in the absence of probable cause—have a reasonable suspicion supported by articulable facts that criminal activity may be afoot?

ANSWER: YES. As was held in *Terry v. Ohio,* 392 *U.S.* 1, 88 *S.Ct.* 1868 (1968), a police officer may "stop and briefly detain a person for investigative purposes if the officer has a reasonable suspicion supported by articulable facts that criminal activity 'may be afoot,' even if the officer lacks probable cause." *Sokolow* at 1585. In addition, the validity of such a stop must be evaluated by considering the "totality of the circumstances—the whole picture." *Sokolow* at 1585.

RATIONALE: In order for an investigative stop of a person to pass constitutional muster, a law enforcement officer must be able to articulate specific and objective facts which, when taken together with the rational inferences from those facts, reasonably lead to the conclusion that criminal activity may be afoot. "The officer, of course, must be able to articulate something more than an 'inchoate and unparticularized suspicion or hunch.' * * * The Fourth Amendment requires 'some minimal level of objective justification' for making the stop. * * * That level of suspicion is considerably less than proof of wrongdoing by a preponderance of the evidence. While the Court has held that probable cause means 'a fair probability that contraband or evidence of a crime will be found,' * * * the level of suspicion required for a *Terry* stop is obviously less demanding than that for probable cause." *Id.* at 1585. [Citations omitted.]

"The concept of *reasonable suspicion*, like probable cause, is not 'readily, or even usefully, reduced to a neat set of legal rules.' " *Id.* [Citation omitted; emphasis added.] Rather, the validity of an investigative stop is more appropriately evaluated by considering the "totality of the circumstances—the whole picture." *Id.*

This case involves a typical attempt to smuggle drugs through one of our Nation's airports. Defendant Sokolow was stopped by Drug Enforcement Administration (DEA) agents upon his arrival at the Honolulu International Airport. The investigative stop led to the discovery of 1,063 grams of cocaine in defendant's carry-on luggage. Prior to conducting the investigative stop, the DEA agents learned that: (1) defendant paid $2,100 for two airplane tickets from a roll of $20 bills; (2) he traveled under a name that did not match the name under which his telephone number was listed; (3) his original destination was Miami, a source city for illicit drugs; (4) he stayed in Miami for only 48 hours, and spent 20 hours of air travel to do so; (5) he appeared nervous during his trip; and (6) he checked none of his luggage. *Id.* at 1583.

While any one of these factors is not by itself proof of any illegal conduct and is quite consistent with innocent travel, all the factors, when taken together, certainly amount to a *reasonable suspicion. Id.* at 1586. [Emphasis added.] In this respect, the Court instructs that there are times when the police may be presented with a set of "circumstances in which wholly lawful conduct may justify the suspicion that criminal activity was afoot." *Id.* Significantly, even the Court in *Terry* was presented with a " 'series of acts, each of them perhaps innocent' if viewed separately, 'but which taken together warranted further investigation.' " *Id.* at 1587 (quoting *Terry* at 22, 88 *S.Ct.* at 1881).

Accordingly, the validity of a stop such as this must be assessed by examining the "totality of the circumstances—the whole picture." *Id.* at 1585 (quoting *United States v. Cortez*, 449 *U.S.* 411, 417, 101 *S.Ct.* 690, 695 (1981)).

"Paying $2,100 in cash for two airplane tickets is out of the ordinary, and it is even more out of the ordinary to pay that sum from a roll of $20 bills containing nearly twice that amount of cash. Most business travelers * * * purchase airline tickets by credit card or check so as to have a record for tax or business purposes, and few vacationers carry with them thousands of dollars in $20 bills." *Id.* Moreover, the Court finds suspicious not only the fact that defendant was traveling under an alias, but the extraordinarily brief period of time he spent in Miami. "While a trip from Honolulu to Miami, standing alone, is not a cause for any sort of suspicion, here there was more: surely," states the Court, "few residents of Honolulu travel from that city for 20 hours to spend 48 hours in Miami during the month of July." *Id.*

Certainly, any one of those circumstances is not proof of illegal conduct; in fact, singularly they could be deemed consistent with normal, or at least innocent travel; but, according to the Court, the totality of those circumstances provided the agents with a reasonable basis to suspect that defendant was transporting illegal drugs. *Id.*

NOTE

1. In *Sokolow, supra,* the defendant also argued that the DEA agents were obligated to use the least intrusive means available to verify or dispel their suspicions that he was smuggling narcotics. In defendant's view, the agents should have simply approached and spoken with him, rather than forcibly detaining him. In support of his contention, defendant cites *Florida v. Royer,* 460 *U.S.* 491, 103 *S.Ct.* 1319 (1983), where Justice White stated that "the investigative methods employed should be the least intrusive means reasonably available to verify or dispel the officer's suspicion in a short period of time." *Royer* at 500, 103 *S.Ct.* at 1325-26. The *Sokolow* Court, however, quickly dispelled defendant's contentions.

Chief Justice Rehnquist, speaking for the Court, explained that the statement in *Royer* "was directed at the *length* of the investigative stop, not at whether the police had a less intrusive means to verify their suspicions before stopping Royer. The reasonableness of the officer's decision to stop a suspect does not turn on the availability of less intrusive investigatory techniques. Such a rule would unduly hamper the police's ability to make swift, on-the-spot decisions * * * and it would require courts to 'indulge in unrealistic second guessing.' " *Sokolow* at 1587.

2. *The drug courier profile.* "The 'drug courier profile' is an abstract of characteristics found to be typical of persons transporting illegal drugs." *Florida v. Royer,* 460 *U.S.* 491, 494 n.2, 103 *S.Ct.* 1319, 1322 n.2 (1983). While not an end in itself, the "drug courier profile" is an effective means or investigative tool utilized by trained law enforcement officers as a systematic method of recognizing characteristics repeatedly found among those who traffic in illicit drugs. The profile has also been described as "the collective or distilled experience of narcotics officers concerning characteristics repeatedly seen in drug smugglers." *Id.* at 525 n.6, 103 *S.Ct.* at 1339 n.6 (Rehnquist, J., dissenting). While conformity with just a few aspects of the profile may not sufficiently support a reasonable and articulable suspicion that criminal activity may be afoot in order to warrant a *Terry* stop of a suspect, *see Reid v. Georgia,* 448 *U.S.* 438, 100 *S.Ct.* 2752 (1980), a police officer is nonetheless entitled to assess the totality of the circumstances surrounding the subject of his or her attention in light of that officer's experience and training, which, of course, may include "instruction on a 'drug courier profile.' " *Royer* at 525 n.6, 103 *S.Ct.* at 1339 n.6.

Thus, while the profile is "not intended to provide a mathematical formula that automatically establishes grounds for a belief that criminal activity is afoot[, b]y the same reasoning, however, simply because these characteristics are accumulated in a 'profile,' [does not mean that] they are [] to be given less weight in assessing whether a suspicion is well founded." *Id.* In this respect, "sheer logic dictates that where certain characteristics repeatedly are found among drug smugglers, the existence of those characteristics in a particular case is to be considered accordingly in determining whether there are grounds to believe that further investigation is appropriate." *Id. See also United States v. Sokolow*, 490 *U.S.* 1, 109 *S.Ct.* 1581, 1587 (1989) ("A court sitting to determine the existence of reasonable suspicion must require the [officer] to articulate the factors leading to the conclusion, but the fact that these factors may be set forth in a 'profile' does not somehow detract from their evidentiary significance"). Consequently, when assessing the reasonableness of an investigative stop on the basis of a well-articulated "drug courier profile," emphasis should be placed "not on the profile *per se*, but on the characteristics common to couriers." *United States v. Quigley*, 890 *F.*2d 1019, 1021 (8th Cir. 1989).

In *Royer*, "the detectives' attention was attracted by the following facts which were considered to be within the profile: (a) Royer was carrying American Tourister luggage, which appeared to be heavy; (b) he was young, apparently between 25-35; (c) he was casually dressed; (d) he appeared pale and nervous, looking around at other people; (e) he paid for his ticket in cash with a large number of bills; and (f) rather than completing the airline identification tag to be attached to checked baggage, which had space for a name, address, and telephone number, he wrote only a name and the destination." *Id.* at 494 n.2, 103 *S.Ct.* at 1322 n.2. Upholding Royer's initial investigatory detention, the Court reasoned that when the officers learned that Royer was traveling under an assumed name, that fact, coupled with the facts already known by the officers which constituted a "drug courier profile"—"paying cash for a one-way ticket, the mode of checking the two bags, and Royer's appearance and conduct in general—were adequate grounds for suspecting Royer of carrying drugs and for temporarily detaining him and his luggage while they attempted to verify or dispel their suspicions." *Id.* at 502, 103 *S.Ct.* at 1326.

See also United States v. Zukas, 843 *F.*2d 179, 182-183 (5th Cir. 1988) ("[While] several of these factors have no independent significance except that they fit the DEA's drug-smuggler profile [and] no single factor would support a reasonable, particularized suspicion[, * * * considered together with Zukas' prior record, the specific activities observed * * * render[] the whole greater than the sum of its parts"); *United States v. Gonzales*, 842 *F.*2d 748, 753 n.2 (5th Cir. 1988) ("[D]rug courier profile characteristics are often useful in focusing the attention of a law enforcement official on a particular individual and may be relied upon, in conjunction with other individualized factors, to support a finding of reasonable suspicion").

UNITED STATES v. TAYLOR
United States Court of Appeals
917 *F.*2d 1402 (6th Cir. 1990)

QUESTION: At what point in the below set of circumstances did the officers develop a reasonable and articulable suspicion sufficient to warrant an investigative detention of defendant Taylor ?

CIRCUMSTANCES:

1. At about 7:00 p.m., in early October, Sergeant Eldridge and Officers Bevel and Roberts of the Memphis Police Department's narcotics task force were stationed at the Memphis International Airport when they observed Taylor deplane a flight arriving from Miami, Florida.

2. Sergeant Eldridge, who, at the time, had been a member of the task force for about six months, described Taylor as a middle-aged black man who appeared much different from the other deplaning passengers. Eldridge stated that the other passengers were neatly dressed in business or vacation attire, but Taylor was shabbily clad in dark slacks, a work shirt and a "dirty black baseball cap" with the military "scrambled eggs" across the front of it. According to Eldridge, while "the rest of the passengers that usually come from Miami [are] either business people or resort type people, people getting off in real casual nice looking clothes," Taylor just stood out "getting off there looking like [he] looked." Eldridge also pointed out that Taylor was the only black individual who had deplaned from this particular flight.

3. Taylor carried what appeared to be a new designer travel bag which he held very tightly to his body.

4. Taylor did not stop at the luggage carousel.

5. Taylor exhibited nervousness and constantly looked over his shoulder as he walked very rapidly through the terminal.

6. As Taylor hurriedly exited the terminal and proceeded toward the parking lot, the officers followed, with Sergeant Eldridge leading the pursuit.

7. Just before Taylor stepped off the sidewalk, Sergeant Eldridge grabbed his arm, pulled him back from the curb, identified himself as a police officer, and advised Taylor that he wanted to speak to him.

8. Eldridge and Officer Bevel stood close to Taylor while Officer Roberts assumed a position across the street between Taylor and the parking lot.

9. After several preliminary questions posed to Taylor by Officer Bevel, such as where he was going and where he was coming from,

Sergeant Eldridge asked to see Taylor's airline ticket and some form of identification, both of which Taylor produced. When Eldridge noticed that the name on Taylor's ticket matched the name on his Missouri driver's license, Officer Bevel asked if she could look inside the bag he was carrying. Taylor did not verbally consent, but unzipped the bag, shuffled papers around in it and said, "There's nothing that you are looking for here."

10. Officer Bevel then took custody of the bag and a closer examination revealed two packages wrapped in brown plastic tape which she recognized as wrapping typically used for the packaging of cocaine.

11. The officers placed Taylor under arrest and led him to the airport security office, where they confirmed that the packages did in fact contain approximately two kilograms of cocaine.

ANSWER: AT NO POINT. The officers in this case failed to demonstrate the existence of "objective observations" which evinced a "common pattern of criminal activity." *Id.* at 1407. While the fact that Taylor met a few characteristics of the drug courier profile may be relevant in deciding the legality of the seizure, "*[m]erely satisfying the drug courier profile [] 'does not, standing alone, justify a seizure.' " Id.* at 1407-08. [Emphasis added; citations omitted.] Rather, the totality of the circumstances must demonstrate that an officer's "objective observations" raise a reasonable and articulable suspicion that the particular individual about to be stopped has been, or is presently, engaged in, or is about to engage in criminal activity. *Id.* at 1408. According to the court, "Taylor's actions were inherently unsuspicious. The totality of the circumstances * * * did not yield particularized suspicions that warranted a seizure[.]" *Id.* at 1410.

RATIONALE: "We recognize that our government is in the midst of waging a 'War on Drugs.' Yet, the valiant effort of our law enforcement officers to rid society of the drug scourge cannot be done in total disregard of an individual's constitutional rights." *Id.* at 1405. As stated in *United States v. Radka*, 904 *F.*2d 357 (6th Cir. 1990):

> "Presently, our nation is plagued with the destructive effects of the illegal importation and distribution of drugs. At this critical time, our Constitution remains a lodestar for the protections that shall endure the most pernicious affronts to our society. ... This drug crisis does *not* license the aggrandizement of governmental power in lieu of civil liberties. Despite the devastation wrought by drug trafficking in communities nationwide, we *cannot* suspend the precious rights guaranteed by the Constitution in an effort to fight the 'War on Drugs.' * * *"

Taylor at 1405 (court's emphasis; quoting *Radka* at 361).

In this case, there is no doubt that *Taylor was seized within the meaning of the Fourth Amendment when, as he was about to cross the street, Sergeant Eldridge grabbed him forcefully by the arm and pulled him back to the sidewalk.* In fact, Eldridge testified at the suppression hearing that Taylor was not free to leave, and if he attempted to leave at any point during the questioning, he would have been pursued. Thus, the critical inquiry here is whether the seizure was constitutionally permissible.

Under the Fourth Amendment, "a brief investigatory detention is permissible if 'supported by a reasonable and articulable suspicion of criminal activity.' * * * The totality of the circumstances are considered in determining which suspicions are 'reasonable and articulable.' " *Id.* Relevant in this regard is the two-part inquiry set forth in *United States v. Cortez*, 449 *U.S.* 411, 417, 101 *S.Ct.* 690, 695 (1981). First, a law enforcement officer "must demonstrate the existence of 'objective observations.' [] This requirement is satisfied by evidence of a common pattern of criminal activity." *Taylor* at 1407. In this case, the fact that Taylor met a few characteristics of the drug courier profile may be relevant in deciding the legality of the seizure. However, *"[m]erely satisfying the drug courier profile [] 'does not, standing alone, justify a seizure.' " Id.* at 1407-08. [Emphasis added; citations omitted.] "Second, under the totality of the circumstances, these 'objective observations' must raise an articulable suspicion that the 'particular' individual" about to be stopped has been, or is presently, engaged in, or is about to engage in, criminal activity. *Id.* at 1408.

The circumstances of this case demonstrate that Taylor "(1) arrived on a plane from Miami, Florida—a drug source city; (2) walked away from the gate nervously, hurriedly and moved faster than the other passengers; (3) constantly looked backwards as he walked; (4) carried a tote bag that he held tightly to his body; and (5) left the terminal walking very fast." *Id.* at 1408. According to the court, those circumstances fail to meet the *Cortez* test.

"The officers failed to meet the first prong of the *Cortez* test because Taylor did not meet the drug courier profile." *Taylor* at 1408. While an officer well-versed in the field of drug trafficking may arguably find the factors set forth above as suspicious, "[i]n this case, however, the officers—particularly Sergeant Eldridge who led the pursuit—had little training in identifying a drug courier." *Id.* Sergeant Eldridge had only been with the narcotics task force for about six months, and on cross-examination admitted that he had had *"little* on-the-job experience with [the drug courier profile]." *Id.* [Emphasis in original.]

Moreover, Eldridge's characterization of Taylor as not belonging— as "appear[ing] 'different' from the other deplaning passengers"—is "flawed" in several respects. *Id.* at 1408, 1409. First, "[t]here is no dress code for passengers taking any flight. People are clad in a wide array of clothing whether or not they are coming from or going to a typical vacation spot." *Id.* at 1409. Next, "[a]t the time he was stopped, Taylor was the *only* black person who had deplaned. In fact, Sergeant Eldridge and Officer Bevel believed Taylor may have been the only black person on the flight." *Id.* [Emphasis in original.] The fact that a black individual is hurrying through an airport supports no basis for suspicion. "Many people, black and white, are constantly hurrying through an airport[.] * * * Walking fast or even running is not uncommon in an airport. Many people do not check-in their luggage to save time. All of these actions constitute perfectly lawful behavior. Yet, when the officers saw Taylor hurrying through the airport, looking around, and not stopping at the baggage area, they determined that he fit the drug courier profile. This determination was inappropriate, because *observing an individual walking quickly through an airport or nervously looking around is insufficient to warrant a search and seizure." Id.* [Emphasis added.]

Accordingly, "[b]ased on the officers' limited experience and the circumstances they observed," this Court determined that "they reasonably could not have suspected, as a matter of law, that Taylor was engaged in criminal activity." *Id.* In this respect, the court stated:

> We find it particularly relevant that the *least* qualified officer, Sergeant Eldridge, led the pursuit. The evidence relied upon— Taylor's arriving on a plane from Miami, Florida, walking quickly through the terminal, clutching luggage—"describes a large category of presumably innocent travelers, who would be subject to virtually random seizures were [this court] to conclude that as little foundation as there was in this case could justify a seizure."

Id. [Citations omitted; emphasis in original.]

Finally, the court concluded that "[t]he officers also failed to meet the second prong of the *Cortez* test because the factors that they relied upon evidenced unsuspicious behavior."

> The mere fact that a black man is observed walking quickly through an airport terminal does not raise the suspicion of criminal activity. Any attempt to detain such an individual, therefore, *must* be conducted within the parameters of the [F]ourth [A]mendment. In this instance, the [F]ourth [A]mendment's protections were ignored. * * *

Taylor at 1409, 1412. [Court's emphasis.]

> We find that Taylor's actions were inherently unsuspicious. The totality of the circumstances in [this] case did not yield particularized suspicions that warranted a seizure[.] * * * Thus, we find Taylor's seizure unconstitutional and the evidence obtained as a result of that seizure must be suppressed.

Id. at 1410.
MERRITT, Chief Judge, concurring.
"I concur in the Court's conclusion about this case. I particularly agree that law enforcement agents cannot make a racial characteristic the predominant feature in the drug courier profile. Like the Court, I can find no real basis for distinguishing this man from the other passengers who deplaned, except for race." * * * *Id.* at 1412.

UNITED STATES v. ROBERSON
United States Court of Appeals
90 *F*.3d 75 (3rd Cir. 1996)

QUESTION: May an anonymous tip that contains only information readily observable at the time the tip is made supply reasonable suspicion for a *Terry* stop in the absence of any suspicious conduct on the part of the subject ?

ANSWER: NO. Reasonable suspicion for a *Terry* stop will not exist in the "absence of observations of suspicious conduct or the corroboration of information from which the police could reasonably conclude that the anonymous tipster's allegation of criminal activity was reliable[.]" *Id.* at 81.

RATIONALE: In late September, just after 7:00 p.m., a Philadelphia Police 911 operator received an anonymous call reporting that "a heavy-set, black male wearing dark green pants, a white hooded sweatshirt, and a brown leather jacket was selling drugs on the 2100 block of Chelten Avenue." *Id.* at 75. The call taker had no information concerning the reliability of the caller or the source of the information.

At about 7:18 p.m., the anonymous tipster's report was relayed over the police radio. Officers Nathan and Hellmuth, who were patrolling the general area in a marked police vehicle, responded. Less than a minute after receiving the call, they arrived at the 2100 block of Chelten and saw a man standing on the corner. The man matched the description provided by the caller. This corner, according to the officers, was a "hot spot" where drugs were sold to passing motorists. "Officer Nathan and the man, later to be identified as the defendant, Lester Roberson, made eye contact. According to Nathan, the defendant then walked 'casually' over to a car parked facing the wrong way on Chelten Avenue and leaned in as if to speak with the vehicle's occupants. The police observed no indicia of drug activity." *Id.* at 76.

At this point, the officers exited their vehicle, "with guns drawn, and ordered the defendant away from the parked car. As they approached him, they observed the butt of a gun protruding from his pants. They patted him down, and seized from his person a 9mm semi-automatic pistol with 13 rounds of ammunition, two plastic bags containing numerous packets of cocaine, a pill bottle containing 47 valium pills, a half-bottle of cough syrup, and $319 in U.S. currency." *Id.* The officers then placed defendant under arrest.

In this appeal, defendant argued that the officers did not have a right to stop him because they did not have a reasonable suspicion that he was involved in criminal activity. *The Court of Appeals for the Third Circuit agreed.*

Preliminarily, the court accepted the district court's unchallenged finding that the officers did not observe the defendant's gun until some time *after* they exited their vehicle with their guns drawn and, for Fourth Amendment purposes, effected a seizure of defendant. Therefore, the observation of the gun could not be used to justify the stop.

In *Terry v. Ohio*, 392 *U.S.* 1, 88 *S.Ct.* 1868 (1968), the United States Supreme Court held that law enforcement officers may, consistent with the Fourth Amendment, stop and temporarily detain citizens short of an arrest, and that such a stop is justified by less than the probable cause necessary for a full-blown arrest. "Under *Terry*, a police officer may detain and investigate citizens when he or she has a reasonable suspicion that 'criminal activity may be afoot.' " *Roberson* at 77 (quoting *Terry* at 30, 88 *S.Ct.* at 1884). In this case, the critical issue was whether the officers had such a reasonable suspicion.

To determine whether the anonymous tip provided a reasonable suspicion of criminal activity, the court relied on two cases: *Illinois v. Gates*, 462 *U.S.* 213, 103 *S.Ct.* 2317 (1983), and *Alabama v. White*, 496 *U.S.* 325, 110 *S.Ct.* 2412 (1990). In *Gates*, the United States Supreme Court determined that, when dealing with probable cause, the "totality of the circumstances" approach should be utilized when an anonymous tip must be evaluated. Thereafter, the Court in *White* adopted the "totality of the circumstances" test to determine whether an anonymous tip could provide the necessary reasonable articulable suspicion for a *Terry* stop. "In concluding that the *Gates* tip provided probable cause and the *White* tip provided reasonable suspicion, the [Supreme] Court stressed two factors: (1) an officer's ability to corroborate significant aspects of the tip, and (2) the tip's ability to predict future events." *Roberson* at 77. Significantly, in *White*, the Court said:

> We think it also important that, as in *Gates*, "the anonymous [tip] contained a range of details relating not just to easily obtained facts and conditions existing at the time of the tip, but to future actions of third parties ordinarily not easily predicted." The fact that the officers found a car precisely matching the caller's description in front of the 235 building is an example of the former. *Anyone could have "predicted" that fact because it was a condition presumably existing at the time of the call. What was important was the caller's ability to predict [White's] future behavior, because it demonstrated inside information—a special familiarity with [White's] affairs.* * * * Because only a small number of people are generally privy to an individual's itinerary, it is reasonable for police to believe that a person with access to such information is likely to also have access to reliable information about that individual's illegal activities.

Id. at 332, 110 *S.Ct.* at 2417. [Emphasis added.]

Here, in *Roberson*, the court ruled that the anonymous tip "indicating that a heavy-set, black man wearing green pants, a brown leather jacket, and a white hooded sweatshirt was selling drugs on the 2100 block of Chelten Avenue—together with the subsequent observations by officers Nathan and Hellmuth"—did not provide the necessary reasonable articulable suspicion under *Alabama v. White* for an investigative stop. *Id.* at 79. The court said:

> [I]n assessing reasonable suspicion for a stop pursuant to an anonymous tip, *Alabama v. White* stressed corroboration and pre-

dictiveness. In [this] situation, it is no doubt true that the officers were able to corroborate most of the tipster's information. But to use the Court's language, "Anyone could have 'predicted' " the facts contained in the tip because they were "condition[s] presumably existing at the time of the call." * * * Indeed, the caller could have been looking out his window at a heavy-set black man in green pants, brown leather jacket, and white hooded sweatshirt at the time of his 911 call.

Id. [Citation omitted.]

Unlike the tipsters in both *Gates* and *White*, the caller in this case did not provide information regarding defendant's future activities.

> The tip * * * contained no "details of future actions of third parties ordinarily not easily predicted." * * * Thus, no future actions could be corroborated, and an important basis for forming reasonable suspicion was absent. Moreover, because they were dealing with an anonymous and bare-bones tip, the police had no basis for assessing either the reliability of the informant or the grounds on which the informant believed that a crime was being committed— * * * important ingredients in the "totality."

Id. at 80.

The court added, however, that these omissions "probably would not have invalidated the stop, if, after corroborating readily observable facts, the police officers had noticed unusual or suspicious conduct on Roberson's part. * * * But they did not." *Id.*

> After their arrival on Chelten Avenue, the police first saw the defendant standing on the corner, and they then observed him walk to a car parked across the street and lean in as if to talk to the vehicle's occupant(s). None of this was unusual. Officer Nathan testified that it was normal for residents of that neighborhood to stand on the corner. * * *

> Furthermore, defendant's walk to the car did not indicate that he was about to engage in drug transactions. First, according to Nathan's own testimony, the defendant walked "casually" to the car—behavior that does not indicate criminal activity. Second, * * * because the defendant had already seen the *marked* police car, it would be "highly unlikely that he would engage in drug transactions at that moment." * * *

> All that the Government is left with then is the fact that the defendant was apprehended on a "hot corner." This is not enough. The 2100 block of Chelten is a residential neighborhood. We simply cannot accept the Government's position that any resident of (or visitor to) that neighborhood who, without otherwise engendering suspicion, is unlucky enough to be the subject of a non-predictive anonymous tip, is subject to a *Terry* stop simply because the neighborhood is known for narcotics sales. * * *

Id. [Court's emphasis.]

Accordingly, the court held that "the police do not have reasonable suspicion for an investigative stop when, as here, they receive a fleshless anonymous tip of drug-dealing that provides only readily observable information, and they themselves observe no suspicious behavior." *Id.* "To hold otherwise," emphasized the court, "would work too great an intrusion on the Fourth Amendment liberties, for any citizen could be subject to police detention pursuant to an anonymous phone call describing his or her present location and appearance and representing that he or she was selling drugs. Indeed, anyone of us could face significant intrusion on the say-so of any anonymous prankster, rival, or misinformed individual. This * * * would be unreasonable." *Id.* at 80-81.

The court did pause to note, however, that

> the police were not powerless to act on the non-predictive, anonymous tip they received. The officers could have set up surveillance of the defendant. * * * If the officers then observed any suspicious behavior or if they had observed suspicious behavior as they approached the defendant in this case, they would have had appropriate cause to stop—and perhaps even arrest—him. This, however, they did not do. In the absence of any observations of suspicious conduct or the corroboration of information from which the police could reasonably conclude that the anonymous tipster's allegation of criminal activity was reliable, we must conclude that there was no reasonable suspicion to stop the defendant.

Id. at 81.

NOTE

The court in *Roberson* did not address whether such an anonymous tip would be sufficient to create a reasonable suspicion when the tip involves an allegation that the suspect is carrying a gun rather than selling drugs. Under those circumstances, a different rule may apply. *See e.g., United States v. Clipper*, 973 *F*.2d 944, 945-46 (D.C.Cir. 1992) (the "element of imminent danger distinguishes a gun tip from one involving possession of drugs"); *United States v. DeBerry*, 76 *F*.3d 884, 885 (7th Cir. 1996) (agreeing with the *Clipper* court that the right of the people "to be protected from *armed* predators" justified the stop and frisk of a man based on an anonymous tip that the man had a gun) (emphasis added).

ILLINOIS v. WARDLOW
United States Supreme Court
528 *U.S.* 119, 120 *S.Ct.* 673 (2000)

QUESTION 1: Will the sudden, unprovoked flight of a person in a high drug-trafficking area, upon sighting a police vehicle, create a reasonable suspicion of criminal activity to support a temporary investigative detention (*Terry* stop) of the person ?

ANSWER: YES. In this case, a caravan of four police vehicles, containing a total of eight police officers, "was converging on an area known for heavy narcotics trafficking, and the officers anticipated encountering a large number of people in the area, including drug customers and individuals serving as lookouts." *Id.* at 676. In this context, as the caravan passed the area where defendant Wardlow was standing and holding an opaque bag, Wardlow looked in the direction of the officers and fled. At that moment, the Court held, the officers were "justified in suspecting that Wardlow was involved in criminal activity[,]" and were permitted to stop him and investigate further. *Id.*

QUESTION 2: Will the Court adopt a bright-line rule authorizing the temporary detention of *anyone* who flees at the mere sight of a police officer ?

ANSWER: NO. The police do not have an automatic right to conduct a temporary detention of *anyone* who flees at the mere sight of an officer. Reasonable suspicion to support such a detention must be determined by "looking to 'the totality of the circumstances—the whole picture.' " *Id.* at 677. (Stevens, J., concurring in part, joined by Souter, Ginsburg, and Breyer, JJ.).

RATIONALE: In the first week of September, Officers Nolan and Harvey of the Chicago Police Department were working as uniformed officers in the special operations section. A few minutes after noon, the officers, while driving the last car of a four-car caravan, converged "on an area known for heavy narcotics trafficking in order to investigate drug transactions. The officers were traveling together because they expected to find a crowd of people in the area, including lookouts and customers." *Id.* at 674.

As the caravan passed a building where defendant, Sam Wardlow, was standing, Officer Nolan noticed him and noticed that he was holding an opaque bag. At that moment, Wardlow looked in the direction of the officers and fled. "Nolan and Harvey turned their car southbound, watched him as he ran through the gangway and an alley, and eventually cornered him on the street." *Id.* at 675. Nolan confronted Wardlow and immediately conducted a protective frisk for weapons "because in his experience it was common for there to be weapons in the near vicinity of narcotics transactions." *Id.* "During the frisk, Officer Nolan squeezed the bag [Wardlow] was carrying and felt a heavy, hard object similar to the shape of a gun. The officer then opened the bag and discovered a .38-caliber handgun with five live rounds of ammunition." *Id.* Wardlow was placed under arrest.

Writing for the Court, Chief Justice Rehnquist observed that this is a case "involving a brief encounter between a citizen and a police officer on a public street." *Id.* The critical issue was whether Officer Nolan had a reasonable suspicion sufficient to justify an investigative stop pursuant to *Terry v. Ohio*, 392 *U.S.* 1, 88 *S.Ct.* 1868 (1968).

In *Terry*, the Court held that "an officer may, consistent with the Fourth Amendment, conduct a brief, investigatory stop when the officer has a reasonable, articulable suspicion that criminal activity is afoot." *Wardlow* at 675. "While 'reasonable suspicion' is a less demanding standard than probable cause[,] * * * [t]he officer must be able to articulate more than an 'inchoate and unparticularized suspicion or "hunch"' of criminal activity." *Id.* at 675-76.

Finding the circumstances of this case sufficient, the Court stated:

> Nolan and Harvey were among eight officers in a four-car caravan that was converging on an area known for heavy narcotics trafficking, and the officers anticipated encountering a large number of people in the area, including drug customers and individuals serving as lookouts. It was in this context that Officer Nolan decided to investigate Wardlow after observing him flee.

Id. at 676.

The Court emphasized that "[a]n individual's presence in an area of expected criminal activity, standing alone, is not enough to support a reasonable, particularized suspicion that the person is committing a crime." *Id.* "But officers are not required to ignore the relevant characteristics of a location in determining whether the circumstances are sufficiently suspicious to warrant further investigation." *Id.* In this respect, the Court has "previously noted the fact that the stop occurred in a 'high crime area' among the relevant contextual considerations in a *Terry* analysis." *Id.*

In this case, it was not merely Wardlow's presence "in an area of heavy narcotics trafficking that aroused the officers' suspicion but his unprovoked flight upon noticing the police." *Id.* And in developing a reasonable articulable suspicion, "nervous, evasive behavior" may be considered as a "pertinent factor." *Id.* The Court said:

> Headlong flight—wherever it occurs—is the consummate act of evasion: it is not necessarily indicative of wrongdoing, but it is certainly suggestive of such. In reviewing the propriety of an officer's conduct, courts do not have available empirical studies dealing with inferences drawn from suspicious behavior, and we cannot reasonably demand scientific certainty from judges or law enforcement officers where none exists.

Id.

Accordingly, "the determination of reasonable suspicion must be based on commonsense judgments and inferences about human behavior." *Id.* The Court concluded, therefore, that "Officer Nolan was justified in suspecting that Wardlow was involved in criminal activity, and, therefore, in investigating further." *Id.*

This holding, noted the Court, is "entirely consistent" with *Florida v. Royer*, 460 *U.S.* 491, 103 *S.Ct.* 1319 (1983), where it was held that "when an officer, without reasonable suspicion or probable cause, approaches an individual, the individual has a right to ignore the police and go about his business. * * * And any 'refusal to cooperate, without more, does not furnish the minimal level of objective justification needed for a detention or seizure.' " *Wardlow* at 676. [Citations omitted.]

> But unprovoked flight is simply not a mere refusal to cooperate. Flight, by its very nature, is not "going about one's business"; in fact, it is just the opposite. Allowing officers confronted with such flight to stop the fugitive and investigate further is quite consistent with the individual's right to go about his business or to stay put and remain silent in the face of police questioning.

Id.

NOTE

In *Wardlow*, Justice Stevens, joined by Justices Souter, Ginsburg and Breyer, filed a concurring and dissenting opinion agreeing with that portion of the majority's opinion which declined to announce "a 'bright-line rule' authorizing the temporary detention of anyone who flees at the mere sight of a police officer." *Id.* at 677. Instead, the Court adhered "to the view that '[t]he concept of reasonable suspicion . . . is not readily, or even usefully, reduced to a neat set of legal rules,' but must be determined by looking to 'the totality of the circumstances—the whole picture.' " *Id.* (quoting *United States v. Sokolow*, 490 *U.S.* 1, 7-8, 109 *S.Ct.* 1581, 1585 (1989)).

UNITED STATES v. HENSLEY
Supreme Court of the United States
469 *U.S.* 221, 105 *S.Ct.* 675 (1985)

QUESTION: May a law enforcement officer stop and briefly detain a person in reliance upon a wanted flyer issued by another department indicating that the person is wanted for questioning pursuant to a felony investigation of a past and completed crime ?

ANSWER: YES. "[W]here police have been unable to locate a person suspected of involvement in a past crime, the ability to briefly stop that person, ask questions, or check identification in the absence of probable cause promotes the strong government interest in solving crimes and bringing offenders to justice." *Id.* at 680. The law enforcement interests promoted by allowing one department to conduct investigative detentions based upon another department's bulletins or flyers are considerable, while the intrusions on a person's Fourth and Fourteenth Amendment rights are minimal. *Id.* at 682.

RATIONALE: To restrain police action until after probable cause is obtained would not only hinder the investigation but might also enable the suspect to flee and remain at large. The law enforcement interests at stake in these circumstances substantially outweigh the individual's right to be free from an investigative detention which is no more intrusive or extensive than permissible in the investigation of imminent or ongoing crimes.

This is the first time the United States Supreme Court specifically addressed the issue of whether the police may stop and detain a person on information from a wanted flyer from another jurisdiction when the investigation is of a past or completed crime. Hensley was wanted for questioning in reference to an armed robbery. The Court held that the justification for the stop did not evaporate merely because the armed robbery was completed.

Therefore, when police have a reasonable suspicion, grounded in specific and articulable facts, that a person they encounter was involved, or wanted, in connection with a completed crime, then a *Terry*-type stop may be made to investigate that suspicion.

If a wanted flyer or bulletin has been issued on the basis of articulable facts supporting a reasonable suspicion that the person wanted has committed an offense, then reliance upon that flyer or bulletin justifies a stop to check identification, to pose questions, or to detain the person briefly while attempting to obtain further information. *Id.* at 682.

In order to evaluate the police officer's actions, the Court set forth an objective test for the officers to follow. It is the objective reading of the flyer or bulletin that determines whether officers from other departments can act in reliance on it. "It is imperative that the facts be judged against the objective standard":

> [W]ould the facts available to the officer at the moment of the [stop and detention] warrant a man of reasonable caution [to believe the] action taken was appropriate[?]

Id.

Therefore, if a police officer makes a *Terry*-type stop in objective reliance upon a flyer or bulletin, the evidence uncovered in the course of the stop is admissible if the police who *issued* the flyer or bulletin possessed a reasonable suspicion, based upon specific and articulable facts, justifying the stop in their own right, and, if the stop which takes place is not significantly more intrusive than what would have been permitted by the issuing department. *Id.*

NOTE

The keynote to the Court's decision is that the stop and detention by the department relying on the flyer from an issuing department is no more intrusive than would have been permitted by that issuing department and to an experienced police officer on an objective reading of the flyer.

UNITED STATES v. SHARPE
Supreme Court of the United States
470 *U.S.* 675, 105 *S.Ct.* 1568 (1985)

QUESTION: Are Investigative Detentions, based upon reasonable suspicion, which last twenty minutes or longer, a violation of the Fourth Amendment's prohibition on unlawful seizures ?

ANSWER: NO. In assessing the effect of the length of an investigative detention, courts will take into account whether the police diligently pursue their investigation, and whether the detention lasts no longer than is necessary to effectuate the purpose of the stop. *Id.* at 1575, 1576.

RATIONALE: "Obviously, if an investigative stop continues indefinitely, at some point it can no longer be justified as an investigative stop." *Id.* at 1575. However, the Court refuses to place a rigid time limitation on *Terry*-type investigatory stops. "While it is clear that the brevity of the invasion of the individual's Fourth Amendment interests is an important factor in determining whether the seizure is so minimally intrusive as to be justifiable on reasonable suspicion," *id.*, courts will also consider the law enforcement purposes to be served by the stop as well as the time reasonably needed to effectuate those purposes.

Therefore, when a court determines whether a detention is too long in duration to be justified as an investigative stop, it will examine whether the police "diligently pursued a means of investigation that was likely to confirm or dispel their suspicions quickly, during which time it was necessary to detain the defendant." *Id.* The court will make this assessment by considering whether the police acted swiftly in developing the situation. The question will not be whether some other alternative was available, but "whether the police acted unreasonably in failing to recognize or to pursue it." *Id.* at 1576.

NOTE

1. "There is no talismanic time beyond which any stop justified on the basis of *Terry* becomes an unreasonable seizure under the [F]ourth [A]mendment." *United States v. McCarthy*, 77 *F.*3d 522, 530 (1st Cir. 1996) (quoting *United States v. Davis*, 768 *F.*2d 893, 901 (7th Cir. 1985)). Rather, in determining whether an investigative stop is too long, "common sense and ordinary human experience must govern over rigid criteria." *United States v. Quinn*, 815 *F.*2d 153, 157 (1st Cir. 1987) (citing *Sharpe* at 685, 105 *S.Ct.* at 1575). In this respect, the court in *McCarthy* observed:

> Indeed, whether a particular investigatory stop is too long turns on a consideration of all relevant factors, including "the law enforcement purposes to be served by the stop as well as the time reasonably needed to effectuate those purposes." * * * Moreover, a court should ask "whether the police diligently pursued a means of inves-

tigation that was likely to confirm or dispel their suspicions quickly, during which time it was necessary to detain the defendant." * * *

Furthermore, time of detention cannot be the sole criterion for measuring the intrusiveness of the detention. Clearly, from the perspective of the detainee, other factors, including the force used to detain the individual, the restrictions placed on his or her personal movement, and the information conveyed to the detainee concerning the reasons for the stop and its impact on his or her rights, affect the nature and extent of the intrusion and, thus, should factor into the analysis. * * *

Id. at 530-31. [Citations omitted.] *See also United States v. Vega,* 72 *F.*3d 507, 514-16 (7th Cir. 1995) (upholding a sixty-two minute stop; "the crux of our inquiry is whether the nature of the restraint meets the Fourth Amendment standard of objective reasonableness").

2. *The "least intrusive means" test.* In *Florida v. Royer,* 460 *U.S.* 491, 500, 103 *S.Ct.* 1319, 1325 (1983), the United States Supreme Court, in a plurality opinion, instructed that a reasonable investigative detention is one that is "temporary," lasting "no longer than is necessary to effectuate the purpose of the stop." The Court then went on to state that "the investigative methods employed should be the least intrusive means reasonably available to verify or dispel the officer's suspicion in a short period of time." *Id.* at 500, 103 *S.Ct.* at 1325-26. "If the detention lasts too long, or if the officers' conduct is too intrusive, then the stop is converted into an arrest." *United States v. Dixon,* 51 *F.*3d 1376, 1380 (8th Cir. 1995). *See also United States v. Bloomfield,* 40 *F.*3d 910, 916-17 (8th Cir. 1994). Since *Royer,* the United States Supreme Court has not emphasized the "least intrusive means" test. Nonetheless, the test is employed by various jurisdictions. *See e.g., Dixon* at 1380 n.3 (8th Circuit continues to employ the "least intrusive means" test).

---

§8.2(c). Transporting suspects.

DUNAWAY v. NEW YORK
Supreme Court of the United States
442 U.S. 200, 99 S.Ct. 2248 (1979)

QUESTION: May a law enforcement officer transport a suspect to police headquarters for questioning, without his consent and without probable cause (for his arrest) ?

ANSWER: NO. Whenever a law enforcement officer removes a suspect from where he is found and transports that suspect to police headquarters for questioning, without his consent and without probable cause (for his arrest), the detention is, in all important respects, indistinguishable from a traditional arrest. Merely because a suspect is not told he is under arrest, is not "booked," and would not have an arrest record if the interrogation proves fruitless, does not make such a detention analogous to the type authorized by *Terry v. Ohio*. Rather, such a "detention for custodial interrogation—regardless of its label—intrudes so severely on interests protected by the Fourth Amendment" that the familiar requirement of probable cause is thereby triggered. *Id.* at 2256, 2258.

RATIONALE: In late March, the proprietor of a pizza parlor in Rochester, New York, was killed during an attempted robbery. By the middle of August, Rochester, police developed reasonable grounds to *suspect* that defendant was involved in the crime. The investigating detective ordered several officers to go out and "pick up" defendant and "bring him in" for questioning. Three detectives located defendant at a neighbor's house, and brought him to police headquarters in a police car. Although defendant "was not told he was under arrest, he would have been physically restrained if he had attempted to leave" *Id.* at 2252. Defendant was placed in an interrogation room, where he was questioned by officers after being given the *Miranda* warnings. During the questioning, defendant made several incriminating admissions which were later used against him at his trial for robbery and felony murder.

Holding that defendant's statements should have been suppressed, the Supreme Court declared that "the Rochester police violated the Fourth and Fourteenth Amendments when, without probable cause to arrest, they took [defendant] into custody, transported him to the police station, and detained him there for interrogation." *Id.* at 2253. According to the Court, "[t]here can be little doubt that [defendant] was 'seized' in the Fourth Amendment sense when he was taken involuntarily to the police station." *Id.*

The State pressed the argument that even if the police lacked probable cause to arrest defendant before his incriminating statements were taken, the seizure of defendant did not amount to an arrest and was therefore permissible under the Fourth Amendment because the police had a "reasonable suspicion" that defendant possessed "intimate knowledge about a serious and unsolved crime." *Id.* at 2254 (relying on *Terry v. Ohio*, 392 *U.S.* 1, 88 *S.Ct.* 1868 (1968)). *The Supreme Court disagreed.*

"*Terry* departed from traditional Fourth Amendment analysis in two respects. First, it defined a special category of Fourth Amendment 'seizures' so substantially less intrusive than arrests that the general rule requiring probable cause to make Fourth Amendment 'seizures' reasonable could be replaced by a balancing test. Second, the application of this balancing test led the Court to approve this narrowly defined less intrusive seizure on grounds less rigorous than probable cause," namely, reasonable suspicion. *Id.* at 2255. The *Terry* standard flowed from the Court's recognition that those "intrusions fell far short of the kind of intrusion associated with arrest." *Id.* at 2256.

In contrast to the type of detention *Terry* authorizes on reasonable suspicion, the detention of defendant "was in important respects indistinguishable from a traditional arrest. *[Defendant] was not questioned briefly where he was found.* Instead, he was taken from a neighbor's home to a police car, transported to a police station, and placed in an interrogation room. *He was never informed that he was 'free to go'*; indeed, he would have been physically restrained if he had refused to accompany the officers or had tried to escape their custody." *Id.* Significantly, "[t]he application of the Fourth Amendment's requirement of probable cause does not depend on whether an intrusion of this magnitude is termed an 'arrest[.]' The mere facts that [defendant] was not told he was under arrest, was not 'booked,' and would not have had an arrest record if the interrogation had proved fruitless, * * * obviously do not make [defendant's] seizure even roughly analogous to the narrowly defined intrusions involved in *Terry*[.]" *Id.* at 2256-57. [Emphasis added.]

"The central importance of the probable cause requirement to the protection of a citizen's privacy afforded by the Fourth Amendment's guarantees cannot be compromised[.]" *Id.* at 2257. Whether deemed a "technical arrest" or characterized by some other term, the treatment of the defendant in this case required probable cause. Accordingly, "detention for custodial interrogation—regardless of its label— intrudes so severely on interests protected by the Fourth Amendment as necessarily to trigger the traditional safeguards against illegal arrest. [Consequently, the Court holds] that the Rochester police violated the Fourth and Fourteenth Amendments when, without probable cause, they seized [defendant] and transported him to the police station for interrogation." *Id.* at 2258.

NOTE

1. In *Kaupp v. Texas*, 538 *U.S.* 626, 123 *S.Ct.* 1843 (2003), the United States Supreme Court reaffirmed that, in the absence of probable cause for arrest, it is unlawful for law enforcement officials to transport a suspect, against his will, to the station for questioning.

In *Kaupp*, during the course of an investigation into the stabbing murder of a 14-year-old girl, Robert Kaupp surfaced as a suspect. Although Kaupp's precise involvement in the murder was uncertain, the authorities suspected that he had somehow assisted the girl's 19-year-old half brother, who had confessed to fatally stabbing his half sister and placing her body in a drainage ditch. In his confession, the girl's brother had mentioned the presence of Kaupp during the crime.

Based on this information, detectives decided to bring Kaupp to headquarters and confront him with what the brother had said. The lead detective, in the company of two other plainclothes detectives and three uniformed officers, went to Kaupp's house the next day, at approximately 3:00 a.m. As soon as Kaupp's father let them in, the officers went to Kaupp's bedroom and awakened him with a flashlight. The lead detective identified himself and said, "We need to go and talk." *Id.*, 123 *S.Ct.* at 1845. Kaupp said, "Okay." The officers then handcuffed Kaupp and led him, shoeless and dressed only in boxer shorts and a T-shirt, out of his house and into a patrol car. At no time was Kaupp told that he was free to decline to go with the officers.

The officers stopped for 5 or 10 minutes where the victim's body had just been found, in anticipation of confronting Kaupp with the brother's confession, and then went on to headquarters. There, they took Kaupp to an interview room, removed his handcuffs, and advised him of his *Miranda* rights. At first, Kaupp denied any involvement in the victim's disappearance, but 10 or 15 minutes into the interrogation, when told of the brother's confession, he admitted having a part in the crime.

Finding the officers' actions improper, the Court declared that it has never allowed "the '*involuntary* removal of a suspect from his home to a police station and his detention there for investigative purposes . . . absent probable cause or judicial authorization.'" *Id.* at 1846. [Citation omitted; emphasis added.] "Such involuntary transport to a police station for questioning is 'sufficiently like arrest to invoke the traditional rule that arrests may constitutionally be made only on probable cause.'" *Id.*

In this case, it was clear that when Kaupp was transported to the station, the officers did not have probable cause. It was also clear to the Court that this encounter was the functional equivalent of an arrest. The Court said:

> A 17-year-old boy was awakened in his bedroom at three in the morning by at least three police officers, one of whom stated, "We need to go and talk." He was taken out in handcuffs, without shoes, dressed only in his underwear in January, placed in a patrol car, driven to the scene of a crime and then to the [station], where he was taken into an interrogation room and questioned. This evidence points to arrest even more starkly than the facts in *Dunaway v. New York* * * *, where the [defendant] "was taken from a neighbor's home to a police car, transported to a police station, and placed in an interrogation room." There we held it clear that the detention was "in important respects indistinguishable from a traditional arrest" and therefore required probable cause or judicial authorization to be legal. The same is, if anything, even clearer here.

Kaupp at 1846-47.

Moreover, Kaupp's reply of, "Okay," in response to the detective's statement is "no showing of consent under the circumstances." *Id.* at 1847. The detective "offered Kaupp no choice, and a group of police officers rousing an adolescent out of bed in the middle of the night with the words 'we need to go and talk' presents no option but 'to go.' " *Id.*

Under the circumstances, there was no reason to believe that Kaupp's answer was anything more than "a mere submission to a claim of lawful authority." *Id.* Moreover, when the detectives began to question Kaupp at the station, "no reasonable person in his situation would have thought he was sitting in the interview room as a matter of choice, free to change his mind and go home to bed." *Id.*

Nor did the Court find it significant that this law enforcement agency "routinely" transported individuals while handcuffed "for safety of the officers," or that Kaupp "did not resist the use of handcuffs or act in a manner consistent with anything other than full cooperation." *Id.* The test is an "objective one," and "stressing the officers' motivation of self-protection does not speak to how their actions would reasonably be understood." *Id.* As for the lack of resistance, a person's failure to resist a group of law enforcement officers should not be interpreted as a waiver of Fourth Amendment rights.

Since Kaupp was arrested before he was questioned, and because the officers did not have probable cause to detain him at that point, the law requires suppression of the confession unless that confession was "an act of free will" sufficient to "purge the primary taint" of the unlawful arrest. *Id.* As a matter of law, the administration of *Miranda* warnings, alone, cannot break the causal connection between the illegal arrest and the confession; and in this case, all other factors point the opposite way. Significantly, there was no indication that "any substantial time passed between Kaupp's removal from his home in handcuffs and his confession after only 10 or 15 minutes of interrogation. Indeed, at no time during this appeal did the prosecution allege "any meaningful intervening event" between the illegal arrest and Kaupp's confession. *Id.* at 1848.

HAYES v. FLORIDA
Supreme Court of the United States
470 *U.S.* 811, 105 *S.Ct.* 1643 (1985)

QUESTION: May a law enforcement officer transport a suspect to the police station for fingerprinting in the absence of probable cause to arrest, consent, or prior judicial authorization ?

ANSWER: NO.   In the absence of probable cause to arrest, consent to the journey to the police station, or judicial authorization for the fingerprinting process, transportation to and investigative detention at the station house "together violate the Fourth Amendment." *Id.* at 1646.

RATIONALE: Defendant, Joe Hayes, was a prime suspect in a series of burglary-rapes that had been committed in Punta Gorda, Florida. At the residence of one of the victims, police found latent fingerprints they believed belonged to the assailant. They also found a herringbone pattern tennis shoe print near the victim's front porch. The officers decided to visit defendant's home to obtain his fingerprints or, if he was uncooperative, to arrest him. At this point in the investigation, the police did not have probable cause for an arrest, nor did they seek judicial authorization for the fingerprinting process.

When the officers arrived at defendant's home, they spoke with him on his front porch. Defendant did not wish to accompany the officers to the station for fingerprinting. When he expressed his reluctance, one of the officers stated that they would therefore arrest him. Defendant then stated that he would rather go with the officers to the station than be arrested. Before they left, one of the officers seized a pair of herringbone pattern tennis shoes that were sitting on the front porch in plain view.

Defendant was taken to the police station, where he was fingerprinted. The police determined that his prints matched those left at the crime scene, and he was then formally arrested.

In this appeal, defendant argued that the fingerprint evidence obtained by the police was inadmissible as the fruit of an illegal detention. *The United States Supreme Court agreed.*

The holding and rationale of *Davis v. Mississippi*, 394 *U.S.* 721, 89 *S.Ct.* 1394 (1969), dictate the outcome of this case. In *Davis*, in the course of investigating a rape, police brought Davis to the station, where he was fingerprinted and briefly questioned. At the time, the police did not have probable cause for an arrest, there was no warrant, and Davis had not consented to the trip to the station. He was later charged with and convicted of the rape. The Court held that Davis' detention for the purpose of fingerprinting was "subject to the constraints of the Fourth Amendment and exceeded the permissible limits of those temporary seizures authorized by *Terry v. Ohio*[.]" *Hayes* at 1645.

"Here, as in *Davis*, there was no probable cause to arrest, no consent to the journey to the police station, and no judicial authorization for such a detention for fingerprinting purposes." *Id.* at 1646. The police action, therefore, violated the rule clearly set forth in *Davis*: "[T]ransportation to and investigative detention at the station house without probable cause or judicial authorization together violate the Fourth Amendment." *Id.*

The Court further explained that "at some point in the investigative process, police procedures can qualitatively and quantitatively be so intrusive with respect to a suspect's freedom of movement and privacy interests as to trigger the full protection of the Fourth and Fourteenth Amendments. * * * [T]he line is crossed when the police, without probable cause or a warrant, forcibly remove a person from his home or other place in which he is entitled to be and transport him to the police station, where he is detained, although briefly, for investigative purposes. * * * [S]uch seizures, at least where not under judicial supervision, are sufficiently like arrests to invoke the traditional rule that arrests may constitutionally be made only on probable cause." *Id.* at 1646-47.

"None of the foregoing implies that a brief detention in the field for the purpose of fingerprinting, where there is only reasonable suspicion not amounting to probable cause, is necessarily impermissible under the Fourth Amendment." *Id.* at 1647. A number of cases have suggested that "the Fourth Amendment would permit seizures for the purpose of fingerprinting, if there is reasonable suspicion that the suspect has committed a criminal act, if there is a reasonable basis for believing that fingerprinting will establish or negate the suspect's connection with that crime, and if the procedure is carried out with dispatch." *Id.*

Moreover, as suggested by *Davis* and *Dunaway*, "under circumscribed procedures, the Fourth Amendment might permit the judiciary to authorize the seizure of a person on less than probable cause and his removal to the police station for the purpose of fingerprinting." *Hayes* at 1647. Indeed, based on *Davis* and *Dunaway*, some states have enacted detailed procedures for judicially authorized seizures for the purpose of fingerprinting.

Accordingly, due to the absence of probable cause and a warrant, consent, or prior judicial authorization, the evidence seized in this case must be suppressed.

---

§8.2(d). The *"Terry* frisk."

ADAMS v. WILLIAMS
Supreme Court of the United States
407 *U.S.* 143, 92 *S.Ct.* 1921 (1972)

QUESTION: Is a protective "pat-down frisk" constitutional when based on an informant's tip that a described suspect seated in a described car at 2:15 a.m. was carrying narcotics and had "a gun at his waist"?

ANSWER: YES. Reasonable suspicion for a stop and frisk need not be based only upon a police officer's personal observations, but may also be based on information supplied by another person. Under these circumstances, a police officer's action in reaching to the spot where the gun was thought to be hidden constituted a limited and reasonable intrusion designed to insure the officer's safety. *Id.* at 1924.

RATIONALE: At approximately 2:15 a.m., Sergeant Connolly of the Bridgeport, Connecticut, Police Department was alone in his patrol car when he was approached by a person known to him. The person stated that "an individual seated in a nearby vehicle was carrying narcotics and had a gun at his waist." *Id.* at 1922. "After calling for assistance on his car radio, Sergeant Connolly approached the vehicle to investigate. Connolly tapped on the car window and asked the occupant, Robert Williams, to open the door. When Williams rolled down the window instead, the sergeant reached into the car and removed a fully loaded revolver from Williams' waistband. The gun had not been visible to Connolly from outside the car, but it was in precisely the place indicated by the informant." *Id.* at 1922-1923. Connolly then placed defendant Williams under arrest for the unlawful possession of the firearm. "A search incident to that arrest was conducted after other officers arrived. They found substantial quantities of heroin on Williams' person and in the car, and they found a machete and a second revolver hidden in the automobile." *Id.* at 1923.

In this appeal, defendant argues that the initial seizure of his gun, upon which rested the later search and seizure of other weapons and narcotics, was "not justified by the informant's tip to Sergeant Connolly. He claims that absent a more reliable informant, or some corroboration of the tip, the police [officer's] actions were unreasonable under the standards set forth in *Terry v. Ohio.*" *Williams* at 1923. *The United States Supreme Court could not agree.*

"The Fourth Amendment does not require a policeman who lacks the precise level of information necessary for probable cause to arrest to simply shrug his shoulders and allow a crime to occur or a criminal to escape. * * * [Rather, a] brief stop of a suspicious individual, in order to determine his identity or to maintain the status quo momentarily while obtaining more information, may be most reasonable in light of the facts known to the officer at the time." *Id.* " 'When an officer is justified in believing that the individual whose suspicious behavior he is investigating at close range is armed and presently dangerous to the officer or others,' " *Terry* permits that officer to " 'conduct a limited protective search for concealed weapons' " *Williams* at 1923 [Citation omitted.] "So long as the officer is entitled to make a forcible stop, and has reason to believe that the suspect is armed and dangerous, he may conduct a weapons search limited in scope to this protective purpose." *Id.*

In this case, Sergeant "Connolly acted justifiably in responding to his informant's tip. The informant was known to him personally and had provided him with information in the past. This is a stronger case than obtains in the case of an anonymous telephone tip. *The informant here came forward personally to give information that was immediately verifiable at the scene." Id.* [Emphasis added.] Thus, while this informant's unverified tip may not have been enough for an arrest or search, the information certainly carried enough reliability to justify the temporary investigative detention of defendant.

Additionally, the information supplied also formed the basis of a reasonable cause to suspect that defendant was armed and presently dangerous. "While properly investigating the activity of a person who was reported to be carrying narcotics and a concealed weapon and who was sitting alone in a car in a high-crime area at 2:15 in the morning, Sergeant Connolly had ample reason to fear for his safety. When Williams rolled down his window, rather than complying with the policeman's request to step out of the car so that his movements could more easily be seen, the revolver allegedly at Williams' waist became an even greater threat. Under these circumstances the policeman's action in reaching to the spot where the gun was thought to be hidden constituted a limited intrusion designed to insure his safety, and [the Court] conclude[s] that it was reasonable. The loaded gun seized as a result of this intrusion was therefore admissible at Williams' trial." *Id.* at 1924.

"Once Sergeant Connolly had found the gun precisely where the informant had predicted, probable cause existed to arrest Williams for unlawful possession of the weapon." *Id.* Because the sergeant found the gun in precisely the place predicted by the informant, the reliability of the informant's report that narcotics may also be found in the vehicle was corroborated. Certainly, defendant had no lawful explanation for the possession of the gun. As a result, the subsequent search of defendant's person and his car were clearly constitutional.

FLORIDA v. J.L.
Supreme Court of the United States
529 U.S. 266, 120 S.Ct. 1375 (2000)

QUESTION: Is an anonymous tip that a person is carrying a gun, without more, sufficient to justify a police officer's stop and frisk of that person ?

ANSWER: NO. To justify a stop based solely on an anonymous tip, police must take steps to establish the reliability of the tip. If the anonymous tip is found to be so lacking in reliability that the constitutional standard of a "reasonable articulable suspicion" of criminal activity has not been satisfied, the stop and frisk will not be justified, even if it alleges "the illegal possession of a firearm." *Id.* at 1380.

RATIONALE: In the middle of October, an anonymous tipster called the Miami-Dade Police and reported that "a young black male standing at a particular bus stop and wearing a plaid shirt was carrying a gun." *Id.* at 1377. Two officers responded to the tip and arrived at the bus stop about six minutes after receiving the dispatch. At the bus stop, the officers noticed three black males "just hanging out." *Id.* One of the three, defendant J.L., was wearing a plaid shirt. "Apart from the tip, the officers had no reason to suspect any of the three of illegal conduct." *Id.* One officer "approached J.L., told him to put his hands up on the bus stop, frisked him, and seized a gun from J.L.'s pocket." *Id.* A second officer frisked the other two individuals, but found nothing.

At the time of the stop, J.L. was "10 days shy of his 16th" birthday. *Id.* He was charged under state law with carrying a concealed firearm without a license and the underage possession of a firearm.

The pivotal issue at the United States Supreme Court was whether it should adopt a "gun exception" to the general rule, originated in *Terry v. Ohio*, which prohibits stops and frisks on the basis of "bare-boned anonymous tips." *Terry v. Ohio* sets forth the fundamental rule that

> where a police officer observes unusual conduct which leads him reasonably to conclude in light of his experience that criminal activity may be afoot and that the persons with whom he is dealing may be armed and presently dangerous, where in the course of investigating this behavior he identifies himself as a policeman and makes reasonable inquiries, and where nothing in the initial stages of the encounter serves to dispel his reasonable fear for his own or others' safety, he is entitled for the protection of himself and others in the area to conduct a carefully limited search of the outer clothing of such persons in an attempt to discover weapons which might be used to assault him.

J.L. at 1378. [Citation omitted.]

Here in *J.L.*, the Court pointed out that the officers' suspicion that J.L. was carrying a concealed weapon arose "not from any observations of their own but solely from a call made from an unknown location by an unknown caller. Unlike a tip from a known informant whose reputation can be assessed and who can be held responsible if her allegations turn out to be fabricated, * * * 'an anonymous tip alone seldom demonstrates the informant's basis of knowledge or veracity[.]' " *Id.* [Citations omitted.] While there certainly are situations in which a sufficiently corroborated anonymous tip will provide enough indicia of reliability to provide reasonable suspicion to make an investigatory stop, the question in this case is "whether the tip pointing to J.L. had those indicia of reliability." *Id.*

According to the Court, there was nothing in this tip to demonstrate that the tipster had any sort of "inside knowledge" about the juvenile. The tip did not predict future movements or actions of J.L., which could have indicated some familiarity with J.L. or "inside knowledge" about him. Without such "predictive information," observed the Court, the officers in this case were left "without means to test the informant's knowledge or credibility." *Id.* at 1379. Moreover, just because the information about the gun turned out to be true "does not suggest," emphasized the Court, "that the officers, prior to the frisks, had a reasonable basis for suspecting J.L." of criminal conduct. *Id.* In this respect,

> [t]he reasonableness of official suspicion must be measured by what the officers knew before they conducted their search. All the police had to go on in this case was the bare report of an unknown, unaccountable informant who neither explained how he knew about the gun nor supplied any basis for believing he had inside information about J.L.

Id.

During the course of this appeal, the prosecution urged that a stop and frisk should be permitted "when (1) an anonymous tip provides a description of a particular person at a particular location illegally carrying a concealed firearm, (2) police promptly verify the pertinent details of the tip except the existence of the firearm, and (3) there are no factors that cast doubt on the reliability of the tip." *Id.* This position, observed the Court, fails to take into account "the reliability needed for a tip to justify a *Terry* stop." The Court elaborated:

> An accurate description of a subject's readily observable location and appearance is of course reliable in this limited sense: It will help the police correctly identify the person whom the tipster means to accuse. Such a tip, however, does not show that the tipster has knowledge of concealed criminal activity. ***The reasonable suspicion here at issue requires that a tip be reliable in its assertion of illegality, not just in its tendency to identify a determinate person.*** * * *

Id. [Emphasis added.]

The prosecution also argued that the standard *Terry* analysis should be modified to permit a "firearm exception." Under such an exception, a tip regarding the possession of an illegal gun should justify a stop and frisk even if the tip did not measure up to the historical requirements set forth by *Terry v. Ohio*. In rejecting this argument, the Court said:

> Firearms are dangerous, and extraordinary dangers sometimes justify unusual precautions. Our decisions recognize the serious threat that armed criminals pose to public safety; *Terry*'s rule, which permits protective police searches on the basis of reasonable suspicion rather than demanding that officers meet the higher standard of probable cause, responds to this very concern. * * * But an automatic firearm exception to our established reliability analysis would rove too far. Such an exception would enable any person seeking to harass another to set in motion an intrusive, embarrassing police search of the targeted person simply by placing an anonymous call falsely reporting the target's unlawful carriage of a gun.

Id. at 1379-80.

The Court did not go so far as to rule that an anonymous tip that a person is in possession of a dangerous instrumentality will never permit a search without a showing of the tip's reliability. For example, the Court would not say that "a report of a person carrying a bomb" need carry with it all the indicia of reliability that is demanded for a report of a person carrying a firearm before the police can constitutionally conduct a frisk. *Id.* Nor would the Court hold that "public safety officials in quarters where the reasonable expectation of Fourth Amendment privacy is diminished, such as airports * * * and schools, cannot conduct protective searches on the basis of information insufficient to justify searches elsewhere." *Id.*

Accordingly, to justify a stop based solely on an anonymous tip, police must take steps to establish the reliability of the tip. If the anonymous tip is found to be so lacking in reliability that the constitutional standard of a "reasonable articulable suspicion" of criminal activity has not been satisfied, the stop and frisk will not be justified, even if it alleges "the illegal possession of a firearm." *Id.*

In a concurring opinion, Justice Kennedy, joined by Chief Justice Rehnquist, further instructed that when the police act on the information contained in an anonymous telephone tip, "there is a second layer of inquiry respecting the reliability of the informant that cannot be pursued. If the telephone call is truly anonymous, the informant has not placed his credibility at risk and can lie with impunity. * * * [T]he risk of fabrication becomes unacceptable." *Id.* at 1381. Here, there was no evidence presented as to whether the receipt of the anonymous tip was formally noted or whether the call was documented by voice recording or through tracing the call to a telephone number.

The concurrence further instructed that a tip might be anonymous in some sense yet contain certain other features that do provide the lawful basis for police action.

One such feature * * * is that the tip predicts future conduct of the alleged criminal. There may be others. For example, if an unnamed caller with a voice which sounds the same each time tells police on two successive nights about criminal activity which in fact occurs each night, a similar call on the third night ought not be treated automatically like the tip in the case now before us. In the instance supposed, there would be a plausible argument that experience cures some of the uncertainty surrounding the anonymity, justifying a proportionate police response. * * *

If an informant places his anonymity at risk, a court can consider this factor in weighing the reliability of the tip. An instance where a tip might be considered anonymous but nevertheless sufficiently reliable to justify a proportionate police response may be when an unnamed person driving a car the police officer later describes stops for a moment and, face to face, informs the police that criminal activity is occurring.

Instant caller identification is widely available to police, and, if anonymous tips are proving unreliable and distracting to police, squad cars can be sent within seconds to the location of the telephone used by the informant. Voice recording of telephone tips might, in appropriate cases, be used by police to locate the caller. It is unlawful to make false reports to the police, * * * and the ability of the police to trace the identity of anonymous telephone informants may be a factor which lends reliability to what, years earlier, might have been considered unreliable anonymous tips.

Id.

Because the anonymous tip in this case carried with it no indicia of reliability, it failed to provide the police with a reasonable articulable suspicion that J.L. was unlawfully in possession of a firearm. Consequently, the Court affirmed the judgment of the Florida Supreme Court which held that the gun unlawfully seized from J.L. had to be suppressed.

NOTE

An unnamed citizen informant's tip plus other circumstances. In *United States v. Thompson,* 234 *F.*3d 725 (D.C.Cir. 2000), at about 3:20 a.m., Officers Holloway and Pope of the Metropolitan Police Department, while in uniform, were approached by a middle-aged male who reported that he "just saw" a man with a gun get out of a sportutility vehicle in the parking lot of a Wendy's restaurant, about 100 yards from where the officers stood. "The informant, who was anxious and agitated, described the suspect as a young Black man wearing dark pants and a bright orange shirt." *Id.* at 727.

Without asking for the man's identity, the officers immediately drove off (in their separate cars) to the Wendy's restaurant, which was closed at the time. As the officers entered the parking lot, they saw a dark colored sport-utility vehicle leaving. Officer Holloway then spotted a Black male, later identified as defendant Thompson, wearing a bright orange shirt and standing by himself at the far end of the parking lot with his back against a fence. At the time, there was no one else in the parking lot. "Thompson was looking around the edge of the fence toward a nightclub called the Mirage * * *, 'sort of peeking around as if he was trying to keep his position concealed.' " *Id.*

In light of the tip and the circumstances, Officer Holloway exited his patrol car with his weapon drawn and approached. Thompson spotted Officer Holloway when the officer was about five to seven feet from him. Holloway told Thompson to raise his hands in the air and to stop, and Thompson complied. "Thompson at that point said something to the effect of 'you got me' and indicated that he would not put up a fight. At Holloway's instruction, he dropped to his knees. As Holloway assisted him to the ground, the officer felt a weapon toward the front of Thompson's person. At that point, Officer Pope arrived and helped to handcuff Thompson. The two officers then rolled Thompson over and retrieved a nine-millimeter semiautomatic pistol, loaded and cocked, that was sticking out of his waistband." *Id.*

Finding the stop and frisk lawful, the court preliminarily observed that the tip in this case carried with it "indicia of reliability beyond those of the anonymous tip in [*Florida v.*] *J.L.*; and the police themselves observed Thompson engaging in suspicious conduct." *Thompson* at 729. The court said:

> First, the tipster here informed the police in person, making his report inherently more trustworthy than that of the unidentified caller in *J.L.* The informant stated that he "just saw" Thompson, indicating that his knowledge was based upon firsthand observation * * *; the recency and the proximity of his claimed observation further suggested that it would prove accurate * * *.

> In addition, the informant in this case was more accountable, and therefore more reliable, than was the anonymous caller in *J.L.* The precise situation here was anticipated by Justice Kennedy, concurring in *J.L.*:

>> If an informant places his anonymity at risk, a court can consider this factor in weighing the reliability of the tip.
>> An instance where a tip might be considered anonymous but nevertheless sufficiently reliable to justify a proportionate police response may be when an unnamed person driving a car the police officer later describes stops for a moment and, face to face, informs the police that criminal activity is occurring.

Thompson at 729 (quoting *J.L.*, 120 *S.Ct.* at 1381).

In this case, the informant "subjected himself to ready identification by the police when he approached them in his car; the police need only have asked for his identification or simply noted the license plate on his car. * * * Had the information he provided proved false, he would have been subject to potential criminal prosecution." *Id.*

591

In addition, the court pointed out that "what the police themselves observed of Thompson's conduct was clearly suspicious. * * * [T]he officers observed Thompson concealing himself behind the fence and peering out toward the street. Moreover, he was doing so in the parking lot of a closed restaurant at three o'clock in the morning." *Id*. Looking at these facts "from the perspective of a reasonable police officer," the court believed that "Thompson's apparent effort to conceal himself behind the fence must be regarded as suspicious[.]" *Id*.

> Thompson's furtive conduct was not merely consistent with the tip that he had a weapon; it would have signaled a reasonable police officer that Thompson was positioning himself to use it, perhaps against someone exiting the nightclub toward which he was looking. To ask more of the police in these circumstances—to require them to investigate still further or to watch from a distance—might well preclude them from interceding before the suspect has accomplished his violent, perhaps lethal, purpose. The requirement of reasonable suspicion does not necessitate such forbearance.

Id. at 729-30.

UNITED STATES v. SMART
United States Court of Appeals
98 *F*.3d 1379 (D.C.Cir. 1996)

QUESTION: In the below set of circumstances, was the stop and frisk proper ?

CIRCUMSTANCES: In the third week of September, Officer Michael Tuz of the Metropolitan Police Department set up an observation post in the area of the 1500 block of Howard Road, S.E., "to investigate illegal narcotic activity." After observing, through binoculars, "an apparent narcotic transaction" in a nearby building, Officer Tuz noticed a man, later identified as Antonio Smart, walk over to a grassy strip near several trees and a building, where he reached down and picked up a plastic bag from the ground alongside the building. The plastic bag contained a "chunk of white—a white substance." Although the officer was about 30 feet away, the binoculars made it appear as though Smart was right next to him.

After Smart picked up the bag, he "walked around the building and into a nearby parking lot, where he was out of Officer Tuz's line of sight. Officer Tuz radioed to a nearby arrest team that the suspect was a black man, wearing a black jacket, black shirt, and a black pair of pants and would be in the first parking lot near the street." Less than a minute later, Officer Chris Huxoll spotted Smart standing "midway" in the parking lot. Although there were a few other people standing in the area, Smart was the only person in the parking lot who matched Officer Tuz's description.

Officer Huxoll drove up to Smart in an unmarked car, identified himself as a police officer and told Smart to put his hands up. Huxoll then walked Smart over to the police car. Before Huxoll could frisk Smart, however, Smart put his hands on his waistband. Officer Huxoll again asked Smart to put up his hands. At first Smart complied; he then immediately put his hands back on his waistband, at which point Officer Huxoll placed his hand on top of Smart's hand. Huxoll felt a hard object and knew it was a gun. A scuffle ensued, and several other officers assisted in taking Smart into custody. The officers recovered a 9-millimeter semi-automatic handgun from Smart. A search incident to Smart's arrest disclosed a bag containing over 25 grams of crack cocaine and 56 small ziplock bags in the pockets of his coat, a pager, and $580 in small bills. While Smart was in the parking lot, Officer Tuz identified him as the individual he had seen earlier.

ANSWER: YES. Based on the "totality of the circumstances," the officers' stop and frisk of Smart was reasonable under the Fourth Amendment. *Id.* at 1384-85.

RATIONALE: Under *Terry v. Ohio*, 392 *U.S.* 1, 88 *S.Ct.* 1868 (1968), "a police officer may, even without probable cause, stop and briefly detain a suspect if the officer has a reasonable suspicion supported by specific, articulable facts that the suspect is involved in some sort of criminal activity. Further, an officer may frisk such a suspect if the officer has a reasonable, articulable suspicion that the suspect in question may be armed and dangerous." *Smart* at 1384.

"The legality of a stop or frisk is evaluated under the totality of the circumstances," *id.*, and in this case, the court determined that under the circumstances, the officers' stop and frisk of Smart was reasonable and proper.

Agreeing with the Government, the court observed:

> The government contends that the "*Terry* stop" was justified because it was based on a reasonable suspicion supported by articulable facts that [Smart] was involved in criminal activity. * * * The reason Officer Tuz set up the observation post at that location was to investigate illegal activity. Prior to observing [Smart] pick up the plastic bag, Officer Tuz had observed an apparent narcotic transaction in the building across the street. Furthermore, Officer Huxoll's subsequent stop of [Smart] was also justified. [Smart] was the only person in the area that matched the description of a black man wearing all black in the exact location specified by Officer Tuz. The inclusion of a specific time and specific location is what makes the government's contention persuasive.

Id. at 1384.

Under *Terry*, officers may also frisk persons that they stop, if they can articulate facts supporting a reasonable belief that "criminal activity may be afoot and that the persons with whom [they are] dealing may be armed and dangerous." *Terry*, 392 *U.S.* at 30, 88 *S.Ct.* at 1884. In the circumstances here, where Officer Tuz had just observed what he believed to be a suspect engaged in a drug transaction, it was reasonable for the officers to suspect that [Smart] had a gun to protect himself and his drugs. Moreover, when Officer Huxoll repeatedly asked [Smart] to raise his hands, [he] moved his hands to his waistband leading the officer to suspect [Smart] was armed. As the Supreme Court [has] noted * * *, *Terry* authorizes "[a] brief stop of a suspicious individual, in order to determine his identity or to maintain the status quo momentarily while obtaining more information," and permits a "limited search . . . not to discover evidence of crime, but to allow the officer to pursue his investigation without fear of violence."

Smart at 1384-85 (quoting *Adams v. Williams*, 407 *U.S.* 143, 146, 92 *S.Ct.* 1921, 1923 (1972)).

Accordingly, the stop and frisk conducted by the officers in this case were entirely proper, and the evidence seized was properly admitted.

NOTE

Questioning a suspect about a bulge felt by an officer conducting a frisk. In *United States v. Chhien*, 266 *F.*3d 1 (1st Cir. 2001), during the course of a motor vehicle stop for an equipment violation, Trooper Holdsworth of the New Hampshire State Police asked the motorist to exit his vehicle and walk to the front of it. The trooper then asked if he could conduct a pat-down search for weapons. The motorist, identified as defendant, Roth Chhien, agreed. During the frisk, Trooper Holdsworth felt something "hard"—a "substantial lump"—in the motorist's right front pants pocket. *Id.* at 4. When he asked about the object, the motorist responded that it was "a large wad of cash, totaling $2,000." *Id.*

Further investigation at the scene of the stop led to the discovery of a quantity of cocaine that was situated in plain view on the front passenger seat of Chhien's vehicle.

In this appeal, Chhien argued that his statements and the evidence should be suppressed because the trooper "exceeded the scope of a permissible traffic stop by conducting an unnecessary, unauthorized pat-down search and wandering far afield in his questioning." *Id.* at 6. Specifically, Chhien contended that the trooper's inquiry about the bulge as he conducted the pat-down was improper because "it did not pertain either to the trooper's safety or to the underlying traffic violations." *Id.*

The court rejected Chhien's contentions, and held that the trooper's actions were proper.

Normally, Holdsworth would have needed some justification (such as a reasonable fear for his own safety) beyond the traffic violation [to conduct the pat-down] * * * In this case, however, [Chhien] explicitly consented to the frisk. * * * There is not a shred of evidence here that Holdsworth tricked, threatened, or bullied [Chhien] into agreeing to the pat-down search. * * * The traffic stop occurred in broad daylight, on a major thoroughfare. At the time of Holdsworth's request, his sidearm was holstered and he was the only trooper present.

Id. at 7-8.

Regarding Chhien's specific contention that the trooper should not have asked about the bulge in Chhien's pocket because he knew that the bulge was not a weapon, the court said:

> This argument misconstrues applicable Fourth Amendment jurisprudence. While an officer may not seize an object during a *Terry* frisk unless he has probable cause, * * * he is not prohibited from inquiring, upon reasonable suspicion, into the nature of that object. So it was here: the origins of the bulge were not readily apparent—it might well have been a weapon—and Holdsworth's question was directly pertinent to the safety concerns that prompted his request for a pat-down search in the first place.

Id. at 8.

The court held, therefore, that "the trooper's inquiry was well within the boundaries set by the Constitution." *Id.* "Consequently, both the bag of crack cocaine and [Chhien's] incriminating statements were lawfully obtained." *Id.* at 10.

UNITED STATES v. GLENNA
United States Court of Appeals
878 *F.*2d 967 (7th Cir. 1989)

QUESTION: Will a law enforcement officer's act of handcuffing a suspect during the course of a *Terry* stop always transform the investigative detention into an arrest?

ANSWER: NO. " '[N]either handcuffing nor other restraints will *automatically* convert a *Terry* stop into a *de facto* arrest requiring probable cause.' * * * [T]he placing of a suspect in handcuffs without probable cause to arrest is [not] always unlawful. If, in a rare case, 'common sense and ordinary human experience' [reasonably convince an officer] that an investigative stop could be effectuated safely only in this manner, * * * [a court should] not substitute [its] judgment for that of the officer[] as to the best methods to investigate." *Id.* at 972. [Citations omitted; emphasis in original.]

RATIONALE: In *Terry v. Ohio*, 392 *U.S.* 1, 88 *S.Ct.* 1868 (1968), the Supreme Court established "a narrowly drawn authority to permit a reasonable search for weapons for the protection of the police officer, where he has reason to believe that he is dealing with an armed and dangerous individual, regardless of whether he has probable cause to arrest the individual for a crime." *Id.* at 27, 88 *S.Ct.* at 1883. The Court authorized such a procedure because of "the need for law enforcement officers to protect themselves and other prospective victims of violence in situations where they may lack probable cause for arrest." *Id.* at 24, 88 *S.Ct.* at 1881. In this respect, the Court observed:

> When an officer is justified in believing that the individual whose suspicious behavior he is investigating at close range is armed and presently dangerous to the officer or to others, it would appear to be clearly unreasonable to deny the officer the power to take necessary measures to determine whether the person is in fact carrying a weapon and to neutralize the threat of physical harm.

Id.

There is, however, "no brightline test" for determining when a lawful *Terry* stop, or investigative detention, is converted into an illegal arrest, "for such a test 'would undermine the . . . important need to allow authorities to graduate their responses to the demands of any particular situation.' " *Glenna* at 971 (quoting *United States v. Sharpe*, 470 *U.S.* 675, 686, 105 *S.Ct.* 1568, 1575 (1985), and *United States v. Place*, 462 *U.S.* 696, 709 n.10, 103 *S.Ct.* 2637, 2646 n.10 (1983)). Rather, when a court must evaluate the reasonableness of an investigative stop, it will "examine first whether the officers' action was justified at its inception and, second, whether it was reasonably related in scope to the circumstances which justified the interference in the first place." *Id.* at 971. [Citations omitted.]

In this case, officers of the Eau Clair, Wisconsin, Police Department received a Teletype from the Indiana State Police informing them that defendant, Wayne Glenna, was enroute to Eau Clair, that he may possibly be involved in "some type of drug deal," and should have in his possession $100,000 in cash, "several small armed weapons" and an "explosive device." *Id.* at 968. The Teletype described Glenna as a white male in his twenties, between 5′9″ and 5′11″ tall and weighing approximately 135 to 150 pounds. According to the Teletype, Glenna's blonde hair, when last seen, was at shoulder length and he was wearing an orange T-shirt and khaki green pants. Glenna was reportedly driving a green Dodge van with no license plates and a motorcycle strapped to the rear.

The following day, a Eau Clair officer spotted a van matching the description given in the Teletype parked in front of a residence on a busy street. A surveillance was set up and within a short period of time, an individual matching Glenna's description was observed walking in the front yard of the residence. Soon thereafter, the van left the residence and traveled south. Officer Tollefson followed the van—planning to stop it for failure to display license plates—but before he had the opportunity, the van turned into a gas station/convenience store. Tollefson parked his car in front of the convenience store. "By the time Tollefson got out of his car, however, the van, which was parked near the gas pumps, was unoccupied. Tollefson, therefore, headed toward the store's entrance where he encountered Glenna who, when asked, told Tollefson that the van was his. Tollefson asked whether Glenna had registration documents for the van. Glenna responded that he had proof of application for title in the van's glove compartment." *Id.* at 968-969. By this point, Tollefson was joined by his "backup," Officer Trapp.

"About eight to ten feet from the van, Tollefson stopped and asked Glenna for some identification. As Glenna reached into a large, military-style pocket of his trousers, Tollefson saw a lump in the pocket which he thought could be a weapon. Tollefson immediately grabbed Glenna's hand and pulled from the pocket a loaded clip for a nine-millimeter firearm." *Id.* at 969. At this point, Glenna was placed in handcuffs. Tollefson then conducted a pat-down frisk of Glenna and found in another pocket a small explosive "cherry bomb."

After conducting the pat-down, Tollefson asked Glenna if he could retrieve the van's registration papers from the glove compartment. When Glenna consented, Tollefson opened the van's front passenger compartment and removed the papers. Upon doing so, the officer noticed between the van's two front bucket seats a box bearing a fireworks label. Tollefson opened the box and found illegal fireworks. After looking in other boxes and bags for fireworks or contraband and finding nothing, Tollefson exited the van and told Glenna that he was under arrest for the possession of illegal fireworks. Glenna was asked whether the van contained any bombs and eventually he responded that there was a bomb in a suitcase behind the driver's seat but that the officers should not worry because it was not activated. Ultimately, with the help of the fire department and the bomb squad, the officers searched the van and seized a cap gun, a knife and, a suitcase which was found to contain a "pipe bomb."

In this appeal, Glenna argued, among other things, that any statements he made and the fruits of all searches of his van following his stop and detention should be suppressed because "he was arrested without probable cause when the officers placed him in handcuffs in the convenience store parking lot[.]" *Id.* at 969. *The United States Court of Appeals for the Seventh Circuit could not agree.*

Initially, Glenna did not challenge Tollefson's seizure of the nine-millimeter clip from his pocket. As the court below concluded, the officer's " 'sensitivity to the presence of a weapon had been elevated by the disquieting Teletype from the Indiana State Police,' and Tollefson's observance of '[t]he protrusion in [Glenna's] pocket could reasonably be seen as an ominous validation of the Teletype.' Tollefson's seizure of the clip, therefore, was precisely the type of graduated response to the demands of a particular situation that the Court [authorized] in *Sharp* and *Place, supra.* Whether what followed—the officers' placing of Glenna in handcuffs—also was a reasonably graduated response to the demands of the situation depends on whether the restraint was temporary and lasted no longer than was necessary to effectuate the purpose of the stop, and whether the methods employed were the least intrusive means reasonably available to verify or dispel the officer's suspicion in a short period of time." *Id.* at 971-972.

While the use of handcuffs "substantially aggravates the intrusiveness of a *Terry* stop," and represents the type of "restraints on freedom of movement normally associated with arrest," this court is "unwilling to hold that under *Terry*, the placing of a suspect in handcuffs without probable cause to arrest is *always* unlawful. If, in a rare case, 'common sense and ordinary human experience' [reasonably convince an officer] that an investigative stop could be effectuated safely only in this manner, * * * [a court should] not 'substitute [its] judgment for that of the officers as to the best methods to investigate.' " *Id.* at 972-973. [Citations omitted; emphasis in original.]

Although it is a close one, this is, in the court's view, just such a case. "Here, Officers Tollefson and Trapp both were aware of the teletype message from the Indiana State Police concerning Glenna. That Teletype, which cited information received from a member of Glenna's own family, indicated that Glenna (1) was driving a van bearing no license plates; (2) possibly was involved in a drug deal; (3) could be carrying $100,000 in cash; (4) was in possession of *several* small armed weapons; and, last but not least, was in possession of an explosive device. This information provided the basis for a reasonable belief that Glenna was armed and dangerous. Tollefson's discovery of the loaded clip, of course, only enhanced the credibility of the teletype's portrayal of Glenna as a well-armed and potentially dangerous individual. As the [court below] found, Tollefson was aware that persons carrying a weapon often carry spare clips. And it was only then that Tollefson and Trapp placed Glenna in handcuffs in order, as Tollefson testified, to preserve their own safety. Tollefson immediately conducted a pat-down search of Glenna for weapons. Although the pat-down yielded no firearms, it did yield a small explosive 'cherry bomb,' which, of course, also corroborated the teletype warning that Glenna was in possession of explosives." *Id.* at 973. [Emphasis in original.]

"At this point, Tollefson had a loaded clip, a cherry bomb, and a reasonable suspicion that Glenna possessed firearms and/or explosives in his van, which happened to be parked next to gasoline pumps. On the other hand, Tollefson had yet to obtain from Glenna any identification and the van's registration papers. Tollefson, therefore, decided not to remove the handcuffs just yet, but to ask Glenna for permission to enter the van and retrieve the registration papers. When Glenna consented, Tollefson entered the van and discovered in plain view the box labeled 'fireworks.' Upon opening the box and observing its contents, Tollefson had probable cause to arrest Glenna for possession of illegal fireworks, which he promptly did." *Id.*

According to the court, the police conduct in this case did not stray "beyond the limits of that contemplated in *Terry*. None of the safeguards taken by the officers in this sequence of events strikes [this court] as unreasonable or out of proportion in relation to the danger posed by the investigatory stop as the officers perceived it." *Id.* Under the circumstances of this case, this court "simply cannot secondguess the officers' belief that, in order to safely effectuate the stop and confirm or dispel their suspicion that Glenna was committing a crime, they had to place Glenna in handcuffs. Moreover, the amount of time Glenna spent in handcuffs in the absence of probable cause for arrest was minimal—no longer than ten or fifteen minutes." *Id.* Consequently, the handcuffing of Glenna did not transform his investigative stop into an unlawful arrest. *Id.*

NOTE

1. *Handcuffing a person during an investigative detention.*

(a) A number of other courts have held that the placing of a person in handcuffs may fall within the permissible scope of a temporary investigative detention under *Terry v. Ohio.* For example, in *United States v. Kapperman,* 764 *F.*2d 786 (11th Cir. 1985), the court noted that:

> neither handcuffing nor other restraints will *automatically* convert a *Terry* stop into a *de facto* arrest requiring probable cause. Just as probable cause to arrest will not justify using excessive force to detain a suspect, the use of a particular method to restrain a person's freedom of movement does not necessarily make police action tantamount to an arrest. The inquiry in either context is reasonableness.

Id. at 790 n.4. [Emphasis added.] *See also United States v. Tilmon,* 19 *F.*3d 1221, 1228 (7th Cir. 1994) ("handcuffing—once highly problematic—is becoming quite acceptable in the context of a *Terry* stop"); *United States v. Perdue,* 8 *F.*3d 1455, 1463 (10th Cir. 1993) (noting "recent trend allowing police to use handcuffs or place suspects on the ground during a *Terry* stop"); *United States v. Purry,* 545 *F.*2d 217, 220 (U.S.App.D.C. 1976) (handcuffing of defendant was reasonable, as a corollary of the lawful *Terry* stop, in order to maintain status quo while the officer sought more information); *United States v. Crittendon,* 883 *F.*2d 326, 329 (4th Cir. 1989) (upholding the use of handcuffs in the context of a *Terry* stop where it was reasonably necessary to protect the officer's safety); *United States v. Taylor,* 716 *F.*2d 701, 709 (9th Cir. 1983) ("use of handcuffs, if reasonably necessary, while substantially aggravating the intrusiveness of an investigatory stop, [does] not necessarily convert a *Terry* stop into an arrest necessitating probable cause").

(b) To determine whether handcuffs are an appropriate temporary restraint during the course of a *Terry* stop, courts will generally ask whether there are serious safety concerns present and whether a reasonable person could conclude that the person detained is "free to leave" once the *Terry* inquiry has ended. *See e.g., United States v. Tilmon, supra,* 19 *F.*3d at 1228 (handcuffing permissible where "the officers had been told by radio dispatch that the bank robber was armed and dangerous"); *United States v. Smith,* 3 *F.*3d 1088 (7th Cir. 1993) (presenting a " 'rare' case wherein common sense and ordinary human experience" convinced the court that the "officer believed reasonably that an investigative stop could be effectuated safely only through the use of handcuffs," in light of "the time of night, the general environment of the investigation and the nature of the alleged offenses"); *United States v. Sanders,* 994 *F.*2d 200 (5th Cir. 1993) (proper to handcuff suspect where officer responding to a "man with a gun" call encountered a male who wore a jacket concealing the area around his waistband and who turned away from the officer, and then refused to lie on the ground when ordered); *In re M.E.B.*, 638 *A*.2d 1123, 1127 (D.C.App. 1993) (because police had reasonable grounds to suspect that defendant and his companion had been involved in a murder that occurred just an hour earlier, the officers' act of handcuffing the two suspects and transporting them to the scene for identification did not transform the temporary detention into a formal arrest); *United States v. Merkley*, 988 *F*.2d 1062, 1064 (10th Cir. 1993) (handcuffing *Terry* detainee permitted where suspect "had threatened to kill someone and was acting violently"); *United States v. Miller*, 974 *F*.2d 953, 957 (8th Cir. 1992) (handcuffing of *Terry* detainee permitted where the police were badly outnumbered). *Reynolds v. State*, 592 *So*.2d 1082, 1084 (Fla. 1992) (upholding the use of handcuffs in the context of a *Terry* stop where it was reasonably necessary to protect the officer's safety); *State v. Reid*, 605 *A*.2d 1050, 1053 (N.H. 1992) (while defendant was "seized" when he was handcuffed and placed in the back of the police cruiser, that seizure did not constitute an arrest); *People v. Allen*, 73 *N.Y*.2d 378, 379-80, 538 *N.E*.2d 323, 324, 540 *N.Y.S*.2d 971, 972 (1989) (use of handcuffs is not dispositive of whether a detention becomes a full-blown arrest because police officers must be permitted to take reasonable steps to assure their safety in rapidly developing and dangerous situations). *But see Baker v. Monroe Tp.*, 50 *F*.3d 1186 (3rd Cir. 1995) (handcuffing was not justified where police had no "reason to feel threatened"); *United States v. Codd*, 956 *F*.2d 1109, 1111 (11th Cir. 1992) (use of handcuffs converted a *Terry* stop into an arrest where the use of handcuffs was not necessary to avoid any sort of tangible threat of violence).

As the court put it in *In re M.E.B.*, "handcuffing the detainee, like the length of the detention, place of detention, and other considerations, is simply one factor, among many, that the trial judge must consider in weighing whether a detention for investigation crossed the line into the realm of arrest." *Id.*, 638 *A*.2d at 1128.

Moreover, the act of patting down a detainee prior to handcuffing and placing him in a police vehicle should not, by itself, affect the character of the detention. Experience has shown that even a careful frisk does not ensure that hidden weapons will be discovered. *See Nelson v. United States*, 601 *A*.2d 582, 587 (D.C.App. 1991) (pat-down by arresting officer discovered no weapon; full-blown search by transporting officer uncovered a knife in the arrestee's pocket); *Lewis v. United States*, 399 *A*.2d 559, 560 (D.C.App. 1979) (frisk by first officer produced no weapon; frisk by second officer uncovered a handgun); *Smith v. United States*, 435 *A*.2d 1066, 1067-68 (D.C.App. 1981) (frisk of defendant revealed no weapon; after transport in police vehicle, a holster was recovered from the seat where he had been sitting).

(c) In *Washington v. Lambert*, 98 *F*.3d 1181 (9th Cir. 1996), the court went so far as to list a few of those "special circumstances" in which handcuffing, although an "especially intrusive means of effecting a stop," should be permissible:

(1) where the suspect is uncooperative or takes action at the scene that raises a reasonable probability of danger or flight;

(2) where the police have information that the suspect is currently armed;

(3) where the stop closely follows a violent crime; and

(4) where the police have information that a crime that may involve violence is about to occur.

In the absence of a continuing threat to officer or citizen safety, the handcuffs should be removed if the protective frisk uncovers no weapons. *See* 4 W. LaFave, *Search and Seizure: A Treatise on the Fourth Amendment* §9.2(d), at 42 (3rd Ed. 1996) (" 'absent other threatening circumstances, once the pat-down reveals the absence of weapons the handcuffs should be removed' ") (footnote omitted).

(d) In *Young v. Prince George's County,* 355 *F.*3d 751 (4th Cir. 2004), on an evening in mid-July, off-duty FBI agent Jerry Young was stopped for a motor vehicle violation by Officer Hines of the Prince George's County Police Department. The violation involved inoperable tail-lights.

After being stopped, Young, and his passenger, Pringle, both exited their vehicle. Pringle remained near the vehicle, as Young approached Officer Hines to ascertain the basis for the stop. "In response, Officer Hines instructed Young and Pringle to sit down on the curb and place their hands on their heads. Both Young and Pringle complied with Officer Hines's instructions. As Officer Hines began to approach Young and Pringle, Young voluntarily informed Officer Hines that he was an off-duty law enforcement officer and that he was armed. Young further informed Officer Hines that his law enforcement credentials were located in his automobile. In response to Young's statement that he was armed, Officer Hines approached and handcuffed Young behind his back in order to prevent him from gaining access to his firearm." *Id.* at 753.

In discussing the officer's use of handcuffs during this investigative detention, the court explained that the law attempts to

strike a delicate balance between "the right of every individual to the possession and control of his own person, free from all restraint or interference of others, unless by clear and unquestionable authority of law," * * * and "the needs of law enforcement officers who constantly place themselves in harm's way."

In an effort to strike this balance, we have held that "[b]rief, even if complete, deprivations of a suspect's liberty do not convert a stop and frisk into an arrest *so long as the methods of restraint used are reasonable to the circumstances.*" * * * As a result, this Court has concluded that police officers may block an automobile and draw their weapons when confronted with a situation in which they have been informed that a passenger fears for his personal safety. * * * We have also held that an officer may handcuff a suspect when "reasonably necessary to maintain the status quo and protect [officer] safety during an investigative stop."

Id. at 755 (quoting *United States v. Crittendon*, 883 *F.*2d at 326, 329 (4th Cir. 1989)). [Court's emphasis.]

Thus, under the totality of the circumstances presented, the court held that the method of restraint used by Officer Hines "did not cross the line between a stop and an arrest." *Id.* The court said:

> In the present case, Officer Hines stopped an automobile carrying two passengers, one of whom admitted he was armed. Given the fact that Young was armed, Officer Hines was entitled to protect his safety by taking reasonable measures designed to disarm Young. We therefore conclude that it was reasonable for Officer Hines to handcuff Young behind his back.

Id.

(e) *See also United States v. Vargas*, 369 *F.*3d 98 (2nd Cir. 2004), where the court explained that "although '[u]nder ordinary circumstances, drawing weapons and using handcuffs are not part of a *Terry* stop[,] intrusive and aggressive police conduct' is *not an arrest* 'when it is a reasonable response to legitimate safety concerns on the part of the investigating officers.'" *Id.* at 102 (quoting *United States v. Miles*, 247 *F.*3d 1009, 1012 (9th Cir. 2001)). [Emphasis added.]

In this case, the officers had reasonable suspicion that Vargas was carrying a weapon. Vargas had demonstrated his unwillingness to cooperate with the officers' investigation by fleeing from them when originally approached and continuing to struggle with the officers following the stop. Immediately upon intercepting Vargas, one of the officers placed him on the ground and handcuffed him. The officer then conducted a frisk for weapons and discovered Vargas's firearm. It was only upon discovering the firearm that Vargas was placed under arrest. Even though the officers used a greater degree of force than is typical of a *Terry* stop, the Court determined that "the force was reasonable under the circumstances and the stop did not become a full arrest until after the officers discovered Vargas was carrying a firearm." *Id.*

2. *Other forms of restraints.* Courts have held that forms of restraints other than the use of handcuffs may fall within the scope of a *Terry* investigative detention.

(a) *Placing suspect in police squad car.* For example, in *Pliska v. City of Stevens Point*, 823 *F.*2d 1168 (7th Cir. 1987), the court determined that the placing of a burglary suspect in a police patrol car during the course of an investigative stop did not transform the detention into an arrest requiring probable cause. According to the court in *Pliska*, the suspect "was detained for the sole purpose of verifying or dispelling [the officer's] suspicion that Pliska was planning a burglary. Such verification represents a substantial and legitimate government interest." *Id.* at 177. Pliska was merely held long enough to determine his identity and his role in the incident, and less than ten minutes went by from the time the officer encountered Pliska until he released him from the squad car.

(b) Holding suspect at gunpoint. Courts have also found that in certain circumstances, the holding of a suspect at gunpoint during the course of an investigative stop will be a reasonable course of action under *Terry*. In *United States v. Serna-Barreto*, 842 *F*.2d 965 (7th Cir. 1988), the court stated, "Although we are troubled by the thought of allowing police [officers] to stop people at the point of a gun when probable cause to arrest is lacking, we are unwilling to hold that an investigative stop is never lawful when it can be effectuated safely only in that manner. It is not nice to have a gun pointed at you by a police [officer] but it is worse to have a gun pointed at you by a criminal, so there is a complex tradeoff involved in any proposal to reduce (or increase) the permissible scope of investigatory stops." *Id.* at 968.

See also United States v. Taylor, 857 *F*.2d 210 (4th Cir. 1988), where the court observed:

> Investigating officers may take such steps as are reasonably necessary to maintain the status quo and to protect their safety during an investigative stop. * * * [In this case, b]locking the progress of [defendant's] automobile with police vehicles and the agents' drawn weapons, for example, were well within the range of permissible police conduct. * * * "The former is a reasonable way of effectuating the stop of a motor vehicle, and the latter is a justified safety precaution." Although blockading an automobile and approaching a suspect with drawn weapons are extraordinary measures, such police procedures have been justified in this circuit as a reasonable means of neutralizing potential danger to police and innocent bystanders. * * * Here the agents were aware that [defendant] had been convicted of assault, assault with intent to murder, robbery, a narcotics violation, and escape. Contrary to [defendant's] assertions, a lawful investigative stop does not become a custodial arrest when circumstances such as these cause police to draw their guns. "A brief but complete restriction of liberty is valid under *Terry*."

Taylor at 213-214 (quoting *United States v. Manbeck*, 744 *F*.2d 360, 377 (4th Cir. 1984), and *United States v. Moore*, 817 *F*.2d 1105, 1108 (4th Cir. 1987)).

In *United States v. Jackson*, 652 *F*.2d 244 (2d Cir. 1981), the Second Circuit reached the same conclusion, and held that it is not unreasonable

> for a police [officer] to draw his gun when he approaches a car whose driver may be an escaping armed bank robber. Although the drawing of a weapon may be a significant factor in determining whether a suspect is under arrest, it is not dispositive of the issue. * * *

To allow such protective measures to transform an investigative stop into an arrest would create a dangerous dilemma for the police officer in those situations, like this one, where suspicion does not rise to the level of probable cause. If the officer approaches a suspected robber with his gun still in his holster, he increases the risk that he will be shot. If, on the other hand, he protects himself by drawing his gun, he increases the risk that a court will set the criminal free by construing his action as an illegal arrest. We decline to impose such a [c]hoice on our law enforcement personnel.

Id. at 249-250.

See also United States v. Maguire, 359 *F*.3d 71, 78 (1st Cir. 2004), where the court emphasized that "the use or display of a weapon does not alone turn an investigatory stop into a *de facto* arrest." The court also noted that physical contact between an officer and a *Terry* detainee will not, even in conjunction with the display of a weapon, transform the detention into a *de facto* arrest. *Id.* (citing *United States v. Hensley*, 469 *U.S.* 221, 235, 105 *S.Ct.* 675, 683-84 (1985) (mere use of force does not convert an investigative stop into an arrest)).

3. *"Are you carrying any needles or syringes?"* In *Commonwealth v. Kondash*, 808 A.2d 943 (Pa.Super. 2002), prior to conducting a pat-down of a suspected intravenous drug user, the officer asked the suspect if he possessed any intravenous needles. The suspect replied that he did, and that the needles were in his jacket pocket inside a pouch. Finding the pat-down and the question proper, the court observed:

The design of a syringe and needle allows for their employment as an easily concealed and potent weapon which can inflict a serious wound. Add to that threat the prospect of contracting hepatitis or HIV from an intravenous drug user's needle, and a needle's capacity to deliver grievous or even deadly injury should not be discounted. It is, therefore, reasonable to subject a suspected intravenous drug user properly detained at an investigatory stop to a limited pat[-]down for needle possession to promote the officer's safety. * * *

In addition, we hold that Officer Zaffutto was permitted to preface the *Terry* search by asking [defendant] if he possessed any needles in his clothing without first informing [him] of his *Miranda* rights, as the dictates of *Miranda* do not attach during an investigatory detention. * * * Indeed, even during a custodial interrogation, the requirements of *Miranda* will be excused where police have reason to fear for their well-being and ask questions to ensure their safety and not to elicit incriminating responses. * * * Therefore, Officer Zaffutto's question was a justifiable means to reduce the risk of puncturing his hand during a *Terry* pat-down of a suspected intravenous drug user and did not constitute interrogation under *Miranda*.

Id. at 948-49 (citing *United States v. Webster*, 162 *F*.3d 308, 332 (5th Cir. 1998) (officer's question whether detainee possessed needles that could injure officer during pat-down was necessary to protect officer and did not constitute interrogation under *Miranda*)).

When defendant replied that he was in possession of needles, his response "not only gave Officer Zaffutto cause under *Terry* to remove the needles for his own safety, it also provided probable cause to believe that the pouch contained illegal paraphernalia subject to immediate lawful seizure." *Id.* at 949.

UNITED STATES v. CAMPBELL
United States Court of Appeals
178 *F*.3d 345 (5th Cir. 1999)

QUESTION: In the below set of circumstances, did the police exceed the permissible scope of an investigative detention by their conduct in ordering defendant, at gunpoint, to lie prone, handcuffing him and then conducting a pat-down ?

CIRCUMSTANCES:

1. In late July, a bank in Olive Branch, Mississippi, was robbed at gunpoint by a black male described as being in his twenties or early thirties, about 6'1" tall, 155 pounds, with long hair and a dark complexion. He escaped with $3,365 in what witnesses described as a late '80s, black Chevrolet Cavalier with Tennessee registration 600-TTP.

2. The following day, FBI Agent Rice learned from Memphis police that the license, which was expired, had been registered to Michael Campbell (defendant's brother), who lived at an address in Olive Branch.

3. At about 5:00 p.m., Agent Rice went to that address with Detective Oliver of the Olive Branch Police Department. Upon arrival, they saw the Cavalier parked in the carport next to the house. With the assistance of Sergeant Gentry, they set up surveillance of the house, which was located in a "high crime" area.

4. Within minutes, three black males emerged from the house and approached the car. As the officers moved in, Michael Campbell and another man entered the car; Billy Campbell was still walking towards the driver's side.

5. Gentry ordered, at gunpoint, all three men to put their hands up. "Moving towards Billy Campbell, Gentry told him to get on the ground. As Campbell did this, Gentry looked to the two men in the car and told them to keep their hands visible. When Agent Rice and Detective Oliver approached the men in the

car, Gentry turned his attention back to Billy Campbell, who had complied with his order to lie down on the concrete surface of the carport." *Id.* at 347. Billy Campbell matched the bank robber's description: he was 24 years old, 6'1" tall, 160 pounds, with a dark complexion and shoulder-length hair.

6. Gentry holstered his weapon, handcuffed Campbell behind his back, and frisked him. "In Campbell's right front pants pocket, Gentry felt a large bulge. Fearing that it might be 'some type of weapon,' Gentry * * * reached into the pocket, pulled its contents out, and laid them on the ground. The contents comprised a large wad of money (more than $1,400), a gold cardboard jewelry box containing a gold chain, and some change." *Id.*

7. A check of several of the $20 bills seized from Billy Campbell revealed that they matched the serial numbers on the list of "bait bills" given to the robber by the bank teller. Billy Campbell was then placed under arrest and advised of his rights. He later confessed to the bank robbery as well as several other armed robberies in the area.

ANSWER: NO. " '[U]sing some force on a suspect, pointing a weapon at a suspect, ordering a suspect to lie on the ground, and handcuffing a suspect—whether singly or in combination—do not automatically convert an investigatory detention into an arrest requiring probable cause.' " *Id.* at 349. [Citation omitted.]

RATIONALE: In this appeal, the court first noted that there was "no doubt that the officers had reasonable suspicion to make an investigatory stop of Campbell." *Id.* at 348. As held in *United States v. Hensley*, 469 *U.S.* 221, 229, 105 *S.Ct.* 675, 680 (1985), "if police have a reasonable suspicion, grounded in specific and articulable facts, that a person they encounter was involved in or is wanted in connection with a completed felony, then a *Terry* stop may be made to investigate that suspicion."

Campbell matched the physical description of the bank robber from the day before and was approaching a car that matched a detailed description of the getaway vehicle and bore the same license plate. These facts were sufficient to warrant further investigation.

Campbell at 348.

During their investigation, the officers were "authorized to 'take such steps as were reasonably necessary to protect their personal safety and to maintain the status quo during the course of the stop.' " *Id.* at 348-49. [Citation omitted.] Courts will also ask "whether the police were unreasonable in failing to use less intrusive procedures to conduct their investigation safely." *Id.* at 349. However, " 'using some force on a suspect, pointing a weapon at a suspect, ordering a suspect to lie on the ground, and handcuffing a suspect—whether singly or in combination—do not automatically convert an investigatory detention into an arrest requiring probable cause.' " *Id.* (quoting *United States v.*

Sanders, 994 *F.*2d 200, 206 (5th Cir. 1993)). While the officers in this case were not met with immediate resistance, and the stop occurred about 30 hours after the bank robbery, those facts do "not mean that the use of drawn guns and handcuffs was unreasonable." *Id.*

In *United States v. Tilmon*, 19 *F.*3d 1221, 1228 (7th Cir. 1994), the court observed: "When a suspect is considered dangerous, requiring him to lie face down on the ground is the safest way for police officers to approach him, handcuff him and finally determine whether he carries any weapons." This is precisely what Sergeant Gentry did.

> Given that Billy Campbell matched the description of the armed bank robber and was walking towards the driver's side of what almost certainly had been the getaway vehicle, there were good reasons to assume that Campbell was armed. * * * Although Campbell had complied with Gentry's order to lie down, this would not have precluded his reaching for a weapon. There were other people in the area and only three officers to control all three suspects. Under the circumstances, it was not unreasonable for Gentry to take the precaution of handcuffing Campbell and frisking him. Nor was it unreasonable * * * to handcuff him before frisking him.

Campbell at 349.

The court also rejected Campbell's argument that the removal of his pocket's contents was unreasonable. In this respect, the court said:

> Gentry testified that he thought the large bulge in Campbell's pocket "was some type of weapon." The combination of change, over $1,400 of currency, and a cardboard box containing a gold chain was no mere "bump." * * * Gentry had not ruled out the possibility that the large bulge was a weapon, and his removal of the pocket's contents was not beyond the scope of a permissible *Terry* frisk.

Id.

The court also found that the totality of the officers' conduct in this case did not constitute an arrest, rather than an investigatory stop. In this respect, the court determined that

> drawn guns and handcuffs do not necessarily convert a detention into an arrest. Nor did it convert the detention into an arrest to leave Billy Campbell handcuffed during the time it took to investigate * * * [and check] the serial numbers on the $20 bills. As the Supreme Court has explained:

> "In assessing whether a detention is too long in duration to be justified as an investigative stop, we consider it appropriate to examine whether the police diligently pursued a means of investigation that was likely to confirm or dispel their suspicions quickly, during which time it was necessary to detain the defendant."

Id. at 349-50 (quoting *United States v. Sharpe*, 470 *U.S.* 675, 686, 105 *S.Ct.* 1568, 1575 (1985)).

In this case, the police had "substantial reasons to suspect Billy Campbell had been the bank robber, and he was detained for no longer than necessary to conduct a cursory check that could provide more conclusory evidence. The entire detention took between 10 and 25 minutes—not an unreasonable amount of time under the circumstances." *Id.* at 350.

Accordingly, the court held that the facts of this case "demonstrate neither an arrest nor unreasonably excessive steps for an investigatory detention." *Id.*

---

§8.3. Investigative detentions of vehicles.

§8.3(a). Introduction.

In *Terry v. Ohio*, 392 *U.S.* 1, 88 *S.Ct.* 1868 (1968), the Supreme Court authorized a temporary investigative detention of a person when a law enforcement officer possesses a reasonable suspicion, based on "specific and articulable facts which, taken together with rational inferences from those facts, reasonably warrant" the belief that criminal activity may be afoot. *Id.* at 21, 88 *S.Ct.* at 1880. Thereafter, in *Delaware v. Prouse*, 440 *U.S.* 648, 99 *S.Ct.* 1391 (1979), the Court extended the rationale of *Terry* to circumstances involving the temporary detention of motor vehicles. The officer in *Prouse* stopped defendant's vehicle merely to check his driver's license and registration. The officer had observed neither traffic nor equipment violations nor any other suspicious activity associated with the vehicle. In applying the exclusionary rule to the seizure of marijuana observed in plain view on the vehicle's floor, the Court held:

> [E]xcept in those situations in which there is at least articulable suspicion that a motorist is unlicensed or that an automobile is not registered, or that either the vehicle or an occupant is otherwise subject to seizure for violation of the law, stopping an automobile and detaining the driver in order to check his driver's license and the registration of the automobile are unreasonable under the Fourth Amendment.

Id. at 663, 99 *S.Ct.* at 1401. *See also United States v. Shabazz*, 993 *F.2d* 431, 434 (5th Cir. 1993) ("It is clear that, as in the case of pedestrians, searches and seizures of motorists who are merely *suspected* of criminal activity are to be analyzed under the framework established in *Terry v. Ohio* * * *."). [Court's emphasis.]

Thus, in Fourth Amendment terms, "a traffic stop entails a seizure of the driver 'even though the purpose of the stop is limited and the resulting detention quite brief.'" *Brendlin v. California*, ___ *U.S.* ___, 127 *S.Ct.* 2400, 2406 (2007). [Citation omitted.] The stop also entails a seizure of every passenger in the vehicle, along with the driver. *Id.*, 127 *S.Ct.* at 2406.

The propriety of conducting motor vehicle stops on the basis of a reasonable and articulable suspicion that an occupant is or has been engaged in criminal activity, including a motor vehicle violation, has been consistently upheld. *See e.g., Ornelas v. United States*, 517 *U.S.* 690, 116 *S.Ct.* 1657, 1660 (1996) ("An investigatory stop is permissible under the Fourth Amendment if supported by reasonable suspicion[.]"); *Alabama v. White*, 496 *U.S.* 325, 110 *S.Ct.* 2412 (1990) (motor vehicle stop on the basis of reasonable suspicion that the driver was in possession of cocaine upheld); *United States v. Cortez*, 449 *U.S.* 411, 101 *S.Ct.* 690 (1981) (totality of the circumstances "must yield a particularized suspicion" that the vehicle or its occupant was engaged in wrongdoing); *United States v. Brignoni-Ponce*, 422 *U.S.* 873, 95 *S.Ct.* 2574 (1975) (motor vehicle stop upheld where officers were "aware of specific and articulable facts, together with rational inferences from those facts, that reasonably warrant suspicion" that the vehicle contains illegal aliens); *New York v. Class*, 475 *U.S.* 106, 106 *S.Ct.* 960 (1986) (upholding stop of defendant for driving above speed limit in a car with a cracked windshield in violation of traffic laws); *Pennsylvania v. Mimms*, 434 *U.S.* 106, 98 *S.Ct.* 330 (1977) (upholding motor vehicle stop where police officers observed expired license plate). *See also United States v. Hensley*, 469 *U.S.* 221, 226, 105 *S.Ct.* 675, 679 (1985) ("law enforcement agents may briefly stop a moving automobile to investigate a reasonable suspicion that its occupants are involved in criminal activity").

In upholding the lawfulness of investigative detentions of vehicles on the basis of a reasonable suspicion, courts have recognized that the physical characteristics of a motor vehicle and its use result in a lessened expectation of privacy therein:

> One has a lesser expectation of privacy in a motor vehicle because its function is transportation and it seldom serves as one's residence or as the repository of personal effects. A car has little capacity for escaping public scrutiny. It travels public thoroughfares where both its occupants and its contents are in plain view.

Cardwell v. Lewis, 417 *U.S.* 583, 590, 94 *S.Ct.* 2464, 2469 (1974).

Moreover, motor vehicles are "justifiably the subject of pervasive regulation by the State. Every operator of a motor vehicle must expect that the State, in enforcing its regulations, will intrude to some extent upon that operator's privacy[.]" *New York v. Class, supra*, 475 *U.S.* at 113, 106 *S.Ct.* at 965. In this respect, the Supreme Court has observed:

> Automobiles, unlike homes, are subject to pervasive and continuing governmental regulation and controls, including periodic inspection and licensing requirements. As an everyday occurrence, police stop and examine vehicles when license plates or inspection stickers have expired, or if other violations, such as exhaust fumes or excessive noise, are noted, or if headlights or other safety equipment are not in proper working order.

South Dakota v. Opperman, 428 *U.S.* 364, 368, 96 *S.Ct.* 3092, 3096 (1976). *See also Cady v. Dombrowski*, 413 *U.S.* 433, 441-442, 93 *S.Ct.*

2523, 2528 (1973); *California v. Carney*, 471 *U.S.* 386, 392, 105 *S.Ct.* 2066, 2069-2070 (1985). It is clear, therefore, that "[a]lthough stopping a car and detaining its occupants constitute a seizure within the meaning of the Fourth Amendment, the governmental interest in investigating an officer's reasonable suspicion, based on specific and articulable facts, may outweigh the Fourth Amendment interest of the driver and passengers in remaining secure from the intrusion." *United States v. Hensley, supra*, 469 *U.S.* at 226, 105 *S.Ct.* at 679.

Nonetheless, "[a]n individual operating or traveling in an automobile does not lose all reasonable expectation of privacy simply because the automobile and its use are subject to government regulation." *Prouse* at 662, 99 *S.Ct.* at 1400.

> Automobile travel is a basic, pervasive, and often necessary mode of transportation to and from one's home, workplace, and leisure activities. Many people spend more hours each day traveling in cars than walking on the streets. Undoubtedly, many find a greater sense of security and privacy in traveling in an automobile than they do in exposing themselves by pedestrian or other modes of travel. Were the individual subject to unfettered governmental intrusion every time he entered an automobile, the security guaranteed by the Fourth Amendment would be seriously circumscribed. As *Terry v. Ohio, supra*, recognized, people are not [stripped] of all Fourth Amendment protection when they step from their homes onto the public sidewalks. Nor are they [stripped] of those interests when they step from the sidewalks into their automobiles.

Prouse at 662-663, 99 *S.Ct.* at 1400-1401.

BROWER v. COUNTY OF INYO
Supreme Court of the United States
489 *U.S.* 593, 109 *S.Ct.* 1378 (1989)

QUESTION: Does a Fourth Amendment "seizure" take place when, during a motor vehicle pursuit of a fleeing suspect, police officials (1) place an unilluminated 18-wheel tractor-trailer across both lanes of a two-lane highway, (2) "effectively conceal" the truck behind a curve in the road in order to, (3) block the path of the fleeing suspect, while at the same time, (4) positioning a police car with its headlights on, between the suspect's oncoming vehicle and the truck, so that the suspect would be "blinded" on his approach, and (5) this official conduct results in the suspect's death when he crashes into the police roadblock ?

ANSWER: YES. A Fourth Amendment "seizure" occurs "when there is a governmental termination of [an individual's] freedom of movement *through means intentionally applied*." *Id.* at 1381 (emphasis in original). "[A] roadblock is not just a significant show of authority to induce a voluntary stop, but is designed to produce a stop by physical impact if voluntary compliance does not occur. * * * [Because t]he complaint here sufficiently alleges that [the officers], under color of law, sought to stop Brower by means of a roadblock and succeeded in doing so[, t]hat is enough to constitute a 'seizure' within the meaning of the Fourth Amendment." *Id.* at 1382, 1383.

RATIONALE: William Caldwell (Brower) "was killed when the stolen car he was driving at high speeds for approximately 20 miles in an effort to elude pursuing police crashed into a police roadblock." *Id.* at 1380. It is alleged that the officers "(1) caused an 18-wheel tractor-trailer to be placed across both lanes of a two-lane highway in the path of Brower's flight, (2) 'effectively concealed' this roadblock by placing it behind a curve and leaving it unilluminated, and (3) positioned a police car, with its headlights on, between Brower's oncoming vehicle and the truck so that Brower would be 'blinded' on his approach." *Id.*

In this appeal, the United States Supreme Court reversed the decision reached by the Court of Appeals for the Ninth Circuit which held that no "seizure," within the meaning of the Fourth Amendment, had occurred.

In *Tennessee v. Garner*, 471 *U.S.* 1, 105 *S.Ct.* 1694 (1985), the Court concluded that "a police officer's fatal shooting of a fleeing suspect constituted a Fourth Amendment 'seizure.'" *Brower* at 1380. Similar to Garner, "Brower's independent decision to continue the chase can no more eliminate the [officers'] responsibility for the termination of his movement effected by the roadblock than Garner's independent decision to flee eliminated the Memphis police officer's responsibility for the termination of his movement effected by the bullet." *Id.*

The Court does acknowledge, however, that a mere police chase, in which a fleeing suspect unexpectedly loses control of his car and crashes, constitutes "no unconstitutional seizure." In this regard, the Court explains:

> Violation of the Fourth Amendment requires an intentional acquisition of physical control. A seizure occurs even when an unintended person or thing is the object of the detention or taking, * * * but the detention or taking itself must be willful. This is implicit in the word "seizure," which can hardly be applied to an unknowing act. * * * In sum, the Fourth Amendment addresses "misuse of power," * * * not the accidental effects of otherwise lawful government conduct.

Id. at 1381. [Citation omitted.]

Therefore, "a Fourth Amendment seizure does not occur whenever there is a governmentally caused termination of an individual's freedom of movement (the innocent passerby), nor even whenever there is a governmentally caused and governmentally *desired* termination of an individual's freedom of movement (the fleeing felon), but only when there is a governmental termination of freedom of movement *through means intentionally applied.*" *Id.* [Emphasis in original.] Thus, in the hypothetical situation where a pursuing police car seeks to stop a fleeing suspect only by show of authority represented by flashing lights and continuing pursuit, no seizure occurs, even if that fleeing suspect loses control of his vehicle and crashes. On the other hand, "[i]f instead of that, the police cruiser had pulled alongside the fleeing car and sideswiped it, producing the crash, then the termination of the suspect's freedom of movement would have been a seizure." *Id.*

"In marked contrast to a police car pursuing with flashing lights, or to a policeman in the road signaling an oncoming car to halt, * * * a roadblock is not just a significant show of authority to induce a voluntary stop, but is designed to produce a stop by physical impact if voluntary compliance does not occur." *Id.* at 1382. Nor does the Court think it possible, "in determining whether there has been a seizure in a case such as this, to distinguish between a roadblock that is designed to give the oncoming driver the option of a voluntary stop (*e.g.*, one at the end of a long straightway), and a roadblock that is designed to produce a collision (*e.g.*, one located just around a bend). * * * [It is] enough for a seizure that a person be stopped by the very instrumentality set in motion or put in place in order to achieve that result. It was enough here, therefore, that * * * Brower was meant to be stopped by the physical obstacle of the roadblock— and that he was so stopped." *Id.* That is enough to constitute a " 'seizure' within [the] meaning of the Fourth Amendment." *Id.* at 1383.

Of course, in this 42 *U.S.C.* §1983 action, (a civil rights action seeking civil damages against the law enforcement authorities), "seizure" alone is not enough for liability; the seizure must be unreasonable. Brower's heirs may only recover for Brower's death if, upon remand, they can establish that the officers precisely set "up the roadblock in such a manner as to be likely to kill him." *Id.*

SCOTT v. HARRIS
Supreme Court of the United States
___ *U.S.* ___, 127 *S.Ct.* 1769 (2007)

QUESTION: Under the Fourth Amendment, can a law enforcement officer attempt to stop a fleeing motorist from continuing his public-endangering flight by ramming the motorist's car from behind?

ANSWER: YES. A law enforcement officer's "attempt to terminate a dangerous high-speed car chase that threatens the lives of innocent bystanders does not violate the Fourth Amendment, even when it places the fleeing motorist at risk of serious injury or death." *Id.* at 1779.

RATIONALE: At 10:42 p.m., Deputy Clinton Reynolds of the Coweta County, Georgia, Sheriff's Department tried to pull Victor Harris over for speeding. At the time, Harris, 19, was driving his Cadillac 73 miles per hour in a 55-mile-per-hour zone. When Harris failed to respond, Deputy Reynolds activated his emergency lights indicating that Harris should pull over. Instead of stopping, Harris sped away, "initiating a chase down what is in most portions a two-lane road, at speeds exceeding 85 miles per hour. The deputy radioed his dispatch to report that he was pursuing a fleeing vehicle, and broadcast its license plate number." *Id.* at 1772-73.

Deputy Timothy Scott heard the radio communication and joined the pursuit along with other officers. Shortly thereafter, Harris "pulled into the parking lot of a shopping center and was nearly boxed in by the various police vehicles." *Id.* at 1773. He "evaded the trap by making a sharp turn, colliding with Scott's police car, exiting the parking lot, and speeding off once again down a two-lane highway." *Id.*

Following the events at the shopping center, Scott took over as the lead pursuit vehicle. "Six minutes and nearly 10 miles after the chase had begun," Scott radioed his supervisor for permission to attempt a "PIT" ("Precision Intervention Technique"), a maneuver in which a police car deliberately bumps a fleeing car at an angle, forcing it to spin to a stop. *Id.* Scott's supervisor authorized the maneuver with the message: "Go ahead and take him out." *Id.* Due to the high rate of speed, however, Scott backed off at the last moment and instead slowed his vehicle and applied his push bumper to the rear of Harris' vehicle. This caused Harris to lose control of his car, swerve off the roadway, and crash.

Now a quadriplegic, Harris sued Scott and others under 42 *U.S.C.* §1983, alleging that the officer had violated his constitutional rights by the use of excessive force resulting in an unreasonable seizure under the Fourth Amendment.

On appeal from Deputy Scott's unsuccessful motion for summary judgment on the basis of qualified immunity, the Eleventh Circuit Court of Appeals determined that a "reasonable jury" could find that the deputy's actions constituted an unreasonable use of "deadly force" under *Tennessee v. Garner*, 471 *U.S.* 1, 105 *S.Ct.* 1694 (1985), and, at the time of the incident, the law was sufficiently clear "to give reasonable law enforcement officers 'fair notice' that ramming a vehicle under these circumstances was unlawful." *Scott* at 1773. [Citation omitted.] *The United States Supreme Court, per Justice Scalia, disagreed and reversed.*

In this case, the main question was whether Deputy Scott's actions violated the Fourth Amendment. To resolve this question, the Court was aided by the existence in the record of a videotape generated from the patrol car's camera. The tape showed Harris' vehicle

> racing down narrow, two-lane roads in the dead of night at speeds that are shockingly fast. We see it swerve around more than a dozen other cars, cross the double-yellow line, and force cars traveling in both directions to their respective shoulders to avoid being hit. We see it run multiple red lights and travel for considerable periods of time in the occasional center left-turn-only lane, chased by numerous police cars forced to engage in the same hazardous maneuvers just to keep up. Far from being [a] cautious and controlled driver * * *, what we see on the video more closely resembles a Hollywood-style car chase of the most frightening sort, placing police officers and innocent bystanders alike at great risk of serious injury.

Id. at 1775-76.

Given this sequence of events, the Court had no doubt that Harris was "driving in such fashion as to endanger human life." *Id.* at 1776. Consequently, the Court found it "quite clear that Deputy Scott did not violate the Fourth Amendment." *Id.* True, his decision to terminate the car chase by ramming his bumper into Harris' vehicle constituted a "seizure"—a governmental "termination of freedom of movement through means intentionally applied." Yet, that seizure was "objectively reasonable." *Id.* [Citations omitted.]

In so ruling, the Court rejected Harris' invitation to analyze this case under the rubric of deadly force, as set forth in *Tennessee v. Garner.* In this regard, Harris insisted that Deputy Scott's actions were *per se* unreasonable, because he failed to meet the preconditions for deadly force: "(1) The suspect must have posed an immediate threat of serious physical harm to the officer or others; (2) deadly force must have been necessary to prevent escape; and (3) where feasible, the officer must have given the suspect some warning." *Id.* at 1777.

Speaking for the Court, Justice Scalia explained:

> *Garner* did not establish a magical on/off switch that triggers rigid preconditions whenever an officer's actions constitute "deadly force." *Garner* was simply an application of the Fourth Amendment's "reasonableness" test * * * to the use of a particular type of force in a particular situation. *Garner* held that it was unreasonable to kill a "young, slight, and unarmed" burglary suspect[,] by shooting him "in the back of the head" while he was running away on foot, and when the officer "could not reasonably have believed that [the suspect] * * * posed any threat," and "never attempted to justify his actions on any basis other than the need to prevent an escape." * * * Whatever *Garner* said about the factors that *might have* justified shooting the suspect in that case, such "preconditions" have scant applicability to this case, which has vastly different facts. "*Garner* had nothing to do with one car striking another or even with car chases in general[.] A police car's bumping a fleeing car is, in fact, not much like a policeman's shooting a gun so as to hit a person." * * * Nor is the threat posed by the flight on foot of an unarmed suspect even remotely comparable to the extreme danger to human life posed by [Harris] in this case. * * * [The standard] in the Fourth Amendment context is * * * "reasonableness." Whether or not Scott's actions constituted application of "deadly force," all that matters is whether Scott's actions were reasonable.

Id. at 1777-78. [Citations omitted.]

In judging whether Scott's actions were reasonable, the Court examined the risk of bodily harm that Scott's actions posed to Harris in light of the threat to the public that Scott was trying to eliminate. It was clear from the videotape that Harris "posed an actual and imminent threat to the lives of any pedestrians who might have been present, to other civilian motorists, and to the officers involved in the chase. * * * It [was] equally clear that Scott's actions posed a high likelihood of serious injury or death to [Harris]—though not the near certainty of death posed by, say, shooting a fleeing felon in the back of the head * * *, or pulling alongside a fleeing motorist's car and shooting the motorist[.]" *Id.* at 1778.

"So how does a court go about weighing the perhaps lesser probability of injuring or killing numerous bystanders against the perhaps larger probability of injuring or killing a single person?" *Id.* In this regard, Justice Scalia explained:

> We think it appropriate in this process to take into account not only the number of lives at risk, but also their relative culpability. It was [Harris], after all, who intentionally placed himself and the public in danger by unlawfully engaging in the reckless, high-speed flight that ultimately produced the choice between two evils that Scott confronted. Multiple police cars, with blue lights flashing and sirens blaring, had been chasing [Harris] for nearly 10 miles, but he ignored their warning to stop. By contrast, those who might have been harmed had Scott not taken the action he did were entirely innocent. *We have little difficulty in concluding it was reasonable for Scott to take the action that he did.*
>
> But wait, says [Harris]: Couldn't the innocent public equally have been protected, and the tragic accident entirely avoided, if the police had simply ceased their pursuit? We think the police need not have taken that chance and hoped for the best. Whereas Scott's action—ramming [Harris] off the road—was *certain* to eliminate the risk that [he] posed to the public, ceasing pursuit was not. First of all, there would have been no way to convey convincingly to [Harris] that the chase was off, and that he was free to go. Had [he] looked in his rear-view mirror and seen the police cars deactivate their flashing lights and turn around, he would have had no idea whether they were truly letting him get away, or simply devising a new strategy for capture. Perhaps the police knew a shortcut he didn't know, and would reappear down the road to intercept him; or perhaps they were setting up a roadblock in his path. * * * Given such uncertainty, [Harris] might have been just as likely to respond by continuing to drive recklessly as by slowing down and wiping his brow.

Id. at 1778-79. [Emphasis added.]

In this case, the Court refused to "lay down a rule requiring the police to allow fleeing suspects to get away whenever they drive *so recklessly* that they put other people's lives in danger. It is obvious the perverse incentives such a rule would create: Every fleeing motorist would know that escape is within his grasp, if only he accelerates to 90 miles per hour, crosses the double-yellow line a few times, and runs a few red lights. The Constitution assuredly does not impose this invitation to impunity-earned-by-recklessness." *Id.* at 1779. [Court's emphasis.]

Here is the more sensible rule: "*A police officer's attempt to terminate a dangerous highspeed car chase that threatens the lives of inno-*

cent bystanders does not violate the Fourth Amendment, even when it places the fleeing motorist at risk of serious injury or death." Id. [Emphasis added.]

The car chase that Harris initiated in this case posed a substantial and immediate risk of serious physical injury to others. Therefore, the Court held that Scott's attempt to terminate the chase by forcing Harris off the road was reasonable.

---

§8.3(b). Roadblocks/highway checkpoints.

MICHIGAN DEPT. OF STATE POLICE v. SITZ
Supreme Court of the United States
496 *U.S.* 444, 110 *S.Ct.* 2481 (1990)

QUESTION: Does the use of highway sobriety checkpoints violate the Fourth and Fourteenth Amendments to the federal Constitution ?

ANSWER: NO. When properly conducted, a State's use of highway sobriety checkpoints does not violate the Constitution. "[T]he balance of the State's interest in preventing drunken driving, the extent to which th[e Michigan] system can reasonably be said to advance that interest, and the degree of intrusion upon individual motorists who are briefly stopped, weighs in favor of th[is State's highway sobriety checkpoint] program." *Id.* at 2488.

RATIONALE: In early 1986, the Michigan Department of State Police and its Director established a sobriety checkpoint pilot program. The Director appointed a Sobriety Checkpoint Advisory Committee made up of representatives of the Michigan State Police, local police, state prosecutors, and the University of Michigan Transportation Research Institute. The work of the Advisory Committee led to the creation of guidelines setting forth procedures governing sobriety checkpoint operations, site selection, and publicity.

"Under the guidelines, checkpoints would be set up at selected sites along state roads. All vehicles passing through a checkpoint would be stopped and their drivers briefly examined for signs of intoxication. In cases where a checkpoint officer detected signs of intoxication, the motorist would be directed to a location out of the traffic flow where an officer would check the motorist's driver's license and car registration and, if warranted, conduct further sobriety tests. Should the field tests and the officer's observations suggest that the driver was intoxicated, an arrest would be made. All other drivers would be permitted to resume their journey immediately." *Id.* at 2484.

"The first—and to date the only—sobriety checkpoint operated under the program was conducted in Saginaw County with the assistance of the Saginaw County Sheriff's Department. During the hour-and-fifteen-minute duration of the checkpoint's operation, 126 vehicles passed through the checkpoint. The average delay for each vehicle was approximately 25 seconds. Two drivers were detained for field sobriety testing, and one of the two was arrested for driving under the influence of alcohol. A third driver who drove through without stopping was pulled over by an officer in an observation vehicle and arrested for driving under the influence." *Id.*

On the day before the operation of the Saginaw County checkpoint, the plaintiffs filed a complaint in the Circuit Court of Wayne County seeking declaratory and injunctive relief from potential subjection to the sobriety checkpoints. Each of the plaintiffs "is a licensed driver in the State of Michigan . . . who regularly travels throughout the State in his automobile." *Id.* After the trial, at which the Circuit Court heard extensive testimony concerning the "effectiveness" of highway sobriety checkpoint programs, the court ruled that the Michigan program violated the Fourth Amendment. The Michigan Court of Appeals affirmed. *The United States Supreme Court, however, disagreed and reversed.*

It is well settled that "a Fourth Amendment 'seizure' occurs when a vehicle is stopped at a checkpoint." *Id.* at 2485. *See e.g., United States v. Martinez-Fuerte*, 428 *U.S.* 543, 556, 96 *S.Ct.* 3074, 3082 (1976) ("It is agreed that checkpoint stops are 'seizures' within the meaning of the Fourth Amendment"); *Brower v. County of Inyo*, 489 *U.S.* 593, 109 *S.Ct.* 1378, 1379 (1989) (Fourth Amendment seizure occurs "when there is a governmental termination of freedom of movement *through means intentionally applied*" (emphasis in original)). The relevant question, therefore, is "whether such seizures are 'reasonable' under the Fourth Amendment[,]" *Sitz* at 2485, and in this case, the Court addresses "only the use of sobriety checkpoints generally," and focuses only on "the initial stop of each motorist passing through a checkpoint and the associated preliminary questioning and observation by checkpoint officers." *Id.* Significantly, the Court does not address the particular treatment of any person *after* an actual detention at a certain checkpoint. "Detention of particular motorists for more extensive field sobriety testing may," according to the Court, "require satisfaction of an individualized suspicion standard." *Id.*

To decide this case, the Court agreed with the Michigan Court of Appeals that the balancing approach of *Brown v. Texas*, 443 *U.S.* 47, 99 *S.Ct.* 2637 (1979), presents the relevant analysis. *Brown* requires " 'balancing the state's interest in preventing accidents caused by drunk drivers, the effectiveness of sobriety checkpoints in achieving that goal, and the level of intrusion on an individual's privacy caused by the checkpoints.' " *Sitz* at 2484. [Citations omitted.] The Supreme Court disagrees, however, with the Michigan court's application of the *Brown* three-prong balancing test.

Preliminarily, Chief Justice Rehnquist, speaking for the Court, points out:

> No one can seriously dispute the magnitude of the drunken driving problem or the States' interest in eradicating it. Media reports of alcohol-related death and mutilation on the Nation's roads are legion. * * * "Drunk drivers cause an annual death toll of over 25,000 and in the same time span cause nearly one million personal injuries and more than five billion dollars in property damage." * * * For

decades, this Court has "repeatedly lamented the tragedy." * * * *See* *Breithaupt v. Abram*, 352 *U.S.* 432, 439, 77 *S.Ct.* 408, 412 [] (1957) ("The increasing slaughter on our highways . . . now reaches the astounding figures only heard of on the battlefield").

Id. at 2485-2486.

On the other side of the scale—"the measure of the intrusion on motorists stopped briefly at sobriety checkpoints—is slight. [This Court] reached a similar conclusion as to the intrusion on motorists subjected to a brief stop at a highway checkpoint for detecting illegal aliens. *See Martinez-Fuerte, supra* at 558, 96 *S.Ct.* at 3083. [There is] virtually no difference between the levels of intrusion on law-abiding motorists from the brief stops necessary to the effectuation of these two types of checkpoints, which to the average motorist would seem identical save for the nature of the questions the checkpoint officers might ask." *Sitz* at 2486.

With respect to what it perceived to be a "substantial subjective intrusion" on motorists, the court below found that "the checkpoints have the potential to generate fear and surprise in motorists. This was so because the record failed to demonstrate that approaching motorists would be aware of their option to make U-turns or turnoffs to avoid the checkpoints. On that basis, the [Michigan] court deemed the subjective intrusion from the checkpoints unreasonable." *Id.*

Disagreeing with the Michigan court's "fear and surprise" analysis, the Chief Justice declared:

> We believe the Michigan courts misread our cases concerning the degree of 'subjective intrusion' and the potential for generating fear and surprise. The 'fear and surprise' to be considered are not the natural fear of one who has been drinking over the prospect of being stopped at a sobriety checkpoint but, rather, the fear and surprise engendered in law abiding motorists by the nature of the stop. This was made clear in *Martinez-Fuerte.* Comparing checkpoint stops to roving patrol stops considered in prior cases, we said, "we view checkpoint stops in a different light because the subjective intrusion—the generating of concern or even fright on the part of lawful travelers—is appreciably less in the case of a checkpoint stop. * * * [And in *United States v. Ortiz*, 422 *U.S.* 891, 95 *S.Ct.* 2585 (1975),] we noted: ' "The circumstances surrounding a checkpoint stop and search are far less intrusive than those attending a roving-patrol stop. Roving patrols often operate at night on seldom-traveled roads, and their approach may frighten motorists. At traffic checkpoints the motorist can see that other vehicles are being stopped, he can see visible signs of the officers' authority, and he is much less likely to be frightened or annoyed by the intrusion." 422 *U.S.* at 894-895[, 95 *S.Ct.* at 2587-2588].' *Martinez-Fuerte*[at] 558, 96 *S.Ct.* at 3083."

Sitz at 2486-2487. In this case, "the checkpoints are selected pursuant to the guidelines, and uniformed police officers stop every approaching vehicle. The intrusion resulting from the brief stop at the sobriety checkpoint is for constitutional purposes indistinguishable from the checkpoint stops [this Court] upheld in *Martinez-Fuerte.*" *Sitz* at 2487.

Addressing next the Michigan court's determination that the checkpoint program failed the "effectiveness" part of the balancing test, the Supreme Court stated: "We think the Court of Appeals was wrong on this point as well." *Id. Brown v. Texas* describes this balancing factor as " 'the degree to which the seizure advances the public interest.' " *Sitz* at 2487 (quoting *Brown* at 51, 99 *S.Ct.* at 2640). "This passage from *Brown* was not meant to transfer from politically accountable officials to the courts the decision as to which among reasonable alternative law enforcement techniques should be employed to deal with a serious public danger. Experts in police science might disagree over which of several methods of apprehending drunken drivers is preferable as an ideal. But for purposes of Fourth Amendment analysis, the choice among such reasonable alternatives remains with the governmental officials who have a unique understanding of, and a responsibility for, limited public resources, including a finite number of police officers." *Id.*

During the sobriety checkpoint operated in this case, "the detention of the 126 vehicles that entered the checkpoint resulted in the arrest of two drunken drivers. Stated as a percentage, approximately 1.5 percent of the drivers passing through the checkpoint were arrested for alcohol impairment. In addition, an expert witness testified at the trial that experience in other States demonstrated that, on the whole, sobriety checkpoints resulted in drunken driving arrests of around 1 percent of all motorists stopped. * * * By way of comparison, the record from one of the consolidated cases in *Martinez-Fuerte*, showed that in the associated checkpoint, illegal aliens were found in only 0.12 percent of the vehicles passing through the checkpoint. * * * The ratio of illegal aliens detected to vehicles stopped (considering that on occasion two or more illegal aliens were found in a single vehicle) was approximately 0.5 percent. * * * [In light of these percentages, the Court] concluded that [the *Martinez-Fuerte*] 'record provide[d] a rather complete picture of the effectiveness of ' [this particular checkpoint, and consequently] sustained its constitutionality." *Sitz* at 2488. And here, in *Sitz*, the Court sees "no justification for a different conclusion[.]" *Id.*

"In sum, the balance of the State's interest in preventing drunken driving, the extent to which this system can reasonably be said to advance that interest, and the degree of intrusion upon individual motorists who are briefly stopped, weighs in favor of the state program." *Id.* Accordingly, the Michigan highway sobriety checkpoint program is consistent with the Fourth and Fourteenth Amendments. *Id.* at 2483, 2488.

NOTE

Many states have had in place, prior to the Court's decision in *Sitz*, judicially crafted guidelines for the implementation of sobriety checkpoints. New Jersey is representative. In *State v. Kirk*, 202 *N.J.Super.* 28 (App.Div. 1985), the court examined the caselaw in New Jersey, as well as nine other jurisdictions, and developed the below guidelines for its law enforcement agencies which, if followed carefully, would overcome any constitutional infirmities.

GUIDELINES GOVERNING ROADSIDE CHECKPOINTS
DWI Roadblocks; Safety Checkpoints; Etc.

1. There must be a social utilitarian purpose—*a legitimate State interest*—for the checkpoint.

2. When establishing the checkpoint, there must be participation of command or supervisory authority in the formulation of an "administrative plan" consisting of explicit, neutral and predetermined limitations on the conduct of officers participating in the checkpoint. Discretion should be minimized by directing checkpoint officers to stop cars at predetermined intervals, *e.g.*, every 5th, 10th, or 15th vehicle, and vehicles having observable violations.

> **a.** The plan must include the selection of the time, place and duration of the checkpoint, which should be based on identifiable statistical data showing the need for the checkpoint at the respective time and place. Consideration should be given to (1) areas known for high incidents of accidents, drunk driving or other traffic violations, (2) traffic volume, and (3) motorist and pedestrian safety.

> **b.** The plan must set forth the required number of checkpoint officers that will be needed to ensure that delays are held to a minimum. If an executive-level officer did not participate in the plan's formulation, it should not be implemented until that officer has reviewed and approved it.

> **c.** Each officer participating in the checkpoint must be provided with a copy of, or instructed in the contents of, the required procedures set forth in the plan.

> **d.** The appropriate prosecuting attorney should be provided with a copy of the administrative plan at least 72 hours prior to the implementation of the roadside checkpoint.

3. To avoid frightening the traveling public, adequate on-the-scene warnings must be given (*for example, a large, obvious sign indicating that the motorist is about to be stopped, the nature of the checkpoint, and that all motorists must pass through; flashing lights; marked police vehicles; and other reflectorized equipment*). In addition, advance general publicity of the checkpoint may be provided to deter drunk drivers from getting in cars in the first place.

4. The checkpoints must be sufficiently staffed by uniformed officers to ensure safety and prevent undue inconvenience to motorists and unreasonable interference with normal traffic flow. A predetermined, safe and convenient "pull over" or parking area should be established and used for vehicles or motorists having violations.

5. Officers participating in the checkpoint should be provided with specified, neutral and courteous procedures to follow when stopping motorists.

6. Carefully planned and predetermined procedures must be in place for operations that will involve the moving of a checkpoint from one location to another.

7. Upon completion of the checkpoint operation, the participating officers should submit, through the appropriate chain of command, full reports in writing of the conduct and results of the checkpoint to the administrative officer(s) who initiated or planned the operation.

[*See State v. Kirk* at 41, 57 (citing *State ex rel. Ekstrom v. Justice Court*, 663 *P*.2d 992, 998-1001 (1983) (Feldman, J., concurring.)]

CITY OF INDIANAPOLIS v. EDMOND
Supreme Court of the United States
31 *U.S.* 32, 121 *S.Ct.* 447 (2000)

QUESTION: Will a roadside checkpoint program, whose primary purpose is the discovery and interdiction of illegal narcotics, violate the Fourth Amendment ?

ANSWER: YES. Roadside checkpoints may not be performed where the program's primary purpose is to "detect evidence of ordinary criminal wrongdoing." *Id.* at 454. In order to conduct a motor vehicle stop for the purpose of discovering or interdicting illegal drugs, police officers must first possess a reasonable articulable suspicion that the motorist or other vehicle occupant is engaged in unlawful activity.

RATIONALE: Between August and November of 1998, the Indianapolis Police Department conducted a series of six roadblocks on Indianapolis roads in an effort to interdict unlawful drugs. In all, 1,161 vehicles were stopped and 104 motorists were arrested. Fifty-five arrests were drug-related and 49 arrests were for offenses unrelated to drugs.

At each roadside checkpoint, there were approximately 30 officers, who were directed to stop a predetermined number of vehicles. Acting in accordance with written directives issued by the chief of police, at least one officer was assigned to approach the stopped vehicle, advise the driver that he or she was being stopped briefly at a drug checkpoint, and ask the driver to produce his or her driving credentials. During the stop, the officer looked for signs of impairment and conducted "an open-view examination of the vehicle from the outside." *Id.*

at 450-51. In addition, a narcotics-detection dog was walked around the outside of each stopped vehicle.

The directives further provided that the officers were not permitted to conduct a search unless they obtained consent or developed a particularized reason to believe that evidence of a crime or contraband would be located within the stopped vehicle. The officers were required to conduct each stop in the same manner; they had "no discretion to stop any vehicle out of sequence." *Id.* at 451. Each checkpoint was operated in such a way as to ensure that the "total duration of each stop, absent reasonable suspicion or probable cause, would be five minutes or less." *Id.*

The checkpoint locations had been "selected weeks in advance based on such considerations as area crime statistics and traffic flow." *Id.* They were generally operated during daylight hours and were identified with lighted signs reading: NARCOTICS CHECKPOINT ___ MILE AHEAD — NARCOTICS K-9 IN USE — BE PREPARED TO STOP. After a group of cars had been stopped, other traffic was permitted to proceed without interruption until all the stopped cars had been processed or diverted for further processing. Overall, the average stop for a vehicle not subject to further processing lasted two to three minutes or less.

James Edmond and Joell Palmer, who were each stopped at one of these checkpoints, filed a lawsuit on behalf of themselves and the class of all motorists who had been stopped or were subject to being stopped at the Indianapolis drug checkpoints. Their primary contention was that these roadside checkpoints, whose primary purpose was drug interdiction, violated the Fourth Amendment. *The United States Supreme Court agreed.*

As a general rule of criminal procedure, a motor vehicle stop is a "seizure" within the meaning of the Fourth Amendment. As such, it must be supported by a reasonable individualized suspicion of wrongdoing. In a series of cases, however, the United States Supreme Court has recognized that there are a certain class of motor vehicle stops that may be permissible in the absence of the usual requirement of reasonable suspicion. For example, in *United States v. Martinez-Fuerte*, 428 *U.S.* 543, 96 *S.Ct.* 3074 (1976), the Court held that brief, suspicionless seizures at Border Patrol checkpoints near the nation's borders for the purpose of intercepting illegal immigrants were constitutional. Similarly, in *Michigan Dept. of State Police v. Sitz*, 496 *U.S.* 444, 110 *S.Ct.* 2481 (1990), the Court held that highway checkpoints conducted for the purpose of combating drunk driving were also constitutional. In addition, in *Delaware v. Prouse*, 440 *U.S.* 648, 99 *S.Ct.* 1391 (1979), the Court suggested that "a similar type of roadblock with the purpose of verifying drivers' licenses and vehicle registrations would be permissible." *Edmond* at 452.

In no case, however, has the Court ever permitted or indicated approval of a roadside checkpoint program whose primary purpose was to "detect evidence of ordinary criminal wrongdoing." *Id.* Writing for the Court, Justice O'Connor emphasized that a roadside checkpoint primarily designed to discover and interdict illegal drugs is nothing more than a police procedure that relates to "ordinary crime control." Id.

In *Martinez-Fuerte*, the Court upheld the roadblock based on considerations specifically related to the need to police the nation's borders, and the "longstanding concern for the protection of the integrity of the border." *Edmond* at 452. In *Sitz*, the Court approved roadblocks designed to detect signs of intoxication and remove impaired drivers from the road. This type of checkpoint program was clearly "aimed at reducing the immediate hazard posed by the presence of drunk drivers on the highways, and there was an obvious connection between the imperative of highway safety and the law enforcement practice at issue. The gravity of the drunk driving problem and the magnitude of the State's interest in getting drunk drivers off the road weighed heavily in [the Court's] determination that the program was constitutional." *Edmond* at 453.

In *Delaware v. Prouse*, the Court invalidated a "discretionary, suspicionless stop for a spot check of a motorist's driver's license and vehicle registration." *Edmond* at 453. Indeed, the officer's conduct in *Prouse* was deemed unconstitutional primarily because of his "exercise of 'standardless and unconstrained discretion.' " *Id.** The *Prouse* Court did acknowledge, however, that the States have a "vital interest in ensuring that only those qualified to do so are permitted to operate motor vehicles, that these vehicles are fit for safe operation, and hence that licensing, registration, and vehicle inspection requirements are being observed." *Id.* [Citation omitted.] Consequently, the Court suggested that the "[q]uestioning of all oncoming traffic at roadblock-type stops" would be a lawful means of serving and protecting this interest in highway safety. *Id.*

Here, in *Edmond*, the Court observed that while there is a "common thread of highway safety" running through *Sitz* and *Prouse*, there is a clear "difference in the Fourth Amendment significance of highway safety interests and the general interest in crime control." *Edmond* at 453. A highway checkpoint designed to discover and interdict illegal narcotics merely furthers the state's general interest in crime control.

In ruling that such checkpoints are unconstitutional, the Court did not hold that the officers' use of the narcotics-detection dog in any way transformed the checkpoint stop into a Fourth Amendment "search." *Id.* at 453. Walking a police K-9 around the exterior of a car so that the dog may conduct an "exterior sniff," is a lawful police procedure which "does not require entry into the car and is not designed to disclose any information other than the presence or absence of narcotics." *Id.* As such, "a sniff by a dog that simply walks around a car is 'much less intrusive than a typical search.' " *Id.* [Citation omitted.] Instead, the reason why the Court held this roadside checkpoint unconstitutional was because of its "primary purpose"—interdicting illegal narcotics. In this regard, the Court said:

---

* The State in *Prouse* also argued that the legitimate state interest of *the apprehension of stolen motor vehicles* justified the officer's discretionary vehicle spot check. The *Edmond* Court addressed this contention by stating that in general, "the governmental interest in controlling automobile thefts is *not distinguishable from the general interest in crime control*." *Id.* at 453. [Emphasis added.] This discussion was presented by the Court as a further example of the "difference in the Fourth Amendment significance of highway safety interests and the general interest in crime control." *Id.*

We have never approved a checkpoint program whose primary purpose was to detect evidence of ordinary criminal wrongdoing. Rather, our checkpoint cases have recognized only limited exceptions to the general rule that a seizure must be accompanied by some measure of individualized suspicion. We suggested in *Prouse* that we would not credit the "general interest in crime control" as justification for a regime of suspicionless stops. * * * Consistent with this suggestion, each of the checkpoint programs that we have approved was designed primarily to serve purposes closely related to the problems of policing the border or the necessity of ensuring roadway safety. *Because the primary purpose of the Indianapolis narcotics checkpoint program is to uncover evidence of ordinary criminal wrongdoing, the program contravenes the Fourth Amendment.* * * * Without drawing the line at roadblocks designed primarily to serve the general interest in crime control, the Fourth Amendment would do little to prevent such intrusions from becoming a routine part of American life.

Id. at 454. [Emphasis added.]

Although the Court was sensitive to the "severe and intractable nature of the drug problem" in the United States today, recognizing that "traffic in illegal narcotics creates social harms of the first magnitude," *id.* at 454, it nonetheless pointed out that the "same can be said of various other illegal activities, if only to a lesser degree." *Id.* at 454-55.

But the gravity of the threat alone cannot be dispositive of questions concerning what means law enforcement officers may employ to pursue a given purpose. Rather, in determining whether individualized suspicion is required, we must consider the nature of the interests threatened and their connection to the particular law enforcement practices at issue. We are particularly reluctant to recognize exceptions to the general rule of individualized suspicion where governmental authorities primarily pursue their general crime control ends.

Nor can the narcotics-interdiction purpose of the checkpoints be rationalized in terms of a highway safety concern similar to that present in *Sitz*. The detection and punishment of almost any criminal offense serves broadly the safety of the community, and our streets would no doubt be safer but for the scourge of illegal drugs. Only with respect to a smaller class of offenses, however, is society confronted with the type of immediate, vehicle-bound threat to life and limb that the sobriety checkpoint in *Sitz* was designed to eliminate.

Id. at 455.

Accordingly, the Court found it clear that the "primary purpose" of the Indianapolis narcotics checkpoints was in the end "to advance 'the general interest in crime control.' " *Id.* The checkpoints were, therefore, held to be unconstitutional. In so ruling, the Court "decline[d] to suspend the usual requirement of individualized suspicion where the police seek to employ a checkpoint primarily for the ordinary enterprise of investigating crimes." *Id.*

During the course of its opinion, the Court did recognize that there are some circumstances that "may justify a law enforcement checkpoint where the primary purpose would otherwise, but for some emergency, relate to ordinary crime control. For example, * * * the Fourth Amendment would almost certainly permit an appropriately tailored roadblock set up to thwart an imminent terrorist attack or to catch a dangerous criminal who is likely to flee by way of a particular route." *Id.*

In this case, the Court did "not limit the purposes that may justify a checkpoint program to any rigid set of categories." *Id.* It merely refused "to approve a program whose primary purpose is ultimately indistinguishable from the general interest in crime control." *Id.*

In several final comments, the Court addressed the argument that it would be improper to focus on a police officer's underlying purpose, or his or her "subjective motivations" in conducting a traffic stop. For example, in *Whren v. United States*, 517 *U.S.* 806, 116 *S.Ct.* 1769 (1996), it was held that "an officer's subjective intentions are irrelevant to the Fourth Amendment validity of a traffic stop that is justified objectively by probable cause to believe that a traffic violation has occurred." *Edmond* at 456. In so holding, however, the *Whren* Court expressly distinguished cases where it had addressed the validity of searches conducted without probable cause.

"*Whren* therefore reinforces the principle that, while '[s]ubjective intentions play no role in ordinary, probable-cause Fourth Amendment analysis,' * * * programmatic purposes may be relevant to the validity of Fourth Amendment intrusions undertaken pursuant to a general scheme without individualized suspicion." *Edmond* at 456. Accordingly, courts will conduct an inquiry into the underlying purpose of police programs such as roadside checkpoints.

In further discussing this "underlying purpose" inquiry, the Court cautioned that a drug interdiction checkpoint will not become constitutional merely by the police deciding to include, as a secondary purpose, a driver's license or sobriety check. In such circumstances, the courts will examine "the available evidence to determine the *primary* purpose of the checkpoint program." *Id.* at 457. [Emphasis added.]

Finally, the Court paused to note that its ruling does not impair "the ability of police officers to act appropriately upon information that they properly learn during a checkpoint stop justified by a lawful primary purpose, even where such action may result in the arrest of a motorist for an offense unrelated to that purpose." *Id.*

As a matter of law, therefore, in order to conduct a motor vehicle stop for the purpose of discovering or interdicting illegal drugs, police officers must first possess a reasonable articulable suspicion that the motorist or other vehicle occupant is engaged in unlawful activity.

NOTE

Stolen vehicle checkpoints. In light of the discussion in *Indianapolis v. Edmond,* characterizing the governmental interest in detecting and deterring automobile thefts as "not distinguishable from the general interest in crime control," *see id.* at 453, local law enforcement officials should not conduct a "stolen vehicle" checkpoint without first consulting with their police legal advisor, prosecutor or district attorney.

ILLINOIS v. LIDSTER
Supreme Court of the United States
540 *U.S.* 419, 124 *S.Ct.* 885 (2004)

QUESTION: Do the police violate the Fourth Amendment by setting up a highway checkpoint for the purpose of stopping and asking motorists for information about a recent, serious crime?

ANSWER: NO.   Brief "information-seeking" highway checkpoints are not unconstitutional *per se.* The police checkpoint in this case involved a brief stop of motorists to ask for information about a recent hit-and-run accident that resulted in a death. The stop's objective was to ask for public assistance in finding the perpetrator of this "specific and known crime." The checkpoint was "appropriately tailored" to this goal; its interference with the liberty of motorists was minimal; and all vehicles were stopped in a systematic and non-discriminatory manner. As such, it was constitutional. *Id.* at 891.

RATIONALE: On Saturday, August 23rd, just after midnight, an unknown motorist traveling eastbound on a highway struck and killed a 70-year-old bicyclist. The motorist drove off without identifying himself. "About one week later at about the same time of night and at about the same place, local police set up a highway checkpoint designed to obtain more information about the accident from the motoring public." *Id.* at 888.
"Police cars with flashing lights partially blocked the eastbound lanes of the highway. The blockage forced traffic to slow down, leading to lines of up to 15 cars in each lane. As each vehicle drew up to the checkpoint, an officer would stop it for 10 to 15 seconds, ask the occupants whether they had seen anything happen there the previous weekend, and hand each driver a flyer. The flyer said 'ALERT – FATAL HIT & RUN ACCIDENT' and requested 'assistance in identifying the vehicle and driver in this accident which killed a 70-year-old bicyclist.'" *Id.*
Defendant, Robert Lidster, drove a minivan toward the checkpoint. As he approached the checkpoint, his van swerved, nearly hitting one of the officers. Investigation at the scene led to Lidster's arrest for drunk driving.
Finding the highway checkpoint constitutional, the Court preliminarily pointed out that its decision in *Indianapolis v. Edmond* does not govern the outcome in this case. The Court said:

> *Edmond* involved a checkpoint at which police stopped vehicles to look for evidence of drug crimes committed by occupants of those vehicles. * * * We found that police had set up this checkpoint primarily for general "crime control" purposes, *i.e.*, "to detect evidence of ordinary criminal wrongdoing." We noted that the stop was made without individualized suspicion. And we held that the Fourth Amendment forbids such a stop, in the absence of special circumstances.

> The checkpoint stop here differs significantly from that in *Edmond*. The stop's primary law enforcement purpose was not to determine whether a vehicle's occupants were committing a crime, but to ask vehicle occupants, as members of the public, for their help in providing information about a crime in all likelihood committed by others. The police expected the information elicited to help them apprehend, not the vehicle's occupants, but other individuals.

Id. at 889.

Here, in *Lidster*, the Court explained that the *Edmond* Court's language of "general interest in crime control" does "not refer to every 'law enforcement' objective." *Id.* The Fourth Amendment does not require a "rule of automatic unconstitutionality to brief, information-seeking highway stops" of the kind performed in this case. *Id.* [Citation omitted.] The Court elaborated:

> [S]pecial law enforcement concerns will sometimes justify highway stops without individualized suspicion. * * * [U]nlike *Edmond*, the context here (seeking information from the public) is one in which, by definition, the concept of individualized suspicion has little role to play. Like certain other forms of police activity, say, crowd control or public safety, an information-seeking stop is not the kind of event that involves suspicion, or lack of suspicion, of the relevant individual. * * *

> [I]nformation-seeking highway stops are less likely to provoke anxiety or to prove intrusive. The stops are likely brief. The police are not likely to ask questions designed to elicit self-incriminating information. And citizens will often react positively when police simply ask for their help as "responsible citizen[s]" to "give whatever information they may have to aid in law enforcement." * * *

> Further, the law ordinarily permits police to seek the voluntary cooperation of members of the public in the investigation of a crime. * * * That, in part, is because voluntary requests play a vital role in police investigatory work. * * *

> The importance of soliciting the public's assistance is offset to some degree by the need to stop a motorist to obtain that help—a need less likely present where a pedestrian, not a motorist, is involved. The difference is significant in light of our determinations that such an involuntary stop amounts to a "seizure" in Fourth

Amendment terms. * * * That difference, however, is not important enough to justify an *Edmond*-type rule here. After all, as we have said, the motorist stop will likely be brief. Any accompanying traffic delay should prove no more onerous than many that typically accompany normal traffic congestion. And the resulting voluntary questioning of a motorist is as likely to prove important for police investigation as is the questioning of a pedestrian. Given these considerations, it would seem anomalous were the law (1) ordinarily to allow police freely to seek the voluntary cooperation of pedestrians but (2) ordinarily to forbid police to seek similar voluntary cooperation from motorists.

Id. at 890. [Citations omitted.]

The Court also did not believe that allowing such checkpoints would result in "an unreasonable proliferation" of them. In this regard, "the Fourth Amendment's normal insistence that the stop be reasonable in context will still provide an important legal limitation on police use of this kind of information-seeking checkpoint." *Id.*

Accordingly, the Court determined that an *Edmond*-type "presumptive rule of unconstitutionality" should not apply in this case. *Id.*

That does not mean the stop is automatically, or even presumptively, constitutional. It simply means that we must judge its reasonableness, hence, its constitutionality, on the basis of the individual circumstances. * * * [I]n judging reasonableness, we look to "the gravity of the public concerns served by the seizure, the degree to which the seizure advances the public interest, and the severity of the interference with individual liberty."

Id. [Citations omitted.]

Turning to the facts in this case, the Court observed:

The relevant public concern was grave. Police were investigating a crime that had resulted in a human death. No one denies the police's need to obtain more information at that time. And the stop's objective was to help find the perpetrator of a specific and known crime, not of unknown crimes of a general sort.

The stop advanced this grave public concern to a significant degree. The police appropriately tailored their checkpoint stops to fit important criminal investigatory needs. The stops took place about one week after the hit-and-run accident, on the same highway near the location of the accident, and at about the same time of night. And police used the stops to obtain information from drivers, some of whom might well have been in the vicinity of the crime at the time it occurred. * * *

Most importantly, the stops interfered only minimally with liberty of the sort the Fourth Amendment seeks to protect. Viewed objectively, each stop required only a brief wait in line a very few minutes at most. Contact with the police lasted only a few seconds.

* * * Police contact consisted simply of a request for information and the distribution of a flyer. * * * Viewed subjectively, the contact provided little reason for anxiety or alarm. The police stopped all vehicles systematically. * * * And there is no allegation here that the police acted in a discriminatory or otherwise unlawful manner while questioning motorists during stops.

Id. at 891.

For the reasons set forth above, the Court held that the checkpoint stop was constitutional.

---

§8.3(c). Motor vehicle stops and the "reasonable articulable suspicion" requirement.

WHREN v. UNITED STATES
Supreme Court of the United States
517 U.S. 806, 116 S.Ct. 1769 (1996)

QUESTION: When a motor vehicle stop is supported by probable cause or reasonable suspicion that the motorist committed a traffic violation, is that stop nonetheless unconstitutional because the officer's underlying motivation was to investigate criminal activity unrelated to the traffic violation ?

ANSWER: NO. The "constitutional reasonableness of traffic stops" does not depend "on the actual motivations of the individual officers involved. * * * Subjective intentions play no role in ordinary, probable-cause Fourth Amendment analysis." *Id.* at 1774.

RATIONALE: Several vice-squad officers of the District of Columbia Metropolitan Police Department were patrolling a "high drug-trafficking" area of the city in an unmarked car when they passed a dark-colored Pathfinder truck with temporary license plates and youthful occupants. The truck was stopped at a stop sign. The officers noticed that the truck's driver was looking down into the lap of the passenger at his right. The truck remained stopped at the intersection for what seemed to be an unusually long time—more than 20 seconds. "When the police car executed a U-turn in order to head back toward the truck, the Pathfinder turned suddenly to its right, without signalling, and sped off at an 'unreasonable' speed." *Id.* at 1772. The officers followed, and quickly caught up with the Pathfinder when it stopped behind other traffic at a red light. They pulled alongside, and Officer Ephraim Soto stepped out and approached the driver's door, identifying himself as a police officer and directing the driver (defendant Brown) to place the truck in park. As Soto positioned himself next to the driver's window, he immediately observed two large plastic bags of what appeared to be crack cocaine in the passenger's (defendant Whren's) hands. Both Brown and Whren were then placed under arrest, and quantities of several types of illicit drugs were confiscated from their vehicle.

In the appeal following their convictions, defendants contended that, even though the officers had probable cause or reasonable suspicion that several provisions of the District of Columbia traffic code had been violated, the stop was nonetheless unconstitutional because a reasonable officer would not have made the stop, based on general or "usual police practices." *The United States Supreme Court rejected defendants' contentions.*

"Temporary detention of individuals during the stop of an automobile by the police, even if only for a brief period and for a limited purpose, constitutes a 'seizure' of 'persons' within the meaning" of the Fourth Amendment. *Id.* "An automobile stop is thus subject to the constitutional imperative that it not be 'unreasonable' under the circumstances. As a general matter, the decision to stop an automobile is reasonable where the police have probable cause to believe that a traffic violation has occurred." *Id.*

The defendants in this case argued that probable cause is not enough. According to defendants, the use of automobiles is so heavily and minutely regulated that "a police officer will almost invariably be able to catch any given motorist in a technical violation." *Id.* at 1773. This, according to defendants, "creates the temptation to use traffic stops as a means of investigating other law violations, as to which no probable cause or even articulable suspicion exists." *Id.* Defendants further contended that "police officers might decide which motorists to stop based on decidedly impermissible factors, such as the race of the car's occupants." *Id.* Thus, defendants urged that the Court adopt an additional requirement for motor vehicle stops, namely, that such a stop is not constitutional unless "a police officer, acting reasonably, *would have* made the stop for the reason given." *Id.* [Emphasis added.] The Court refused to add such an additional requirement.

Prior cases have never endorsed the principle, "that ulterior motives can invalidate police conduct that is justifiable on the basis of probable cause to believe that a violation of law has occurred." *Id.* In this respect, the Court said:

> Not only have we never held, outside the context of an inventory search or administrative inspection * * *, that an officer's motive invalidates objectively justifiable behavior under the Fourth Amendment; but we have repeatedly held and asserted the contrary.

Id. at 1774. *See, e.g., Scott v. United States,* 436 *U.S.* 128, 138, 98 *S.Ct.* 1717, 1723 (1978) ("[s]ubjective intent alone . . . does not make otherwise lawful conduct illegal or unconstitutional"; "the fact that the officer does not have the state of mind which is hypothecated by the reasons which provide the legal justification for the officer's action does not invalidate the action taken as long as the circumstances, viewed objectively, justify that action"). *See also United States v. Robinson,* 414 *U.S.* 218, 236, 94 *S.Ct.* 467, 477 (1973).

Consequently, "the constitutional reasonableness of traffic stops" does not depend "on the actual motivations of the individual officers involved. * * * Subjective intentions play no role in ordinary, probable-cause Fourth Amendment analysis." *Whren* at 1774.

The standard that defendants forward—"whether the officer's conduct deviated materially from usual police practices, so that a reasonable officer in the same circumstances would not have made the stop for the reasons given"—is "plainly and indisputably driven by subjective considerations." *Id.*

> Its whole purpose is to prevent the police from doing under the guise of enforcing the traffic code what they would like to do for different reasons. *[Defendants'] proposed standard may not use the word "pretext," but it is designed to combat nothing other than the perceived "danger" of the pretextual stop * * *.*

> While police manuals and standard procedures may sometimes provide objective assistance, ordinarily one would be reduced to speculating about the hypothetical reaction of a hypothetical [police officer]—an exercise that might be called virtual subjectivity.

> Moreover, police enforcement practices, even if they could be practicably assessed by a judge, vary from place to place and from time to time. We cannot accept that the search and seizure protections of the Fourth Amendment are so variable, * * * and can be made to turn upon such trivialities.

Id. at 1774-75. [Emphasis added.]

Where probable cause has existed, the only cases in which the Court found it necessary to add an extra layer of analysis are those cases that involved "searches or seizures conducted in an extraordinary manner, usually harmful to an individual's privacy or even physical interests." *Id.* at 1776. *See e.g., Tennessee v. Garner,* 471 *U.S.* 1, 105 *S.Ct.* 1694 (1985) (seizure by means of deadly force); *Wilson v. Arkansas,* 514 *U.S.* 927, 115 *S.Ct.* 1914 (1995) (unannounced entry into a home); *Welsh v. Wisconsin,* 466 *U.S.* 740, 104 *S.Ct.* 2091 (1984) (entry into a home without a warrant); *Winston v. Lee,* 470 *U.S.* 753, 105 *S.Ct.* 1611 (1985) (physical penetration into the body). "The making of a traffic stop out-of-uniform," observed the Court, "does not remotely qualify as such an extreme practice, and so is governed by the usual rule that probable cause to believe the law has been broken 'outbalances' private interest in avoiding police contact." *Whren* at 1777.

Accordingly, because the officers in this case had probable cause to believe that the defendants had violated the traffic code, the stop was reasonable under the Fourth Amendment, and the evidence discovered thereby admissible. *Id.*

NOTE

1. During the course of its opinion in *Whren,* the Court noted its agreement with the defendants that "the Constitution prohibits selective enforcement of the law based on considerations such as race." *Id.* at 1774. The Court emphasized, however, that "the constitutional ba-

sis for objecting to intentionally discriminatory application of laws is the Equal Protection Clause, not the Fourth Amendment." *Id.*

2. Regarding the Court's use of the phrase, "probable cause to believe" a traffic violation has occurred, *id.* at 808, 819, 116 *S.Ct.* at 1771, 1777, subsequent cases have made clear that the Fourth Amendment standard for a lawful motor vehicle stop is no more than a reasonable suspicion. *See United States v. Lopez-Soto*, 205 *F.*3d 1101 (9th Cir. 2000) ("none of our sister circuits, either before or after *Whren*, has concluded that a traffic stop must be justified by more than reasonable suspicion," and "some circuits have explicitly held, post-*Whren*, that reasonable suspicion is all the Fourth Amendment requires").

3. *Advising motorist of the end of the motor vehicle stop.* In *Ohio v. Robinette*, 519 *U.S.* 33, 117 *S.Ct.* 417 (1996), the United States Supreme Court made it clear that there is no requirement under the Fourth Amendment that police, during the course of a motor vehicle stop or other investigative detention, advise the person detained that he or she is "free to go" before a consent to search may be lawfully obtained. *Id.* at 419. The Court wholly rejected the Ohio Supreme Court's requirement that "any attempt at consensual interrogation must be preceded by the phrase, 'At this time you legally are free to go,' or words of similar import." *Id.* at 420 (quoting *State v. Robinette*, 653 *N.E.*2d 695, 696 (Ohio 1995)). According to the Court, during the course of a motor vehicle stop, "it would be unrealistic to require police officers to always inform detainees that they are free to go before a consent to search may be deemed voluntary." *Id.* at 421.

4. *Police questioning on matters unrelated to the initial purpose of the traffic stop.* The Court, in *Terry v. Ohio*, emphasized that "[t]he scope of a search must be 'strictly tied to and justified by' the circumstances which rendered its initiation permissible." 392 *U.S.* at 19, 88 *S.Ct.* at 1878. [Citation omitted.] This aspect of *Terry*, sometimes called *Terry*'s "second prong," has been applied to police questioning, taking place during the course of a routine motor vehicle stop, that focuses on matters wholly unrelated to the initial justification for the stop.

(a) *A restrictive approach.*

(1) In *United States v. Guzman*, 864 *F.*2d 1512, 1515 (10th Cir. 1988), a New Mexico police officer stopped Guzman, the driver of a rented Cadillac with Florida license plates, and his wife for seat belt violations. Guzman provided the officer with his license, registration and a car rental agreement. The officer examined the documents and concluded that they were in order. At that point, rather than merely issuing a warning or citation, the officer investigated further by examining the odometer and extensively questioning Guzman and his wife. The officer then asked if the two were carrying contraband. Guzman denied the allegation and invited the officer to search the car. The

search uncovered a quantity of cocaine concealed in the car, whereupon Guzman and his wife were arrested.

Holding that the officer's actions violated the Fourth Amendment, the court stated:

> An officer conducting a routine traffic stop may request a driver's license and vehicle registration, run a computer check, and issue a citation. When the driver has produced a valid license and proof that he is entitled to operate the car, he must be allowed to proceed on his way, without being subject to further delay by police for additional questioning. In order to justify a temporary detention for questioning, the officer must also have reasonable suspicion of illegal transactions in drugs or of any other serious crime.

Id. at 1519. *See also United States v. Kelley*, 981 *F.*2d 1464, 1470 (5th Cir. 1993) ("under appropriate circumstances, excessive questioning about matters wholly unrelated to the purpose of a routine traffic stop may violate the Fourth Amendment").

(2) In *United States v. Holt*, 229 *F.*3d 931 (10th Cir. 2000), the court emphasized that, in the context of a nonconsensual police-citizen encounter, police questioning on matters unrelated to the purpose of the initial stop can be so intrusive that the questioning can violate the Fourth Amendment.

The vehicle Holt was driving was stopped at a checkpoint set up by the Oklahoma Highway Patrol and the Muldrow Police Department within the city limits of Muldrow. At approximately 10:30 p.m., Holt's Ford Ranger truck approached the checkpoint and Holt was stopped because he was not wearing a seatbelt. The officer asked to see Holt's driver's license and also asked him why he was not wearing a seatbelt. Holt replied that he lived in the area and pointed toward his house. Holt was asked to pull over to the side of the road and to sit in a patrol car, where an officer proceeded to write a warning for the seatbelt violation. While doing so, the officer asked Holt if "there was anything in [his] vehicle" that the officer "should know about such as loaded weapons." Holt told the officer that there was a loaded handgun behind the passenger seat of the truck. The officer then asked Holt if there was anything else in the vehicle that the officer should know about. Holt replied, "I know what you are referring to" but "I don't use them anymore." *Id.* at 933. The officer then asked Holt for consent to search his truck, and Holt agreed. During the questioning, the officer held Holt's driver's license in his possession.

A search of the truck produced a loaded pistol from behind the passenger seat. Inside the camper shell on the back of the truck, the officers found a small bag containing spoons, syringes, loose matches, and a white powdery substance in separate bags.

Finding the scope of the officer's questions unreasonable, the court first reiterated that the reasonableness of an investigative detention is determined by a two-part inquiry. First, a court will ask "whether the officer's action was justified at its inception," and second "whether it was reasonably related in scope to the circumstances which justified the interference in the first place." *Id.* at 934. [Citations and internal quotes omitted.] Since it was clear to the court that the initial traffic stop was justified at its inception because of the observation of Holt driving without a seatbelt, the focus of this case was on the issue whether the officer's questioning of Holt regarding the presence of weapons in his vehicle was reasonably related in scope to the initial reason for the detention.

In *Florida v. Royer*, 460 *U.S.* 491, 500, 103 *S.Ct.* 1319, 1325-26 (1983), the United States Supreme Court, in discussing the permissible scope of an investigatory detention, held that the detention must "last no longer than is necessary to effectuate the purpose of the stop" and "be carefully tailored to its underlying justification."

There are limits, noted the *Holt* court, on "the length and the manner of the detention." *Id.* at 936. In this respect, in *Royer*, the Court emphasized that "the investigative methods employed should be the *least intrusive means* reasonably available to verify or dispel the officer's suspicion in a *short period of time.*" *Holt* at 936. [Court's emphasis; citation omitted.] In addition, it is the government's burden to demonstrate that an investigative detention "was sufficiently limited in scope and duration." *Id.*

In rejecting the holding of *United States v. Shabazz, infra*, the court pointed out that, in contrast to the Fifth Circuit, the Tenth Circuit has already held that "an officer conducting a routine traffic stop may not ask the detainee questions unrelated to the purpose of the stop, even if the questioning does not extend the normal length of the stop, unless the officer has reasonable suspicion of illegal activity." *Id.* (citing *United States v. Jones*, 44 *F.*3d 860, 872 (10th Cir. 1995). *See also United States v. Turner*, 928 *F.*2d 956, 959 (10th Cir.1991) ("if the officer retains the driver's license, he or she must have reasonable and articulable suspicion to question the driver about drugs or weapons").

While the court would not hold that all questioning that is seemingly unrelated to a stop is improper, for example, asking a detainee about the origin of his trip, his destination and travel plans, the court was not convinced that the question in this case posed by the officer to Holt—which would require an incriminatory answer or an answer which would directly lead to a search of Holt's vehicle—was proper. Rather, questions about weapons or contraband," held the court, "must be precipitated by reasonable suspicion." *Id.* at 937.

Accordingly, the court concluded that the officer in this case "exceeded the reasonable scope of the detention by questioning Holt about the possession of contraband, including loaded weapons. Although the questioning occurred while [the officer] was writing out the citation, it is essentially uncontroverted that the questioning was unrelated to the purpose of the stop (*i.e.*, the seatbelt violation). Further, there [was no showing that the officer's] questioning was prompted by a reasonable suspicion of illegal activity on the part of Holt * * * [or] that the questioning was motivated by safety concerns." *Id.* at 940.

The court remanded the case for further proceedings to determine whether the consent to search, provided by Holt, was voluntary, notwithstanding the improper nature of the officer's questions.

(b) A more expansive approach.

(1) In United States v. Shabazz, 993 F.2d 431 (5th Cir. 1993), where the court rejected "any notion that a police officer's questioning, even on a subject unrelated to the purpose of [a motor vehicle] stop, is itself a Fourth Amendment violation." *Id.* at 436. "Mere questioning," explained the court,

> is neither a search nor a seizure. * * * Rather, *Terry*'s second prong is concerned with detentions, in other words, seizures. * * * This is not to say that questioning is unrelated to the determination that a detention has exceeded its lawful duration. In a garden variety *Terry* stop, the nature of the questioning during a later portion of the detention may indicate that the justification for the original detention no longer supports its continuation. Thus, when a police officer reasonably suspects only that someone is carrying a gun and stops and frisks that person, the officer, after finding nothing in a pat down, may not thereafter further detain the person merely to question him about a fraud offense. This is not because the questioning itself is unlawful, but because at that point suspicion of weapons possession has evaporated and no longer justifies further detention.

> [In this case, the defendants] cannot successfully claim that the detention exceeded its original scope. * * * [I]n a valid traffic stop, an officer can request a driver's license, insurance papers, vehicle registration, run a computer check thereon, and issue a citation. * * * In this case, Officer LaChance asked Shabazz to exit the vehicle and produce his driver's license. He then called in for a computer check of the license. The questioning that took place occurred while the officers were waiting for the results of the computer check. Therefore, the questioning did nothing to extend the duration of the initial, valid seizure. Because the officers were still waiting for the computer check at the time that they received consent to search the car, the detention to that point continued to be supported by the facts that justified its initiation.

Id. at 436-37.

(2) Permissible questions for a "typical" motor vehicle stop. In *State v. Chapman,* 332 N.J.Super. 452, 753 A.2d 1179 (App.Div. 2000), the court also explored the proper scope of a "typical" motor vehicle stop and the types of questions that an officer may ask the motorist.

At 2:13 p.m., in late January, Trooper Ocetnik was patrolling Route 80 when he observed a Ford pickup truck with California license plates weaving between lanes and fluctuating in speed. Suspecting that the driver was either intoxicated or fatigued, the officer activated his overhead lights, directing the vehicle to stop.

Shortly after the stop, Troopers Kratzer and Hanley arrived at the scene. Defendant Chapman was seated in the driver's seat and Scott Curran was seated in the front passenger seat. Ruben and Roberto

Velez were in the rear seat. "Trooper Ocetnik asked Chapman for his license and registration. Chapman produced a registration identifying him as the owner of the pickup truck, but told Ocetnik that he had 'lost' his driver's license. At this point, Ocetnik was no longer concerned that Chapman was intoxicated. He nevertheless asked all the passengers to produce identification, preferably their drivers' licenses, because Chapman could not legally operate the vehicle. Each produced a California driver's license." *Id.*, 332 *N.J.Super.* at 456.

Upon request, Chapman stepped out of the truck. The trooper explained his reason for stopping him, pointing out that he suspected there was a problem with intoxication or fatigue. Chapman admitted that he was fatigued and answered the trooper's questions regarding the travelers' destination and the location from which they had come. Chapman then admitted that his driver's license was suspended. Trooper Ocetnik told him that he intended to issue a summons for that offense, and that one of the passengers might be required to take over as driver.

While Chapman was being questioned, Curran was questioned by Trooper Kratzer. Curran contradicted Chapman's account. In addition, when questioned, Roberto Velez's account contradicted the earlier statements made by Chapman and Curran. After talking to Roberto, Ocetnik directed him to sit in the driver's seat in order to be the designated driver. Ocetnik also questioned Ruben Velez, who was " 'dripping' with perspiration despite the frigid January weather." *Id.* at 457. Ruben stated that he and his brother were originally from Colombia.

Trooper Ocetnik ran a computer check on the subjects' drivers' licenses, and prepared a summons for driving with a revoked license and a warning for careless driving. He also prepared a consent-to-search form. Ocetnik then approached Chapman and advised him that he had issued a summons for driving with a revoked license and a warning for careless driving. He read aloud to Chapman the consent-to-search form, including the "right to refuse" portion. Chapman asked the trooper, "I'm not signing * * * myself away when I sign this thing?" *Id.* at 459. Ocetnik replied that "the request to search form was not an admission of guilt, but rather a consent to examine the pickup truck." *Id.* Once Chapman signed and dated the form, the trooper began to search the truck. Inside the cargo area, he found two large suitcases. "When Ocetnik slid one of the suitcases out, Kratzer immediately detected a strong odor of raw marijuana. Ocetnik noticed the same smell. Each individual was asked whether he owned the suitcase. They all disclaimed ownership. Ocetnik then opened the suitcases. In one, he found twenty-eight packages of suspected marijuana and an open box of baking soda." *Id.* Approximately 45 minutes had elapsed from the time of the initial stop to the discovery of the contraband.

In the appeal following the denial of defendants' motion to suppress evidence, defendants conceded that the initial stop of Chapman's pickup truck was lawful. They argued, however, that the continued detention that followed the stop was unlawful, for it was not based upon an articulable suspicion of criminal activity or other justification, and that the consent to search was involuntary. The Appellate Division disagreed and affirmed.

The critical question on appeal was whether the 45-minute detention that followed the traffic stop was sufficiently limited in scope to be upheld as constitutional. While the court would not "endorse all of the questions propounded by the troopers to the occupants of the vehicle," it held that "the duration of the detention and the degree of intrusion" did not exceed constitutional bounds. *Id.* at 461.

Preliminarily, the court reminded that an investigative stop of a vehicle and its occupants will become " 'a *de facto* arrest when the officers' conduct is more intrusive than necessary' to fulfill the legitimate demands of law enforcement." *Id.* The reasonableness of a detention is not, however, "limited to investigating the circumstances of the [initial] traffic stop. * * * If, during the course of the stop or as a result of the reasonable inquiries initiated by the officer, the circumstances 'give rise to suspicions unrelated to the traffic offense, an officer may broaden [the] inquiry and satisfy those suspicions.' " *Id.* at 462 (quoting *State v. Dickey*, 152 *N.J.* at 479-80).

"The question is what inquiries may a police officer lawfully propound to an individual who has been stopped for a traffic infraction." *Id.* In answering this question, the court used a bit of "common sense and ordinary human experience," while at the same time according " 'appropriate deference to the ability of trained law enforcement officer[s] to distinguish between innocent and suspicious actions.' " *Id.* [Citations omitted.]

The court held that during the course of a typical traffic stop, an officer:

1. May request the motorist's driving credentials;

2. Should advise the motorist of the reason for the traffic stop;

3. May run a computer check;

4. May ask questions reasonably related to the reason for the traffic stop; and

    [Inconsistent or contradictory answers provided by the vehicle's occupants may then permit an officer to broaden the inquiry and ask more intrusive questions designed to confirm or dispel suspicions of criminal activity.]

5. May issue a citation.

Id. at 463.

Under ordinary circumstances, when "the driver has produced a valid license and proof that he is entitled to operate the car, he must be allowed to proceed on his way, without being subject to further delay by [the] police for additional questioning." *Id.* [Citations and internal quotes omitted.] A law enforcement officer "may not engage in excessive questioning about matters wholly unrelated to the purpose of a routine traffic stop * * *." *Id.*

In this case, the court was satisfied that the trooper's initial questions "concerning where the defendants had been and where they were going were reasonably related to the reason for the traffic stop. These inquiries had a substantial nexus to ascertaining the reasons for Chapman's erratic driving and whether he and his passengers posed a danger to others on the road. It will be recalled that Trooper Ocetnik suspected the driver's intoxication or fatigue caused the pickup truck to weave between lanes and fluctuate in speed. Upon stopping the vehicle and observing Chapman's behavior, Ocetnik immediately discounted the possibility that Chapman was drunk. He nevertheless remained concerned about the possibility of fatigue. Because Chapman did not have a valid driver's license, Ocetnik was duty-bound to inquire into whether one of the passengers could safely and lawfully drive the vehicle." *Id.*

In addition, the "community caretaking function" of the police, considering the circumstances confronting Trooper Ocetnik, would permit "questions pertaining to the nature and purpose of the trip, the recent whereabouts of the driver and passengers, their destination, and their relationship to each other." These questions "were reasonably related to the purpose of the stop." *Id.* at 463, 464.

"Because Chapman, Curran and Roberto Velez gave inconsistent statements concerning their recent whereabouts, the troopers were entitled to expand the scope of the stop and ask additional, more intrusive questions. * * * The fact that these individuals could not agree on where they had just been reasonably aroused the troopers' suspicions. Moreover, the troopers' observations of Ruben Velez—specifically the fact that he was perspiring profusely despite the frigid January weather—constituted an additional basis for further investigation." *Id.* at 464-65.

"Beyond this, it appears that most, if not all, of the troopers' questioning occurred while Ocetnik was awaiting a computer check to verify the information Chapman and his passengers had given pertaining to the status of their California drivers' licenses. It is at least arguable that the questioning did nothing to extend the duration of the initial, valid seizure. It appears that the troopers were waiting for the results of the computer check until shortly before they received Chapman's consent to search the car. This case thus 'does not involve any delay unnecessary to the legitimate investigation of the law enforcement officers.' * * * The detention up to the point the troopers obtained Chapman's consent 'continued to be supported by the facts that justified its initiation.' " *Id.* at 465. [Citations omitted.]

Accordingly, the court held that this detention did not turn into an invalid *de facto* arrest. The defendants' detention was supported by "an articulable suspicion that criminal activity might be afoot." *Id.* at 466.

In addition, the court determined that the consent provided by Chapman was voluntary. Beyond that, the troopers "clearly had the right to search the unclaimed suitcases." *Id.* at 471. None of the vehicle's occupants claimed ownership of the suitcases. As a result, they "objectively relinquished" their expectation of privacy in the objects searched. *Id.* "In any event, Troopers Ocetnik and Kratzer detected the odor of marijuana before opening and searching the suitcases. The search was thus supported by probable cause and exigent circumstances." *Id.*

See also United States v. Walker, 933 F.2d 812 (10th Cir. 1991), where the court indicated that its "determination that the defendant was unlawfully detained might be different if the questioning by the officer did not delay the stop beyond the measure of time necessary to issue a citation." *Id.* at 816 n.2. In this respect, the court noted, "this case would be changed significantly if the officer asked the same questions while awaiting the results of an NCIC [] license or registration inquiry." *Id.*

5. *Running a check of driving credentials after the original reason for the stop ceases to exist.* In *State v. Gulick*, 759 A.2d 1085 (Me. 2000), at 2:53 a.m., Officer Sheehan watched a car drive into a parking lot of an emergency care medical facility that operated only during the day. Concerned that the vehicle's occupants might be looking for emergency medical treatment, Sheehan followed the car, parked behind it, approached its driver and asked if everything was okay. The driver, Tanner Gulick, replied that "everything was fine." *Id.* at 1086. Officer Sheehan then asked to see Guilick's driver's license. Guilick told the officer that he did not have the license with him because "he had been to a rock concert and had left his license at home for fear that it would be stolen." *Id.* at 1087 n.1. Suspicious of Gulick's explanation, the officer obtained Gulick's name and date of birth and ran a computer check on the status of his license. Upon learning that the license was suspended, Sheehan issued him a summons for that violation.

Gulick moved to suppress all evidence resulting from Sheehan's request for his license, arguing that the officer lacked a reasonable articulable suspicion to justify detaining him. The Supreme Judicial Court of Maine disagreed.

Preliminarily, the court pointed out that Officer Sheehan's initial approach and inquiry of the vehicle's occupants did not constitute a "seizure." However, the officer's actions following his approach of the car, namely, asking for the license, followed up by a request for identifying information for a computer check, did constitute a "seizure" for Fourth Amendment purposes. *Id.* at 1088.

Finding the seizure lawful, the court said:

> When Sheehan approached the vehicle he had a clearly articulated and objectively reasonable concern for the occupants' safety. "[S]afety reasons alone can be sufficient" to allow the detention of a driver if they are based on "specific and articulable facts." * * * [This is] the police officer's legitimate role as a public servant to assist those in distress and to maintain and foster public safety." Thus, Sheehan's concern for the safety of the car's occupants was sufficient to justify a brief detention of those occupants.

> After an officer stops a vehicle, he may request verification of the operator's right to drive, even when the original reason for a stop has disappeared, or evaporated, before the request is made. * * * For instance, in [*State v. Hill*, 606 A.2d 793 (Me. 1992)], the defendant's vehicle was stopped because the officer believed it did

not have a visible license plate * * *. As the officer approached the defendant's truck, however, he observed an unilluminated license plate in the car's rear window. * * * The officer nevertheless approached the driver to request his license and registration. * * * After making the request, the officer observed that Hill appeared to be intoxicated. * * * We concluded that the officer's request to see the defendant's license was a "minimal further intrusion," and rejected the defendant's argument that the request itself must be supported independently by a reasonable articulable suspicion. * * * Because Hill had been validly stopped as a result of the officer's belief that the vehicle had no license plate, we concluded that the subsequent police action, although not independently supported by reasonable articulable suspicion, was justified.

Gulick at 1088-89. [Court's emphasis; citations omitted.]

Because Officer Sheehan was justified in approaching the driver, "it was reasonable for the officer to request verification of his license to operate, before allowing the driver to proceed." *Id.* at 1089-90. A police officer is not required "to justify his inquiry on a question-by-question basis." *Id.* at 1090. In this respect, the court observed:

> The State's efforts to assure that only licensed operators are present on our roads is crucial to the safety of the public. The Legislature has therefore required that any person who operates a motor vehicle on public ways must be licensed to operate that vehicle and must carry evidence of that license on him or her when driving the vehicle. * * * When balancing the significance of the public concern served by the license check against the relatively minimal intrusion of the driver's liberty interests, * * * we conclude that Sheehan's actions did not exceed the scope justified under the circumstances.

Id.

The court held, therefore, that "a detention related to a request by a law enforcement official that a motor vehicle operator demonstrate that the operator is licensed to drive is not an unreasonable intrusion *when the officer's initial contact with the operator is based on reasonable and articulable facts of concern for safety or wrongdoing*, whether or not the initial contact itself constituted a seizure." *Id.* [Emphasis added.]

6. *The "pretext" defense revisited.* In *Arkansas v. Sullivan*, 532 *U.S.* 769, 121 *S.Ct.* 1876 (2001), the United States Supreme Court rejected defendant Sullivan's argument that his arrest was merely a "pretext and sham to search" him and, therefore, violated the Fourth Amendment.

Sullivan was stopped by the police for speeding and for having an improperly tinted windshield. During the stop, Officer Taylor asked Sullivan to produce his driving credentials. Upon seeing Sullivan's license, Taylor recalled learning of some "intelligence" on Sullivan "regarding narcotics." *Id.*, 121 *S.Ct.* at 1877. "When Sullivan opened his car door in an (unsuccessful) attempt to locate his registration and insurance papers, Taylor noticed a rusted roofing hatchet on the car's floorboard. Taylor then arrested Sullivan for speeding, driving without his registration and insurance documentation, carrying a weapon (the roofing hatchet), and improper window tinting." *Id.*, 121 *S.Ct.* at 1877. Thereafter, an inventory search of Sullivan's vehicle uncovered suspected methamphetamine as well as numerous items of suspected drug paraphernalia.

Finding the motor vehicle stop and Sullivan's arrest proper, the Court, relying on *Whren v. United States,* held that the state supreme court erred when it ruled that Officer Taylor's "arrest of Sullivan, although supported by probable cause, nonetheless violated the Fourth Amendment because Taylor had an improper subjective motivation for making the stop." *Id.* at 1878. The Court said:

> The Arkansas Supreme Court's holding to that effect cannot be squared with our decision in *Whren,* in which we noted our "unwilling[ness] to entertain Fourth Amendment challenges based on the actual motivations of individual officers," and held unanimously that "[s]ubjective intentions play no role in ordinary, probable-cause Fourth Amendment analysis." * * * That *Whren* involved a traffic stop, rather than a custodial arrest, is of no particular moment * * *.

Id. [Citation omitted.]

ALABAMA v. WHITE
Supreme Court of the United States
496 *U.S.* 325, 110 *S.Ct.* 2412 (1990)

QUESTION: May a sufficiently corroborated "anonymous tip" provide police with a reasonable suspicion for an investigatory stop ?

ANSWER: YES. When an anonymous caller provides police with information consisting of " 'a range of details relating not just to easily obtained facts and conditions existing at the time of the tip, but to *future actions* of third parties ordinarily not easily predicted,' " the information contained in the tip demonstrates "inside information," and the anonymous informant's "special familiarity with the suspect's affairs." Thereafter, when significant aspects of the information and predictions in the anonymous tip are verified by independent police investigation, reason may then exist "to believe not only that the caller was honest but also that he was well informed, at least well enough to justify * * * [an] investigatory stop[.]" *Id.* at 2417. [Emphasis added.]

RATIONALE: At about 3:00 on an April afternoon, Corporal Davis of the Montgomery Police Department "received a telephone call from an anonymous person, stating that Vanessa White would be leaving 235-C Lynwood Terrace Apartments at a particular time in a brown Plymouth station wagon with the right taillight lens broken, that she would be going to Dobey's Motel, and that she would be in possession of about an ounce of cocaine inside a brown attache case. Corporal Davis and his partner, Corporal P.A. Reynolds, proceeded to the Lynwood Terrace Apartments. The officers saw a brown Plymouth station wagon with a broken right taillight in the parking lot in front of the 235 building. The officers observed [defendant] leave the 235 building, carrying nothing in her hands, and enter the station wagon. They followed the vehicle as it drove the most direct route to Dobey's Motel." *Id.* at 2414.

"When the vehicle reached the Mobile Highway, on which Dobey's Motel is located, Corporal Reynolds requested a patrol unit to stop the vehicle. The vehicle was stopped at approximately 4:18 p.m., just short of Dobey's Motel. Corporal Davis asked [defendant] to step to the rear of her car, where he informed her that she had been stopped because she was suspected of carrying cocaine in the vehicle. He asked if they could look for cocaine and [defendant] said they could look. The officers found a locked brown attache case in the car and, upon request, [defendant] provided the combination to the lock. The officers found marijuana in the attache case and placed [defendant] under arrest. During processing at the station, the officers found three milligrams of cocaine in [defendant's] purse." *Id.* at 2414-2415.

In the appeal which followed the denial of defendant's motion to suppress evidence, the Alabama Court of Criminal Appeals held that the marijuana and cocaine should have been suppressed as fruits of defendant's unconstitutional detention because the officers did not have a reasonable and articulable suspicion—required by *Terry v. Ohio*—to justify the investigatory stop of defendant's car. *The United States Supreme Court disagreed and reversed.*

In *Illinois v. Gates*, 462 *U.S.* 213, 103 *S.Ct.* 2317 (1983), the Court dealt with an anonymous tip in the probable cause context. *Gates* established the "totality-of-the-circumstances" approach to determine whether an informant's tip establishes probable cause. In addition, *Gates* made clear that "an informant's 'veracity,' 'reliability,' and 'basis of knowledge' [] remain 'highly relevant in determining the value of his report.'" *White* at 2415 (quoting *Gates* at 230, 103 *S.Ct.* at 2328). "These factors are also relevant in the reasonable suspicion context, although allowance must be made in applying them for the lesser showing required to meet that standard." *Id.*

"The opinion in *Gates* recognized that an anonymous tip alone seldom demonstrates the informant's basis of knowledge or veracity inasmuch as ordinary citizens generally do not provide extensive recitation of the basis of their everyday observations and given that the veracity of persons supplying anonymous tips is 'by hypothesis largely unknown, and unknowable.' * * * This is not to say that an anonymous caller could never provide the reasonable suspicion necessary for a *Terry* stop. But the tip in *Gates* was not an exception to the general rule, and the anonymous tip in this case is like the one in *Gates*: '[it] provides virtually nothing from which one might conclude that [the caller] is either honest or his information reliable; likewise, the [tip] gives absolutely no indication of the basis for the [caller's] predictions regarding [Vanessa White's] criminal activities.'" *White* at 2415 (quot-

ing *Gates* at 227, 103 *S.Ct.* at 2326). Here, as in *Gates*, something more
is required. In *Adams v. Williams*, 407 *U.S.* 143, 147, 92 *S.Ct.* 1921,
1924 (1972), this Court observed that, " 'Some tips, completely lacking
in indicia of reliability, would either warrant no police response or require further investigation before a forcible stop of a suspect would be
authorized.' * * * Simply put, a tip such as this one, standing alone,
would not ' "warrant a man of reasonable caution in the belief" that [a
stop] was appropriate.' " *White* at 2416. [Citations omitted.]

Similar to the circumstances in *Gates*, in this case we have more
than the tip itself. Although the tip is not as detailed or as corroborated as the tip was in *Gates*, "the required degree of suspicion [is]
likewise not as high." *White* at 2416. In this context, "[r]easonable
suspicion is a less demanding standard than probable cause not only
in the sense that reasonable suspicion can be established with information that is different in quantity or content than that required to
establish probable cause, but also in the sense that reasonable suspicion can arise from information that is less reliable than that required
to show probable cause. * * * Reasonable suspicion, like probable
cause, is dependent upon both the content of the information possessed by police and its degree of reliability. Both factors—quantity
and quality—are considered in the 'totality of the circumstances—the
whole picture' * * * that must be taken into account when evaluating
whether there is reasonable suspicion. Thus, if a tip has a relatively
low degree of reliability, more information will be required to establish
the requisite quantum of suspicion than would be required if the tip
were more reliable." *Id.* [Citations omitted.]

The totality of the circumstances test applied in *Gates* takes "into
account the facts known to the officers from personal observation, and
giv[es] the anonymous tip the weight it deserve[s] in light of its indicia
of reliability as established through independent police work. The
same approach applies in the reasonable suspicion context, the only
difference being the level of suspicion that must be established." *Id.*

In light of these principles, the Court "conclude[s] that when the
officers stopped [defendant], the anonymous tip had been sufficiently
corroborated to furnish reasonable suspicion that [defendant] was engaged in criminal activity and that the investigative stop therefore
did not violate the Fourth Amendment." *Id.* While it is true that "not
every detail mentioned by the tipster was verified, such as the name
of the woman leaving the building or the precise apartment from
which she left[,] the officers did[, nonetheless] corroborate that a
woman left the 235 building and got into the particular vehicle that
was described by the caller. With respect to the time of the departure
predicted by the informant, Corporal Davis testified that the caller
gave a particular time when the woman would be leaving, * * * but he
did not state what the time was. He did testify that, after the call, he
and his partner proceeded to the Lynwood Terrace Apartments to put
the 235 building under surveillance * * *. Given the fact that the officers proceeded to the indicated address immediately after the call and
that [defendant] emerged not too long thereafter, it appears * * * that
[defendant's] departure from the building was within the time frame
predicted by the caller. As for the caller's prediction of [defendant's]

destination, it is true that the officers stopped her just short of Dobey's Motel and did not know whether she would have pulled in or continued on past it. But given that the four-mile route driven by [defendant] was the most direct route possible to Dobey's Motel[, it is reasonable to conclude that defendant's] destination was significantly corroborated." *Id.* at 2416-2417.

Credit must also be given "to the proposition that because an informant is shown to be right about some things, he is probably right about other facts that he has alleged, including the claim that the object of the tip is engaged in criminal activity. * * * Thus, it is not unreasonable to conclude in this case that the independent corroboration by the police of significant aspects of the informer's predictions imparted some degree of reliability to the other allegations made by the caller." *Id.* at 2417.

Finally, the Court finds it significant that, "as in *Gates*, 'the anonymous [tip] contained a range of details relating not just to easily obtained facts and conditions existing at the time of the tip, but to future actions of third parties ordinarily not easily predicted.' * * * The fact that the officers found a car precisely matching the caller's description in front of the 235 building is an example of the former. Anyone could have 'predicted' that fact because it was a condition presumably existing at the time of the call. *What was important was the caller's ability to predict [defendant's] future behavior, because it demonstrates inside information—a special familiarity with [defendant's] affairs.* The general public would have had no way of knowing that [defendant] would shortly leave the building, get in the described car, and drive the most direct route to Dobey's Motel. *Because only a small number of people are generally privy to an individual's itinerary, it is reasonable for the police to believe that a person with access to such information is likely to also have access to reliable information about that individual's illegal activities.* * * * When significant aspects of the caller's predictions were verified, there was reason to believe not only that the caller was honest but also that he was well informed, at least well enough to justify the stop." *Id.* [Citations omitted; emphasis added.]

Accordingly, under the "totality of the circumstances," the anonymous tip, as corroborated, "exhibited sufficient indicia of reliability to justify the investigatory stop of [defendant's] car." *Id.*

NOTE

1. *See also United States v. Hill*, 91 *F.*3d 1064, 1069 (8th Cir. 1996), where the court similarly emphasized the importance of an informant's ability to predict the target's future behavior, for the purpose of establishing a reasonable suspicion for an investigative detention.

2. *911 calls.* "Within modern police departments, the officer who receives information justifying an individual's detention often is not the officer who acts on the information. Daily bulletins, computer messages and radio broadcasts alert officers in the field about those suspected of criminal activity." *United States v. Cutchin*, 956 *F.*2d 1216, 1217 (D.C. Cir. 1992). In *Cutchin*, at about 1:00 a.m., "a police dis-

patcher, apparently acting on a tip from a 911 call, radioed Officer []
Taylor to look for a brown car 'with a loud muffler' that had been reported racing near Fourth and W Streets, N.W. In response, Officer
Taylor stopped a brown car in the area but did not detain it." *Id.* at
1217. Shortly thereafter, the dispatcher radioed another message,
"this time regarding an old white station wagon with a dragging muffler making a loud noise that had been racing in the same vicinity.
* * * Officer Taylor soon came upon a 1981 white station wagon driven
by Cutchin. The car was not speeding, its muffler was not dragging
and Officer Taylor did not hear any loud noises coming from it. Traffic
was light. Seeing no other cars matching the dispatcher's description,
Officer Taylor pulled Cutchin over[.]" *Id.* The motor vehicle stop produced evidence which led to Cutchin's arrest for operating without a
driver's license and the unlawful possession of a sawed-off shotgun
and .38 caliber handgun.

Finding the record insufficient to determine whether the motor
vehicle stop was sufficiently supported by a reasonable and articulable
suspicion, the court explained:

> Investigatory stops of vehicles must be supported by "a particular-
> ized and objective basis for suspecting" criminal conduct. * * * This
> can be supplied on the basis of a 911 call alone if it has sufficient
> indicia of reliability. *See Alabama v. White* * * *. If so, a dispatcher
> may alert other officers by radio, who may then rely on the report,
> * * * even though they cannot vouch for it. * * * Without such indi-
> cia of reliability the stop will be illegal unless the officers acting on
> the report have "sufficiently corroborated [the report] to furnish
> reasonable suspicion that [the subject] was engaged in criminal ac-
> tivity" or had been so engaged.

Cutchin at 1217-18. [Citations omitted.]

In this case, Cutchin did not challenge Officer Taylor's version of
what the dispatcher said in the second broadcast. Instead, he argued
that the dispatcher had no basis for alerting the officer about a white
station wagon "because the only 911 calls the dispatcher received related to a brown car." *Id.* at 1218.

It was clear to the court that the 911 tape should have been admitted in evidence. "What the tape itself revealed," said the court, "went
directly to the issue whether the dispatcher had reasonable, articulable suspicion, without which Officer Taylor's stop of Cutchin's car
might not have been legal." *Id.*

> That the tape was hearsay was not a sufficient ground[] for ex-
> cluding it in the suppression hearing. * * * Therefore, we are com-
> pelled to remand for a new suppression hearing, so that the parties
> can present evidence, including the tape, pertaining to the dis-
> patcher's justification for the radio broadcast.

Id.

---

§8.3(d). Removing drivers or passengers from the motor vehicle.

PENNSYLVANIA v. MIMMS
Supreme Court of the United States
434 U.S. 106, 98 S.Ct. 330 (1977)

QUESTION: May the police order the occupant(s) of an automobile out of the car during a routine motor vehicle stop for a traffic violation in the absence of suspicion of criminal activity or a reasonable belief that the occupants pose a threat to police safety ?

ANSWER: YES. The police may order persons out of an automobile during a routine motor vehicle stop for a traffic violation even in the absence of suspicion of criminal activity or a reasonable belief that those persons pose a threat to police safety. *Id.* at 333.

RATIONALE: While on patrol, two Philadelphia police officers observed defendant driving an automobile with an expired license plate. "The officers stopped the vehicle for the purpose of issuing a traffic summons. One of the officers approached and asked [defendant] to step out of the car and produce his owner's card and operator's license." *Id.* at 331. As the defendant alighted from the car, one of the officers noticed a large bulge under his sports jacket. "Fearing that the bulge might be a weapon, the officer frisked [defendant] and discovered in his waistband a .38 caliber revolver loaded with five rounds of ammunition." *Id.*

In this appeal, the United States Supreme Court focused on the "narrow question of whether the order to get out of the car, issued after the driver was lawfully detained, was reasonable and thus permissible under the Fourth Amendment." *Id.* at 332. According to the Court: "This inquiry must therefore focus not on the intrusion resulting from the request to stop the vehicle or from the later 'pat down,' but on the incremental intrusion resulting from the request to get out of the car once the vehicle was lawfully stopped." *Id.*

Here, the State "freely concede[d] the officer had no reason to suspect foul play from the particular driver at the time of the stop, there having been nothing unusual or suspicious about his behavior. It was apparently his practice to order all drivers out of their vehicles as a matter of course whenever they had been stopped for a traffic violation. The State argue[d] that this practice was adopted as a precautionary measure to afford a degree of protection to the officer and that it may be justified on that ground. Establishing a face-to-face confrontation diminishes the possibility, otherwise substantial, that the driver can make unobserved movements; this in turn, reduces the likelihood that the officer will be the victim of an assault." *Id.* at 333.

The Court agreed that "the State's proffered justification—the safety of the officer—is both legitimate and weighty." *Id.* " 'Certainly it would be unreasonable to require that police officers take unnecessary risks in the performance of their duties.' " *Id.* (quoting *Terry v. Ohio,*

392 *U.S* 1, 23, 88 *S.Ct.* 1868, 1881 (1968)). The Court also "recognize[d] the inordinate risk confronting an officer as he approaches a person seated in an automobile. 'According to one study, approximately 30% of police shootings occurred when a police officer approached a suspect seated in an automobile.'" *Mimms* at 333. [Citations omitted.]

Moreover, "[t]he hazard of accidental injury from passing traffic to an officer standing on the driver's side of the vehicle may also be appreciable in some situations. Rather than conversing while standing exposed to moving traffic, the officer prudently may prefer to ask the driver of the vehicle to step out of the car and off onto the shoulder of the road where the inquiry may be pursued with greater safety to both." *Id.*

The Court then proceeded to weigh these significant law enforcement interests against "the intrusion into the driver's personal liberty occasioned not by the initial stop of the vehicle, which was admittedly justified, but by the order to get out of the car." *Id.* This "additional intrusion," stated the Court, "can only be described as *de minimis* * * * it hardly rises to the level of a 'petty indignity.'" *Id.* [Citation omitted.]

Accordingly, a police officer may order persons out of an automobile during a routine motor vehicle stop for a traffic violation even in the absence of suspicion of criminal activity or a reasonable belief that those persons posed a threat to the officer's safety. "What is at most a mere inconvenience cannot prevail when balanced against legitimate concerns for the officer's safety." *Id.*

MARYLAND v. WILSON
Supreme Court of the United States
519 *U.S.* 408, 117 *S.Ct.* 882 (1997)

QUESTION: Does the rule of *Pennsylvania v. Mimms*—that a police officer may, as a matter of course, order the driver of a lawfully stopped car to exit his vehicle—extend to passengers?

ANSWER: YES. The "danger to an officer from a traffic stop is likely to be greater when there are passengers in addition to the driver in the stopped car." *Id.* at 886. Because "the additional intrusion on the passenger is minimal[,] * * * an officer making a traffic stop may order passengers to get out of the car pending completion of the stop." *Id.*

RATIONALE: At about 7:30 p.m., Trooper David Hughes of the Maryland State Police noticed a passenger car traveling southbound on I-95 in Baltimore County at a speed of 64 miles per hour. "The posted speed limit was 55 miles per hour, and the car had no regular license tag; there was a torn piece of paper reading 'Enterprise Rent-A-Car' dangling from its rear. Hughes activated his lights and sirens, signaling the car to pull over, but it continued driving for another mile and a half until it finally did so." *Id.* at 884.

Hughes noticed that the car contained three occupants; and that the two passengers turned around to look at him several times, "repeatedly ducking below sight level and then reappearing." *Id.* When the car stopped, its driver met Trooper Hughes halfway between the two vehicles. The driver was trembling and appeared extremely nervous. After the driver produced a valid Connecticut driver's license, Hughes instructed him to return to the car and retrieve the vehicle's rental documents. The driver complied. In the meantime, the trooper noticed that the front-seat passenger, defendant Jerry Lee Wilson, was sweating and also appeared very nervous. Based on this observation, while the driver sat in the car and looked for the rental papers, the trooper ordered Wilson out of the car. As Wilson stepped out of the car, a quantity of crack cocaine fell to the ground. Trooper Hughes then placed Wilson under arrest and charged him with the possession of cocaine with intent to distribute.

In this appeal, the Court addressed the question whether the trooper's order—directing Wilson to step out of the car—constituted an unreasonable seizure under the Fourth Amendment.

In *Pennsylvania v. Mimms*, this Court explained that:

> "[t]he touchstone of our analysis under the Fourth Amendment is always 'the reasonableness of the particular governmental invasion of a citizen's personal security,' * * * and that reasonableness depends 'on a balance between the public interest and the individual's right to personal security free from arbitrary interference by law officers[.]' "

Id. at 884-85 (quoting *Mimms* at 108-9, 98 *S.Ct.* at 332).

"On the public interest side of the balance," the Court pointed out that in *Mimms*, it was the police officer's practice to order all drivers stopped in traffic stops out of their vehicles "as a matter of course" as a "precautionary measure" to protect the officer's safety. The officer's concerns prompting such a practice, held the court, were "both legitimate and weighty." *Id.* at 885 (quoting *Mimms* at 110, 98 *S.Ct.* at 333). In addition, the Court observed that "the danger to the officer of standing by the driver's door and in the path of oncoming traffic might also be 'appreciable.' " *Id.*

"On the other side of the balance, [the Court considered] the intrusion into the driver's liberty occasioned by the officer's ordering him out of the car. Noting that the driver's car was already validly stopped for a traffic infraction, [the Court] deemed the additional intrusion of asking him to step outside his car '*de minimis.*' " *Id.* (quoting *Mimms* at 111, 98 *S.Ct.* at 333). The *Mimms* Court concluded, therefore, that " 'once a motor vehicle has been lawfully detained for a traffic violation, the police officers may order the driver to get out of the vehicle without violating the Fourth Amendment * * *.' " *Id.*

Here, in *Wilson*, the Court extended the *Mimms* "*per se* rule" to passengers.

On the public interest side of the balance, the same weighty interest in officer safety is present regardless of whether the occupant of the stopped car is a driver or passenger. Regrettably, traffic stops may be dangerous encounters. In 1994 alone, there were 5,762 officer assaults and 11 officers killed during traffic pursuits and stops. * * * In the case of passengers, the danger of the officer's standing in the path of oncoming traffic would not be present except in the case of a passenger in the left rear seat, but the fact that there is more than one occupant of the vehicle increases the possible sources of harm to the officer.

On the personal liberty side of the balance, the case for the passengers is in one sense stronger than that for the driver. There is probable cause to believe that the driver has committed a minor vehicular offense, but there is no such reason to stop or detain the passengers. But, as a practical matter, the passengers are already stopped by virtue of the stop of the vehicle. The only change in their circumstances which will result from ordering them out of the car is that they will be outside of, rather than inside of, the stopped car. Outside the car, the passengers will be denied access to any possible weapon that might be concealed in the interior of the passenger compartment. It would also seem that the possibility of a violent encounter stems not from the ordinary reaction of a motorist stopped for a speeding violation, but from the fact that evidence of a more serious crime might be uncovered during the stop. And the motivation of a passenger to employ violence to prevent apprehension of such a crime is every bit as great as that of the driver.

Id. at 885-86.

The Court concluded, therefore, that the "danger to an officer from a traffic stop is likely to be greater when there are passengers in addition to the driver in the stopped car. While there is not the same basis for ordering the passengers out of the car as there is for ordering the driver out, the additional intrusion on the passenger is minimal." *Id.* at 886.

Accordingly, "an officer making a traffic stop may order passengers to get out of the car pending completion of the stop." *Id.*

NOTE

1. During the course of its opinion in *Wilson*, the Court emphasized that it was *not deciding* whether a police officer may forcibly detain a passenger for the entire duration of the motor vehicle stop. Because that precise issue was not presented by this case, the Court "express[ed] no opinion upon it." *Id.* at 886 n.3. While it may seem like a legitimate law enforcement procedure—requesting the vehicle's passenger(s) to remain at the scene of the stop for a reasonable time while the officer completes the inquiry—the validity of such a procedure remains an open question under the Fourth Amendment.

2. *Ordering a passenger to reenter a motor vehicle during a traffic stop.* May a law-enforcement officer briefly detain and order a passen-

ger to reenter an automobile to protect the officer's safety while the officer investigates a crime committed in his presence by two associates of the passenger? In *United States v. Clark*, 337 F.3d 1282 (11th Cir. 2003), the court said *yes*.

In mid-April, at approximately 9:30 p.m., Huff was patrolling alone in a marked Atlanta Police Department vehicle. In front of a train station, he observed two men fighting or wrestling in the middle of the street. "An automobile was stopped on the wrong side of the street with its lights on and with one door open. The engine was running. Officer Huff had patrolled that area for approximately four years. During that time, he had received a 'lot of calls involving violence' in that area." *Id.* at 1283.

Officer Huff activated his patrol car's lights, alighted from his vehicle, and ordered the two men to stop fighting. Huff then observed a person, later identified as defendant, John Clark, standing on the sidewalk watching the fight. At the time, Clark was not engaged in any criminal activity. "Officer Huff asked the three men if the vehicle belonged to one of them. One of the combatants replied that it was his car. Officer Huff asked the other two men whether they had been passengers in the car. Mr. Clark admitted that he had been a passenger." *Id.*

In order to gain control of the situation, and for safety reasons, Officer Huff ordered "all three men to reenter the vehicle and told them to sit where they had previously been sitting and to keep their hands where he could see them. The three men did so without resistance. Mr. Clark seated himself in the front passenger seat." *Id.*

To facilitate the investigation, Officer Huff ordered the driver to alight from the automobile. The officer placed handcuffs on the driver and directed him to sit on the curb. He next asked the passenger in the back seat to step out of the vehicle. At this time, Officer Bilak arrived at the scene as back-up. As Officer Bilak approached, he saw Clark "fumbling around under the seat." *Id.* Bilak ordered Clark to "put his hands back on the dashboard. When Officer Huff opened the passenger door to remove Mr. Clark from the vehicle, an Uzi America, Model Eagle, .40 caliber semi-automatic assault weapon fell onto the street. One of the officers seized the weapon. Mr. Clark was placed under arrest. In searching the inside of the vehicle, the officers found a weapon under the front seat and another in the back seat area." *Id.*

In this appeal, the Government contended that "it is constitutionally permissible to detain a passenger who is not suspected of wrongdoing in order to protect an officer from the possibility that the passenger will assist the driver in attempting to escape or in attacking the officer." *Id.* at 1284. The Court of Appeals for the Eleventh Circuit *agreed*.

In *Maryland v. Wilson*, 519 U.S. 408, 117 S.Ct. 882 (1997), the United States Supreme Court held that an officer may order a passenger out of a vehicle during a stop for a traffic infraction without violating the Fourth Amendment, although there is no articulable reason to detain the passenger. The Court reasoned:

"[D]anger to an officer from a traffic stop is likely to be greater when there are passengers in addition to the driver in the stopped car. While there is not the same basis for ordering the passengers out of the car as there is for ordering the driver out, the additional intrusion on the passenger is minimal. We therefore hold that an officer making a traffic stop may order the passengers to get out of the car pending completion of the stop."

Clark at 1285 (quoting *Wilson* at 414-15).

The *Wilson* Court explained that passengers pose as great a danger to police officers as do drivers during traffic stops because

the possibility of a violent encounter stems not from the ordinary reaction of a motorist stopped for a speeding violation, but from the fact that evidence of a more serious crime might be uncovered during the stop. And the motivation of a passenger to employ violence to prevent apprehension of such a crime is every bit as great as that of the driver.

Id. (quoting *Wilson* at 414).

"The Court's approval in *Maryland v. Wilson* of officer control of passengers in a traffic stop stems from the 'legitimate and weighty' need for officer safety." *Clark* at 1286. [Citation omitted.] Thus, "the interest in officer safety outweighs the liberty interest of a passenger who is not suspected of violating the law." *Id.* And in other contexts, this court has held that " 'a police officer performing his lawful duties may direct and control—to some extent—the movements and location of persons nearby, even persons that the officer may have no reason to suspect of wrongdoing.' " *Id.* at 1286-87. [Citations omitted.]

"The District of Columbia Circuit and the Third Circuit have each relied on *Maryland v. Wilson* in holding that a police officer may detain a passenger, who is not suspected of wrongdoing, during a lawful traffic stop. In *Rogala v. District of Columbia*, 161 *F*.3d 44 (D.C. Cir. 1998), a police officer ordered a passenger to return to the car while he investigated the driver. ✳ ✳ ✳ In upholding the reasonableness of the detention, the court held 'that in the circumstances presented, it follows from *Maryland v. Wilson* that a police officer has the power to reasonably control the situation by requiring a passenger to remain in a vehicle during a traffic stop, particularly where, as here, the officer is alone and feels threatened.' " *Clark* at 1287 (quoting *Rogala* at 53).

In *United States v. Moorefield*, 111 *F*.3d 10, 12-13 (3rd Cir. 1997), the Third Circuit held that it was constitutionally permissible for officers to order a passenger who was not suspected of criminal activity "to remain in the car with his hands in the air." *Id.*, 111 *F*.3d at 13. The Third Circuit reasoned:

Just as the Court in *Wilson* found ordering a passenger out of the car to be a minimal intrusion on personal liberty, we find the imposition of having to remain in the car with raised hands equally minimal. We conclude that the benefit of added officer protection far outweighs this minor intrusion.

Id.

Here, in *Clark,* the court concluded that Officer Huff's conduct was reasonable in light of the totality of the circumstances facing him. The court observed:

> One. Officer Huff observed a violent confrontation between two men fighting in the street. Two. The combatants were next to an automobile that was on the wrong side of the street. Three. The door to the vehicle was open, the engine was running, and the lights were on. Four. Officer Huff had responded to numerous reports of violence in that vicinity. Five. Mr. Clark informed Officer Huff that he had been a passenger in the automobile. Six. Officer Huff was alone at night facing three men who were associates.

Id. at 1287.

Clearly, an individual's "proximity to illegal activity" may be considered when determining whether there were reasonable grounds to justify a detention. *Id.* Street encounters put officers in danger. "Although Mr. Clark had alighted from the automobile in which he had been a passenger before Officer Huff arrived on the scene, his admitted relationship to the parties whom Officer Huff was investigating made him 'every bit as great' a danger as the combatants." *Id.* at 1287-88. [Citation omitted.]

> The need for an officer to take command and control persons during a criminal investigation is "particularly [true] where the officer is alone and feels threatened." * * * While acting alone, Officer Huff observed two men engaged in violent criminal conduct. Officer Huff testified that Mr. Clark informed him that Mr. Clark was a passenger in the vehicle that was next to the two men who were fighting. He testified that he detained Mr. Clark and the other persons in order to control the situation to protect his safety. Under the circumstances presented by this case, Mr. Clark's liberty interest was outweighed by the necessity for Officer Huff to control the movement of the three associates and to detain them briefly to ensure his safety while he conducted a criminal investigation.

Id. at 1288.

The court concluded, therefore, that "Officer Huff did not violate the Fourth Amendment in briefly detaining Mr. Clark after learning that he was not a mere bystander but, instead and notably, had been a passenger in the automobile and an associate of two persons being investigated for criminal activities." *Id.* In reaching this conclusion, the court paused to observe that this was "not a case where a law enforcement officer detained an individual who was in no way associated with any criminal wrongdoing, but rather was simply an unrelated bystander to a traffic violation or to an altercation between other persons." *Id.* In that circumstance, a different result might be reached.

3. *Traffic stops and the "seizure" of passengers.* When a police officer makes a traffic stop, the driver of the car is seized within the meaning of the Fourth Amendment. In *Brendlin v. California,* ___

U.S. ___, 127 *S.Ct.* 2400 (2007), the United States Supreme Court determined that the same holds true for passengers. Writing for the Court, Justice Souter held that, during the course of a traffic stop, like the driver, "a passenger is seized," and so may challenge the constitutionality of the stop. *Id.*, 127 *S.Ct.* at 2403.

The circumstances of *Brendlin* unfolded in late November, in the early morning hours, when a deputy sheriff and his partner noticed a parked Buick with expired registration tags. After checking with dispatch, the deputy learned that an application for renewal of registration was being processed. Shortly thereafter, the officers saw the car again on the road, and this time the deputy noticed its display of a temporary operating permit with the number "11," indicating it was legal to drive the car through November. Even though there were no grounds to stop the vehicle, the officers decided to pull the Buick over to verify credentials.

During the stop, the deputy asked the driver, Karen Simeroth, for her license and saw a passenger in the front seat, Bruce Brendlin, who he believed had dropped out of parole supervision. A further check with dispatch revealed that Brendlin "was a parole violator with an outstanding no-bail warrant for his arrest." *Id.* at 2404. Once backup officers arrived, the deputy went to the passenger side of the Buick, ordered Brendlin out of the car at gunpoint, and placed him under arrest. A search incident to arrest uncovered an orange syringe cap on Brendlin's person. In the vehicle, the officers discovered various items of drug paraphernalia.

Charged with drug-related offenses, Brendlin moved to suppress the evidence seized during the searches of his person and the car, arguing that the officers lacked the proper grounds to make the traffic stop, and therefore the traffic stop was "an unlawful seizure of his person." *Id.*

At the state level, the California Supreme Court held that suppression was unwarranted because Brendlin was not "seized" by the traffic stop, primarily because the driver (Simeroth) was the officers' exclusive target, and, "once a car has been pulled off the road, a passenger would feel free to depart or otherwise to conduct his or her affairs as though the police were not present." *Id.* at 2405. Consequently, the state court determined that Brendlin did not have standing to challenge the admissibility of the evidence seized. *The United States Supreme Court disagreed.*

In the typical case, when a law enforcement officer conducts a motor vehicle stop, he or she directs authority at the driver because the driver has initial control of the vehicle. The passenger is simply along for the ride. In the past, this had created confusion under the usual test for "seizing" a person because the officer is causing a seizure by conduct not actually directed at the passenger. At issue in this case is "whether a traffic stop subjects a passenger, as well as the driver, to Fourth Amendment seizure." *Id.*

Under the Fourth Amendment, a person is seized by the police and "thus entitled to challenge the government's action" when the officer, "by means of physical force or show of authority," terminates or restrains the person's freedom of movement, "through means intentionally applied." Thus, even an "unintended person" may be the object of the detention, "so long as the detention is 'willful' and not merely the consequence of 'an unknowing act.' " *Id.* [Citations omitted.]

"The law is settled that in Fourth Amendment terms a traffic stop entails a seizure of the driver, 'even though the purpose of the stop is limited and the resulting detention quite brief.' " *Id.* at 2406 (quoting *Delaware v. Prouse,* 440 *U.S.* 648, 653, 99 *S.Ct.* 1391, 1396 (1979)). And although the Court has not, until this case, "squarely answered the question whether a passenger is also seized," it has held that "during a traffic stop an officer seizes everyone in the vehicle, not just the driver." *Id.* [Citations omitted.]

In this case, the prosecution conceded that the police had no adequate justification to pull the car over, but argued that "the passenger was not seized and thus cannot claim that the evidence was tainted by an unconstitutional stop." *Id.* To resolve this question, the Court focused on the question "whether a reasonable person in Brendlin's position when the car stopped would have believed himself free to 'terminate the encounter' between the police and himself." Said the Court:

> We think that in these circumstances any reasonable passenger would have understood the police officers to be exercising control to the point that no one in the car was free to depart without police permission.
>
> A traffic stop necessarily curtails the travel a passenger has chosen just as much as it halts the driver, diverting both from the stream of traffic to the side of the road, and the police activity that normally amounts to intrusion on "privacy and personal security" does not normally (and did not here) distinguish between passenger and driver. * * *
>
> An officer who orders one particular car to pull over acts with an implicit claim of right based on fault of some sort, and a sensible person would not expect a police officer to allow people to come and go freely from the physical focal point of an investigation into faulty behavior or wrongdoing. If the likely wrongdoing is not the driving, the passenger will reasonably feel subject to suspicion owing to close association; but even when the wrongdoing is only bad driving, the passenger will expect to be subject to some scrutiny, and his attempt to leave the scene would be so obviously likely to prompt an objection from the officer that no passenger would feel free to leave in the first place. * * * It is also reasonable for passengers to expect that a police officer at the scene of a crime, arrest, or investigation will not let people move around in ways that could jeopardize his safety.

Id. at 2406-07.

According to the Court, during a lawful traffic stop, there is a "societal expectation of 'unquestioned [police] command' " which is "at odds with any notion that a passenger would feel free to leave, or to terminate the personal encounter any other way, without advance permission." *Id.* at 2407.

In so ruling, the Court rejected the lower court's reasoning that Brendlin was not seized by the stop because the officer only intended to investigate the driver (Simeroth), and did not direct a show of authority toward Brendlin. Rather, the test is an "objective" one, that is, "whether a reasonable passenger would have perceived that the show of authority was at least partly directed at him, and that he was thus not free to ignore the police presence and go about his business." *Id.* at 2408. In this regard, the Court paused to note that, as a matter of law, the police are authorized to stop a car solely to investigate a passenger's conduct, for example, a violation of the state's seatbelt law, or a violation of a local littering ordinance. Therefore, "a passenger cannot assume, merely from the fact of a traffic stop, that the driver's conduct is the cause of the stop." *Id.* at 2407 n.3.

Accordingly, "Brendlin was seized from the moment Simeroth's car came to a halt on the side of the road," and it was error for the lower court to deny his suppression motion on the ground that seizure occurred only at the formal arrest. *Id.* at 2410.

4. *Tinted windows.* In *United States v. Stanfield*, 109 *F.*3d 976 (4th Cir. 1997), the court held that "the government's substantial interest in officer safety during a lawful traffic stop outweighs the intrusion on the privacy interests of the vehicle's occupants which results when, because of heavily tinted windows that prevent the interior compartment from being viewed, an officer opens a door of the vehicle in order to ensure that the vehicle's driver is unarmed, and that there are no other occupants who might threaten his safety during the investigatory stop." *Id.* at 978.

In this case, three Baltimore City police officers were patrolling a high crime area in West Baltimore known for its open narcotics trafficking when they saw a late model, black Nissan Pathfinder with heavily tinted windows illegally parked in the middle of the street. At the time, the vehicle was blocking traffic. The officers circled the block, and when the driver of the Pathfinder made no attempt to move his vehicle to allow a free flow of traffic, the officers parked their unmarked vehicle in front of the Pathfinder. Upon exiting their vehicle, the officers noticed that the Pathfinder's driver was talking to a man leaning from a second story window. The officers recognized the man as a known drug dealer.

The officers (each in uniform) approached the Pathfinder from both the driver and passenger sides, and as they did so, they noticed that the front driver's side window was down, but that the front passenger side window was up. The tinting on the Pathfinder's windows was so dark that the officer who approached on the passenger's side could not see into the vehicle. As a result, the officer opened the front passenger side door to determine if the driver was armed or had access to weapons and whether he was alone in the vehicle. When the officer opened the door, he saw in plain view, from his vantage point outside the vehicle, a clear plastic bag of cocaine on the back seat of the Pathfinder. A further search of the vehicle uncovered a nine-millimeter semi-automatic handgun, numerous empty vials, two pagers and over 200 grams of cocaine.

Finding the evidence admissible under the plain view doctrine, the court ruled:

> [W]henever, during a lawful traffic stop, officers are required to approach a vehicle with windows so heavily tinted that they are unable to view the interior of the stopped vehicle, they may, when it appears in their experienced judgment prudent to do so, open at least one of the vehicle's doors and, without crossing the plane of the vehicle, visually inspect its interior in order to ascertain whether the driver is armed, whether he has access to weapons, or whether there are other occupants of the vehicle who might pose a danger to the officers. Indeed, it seems to us that a contrary holding would not only be irreconcilable with, but arguably undermine altogether, the caselaw from the Supreme Court that was developed specifically for the purpose of protecting officer safety during what are, in today's society, frighteningly perilous encounters.

* * * *

> When, during already dangerous traffic stops, officers must approach vehicles whose occupants and interiors are blocked from view by tinted windows, the potential harm to which the officers are exposed increases exponentially, to the point, we believe, of unconscionability. *Indeed, we can conceive of almost nothing more dangerous to a law enforcement officer in the context of a traffic stop than approaching an automobile whose passenger compartment is entirely hidden from the officer's view by darkly tinted windows.* As the officer exits his cruiser and proceeds toward the tinted-windowed vehicle, he has no way of knowing whether the vehicle's driver is fumbling for his driver's license or reaching for a gun; he does not know whether he is about to encounter a single law-abiding citizen or to be ambushed by a car-full of armed assailants. * * * In fact, it is out of recognition of just such a danger that at least twenty-eight States * * * have now enacted laws either regulating or altogether prohibiting the use of tinted windows on vehicles in their states.

Id. at 981-82. [Court's emphasis; footnote omitted.]

Accordingly, this court was convinced that "the presence of windows so tinted that the vehicle's interior compartment is not visible is, in itself, a circumstance that would cause an officer reasonably to believe that his safety might be in danger[.]" *Id.* at 984.

---

§8.3(e). The *"Terry* frisk" of the vehicle's passenger compartment.

MICHIGAN v. LONG
Supreme Court of the United States
463 *U.S.* 1032, 103 *S.Ct.* 3469 (1983)

QUESTION: May a law enforcement officer conduct a *Terry*-type protective "frisk" of the passenger compartment of a motor vehicle during a lawful investigatory stop of the occupant of the vehicle ?

ANSWER: YES. A police officer may conduct a *Terry*-type protective "frisk" of the passenger compartment of a motor vehicle, limited to those areas in which a weapon may be placed or hidden "if the officer possesses a reasonable belief based on specific and articulable facts which, when taken together with the rational inferences from those facts, reasonably warrant the officer * * * in believing that the suspect is dangerous and the suspect may gain immediate control of weapons." *Id.* at 3480.

RATIONALE: The significant question here, as was raised in *Terry v. Ohio*, 392 *U.S.* 1, 88 *S.Ct.* 1868 (1968), is whether a reasonably prudent person in the circumstances would believe that his or her safety or the safety of others was in danger.

The Court analogizes the investigatory stop of the occupant of a motor vehicle and a subsequent search of the passenger compartment with the investigatory stop of an individual on the street and the subsequent *Terry*-type frisk or pat-down of the person's outer clothing for weapons which might be used to harm the officer or others.

In *Terry v. Ohio, supra*, the Supreme Court upheld the validity of a protective search for weapons in the absence of probable cause to arrest because "it is unreasonable to deny a police officer the right to neutralize the threat of physical harm," *Terry* at 24, when he possesses a specific and articulable suspicion that an individual is armed and dangerous. *Long* at 3472.

Here, Long was convicted for possession of marijuana found by police in the passenger compartment of the automobile he was driving. The police conducted a protective frisk of the passenger compartment because they had reason to believe that the vehicle contained weapons potentially dangerous to the officers. Due to this, the High Court held that the protective search of the passenger compartment was reasonable in light of the principles set forth in *Terry. Long* at 3472.

The Court re-examined the reasonableness of the officer's conduct in *Terry*, where it held that there is "no ready test for determining reasonableness other than by balancing the need to search [or seize] against the invasion which the search [or seizure] entails." *Long* at 3479. Although the actions of the officer in *Terry* encompassed a significant, albeit brief intrusion upon personal security, the Court found the conduct reasonable when it "weighed the interest of the individual against the legitimate interest in crime prevention and detection[,] and the need for law enforcement officers to protect themselves and other prospective victims of violence in situations where they lack probable cause for arrest." *Id.*

As a result, when a police officer has a reasonable belief, which he can base upon specific and articulable facts, that the individual whose suspicious conduct he is investigating at close range is armed and possibly dangerous to the officer or others, the Court, through Justice O'Connor, concludes that it would be clearly unreasonable to deny the officer the ability to take necessary measures to determine whether the person is, in fact, carrying a weapon on his person or has easy access to a weapon located in the passenger compartment of his vehicle, and to neutralize the threat of physical harm.

"If a suspect is dangerous, he is no less 'dangerous' simply because he is not arrested." *Id.* at 3481. In addition, should an officer, as in the present case, find contraband instead of, or in addition to, weapons during the course of a legitimate *Terry*-type frisk of the passenger compartment of an automobile, "he clearly cannot be required to ignore the contraband, and the Fourth Amendment does not require its suppression in such circumstances." *Id.*

Thus, the balancing test set forth in *Terry, supra*, and extended here in *Long*, clearly weighs in favor of allowing the police to conduct an area search of the passenger compartment of an automobile to uncover weapons, as long as the officers possess a specific, articulable, and objectively reasonable suspicion that the suspect is potentially armed and dangerous or able to arm himself by gaining immediate access to a weapon.

NOTE

1. Law enforcement officers are, of course, not permitted to conduct automobile searches whenever they conduct an investigative stop. The *Terry* frisk is not justified by the need to prevent the disappearance or destruction of evidence of a crime. Rather, "the sole justification for the search is the protection of the police officers and others nearby." *Terry*, 392 *U.S.* at 29, 88 *S.Ct.* at 1884. Therefore, officers who conduct area searches during investigative detentions must do so only when they have a reasonable suspicion that the person or persons detained may be armed or able to gain immediate control of a dangerous weapon. When officers have this level of belief, they may search the passenger compartment of the automobile, limited to those areas and closed containers in which a weapon may be placed or hidden.

2. As in other areas of criminal procedure, state courts are free to rely on their state constitutions to provide greater protection to their citizens' liberty interests than that afforded by the United States Supreme Court interpreting parallel provisions of the federal Constitution. For example, in *People v. Torres*, 74 *N.Y.*2d 224, 543 *N.E.*2d 61 (1989), the New York Court of Appeals held, despite the Supreme Court's authorization in *Michigan v. Long*, that a *Terry* protective "frisk" of the passenger compartment of an automobile is prohibited under the "more protective State constitutional provision[]" found in

Article I, Section 12, when the sole justification for the procedure stems from the rationale that, "if the suspect is not placed under arrest, he will be permitted to reenter his automobile, and will then have access to any weapons inside." *Id.*, 543 *N.E.*2d at 62.

Finding the "expansive view" of the *Terry*-"frisk" procedure adopted in *Long* to be inconsistent with the New York Constitution, the *Torres* court observed that

> although the history and identical language of the State and Federal constitutional privacy guarantees (*U.S.*Const. 4th Amend.; N.Y. Const. art. I, §12) generally support a "policy of uniformity," this court has demonstrated its willingness to adopt more protective standards under the State Constitution "when doing so best promotes 'predictability and precision in judicial review of search and seizure cases and the protection of the individual rights of our citizens.'" * * *

> A police officer's entry into a citizen's automobile and his inspection of personal effects located within are significant encroachments upon that citizen's privacy interests[.] * * *

> In this instance, for example, the suspects had already been removed from the car * * *. Further, the suspects had been patted down without incident. At that point, there was nothing to prevent these two armed detectives from questioning the two suspects with complete safety to themselves, since the suspects had been isolated from the interior of the car * * *. Any residual fear that the detectives might have had about the suspects' ability to break away and retrieve [a weapon from the car] could have been eliminated by taking the far less intrusive step of asking the suspects to move away from the vicinity of the car[.] * * * Finally, it is unrealistic to assume, as the Supreme Court did in *Michigan v. Long*[,] that having been stopped and questioned without incident, a suspect who is about to proceed on his way would, upon reentry into his vehicle, reach for a concealed weapon and threaten the departing police officer's safety. Certainly, such a far-fetched scenario is an insufficient basis upon which to predicate the substantial intrusion that occurred here[.]

Id. at 63, 65. [Citations omitted.]

3. *Suspicious / threatening bulges.* In *United States v. Baker*, 78 *F.*3d 135 (4th Cir. 1996), United States Park Police Officer Pope noticed four automobiles, which appeared to be traveling together, go through a red light "in close succession." As the officer began following the vehicles, the driver of the last car decreased his speed and began swerving back and forth in an apparent attempt to prevent the officer from overtaking the other three vehicles. As soon as a back-up officer arrived, however, Officer Pope was able to pass the last car and pur-

sue the others. Ultimately, Pope effected a motor vehicle stop of two of the four automobiles.

"In response to a question from Officer Pope, the driver of the first automobile related that the four drivers knew each other and were travelling together. He then moved to Baker's vehicle and repeated the question. Baker denied knowing the other three drivers. During this conversation, Officer Pope observed a triangular-shaped bulge underneath the front of Baker's shirt, near the waistband of his pants. In order to determine whether Baker was carrying a concealed weapon, Officer Pope ordered Baker to lift his shirt above the bulge. Twice, he quickly raised his shirt approximately an inch and then dropped it, preventing the officer from observing what was concealed underneath. Finally, Baker lifted his shirt sufficiently to permit Officer Pope to see a handgun tucked into the waistband of his pants." *Id.* at 136.

"Ordering Baker to raise his hands, Officer Pope drew his weapon and requested assistance via his radio. After initially complying with the officer's request, Baker slowly dropped his hands and pushed the door of the vehicle into Officer Pope, who quickly kicked it shut. Baker then exited the automobile on the passenger side and moved toward the rear of the vehicle. He removed the weapon from his waistband and, after lifting it approximately to shoulder height, dropped it, turned and ran." *Id.* He was apprehended several months later.

In this appeal, Baker argued that the lower court was correct in ruling that a "bulge alone" does not give an officer a reasonable suspicion that a person may be armed and dangerous. The Court of Appeals for the Fourth Circuit disagreed. The court said:

> The district court was in error in concluding that Officer Pope lacked a proper basis to conduct a protective search. Because of the hazards involved in a roadside encounter with a suspect, a law enforcement officer may conduct a protective search aimed at uncovering concealed weapons after making a proper traffic stop if the officer "possesses a reasonable belief based on 'specific and articulable facts which, taken together with the rational inferences from those facts, reasonably warrant' the officer in believing that the suspect is dangerous." * * * An officer's belief must be based not on subjective hunches but on information sufficient to cause a reasonably prudent person under the circumstances to believe that either his safety or that of others is in danger. * * *

> The question of whether Officer Pope possessed a reasonable belief that Baker was armed and dangerous need not detain us long. Based on the inordinate risk of danger to law enforcement officers during traffic stops, *observing a bulge that could be made by a weapon in a suspect's clothing reasonably warrants a belief that the suspect is potentially dangerous, even if the suspect was stopped only for a minor violation. Pennsylvania v. Mimms*, 434 *U.S.* 106, 112, 98 *S.Ct.* 330, 333 [] (1977) (*per curiam*) (The bulge in the jacket permitted the officer to conclude that the suspect "was armed and thus posed a serious and present danger to the safety of the officer.").

Id. at 137. [Citations omitted; emphasis added.]

The court also determined that the manner in which Officer Pope conducted the "frisk" of Baker was entirely proper. In this respect, the court explained:

> Determining the reasonableness of a protective search involves balancing the officer's interest in self-protection against the intrusion on individual rights necessitated by the search. * * * A police officer's interest in self-protection arises when he reasonably believes that a suspect is armed and dangerous; at that point, he has an interest in "taking steps to assure himself that the person with whom he is dealing is not armed with a weapon that could unexpectedly and fatally be used against him."

> In finding that Officer Pope was restricted to conducting a patdown frisk, the district court erroneously concluded that a patdown frisk was the only permissible method of conducting a *Terry* search. The reasoning is incorrect because the reasonableness of a protective search depends on the factual circumstances of each case. * * * *[A] patdown frisk is but one example of how a reasonable protective search may be conducted.* * * *

> Balancing the officer's interest in self-protection against the resulting intrusion upon Baker's personal security, we hold that Officer Pope's direction was reasonable under the circumstances. Having formed a reasonable belief that Baker was carrying a weapon, Officer Pope had an immediate interest in determining whether Baker actually was armed and, if so, neutralizing any potential threat without assuming unnecessary risks. * * * Directing that he raise his shirt required little movement by Baker and allowed Officer Pope to immediately determine whether Baker was armed without having to come in close contact with him. And, it minimized the risk that he could draw his weapon before Officer Pope could attempt to neutralize the potential threat. * * * Indeed, this act was less intrusive than the patdown sanctioned in *Terry*. * * * In sum, based on a balancing of the necessity for the search against the intrusion caused by the search, directing that Baker raise his shirt constituted a reasonable search limited to discovering whether he was carrying a concealed weapon. * * *

Id. at 137-38. [Citations omitted; emphasis added.]

§8.4. Investigative detentions of property.

UNITED STATES v. PLACE
Supreme Court of the United States
462 U.S. 696, 103 S.Ct. 2637 (1983)

QUESTION 1: Does the Fourth Amendment prohibit law enforcement officials from temporarily detaining an individual's personal luggage for exposure to a trained narcotics detection dog on the basis of a reasonable suspicion that the luggage contains narcotics ?

ANSWER: NO. "Given the enforcement problems associated with the detection of narcotics trafficking and the minimal intrusion that a properly limited detention would entail, * * * the Fourth Amendment does not prohibit such a detention." *Id.* at 2639. When an officer's observations provide him or her with a reasonable and articulable suspicion that a traveler is carrying luggage that contains narcotics, the principles of *Terry v. Ohio* "would permit the officer to detain the luggage briefly to investigate the circumstances that aroused his [or her] suspicion, provided that the investigative detention is properly limited in scope." *Id.* 2644. Thus, "the limitations applicable to investigative detentions of the person should define the permissible scope of an investigative detention of the person's luggage on less than probable cause." *Id.* at 2645.

QUESTION 2: Will a 90-minute detention of personal luggage for the purpose of arranging its exposure to a narcotics detection dog violate the Fourth Amendment when (1) it is supported only by a reasonable, articulable suspicion, and (2) the detaining officers, although having ample time to do so, failed to diligently pursue a means of investigation which would have greatly minimized the length of the detention ?

ANSWER: YES. The detention of defendant's luggage in this case "went beyond the narrow authority possessed by police to detain briefly luggage reasonably suspected to contain narcotics." *Id.* at 2646. Although the Court would not in this case "adopt any outside time limitation for a permissible *Terry* stop, [it has] never approved a seizure of the person for the prolonged 90-minute period involved here[.]" *Id.* Therefore, based on the facts presented, the Court concluded that the length of the detention of defendant's luggage *alone* made the seizure unreasonable in the absence of probable cause. *Id.* at 2645.

RATIONALE: "The Fourth Amendment protects the 'right of the people to be secure in their persons, houses, papers, *and effects*, against unreasonable searches and seizures.' Although in the context of personal property, and particularly containers, the Fourth Amendment challenge is typically to the subsequent search of the container rather than to its initial seizure by the authorities, [there are] some general principles regarding seizures. In the ordinary case, th[is] Court has viewed a seizure of personal property as *per se* unreasonable within the meaning of the Fourth Amendment unless it is accomplished pursuant to a judicial warrant issued upon probable cause and particularly describing the items to be seized. * * * Where law enforcement authorities have probable cause to believe that a container holds contraband or evidence of crime, but have not secured a warrant, the Court has interpreted the Amendment to permit seizure of the property, pending issuance of a warrant to examine its contents, if the exigencies of the circumstances demand it or some other recognized exception to the warrant requirement is present." *Id.* at 2641. [Citations and footnotes omitted; Court's emphasis.]

In this case, the first critical question addressed by the Court is whether, under the Fourth Amendment, the warrantless seizure of personal property on the basis of less than probable cause could, when properly limited in scope, be reasonable.

The record revealed that law enforcement authorities at the Miami International Airport developed a reasonable and articulable suspicion that defendant Raymond Place was engaged in drug-trafficking activity. After Place boarded his flight to New York's La Guardia Airport, the Miami officials called the Drug Enforcement Administration (DEA) authorities in New York to relay their information about him.

"Two DEA agents waited for Place at the arrival gate at La Guardia Airport in New York. There again, his behavior aroused the suspicion of the agents. After he had claimed his two bags and called a limousine, the agents decided to approach him. They identified themselves as federal narcotics agents, to which Place responded that he knew they were 'cops' and had spotted them as soon as he had deplaned. One of the agents informed Place that, based on their own observations and information obtained from the Miami authorities, they believed that he might be carrying narcotics. * * * When Place refused to consent to a search of his luggage, one of the agents told him that they were going to take the luggage to a federal judge to try to obtain a search warrant and that Place was free to accompany them. Place declined, but obtained from one of the agents telephone numbers at which the agents could be reached." *Id.* at 2640.

"The agents then took the bags to Kennedy Airport, where they subjected the bags to a 'sniff' test by a trained narcotics detection dog. The dog reacted positively to the smaller of the two bags[.] Approximately 90 minutes had elapsed since the seizure of [Place's] luggage. Because it was late on a Friday afternoon, the agents retained the luggage until Monday morning, when they secured a search warrant from a Magistrate for the smaller bag. Upon opening that bag, the agents discovered 1,125 grams of cocaine." *Id.*

At the Supreme Court, Place argued that the rationale for a *Terry* stop of the person should not apply to investigative detentions of a person's property. In this respect, Place urged that in the "property context," there are "no degrees of intrusion," and in the absence of some special law enforcement interest such as officer safety, an investigative detention of personal property must be based on probable cause. *Id.* at 2643. Rejecting these contentions, the Court agreed with the Government that the "warrantless seizure[] of personal luggage from the custody of the owner on the basis of less then probable cause, for the purpose of pursuing a limited course of investigation, short of opening the luggage, that would quickly confirm or dispel the authorities' suspicion" is reasonable under the Fourth Amendment. *Id.* at 2642. According to the Court, the principles of *Terry* "permit such seizures on the basis of reasonable, articulable suspicion, premised on objective facts, that the luggage contains contraband or evidence of a crime." *Place* at 2642.

In *Terry v. Ohio*, 392 *U.S.* 1, 88 *S.Ct.* 1868 (1968), the Court explained that the exception to the probable-cause requirement for limited, temporary seizures of the person "rests on a balancing of the competing interests to determine the reasonableness of the type of seizure involved[.]" *Place* at 2642.

> We must balance the nature and quality of the intrusion on the individual's Fourth Amendment interests against the importance of the governmental interests alleged to justify the intrusion. When the nature and extent of the detention are minimally intrusive of the individual's Fourth Amendment interests, the opposing law enforcement interests can support a seizure on less than probable cause.

Id.

Examining first "the governmental interest offered as a justification for a brief seizure of luggage from [a] suspect's custody for the purpose of pursuing a limited course of investigation[,]" *id.*, the Court agreed that, "where the authorities possess specific and articulable facts warranting a reasonable belief that a traveler's luggage contains narcotics, the governmental interest in seizing the luggage briefly to pursue further investigation is substantial. As observed in *United States v. Mendenhall*, 446 *U.S.* 544, 561, 100 *S.Ct.* 1870, 1880 [] (1980) [], '[t]he public has a compelling interest in detecting those who would traffic in deadly drugs for personal profit.' " *Place* at 2642-43. In *Terry*, the Court "described the governmental interests supporting the initial seizure of the person as 'effective crime prevention and detection; it is this interest which underlies the recognition that a police officer may in appropriate circumstances and in an appropriate manner approach a person for purposes of investigating possibly criminal behavior even though there is no probable cause to make an arrest.' * * * The test is whether those interests are sufficiently 'substantial,' * * * not whether they are independent of the interest in investigating crimes effectively and apprehending suspects. * * * Because of the inherently transient nature of drug courier activity at airports, allowing police to make brief investigative stops of persons at airports on reasonable suspicion of drug-trafficking substantially enhances the likelihood that police will be able to prevent the flow of narcotics into distribution channels." *Id.* at 2643. [Citations and footnote omitted.]

"Against this strong governmental interest, we must weigh the nature and extent of the intrusion upon the individual's Fourth Amendment rights when the police briefly detain luggage for limited investigative purposes." *Id.* According to the Court, "[t]he intrusion on possessory interests occasioned by a seizure of one's personal effects can vary both in its nature and extent. The seizure may be made after the owner has relinquished control of the property to a third party or, as here, from the immediate custody and control of the owner. Moreover, the police may confine their investigation to an on-the-spot inquiry— for example, immediate exposure of the luggage to a trained narcotics detection dog—or transport the property to another location. Given the fact that seizures of property can vary in intrusiveness, some brief detentions of personal effects may be so minimally intrusive of Fourth Amendment interests that strong countervailing governmental interests will justify a seizure based only on specific articulable facts that the property contains contraband or evidence of crime." *Id.* at 2643-44. [Footnotes omitted.]

Accordingly, "when an officer's observations lead him reasonably to believe that a traveler is carrying luggage that contains narcotics, the principles of *Terry* and [the cases interpreting *Terry*] would permit the officer to detain the luggage briefly to investigate the circumstances that aroused his suspicion, provided that the investigative detention is properly limited in scope." *Id.* at 2644.

The investigation in this case was, however, not properly limited in scope. Place's luggage was seized for the purpose of arranging its exposure to a narcotics detection dog. As observed in *Terry*, " '[t]he manner in which [a] seizure [is] conducted is, of course, as vital a part of the inquiry as whether [it was] warranted at all.' " *Place* at 2645 (quoting *Terry* at 28, 88 *S.Ct.* at 1883). "[W]hen the police seize luggage from the suspect's custody, [] the limitations applicable to investigative detentions of the person should define the permissible scope of an investigative detention of the person's luggage on less than probable cause." *Id.* Under this standard, the Court found it "clear that the police conduct here exceeded the permissible limits of a *Terry*-type investigative stop." *Id.*

> The length of the detention of [Place's] luggage alone precludes the conclusion that the seizure was reasonable in the absence of probable cause. * * * [T]he brevity of the invasion of the individual's Fourth Amendment interests is an important factor in determining whether the seizure is so minimally intrusive as to be justifiable on reasonable suspicion. Moreover, in assessing the effect of the length of the detention, we take into account whether the police diligently pursue their investigation. We note that here the New York agents knew the time of Place's scheduled arrival at La Guardia, had ample time to arrange for their additional investigation at that location, and thereby could have minimized the intrusion on [Place's] Fourth Amendment interests. Thus, although we decline to adopt any outside time limitation for a permissible *Terry* stop, we have never approved a seizure of the person for the prolonged 90-minute period involved here and cannot do so on the facts presented by this case. * * *
>
> [W]e hold that the detention of [Place's] luggage in this case went beyond the narrow authority possessed by police to detain briefly luggage reasonably suspected to contain narcotics. * * * Consequently, the evidence obtained from the subsequent search of his luggage was inadmissible, and Place's conviction must be reversed.

Id. at 2645-46.

NOTE

1. In addition to declaring that the 90-minute detention of Place's luggage *alone* was sufficient to render the seizure unreasonable, the Court noted that "the violation was exacerbated by the failure of the agents to accurately inform [him] of the place to which they were transporting his luggage, of the length of time he might be dispossessed, and what arrangements would be made for the return of the luggage if the investigation dispelled the suspicion." *Id.* at 2646.

2. *A trained "sniff" by a "canine cannabis connoisseur."* *

(a) Not a search under the Fourth Amendment. During the course of its opinion in *Place*, the Court had occasion to address the constitutionality of employing a narcotics-detection dog for the purpose of determining whether a particular item of property contains a controlled substance. Writing for the Court, Justice O'Connor instructed:

> We have affirmed that a person possesses a privacy interest in the contents of personal luggage that is protected by the Fourth Amendment. * * * A "canine sniff" by a well-trained narcotics detection dog, however, does not require opening the luggage. It does not expose noncontraband items that otherwise would remain hidden from public view, as does, for example, an officer's rummaging through the contents of the luggage. Thus, the manner in which information is obtained through this investigative technique is much less intrusive than a typical search. Moreover, the sniff discloses only the presence or absence of narcotics, a contraband item. Thus, despite the fact that the sniff tells the authorities something about the contents of the luggage, the information obtained is limited. This limited disclosure also ensures that the owner of the property is not subject to the embarrassment and inconvenience entailed in less discriminate and more intrusive investigative methods.
>
> In these respects, the canine sniff is *sui generis* [*i.e.*, in its own class]. We are aware of no other investigative procedure that is so limited both in the manner in which the information is obtained and in the content of the information revealed by the procedure. *Therefore, we conclude that the particular course of investigation that the agents intended to pursue here—exposure of [defendant's] luggage, which was located in a public place, to a trained canine—did not constitute a "search" within the meaning of the Fourth Amendment.*

Id. at 2644-45. [Emphasis added.] *See also United States v. Jacobsen,* 466 *U.S.* 109, 104 *S.Ct.* 1652 (1984), where the Court gave *Place* a broad interpretation and concluded that a police investigatory tool is not a "search" if it merely discloses the presence or absence of contraband. According to the *Jacobsen* Court, similar to the *Place* canine sniff, the likelihood that chemical tests (which merely disclose whether or not a certain substance is an illicit drug), "will actually

---

* *People v. Evans,* 65 *Cal.App.*3d 924, 134 *Cal.Rptr.* 436 (1977).

compromise any legitimate interest in privacy seems much too remote to characterize the testing as a search subject to the Fourth Amendment." *Jacobsen* at 122-24, 104 *S.Ct.* at 1661-62. *And see United States v. Lingenfelter*, 997 *F.*2d 632, 638-39 (9th Cir. 1993) (sniff test of the door of defendant's warehouse held not to be a search requiring probable cause); *United States v. Dicesare*, 765 *F.*2d 890, 897 (9th Cir.) (sniff test of automobile trunk not a search requiring probable cause), *amended*, 777 *F.*2d 543 (9th Cir. 1985); *United States v. Beale*, 736 *F.*2d 1289, 1291-92 (9th Cir. 1984) (*en banc*) (subjecting luggage to a sniff test by a trained narcotics dog held not to be a search).

Although the *Place* Court held that a canine sniff of personal property located in a public place by a trained scent-detection dog does not constitute a Fourth Amendment "search," if the property is to be "detained" for purposes of arranging its exposure to the dog, that detention must be constitutionally justified by a reasonable and articulable suspicion, based on objective facts, that the property to be detained contains contraband or evidence of a crime. *Id.* at 2642. *See also United States v. Nurse*, 916 *F.*2d 20, 24 (D.C.Cir. 1990) (officer developed the requisite "reasonable suspicion of Nurse's illicit drug activity to justify his detention of the bag for a canine sniff"). Thereafter, if the canine sniff results in a positive "alert" or indication that the particular piece of property contains contraband or evidence of a suspected crime, this trained canine's reaction elevates the reasonable suspicion to probable cause, and thus provides the necessary justification for the issuance of a search warrant or for a search under an applicable exception to the warrant requirement. *See United States v. Ludwig*, 10 *F.*3d 1523 (10th Cir. 1993) (a dog alert, by itself, provides probable cause for a search and seizure, unless the particular dog had a poor accuracy record).

(i) Amtrak sleeper compartments. In *United States v. Colyer*, 878 *F.*2d 469 (D.C.Cir. 1989), the court held that using a trained narcotics-detection dog to "sniff" a sleeper compartment of an Amtrak train for narcotics, from a vantage point located in the public corridor outside the compartment, does not constitute a search within the meaning of the Fourth Amendment. The court reasoned that the canine "sniff" caused virtually no annoyance to the defendant. It was conducted in such a manner and location that the defendant was not subjected to the embarrassment and inconvenience entailed in less discriminate and more intrusive investigative methods. In addition, the court noted that a sniff by a trained narcotics-detection dog reveals only whether a particular container or area is concealing narcotics. Because it reveals no other "private" fact, it does not compromise any legitimate expectation of privacy. As the Supreme Court noted in *United States v. Jacobsen*, 466 *U.S.* 109, 104 *S.Ct.* 1652 (1984), governmental conduct that can "reveal nothing about noncontraband items," *id.* at 124 n.24, 104 *S.Ct.* 1662 n.24, interferes with no legitimate privacy expectation. Finding that the canine sniff constituted no search within the meaning of the Fourth Amendment, the *Colyer* court also held that in light of this determination, canine officers do not need to demonstrate a preliminary showing of a reasonable and articulable suspicion prior to summoning the narcotics detection dog.

(ii) Removing luggage from a bus' overhead baggage area.
In *United States v. Harvey*, 961 *F*.2d 1361 (8th Cir. 1992), defendants
Harvey and Flagella were traveling across country on a Greyhound
bus. At a scheduled stopover, a number of passengers, including Harvey and Flagella, left the bus. Thereafter, two Little Rock, Arkansas,
police detectives boarded the bus with Jupp, a narcotics detection dog.
As Jupp was walked down the aisle he lifted "his head and * * *
sniff[ed] high" indicating "that the odor of narcotics [was] above his
head level." *Id.* at 1362. "At that point, the detectives opened some of
the doors to the overhead baggage area, removed some of the bags,
placed them at Jupp's level, and allowed Jupp to sniff them. Jupp
'alerted' to two bags. The detectives then returned all of the bags to
the overhead storage area and exited the bus." *Id.*

"The overhead baggage area was described as similar to those
found on airplanes. Unlike airplanes, however, the baggage area is not
compartmentalized; there are no inner walls dividing the baggage
area into individualized compartments[, and the] doors cannot be
locked[.]" *Id.*

When Harvey, Flagella and the other passengers returned to their
seats, the detectives entered the bus, retrieved the bags to which Jupp
alerted, and asked who owned them. Harvey and Flagella claimed
ownership to the bags. Subsequently, the detectives secured Harvey's
and Flagella's consent to search the bags. Inside each they discovered
approximately five pounds of marijuana.

In this appeal Harvey and Flagella (defendants) argued that even
if the canine sniff is not a search within the meaning of the Fourth
Amendment, "the initial removal of their bags from the overhead baggage area," constituted an unlawful seizure. *Id.* at 1363. The court
disagreed.

In *United States v. Jacobsen, supra*, the Court defined a "seizure"
of property as "some meaningful interference with an individual's possessory interests in that property." *Id.* at 113, 104 *S.Ct.* at 1656. Here,
in *Harvey*, the court observed that "when Jupp stopped and 'air
sniffed' while moving down the aisle, the detectives had a reasonable
suspicion that contraband existed in the overhead baggage area." *Id.*
at 1363. Thus, this is not a case where "the defendants' baggage was
taken directly from their custody to facilitate the canine sniff test." *Id.*
Rather, defendants' baggage was "moved from one public area, the
overhead baggage area, to another, the aisle. [Defend]ants had left
their baggage unattended, and the temporary removal of the bags
caused no delay to [their] travel." *Id.* at 1363-64.

The court concluded, therefore, that "because there was no meaningful interference with [defend]ants' possessory interests in their
baggage, * * * no seizure occurred." *Id.* at 1364. The court elaborated:

> [T]he removal of the baggage from the overhead compartment was
> completely related to the lawful purpose for which the detective[s]
> boarded the bus. After boarding the bus and seeing Jupp "alert,"
> the detective[s] clearly had reasonable suspicion to conclude that
> narcotics were located somewhere in the overhead compartment.
> Passengers have no objective, reasonable expectation that their

baggage will never be moved once placed in an overhead compartment. It is not uncommon for the bus driver or a fellow passenger to rearrange the baggage in the overhead compartment or to temporarily remove the baggage and place it in a seat or in the aisle in order to rearrange and maximize the use of limited compartment space. [Moreover,] the movement of the unattended luggage revealed nothing of independent evidentiary value[.]

Id.

(b) *The canine "sniff" under state law.* State officials are reminded that a State is free to rely on its own constitution to provide its citizens with additional protection in this area. For example, in *State v. Pellicci*, 580 A.2d 710 (N.H. 1990), the New Hampshire Supreme Court determined that the use of a drug detection dog to sniff the exterior of a suspect's automobile for controlled substances is a "search" within the meaning of part I, article 19 of the New Hampshire Constitution. *Id.* at 716. According to the *Pellicci* court, under the New Hampshire Constitution, " 'a search ordinarily implies a quest by an officer of the law, a prying into hidden places for that which is concealed.' * * * Employing a trained canine to sniff a person's private vehicle in order to determine whether controlled substances are concealed inside is certainly a search in these terms." *Id.*

The drug detection dog discerned something not otherwise apparent to the officers through their own senses, aided or unaided, and advised them of what the dog had discovered by means the officers could perceive. The very purpose of bringing the dog to the vehicle was to have it detect any contraband that might be hidden inside. The sniff, in short, was a prying by officers into the contents of Pellicci's possession[s], which, concealed as they were from public view, could not have been evident to the officers before the prying began. However limited the information it provided, [this court] believe[s] that it is proper to categorize this dog sniff as a search, and it was therefore subject to the strictures of part I, article 19.

Id. [Citations omitted.]

Determining that a canine sniff is a search within the meaning of a state constitutional provision does not, however, end the inquiry. A finding must also be made as to the appropriate level of constitutional justification required to support such a search. In this respect, the New Hampshire Supreme Court determined that "a canine sniff differs from the traditional search in that it discloses only limited information and likely entails less embarrassment or inconvenience." *Id.* Thus, rather than holding the police to a probable-cause standard of justification, the court concluded that, "where, as here, a canine sniff: (1) is part of an investigative stop based on a reasonable and articulable suspicion of imminent criminal activity involving controlled substances; (2) is employed to search a vehicle; (3) in no way increases the time necessary for the [investigative stop]; and (4) is itself based on a reasonable and articulable suspicion that the property searched contains controlled substances, it satisfies [state constitutional] requirements[.]" *Id.* at 717.

See also *Pooley v. State*, 705 *P*.2d 1293, 1310-11 (Alaska App. 1985) (canine sniff is a "search" within the meaning of the Alaska Constitution, but its limited nature justifies its employment on the basis of a reasonable suspicion); *People v. Boylan*, 854 *P*.2d 807 (Colo. 1993) (use of a drug-sniffing dog to determine the contents of a package or area in which a reasonable expectation of privacy exists is a search under Article II, section 7, of the Colorado Constitution; such a sniff, however, need only be justified by a reasonable suspicion, rather than probable cause); *People v. Dunn*, 77 *N.Y*.2d 19, 564 *N.E*.2d 1054 (1990) (While the use of "canine cannabis connoisseurs" does not implicate the protections of the Fourth Amendment, Article I, Section 12 of the New York Constitution "requires that the police have at least a reasonable suspicion that a residence contains illicit contraband before this investigative technique may be employed"; "the use of the trained canine outside defendant's apartment constituted a search" within the meaning of the state constitution); *Commonwealth v. Johnston*, 530 *A*.2d 74, 79-80 (Pa. 1987) (canine sniff is a "search" within the meaning of the Pennsylvania Constitution, but to employ the use of a trained canine, the police need only possess a reasonable and articulable suspicion that drugs may be present in the *place* they seek to test); *Commonwealth v. Martin*, 626 *A*.2d 556, 560 (Pa. 1993) (When the canine sniff is directed to a *person*, "police must have probable cause to believe that a canine search of [the suspect] will produce contraband or evidence of crime.").

2. *Reasonable suspicion permits a brief detention, but not a search, of property.* In *Smith v. Ohio*, 494 *U.S.* 541, 110 *S.Ct.* 1288 (1990), defendant was approached by two plain-clothes officers of the Ashland, Ohio, Police Department on a June evening as he and an associate exited a private residence and entered the parking lot of a YMCA. The officers were driving an unmarked police vehicle. According to the officers, defendant was "gingerly" carrying a brown paper grocery bag with the words "Kash 'n Karry" and "Loaded with Low Prices" printed on the outside. Officer Thomas alighted from the vehicle and, without identifying himself, asked defendant to "come here a minute." Defendant did not respond and kept walking. Immediately thereafter, Officer Thomas walked closer to defendant and identified himself as a police officer; defendant responded by throwing the grocery bag he was carrying onto the hood of his car and turned to face Thomas. When Officer Thomas asked defendant what was in the bag, defendant did not respond. The officer then overcame defendant's attempt to protect the bag, pushed defendant's hand away and opened it. Inside, the officer found an assortment of drug paraphernalia. This discovery formed the basis for defendant's arrest. Significantly, at no time during the course of the proceedings which followed, did the State contend that the officer's reaching for the bag involved a self-protective action necessary for the officer's safety.

Finding the search of defendant's property violative of the Fourth and Fourteenth Amendments, the Court explained:

> Although the Fourth Amendment may permit the detention for a brief period of property on the basis of only "reasonable, articulable suspicion" that it contains contraband or evidence of criminal activity, *United States v. Place*, * * * it proscribes—except in certain well-defined circumstances—the search of that property unless accomplished pursuant to a judicial warrant issued upon probable cause. * * * That guarantee protects alike the "traveler who carries a toothbrush and a few articles of clothing in a paper bag" and "the sophisticated executive with the locked attache case."

Smith, 110 *S.Ct.* at 1289 (quoting *United States v. Ross*, 456 *U.S.* 798, 822, 102 *S.Ct.* 2157, 2171 (1982)).

UNITED STATES v. DIAZ
United States Court of Appeals
25 *F.*3d 392 (6th Cir. 1994)

QUESTION: May the police rely on a trained and certified narcotics detection dog as probable cause for a search ?

ANSWER: YES. "[T]he police properly may rely on a trained and certified dog as probable cause for a search." *Id.* at 393. "A positive indication by a properly-trained dog is sufficient to establish probable cause for the presence of a controlled substance." *Id.* at 393-94. If, however, a positive dog reaction is to support a determination of probable cause, "the training and reliability of the dog must be established." *Id.* at 394.

RATIONALE: Acting on information received from a suspected drug courier at the Detroit airport, drug agents located Diaz's car at the Colonial Motel in Taylor, Michigan. Wayne County Deputy Sheriff Kris Dennard responded to the motel's parking lot with her partner, "Dingo," a narcotics detection dog. Dingo "alerted" on the car, and a subsequent search uncovered one hundred pounds of marijuana located in the car's trunk.

In the appeal following his unsuccessful motion to suppress, Diaz contended that "the government failed to establish the dog's training and reliability," and thus the agents lacked probable cause to search the car. *The United States Court of Appeals for the Sixth Circuit disagreed.*

"A positive indication by a properly-trained dog is sufficient to establish probable cause for the presence of a controlled substance." *Id.* at 393-94. In this case, Diaz does not challenge the proposition that a narcotics detection dog's alert can establish probable cause, but challenges the training and reliability of the drug detection dog, Dingo.

"For a positive dog reaction to support a determination of probable cause, the training and reliability of the dog must be established." *Id.* at 394. Because the courts "have not definitively addressed the issue of the quality or quantity of evidence necessary to establish a drug detection dog's training and reliability[,]" this court looked to "analogous principles of evidence law for guidance on this issue." *Id.*

> As with evidence generally, trial judges have broad discretion in determining the admissibility of expert evidence. * * * Similarly, an expert's qualification is a question that lies within the trial judge's discretion. * * * The court considers the proffered expert's education and experience in determining if he is qualified. * * * Formal education is not always necessary to qualify an expert; practical skill and experience may suffice. [Above all,] "the expert's knowledge of the subject matter [must be] such that his opinion will likely assist the trier of fact in arriving at the truth." * * * When an expert has been qualified, other evidence, including the testimony of other experts, that contradicts or undermines the testimony of the expert affects that expert's credibility, not his qualifications to testify.

Id. [Citations omitted.]

Those principles, found the court, are "useful guides in evaluating the training and reliability of a drug detection dog for the purpose of determining if probable cause exists based on the results of the dog's sniff." *Id.*

> When the evidence presented, whether testimony from the dog's trainer or records of the dog's training, establishes that the dog is generally certified as a drug detection dog, any other evidence, including the testimony of other experts, that may detract from the reliability of the dog's performance properly goes to the "credibility" of the dog. Lack of additional evidence, such as documentation of the exact course of training, similarly would affect the dog's reliability. As with the admissibility of evidence generally, the admissibility of evidence regarding a dog's training and reliability is committed to the trial court's sound discretion.

Id.

At the hearing on Diaz's motion to suppress, Deputy Sheriff Dennard, Dingo's trainer and handler, testified that

> she and Dingo successfully attended an eight-week training school in which both learned techniques for the detection of controlled substances, including marijuana, cocaine, and heroin; that as part of the training, Dingo was subjected to "live" search tests (in which drugs were present) and "dead" search tests (in which drugs were not present, but plastic bags and live animals sometimes were); that to gain certification, Dingo was required to successfully "indicate" narcotics on fourteen "live" targets; that Dingo would "indi-

cate" by barking, biting, and scratching, but occasionally would "alert" by coming to a standstill in order to scent more intently; that Dingo was certified; that she and Dingo have passed recertification tests every year since their original training in 1989; that she and Dingo have had occasion to search for the presence of drug odors on approximately 1500 occasions; that on at least one occasion, Dingo indicated the presence of illegal substances but none was found, although there was evidence that drugs had been present among the items to which Dingo had positively responded; that she ran Dingo around a test car before scenting Diaz's car to avoid unduly suggesting to the dog a specific place to indicate; and that Dingo indicated on Diaz's car but not on the test car. The district court found Dennard's testimony to be credible.

Id. at 394-95.

Diaz presented the testimony of a former police officer who trains drug detection dogs and their handlers and who has testified on a number of occasions regarding the reliability of dog sniffs. This "expert" relied on defense counsel's description of Dennard's testimony. "He never visited Dingo's school, never spoke with Dingo's trainer or with Dennard, and had never seen Dingo in action." *Id.* at 395. Diaz's expert testified that "barking and biting may indicate a dog's frustration over not detecting any drug odors; that Dingo's reliability was compromised by [according to this expert's knowledge of Dingo's training] failing to be trained on 'dead' targets; and that, because Dennard knew which car was suspected, she may have unconsciously cued Dingo, and thus Dingo's indication might have been tainted." *Id.*

Diaz therefore contended that the finding by the court below "that Dingo was a reliable drug detection dog was clearly erroneous * * *." *Id.* Diaz argued that "the government could not establish Dingo's reliability because Dennard failed to bring the dog's training and performance records to court and so was unable to answer precisely how many searches Dingo had done and how many times drugs were or were not discovered when Dingo indicated." *Id.* He further contended that "the search was unreliable because of the possibility * * * of unconscious cuing by Dennard. Finally, Diaz argue[d] that Dennard and Dingo were improperly trained, as evidenced by Dennard's taking Dingo's barking and biting as a positive indication when [his expert] says it may mean frustration at the failure to detect odors and by Dennard's failure to define 'alert' and 'dead target' in the same manner as [his expert]." *Id.* The court found Diaz's contentions unpersuasive.

> Dennard testified as to her and Dingo's training, certification, and experience. The district judge heard the testimony and made a credibility determination: Dennard was believable. Her testimony supports a finding that Dingo was trained and reliable. After reviewing the testimony, we are not left with a definite and firm conviction that a mistake has been made.

Furthermore, [the defense expert's] objections simply appear unpersuasive. The fact that [he] is a former police officer and now a drug detection trainer does not detract from Dennard's qualifications. As to the issue of false positive indications, Dennard admitted that there had been times when Dingo had alerted yet no drugs were found. She then described one such instance at an airport search. She explained that although there were no drugs present, the owner of the suitcase on which Dingo had alerted admitted that she had been smoking "weed" all weekend and that the scent could have remained in her clothing found in the suitcase. Diaz infers from this that there had been false positive indications and that therefore Dingo was not reliable. [This court disagrees. B]ased on Dennard's testimony, Dingo was reliable and the single incident described did not detract from this reliability. *In any event, a very low percentage of false positives is not necessarily fatal to a finding that a drug detection dog is properly trained and certified.* * * *

Regarding the failure to prove Dingo's training and reliability with training and performance records, this court has indicated that testimony is sufficient to establish a dog's reliability in order to support a valid sniff. * * * While training and performance documentation would be useful in evaluating a dog's reliability, here the testimony of Dennard, Dingo's handler, sufficiently established the dog's reliability.

United States v. Trayer, 898 *F*.2d 805, 809 (D.C.Cir. * * * 1990), noted that "less than scrupulously neutral procedures, which create at least the possibility of unconscious 'cuing,' may well jeopardize the reliability of dog sniffs," but upheld the district court's determination that cuing had in fact not occurred. Here, similarly, although there was a possibility of unconscious cuing because Dennard knew which was the suspected car, the district court found that Dennard had not done anything differently between the sniffs of the test car and the suspected car and thus the chance of cuing was reduced. * * *

Finally, Dennard did define "alert" and testified that Dingo was in fact trained with "dead targets," although she did not use term "dead target." She also explained that Dingo was trained to bark, bite, and scratch when he indicated. In any event, she testified that, on this search, Dingo indicated by scratching alone. This supports the district judge's finding that Dingo was not frustrated as Diaz contends, but, instead, reliable.

Id. at 395-96. [Emphasis added.]

Accordingly, this court accepted the findings of the court below that "Dingo was trained and reliable." *Id.* at 396. "Therefore, there was probable cause to search Diaz's car, because a valid dog sniff indicated the presence of a controlled substance." *Id.*

See also United States v. Dovali-Avila, 895 *F.*2d 206, 207 (5th Cir. 1990) (a "dog alert" is sufficient to create probable cause to conduct a warrantless vehicle search).

ILLINOIS v. CABALLES
Supreme Court of the United States
543 *U.S.* 404, 125 *S.Ct.* 834 (2005)

QUESTION: Does the Fourth Amendment require a reasonable, articulable suspicion to justify using a drug-detection dog to sniff a vehicle during a legitimate traffic stop ?

ANSWER: NO. A lawful traffic stop does not become an unlawful seizure solely as a result of a canine sniff. "A dog sniff conducted during a [] lawful traffic stop that reveals no information other than the location of a substance that no individual has any right to possess does not violate the Fourth Amendment." *Id.* at 838.

RATIONALE: Illinois State Trooper Daniel Gillette stopped defendant, Roy Caballes, for speeding on an interstate highway. When Gillette called in the stop, a second trooper, Craig Graham, a member of the state's Drug Interdiction Team, overheard the transmission and immediately headed for the scene with his narcotics-detection dog. Upon Graham's arrival, defendant's car was on the shoulder of the road and defendant was sitting in Trooper Gillette's patrol car. As Gillette wrote out a warning for the motor vehicle violation, Trooper Graham walked his dog around defendant's car. The dog alerted at the trunk. Based on that alert, the officers searched the trunk, found marijuana, and placed defendant under arrest. The entire incident lasted less than 10 minutes.

Finding the use of the drug-detection dog lawful, the Court preliminarily noted that the initial traffic stop was constitutional based on the officer's observation of defendant speeding. Nonetheless, "a seizure that is lawful at its inception can violate the Fourth Amendment if its manner of execution unreasonably infringes interests protected by the Constitution." *Id.* at 837. A motor vehicle stop that is justified solely by the interest in issuing a warning or a ticket to the driver can become an unlawful seizure if it is prolonged beyond the time reasonably required to complete that mission. Thus, the use of a drug-detection dog during an "unreasonably prolonged traffic stop" may lead to the suppression of evidence if the dog sniff is conducted while the motorist is being unlawfully detained.

In this case, a careful review of the details of Trooper Gillette's conversations with defendant and the precise timing of his radio transmissions to the dispatcher revealed that the duration of the motor vehicle stop was not unreasonably prolonged. Rather, the duration of the stop "was entirely justified by the traffic offense and the ordinary inquiries incident to such a stop." *Id.*

In the proceedings below, the Illinois Supreme Court held that the initially lawful traffic stop became an unlawful seizure solely as a result of the canine sniff. That court determined that the use of the dog converted the police-citizen encounter from a lawful traffic stop into a drug investigation, and because the shift in purpose was not supported by any reasonable suspicion that defendant possessed narcotics, it was unlawful. *The United States Supreme Court disagreed.*

Speaking for the Court, Justice Stevens said:

> In our view, conducting a dog sniff would not change the character of a traffic stop that is lawful at its inception and otherwise executed in a reasonable manner, unless the dog sniff itself infringed [defendant's] constitutionally protected interest in privacy. Our cases hold that it did not.

Id.

In *United States v. Place*, 462 *U.S.* 696, 103 *S.Ct.* 2637 (1983), the Court "treated a canine sniff by a well-trained narcotics-detection dog as '*sui generis*' because it 'discloses only the presence or absence of narcotics, a contraband item.'" *Caballes* at 838. [Citation omitted.] And here, as found by the trial judge, "the dog sniff was sufficiently reliable to establish probable cause to conduct a full-blown search of the trunk." *Id.*

"Accordingly, the use of a well-trained narcotics-detection dog—one that 'does not expose non-contraband items that otherwise would remain hidden from public view,' * * * —during a lawful traffic stop, generally does not implicate legitimate privacy interests. In this case, the dog sniff was performed on the exterior of [defendant's] car while he was lawfully seized for a traffic violation. Any intrusion on [his] privacy expectations does not rise to the level of a constitutionally cognizable infringement." *Id.* [Citation omitted.]

The Court held, therefore, that "[a] dog sniff conducted during a [] lawful traffic stop that reveals no information other than the location of a substance that no individual has any right to possess does not violate the Fourth Amendment." *Id.*

NOTE

1. *Lawfully in the "sniffing" area.* Naturally, once a narcotics-detection dog arrives at the scene of the investigation, officers may not permit the dog to intrude into private areas in order to effectuate the "sniff." Stated another way, officers may not violate the Fourth Amendment by allowing the dog to enter a particular vantage point which itself harbors Fourth Amendment protection, and thereafter direct the canine to conduct the "sniff." *See United States v. Ludwig*, 10 *F.*3d 1523, 1527 n.1 (10th Cir. 1993) ("Of course, the government agent may not unlawfully enter an area in order to conduct such a dog sniff. The physical entry may intrude on a legitimate expectation of privacy. This requires separate analysis * * *."). *Cf. Horton v. California*, 496 *U.S.* 128, 110 *S.Ct.* 2301, 2309 (1990) (an officer's access to an

item or place must be lawful); *Texas v. Brown,* 460 *U.S.* 730, 737, 103 *S.Ct.* 1535, 1540 (1983) (the officer's "initial intrusion"—which permits a first-hand perception of the property in question—must be lawful); *United States v. Curran,* 498 *F.*2d 30, 33 (9th Cir. 1974) (before an officer may rely on his or her sense of smell for probable cause, the officer would have to justify his or her presence at the place from which the odor could be plainly detected).

2. *Drug detection versus accelerant detection. See State v. Buller,* 517 *N.W.*2d 711 (Iowa 1994), where the court noted the existence of two types of cases involving police dogs. "The first involves the use of dogs to search for hidden drugs and explosives. * * * In these cases, the evidence was used to establish probable cause for a search and seizure, but does not speak directly to the guilt or innocence of the party." *Id.* at 712. "The second line of cases deals with testimony concerning the tracking ability of dogs and the use of that testimony to identify a suspect." *Id.*

Here in *Buller,* following a fire in his apartment, the defendant was charged with, and convicted of first-degree arson. In this appeal, he argued that it was error to admit testimony describing the dog's actions that indicated that it detected the scent of a fire accelerant. This evidence was offered to show that the fire was cause by arson.

Finding the testimony proper, the court explained:

> Dog tracking evidence, like accelerant detection, is evidence of a defendant's ultimate guilt. Drug and explosive detection evidence is almost exclusively used to analyze probable cause in the context of a search and seizure.

Id. At the time of this court decision, a 32-state majority had "taken the view that evidence of trailing by dogs of one charged with a criminal offense is admissible to prove identity in a criminal prosecution, provided the proper foundation is laid." *Id.* at 713 (citing cases).

The court concluded that the evidence in this case qualified as expert testimony and was admissible under the rules of evidence.

> Evidence of the reaction at a fire scene of a dog trained in accelerant detection is a type of specialized information that will assist [the jury]. Accelerant detection by a trained dog is probative in arson cases in that it provides direct evidence that a crime has been committed.

Id.

The final aspect of the court's decision focused on the accelerant detection dog's training and experience, noting that a proper foundation would include: "(1) the dog handler's expertise; (2) the dog's training; and (3) the general accuracy of the dog's reaction during investigations." *Id.* at 714.

3. *The failure to alert.* The fact that a narcotics detection dog does not alert to a particular item does not necessarily mean that the item

is free of narcotics. For example, in *United States v. Frost*, 999 *F*.2d 737 (3rd Cir. 1993), the police developed probable cause to believe that Frost's suitcase contained illicit drugs. The officers summoned a narcotics detection dog for the purpose of subjecting the suitcase to the K-9's sniff. The dog was exposed to, but did not alert to the suitcase. Subsequently, a search warrant was obtained and the suitcase was found to contain ten one-kilogram packages of cocaine. "Each package was sealed in a plastic bag, covered with tape, sealed in another plastic bag, wrapped in a layer of aluminum foil and a layer of duct tape, smeared with axle grease, and wrapped in yet another layer of plastic wrap and duct tape." *Id.* at 739.

At defendant's suppression hearing, one of the officers testified that in his experience, "drug couriers often mask the scent of drugs by packaging the drugs in materials such as coffee or pepper or, as in this case, axle grease." *Id.* at 743. Relying heavily on this testimony, the Court of Appeals concluded that the probable cause—obtained prior to the employment of the narcotics detection dog—did not dissolve merely because the dog did not alert to the suitcase.

> When one includes both the fact that the drug sniffing dog did not alert to the suitcase and the fact that drug couriers often mask the scent of drugs in suitcases so that a drug sniffing dog will not alert, the failure to alert to the suitcase is not inconsistent with the substantial probative thrust of information which [the officers had prior to the use of the dog]. Probable cause thus remains[.]

Id. at 744.

CHAPTER 9

THE INDEPENDENT SOURCE DOCTRINE AND THE INEVITABLE DISCOVERY RULE

Section
9.1   Cases and materials

§9.1. Cases and materials.

NIX v. WILLIAMS
Supreme Court of the United States
467 U.S. 431, 104 S.Ct. 2501 (1984)

QUESTION: When law enforcement officers violate a defendant's Sixth Amendment right to counsel by eliciting incriminating statements from him in his counsel's absence, must the fruits of such violation be suppressed when it can be shown that the evidence would have inevitably or ultimately been discovered even if the incriminating statements had not been elicited ?

ANSWER: NO. "If the prosecution can establish by a preponderance of the evidence* that the information ultimately or inevitably would have been discovered by lawful means, * * * that * * * evidence should be received." *Id.* at 2509.

RATIONALE: Defendant Williams, a recent escapee from a mental hospital, abducted and murdered a 10-year-old girl. Acting on the advice of his lawyer, Williams turned himself in to the Davenport, Iowa, police. The abduction took place in Des Moines, Iowa, and the Des Moines police informed Williams' lawyer that they would pick him up in Davenport and return him to Des Moines without questioning him. Two Des Moines police detectives then drove to Davenport, took the defendant into custody, and started the drive back to Des Moines.

During the return trip, one of the detectives began conversation by saying:

> I want to give you something to think about while we're traveling down the road. . . . They are predicting several inches of snow for tonight, and I feel that you yourself are the only person that knows where this little girl's body is . . . and if you get a snow on top of it you yourself may be unable to find it. And since we will be going right past the area [where the body is] on the way into Des Moines, I feel that we could stop and locate the body, that the parents of this little girl should be entitled to a Christian burial for the little girl

---

* *See* §1.1; Fig. 1.1.

679

who was snatched away from them on Christmas [E]ve and murdered. . . . [A]fter a snow storm [we may not be] able to find it at all.

Id. at 2505.

As they approached Mitchellville, a town between Davenport and Des Moines, Williams offered to direct the detectives to the child's body.

Meanwhile, a large scale search party consisting of two hundred volunteers had been combing the area. The detectives called off the search when they believed Williams would lead them to the little girl's body. The child's body was found in a ditch beside a gravel road in Polk County about two miles south of Interstate 80. The location was essentially within the area to be searched. In fact, the body was found approximately two and one half miles from where the search had stopped.

At the defendant's first set of Iowa murder proceedings, he contended that his Sixth Amendment right to counsel had been violated and the Exclusionary Rule (attaching to the Sixth Amendment) should bar the use of the evidence so obtained. Nonetheless, Williams was found guilty of first-degree murder.

Upon first review by the United States Supreme Court, it was held that the defendant's right to counsel was, in fact, violated. The police detective had obtained incriminatory statements from the defendant "by what was viewed as interrogation in violation of his right to counsel." *Id.* at 2506. However, the Court sent the case back to the Iowa court with directions to see if "evidence of the body's location and condition might well be admissible on the theory that the body would have been discovered in any event, even had incriminating statements not been elicited from Williams." *Id.* at 2506 (quoting from its first review of this case, *Brewer v. Williams*, 430 *U.S.* 387, 407 n.12, 97 *S.Ct.* 1232, 1243 n.12 (1977)).

In the second set of court proceedings, Williams was again found guilty of first-degree murder. Here, the prosecution was not permitted to use evidence of Williams' statements which led to the recovery of the body, but it was permitted to present evidence as to the condition of the body as it was found, articles and photos of the child's clothing, and medical examiner's findings. However, upon appeal, the higher courts misapplied the standard for assessing the "ultimate or inevitable discovery exception to the Exclusionary Rule." *Nix* at 2510.

The United States Supreme Court again granted *certiorari* and held that "[if] the prosecution can establish by a preponderance of the evidence that the information ultimately would have been discovered by lawful means—here the volunteers' search—then the deterrence rationale [of the Exclusionary Rule] has so little basis that the evidence should be received." *Id.* at 2509.

When the government proves that "evidence would have been obtained inevitably and, therefore would have been admitted regardless of any overreaching by the police, there is no rational basis to keep that evidence from the jury[.]" *Id.* at 2511.

Thus, when "the evidence in question would inevitably have been discovered without reference to the police error or misconduct * * * the evidence is admissible." *Id.*

NOTE

1. *See also United States v. Whitehorn*, 829 *F*.2d 1225 (2nd Cir. 1987), where the court emphasized that the inevitable discovery rule, as an "exception to the exclusionary rule," allows the introduction of evidence initially detected as the result of unlawful government conduct "so long as the 'prosecution can establish by a preponderance of the evidence that the information ultimately or inevitably would have been discovered by lawful means.'" *Id.* at 1230 (quoting *Nix* at 444, 104 *S.Ct.* at 2509). This exception, according to the *Whitehorn* court, is "not a revolutionary concept but rather the logical extension of another, the independent source doctrine." *Id.* Both exceptions are considered necessary to ensure that " 'the interest of society in deterring unlawful police conduct and the public interest in having juries receive all probative evidence of a crime are properly balanced by putting the police in the same, not a *worse*, position that they would have been in if no police error or misconduct had occurred.' " *Id.* (quoting *Nix* at 443, 104 *S.Ct.* at 2509) (emphasis in original).

2. *See United States v. Rahman*, 189 *F*.3d 88 (2nd Cir. 1999), where the court held that forged passports were admissible, though found during an unlawful frisk for weapons, where the law enforcement agents already had probable cause to arrest the defendant for his assaults on them, and such arrest would have inevitably led to the discovery of the passports in defendant's pockets as a result of a search incident to arrest.

3. *Burden of proof.* Under federal law, the Government bears the burden of establishing by *the preponderance of the evidence* that (1) proper, normal, and specific investigatory procedures would have been pursued in order to complete the investigation in the particular case, regardless of the initial, improper action; (2) under all the circumstances, the pursuit of those procedures would have inevitably resulted in the discovery of the evidence in question; and (3) the discovery of the evidence through the use of such procedures would have occurred wholly independently of the discovery of such evidence by the initial, improper means.

State officers are reminded that state courts are free in this area of the law, as in other areas of criminal procedure, to rely on their own state constitutions to provide increased protection to the personal liberties of their citizens. The burden of proof, therefore, under certain state law, may be greater than a preponderance of the evidence. The next New Jersey case is illustrative.

MURRAY v. UNITED STATES
Supreme Court of the United States
487 U.S. 533, 108 S.Ct. 2529 (1988)

QUESTION: Will a police officer's unlawful entry upon private premises require suppression of evidence subsequently discovered at those premises pursuant to an independently obtained search warrant issued on the basis of information wholly unconnected with the prior illegal entry ?

ANSWER: NO. "[T]he 'independent source' exception to the exclusionary rule may justify admitting evidence discovered during an illegal warrantless search that is later 'rediscovered' * * * during a search pursuant to a warrant obtained * * * after the illegal search" so long as "the warrantless entry in no way contributed * * * either to the issuance of [the] warrant or to the discovery of the evidence during the lawful search that occurred pursuant to the warrant." *Id.* at 2536.

RATIONALE: During the course of a narcotics investigation, federal law enforcement agents developed probable cause to believe that a significant quantity of marijuana was located in a particular warehouse in South Boston. Prior to obtaining a search warrant, several of the agents forcibly entered the warehouse and discovered "in plain view numerous burlap-wrapped bales that were later found to contain marijuana. They left without disturbing the bales, kept the warehouse under surveillance, and did not reenter it until they had a search warrant. In applying for the warrant, the agents did not mention the prior entry, and did not rely on any observations made during that entry. When the warrant was issued— * * * approximately eight hours after initial entry—the agents immediately reentered the warehouse and seized 270 bales of marijuana and notebooks listing customers for whom the bales were destined." *Id.* at 2532.

In this appeal, defendants argue "that the warrant was invalid because the agents did not inform the magistrate about their prior warrantless entry, and that the warrant was tainted by that entry." *Id.* *The United States Supreme Court, per Justice Scalia, disagreed.*

As a general rule, "[t]he exclusionary rule prohibits introduction into evidence of tangible materials seized during an unlawful search, * * * and testimony concerning knowledge acquired during an unlawful search[.] * * * Beyond that, the exclusionary rule also prohibits the introduction of derivative evidence, both tangible and testimonial, that is the product of the primary evidence, or that is otherwise acquired as an indirect result of the unlawful search, up to the point at which the connection with the unlawful search becomes 'so attenuated as to dissipate the taint.' " *Id.* at 2532-2533. [Citations omitted.]

As the exclusionary rule developed in our law, there also developed a legal principle which has come to be known as the "independent source" doctrine. This "doctrine," which has been applied to evidence acquired not only through Fourth Amendment violations but also through Fifth and Sixth Amendment violations, has * * * been described as follows:

[T]he interest of society in deterring unlawful police conduct and the public interest in having juries receive all probative evidence of a crime are properly balanced by putting the police in the same, not a *worse*, position that they would have been in if no police error or misconduct had occurred. ... When the challenged evidence has an independent source, exclusion of such evidence would put the police in a worse position than they would have been in absent any error or violation.

Id. at 2533 (quoting *Nix v. Williams,* 467 *U.S.* 431, 443, 104 *S.Ct.* 2501, 2509 (1984)). [Emphasis in original.]

Defendants acknowledge the import of the independent source doctrine but contend that its scope is limited "to evidence obtained for the first time during an independent lawful search. The Government argues that it applies also to evidence initially discovered during, or as a consequence of, an unlawful search, but later obtained independently from activities untainted by the initial illegality[; and this view, according to the Court] has better support in both precedent and policy." *Id.* at 2533.

" 'In the classic independent source situation, information which is received through an illegal source is considered to be cleanly obtained when it arrives through an independent source.' " *Id.* at 2534. Thus, in *Nix v. Williams, supra,* incriminating statements obtained in violation of defendant's right to counsel which had led police to the victim's body did not automatically cause the exclusion of evidence concerning the body. There, it was held that "evidence concerning the body was nonetheless admissible because a search had been under way which would have discovered the body, had it not been called off because of the discovery produced by the unlawfully obtained statements." *Id.* In this respect, the " 'inevitable discovery' doctrine obviously assumes the validity of the independent source doctrine as applied to evidence initially acquired unlawfully. * * * [Therefore, t]he inevitable discovery doctrine, with its distinct requirements, is in reality an extrapolation from the independent source doctrine: *Since* the tainted evidence would be admissible if in fact discovered through an independent source, it should be admissible if it inevitably would have been discovered." *Id.*

In this case, "[k]nowledge that the marijuana was in the warehouse was assuredly acquired at the time of the unlawful entry. But it was also acquired at the time of entry pursuant to the warrant, and if the later acquisition was not the result of the earlier entry there is no reason why the independent source doctrine should not apply. Invoking the exclusionary rule would put the police (and society) not in the *same* position they would have occupied if no violation occurred, but in a *worse* one." *Id.* at 2535. [Emphasis added.]

Accordingly, "so long as a later, lawful [search and] seizure is genuinely independent of an earlier, tainted one," the "independent source" doctrine may permit the introduction of the evidence acquired pursuant to the lawful police activity. *Id.* The case is remanded to the Court of Appeals for the First Circuit to determine whether the warrant-authorized search of the warehouse was, in fact, a genuinely independent source of the information and tangible evidence here at issue.

NOTE

At one point in the Court's opinion in *Murray, supra*, defendants argued that the Court's ruling "will remove all deterrence to, and indeed positively encourage unlawful police searches, * * * [that] law enforcement officers will routinely enter without a warrant to make sure that what they expect to be on the premises is in fact there. If it is not, they will have spared themselves the time and trouble of getting a warrant; if it is, they can get the warrant and use the evidence despite the unlawful entry." *Id.* at 2534. The Supreme Court, however, saw the incentives differently:

> An officer with probable cause sufficient to obtain a warrant would be foolish to enter the premises first in an unlawful manner. By doing so, he would risk suppression of all evidence on the premises, both seen and unseen, since his action would add to the normal burden of convincing a magistrate that there is probable cause the much more onerous burden of convincing a trial court that no information gained from the illegal entry affected either the law enforcement officer's decision to seek a warrant or the magistrate's decision to grant it. * * * Nor would the officer *without* sufficient probable cause to obtain a search warrant have any added incentive to conduct an unlawful entry, since whatever he finds cannot be used to establish probable cause before a magistrate.

Id.

CHAPTER 10

GOOD FAITH AND THE EXCLUSIONARY RULE

Section
10.1   Cases and materials

§10.1. Cases and materials.

UNITED STATES v. LEON
Supreme Court of the United States
468 *U.S.* 897, 104 *S.Ct.* 3405 (1984)

QUESTION: When a police officer acts in reasonable reliance on a search warrant issued by a detached and neutral magistrate or judge, and that warrant is ultimately found to be defective, does the Fourth Amendment Exclusionary Rule bar the use of the officer's evidence so obtained ?

ANSWER: NO. A search warrant subsequently found to be defective will not act as a bar to the admissibility of evidence obtained from the execution of such warrant if the court finds that the officer was acting with objective good faith in reasonable reliance on the search warrant issued by a detached and neutral magistrate.

RATIONALE: In creating a "good faith" exception to the exclusionary rule, the Court re-examined the competing goals of, on the one hand, deterring police misconduct, and on the other, creating procedures under which criminal defendants are acquitted or convicted on the basis of all the evidence which tends to shed the appropriate light on the truth.

The Court concluded that the costs of excluding trustworthy evidence obtained in objective and reasonable reliance upon a search warrant issued by a detached and neutral magistrate which is subsequently found to be defective far outweighs the benefits to be achieved from such exclusion. Such costs include:

1. An unacceptable impediment to the truth-finding functions of the judge and jury;

2. Unnecessary interference with the Criminal Justice System which would result in some guilty defendants going free while others receive reduced sentences;

3. A particular cost where police officers have acted in objective good faith or their mistakes have been so relatively minor, that the magnitude of the benefit conferred upon such guilty defendants offends basic concepts of the Criminal Justice System; and

4. Arbitrary and indiscriminate applications of the Exclusionary Rule giving rise to disrespect for the law and the judicial administration of justice.

Id. at 3428.

The basic purpose of the Exclusionary Rule is to deter police misconduct, not to punish the errors of judges and magistrates. It is neither intended nor able to cure the invasion of the defendant's rights which he has suffered. The rule thus operates as a judicially drafted remedy designed to safeguard, through its deterrent effect on the police, Fourth Amendment rights generally rather than as a personal constitutional right of the person so affected.

Therefore, when a police officer, acting in objective good faith, has obtained a search warrant from a judge and has acted within its scope, there is no police misconduct, and thus, nothing to deter. *Id.* at 3431. Penalizing the police officer for the judge's error cannot logically contribute to the deterrence of Fourth Amendment violations. *Id.*

Finally, it is important to note that the police officer's reliance on the judge's probable-cause determination and on the technical sufficiency of the search warrant he issues *must be objectively reasonable.* In other words, if the officer's affidavit for the search warrant contains assertions which are less than truthful, the evidence obtained by the execution of the resulting warrant will ultimately be suppressed.

MASSACHUSETTS v. SHEPPARD
Supreme Court of the United States
468 *U.S.* 981, 104 *S.Ct.* 3424 (1984)

QUESTION: Should the Exclusionary Rule bar the admission of evidence in court when law enforcement officers obtain that evidence by acting in objectively reasonable reliance on a warrant issued by a detached and neutral magistrate which is later found to be invalid because of a technical error in the warrant's form ?

ANSWER: NO. The Exclusionary Rule should not serve as a bar to the admissibility of evidence seized by law enforcement officers pursuant to a warrant later found to be invalid "because of a technical error on the part of the issuing judge." *Id.* at 3426.

RATIONALE: This case was decided the same day as *United States v. Leon*, 468 *U.S.* 897, 104 *S.Ct.* 3405 (1984). *Leon* had established a "good faith" exception to the Exclusionary Rule when officers seize evidence pursuant to a warrant which is subsequently found to be invalid because of an underlying deficiency in probable cause.

Here, in *Sheppard*, the defendant challenged the officer's warrant which appeared to be defective in form. It seems that the officer could not find a proper affidavit and search warrant form. It was Sunday and the necessary offices which contained such forms were closed. The officer then proceeded to use a warrant form from another district. The form was a standard "controlled substances" search warrant. Since the officer's probable cause led him to believe that the premises to be searched contained evidence of a recent homicide, he had to alter the form to properly depict the object of his search.

The officer presented the affidavit to the district attorney's assistants who concluded that the probable cause was sufficient. The officer then presented the affidavit and warrant form to a judge and explained the problem he had and the alterations he made. After failing to find a better form, the judge informed the officer that he would make any necessary changes in form so as to provide a proper search warrant.

Changes were made, the warrant was signed, and the officer effected the search and seized several incriminating pieces of evidence. The defendant was charged with first degree murder.

The Massachusetts courts suppressed the evidence because "the warrant failed to conform to the commands of the Fourth Amendment because it did not particularly describe the items to be seized." *Id.* at 3428.

The United States Supreme Court disagreed and reversed.

Since the Court in *Leon* established that "the Exclusionary Rule should not be applied when the officer conducting the search acted in objectively reasonable reliance on a warrant issued by a detached and neutral magistrate that is subsequently found to be invalid", *Sheppard* at 3428, the main question in this case "is whether there was an objectively reasonable basis for the officer's mistaken belief." *Id.* at 3428, 3429.

"The officers in this case took every step that could reasonably be expected of them." *Id.* at 3429. If the judge told the officer that the warrant form was invalid, the officer must accept that judgment. Then again, if the judge told the officer (as he did) that the warrant form was acceptable, there is no reason for the officer not to accept that judgment. "[T]he [E]xclusionary [R]ule was adopted to deter unlawful searches by police, not to punish the errors of magistrates and judges." *Id.* 3429 (quoting *Illinois v. Gates*, 462 *U.S.* 213, 103 *S.Ct.* 2317, 2345 (1983) (White, J., concurring)).

NOTE

1. The keynote to the *Leon* and *Sheppard* cases is that the officer's reliance must be objectively reasonable. If a judge issues a warrant to an officer which is later found to be defective because of blatant or outrageous misstatements of fact, that warrant will not be upheld, for the absence of good faith will be readily apparent. Good faith will be displayed when other prudent and reasonably well-trained officers, objectively viewing the warrant, could not at once say that given the underlying investigation and information received, the warrant on its face does not appear perfectly valid.

2. In earlier Sections, state officers have been reminded that state courts are free, and indeed encouraged, to rely on their own constitutions to provide greater protection to the privacy interest of their

citizens than that afforded under parallel provisions of the United States Constitution. Naturally, when a state goes beyond the federal "floor of protection," and provides more expansive individual liberties on the basis of its state constitution, law enforcement in that state is thereby counteractively restricted. Keeping this principle in mind, state officers should be aware that the "good-faith exception" to the exclusionary rule, adopted in *United States v. Leon*, and *Massachusetts v. Sheppard*, has been receiving mixed treatment at the state level.

For example, New Jersey, a state which relies heavily on its own constitution to provide its citizens enhanced individual liberties, has refused to adopt a "good-faith exception" to the exclusionary rule when the defect in the warrant is a deficiency in the underlying probable cause. *See State v. Novembrino*, 105 *N.J.* 95, 157-158 (1987) ("the good-faith exception * * * would tend to undermine the constitutionally-guaranteed standard of probable cause" found in article I, paragraph 7 of the New Jersey Constitution). When the defect in the warrant is only in its form, however, New Jersey endorses the "good-faith" exception set forth in *Massachusetts v. Sheppard*. *See generally State v. Brooks*, 201 *N.J.Super.* 10 (App.Div. 1985).

See also State v. Marsala, 216 *Conn.* 150, 151, 579 *A.2d* 58, 59 (1990) (the " 'good faith' exception to the exclusionary rule is incompatible with the constitution of Connecticut, article first, §7"); *Mason v. State*, 534 *A.2d* 242 (Del. 1987) (rejecting federal good-faith exception on statutory grounds); *State v. Guzman*, 122 *Idaho* 981, 842 *P.2d* 660 (1992) (rejecting as a matter of state constitutional law the federal good-faith exception); *Commonwealth v. Upton*, 394 *Mass.* 363, 476 *N.E.2d* 548, 554 n.5 (1985) (good-faith exception rejected on statutory grounds); *People v. Sundling*, 153 *Mich. App.* 277, 292, 395 *N.W.2d* 308 (1986), *appeal denied*, 428 *Mich.* 887 (1987) ("good faith" exception rejected on the basis of state constitutional law); *State v. Canelo*, 653 *A.2d* 1097, 1105 (N.H. 1995) ("[T]he good faith exception is incompatible with and detrimental to our citizens' strong right of privacy inherent in part I, article 19" of the New Hampshire Constitution "and the prohibition against the issuance of warrants without probable cause."); *State v. Gutierrez*, 863 *P.2d* 1052, 1053 (N.M. 1993) ("the good-faith exception is incompatible with the guarantees of the New Mexico Constitution"); *People v. Bigelow*, 66 *N.Y.2d* 417, 427, 497 *N.Y.S.2d* 630, 488 *N.E.2d* 451, 458 (1985) ("good-faith" exception not recognized under the New York Constitution); *State v. Carter*, 322 *N.C.* 709, 724, 370 *S.E.2d* 553 (1988) ("good-faith" exception rejected on basis of state constitutional law); *Commonwealth v. Edmunds*, 526 *Pa.* 374, 586 *A.2d* 887, 905-906 (1991) ("Article I, Section 8 of the Pennsylvania Constitution does not incorporate a 'good faith' exception to the exclusionary rule."); *State v. Oakes*, 157 *Vt.* 171, 598 *A.2d* 119 (1991) (*Leon* standard held incompatible with Chapter I, Article 11 of the Vermont Constitution). *See also Stringer v. State*, 491 *So.2d* 837, 841 (Miss. 1986) (Robertson, J., concurring).

In a number of states, however, the *Leon* "good-faith exception" has been endorsed. *See e.g., Jackson v. State*, 291 *Ark.* 98, 722 *S.W.2d* 831 (1987) (embracing the federal good-faith exception); *People v. Camarella*, 54 *Cal.3d* 592, 286 *Cal.Rptr.* 780, 818 *P.2d* 63 (1991) (good-faith exception endorsed and applied); *State v. Bernie*, 472 *So.*2d 1243, 1248 (Fla.App. 1985), *approved*, 524 *So.*2d 988 (Fla. 1988) (good-faith exception accepted and applied); *State v. Kingston*, 617 *So.*2d 414 (Fla.Ct.App. 1993) (applying good-faith exception under Florida constitution which expressly applies federal standards); *People v. Stewart*, 104 *Ill.*2d 463, 477, 473 *N.E.*2d 1227 (1984) (good-faith exception endorsed and applied); *Mers v. State*, 482 *N.E.*2d 778, 783 (Ind.App. 1985) (*same*); *State v. Huber*, 10 *Kan.App.*2d 560, 704 *P.*2d 1004, 1011 (1985) (*same*); *Crayton v. Commonwealth*, 846 *S.W.*2d 684 (Ky. 1992) (*same*); *State v. Shannon*, 472 *So.*2d 286, 291 (La.App.), *cert. denied*, 476 *So.*2d 349 (La. 1985) (*same*); *Connelly v. State*, 322 *Md.* 719, 589 *A.*2d 958, 966 (1991) ("applying *Leon's* objectively reasonable good faith test"); *State v. Sweeney*, 701 *S.W.*2d 420, 426 (Mo. 1985) ("good-faith" exception recognized under state law); *State v. Brown*, 708 *S.W.*2d 140, 145 (Mo. 1986) (*same*); *State v. Wilmoth*, 22 *Ohio* St.3d 251, 266-267, 490 *N.E.*2d 1236 (1986) ("good-faith" exception accepted and applied).

UNITED STATES v. BOWLING
United States Court of Appeals
900 *F.*2d 926 (6th Cir. 1990)

QUESTION: When the police learn, just as they are about to execute a search warrant, that a fruitless consent search had been conducted prior to their arrival at the target premises, will the officers' knowledge of such an event be relevant to the determination of whether they relied on the warrant in good faith ?

ANSWER: YES. "Where officers become aware after a warrant's issuance that a fruitless consent search has been conducted, the officers' knowledge of such an event is relevant to a determination of whether they relied on the warrant in good faith." *Id.* at 932. If an "initial fruitless consent search dissipates the probable cause that justified the warrant, new indicia of probable cause must exist to repeat a search of the same premises pursuant to the warrant." *Id.* Thus, an officer's good-faith belief that the warrant is valid must exist, not only at the time of its issuance but also at the time of its execution.

RATIONALE: During the course of a marijuana cultivation investigation, agents of the United States Forest Service developed probable cause to believe that additional quantities of marijuana and paraphernalia could be found in a trailer home owned by defendants, Delbert and Idell Bowling. The agents secured the assistance of the Clay County, Kentucky, Sheriff's Department in securing a search warrant.

Several Forest Service officers remaining at the site near defendants' trailer were advised that a search warrant was in the process of being procured. As the officers awaited the arrival of the warrant, one of them, Officer Dees, engaged Delbert Bowling in a conversation and advised him that a warrant to search his trailer was being obtained.

Delbert immediately advised the officer that he could search the trailer without a warrant. Officer Dees then called in over the radio and advised "someone" of Delbert's consent, and stated that "he was going to go on in and search the trailer," and that they should "bring the warrant on." *Id.* at 929.

Although it is unclear as to how thorough the consent search was, Officer Dees testified at the suppression hearing that a "very quick search" of each room of the trailer was conducted, but only the bedroom was "examined in detail." *Id.* The consent search, which lasted only about fifteen minutes, did not include the Bowlings' automobile which was located behind the trailer. No incriminating evidence was found. Significantly, the judge who was about to issue the search warrant was never apprised of the results of the consent search, and "it is disputed whether the search warrant affiant or anyone else who participated in securing the warrant was informed about the consent search[.]" *Id.*

About two hours later, several sheriff's officers and federal agents arrived at the trailer with the search warrant. As they entered the trailer, Officer Dees advised them of the "preliminary" fruitless consent search which had been conducted. The second search, conducted under the authority of the search warrant, produced a number of incriminating items, including ammunition, plant food, marijuana, and marijuana residue. The warrant also authorized a search of the automobile located behind the trailer in which the officers found a bottle of marijuana seeds.

At their suppression hearing, defendants argued that "the second search was illegal because the consent search performed a few hours before it eliminated probable cause to issue a warrant." *Id.* at 929-30. Additionally, defendants urged that "the second search of their trailer was not made in good faith reliance on the search warrant because the officers performing that search were informed of the prior consent search before the warrant was executed." *Id.* at 930-31. The government, on the other hand, argued that "the time relevant to a determination of whether the second search was made in good faith is the point at which the warrant was obtained." *Id.* at 931. "The revelation after the issuance of the warrant that a fruitless consent search had already been conducted," according to the prosecution, should "not affect the probable cause for the second search or render its execution violative of *Leon*." *Id.*

Agreeing with the Government's contention, the district court ruled that "as long as the officers who obtained the warrant were unaware at the time of the warrant's issuance that a prior consent search had been performed, the officers had a right to execute the warrant." *Id.* at 930. According to the district court, "because neither the magistrate nor the officers obtaining the warrant knew at the time of the warrant's issuance that a fruitless consent search had been conducted, bad faith cannot be inferred from the officers' execution of the warrant." *Id.* at 931. Thus, the court concluded that "the initial search had no bearing on a determination of the second search's validity." *Id. The Court of Appeals for the Sixth Circuit, however, disagreed.*

Preliminarily, the court pointed out that *Leon* stands for the proposition that

> where officers rely in an objectively reasonable fashion on a search warrant issued by a neutral magistrate that is subsequently found to be invalid, the Fourth Amendment exclusionary rule does not require suppression of the fruits of the search. * * * *Leon's* good faith inquiry "is confined to the objectively ascertainable question whether a reasonably well trained officer would have known that the search was illegal *despite the magistrate's authorization.* In making this determination, *all of the circumstances . . .* may be considered."

Bowling at 931 (quoting *Leon* at 922-23 n.23, 104 *S.Ct.* at 3420 n.23) (court's emphasis). Thus, based on *Leon*, the Sixth Circuit determined that the district court erred in two respects:

> First, in light of the language in *Leon* instructing courts to view "all of the circumstances" and to ascertain whether an officer acted in good faith "despite the magistrate's authorization," the district court misstated the law in holding that "once the [] judge issued [the warrant], the agents had a right to depend upon it under the *Leon* case." * * * Second, the district court erred by failing to consider the conduct of *all* officers involved in the search—both those who obtained the search warrant and those who remained behind and conducted a consent search with knowledge that a warrant was being obtained.

Id. at 931. [Emphasis in original.]

Respecting the first error, it is clear that "probable cause may dissipate between the time of a warrant's issuance and its execution." *Id.* Circumstances can, and often do, arise after the issuance of a search warrant, which directly affect the probable cause set forth in the supporting affidavit. Moreover, closely related to the concern regarding "continuing probable cause" is the courts' "disfavor of repeated searches of the same premises where the same set of facts constitute the probable cause for each search." *Id.* at 932.

As a result, "where an initial fruitless consent search dissipates the probable cause that justified a warrant, new indicia of probable cause must exist to repeat a search of the same premises pursuant to the warrant." *Id.* The district court was, therefore, in error when it gave primacy to the time of the warrant's issuance over the time of its execution. "The law is clear that probable cause must exist at both points in time. *Where officers become aware after a warrant's issuance that a fruitless consent search has been conducted, the officers' knowledge of such an event is relevant to a determination of whether they relied on the warrant in good faith.*" *Id.* [Emphasis added.]

Respecting the district court's second error, "[i]t is not dispositive of the good faith inquiry that the officers obtaining the warrant * * * did not know at the time of the warrant's issuance that a fruitless consent search had been performed. *Leon* counsels that we evaluate the objective reasonableness of all officers actively involved in the entire search warrant process, not merely those who obtained the search warrant." *Bowling* at 932. As the *Leon* Court noted:

> "References to 'officer' throughout this opinion should not be read too narrowly. It is necessary to consider the objective reasonableness, not only of the officers who eventually executed a warrant, but also of the officers who originally obtained it or who provided information material to the probable-cause determination."

Bowling at 932 (quoting *Leon* at 923 n.24, 104 *S.Ct.* at 3420 n.24.). In this case, however, there is more. Once the sheriff's officers and federal agents arrived at (and entered) defendants' trailer to conduct the search pursuant to the warrant, Officer Dees informed them that a "preliminary search of the trailer" had already been made under the authority of Delbert Bowling's consent. Thus, "knowledge of the prior consent search may be fairly imputed to all officers involved." *Id.* at 933.

Moreover, Officer Dees' characterization of the prior consent search to the officers and agents about to engage in the second search as " 'preliminary,' should not have constituted a license to proceed with a search whose continuing probable cause was at the very least questionable. '[I]t is the magistrate who must determine independently whether there is probable cause.' " *Id.* [Citation omitted.]

Similar to a warrantless search situation, in the absence of exigent circumstances, "officers should not rely on their own discretion, but should instead resort to a neutral magistrate, to determine whether probable cause exists." *Id. Where, as here, no emergency exists and "officers possess a warrant but are alerted to circumstances which affect the probable cause for its execution[,]" they should refrain from conducting the search "until a neutral magistrate determine[s] that probable cause continue[s] to exist." Id.* [Emphasis added.]

Significantly, notwithstanding the officers' failure in this case to resort to a magistrate for the purpose of obtaining a neutral and independent determination as to whether probable cause continued to exist at the time of the second search, the court held that the fruits of the second search need not be suppressed if it could conclude that "a neutral magistrate *would have determined that probable cause existed* to conduct a second search despite the prior fruitless consent search." *Id.* [Emphasis added.] The relevant inquiry in this respect "is whether the first search was so broad as to dissipate probable cause for the second. If it was, and if knowledge of the initial fruitless search may fairly be imputed to those officers conducting the second search, bad faith may be inferred and the evidence must be suppressed." *Id.* at 934.

Applying the above standard, the court held:

> [W]e decline to suppress the second search's fruits because we believe that even if a neutral magistrate were apprised of the prior fruitless consent search, probable cause for a second search would still have existed. Two facts sway us to this conclusion. First, although [the consent search] spanned every room and was detailed

at points, it was not overall as intricate as the search under the warrant. This is evidenced by the fact that it lasted only fifteen minutes or so. Second, a principal incriminating item, the marijuana seeds, was found in the car located behind the trailer. This car was not searched during the consent search. Thus, although we hold that police officers may not take the probable cause determination into their own hands when presented with nonexigent circumstances such as the ones in this case, the consent search here was not so broad as to dissipate probable cause or imply bad faith. We therefore affirm the denial of suppression.

Id. at 934.

ILLINOIS v. KRULL
Supreme Court of the United States
480 *U.S.* 340, 107 *S.Ct.* 1160 (1987)

QUESTION: Does the Fourth Amendment exclusionary rule apply to evidence obtained by police who act in objectively reasonable reliance upon a statute authorizing warrantless administrative searches, when that statute is subsequently found to violate the Fourth Amendment ?

ANSWER: NO. The United States Supreme Court now creates a "good-faith" exception to the Fourth Amendment's exclusionary rule "when an officer's reliance on the constitutionality of a statute is objectively reasonable, but the statute is subsequently declared unconstitutional." *Id.* at 1165, 1167.

RATIONALE: Chicago Police Detective McNally seized four automobiles from a wrecking yard—three of which were stolen and the fourth missing a VIN—and arrested the yard's operator and licensee. Illinois law at the time required licensed motor vehicle and vehicular parts sellers to permit state officials to inspect their business records "at any reasonable time during the night or day" and to allow "examination of the premises of the licensee's established place of business for the purpose of determining the accuracy of [the] required records." *Id.* at 1163 (quoting *Ill.Rev. Stat.* ch. 95 ½, para. 5-401(e) (1981)). Because the statute was later found to be unconstitutional by the Illinois Supreme Court, the Illinois trial court suppressed the automobiles seized by Detective McNally.

The United States Supreme Court granted the State's petition for *certiorari* "to consider whether a good-faith exception to the Fourth Amendment exclusionary rule applies when an officer's reliance on the constitutionality of a statute is objectively reasonable, but the statute is subsequently declared unconstitutional." *Id.* at 1165.

As a general rule, "[w]hen evidence is obtained in violation of the Fourth Amendment, the judicially developed exclusionary rule usually precludes its use in a criminal proceeding against the victim of

the illegal search and seizure." *Id.* The "prime purpose" of the exclusionary rule "is to deter unlawful police conduct and thereby effectuate the guarantee of the Fourth Amendment against unreasonable
searches and seizures." *Id.* (quoting *United States v. Calandra*, 414
U.S. 338, 347 (1974)). The rule's application "is neither intended nor
able to 'cure the invasion of the defendant's rights which he has already suffered.'" *United States v. Leon*, 468 *U.S.* 897, 906 (1984)
(quoting *Stone v. Powell*, 428 *U.S* 465, 540 (1976) (WHITE, J. dissenting)). *Krull* at 1166. Instead, the rule "operates as 'a judicially created
remedy designed to safeguard Fourth Amendment rights generally
through its deterrent effect, rather than a personal constitutional
right of the party aggrieved.'" *Krull* at 1166. [Citations omitted.]

"As with any remedial device, application of the exclusionary rule
properly has been restricted to those situations in which its remedial
purpose is effectively advanced." *Id.* Whether the rule's deterrent effect will be achieved will be determined by weighing "the likelihood of
such deterrence against the costs of withholding reliable information
from the truthseeking process." *Id.*

In *Leon*, the Court found that "a deterrent effect was particularly
absent when an officer, acting in objective good faith, obtained a
search warrant from a magistrate and acted within its scope. 'In most
such cases, there is no police illegality and thus nothing to deter.'"
Krull at 1167 (quoting *Leon* at 920-921).

As a result, the approach used in *Leon* is equally applicable here.
"The application of the exclusionary rule to suppress evidence obtained by an officer acting in objectively reasonable reliance on a statute would have as little deterrent effect on the officer's actions as
would the exclusion of evidence when an officer acts in objectively reasonable reliance on a warrant. Unless a statute is clearly unconstitutional, an officer cannot be expected to question the judgment of the
legislature that passed the law. If the statute is subsequently declared
unconstitutional, excluding evidence obtained pursuant to it prior to
such a judicial declaration will not deter future Fourth Amendment
violations by an officer who has simply fulfilled his responsibility to
enforce the statute as written." *Krull* at 1167. "'Penalizing the officer
for the (legislature's) error, rather than his own, cannot logically contribute to the deterrence of Fourth Amendment violations.'" *Id.* (para-
phrasing *Leon* at 921).

An officer's reliance upon a statute will not be objectively reasonable, however, "if, in passing the statute, the legislature wholly abandoned its responsibility to enact constitutional laws. Nor can a law enforcement officer be said to have acted in good-faith reliance upon a
statute if its provisions are such that a reasonable officer should have
known that the statute was unconstitutional." *Krull* at 1170. As emphasized in *Leon*, "the standard of reasonableness * * * is an objective
one; the standard does not turn on the subjective good faith of individual officers." *Id.* [*Leon* at 919 n.20.]

In this case, "Detective McNally's reliance on the Illinois statute
was objectively reasonable." *Id.* at 1171. The Illinois Supreme Court
found the statute unconstitutional solely because it "vested State offi-

cials with too much discretion to decide who, when, and how long to search." *Id.* at 1172 (citation omitted). But the additional restrictions on discretion that might be necessary to establish the statute's constitutionality "are not so obvious that an objectively reasonable police officer would have realized the statute was unconstitutional without them." *Id.* at 1172.

Accordingly, under the "new" good-faith exception for statutes, "Detective McNally relied, in objective good faith, on a statute that appeared legitimately to allow a warrantless administrative search of [the wrecking yard,]" *id.*, and as a result, the automobiles seized are admissible as evidence.

NOTE

1. *See also Michigan v. DeFillippo*, 443 *U.S.* 31, 99 *S.Ct.* 2627 (1979), where the United States Supreme Court addressed the question "whether an arrest made in good-faith reliance on an ordinance, which at the time had not been declared unconstitutional, is valid regardless of a subsequent judicial determination of its unconstitutionality." *Id.* at 33, 99 *S.Ct.* at 2629. In upholding the validity of the arrest, the Court reasoned that the "prudent officer, in the course of determining whether [a suspect] has committed an offense under all the circumstances [of the encounter], should not [be] required to anticipate that a court would later hold the ordinance unconstitutional." *Id.* at 37-38, 99 *S.Ct.* at 2632. According to the Court: "Police officers are charged to enforce laws until and unless they are declared unconstitutional. The enactment of a law forecloses speculation by enforcement officers concerning its constitutionality—with the possible exception of a law so grossly and flagrantly unconstitutional that any person of reasonable prudence would be bound to see its flaws. Society would be ill-served if its police officers took it upon themselves to determine which laws are and which are not constitutionally entitled to enforcement." *Id.* at 38, 99 *S.Ct.* at 2632. As Chief Justice Warren observed in *Pierson v. Ray*, 386 *U.S.* 547, 555, 87 *S.Ct.* 1213, 1218 (1967), "[a] police [officer's] lot is not so unhappy that he must choose between being charged with dereliction of duty if he does not arrest when he has probable cause, and being [sued for money] damages if he does."

2. *Good faith and reasonable reliance on computer-generated records.* In *Arizona v. Evans*, 514 *U.S.* 1, 115 *S.Ct.* 1185 (1995), the Court addressed the question whether "evidence seized in violation of the Fourth Amendment by an officer who acted in reliance on a police record indicating the existence of an outstanding warrant—a record that is later determined to be erroneous—must be suppressed by virtue of the exclusionary rule regardless of * * * whether police personnel or court personnel were responsible for the record's continued presence in the police computer." *Id.*, 115 *S.Ct.* at 1187-88, 1189.

In January, Phoenix police officer Bryan Sargent observed defendant Evans driving the wrong way on a one-way street in front of the police station. The officer stopped Evans and asked to see his driver's license.

When Evans told Sargent that his license had been suspended, the officer entered Evans' name into a computer data terminal located in Sargent's patrol car. The computer inquiry confirmed that Evans' license had been suspended and also indicated that there was an outstanding misdemeanor warrant for his arrest. On the strength of the outstanding warrant, Sargent placed Evans under arrest. While being handcuffed, Evans dropped a hand-rolled cigarette that the officer determined smelled like marijuana. Immediately thereafter, a search of Evans' car uncovered a bag of marijuana under the passenger's seat.

Evans was charged with possession of marijuana. "When the police notified the Justice Court that they had arrested him, the Justice Court discovered that the arrest warrant previously had been quashed and so advised the police." *Id.* at 1188.

In this appeal, Evans argued that "because his arrest was based on a warrant that had been quashed 17 days prior to his arrest, the marijuana seized incident to the arrest should be suppressed as the fruit of an unlawful arrest. [Evans] also argued that '[t]he "good faith" exception to the exclusionary rule [was] inapplicable . . . because it was police error, not judicial error, which caused the invalid arrest.' " *Id.* The United States Supreme Court disagreed. The Court reasoned:

> "The question whether the exclusionary rule's remedy is appropriate in a particular context has long been regarded as an issue separate from the question whether the Fourth Amendment rights of the party seeking to invoke the rule were violated by police conduct." * * * The exclusionary rule operates as a judicially created remedy designed to safeguard against future violations of Fourth Amendment rights through the rule's general deterrent effect. * * * As with any remedial device, the rule's application has been restricted to those instances where its remedial objectives are thought most efficaciously served. * * * Where "the exclusionary rule does not result in appreciable deterrence, then, clearly, its use . . . is unwarranted." * * *

> The Arizona Supreme Court determined that it could not "support the distinction drawn . . . between clerical errors committed by law enforcement personnel and similar mistakes by court employees," * * * and that "even assuming . . . that responsibility for the error rested with the justice court, it does not follow that the exclusionary rule should be inapplicable to these facts."

> [The Arizona Supreme Court's] holding is contrary to the reasoning of *Leon, supra; Massachusetts v. Sheppard[, supra]*; and *Illinois v. Krull, supra.* If court employees were responsible for the erroneous computer record, the exclusion of evidence at trial would not sufficiently deter future errors so as to warrant such a severe sanction. First, as we noted in *Leon,* the exclusionary rule was historically designed as a means of deterring police misconduct, not mistakes by court employees. * * * Second, [Evans] offers no evi-

dence that court employees are inclined to ignore or subvert the Fourth Amendment or that lawlessness among these actors requires application of the extreme sanction of exclusion. * * * To the contrary, the Chief Clerk of the Justice Court testified at the suppression hearing that this type of error occurred once every three or four years. * * *

Finally, and most important, there is no basis for believing that application of the exclusionary rule in these circumstances will have a significant effect on court employees responsible for informing the police that a warrant has been quashed. Because court clerks are not adjuncts to the law enforcement team engaged in the often competitive enterprise of ferreting out crime, * * * they have no stake in the outcome of particular criminal prosecutions. * * * The threat of exclusion of evidence could not be expected to deter such individuals from failing to inform police officials that a warrant had been quashed. * * *

If it were indeed a court clerk who was responsible for the erroneous entry on the police computer, application of the exclusionary rule also could not be expected to alter the behavior of the arresting officer. As the trial court in this case stated: "I think the police officer [was] bound to arrest. I think he would [have been] derelict in his duty if he failed to arrest." * * * The Chief Clerk of the Justice Court testified that this type of error occurred "on[c]e every three or four years." * * * In fact, once the court clerks discovered the error, they immediately corrected it[,] and then proceeded to search their files to make sure that no similar mistakes had occurred[.] There is no indication that the arresting officer was not acting objectively reasonably when he relied upon the police computer record. Application of the *Leon* framework supports a categorical exception to the exclusionary rule for clerical errors of court employees.

Id. at 1191, 1193-94. [Citations omitted.]

In a concurring opinion, Justice O'Connor, joined by Justices Souter and Breyer, emphasized that the evidence in this case strongly suggested that

it was a court employee's departure from established recordkeeping procedures that caused the record of [Evans'] arrest warrant to remain in the computer system after the warrant had been quashed. * * *

The Court does not hold that the court employee's mistake in this case was necessarily the *only* error that may have occurred and to which the exclusionary rule might apply. While the police were innocent of the court employee's mistake, they may or may not have acted reasonably in their reliance *on the recordkeeping system itself.* Surely it would *not* be reasonable for the police to rely, say, on a recordkeeping system, their own or some other agency's, that has no mechanism to ensure its accuracy over time and that routinely leads to false arrests, even years after the probable cause for any such arrest has ceased to exist (if it ever existed). * * *

In recent years, we have witnessed the advent of powerful, computer-based recordkeeping systems that facilitate arrests in ways that have never before been possible. The police, of course, are entitled to enjoy the substantial advantages this technology confers. They may not, however, rely on it blindly. With the benefits of more efficient law enforcement mechanisms comes the burden of corresponding constitutional responsibilities.

Id. at 1194-95. [Court's emphasis.]

PART II

INTERVIEWS AND CONFESSIONS; EYEWITNESS IDENTIFICATION; AND THE SIXTH AMENDMENT RIGHTS TO COUNSEL AND CONFRONTATION

CHAPTER 11

INTERVIEWS; CONFESSIONS; AND *MIRANDA*

§11.1. Introduction.

The **Fifth Amendment** to the Federal Constitution provides in pertinent part:

> No person * * * shall be compelled in any criminal case to be a witness against himself * * *

This provision represents the constitutional right which has come to be recognized as the "privilege against self-incrimination." It has been made applicable to the states through the Fourteenth Amendment by the United States Supreme Court's decision in *Malloy v. Hogan*, 378 *U.S.* 1, 84 *S.Ct.* 1489 (1964). In *Malloy*, the Court ruled that the privilege against self-incrimination is a "fundamental right," and, as such, is binding upon the states in the same manner the Fifth Amendment safeguards persons from the federal government. The Court employed the Fourteenth Amendment's Due Process Clause as the vehicle through which the privilege was made binding upon the states. In pertinent part, the Due Process Clause provides:

> * * * *No State* shall * * * deprive any person of life, liberty, or property, without *due process of law*; * * * (emphasis added).

The privilege to be free from self-incrimination has been described as the "essential mainstay of our adversary system," and "the constitutional foundation underlying the privilege is the respect a government—state or federal—must accord to the dignity and integrity of its citizens." *Miranda v. Arizona*, 384 *U.S.* 436, 460, 86 *S.Ct.* 1602, 1620 (1966).

The Supreme Court in *Miranda* perceived an intimate connection between the constitutional privilege against self-incrimination and "police custodial questioning" which takes place in a "police dominated atmosphere." *Id.* at 458, 86 *S.Ct.* at 1619.

Miranda dealt with "the admissibility of statements obtained from an individual who is subjected to custodial police interrogation and the necessity for procedures which assure that the individual is accorded his privilege under the Fifth Amendment to the Constitution not to be compelled to incriminate himself." *Id.* at 439, 86 *S.Ct.* at 1609.

Chief Justice Warren, speaking for the Court, concluded that "the privilege is fulfilled only when the person is guaranteed the right 'to remain silent unless he chooses to speak in the unfettered exercise of his own free will.'" *Id.* at 460, 86 *S.Ct.* at 1620 (quoting *Malloy v. Hogan, supra* at 8, 84 *S.Ct.* at 1493).

"Coercive" custodial interrogation is the evil which the Court addressed in *Miranda*. "Custodial interrogation" is defined as "questioning initiated by law enforcement officers after a person has been taken into custody or otherwise deprived of his freedom of action in any significant way." *Id.* at 444, 86 *S.Ct.* at 1612. This concept of custodial interrogation is what the Court had in mind when it previously "spoke of an investigation which had focused on an accused." *Id.* at note 4 (referring to *Escobedo v. Illinois*, 378 *U.S.* 478, 84 *S.Ct.* 1758 (1964)).

The necessary procedural safeguards emanating from *Miranda* are as follows:

> Prior to any questioning, the person must be warned that he has the right to remain silent, that any statement he does make [can and will] be used [against him in a court of law], and that he has a right to the presence of an attorney, * * * and that if he cannot afford an attorney one will be appointed for him prior to any questioning if he so desires.

Id. at 444, 479, 86 *S.Ct.* at 1612, 1630. Good practice dictates that the individual also be clearly informed that he or she may ask for counsel at any time during custodial questioning, and, in addition, that the questioning will cease at any time the person desires counsel. Thereafter, if the individual

> *indicates in any manner* and at any stage of the process that he wishes to consult with an attorney before speaking there can be no questioning. Likewise, if the individual is alone and *indicates in any manner* that he does not wish to be interrogated, the police

may not question him. The mere fact that he might have answered some questions on his own does not deprive him of the right to refrain from answering any further inquiries until he has consulted with an attorney and thereafter consents to be questioned.

Id. at 444-45, 86 *S.Ct.* at 1612. [Emphasis added.]

Thus, as a general matter, the prosecution must demonstrate that the *Miranda* warnings were administered to the accused prior to any custodial interrogation. At the time of questioning, the accused may, of course, waive his or her *Miranda* rights, provided the waiver is made *voluntarily, knowingly, and intelligently. Id.* Failure to establish adherence to *Miranda*'s procedural safeguards—the administration of the warnings and receipt of an appropriate waiver—renders any and all statements obtained from an accused in any ensuing custodial interrogation inadmissible at trial, at least in the prosecution's case-in-chief. *See Michigan v. Tucker*, 417 *U.S.* 433, 444, 94 *S.Ct.* 2357, 2364 (1974) (recognizing that *Miranda*'s "procedural safeguards were not themselves rights protected by the Constitution but were instead measures to insure that the right against compulsory self-incrimination was protected").

"The *Miranda* Court did of course caution that the Constitution requires no 'particular solution for the inherent compulsions of the interrogation process,' and left it open to a State to meet its burden by adopting 'other procedures * * * at least as effective in apprising accused persons' of their rights. * * * The Court indeed acknowledged that, in barring introduction of a statement obtained without the required warnings, *Miranda* might exclude a confession that [] would not [be] condemn[ed] as 'involuntary in traditional terms,' * * * and for this reason [the Court has] sometimes called the *Miranda* safeguards 'prophylactic' in nature." *Withrow v. Williams*, 507 *U.S.* 680, 113 *S.Ct.* 1745, 1752 (1993) (quoting *Miranda* at 457, 467, 86 *S.Ct.* at 1618, 1624).

In *Dickerson v. United States*, 530 *U.S.* 428, 120 *S.Ct.* 2326 (2000), the Court, for the first time since *Miranda v. Arizona* was decided, had occasion to determine whether it should overrule *Miranda* and replace it with a test of "voluntariness" as the touchstone of a confession's admissibility, with the now-familiar warnings being just one factor in the analysis.

The *Dickerson* case addressed whether a federal statute, 18 *U.S.C.* §3501, enacted two years after *Miranda* was decided, was an unconstitutional attempt by Congress to legislatively overrule *Miranda*. To nullify *Miranda*, Section 3501 set forth a rule providing that the admissibility of an accused's confession or admission should turn only on whether or not it was voluntarily made. In a seven-to-two opinion, the *Dickerson* Court declared that

Miranda, being a constitutional decision of this Court, may not be in effect overruled by an Act of Congress, and we decline to overrule *Miranda* ourselves. We therefore hold that *Miranda* and its progeny in this Court govern the admissibility of statements made during custodial interrogation in both state and federal courts.

Id., 120 *S.Ct.* at 2329-30.

The *Dickerson* Court reemphasized that *Miranda* "laid down 'concrete constitutional guidelines for law enforcement agencies and courts to follow.'" *Id.* at 2331. [Citation omitted.] Those guidelines mandate the administration of four warnings which have now "come to be known colloquially as '*Miranda* rights.'" *Id.*

The *Miranda* warnings, held the *Dickerson* Court, are constitutional in dimension, and "Congress may not legislatively supersede [the Court's] decisions interpreting and applying the Constitution." *Id.* at 2332. The *Dickerson* Court would not, however, go so far as to rule that the *Miranda* warnings are *directly* required by the Constitution (a ruling thought necessary by dissenting Justices Scalia and Thomas). In this respect, the Court said:

> [W]e need not go farther than *Miranda* to decide this case. In *Miranda*, the Court noted that reliance on the traditional totality-of-the-circumstances test raised a risk of overlooking an involuntary custodial confession, * * * a risk that the Court found unacceptably great when the confession is offered in the case in chief to prove guilt. The Court therefore concluded that something more than the totality test was necessary. * * *

> We do not think there is [a] justification for overruling *Miranda*. *Miranda* has become embedded in routine police practice to the point where the warnings have become part of our national culture. * * *

Id. at 2335-36.

THE FORMULA

From the foregoing discussion, it is clear that prior to any custodial interrogation, law enforcement officers are required to administer the *Miranda* warnings to the person about to be questioned. The formula should be as easy as $1 + 1 = 2$; that is, "custody" + "interrogation" = the requirement that *Miranda* warnings be given. As the materials in this chapter will demonstrate, however, the formula is easier to recite than to apply. For law enforcement, the desired, ultimate result is the acquisition of a valid confession, fully admissible at trial. In order for that to occur, officers are at all times required to scrupulously honor each of the rights contained within the *Miranda* warnings.

Assuming that a criminal suspect is "in custody" and that law enforcement officials have administered the appropriate warnings, there are several courses that the interview may take. The first, and perhaps most straightforward, course that an interview session may take is: (1) a custodial suspect, (2) is given *Miranda* warnings, and thereafter (3) voluntarily, knowingly and intelligently waives his or her rights, and (4) gives a full confession.

Second, a custodial suspect may blurt out a confession before the authorities have an opportunity to administer the *Miranda* warnings.

A third direction in which an interview session may head is illustrated by the following: (1) a custodial suspect, (2) is given *Miranda* warnings, and thereafter (3) indicates that he or she does not want to talk—the suspect invokes his or her right to remain silent.

Fourth, an interview session may proceed as follows: (1) a custodial suspect, (2) is given *Miranda* warnings, and thereafter (3) indicates that he or she wants a lawyer—the suspect invokes his or her right to counsel.

Fifth, the suspect may change his or her mind; in this instance, (1) a custodial suspect, (2) is given *Miranda* warnings, and (3) indicates that he or she wants (a) to remain silent, or (b) a lawyer, but (4) sometime thereafter changes his or her mind and indicates a desire to communicate with the authorities, to open up a dialogue about the investigation.

Sixth, outside influences may interrupt or affect an interview; for example, where (1) a custodial suspect, (2) is given *Miranda* warnings, and (3) voluntarily, knowingly and intelligently waives his or her rights, but at some time during the process (4) an attorney, family member or close friend of the suspect (a) notifies the authorities of his or her pending or actual arrival at the station house, and / or (b) advises the authorities not to question the suspect.

The following sections explore each of the above-described paths down which an interview or questioning session may travel. There are, however, several preliminary issues that need to be addressed. For example, "What constitutes custody?" "What constitutes interrogation?" and, "Is a validly obtained confession, by itself, sufficient to support a criminal conviction?"

---

§11.2. Interviews and confessions.

Lawfully obtained admissions and confessions continue to play an integral role in the law enforcement scheme, and are extremely persuasive at trial. The ability of law enforcement to obtain a valid, uncoerced confession has been described as "not an evil but an unmitigated good." *McNeil v. Wisconsin*, 501 *U.S.* 171, 111 *S.Ct.* 2204, 2210 (1991). As the Court observed in *McNeil*, "[a]dmissions of guilt resulting from valid *Miranda* waivers 'are more than merely "desirable"; they are essential to society's compelling interest in finding, convicting, and punishing those who violate the law.' " *Id.* [Citation omitted.] The introduction of an admission or a confession at trial

> is like no other evidence. Indeed, "the defendant's own confession is probably the most probative and damaging evidence that can be admitted against him. * * * [T]he admissions of a defendant come from the actor himself, the most knowledgeable and unimpeachable source of information about his past conduct. Certainly, confessions have profound impact on the jury * * *."

Arizona v. Fulminante, 499 *U.S.* 279, 111 *S.Ct.* 1246, 1257 (1991) (quoting *Bruton v. United States*, 391 *U.S.* 123, 139-140, 88 *S.Ct.* 1620, 1630 (1968) (White, J., dissenting)).

---

§11.2(a). Preliminary issues.

STATE v. LUCAS
Supreme Court of New Jersey
30 N.J. 37, 152 A.2d 50 (1959)

QUESTION: Can an uncorroborated confession obtained by a law enforcement officer provide the evidential basis sufficient to sustain a criminal conviction ?

ANSWER: NO. "[A] confession without more cannot sustain a conviction[.]" *Id., 30 N.J.* at 51.

RATIONALE: "The rule * * * that a confession without more cannot sustain a conviction can be traced back through the decisional law to as early as 1818." *Id.* While the rule requiring corroboration is well settled, the question then becomes: What is the *quantum* of proof independent of the confession that the State must introduce before the confession may be considered as evidential ? *Id.* at 52.
   The Court answers that question by requiring that

> the State must introduce independent proof of facts and circumstances which strengthen or bolster the confession and tend to generate a belief in its trustworthiness, plus independent proof of loss or injury[.]

Id. at 56. With regard to this standard, the Court further observes:

> Confessions, like other admissions against interest, stand high in the probative hierarchy of proof. It is for this reason that the law imposes various safeguards designed to assure that the confession is true. But safeguards for the accused should not be turned into obstacles whereby the guilty can escape punishment. No greater burden should be required of the State than independent corroborative proof tending to establish that when the defendant confessed, he was telling the truth, plus independent proof of the loss or injury.

Id. at 57-58.

   Not all admissions or confessions obtained in the absence of *Miranda* warnings are inadmissible. The formula set forth in the preceding section—*custody* + *interrogation* = the requirement that *Miranda* warnings be given—teaches that law enforcement officials may, without the administration of *Miranda* warnings, question a criminal suspect who is not in custody. Moreover, officers may utilize any admission or confession volunteered by an in-custody criminal suspect when no interrogation (express or implied) has taken place. In this respect, the Court in *Miranda* emphasized that "[a]ny statement given freely and voluntarily without any compelling influences is, of course, admissible in evidence." *Miranda* at 478, 86 *S.Ct.* at 1630. Law enforcement officials are by no means required to stop people from speaking when they step forward to confess to a crime. "Volunteered statements of any kind are not barred by the Fifth Amendment and their admissibility [has] not been affected by" the Court's ruling in *Miranda*. *Id.*

---

§11.2(b). What constitutes custody?

In *Miranda v. Arizona,* the Court held that pre-interrogation warnings are required in the context of custodial interrogations, given "the compulsion inherent in custodial surroundings." 384 *U.S.* at 458, 86 *S.Ct.* at 1619. The Court defined "custodial interrogation" as "questioning initiated by law enforcement officers after a person has been taken into custody or otherwise deprived of his freedom of action in any significant way." *Id.* at 444, 86 *S.Ct.* at 1612.

Since *Miranda*, recent decisions of the Court instruct that "custody must be determined based on how a reasonable person in the suspect's situation would perceive his circumstances." *Yarborough v. Alvarado,* 541 *U.S.* 652, 662, 124 *S.Ct.* 2140, 2148 (2004). The "initial determination of custody depends on the objective circumstances of the interrogation, not on the subjective views harbored by either the interrogating officers or the person being questioned." *Stansbury v. California,* 511 *U.S.* 318, 323, 114 *S.Ct.* 1526, 1529 (1994). Thus, a "noncustodial setting," will not be transformed into a "custodial" one, even where the police investigation has focused on a particular suspect as a primary target. *See Beckwith v. United States,* 425 *U.S.* 341, 347-47, 96 *S.Ct.* 1612, 1616 (1976). *See also Minnesota v. Murphy,* 465 *U.S.* 420, 431, 104 *S.Ct.* 1136, 1144 (1984) ("The mere fact that an investigation has focused on a suspect does not trigger the need for *Miranda* warnings in noncustodial settings."); *Stansbury v. California, supra* at 323, 114 *S.Ct.* at 1528-29 ("a police officer's subjective view that an individual under questioning is a suspect, if undisclosed, does not bear upon the question whether the individual is in custody for purposes of *Miranda*.").

In *Thompson v. Keohane,* 516 *U.S.* 99, 116 *S.Ct.* 457 (1995), the Court provided the following description of the *Miranda* custody test:

> Two discrete inquiries are essential to the determination: first, what were the circumstances surrounding the interrogation; and second, given those circumstances, would a reasonable person have felt he or she was not at liberty to terminate the interrogation and leave. Once the scene is set and the players' lines and actions are reconstructed, the court must apply an objective test to resolve the ultimate inquiry: was there a formal arrest or restraint on freedom of movement of the degree associated with a formal arrest.

Id. at 112, 116 *S.Ct.* at 465.

Although a suspect's age and experience with law enforcement and the criminal justice system may be significant in other contexts, the United States Supreme Court has yet to hold that "a suspect's age or experience is relevant to the *Miranda* custody analysis." *Yarborough* at 666, 124 *S.Ct.* at 2150. "The *Miranda* custody inquiry is an objective test," which does not require the police to analyze a suspect's individual characteristics, including his age and criminal history. *Id.* at 667-68, 124 *S.Ct.* at 2151.

UNITED STATES v. BOOTH
United States Court of Appeals
669 *F*.2d 1231 (9th Cir. 1981)

QUESTION: What factors will a court examine to determine whether a person is "in custody" or has been significantly deprived of his freedom of action so as to trigger the requirement that *Miranda* warnings be given?

ANSWER: When a court must decide whether a person is "in custody" for *Miranda* purposes, it will analyze "the totality of circumstances," specifically examining such pertinent factors as: (1) the duration of the detention; (2) the nature and degree of the pressure applied to detain the individual; (3) the physical surroundings of the questioning; and (4) the language used by the officer.

RATIONALE: Generally, "the requirements of *Miranda* are not implicated when the detention and questioning of a suspect is part of an investigatory procedure rather than a custodial interrogation," *id.* at 1237, or where the restriction on a defendant's freedom is not of such significance as to render him "in custody."

The reasonableness of brief, on-the-scene detention for a limited investigative inquiry is generally tested by

> [T]he seriousness of the offense, the degree of likelihood that the person detained may have witnessed or been involved in the offense, the proximity in time and space from the scene of the crime, the urgency of the occasion, the nature of the detention and its extent, the means and procedures employed by the officer, [or] the presence of any circumstances suggesting harassment[.]

Arnold v. United States, 382 *F*.2d 4, 7 (9th Cir. 1967).

Overall, the determinative consideration is whether a reasonable, innocent person under the circumstances would conclude that after brief questioning, he or she would or would not be free to leave. *Booth* at 1235.

NOTE

Custody for Miranda purposes. In *United States v. Bengivenga,*
845 *F.*2d 593 (5th Cir. 1988) (en banc), the court summarized the concept of "custody" in the *Miranda* context. According to the court:

> A suspect is [] "in custody" for Miranda purposes when placed
> under arrest or when a reasonable person in the suspect's position
> would have understood the situation to constitute a restraint on
> freedom of movement of the degree which the law associates with
> formal arrest. The reasonable person through whom we view the
> situation must be neutral to the environment and to the purposes
> of the investigation—that is, neither guilty of criminal conduct and
> thus overly apprehensive nor insensitive to the seriousness of the
> circumstances.

Id. at 596. [Emphasis added.]

OREGON v. MATHIASON
Supreme Court of the United States
429 *U.S.* 492, 97 *S.Ct.* 711 (1977)

QUESTION: Are *Miranda* warnings required when law enforcement
officers question a suspect who is not under arrest nor "in custody"
when such questioning takes place within the confines of the police
station house ?

ANSWER: NO. "[P]olice officers are not required to administer
Miranda warnings to everyone whom they question. Nor is the requirement of warnings to be imposed simply because the questioning
takes place in the station house, or because the questioned person is
one whom the police suspect. *Miranda* warnings are required only
where there has been such a restriction on a person's freedom as to
render him 'in custody.' " *Id.* at 714.

RATIONALE: During the investigation of a Pendleton residential
burglary, an Oregon State Police officer gained information which
formed the basis of his suspicion of defendant, Mathiason. After three
or four unsuccessful attempts to contact defendant, the officer (25 days
after the burglary) left his card at defendant's apartment with a note
asking him to call because "I'd like to discuss something with you."
　"The next afternoon the defendant did call. The officer asked
where it would be convenient to meet. The defendant had no preference; so the officer asked if the defendant could meet him at the state
patrol office in about an hour and a half, about 5 p.m. The patrol office
was about two blocks from defendant's apartment." *Id.* at 713.
　At the patrol office, defendant met with the officer, shook hands,
and was led into an office. "The defendant was told he was not under
arrest. The door was closed. * * * The officer told defendant he wanted

to talk to him about a burglary and that his truthfulness would possibly be considered by the district attorney or judge. The officer further advised that the police believed defendant was involved in the burglary and (falsely stated that) defendant's fingerprints were found at the scene. The defendant sat for a few minutes and then said he had taken the property." *Id.* Defendant was then advised of his *Miranda* rights and gave a full confession, which the officer recorded.

At the conclusion of the taped interview, "the officer told defendant he was not arresting him at this time; he was released to go about his job and return to his family. The officer said he was referring the case to the district attorney for him to determine whether criminal charges would be brought." *Id.*

At the suppression hearing, defendant argued that his confession should be suppressed "as the fruit of questioning by the police not preceded by the warnings required in *Miranda*[.]" *Id.* at 712. The motion judge refused to exclude the confession "because [he] found that Mathiason was not in custody at the time of the confession." *Id.* While the Oregon Supreme Court reversed the motion judge's ruling, finding that the interrogation at the police station house took place "in a 'coercive environment' of the sort to which *Miranda* was intended to apply[,]" *the United States Supreme Court disagreed, and reinstated the lower judge's order. Id. at 712, 713.*

Miranda generally embraces a "police procedure applicable to 'custodial interrogation.' 'By custodial interrogation [the Court refers to] questioning initiated by a law enforcement officer after a person has been taken into custody or otherwise deprived of his freedom of action in any significant way.'" *Id.* at 713. [Citation omitted.] Thus, *Miranda* applies to "questioning which takes place in a prison setting during a suspect's term of imprisonment on a separate offense, * * * and to questioning taking place in a suspect's home, after he has been arrested and is no longer free to go where he pleases[.]" *Id.* at 713-714. [Citations omitted.]

Here, Mathiason's questioning did not take "place in a context where [his] freedom to depart was restricted in any way. He came voluntarily to the police station, where he was immediately informed that he was not under arrest. At the close of a -hour interview [Mathiason] did in fact leave the police station without hindrance. It is clear from these facts that Mathiason was not in custody 'or otherwise deprived of his freedom of action in any significant way.'" *Id.* at 714.

Such an atmosphere, *i.e.*, a noncustodial environment, "is not converted into one in which *Miranda* applies simply because a reviewing court concludes that, even in the absence of any formal arrest or restraint on freedom of movement, the questioning took place in a 'coercive environment.' Any interview of one suspected of a crime by a police officer will have coercive aspects to it, simply by virtue of the fact that the police officer is part of a law enforcement system which may ultimately cause the suspect to be charged with a crime." *Id.*

Accordingly, law enforcement "officers are not required to administer *Miranda* warnings to everyone whom they question. Nor is the requirement of warnings to be imposed simply because the questioning takes place in the station house, or because the questioned person is one whom the police suspect. *Miranda* warnings are required only where there has been such a restriction on a person's freedom as to render him 'in custody.' It is *that* sort of coercive environment to which *Miranda* by its terms was made applicable, and to which it is limited." *Id.* [Emphasis added.]

NOTE

The Supreme Court briefly mentions the Oregon State Police officer's false statement about having discovered defendant Mathiason's fingerprints at the scene of the burglary. Although the Oregon Supreme Court found this to be another circumstance contributing to the coerciveness of the environment, the United States Supreme Court promptly and summarily dismissed this aspect of the interview, stating: "Whatever relevance this fact may have to other issues in the case, it has nothing to do with whether [Mathiason] was in custody for purposes of the *Miranda* rule." *Mathiason* at 714.

CALIFORNIA v. BEHELER
Supreme Court of the United States
463 *U.S.* 1121, 103 *S.Ct.* 3517 (1983)

QUESTION: Were *Miranda* warnings necessary in the below set of circumstances ?

CIRCUMSTANCES: Defendant, Jerry Beheler, and his stepbrother, Danny Wilbanks, attempted to steal a quantity of hashish from Peggy Dean, who was selling the drug in the parking lot of a liquor store. When Dean refused to turn over the hashish, Wilbanks shot and killed her. Shortly thereafter, Beheler called the police, told them that Wilbanks had killed Dean and that the gun was hidden in his backyard. "Beheler gave consent to search the yard and the gun was found. Later that evening, Beheler voluntarily agreed to accompany police to the station house, although the police specifically told Beheler that he was not under arrest." *Id.* at 3518.

While at the station house, Beheler agreed to talk to police about the murder, and the conversation proceeded for approximately 30 minutes without the administration of the *Miranda* warnings. The 30-minute interview resulted in Beheler's confession. He was then advised that his statement would be evaluated by the district attorney, and was permitted to go home. Five days later Beheler was arrested in connection with the Dean murder and was subsequently convicted of aiding and abetting first-degree murder.

ANSWER: NO. "The police are required to give *Miranda* warnings only 'where there has been such a restriction on a person's freedom as to render him *in custody*.' " *Id.* at 3519. [Citation omitted; emphasis added.]

RATIONALE: "Although the circumstances of each case must certainly influence a determination of whether a suspect is 'in custody' for purposes of receiving *Miranda* protection, the ultimate inquiry is simply whether there is a 'formal arrest or restraint on freedom of movement' of the degree associated with a formal arrest." *Id.* at 3520. [Citations omitted.] As recognized in *Oregon v. Mathiason*, 429 *U.S.* 492, 97 *S.Ct.* 711 (1977), "*Miranda* warnings are not required simply because the questioning takes place in the station house, or because the questioned person is one whom the police suspect." *Id.* at 495, 97 *S.Ct.* at 714.

While the lower court distinguished the facts in *Mathiason* from this case, finding that Mathiason was not questioned by police until some 25 days after the burglary and here Beheler was interviewed shortly after the crime was committed, the Supreme Court found that "the length of time that elapsed between the commission of the crime and the police interview has no relevance to the [*Miranda*] inquiry." *Beheler* at 3520. Additionally, the lower court "observed that the police had a great deal more information about Beheler before their interview than did the police in *Mathiason*." *Id.* The Supreme Court found, however, that the fact that "the police knew more about Beheler before his interview than they did about Mathiason before his is irrelevant, * * * especially because it was Beheler himself who had initiated the earlier communication with police." *Id.*

Accordingly, because there was no restraint on Beheler's " 'freedom of movement' of the degree associated with formal arrest" during his questioning, the police were not required to administer the *Miranda* warnings.

NOTE

See also Thompson v. Keohane, 516 *U.S.* 99, 116 *S.Ct.* 457, 465 (1995), where the Court instructed that the ultimate "in custody" determination for *Miranda* purposes requires two discrete inquiries: "first, what were the circumstances surrounding the interrogation; and second, given those circumstances, would a reasonable person have felt that he or she was not at liberty to terminate the interrogation and leave." The ultimate inquiry requires courts to employ an objective test: Was there "a 'formal arrest or restraint on freedom of movement of the degree associated with a formal arrest.' " *Id.*, 116 *S.Ct.* at 465 (quoting *Beheler* at 1125, 103 *S.Ct.* at 3520).

---

§11.2(c). What constitutes interrogation ?

One of the many recurring problems in this area is the question of what particular type of police conduct constitutes "interrogation." *Miranda* suggested that "interrogation" referred only to actual "questioning initiated by law enforcement officers." 383 *U.S.* 436, 444, 86 *S.Ct.* 1602, 1612. But what of the concern about the coerciveness of the "interrogation environment" ? There are times that the creative and inventive officer may subjugate the will of the individual questioned *without asking any questions whatsoever*. It is this type of "psychological ploy" which necessarily undermines the privilege against compulsory self-incrimination, and, such ploys may thereby be treated as the "functional equivalent" of interrogation.

Interestingly, to determine whether an interrogation has taken place, the first question to ask is not, "What did the officer say or do ?" That question comes second. The first question is: "At what stage of the criminal proceedings is the officer-defendant interaction occurring ?" The answer to this question is critical for it may change the definition of the term "interrogation." Indeed, under the law of some states, it may even determine whether a criminal defendant may be questioned at all.

In determining what stage of the criminal proceedings the officer-defendant interaction is occurring, there are two time periods with which to be concerned. The first covers those events occurring *prior* to the initiation of formal criminal charges. The second time period begins at the initiation of formal charges and continues at least through trial. Once formal criminal charges have been initiated, any confrontational law-enforcement procedure involving the defendant (for example, an in-person lineup or an interrogation) is generally called a "critical stage" in the prosecution. The term "critical stage" is used because, at the moment formal criminal charges are initiated, the defendant's Sixth Amendment right to counsel attaches.

Thus, any law enforcement procedures involving a particular defendant which occur prior to the initiation of formal charges take place in what the courts call the "Fifth-Amendment setting." Procedures occurring after formal charges take place in a "Sixth-Amendment setting." For purposes of defining the term "interrogation" in a Fifth-Amendment setting, the focus will be upon the perceptions of the suspect, rather than on the intent or design of the police. The critical question will be whether the police used any words or actions that they *knew or should have known* were "reasonably likely to elicit an incriminating response from the suspect." *Rhode Island v. Innis*, 446 *U.S.* 291, 301, 100 *S.Ct.* 1682, 1689-90 (1980). In the Sixth-Amendment setting, the focus is upon the intent or design of the police, and the critical question will be whether officers *deliberately elicited* incriminating information from a defendant in the absence of counsel after a formal charge against the defendant had been filed. *Massiah v. United States*, 377 *U.S.* 201, 206, 84 *S.Ct.* 1199, 1203 (1964).

THE FIFTH AMENDMENT SETTING

RHODE ISLAND v. INNIS
Supreme Court of the United States
446 *U.S.* 291, 100 *S.Ct.* 1682 (1980)

QUESTION: In the following set of circumstances, was the defendant "interrogated" in violation of his right under *Miranda* to remain silent until he had consulted with an attorney ?

CIRCUMSTANCES: In 1975, a Providence, Rhode Island, taxicab driver's body was discovered buried in a shallow grave in Coventry, R.I. He had died from what appeared to be a shotgun blast to the back of his head. The next day, Providence police received a call from a taxicab driver reporting that he had just been robbed by a "man wielding a sawed-off shotgun." While at police headquarters and waiting to give a statement describing the robbery, the driver noticed a picture of his assailant on a bulletin board. He notified the investigating officer and then picked out the same assailant from a photo line-up prepared by that officer. Shortly thereafter, the Providence police began searching for the assailant.

Within a few hours the assailant (hereafter, defendant) was spotted, arrested, and advised of his *Miranda* rights several times by several officers. Defendant stated that he understood his rights and wanted to speak to an attorney. The captain of police at the scene of the arrest ordered the officers to place defendant in a "caged wagon," a four-door police car with a wire screen mesh between the front and rear seats, and drive him to headquarters. The three officers assigned to transport defendant to the station were then instructed by the captain not to question defendant or intimidate or coerce him in any way. Defendant was unarmed at the time of his arrest.

En route to the police station, the following conversation took place among the officers:

> . . . I frequent this area while on patrol and there's a lot of handicapped children running around in this area, and God forbid one of them might find a weapon with shells and they might hurt themselves . . . it would be too bad if the little girl would pick up the gun, maybe kill herself.

Defendant then interrupted the conversation and requested that the officers turn the patrol car around so he could show them where the gun was located. Upon return to the scene of the arrest, the captain again advised defendant of his *Miranda* rights. Defendant stated that he understood his rights, but he "wanted to get the gun out of the way because of the kids in the area in the school." Defendant then directed the police to a nearby field and pointed out the hidden shotgun.

ANSWER: NO. Defendant's incriminating response was not the product of words or actions on the part of the police that they *should*

712

have known were reasonably likely to elicit an incriminating response.
Id. at 1691.

RATIONALE: The Court in *Miranda v. Arizona* instructed:

> Once warnings have been given, the subsequent procedure is clear.
> * * * If the individual states that he wants an attorney, the inter-
> rogation must cease until an attorney is present. At that time, the
> individual must have an opportunity to confer with the attorney
> and to have him present during any subsequent questioning. If the
> individual cannot obtain an attorney and he indicates that he
> wants one before speaking to police, they must respect his decision
> to remain silent.

Innis at 1688 (quoting *Miranda* at 473-474, 86 *S.Ct.* at 1627-28).

Here, in *Innis*, the parties are in agreement that defendant was
fully informed of his *Miranda* rights and that he invoked his right to
counsel. It is also understood that defendant was "in custody" while en
route to police headquarters.

Thus, the central question is whether defendant was "interrogated" by the police officers in violation of his *Miranda* right to remain
silent until he had consulted with an attorney.

As a starting point, we must refer to the *Miranda* decision where
the Court observed that "[b]y custodial interrogation, we mean *questioning* initiated by law enforcement officers after a person has been
taken into custody or otherwise deprived of his freedom of action in
any significant way." *Id.* at 1688 (quoting *Miranda* at 444, 86 *S.Ct.* at
1612) (emphasis supplied by the *Innis* Court). Here, the concern was
that the "interrogation environment" created by the interplay of interrogation and custody would "subjugate the individual to the will of his
examiner" and thereby undermine the privilege against compulsory
self-incrimination. *Id.* "The fundamental import of the privilege [to be
free from compulsory self-incrimination] while an individual is in custody is not whether he is allowed to talk to the police without the
benefit of warnings and counsel, but whether he can be interrogated."
Id. at 1689. [Citation omitted.]

As a result, the *Innis* Court concluded that " 'interrogation,' as
conceptualized in the *Miranda* opinion, must reflect a measure of
compulsion above and beyond that inherent in custody itself." *Id.*
Thus, "*Miranda* safeguards come into play whenever a person in custody is subjected to either express questioning or its functional
equivalent." *Id.* Interrogation shall now include not only "express
questioning," but also "any words or actions on the part of the police
(other than those normally attendant to arrest and custody) that the
*police should know are reasonably likely to elicit an incriminating re-
sponse from the suspect.*" *Id.* at 1689-90. [Emphasis added.] "Incriminating response" refers to "any response—whether inculpatory or exculpatory—that the prosecution may seek to introduce at trial." *Id.* at
1690 n.5. The *reasonably-likely-to-elicit standard* thus "focuses primarily upon the perceptions of the suspect, rather than the intent of

the police. This focus reflects the fact that the *Miranda* safeguards
were designed to vest a suspect in custody with an added measure of
protection against coercive police practices, without regard to objective proof of the underlying intent of the police.[a]

A practice that the police should know is reasonably likely to evoke
an incriminating response from a suspect thus amounts to interrogation." *Id.* at 1690. The Court, however, does acknowledge that "since
the police surely cannot be held accountable for the unforeseeable results of their words or actions, the definition of interrogation can extend only to words or actions on the part of police officers that they
*should have known were reasonably likely to elicit an incriminating
response." Id.* (emphasis supplied by the Court).[b]

In the present case, there was no express questioning of the defendant, and, it cannot be fairly concluded that the defendant was subjected to the "functional equivalent" of questioning. Additionally, there
is no evidence in the record suggesting that these law enforcement officers were aware that the defendant "was peculiarly susceptible to an
appeal to his conscience concerning the safety of handicapped children. Nor is there anything in the record to suggest that the police
knew that the [defendant] was unusually disoriented or upset at the
time of his arrest." *Id.* Thus, it cannot be said that these officers
should have known that defendant would suddenly be moved to give a
self-incriminating response.

Accordingly, because it was not established that defendant's incriminating response was the product of words or actions on the part
of the police that they should have known were reasonably likely to
elicit an incriminating response, their actions did not constitute "interrogation" within the meaning of *Miranda*.

NOTE

1. *Conduct not "reasonable likely to elicit" an incriminating response.* In *United States v. Morton*, 391 *F.*3d 274 (D.C. Cir. 2004), at
about 2:00 a.m., Officers Hays and Beyer of the Metropolitan Police
Department pulled a vehicle over for running a stop sign. "Morton,
the driver, did not have a valid driver's license. After the officers ordered Morton and the passenger out of the vehicle, Officer Beyer noticed the tip of a gun underneath the cushion on which Morton had
been sitting. Officer Hays then arrested Morton and called Officer

---

[a] The *Innis* right to counsel issue is based upon the Fifth and Fourteenth Amendments as
interpreted by the *Miranda* decision. It is a different standard than that embraced in *Massiah v. United States*, 377 *U.S.* 201 (1964) and *Brewer v. Williams*, 430 *U.S.* 387 (1977),
which prohibits law enforcement officers from "deliberately eliciting" incriminating information from a defendant in the absence of an attorney after formal charges have been filed. *See
also United States v. Henry*, 447 *U.S.* 264 (1980), *Maine v. Moulton*, 474 *U.S.* 159, 106 *S.Ct.*
447 (1985), *Kuhlmann v. Wilson*, 477 *U.S.* 436, 106 *S.Ct.* 2616 (1986), and *Michigan v. Jackson*, 475 *U.S.* 625, 106 *S.Ct.* 1404 (1986) for the right to counsel issue based upon the Sixth
and Fourteenth Amendments.

[b] Any knowledge the police may have had concerning the unusual susceptibility of a defendant to a particular form of persuasion might be an important factor in determining
whether the police should have known that their words or actions were reasonably likely to
elicit an incriminating response from the suspect." *Id.* at 1690 n.8.

Parker to transport her to the police station. The officers questioned the passenger but did not place him under arrest." *Id.* at 275.

"On the way to the station, Morton expressed concern over what would happen to her vehicle. Officer Parker said her vehicle would be impounded. Morton then became upset. She told Officer Parker she would be released in the morning. Officer Parker responded that she had been arrested for a serious charge and that 'she might not be getting out as quickly as she thinks.' Morton told Officer Parker that her lawyer would help her 'beat the charge,' and when she did get out, 'she would be back down in the same area riding around with another gun' that she kept at home. Morton also stated she did not like the police, and 'that's why police officers get killed.' " *Id.* at 275-76.

In the appeal following her unsuccessful motion to suppress her statements, Morton argued that Officer Parker's conduct was the "functionally equivalent" to interrogation because Officer Parker should have known that his comments were "reasonably likely to elicit an incriminating response" from her. The court disagreed.

" 'Interrogation,' as conceptualized in the *Miranda* opinion, requires a measure of compulsion above and beyond that inherent in custody itself.' " *Id.* at 276 (quoting *Rhode Island v. Innis*, 446 *U.S.* 291, 300, 100 *S.Ct.* 1682, 1689 (1980)). In this case, "Officer Parker did not 'compel' or even encourage Morton to incriminate herself. Officer Parker's statements—that Morton's vehicle would be impounded and that she had been arrested on a serious charge and might not be released as quickly as she thought—were directly responsive to what Morton had said and were not reasonably likely to elicit an incriminating response." *Id.*

Accordingly, although Morton was in custody, she was not subject to interrogation or its "functional equivalent" within the meaning of *Rhode Island v. Innis*. Officer Parker did not "coerce her into making any incriminating statement." *Id.*

ARIZONA v. MAURO
Supreme Court of the United States
481 *U.S.* 520, 107 *S.Ct.* 1931 (1987)

QUESTION: After an arrestee has asserted his right to counsel, does a law enforcement officer subject him to interrogation or its functional equivalent by allowing the arrestee's wife to speak with him in the presence of an officer who tape records the conversation ?

ANSWER: NO. The actions of the officers in this case did not rise to the level of interrogation or its functional equivalent within the meaning of *Miranda v. Arizona* and *Rhode Island v. Innis*.

RATIONALE: Officers of the Flagstaff, Arizona Police Department were summoned to a local K-Mart store when defendant, Mauro, entered the store and informed the clerk that he had just killed his son. Upon arrival of the officers, Mauro freely admitted that he had killed his son, and, he directed the officers to the location of the child's body. At this point, Mauro was placed under arrest and was advised of his *Miranda* rights. At police headquarters, Mauro was again advised of his rights, and this time he told the police that he did not wish to make any more statements without the presence of an attorney. Because the Flagstaff Police Department did not have a secure detention area, Mauro was detained in the police captain's office.

When Mauro's wife arrived, she spoke briefly to the investigating detective, and then insisted that she be permitted to speak to her husband. The detective's supervisor permitted the conversation between Mauro and his wife, but instructed the detective to remain present during the meeting and to tape record the entire conversation. Both Mr. and Mrs. Mauro were informed that they could speak together only if an officer was present to observe and hear what was going on. The officer sat down in the room with them and placed a tape recorder on a desk in front of the Mauros, in full view. Subtle admissions seemed to flow from their conversation and, during the conversation, Mauro repeatedly told his wife not to answer any questions until an attorney was present.

At trial, the prosecution attempted to rebut Mauro's defense of insanity by playing the tape of the meeting between Mauro and his wife. Mauro argued that the recording should be suppressed because it was the product of police interrogation in violation of his *Miranda* rights.

The Supreme Court disagreed with Mauro and held that he was not subjected to interrogation or its functional equivalent when the police allowed his wife to speak to him in the presence of an officer who tape recorded the entire conversation.

The pivotal issue here "is whether, in the circumstances of this case, officers interrogated [defendant] in violation of the Fifth and Fourteenth Amendments when they allowed him to speak with his wife in the presence of a police officer." *Id.* at 1932.

In *Rhode Island v. Innis*, 446 *U.S.* 291, 100 *S.Ct.* 1682 (1980), the Court concluded that the safeguards embraced by *Miranda* extended not only to express questioning, but also to "its functional equivalent." The *Innis* Court explained the phrase "functional equivalent" of interrogation as including "any words or actions on the part of the police (other than those normally attendant to arrest and custody) that the police should know are reasonably likely to elicit an incriminating response from the suspect." *Mauro* at 1935 (quoting *Innis* at 301, 100 *S.Ct.* at 1689-90).

Here, the officers advised Mauro of his *Miranda* rights and Mauro indicated that he wanted a lawyer. However, "the tape recording of the conversation between Mauro and his wife shows that [the detective] asked Mauro no questions about the crime or his conduct. Nor is it suggested—or even supported by any evidence—that [the detective sergeant's] decision to allow Mauro's wife to see him was the kind of psychological ploy that properly could be treated as the functional equivalent of interrogation." *Mauro* at 1935. Further, "there is no evidence that the officers sent Mrs. Mauro in to see her husband for the purpose of eliciting incriminating statements. * * * We doubt that a suspect, told by officers that his wife will be allowed to speak to him, would feel that he was being coerced to incriminate himself in any way. * * * Officers do not interrogate a suspect simply by hoping that he will incriminate himself." *Id.* at 1936.

As a result, the Court, speaking through Justice Powell, concludes that "Mauro was not subjected to compelling influences, psychological ploys, or direct questioning. Thus, his volunteered statements cannot properly be considered the result of police interrogation." *Id.* Justice Powell then instructs:

> In deciding whether particular police conduct is interrogation, we must remember the purpose behind our decisions in *Miranda* and *Edwards:* preventing government officials from using the coercive nature of confinement to extract confessions that would not be given in an unrestrained environment. The government actions in this case do not implicate this purpose in any way. Police departments need not adopt inflexible rules barring suspects from speaking with their spouses, nor must they ignore legitimate security concerns by allowing spouses to meet in private. In short, the officers in this case acted reasonably and lawfully by allowing Mrs. Mauro to speak with her husband. In this situation, the Federal Constitution does not forbid use of Mauro's subsequent statements at his criminal trial.

Id. at 1936-1937.

UNITED STATES v. BENTON
United States Court of Appeals
996 *F.*2d 642 (3rd Cir. 1993)

QUESTION: At the scene of an armed-robbery arrest, will an officer's comment to the arrestee that the officer intends to lodge charges against him, along with the additional comment that, just prior to the arrest, the officer observed the arrestee bend over in the area where the gun was found, constitute interrogation ?

ANSWER: **NO.** An officer's comment to an arrestee as to why he is being arrested, along with an additional comment describing the arrestee's conduct just prior to the arrest, does not constitute interrogation or the functional equivalent of interrogation. *Id.* at 644.

RATIONALE: In the middle of September, Officer Patterson received a radio communication that defendant, Brian Benton, had robbed someone at gunpoint at a tavern in Harrisburg, Pennsylvania. When several other officers arrived at the scene, Benton fled. Patterson, who knew Benton, spotted him on Peffer Street and noticed him bend down by a wooden door which opened into Peffer Street from the storage area of another tavern. Benton then stood up and walked back in the direction from which he had come. At that point, Benton was confronted by Officer Cesari, who drew his gun and ordered Benton to stand against a wall. Officer Patterson searched Benton for weapons but found none. During the pat-down, Benton asked Patterson what was going on. Patterson told Benton that the police had received a call advising that he had robbed someone with a gun and that they were looking for the gun. The officer then handcuffed Benton and placed him in the back seat of a patrol car.

Officer Patterson easily located the gun, a loaded semi-automatic, by the wooden door where Benton had bent down. When the officer went back to the patrol car, Benton again asked what was going on. The officer told Benton that he was going to be charged, and that he had seen Benton bend over, referring to Benton's conduct near the door where the gun was found. At that point, Benton said that no one had seen him throw away the gun.

At the conclusion of Benton's motion to suppress, the district court concluded that the statement was the product of custodial interrogation, and, because Benton was not given the *Miranda* warnings, the statement must be suppressed. According to the district court, it was "unnecessary to the arrest for Officer Patterson to tell [Benton] that he saw him bend over at the door." In the district court's view, "Patterson's statement was not an answer to Benton's question of what was going on. Rather, it was a declaration to Benton that the police had evidence 'linking him to the gun' which was likely to elicit" an incriminating response. *Id.* at 644. *The Court of Appeals for the Third Circuit, disagreed and reversed.*

It is clear that by using psychological ploys and subtle coercion, the police can effectively conduct custodial interrogations. "Thus, it is important to consider this case with reference to the circumstances at the time Benton made his statement." *Id.*

> Obviously, this case did not involve a contrived situation in which a suspect, arrested after a significant time interval following an offense, was brought to a police station and told of information which the police had accumulated linking him to the crime. Rather, Benton made his statement following his on-the-spot arrest by officers directed to the scene of the crime.

Id.

The court concluded, therefore, that the officers in this case did not intentionally create circumstances likely to elicit a statement from Benton. In this respect, the court stated:

> Patterson did nothing more than tell Benton why he was being arrested. While we do not doubt that he lawfully could have told Benton the charge against him and have said nothing more, we do not think that Patterson's act of describing an observation he made prior to the arrest constituted the functional equivalent of a custodial interrogation. Rather, this was a case in which Benton's remarks were unforeseeable. * * *

Finally, we point out that this is not a situation in which a suspect would have felt compelled to respond to the arresting officer's statement. This was not, for example, a case in which the police suggested that other members of Benton's family were implicated in the crime, thus encouraging him to speak to accept sole responsibility. Nor did the police tell Benton that they had inculpatory information from a witness which Benton might want to deny. Furthermore, the police did not attempt to induce Benton to incriminate himself by confronting him with a partner in crime who had confessed. * * * In the circumstances, it is clear that Patterson's remarks gave Benton no incentive to say that no one had seen him throw away the gun. Thus, even if we disregarded the fact that Benton had asked what was going on, we would conclude that *the police did not conduct a custodial interrogation or its functional equivalent.* Rather, Benton's statement was simply gratuitous.

Id. [Emphasis added.]

NOTE

Consent searches. As a general rule, a police officer's request for consent to search a particular area is not "interrogation" within the meaning of *Miranda,* and an individual's subsequent response granting or denying consent is not "testimonial" for purposes of the Fifth Amendment privilege against self-incrimination. *United States v. Glenna,* 878 *F.*2d 967, 971 (7th Cir. 1989). *See also United States v. LeGrone,* 43 *F.*3d 332 (7th Cir. 1994) ("[B]ecause requesting consent to search is not likely to elicit an incriminating statement, such questioning is not interrogation, and thus *Miranda* warnings are not required."); *United States v. Rodriguez-Garcia,* 983 *F.*2d 1563 (10th Cir. 1993) (*same*); *Cody v. Solem,* 755 *F.*2d 1323, 1330 (8th Cir. 1985) ("Simply put, a consent to search is not an incriminating statement."); *Smith v. Wainwright,* 581 *F.*2d 1149, 1152 (5th Cir. 1978) ("A consent to search is not a self-incriminating statement."); *United States v. Lemon,* 550 *F.*2d 467, 472 (9th Cir. 1977) ("A consent to search is not the type of incriminating statement toward which the fifth amendment is directed. It is not in itself 'evidence of a testimonial or communicative nature.'"); *United States v. Faruolo,* 506 *F.*2d 490, 495 (2d Cir. 1974) ("There is no possible violation of fifth amendment rights since the consent to search is not 'evidence of a testimonial or communicative nature.'").

THE SIXTH AMENDMENT SETTING

BREWER v. WILLIAMS
Supreme Court of the United States
430 *U.S.* 387, 97 *S.Ct.* 1232 (1977)

QUESTION: In the below circumstances, was defendant Williams "interrogated" in violation of his Sixth Amendment right to counsel?

CIRCUMSTANCES: On the afternoon of December 24th, 10-year-old Pamela Powers went with her family to the YMCA in Des Moines, Iowa, to watch a wrestling tournament in which her brother was participating. When she failed to return from a trip to the washroom, an unsuccessful search for her began.

"Robert Williams, who had recently escaped from a mental hospital, was a resident of the YMCA. Soon after the girl's disappearance, Williams was seen in the YMCA lobby carrying some clothing and a large bundle wrapped in a blanket. He obtained help from a 14-year-old boy in opening the street door of the YMCA and the door to his automobile parked outside. When Williams placed the bundle in the front seat of his car, the boy 'saw two legs in it and they were skinny and white.' Before anyone could see what was in the bundle, Williams drove away. His abandoned car was found the following day in Davenport, Iowa, roughly 160 miles east of Des Moines. A warrant was then issued in Des Moines for his arrest on a charge of abduction." *Id.*, 430 *U.S.* 390.

On the morning of December 26th, acting on the advice of an attorney, Williams turned himself in to the Davenport police, where he was booked on the charge specified in the arrest warrant. After advising Williams of his *Miranda* rights, the Davenport police telephoned representatives of the Des Moines Police Department and advised them that Williams had surrendered. At the time, Williams' attorney was still at Des Moines police headquarters. The attorney spoke with Williams on the telephone and, in the presence of the Des Moines chief of police and a police detective named Leaming, the attorney advised Williams that Des Moines police officers would be driving to Davenport to pick him up, that the officers would not interrogate him or mistreat him, and that Williams was not to talk to the officers about Pamela Powers until after consulting with him upon his return to Des Moines.

As a result of these conversations, it was agreed Detective Leaming and a fellow officer would drive to Davenport to pick up Williams, that they would bring him directly back to Des Moines, and that they would not question him during the trip. "In the meantime Williams was arraigned before a judge in Davenport on the outstanding arrest warrant. The judge advised him of his *Miranda* rights and committed him to jail[.] Before leaving the courtroom, Williams conferred with a lawyer named Kelly, who advised him not to make any statements until consulting with [his attorney] back in Des Moines." *Id.* at 391.

Detective Leaming and his fellow officer arrived in Davenport at about noon to pick up Williams and return him to Des Moines. Detective Leaming repeated the *Miranda* warnings and was again told by Mr. Kelly that "Williams was not to be questioned about the disappearance of Pamela Powers until after he had consulted with [his attorney] back in Des Moines." *Id.* at 392.

The two detectives, along with Williams, then set out on the 160-mile drive. During the drive, Williams stated several times that "[w]hen I get to Des Moines and see [my attorney], I am going to tell you the whole story." *Id.*

"Detective Leaming knew that Williams was a former mental patient, and knew also that he was deeply religious. The detective and his prisoner soon embarked on a wide-ranging conversation covering a variety of topics, including the subject of religion. Then, not long after leaving Davenport and reaching the interstate highway, Detective Leaming delivered what has been referred to * * * as the 'Christian burial speech.' " *Id.*

Addressing Williams as "Reverend," the detective said:

> I want to give you something to think about while we're traveling down the road. . . . Number one, I want you to observe the weather conditions, it's raining, it's sleeting, it's freezing, driving is very treacherous, visibility is poor, it's going to be dark early this evening. They are predicting several inches of snow for tonight, and I feel that you yourself are the only person that knows where this little girl's body is, that you yourself have only been there once, and if you get a snow on top of it, you yourself may be unable to find it. And, since we will be going right past the area on the way into Des Moines, I feel that we could stop and locate the body, that the parents of this little girl should be entitled to a Christian burial for the little girl who was snatched away from them on Christmas Eve and murdered. And I feel we should stop and locate it on the way in, rather than waiting until morning and trying to come back out after a snow storm and possibly not being able to find it at all.

Id. at 392-93.

"Williams asked Detective Leaming why he thought their route to Des Moines would be taking them past the girl's body, and Leaming responded that he knew the body was in the area of Mitchellville—a town they would be passing on the way to Des Moines. Leaming then stated: 'I do not want you to answer me. I don't want to discuss it any further. Just think about it as we're riding down the road.' " *Id.* at 393. As they continued towards Des Moines, just as they approached Mitchellville, "Williams said that he would show the officers where the body was. He then directed the police to the body of Pamela Powers." *Id.*

ANSWER: YES. The police detective "deliberately and designedly set out to elicit information from Williams just as surely as—and perhaps more effectively than—if he had formally interrogated him." *Id.* at 399. The detective's "Christian burial speech" was "tantamount to interrogation." *Id.* Because the detective did not obtain from Williams a waiver of his right to counsel prior to that "interrogation," neither "Williams' incriminating statements themselves nor any testimony describing his having led the police to the victim's body can constitutionally be admitted into evidence." *Id.* at 406 n.12.

RATIONALE: The right to the "assistance of counsel," guaranteed by the Sixth and Fourteenth Amendments,

> is indispensable to the fair administration of our adversary system of criminal justice. * * * Whatever else it may mean, the right to counsel granted by the Sixth and Fourteenth Amendments means at least that a person is entitled to the help of a lawyer at or after the time that judicial proceedings have been initiated against him—"whether by way of formal charge, preliminary hearing, indictment, information, or arraignment." * * *

Id. at 399. [Citations omitted.]

There can be no doubt in the present case that judicial proceedings had been initiated against Williams before the start of the automobile ride from Davenport to Des Moines. A warrant had been issued for his arrest, and he had been arraigned on that warrant before a judge in a Davenport courtroom. "There can be no serious doubt, either, that Detective Leaming deliberately and designedly set out to elicit information from Williams just as surely as—and perhaps more effectively than—if he had formally interrogated him." *Id.* Detective Leaming was fully aware before departing for Des Moines that Williams was represented by counsel and had been arraigned in court. Yet he purposely set out to obtain from Williams as much incriminating information as possible. Indeed, Detective Leaming conceded as much when he testified at trial:

> Q. In fact, Captain, whether he was a mental patient or not, you were trying to get all the information you could before he got to his lawyer, weren't you?
>
> A. I was sure hoping to find out where that little girl was, yes, sir.

Id.

What is clear in this case is that Detective Leaming's "Christian burial speech" had been "tantamount to interrogation." *Id.* at 400. Consequently, Williams was entitled to the assistance of counsel at the time he made the incriminating statements. "Yet no such constitutional protection would have come into play if there had been no interrogation." *Id.*

Moreover, the statements were obtained from Williams "only after Detective Leaming's use of psychology on a person whom he knew to be deeply religious and an escapee from a mental hospital— with the specific intent to elicit incriminating statements. In the face of this evidence, the State has produced no affirmative evidence whatsoever to [demonstrate] * * * a knowing and intelligent waiver of Sixth Amendment rights." *Id.* at 403. [Citations and internal quotes omitted.] While it is true that "an accused can voluntarily, knowingly and intelligently waive his right to have counsel present at an interrogation after counsel has been appointed[, t]he prosecution, however, has the weighty obligation to show that the waiver was knowingly and intelligently made." *Id.*

Knowing that Williams had been arraigned in court and was represented by counsel, Detective Leaming nonetheless deliberately and designedly proceeded to elicit incriminating statements from him. "Leaming did not preface this effort by telling Williams that he had a right to the presence of a lawyer, and made no effort at all to ascertain whether Williams wished to relinquish that right." *Id.* at 405. Because the detective did not obtain from Williams a waiver of his right to counsel prior to embarking on the so-called "Christian burial speech," neither "Williams' incriminating statements themselves nor any testimony describing his having led the police to the victim's body can constitutionally be admitted into evidence." *Id.* at 406 n.12.

NOTE

1. During the course of its opinion, the Court noted that its decision did not touch upon the issue of what evidence, if any, beyond the incriminating statements themselves must be excluded as "fruit of the poisonous tree." *Id.* at 406 n.12. Said the Court: "While neither Williams' incriminating statements themselves nor any testimony describing his having led the police to the victim's body can constitutionally be admitted into evidence, evidence of where the body was found and of its condition might well be admissible on the theory that the body would have been discovered in any event, even had incriminating statements not been elicited from Williams." *Id.* For subsequent treatment of this issue and the "Inevitable Discovery Rule, *see Nix v. Williams*, 467 *U.S.* 431, 104 *S.Ct.* 2501 (1984), at Chapter 9.

2. *See also Fellers v. United States*, 540 *U.S.* 519, 524, 124 *S.Ct.* 1019, 1022 (2004) (reaffirming application of the "deliberate-elicitation standard" for Sixth Amendment cases) (citing *United States v. Henry*, 447 *U.S.* 264, 270, 100 *S.Ct.* 2183 (1980) ("The question here is whether under the facts of this case a Government agent 'deliberately elicited' incriminating statements"). The *Fellers* Court also "expressly distinguished this standard from the Fifth Amendment custodial-interrogation standard." *Id.*, 124 *S.Ct.* at 1023 (citing *Rhode Island v. Innis* 446 *U.S.* 291, 100 *S.Ct.* 1682 (1980)).

In *Fellers*, after a grand jury indicted defendant on drug charges, two officers went to his home in Lincoln, Nebraska, to arrest him. The officers knocked on defendant's door and, when he answered, identified themselves and asked if they could come in. Defendant invited the officers into his living room. The officers advised defendant they had come to discuss his involvement in methamphetamine distribution. They informed him that they had a federal warrant for his arrest and that a grand jury had indicted him for conspiracy to distribute methamphetamine. The officers advised defendant that the indictment referred to "his involvement with certain individuals, four of whom they named." *Id.* at 1021. Defendant then admitted that "he knew the four people and had used methamphetamine during his association with them." *Id.* About fifteen minutes later, the officers transported defendant to jail where, for the first time, they advised him of his *Miranda* rights. After signing a *Miranda* waiver form, defendant "reiterated the inculpatory statements he had made earlier, admitted to having associated with other individuals implicated in the charged conspiracy, and admitted to having loaned money to one of them even though he suspected that she was involved in drug transactions." *Id.*

Finding a violation of the Sixth Amendment right to counsel, the Court said:

> [T]here is no question that the officers in this case "deliberately elicited" information from [defendant]. Indeed, the officers, upon arriving at [defendant's] house, informed him that their purpose in coming was to discuss his involvement in the distribution of methamphetamine and his association with certain charged co-conspirators. Because the ensuing discussion took place after [defendant] had been indicted, outside the presence of counsel, and in the absence of any waiver of [defendant's] Sixth Amendment rights, the * * * officers' actions [violated] Sixth Amendment standards[.]

Id. at 1023.

PATTERSON v. ILLINOIS
Supreme Court of the United States
487 U.S. 285, 108 S.Ct. 2389 (1988)

QUESTION 1: Once a defendant's Sixth Amendment right to counsel arises with his indictment, are the police prohibited from initiating communication, exchanges, or conversations with him ?

ANSWER: NO. The police are not barred from initiating communication, exchanges, or conversations with a defendant whose Sixth Amendment right to counsel has arisen with his indictment. Such a defendant should not be equated with a preindictment suspect who, while being questioned, asserts his Fifth Amendment right to counsel which, under the *Edwards* rule, would bar further questioning of such suspect unless he initiates the meeting. *Id.* at 2394.

RATIONALE: The mere fact that a defendant's Sixth Amendment right to counsel "came into existence with his indictment, *i.e.*, that he had such a right at the time of his questioning, does not distinguish him from the preindictment interrogatee whose right to counsel is in existence and available for his exercise while he is questioned." *Id.* Like the preindictment setting, the request for an attorney in the post-indictment setting would also prohibit the police from any further questioning unless the accused himself initiates further communication. *See Edwards v. Arizona*, 451 *U.S.* 477, 484-485, 101 *S.Ct.* 1880, 1884-85 (1981) (for the preindictment, Fifth Amendment setting) and

Michigan v. Jackson, 475 *U.S.* 625, 629-630, 106 *S.Ct.* 1404, 1407-1408 (1986) (for the postindictment, Sixth Amendment setting).

QUESTION 2:   Are *Miranda* warnings adequate, in a Sixth Amendment, postindictment setting, to sufficiently apprise an accused of the nature of his Sixth Amendment rights and the consequences of abandoning them ?

ANSWER: YES.   In a Sixth Amendment, postindictment setting, an accused who is admonished with the warnings prescribed by *Miranda* "has been sufficiently apprised of the nature of his Sixth Amendment rights, and of the consequences of abandoning those rights, so that his waiver on this basis will be considered a knowing and intelligent one." *Patterson* at 2397.

RATIONALE: In this appeal, defendant argues that "he had not 'knowingly and intelligently' waived his Sixth Amendment right to counsel before he gave his uncounseled postindictment confessions." *Id.* at 2393. Moreover, defendant contends that the warnings he received, while adequate for the purpose of protecting his *Fifth* Amendment rights as guaranteed by *Miranda*, did not adequately inform him of his Sixth Amendment right to counsel. *Id.*

The United States Supreme Court rejected defendant's contentions, thereby affirming the holding of the Illinois Supreme Court "that *Miranda* warnings were sufficient to make a defendant aware of his Sixth Amendment right to counsel during postindictment questioning." *Id.*

As a general rule, "a waiver of the Sixth Amendment right to counsel is valid only when it reflects 'an intentional relinquishment or abandonment of a known right or privilege.' " *Id.* at 2395 (quoting *Johnson v. Zerbst,* 304 *U.S.* 458, 464, 58 *S.Ct.* 1019, 1023 (1938)). This requires the accused to be fully aware of what he is doing "so that 'his choice is made with eyes open.' " *Id.* [Citation omitted.]

In a Fifth Amendment setting, this requirement is described "as 'a full awareness (of) both the nature of the right being abandoned and the consequences of the decision to abandon it.' *Moran v. Burbine,* 475 *U.S.* 412, 421, 106 *S.Ct.* 1135, 1141 (1986). Whichever of these formulations is used, the key inquiry in a case such as this one must be: Was the accused, who waived his Sixth Amendment rights during postindictment questioning, made sufficiently aware of his right to have counsel present during the questioning, and of the possible consequences of a decision to forgo the aid of counsel ?" *Patterson* at 2395.

The *Miranda* warnings satisfy this inquiry. Such warnings not only convey to an accused "the sum and substance of the rights that the Sixth Amendment provide[s]," but also "serve[] to make [an accused] aware of the consequences of a decision by him to waive his Sixth Amendment rights during postindictment questioning." *Id.* "By knowing what could be done with any statements he might make, and therefore, what benefit could be obtained by having the aid of counsel while making such statements, [a defendant is] essentially informed of the possible consequences of going without counsel during questioning. If [a defendant] nonetheless lack[s] 'a full and complete appreciation of all the consequences flowing' from his waiver, it does not defeat the State's showing that the information it provided to him satisfied the constitutional minimum." *Id.* at 2396.

Accordingly, "an accused who is admonished with the warnings prescribed by [*Miranda*] has been sufficiently apprised of the nature of his Sixth Amendment rights, and of the consequences of abandoning those rights, so that his waiver on this basis will be considered a knowing and intelligent one." *Id.* at 2396-2397. The Court further finds that its conclusion reached in a Fifth Amendment setting "is equally apposite here: 'Once it is determined that a suspect's decision not to rely on his rights was uncoerced, that he at all times knew he could stand mute and request a lawyer, and that he was aware of the State's intention to use his statement to secure a conviction, the analysis is complete and the waiver is valid as a matter of law.' " *Id.* at 2397 (quoting *Moran v. Burbine, supra,* 475 *U.S.* at 422-423, 106 *S.Ct.* at 1142). "So long as the accused is made aware of the 'dangers and disadvantages of self-representation' during postindictment questioning by use of the *Miranda* warnings, his waiver of his Sixth Amendment right to counsel at such questioning is 'knowing and intelligent.' " *Patterson* at 2399.

NOTE

1. During the course of the opinion in *Patterson, supra,* the Court rejected the contention that "since 'the sixth amendment right (to counsel) is far superior to that of the fifth amendment right' and since '(t)he greater the right the greater the loss from a waiver of that right,' waiver of an accused's Sixth Amendment right to counsel should be 'more difficult' to effectuate than waiver of a suspect's Fifth Amendment rights." *Id.* at 2397. [Citation omitted.] In this respect the Court explained:

> While our cases have recognized a "difference" between the Fifth Amendment and Sixth Amendment rights to counsel, and the "policies" behind these Constitutional guarantees, we have never suggested that one right is "superior" or "greater" than the other, nor is there any support in our cases for the notion that because a Sixth Amendment right may be involved, it is more difficult to waive than the Fifth Amendment counterpart.

> Instead, we have taken a more pragmatic approach to the waiver question—asking what purposes a lawyer can serve at the particular stage of the proceedings in question, and what assistance he could provide to an accused at that stage—to determine the scope of the Sixth Amendment right to counsel, and the type of warnings and procedures that should be required before a waiver of that right will be recognized. * * * [W]e have defined the scope of the right to counsel by a pragmatic assessment of the usefulness of counsel to the accused at the particular proceeding, and the dangers to the accused of proceeding without counsel. An accused's waiver of his right to counsel is "knowing" when he is made aware of these basic facts.

Id. at 2397-2398. Using this approach, the Court took the view that "whatever warnings suffice for *Miranda's* purposes will also be sufficient in the context of postindictment questioning. * * * [Thus, with respect to this inquiry, the Court did] 'not discern a substantial difference between the usefulness of a lawyer to a suspect during custodial interrogation, and his value to an accused at postindictment questioning.' " *Id.* at 2398.

2. *See also Michigan v. Harvey,* 494 *U.S.* 344, 110 *S.Ct.* 1176 (1990), where the Court observed: "Although a defendant may sometimes later regret his decision to speak with police, the Sixth Amendment does not disable a criminal defendant from exercising his free will. To hold that a defendant is inherently incapable of relinquishing his right to counsel once it is invoked would be 'to imprison a man in his privileges and call it the Constitution.' " *Id.,* 110 *S.Ct.* at 1182 (quoting *Adams v. United States ex rel. McCann,* 317 *U.S.* 269, 280, 63 *S.Ct.* 236, 242 (1942)).

3. The dissenting justices in *Patterson* placed far greater significance on the return of the indictment. These justices emphasized:

> "The initiation of judicial criminal proceedings is far from a mere formalism. It is the starting point of our whole system of adversary criminal justice. For it is only then that the government has committed itself to prosecute, and only then that the adverse positions of government and defendant have solidified. It is then that a defendant finds himself faced with the prosecutorial forces of organized society, and immersed in the intricacies of substantive and procedural criminal law. It is this point, therefore, that marks the commencement of the 'criminal prosecutions' to which alone the explicit guarantees of the Sixth Amendment are applicable."

Patterson at 304, 108 *S.Ct.* at 2401. [Citations omitted.] Noting the "strong presumption against waiver of Sixth Amendment protections," the dissent concluded that *Miranda* warnings were inadequate to satisfy the high standard placed on the defendant's right to counsel. *Id.* at 307, 108 *S.Ct.* at 2402-03. Speaking for the dissent, Justice Stevens found that the *Miranda* warnings amounted to a "gross understatement of the disadvantage of proceeding without a lawyer and an understatement of what a defendant must understand to make a knowing waiver." *Id.* at 307-08, 108 *S.Ct.* at 2403.

MAINE v. MOULTON
Supreme Court of the United States
474 U.S. 159, 106 S.Ct. 477 (1985)

QUESTION: Does the Sixth Amendment prohibit the use (at trial) of post-indictment statements made to a police informant, when those statements were recorded as part of a good faith investigation of entirely separate crimes ?

ANSWER: YES. An indicted defendant's Sixth Amendment Right to Counsel is violated when the police arrange the recording of conversations between the defendant and his codefendant-turned-police-informant at a meeting where both defendants, without counsel, planned to discuss defense strategy and which the police knew or should have known would produce incriminating statements concerning the defendant's pending charges. *Id.* at 487-488.

RATIONALE: Defendant Moulton and his codefendant Colson were indicted for receiving stolen property contrary to Maine's statutory law. At arraignment, both defendants, represented by counsel, pled not guilty and were released on bail pending trial.

Subsequently, defendant Colson decided to turn State's evidence and agreed to be equipped with a body wire transmitter which he agreed to wear at a meeting between defendant Moulton and himself. Colson had previously set up the meeting, but now, as a police informant, agreed to have the police monitor and record the conversation through the hidden wire.

At the meeting, Colson elicited numerous incriminating statements from Moulton concerning the charges pending under the indictment. The State used the statement against Moulton at trial and defended its actions by asserting that the police had other legitimate reasons for listening to Moulton's conversations with Colson. [Such as ensuring Colson's safety and investigating an alleged plan of Moulton to kill a State's witness.]

The Supreme Court rejected the State's argument and held that the police "violated Moulton's Sixth Amendment right when it arranged to record conversations between Moulton and its undercover informant, Colson." *Id.* at 487. The Court reasoned that the police knew or should have known that Moulton and Colson were meeting to discuss the pending charges and their plans for defense strategy. Accordingly, the Court concluded that the police knew or should have known that Moulton would probably make statements that he had a constitutional right not to make to a police-undercover-informant without the presence of a lawyer.

"By concealing the fact that Colson was an agent of the State, the police denied Moulton the opportunity to consult with counsel and thus denied him the assistance of counsel guaranteed by the Sixth Amendment." *Id.* at 488.

The right to the assistance of counsel "attaches at earlier 'critical' stages in the criminal justice process 'where the results might settle the accused's fate and reduce the trial to a mere formality.'" *Id.* at 484.

The right to counsel guaranteed by the Sixth Amendment and made applicable to the states via the Fourteenth Amendment "means at least that a person is entitled to the help of a lawyer at or after the time that judicial proceedings have been initiated against him, [and,] at the very least, the prosecutor and the police have an affirmative obligation not to act in a manner that circumvents and thereby dilutes the protection afforded by the right to counsel." *Id.*

The Court does note, however, that the Sixth Amendment will not be violated if "by luck or happenstance" the police obtain incriminating statements from the accused after the right to counsel has attached. *Id.* at 487. Nonetheless, whenever the police take advantage of an opportunity to engage in a knowing exploitation by confronting the accused without the presence of counsel, the Court will find this to be a "breach of the State's obligation not to circumvent the right to the assistance of counsel as is the intentional creation of such an opportunity." *Id.*

As a result, a Sixth Amendment violation will arise when the police obtain "incriminating statements from an accused by knowingly circumventing the accused's right to have counsel present in a confrontation between the accused and a [police] agent," *id.*, "notwithstanding the fact that the police were also investigating other crimes[.]" *Id.* at 489. However, evidence pertaining to charges as to which the Sixth Amendment right to counsel had not yet attached at the time the evidence was obtained will be deemed admissible. *Id.*

KUHLMANN v. WILSON
Supreme Court of the United States
477 U.S. 436, 106 S.Ct. 2616 (1986)

QUESTION: Does the Sixth Amendment prohibit the admission in evidence of an accused's post-arraignment statements to a jailhouse informant who was placed in close proximity to the accused but made no effort to stimulate conversations about the crime charged ?

ANSWER: NO. A defendant does not make out a Sixth Amendment right to counsel violation "simply by showing that a [police] informant, either through prior arrangement or voluntarily, reported his incriminating statements to the police. Rather, the defendant must demonstrate that the police and their informant took some action, beyond merely listening, that was designed deliberately to elicit incriminating remarks." *Id.* at 2630.

RATIONALE: Defendant Wilson was arrested for his involvement in the robbery of the Star Taxicab Garage in the Bronx, New York, and the murder of the night dispatcher. "After his arraignment, [Wilson] was confined in the Bronx House of Detention, where he was placed in a cell with a prisoner named Benny Lee. Unknown to [Wilson], Lee had agreed to act as police informant." *Id.* at 2619. Lee was instructed by Detective Cullen not to ask Wilson any questions, "but simply to 'keep his ears open' for the names of the other perpetrators." *Id.* Lee followed these directions; he "at no time asked any questions with respect to the crime, and * * * only listened to [Wilson] and made notes regarding what [Wilson] had to say." *Id.* at 2620.

At the motion to suppress, Wilson argued that the incriminating statements made to Lee [and turned over to the police] were obtained in violation of his Sixth Amendment right to counsel, and as such, should be suppressed.

The United States Supreme Court disagreed. In *Massiah v. United States*, 377 *U.S.* 201, 84 *S.Ct.* 1199 (1964), it was held that "once a defendant's Sixth Amendment right to counsel has attached, he is denied that right when federal agents 'deliberately elicit' incriminating statements from him in the absence of his lawyer." *Wilson* at 2629 (quoting *Massiah* at 206, 84 *S.Ct.*, at 1203). "The defendant in *Massiah* made the incriminating statements in a conversation with one of his confederates, who had secretly agreed to permit government agents to listen to the conversation over a radio transmitter. The agents instructed the confederate to 'engage Massiah in conversation relating to the alleged crimes.'" *Wilson* at 2629 n.20. [Citation omitted.]

Sixteen years later, the Court in *United States v. Henry*, 447 *U.S.* 264, 100 *S.Ct.* 2183 (1980), applied the test set forth in *Massiah* to suppress a defendant's statements made to a paid jailhouse informant. In *Henry*, a violation of *Massiah* was found "because the informant had engaged the defendant in conversations and 'had developed a relationship of trust and confidence with the defendant such that the defendant revealed incriminating information.'" *Wilson* at 2629. [Citations omitted.] While the *Henry* informant did not question the defendant, he nonetheless "stimulated" conversations with him in order to "elicit" incriminating information. Thus, the situation in *Henry*, like the situation in *Massiah*, "amounted to 'indirect and surreptitious interrogation' of the defendant." *Wilson* at 2629. [Citations omitted.]

In the present case, Detective Cullen specifically instructed Lee only to listen to Wilson for the limited purpose of ascertaining the identities of the other participants in the robbery and murder. Lee, in fact, followed those instructions; he did not question Wilson concerning the pending charges, but "only listened" to Wilson's "spontaneous" and "unsolicited" statements. *Id.* at 2630. As Chief Justice Burger pointed out, "[t]here is a vast difference between placing an 'ear' in the suspect's cell and placing a voice in the cell to encourage conversations for the 'ear' to record." *Id.* at 2631 (Burger, C.J., concurring).

As was recognized in *Maine v. Moulton, supra*, "the primary concern of the *Massiah* line of decisions is secret interrogation by investigatory techniques that are the equivalent of direct police interrogation. Since 'the Sixth Amendment is not violated whenever—by luck or happenstance—the State obtains incriminating statements from the accused after the right to counsel has attached,' * * * a defendant does not make out a violation of that right simply by showing that an informant, either through prior arrangement or voluntarily, reported his incriminating statements to the police. Rather, the defendant must demonstrate that the police and their informant took some action, beyond merely listening, that was designed deliberately to elicit incriminating remarks." *Id.* at 2630. [Citations omitted.]

§11.3. Miranda.

§11.3(a). Administration; when to advise.

DUCKWORTH v. EAGAN
Supreme Court of the United States
492 U.S. 195, 109 S.Ct. 2875 (1989)

QUESTION: Does the procedure of informing a suspect that an attorney would be appointed for him "if and when you go to court" render the *Miranda* warnings inadequate ?

ANSWER: NO. The Court has "never insisted that *Miranda* warnings be given in the exact form described in [the *Miranda* decision itself]. * * * The inquiry is simply whether the warnings reasonably 'conve(y) to (a suspect) his rights as required by *Miranda*.' " *Id.* at 2879, 2880. [Citation omitted.]

RATIONALE: Defendant confessed to stabbing a woman nine times after she refused to have sexual relations with him. Before confessing, defendant was provided with, and asked to sign an "Advice of Rights" form which provided:

> Before we ask you any questions, you must understand your rights. You have the right to remain silent. Anything you say can be used against you in court. *You have the right to talk to a lawyer for advice before we ask you any questions, and to have him with you during questioning.* You have this right to the advice and presence of a lawyer even if you cannot afford to hire one. *We have no way of giving you a lawyer, but one will be appointed for you, if you wish, if and when you go to court.* If you wish to answer questions now without a lawyer present, you have the right to stop answering at any time until you have talked to a lawyer.

Id. at 2877. [Emphasis in original.]

The United States Circuit Court of Appeals for the Seventh Circuit held that this warning did not comply with the strict requirements of *Miranda*, reasoning that the advice that counsel would be appointed "if and when you go to court," "was 'constitutionally defective because it denies an accused indigent a clear and unequivocal warning of the right to appointed counsel before an interrogation,' and 'link(s) an indigent's right to counsel before interrogation with a future event.' " *Id.* at 2878. [Citation omitted.]

The United States Supreme Court granted *certiorari*, to decide "whether informing a suspect that an attorney would be appointed for him 'if and when you go to court' renders *Miranda* warnings inadequate. [The Court now holds] that it does not." *Id.* at 2878-2879.

In *Miranda v. Arizona*, 384 *U.S.* 436, 86 *S.Ct.* 1602 (1966), "the court established certain procedural safeguards that require police to advise criminal suspects of their rights under the Fifth and Fourteenth Amendments before commencing custodial interrogation. In now familiar words, the Court said that the suspect must be told that

> he has the right to remain silent, that anything he says can be used against him in a court of law, that he has the right to the presence of an attorney, and that if he cannot afford an attorney, one will be appointed for him prior to any questioning if he so desires."

Id. at 2879 (quoting *Miranda* at 479, 86 *S.Ct.* at 1630).

The Court has never, however, "insisted that *Miranda* warnings be given in the exact form described in the decision. In *Miranda* itself, the Court said that '(t)he warnings required and the waiver necessary in accordance with our opinion today are, *in the absence of a fully effective equivalent*, prerequisites to the admissibility of any statement made by a defendant.'" *Id.* at 2879. [Citation omitted; emphasis supplied.] In this respect, the Court, in *California v. Prysock*, 453 *U.S.* 355, 101 *S.Ct.* 2806 (1981), has declared:

> [T]he "rigidity" of *Miranda* (does not) exten(d) to the precise formulation of the warnings given a criminal defendant, [and that] no talismanic incantation (is) required to satisfy its strictures.

Prysock at 359, 101 *S.Ct.* at 2809.

Naturally, *Miranda* has not been limited to "stationhouse" questioning, "and the officer in the field may not always have access to printed *Miranda* warnings, or he may inadvertently depart from routine practice, particularly if a suspect requests an elaboration of the warnings." *Eagan* at 2879-2880. Significantly, the Court emphasizes that "[t]he prophylactic *Miranda* warnings are 'not themselves protected by the Constitution but (are) instead measures to insure that the right against compulsory self-incrimination (is) protected.'" *Id.* at 2880. [Citation omitted.] Therefore, reviewing courts are instructed that they "need not examine *Miranda* warnings as if construing a will or defining the terms of [a similar legal document]. The inquiry is simply whether the warnings reasonably 'conve(y) to (a suspect) his rights as required by *Miranda.*'" *Id.* at 2880 (quoting *Prysock* at 361, 101 *S.Ct.* at 2810).

The warnings given to defendant in this case "touched all the bases required by *Miranda.*" *Id.* at 2880. Moreover, the warnings "accurately described the procedure for the appointment of counsel in Indiana." *Id.* According to the Court, "*Miranda* does not require that attorneys be producible on call, but only that the suspect be informed, as here, that he has the right to an attorney before and during questioning, and that the attorney would be appointed for him if he could not afford one." *Id.* There was no suggestion in *Miranda* that each police department must have a "stationhouse lawyer" present at all times to advise prisoners. *Id.*

Accordingly, "the initial warnings given to [defendant], in their totality, satisfied *Miranda,*" *id.* at 2880-2881, and therefore defendant's confession was properly admitted into evidence.

STATE v. GOSSER
Supreme Court of New Jersey
50 *N.J.* 438, 236 *A.*2d 377 (1967)

QUESTION: Is the administration of *Miranda* warnings absolutely required prior to an officer's engaging in "on-the-scene questioning" as to the facts surrounding a crime ?

ANSWER: NO. In addition to recognizing that uncoerced, freely-volunteered statements are admissible at trial even in the absence of *Miranda*, courts also recognize an exception to the *Miranda* exclusionary rule which permits the introduction of a suspect's responses to an officer's "on-the-scene questioning as to the facts surrounding a crime." *Id.*, 50 *N.J.* at 446.

RATIONALE: Sea Isle City police responded to defendant's home after receiving a call from a friend of defendant's wife. She informed police officials that defendant stated to her that "something terrible had happened," and that he was requesting her presence at his house. Upon arrival at defendant's home, the patrol officer knocked on the door. When defendant opened the door "[h]e appeared groggy, upset and crying, with caked blood on his pajamas and his face. The officer asked what the trouble was and he said that he had killed his wife. He was directed to sit on the couch in the living room and remain there. The officer returned to the patrol car in front of the home and radioed to headquarters for assistance." *Id.* at 443. The officer waited outside for his backup, and upon the arrival of a sergeant and another patrol officer, he again knocked on the door, calling for defendant.

When defendant again appeared at the door, the sergeant asked what had happened. "Defendant said he had shot his wife. When asked where she was, he replied, 'upstairs.' The three then entered the house and the sergeant and one of the officers raced upstairs and searched from room to room. The other patrolmen * * * remained downstairs to watch the defendant[.]" *Id.* at 444. Defendant then "started complaining to this officer, without being questioned, about his wife's nagging and said that 'all of a sudden something just snapped' and 'I ought to get the electric chair for this.' He also volunteered that he had taken a box of pills and wanted a glass of water." *Id.*

The officers found Mrs. Gosser's body in an upstairs bedroom, "lying on the floor near the bed in her night clothing, with a gaping wound in the abdomen[,]" *id.*, obviously dead.

After the discovery of the body (and the shotgun), the sergeant advised defendant that he was under arrest and placed him in handcuffs. He then called the prosecutor's office for assistance and a local physician for the pronouncement of death and examination or treatment of defendant.

First to arrive was the physician, who pronounced Mrs. Gosser dead. Shortly thereafter, as defendant was being examined by the doctor, an assistant prosecutor and a county detective arrived. During his examination, defendant stated to the doctor that he had taken 17 sleeping pills, and then, "without any prompting or interrogation, made rambling statements [which included] * * * that he didn't mean to do it, his wife was always on his neck; that he wanted to go to the state mental hospital; that he was having hallucinations and delusions and had nightmares all night; and that he had put two shells in the gun, one to use on himself, [but] then used the pills instead." *Id.* at 445.

Defendant was convicted of second-degree murder. In this appeal, he contends that the testimony of the physician and county detective of the statements made by him during his physical examination should not have been admitted due to the failure of the officers to administer the *Miranda* warnings. The New Jersey Supreme Court rejected this contention, and in so doing also addressed the propriety of an officer's on-the-scene questioning of a suspect as to the facts surrounding a crime.

As a general rule, *Miranda's* exclusionary rule "bars from evidence statements of a defendant made during in-custody interrogation unless he has been advised [of his constitutional rights] and has knowingly and intelligently waived such rights." *Id.* at 445-446. The Court in *Miranda* "recognized, however, at least two exceptions. One is general on-the-scene questioning as to facts surrounding a crime, and the other, statements freely volunteered without compelling influences." *Id.* at 446. (citing *Miranda v. Arizona*, 384 *U.S.* 436, 477-478, 86 *S.Ct.* 1602, 1629 (1966)).

Defendant's statements to the first-arriving Sea Isle City police officer—that he had killed or shot his wife—and then repeated to the sergeant "clearly fall in the first category[,]" that of on-the-scene questioning as to facts surrounding a crime and, accordingly, are clearly admissible notwithstanding the absence of *Miranda* warnings. *Gosser* at 446. As to the second category, it is true that defendant's statements to the physician and county detective were made "while in custody"; however, it is clear "that they were completely volunteered and not the product of any interrogation[.]" *Id.*

The Court also rejected defendant's argument that the statements were not truly "voluntary" in the fundamental fairness sense due to his situation and physical and mental condition at the time. Here, the Court explains "that defendant thoroughly understood his situation and that the statements were completely unsolicited expressions of remorse or attempts at explanation and rationalization of what he fully realized he had done." *Id.*

Accordingly, defendant's conviction for second-degree murder in the shotgun slaying of his wife is affirmed.

NOTE

Volunteered statements and follow-up questions. There are some volunteered statements that beg the use of follow-up questions. For example, an individual walks up to a uniformed officer and says, "I did it." The officer responds with a natural follow-up question, "Did what ?" So long as the nature of the officer's follow-up questions may be deemed a "continuation of the volunteered statement," the questions will not rise to the level of "interrogation" within the meaning of *Miranda*. Thus, questions designed to clarify what has been volunteered, or to ascertain if an individual is in need of medical attention, are not the type of questions that must be preceded by *Miranda* warnings. On the other hand, questions designed to elicit incriminating responses, enhance the suspect's guilt, or raise the degree of a suspected offense are dangerous follow-up questions and should only be asked after the subject has been properly warned.

In *State v. Gravel*, 601 A.2d 678 (N.H. 1991), the defendant was arrested for drunk driving and transported to the police station. At the station, the police learned that defendant's license had been revoked and that active bench warrants for his arrest for an unrelated offense were outstanding. During the ride to the county jail, the following conversation took place between the state trooper and defendant.

Defendant: "Is there a doctor at the jail ?"

Trooper: "Well, do you want to go to the hospital ?"

Defendant: "No. But I am going to need to see somebody."

Trooper: "Why ?"

Defendant: "Well, I am going to be coming down in a few hours, and I am going to need something."

Trooper: "Well, what are you coming down from ?"

Defendant: "Coke. What do you think ?"

[Trooper: "How much ?"]

[Defendant: "I freebased an eightball of cocaine earlier in the day."]

Trooper: "Oh. . . . Well, do you have any more drugs on you ?"

Defendant: "No. I am not stupid enough to get caught carrying it."

Trooper: "Well, where do you do your drugs ?"

Defendant: "I do everything in my bedroom."

Id. at 679. The defendant went on to say that he had used the drugs that day in his bedroom. Based on the information defendant provided, the trooper sought and obtained a warrant to search defendant's bedroom. The search uncovered drug paraphernalia and trace amounts of cocaine.

The threshold question, according to the court, was whether, at the time the defendant made the incriminating remarks, he was entitled to *Miranda* warnings. There was no dispute that at the time of the exchange, the defendant was "in custody." Thus, the critical inquiry was whether defendant was "interrogated" within the meaning of *Miranda*.

The state contended that defendant "was not being questioned, as he in fact initiated the conversation and volunteered the incriminating comments." *Id.* at 681. The court could not agree.

> In this case, although the defendant initiated the conversation "in the ordinary dictionary sense of that word," * * * Trooper Quinn extended it with express questions of his own[.] The defendant clearly opened the dialogue by asking if there would be a doctor at the jail, but it was Trooper Quinn who shifted the direction and altered the character of the conversation. *While the officer's initial queries into the type of drug used, the method employed, and the amount ingested were follow-up questions germane to determining whether medical care would be required, his subsequent questions pertaining to the location where the drug was used sought only to elicit incriminating evidence and, thus, constituted interrogation.*

> * * * We hold that once the focus of the colloquy shifted from the potential need for medical care to an inquiry concerning the location of the defendant's drug use, it constituted custodial interrogation within the meaning of *Miranda*.

Id. [Emphasis added.]

STANSBURY v. CALIFORNIA
Supreme Court of the United States
511 *U.S.* 318, 114 *S.Ct.* 1526 (1994)

QUESTION: Is a person's right to receive *Miranda* warnings triggered when he or she becomes a suspect in, or the focus of, an officer's investigation?

ANSWER: NO. A law enforcement officer's obligation to administer *Miranda* warnings attaches *only* where there has been such a restriction on a person's freedom as to render him or her "in custody." *Id.* at 1528. A person's *Miranda* rights are not triggered by virtue of the fact that he or she has become the focus of an officer's suspicions. *Id.* at 1530. Case law "makes clear, in no uncertain terms, that any inquiry into whether the interrogating officers have focused their suspicions upon the individual being questioned (assuming those suspicions remain undisclosed) is not relevant for purposes of *Miranda*." *Id.*

RATIONALE: To determine whether an individual was in custody during police questioning, courts will examine "all of the circumstances surrounding the interrogation, but 'the ultimate inquiry is simply whether there [was] a "formal arrest or restraint on freedom of movement" of the degree associated with a formal arrest.'" *Id.* at 1528-29. [Citations omitted.]

"[T]he initial determination of custody depends on the objective circumstances of the interrogation, not on the subjective views harbored by either the interrogating officers or the person being questioned." *Id.* at 1529. This was made clear in *Beckwith v. United States*, 425 *U.S.* 341, 96 *S.Ct.* 1612 (1976), where the Court rejected the defendant's contention that *Miranda* " 'be extended to cover interrogation in non-custodial circumstances after a police interrogation has focused on the suspect.' " *Stansbury* at 1529. [Citation omitted.] According to the *Beckwith* Court, it " 'was the compulsive aspect of custodial interrogation, and not the strength of the government's suspicions at the time the questioning was conducted, which led the Court to impose the *Miranda* requirements with regard to custodial questioning.' " *Stansbury* at 1529 (quoting *Beckwith* at 346-47, 96 *S.Ct.* at 1616).

"It is well settled, then, that a police officer's subjective view that the individual under questioning is a suspect, if undisclosed, does not bear upon the question whether the individual is in custody for purposes of *Miranda*. * * * The same principle obtains if an officer's undisclosed assessment is that the person being questioned is not a suspect. In either instance, one cannot expect the person under interrogation to probe the officer's innermost thoughts." *Id.* at 1529-30. Except when they are communicated or otherwise made known to the person being questioned, "an officer's evolving but unarticulated suspicions do not affect the objective circumstances of an interrogation or interview, and thus cannot affect the *Miranda* custody inquiry. 'The threat to a citizen's Fifth Amendment rights that *Miranda* was designed to neutralize has little to do with the strength of an interrogating officer's suspicions.' " *Id.* at 1530. [Citation omitted.]

On the other hand, "[a]n officer's knowledge or beliefs may bear upon the custody issue if they are conveyed, by word or deed, to the individual being questioned. * * * Those beliefs are relevant only to the extent they would affect how a reasonable person in the position of the individual being questioned would gauge the breadth of his or her 'freedom of action.' " *Id.*

> Even a clear statement from the officer that the person under interrogation is a prime suspect is not, in itself, dispositive of the custody issue, for some suspects are free to come and go until the police decide to make an arrest. The weight and pertinence of any communications regarding the officer's degree of suspicion will depend upon the facts and circumstances of the particular case.

Id.

"In sum, an officer's views concerning the nature of an interrogation, or beliefs concerning the potential culpability of the individual being questioned, may be one among many factors that bear upon the assessment whether that individual was in custody." *Id.* But those views alone are not dispositive. "(Of course, instances may arise in which the officer's undisclosed views are relevant in testing the credibility of his or her account of what happened during an interrogation;

but it is the objective surroundings, and not any undisclosed views, that control the *Miranda* custody inquiry.)" *Id.*

ILLINOIS v. PERKINS
Supreme Court of the United States
496 *U.S.* 292, 110 *S.Ct.* 2394 (1990)

QUESTION: Must an undercover law enforcement officer, posing as a fellow inmate, administer *Miranda* warnings to an incarcerated suspect before asking questions that may elicit an incriminating response?

ANSWER: NO. *Prior to the filing of formal charges,** "[c]onversations between suspects and undercover agents do not implicate the concerns underlying *Miranda*. The essential ingredients of a 'police-dominated atmosphere' and compulsion are not present when an incarcerated person speaks freely to someone that he believes to be a fellow inmate." *Id.* at 2397. Thus, "an undercover law enforcement officer posing as a fellow inmate need not give *Miranda* warnings to an incarcerated suspect before asking questions that may elicit an incriminating response." *Id.* at 2399.

RATIONALE: Police authorities learned through a reliable source that defendant, Lloyd Perkins, was boasting about his role in the murder of Richard Stephenson while Perkins was incarcerated in the Graham Correctional Facility. The police proceeded to follow up the information but soon discovered that Perkins had been released from Graham. They traced Perkins to a jail in Montgomery County, Illinois, where he was being held pending trial on an assault charge, unrelated to the Stephenson murder.

In order to further investigate Perkins' connection with the Stephenson murder, investigators decided to place an undercover agent and an informant (known to Perkins) in the cellblock with Perkins. The plan was for the informant and undercover agent John Parisi to pose as escapees from a work release program who had been arrested in the course of a burglary. Parisi and the informant were instructed "to engage [Perkins] in casual conversation and report anything he said about the Stephenson murder." *Id.* at 2396.

Using the alias "Vito Bianco," Parisi entered the cellblock at the Montgomery County jail with the informant by his side, both clothed

---

* In the absence of formal charges, the interaction between an undercover officer and a defendant does not represent a "critical stage" of the proceedings. Consequently, the Court's Sixth Amendment decisions in *Massiah v. United States*, 377 *U.S.* 201, 84 *S.Ct.* 1199 (1964), *United States v. Henry*, 447 *U.S.* 264, 100 *S.Ct.* 2183 (1980), and *Maine v. Moulton*, 474 *U.S.* 159, 106 *S.Ct.* 477 (1985), do not apply. The Court "held in those cases that the government may not use an undercover agent to circumvent the Sixth Amendment right to counsel once a suspect has been charged with a crime. After charges have been filed, the Sixth Amendment prevents the government from interfering with the accused's right to counsel." *Perkins* at 2398-2399. Because "no [formal] charges had been filed [against Perkins] *on the subject of the interrogation,* [the Court's] Sixth Amendment precedents are not applicable." *Id.* at 2399. [Emphasis added.]

in jail garb. Perkins greeted the informant who, after a brief conversation with Perkins, introduced Parisi by his alias. Parisi told Perkins that he "wasn't going to do any more time," and suggested that the three of them escape. Perkins replied that the Montgomery County jail was "rinky-dink" and that they could "break out." Later that evening, the three met in Perkins' cell, after the other inmates were asleep, to refine their plan. Perkins said that his girlfriend could smuggle in a pistol. The informant then replied, "Hey, I'm not a murderer, I'm a burglar. That's your guys' profession." After telling the informant that he would be responsible for any murder that occurred, Parisi asked Perkins if he had ever "done" anybody. Perkins stated that he had, and proceeded to describe at length the events of the Stephenson murder. Parisi and Perkins then engaged in some casual conversation before Perkins went to sleep. At no time did Parisi give Perkins *Miranda* warnings.

In this appeal, Perkins argued that the statements he made "should be inadmissible because he had not been given *Miranda* warnings by the agent." *Id.* at 2396. *The United States Supreme Court disagreed, holding that the statements were admissible* because, in this context, "*Miranda* warnings are not required when the suspect is unaware that he is speaking to a law enforcement officer and gives a voluntary statement." *Id.*

"The warning mandated by *Miranda* was meant to preserve the privilege [against self-incrimination] during 'incommunicado interrogation of individuals in a police-dominated atmosphere.' * * * That atmosphere is said to generate 'inherently compelling pressures which work to undermine the individual's will to resist and to compel him to speak where he would not otherwise do so freely.' " *Id.* at 2397. [Citations omitted.]

"Conversations between suspects and undercover agents do not implicate the concerns underlying *Miranda*. The essential ingredients of a 'police-dominated atmosphere' and compulsion are not present when an incarcerated person speaks freely to someone that he believes to be a fellow inmate." *Id.* In this respect, "[c]oercion is determined from the perspective of the suspect." *Id.* "When a suspect considers himself in the company of cellmates and not officers, the coercive atmosphere is lacking[, and there is no] basis for the assumption that a suspect speaking to those whom he assumes are not officers will feel compelled to speak by the fear of reprisal for remaining silent or in the hope of more lenient treatment should he confess." *Id.*

While "the premise of *Miranda* [is] that the danger of coercion results from the interaction of custody and official interrogation[, the Court] reject[s] the argument that *Miranda* warnings are required whenever a suspect is in custody in a technical sense and converses with someone who happens to be a government agent. Questioning by captors, who appear to control the suspect's fate, may create mutually reinforcing pressures that the Court has assumed will weaken the suspect's will, but where a suspect does not know that he is conversing with a government agent, these pressures do not exist. * * * When the suspect has no reason to think that the listeners have official power over him, it should not be assumed that his words are motivated by the reaction he expects from his listeners." *Id.*

"[W]hen the agent carries neither badge nor gun and wears not 'police blue,' but the same prison gray" as the suspect, there is no "*interplay* between police interrogation and police custody."

Id. [Citation omitted; emphasis in original.]

According to the Court, "*Miranda* forbids coercion, not mere strategic deception by taking advantage of a suspect's misplaced trust in one he supposes to be a fellow prisoner. * * * Ploys to mislead a suspect or lull him into a false sense of security that do not rise to the level of compulsion or coercion to speak are not within *Miranda's* concerns." *Id. Cf. Oregon v. Mathiason*, 429 *U.S.* 492, 495-496, 97 *S.Ct.* 711, 714 (1977) (officer's falsely telling suspect that suspect's fingerprints had been found at crime scene did not render interview "custodial" under *Miranda*).

"*Miranda* was not meant to protect suspects from boasting about their criminal activities in front of persons whom they believe to be their cellmates. This case is illustrative. [Perkins] had no reason to feel that undercover agent Parisi had any legal authority to force him to answer questions or that Parisi could affect [Perkins'] future treatment. [Perkins] viewed the cellmate-agent as an equal and showed no hint of being intimidated by the atmosphere of the jail. In recounting the details of the Stephenson murder, [Perkins] was motivated solely by the desire to impress his fellow inmates. He spoke at his own peril." *Id.* at 2398.

"The tactic employed here to elicit a voluntary confession from a suspect does not violate the Self-Incrimination Clause. * * * Where the suspect does not know that he is speaking to a government agent there is no reason to assume the possibility that the suspect might feel coerced." *Id.*

Contrary to Perkins' contention, "[l]aw enforcement officers will have little difficulty putting into practice [the ruling herein] that undercover agents need not give *Miranda* warnings to incarcerated suspects. The use of undercover agents is a recognized law enforcement technique, often employed in the prison context to detect violence against correctional officials or inmates, as well as for the purposes served here. The interests protected by *Miranda* are not implicated in these cases, and the warnings are not required to safeguard the constitutional rights of inmates who make voluntary statements to undercover agents." *Id.* at 2399.

Accordingly, "an undercover law enforcement officer posing as a fellow inmate need not give *Miranda* warnings to an incarcerated suspect before asking questions that may elicit an incriminating response. The statements at issue in this case were voluntary, and there is no federal obstacle to their admissibility at trial." *Id.*

NOTE

Probation officers. Generally, the required meeting which routinely takes place between a probation officer and a probationer does not rise to the level of "custody" within the meaning of *Miranda*. *Minnesota v. Murphy*, 465 *U.S.* 420, 104 *S.Ct.* 1136 (1984). In this respect, the Court in *Murphy* emphasized that at such a meeting, the probationer is "not 'in custody' for purposes of receiving *Miranda* protection since there [is] no ' "formal arrest or restraint on freedom of movement" of the degree associated with a formal arrest.' " *Murphy* at 430, 104 *S.Ct.* at 1144. [Citations omitted.] "Custodial interrogation," for purposes of *Miranda*, conveys "to the suspect a message that he has no choice but to submit to the officers' will and to confess. * * * It is unlikely that a probation interview, arranged by appointment at a mutually convenient time, would give rise to a similar impression." *Id.* at 433, 104 *S.Ct.* at 1145.

Moreover, "the general obligation to appear and answer questions truthfully d[oes] not in itself convert [a probationer's] otherwise voluntary statements into compelled ones." *Id.* at 427, 104 *S.Ct.* at 1142. It is true that a probation officer may compel a probationer to attend periodic meetings and to answer questions truthfully. This does not, however, transform "a routine interview into an inherently coercive setting." *Id.* at 431, 104 *S.Ct.* at 1144. During the course of the meeting, a probation officer may even consciously seek incriminating evidence. Yet, "[t]he mere fact that an investigation has focused on a suspect does not trigger the need for *Miranda* warnings in noncustodial settings, * * * and the probation officer's knowledge and intent have no bearing" in this regard. *Id.* "[T]he nature of probation is such that probationers should expect to be questioned on a wide range of topics," even those "related to their past criminality." *Id.* at 432, 104 *S.Ct.* at 1144.

"A probationer cannot pretend ignorance of the fact that his probation officer 'is a peace officer, and as such is allied to a greater or lesser extent, with his fellow peace officers.' * * * Absent some express or implied promise to the contrary, he may also be charged with knowledge that 'the probation officer is duty bound to report wrongdoing by the [probationer] when it comes to his attention, even if by communication from the [probationer] himself.' " *Id.* at 432, 104 *S.Ct.* at 1145. [Citation omitted.]

While a probation officer may require a probationer to appear and discuss matters that touch and concern his probationary status, a different result may obtain "if the questions put to the probationer, however relevant to his probationary status, call for answers that would incriminate him in a pending or later criminal prosecution." *Id.* at 435, 104 *S.Ct.* at 1146. In this respect, the *Murphy* Court noted that while a probation officer "may insist on answers to even incriminating questions," the officer must recognize that compelling answers *under the threat of probation revocation* will result in the suppression of those answers in a subsequent criminal proceeding. *Id.* at 435 n.7, 104 *S.Ct.* at 1146 n.7. It is clear, therefore, that rather than answering questions designed to elicit incriminating responses concerning a separate criminal proceeding, the probationer may assert his or her right to remain silent; and the legitimate exercise of the Fifth Amendment privilege may not be used to revoke probation. *Id.* at 438, 104 *S.Ct.* at 1148. On the other hand, when a probationer reveals incriminating information instead of timely asserting his or her right to remain silent, and when no penalty has been threatened for the legitimate exercise of the Fifth Amendment privilege, the probationer's disclosures will not be considered "compelled incriminations," and they may be used against the probationer in a subsequent criminal prosecution. *Id.* at 440, 104 *S.Ct.* at 1149.

---

§11.3(b). *Miranda* and motor vehicle offenses.

BERKEMER v. McCARTY
Supreme Court of the United States
468 *U.S.* 420, 104 *S.Ct.* 3138 (1984)

QUESTION 1: When a law enforcement officer places a motorist under arrest for a traffic violation, must the officer advise the motorist of his *Miranda* rights prior to any interrogation ?

ANSWER: YES. Prior to interrogation, a person must be advised of his *Miranda* rights if his freedom of action is curtailed to a degree associated with a formal arrest. Moreover, "a person subjected to custodial interrogation is entitled to the benefit of the [*Miranda* warnings] regardless of the nature or severity of the offense of which he is suspected or for which he was arrested." *Id.* at 3148.

QUESTION 2: Must a law enforcement officer administer *Miranda* warnings during the course of a traffic stop where the officer temporarily detains a motorist in order to ask a few brief questions and issue a traffic citation ?

ANSWER: NO. An ordinary traffic stop, by its very nature "is presumptively temporary and brief," lasting "only a few minutes." *Id.* at 3149. It generally involves no more than a check of credentials and issuance of citations for violations observed. Therefore, "persons temporarily detained pursuant to such stops are not 'in custody' for the purposes of Miranda." *Id.* at 3151.

QUESTION 3: At what point in the below set of circumstances was the officer required to give defendant McCarty *Miranda* warnings ?

CIRCUMSTANCES:

1. In late March, Ohio State Trooper Williams stopped the car Richard McCarty was driving for weaving in and out of his lane of travel.

2. As soon as McCarty stopped, Trooper Williams asked him to step out of the car. McCarty had difficulty standing as he stepped out of the vehicle.

3. At this point, Trooper Williams concluded that McCarty would be charged with a traffic offense and, therefore, his freedom to leave the scene was terminated. McCarty was not told, however, that he would be taken into custody.

4. Trooper Williams asked McCarty to perform a field sobriety test—a balancing test—which McCarty could not perform without falling.

5. The trooper asked McCarty if he had been using any intoxicants. McCarty replied that he "had consumed two beers and had smoked several joints of marijuana a short time before."

6. As McCarty spoke to Williams, the trooper noticed that McCarty's speech was slurred and that it was difficult to understand him.

7. Trooper Williams formally placed McCarty under arrest and transported him to the Franklin County, Ohio, jail.

8. At the jail, after a breath test did not reveal any concentration of alcohol in McCarty's blood, Trooper Williams continued questioning him to obtain information for the Alcohol Influence Report. When asked if he was under the influence of alcohol, McCarty answered, "I guess, barely." McCarty then reported that there was no angel dust or PCP in the marijuana that he had smoked.

ANSWER: AFTER POINT 7.   Under the circumstances presented, the Court held that McCarty was not entitled to *Miranda* warnings "at any point prior to the time Trooper Williams placed him under arrest." *Id.* at 3151. The initial motor vehicle stop did not, by itself, render McCarty "in custody." *Id.* In addition, the Court ruled that McCarty "failed to demonstrate that, at any time between the initial stop and the arrest, he was subjected to restraints comparable to those associated with a formal arrest." *Id.*

RATIONALE: Preliminarily, the Court held that the requirement that law enforcement officers administer *Miranda* warnings prior to custodial interrogation clearly applies to interrogations involving minor offenses as well as serious offenses. Once a person is subjected to "custodial interrogation," he is entitled to the benefit of the procedural safeguards set forth in *Miranda*, "regardless of the nature or severity of the offense of which he is suspected or for which he was arrested." *Id.* at 3148.

The Court held, however, that McCarty was not "in custody" until "he was formally placed under arrest and instructed to get into the police car." *Id.* During the course of its opinion, the Court noted that a traffic stop significantly curtails the "freedom of action" of the driver and the passengers, if any, of the detained vehicle. Moreover, under the Fourth Amendment, the stopping of a motor vehicle and the detaining of its occupants is a "seizure" which requires a constitutional justification. *Id.* at 3149 (citing *Delaware v. Prouse*, 440 *U.S.* 648, 653, 99 *S.Ct.* 1391, 1396 (1979)). This temporary stop, however, like the *Terry* stop, does not constitute "custody" for purposes of *Miranda*.

Two features of the ordinary traffic stop militate against a finding that the attendant roadside questioning should be considered "custodial interrogation."

> First, detention of a motorist pursuant to a traffic stop is presumptively temporary and brief. The vast majority of roadside detentions last only a few minutes. * * *

> Second, circumstances associated with the typical traffic stop are not such that the motorist feels completely at the mercy of the police. * * * [T]he typical traffic stop is public, at least to some degree. Passersby, on foot or in other cars, witness the interaction of officer and motorist. * * * In short, the atmosphere surrounding an ordinary traffic stop is substantially less "police dominated" than that surrounding the kinds of interrogation at issue in *Miranda* itself[.] * * *

Id. at 3149-50.

As in the case of the typical *Terry* stop, which is not subject to the dictates of *Miranda*, "[t]he similarly noncoercive aspect of ordinary traffic stops [prompted the Court to hold] that persons temporarily detained pursuant to such stops are not 'in custody' for the purposes of *Miranda*." *Id.* at 3151.

It is well settled, however, that "as soon as a suspect's freedom of action is curtailed to a 'degree associated with formal arrest,'" the *Miranda* safeguards come into play. *Id.* [Citations omitted.] "If a motorist who has been detained pursuant to a traffic stop thereafter is subjected to treatment that renders him 'in custody' for practical purposes, he will be entitled to" *Miranda* warnings. *Id.*

In this case, the Court could find nothing in the facts that indicated that McCarty should have been given *Miranda* warnings "at any point prior to the time Trooper Williams placed him under arrest." *Id.* Nor do the circumstances demonstrate that, "at any time between the initial stop and the arrest," McCarty was "subjected to restraints comparable to those associated with a formal arrest." *Id.*

"Although Trooper Williams apparently decided as soon as [McCarty] stepped out of his car that [he] would be taken into custody and charged with a traffic offense, Williams never communicated his intention to [McCarty]. A police[officer's] unarticulated plan has no bearing on the question of whether a suspect was 'in custody' at a particular time; the only relevant inquiry is how a reasonable [person] in the suspect's position would have understood his situation." *Id.* at 3152.

Accordingly, the Court concluded that McCarty "was not taken into custody for purposes of *Miranda* until Williams arrested him. Consequently, the statements [McCarty] made prior to that point were admissible against him." *Id.* Because he was not advised of his constitutional rights after his arrest, his subsequent admissions should not have been used against him. *Id.* at 3148.

PENNSYLVANIA v. BRUDER
Supreme Court of the United States
488 *U.S.* 9, 109 *S.Ct.* 205 (1988)

QUESTION: Is a motorist "in custody" for *Miranda* purposes when he or she is detained for an ordinary traffic stop ?

ANSWER: NO. The " 'noncoercive aspect of ordinary traffic stops' " leads to the conclusion that " 'persons temporarily detained pursuant to such stops are *not in custody* for the purposes of *Miranda.*' " *Id.* at 206 (quoting *Berkemer v. McCarty*, 468 *U.S.* 420, 440). [Emphasis added.]

RATIONALE: Officer Steve Shallis of the Newton Township, Pennsylvania, Police Department observed defendant, Thomas Bruder, driving very erratically along State Highway 252 and pass a red light. When the officer effected the motor vehicle stop, Bruder stepped out of his car and approached the patrol vehicle. When asked for his registration card, Bruder returned to his car to obtain it. During this time, the officer smelled the odor of an alcoholic beverage and observed Bruder's stumbling movements. The officer asked Bruder whether he had been drinking and Bruder stated that he had. The officer then asked Bruder where he was going and Bruder answered that he was going home. Bruder was also requested to walk a straight line, heel-to-toe, which he was unable to do, and to recite the alphabet, which he was also unable to do. Officer Shallis then arrested him, placed him in the patrol car and gave him his *Miranda* warnings. Bruder was convicted of driving while under the influence.

In an appeal to the Pennsylvania Superior Court, defendant argued that the "statements that he made after he was stopped, as well as the results of the field sobriety test, should have been suppressed." *Commonwealth v. Bruder*, 365 *Pa.Super.* 106, 110 (1987). Except for the line-walk, heel-to-toe, the Superior Court agreed with Bruder, holding that the statements Bruder uttered during the roadside questioning were elicited through custodial interrogation and should have been suppressed for lack of *Miranda* warnings. *The United States Supreme Court granted the Commonwealth's writ, and reversed.*

"In *Berkemer v. McCarty, supra,* which involved facts strikingly similar to those in this case, the Court concluded that the 'noncoercive aspect of ordinary traffic stops prompts us to hold that persons temporarily detained pursuant to such stops are not *in custody* for purposes of *Miranda*.' " *Bruder* at 206 (quoting *Berkemer* at 440). [Emphasis added.] In this respect, "[t]he Court reasoned that although the stop was unquestionably a seizure within the meaning of the Fourth Amendment, such traffic stops typically are brief, unlike a prolonged station house interrogation. Second, the Court emphasized that traffic stops commonly occur in the 'public view,' in an atmosphere far 'less "police dominated" than that surrounding the kinds of interrogation at issue in *Miranda* itself.' * * * The detained motorist's freedom of action (was not) curtailed to 'a degree associated with formal arrest.' " *Bruder* at 206. [Citations omitted.] Accordingly, such a motorist is "not entitled to a recitation of his constitutional rights prior to arrest, and his roadside responses to questioning [are] admissible." *Id.* at 206-207.

The facts here in *Bruder* "reveal the same noncoercive aspects as the *Berkemer* detention: 'a single police officer ask(ing) [the motorist] a modest number of questions and request(ing) him to perform a simple balancing test at a location visible to passing motorists.' * * * Accordingly, *Berkemer's* rule, that ordinary traffic stops do not involve custody for purposes of *Miranda*, governs this case. The judgment of the Pennsylvania Superior Court that evidence was inadmissible for lack of *Miranda* warnings is reversed." *Id.* at 207.

NOTE

1. The *Bruder* decision should not be read as an absolute rule for all motorist detentions. Police must be vigilant to avoid undue "delay [in] formally arresting detained motorists, and . . . subject[ing] them to sustained and intimidating interrogation at the scene of their initial detention." *Berkemer* at 440, 104 *S.Ct.* at 3150.

For example, in *Commonwealth v. Meyer*, 488 *Pa.* 297 (1980), the motorist was detained for over one-half an hour, and subjected to questioning while in the patrol car. It was this "unusual prolonged detention" which caused the Pennsylvania Supreme Court to hold that *Miranda* warnings were necessary: "[C]ustodial interrogation does not require that police make a formal arrest, nor that the police intend to make an arrest . . . . Rather, the test of custodial interrogation is whether the individual being interrogated reasonably believes his freedom of action is being restricted." *Id.* at 307. In a discussion of *Meyer*, the United States Supreme Court stated, "*Meyer* involved facts which * * * might properly remove its result from *Berkemer's* application to ordinary traffic stops; specifically, the motorist in *Meyer* could be found to have been placed in custody for purposes of *Miranda* safeguards." *Bruder, supra*, 109 *S.Ct.* at 207 n.2.

2. The Superior Court, in *Commonwealth v. Bruder*, 365 *Pa.Super.* 106 (1987), also ruled that the results of Bruder's physical field sobriety test, *i.e.*, walking in a straight line, heel-to-toe, did " 'not violate the privilege against self-incrimination because the evidence procured is of a physical nature rather than testimonial, and therefore, no

Miranda warnings are required.' " *Id.* at 113 (quoting *Commonwealth v. Benson*, 280 *Pa.Super.* 20, 29 (1980)).

Bruder's recitation of the alphabet, however, is another matter. In this respect, the Superior Court found that "[w]hereas the constitutional protection against self-incrimination which *Miranda* was designed to protect does not encompass physical evidence, it does refer to testimonial evidence. * * * 'Testimonial evidence is communicative evidence as distinguished from demonstrative or physical evidence.' " *Id.* at 113 (quoting *Commonwealth v. Fernandez*, 333 *Pa.Super.* 279, 284 (1984)). Because the Superior Court viewed "the recitation of the alphabet as essentially communicative in nature[,]" it held that the recitation, in response to custodial interrogation, should be inadmissible in the absence of *Miranda*. *Id.* at 114. Since the United States Supreme Court, in *Pennsylvania v. Bruder, supra*, held that *Berkemer's* rule, that ordinary traffic stops do not involve custody for purposes of *Miranda*, governs the case, it did not reach the issue of whether recitation of the alphabet in response to custodial questioning is testimonial and hence inadmissible under *Miranda*. *Bruder*, 109 S.Ct. at 207 n.3.

PENNSYLVANIA v. MUNIZ
Supreme Court of the United States
496 *U.S.* 582, 110 *S.Ct.* 2638 (1990)

QUESTION 1: When a drunk-driving suspect slurs his speech and exhibits a lack of muscular coordination in response to custodial police questioning, are the responses "testimonial" in nature such that, if elicited in the absence of *Miranda* warnings, they will be deemed inadmissible ?

ANSWER: NO. A drunk driving defendant's responses to custodial police questioning "are not rendered inadmissible by *Miranda* merely because the slurred nature of his speech was incriminating. The physical inability to articulate words in a clear manner due to 'the lack of muscular coordination of his tongue and mouth' * * * is not itself a testimonial component of [an intoxicated motorist's] responses to [an officer's] questions. * * * Requiring a suspect to reveal the physical manner in which he articulates words, like requiring him to reveal the physical properties of the sound produced by his voice * * * does not, without more, compel him to provide a 'testimonial' response for purposes of the privilege [to be free from compelled self-incrimination]." *Id.* at 2644-2645.

QUESTION 2: Does the question, "Do you know what the date was of your sixth birthday ? " asked of a drunk-driving defendant while in custody constitute "interrogation" within the meaning of *Miranda* ?

ANSWER: YES. In this case, defendant's answer to the "sixth birthday" question constituted a "testimonial response," *id.* at 2649, and "was incriminating, not just because of his delivery, but also because of his answer's *content*; [one could] infer from [an intoxicated motorist's] answer (that he did not *know* the proper date) that his mental state was confused." *Id.* at 2645. [Emphasis in original.] In this context, the definition of "testimonial" evidence must encompass "all responses to questions that, if asked of a sworn suspect during a criminal trial, could place the suspect in a 'cruel trilemma[,]' " which would require him to choose whether he should (a) remain silent, (b) answer "untruthfully by reporting a date that he did not then believe to be accurate (an incorrect guess would be incriminating as well as untruthful)," or (c) incriminate himself by answering truthfully that he did not know the correct date, which would thereby support "an inference that his mental faculties were impaired[.]" *Id.* at 2648, 2649. Significantly, "the incriminating inference of impaired mental faculties stem[s], not just from the fact that [the accused] slurred his response, but also from a testimonial aspect of that response." *Id.* at 2649. Consequently, police questioning in this regard constitutes "interrogation" within the meaning of *Miranda*.

QUESTION 3: Must an in-custody accused's responses to routine booking questions, such as, "What is your name? Address? Height? Weight? Eye color? Date of birth? and Current age?" be suppressed when asked without prior administration of *Miranda* warnings ?

ANSWER: NO. While a law enforcement officer's custodial questions regarding an accused's name, address, height, weight, eye color, date of birth, and current age do in fact constitute "custodial interrogation" within the meaning of *Miranda*, the responses to such questions in the absence of *Miranda* "are nonetheless admissible because the questions fall within [the] 'routine booking question' exception which exempts from *Miranda's* coverage questions to secure the ' biographical data necessary to complete booking or pretrial services.' " *Id.* at 2650. These types of questions are asked for "record-keeping purposes only," and therefore "appear reasonably related to the police's administrative concerns." *Id.*

QUESTION 4: Once a suspected drunk driver is in custody, will the police request that he perform physical sobriety tests or submit to a breathalyzer examination constitute "interrogation" within the meaning of *Miranda* ?

ANSWER: NO. When an officer's dialogue with a drunk-driving suspect concerning physical sobriety tests consists primarily of carefully scripted instructions as to how the tests are to be performed, the request and the instructions are "not likely to be perceived as calling for any verbal response and therefore [are] not 'words or actions' constituting custodial interrogation." *Id.* at 2651. Similarly, "*Miranda* does not require suppression of [volunteered statements] made when [a suspected intoxicated motorist is] asked to submit to a breathalyzer examination." *Id.* at 2652. Requesting a suspected drunk driver to perform several balance tests, or take a breathalyzer test does not constitute "interrogation within the meaning of *Miranda.*" *Id.*

RATIONALE: During the course of a motor vehicle stop, a patrol officer developed reasonable grounds to suspect that defendant Muniz had been operating his automobile while under the influence of alcohol. The officer smelled alcohol on Muniz's breath and observed that Muniz's eyes were glazed and bloodshot and his face was flushed. Subsequently, the officer asked Muniz to perform "three standard field sobriety tests: 'a horizontal gaze nystagmus' test,[a] a 'walk and turn' test,[b] and a 'one leg stand' test.[c] Muniz performed the tests poorly, and he informed the officer that he had failed the tests because he had been drinking." *Id.* at 2641-2642.

Muniz was placed under arrest and transported to the County Central Booking Center where, following its routine practice for receiving persons suspected of driving while intoxicated, the Booking Center videotaped the events which followed. At this time, Muniz was informed that he was being recorded, but he was not (nor had he been previously) given the *Miranda* warnings. Preliminarily, Officer Hosterman "asked Muniz his name, address, height, weight, eye color, date of birth, and current age. He responded to each of these questions, stumbling over his address and age. The officer then asked Muniz, 'Do you know what the date was of your sixth birthday?' After Muniz offered an inaudible reply, the officer repeated, 'When you turned six years old, do you remember what the date was?' Muniz responded, 'No I don't.'" *Id.* at 2642.

"Officer Hosterman next requested Muniz to perform each of the three sobriety tests that Muniz had been asked to perform earlier during the initial roadside stop. The videotape reveal[ed] that his eyes jerked noticeably during the gaze test, that he did not walk a very straight line, and that he could not balance himself on one leg for more than several seconds. During the latter two tests, he did not complete the requested verbal counts from one to nine and from one to thirty. Moreover, while performing these tests, Muniz 'attempted to explain his difficulties in performing the various tasks, and often requested further clarification of the tasks he was to perform.'" *Id.*

Finally, Muniz was asked to submit to a breathalyzer test. He was read Pennsylvania's Implied Consent Law and informed of the legal consequences that would ensue should he refuse. "Muniz asked a

---

[a] "The 'horizontal gaze nystagmus' test measures the extent to which a person's eyes jerk as they follow an object moving from one side of the person's field of vision to the other. The test is premised on the understanding that, whereas everyone's eyes exhibit some jerking while turning to the side, when the subject is intoxicated, 'the onset of the jerking occurs after fewer degrees of turning, and the jerking at more extreme angles becomes more distinct.'" *Id.* at 2641 n.1. [Citation omitted.]

[b] "The 'walk and turn' test requires the subject to walk heel-to-toe along a straight line for [a stated number of] paces, pivot, and then walk back heel-to-toe along the line for [a stated number of] paces. The subject is required to count each pace aloud[.]" *Id.* Muniz was asked to walk nine paces in each direction.

[c] "The 'one leg stand' test requires the subject to stand on one leg with the other leg extended in the air for 30 seconds, while counting aloud from one to thirty." *Id.*

number of questions about the law, commenting in the process about his state of inebriation. Muniz ultimately refused to take the breath test. At this point, Muniz was for the first time advised of his *Miranda* rights. Muniz then signed a statement waiving his rights and admitted in response to further questioning that he had been driving while intoxicated." *Id.*

In this appeal, Muniz contends that his "testimony relating to the field sobriety tests and the videotape taken at the Booking Center" should be suppressed "because they were incriminating and completed prior to [his] receiving his *Miranda* warnings." *The Supreme Court herein rejects all but one of Muniz's contentions, and holds that, except for the "sixth birthday question," all other evidence of Muniz's intoxication is admissible.*

As a preliminary matter, the Court emphasizes that the privilege set forth in the Fifth Amendment protects an individual from being " 'compelled in any criminal case to be a witness against himself.' " *Id.* at 2643. It is well-established law, however, "that the privilege does not protect a suspect from being compelled by the State to produce 'real or physical evidence.' * * * Rather, the privilege 'protects an accused only from being compelled to testify against himself, or otherwise provide the State with evidence of a testimonial or communicative nature.' * * * [I]n order to be testimonial, an accused's communication must itself, explicitly or implicitly, relate a factual assertion or disclose information. Only then is a person compelled to be a "witness" against himself.' " *Id.* [Citations omitted.]

In *Miranda*, the Court determined that "the privilege against self-incrimination protects individuals not only from legal compulsion to testify in a criminal courtroom but also from 'informal compulsion,' exerted by law-enforcement officers during in-custody questioning." *Id.* at 2644. "This case implicates both the 'testimonial' and 'compulsion' components of the privilege against self-incrimination in the context of pretrial questioning. Because Muniz was not advised of his *Miranda* rights until after the videotaped proceedings at the Booking Center, any verbal statements that were both testimonial in nature and elicited during custodial interrogation [other than those normally attendant to arrest and custody must] be suppressed." *Id.*

Slurred speech. The Court agrees "with the Commonwealth's contention that Muniz's answers are not rendered inadmissible by *Miranda* merely because the slurred nature of his speech was incriminating. The physical inability to articulate words in a clear manner due to 'the lack of muscular coordination of his tongue and mouth,' * * * is not itself a testimonial component of Muniz's responses to Officer Hosterman's introductory questions." *Id.* Prior cases teach that " '[t]he prohibition of compelling a man in a criminal court to be witness against himself is a prohibition of the use of physical or moral compulsion to extort communications from him, not an exclusion of his body as evidence when it may be material.' " *Id.* at 2644-2645. [Citations omitted.] Thus, "*any slurring of speech* and other *evidence of lack of muscular coordination* revealed by Muniz's responses to Officer

Hosterman's direct questions constitute *nontestimonial components of those responses.* Requiring a suspect to reveal the physical manner in which he articulates words, like requiring him to reveal the physical properties of the sound produced by his voice, * * * does not, without more, compel him to provide a 'testimonial' response for purposes of the privilege." *Id.* at 2645. [Emphasis added.]

The "sixth birthday" question. According to the Court, Muniz's answer to the sixth birthday question was incriminating, "not just because of his delivery, but also because of his answer's *content*; [one could] infer from Muniz's answer (that he did not *know* the proper date) that his mental state was confused." *Id.* at 2445. [Emphasis in original.] The critical inquiry is "whether the incriminating inference of mental confusion is drawn from a testimonial act or from physical evidence," *id.* at 2446, and in this respect, the Court defines "testimonial" evidence as "encompass[ing] all responses to questions that, if asked of a sworn suspect during a criminal trial, could place the suspect in the 'cruel trilemma' * * * of truth, falsity, or silence and hence the response (whether based on truth or falsity) contains a testimonial component." *Id.* at 2648.

"[T]he sixth birthday question in this case required a testimonial response. When Officer Hosterman asked Muniz if he knew the date of his sixth birthday and Muniz, for whatever reason, could not remember or calculate that date, he was confronted with the trilemma. By hypothesis, the inherently coercive environment created by the custodial interrogation precluded the option of remaining silent[.] Muniz was left with the choice of incriminating himself by admitting that he did not then know the date of his sixth birthday, or answering untruthfully by reporting a date that he did not then believe to be accurate (an incorrect guess would be incriminating as well as untruthful). The content of his truthful answer supported an inference that his mental faculties were impaired," for a law enforcement officer (or a court) "might reasonably have expected a lucid person to provide" the correct date. "Hence, the incriminating inference of impaired mental faculties stemmed, not just from the fact that Muniz slurred his response, but also from a testimonial aspect of that response." *Id.* at 2649. Accordingly, because "Muniz's response to the sixth birthday question was testimonial, the response should have been suppressed." *Id.*

The "routine booking question" exception to Miranda. "The Commonwealth argues that the seven questions asked by Officer Hosterman just *prior* to the sixth birthday question—regarding Muniz's name, address, height, weight, eye color, date of birth, and current age" did not constitute custodial interrogation. In *Miranda*, "the Court referred to 'interrogation' as actual 'questioning initiated by law enforcement officers.' [Since *Miranda*, the Court has] clarified that definition, finding that the 'goals of the *Miranda* safeguards could be effectuated if those safeguards extended not only to express questioning, but also to "its functional equivalent." ' " *Id.* at 2650. Thus, interrogation includes not only express questioning but " 'any words or actions on the part of the police (other than those normally attendant to arrest and custody) that the police should know[—given the officer's knowledge of any special susceptibilities of the suspect]— are reasonably likely to elicit an incriminating response from the suspect.' " *Id.* [Citations omitted.]

In light of these principles, the Court disagrees with the Commonwealth's contention that Officer Hosterman's first seven questions regarding Muniz's name, address, height, weight, eye color, date of birth, and current age do not qualify as "custodial interrogation." *Id.* Nonetheless, the Court holds that Muniz's answers to these first seven questions are "admissible because the questions fall within a *'routine booking question' exception* which exempts from *Miranda's* coverage questions to secure the 'biographical data necessary to complete booking or pretrial services.' " *Id.* [Emphasis added.] These types of questions are asked for "record-keeping purposes only," and therefore "appear reasonably related to the police's administrative concerns. In this context, therefore, the first seven questions asked at the Booking Center fall outside the protections of *Miranda* and the answers thereto need not be suppressed." *Id.*

Requesting performance of physical sobriety tests and submission to a breathalyzer examination. "During the second phase of the videotaped proceedings, Officer Hosterman asked Muniz to perform the same three sobriety tests that he had earlier performed at roadside prior to his arrest * * *. While Muniz was attempting to comprehend Officer Hosterman's instructions and then perform the requested sobriety tests, Muniz made several audible and incriminating statements." *Id.* at 2650-2651. Here, the officer's "dialogue with Muniz concerning the physical sobriety tests consisted primarily of carefully scripted instructions as to how the tests were to be performed. These instructions were not likely to be perceived as calling for any verbal response and therefore were not 'words or actions' constituting custodial interrogation, with two narrow exceptions not relevant here.[d] The dialogue also contained limited and carefully worded inquiries as to whether Muniz understood those instructions, but these focused inquiries were necessarily 'attendant to' the police procedure [which the Court accepts as] legitimate. Hence, Muniz's incriminating utterances during this phase of the videotaped proceedings were 'voluntary' in the sense that they were not elicited in response to custodial interrogation." *Id.* at 2651.

Similarly, the Court concludes "that *Miranda* does not require suppression of the statements Muniz made when asked to submit to a breathalyzer examination." *Id.* at 2652. The officer "read Muniz a prepared script explaining how the test worked, the nature of Pennsylvania's Implied Consent Law, and the legal consequences that would ensue should he refuse. [Muniz was then asked] whether he under-

---

d "The two exceptions consist of Officer Hosterman's requests that Muniz count aloud from one to nine while performing the 'walk-the-line' test and that he count aloud from one to thirty while balancing during the 'one leg stand' test. Muniz's counting at the officer's request qualifies as a response to custodial interrogation." *Id.* at 2651 n.17. The Court does not decide, however, whether Muniz's counting itself was "testimonial" within the meaning of the Fifth Amendment privilege. *Id.*

stood the nature of the test and the law and whether he would like to submit to the test. Muniz asked * * * several questions concerning the legal consequences of the refusal, which [the officer] answered directly, and Muniz then commented upon his state of inebriation." *Id.* Muniz ultimately refused to take the test.

With respect to both requests, the Court held that "Muniz's statements were not prompted by an interrogation within the meaning of *Miranda*, and therefore the absence of *Miranda* warnings does not require suppression of these statements at trial." *Id.* at 2652. As was The Case With The Administration Of The Three Physical Sobriety Tests, The Officer Provided Direct Relevant Information About The breathalyzer and the implied consent law. The officer questioned Muniz only as to whether he understood the instructions and wished to submit to the test. "These limited and focused inquiries were necessarily 'attendant to' the legitimate police procedure, * * * and were not likely to be perceived as calling for any incriminating response." *Id.* at 2652.

In sum, *Miranda* requires the suppression of Muniz's response to the question regarding the date of his sixth birthday. In all other respects, the evidence of his intoxication is admissible. *Id.*

NOTE

1. Justices White, Blackmun and Stevens, along with Chief Justice Rehnquist, disagreed with the majority's conclusion that the "sixth birthday question" should have been suppressed, and in addition, rejected the majority's characterization that the seven "booking" questions constitute "interrogation" within the meaning of *Miranda*. The dissenters believed that "[t]he sixth birthday question here was an effort on the part of the police to check how well Muniz was able to do a simple mathematical exercise." *Id.* at 2653. Speaking for the minority, the Chief Justice opined, "If the police may require Muniz to use his body in order to demonstrate the level of his physical coordination, there is no reason why they should not be able to require him to speak or write in order to determine his mental coordination. That was all that was sought here." *Id.*

"For substantially the same reasons," the justices in the minority would have held that "Muniz's responses to the videotaped 'booking' questions were not testimonial and do not warrant application of the privilege." *Id.* at 2654. As a result, the issue whether the questions fell within the "routine booking question" exception to *Miranda* should never have been reached. *Id.* (Opinion by Rehnquist, C.J., joined by White, Blackmun, and Stevens, J.J.).

2. Prior to the Court's decision in *Muniz*, several courts had recognized that "the taking of basic information such as name, age, and place of birth is a ministerial duty incident to arrest and custody which does not constitute 'interrogation or its functional equivalent, "reasonably likely to elicit an incriminating response."'" *United States v. Taylor*, 799 *F*.2d 126, 128 (4th Cir. 1986). [Citations omitted.] *See United States*

v. Morrow, 731 *F*.2d 233, 237 (4th Cir.), *cert. denied*, 467 *U.S.* 1230, 104 *S.Ct.* 2689 (1984) (taking basic personal information such as one's name, age or place of birth for an "M.O. card" is a ministerial duty and does not constitute interrogation or its functional equivalent); *United States v. Booth*, 669 *F*.2d 1231, 1238 (9th Cir. 1981) (routine gathering of background or "booking" information ordinarily does not constitute interrogation); *United States Ex Rel. Hines v. LaValle*, 521 *F*.2d 1109, 1113 (2d Cir. 1976) (rape suspect's response to arresting officer's question that suspect had been married 11 years and had two children constituted "merely basic identification required for booking purposes").

But see United States v. Disla, 805 *F*.2d 1340 (9th Cir. 1986) (although routine booking information ordinarily does not constitute "interrogation," questioning defendant as to his residence subjected him to interrogation within meaning of *Miranda* where officer knew that a large quantity of cocaine and cash had been found at a particular apartment and that the residents of that apartment had not been identified, and question as to where defendant lived was relevant to an element of the crime in which defendant was a suspect).

3. *Asking the arrestee to recite, out of ordinary sequence, the alphabet or numbers.* In *Allred v. State*, 622 *So*.2d 984 (Fla. 1993), the court held that a police officer's request that a drunk-driving arrestee recite the alphabet from "c" to "w" and count from 1001 to 1030 is an attempt to elicit an incriminating testimonial response within the privilege and protection of the self-incrimination clause of the Florida Constitution. According to the Florida Supreme Court, a person is "interrogated" when he or she is asked to recite, out of ordinary sequence, the alphabet or numbers. *Id.* at 987. The court observed that "[a] reasonable person would conclude that the request to recite, out of ordinary sequence, letters and numbers," was a request that "was designed to lead to an incriminating response." *Id.* The failure to "accurately recite the alphabet 'discloses information' beyond possible slurred speech; it is the *content* (incorrect recitation) of the speech that is being introduced, rather than merely the *manner* (slurring) of speech." *Id.* [Court's emphasis.] Thus, the defendants' responses in this case, given without the benefit of the *Miranda* warnings, violated their Florida constitutional protection against self-incrimination.

---

§11.3(c). Public safety exception.

NEW YORK v. QUARLES
Supreme Court of the United States
467 U.S. 649, 104 S.Ct. 2626 (1984)

QUESTION: Does the need for answers to questions in situations which pose a significant threat to the public safety justify a law enforcement officer's delay in advising an arrestee of his *Miranda* rights ?

ANSWER: YES. There is now a *"public safety exception"* to the requirement that *Miranda* warnings be administered before a suspect's answers may be admitted into evidence, and the availability of this exception does not depend upon the subjective motivation of the individual police officers involved.

RATIONALE: Officers were stopped while on patrol by a female who advised the officers that she was just raped. The female gave a particularized description of the suspect and further stated that he ran into an A & P Supermarket located nearby and was carrying a gun. The officers located the suspect in the A & P and proceeded to stop and frisk him. The frisk revealed a concealed shoulder holster, which was empty. At this point, the officers placed the suspect under arrest, handcuffed him, and then asked him one question: "Where is the gun ?" The arrestee motioned to the gun's location and the officers immediately recovered a loaded .38 caliber revolver from an empty carton. At this point the officers read the arrestee his rights as required by *Miranda*.

The circumstances in this case present overriding considerations of public safety to justify the officers' failure to administer *Miranda* warnings before they asked a question devoted to locating the abandoned gun. "Public safety must be paramount to adherence to the literal language of the prophylactic rules enunciated in *Miranda*." *Id.* at 812. Here, the police were presented with the immediate necessity of ascertaining the location of a gun which they had every reason to believe the suspect had just removed from his holster and discarded in the supermarket. So long as the gun was concealed somewhere in the supermarket, with its whereabouts unknown, it posed many significant dangers to the public safety. Administration of *Miranda* in such circumstances might deter a suspect from responding and have a result of creating a significant danger to the public—that of a concealed loaded gun in a public area.

Therefore, a suspect's Fifth Amendment privilege to be free from self-incrimination must give way when the need for an immediate answer is necessary to protect the lives and safety of the general public. *Id.* at 812, 813.

NOTE

The public safety exception and "officer safety." In *United States v. Reilly*, 224 *F*.3d 986 (9th Cir. 2000), F.B.I. agents, accompanied by several police officers, entered the motel room where Reilly was reportedly staying with a woman, Doris Lang. At the time, Reilly was wanted in connection with twenty-seven bank robberies in twenty-three cities in ten different states. Officers also considered him a prime suspect in a recent armed carjacking. Prior to entry, the officers conducted a surveillance of the motel room. A woman, later identified as Lang, eventually emerged from the room and was confronted by the officers. While outside, she yelled a warning to Reilly.

Upon hearing Lange's cry, agents and officers forcibly entered the motel room and found Reilly sitting on the couch. Reilly was ordered to lay face-down on the floor, which he did. As additional agents entered the unit, Reilly was ordered to spread his arms out on the ground. While in this position, however, Reilly began to bring his hands down to his front waistband. An agent then ordered Reilly to reposition his hands, and, as he handcuffed Reilly, the agent asked, "Where is the gun?" *Id.* at 990. Reilly responded that the gun was in a black bag in the bedroom. At this point, Reilly had received no *Miranda* warning. Agents immediately entered the bedroom, where a black leather briefcase containing a large amount of money was located. The gun was found in a black bag on the night stand.

According to the court, because "the officers had an objectively reasonable suspicion that their safety was threatened," *Miranda*'s "public safety" exception applied to warrant the admission of Reilly's statement and his weapon into evidence. *Id.* at 995. In this respect, the court observed:

> Under *Quarles*, an officer's questioning of a suspect before giving a *Miranda* warning is acceptable if it "relate[s] to an objectively reasonable need to protect the police or the public from any immediate danger associated with the weapon."

Reilly at 992 (quoting *Quarles*, 467 *U.S.* at 659 n.8).

In holding that the public safety exception applied in this case, the court reasoned that the agent's question, "Where is the gun?" was not "investigatory in nature and was sufficiently limited in scope to allow the officers to quell the volatile situation they faced." *Id.* "[T]he danger and instability of the situation" excused "the pre-*Miranda* questioning." *Id.* at 992-93. At the time the question was asked, noted the court, the motel room

> had not been secured. The couch on which Reilly was seated had not been searched, and a gun could have been hidden nearby. [Although] Reilly was surrounded by officers with loaded weapons pointed at him, he was not yet handcuffed and still had the capacity to reach and grab any nearby objects. Factors such as these are relevant when deciding whether to apply the public safety doctrine. * * *

"The *Quarles* exception rests on the ease with which police officers can and will distinguish almost instinctively between questions necessary to secure their own safety or the safety of the public and questions designed solely to elicit testimonial evidence from a suspect." * * * Given the circumstances of this case, the question "Where is the gun?" falls more cleanly into the former category of questions. There was an objectively reasonable need on the part of the officers to protect themselves given the volatility of the situation with which they were faced.

Id. at 993-94.

Accordingly, the testimonial and physical evidence gained as a result of Reilly's response was held to be admissible.

---

§11.3(d). Impeachment exception.

The "impeachment exception" to *Miranda*'s exclusionary rule provides the prosecution with a means to rebut a defendant's false or fabricated testimony, or attack the credibility of a defendant who offers testimony that contradicts a previously given, albeit inadmissible, statement.

Historically, the fundamental remedy for violations of constitutional rights resulting from a law enforcement officer's acquisition of evidence is "exclusion" of that evidence. As originally set forth, the exclusionary rule prohibited the prosecution from using evidence obtained in violation of a defendant's constitutional rights for any purpose. *See Weeks v. United States*, 232 *U.S.* 383, 34 *S.Ct.* 341 (1914). *See also Mapp v. Ohio*, 367 *U.S.* 643, 655, 81 *S.Ct.* 1684, 1691 (1961) (evidence obtained "in violation of the Constitution is, by that same authority, inadmissible in a state court").

In *Walder v. United States*, 347 *U.S.* 62, 74 *S.Ct.* 354 (1954), the Supreme Court carved out an exception to the exclusionary rule for purposes of impeaching a defendant's credibility at trial. The Court explained:

It is one thing to say that the Government cannot make an affirmative use of evidence unlawfully obtained. It is quite another to say that the defendant can turn the illegal method by which evidence in the Government's possession was obtained to his own advantage, and provide himself with a shield against contradiction of his untruths.

Id. at 65, 74 *S.Ct.* at 356.

The impeachment exception was further anchored in *Harris v. New York*, 401 *U.S.* 222, 91 *S.Ct.* 643 (1971). The defendant's statement in *Harris*, obtained after his arrest, was suppressed at trial because it was obtained without warning the defendant of his right to counsel, and therefore, in violation of *Miranda*'s prophylactic rule. Nonetheless, the Supreme Court determined that the statement could be used by the prosecution for impeachment purposes. The Court said:

"The shield provided by *Miranda* cannot be perverted into a license to use perjury by way of a defense, free from the risk of confrontation with prior inconsistent utterances." *Id.* at 226, 91 *S.Ct.* at 646. Significantly, the illegally-obtained statement in *Harris* directly contradicted the defendant's trial testimony. The *Harris* Court explained:

> The impeachment process here undoubtedly provided valuable aid to the jury in assessing [the defendant's] credibility, and the benefits of this process should not be lost, in our view, because of the speculative possibility that impermissible police conduct will be encouraged thereby. * * * Every criminal defendant is privileged to testify in his own defense or to refuse to do so. But that privilege cannot be construed to include the right to commit perjury.

Id. at 225, 91 *S.Ct.* at 645-46. According to the Court, exclusion of the unlawfully obtained statement from the prosecution's case-in-chief provided sufficient deterrence of police misconduct. *Id.* at 225, 91 *S.Ct.* at 654.

In *Oregon v. Haas*, 420 *U.S.* 714, 723, 95 *S.Ct.* 1215, 1223 (1975), the Court further extended the impeachment exception to cover statements obtained not only through violations of *Miranda*'s prophylactic rules but also statements taken in violation of the constitutional privilege against self-incrimination. The Court in *Haas* emphasized the ultimate truth seeking process of a criminal trial, and found that process secured by the use of impeachment evidence that is "trustworthy" and not "involuntary or coerced." *Id.* at 722, 95 *S.Ct.* at 1221.

Accordingly, the impeachment exception applies not just to violations of *Miranda*'s prophylactic rules, but also to constitutional violations.

Application of the impeachment exception should be limited to situations in which the suppressed statement is trustworthy and reliable, in that it was given freely and voluntarily without compelling influences. Normally, the question whether a statement was voluntary is a "question of fact," which courts will explore by reference to the totality of the circumstances surrounding the interrogation. Such an inquiry takes into account the characteristics of the suspect, as well as the specifics of the interrogation. Relevant factors include the suspect's age, education and intelligence; the suspect's previous encounters with the law; how and by what method the suspect was advised of his constitutional rights; the length of the detention; the nature of the questioning and whether it was repeated or prolonged; and whether physical or mental punishment, coercive police activity or mental exhaustion was involved. *See Colorado v. Spring*, 479 *U.S.* 564, 573-574, 107 *S.Ct.* 851, 857 (1987); *Oregon v. Elstad*, 470 *U.S.* 298, 312, 105 *S.Ct.* 1285, 1295 (1985); *Schneckloth v. Bustamonte*, 412 *U.S.* 218, 226, 93 *S.Ct.* 2041, 2047-48 (1973). *See also Colorado v. Connelly*, 479 *U.S.* 157, 167, 107 *S.Ct.* 515, 522 (1986) ("coercive police activity is a necessary predicate to the finding that a confession is not voluntary").

As pointed out in *Oregon v. Haas*, a statement can be voluntary as a matter of fact even in the face of a constitutional violation of the suspect's right to remain silent or his right to counsel. *Id.* at 714, 95 *S.Ct.* at 1215. Thus, a statement that is given freely and voluntarily given without any compelling influences after a violation of a suspect's

Fifth Amendment rights is admissible for impeachment purposes—that is, to impeach the credibility of a defendant who takes the witness stand and offers testimony that is at variance with the earlier statement. Indeed, if a defendant should falsely testify about a matter to which the Government has contrary evidence, then the prosecution need not sit idly by.

The impeachment exception is, however, subject to certain limitations. As a fundamental prerequisite, the previously-suppressed statement must be "voluntary" and "trustworthy." *See Hass* at 722, 95 *S.Ct.* at 1220. *See also Mincey v. Arizona*, 437 *U.S.* 385, 397-98, 98 *S.Ct.* 2408, 2416 (1978) (while a statement obtained in violation of *Miranda* is admissible for impeachment if otherwise trustworthy, the Constitution prohibits "*any* criminal trial use against a defendant of his *involuntary* statement") (Court's emphasis). A statement is not "trustworthy," and therefore will be deemed compelled or involuntary as a "matter of law," if it is obtained by law enforcement officials in direct violation of a criminal suspect's asserted *Miranda* right to silence or counsel. *See e.g., Cooper v. Dupnik*, 963 *F.*2d 1220 (9th Cir. 1992) (intentional violation of *Miranda*'s requirements to obtain statement for impeachment purposes is conduct that "shocked the conscience" and violated Due Process); *California Attorneys for Criminal Justice v. Butts*, 195 *F.*3d 1039 (9th Cir. 1999) (officers' continued interrogation of suspects despite their invocation of their right to remain silent and their requests for an attorney violated core values of *Miranda*; officers "who intentionally violate the rights protected by *Miranda* must expect to have to defend themselves in civil actions"). *See also Cooper* at 1242 (officers may not trick a suspect "into foregoing his rights by turning the *Miranda* advisement into a farce").

Next, the defendant should be informed prior to taking the witness stand whether the prosecution will seek to admit a suppressed statement, and, the jury should be instructed that the prior statement is admitted for the limited purpose of impeaching the defendant's credibility and that it cannot be used as evidence of the defendant's guilt.

---

§11.4. Events surrounding the interrogation process.

§11.4(a). Invocation of rights.

Two corollaries which flow from *Miranda*'s prophylactic safeguards embody the principle that a defendant's assertion of his right to remain silent and his right to the assistance of counsel must be honored *scrupulously* by the law enforcement authorities. The Fifth Amendment privilege to be free from self-incrimination requires that law enforcement officials inform a criminal suspect of his right to remain silent and of his right to have the assistance of an attorney. The basis for this prophylactic requirement is the inherently coercive nature of interrogation which takes place in a police-dominated, custodial atmosphere. According to the *Miranda* Court, "without the proper safeguards, the process of in-custody interrogation of persons suspected or accused of crime contains inherently compelling pressures which work to undermine the individual's will to resist and to compel him to speak where he would not otherwise do so freely." *Miranda v. Arizona*, 384 *U.S.* 436, 467, 86 *S.Ct.* 1602, 1624 (1966).

What *Miranda* did not address, however, are the circumstances in which law enforcement officials may resume questioning when a criminal suspect has invoked his right to remain silent or his right to the assistance of counsel. Subsequent cases have, however, demonstrated that the law enforcement response will vary with the nature of the particular right asserted.

---

§11.4(a)(1). The right to remain silent.

The Court in *Miranda v. Arizona* was very clear in its command that once a suspect invokes his or her right to remain silent, "all questioning must cease." *Miranda* did not discuss, however, whether, and under what circumstances, law enforcement authorities may resume questioning the suspect. In *Michigan v. Mosley*, 423 *U.S.* 96, 96 *S.Ct.* 321 (1975), the Court revisited this issue and noted that a strict, literal reading of the phrase "all questioning must cease" would lead to "absurd and unintended results." *Id.* at 102, 96 *S.Ct.* at 325. According to the Court, "a blanket prohibition against the taking of voluntary statements or a permanent immunity from further interrogation, regardless of the circumstances, would transform the *Miranda* safeguards into wholly irrational obstacles to legitimate police investigative activity, and deprive suspects of an opportunity to make informed and intelligent assessments of their interests." *Id.*

Accordingly, the *Mosley* Court concluded that *Miranda* did not impose an absolute ban on the resumption of questioning following an invocation of the right to remain silent by a person in custody. The Court held that "the admissibility of statements obtained after the person in custody has decided to remain silent depends under *Miranda* on whether his 'right to cut off questioning' was 'scrupulously honored.'" *Id.* at 102-03, 96 *S.Ct.* at 326. Mosley's expression of his desire to remain silent was deemed "scrupulously honored" based on the facts that (1) Mosley had been advised of his *Miranda* rights before both interrogations; (2) the officer conducting the first interrogation immediately ceased all questioning when Mosley expressed his desire to remain silent; (3) the second interrogation occurred after a significant time lapse; (4) the second interrogation was conducted in another location, (5) by another officer, and (6) it related to a different offense.

STATE v. HARTLEY
Supreme Court of New Jersey
103 *N.J.* 252, 511 *A.2d* 80 (1986)

QUESTION: Before an accused's previously-asserted right to remain silent may be deemed to have been "scrupulously honored," must law-enforcement authorities, at a minimum, readminister the *Miranda* warnings before any subsequent interrogation takes place ?

ANSWER: YES. "[B]efore an accused's previously-asserted right to remain silent may be deemed to have been 'scrupulously honored,' law-enforcement authorities must, at a minimum, readminister the *Miranda* warnings. In the absence of those renewed warnings any inculpatory statement given in response to police-initiated custodial interrogation after the right to silence has been invoked is inadmissible." *Id.*, 103 *N.J.* at 256.

RATIONALE: Defendant, Terrence Hartley, was convicted of one count of first-degree robbery and two counts of felony murder. The convictions stemmed from the armed robbery of the Holst Jewelry Store in Atlantic City, New Jersey. During the course of the robbery, the owner and his aunt were shot and killed.

Investigation led to warrants issued for the arrest of Hartley, which were executed at his Brooklyn, New York, apartment at 7:30 a.m. on February 5, 1981. Executing the warrants were members of the Atlantic City Police Department, the FBI, the Atlantic County Prosecutor's Office, and the New York City Police Department. At the time of the arrest, Hartley was read his *Miranda* rights by Special Agent Robley of the FBI, and was then transported to the Brooklyn-Queens FBI office. At 9:16 a.m., Hartley was readvised of his rights and responded by invoking his right to remain silent. Hartley was then processed for identification and, at 10:43 a.m., Special Agent Frieberg of the FBI approached Hartley and resumed questioning without readministering the *Miranda* warnings. Hartley gave what amounted to a full confession, but refused to sign the finished typed version.

After being questioned by the FBI agents, Hartley was approached by the New York and New Jersey police officials, was read his *Miranda* rights, and, in essence, made additional inculpatory statements. This questioning was conducted primarily by Detective Dennis Mason of the Atlantic City Police Department. Again, Hartley refused to sign the typed description of this interview.

Although the trial court disallowed admission of Hartley's unsigned typewritten statements, it nonetheless permitted the testimony of the FBI agents and the State authorities as to the contents of the oral statements made to them. Hartley appealed his convictions, "alleging error in the trial court's failure to have suppressed 'statements attributed to [him] in violation of federal and state constitutions.' " *Id.* at 259. The Appellate Division affirmed, finding no violation of Hartley's right to remain silent.

The Supreme Court of New Jersey disagreed and reversed.

The focus of this case centers upon "the admissibility, on the State's case-in-chief, of defendant's two inculpatory statements given during custodial interrogations by separate branches of law enforcement, who were pursuing a 'joint' investigation." *Id.* at 255. At the Brooklyn-Queens office, when Hartley was advised of his rights, he responded by unequivocally asserting his right to remain silent. "Sometime later he made the statements in question, the first in response to interrogation by federal authorities, who did not give [him] the *Miranda* warnings anew, and the second, to New Jersey authorities after [he] had been re-informed of his *Miranda* rights." *Id.* Therefore, the issues boil down to "whether the federal authorities 'scrupulously honored' defendant's pre-viously-invoked right to silence, * * *; and if not, whether the statement to the New Jersey authorities is tainted because of its relationship to the 'federal' statement." *Id.* at 255-256. [Citation omitted.]

"In *Miranda*, the Court made clear that the requirement that the police 'scrupulously honor' the suspect's assertion of his right to remain silent is independent of the requirement that any waiver be knowing, intelligent, and voluntary." *Id.* at 261. The question of waiver will not be reached if it is found that government officials failed to honor a previ-ously-invoked right to remain silent. Such a failure "renders unconstitu-tionally compelled any resultant incriminating statement made in re-sponse to custodial interrogation[.]" *Id.*

As a result, this Court holds that "before an accused's previously-asserted right to remain silent may be deemed to have been 'scrupu-lously honored,' law-enforcement authorities must, at a minimum, re-administer the *Miranda* warnings. In the absence of those renewed warnings any inculpatory statement given in response to police-initiated custodial interrogation after the right to remain silent has been invoked is inadmissible." *Id.* at 256. Additionally, the failure of the police to scru-pulously honor "an accused's earlier-invoked right to silence amounts to a violation not simply of *Miranda's* prophylactic rules but of the ac-cused's privilege against self-incrimination. Therefore, any statement that a suspect may make after his right to silence has not been scrupu-lously honored is unconstitutionally compelled as a matter of law." *Id.*

Accordingly, the Court declares "as indispensible to a permissible resumption of custodial interrogation of a previously warned suspect the furnishing of fresh *Miranda* warnings. Unless the police follow this 'bright-line,' inflexible, minimum requirement, a defendant's statement made in the above stated circumstances cannot be admitted into evidence as part of the prosecution's case-in-chief." *Id.* at 267.

Here, "the federal authorities' failure scrupulously to honor defen-dant's announced intention not to make a statement requires the ex-clusion, on the State's case, not only of defendant's confession to agents of the FBI, but also of defendant's second statement, made to state and municipal authorities." *Id.* at 256. The result is mandated because the FBI agent's "failure to readminister *Miranda* warnings was a violation of the obligation scrupulously to honor Hartley's as-serted right to silence, and therefore amounted to a violation of [his] fifth-amendment and state common-law right not to be compelled to be a witness against himself." *Id.* at 278.

Since the second (State) statement came "as it did on the heels of—if not in tandem with—the first, unconstitutionally-obtained, compelled statement, [it] was unavoidably tainted[, and even the most generous reading] of the record cannot generate a conclusion of sufficient attenuation between the first and second interrogations to dissipate the taint." *Id.* at 284.

In sum, the Court holds that "(1) failure to readminister *Miranda* warnings before interrogating an accused who has previously invoked the right to silence will invariably result in a finding that the right has not been 'scrupulously honored'; and (2) any statement thus obtained is unconstitutionally compelled, and hence inadmissible, as having been obtained in violation of the fifth-amendment and of the state common-law right against self-incrimination." *Id.* at 278-279. [This latter rationale means that the suppression of the statement in this case by the New Jersey Supreme Court may continue to be a stricter interpretation than Federal or other States' guidelines, and must be made known to cooperating agencies working with New Jersey law enforcement personnel in the course of investigations which may result in prosecutions in New Jersey courts.]

NOTE

1. During the discussion of the inadmissibility of the second statement, the Court had occasion to discuss the factors which may come into consideration when assessing the admissibility of such a statement. These factors center around the question of whether the prosecution could establish either that the second statement was not the *product* of the first, or that the "taint" of the first statement was attenuated. "Factors relevant to this determination include the time between confessions, any intervening circumstances, whether there was a change in place, whether defendant received an adequate warning of his rights, whether the defendant initiated the second confession, the effect of his having previously made a confession, and the 'purpose and flagrancy of police misconduct.'" *Hartley*, 103 *N.J.* at 283. [Citations omitted.]

2. The ruling in *Hartley* flowed from questioning initiated after an accused has already invoked his right to remain silent. In *State v. Magee*, 52 *N.J.* 352 (1968), *cert. den.*, 393 *U.S.* 1097, 89 *S.Ct.* 891 (1969), a question arose whether fresh *Miranda* warnings were required after every successive interview when defendant has *not* invoked his right to remain silent. In *Magee*, defendant was arrested and given *Miranda* warnings, at which point he waived his rights and gave a brief statement to the authorities. Two days later, prior to his arraignment on narcotics charges, defendant made *unsolicited* statements implicating his involvement in a murder, which immediately thereafter led to a full confession. Defendant argued that the police were mandated to repeat the *Miranda* warnings before accepting defendant's admissions. Finding "no such *mandate,*" the Court held: "Once *Miranda*'s rule has been complied with at the threshold of the questioning it is not necessary as a matter of law to repeat the warnings at each successive interview." *Id.* at 374. Moreover, the Court found that adopting "'an automatic second-warning requirement

would be to add a perfunctory ritual to police procedures rather than providing the meaningful set of procedural safeguards envisioned by *Miranda.*'" *Id.* [Citation omitted.]

Critical elements in this area include whether the accused understood that he had the right to remain silent, the consequences of giving up that right, and that he had the right to counsel before doing so, if he so desired. An additional element is the period of time between the initial warnings and the subsequent admission or confession. Naturally, as more time elapses, the more likely that fresh *Miranda* warnings would be necessary. Finally, the party who initiates the second or subsequent interview is also relevant here.

3. *Remaining silent during the course of booking or pedigree questioning.* May an accused be deemed to have invoked his Fifth Amendment privilege simply by remaining silent during pedigree questioning? In *United States v. Montana*, 958 *F.*2d 516 (2nd Cir. 1992), the court said yes.

Generally, after receiving the *Miranda* warnings, an accused's silence in the face of repeated questioning "has been held sufficient to invoke the Fifth Amendment privilege, * * * or at least sufficient to create an ambiguity requiring the authorities either to cease interrogation or to limit themselves to clarifying questions[.]" *Id.* at 518. [Citations omitted.] Here, in *Montana*, the court could see "no basis for distinguishing silence in the face of pedigree questions from silence in the face of more substantive interrogation." *Id.* "If a suspect refuses to answer even non-incriminating pedigree questions," reasoned the court, "the interrogating officer cannot reasonably conclude that he will immediately thereafter consent to answer incriminating ones." *Id.* The court held, therefore, that an in-custody accused invokes his right to remain silent by declining to answer pedigree questions. *Id.* at 517.

---

§11.4(a)(2). The right to counsel.

When an in-custody suspect requests counsel, all questioning must stop. This was made clear by the United States Supreme Court in *Edwards v. Arizona*, 451 *U.S.* 477, 101 *S.Ct.* 1880 (1981). *Edwards* held that once a suspect invokes the right to counsel, "a valid waiver of that right cannot be established by showing only that he responded to further *police initiated* custodial interrogation even if he has been advised of his rights." *Id.* at 484, 485, 101 *S.Ct.* at 1884, 1885. [Emphasis added.]

Although the Fifth Amendment privilege against self-incrimination does not expressly provide for the right to counsel, courts construe that right as implicitly existing in the Fifth-Amendment setting as a "preventative measure" that protects an accused from self-incrimination. The correlative right to counsel found in the *Miranda* warnings is said to be necessary "to make the process of police interrogation conform to the dictates of the [Fifth Amendment] privilege." *Miranda v. Arizona*, 384 *U.S.* 436, 466, 86 *S.Ct.* 1602, 1623 (1966).

The assertion of a suspect's right to an attorney while being questioned in police custody is "an invocation of his Fifth Amendment rights, requiring that all interrogation must cease." *Edwards* at 485, 101 *S.Ct.* at 1885. If the accused indicates in any manner that he may desire a lawyer, the police may not ask him any further questions or reinitiate questioning "until counsel has been made available to him, *unless the accused himself initiates further communication, exchanges or conversations with the police.*" *Id.* [Emphasis added.] In these circumstances, courts will question first whether the accused invoked his right to counsel. If so, the inquiry next addresses whether the accused or the police initiated further communications or exchanges about the investigation. If it is determined that the police initiated further questioning after a previous assertion of the right to counsel, any statements made by the accused will be inadmissible at trial unless, at the time of the second or subsequent questioning, the accused had been given an opportunity "to confer with [an] attorney and to have him present during" the second or subsequent questioning session. *Id.* at 485, 101 *S.Ct.* at 1885. *See also Minnick v. Mississippi*, 498 *U.S.* 146, 111 *S.Ct.* 486, 491 (1990) ("when counsel is requested, interrogation must cease, and officials may not reinitiate interrogation without counsel present, whether or not the accused has consulted with his attorney"). If, however, it is determined that the accused himself initiated further communication, exchanges or conversations about the investigation, the inquiry would then be whether, after providing the accused with a fresh set of *Miranda* warnings, the police received "a valid waiver of the right to counsel and the right to silence[,]" that is, whether the accused voluntarily, knowingly and intelligently waived his rights based on "the totality of the circumstances, including the necessary fact that the accused, not the police, reopened the dialogue with the authorities." *Edwards* at 486 n.9, 101 *S.Ct.* at 1885 n.9.

THE FIFTH AMENDMENT SETTING

MINNICK v. MISSISSIPPI
Supreme Court of the United States
498 *U.S.* 146, 111 *S.Ct.* 486 (1990)

QUESTION: Once an accused requests counsel during custodial interrogation and is then given the opportunity to consult with an attorney, may police thereafter initiate further questioning without the attorney present?

ANSWER: NO. "[W]hen counsel is requested, interrogation must cease, and officials may not reinitiate interrogation without counsel present, whether or not the accused has consulted with his attorney." *Id.* at 491.

RATIONALE: *Miranda v. Arizona* "protect[s] the privilege against self-incrimination guaranteed by the Fifth Amendment [by the requirement] that the police must terminate interrogation of an accused in custody if the accused requests the assistance of counsel. * * * [The Court] reinforced the protections of *Miranda* in *Edwards v. Arizona*[,] which held that once the accused requests counsel, officials may not reinitiate questioning 'until counsel has been made available' to him. The issue in this case * * * is whether *Edwards'* protection ceases once the suspect has consulted with an attorney." *Minnick* at 488.

Ruling that "the Fifth Amendment protection of *Edwards* is not terminated or suspended by consultation with counsel[,]" *id.* at 489, the Court here in *Minnick* focuses on that language in *Miranda* which makes clear that "once an individual in custody invokes his right to counsel, interrogation 'must cease until an attorney is present'; at that point, 'the individual must have an opportunity to confer with the attorney and to have him present during any subsequent questioning.'" *Minnick* at 489. [Citation omitted.] Further, the Court in *Miranda* noted that " '[e]ven preliminary advice given to the accused by his own attorney can be swiftly overcome by the secret interrogation process. Thus, the need for counsel to protect the Fifth Amendment privilege comprehends not merely a right to consult with counsel prior to questioning, but also to have counsel present during any questioning if the defendant so desires.'" *Minnick* at 491. [Citation omitted.]

Edwards fortified these requirements by the further direction that once an accused requests an attorney, " 'having expressed his desire to deal with the police only through counsel, [he] is not subject to further interrogation by the authorities until counsel has been made available to him, unless the accused himself initiates further communications, exchanges, or conversations with the police.'" *Minnick* at 489. [Citation omitted.] "*Edwards* is 'designed to prevent police from badgering a defendant into waiving his previously asserted *Miranda* rights' * * * The rule ensures that any statement made in subsequent interrogation is not the result of coercive pressures. [Moreover, t]he merit of the *Edwards* decision lies in the clarity of its command and the certainty of its application. * * * [T]he *Edwards* rule provides ' "clear and unequivocal" guidelines to the law enforcement profession.'" *Minnick* at 489-490. [Citations omitted.]

Therefore, the "statement in *Edwards* that an accused who invokes his right to counsel 'is not subject to further interrogation by the authorities until counsel has been made available to him[,' should not be interpreted] to mean * * * that the protection of *Edwards* terminates once counsel has consulted with the suspect. In context, the requirement that counsel be 'made available' to the accused refers to more than an opportunity to consult with an attorney outside the interrogation room." *Minnick* at 490. The requirement dictates that counsel be *present* during the interrogation.

Accordingly, the *Edwards* rule must be interpreted "to bar *police-initiated* interrogation unless the accused has counsel with him at the time of questioning. * * * [W]hen counsel is requested, interrogation must cease, and officials may not reinitiate interrogation without counsel present, whether or not the accused has consulted with his attorney. * * * [In this respect, the Court declines] to remove protection from *police-initiated* questioning based on isolated consultations with counsel who is absent when the interrogation resumes." *Minnick* at 491. [Emphasis added.]

NOTE

Minnick involved "police-initiated" questioning following an accused's request for counsel. The Court did not, however, change the law surrounding those circumstances in which the accused himself initiates further communications after an earlier request for counsel. In this respect, the Court stated: *"Edwards* does not foreclose finding a waiver of Fifth Amendment protections after counsel has been requested, provided the accused has initiated the conversation or discussion with the authorities[.]" *Id.* at 492.

SMITH v. ILLINOIS
Supreme Court of the United States
469 *U.S.* 91, 105 *S.Ct.* 490 (1984)

QUESTION: In the below set of circumstances, did defendant Smith invoke his right to counsel within the meaning of *Miranda v. Arizona* and *Edwards v. Arizona* ?

CIRCUMSTANCES:
Shortly after his arrest for armed robbery, defendant, 18-year-old Steven Smith was taken to an interrogation room at the Logan County Safety Complex for questioning by two police detectives. The session began as follows:

"Q-1. Steve, I want to talk with you in reference to the armed robbery that took place at McDonald's restaurant on the morning of the 19th. Are you familiar with this ?

"A. Yeah. My cousin Greg was.

"Q-2. Okay. But before I do that I must advise you of your rights. Okay ? You have a right to remain silent. You do not have to talk to me unless you want to do so. Do you understand that ?

"A. Uh. [I was] told [] to get my lawyer. [I was told] you guys would railroad me.

"Q-3. Do you understand that as I gave it to you, Steve ?

"A. Yeah.

"Q-4. If you do want to talk to me I must advise you that
whatever you say can and will be used against you in
court. Do you understand that ?

"A.   Yeah.

"Q-5. You have a right to consult with a lawyer and to have a
lawyer present with you when you're being questioned.
Do you understand that ?

"A.   Uh, yeah. I'd like to do that.

"Q-6. Okay. If you want a lawyer and you're unable to pay for
one a lawyer will be appointed to represent you free of
cost, do you understand that ?

"A.   Okay.

"Q-7. Do you wish to talk to me at this time without a lawyer
being present ?

"A.   Yeah and no, uh, I don't know what's what, really.

"Q-8. Well. You either have [to agree] to talk to me this time
without a lawyer being present and if you do agree to
talk with me without a lawyer being present you can
stop at any time you want to.

"A.   All right. I'll talk to you then.

Id. at 491. "Smith then told the detectives that he knew in advance
about the planned robbery, but contended that he had not been a
participant. After considerable probing by the detectives, Smith confessed[.]" *Id.*

ANSWER: YES. Under *Miranda* and *Edwards*, there is no question that Smith invoked his right to counsel in his response to the detective's *fifth* question. Moreover, under both of those cases, "an accused's postrequest responses to further interrogation may not be used
to cast doubt on the clarity of his initial request for counsel." *Smith* at
491.

RATIONALE: "An accused in custody, 'having expressed his desire
to deal with the police only through counsel, is not subject to further
interrogation by the authorities until counsel has been made available
to him,' unless he validly waives his earlier request for the assistance
of counsel." *Id.* at 492 (quoting *Edwards v. Arizona*, 451 *U.S.* at 477,
484-485, 101 *S.Ct.* 1880, 1885 (1981)). "This 'rigid' prophylactic rule,
* * * embodies two distinct inquiries. First, courts must determine
whether the accused actually invoked his right to counsel. * * * Second, if the accused invoked his right to counsel, courts may admit his

responses to further questioning only on finding that he (a) initiated further discussions with the police, and (b) knowingly and intelligently waived the right he had invoked." *Id.* at 492-493.

"This case concerns the threshold inquiry: whether Smith invoked his right to counsel in the first instance. On occasion, an accused's asserted request for counsel may be ambiguous or equivocal." *Id.* at 493. But in this case, no one has pointed to anything Smith previously had said that might have cast doubt on the meaning of his statement, "I'd like to do that," upon learning that he had the right to his counsel's presence. Nor is there anything in that statement itself which would suggest anything inherently ambiguous or equivocal. *Id.*

"Where nothing about the request for counsel or the circumstances leading up to the request would render it ambiguous, all questioning must cease. In these circumstances, an accused's subsequent statements are relevant only to the question whether the accused waived the right he had invoked. Invocation and waiver are entirely distinct inquiries, and the two must not be blurred by merging them together." *Id.* at 494.

"The importance of keeping the two inquiries distinct is manifest. *Edwards* set forth a 'bright-line rule' that *all* questioning must cease after an accused requests counsel. * * * With respect to the waiver inquiry, [the Court] emphasize[s] that a valid waiver 'cannot be established by showing only that [the accused] responded to further police-initiated custodial questioning.' * * * Using an accused's subsequent responses to cast doubt on the adequacy of the initial request itself is even more intolerable. 'No authority, and no logic, permits the interrogator to proceed * * * on his own terms and as if the defendant had requested nothing, in the hope that the defendant might be induced to say something casting retrospective doubt on his initial statement that he wished to speak through an attorney or not at all.'" *Smith* at 494. [Citations omitted; emphasis in original.]

Though the Court does not herein decide the appropriate procedure when an accused's request for counsel may be characterized as ambiguous or equivocal, it does hold that "an accused's *postrequest* responses to further interrogation may not be used to cast retrospective doubt on the clarity of the initial request itself. Such subsequent statements are relevant only to the distinct question of waiver." *Id.* at 495. [Emphasis in original.]

NOTE

A request for counsel during non-custodial questioning. In *McNeil v. Wisconsin*, 501 *U.S.* 171, 111 *S.Ct.* 2204 (1991), the Court noted:

We have in fact never held that a person can invoke his *Miranda* rights anticipatorily, in a context other than "custodial interrogation[.]" * * * If the *Miranda* right to counsel can be invoked at a preliminary hearing, it could be argued, there is no logical reason why it could not be invoked by a letter prior to arrest, or indeed even prior to identification as a suspect. Most rights must be asserted when the government seeks to take the action they protect against. The fact that we have allowed the *Miranda* right to counsel, once asserted, to be effective with respect to future custodial interrogation *does not necessarily mean that we will allow it to be asserted initially outside the context of custodial interrogation, with similar effect.*

Id., 111 *S.Ct.* at 2211 n.3. [Emphasis added.]

(a) In a pre-*McNeil* decision, the court in *Tukes v. Dugger,* 911 *F.*2d 508 (11th Cir. 1990), concluded that where a suspect "is not in custody, the *Edwards* and *Roberson* concerns are not triggered because the non-custodial defendant is free to refuse to answer police questions, free to leave the police station and go home, and free to seek out and consult a lawyer." *Id.* at 515. According to the Eleventh Circuit, when the interrogation is not "custodial," the "danger of coercion is lessened because the suspect is free to quit the coercive environment." *Id.* The court held, therefore, that Tukes could not rely on *Edwards* to invalidate a search of his home conducted on the basis of his consent obtained by the police after a previous non-custodial, equivocal request for a lawyer.

In this case, Tukes was not in custody at the time he gave his consent to the search. He voluntarily accompanied the police to the stationhouse, and voluntarily remained there. At the time he consented to the search of his home, his freedom of action had not been restricted: he was free to leave, and no reasonable person would have felt otherwise. Therefore, because Tukes was not in custody, he may not obtain relief under *Edwards.* Finding that Tukes was not in custody, we need not reach the question of whether his prior equivocal invocation of counsel at his home would have been sufficient to cut off questioning had Tukes been placed in custody.

Id. at 515-16.

(b) In *Commonwealth v. Lewis,* 407 *Pa.Super.* 186, 595 A.2d 593 (1991), Amtrak police approached defendant and his companion after they disembarked a train arriving at Harrisburg from New York City. Believing the two men fit the "drug courier profile," the officers began to question them. Defendant immediately requested a lawyer. In response to defendant's request, one of the officers asked why he wanted a lawyer "when he was not even under arrest." The questioning continued and defendant and his companion made several incriminating remarks. A subsequent pat-down search uncovered a gun from the waistband of defendant's companion, and a search incident to arrest produced a packet of cocaine from defendant's sock. At this point, both arrestees were given the *Miranda* warnings, and, thereafter, both provided the police with incriminating statements.

Rejecting defendant's claim that the police were required to cease all questioning after he asked for a lawyer, the court held that a request for a lawyer stops further questioning by police only in instances where the right to counsel has been invoked during *custodial* interrogation. *Id.,* 595 A.2d at 597. Relying on *McNeil's* footnote 3 (set forth above), the *Lewis* court concluded that defendant and his companion were not "in custody" when they were first approached by the Amtrak officers, and,

> [c]onsequently, [defendant's] request for counsel when the officers approached him did not serve to terminate further questions by police or mandate suppression of the responses made by either [defendant or his companion]; nor does it compel suppression of the resulting arrest and the evidence seized as a consequence of the arrest.

Id. at 598 (citing *McNeil*, 111 *S.Ct.* at 2211 n.3). *See also Minnesota v. Murphy*, 465 *U.S.* 420, 430, 104 *S.Ct.* 1136, 1143-44 (1984) (*Miranda's* "extraordinary safeguard 'does not apply outside the context of the inherently coercive custodial interrogations for which it was designed' ") (quoting *Roberts v. United States*, 445 *U.S.* 552, 560, 100 *S.Ct.* 1358, 1364 (1980)).

　　(c) A different result may be in order, however, if interrogation continues after a suspect invokes the right to counsel during *non-custodial* questioning, *as a direct result of* being advised of his or her *Miranda* rights. If a government officer advises a criminal suspect that he or she has the right to counsel, retained or appointed, but is then free to continue interrogating despite such a request, with the justification being that the suspect was not actually in custody, the suspect would be led to believe that no request for counsel would ever be honored. In such circumstances, the integrity of the process becomes tainted and the trustworthiness of the government's assurances to respect the suspect's constitutional rights is thereby impugned. While the continued, non-custodial interrogation of a criminal suspect under these circumstances does not immediately appear to violate the letter of the prophylactic safeguards of *Miranda* and *Edwards*, it may touch on due process concerns which require government officials to "respect certain decencies of civilized conduct" by avoiding "methods that offend a 'sense of justice.' " *Rochin v. California*, 342 *U.S.* 165, 172, 72 *S.Ct.* 205, 209 (1952).

ALSTON v. REDMAN
United States Court of Appeals
34 *F.*3d 1237 (3rd Cir. 1994)

QUESTION: May the *Miranda* right to counsel be invoked outside the context of custodial interrogation, in anticipation of a future interrogation ?

ANSWER: NO. "[T]o be effective, a request for *Miranda* counsel must be made within 'the context of custodial interrogation' and no sooner." *Id.* at 1246. [Citations omitted.]

RATIONALE: In the summer of 1985, police were investigating a number of robberies that had taken place in and around Wilmington, Delaware. The investigation linked defendant, Harold Alston, to one of those robberies, that of Allen Medkeff and Michelle Sands (the "Medkeff-Sands robberies"). A warrant issued for Alston's arrest, charging him with first-degree robbery and second-degree conspiracy. On August 23rd, Alston was taken into custody by the Delaware authorities and given his *Miranda* rights. Alston waived his rights and was questioned. He admitted to participating in the Medkeff-Sands robberies, as well as six other robberies committed during the summer of 1985. Thereafter, Alston was taken before a Justice of the Peace on the robbery and conspiracy charges and was committed to the Gander Hill facility for pretrial detention.

Three days later, on August 26th, Alston was interviewed by an investigator from the Public Defender's office. During the course of this interview, Alston signed the following form letter, addressed to the warden of the prison:

Dear Sir:
    I am presently a detainee in this institution and I will not speak to any police officer, law enforcement officers, their agents, or representatives from the Department of Justice, of any jurisdiction, without a Public Defender being present at such a meeting
    I further do not wish to be removed from my [cell] and brought to a meeting with the above-mentioned officers for the purpose of discussing a waiver of my constitutional rights in this regard.

Signed /s/ Harold S. Alston
Date 8-26-85

Id. at 1240. "The letter was never actually delivered to Gander Hill's warden, since the established practice at Gander Hill was that someone from the warden's office would call the Public Defender's office when officers sought to question a prisoner, and inquire whether such a form letter had been executed." *Id.* at 1240-41.

Alston was indicted for the Medkeff-Sands robberies on August 28th. On August 29th, he was taken from his cell to the Wilmington Police Department for processing on the new charges stemming from the six other robberies to which he had confessed on the 23rd and for additional questioning. No inquiry was made of the Public Defender as to whether Alston had signed the invocation of counsel form. At the police station, Alston was read his *Miranda* rights. After waiving his rights, he was again questioned. During this second questioning session, occurring six days after his August 23rd interrogation, "Alston confirmed his prior confessions, and, after prompting by one interrogator, confessed to another robbery that he had not mentioned before." *Id.* at 1241.

Alston was convicted of seven counts of robbery and nine counts of conspiracy. In the appeal following an unsuccessful petition for a writ of *habeas corpus*, Alston contended that the statement he made during the August 29th interrogation violated his Sixth Amendment right to counsel. *The Third Circuit disagreed*, holding that Alston's "invocation of his *Miranda* right to counsel was anticipatory since it was made outside of the context of custodial interrogation, and was thus ineffective[.]" *Id.* at 1240.

The United States Supreme Court has made clear that once a suspect has requested counsel during custodial interrogation, that suspect "cannot be questioned concerning *any* crime, not just the one that put him in custody." *Id.* at 1243 (court's emphasis) (citing *Miranda v. Arizona* and *Edwards v. Arizona*). Moreover, "officers who interrogate a suspect after the suspect has invoked his right to counsel are charged with the knowledge of the prior invocation." *Id.*

Miranda's role in protecting the Fifth Amendment privilege, however, is triggered only when an interrogation occurs in a custodial setting. "Because the presence of *both* a custodial setting and official interrogation is required to trigger the *Miranda* right-to-counsel pro[tection], absent one or the other, *Miranda* is not implicated." *Id.* at 1244. *See e.g., Illinois v. Perkins*, 496 *U.S.* 292, 297, 110 *S.Ct.* 2394, 2397 (1990) ("It is the premise of *Miranda* that the danger of coercion results from the interaction of custody and official interrogation.").

In this case, Alston's execution of the "invocation of counsel" form "was insufficient to trigger his *Miranda* right to counsel[,]" for it "was made outside of the context of custodial interrogation, and was thus ineffective." *Alston* at 1244. At the time Alston requested counsel, he was not being interrogated nor was interrogation imminent. He was questioned on August 23rd and again on August 29th. There is no evidence to suggest that he had been questioned on the 26th, the date on which he made his request for counsel. "His putative invocation of his right to counsel on August 26th was made while he was sitting in his jail cell speaking with a representative of the Public Defender's office, far removed from the strictures of custodial interrogation feared by the *Miranda* Court." *Id.* at 1245. Absent the "interaction of custody and interrogation," Alston's "*Miranda* right to counsel had simply not attached when [he] signed the invocation form in his cell." *Id.*

In essence, Alston asks this Court to adopt, as an extension of the reach of *Miranda*, a rule allowing a suspect to invoke the right to counsel in cases where the suspect is in custody, has already been interrogated, and may be reinterrogated at some point in the future. We decline the invitation.

Id.

In *McNeil v. Wisconsin*, 501 *U.S.* 171, 111 *S.Ct.* 2204 (1991), the Supreme Court noted that it had "in fact never held that a person can invoke his *Miranda* rights anticipatorily, in a context other than 'custodial interrogation.' * * * Most rights must be asserted when the government seeks to take the action they protect against." *McNeil* at 182 n.3, 111 *S.Ct.* at 2211 n.3. This language, observed the *Alston* court, "strongly supports the proposition that, to be effective, a request for *Miranda* counsel must be made within 'the context of custodial interrogation' and no sooner." *Alston* at 1246.

> The *Miranda* right to counsel is a prophylactic rule that does not operate independent from the danger it seeks to protect against—"the compelling atmosphere inherent in the process of in-custody interrogation"—and the effect that danger can have on a suspect's privilege to avoid compelled self-incrimination. * * * To allow an individual to interpose *Miranda* in a situation outside the custodial interrogation context would represent an unwarranted extension of *Miranda*'s procedural safeguards * * *.

Id. [Citations omitted.]
The "true protection of *Miranda*," noted the court,

> only arises if the state chooses to question a suspect without providing the *Miranda* warnings and attempts to introduce those statements in evidence. * * * Until the attempt is made, the *Miranda* right, and the corresponding Fifth Amendment right it prophylactically protects, essentially lies dormant. If the state never interrogates a suspect, *Miranda* is not implicated.

Id. at 1247 n.10.
Accordingly, "[g]iven that Alston was not being interrogated when he signed the invocation form, and that no interrogation was impending or imminent," the court held that the statement taken from him on August 29th was admissible. *Id.* at 1249.

NOTE

1. During the course of its opinion, the *Alston* court also observed that the method used by Alston, *i.e.*, advising the warden of his decision, was insufficient to trigger the protections of *Miranda, Edwards,* and *Arizona v. Roberson*, 486 *U.S.* 675, 108 *S.Ct.* 2093 (1988). The Supreme Court's opinion in *Roberson* emphasized that "custodial interrogation must be conducted pursuant to established procedures, and those procedures in turn must enable an officer who proposes to initiate an interrogation to determine whether the suspect has previously requested counsel." *Id.* at 687, 108 *S.Ct.* at 2101. Thus, later interrogators are "charged with the knowledge of what occurred during prior

interrogations, not what occurred during other time periods, *i.e.*, while the suspect was sitting in his cell speaking with a representative from the Public Defender's office." *Alston* at 1250. "The practical implication of this conclusion," ruled the *Alston* court,

> is that noninvestigatory officials charged with the mere custody or care of a suspect, *e.g.*, jailers, doctors, vocational instructors, should not be considered state agents capable of accepting a suspect's invocation of his *Miranda* rights. Any other interpretation of *Roberson* would not provide serviceable guidance to law enforcement officials seeking to administer the *Miranda-Edwards* protections, since, in effect, they would become absolutely liable for any statement made by an incarcerated suspect to his jailer. This conclusion is consistent with our rejection [] of anticipatory invocations. If Alston cannot assert his *Miranda* rights anticipatorily, it would make little sense to permit him to assert them to the warden, a noninvestigatory state official. * * *

> We conclude that knowledge of the letter "sent" by Alston to the warden of the Gander Hill facility cannot be imputed to the police officers who interrogated Alston on the 29th, and that the interrogation was therefore not violative of *Miranda, Edwards,* or *Roberson.*

> We decline to extend the reach of *Miranda-Edwards* to encompass a suspect sitting in his cell, free of any interrogation, impending or otherwise. As the Supreme Court stated, * * * "[i]f a suspect does not wish to communicate with the police except through an attorney, he can simply tell them when they give him the *Miranda* warnings."

Alston at 1251. [Citation omitted.]

2. *Requesting counsel prior to giving the police consent to search.* In *United States v. LaGrone*, 43 F.3d 332 (7th Cir. 1994), the court rejected the defendant's contention that his request to speak to his attorney about the police request for consent to search barred any subsequent questioning later at the station house.

Preliminarily, the court noted that a police request for consent to search is not "interrogation" within the meaning of *Miranda.* Therefore, at the time defendant asked to talk to his attorney, "he was not in a custodial interrogation atmosphere." *Id.* at 337. The court elaborated:

> The *Miranda* right to counsel attaches only in the context of custodial interrogation. LaGrone apparently argues that once a defendant's right to counsel under *Miranda* is triggered, it is like the Energizer Bunny—it keeps going, and going, and going. . . . While this is true of the Sixth Amendment right to counsel—once the government initiates formal charges against the defendant, he has a right to counsel at all future "critical stages," * * *—we believe that there are certain "windows of opportunity" in which a defendant must assert his *Miranda* right to counsel. A defendant must

clearly invoke his right to counsel from each constitutional source, at a time when the right is available. * * *

We agree with the Third Circuit that in order for a defendant to invoke his *Miranda* rights the authorities must be conducting interrogation, or interrogation must be imminent. Such a requirement advances the twin goals of *Miranda*: providing an opportunity for the defendant to dissipate the compulsion and allowing law enforcement the ability to conduct investigations. We believe that not allowing a defendant to invoke his *Miranda* rights anticipatorily does not place an arduous burden on the defendant—all he needs to do is invoke his right in response to or just before interrogation.

Id. at 338-40.

DAVIS v. UNITED STATES
Supreme Court of the United States
512 U.S. 452, 114 S.Ct. 2350 (1994)

QUESTION: In the below set of circumstances, did defendant Davis invoke his right to counsel within the meaning of *Miranda* and *Edwards* ?

CIRCUMSTANCES: Defendant, Robert Davis, a member of the United States Navy, was suspected of beating Keith Shackleford, another sailor, to death with a pool cue. The investigation was conducted by the Naval Investigative Service (NIS). Defendant was interviewed at the NIS office. As required by military law, NIS agents advised defendant that he was a suspect in the killing, that he was not required to make a statement, that any statement could be used against him at a trial by court-martial, and that he was entitled to speak with an attorney and have an attorney present during questioning. Defendant waived his rights, both orally and in writing.

Approximately an hour and a half into the interview, defendant said, "Maybe I should talk to a lawyer." At this point, the interviewing agent

> "[m]ade it very clear that we're not here to violate his rights, that if he wants a lawyer, then we will stop any kind of questioning with him, that we weren't going to pursue the matter unless we have it clarified is he asking for a lawyer or is he just making a comment about a lawyer, and he said, 'No, I'm not asking for a lawyer,' and then he continued on, and said, 'No, I don't want a lawyer.'"

Id. at 2353.

After a short break, the NIS agents reminded defendant of his rights and continued with the interview.

ANSWER: NO. Defendant's "remark to the NIS agents—'Maybe I should talk to a lawyer'—was not a request for counsel[.] * * * The NIS agents therefore were not required to stop questioning [defendant], though it was entirely proper for them to clarify whether [defendant] in fact wanted a lawyer." *Id.* at 2357. "[A]fter a knowing and voluntary waiver of the *Miranda* rights, law enforcement officers may continue questioning until and unless the suspect *clearly requests* an attorney." *Id.* at 2356. [Emphasis added.]

RATIONALE: In *Edwards v. Arizona,* 451 *U.S.* 477, 101 *S.Ct.* 1880 (1981), the Court held that "law enforcement officers must immediately cease questioning a suspect who has clearly asserted his right to have counsel present during custodial interrogation." *Davis* at 2352. In this case, the Court addressed the question of "how law enforcement officers should respond when a suspect makes a reference to counsel that is insufficiently clear to invoke the *Edwards* prohibition on further questioning." *Id.*

"The right to counsel recognized in *Miranda* is sufficiently important to suspects in criminal investigations, * * * that it 'requir[es] the special protection of the knowing and intelligent waiver standard.' * * * If the suspect effectively waives his right to counsel after receiving *Miranda* warnings, law enforcement officers are free to question him. * * * But if a suspect requests counsel at any time during the interview, he is not subject to further questioning until a lawyer has been made available or the suspect himself reinitiates conversation." *Id.* at 2354-55 (citing *Edwards v. Arizona*). This second layer of protection for the *Miranda* right to counsel is " 'designed to prevent police from badgering a defendant into waiving his previously asserted *Miranda* rights.' " *Id.* at 2355. [Citation omitted.]

The applicability of the *Edwards* rule requires courts "to 'determine whether the accused *actually invoked* his right to counsel.' * * * To avoid difficulties of proof and to provide guidance to officers conducting interrogations, this is an objective inquiry. * * * Invocation of the *Miranda* right to counsel 'requires, at a minimum, some statement that can reasonably be construed to be an expression of the desire for the assistance of an attorney.' " *Davis* at 2355. [Court's emphasis; citations omitted.] "But if a suspect makes a reference to an attorney that is ambiguous or equivocal in that a reasonable officer would have understood only that the suspect *might* be invoking the right to counsel, [officer's are] not require[d] [to cease] questioning." *Id.* [Court's emphasis.]

"Rather, the suspect must unambiguously request counsel." *Id.* As emphasized in *Smith v. Illinois,* 469 *U.S.* 91, 97-98, 105 *S.Ct.* 490, 494 (1984), " 'a statement either is such an assertion of the right to counsel or it is not.' " *Davis* at 2355.

Although a suspect need not "speak with the discrimination of an Oxford don," * * * he must articulate his desire to have counsel present sufficiently clearly that a reasonable police officer in the circumstances would understand the statement to be a request for an attorney. If the statement fails to meet the requisite level of clarity, *Edwards* does not require that the officers stop questioning the suspect. * * *

We decline [defendant's] invitation to extend *Edwards* and require law enforcement officers to cease questioning immediately upon the making of an ambiguous or equivocal reference to an attorney. * * * The rationale underlying *Edwards* is that the police must respect a suspect's wishes regarding his right to have an attorney present during custodial interrogation. But when the officers conducting the questioning reasonably do not know whether or not the suspect wants a lawyer, a rule requiring the immediate cessation of questioning "would transform the *Miranda* safeguards into wholly irrational obstacles to legitimate police investigative activity," * * * because it would needlessly prevent the police from questioning a suspect in the absence of counsel even if the suspect did not wish to have a lawyer present.

Id. at 2355-56.

Accordingly, the *Miranda* right to counsel "must be affirmatively invoked by the suspect." *Id.* at 2356. "[A]fter a knowing and voluntary waiver of the *Miranda* rights, law enforcement officers may continue questioning until and unless the suspect clearly requests an attorney." *Id.*

Of course, when a suspect makes an ambiguous or equivocal statement it will often be good police practice for the interviewing officers to clarify whether or not he actually wants an attorney. That was the procedure followed by the NIS agents in this case. Clarifying questions help protect the rights of the suspect by ensuring that he gets an attorney if he wants one, and will minimize the chance of a confession being suppressed due to subsequent judicial second-guessing as to the meaning of the suspect's statement regarding counsel. But [this Court] decline[s] to adopt a rule requiring officers to ask clarifying questions. If the suspect's statement is not an unambiguous or unequivocal request for counsel, the officers have no obligation to stop questioning him. [In other words, u]nless the suspect actually requests an attorney, questioning may continue.

Id. at 2356-57.

Applying the standard set forth above to the circumstances of this case, the Court determined that defendant Davis's remark to the NIS agents—"Maybe I should talk to a lawyer"—was not a request for counsel. "The NIS agents therefore were not required to stop questioning [defendant], though it was entirely proper for them to clarify whether [he] in fact wanted a lawyer." *Id.* at 2357.

Justice SOUTER, with whom Justice BLACKMUN, Justice STEVENS, and Justice GINSBURG join, concurring in the judgment.

"In the midst of his questioning by naval investigators, [defendant] said 'maybe I should talk to a lawyer.' The investigators promptly stopped questioning Davis about the killing of Keith Shackleford and instead undertook to determine whether he meant to invoke his right to counsel * * *.

"I agree with the majority that the Constitution does not forbid law enforcement officers to pose questions (like those directed at Davis), aimed solely at clarifying whether a suspect's ambiguous reference to counsel was meant to assert his Fifth Amendment right. Accordingly, I concur in the judgment affirming Davis's conviction, resting partly on evidence of statements given after agents ascertained that he did not wish to deal with them through counsel. I cannot, however, join in my colleagues' further conclusion that if the investigators here had been so inclined, they were at liberty to disregard Davis's reference to a lawyer entirely, in accordance with a general rule that interrogators have no legal obligation to discover what a custodial subject meant by an ambiguous statement that could reasonably be understood to express a desire to consult a lawyer. * * *

" * * * The concerns of fairness and practicality that have long anchored the *Miranda* case law [require the following] response: when law enforcement officials 'reasonably do not know whether or not the suspect wants a lawyer,' * * * they should stop their interrogation and ask him to make his choice clear[;] * * * questions should be confined to verifying whether the individual meant to ask for a lawyer." *Id.* at 2358-59, 2364.

CONNECTICUT v. BARRETT
Supreme Court of the United States
479 U.S. 523, 107 S.Ct. 828 (1987)

QUESTION: May a law enforcement officer continue questioning a suspect after the suspect states that he would not give a written statement unless his attorney was present but has "no problem" talking about the incident?

ANSWER: YES. Defendant "Barrett's limited requests for counsel * * * were accompanied by affirmative announcements of his willingness to speak with the authorities. The fact that officials took the opportunity provided by Barrett to obtain an oral confession is quite consistent with the Fifth Amendment." *Id.* at 832.

RATIONALE: Defendant Barrett, a suspect in a sexual assault, was transported to the Wallingford, Connecticut, police station for questioning. After being read his *Miranda* rights several times, Barrett signed a card acknowledging that he had been read the warnings and stated that he understood his rights. Barrett then told the officers that he would not give a written statement unless his attorney was present, but had "no problem" talking about the incident. He then gave an oral statement admitting his involvement in the sexual assault.

Although the trial court held that the statement was admissible, finding that Barrett voluntarily waived his right to counsel, the Connecticut Supreme Court reversed the conviction, holding that Barrett invoked his right to counsel under the Fifth and Fourteenth Amendments, and because he had not initiated further discussions with police, his statement should have been suppressed.

The United States Supreme Court, per Chief Justice Rehnquist, disagreed, finding "that the Connecticut Supreme Court erred in holding that the United States Constitution required suppression of Barrett's statement." *Id.* at 831.

"Barrett made clear to police his willingness to talk about the crime for which he was a suspect. The trial court found that this decision was a voluntary waiver of his rights, and there is no evidence that Barrett was 'threatened, tricked, or cajoled' into this waiver." *Id.* [Citation omitted.] Thus, states the Court, "we know of no constitutional objective that would be served by suppression in this case." *Id.* at 832.

"The fundamental purpose of the Court's decision in *Miranda* was 'to assure that *the individual's right to choose* between speech and silence remains unfettered throughout the interrogation process.'" *Id.* at 831 (emphasis supplied). "To this end, the *Miranda* Court adopted prophylactic rules designed to insulate the exercise of Fifth Amendment rights from the government 'compulsion, subtle or otherwise,' that 'operates on the individual to overcome free choice in producing a statement after the privilege has been once invoked.' * * * One such rule requires that, once the accused 'states that he wants an attorney, the interrogation must cease until an attorney is present.' * * * It remains clear, however, that this prohibition on further questioning—like other aspects of *Miranda*—is not itself required by the Fifth Amendment's prohibition on coerced confessions, but is instead justified only by reference to its prophylactic purpose. * * * By prohibiting further interrogation after the invocation of these rights, we erect an auxiliary barrier against police coercion." *Id.* at 832. [Citations omitted.]

In the present case, "[i]t is undisputed that Barrett desired the presence of counsel before making a written statement. Had the police obtained such a statement without meeting the waiver standards of *Edwards*, it would clearly be inadmissible. Barrett's limited requests for counsel, however, were accompanied by affirmative announcements of his willingness to speak with the authorities. The fact that officials took the opportunity provided by Barrett to obtain an oral confession is quite consistent with the Fifth Amendment. *Miranda* gives the defendant a right to choose between speech and silence, and Barrett chose to speak." *Id.*

Accordingly, Barrett's oral confession was found to be admissible.

NOTE

In *United States v. Quiroz*, 13 *F.*3d 505 (2nd Cir. 1993), after the defendant's arrest for money laundering and conspiracy to distribute cocaine base, he was read his rights by a Customs Special Agent from printed forms in English and Spanish. Each form contained a "Statement of Rights" and a section providing for a formal waiver. The agent asked defendant whether he understood the forms, and defendant nodded affirmatively. When the agent asked defendant to sign the forms, defendant stated, "Before I sign anything, I want to speak to my attorney." *Id.* at 509. The agent wrote on the forms that "defendant refused to sign copy until he called his attorney." *Id.* The agent then asked defendant if he would mind answering a few questions. Defendant replied, "[N]o not at all, go right ahead." In response to those questions, defendant made several statements regarding the cocaine charge.

Holding that defendant's post-arrest statements should have been suppressed, the court stated:

> The courts must [] "give a broad, rather than narrow, interpretation to a defendant's request for counsel." * * *
>
> Unlike the statement of the suspect in *Barrett*, Quiroz's refusal to give an uncounseled signature was not accompanied by a volunteered statement that he was willing to answer questions orally. Further, under the holding in *Smith [v. Illinois]*, Quiroz's response to [the agent's] inquiry as to whether Quiroz would answer questions orally cannot be used to determine whether his initial response was limited. Looking only to Quiroz's initial statement that he wished to consult with counsel before signing, we do not see any intended limitation, for that statement was a direct and complete response to the precise question Quiroz had been asked. * * *
>
> The record reveals [] that [the agent] did not ask Quiroz orally and directly whether he was willing to waive his rights. Rather, [the agent] asked Quiroz to read the advice-of-rights forms, asked whether he understood the forms, and simply asked Quiroz to sign them. We have no doubt whatever that, had Quiroz signed, [the agent] would have viewed that act as a complete waiver of Quiroz's rights. We can see no good reason not to treat Quiroz's refusal to sign forms in the absence of counsel as a refusal that was coextensive with the waiver [the agent] sought.
>
> In sum, we do not view Quiroz's refusal to sign the forms as a limited request for counsel any more than [the agent's] request to sign the forms was a request for a limited waiver. Since we do not view Quiroz's statement as narrower than the agent's request, we see no ambiguity. In the absence of ambiguity, further questions by the authorities were prohibited, for there was nothing to clarify. Quiroz's request for counsel should have concluded [the agent's] questioning.

Id. at 511-12. [Citations omitted.]

OREGON v. BRADSHAW
Supreme Court of the United States
462 *U.S.* 1039, 103 *S.Ct.* 2830 (1983)

QUESTION: After an accused has been advised of his *Miranda* rights and requests counsel, does his subsequent question of "Well, what is going to happen to me now ?", constitute a sufficient *initiation* of further conversation so as to satisfy the rule set forth in *Edwards v. Arizona,* 451 *U.S.* 477, 101 *S.Ct.* 1880 (1981) ?

ANSWER: YES. The defendant's question, "Well what is going to happen to me now ?", constitutes a sufficient *initiation* of further conversation so as to satisfy the *Edwards* rule.

RATIONALE: The Supreme Court in *Edwards v. Arizona, supra,* held that "after the right to counsel had been asserted by an accused, further interrogation should not take place 'unless the accused himself *initiates* further communication, exchanges, or conversations with the police.'" *Bradshaw* at 2834 (quoting *Edwards* at 485, 101 *S.Ct.* at 1885). [Emphasis added.]

This rule was "designed to safeguard an accused in police custody from being badgered by police officers in the manner in which the defendant in *Edwards* was." In *Edwards,* the accused had first voluntarily answered some questions posed by police detectives but after a number of responses requested a lawyer. The next day, other detectives visited the defendant in his jail cell, initiated additional questioning, and, when the defendant stated that he did not wish to speak to the detectives, he was told he "had to talk."

This *Edwards* rule has later been interpreted by the Court to prohibit subjecting an accused to further custodial interrogation after he requests an attorney, unless the police demonstrate that the accused himself initiated "dialogue with the authorities." *Wyrick v. Fields,* 459 *U.S.* 42, 103 *S.Ct.* 394, 395 (1982).

Once the *Edwards* rule is satisfied, *i.e.,* that it is shown that the accused initiated further conversation with the law enforcement authorities, there is a second inquiry that will be made by the courts. The courts will then require the police and the prosecution to demonstrate that "subsequent events indicated a waiver of the Fifth Amendment right to have counsel present during the interrogation." *Bradshaw* at 2834. The question then becomes whether the accused voluntarily, knowingly and intelligently waived his right to counsel and right to remain silent. Here, courts will make the assessment by examining "the totality of the circumstances, including the necessary fact that the accused, not the police, reopened the dialogue." *Id.*

As a final note of caution, there are certain inquiries which an accused may make in the course of the routine custodial relationship which may *not* be considered an "initiation of further dialogue." Such examples may include a request for a phone call, for a drink of water, to use the bathroom, etc. These are considered "so routine that they cannot be fairly said to represent a desire on the part of an accused to open up a more generalized discussion relating directly or indirectly to the investigation." *Id.* at 2835.

NOTE

This was a plurality opinion [*See* Glossary] which has been subject to much subsequent criticism. As Justice Powell observes in his concurring opinion, the better analysis is whether the accused in fact effected a voluntary, knowledgeable and intelligent waiver rather than getting caught up in a "who said what first" bandy. *Bradshaw* at 2838 (Powell, J., concurring).

ARIZONA v. ROBERSON
Supreme Court of the United States
486 *U.S.* 675, 108 *S.Ct.* 2093 (1988)

QUESTION: Once a suspect has requested the assistance of counsel during custodial interrogation, may the police subject that suspect to further questioning about an offense that is wholly unrelated to the subject of their initial interrogation ?

ANSWER: NO.   Once a suspect has requested an attorney during custodial interrogation, the police are prohibited from subjecting that suspect to further questioning—regardless of whether that questioning concerns the offense at issue or a wholly unrelated offense—" 'unless the [suspect] himself initiates further communication, exchanges, or conversations with the police.' " *Id.* at 2096. [Citation omitted.]

RATIONALE: At the scene of defendant's burglary arrest, the arresting officer advised him of his *Miranda* rights. Defendant "replied that he 'wanted a lawyer before answering any questions[,' and t]his fact was duly recorded in the officer's written report of the incident." *Id.* at 2096.
    Three days later, while defendant was still in custody pursuant to the burglary arrest, a different officer questioned him about a different burglary, one that occurred on April 15. "That officer was not aware of the fact that [defendant] had requested the assistance of counsel three days earlier. After advising [defendant] of his rights, the officer obtained an incriminating statement concerning the April 15th burglary." *Id.* In the prosecution for that offense, the Arizona trial court suppressed that statement, finding that " 'the accused was continuously in police custody from the time of asserting his Fifth Amendment right through the time of the impermissible questioning. The coercive environment never dissipated.' " *Id.* at 2096-2097. [Citation omitted.]
    In *Edwards v. Arizona*, 451 *U.S.* 477, 484-485, 101 *S.Ct.* 1880, 1884-1885 (1981), the United States Supreme Court held that a suspect who has "expressed his desire to deal with the police only through counsel is not subject to further interrogation by the authorities until counsel has been made available to him, unless the accused himself

initiates further communication, exchanges, or conversations with the police." In this case, the State of Arizona asks the Court "to craft an exception to that rule for cases in which the police want to interrogate a suspect about an offense that is unrelated to the subject of their initial interrogation." *Roberson* at 2096. "Several years ago the Arizona Supreme Court considered, and rejected, a similar argument," finding that " '[t]he only difference between Edwards and [defendant] is that Edwards was questioned about the same offense after a request for counsel while [defendant] was reinterrogated about an unrelated offense.' " *Id.* [Citations omitted.] As a result, the Arizona Supreme Court concluded, and the United States Supreme Court agrees, " 'that this factual distinction holds [no] legal significance for [F]ifth [A]mendment purposes.' " *Id.*

"A major purpose of the Court's opinion in *Miranda* * * * was 'to give concrete constitutional guidelines for law enforcement agencies and courts to follow.' * * * The rule of the *Edwards* case came as a corollary to *Miranda's* admonition that '(i)f the individual states that he wants an attorney the interrogation must cease until an attorney is present.' " *Roberson* at 2097. [Citations omitted.] Additionally, *Edwards* emphasized "that it is inconsistent with *Miranda* and its progeny for the authorities, at their instance, to reinterrogate an accused in custody if he has clearly asserted his right to counsel." 451 *U.S.* at 485, 101 *S.Ct.* at 1885. Thus, the *Edwards* Court "concluded that reinterrogation may only occur if 'the accused himself initiates further communication, exchanges, or conversations with the police.' " *Id.* Moreover, the Court here recognizes that:

> [T]he prophylactic protections that *Miranda* warnings provide to counteract the "inherent compelling pressures" of custodial interrogation and to "permit a full opportunity to exercise the privilege against self-incrimination," 384 *U.S.*, at 467, 86 *S.Ct.*, at 1624, are implemented by the application of the *Edwards* corollary that if a suspect believes that he is not capable of undergoing such questioning without advice of counsel, then it is presumed that any subsequent waiver that has come at the authorities' behest, and not at the suspect's own instigation, is itself the product of the "inherently compelling pressures" and not the purely voluntary choice of the suspect.

Roberson at 2097-2098. [Citations omitted.]

As a result, the *Edwards* rule "serves the purpose of providing 'clear and unequivocal' guidelines to the law enforcement profession. Surely there is nothing ambiguous about the requirement that after a person in custody has expressed his desire to deal with police only through counsel, he 'is not subject to further interrogation by the authorities until counsel has been made available to him, unless the accused himself initiates further communication, exchanges, or conversations with the police.' " *Roberson* at 2098. [Citation omitted.]

Accordingly, the Court totally rejects the State's contention "that the bright-line, prophylactic *Edwards* rule should not apply when the police-initiated interrogation following a suspect's request for counsel occurs in the context of a separate investigation." *Id.* While it is true that "a suspect may have good reasons for wanting to speak with the police about the offenses involved in the new investigation, or at least to learn from the police what the new investigation is about * * *[, t]he simple answer is that the suspect, having requested counsel, can determine how to deal with the separate investigations with counsel's advice." *Id.* at 2101. [Citation omitted.]

Finally, the Court attaches "no significance to the fact that the officer who conducted the second interrogation did not know that [defendant] had made a request for counsel. In addition to the fact that *Edwards* focuses on the state of mind of the suspect and not of the police, custodial interrogation must be conducted pursuant to established procedures, and those procedures in turn must enable an officer who proposes to initiate an interrogation to determine whether the suspect has previously requested counsel. In this case [defendant's] request had been properly memorialized in a written report but the officer who conducted the interrogation simply failed to examine that report." *Id.*

Consequently, "[w]hether a contemplated reinterrogation concerns the same or a different offense, or whether the same or different law enforcement authorities are involved in the second investigation, the same need to determine whether the suspect has requested counsel exists. The police department's failure to honor that request cannot be justified by the lack of diligence of a particular officer." *Id.*

NOTE

See also Tukes v. Dugger, 911 *F.*2d 508, 515 (11th Cir. 1990) ("once a prisoner in custody requests counsel, he may not be interrogated about additional offenses, even if the interrogator does not have actual notice of the prisoner's prior invocation of his right to counsel").

THE SIXTH AMENDMENT SETTING

MICHIGAN v. JACKSON
Supreme Court of the United States
475 *U.S.* 625, 106 *S.Ct.* 1404 (1986)

QUESTION: Does a Sixth Amendment right to counsel violation occur when law enforcement officers initiate further interrogation of a defendant after that defendant, at an arraignment or similar proceeding, has requested a lawyer ?

ANSWER: YES. Postarraignment confessions or responses to police-initiated interrogation shall be held inadmissible in court as a Sixth Amendment right to counsel violation in circumstances where the defendant requests counsel at an arraignment or similar proceeding, but is not afforded an opportunity to consult with counsel before police initiate further interrogation. The ultimate result is that "any waiver of [that] defendant's right to counsel for that police-initiated interrogation is invalid." *Id.* at 1411.

RATIONALE: For purposes of this opinion, the Supreme Court consolidated two Michigan cases in which the defendants in each were charged with murder. Each defendant, at his arraignment, asserted his Sixth Amendment right to counsel, and, present at each arraignment, were the detectives in charge of the respective investigations.

After the arraignments, the officers confronted the defendants and initiated interrogation. Each defendant, prior to any questioning, was advised of his *Miranda* rights, and each executed a waiver. Incriminating statements were obtained.

In a sharply split decision, *the United States Supreme Court, per Justice Stevens, held that the waivers obtained by the officers were invalid, and the statements received were inadmissible.*

Although the circumstances indicate that the questioning took place *after* the "initiation of adversary judicial proceedings," and although any subsequent deliberate elicitation of information from an accused has been deemed a "critical stage" at which the Sixth Amendment right to counsel applies, *Maine v. Moulton*, 474 *U.S.* 159, 106 *S.Ct.* 477 (1985), the Court, nonetheless, invoked a Fifth Amendment rationale to question whether the defendants "validly waived their right to counsel at the postarraignment custodial interrogations." *Jackson* at 1408.

In *Edwards v. Arizona*, 451 *U.S.* 477, 101 *S.Ct.* 1880 (1981), a Fifth Amendment case, the Court "held that an accused person in custody who has 'expressed his desire to deal with the police only through counsel, is not subject to further interrogation by the authorities until counsel has been made available to him, unless the accused himself initiates further communication, exchanges, or conversations with the police.'" *Jackson* at 1405 (quoting *Edwards* at 484-485, 110 *S.Ct.* at 1884-85). In addition, the Court re-emphasized this "bright-line" principle in *Solem v. Stumes*, 465 *U.S.* 638, 104 *S.Ct.* 1338 (1984), as a "safeguard [of] pre-existing rights." There, the Court reiterated that "once a suspect has invoked the right to counsel, any subsequent conversation must be initiated by him." *Jackson* at 1406. [Citation omitted.]

Here, in *Jackson*, the Court utilized the Fifth Amendment *Edwards-Stumes* analysis in a Sixth Amendment setting and reasoned that the prohibition on "interrogation of an uncounseled prisoner who has asked for the help of a lawyer [is] even stronger after he has been formally charged with an offense than before." *Id.* at 1408. Indeed, "the Sixth Amendment right to counsel at a post-arraignment interrogation requires at least as much protection as the Fifth Amendment right to counsel at any custodial interrogation." *Id.* at 1408-09.

Accordingly, "after a formal accusation has been made—and a person who had previously been just a 'suspect' has become an 'accused' within the meaning of the Sixth Amendment—the constitutional right to the assistance of counsel is of such importance that the police may no longer employ techniques for eliciting information from an uncounseled defendant that might have been entirely proper at an earlier stage of their investigation." *Id.* at 1409. For example, the "surreptitious employment of a cellmate" (*United States v. Henry*, 447 U.S. 264, 100 S.Ct. 2183 (1980)), or the "electronic surveillance of conversations with third parties" (*Maine v. Moulton*, 474 U.S. 159, 106 S.Ct. 477 (1985); *Massiah v. United States*, 377 U.S. 201, 84 S.Ct. 1199 (1964)), "may violate the defendant's Sixth Amendment right to counsel even though the same methods of investigation might have been permissible before arraignment or indictment." *Jackson* at 1409.

As a result, "[j]ust as written waivers are insufficient to justify police-initiated interrogation after the request for counsel in a Fifth Amendment analysis, so too they are insufficient to justify police-initiated interrogations after the request for counsel in a Sixth Amendment analysis." *Id.* at 1410-11.

Thus, if a law enforcement officer initiates "interrogation after a defendant's assertion, at an arraignment or similar proceeding, of his right to counsel, any waiver of the defendant's right to counsel for that police-initiated interrogation is invalid." *Id.* at 1411.

NOTE

1. *Imputing State's knowledge from one actor to another.* In *Jackson, supra,* the police detectives in charge of the respective investigations were, in fact, present at the defendants' arraignments. However, the State pointed out that there are times, perhaps more times than not, that the investigating officer would not be at the arraignment, and, as a result, may not know of the defendant's request for counsel at the arraignment.

The Court rejected this argument and held that for Sixth Amendment purposes, a court should impute State's knowledge from one state actor to another. "[T]he Sixth Amendment concerns the confrontation between the State and the individual. One set of state actors [the police] may not claim ignorance of defendant's unequivocal request for counsel to another state actor [the court]." *Jackson* at 1410.

2. *Invoking the right to counsel in a Sixth Amendment setting.* An accused's invocation of his Sixth Amendment right to counsel does not

apply to all future prosecutions, for the right does not attach until a prosecution is commenced, *i.e.*, " 'at or after the initiation of adversary judicial criminal proceedings—whether by way of formal charge, preliminary hearing, indictment, information, or arraignment.' " *United States v. Gouveia*, 467 *U.S.* 180, 188, 104 *S.Ct.* 2292, 2297 (1984). [Citation omitted.] Similar to the Sixth Amendment right to counsel, the *Michigan v. Jackson* rule may be considered "offense specific," *McNeil v. Wisconsin*, 501 *U.S.* 171, 111 *S.Ct.* 2204, 2207 (1991), that is, "after the Sixth Amendment right to counsel attaches and is invoked, any statements obtained from the accused during subsequent police-initiated custodial questioning *regarding the charge at issue* (even if the accused purports to waive his rights) are inadmissible." *Id.*, 111 *S.Ct.* at 2209. [Emphasis added.]

Incriminating statements produced during custodial interview "pertaining to other crimes, as to which the Sixth Amendment right has not yet attached, are, of course, admissible at a trial of those offenses." *Maine v. Moulton*, 474 *U.S.* 159, 179-180 & n.16, 106 *S.Ct.* 477, 488-489 & n.16 (1985).

3. *A request for counsel requires the "presence" of counsel.* In a Fifth or Sixth Amendment setting, once an accused invokes his right to counsel, there can be no further questioning until an attorney has been made available to him. In *Minnick v. Mississippi*, 498 *U.S.* 146, 111 *S.Ct.* 486 (1990), the Court made clear that this requisite is not satisfied by the mere provision of "an opportunity to consult with an attorney outside the interrogation room." *Id.*, 111 *S.Ct.* at 490. Although the *Minnick* Court did not reach the "Sixth Amendment implications in the case," *id.* at 489, it is fair to conclude that an accused's request for counsel at an arraignment or similar proceeding precludes any subsequent police-initiated questioning about that particular offense without the provision and *presence* of an attorney. *See id.* at 490.

A different result obtains, however, when the subsequent questioning follows a "defendant-initiated" communication, exchange or conversation. *See e.g., Edwards v. Arizona*, 451 *U.S.* 477, 484-485, 101 *S.Ct.* 1880, 1885 (1981). In this respect, the *Minnick* Court stated, "*Edwards* does not foreclose finding a waiver of Fifth Amendment protections after counsel has been requested, provided the accused has initiated the conversation or discussions with the authorities[.]" *Minnick* at 492.

4. *Impeachment purposes.* Is a statement to police taken in violation of the rule in *Jackson* nonetheless admissible to impeach a defendant's false or inconsistent trial testimony ? According to the Court, in *Michigan v. Harvey*, 494 *U.S.* 344, 110 *S.Ct.* 1176, 1178 (1990), the answer is yes.

In *Michigan v. Jackson*, it was held that statements taken in violation of its terms "may not be admitted as substantive evidence in the prosecution's case-in-chief." *Harvey*, 110 *S.Ct.* at 1177 (citing *Jackson* at 636, 106 *S.Ct.* at 1411). While based on the Sixth Amendment, the underlying rationale of *Jackson* stems from the Court's *Miranda* and *Edwards* line of decisions. "*Jackson* simply superimposed the Fifth Amendment analysis of *Edwards* onto the Sixth Amendment." *Harvey* at 1180.

The Court has already determined "that although statements taken in violation of only the prophylactic *Miranda* rules may not be used in the prosecution's case-in-chief, they are admissible to impeach conflicting testimony by the defendant." *Id.* (citing *Harris v. New York*, 401 *U.S.* 222, 91 *S.Ct.* 643 (1971), and *Oregon v. Hass*, 420 *U.S.* 714, 95 *S.Ct.* 1215 (1975)). In this regard, "[i]f a defendant exercises his right to testify on his own behalf, he assumes a reciprocal 'obligation to speak truthfully and accurately[.' He may not] ' "turn the illegal method by which evidence in the Government's possession was obtained to his own advantage, and provide himself with a shield against contradiction of his untruths." ' " *Id.* [Citations omitted.]

Thus, the *Harvey* Court concluded:

> There is no reason for a different result in a *Jackson* case, where the prophylactic rule is designed to ensure voluntary, knowing, and intelligent waivers of the Sixth Amendment right to counsel rather than the Fifth Amendment privilege against self-incrimination or "right to counsel." * * *

Id. at 1181.

> Both *Jackson* and *Edwards* establish prophylactic rules that render some otherwise valid waivers of constitutional rights invalid when they result from police-initiated interrogation, and in neither case should "the shield provided by [the prophylactic rule] be perverted into a license to use perjury by way of a defense, free from the risk of confrontation with prior inconsistent utterances."

Id. at 1182 (quoting *Harris* at 226, 91 *S.Ct.* at 646).

5. Represented defendants.

(a) A defendant who is represented by counsel on one matter is not wholly "off-limits" when it comes to police questioning about a different, unrelated investigation. In this respect, a Sixth Amendment waiver of counsel may be effective, even when a defendant is represented by counsel in other criminal proceedings, so long as the right to counsel has not yet attached to the criminal offense which is the subject of the waiver. Thus, when a defendant is incarcerated on one charge, and is represented by counsel on that charge, he may effectively waive his or her right to counsel on a second, unrelated charge to which the right to counsel has not yet attached. As the Court stated in *Cobb v. State*, 85 *S.W.*3d 258 (Tex.Crim.App. 2002):

> If a person has already been charged with an offense and has an attorney representing him on that charge, that attorney can tell his client not to talk to the police if questioned about *anything*. It is then up to the accused to decide whether or not to follow his counsel's advice. If law enforcement officers subsequently approach the

suspect about another offense, whether related to the charged offense or not, and administer *Miranda* warnings, neither the federal nor the Texas constitution prevents the suspect from voluntarily waiving his privilege and speaking to the officers about his other offense, even without the benefit of his counsel's assistance.

Id. at 269. [Court's emphasis.]

(b) In *Texas v. Cobb*, 532 *U.S.* 162, 121 *S.Ct.* 1335 (2001), Chief Justice Rehnquist, speaking for a majority of the United States Supreme Court, rejected the dissent's suggestion that the Sixth Amendment right to counsel carries with it the principle that once the right to counsel attaches, law enforcement authorities may only deal with the defendant through counsel, rather than directly. In this respect, the dissenting justices implied that, just as Rule 4.2 of the *ABA Model Rules of Professional Conduct* generally prohibits a lawyer from communicating with a person known to be represented by counsel "about the subject of the representation" without counsel's "consent," that same rule may also apply to the police. The majority of the Court disagreed. The Court said:

> * * * [C]ontrary to the dissent's suggestion, * * * there is no "background principle" of our Sixth Amendment jurisprudence establishing that there may be no contact between a defendant and police without counsel present. The dissent would expand the Sixth Amendment right to the assistance of counsel in a criminal prosecution into a rule which "'exists to prevent lawyers from taking advantage of uncounseled lay persons and to preserve the integrity of the lawyer-client relationship.'" * * * Every profession is competent to define the standards of conduct for its members, but such standards are obviously not controlling in interpretation of constitutional provisions. The Sixth Amendment right to counsel is personal to the defendant and specific to the offense.

Id. at 1342-43 n.2 (quoting *ABA Ann. Model Rule of Professional Conduct* 4.2).

6. *When the "right to counsel" attaches.* In *Rothgery v. Gillespie County, Texas* ___ *U.S.* ___, 128 *S.Ct.* 2578 (2008), the United States Supreme Court reaffirmed that a defendant's right to counsel, guaranteed by the Sixth Amendment, attaches "at the first appearance before a judicial officer at which a defendant is told of the formal accusation against him and restrictions are imposed on his liberty." *Id.*, 128 *S.Ct.* at 2581. Moreover, the attachment of the right does not require that a public prosecutor be aware of that initial proceeding or involved in its conduct. *Id.*

"The Sixth Amendment right of the 'accused' to assistance of counsel in 'all criminal prosecutions' is limited by its terms: 'it does not attach until a prosecution is commenced.'" *Id.* at 2583. [Citations omitted.] As a general rule, the prosecution "has commenced" at the "initiation of adversary judicial criminal proceedings — whether by way of formal charge, preliminary hearing, indictment, information, or arraignment." *Id.* According to the Court, the rule is "not 'mere formalism,' but a recognition of the point at which 'the government has committed itself to prosecute,' 'the adverse positions of government and defendant have solidified,' and the accused 'finds himself faced with the prosecutorial forces of organized society, and immersed in the intricacies of substantive and procedural criminal law.'" *Id.* [Citation omitted.]

As a matter of law, it does not matter that the prosecutor did not take part in the accused's initial court appearance, or was even aware of it. Prosecutorial awareness is not the standard. In this regard, the Court noted that "an attachment rule that turned on determining the moment of a prosecutor's first involvement would be 'wholly unworkable and impossible to administer.'" *Id.* at 2588. [Citation omitted.] Rather, the right to counsel attaches at the first, initial appearance before a judicial officer. Known also as the "preliminary arraignment," or "arraignment on the complaint," this is the first time the accused appears before a court; it is "generally the hearing at which 'the magistrate informs the defendant of the charge in the complaint, and of various rights in further proceedings,' and 'determine[s] the conditions for pretrial release.'" *Id.* at 2584. Such "an initial appearance following a charge signifies a sufficient commitment to prosecute regardless of a prosecutor's participation[.]" *Id.* at 2590.

Once the right to counsel attaches, "the accused at least is entitled to the presence of appointed counsel during any 'critical stage' of the postattachment proceedings; what makes a stage critical is what shows the need for counsel's presence. Thus, counsel must be appointed within a reasonable time after attachment to allow for adequate representation at any critical stage before trial, as well as at trial itself." *Id.* at 2591.

Accordingly, "a criminal defendant's initial appearance before a judicial officer, where he learns the charge against him and his liberty is subject to restriction, marks the start of adversary judicial proceedings that trigger attachment of the Sixth Amendment right to counsel." *Id.* at 2592.

McNEIL v. WISCONSIN
Supreme Court of the United States
501 *U.S.* 171, 111 *S.Ct.* 2204 (1991)

QUESTION: Does an accused's Sixth Amendment request for counsel at an initial appearance or other judicial proceeding on a charged offense constitute an invocation of his "Fifth Amendment" (*Miranda*) right to counsel that precludes any subsequent police-initiated interrogation on unrelated, uncharged offenses ?

ANSWER: NO. The Sixth Amendment right to counsel and *Miranda's* "Fifth Amendment" right to counsel are fundamentally different. The Sixth Amendment right is "offense-specific." The right "cannot be invoked once for all future prosecutions, for it does not attach until a prosecution is commenced[.]" *Id.* at 2207. The *Miranda-Edwards* rule, however, "is *not* offense-specific: once a suspect invokes the *Miranda* right to counsel for interrogation regarding one offense, he may not be reapproached regarding *any* offense unless counsel is present." *Id.* at 2208. [Emphasis in original.] Thus, "[t]he purpose of the Sixth Amendment counsel guarantee—and hence the purpose of invoking it—is to 'protect the unaided layman at critical confrontations' with his 'expert adversary,' the government, *after* [the initiation of adversary judicial criminal proceedings]." *Id.* at 2208-09. [Citation omitted.] "The purpose of the *Miranda-Edwards* guarantee, on the other hand—and hence the purpose of invoking it—is to protect a quite different interest: the suspect's 'desire to deal with the police only through counsel[.]' " *McNeil* at 2209. [Citation omitted.] As a result, "[t]o invoke the Sixth Amendment interest is, as a matter of *fact, not* to invoke the *Miranda-Edwards* interest. One might be quite willing to speak to the police without counsel present concerning many matters, but not the matter under prosecution." *Id.* [Emphasis in original.]

RATIONALE: Defendant, Paul McNeil, was arrested in Omaha, Nebraska, for an armed robbery which took place in West Allis, Wisconsin. After his arrest, McNeil was taken back to Wisconsin where he was brought before a county court for an initial appearance and a bail hearing. At the hearing, he was represented by a public defender.

Later that evening, a detective visited McNeil in jail and questioned him concerning a murder, attempted murder, and armed burglary which occurred in Caledonia, Wisconsin. McNeil did not deny knowledge of the crimes, but said that he was not involved. At a second interview, two days later, the detective again questioned McNeil about the Caledonia crimes. As in the first interview, prior to any questioning, the detective advised McNeil of his *Miranda* rights. McNeil signed a written waiver and, this time, "admitted that he had been involved in the Caledonia crimes, which he described in detail" in a written statement. *Id.* at 2207. At a third interview, after again being advised of his *Miranda* rights, defendant waived his rights and provided the authorities with another incriminating written statement.

McNeil was formally charged with the Caledonia crimes. After the trial court denied his motion to suppress the three incriminating statements, McNeil was convicted of second-degree murder, attempted first-degree murder, and armed robbery. On appeal, McNeil contended "that his courtroom appearance with an attorney for the West Allis crime constituted an invocation of the *Miranda* right to counsel, and that any subsequent waiver of that right during police-initiated questioning regarding *any* offense was invalid." *Id.* at 2207. The Wisconsin Supreme Court rejected McNeil's contention, and *the United States Supreme Court affirmed.*

In *Michigan v. Jackson*, 475 *U.S.* 625, 106 *S.Ct.* 1404 (1986), the Court held that once the Sixth Amendment "right to counsel has attached and has been invoked, any subsequent waiver during a police-initiated custodial interview is ineffective[,]" and, for purposes of its decision here in *McNeil*, the Court determined that "at the time [McNeil] provided the incriminating statements at issue, his Sixth Amendment right had attached and had been invoked with respect to the *West Allis armed robbery*, for which he had been formally charged." *McNeil* at 2207. [Emphasis in original.] Significantly, the issue in *Jackson* focused upon "any statements obtained from the accused during subsequent police-initiated custodial questioning *regarding the charge at issue*," *id.* at 2209, and whether any purported waiver of the Sixth Amendment right to counsel on that particular charge could be effective. [Emphasis added.]

The Sixth Amendment right to counsel and the *Michigan v. Jackson* effect of invalidating subsequent waivers in police-initiated interviews are both "offense-specific." *McNeil* at 2207. The Sixth Amendment right "cannot be invoked once for all future prosecutions, for it does not attach until a prosecution is commenced," that is, " 'at or after the initiation of adversary judicial criminal proceedings—whether by way of formal charge, preliminary hearing, indictment, information, or arraignment.' " *Id.* (quoting *United States v. Gouveia*, 467 *U.S.* 180, 188, 104 *S.Ct.* 2292, 2297 (1984) (citation omitted)). Moreover, " '[t]he police have an interest * * * in investigating new or additional crimes [after an individual is formally charged with one crime.] * * * [T]o exclude evidence pertaining to charges as to which the Sixth Amendment right to counsel had not attached at the time the evidence was obtained, simply because other charges were pending at that time, would unnecessarily frustrate the public's interest in the investigation of criminal activities[.]' * * * 'Incriminating statements pertaining to other crimes, as to which the Sixth Amendment right has not yet attached, are, of course, admissible at a trial of those offenses.' " *Id.* at 2207-08. [Citations omitted.] "Because [McNeil] provided the statements at issue here before his Sixth Amendment right to counsel with respect to the *Caledonia offenses* had been (or even could have been) invoked, that right poses no bar to the admission of the statements in this case." *Id.* at 2208. [Emphasis in original.]

McNeil argued that the police violated his right to counsel, not as found in the text of the Sixth Amendment, but in the case law relating to the Fifth Amendment privilege against compelled self-incrimination. In this respect, *Miranda v. Arizona*, 384 *U.S.* 436, 86 *S.Ct.* 1602 (1966), "established a number of prophylactic rights designed to counteract the 'inherently compelling pressures' of custodial interrogation, including the right to have counsel present." *McNeil* at 2208. In *Edwards v. Arizona*, 451 *U.S.* 477, 101 *S.Ct.* 1880 (1981), the Court added a "second layer" of protection for the *Miranda* right to counsel: "once a suspect asserts the right, not only must the current interrogation cease, but he may not be approached for further interrogation 'until counsel has been made available to him,' * * * which means * * * that counsel must be present[.]" *McNeil* at 2208. [Citations omitted.] "If the police do subsequently initiate an encounter in the absence of counsel (assuming there has been no break in custody), the suspect's statements are presumed involuntary and therefore inadmissible as substantive evidence at trial, even where the suspect executes a waiver and his statements would be considered voluntary under traditional standards. This is 'designed to prevent police from badgering a defendant into waiving his previously asserted *Miranda* rights[.]' " *Id.* [Citation omitted.] "The *Edwards* rule, moreover, is not offense-specific: once a suspect invokes the *Miranda* right to counsel for interrogation regarding one offense, he may not be reapproached regarding *any* offense unless counsel is present." *McNeil* at 2208 (citing *Arizona v. Roberson*, 486 *U.S.* 675, 108 *S.Ct.* 2093 (1988)). [Emphasis in original.]

McNeil's attempt to combine the Sixth Amendment right to counsel and the *Miranda-Edwards* "Fifth Amendment" right to counsel, by asserting that "his prior invocation of the offense-specific Sixth Amendment right with regard to the West Allis burglary was also an invocation of the non-offense-specific *Miranda-Edwards* right[,] * * * is false as a matter of fact and inadvisable" as a matter of policy. *McNeil* at 2208.

"The purpose of the Sixth Amendment counsel guarantee—and hence the purpose of invoking it—is to 'protec[t] the unaided layman at critical confrontations' with his 'expert adversary,' the Government, *after* [the initiation of adversary judicial criminal proceedings]." *Id.* at 2209. [Citation omitted.] "The purpose of the *Miranda-Edwards* guarantee, on the other hand—and hence the purpose of invoking it—is to protect quite a different interest: the suspect's 'desire to deal with the police only through counsel[.]' " *McNeil* at 2209. [Citation omitted.] The *Miranda-Edwards* "Fifth Amendment" right to counsel

> is in one respect narrower than the interest protected by the Sixth Amendment guarantee (because it relates only to custodial interrogation) and in another respect broader (because it relates to interrogation regarding *any* suspected crime and attaches whether or not the 'adversarial relationship' produced by a pending prosecution has yet arisen).

McNeil at 2209. [Emphasis in original.] "To invoke the Sixth Amendment interest is, as a matter of *fact, not* to invoke the *Miranda-Edwards* interest. One might be quite willing to speak to the police without counsel present concerning many matters, but not the matter under prosecution." *Id.* [Emphasis in original.] The *Edwards* rule "applies only when the suspect 'ha[s] *expressed*' his wish for the particular sort of lawyerly assistance that is the subject of *Miranda*. * * * It requires, at a minimum, some statement that can reasonably be construed to be an expression of a desire for the assistance of an attorney *in dealing with custodial interrogation by the police.* Requesting the assistance of an attorney at [an initial appearance or] a bail hearing does not bear that construction. '[T]o find that [the defendant] invoked his Fifth Amendment right to counsel on the present charges merely by requesting the appointment of counsel at his arraignment on the unrelated charge is to disregard the ordinary meaning of that request.' " *Id.* [Emphasis added; citations omitted.]

McNeil's proposed rule would "seriously impede effective law enforcement. The Sixth Amendment right to counsel attaches at the first formal proceeding against an accused, and in most States, at least with respect to serious offenses, free counsel is made available at that time and ordinarily requested." *Id.* at 2210.

> Thus, if we were to adopt [McNeil's proposed] rule, most persons in pretrial custody for serious offenses would be *unapproachable* by police officers suspecting them of involvement in other crimes, *even though they have never expressed any unwillingness to be questioned.* Since the ready ability to obtain uncoerced confessions is not an evil but an unmitigated good, society would be the loser. Admissions of guilt resulting from valid *Miranda* waivers "are more than merely 'desirable'; they are essential to society's compelling interest in finding, convicting, and punishing those who violate the law."

Id. [Citation omitted; emphasis in original.]

NOTE

During the course of its opinion in *McNeil,* the Court's majority rejected the dissent's prediction that the rule announced will be routinely circumvented when, "[i]n future preliminary hearings, competent counsel * * * make sure that they, or their clients, make a statement on the record" invoking the *Miranda* right to counsel. *Id.* at 2212 (Stevens, J., dissenting). Writing for the majority, Justice Scalia noted:

> We have in fact never held that a person can invoke his *Miranda* rights anticipatorily, in a context other than "custodial interrogation"—which a preliminary hearing will not always, or even usually, involve[.] * * * If the *Miranda* right to counsel can be invoked at a preliminary hearing, it could be argued, there is no logical reason why it could not be invoked by a letter prior to arrest, or indeed even prior to identification as a suspect. Most rights must be asserted when the government seeks to take the action they protect against. The fact that we have allowed the *Miranda* right to counsel, once asserted, to be effective with respect to future custodial interrogation does not necessarily mean that we will allow it to be asserted initially outside the context of custodial interrogation, with similar future effect.

Id. at 2211 n.3.

TEXAS v. COBB
Supreme Court of the United States
532 *U.S.* 162, 121 *S.Ct.* 1335 (2001)

QUESTION: Does a criminal defendant's Sixth Amendment right to counsel attach *not only* to the offense with which he or she is charged, but to other *uncharged* offenses "closely related factually" to the charged offense ?

ANSWER: NO. The Sixth Amendment right to counsel is "offense specific." *Id.* at 1340. When the right to counsel attaches, it will encompass uncharged offenses *only when* each of those offenses may be considered the same "offense," as that term is defined by case law. The applicable rule is that "where the same act or transaction constitutes a violation of two distinct statutory provisions, the test to be applied to determine whether there are two offenses or only one, is whether each provision requires proof of a fact which the other does not." *Id.* at 1343. [Citation & internal quotes omitted.] In this case, Cobb had been indicted for burglary at the time he was questioned by the police. When he confessed to the murder of two residents of the burglarized home, he had not yet been charged with murder. Since burglary and murder are not the "same offense"—each requiring proof of a different element—the Sixth Amendment right to counsel did not bar police from interrogating Cobb regarding the murders.

RATIONALE: While under arrest (for an unrelated offense), defendant, Raymond Cobb, was questioned about a December 1993 burglary of a home located across the street from his home in Walker County, Texas. The burglary had been reported to the police by Lindsey Owings, who also reported that his wife, Margaret, and their 16-month-old daughter were missing. Cobb confessed to the burglary, but denied any knowledge of the disappearances. In August of 1994, Cobb was indicted on the burglary charge, and attorney Hal Ridley was appointed to represent him on that charge.

After Ridley's appointment as Cobb's attorney, investigators asked and received his permission to question Cobb, on two occasions, about the disappearances. Cobb denied any involvement.

In November 1995, while free on bail on the burglary charge, Cobb was living with his father in Odessa, Texas. Cobb's father contacted the law enforcement authorities and reported that his son had confessed to him that he killed Margaret Owings in the course of the burglary. After obtaining a statement from Cobb's father, the police secured a warrant for Cobb's arrest, took him into custody, and read him his *Miranda* warnings.

Cobb waived his rights and confessed to murdering both Margaret and her 16-month-old daughter. Cobb explained that "when Margaret confronted him as he was attempting to remove the Owings' stereo, he stabbed her in the stomach with a knife he was carrying." *Id.* at 1339. He told the police that he "dragged her body to a wooded area a few hundred yards from the house." *Id.* Cobb then stated:

796

"I went back to her house and I saw the baby laying on its bed. I took the baby out there and it was sleeping the whole time. I laid the baby down on the ground four or five feet away from its mother. I went back to my house and got a flat edge shovel. That's all I could find. Then I went back over to where they were and I started digging a hole between them. After I got the hole dug, the baby was awake. It started going toward its mom and it fell in the hole. I put the lady in the hole and I covered them up. I remember stabbing a different knife I had in the ground where they were. I was crying right then."

Id. at 1339-40.

Cobb ultimately led the officers to the location where he had buried the victims' bodies. He was later convicted of capital murder and was sentenced to death.

In this appeal, Cobb argued, among other things, that "his confession should have been suppressed because it was obtained in violation of his Sixth Amendment right to counsel." *Id.* at 1340. Relying on *Michigan v. Jackson*, 475 *U.S.* 625, 106 *S.Ct.* 1404 (1986), Cobb contended that his right to counsel had attached when he accepted Ridley's appointment as counsel in the burglary case and that the police "were therefore required to secure Ridley's permission before proceeding with the interrogation." *Cobb* at 1340. *The United States Supreme Court disagreed.*

In McNeil v. Wisconsin, 501 U.S. 171, 111 S.Ct. 2204 (1991), the Court explained that the Sixth Amendment right to counsel

"is offense specific. It cannot be invoked once for all future prosecutions, for it does not attach until a prosecution is commenced, that is, at or after the initiation of adversary judicial criminal proceedings—whether by way of formal charge, preliminary hearing, indictment, information, or arraignment."

Cobb at 1340 (quoting *McNeil* at 175, 111 *S.Ct.* at 2207). The *McNeil* Court held, therefore, that a defendant's statements regarding offenses for which he had not been charged were admissible notwithstanding the attachment of his Sixth Amendment right to counsel on other charged offenses.

Recently, some courts have read into *McNeil's* offense-specific definition an exception for *uncharged* crimes that are "factually related" to a charged offense. Yet, even prior to *McNeil*, the Supreme Court, in *Maine v. Moulton*, 474 *U.S.* 159, 106 *S.Ct.* 477 (1985), observed:

"The police have an interest in the thorough investigation of crimes for which *formal charges* have already been filed. They also have an interest in investigating new or additional crimes. Investigations of either type of crime may require surveillance of individuals already under indictment. Moreover, law enforcement officials investigating an individual suspected of committing one crime and *formally charged* with having committed another crime obviously seek to discover evidence useful at trial of either crime.

> In seeking evidence pertaining to *pending charges*, however, the Government's investigative powers are limited by the Sixth Amendment rights of the accused. * * * On the other hand, *to exclude evidence pertaining to charges as to which the Sixth Amendment right to counsel had not attached at the time the evidence was obtained, simply because other charges were pending at that time, would unnecessarily frustrate the public's interest in the investigation of criminal activities.*"

Cobb at 1342. [Citation omitted; emphasis added.]

During this course of these proceedings, Cobb urged that without such an exception, the offense-specific rule "will prove 'disastrous' to suspects' constitutional rights and will 'permit law enforcement officers almost complete and total license to conduct unwanted and uncounseled interrogations.' " *Id.* In rejecting this argument, the Court said:

> Besides offering no evidence that such a parade of horribles has occurred in those jurisdictions that have not enlarged upon *McNeil*, he fails to appreciate the significance of two critical considerations. First, there can be no doubt that a suspect must be apprised of his rights against compulsory self-incrimination and to consult with an attorney before authorities may conduct custodial interrogation.[*] . . . In the present case, police scrupulously followed *Miranda*'s dictates when questioning [Cobb]. Second, it is critical to recognize that the Constitution does not negate society's interest in the ability of police to talk to witnesses and suspects, even those who have been charged with other offenses.
>
> "Since the ready ability to obtain uncoerced confessions is not an evil but an unmitigated good, society would be the loser. Admissions of guilt resulting from valid *Miranda* waivers 'are more than merely "desirable"; they are essential to society's compelling interest in finding, convicting, and punishing those who violate the law.' "

Id. at 1342-43. [Citations omitted.]

Thus, it is clear that the Sixth Amendment right to counsel attaches only to charged "offenses." *Id.* at 1343. In the remaining part of its opinion, the Court went on to set forth the contours of the definition of "offense" for Sixth Amendment purposes.

In the Fifth Amendment context, the Double Jeopardy Clause prevents multiple or successive prosecutions for the "same offense." In this respect, the Court has held that " 'where the same act or transaction constitutes a violation of two distinct statutory provisions, the test to be applied to determine whether there are two offenses or only one,' " is the *Blockburger* test—whether each statutory provision " 'requires proof of a fact which the other does not.' " *Id.* (quoting *Blockburger v. United*

---

[*] In this respect, the Court noted that "[e]ven though the Sixth Amendment right to counsel has not attached to uncharged offenses, defendants retain the ability under *Miranda* to refuse any police questioning, and, indeed, charged defendants presumably have met with counsel and have had the opportunity to discuss whether it is advisable to invoke those Fifth Amendment rights." *Id.* at 1342 n.2.

States, 284 *U.S.* 299, 304, 52 *S.Ct.* 180 (1932)). Under the *Blockburger* test, for there to be two separate offenses, it is important that *each* statutory provision requires something that the other does not. Here, in *Cobb*, the Court held that this test should also be used in the context of the Sixth Amendment right to counsel, for it could perceive "no constitutional difference between the meaning of the term 'offense' in the contexts of double jeopardy and of the right to counsel." *Id.*

Thus, if during a single course of conduct, a defendant commits two statutory offenses, but is formally charged with only one of those offenses, the applicable rule provides that if each statutory provision requires proof of an additional fact which the other does not, the offenses are not the same under the *Blockburger* test. On the other hand, if only one, or if neither statutory provision requires proof of an additional fact, the offense is the same; and for purposes of the Sixth Amendment, when the right to counsel attaches to the charged offense, the Court ruled that it *will also* "encompass offenses that, even if not formally charged, would be considered the same offense under the Blockburger test." *Cobb* at 1343. [Emphasis added.]

In this case, at the time Cobb confessed to the police, he "had been indicted for burglary of the Owings residence, but he had not been charged in the murders of Margaret and [her daughter]. As defined by Texas law, burglary and capital murder are not the same offense under *Blockburger*[.]" *Id.* at 1344.

"Accordingly, the Sixth Amendment right to counsel did not bar police from interrogating [Cobb] regarding the murders, and [his] confession was therefore admissible." *Id.*

---

§11.4(b). Waiver of rights.

To be valid, a criminal defendant's waiver of his or her rights must be made voluntarily, knowingly, and intelligently, and the government bears the burden of proof. Under the federal Constitution, the prosecution must prove waiver by a "preponderance of the evidence." *Colorado v. Connelly*, 479 *U.S.* 157, 107 *S.Ct.* 515, 523 (1986). A state court is free, however, to require a higher standard under its state constitution. *See e.g., State v. Galloway*, 133 *N.J.* 631, 654, 628 *A.2d* 735 (1993) (prosecution must prove waiver "beyond a reasonable doubt"). This is yet another example of the established principle of our federalist system that a state may provide individual liberties more expansive than those afforded under federal law.

When a court assesses the voluntariness of a waiver of rights, it considers the characteristics of the suspect and the totality of the circumstances surrounding the interrogation. Relevant factors will include, but not be limited to:

1. The suspect's age, education and intelligence;

2. How and by what method the suspect was advised of his constitutional rights;

3. The length of the detention;

4. The nature of the questioning and whether it was repeated or prolonged;

5. Whether physical or mental punishment, coercive police activity, or mental exhaustion was involved;

6. Whether law enforcement officials made an express promise of leniency or sentence;

7. The suspect's previous encounters with the law.

See Colorado v. Connelly, supra, 107 *S.Ct.* at 522; *Schneckloth v. Bustamonte,* 412 *U.S.* 218, 226, 93 *S.Ct.* 2041, 2047-48 (1973). *See also Green v. Scully,* 850 *F.*2d 894, 901 (2nd Cir. 1988) ("the presence of a direct or implied promise of help or leniency alone has not barred the admission of a confession where the totality of the circumstances indicates it was the product of a free and independent decision").

NORTH CAROLINA v. BUTLER
Supreme Court of the United States
441 *U.S.* 369, 99 *S.Ct.* 1755 (1979)

QUESTION: Must a statement of an accused made during the course of police custodial interrogation *always* be deemed inadmissible when, at the time the statement is made, the accused did not "expressly" waive his *Miranda* rights ?

ANSWER: NO. The Court in *Miranda* "did not hold that [an express statement of waiver] is indispensable to a finding of waiver." *Id.* at 1757. "An express written or oral statement" by an accused waiving his right to remain silent or right to counsel "is usually strong proof of the validity of that waiver, but is not inevitably either necessary or sufficient to establish waiver. The question is not one of form, but rather whether the defendant in fact knowingly and voluntarily waived the rights delineated in the *Miranda* case." *Id.*

RATIONALE: Shortly after defendant's arrest for kidnapping, armed robbery, and felonious assault, FBI agents fully advised him of his rights according to *Miranda.* When it was determined that defendant had an 11th grade education and was literate, he was given the Bureau's "Advice of Rights" form, which he read. When asked if he understood his rights, defendant replied that he did. Defendant then refused to sign the waiver at the bottom of the form. "He was told that he need neither speak nor sign the form, but that the agents would like him to talk to them." *Id.* at 1756. Defendant stated, "I will talk to you but I am not signing any form." *Id.* Shortly thereafter, defendant made several incriminating statements.

In the appeal which followed the denial of defendant's motion to suppress his statements, the North Carolina Supreme Court held "[i]n evident conflict with the present view of every other court that has considered the issue, * * * that *Miranda v. Arizona* * * * requires that no statement of a person under custodial interrogation may be admitted in evidence against him unless, at the time the statement was made, he explicitly waived the right to the presence of a lawyer." *Id.* at 1755-1756. *The United States Supreme Court disagreed,* ruling that "the North Carolina Supreme Court has gone beyond the requirements of federal [] law," by "creating an inflexible rule that no implicit waiver can ever suffice[.]" *Id.* at 1759.

In *Miranda v. Arizona,* 384 *U.S.* 436, 86 *S.Ct.* 1602 (1966), the Court stated:

> "If the interrogation continues without the presence of an attorney and a statement is taken, a heavy burden rests on the government to demonstrate that the defendant knowingly and intelligently waived his privilege against self-incrimination and his right to retained or appointed counsel."

Butler at 1757 (quoting *Miranda* at 475, 86 *S.Ct.* at 1628). The *Miranda* opinion goes on to say, however, that,

> "An express statement that the individual is willing to make a statement and does not want an attorney followed closely by a statement could constitute a waiver. But a valid waiver will not be presumed simply from the silence of the accused after warnings are given or simply from the fact that a confession was in fact eventually obtained."

Id.

Thus, *Miranda* stands for the proposition that "an express statement can constitute a waiver, and that silence alone after such warnings cannot do so. But the Court did not hold that such an express statement is indispensable to a finding of waiver." *Butler* at 1757.

"An express written or oral statement of waiver of the right to remain silent or of the right to counsel is usually strong proof of the validity of that waiver, but is not inevitably either necessary or sufficient to establish waiver. The question is not one of form, but rather whether the defendant in fact knowingly and voluntarily waived the rights delineated in the *Miranda* case. As was unequivocally said in *Miranda,* mere silence is not enough. That does not mean that the defendant's silence, coupled with an understanding of his rights and a course of conduct indicating waiver, may never support a conclusion that a defendant has waived his rights. The courts must presume that a defendant did not waive his rights; the prosecution's burden is great; but in at least some cases waiver can be clearly inferred from the actions and words of the person interrogated." *Id.*

In this case, it is clear that defendant was adequately and effectively apprised of his rights. "The only question is whether he waived the exercise of one of those rights, the right to the presence of a lawyer."

Id. at 1758. Based on the totality of the "particular facts and circumstances surrounding th[is] case, including the background, experience, and conduct of the accused[,]" the Court finds that he validly, though implicitly, provided the authorities with a waiver of *Miranda. Id.*

At the time of this opinion, "[t]en of the eleven United States Courts of Appeals and the courts of at least 17 States have held that an explicit statement of waiver is not invariably necessary to support a finding that the defendant waived the right to remain silent or the right to counsel guaranteed by the *Miranda* case. By creating an inflexible rule that no implicit waiver can ever suffice, the North Carolina Supreme Court has gone beyond the requirements of federal organic law. It follows that its judgment cannot stand[.]" *Id.* at 1759.

NOTE

1. In *Johnson v. Zerbst*, 304 *U.S.* 458, 464, 58 *S.Ct.* 1019, 1023 (1938), the Court established a strict standard for determining whether a criminal defendant has voluntarily, knowingly and intelligently waived a fundamental constitutional *trial* right. The standard requires the prosecution to demonstrate an "intentional relinquishment or abandonment of a known right or privilege." "Almost without exception, the requirement of a knowing and intelligent waiver has been applied only to those rights which the Constitution guarantees to a criminal defendant in order to preserve a fair trial," *e.g.*, waiving the right to counsel either at trial or upon a guilty plea. *Schneckloth v. Bustamonte*, 412 *U.S.* 218, 235-237, 93 *S.Ct.* 2041, 2052-2053 (1973).

In his concurring opinion in *Butler*, Justice Blackmun stressed that the formula *Zerbst* articulated for the waiver of fundamental constitutional rights has no "relevance in determining whether a defendant has waived his 'right to the presence of a lawyer,' * * * under *Miranda*'s prophylactic rule." *Butler* at 1759 (Blackmun, J., concurring). *See also Schneckloth* at 235, 93 *S.Ct.* at 2052 (*Zerbst* standard was enunciated "in the context of the safeguards of a fair criminal trial," and has no relevance in the context of a suspect's provision of his consent to search).

2. State officials are reminded that as a matter of local constitutional law, a state is free to rely on its own constitution to provide its citizens with more protection than that afforded by the United States Supreme Court's decision in *North Carolina v. Butler. See e.g., Commonwealth v. Bussey*, 486 *Pa.* 221, 230-31, 404 *A.2d* 1309 (1979) (Under the Pennsylvania Constitution, before any statement made by an accused in response to custodial interrogation may be used at trial, "an explicit waiver is a mandatory requirement.").

3. *Voluntariness—a two-step analysis.* As a general proposition, the admissibility of a confession "depends upon whether it was voluntarily made. The ultimate issue remains that which has been the only clearly established test in Anglo-American courts for two hundred years: the test of voluntariness. Is the confession the product of an essentially free and unconstrained choice by its maker? If it is, if he has willed to confess, it may be used against him. If it is not, if his will has

been overborne and his capacity for self-determination critically impaired, the use of his confession offends due process.'" *Arizona v. Fulminante*, 499 *U.S.* 279, 111 *S.Ct.* 1246, 1261 (1991) (opinion of Rehnquist, C.J., dissenting in part) (quoting *Culombe v. Connecticut*, 367 *U.S.* 568, 602, 81 *S.Ct.* 1860, 1879 (1961)). *See also Blackburn v. Alabama*, 361 *U.S.* 199, 206, 80 *S.Ct.* 274, 279 (1960) ("coercion can be mental as well as physical, and ∗ ∗ ∗ the blood of the accused is not the only hallmark of an unconstitutional inquisition"). Unlike the use of physical coercion, however, use of psychologically-oriented methods during questioning are not inherently coercive. The critical inquiry in such cases is whether the person's decision to confess results from a free and self-directed choice rather than from an overbearing of the suspect's will. See *Arizona v. Fulminante, supra*, 111 *S.Ct.* at 1252-53 (confession held involuntary where defendant, an alleged child murderer in danger of physical violence from other inmates, was motivated to confess when a fellow inmate (a government agent) promised to protect him in exchange for the confession); *Payne v. Arkansas*, 356 *U.S.* 560, 561, 78 *S.Ct.* 844, 846 (1958) (confession held to be coerced because the interrogating officer had promised that if the accused confessed, the officer would protect him from an angry mob outside the jailhouse door).

   (a) A free and unconstrained choice; inducements to confess. Police are not permitted to employ unreasonable or improper inducements which impair a suspect's decision whether to give a statement or seek legal counsel. The rule applies to those situations where the police prompt an admission or confession by suggesting a benefit if the suspect forgoes his or her rights. This reasoning was first announced in *Bram v. United States*, 168 *U.S.* 532, 542-43, 18 *S.Ct.* 183, 187 (1897), where the United States Supreme Court declared: "[A] confession, in order to be admissible, must be free and voluntary: that is, [it] must not be extracted by any sort of threats of violence, nor obtained by any direct or implied promises, however slight, nor by exertion of any improper influence[.]"

   (i) In *Commonwealth v. Gibbs*, 520 *Pa.* 151, 553 *A.2d* 409, *cert. denied*, 493 *U.S.* 963, 110 *S.Ct.* 403 (1989), the statement found to be an improper inducement was made to the defendant after he was read his rights and after he commented, "Maybe I should talk to a lawyer. What good would it do me to tell you?" The detective's response of a possible benefit, that he would "tell the District Attorney [defendant] cooperated," was held to be an improper inducement to confess, and "thereby tainted" defendant's admissions. The Court reasoned: "By conveying the distinct impression that the district attorney would be told of his cooperation in giving a confession on the spot, there occurred an inescapable inducement which cannot be condoned under our law." *Id.* at 155, 553 *A.2d* at 410-11. According to the Court,

   criminal suspects have a constitutional right to make up their own minds as to whether they want the *Miranda* protections. Promises of benefits or special considerations, however benign in intent, comprise the sort of persuasions and trickery which easily can mislead suspects into giving confessions. The process of rendering *Miranda* warnings should proceed freely without any intruding frustration by the police. * * * Misleading statements and promises by the police choke off the legal process at the very moment which *Miranda* was designed to protect.

Id. at 155, 553 *A.*2d at 411.

(*ii*) When, however, an officer's comment is not a promise of benefits or special consideration designed to mislead or induce a defendant to confess, courts have found no improper inducement. *See e.g., United States v. Fraction*, 795 *F.*2d 12, 15 (3rd Cir. 1986), where a bank robbery suspect, after receiving his *Miranda* warnings, asked an FBI agent what he would receive in return for his cooperation. The agent replied that he "would not be able to promise him anything in terms of help other than to notify the U.S. Attorney and a sentencing judge that he had cooperated in the matter." Finding no causal connection between the FBI agent's promise to bring the suspect's cooperation to the authorities' attention and the suspect's decision to confess, the Third Circuit noted that the circuit courts of appeal have uniformly rejected the contention that a promise to bring a suspect's cooperation to the attention of the authorities suffices to render a confession involuntary.

(*iii*) In more recent opinions, the United States Supreme Court has backed off from the idea that a suspect's statement is always or inherently involuntary if induced by a promise. Rather, the proper inquiry is whether, under the totality of the circumstances, the defendant's "will has been overborne and his capacity for self-determination critically impaired." *Arizona v. Fulminante, supra,* 111 *S.Ct.* at 1251. As a result, so long as an officer's comment is "not a promise of benefits or special consideration designed to mislead or induce [a defendant] into confessing," courts have found no improper inducement. *Commonwealth v. Purnell*, 412 *Pa.Super.* 462, 603 *A.*2d 1028 (1992). So long as it may be concluded that any promise made was not in any way causally connected to a subsequent confession, the promise should not be interpreted as an improper inducement. *See Purnell* at 1030 (no improper inducement found where, in response to defendant's questions about securing bail, the officer explained the arraignment's procedure and simply stated that he "would tell the judge that [defendant was] cooperative"). The court's rationale in *Purnell* stemmed in large part from the recognition that

> many states also agree that a promise to bring a suspect's cooperation to the attention of the authorities (when accompanied by no other coercive tactics) does not render his confession involuntary. * * *

Id. at 1031. (Cataloging representative cases). Consequently, the *Purnell* court determined that it would "follow the lead of the Federal judiciary and our sister states and hold that under the facts [of the case, the officer's] promise to inform the authorities of [defendant's] cooperation was insufficient to render [his] confession involuntary." *Id.*

In *State v. Roberts*, 631 A.2d 835 (Vt. 1993), an officer told an in-custody suspect that if the suspect gave a statement it might result in reduced bail. Finding the ensuing statement voluntarily given, the court observed:

> While the influence of a promise will render a confession inadmissible, * * * mere predictions regarding the value of cooperation are not sufficiently coercive to render a subsequent confession involuntary.
> * * *
>
> The statement here under scrutiny—that the judge responsible for setting bail "would probably consider" defendant's statement— makes a prediction rather than a promise. The officer did not personally promise to provide any benefit to defendant, other than to convey the fact of defendant's cooperation to the judge and indicate that the judge might consider, when setting bail, that defendant had given a statement. * * * Because the officer made no promise, his statement regarding bail did not render the confession here involuntary.

Id. at 837, 838. *See also United States v. Hart*, 619 F.2d 325, 326 (4th Cir. 1980) (officer's statement that cooperation could have an effect on bond reduction did not render the confession involuntary); *United States v. Ferrara*, 377 F.2d 16, 18 (2nd Cir. 1967) (absent prolonged interrogation or threats, statement to defendant that if he cooperated he would likely get out on reduced bail did not make confession involuntary).

Compare State v. Watford, 261 N.J.Super. 151, 618 A.2d 358 (App.Div. 1992), where an assistant prosecutor promised Watford a "package deal" of "20 years," "7 years without parole," if he "cooperated" with the police. After *Miranda* warnings were readministered, Watford confessed to stabbing the victim three times with a knife. Holding the confession invalid as a matter of State law, the court declared:

> This case involves neither a discussion about what the prosecutor would recommend, by way of sentence or otherwise, to a judge incident to a plea, or how the prosecutor would exercise his own jurisdiction in the filing of charges, if defendant cooperated in the investigation. Rather, this case involves a statement made on the basis of a promise of a specific sentence which the prosecutor could not guarantee. * * * Given the Judiciary's responsibility for sentencing and our State's firm policy concerning the impact of a sentence recommendation by the prosecutor, we adopt a 'bright line' approach to the admissibility against a defendant of a statement made in exchange for a sentence recommendation by the

prosecutor, and hold such statements inadmissible in the absence of counsel on an indictable charge. * * *

Id., 261 *N.J.Super.* at 158. Thus, as a matter of State law, "an uncounselled statement made incident to, or in exchange for, a sentence recommendation or sentence promise by the prosecutor to the defendant on an indictable offense, is inadmissible." *Id.* at 159.

     (iv) Threatening harsher treatment if rights are asserted. While "it is permissible for an interrogating officer to represent, under some circumstances, that the fact that the defendant cooperates will be communicated to the proper authorities, the same cannot be said of a representation that a defendant's failure to cooperate will be communicated to a prosecutor. Refusal to cooperate is every defendant's right under the fifth amendment." *United States v. Tingle*, 658 *F.*2d 1332, 1336 n.5 (9th Cir. 1981). *See also California Attorneys for Criminal Justice v. Butts*, 195 *F.*3d 1039 (9th Cir. 1999) (interrogating officer cannot "threaten a suspect with harsher treatment as a result of a suspect's decision to remain silent and not cooperate"). *United States v. Guerrero*, 847 *F.*2d 1363, 1366 & n.2 (9th Cir. 1988) (recommendations of leniency as a result of cooperation are appropriate, but "threatening to inform the prosecutor of a suspect's refusal to cooperate violates her fifth amendment right to remain silent").

     (b) A knowing and intelligent choice. The question whether a waiver of rights was the product of force, threat, duress, improper influence, or any other type of coercive police activity is only half the equation. The second step in the inquiry questions whether the waiver was given "knowingly and intelligently." Among other things, this requires that the administration of the *Miranda* warnings be more than a mere perfunctory exercise.

PEOPLE v. BERNASCO
Supreme Court of Illinois
138 *Ill.*2d 349, 150 *Ill.Dec.* 155, 562 *N.E.*2d 958 (1990)

QUESTION: May a defendant's waiver of *Miranda*, though not a product of coercion or police overreaching, nonetheless be invalid due to an intelligence level so low that the defendant could not reasonably provide it "knowingly and intelligently"?

ANSWER: YES. "[A] valid waiver of *Miranda* must be knowing and intelligent in addition to being free from coercion or other misconduct." *Id.* at 959, 961. "[W]here a defendant confesses after being given *Miranda* warnings[,] both intelligent knowledge and voluntariness remain requirements for assuring that a defendant's *Miranda* waiver reflects *Miranda*'s 'carefully drawn approach': its 'subtle balance' between the need for police questioning and the coercive pressures inherent in such questioning." *Id.* at 961.

RATIONALE: After receiving *Miranda* warnings, defendant, 17-year-old Brian Bernasco, confessed to his involvement in several residential burglaries. In this appeal, he defends the circuit court's suppression of his confession, asserting that the confession was the product of an invalid waiver of his *Miranda* rights. The circuit court found that defendant "was of subnormal intelligence and was questioned by police outside his father's presence and on the assumption that he could understand *Miranda* warnings." *Id.* at 959. At trial, it was established that defendant had "no prior criminal experience and had a beginning fourth-grade reading and comprehension level that prevented him from 'understand[ing] what was happening'" during the interrogation process. *Id.* at 963. "A psychologist testified that defendant could not understand certain *Miranda* terminology and that he would probably have agreed to almost anything said to him if doing so would end his interrogation." *Id.* at 959. Finally, defendant testified that he "had not been paying attention to his *Miranda* waiver form, had not understood it, and had been scared." *Id.*

Finding defendant's waiver of his Miranda rights invalid due to the absence of "intelligent knowledge," the Illinois Supreme Court held that, in addition to being free from coercion or other misconduct, "a valid waiver of *Miranda* must be knowing and intelligent." *Id.* at 959, 961.

Preliminarily, the court pointed out that in *Colorado v. Connelly,* 479 *U.S.* 157, 107 *S.Ct.* 515 (1986), the federal Supreme Court "rejected any conclusion that, 'by itself and apart from its relation to official coercion,' a defendant's mental condition might determine constitutional voluntariness." *Bernasco* at 959 (quoting *Connelly* at 164, 107 *S.Ct.* at 520). According to the *Connelly* Court, however, "any voluntariness inquiries into a confessing defendant's state of mind, 'inquiries quite divorced from any coercion brought to bear on the defendant by the State,' should be left for resolution by State evidence rules pertaining to reliability; such matters are not governed by the fourteenth amendment's due process clause." *Bernasco* at 959-60 (quoting *Connelly* at 166-67, 107 *S.Ct.* at 522). Thus, a fair reading of *Connelly* indicates that "a confession, made after a *Miranda* waiver, might still be suppressed on grounds that *Miranda's* protections had not been intelligently and knowingly waived[.]" *Bernasco* at 960.

Here in *Bernasco,* the court explained:

> *Connelly* merely means that, in general, issues of intelligent knowledge are separate from issues of voluntariness. The *Connelly* opinion was actually addressing (1) an initial confession given under circumstances requiring no *Miranda* warning (hence involving no question of waiver), the voluntariness of the confession being at issue, and (2) subsequent confessions given after *Miranda* warnings, the voluntariness of the *Miranda* waivers being at issue. Thus—in a narrower vein than that in which the opinion's opening sentences might cursorily be read—the Court continued that, *in determining whether a confession is voluntary* where there has been no official coercion, inquiries into the state of a confessing defendant's mind, when "divorced from any coercion * * * by the

State," are to be resolved by State evidence law rather than by the due process clause of the fourteenth amendment. * * *

We observe that at no point did the *Connelly* Court overrule [any other of the Court's cases which require] that a *Miranda* waiver be intelligent and knowing as well as voluntary. * * *

Id. at 961. [Citations omitted; court's emphasis.]

In *Moran v. Burbine*, 475 *U.S.* 412, 106 *S.Ct.* 1135 (1986), the Court clarified that "an inquiry into *Miranda* waiver has 'two distinct dimensions': (1) whether there was a free, uncoerced choice, and (2) whether there was awareness of the right and the consequences of abandoning it. * * * A valid *Miranda* waiver would thus require '*both* an uncoerced choice *and* the requisite level of comprehension.'" *Bernasco* at 960 (court's emphasis) (quoting *Burbine* at 421, 106 *S.Ct.* at 1141). The *Burbine* Court determined that the unethical failure of the police to inform Burbine that an attorney, whom his sister had attempted to retain for him, had telephoned the police less than an hour before the police questioning, did not compromise Burbine's ability to comprehend the full panoply of *Miranda* rights and the consequences of waiving them. Accordingly, because Burbine's "'voluntary decision to speak was made with full awareness and comprehension of all the information *Miranda* requires the police to convey,' his *Miranda* waivers were valid." *Bernasco* at 960 (quoting *Burbine* at 424, 106 *S.Ct.* at 1142).

From a federal constitutional viewpoint, therefore, "only voluntariness, rather than intelligent knowledge, ordinarily need be shown in the case of a confession * * * that is given under circumstances not requiring a *Miranda* warning. But, where a defendant confesses after being given *Miranda* warnings[,] both intelligent knowledge and voluntariness remain requirements for assuring that a defendant's *Miranda* waiver reflects *Miranda*'s 'carefully drawn approach': its 'subtle balance' between the need for police questioning and the coercive pressures inherent in such questioning." *Id.* at 961. [Citation omitted.] *See also Colorado v. Spring*, 479 *U.S.* 564, 572, 107 *S.Ct.* 851, 857 (1987) (*Miranda* waiver must be made "'voluntarily, knowingly and intelligently'").

"There remains a world of difference between voluntariness and intelligent knowledge. [For example,] a mentally ill person may 'confess' at length quite without external compulsion but not intelligently and knowingly, while a perfectly rational person on the torture rack may confess intelligently and knowingly but without free will." *Bernasco* at 962.

For constitutional purposes, however, "a distinction does need to be made between two types of awareness in interpreting the *Miranda*-derived waiver requirement of intelligent knowledge." *Id.* The first type of awareness goes far beyond what is required for a valid waiver of *Miranda*. This type involves knowing and understanding "'every possible consequence of a waiver of the Fifth Amendment privilege[,]'" *Spring* at 574, 107 *S.Ct.* at 857, "being 'totally rational and properly motivated' when confessing," *Connelly* at 166, 107 *S.Ct.* at 521, "or having all information that might be 'useful' or 'might * * * affec[t one's] decision to confess[,]' " *Burbine* at 422, 106 *S.Ct.* at 1141, "such as a list of 'all the possible subjects of questioning in advance of interrogation.' " *Bernasco* at 962 (quoting *Spring* at 577, 107 *S.Ct.* at 859). In the cases cited, "the Supreme Court held that this mental state is not necessary for a valid *Miranda* waiver. The Constitution does not demand 'that the police supply a suspect with a flow of information to help him calibrate his self-interest in deciding to speak or stand by his rights[.]' " *Id.* (quoting *Burbine* at 422, 106 *S.Ct.* at 1141). Moreover, "there is no federal constitutional right to confess only when in possession of information that 'could affect only the wisdom of a *Miranda* waiver, not its essential voluntary and knowing nature[.]' " *Id.* (quoting *Spring* at 577, 107 *S.Ct.* at 859).

"The second type of awareness involves simply being cognizant at all times of 'the State's intention to use [one's] statements to secure a conviction' and of the fact that one can 'stand mute and request a lawyer.' " *Id.* (quoting *Burbine* at 422, 106 *S.Ct.* at 1141). It is this type of mental awareness which is "necessary for a valid waiver of *Miranda*." *Id.* To satisfy this level of awareness, it is sufficient that a defendant had been aware that, in addition to his right to remain silent, "(1) he had a right to consult with an attorney, to have an attorney present during questioning, and to have an attorney appointed if he could not afford to retain one privately; and (2) any statement that he made could be used against him in criminal proceedings, and an attorney's presence during questioning could serve him by affording him advice on making any statements." *Id.* at 963.

Accordingly, "this second type of awareness on a defendant's part is necessary in order to constitute the intelligent knowledge that in turn is required for blunting the coercive effects of police interrogation in a *Miranda* waiver context." *Id.*

In this case, the circuit court found that defendant did not understand the "fundamental terms contained in the *Miranda* warnings," or the rights conveyed by the warnings. *Id.* at 964. Defendant did not have a normal ability to understand "relatively routine questions" and "simple concepts," and he was substantially "limited in his comprehension of single words." *Id.* The circuit court was also convinced "from the psychological testimony that defendant would have agreed to and signed almost anything given to him during interrogation." *Id.* Those findings, amply supported by the record, "are sufficient to warrant the conclusion that defendant did not waive his *Miranda* rights knowingly and intelligently, and hence [] justif[ied the] suppress[ion of] his confession." *Id.*

"If intelligent knowledge in the *Miranda* context means anything, it means the ability to understand the very words used in the warnings. It need not mean the ability to understand far-reaching legal and strategic effects of waiving one's rights, or to appreciate how widely or deeply an interrogation may probe, or to withstand the influence of stress or fancy; but to waive rights intelligently and knowingly, one must at least understand basically what those rights encompass and minimally what their waiver will entail. * * * *See* Note, *Constitutional*

Protection of Confessions Made by Mentally Retarded Defendants, 14 Am.J.L.Med. 431, 432-33, 440-44 (1989) (discussing mentally retarded persons' limited intellectual ability to make knowing and intelligent *Miranda* waivers); *cf.* Holtz, *Miranda in a Juvenile Setting: A Child's Right to Silence*, 78 J.Crim.L. & Criminology 534, 536-37, 546-56 (1987) (citing evidence that most youths lack proper comprehension of rights under police interrogation; proposing use of simplified version of *Miranda* warnings)." *Bernasco* at 964.

NOTE

1. *Compare Reno v. Flores*, 507 *U.S.* 292, 113 *S.Ct.* 1439, 1451 (1993) ("juveniles are capable"—at least 16- and 17-year-olds—"of 'knowingly and intelligently' waiving their right against self-incrimination") (citing *Fare v. Michael C.*, 442 *U.S.* 707, 724-27, 99 *S.Ct.* 2560, 2571-73 (1979), and *United States v. Saucedo-Velasquez*, 843 *F.*2d 832, 835 (5th Cir. 1988) (applying *Fare* to an alien juvenile).

2. *Impaired defendants. See United States v. Andrews*, 22 *F.*3d 1328, 1337 (5th Cir. 1994), where the court found the defendant's waiver of *Miranda* rights "knowing and intelligent" notwithstanding defendant's assertion that at the time he waived his rights "he was too drunk to understand those rights and the consequences of relinquishing them." The court found that defendant's contention was sufficiently contradicted by the testimony of the interrogating agents that established that defendant did not appear inebriated at the time of questioning, and that although it appeared that he had been drinking, "he seemed pretty reasonable" and "aware of his surroundings." *Id.* at 1340. Defendant was read his *Miranda* warnings and he indicated that he understood them; and, according to one agent, defendant appeared to be "able to reason and understand what [they] were discussing." *Id.*

See also Commonwealth v. Edwards, 521 *Pa.* 134, 555 *A.*2d 818, 826 (1989) (the fact that defendant "had been drinking before his arrest does not automatically render his statements inadmissible"); *Commonwealth v. McFadden*, 384 *Pa.Super.* 444, 559 *A.*2d 58, 60 (1989) (evidence of alcohol consumption "only affects the weight to be accorded to the confession").

COLORADO v. SPRING
Supreme Court of the United States
479 *U.S.* 564, 107 *S.Ct.* 851 (1987)

QUESTION: Must a suspect be informed of all the crimes about which he may be questioned before his waiver of *Miranda* will be considered valid ?

ANSWER: NO. "[A] suspect's awareness of all the possible subjects of questioning in advance of interrogation is not relevant to determining whether the suspect voluntarily, knowingly, and intelligently waived his Fifth Amendment privilege." *Id.* at 859.

RATIONALE: On March 30, 1979, agents from the Bureau of Alcohol, Tobacco, and Firearms arrested defendant Spring, charging him with the interstate transportation of stolen firearms. At the scene of the arrest, Spring was advised of his *Miranda* rights and, when transported to the ATF office in Kansas City, was advised a second time. After Spring signed a rights waiver form, the ATF agents questioned him about the firearms transactions that led to his arrest. In addition, the agents questioned Spring about a Colorado murder of which, unbeknownst to Spring, he was also a suspect. Although Spring did make some admissions, he did not expressly admit any involvement in the Colorado murder.

Approximately two months later, on May 26, Colorado law enforcement officials visited defendant while he was in jail in Kansas City pursuant to his arrest on the firearms offenses. Defendant was advised of his *Miranda* rights and, after signing a written waiver form, confessed to the Colorado murder.

Defendant moved to suppress his statements, arguing that the waiver of *Miranda* rights before the March 30 statement was invalid because he was not informed that he would be questioned about the Colorado murder. Moreover, contends defendant, because of the invalidity of the March 30 waiver, the May 26 confession should be inadmissible as an "illegal fruit" of the poisonous March 30 statement.

The United States Supreme Court disagreed. "A confession cannot be 'fruit of the poisonous tree' if the tree itself is not poisonous." *Id.* at 856.

It is well settled that "a suspect may waive his Fifth Amendment privilege, 'provided the waiver is made voluntarily, knowingly and intelligently.' In this case, the law enforcement officials twice informed Spring of his Fifth Amendment privilege in precisely the manner specified by *Miranda*. * * * Spring indicated that he understood the enumerated rights and signed a written form expressing his intention to waive his Fifth Amendment privilege." *Id.* at 857. [Citations omitted.] The trial court specifically found that there was no element of duress or coercion used to induce Spring's statement. Nonetheless, Spring "argues that his March 30 statement was in effect compelled in violation of his Fifth Amendment privilege because he signed the waiver form without being aware that he would be questioned about the Colorado homicide. Spring's argument strains the meaning of compulsion past the breaking point." *Id.*

As a general rule, "[a] statement is not 'compelled' within the meaning of the Fifth Amendment if an individual 'voluntarily, knowingly and intelligently' waives his constitutional privilege. The inquiry whether a waiver is coerced 'has two distinct dimensions.' " *Id.* [Citations omitted.] "First, the relinquishment of the right must have been voluntary in the sense that it was the product of a free and deliberate choice rather than intimidation, coercion, or deception. Second, the waiver must have been made with a full awareness both of the nature of the right being abandoned and the consequences of the decision to abandon it. Only if the 'totality of the circumstances surrounding the interrogation' reveal both an uncoerced choice and the requisite level of comprehension may a court properly conclude that the *Miranda* rights have been waived." *Id.* [Citation omitted.]

In this case, "[t]here is no doubt that Spring's decision to waive his Fifth Amendment privilege was voluntary. He alleges no 'coercion of a confession by physical violence or other deliberate means calculated to break (his) will[.]' * * * His allegation that the police failed to supply him with certain information does not relate to any of the traditional indicia of coercion: 'the duration and conditions of detention . . ., the manifest attitude of the police toward him, his physical and mental state, the diverse pressures which sap or sustain his powers of resistance and self-control.' * * * Absent evidence that Spring's 'will (was) overborne and his capacity for self-determination critically impaired' because of coercive police conduct, * * * his waiver of his Fifth Amendment privilege was voluntary under this Court's decision in *Miranda.*" *Id.* [Citations omitted.]

"There is also no doubt that Spring's waiver of his Fifth Amendment privilege was knowingly and intelligently made: that is, Spring understood that he had the right to remain silent and that *anything* he said could be used as evidence against him. The Constitution does not require that a criminal suspect know and understand every possible consequence of a waiver of the Fifth Amendment privilege." *Id.* [Emphasis added.]

Defendant Spring also contends that the failure of the ATF agents to inform him of the potential subjects of interrogation constitutes the police trickery and deception condemned in *Miranda*, thereby rendering his waiver of *Miranda* invalid.

This argument is not persuasive. First, the Colorado courts made no finding of official trickery. But more significantly, "[t]his Court has never held that mere silence by law enforcement officials as to the subject matter of an interrogation is 'trickery' sufficient to invalidate a suspect's waiver of *Miranda* rights, and we expressly decline so to hold today." *Id.* at 858.

"[A] valid waiver does not require that an individual be informed of all information 'useful' in making his decision or all information that 'might . . . affec(t) his decision to confess. [The police are not required to] supply a suspect with a flow of information to help him calibrate his self-interest in deciding whether to speak or stand by his rights.'" *Id.* at 859. [Citation omitted.]

"*Miranda* specifically require[s] that the police inform a criminal suspect that he has the right to remain silent and that *anything* he says may be used against him. * * * The warning * * * conveys to a suspect the nature of his constitutional privilege and the consequences of abandoning it. Accordingly, * * * a suspect's awareness of all the possible subjects of questioning in advance of interrogation is not relevant to determining whether the suspect voluntarily, knowingly, and intelligently waived his Fifth Amendment privilege." *Id.* (emphasis supplied).

NOTE

1. *The wisdom of a waiver.* The imprudence of a defendant's waiver of *Miranda* should not alter the conclusion that the waiver was otherwise knowingly and intelligently given. As one court put it: "A defendant's waiver is not unintelligent merely because it is unwise." *State v. Adams*, 127 *N.J.* 438, 449, 605 *A.*2d 1097 (1992).

2. *Lying to a suspect.* Lying to a suspect will not, by itself, render a confession involuntary.

(a) In *Frazier v. Cupp*, 394 *U.S.* 731, 89 *S.Ct.* 1420 (1969), the Court held that the defendant's confession was admissible notwithstanding the fact that the police falsely told him that another person had confessed. The Court noted that the defendant was a mature person of normal intelligence and that the questioning session lasted only slightly over an hour. *Id.* at 739, 89 *S.Ct.* at 1425.

(b) The defendant in *State v. Miller*, 76 *N.J.* 392 (1978), was assured by the interrogating officer that he was acting solely in the defendant's best interest. The officer told the defendant that the person who killed the victim was not a criminal who should be punished, but rather a person needing medical treatment, and that the officer would help him with his problem if he told the truth. The Court found the defendant's ensuing confession admissible, noting that the questioning session lasted for only about an hour, defendant was an adult, 32 years old, and had a prior conviction. The Court stated defendant "was in no way deluded or misled into believing that the state trooper was acting in any capacity other than as an interrogating police officer in the investigation of a serious crime." *Id.* at 404.

(c) In *State v. Galloway, supra*, 133 *N.J.* 631, 628 *A.*2d 735 (1993), defendant confessed to shaking a three-month-old child very hard several times, thereby injuring the child and causing his eventual death. The interrogating officer told defendant that the baby was seriously injured, and asked defendant to describe exactly what he had done to the baby so the doctors could treat the child accordingly. The Court described the officer's conduct as "a deliberate act of deception to secure a confession." *Id.* at 653. Nonetheless, the Court ruled that the officer's actions did not rise to an improper level of psychological pressure warranting suppression of defendant's confession. The Court stated:

> The police had no reason to believe that defendant would be particularly vulnerable to interrogation. At the time of the arrest, defendant was twenty-seven years old. He had a tenth grade education, but had received a G.E.D. Psychological testing shows that defendant's IQ is "dull normal." Defendant had served in the Army for three years, receiving (according to defendant) an honorable discharge. Defendant had some minimal experience with the police, from a prior arrest and conviction for writing bad checks. Moreover, at the police station, defendant was not deprived of food or drink. * * * [H]e did not appear tired. Defendant appeared to be under stress and was crying. However, the fact that defendant was distressed and emotional is not by itself sufficient to render his confession involuntary. * * *
> * * * [H]e was repeatedly told pursuant to *Miranda* that whatever he said would be used against him. * * * [D]efendant was aware of the purpose of the interrogation[.]

Id. at 656-57.

The Court concluded, therefore, that "the interrogation that elicited defendant's confession did not violate his rights against self-incrimination, and that his confession was the result of a knowing, voluntary, and intelligent waiver of those rights[.]" *Id.* at 657.

OREGON v. ELSTAD
Supreme Court of the United States
470 *U.S.* 298, 105 *S.Ct.* 1285 (1985)

QUESTION: Does an initial failure of a law enforcement officer to administer *Miranda* warnings "taint" subsequent admissions made after a suspect has been fully advised of, and has waived, his constitutional rights ?

ANSWER: NO. "[A] suspect who has once responded to unwarned yet uncoercive questioning is not thereby disabled from waiving his rights and confessing after he has been given the requisite *Miranda* warnings." *Id.* at 1298.

RATIONALE: When police ask questions of a suspect in custody without giving the required warnings, *Miranda* will exclude the use of the suspect's admissions. Even when the admissions are in no way coerced, *Miranda* raises a presumption of coercion. *Id.* at 1297.

However, the Court states that it is "an unwarranted extension of *Miranda*" to hold that a mere failure to administer the warnings, unaccompanied by any actual coercion or other circumstances calculated to disrupt the suspect's ability to exercise his free will, so taints the investigative process that a subsequent voluntary and "informed" waiver is ineffective. *Id.* at 1293.

Therefore, "[a] subsequent administration of *Miranda* warnings to a suspect who has given a voluntary but unwarned statement ordinarily should suffice to remove the conditions that precluded admission of the earlier statement." *Id.* at 1296. The result is that the previous unwarned admission is excluded, but all admissions made after the proper *Miranda* warnings are given are valid and admissible.

NOTE

1. *Deliberate "end runs" around Miranda.*

(a) In *Missouri v. Seibert,* 542 *U.S.* 600, 124 *S.Ct.* 2601 (2004), in a plurality opinion, the United States Supreme Court addressed the technique of interrogating in successive, unwarned and warned phases. At the trial court level, one of the officers testified that the strategy of withholding *Miranda* warnings until after interrogating and drawing out a confession was promoted not only by his own department, but by a national police training organization. The object of "question first" is to render *Miranda* warnings ineffective by waiting for a particularly opportune time to give them, after the suspect has already confessed.

Finding such a practice *improper*, the Court said:

> By any objective measure, * * * it is likely that if the interrogators employ the technique of withholding warnings until after interrogation succeeds in eliciting a confession, the warnings will be ineffective in preparing the suspect for successive interrogation, close in time and similar in content. After all, the reason that question-first is catching on is as obvious as its manifest purpose, which is to get a confession the suspect would not make if he understood his rights at the outset; the sensible underlying assumption is that with one confession in hand before the warnings, the interrogator can count on getting its duplicate, with trifling additional trouble.

> Upon hearing warnings only in the aftermath of interrogation and just after making a confession, a suspect would hardly think he had a genuine right to remain silent, let alone persist in so believing once the police began to lead him over the same ground again. A more likely reaction on a suspect's part would be perplexity about the reason for discussing rights at that point, bewilderment being an unpromising frame of mind for knowledgeable decision. What is worse, telling a suspect that "anything you say can and will be used against you," without expressly excepting the statement just given, could lead to an entirely reasonable inference that what he has just said will be used, with subsequent silence being of no avail. Thus, when *Miranda* warnings are inserted in the midst of coordinated and continuing interrogation, they are likely to mislead and deprive a defendant of knowledge essential to his ability to understand the nature of his rights and the consequences of abandoning them.

Id., 124 *S.Ct.* at 2610-11.

The Court also rejected the prosecution's argument that a confession repeated at the end of an interrogation sequence envisioned in a question-first strategy is admissible on the authority of *Oregon v. Elstad*. In *Elstad*, the failure to preliminarily provide the *Miranda* warnings was, at most, an "oversight." The *Elstad* questioning session had "none of the earmarks of coercion." *Seibert* at 2611. Thus it is fair to read *Elstad* as treating the officer's failure to first administer the warnings as "a good-faith *Miranda* mistake, not only open to correction by careful warnings before systematic questioning in that particular case, but posing no threat to warn-first practice generally." *Id.* at 2612.

Here, in *Seibert*, the facts "reveal a police strategy adapted to undermine the *Miranda* warnings. The unwarned interrogation was conducted in the station house, and the questioning was systematic, exhaustive, and managed with psychological skill. When the police were finished there was little, if anything, of incriminating potential left unsaid." *Id.*

Accordingly, "[b]ecause the question-first tactic effectively threatens to thwart *Miranda*'s purpose of reducing the risk that a coerced confession would be admitted, and because the facts here do not reasonably support a conclusion that the warnings given could have served their purpose," the Court held that Seibert's postwarning statements were inadmissible. *Id.* at 2613.

(b) The analytical framework for analyzing whether a second, post-warning confession is admissible. In *Seibert*, Justice Kennedy, whose concurrence supplied the fifth vote necessary to overturn Seibert's conviction, agreed that the technique of intentionally interrogating in successive, unwarned and warned phases was a deliberate violation of *Miranda*. Justice Kennedy disapproved of the tactic whereby the officer interrogating Seibert used her inadmissible incriminating pre-warning statement to extract a post-warning confession.

In outlining an analytical framework for analyzing whether a second, post-warning confession is admissible, Justice Kennedy recommended its use

> only in the infrequent case, such as we have here, in which the two-step interrogation technique was used in a calculated way to undermine the *Miranda* warning. The admissibility of post-warning statements should continue to be governed by the principles of [*Oregon v. Elstad, supra,*] unless the deliberate two-step strategy was employed. If the deliberate two-step strategy has been used, post-warning statements that are related to the substance of pre-warning statements must be excluded unless curative measures are taken before the post-warning statement is made. Curative measures should be designed to ensure that a reasonable person in the suspect's situation would understand the import and effect of the *Miranda* warning and of the *Miranda* waiver. For example, a substantial break in time and circum-

stances between the pre-warning statement and the *Miranda* warning may suffice in most circumstances, as it allows the accused to distinguish the two contexts and appreciate that the interrogation has taken a new turn. * * * Alternatively, an additional warning that explains the likely inadmissibility of the pre-warning custodial statement may be sufficient. No curative steps were taken in this case, however, so the post-warning statements are inadmissible and the conviction cannot stand.

Seibert at 622, 124 *S.Ct.* at 2616 (Kennedy, J., concurring).

Because Justice Kennedy concurred with the plurality on the narrowest grounds, the reasoning expressed in his concurrence is the holding of the Court.

2. *Physical evidence obtained as a result of a voluntary but unwarned statement.* In *United States v. Patane,* 542 *U.S.* 630, 124 *S.Ct.* 2620 (2004), a plurality of the Supreme Court held that an officer's failure to give a suspect the complete *Miranda* warnings does not require the suppression of physical evidence obtained as a result of the suspect's "unwarned but voluntary statements." *Id.,* 124 *S.Ct.* at 2624.

In *Patane,* officers were in the process of investigating a violation of a domestic violence restraining order by defendant, a convicted felon. During the investigation, it was learned that defendant illegally possessed a Glock handgun. Officers responded to defendant's residence and, upon making entry, arrested him for violating the restraining order. Immediately thereafter, an officer attempted to advise defendant of his *Miranda* rights but got no further than the right to remain silent. At that point, defendant interrupted the officer and asserted that he knew his rights. The officer did not attempt to complete the warning. The officer then asked defendant about the Glock. After some reluctance to discuss the matter, defendant told the officer that the gun was in his bedroom, and gave the officer permission to retrieve it. The officer found the gun and seized it.

Finding the gun admissible, the Court reasoned:

> [T]he *Miranda* rule is a prophylactic employed to protect against violations of the Self-Incrimination Clause. The Self-Incrimination Clause, however, is not implicated by the admission into evidence of the physical fruit of a voluntary statement. Accordingly, there is no justification for extending the *Miranda* rule to this context. And just as the Self-Incrimination Clause primarily focuses on the criminal trial, so too does the *Miranda* rule. The *Miranda* rule is not a code of police conduct, and police do not violate the Constitution (or even the *Miranda* rule, for that matter) by mere failures to warn. For this reason, the exclusionary rule * * * does not apply.

Id., 124 *S.Ct.* at 2626.

Since the "core protection" afforded by the Self-Incrimination Clause of the Fifth Amendment is "a prohibition on compelling a criminal defendant to testify against himself at trial," the Clause "cannot be violated by the introduction of nontestimonial evidence obtained as a result of voluntary statements." *Id.*

It follows that police do not violate a suspect's constitutional rights (or the *Miranda* rule) by negligent or even deliberate failures to provide the suspect with the full panoply of warnings prescribed by *Miranda*. Potential violations occur, if at all, only upon the admission of unwarned statements into evidence at trial. And, at that point, "[t]he exclusion of unwarned statements . . . is a complete and sufficient remedy" for any perceived *Miranda* violation. * * *

Thus, unlike unreasonable searches under the Fourth Amendment or actual violations of the Due Process Clause or the Self-Incrimination Clause, there is, with respect to mere failures to warn, nothing to deter. There is therefore no reason to apply the "fruit of the poisonous tree" doctrine[.] * * *

Id. at 2629.

---

§11.4(b)(1). Illegal detention.

The United States Supreme Court has held that a confession made by an accused during a period of illegal detention is inadmissible. *Mallory v. United States*, 354 *U.S.* 449, 455, 77 *S.Ct.* 1356, 1360 (1957); *McNabb v. United States*, 318 *U.S.* 332, 344-45, 63 *S.Ct.* 608, 615 (1943). The rule is based, in part, on the notion that an unlawful or "unwarranted detention" may lead "to tempting utilization of intensive interrogation, easily gliding into the evils of 'the third degree.'" *Mallory* at 453, 77 *S.Ct.* at 1358. The mandate of what is now known as "the *McNabb-Mallory* rule," was handed down by the Court in the context of its supervisory authority over the federal courts, and for the purpose of adequately enforcing "the congressional requirement of prompt arraignment." *Id.* at 463, 77 *S.Ct.* at 1359. It is not, therefore, constitutionally compelled.

Not all state courts follow the *McNabb-Mallory* rule. For example, in *State v. Tucker*, 137 *N.J.* 259, 645 *A.2d* 111 (1994), in violation of federal precedent, the defendant was not afforded a probable cause hearing until some 72 hours after his arrest. Notwithstanding the "unlawful detention," the court rejected the defendant's contention that his statements—obtained during the course of that unlawful detention—should be suppressed. The court elaborated:

This Court consistently has declined to adopt the practice set forth in *Mallory*. * * *

Our cases hold that delay in affording a defendant a probable-cause determination is a factor that courts should weigh, in the totality of the circumstances, in determining whether a confession during the period of detention was voluntary.

Id., 137 *N.J.* at 272. By itself, however, the delay does not demand exclusion of an otherwise voluntary confession. As the court below determined:

> Voluntariness equates to a free and unconstrained choice. * * *
> In determining voluntariness, we consider the totality of the circumstances with particular attention to the characteristics of the accused and the details of the interrogation. * * *
>
> In the context of the Fourth Amendment, the failure to afford a defendant a probable cause hearing before a judicial officer should not *per se* be the basis for suppression of his incriminatory statements. * * *
>
> Instead, the requirement of a prompt probable cause hearing should be anchored to the reason for its existence, *i.e.*, to prevent unlawful detention. Here, defendant was detained lawfully [that is, on a clear showing of probable cause] and his voluntary statements made during that detention were properly admitted.

Id., 265 *N.J.Super.* 296, 314-16.

TAYLOR v. ALABAMA
Supreme Court of the United States
457 *U.S.* 687, 102 *S.Ct.* 2664 (1982)

QUESTION: Will the exclusionary rule prohibit the use of an accused's confession obtained through custodial interrogation after an arrest effectuated without probable cause ?

ANSWER: YES. "[A] confession obtained through custodial interrogation after an illegal arrest should be excluded unless intervening events break the causal connection between the illegal arrest and confession so that the confession is sufficiently an act of free will to [remove] the [initial illegality]." *Id.* at 2667.

RATIONALE: In 1978, Montgomery, Alabama, had been plagued with a number of robberies in the area of a particular grocery store. The police effected an extensive "manhunt" in an attempt to find the robbers. During this time, a person (who happened to be in jail at the time on an unrelated charge) told a police officer that "he heard" that (defendant) Taylor was involved in the robberies. However, this informant, a stranger to the officer, failed to elaborate on where or how he came upon this information, nor did the officer follow up the tip for corroboration. The officer did, however, arrest defendant, Taylor, without a warrant, and, as it appears, without probable cause.

Taylor was taken to the police station where he was advised of his *Miranda* rights. He signed a waiver of those rights and then gave a full written confession.

In a five to four opinion, *the United States Supreme Court ruled the confession to be invalid as a poisonous fruit of the initial illegal arrest.*

Justice Marshall, speaking for the Court, found that "the police effected an investigatory arrest without probable cause, based upon an uncorroborated informant's tip, and involuntarily transported [the defendant] to the station for interrogation in the hope that something would turn up." *Id.* at 2668. It was further explained that although the confession was voluntary for Fifth Amendment purposes, this "does not cure the illegality of the initial arrest." *Id.* at 2669.

Here, it is clear that the interests and policies to be protected by the Fourth Amendment's Exclusionary Rule [deterrence of unreasonable searches and seizures] are separate and distinct from those protected by the Fifth Amendment's Exclusionary Rule [deterrence of unlawfully coercive custodial interrogation leading to a likelihood of unreliable incriminating responses]. The Court held that the administration of *Miranda* warnings will not act as a "cure" for all Fourth Amendment violations. This would reduce "the constitutional guarantee against unlawful searches and seizures * * * to a mere 'form of words.'" *Id.* at 2667 (quoting from *Brown v. Illinois*, 422 *U.S.* 590, 601, 95 *S.Ct.* 2254, 2260 (1975)).

As a result, "a confession obtained through custodial interrogation after an illegal arrest should be excluded unless intervening events break the causal connection between the illegal arrest and the confession so that the confession is sufficiently an act of free will to purge [or remove] the primary taint [or illegality]." *Id.* [Citations omitted.]

Factors which will be considered as to whether the confession has been "purged of the taint of the illegal arrest" include:

[1] An inquiry into whether the defendant was properly advised of his *Miranda* rights and whether his waiver was voluntary, knowledgeable, and intelligent;

[2] An inquiry into the amount of time which separated the arrest and the confession;

[3] An inquiry into whether the arrest was effected with violence, or whether it was designed to cause surprise, fright, or confusion; and

[4] An inquiry into whether significant intervening circumstances separated the arrest and the confession.

Id. at 2667, 2672.

NOTE

1. It is interesting to note that the four dissenters, Chief Justice Burger, Justice O'Connor, Justice Rehnquist, and Justice Powell did not disagree with nor reject the underlying law of this case. The dissenting opinions centered upon the assertion that the majority of the Court misapplied the four determining inquiries to the facts of this case.

2. *The causal connection between the illegal arrest and the confession.* In *Brown v. Illinois*, 422 *U.S.* 590, 603, 95 *S.Ct.* 2254 (1975), the

Court held that *Miranda* warnings alone cannot always make a suspect's act of confessing a sufficient product of free will to break, for Fourth Amendment purposes, the causal connection between the initial illegality (the primary taint) and the confession (the fruit thereof). In this regard, a court must determine whether statements made after the administration of appropriate *Miranda* warnings were not only "voluntary" for purposes of the Fifth Amendment but in addition, whether they were obtained by exploitation of the unlawful arrest under the Fourth Amendment. Two policies behind the use of the exclusionary rule to effectuate the Fourth Amendment are reflected in *Brown's* focus on "the causal connection between the illegality and the confession." First, when a close causal connection exists between the illegal seizure and the confession, the exclusion of the confession is more likely to deter law enforcement officers from such misconduct in the future. Second, when a confession constitutes an exploitation of a prior illegality, the use of such evidence is more likely to compromise the integrity of the courts.

Brown set forth three factors for determining whether an accused's statements were obtained by the exploitation of an illegal arrest:

(1) the temporal proximity of the statements and the arrest;

(2) the presence of any intervening circumstances; and

(3) the purpose and flagrancy of the official misconduct.

Id. at 603-604, 95 *S.Ct.* at 2261-2262. The first two factors, "temporal proximity" and "the presence of intervening circumstances," "clearly pertain to the determination of whether the defendant supplied the evidence of his own free will, apart from any compulsion by the illegal detention. The attenuation which we analyze is the degree of causal remoteness between the illegal detention and the evidence obtained from the defendant." *United States v. Johnson*, 626 *F.*2d 753, 758 (9th Cir. 1980). "The third factor, 'the purpose and flagrancy of the official misconduct,' could arguably be viewed as a broad general factor utilized to assess whether the flagrancy of police misconduct justifies the exclusion of the evidence in light of the deterrence rationale of the exclusionary rule. However, the [Supreme] Court appears instead, to apply the third factor along with the first two factors in determining the degree of causal remoteness." *Id.* at 758. Thus, in *Dunaway v. New York*, 442 *U.S.* 200, 99 *S.Ct.* 2248 (1979), Justice Stevens emphasized: "The flagrancy of the official misconduct is relevant, in my judgment, only insofar as it has a tendency to motivate the defendant. * * * [I]f the Fourth Amendment is violated, the admissibility question will turn on the causal connection between the violation and the defendant's subsequent confession." *Id.*, 99 *S.Ct.* at 2260 (Stevens, J., concurring).

In *Dunaway v. New York, supra*, 442 *U.S.* at 216-219, 99 *S.Ct.* at 2258-60, the Court applied the standards set forth in *Brown v. Illinois* to suppress statements received from a suspect involuntarily transported to police headquarters for "questioning." In *Dunaway*, the Court characterized the *Brown* factors as a two-part test for determining whether an unconstitutional seizure invalidates a subsequent confession obtained from the person seized. First, the threshold inquiry concerns the issue whether the Fifth Amendment has been satisfied. Naturally, this mandates the proper administration of the warnings required by *Miranda* and the receipt of a voluntary, knowing and intelligent waiver. The second inquiry questions whether any statements obtained after the warnings and waiver constituted an exploitation of the illegality of the initial seizure. Here, the focus is on the causal connection between the illegality and the confession. Then, it is only where sufficient intervening events break the causal connection between an individual's unlawful seizure and his confession that it may be said that receipt of the confession "is sufficiently attenuated to permit [its] use [at trial]." *Dunaway* at 216, 99 *S.Ct.* at 2258 (citing *Wong Sun v. United States*, 371 *U.S.* 471, 83 *S.Ct.* 407 (1963)).

NEW YORK v. HARRIS
Supreme Court of the United States
495 *U.S.* 14, 110 *S.Ct.* 1640 (1990)

QUESTION: Where the police have probable cause to arrest a suspect, will the exclusionary rule bar the use of a statement made by him outside of his home, when the statement is taken after an arrest made in the home in violation of *Payton v. New York* ?

ANSWER: NO. The rule in *Payton*—requiring the police to obtain a warrant prior to effecting a routine felony arrest in an individual's home—is imposed to protect the home, and anything incriminating the police gather from effecting a warrantless arrest in an accused's home, rather than elsewhere, will be excluded. The rule is not furthered by suppressing statements taken from an accused *outside* his home. Thus, "where the police have probable cause to arrest a suspect, the exclusionary rule does not bar the State's use of a statement made by the [suspect] outside of his home, even though the statement is taken after an arrest made in the home in violation of *Payton*." *Harris* at 1644-1645.

RATIONALE: In *Payton v. New York*, 445 *U.S.* 573, 100 *S.Ct.* 1371 (1980), the Court held that "the Fourth Amendment prohibits the police from effecting a warrantless and nonconsensual entry into a suspect's home in order to make a routine felony arrest. * * * [T]he rule in *Payton* was designed to protect the physical integrity of the home[.]" *Harris* at 1642, 1643. In this case, the Court addressed the question whether a violation of the rule in *Payton* requires suppression of all statements taken from an accused after the violation.

In the middle of January, New York City police found the body of Thelma Staton murdered in her apartment. Subsequent investigation provided the police with probable cause to believe defendant Harris had killed Staton. As a result, three officers went to Harris' apartment to take him into custody. They did not, however, first obtain an arrest warrant.

Upon arrival at Harris' apartment, the officers knocked on the door, displayed their guns and badges, and Harris let them in. "Once inside, the officers read Harris his *Miranda* rights. Harris acknowledged that he understood the warnings, and agreed to answer the officers' questions. At that point, he reportedly admitted that he had killed Ms. Staton." *Id.* at 1642.

Harris was then placed under arrest and transported to the station house where he again was informed of his *Miranda* rights. Harris provided the officers with a signed, written incriminating statement. "The police subsequently read Harris the *Miranda* warnings a third time and videotaped an incriminating interview between Harris and a district attorney, even though Harris had indicated that he wanted to end the interrogation." *Id.*

"The trial court suppressed Harris' first and third statements; the State does not challenge those rulings. The sole issue in this case is whether Harris' second statement—the written statement made at the station house—should have been suppressed because the police, by entering Harris' home without a warrant and without his consent, violated *Payton v. New York[.]" Harris* at 1642.

Preliminarily, the Court pointed out that it accepted the lower court's finding that Harris did not consent to the police officers' entry into his home and the conclusion that the police had probable cause to arrest him. According to the Court, "[i]t is also evident, in light of *Payton*, that arresting Harris in his home without an arrest warrant violated the Fourth Amendment." *Harris* at 1642. Yet, the penalties which are " 'visited upon the Government, and in turn upon the public, because its officers have violated the law must bear some relation to the purposes which the law is to serve.' " *Id.* at 1642-1643. [Citation omitted.] Thus, the Court "decline[d] to apply the exclusionary rule in this context because the rule in *Payton* was designed to protect the physical integrity of the home; it was not intended to grant criminal suspects, like Harris, protection for statements made outside their premises where the police have probable cause to arrest the suspect for committing a crime." *Harris* at 1643.

Significantly, nothing in *Payton* "suggests that an arrest in a home without a warrant but with probable cause somehow renders unlawful continued custody of the suspect once he is removed from the house. There could be no valid claim here that Harris was immune from prosecution because his person was the fruit of an illegal arrest. * * * Nor is there any claim that the warrantless arrest required the police to release Harris or that Harris could not be immediately rearrested if momentarily released. Because the officers had probable cause to arrest Harris for a crime, Harris was not unlawfully in custody when he was removed to the station house, given *Miranda* warnings and allowed to talk. For Fourth Amendment purposes, the legal issue is the same as it would be had the police arrested Harris on his door step, illegally entered his home to search for evidence, and later interrogated Harris at the station house. Similarly, if the police had made a warrantless entry into Harris' home, not found him there, but arrested him on the street when he returned, a later statement made by him after proper warnings would no doubt be admissible." *Id.*

"This case is therefore different from *Brown v. Illinois*, 422 *U.S.* 590, 95 *S.Ct.* 2254 [] (1975), *Dunaway v. New York*, 442 *U.S.* 200, 99 *S.Ct.* 2248 [] (1979), and *Taylor v. Alabama*, 457 *U.S.* 687, 102 *S.Ct.* 2664 [] (1982). In each of those cases, evidence obtained from a criminal defendant following arrest was suppressed because the police lacked probable cause. The three cases stand for the familiar proposition that the indirect fruits of an illegal search or arrest should be suppressed when they bear a sufficiently close relationship to the underlying illegality." *Harris* at 1643 (citing *Wong Sun v. United States*, 371 *U.S.* 471, 83 *S.Ct.* 407 (1963)). In this respect, the initial arrest, along with the continuing detention, is itself unlawful for " 'the "illegality" is the absence of probable cause and the wrong consists of the police's having control of the defendant's person at the time he made the challenged statement. In these cases, the "challenged evidence"—*i.e.*, the post-arrest confession—is unquestionably "the product of [the] illegal governmental activity"—*i.e.*, the wrongful detention.' " *Harris* at 1643-1644. [Citation omitted.]

"Harris' statement taken at the police station was not the product of being in unlawful custody. Neither was it the fruit of having been arrested in the home rather than someplace else. * * * [T]he police had a justification to question Harris prior to his arrest; therefore his subsequent statement was not an exploitation of the illegal entry into [his] home." *Id.* at 1644. Thus, Harris' station-house statement is admissible because he "was in legal custody," *and* "because the statement, while the product of an arrest and being in custody, was not the fruit of the fact that the arrest was made in the house rather than someplace else." *Id.*

Moreover, "suppressing the statement taken outside the house would not serve the purpose of the rule that made Harris' in-house arrest illegal. The warrant requirement for an arrest in the home is imposed to protect the home, and anything incriminating the police gathered from arresting Harris in his home, rather than elsewhere, has been excluded, as it should have been; the purpose of the rule has thereby been vindicated." *Id.* The Constitution does not require the further step of suppressing statements later made by Harris in order to deter police from violating *Payton*, for "the principal incentive to obey *Payton* still obtains: the police know that a warrantless entry will lead to suppression of any evidence found or statements taken inside the home. * * * Given that the police have probable cause to arrest a suspect in Harris' position, they need not violate *Payton* in order to interrogate the suspect. It is doubtful therefore that the desire to secure a statement from a criminal suspect would motivate the police to violate *Payton*. As a result, suppressing a station-house statement obtained after a *Payton* violation will have little effect on the [actions of police officers], one way or another." *Id.*

Consequently, "where the police have probable cause to arrest a suspect, the exclusionary rule does not bar the State's use of a statement made by the defendant outside of his home, even though the statement is taken after an arrest made in the home in violation of *Payton.*" *Harris* at 1644-1645.

NOTE

Coerced confessions and the "harmless error" rule. In *Arizona v. Fulminante*, 499 *U.S.* 279, 111 *S.Ct.* 1246 (1991), the Court overruled a "vast body of precedent," *id.*, 111 *S.Ct.* at 1254, and abandoned what Justice White described as "the 'axiomatic [proposition] that a defendant in a criminal case is deprived of due process of law if his conviction is founded, in whole or in part, upon an involuntary confession, * * * even though there is ample evidence aside from the confession to support the conviction.'" *Id.* at 1253 (White, J., dissenting in part) (quoting *Jackson v. Denno*, 378 *U.S.* 368, 376, 84 *S.Ct.* 1774, 1780 (1964)). Prior to the decision here in *Fulminante*, the admission of a coerced confession, over objection, had been considered a "structural defect[] in the constitution of the trial mechanism, which def[ies] analysis by 'harmless-error' standards[,]" particularly because "'no one can say what credit and weight the jury gave to the confession.'" *Id.* at 1264, 1265 (quoting *Payne v. Arkansas*, 356 *U.S.* 560, 567-568, 78 *S.Ct.* 844, 850 (1958)). Writing for the *Fulminante* majority on this issue, Chief Justice Rehnquist held that "the admission of an 'involuntary' confession at trial [should now be] subject to harmless error analysis." *Id.* at 1261.

In the landmark case of *Chapman v. California*, 386 *U.S.* 18, 87 *S.Ct.* 824 (1967), the Court "adopted the general rule that a constitutional error does not automatically require reversal of a conviction." *Fulminante* at 1263. Before a constitutional error may be deemed "harmless," however, a "court must be able to declare a belief that it was harmless beyond a reasonable doubt." *Chapman* at 24, 87 *S.Ct.* at 828. This requires the State to meet its burden of establishing that the admission of the evidence did not contribute to the defendant's conviction. *See id.* at 26, 87 *S.Ct.* at 829.

Since *Chapman*, "the Court has applied harmless error analysis to a wide range of errors and has recognized that most constitutional errors can be harmless." *See Fulminante* at 1263 (listing a host of cases applying the harmless error rule). According to the Chief Justice, the "common thread" connecting the prior cases "is that each involved 'trial error'—error which occurred during the presentation of the case to the jury, and which may therefore be quantitatively assessed in the context of other evidence presented in order to determine whether its admission was harmless beyond a reasonable doubt." *Id.* at 1264.

Concluding that an involuntary statement or coerced confession "is a 'trial error,' similar in both degree and kind to the erroneous admission of other types of evidence[,]" *id.* at 1265, the *Fulminante* Court reasoned:

> The evidentiary impact of an involuntary confession, and its effect upon the composition of the record, is indistinguishable from that of a confession obtained in violation of the Sixth Amendment—of evidence seized in violation of the Fourth Amendment—or of a

prosecutor's improper comment on a defendant's silence at trial in violation of the Fifth Amendment. When reviewing the erroneous admission of an involuntary confession, the appellate court, as it does with the admission of other forms of improperly admitted evidence, simply reviews the remainder of the evidence against the defendant to determine whether the admission of the confession was harmless beyond a reasonable doubt.

Id. Nonetheless, in the case of a coerced confession, "the risk that the confession is unreliable, coupled with the profound impact that the confession has upon the jury, requires a reviewing court to exercise extreme caution before determining that the admission of the confession at trial was harmless." *Id.* at 1258.

---

§11.4(b)(2). Outside influences.

Many times in the interrogation process, factors outside or extrinsic to the actual questioning session may work to undermine the integrity of the process or the voluntariness of the defendant's responses. How an officer deals with such outside influences will, in many cases, determine the admissibility of any statements the defendant may make.

MORAN v. BURBINE
Supreme Court of the United States
475 U.S. 412, 106 S.Ct. 1135 (1986)

QUESTION: May law enforcement officers question a person who is in custody and who has properly waived his *Miranda* rights without telling him that a lawyer (who was contacted by his sister) has been trying to reach him ?

ANSWER: YES. The conduct of the police in failing to advise a suspect in custody that a lawyer (who was contacted by the suspect's sister) has been trying to reach him has no bearing on the validity of the waiver of his *Miranda* rights. "Events occurring outside of the presence of the suspect and entirely unknown to him surely can have no bearing on the capacity to comprehend and knowingly relinquish a constitutional right." *Id.* at 1411.

RATIONALE: Defendant Burbine was arrested with two others by the Cranston, Rhode Island, police in connection with a local burglary. While in custody for the burglary, Cranston officers learned that Burbine may have been involved in a murder in Providence, Rhode Island. The Cranston police advised Burbine of his *Miranda* rights and then called the Providence police to relay the information concerning the possible murder involvement.

During this time, and unbeknownst to Burbine, his sister had attempted to retain a lawyer to represent him [for the burglary charges]. The attorney contacted the Cranston police by telephone, and was assured that the Cranston police would not be questioning Burbine, and, they were through with him for the night. However, the attorney was not informed of the possible murder involvement nor of the fact that three Providence police officers had arrived at the Cranston police department to question Burbine about the murder.

Within an hour of the phone call, the Providence police began to conduct questioning sessions with Burbine. Prior to each session, he was informed of his *Miranda* rights, "and on three separate occasions, he signed a written form acknowledging that he understood his right to the presence of an attorney and explicitly indicating that he '(did) not want an attorney called or appointed for (him)' before he gave a statement." *Id.* at 1139. [Citations omitted.] Within a short period of time, Burbine confessed to the murder and signed three written statements admitting his guilt.

In a six to three opinion, *the United States Supreme Court held, per Justice O'Connor, that Burbine's confession may be used against him.*

Burbine's first contention was that the confession "must be suppressed because the police's failure to inform him of the attorney's telephone call deprived him of information essential to his ability to knowingly waive his Fifth Amendment rights." *Id.* at 1140.

The Court rejected this contention, reasoning that the Constitution does not require the police to "supply a suspect with a flow of information to help him calibrate his self-interest in deciding whether to speak or stand by his rights." *Id.* at 1141. The relative inquiry is whether the suspect, himself, "voluntarily, knowingly and intelligently" waived effectuation of the rights conveyed in the *Miranda* warnings. *Id.* "Events occurring outside the presence of the suspect and entirely unknown to him surely can have no bearing on the capacity to comprehend and knowingly relinquish a constitutional right." *Id.*

> First, the relinquishment of the right must have been voluntary in the sense that it was the product of a free and deliberate choice rather than intimidation, coercion, or deception. Second, the waiver must have been made with a full awareness of both the nature of the right being abandoned and the consequences of the decision to abandon it. Only if the "totality of the circumstances surrounding the interrogation" reveal both an uncoerced choice and the requisite level of comprehension may a court properly conclude that the *Miranda* rights have been waived. [Citations omitted.]

Id. The Court concluded, therefore, that on the facts presented, Burbine "validly waived his right to remain silent and to the presence of counsel." *Id.*

Next, Burbine argued that the intentional or "reckless conduct of the police, in particular their failure to inform [him] of the telephone call, fatally undermined the validity of the otherwise proper waiver." *Id.*

The Court quickly disposed of this contention, reasoning that "the state of mind of the police is irrelevant to the question of the intelligence and voluntariness of [Burbine's] election to abandon his rights." *Id.* at 1142. Although the intentional or reckless withholding of advantageous information is highly inappropriate, "such conduct is only relevant to the constitutional validity of a waiver if it deprives a defendant of knowledge essential to his ability to understand the nature of his rights and the consequences of abandoning them." *Id.* However, Burbine's decision to speak was voluntary and made "with full awareness and comprehension of all the information *Miranda* requires the police to convey, [and, as such] the waivers were valid." *Id.*

Burbine also argued that his conviction should be reversed because the police were not totally forthright with an attorney who was attempting to contact him.

What Burbine failed to understand, however, is that "[t]he purpose of the *Miranda* warnings * * * is to dissipate the compulsion inherent in custodial interrogation and, in so doing, guard against abridgement of the suspect's Fifth Amendment rights. Clearly, a rule that focuses on how the police treat an attorney—conduct that has no relevance at all to the degree of compulsion experienced by the defendant during interrogation—would ignore both *Miranda's* mission and its only source of legitimacy." *Id.* at 1143. Such a rule would serve only to confuse and muddy the otherwise "relatively clear waters" in which *Miranda* operates. *Id.*

Finally, Burbine contended that the police violated his Sixth Amendment right to counsel by disallowing the presence of "his" attorney during the interrogation.

"[A]bsent a valid waiver, the defendant has the right to the presence of an attorney during any interrogation occurring after the first formal charging proceeding, the point at which the Sixth Amendment right to counsel initially attaches." *Id.* at 1144. When that right has attached, "the police may not interfere with the efforts of a defendant's attorney to act as a 'medium between (the suspect) and the State' during the interrogation." *Id.* (quoting *Maine v. Moulton*, 474 *U.S.* 159, 176, 106 *S.Ct.* 477, 487 (1985)). However, the questioning sessions which produced Burbine's confession occurred *before* the initiation of "adversary judicial proceedings." *Id.* at 1145. [Citations omitted.] "The Sixth Amendment's intended function * * * is to assure that in any 'criminal prosecution,' * * * the accused shall not be left to his own devices in facing the 'prosecutorial forces of organized society.'" *Id.* at 1145-46. [Citation omitted.] Its application is necessitated when the "government's role shifts from investigation to accusation," and, it is the initiation of adversary judicial proceedings [*i.e.*, the initiation of formal charges] which invokes the application of the Sixth Amendment right to counsel. *Id.* at 1146. "[U]ntil such time as the 'government has committed itself to prosecute, and . . . the adverse positions of government and defendant have solidified,' the Sixth Amendment right to counsel does not attach." *Id.* [Citations omitted.]

Since Burbine's confession came before "the formal initiation of adversary judicial proceedings, * * * the conduct of the police [did not violate] his rights under the Sixth Amendment." *Id.*

Accordingly, the Constitution does not require the exclusion of his confession.

NOTE

1. It is significant to note that Burbine never asked for the services of an attorney, despite being given appropriate warnings and an opportunity to seek an attorney's assistance. Moreover, there was no evidence that the police conduct at issue actually interfered with any attorney-client relationship; Burbine had chosen to waive his right to counsel, and the attorney who telephoned had never been asked by Burbine to represent him.

2. A state court is free, of course, to rely on its own state constitution to provide greater protection to a suspect in circumstances where an attorney makes it known to the police that he or she has been retained by a family member or friend, and is ready, willing and able to provide representation.

(a) A prime example is *State v. Reed*, 133 *N.J.* 237, 627 *A.2d* 630 (1993). In *Reed*, the defendant was questioned at the county prosecutor's office regarding the stabbing death of his friend and co-worker, S.G. When he arrived at the office, he was accompanied by his girlfriend, Fran Varga. "The detectives isolated defendant in an interrogation room, and asked Varga to remain in the waiting room." *Id.*, 133 *N.J.* at 241. As soon as defendant was taken away by the investigators, Varga called her aunt, who gave her the name of an attorney. Varga then called the attorney and told him that she and defendant were at the prosecutor's office, that the investigators were about to question defendant, and that she and defendant "needed an attorney." The attorney told Varga that he would immediately send William Aitken, an associate from the law office.

Varga immediately advised one of the officers that an attorney was on his way and asked that defendant not be questioned until the attorney arrived. The officer, according to Varga, nodded that he understood.

When Aitken arrived at the prosecutor's office, Varga met him and explained that defendant had been taken into an office for questioning. "Aitken approached the prosecutor who would eventually present the case against defendant. Aitken told the prosecutor that he was there to represent both Varga and defendant. The prosecutor informed Aitken that * * * Aitken had 'no right to walk into an investigation.' * * * [T]he prosecutor assured Aitken that the police would call him if and when defendant requested an attorney." *Id.* at 242-43. "No one informed the defendant that a lawyer retained by Varga was waiting to see him." *Id.* at 243.

After waiving his *Miranda* rights (for a third time), defendant confessed to the murder. The (taped) confession was given almost five hours from the time defendant had been taken into custody, and nearly four and one-half hours from the time law-enforcement officials had refused to permit an attorney, who had been retained for the defendant, to speak with him, or inform defendant of the attorney's presence. The critical issue in this case, according to the Court, is whether that refusal "violated defendant's constitutional rights, including the privilege against self-incrimination, and therefore rendered defendant's confession inadmissible." *Id.* at 240.

Under federal constitutional law, defendant's confession would be admissible. *Moran v. Burbine* made clear that the failure of the police to inform a suspect under questioning that an attorney was available to assist him "was irrelevant to the question whether he had knowingly waived his rights." *Reed* at 247. At the time *Burbine* was decided, however, "many courts had held that when the police fail to inform a suspect that an attorney is actually available and seeking to render assistance, any subsequent waiver of the suspect's *Miranda* rights was invalid." *Reed* at 248. "Those decisions likely prompted the Supreme Court in [*Burbine*] to state explicitly: 'Nothing we say today disables the States from adopting different requirements for the conduct of their employees and officials as a matter of State law.' " *Reed* at 249 (quoting *Burbine* at 428, 106 *S.Ct.* at 1144).

Accordingly, the Court here in *Reed* parted company with the federal Supreme Court's ruling in *Moran v. Burbine*, and proceeded to look to New Jersey State law

> to determine the standards that should govern the conduct of law-enforcement officers in undertaking the custodial interrogation of a suspect, and, specifically, to determine whether law-enforcement officers in conducting such interrogation must inform the suspect that an attorney retained on his or her behalf is present and seeks to provide assistance.

Id. at 249-50.

"In New Jersey, the right against self-incrimination is founded on a common-law and statutory—rather than a constitutional—basis. * * * From its beginnings as a State, New Jersey has recognized the right against self-incrimination and has consistently and vigorously protected that right. * * * The right against self-incrimination is an integral and essential safeguard in the administration of criminal justice. The common law right against self-incrimination was first codified in New Jersey in 1855. *L.* 1855, *c.*236, §4. * * * Subsequently, the Legislature incorporated the right against self-incrimination in its enactment of the Rules of Evidence. * * * Thus, although lacking a constitutional provision expressly establishing the right, '[t]he privilege against self-incrimination has been an integral thread in the fabric of New Jersey common law.' " *Id.* at 250. [Citations omitted.]

A suspect has an absolute right to remain silent and to the assistance of counsel while under police interrogation, and "[w]aiver of that right must be knowing, intelligent, and voluntary. * * * In demonstrating that a defendant has waived his or her right against self-incrimination the government bears the burden of proof and that burden is a heavy one." *Id.* at 250-51.

"Many state courts, as already noted, have interpreted their respective state constitutions to require that a suspect exposed to custodial interrogation be apprised of the presence of an attorney seeking to render assistance." *Id.* at 253-54. While those courts "may differ on the rationale for imposing the duty to inform a suspect that an attorney is waiting to confer, they agree on one supervening principle: the atmosphere of custodial interrogation is inherently coercive and protecting the right against self-incrimination entails counteracting that coercion. Thus, although 'knowledge' is always a relevant factor in assessing the validity of a waiver of the right against self-incrimination, because the right is against *compelled* self-incrimination, 'knowledge' can best be understood as a condition of 'voluntariness,' which itself denotes the absence of 'compulsion.' Consequently, standards [] imposed to enhance a suspect's 'knowledge' of the *Miranda* rights also counteract coercion and assure 'voluntariness.'" *Id.* at 255-56. [Court's emphasis.]

This Court believes "that requiring the police to inform the suspect of an attorney's presence will greatly reduce the temptation, on law enforcement authorities, to pressure the suspect into a confession before the attorney gains access to the suspect." *Id.* at 257. As this "case well illustrates, by allowing police to withhold the information that an attorney is available to see the suspect, enormous pressure is created, on the police, to secure a confession before either the suspect exercises the right to an attorney, or a break in the interrogation presents the opportunity for the suspect to contact family or friends who will surely tell the suspect of the attorney's presence." *Id.* at 257-58. The ruling in this case eliminates that temptation.

The new rule announced in this case, according to the Court, should be governed by a two-fold purpose:

> to enhance the reliability of confessions by reducing the inherent coercion of custodial interrogation and diminish the likelihood of unreasonable police conduct in those situations where police, knowing that an attorney has been retained for the suspect and is asking for contact with his or her client, are desperate to acquire a confession before the suspect speaks with the attorney.

Id. at 260.

Regarding the existence of an "attorney-client relationship," the Court held that the relationship between the suspect and the attorney should be deemed to exist "when the suspect's family or friends have retained the attorney or where the attorney has represented or is representing the suspect on another matter." *Id.* at 261. "When, to the knowledge of the police, such an attorney is present or available, and the attorney has communicated a desire to confer with the suspect, the police must make that information known to the suspect before custodial interrogation can proceed or continue. Further, * * * the failure of the police to give the suspect that information renders the suspect's subsequent waiver of the privilege against self-incrimination invalid *per se*." *Id.* at 261-62.

The Court in this case places an "additional responsibility" upon the police in their conduct toward criminal defendants. "The duty to inform * * * is narrow and specific. It arises only where counsel has made known that he or she has been retained to represent the person held in custody, is present or readily available, and makes a request to consult with the suspect in 'a reasonably diligent, timely and pertinent' fashion." *Id.* at 263-64. The attorney need not communicate directly with the interrogating officers. "That communication will not, most times, be possible. Rather, whenever the attorney has communicated his presence and desire to confer with the suspect to an agent of the State in a position to contact the interrogating officers, [this Court] will impute to those officers knowledge of the attorney's presence and desire to confer with the suspect. Thus, the police need do no more than receive and convey what has already been communicated: that an identified attorney retained for a person in custody is available to assist that person if he or she requests such assistance." *Id.* at 264.

In this case, "the failure of the police to inform defendant that an attorney was present and asking to speak with him violated defendant's State privilege against self-incrimination." *Id.* at 268.

Accordingly, "when, to the knowledge of law enforcement officers, an attorney has been retained on behalf of a person in custody on suspicion of crime and is present or readily available to assist that person, the communication of that information to the suspect is essential to making a knowing waiver of the privilege against self-incrimination, and withholding that information renders invalid the suspect's waiver of the privilege against self-incrimination." *Id.* at 269.

(b) The standard adopted by the Court in *Reed* declares that certain police acts or omissions will work to invalidate a suspect's waiver of *Miranda* rights. In short, a criminal suspect's waiver of *Miranda* rights without being advised of the presence or ready availability of counsel is invalid. *Reed* at 264. The *Reed* Court also emphasized that interrogating officials will be deemed to know of an attorney's presence or ready availability when that information has been communicated to any "State agent" in "a position to contact the interrogating officers." Consequently, law enforcement officials would be well advised to inform clerks, secretaries, receptionists, and similar personnel of this standard.

COLORADO v. CONNELLY
Supreme Court of the United States
479 *U.S.* 157, 107 *S.Ct.* 515 (1986)

QUESTION: Will a suspect's confession be held "involuntary" on Due Process grounds when it results from the suspect's internal compulsion caused by a mental illness rather than from police overreaching ?

ANSWER: NO. "[C]oercive police activity is a necessary predicate to the finding that a confession is not 'voluntary' within the meaning of the Due Process Clause of the Fourteenth Amendment." *Id.* at 522.

RATIONALE: In August of 1983, defendant Connelly approached a Denver, Colorado, police officer and, without any prompting, stated that he had murdered someone and wanted to talk about it. The officer immediately advised Connelly of his *Miranda* rights. Connelly responded by saying that he understood his rights, but wanted to talk anyway because his conscience was bothering him.

Within a short period, a homicide detective was summoned and Connelly was readvised of his *Miranda* rights. The detective then asked him "what he had on his mind." *Id.* at 518. Connelly stated "that he had come all the way from Boston to confess to the murder of Mary Ann Junta, a young girl whom he had killed in Denver sometime during November 1982." *Id.*

Connelly was then taken to police headquarters where his story was confirmed. During this time, Connelly appeared to the officer to understand fully the nature of his acts. The detective perceived no indication whatsoever that Connelly was suffering from any kind of mental illness, although Connelly had previously told the officer that he had been a patient in several mental hospitals.

The next day, when Connelly met with the public defender, he became disoriented, and for the first time, stated that " 'voices' had told him to come to Denver and that he had followed the directions of these voices in confessing." *Id.* at 519.

At the preliminary hearing, Connelly moved to suppress his confession. Psychiatric testimony indicated that he was suffering from "chronic schizophrenia" and that Connelly believed he was following the "voice of God," which instructed him to fly to Denver and "either confess to the killing or to commit suicide. Reluctantly following the command of the voices, [Connelly] approached the [Denver police officer] and confessed." *Id.*

The Colorado courts found Connelly's statements involuntary and inadmissible because they were not a product of "rational intellect and free will." *Id.* "Although the [lower] court found that the police had done nothing wrong or coercive in securing [the] confession, Connelly's illness [not only] destroyed his volition and compelled him to confess[, but also] vitiated his attempted waiver of the right to counsel and the privilege against compulsory self-incrimination." *Id.*

The United States Supreme Court disagreed and reversed.

The Court began with a Fourteenth Amendment, Due Process Clause, analysis, and recognized that "by virtue of the Due Process

Clause, 'certain interrogation techniques, either in isolation or as applied to the unique characteristics of a particular suspect, are so offensive to a civilized system of justice that they must be condemned.' " *Id.* at 520. [Citations omitted.] However, the crucial element is *coercive government misconduct.* "Absent police conduct causally related to the confession, there is simply no basis for concluding that any state actor has deprived a criminal defendant of due process of law." *Id.* The mental state of the defendant, by itself and apart from its relation to official coercion, does not dispose of the constitutional "voluntariness" issue. Rather, what is needed is "some sort of 'state action' to support a claim of violation of the Due Process Clause of the Fourteenth Amendment." *Id.* at 521. While statements given by one in Connelly's condition might prove to be unreliable, "this is a matter to be governed by the [State's] evidentiary laws * * *, and not by the Due Process Clause of the Fourteenth Amendment." *Id.* at 522. Thus, "coercive police activity is a necessary predicate to the finding that a confession is not 'voluntary' within the meaning of the Due Process Clause[. Accordingly,] the taking of [Connelly's] statements, and their admission into evidence constitute no violation of that clause." *Id.*

The Court also held that the Colorado court was in error when it found that the State did not meet its burden of proving that Connelly waived his right to counsel and his right to remain silent by "clear and convincing" evidence.[*] Here, the Court reaffirmed *Lego v. Twomey*, 404 *U.S.* 477, 92 *S.Ct.* 619 (1972), and holds: "Whenever the State bears the burden of proof in a motion to suppress a statement that the defendant claims was obtained in violation of our *Miranda* doctrine, the State must prove waiver only by a preponderance of the evidence."[*] *Connelly* at 523. Since the voluntariness of a confession need be established only by a preponderance of the evidence, then "a waiver of the auxiliary protections [*e.g.*, right to remain silent, right to counsel] established in *Miranda* should require no higher burden of proof." *Id.*

Finally, the Court determined that the Colorado court was in error when it ruled that Connelly did not effectively waive his *Miranda rights.*

In this respect, the Court reasoned that the:

> Supreme Court of Colorado erred in importing into the area of constitutional law notions of "free will" that have no place there. There is obviously no reason to require more in the way of a "voluntariness" inquiry in the *Miranda* waiver context than in the Fourteenth Amendment context. The sole concern of the Fifth Amendment, on which *Miranda* was based, is governmental coercion. * * * Indeed, the Fifth Amendment privilege is not concerned "with moral and psychological pressures to confess emanating from sources other than official coercion." * * * The voluntariness of a waiver of this privilege has always depended on the absence of police overreaching, not on "free choice" in any broader sense of the word.

---

[*] *See* §1.1, Fig. 1.1.

Id. Accordingly, *"Miranda* protects defendants against government coercion leading them to surrender rights protected by the Fifth Amendment; it goes no further than that. [Connelly's] perception of coercion flowing from the 'voice of God,' however important or significant such a perception may be in other disciplines, is a matter to which the United States Constitution does not speak." *Id.* at 524.

NOTE

It is still a dangerous law-enforcement practice to rely upon "waivers" of constitutional rights by a person who is *clearly* unable to make such an "intelligent" decision, as Connelly was found to be by the Colorado Supreme Court. As Justice Brennan, joined by Justice Marshall, stated, "Because I believe that the use of a mentally ill person's involuntary confession is antithetical to the notion of fundamental fairness embodied in the Due Process Clause, I dissent." *Id.* at 526.

CHAPTER 12

EYEWITNESS IDENTIFICATION

§12.1. Introduction.

As a general principle of constitutional criminal procedure, the Fifth Amendment command that "[n]o person * * * shall be compelled in any criminal case to be a witness against himself[,]" "does not protect a suspect from being compelled by the State to provide 'real or physical evidence.'" *Pennsylvania v. Muniz*, 496 *U.S.* 582, 110 *S.Ct.* 2638, 2643 (1990). Instead, the privilege against self-incrimination "protects an accused only from being compelled to testify against himself, or otherwise provide the State with evidence of a testimonial or communicative nature." *Schmerber v. California*, 384 *U.S.* 757, 761, 86 *S.Ct.* 1826, 1830 (1966). In order "to be testimonial, an accused's communication must itself, explicitly or implicitly, relate a factual assertion or disclose information. Only then is a person compelled to be a 'witness' against himself." *Doe v. United States*, 487 *U.S.* 201, 210, 108 *S.Ct.* 2341, 2347 (1988).

Over time, the United States Supreme Court has held that certain acts, though incriminating, are not within the Fifth Amendment privilege. For example, a suspect may be compelled to furnish a blood sample, *Schmerber, supra*, 384 *U.S.*, at 765, 86 *S.Ct.*, at 1832; to provide a handwriting exemplar, *Gilbert v. California*, 388 *U.S.* 263, 266-267, 87 *S.Ct.* 1951, 1953 (1967), or a voice exemplar, *United States v. Dionisio*, 410 *U.S.* 1, 7, 93 *S.Ct.* 764, 768 (1973); to stand in a line-up, *United States v. Wade*, 388 *U.S.* 218, 221-222, 87 *S.Ct.* 1926, 1929 (1967); and to wear particular clothing, *Holt v. United States*, 218 *U.S.* 245, 252-253, 31 *S.Ct.* 2, 6 (1910). In each of these cases, the Court held that the Fifth Amendment privilege was not implicated because the suspect was not required "to disclose any knowledge he might have," or "to speak his guilt." *Wade* at 222-223, 87 *S.Ct.* at 1929-1930. Rather, "[i]t is the 'extortion of information from the accused,' * * * the attempt to force him 'to disclose the contents of his own mind,' * * * that implicates the Self-Incrimination Clause." *Doe*, 108 *S.Ct.* at 2348. [Citations omitted.]

Accordingly, the Fifth Amendment privilege to be free from self-incrimination is a "bar against compelling 'communications' or 'testimony,' but * * * compulsion which makes a suspect or accused the source of 'real or physical evidence' does not violate it." *Schmerber* at 764, 86 *S.Ct.* at 1832. For purposes of this chapter, then, causing a suspect or an accused to stand for a show-up or line-up, or placing a photograph of a suspect or an accused in a photographic array, does not implicate the Fifth Amendment privilege to be free from self-incrimination. The method or procedure, however, if employed in an unnecessarily suggestive manner, can nonetheless have constitutional ramifications.

The Fourteenth Amendment to the United States Constitution provides in pertinent part that:

> No State shall * * * deprive any person of life, liberty, or property, without *due process of law;* * * * [Emphasis added.]

and it is this Due Process Clause which will invalidate an unnecessarily suggestive eyewitness identification.

While each case will be considered on its own facts, a court will nonetheless invalidate an in-court eyewitness identification when it follows a pretrial identification procedure which was "so impermissibly suggestive as to give rise to a very substantial likelihood of irreparable misidentification." *Simmons v. United States*, 390 *U.S.* 377, 384, 88 *S.Ct.* 967, 971 (1968). Here, the relationship between suggestiveness and misidentification becomes significant, for as the degree of suggestiveness increases, the likelihood of misidentification similarly increases.

The "very substantial likelihood of irreparable misidentification" standard is the general determining factor of whether an "in-court identification would be admissible in the wake of a suggestive out-of-court identification[.]" *Neil v. Biggers*, 409 *U.S.* 188, 198, 93 *S.Ct.* 375, 381 (1972). When the word "irreparable" is deleted, we come to the "standard for the admissibility of testimony concerning the out-of-court identification itself." *Id.* at 198, 93 *S.Ct.* at 381. Thus, it is this substantial "likelihood of misidentification which violates a defendant's right to due process [which then forms the basis for the exclusion of the identification as evidence in court]." *Id.* at 198, 93 *S.Ct.* at 381, 382.

The admissibility of eyewitness identification evidence may be challenged by a defendant prior to trial, or outside the presence of the jury, at a proceeding called a *"Wade* hearing." (*United States v. Wade*, 388 *U.S.* 218, 87 *S.Ct.* 1926 (1967)). It is the defendant's burden, however, to establish the need for such a hearing. The defendant must preliminarily show the court "some evidence" of impermissible suggestiveness before he or she would be entitled to the hearing. *Watkins v. Sowders*, 449 *U.S.* 341, 101 *S.Ct.* 654 (1981). If the defendant satisfies his or her preliminary burden of producing some evidence of impermissible suggestiveness, a *Wade* hearing is held and the judge must first decide whether the suggestive out-of-court identification procedure was in fact "impermissibly" suggestive. If it is determined that the identification procedure was impermissibly suggestive, the state has the burden of proving that the identification had a source independent of the police-conducted identification procedure. The court must then decide, based on the factors listed below, whether the suggestive out-of-court identification procedure will result in a very substantial likelihood of misidentification in court. If so, the court will disallow any evidence related to, or testimony concerning, the out-of-court identification. Moreover, if the court determines that the eyewitness' identification has no independent origin—that the eyewitness' identification of the defendant flows only from the identification procedure employed by the law enforcement officials and not from the witness' observation of the defendant at the time of the crime—the court will disallow any in-court identification by the eyewitness.

The ultimate inquiry will always turn on whether the eyewitness identification, in light of the totality of the circumstances, was "reliable." *Id.* at 198, 93 *S.Ct.* at 382. "Reliability," then, is "the linchpin in determining the admissibility of identification testimony[,]" *Manson v. Brathwaite*, 432 *U.S.* 98, 114, 93 *S.Ct.* 2243, 2253 (1977), and it may be assessed by examining such factors as:

[1 T]he opportunity of the witness to view the criminal at the time of the crime [including items such as length of time viewed, lighting, whether face-to-face or side view, or, whether casual observer or direct victim of the crime[;]

[2 T]he witness' degree of attention[;]

[3 T]he accuracy of the witness' prior description of the criminal[;]

[4 T]he level of certainty demonstrated by the witness at the confrontation[;] and

[5 T]he length of time between the crime and the confrontation.

Biggers at 199, 93 *S.Ct.* at 382.

Although many commentators explain "that eyewitness evidence is inherently suspect and that suggestive procedures may prejudicially affect the ultimate identification," it is also true that in criminal actions an eyewitness' identification may be the most crucial evidentiary part of the case. W. LaFave & J. Israel, *Criminal Procedure*, §7.4 at 320 (1985). Significantly, many prosecutions can be proved *only* through the use of the testimony of an eyewitness.

---

§12.2. Preliminary issues.

The eyewitness may be the single most common form of witness in many criminal trials. Eyewitness identifications are often considered direct evidence of guilt, and therefore are accorded great importance by juries. Most jurors likely will believe eyewitness testimony, particularly when it is offered with a high level of confidence. Indeed, "there is almost *nothing more convincing* than a live human being who takes the stand, points a finger at the defendant, and says, 'That's the one!'" *Watkins v. Sowders*, 449 *U.S.* 341, 352, 101 *S.Ct.* 654, 661 (1981) (Brennan, J. dissenting). Consequently, law enforcement officers must exercise particular care in respect of this powerful evidence—the eyewitness.

An eyewitness identification takes place when a person, place or object is later recognized, or "identified," by one or more persons as being the same person, place or object which had been previously drawn into question. The subsequent recognition or identification may be made by:

(1) a direct one-on-one examination of the actual person, place or object—the "showup";

(2) a viewing of a photographic array—the "photo lineup"; or

(3) a viewing of a corporeal group of individuals—the "in-person lineup."

Significantly, whether the identification procedure is conducted live or by means of photographs, the law will focus upon, as §12.1 has illustrated, two concepts: "reliability" and "suggestiveness."

Another preliminary issue concerns the documentation of an eyewitness identification procedure. Whether or not an identification is made, law enforcement officials should make a complete record of the identification procedure to the end that the event may, if necessary, be reconstructed at court. The identity of persons participating in a lineup should be recorded, and the lineup itself should be photographed. In addition, whenever an identification is made or attempted on the basis of photographs, a record should be made of the photographs exhibited, and, where feasible, the entire photographic array should be preserved intact. This practice permits the prosecution to address or combat any subsequent allegations of impropriety during the eyewitness identification process. *See e.g., Branch v. Estelle,* 631 *F.*2d 1229, 1234 (5th Cir. 1980); *United States v. Sonderup,* 639 *F.*2d 294, 298-99 (5th Cir. 1981).

UNITED STATES v. CREWS
Supreme Court of the United States
445 *U.S.* 463, 100 *S.Ct.* 1244 (1980)

QUESTION: Will evidence of an out-of-court identification procedure be admissible in court when it is obtained from an eyewitness' viewing of a photo array containing a picture of the defendant which was taken during the course of an unlawful arrest?

ANSWER: NO. A pretrial identification obtained through the use of a photograph taken during the defendant's illegal arrest cannot be introduced in evidence at trial. The "in court" identification of the defendant may, however, be admissible if the police's knowledge of the defendant's identity and the victim's independent recollection of him both developed before the unlawful arrest and were untainted by the constitutional violation. *Id.* at 1253.

RATIONALE: During the course of an investigation into several armed robberies occurring in the women's restroom on the grounds of the Washington Monument, police developed grounds to suspect that defendant, 16-year-old Keith Crews, was the perpetrator. Under the pretense of taking him into custody as a suspected truant, an officer of the United States Park Police transported him to police headquarters, where officers questioned Crews, took his picture, telephoned his school, and then released him. Crews was not formally arrested at this time, nor was he charged with any offense.

The next day, the police showed the first robbery victim an array of eight photographs, including one of Crews. Although she had previously viewed over 100 pictures of possible suspects without identifying any of them as her assailant, she immediately selected Crews' photograph as that of the man who had robbed her. Three days later, one of the other victims made a similar identification. Prior to the photo-lineup procedures (immediately after the crimes), the robbery victims provided the police with detailed descriptions of their assailants. Each description matched the physical appearance of Crews. Crews was again taken into custody, and at a court-ordered lineup was positively identified by the two women who had made the photographic identifications.

At trial, the court disallowed the introduction by the government of any evidence related to the photographic and lineup identifications, ruling that each was the product of an arrest without probable cause.

The critical issue, according to the United States Supreme Court, was "whether in the circumstances of this case an in-court identification of the accused by the victim of a crime should be suppressed as the fruit of defendant's unlawful arrest." *Id.* at 1246.

As a general rule, the exclusionary rule operates to prohibit the use at trial of direct, as well as indirect, products of Fourth Amendment violations. "[T]he exclusionary sanction applies to any 'fruits' of a constitutional violation—whether such evidence be tangible, physical material actually seized in an illegal search, items observed or words overheard in the course of the unlawful activity, or confessions or statements of the accused obtained during an illegal arrest and detention." *Id.* at 1249.

"In the typical 'fruit of the poisonous tree' case, however, the challenged evidence was acquired by the police *after* some initial Fourth Amendment violation[.] * * * Thus, most cases begin with the premise that the challenged evidence is in some sense the product of illegal governmental activity." *Id.* at 1249-50. [Emphasis added.]

Eyewitness identification cases are, however, a bit different. "A victim's in-court identification of the accused has three distinct elements. First, the victim is present at trial to testify as to what transpired between her and the offender, and to identify the defendant as the culprit. Second, the victim possesses knowledge of and the ability to reconstruct the prior criminal occurrence and to identify the defendant from her observations of him at the time of the crime. And third, the defendant is also physically present in the courtroom, so that the victim can observe him and compare his appearance to that of the offender." *Id.* at 1250. In this case, the Court concluded that none of these three elements has come into existence through the exploitation of Crews' unlawful arrest. *Id.* The Court elaborated:

> In this case, the robbery victim's presence in the courtroom at [defendant's] trial was surely not the product of any police misconduct. She had notified the authorities immediately after the attack and had given them a full description of her assailant. The very next day, she went to the police station to view photographs of possible suspects, and she voluntarily assisted the police in their investigation at all times. Thus, this is not a case in which the witness' identity was discovered or her cooperation secured only as a result of an unlawful search or arrest of the accused. Here, the victim's identity was known long before there was any official misconduct, and her presence in court is thus not traceable to any Fourth Amendment violation.
>
> Nor did the illegal arrest infect the victim's ability to give accurate identification testimony. Based upon her observations at the time of the robbery, the victim constructed a mental image of her assailant. At trial, she retrieved this mnemonic representation, compared it to the figure of the defendant, and positively identified him as the robber. [As the Government put it, the witness' mental image may be compared to "an undeveloped photograph of the robber that is given to the police immediately after the crime, but which becomes visible only at the trial."] No part of this process was affected by [defendant's] illegal arrest.
>
> This is not to say that the intervening photographic and lineup identifications—both of which are conceded to be suppressible fruits of the Fourth Amendment violation—could not under some circumstances affect the reliability of the in-court identification and render it inadmissible as well. Indeed, given the vagaries of human memory and the inherent suggestibility of many identification procedures, just the opposite may be true. But in the present case[,] * * * the witness' courtroom testimony rested on an independent recollection of her initial encounter with the assailant, uninfluenced by the pretrial identifications[.] * * * In short, the victim's capacity to identify her assailant in court neither resulted from nor was biased by the unlawful police conduct committed long after she had developed that capacity.

Id. at 1250-51 & n.16.

Defendant cannot claim that he is immune from prosecution simply because his appearance in court was precipitated by an arrest without probable cause. "An illegal arrest, without more, has never been viewed as a bar to subsequent prosecution, nor as a defense to a valid conviction." *Id.* at 1251. Defendant "is not himself a suppressible 'fruit,' and the illegality of his detention cannot deprive the Government of the opportunity to prove his guilt through the introduction of evidence wholly untainted by the police misconduct." *Id.* at 1251. In this respect, "a defendant's face can[not] be a suppressible fruit of an illegal arrest." *Id.* at 1253.

[I]n this case the record plainly discloses that prior to his illegal arrest, the police both knew [defendant's] identity and had some basis to suspect his involvement in the very crimes with which he was charged. * * * In short, the Fourth Amendment violation in this case yielded nothing of evidentiary value that the police did not already have in their grasp. Rather, [defendant's] unlawful arrest served merely to link together two extant ingredients in his identification. *The exclusionary rule enjoins the Government from benefiting from evidence it has unlawfully obtained; it does not reach backward to taint information that was in official hands prior to any illegality.*

Id. at 1252. [Emphasis added.]

Accordingly, the pretrial identification obtained through use of the photograph taken during defendant's illegal arrest cannot be introduced in evidence; "but the in-court identification is admissible * * * because the police's knowledge of [defendant's] identity and the victim's independent recollection[] of him both antedated the unlawful arrest and were thus untainted by the constitutional violation." *Id.* at 1253.

---

§12.3. Showups and lineups.

§12.3(a). Showups.

NEIL v. BIGGERS
Supreme Court of the United States
409 U.S. 188, 93 S.Ct. 375 (1972)

QUESTION: In the wake of a suggestive showup procedure, what factors will a court consider to determine whether the suggestive nature of the showup created a substantial likelihood of misidentification, thereby requiring the exclusion at trial of any evidence relating to the showup ?

ANSWER: Under the totality of the circumstances, a witness' identification may be deemed "reliable" even though the showup procedure was suggestive. In order to determine whether a suggestive out-of-court confrontation gave rise to a likelihood of misidentification, a court will consider such factors as:

    (1) "the opportunity of the witness to view the criminal at the time of the crime,"

    (2) "the witness' degree of attention,"

    (3) "the accuracy of the witness' prior description of the criminal,"

    (4) "the level of certainty demonstrated by the witness at the confrontation,"

(5) "the length of time between the crime and the confrontation," and

(6) whether the witness was a "casual observer" or the victim of the crime.

Id. at 382.

RATIONALE: Whenever a suggestive out-of-court identification procedure is challenged by a defendant, a court will conduct an inquiry into whether the suggestive procedure gave rise to a likelihood of misidentification at a future court proceeding. If the court determines that the showup procedure was unnecessarily suggestive and the likelihood of misidentification is substantial, it may disallow the admission of the out-of-court identification, along with any evidence relating to it, at trial, in order to safeguard the defendant's right to due process of law. Respecting the relationship between "suggestiveness" and "misidentification," the Court states that "the primary evil to be avoided is 'a very substantial likelihood of irreparable misidentification.' While the phrase was coined as a standard for determining whether an in-court identification would be admissible in the wake of a suggestive out-of-court identification, with the deletion of 'irreparable' it serves equally well as a standard for the admissibility of testimony concerning the out-of-court identification itself. It is the likelihood of misidentification which violates a defendant's right to due process[.] * * * Suggestive confrontations are disapproved because they increase the likelihood of misidentification, and unnecessarily suggestive ones are condemned for the further reason that the increased chance of misidentification is [a given]." *Id.* at 381-382.

"[T]he admission of evidence of a showup without more," however, "does not violate due process." *Id.* at 382. Moreover, "unnecessary suggestiveness alone" does not automatically require the exclusion of the out-of-court identification procedure. *Id.* Rather, the central question is whether, "under the 'totality of the circumstances[,]' the identification was *reliable* even though the confrontation procedure was suggestive." *Id.* [Emphasis added.]

In this case, defendant was convicted of rape and sentenced to 20 years' imprisonment. The evidence presented at two separate hearings* established that on January 22, the victim, a practical nurse, was accosted by defendant in her home at the doorway leading to her kitchen. The victim testified that a youth with a butcher knife:

"* * * grabbed me from behind, and grappled—twisted me on the floor. Threw me down on the floor.
"Q. And there was no light in that kitchen ?
"A. Not in the kitchen.
"Q. So you couldn't have seen him then ?
"A. Yes, I could see him, when I looked up in his face.

---

* To decide this case, the Supreme Court considered the evidence which was presented at defendant's jury trial and at his habeas corpus hearing.

"Q. In the dark ?

"A. He was right in the doorway—it was enough light from the bedroom shining through. Yes, I could see who he was."

Id. at 379.

"When the victim screamed, her 12-year-old daughter came out of her bedroom and also began to scream. The assailant directed the victim to 'tell her [the daughter] to shut up, or I'll kill you both.' She did so, and was then walked at knifepoint about two blocks along a railroad track, taken into a woods, and raped there. She testified that 'the moon was shining brightly, full moon.' After the rape, the assailant ran off, and she returned home, the whole incident having taken between 15 minutes and half an hour." *Id.*

Subsequently, the victim described her attacker to the police as "being fat and flabby with smooth skin, bushy hair and a youthful voice." *Id.* at 380. She reported that he was "between 16 and 18 years old and between five feet ten inches and six feet tall, as weighing between 180 and 200 pounds, and as having a dark brown complexion." *Id.*

"On several occasions over the course of the next seven months, she viewed suspects in her home or at the police station, some in lineups and others in showups, and was shown between 30 and 40 photographs." *Id.* At no time did she positively identify any of the individuals that were shown to her. Thereafter, on August 17, almost seven months after the attack, the police called the victim to the station to view defendant, who was being detained on another charge. "In an effort to construct a suitable lineup, the police checked the city jail and the city juvenile home. Finding no one at either place fitting [defendant's] unusual physical description, they conducted a showup instead." *Id.*

The showup itself consisted of two detectives walking defendant past the victim. At the completion of the showup, the victim positively identified the defendant as the rapist. According to the victim's testimony, she had "no doubt" about her identification. *Id.*

"A. That I have no doubt, I mean that I am sure that when I—see, when I first laid eyes on him, I knew that it was the individual, because his face—well, there was just something that I don't think I could ever forget. * * *"

During the course of the procedure (it is unclear from the trial testimony when) the victim requested the police to direct the defendant to say, "shut up or I'll kill you." According to the victim:

"Q. What physical characteristics, if any, caused you to be able to identify him ?

"A. First of all,—uh—his size,—next I could remember his voice.

"Q. What about his voice ? Describe his voice to the Jury.

"A. Well, he has the voice of an immature youth—I call it an immature youth. I have teenage boys. And that was the first thing that made me think it was the boy."

The "central question" in this case, according to the Supreme Court, is "whether under the 'totality of the circumstances' the [nurse's] identification [of defendant] was reliable even though the confrontation procedure was suggestive." *Id.* at 382.

Preliminarily, the Court notes that "the police did not exhaust all possibilities in seeking persons physically comparable to [defendant]" in order to conduct an appropriate in-person lineup. *Id.* Nonetheless, it concludes that the evidence of the showup need not be excluded so long as the suggestive procedure did not give rise to a "substantial likelihood of misidentification." *Id.*

"[T]he factors to be considered in evaluating the likelihood of misidentification include the opportunity of the witness to view the criminal at the time of the crime, the witness' degree of attention, the accuracy of the witness' prior description of the criminal, the level of certainty demonstrated by the witness at the confrontation, and the length of time between the crime and the confrontation." *Id.*

Applying and weighing all of the factors, the Court stated:

> The victim spent a considerable period of time with her assailant, up to half an hour. She was with him under adequate artificial light in her house and under a full moon outdoors, and at least twice, once in the house and later in the woods, faced him directly and intimately. She was no casual observer, but rather the victim of one of the most personally humiliating of all crimes. Her description to the police, which included the assailant's approximate age, height, weight, complexion, skin texture, build, and voice * * * was more than ordinarily thorough. She had "no doubt" that [defendant] was the person who raped her. In the nature of crime, there are rarely witnesses to a rape other than the victim, who often has a limited opportunity of observation. The victim here, a practical nurse by profession, had an unusual opportunity to observe and identify her assailant. She testified [at one point in the proceedings] that there was something about his face "I don't think I could ever forget."

Id. at 382-383.

There was, of course, a lapse of seven months between the rape and the confrontation. According to the Court, "[t]his would be a seriously negative factor in most cases. Here, however, the testimony is undisputed that *the victim made no previous identification at any of the showups, lineups, or photographic showings. Her record for reliability was thus a good one, as she had previously resisted whatever suggestiveness inheres in a showup.*" *Id.* at 383. [Emphasis added.]

Accordingly, "[w]eighing all the factors, [the Court] find[s] no substantial likelihood of misidentification. The evidence was properly allowed to go to the jury." *Id.*

STOVALL v. DENNO
Supreme Court of the United States
388 *U.S.* 293, 87 *S.Ct.* 1967 (1967)

QUESTION: In the below set of circumstances, was the showup procedure performed by the police so unnecessarily suggestive that any identification made by the eyewitness must be deemed unreliable and therefore inadmissible at trial ?

CIRCUMSTANCES: Dr. Paul Behrendt was stabbed to death in the kitchen of his home at about midnight on the 23rd of August. His wife, also a physician, had followed her husband to the kitchen and jumped at the assailant who immediately knocked her to the floor and stabbed her 11 times. The police found a shirt on the kitchen floor and keys in a pocket which they traced to defendant Stovall. They arrested Stovall on the afternoon of August 24th.

On August 25th, the day after Mrs. Behrendt's surgery, the police arranged with her surgeon to permit them to bring Stovall to her hospital room for a showup. Stovall was handcuffed to one of five police officers who, with two members of the staff of the District Attorney, brought him to the hospital room. Stovall was the only black male in the room. "Mrs. Behrendt identified him from her hospital bed after being asked by an officer whether he 'was the man' and after [Stovall] repeated at the direction of the officer a 'few words for voice identification.' "

Mrs. Behrendt and the officers testified at the trial to her identification of Stovall in the hospital room, and Mrs. Behrendt also identified Stovall in the courtroom.

ANSWER: NO.   On the facts of this case Stovall "was not deprived of due process of law in violation of the Fourteenth Amendment." *Id.* at 1969.

RATIONALE: Using a well-recognized ground of attack upon his conviction, defendant asserts that the confrontation (showup) conducted in Mrs. Behrendt's hospital room "was so unnecessarily suggestive and conducive to irreparable mistaken identification that he was denied due process of law." *Id.* at 1972. *The United States Supreme Court disagreed.*

"The practice of showing suspects singly to persons for the purpose of identification, and not as part of a lineup, has been widely condemned. However, a claimed violation of due process of law in the conduct of a confrontation depends on the totality of the circumstances surrounding it, and the record in the present case reveals that the showing of Stovall to Mrs. Behrendt in an immediate hospital confrontation was imperative." *Id.* Accepting the reasoning of the court below, the Supreme Court reiterated:

"Here was the only person in the world who could possibly exonerate Stovall. Her words, and only her words, 'He is not the man' could have resulted in freedom for Stovall. The hospital was not far distant from the courthouse and jail. No one knew how long Mrs. Behrendt might live. Faced with the responsibility of identifying the attacker, with the need for immediate action and with the knowledge that Mrs. Behrendt could not visit the jail, the police followed the only feasible procedure and took Stovall to the hospital room. Under these circumstances, the usual police station line-up, which Stovall now argues he should have had, was out of the question."

Id. at 1972-73.

NOTE

1. *Transporting the suspect to the victim.* An officer conducting an investigative detention for eyewitness identification should use the least intrusive investigative techniques reasonably available to confirm or dispel his suspicions quickly. *See United States v. Sharpe*, 470 *U.S.* 675, 684-88, 105 *S.Ct.* 1568, 1574-76 (1985); *United States v. Place*, 462 *U.S.* 696, 709, 103 *S.Ct.* 2637, 2645 (1983); *Florida v. Royer*, 460 *U.S.* 491, 500, 103 *S.Ct.* 1319, 1325 (1983). This principle mandates that, in the absence of exigent circumstances or consent, the victim should be called or escorted to the place where the suspect is being detained for the showup. It contemplates probable cause that an offense has occurred and reasonable suspicion that the person to be detained was a criminal participant. Exigent circumstances may be shown where, for example, "the victim of an assault or other serious offense was injured or otherwise physically unable to be taken promptly to view the suspect, or a witness was [otherwise] incapacitated." *See People v. Harris*, 15 *Cal.*3d 384, 124 *Cal.Rptr.* 536, 540 *P.*2d 632 (1975). *See also State v. Mitchell*, 204 *Conn.* 187, 527 *A.*2d 1168 (1987) (transportation of sexual assault suspects to hospital for viewing by victim upheld as a "means of investigation that was likely to confirm or dispel their suspicions quickly"); *Buckingham v. State*, Del.Supr., 482 *A.*2d 327 (1984) (bringing robbery suspect back to the grocery store for identification upheld for it did not "unduly prolong the detention"). *Cf. State v. Salaam*, 225 *N.J.Super.* 66 (App.Div. 1988) (transportation of robbery suspect back to the victim, a convenience store cashier, within 30 minutes of the robbery, not an issue in the case).

2. *Inadvertent courtroom corridor encounters.* Accidental courtroom encounters are not unduly suggestive *per se*. For example, in *State v. Mance*, 300 *N.J.Super.* 37, 691 *A.*2d 1369 (App.Div. 1997), Captain Johnston of the New Jersey State Prison was waiting outside the courtroom to testify as to the events taking place at a prison riot. When the trial broke for lunch, the defendants, in shackles, were brought past him as they were being taken to eat. Johnston identified two defendants as the men who had attacked him on the morning of the prison riot. Earlier, Captain Johnston had been unable to identify his attackers through a photo array shown to him at the hospital, five days after the riot, at a time when he was heavily sedated. He did in-

dicate at that time, however, that if he saw his assailants in person, he believed he could identify them.

According to the court, "the exposure of the defendants to Johnston was 'inadvertent,' " and therefore, not "so suggestive as to result in a substantial likelihood of misidentification." *Id.*, 300 *N.J.Super.* at 58, 59. Significantly, at the time of the inadvertent confrontation, no one had said or done anything to influence Johnston's identifications. The court elaborated:

> Since the encounter in the courtroom corridor was inadvertent, *Wade* is not implicated even though defense counsel was absent. * * * Nor are such accidental courthouse encounters unduly suggestive *per se. See e.g., United States v. Colclough*, 549 *F.*2d 937, 941-42 (4th Cir. 1977). Here, seven shackled defendants passed by the witness. Although he obviously knew they were the defendants in this case, there was nothing to indicate which of them were the men who attacked him. Therefore, there was no suggestibility with regard to his specific identifications of two of the seven as his attackers.

Id. at 58-59.

§12.3(b). Lineups.

A pretrial confrontation for the purpose of identification may take place by means of an in-person "lineup" or "identification parade." The in-person lineup is normally conducted by the presentation of a group of at least five individuals, including the suspect, for an eyewitness' viewing. Each of the individuals in the lineup must be of the same race and sex, and should have similar physical appearances. In this respect, courts have not required a "substantial" degree of similarity; rather, "a reasonable effort to harmonize the lineup is normally all that is required."[1]

Recent research conducted by the National Institute of Justice (NIJ)[2] suggests that the nonsuspects in the lineup—the "fillers"—should be

---

[1] *See United States v. Lewis*, 547 *F.*2d 1030, 1035 (8th Cir. 1976) (police stations "are not theatrical casting offices"), *cert. denied*, 429 *U.S.* 1111, 97 *S.Ct.* 1149 (1977). *See also Herrera v. State*, 682 *S.W.*2d 313, 319 (Tex.Crim.App. 1984) ("While the better practice may be to get as many individuals as possible who fit the defendant's description, it is not essential that all the individuals be identical; 'neither due process nor common sense' requires such exactitude.") (citation omitted).

[2] In 1998, the NIJ convened the Technical Working Group for Eyewitness Evidence. The group consisted of law enforcement, legal, and psychological research professionals, who joined forces and shared information with the goal of developing improved procedures for collecting and preserving accurate and reliable eyewitness identification evidence. The findings of the Working Group were published in October 1999, in a document titled *Eyewitness Evidence: A Guide for Law Enforcement*. One key principle drawn from all the research was that the memory of an eyewitness should be viewed as "trace evidence," subject to possible contamination, and requiring "rigorous criteria for handling eyewitness evidence that are as demanding as those governing the handling of physical trace evidence." National Institute of Justice, *Eyewitness Evidence: A Guide for Law Enforcement* (1999), at 2.

chosen to match the eyewitness' description of the perpetrator rather than the features of an individual the police may have apprehended as the suspect in the case. Lineups created by selecting fillers that all look substantially like the suspect tend to be unfair to the suspect as well as the witness, particularly when the police are not entirely sure that the suspect is in fact the perpetrator. This process tends to narrow the universe of options for the witness, while also creating a subtle suggestion as to what the police think the suspect looks like. If, however, the witness is unable to provide an adequate description of the perpetrator, the fillers should resemble the suspect's significant features.

At no time should the lineup administrator inform a witness that the police "have a suspect" or that the perpetrator is in the lineup. Rather, the witness should be instructed that the actual suspect might not even be present in the lineup, and therefore the witness should not feel compelled to make a selection. The witness should understand that the lineup procedure is important not just to identify the guilty, but to clear the innocent as well. By informing the witness that the person who committed the crime *may or may not be in the lineup,* the police guard against a witness selecting an individual who looks *most like* the one who committed the crime, hoping that this will help move the investigation along, even if they are not certain, and even if the individual is not the actual perpetrator.

It is also a good practice to display the lineup participants one at a time—sequentially—rather than in a line at the same time. This process guards against the tendency of an eyewitness to compare one member of a lineup to another, making relative judgments as to which person looks most like the perpetrator. By viewing the lineup participants separately, rather than simultaneously, the witness is in a better position to make an identification by comparing each person to his or her own memory of the crime. This lessens the witness' opportunity to engage in a process of elimination, because there is no opportunity to simultaneously compare the relative appearance of all of the lineup participants.

Moreover, it is impermissible to allow more than one witness to view the lineup at the same time; and it is also impermissible for a witness to know that a suspect in the lineup has already been identified by another witness at a previous viewing. If a witness identifies an individual in the lineup, the police should not indicate to the witness that he or she "picked the right person," or that the witness' identification "was correct" or "very helpful," or that the police "also think that the right person has been selected." The danger of making such suggestive comments lies in the fact that the opinion of the police that the individual identified by the eyewitness is, in fact, the perpetrator of the crime creates a risk that any future identifications that may need to be made by the witness would be unduly influenced by the official "stamp of approval." In this regard, the witness should be assured that the investigation will continue, whether or not the witness is able to identify anyone as the actual perpetrator.

To further enhance the reliability of the procedure, the lineup should be administered by an officer who does not know which lineup member is the suspect. This "blind" assignment technique helps avoid any inadvertent body signals or cues which may adversely impact a witness' ability to make a reliable identification. Even when unintended, verbal or nonverbal cues are sometimes given to witnesses when the identity of the actual suspect is known to the officer conducting the procedure.

As with other identification procedures, the lineup must be carefully documented, regardless of whether an identification is made. As a final precaution, the in-person lineup should be photographed or videotaped in case it becomes necessary at a future proceeding to examine or recreate the lineup.

UNITED STATES v. WADE
Supreme Court of the United States
388 *U.S.* 218, 87 *S.Ct.* 1926 (1967)

QUESTION: Is a *post-indictment*, pretrial lineup at which the accused is exhibited to identifying witnesses a "critical stage" of the criminal prosecution at which the accused has the right to the assistance of counsel?

ANSWER: YES. A *post-indictment*, pretrial lineup at which the accused is exhibited to identifying witnesses is a "critical stage" of the prosecution; the police conduct of such a lineup without notice to and in the absence of his counsel denies the accused his Sixth Amendment right to counsel and seriously calls into question the admissibility at trial of any subsequent in-court identification of the accused by witnesses who attended the lineup. *Id.* at 1937. At trial, no evidence of an eyewitness' identification which flows from an uncounseled post-indictment lineup may be admitted. The absence of counsel at the lineup does not, however, automatically mean that no in-court identification will be permitted. In these circumstances, the Government has an opportunity to establish by clear and convincing evidence, at a pretrial hearing, that the prospective in-court identification will be "based upon observations of the suspect other than the lineup identification." *Id.* at 1939. If the Government is successful, courtroom identification is permissible. *Id.* at 1939, 1940.

RATIONALE: The Sixth Amendment guarantees an accused the right to the assistance of counsel for his defense; and since *Powell v. Alabama*, 287 *U.S.* 45, 53 *S.Ct.* 55 (1964), the Court has "recognized that the period from arraignment to trial [is] 'perhaps *the most critical period of the [criminal] proceedings'* * * * during which the accused 'requires the guiding hand of counsel,' * * * if the guarantee is not to prove [to be] an empty right." *Wade* at 1931 (quoting *Powell* at 57, 69, 53 *S.Ct.* at 59, 64). [Emphasis added.] That principle has since been applied to require the assistance of counsel at an arraignment or similar proceeding, or at other *critical* pretrial confrontations which, as the trial itself, "operates to assure that the accused's interests will be protected consistently with our adversary theory of criminal prosecution." *Id.* at 1932.

"A major factor contributing to the high incidence of miscarriage of justice from mistaken identification has been the degree of suggestion inherent in the manner in which the prosecution presents the suspect to witnesses for pretrial identification. * * * Suggestion can be created intentionally or unintentionally in many subtle ways. And the dangers for the suspect are particularly grave when the witness' opportunity for observation was insubstantial, and thus his susceptibility to suggestion the greatest." *Id.* at 1933.

"Moreover, '[i]t is a matter of common experience that, once a witness has picked out the accused at the lineup, he is not likely to go back on his word later on, so that in practice the issue of identity may (in the absence of other relevant evidence) for all practical purposes be determined there and then, before the trial.'" *Id.* [Citation omitted.]

"Since it appears that there is grave potential for prejudice, intentional or not, in the pretrial lineup, which may not be capable of reconstruction at trial, and since presence of counsel itself can often avert prejudice and assure a meaningful confrontation at trial, there can be little doubt that [a] * * * post-indictment lineup [is] a critical stage of the prosecution at which [an accused is entitled to the assistance of counsel]." *Id.* at 1937. In this case, "both Wade and his counsel should have been notified of the impending lineup, and counsel's presence should have been a requisite to conduct of the lineup, absent an 'intelligent waiver.'" *Id.*

According to the Court, requiring counsel at a post-indictment lineup will not impede legitimate law enforcement; "on the contrary, * * * law enforcement may be assisted by preventing the infiltration of taint in the prosecution's identification evidence. That result cannot help the guilty avoid conviction but can only help assure that the right man has been brought to justice." *Id.* at 1938.

In this case, Wade moved to strike the in-court identification by the witnesses because of the absence of counsel at the pretrial lineup. This disposition, stated the Court, cannot "be justified without first giving the Government the opportunity to establish by clear and convincing evidence that the in-court identifications were based upon observations of the suspect other than the lineup identification. * * * Where, as here, the admissibility of evidence of the lineup identification itself is not involved, a *per se* rule of exclusion of courtroom identification would be unjustified." *Id.* at 1939. Quoting *Wong Sun v. United States*, 371 *U.S.* 471, 488, 83 *S.Ct.* 407, 417 (1963), the Court held that "the proper test to be applied in these situations" is: "'[W]hether, granting establishment of the primary illegality, the evidence to which [] objection is made has been come at by exploitation of that illegality or instead by means sufficiently distinguishable to be purged of the primary taint.'" *Wade* at 1939.

"Application of this test * * * requires consideration of various factors; for example, the prior opportunity to observe the alleged criminal act, the existence of any discrepancy between any pre-lineup description and the defendant's actual description, any identification prior to lineup of another person, the identification by picture of the defendant prior to the lineup, failure to identify the defendant on a prior occasion, and the lapse of time between the alleged act and the lineup identification. It is also relevant to consider those facts which, despite the absence of counsel, are disclosed concerning the conduct of the lineup." *Id.* at 1940.

As a result, Wade's conviction was vacated and the case remanded to provide the Government an opportunity to establish at a hearing that the in-court identification had a separate and independent source, *i.e.*, a basis unrelated to the improper out-of-court lineup.

NOTE

1. *The Wade hearing.* When a defendant presents "some evidence of impermissible suggestiveness" in the identification process, a *"Wade hearing"* should be conducted by the trial court. At the hearing, the first issue to be decided is whether the procedure utilized by the police was in fact "impermissibly suggestive." However, suggestiveness alone is not fatal. If suggestiveness is found, the second issue to be decided is whether the objectionable procedure resulted in a "very substantial likelihood of irreparable misidentification." The essence of the second inquiry is reliability, that is, whether the identification was prompted by the eyewitness' own recollection of the crime or by the suggestive manner in which the identification procedure was conducted.

2. *Pre-indictment identification procedures.* The Court, in *United States v. Wade*, made clear that a post-indictment, pretrial lineup at which the accused is exhibited to an identifying witness is a "critical stage" of the criminal prosecution. Police conduct of such a lineup, without notice to, and in the absence of, the accused's attorney violates the accused's right to counsel and calls into question the admissibility at trial of the in-court identification of the accused by the witness who attended the lineup. In *Gilbert v. California*, 388 *U.S.* 263, 87 *S.Ct.* 1951 (1967), the Court further emphasized that no in-court identification will be admissible in evidence if its "source" is a lineup conducted in violation of the *Wade* constitutional standard. This acts as a *per se* rule of exclusion "to assure that law enforcement authorities will respect the accused's constitutional right to the presence of counsel at the critical lineup." *Gilbert* at 273, 87 *S.Ct.* at 1957.

In *Kirby v. Illinois*, 406 *U.S.* 682, 92 *S.Ct.* 1877 (1972), the defendant argued that the *Wade-Gilbert per se* exclusionary rule should be extended "to identification testimony based upon a police station showup that took place *before* the defendant had been indicted or otherwise formally charged with any criminal offense." *Id.* at 684, 92 *S.Ct.* at 1879. [Court's emphasis.]

During an investigative detention conducted by Chicago police officers, Kirby was found to be in possession of three traveler's checks and a Social Security card, all bearing the name of Willie Shard, a victim of a robbery that had been perpetrated the day before. Kirby was taken to the police station and a police cruiser was dispatched to locate and bring the robbery victim to the station. Immediately upon entering the room in the police station where Kirby was seated, Shard positively identified him as the robber. No lawyer was present in the room, nor had Kirby asked for legal assistance, or been advised of any right to the presence of counsel.

Finding no constitutional violation, the Court explained that the *Wade-Gilbert* exclusionary rule stems from the constitutional guarantee of the right to counsel contained in the Sixth and Fourteenth Amendments, which "attaches only at or after the time that adversary judicial proceedings have been initiated against" the accused, "by way of formal charge, preliminary hearing, indictment, information, or arraignment." *Id.*, 92 *S.Ct.* at 1881, 1882. "The initiation of judicial criminal proceedings * * * marks the commencement of the 'criminal prosecutions' to which alone the explicit guarantees of the Sixth Amendment are applicable." *Id.*

Accordingly, the Court refused to inject

> into a routine police investigation an absolute constitutional guarantee historically and rationally applicable only after the onset of formal prosecutorial proceedings. * * * "[A]n accused is entitled to counsel at any 'critical stage of the *prosecution*,' and [] a post-indictment lineup is such a 'critical stage.'" [This Court] decline[s] to depart from that rationale today by imposing a *per se* exclusionary rule upon testimony concerning an identification that took place long before the commencement of any prosecution whatever.

Id. at 1882-83. [Court's emphasis.]

3. *Voice exemplars for identification purposes.* In *Burnett v. Collins*, 982 *F.*2d 922 (5th Cir. 1993), the court rejected Burnett's contention that "his compelled voice exemplar before the jury was a violation of his Fifth Amendment rights because he was required to repeat the exact words of the armed robber, even though he chose not to testify during trial." *Id.* at 925. The court explained that the Fifth Amendment privilege against self-incrimination "protects a defendant from being compelled to provide information against himself, *of a testimonial or communicative nature.* * * * It does not protect him from being compelled to produce real or physical evidence." *Id.* [Court's emphasis.] "A voice exemplar does not violate one's Fifth Amendment privilege against self-incrimination because the exemplar is merely a source of physical evidence." *Id.*

For identification purposes, a voice exemplar may even consist of the exact words spoken at the time of the crime. *See e.g., United States v. Wade, supra*, 388 *U.S.* at 220, 222-23, 87 *S.Ct.* at 1929, 1930 (requiring the defendant to repeat the words, "put the money in the bag," was not a compulsion to utter statements of a "testimonial" nature; defendant was merely "required to use his voice as an identifying characteristic, not to speak his guilt"); *Burnett v. Collins, supra* at 924 n.1, 927 (requiring Burnett to repeat before the jury the words, "open the register," "lay down on the floor," "you f...ing whores, I'll be back, I'll be back," and "don't touch the bat," did not violate his Fifth Amendment privilege against self-incrimination); *United States v. Domina*, 784 *F.*2d 1361, 1371 (9th Cir. 1986) (requiring defendant to repeat before the jury the words, "Ladies, this is a holdup" and "Put all the money in the bag," found not to be unduly prejudicial); *United States v. Brown*, 644 *F.*2d 101, 103 (2nd Cir. 1981) (requiring defendant to repeat before the jury the words, "Give me your money or I am going to blow you up," found appropriate). *See also United States v. Williams*, 704 *F.*2d 315 (6th Cir. 1983) (requiring defendant to read a neutral passage from *Time Magazine* to allow jury to hear his voice found appropriate).

FOSTER v. CALIFORNIA
Supreme Court of the United States
394 *U.S.* 440, 89 *S.Ct.* 1127 (1969)

QUESTION: Did the lineup procedure conducted by the police in the below set of circumstances violate defendant's rights under the Due Process Clause of the Fourteenth Amendment?

CIRCUMSTANCES: The day after an armed robbery of a Western Union office, one of the robbers, Clay, surrendered to the police and implicated Foster and Grice. According to Clay, he and Foster entered and robbed the Western Union office while Grice waited in a nearby car. Except for the robbers themselves, the only witness to the crime was the late-night manager of the Western Union office, Joseph David. David was called to the police station to view a police lineup. "There were three men in the lineup. One was [Foster]. He is a tall man—close to six feet in height. The other two men were short—five feet, five or six inches. [Foster] wore a leather jacket which David said was similar to the one he had seen underneath the coveralls worn by the robber."

After viewing the lineup, David could not positively identify Foster as the robber. He "thought" he was the man, but he was not sure. David then asked to speak to Foster. Shortly thereafter, Foster was brought into an office and sat across from David at a table. Except for the law enforcement officials, there was no one else in the room. Even after this one-to-one confrontation, David still was uncertain whether Foster was one of the robbers.

About a week to ten days later, the police called David and asked him to come to the police department to view a second lineup. There were five men in the lineup, including Foster, who was the only person in this second lineup who had appeared in the first lineup. This time, David was "convinced" that Foster "was the man."

At trial, David testified to his identification of Foster as summarized above. He also made an in-court identification of him. Foster was convicted.

ANSWER: YES. Under the totality of the circumstances, the identification procedures conducted by the police in this case were " 'so unnecessarily suggestive and conducive to irreparable mistaken identification,' " that the resulting identification is constitutionally defective as a matter of law. *Id.* at 1128, 1128 n.2. [Citations omitted.]

RATIONALE: "[I]n some cases the procedures leading to an eyewitness identification may be so defective as to make the identification constitutionally inadmissible as a matter of law." *Id.* at 1128 n.2. This case "presents a compelling example of [such an] unfair lineup procedure[]." *Id.* at 1128.

In the first lineup arranged by the police, Foster "stood out from the other two men by the contrast of his height and by the fact that he was wearing a leather jacket similar to that worn by the robber. * * * When this did not lead to positive identification, the police permitted a one-to-one confrontation between [Foster] and the witness. * * * Even after this, the witness' identification of [Foster] was tentative. So some days later another lineup was arranged. [Foster] was the only person in this lineup who had also participated in the first lineup. * * * This finally produced a definite identification." *Id.* at 1128-1129.

"The suggestive elements in this identification procedure made it all but inevitable that David would identify [Foster] whether or not he was in fact 'the man.' * * * In effect, the police repeatedly said to the witness, 'This is the man.' " *Id.* at 1129. It is clear, therefore, that "the pretrial confrontations" were "so arranged as to make the resulting identifications virtually inevitable." *Id.* "This procedure so undermined the reliability of the eyewitness identification as to violate due process of law." *Id.*

NOTE

1. *Group viewings prohibited.* In *Gilbert v. California*, 388 *U.S.* 263, 87 *S.Ct.* 1951 (1967), Gilbert was identified by eyewitnesses in a Los Angeles auditorium. Between ten and thirteen prisoners were placed on the auditorium's stage behind bright lights which prevented those in the line from seeing the audience. "Upwards of 100 persons were in the audience, each an eyewitness to one of the several robberies charged to Gilbert." *Id.*, 87 *S.Ct.* at 1955. "State and federal officers were also present and one of them acted as 'moderator' of the proceedings." *Id.* at 1955 n.2. "Each man in the lineup was identified by number, but not by name. Each man was required to step forward into a marked circle, to turn, presenting both profiles as well as a face and back view, to walk, to put on or take off certain articles of clothing. When a man's number was called and he was directed to step into the circle, he was asked certain questions: where he was picked up, whether he owned a car, whether, when arrested, he was armed, where he lived. Each was also asked to repeat certain phrases, both in a loud and in a soft voice, phrases that witnesses to the crimes had heard the robbers use: 'Freeze, this is a stickup'; 'this is a holdup'; 'empty your cash drawer'; 'this is a heist'; 'don't anybody move.' * * * [T]he assembled witnesses were asked if there were any that they would like to see again, and told that if they had doubts, now was the time to resolve them. Several gave the numbers of men they wanted to see, including Gilbert's. * * * After the lineup, the witnesses talked to each other[, and] in each other's presence, call[ed] out the number of [each man] they could identify." *Id.* Gilbert's number was called by eleven witnesses.

Almost without discussion, the Court held the conduct of the auditorium identification wholly "illegal," and any evidence of the procedure clearly inadmissible. *Id.* at 1956-1957.

2. *Significant age differences.* In *Swicegood v. State of Alabama*, 577 *F.*2d 1322 (5th Cir. 1978), Birmingham police arranged an in-person lineup consisting of six white males, including defendant Swicegood. All participants were dressed in "street clothes," their height ranged from 5'7" to 5'11" and weight from 125 to 150 pounds. Some had moustaches and some did not, and their hair color varied. All of the men in the lineup were 26 years of age or younger, except Swicegood, who was 35 at the time. After a second viewing, both strong-armed robbery victims identified Swicegood. Significantly, the identification occurred after the men in the lineup were directed to speak the phrases uttered by the intruders on the night of the robbery.

With respect to the difference in age, the court stated:

> First, there was a considerable difference in the ages of the lineup participants, with Swicegood being nine years older than the next-oldest man and 15 years older than the youngest. Although age generally manifests itself in appearance-related characteristics and courts often treat age as a physical attribute, * * * we think it should be treated as an independent element in this case. A person's age, for example, often has a decided effect on his vernacular, speech patterns, or voice characteristics, and both Mr. and Mrs. Carter identified Swicegood on the basis of his voice. * * * Further, a significant disparity in the ages of the lineup participants could influence a witness who believed that the culprit was an "older" person. Thus, a lineup with only one "older" person could impermissibly point the finger at that individual, albeit in a much more subtle fashion than in other situations.

Id. at 1327.

---

§12.4. Photo arrays.

Ideally, photographic arrays should be prepared, exhibited, and preserved by means of a standard procedure which demonstrates reliability and the absence of undue suggestiveness. In addition to the photograph of the suspect, at least five additional photographs are normally incorporated, producing an array of six. The photographs chosen for the array should depict individuals of the same race and sex, and having reasonably similar physical characteristics. Care should be exercised to avoid significant age differences, facial hair differences, and significant height differences, with particular attention given to the absence or presence of mustaches, eyeglasses, wild haircuts, closed eyes, etc.

Recent research conducted by the National Institute of Justice (NIJ)[3] suggests that the nonsuspects in the photo array—the "fillers"—should be chosen to match the eyewitness' description of the perpetrator rather than the features of an individual the police may have apprehended as the suspect in the case. Lineups created by selecting fillers that all look substantially like the suspect tend to be unfair to the suspect as well as the witness, particularly when the police are not entirely sure that the suspect is in fact the perpetrator. This process tends to narrow the universe of options for the witness, while also creating a subtle suggestion as to what the police think the suspect looks like. If, however, the witness is unable to provide an adequate description of the perpetrator, the fillers should resemble the suspect's significant features.

With respect to the type of photograph used, black and white pictures should not be mixed with color photographs, and "mugshots" should not be mixed with "snapshots." If one or more of the photographs portray some type of identifying information—either on the front or the back—the printed material should be covered to prevent sending an inappropriate suggestion to a witness. Moreover, if it becomes necessary to partially cover one photograph to eliminate printed material, all the photographs in the array should be treated similarly, regardless of whether they do or do not have identifying material on them. The photographs in the array are then numbered in sequence and the entire procedure is meticulously documented.

At no time should police inform a witness that the perpetrator's picture is in the photo lineup. Rather, the witness should be instructed that the actual suspect might not even be present in the array, and therefore the witness should not feel compelled to make a selection. The witness should understand that the photo lineup procedure is important not just to identify the guilty, but to clear the innocent as well. By informing the witness that the person who committed the crime may or may not be in the photo lineup, the police guard against a witness selecting an individual who looks *most like* the one who committed the crime, hoping that this will help move the investigation along, even if he or she is not certain.

It is also a good practice to display the photographs one at a time—sequentially—rather than simultaneously. This process guards against the tendency of an eyewitness to compare one photo to another, making relative judgments as to which person looks most like the perpetrator. By viewing the photographs separately, rather than simultaneously, the witness is in a better position to make an identification by comparing

---

[3] In 1998, the NIJ convened the Technical Working Group for Eyewitness Evidence. The group consisted of law enforcement, legal, and psychological research professionals, who joined forces and shared information with the goal of developing improved procedures for collecting and preserving accurate and reliable eyewitness identification evidence. The findings of the Working Group were published in October 1999, in a document titled *Eyewitness Evidence: A Guide for Law Enforcement*. One key principle drawn from all the research was that the memory of an eyewitness should be viewed as "trace evidence," subject to possible contamination, and requiring "rigorous criteria for handling eyewitness evidence that are as demanding as those governing the handling of physical trace evidence." National Institute of Justice, *Eyewitness Evidence: A Guide for Law Enforcement* (1999), at 2.

each person to his or her own memory of the crime. This lessens the witness' opportunity to engage in a process of elimination, because there is no opportunity to simultaneously compare the relative appearance of all of the photographs in the array.

As in the case of the in-person lineup, only one witness at a time may view the photo array, and at no time should an officer suggest to the witness which photograph to pick. It is also highly inappropriate for an officer to even suggest that the perpetrator's photograph may be in the array or that someone else has already identified one of the individuals portrayed in the array as the perpetrator. If a witness identifies an individual in the photo lineup, the police should not indicate to the witness that he or she "picked the right person," selected the "right photograph," or that the witness' identification "was correct" or "very helpful," or that the police "also think that the right person has been selected." Here, again, the danger of making such suggestive comments lies in the fact that the opinion of the police that the individual identified by the eyewitness is, in fact, the perpetrator creates a risk that any future identifications that may need to be made by the witness would be unduly influenced by the official "stamp of approval." In this regard, the witness should be assured that the investigation will continue, whether or not the witness is able to identify anyone as the actual perpetrator.

To further enhance the reliability of the procedure, the photo lineup should be administered by an officer who does not know which photograph depicts the suspect. This "blind" assignment technique helps avoid any inadvertent body signals or cues which may adversely impact a witness' ability to make a reliable identification. Even when unintended, verbal or nonverbal cues are sometimes given to witnesses when the identity of the actual suspect is known to the officer conducting the photo lineup procedure.

As with other identification procedures, the photo lineup must be carefully documented, regardless of whether an identification is made. The presentation order of the photo lineup should be preserved, and the photographs themselves should be preserved in their original condition.

While the procedures appear to be clear, problems nonetheless arise in the preparation (creation), exhibition, or preservation of investigative photographic arrays.

SIMMONS v. UNITED STATES
Supreme Court of the United States
390 *U.S.* 377, 88 *S.Ct.* 967 (1968)

QUESTION: What standard will a court use to determine whether a criminal defendant's conviction should be set aside because of the improper use of a photographic array ?

ANSWER: Proceeding on a case-by-case basis, "convictions based on eyewitness identification at trial following a pretrial identification by photograph will be set aside on that ground only if the photographic identification procedure was so *impermissibly suggestive* as to give rise to a *very substantial likelihood of irreparable misidentification.*" *Id.* at 971. [Emphasis added.]

RATIONALE: "[I]mproper employment of photographs by police may sometimes cause witnesses to err in identifying criminals. A witness may have obtained only a brief glimpse of a criminal, or may have seen him under poor conditions. Even if the police subsequently follow the most correct photographic identification procedures and show him the pictures of a number of individuals without indicating whom they suspect, there is some danger that the witness may make an incorrect identification. This danger will be increased if the police display to the witness only the picture of a single individual who generally resembles the person he saw, or if they show him the pictures of several persons among which the photograph of a single individual recurs or is in some way emphasized." *Id.*

"The chance of misidentification is also heightened if the police indicate to the witness that they have other evidence that one of the persons pictured committed the crime. Regardless of how the initial misidentification comes about, the witness thereafter is apt to retain in his memory the image of the photograph rather than of the person actually seen, reducing the trustworthiness of subsequent lineup or courtroom identification." *Id.*

"Despite the hazards of initial identification by photograph, this procedure has been used widely and effectively in criminal law enforcement, from the standpoint both of apprehending offenders and of sparing innocent suspects the [stigma] of arrest by allowing eyewitnesses to exonerate them through scrutiny of photographs." *Id.* As a result, the Court is "unwilling to prohibit its employment, either in the exercise of [its] supervisory power or, still less, as a matter of constitutional requirement. Instead, * * * each case must be considered on its own facts, and [] convictions based on eyewitness identification at trial following a pretrial identification by photograph will be set aside on that ground only if the photographic identification procedure was so impermissibly suggestive as to give rise to a very substantial likelihood of irreparable misidentification." *Id.*

NOTE

1. *Improper notations attached to the photographs.* During the course of defendant's trial in *State v. Onysko,* 226 *N.J.Super.* 599 (App.Div. 1988), the State introduced into evidence a photographic line-up which included a photograph of defendant. The photograph was a mug shot which on the reverse side contained the following information:

MAHWAH POLICE DEPT.
Mahwah, N.J.

NAME	ROBERT J. ONYSKO	
ALIAS	Timothy Eggers	
CRIME	Violation of Probation	
AGE	39	HEIGHT 5'10"
WEIGHT	170	BUILD thin
HAIR	brown	EYES brown
COMP	Superior Ct. Bergen County	
BORN	Jersey City 4/25/46	
OCCUP.	burglar	
DATE OF ARREST	7/31/85	
OFFICER	McGill	
REMARKS		

Id. at 601-602. After the trial, in which defendant elected not to testify, it was learned that at least one juror had read the information appearing on the reverse side of defendant's photograph. In the appeal which thereafter followed, the Superior Court, Appellate Division granted defendant a new trial. The court agreed with defendant that the information disclosed improperly "characterized him as a professional burglar by listing his occupation as 'burglar,' and that the use of an alias reflected the magnitude of his criminal propensities." *Id.* at 605. According to the court, "[i]njection of his prior use of aliases and that he is characterized by the police as having an occupation as a 'burglar' clearly reveals to the jury precisely that, that he is a 'burglar' and thus guilty of the offense charged." *Id.* The officers in this case should have made some effort to at least cover the information on the back of defendant's photograph. *Id.* at 603.

2. *The number of photographs used.* Courts have recognized that the size of the photo array, in terms of the number of photographs in it, is a factor in determining the array's constitutionality. *United States v. Sanchez,* 24 *F.*3d 1259, 1262 (10th Cir. 1994). *See e.g., United States v. Rosa,* 11 *F.*3d 315, 330 (2nd Cir. 1993) (six pictures upheld); *United States v. Bennett,* 409 *F.*2d 888, 898 (2nd Cir. 1969) (*same*). *See also United States v. Smith,* 551 *F.*2d 348, 355 n.13 (D.C.Cir. 1976) (noting that photo arrays in England usually contain at least eight photographs and the range is fifteen to twenty photographs in France). The courts have been less than clear, however, as to the extent to which the size of an array impacts on the inquiry into whether the array is impermissibly suggestive.

In *United States v. Sanchez, supra,* the court held that "the number of photographs in an array is not itself a substantive factor, but instead is a factor that merely affects the *weight* given to other alleged problems or irregularities in an array." *Id.* at 1262. [Court's emphasis.] The court suggested that

> [t]he larger the number of pictures used in an array, the less likely it is that a minor difference, such as background color or texture, will have a prejudicial effect on selection. In such a case, the differences become diluted and less obvious among the large number of images, each of which are likely to contain some sort of minor idiosyncratic aberration. * * * This is not to say that one color picture cannot stand out in an array of one thousand black and white pictures, but on the whole, minor irregularities will be less noticeable as the number of photographs increase.
>
> Conversely, when a relatively low number of photographs are used in an array, minor differences such as background color can make a picture stand out, and can act to repeatedly draw a witness's eyes to that picture. Common sense dictates that slight irregularities are more likely to "jump out" at a witness reviewing a single sheet of paper with only six photographs on it than at a witness reviewing a large mug book containing hundreds of pictures. Upon continued inspection, the witness may begin to believe that the "oddball" picture was taken under different circumstances than the others. This fact can suggest a number of things to a witness, the most dangerous of which is that the similar pictures were taken together to form a pool or control group, and that the one picture that stands out is the suspect. Thus, the number of pictures in an array relates to a fixed point on a sliding scale that can be used to determine the effect that irregularities in a picture may have had on its viewer. The lower the number of photographs used by officers in a photo array, the closer the array must be scrutinized for suggestive irregularities.

Id. at 1262-63.

In applying the above analysis, the *Sanchez* court concluded that, under the circumstances of the case, the six-picture photo array shown to the eyewitnesses was not impermissibly suggestive, notwithstanding the fact that defendant was the only man pictured in the photo array with his eyes closed. *Id.* at 1263.

3. Officer's testimony describing defendant's photograph as a "mug shot." At trial, it is improper for a witness to refer to the photo array as a group of "mug shots," or accentuate the fact that the defendant's photograph is a mug shot. "Identification of photos of a defendant as mug shots has resulted in reversal of convictions on appeal because they imply [that the defendant has] a criminal history." *State v. Cribb,* 281 *N.J.Super.* 156, 160, 656 *A.*2d 1279 (App.Div. 1995). *See also United States v. Torres-Flores,* 827 *F.*2d 1031, 1035-39 (5th Cir. 1987); *Barnes v. United States,* 365 *F.*2d 509, 512 (D.C.Cir. 1966). Even a fleeting reference to a mug shot by a witness would require the trial court to give the jury a "curative instruction."

Where identification is at issue, mug shots may be admissible. But they must be presented in an impartial and neutral manner. Testifying officers should, therefore, refrain from characterizing photo arrays as "mug shots," "mug books," photographs from a "police file," photographs from "our gallery," or any other type of reference that would reasonably suggest to the jury that the photographs were obtained as a result of the defendant's prior criminal activity. Testimony that refers to these arrays merely as "photographs" has been consistently interpreted as neutral, and upheld as proper.

MANSON v. BRATHWAITE
Supreme Court of the United States
432 U.S. 98, 97 S.Ct. 2243 (1977)

QUESTION: Should evidence of a photographic identification automatically be excluded from evidence, regardless of "reliability," when the identification procedure consists of a police officer's examination of a single photograph after an undercover buy of narcotics ?

ANSWER: NO. Although in this case the police procedure of examining a single photograph "was both suggestive and unnecessary," *id.* at 2245, the " 'central question' " is " 'whether under the "totality of the circumstances" the identification was reliable even though the confrontation procedure was suggestive.' " *Id.* at 2249. [Citation omitted.] "The admission of testimony concerning a suggestive and unnecessary identification procedure does not violate due process so long as the identification possesses sufficient aspects of reliability." *Id.* In fact, *"reliability is the linchpin in determining the admissibility of identification testimony[.]" Id.* at 2253. [Emphasis added.]

RATIONALE: At about 7:45 p.m. on May 5, Trooper Glover of the Connecticut State Police Narcotics Division, accompanied by Henry Brown, an informant, went to an apartment building at 201 Westland, in Hartford, for the purpose of purchasing narcotics from "Dickie Boy" Cicero, a known narcotics dealer. Glover and Brown were both wearing ordinary street clothes. Upon arrival at the apartment building, Glover and Brown walked up the stairs and knocked on the door of one of the third-floor apartments where it was believed that Cicero was living. The area outside the apartment was illuminated by natural light from a window in the third floor hallway. In response to Glover's knock, the door opened 12 to 18 inches, and Glover observed a man standing at the door and, behind him, a woman. Brown identified himself and Glover asked for "two things" of narcotics. "The man at the door held out his hand, and Glover gave him two $10 bills. The door closed. Soon the man returned and handed Glover two glassine bags. While the door was open, Glover stood within two feet of the person from whom he made the purchase and observed his face. Five to seven minutes elapsed from the time the door first opened until it closed the second time." *Id.* at 2246. The seller was not Cicero.

Within approximately eight minutes of their arrival, Glover and Brown left the building. Glover drove to headquarters, where he described the seller to two other investigators. At the time, Glover did not know the identity of the seller. He described him as a black male, about five feet eleven inches tall, heavy build, dark complexion, black hair cut in a short Afro, and having high cheekbones. At the time of the sale, the suspect was wearing blue pants and a plaid shirt. One of the other investigators, suspecting that defendant, Nowell Brathwaite, was the seller, obtained a photograph of Brathwaite from the Records Division of the Hartford Police Department. The photograph was left at Glover's office. On May 7, while alone, Glover viewed the photograph; "he identified the person shown as the one from whom he had purchased the narcotics." *Id.*

Subsequently, Brathwaite was arrested at the apartment at which the narcotics sale had taken place. At his trial for the possession and sale of heroin, the photograph from which Glover had identified Brathwaite was received in evidence. Glover also testified that, although he had not seen Brathwaite in the eight months that had elapsed since the sale, "there [was] no doubt whatsoever" in his mind that the person in the photograph was Brathwaite. *Id.* at 2247. Glover also made a positive in-court identification. "No explanation was offered by the prosecution for the failure to utilize a photographic array or to conduct a lineup." *Id.* Brathwaite was convicted on both counts and the Connecticut Supreme Court affirmed.

Fourteen months later, Brathwaite brought a petition for habeas corpus in federal court, contending that "the admission of the identification testimony at his state trial deprived him of due process of law to which he was entitled under the Fourteenth Amendment." *Id.* Though the petition was unsuccessful at the District Court level, the Second Circuit Court of Appeals agreed with Brathwaite and held that "evidence as to the photograph should have been excluded, regardless of reliability, because the examination of the single photograph was unnecessary and suggestive." *Id. The United States Supreme Court disagreed and reversed.*

Although in this case the police procedure of examining a single photograph "was both suggestive [because only one photograph was used] and unnecessary" [because there was no emergency or exigent circumstance], *id.* at 2245, 2250, the " 'central question' " is " 'whether under the "totality of the circumstances" the identification was reliable even though the confrontation procedure was suggestive.' " *Id.* at 2249. [Citation omitted.] "The admission of testimony concerning a suggestive and unnecessary identification procedure does not violate due process so long as the identification possesses sufficient aspects of reliability." *Id.*

The standard, as required by the Due Process Clause of the Fourteenth Amendment, "is that of fairness," *id.* at 2252, and for determining the admissibility of eyewitness identification testimony, "reliability is the linchpin[.]" *Id.* at 2253. To determine whether an eyewitness identification is reliable, several factors may be considered: (1) "the opportunity of the witness to view the criminal at the time of the crime," (2) "the witness' degree of attention," (3) "the accuracy of his prior description of the criminal," (4) "the level of certainty demonstrated at the confrontation," and (5) "the time between the crime and the confrontation." *Id.* "Against these factors is to be weighed the corrupting effect of the suggestive identification itself." *Id.*

Applying the above criteria to the facts of this case:

1. *The opportunity of the witness to view.* Glover testified that for two to three minutes he stood at the apartment door, within two feet of Brathwaite. The door opened twice, and each time Brathwaite stood at the door Glover looked directly at him. Natural light from outside entered the hallway through a window, as well as from inside the apartment. *Id.* at 2253.

2. *The witness' degree of attention.* Glover was not a casual or passing observer; he was a trained police officer on duty, engaged in a specialized and dangerous undercover buy of narcotics. "As a specially trained, assigned, and experienced officer, he could be expected to pay scrupulous attention to detail, for he knew that subsequently he would have to find and arrest his vendor. In addition, he knew that his claimed observations would be subject later to close scrutiny and examination at any trial." *Id.* Additionally, Trooper Glover was of the same race as Brathwaite and was therefore able to perceive more than mere "general features." *Id.*

3. *The accuracy of the description.* Within minutes of the undercover buy of narcotics, Glover described Brathwaite's race, height, build, color and style of hair, and the high cheekbone facial features. The description also included the clothing Brathwaite was wearing. No claim is made that the description did not match Brathwaite's, and significantly, another investigator was able to call for Brathwaite's picture from Glover's description. *Id.*

4. *The witness' level of certainty.* "There is no dispute that the photograph in question was that of [Brathwaite]. Glover, in response to a question whether the photograph was that of the person from whom he made the purchase, testified: 'There is no question whatsoever.'" *Id.*

5. *The time between the crime and the confrontation.* Within minutes of the crime, Glover gave a description of Brathwaite to a second investigator. "The photographic identification took place only two days later. We do not have here the passage of weeks or months between the crime and the viewing of the photograph." *Id.* at 2253-2254.

"These indicators of Glover's ability to make an accurate identification are hardly outweighed by the corrupting effect of the challenged identification itself. Although identifications arising from single-photograph displays may be viewed in general with suspicion, * * * [the Court finds in this] case little pressure on the witness to acquiesce in the suggestion that such a display entails. * * * And since Glover examined the photograph alone, there was no coercive pressure to make an identification arising from the presence of another. The identification was made in circumstances allowing care and reflection." *Id.* at 2254.

Accordingly, the totality of the circumstances of this case do not present a "very substantial likelihood of irreparable misidentification." *Id.* The criteria or factors for determining the admissibility of an eyewitness' identification set forth above have been "satisfactorily met and complied with here." *Id.*

NOTE

1. *Officer's "post-buy" viewing of suspect's photograph.* The Court in *Manson v. Brathwaite* instructed that it would have been better had Glover been presented with a photographic array including "so far as practicable * * * a reasonable number of persons similar to any person then suspected whose likeness is included in the array." *Id.* at 2254. "The use of that procedure," according to the Court, "would have enhanced the force of the identification at trial and would have avoided the risk that the evidence would be excluded as unreliable." *Id.*

(a) In *State v. Matthews*, 233 *N.J.Super.* 291 (App.Div. 1989), defendant argued that it was error for the trial "court to admit testimony and photographs concerning an investigator's pre-trial identification." *Id.* at 294. Finding defendant's argument "clearly without merit," the Appellate Division noted "that this case did not involve an identification in the traditional sense. Rather, it dealt with review of two photographs by the undercover investigator in order to obtain the name of the person who sold him cocaine on [a particular date]. The undercover investigator indicated that he was 'unaware of the name,' not the identity, of the individual who sold him cocaine, and that he looked at the pictures so that the investigators could ascertain the name." *Id.* at 294-295.

According to the court, "there was no showing of impermissible suggestiveness in these circumstances, and that, in any event, the State showed by clear and convincing evidence that the in-court identification was not tainted by any out-of-court identification because there was never a question on the part of the undercover investigator as to the person, as opposed to the name of the person, from whom he bought drugs." *Id.* at 295.

(b) It is improper for investigators to tell an undercover officer that the photo array he or she is about to view contains a photograph of the person arrested at the time of warrant execution, or of the person from whom the officer had purchased narcotics on an earlier occasion. This may result in a court concluding that the identification procedure was "impermissibly suggestive." *See State v. Little*, 296 *N.J.Super.* 573, 579 (App.Div. 1997). *See also United States v. Lewin*, 900 *F.*2d 145, 149 (8th Cir. 1990). The in-court identification in *Little* was salvaged, however, in light of the specific facts of the case. In this respect, the court observed:

> There can be no dispute that a trained undercover police officer has heightened awareness of the need for proper identification of persons who engage in drug purveyance. Vitkosky was a trained and experienced illicit-drug-activity investigator. As an undercover officer, he was not only trained to be observant but also had a strong incentive to be observant. Vitkosky had significant opportunity to observe defendant close up during the very early evening hours of the July date in question. During the five to seven minutes it took to arrange and complete the undercover sale of cocaine, Vitkosky had at least three face-to-face unhindered opportunities to view defendant: when they first met to set up the transaction; when they met in the alleyway to carry it out; and during the entire duration the sale took place when defendant continually solicited his $5 fee for arranging the buy. When these opportunities are considered with the degree of attention and the level of the officer's certainty in his identification, any corrupting effect of the out-of-court identification is eradicated. On the record before us, we are satisfied the circumstances demonstrate the reliability of the in-court identification independent of the photographs reviewed pretrial. *See Lewin, supra*, 900 *F*.2d at 149. There was no substantial likelihood of misidentification.

Little at 580.

2. *Voice identification.* Generally, the constitutional safeguards that apply to visual identification evidence also apply to "voice identification." A voice identification will be admissible in court "so long as its reliability is not outweighed by the suggestiveness of the identification procedure." *See e.g. State v. Clausell*, 121 *N.J.* 298, 328, 580 *A*.2d 221 (1990). "Reliability depends on such factors as the witness's opportunity to hear the accused and the consistency with prior voice identifications." *Id.* This means that the witness must have had a substantial basis for comparing the voice of the accused with the voice he or she identified as the voice of the assailant.

(a) In *Government of Virgin Islands v. Sanes*, 57 *F*.3d 338 (3rd Cir. 1995), a rape victim identified her attacker through a voice identification procedure similar to that used by police when conducting a photo array identification procedure. Using the five-part test set forth by the Supreme Court in *Neil v. Biggers* and *Manson v. Brathwaite*, the court found no evidence that the voice identification procedure was impermissibly suggestive or that there was a substantial likelihood of misidentification. In this respect, the court observed:

> Although voice identification obviously differs from eyewitness identification (for example, what is at issue in the first part of the *Neil* and *Manson* test is opportunity to view rather than opportunity to hear), we conclude that the *Neil* and *Manson* eyewitness

identification test, adapted to voice identification, provides a standardized source of guidance * * * for assessing the reliability of voice identification as well.

Id. at 340.

The victim in this case was attacked on two different occasions, and on each occasion, she conversed with her attacker for ten minutes. Not only did she listen to her attacker for this considerable period of time, but she testified "that she engaged him in conversation in the hope that she could identify his voice[.]" *Id.* at 341. The court found that the victim was alert and had a sufficient opportunity to view or hear her attacker on both occasions, and she presented an accurate description of Sanes and his clothing. She identified the items taken from Sanes as looking like items the attacker had worn. In addition, she stated that she was certain that Sample No. 4 was the voice of her attacker. "During the voice identification procedure, she listened to the voice array three times. She was ready to identify Sample No. 4 after the second time, but was encouraged by the police to listen to the tape one more time. [She] then positively identified the fourth voice as that of her attacker. Sample No. 4 was Sanes' voice." *Id.* at 340. "Finally, although there was a six-month period between the incidents, only fifteen days elapsed between the last attack and her positive voice identification." *Id.* at 340-41.

The court concluded, therefore, that "the district court properly applied the *Neil/Manson* factors and properly denied Sanes' motion to suppress the voice identification." *Id.* at 341.

(b) In *United States v. Schultz,* 698 F.2d 365 (8th Cir. 1983), the F.B.I. conducted a pretrial voice lineup. The defendant contended that the recording of his voice sounded halting and uneducated with an accent while the voices of the five F.B.I. agents who participated in the lineup sounded educated and highly trained. The court observed that the difference in accent and vocal style was not so pronounced as to result in impermissible suggestiveness, but the discrepancy in volume and sound resolution when defendant's voice was played did amount to impermissible suggestiveness. *Id.* at 367-68. Nonetheless, the court determined that the in-court identification was admissible because the witnesses paid careful attention to the extortionist's voice even though they only heard it for a short period of time, neither witness equivocated in the identification of the defendant even though neither provided a description of the extortionist's voice prior to trial, and the three months that elapsed between the crime and the lineup did not render the identifications unreliable. *Id.* at 368.

(c) In *United States v. Patton,* 721 F.2d 159, 162-63 (6th Cir. 1983), the court found that the in-court voice identification was admissible in light of the facts that (a) the witness received threats on four separate occasions, (b) her ability to repeat the threats demonstrated a high level of concentration, and (c) her exposure to the defendant's voice during the pretrial lineup was minimal. Moreover, only three weeks elapsed between the commission of the crime and the pretrial

lineup. And upon hearing defendant's voice, the witness "immediately recoiled" indicating a familiarity with the voice from the four threatening phone calls. *Id.* at 162.

See also United States v. Duran, 4 *F.*3d 800, 803 (9th Cir. 1993), where the court held that an in-court voice identification was reliable because the witnesses (bank tellers) had a sufficient opportunity to hear the bank robber who shouted several commands and threats, the tellers were quite attentive due to the presence of a weapon accompanied by threats, they provided accurate descriptions of defendant's distinctive voice, and neither witness equivocated in her identification of defendant.

CHAPTER 13

THE RIGHT TO COUNSEL AND OTHER SIXTH AMENDMENT ISSUES

Section
13.1   Introduction
13.2   Effective assistance of counsel
13.3   [*Reserved for supplementary material*]
13.4   Right of Confrontation

§13.1. Introduction.

The **Sixth Amendment** to the Federal Constitution provides in pertinent part that:

> In all criminal prosecutions, the accused shall enjoy the right * * * to have the *Assistance of Counsel* for his defense. [Emphasis added.]

This provision depicts a guarantee that "the conviction of the accused will be the product of an adversarial process, rather than the *ex parte* investigation and determination by the prosecutor." *Nix v. Williams*, 467 *U.S.* 431, 453, 104 *S.Ct.* 2501, 2514 (1984) (Stevens J., concurring). This adversary process in America is grounded at the foundation of a system of criminal procedure which is accusatorial in nature. It is accusatorial in that the government accuses and then bears the burden of proving an individual guilty of a crime.

Our Adversary System of Jurisprudence (or science of law) may be likened to a 1000-meter rowing race wherein the defendant's shell is sitting on the water at the 700-meter mark. At the 0-meter mark we find the prosecutor's shell standing ready to row. It now becomes readily apparent that the prosecutor has a heavy burden at the start of the race. He must catch up with the defendant's shell, overtake it, and cross the finish line first. He must have and carry this burden throughout the race—a demand for great oarsmanship!

Such is the burden the prosecutor has at trial. The prosecutor must have and carry through trial the burden of proving the defendant *guilty beyond a reasonable doubt*. The defendant's lead at trial is premised upon an important presumption which constitutes the mainstay of our adversarial system. The presumption is that *the defendant is innocent until proven guilty beyond a reasonable doubt*.

The prosecution is not required, however, to prove its case beyond all possible doubt or to a mathematical certainty, nor must it demonstrate the complete impossibility of innocence. Reasonable doubt contemplates neither a "grave uncertainty" nor an "actual substantial doubt." *Cage v. Louisiana*, 498 *U.S.* 39, 111 *S.Ct.* 328, 329 (1990). Moreover, it may not be an imaginary or fanciful doubt invented by a factfinder for the purpose of avoiding an unpleasant verdict. Rather, reasonable doubt must take on the form of an honest doubt for which a reason can be articulated; a doubt which arises from the evidence or lack of evidence presented. It is, therefore, that type of doubt which would cause a reasonably cautious and sensible person to hesitate or refrain from acting on a matter of the highest importance to himself.

The United States Supreme Court has emphasized that the "reasonable doubt standard"

> plays a vital role in the American scheme of criminal procedure. It is a prime instrument for reducing the risk of convictions resting on factual error. The standard provides concrete substance for the presumption of innocence—that bedrock "axiomatic and elementary" principle whose "enforcement lies at the foundation of the administration of our criminal law."

In re Winship, 397 *U.S.* 358, 363, 90 *S.Ct.* 1068, 1072 (1970). [Citation omitted.]

> The accused during a criminal prosecution has at stake interests of immense importance, both because of the possibility that he may lose his liberty upon conviction and because of the certainty that he would be stigmatized by the conviction. Accordingly, a society that values the good name and freedom of every individual should not condemn a man for commission of a crime when there is reasonable doubt about his guilt.

Id. at 363, 364, 90 *S.Ct.* at 1072-73. *See also Sullivan v. Louisiana,* 508 *U.S.* 275, 113 *S.Ct.* 2078, 2080 (1993) ("prosecution bears the burden of proving all elements of the offense charged * * * and must persuade the factfinder 'beyond a reasonable doubt' of the facts necessary to establish each of those elements"); *Cage v. Louisiana, supra,* 111 *S.Ct.* at 329 ("In state criminal trials, the Due Process clause of the Fourteenth Amendment 'protects the accused against conviction except upon proof beyond a reasonable doubt of every fact necessary to constitute the crime with which he is charged.' ") (quoting *Winship* at 364, 90 *S.Ct.* at 1073).

The Sixth Amendment guarantees that these important fundamental interests shall be protected through the assistance of counsel. *See e.g., Lockhart v. Fretwell,* 506 *U.S.* 364, 113 *S.Ct.* 838, 842 (1993) ("the Sixth Amendment right to counsel exists 'in order to protect the fundamental right to a fair trial' ") (citation omitted). Moreover, courts have consistently interpreted this provision to not only mean assistance of counsel, but "effective assistance." *McMann v. Richardson,* 397 *U.S.* 759, 90 *S.Ct.* 1441 (1970). Here, the right to effective, unhindered assistance of counsel has long been treated as among those "immutable principles of justice which inhere in the very idea of free government." *Powell v. Alabama,* 287 *U.S.* 45, 71-72 (1932) (quoting *Holden v. Hardy,* 169 *U.S.* 366, 389 (1897)).

Although *Powell* and other early cases ensured effective assistance of counsel through a Fifth Amendment due process standard, *Johnson v. Zerbst,* 304 *U.S.* 458 (1938), brought to bear the Sixth Amendment's provision of the right to counsel by holding this fundamental Sixth

Amendment right applicable to the states through the Fourteenth Amendment. Thus, the Sixth Amendment itself became the significant constitutional source influencing the right to effective assistance of counsel.

In 1984, the United States Supreme Court in *Strickland v. Washington*, 466 *U.S.* 668, distinguished between two types of right-to-counsel cases. The first type covers cases "based on actual or constructive denial of the right to counsel altogether, including claims based on state interference with the ability of counsel to render effective assistance to the accused," *Id.* at 683, while the second type governs cases in which counsel "simply fail[ed] to render 'adequate legal assistance', or 'actual ineffectiveness.' " *Id.* at 686.

As to the first type of case, police officers as well as prosecutors must not interfere with nor deprive an accused of his fundamental right to the effective assistance of counsel at any "critical stage" of the criminal case. In this regard, Justice Douglas so aptly questioned:

> [What] use is a defendant's right to effective counsel at every stage of a criminal case if, while he is held awaiting trial, he can be questioned in the absence of counsel until he confesses ? In that event the secret trial in the police precincts effectively supplants the public trial guaranteed by the Bill of Rights.

Spano v. New York, 360 *U.S.* 315, 326 (1959) (Douglas J., concurring, joined by Black and Brennan, J.J.).

With regard to the second type of case, *Strickland* provides a two-part test for evaluating claims of "actual ineffectiveness" of counsel:

> First, the defendant must show that counsel's performance was deficient. This requires showing that counsel made errors so serious that counsel was not functioning as the "counsel" guaranteed the defendant by the Sixth Amendment. Second, the defendant must show that the deficient performance prejudiced the defense. This requires showing that counsel's errors were so serious as to deprive the defendant of a fair trial, a trial whose result is reliable. Unless defendant makes both showings, it cannot be said that the conviction * * * resulted from a breakdown in the adversary process that renders the result unreliable.

Strickland at 687. Thus, we have the *Strickland* two-pronged inquiry into ineffective assistance of counsel claims: "Performance and Prejudice." As to the second prong, the prejudice generally must be proved; it is not presumed. *Id.* at 692-693. A defendant alleging ineffective assistance of counsel must show that there is "a reasonable probability that, but for counsel's unprofessional errors, the result of the proceeding would have been different. A reasonable probability is a probability sufficient to undermine confidence in the outcome." *Id.* at 694. *See also Kimmelman v. Morrison*, 477 *U.S.* 365, 374, 106 *S.Ct.* 2574, 2582 (1986) ("The essence of an ineffective-assistance claim is that counsel's unprofessional errors so upset the adversarial balance between defense and prosecution that the trial was rendered unfair and the verdict rendered suspect."). The analysis of the ineffective-assistance claim must not, however, focus solely on the outcome of the proceeding, "without attention to whether the result of the proceeding was fundamentally unfair or unreliable." *Lockhart v. Fretwell, supra,* 113 *S.Ct.* at 842. *See also id.* at 843 ("To set aside a conviction or sentence solely because the outcome would have been different but for counsel's error may grant the defendant a windfall to which the law does not entitle him.").

There are some cases, however, that present "circumstances that are so likely to prejudice the accused that the cost of litigating their effect in a particular case is unjustified." *United States v. Cronic,* 466 *U.S.* 648, 658 (1984). In such cases, presenting circumstances involving the complete denial of the right to counsel—actual or constructive—prejudice to the defendant may be presumed.

---

§13.2. Effective assistance of counsel.

NIX v. WHITESIDE
Supreme Court of the United States
475 *U.S.* 157, 106 *S.Ct.* 988 (1986)

QUESTION: Is the Sixth Amendment right of a criminal defendant to assistance of counsel violated when an attorney refuses to cooperate with the defendant in presenting perjured testimony at his trial?

ANSWER: NO. The Sixth Amendment right of a criminal defendant to assistance of counsel is not violated when an attorney refuses to cooperate with the defendant in presenting perjured testimony at his trial. "Although counsel must take all reasonable lawful means to attain the objectives of the client, counsel is [prohibited] from taking steps or in any way assisting the client in presenting false evidence or otherwise violating the law." *Id.* at 994.

RATIONALE: Defendant, Emanuel Charles Whiteside, was charged with a Cedar Rapids, Iowa, murder. During his trial preparation, Whiteside informed his attorney, Gary L. Robinson, that he had stabbed one Calvin Love during an argument over the purchase of marihuana. Whiteside stated that he had stabbed Love just as Love "was pulling a pistol from underneath the pillow on the bed." *Id.* at 991. Whiteside further stated that although he had not actually seen a gun, he was convinced that Love possessed a gun from prior dealings with him. A police search of the crime scene (Calvin Love's apartment) revealed no weapon at all.

Robinson informed Whiteside that the existence of a gun was not absolutely necessary to establish his self-defense argument; all that was necessary was that Whiteside have a reasonable belief that Love had a gun nearby.

Shortly before trial, during preparation for direct examination, Whiteside—for the first time—told Robinson that he had seen something "metallic" in Love's hand. *Id.* When Robinson questioned Whiteside about this, Whiteside stated: "If I don't say I saw a gun, I'm dead." *Id.* Robinson informed Whiteside that this type of testimony at trial would be perjury. If he did decide to testify that way, Robinson stated that it would be his duty to tell the court of what he (Whiteside) was doing, that such testimony was perjury, and that Robinson would probably be allowed to impeach or attack that particular testimony. Robinson also stated that he would attempt to withdraw from representing him if he insisted on committing perjury.

Whiteside did not commit perjury. The jury convicted him of second-degree murder.

After exhausting his State remedies, Whiteside petitioned for a writ of habeas corpus claiming he had been denied effective assistance of counsel. He also asserted that his right to present a defense was denied by his attorney's refusal to allow him to testify as he had originally so desired.

Although the United States Court of Appeals for the Eighth Circuit directed that the writ of habeas corpus be granted, *the United States Supreme Court disagreed and reversed.*

In *Strickland v. Washington*, the Supreme Court held that to obtain relief by way of a writ of federal habeas corpus on a claim of a denial of effective assistance of counsel under the Sixth Amendment, the petitioning party "must establish both serious attorney error and prejudice." *Id.* at 993. "To show such error, it must be established that the assistance rendered by counsel was constitutionally deficient in that 'counsel made errors so serious that counsel was not functioning as *counsel* guaranteed the defendant by the Sixth Amendment.'" *Id.* [Citation omitted.] "To establish prejudice, it must be established that the claimed lapses in counsel's performance rendered the trial unfair so as to 'undermine confidence in the outcome' of the trial." *Id.* [Citation omitted.] As a general rule, the "Sixth Amendment inquiry is into whether the attorney's conduct was 'reasonably effective.'" *Id.*

Here, the overriding issue focused upon "the definition of the range of 'reasonable professional' responses to a criminal defendant client who informs counsel that he will perjure himself on the stand." *Id.* at 994. While the Court has recognized a lawyer's duty of loyalty and his or her "overreaching duty to advocate the defendant's cause," the Court nonetheless emphasized that "that duty is limited to legitimate, lawful conduct compatible with the very nature of a trial as a *search for truth.*" *Id.* [Emphasis added.] "Although counsel must take all reasonable lawful means to attain the objectives of the client, counsel is [prohibited] from taking steps or in any way assisting the client in presenting false evidence or otherwise violating the law." *Id.* At the bare minimum, the attorney should, as his "first duty when confronted with a proposal for perjurious testimony[,] attempt to dissuade the client from the unlawful course of conduct." *Id.* at 995. In this case, the American Bar Association (ABA) agreed "that under no circumstances may a lawyer either advocate or passively tolerate a client's giving false testimony." *Id.* This, stated the Court, "is consistent with the governance of trial conduct in what we have long called 'a search for the truth.'" *Id.* at 995.

The Court therefore held that Whiteside's attorney did absolutely nothing wrong or violative of the Sixth Amendment right to assistance of counsel, nor did he violate the Supreme Court's additional requirement that such assistance be *effective.* "Robinson's representation of Whiteside f[ell] well within accepted standards of professional conduct and the range of reasonable professional conduct acceptable under [United States Supreme Court standards]." *Id.* at 996. At most, the only deprivation here involved Robinson's depriving Whiteside of his contemplated perjury.

As a result, the Court ruled—as a matter of law—that Robinson's "conduct complained of here cannot establish the prejudice required for relief under the second strand of the *Strickland*[, *supra*,] inquiry." *Id.* at 998. "Although a defendant need not establish that the attorney's deficient performance more likely than not altered the outcome in order to establish prejudice under *Strickland*, a defendant must show 'that there is a reasonable probability that, but for counsel's unprofessional errors, the result of the proceeding would have been different.'" *Id.* [Citation omitted.] "Reasonable probability" is "a probability sufficient to undermine confidence in the outcome [of the trial proceeding]." *Id.* [Citations omitted.]

Finally, the Court observed: "[T]he responsibility of an ethical lawyer, as an officer of the court and key component of a system of justice, dedicated to a search for truth, is essentially the same whether the client announces an intention to bribe or threaten witnesses or jurors or to commit or procure perjury. No system of justice worthy of the name can tolerate a lesser standard." *Id.*

---

§13.3. [Reserved for supplementary material.]

---

§13.4. Right of confrontation.

The United States Constitution guarantees criminal defendants the right to confront their accusers. In this respect, the Confrontation Clause of the Sixth Amendment provides: "In all criminal prosecutions, the accused shall enjoy the right * * * to be confronted with the witnesses against him." *U.S.Const.* amend. VI. *See also Pointer v. Texas*, 380 *U.S.* 400, 85 *S.Ct.* 1065 (1965).

The primary interests protected by the right of confrontation are the right of defendants to physically face those who testify against them (their accusers), and the right to conduct cross-examination. *Pennsylvania v. Richie*, 480 *U.S.* 39, 51, 107 *S.Ct.* 989, 998 (1987). The components of the constitutional right of confrontation have been interpreted to afford a criminal defendant: (1) a meaningful opportunity for a face-to-face courtroom meeting with the witnesses against him; (2) the right not to have undue restrictions placed on questions defense counsel may ask during cross-examination; (3) the right to elicit favorable testimony through the cross-examination of witnesses testifying against him; and (4) a meaningful opportunity to present a complete defense. *Richie* at 52, 107 *S.Ct.* at 999; *Davis v. Alaska*, 415 *U.S.* 308, 318, 94 *S.Ct.* 1105, 1111 (1974); *Crane v. Kentucky*, 476 *U.S.* 683, 690, 106 *S.Ct.* 2142, 2146 (1986).

Time and time again, the courts have made it clear that the right to confront and cross-examine accusing witnesses is "among the minimum essentials of a fair trial." *Chambers v. Mississippi*, 410 *U.S.* 284, 294-95, 93 *S.Ct.* 1038, 1045 (1973); *In re Oliver*, 333 *U.S.* 257, 273, 68 *S.Ct.* 499, 507 (1948). The right to meet one's accuser "face-to-face" before the trier of fact forms the heart of the values upon which the Confrontation Clause rests. *See Crawford v. Washington*, 541 *U.S.* 36, 124 *S.Ct.* 1354 (2004). The right is applicable to the states by reason of the Fourteenth Amendment. *Pointer v. Texas, supra.*

COY v. IOWA
Supreme Court of the United States
487 *U.S.* 1012, 108 *S.Ct.* 2798 (1988)

QUESTION: Does the placement of a large screen between the defendant and his two 13-year-old victims at trial, which had the effect of blocking the defendant from the sight of the victims and obscuring the defendant's view of the victims, violate the defendant's Sixth Amendment right to confront the witnesses against him ?

ANSWER: YES. "[T]he Confrontation Clause guarantees the defendant a face-to-face meeting with witnesses appearing before the trier of fact. * * * The screen at issue was specifically designed to enable the complaining witnesses to avoid viewing [defendant] as they gave their testimony," and according to the Court, "[i]t is difficult to imagine a more obvious or damaging violation of the defendant's right to a face-to-face encounter." *Id.* at 2800, 2802.

RATIONALE: Defendant "was convicted of two counts of lascivious acts with a child after a jury trial in which a screen placed between him and the two complaining witnesses blocked him from their sight." *Id.* at 2799. The evidence adduced at trial established that defendant sexually assaulted two 13-year-old girls while they were camping out in the backyard of the house next door to him.

At trial, the State invoked a recent Iowa statute which permits complaining witnesses in such cases "to testify either via closed-circuit television or behind a screen. * * * The trial court approved the use of a large screen to be placed between [defendant] and the witness stand during the girls' testimony. After certain lighting adjustments in the courtroom, the screen would enable [defendant] dimly to perceive the witnesses, but the witnesses [could not see defendant] at all." *Id.* at 2799.

In this appeal, defendant argues, among other things, that the procedure employed at trial, although authorized by state statute, "violated his Sixth Amendment right to confront the witnesses against him." *Id. The United States Supreme Court agreed.*

"The Sixth Amendment gives a criminal defendant the right 'to be confronted with the witnesses against him.' " *Id.* at 2800. Known as the "Confrontation Clause," this provision "guarantees the defendant a face-to-face meeting with witnesses appearing before the trier of fact." *Id.*

Historically, it has been recognized that " 'a fact which can be primarily established only by witnesses cannot be proved against an accused . . . except by witnesses who confront him at the trial, upon whom he can look while being tried, whom he is entitled to cross-examine, and whose testimony he may impeach in every mode authorized by the established rules governing the trial or conduct of criminal cases.' " *Id.* at 2800-2801 (quoting *Kirby v. United States,* 174 *U.S.* 47, 55, 19 *S.Ct.* 574, 577 (1989)). Thus, the Sixth Amendment's guarantee of a "face-to-face encounter between witness and accused serves ends related both to appearances and to reality." *Coy* at 2801. In this respect, the Court notes that "there is something deep in human nature that regards face-to-face confrontation between accused and accuser as 'essential to a fair trial in criminal prosecutions.' " *Id.* [Citation omitted.] "A witness 'may feel quite differently when he has to repeat his story looking at the man whom he will harm greatly by distorting or mistaking the facts.' * * * It is always more difficult to tell a lie about a person 'to his face' than 'behind his back.' " *Id.* at 2802. [Citations omitted.]

Naturally, the Confrontation Clause does not "compel the witness to fix his eyes upon the defendant; he may studiously look elsewhere, but the trier of fact will draw its own conclusions. Thus, the right to face-to-face confrontation serves much the same purpose as * * * the right to cross-examine the accuser; both 'ensur(e) the integrity of the fact-finding process.' " *Id.* [Citation omitted.] The Court does, however, recognize that "face-to-face presence may, unfortunately, upset the truthful rape victim or abused child; but by the same token it may confound and undo the false accuser, or reveal the child coached by a malevolent adult. It is a truism that constitutional protections have costs." *Id.*

In this case, defendant's "constitutional right to face-to-face confrontation was violated[.]" *Id.* at 2903. "The screen at issue was specifically designed to enable the complaining witnesses to avoid viewing [defendant] as they gave their testimony, and the record indicates that it was successful in this objective. It is difficult to imagine a more obvious or damaging violation of the defendant's right to a face-to-face encounter." *Id.* at 2802.

Since defendant's constitutional right to face-to-face confrontation was violated, the judgment of the Iowa Supreme Court affirming defendant's conviction is reversed.

NOTE

1. In *Maryland v. Craig,* 497 *U.S.* 836, 110 *S.Ct.* 3157, 3160 (1990), the Court held that the Confrontation Clause does not categorically prohibit a child witness in a child abuse case from testifying against a defendant at trial, outside the defendant's physical presence, by one-way closed circuit television. According to the Court, "if the State

makes an adequate showing of necessity, the state interest in protecting child witnesses from the trauma of testifying in a child abuse case is sufficiently important to justify the use of a special procedure that permits a child witness in such cases to testify at trial against a defendant in the absence of face-to-face confrontation with the defendant." *Id.*, 110 *S.Ct.* at 3169. The Court explained:

> The requisite finding of necessity must of course be a case-specific one: the trial court must hear evidence and determine whether use of the one-way closed circuit television procedure is necessary to protect the welfare of the particular child witness who seeks to testify. * * * The trial court must also find that the child witness would be traumatized, not by the courtroom generally, but by the presence of the defendant. * * * Finally, the trial court must find that the emotional distress suffered by the child witness in the presence of the defendant is more than *de minimis, i.e.,* more than "mere nervousness or excitement or some reluctance to testify[.]" We need not decide the minimum showing of emotional trauma required for use of the special procedure, however, because the Maryland statute, which requires that the child witness will suffer "serious emotional distress such that the child cannot reasonably communicate," * * * clearly suffices to meet constitutional standards. * * *
>
> In sum, we conclude that where necessary to protect a child witness from trauma that would be caused by testifying in the physical presence of the defendant, at least where such trauma would impair the child's ability to communicate, the Confrontation Clause does not prohibit use of a procedure that, despite the absence of face-to-face confrontation, ensures the reliability of the evidence by subjecting it to rigorous adversarial testing and thereby preserves the essence of effective confrontation.

Id. at 3169-70. [Citations omitted.]

2. *Out-of-court statements by a child relating a sexual assault.* In *White v. Illinois*, 502 *U.S.* 346, 112 *S.Ct.* 736 (1992), the Court addressed the question whether the Confrontation Clause of the Sixth Amendment requires that, before a trial court admits testimony of persons to whom a four-year-old child related a sexual assault under the "spontaneous declaration" and "medical examination" exceptions to the hearsay rule, the prosecution must either produce the child at trial or demonstrate that the child is legally "unavailable" to testify.

In the early morning hours of April 16, 1988, Tony DeVore, 4-year-old S.G.'s babysitter, was awakened by S.G.'s scream. DeVore went to S.G.'s bedroom and witnessed defendant leaving the room, and then leaving the house. "DeVore asked S.G. what had happened. According to DeVore's trial testimony, S.G. stated that [defendant] had put his hand over her mouth, choked her, threatened to whip her if she screamed, and had 'touch[ed] her in the wrong places.' Asked by DeVore to point to where she had been touched, S.G. identified the vaginal area." *Id.*, 112 *S.Ct.* at 736. When S.G.'s mother, Tammy Grigsby, returned home, she questioned S.G. At trial, Grigsby testified that S.G. repeated her claims that defendant had choked and threatened her. Grigsby also testified that S.G. stated that defendant "put his mouth on her front part." *Id.*

Approximately 45 minutes after S.G.'s scream had first awakened DeVore, Officer Terry Lewis arrived and questioned S.G. alone in the kitchen. Officer Lewis' trial testimony relayed essentially the same account provided by DeVore and Grigsby, including a statement that defendant had "used his tongue on her in her private part." *Id.* After Lewis concluded his investigation, S.G. was taken to the hospital, where she was examined by an emergency room nurse, Cheryl Reents, and by Dr. Michael Meinzen. Each testified at trial and related an account of the events that was essentially the same as that provided by DeVore, Grigsby, and Lewis. S.G. never testified, nor did the prosecution demonstrate that she was legally "unavailable" to testify. Moreover, the trial court did not make, nor was it asked to make, a finding that S.G. was unavailable to testify.

Finding no Confrontation Clause violation, the Court rejected the defendant's contention that, as a necessary precondition to the introduction of testimony under the "spontaneous declaration" and "medical examination" exceptions to the hearsay rule, the prosecution must either produce the declarant or show that the declarant is unavailable. In this respect, the Court reaffirmed that there is no *per se* rule "that 'no out-of-court statement would be admissible without a showing of unavailability'" of the declarant. *Id.* at 741. Rather, the "unavailability analysis is a necessary part of the Confrontation Clause inquiry only when the challenged out-of-court statements were made in the course of a prior judicial proceeding." *Id.* (quoting *United States v. Inadi*, 475 *U.S.* 387, 392, 106 *S.Ct.* 1121, 1124 (1986)).

> [T]he evidentiary rationale for permitting hearsay testimony regarding spontaneous declarations and statements made in the course of receiving medical care is that such out-of-court declarations are made in contexts that provide substantial guarantees of their trustworthiness. But those same factors that contribute to the statements' reliability cannot be recaptured by later in-court testimony. A statement that has been offered in a moment of excitement—without the opportunity to reflect on the consequences of one's exclamation—may justifiably carry more weight with a trier of fact than a similar statement offered in the relative calm of the courtroom. Similarly, a statement made in the course of procuring medical services, where the declarant knows that a false statement may cause misdiagnosis or mistreatment, carries special guarantees of credibility that a trier of fact may not think replicated by courtroom testimony. [Such statements] are thus materially different from * * * out-of-court statements sought to be introduced [which] were themselves made in the course of a judicial proceeding, and where there was consequently no threat of lost evidentiary value if the out-of-court statements were replaced with live testimony.

The preference for live testimony in the case of statements [which were originally made at a prior judicial proceeding] is because of the importance of cross examination, "the greatest legal engine ever invented for the discovery of truth." * * * Thus, courts have adopted the general rule prohibiting the receipt of hearsay evidence. But where the proffered hearsay has sufficient guarantees of reliability to come within a firmly rooted exception to the hearsay rule, the Confrontation Clause is satisfied.

We therefore think it clear that the out-of-court statements admitted in this case had substantial probative value, value that could not be duplicated simply by the declarant later testifying in court. To exclude such probative statements under the strictures of the Confrontation Clause would be the height of wrong-headedness, given that the Confrontation Clause has as a basic purpose the promotion of the " 'integrity of the factfinding process.' " * * * Given the evidentiary value of such statements, their reliability, and that establishing a generally applicable unavailability rule would have few practical benefits while imposing pointless litigation costs, we see no * * * basis * * * for excluding from trial, under the aegis of the Confrontation Clause, evidence embraced within such exceptions to the hearsay rule as those for spontaneous declarations and statements made for medical treatment.

Id. at 742-43. [Citations and footnote omitted.]
The Court also rejected defendant's contention that before the child's statements could be repeated at trial, *Coy v. Iowa, supra,* and *Maryland v. Craig, supra,* require a preliminary showing of "necessity," that is, a preliminary showing that the procedure is "necessary to protect the child's physical and psychological well-being." *White* at 743. According to the Court, defendant's reliance on *Coy* and *Craig*

is misplaced. *Coy* and *Craig* involved only the question of what *in-court* procedures are constitutionally required to guarantee a defendant's confrontation right once a witness is testifying. Such a question is quite separate from that of what requirements the Confrontation Clause imposes as a predicate for the introduction of out-of-court declarations. *Coy* and *Craig* did not speak to the latter question. As we recognized in *Coy,* the admissibility of hearsay statements raises concerns lying at the periphery of those that the Confrontation Clause is designed to address * * *. There is thus no basis for importing the "necessity requirement" announced in those cases into the much different context of out-of-court declarations admitted under established exceptions to the hearsay rule.

Id. at 743-44. [Citations omitted; Court's emphasis.]

UNITED STATES v. OWENS
Supreme Court of the United States
484 *U.S.* 554, 108 *S.Ct.* 838 (1988)

QUESTION: Does the Sixth Amendment Confrontation Clause prohibit the admission at trial of testimony concerning a prior, out-of-court identification when the identifying witness is unable, because of memory loss, to explain the basis for the identification ?

ANSWER: NO. "[T]he Confrontation Clause is not violated by admission of an identification statement of a witness who is unable, because of memory loss, to testify concerning the basis for the identification." *Id.* at 845. This "Clause guarantees only 'an *opportunity* for effective cross-examination, not cross-examination that is effective in whatever way, and to whatever extent, the defense might wish.' " *Id.* at 842. [Citation omitted; emphasis in original.]

RATIONALE: At the federal prison in Lompoc, California, John Foster, a correctional counselor, was attacked and brutally beaten with a pipe. The assailant fractured Foster's skull, and inflicted other injuries which necessitated Foster's hospitalization for almost a month.

Agent Mansfield of the FBI first attempted to interview Foster one week after the attack; "he found Foster lethargic and unable to remember the attacker's name." *Id.* at 841. Sixteen days later, Mansfield again attempted to interview Foster, "who was much improved and able to describe the attack." *Id.* Foster named James Owens (the defendant herein) as his attacker and then identified Owens from an array of photographs.

At trial, "Foster recounted his activities just before the attack, and described feeling the blows to his head and seeing blood on the floor. He testified that he clearly remembered identifying [defendant] as his assailant during his * * * interview with Mansfield." *Id.* When cross-examined, however, Foster "admitted that he could not remember seeing his assailant. He also admitted that, although there was evidence that he had received numerous visitors in the hospital, he was unable to remember any of them except Mansfield, and could not remember whether any of these visitors had suggested that defendant was the assailant." *Id.* Foster's attorney was unsuccessful in his attempt to refresh Foster's recollection. Nonetheless, defendant was convicted of assault with intent to commit murder, contrary to 18 *U.S.C.* §113(a).

In this appeal, defendant argued that the testimony of Foster concerning his prior, out-of-court identification should not be admitted at trial because of his inability, due to his memory loss, to explain the basis for the identification.

The United States Supreme Court, per Justice Scalia, disagreed. "The Confrontation Clause of the Sixth Amendment gives the accused the right 'to be confronted with the witnesses against him.' This has long been read as an adequate opportunity to cross-examine adverse witnesses." *Owens* at 841. The Court, however, "has never held," and does not so hold in this case, "that a Confrontation Clause violation can be founded upon a witness's loss of memory[.]" *Id.* As stated in *Delaware v. Fensterer*, 474 *U.S.* 15, 106 *S.Ct.* 292 (1985), "the Confrontation Clause is generally satisfied when the defendant is given a full and fair opportunity to probe and expose [a witness' infirmities such as forgetfulness, confusion, or evasion] through cross-examination, thereby calling to the attention of the factfinder the reasons for giving scant weight to the witness' testimony." *Id.*, 474 *U.S.*, at 21-22, 106 *S.Ct.*, at 296.

Thus, " 'the Confrontation Clause guarantees only an *opportunity* for effective cross-examination, not cross-examination that is effective in whatever way, and to whatever extent, the defense might wish.' " *Owens* at 842. [Citations omitted; emphasis in original.] Consequently, "that opportunity is not denied when a witness testifies as to his current belief but is unable to recollect the reasons for that belief. It is sufficient that the defen[se] has the opportunity to bring out such matters as the witness' bias, his lack of care and attentiveness, his poor eyesight, and even (what is often a prime objective of cross-examination) the very fact that he has a bad memory." *Id.* at 842. Moreover, the Court reasoned that "[i]f the ability to inquire into these matters suffices to establish the constitutionally requisite opportunity for cross-examination when a witness testifies as to his current belief, the basis for which he cannot recall, we see no reason why it should not suffice when the witness' [] past belief is introduced and he is unable to recollect the reason for that past belief. In both cases, the foundation for the belief (current or past) cannot effectively be elicited, but other means of impugning the belief are available." *Id.*

Accordingly, the Confrontation Clause is not "violated by admission of an identification statement of a witness who is unable, because of memory loss, to testify concerning the basis for the identification." *Id.* at 845.

PART III

CHAPTER 14

NARCOTIC DRUGS:
POSSESSION AND DISTRIBUTION

§14.1. [Reserved for supplementary material.]

---

§14.2. Possessory issues: actual, constructive and joint.

UNITED STATES v. CABALLERO
United States Court of Appeals
712 F.2d 126 (5th Cir. 1983)

QUESTION: Will a defendant's mere presence or association with those who actually possess or control the illegal substance support that defendant's conviction for the unlawful "constructive" possession of marihuana ?

ANSWER: NO. Mere presence or association with those who control or possess illegal drugs will not automatically give rise to *constructive possession*. Rather, "constructive possession" must "be proved by 'ownership, dominion or control over the contraband itself, or dominion or control over the premises or vehicle in which the contraband was concealed.' " *Id.* at 129. [Citation omitted.] " 'In essence, constructive possession is the ability to reduce an object to actual possession.' " *Id.* (quoting *United States v. Martinez*, 588 *F.*2d 495, 498 (5th Cir. 1979)).

RATIONALE: Defendants, Conrado Caballero, Juan Rodriguez, Daniel Gonzalez and Juan Caceres bring this appeal, contending that the Government presented insufficient evidence at trial to support their convictions for possession with the intent to distribute marihuana, in violation of 21 *U.S.C.* §841(a)(1). "The charges against defendants arose from a Drug Enforcement Administration (DEA) investigation into the suspected narcotics operations of David Punch. That investigation was conducted primarily by one DEA agent, Paul Herring, who posed as an individual involved in the business of importing and storing marihuana. Herring was assisted in his investigation by a number of DEA agents, including Agent Arturo Ramirez, who entered the investigation in late February and was present during the negotiations of the specific transaction for which defendants were indicted." *Id.* at 128.

"Agent Herring was introduced to Punch by a DEA informer in October[.] Over the course of the next few months, the two had numerous discussions about narcotics operations." *Id.* At one point, Herring negotiated the purchase of ten tons of marihuana, but the vessel carrying the shipment was seized by the Government, eliminating the possibility of that sale. "In February, Agent Herring accompanied Punch to Florida for a meeting with his contacts in the smuggling business. This led to renewed negotiations about the importation of a large amount of marihuana[,]" *id.*, and to Herring's purchase of a substantial quantity of the drug. Punch informed Agents Herring and Ramirez that he knew someone interested in selling 15,000 pounds of marihuana. "The agents expressed interest and generally discussed the idea with Punch for two weeks. These discussions solidified on March 19 when the agents met with Punch at his Galveston home. At that meeting, the agents met Ezell Minton who told them that he had 15,000 pounds of marihuana stored in a warehouse located between Galveston and Houston." *Id.* Minton produced a two-pound sample of the marihuana, and the agents made an offer to purchase conditioned upon their ability to inspect the entire load.

"The next day, the same parties held another meeting for the purpose of discussing specifics of the sale. Ezell Minton left for a short while during the meeting and returned with defendant Juan Caceres. Later, the agents again insisted on inspecting the marihuana; Caceres explained that this would have to be done in Houston. The five left Punch's home and proceeded to the Candlelight Lounge [where arrangements were to be made]. Caceres arrived twenty-five minutes after the rest of the group." *Id.* At the lounge, additional details were ironed out.

"When Caceres informed the group that his associates had arrived, Herring suggested that Ramirez go to inspect the marihuana. This was consistent with Ramirez' role as one of Herring's associates. Ramirez then left the lounge with Caceres, who introduced him to defendants Daniel Gonzalez and Conrado Caballero, and told the agent that the two had a financial interest in the marihuana. Gonzalez questioned Ramirez about his ability to purchase such a large amount of marihuana; Caceres immediately assured Gonzalez and Caballero that the two had sufficient funds." *Id.*

"After this brief exchange, Gonzalez told Caballero to go get the men who were to accompany Ramirez to the warehouse. Ramirez interjected that he could only fit one other person in his small car. Caballero returned from the lounge with defendant Juan Rodriguez. The inspection tour was now set to begin, and Caballero reminded Gonzalez that Rodriguez needed the keys. Gonzalez fished the keys from his pocket and handed them to Caballero who, in turn, handed them to Rodriguez." *Id.* at 128-129.

"Rodriguez and Ramirez proceeded to the warehouse which was located about 10-12 miles from the lounge. * * * Inside the warehouse was a yellow van container which Rodriguez unlocked to reveal between 10,000-15,000 pounds of marihuana. Ramirez examined the marihuana briefly and then the two returned to the Candlelight Lounge. They found Gonzalez and Caballero waiting for them outside the lounge. Caballero asked if the marihuana was satisfactory[, and was informed that it was fine]. Gonzalez said that he had spoken with someone at the warehouse who had assured him that it would remain open until Ramirez finished loading the marihuana." *Id.* at 129. At this point, Ramirez stepped inside the lounge and indicated to Herring that he had seen the marihuana. "Herring made the necessary phone call, and defendants were arrested shortly thereafter." *Id.*

SUFFICIENCY OF THE EVIDENCE.

Defendants contend that the evidence presented at trial (as set forth above) was insufficient to support their convictions for the possession of marihuana with intent to distribute, in violation of 21 *U.S.C.* §841(a)(1). The United States Court of Appeals for the Fifth Circuit *disagreed.*

While mere presence or association with those who actually possess or control a quantity of illegal drugs is insufficient to support a conviction for the possession of a controlled dangerous substance, the extent of defendants' involvement here goes well beyond "mere presence or association." Possession of illegal drugs "may be constructive as well as actual and may be joint among several defendants. * * * Constructive possession may be proved by 'ownership, dominion or control over the contraband itself, or dominion or control over the premises or vehicle in which the contraband was concealed.' " *Id.* at 129 (quoting *United States v. Salinas-Salinas*, 555 *F.*2d 470, 473 (5th Cir. 1979)). " '*In essence, constructive possession is the ability to reduce an object to actual possession.*' " *Id.* (quoting *United States v. Martinez*, 588 *F.*2d 495, 498 (5th Cir. 1979)). [Emphasis added.]

The evidence presented in this case provides an ample basis to support each defendant's conviction for the constructive possession of marihuana. "Defendant Gonzalez had the keys to the vanload of marihuana when Agent Ramirez met him. This clearly gave him dominion and control over the marihuana. His participation in discussions about the marihuana shows his knowledge about the whereabouts of the drugs. Defendant Juan Rodriguez took this ability to have dominion and control over the marihuana one step further when he used the keys to open the van containing the controlled substance. He obviously did have actual possession of the marihuana." *Id.* at 129-130.

"Defendant Caballero, who reminded Gonzalez to give the keys to Rodriguez, only held the keys briefly as he passed them between the two defendants. His comment about the keys indicates, however, both knowledge of and ability to obtain dominion and control over the substance. In addition, defendant Caceres introduced both Gonzalez and Caballero to Agent Ramirez as individuals who had a financial interest in the transaction. * * * [T]hese two remarks [certainly could lead to the conclusion reached by the jury] that Caballero constructively possessed the marihuana." *Id.* at 130.

Although defendant Caceres is the only one of the four defendants whom the agents did not see in possession of the keys, the evidence presented at the trial about his role "leads to only one possible conclusion: Caceres was properly convicted of possession of marihuana. At the March 20 meeting where he met Agents Herring and Ramirez, Caceres immediately asked for a clarification of the financial terms of the marihuana sale. When Agent Herring expressed his concern about the quality of the marihuana, Caceres assured him that the marihuana was [fine]. He also stated that he had made arrangements for the agents to inspect the marihuana that afternoon[.]" *Id.* At the Candlelight Lounge meeting, Caceres arranged for his associates to take Ramirez to the warehouse where the marihuana was stored. These "conversations indicate not only Caceres' financial interest in the marihuana and knowledge of its storage location, but most importantly his ability to direct others to take Ramirez to the storage facility. Since the very essence of constructive possession is the ability to reduce the marihuana to actual possession, the power to direct his assistants to show Ramirez the marihuana demonstrates the consequent power to exercise dominion and control over the marihuana personally." *Id.* at 130-131.

Accordingly, the evidence in this case sufficiently connects all four defendants to the marihuana by either actual or constructive possession. *Id.* at 131.

NOTE

1. The mere presence of a person at a residence, or simply his proximity to the drug, is alone insufficient to establish constructive possession. To establish constructive possession, the government must show not only that the individual knew of the presence of the drugs, "but that he was in a position to exercise dominion and control over them." *United States v. Dingle*, 114 *F.*3d 307, 310 (D.C. Cir. 1997). "There must be some action, some word, or some conduct that links the individual to the narcotics and indicates that he had some stake in them, some power over them." *United States v. Pardo*, 636 *F.*2d 535, 549 (D.C. Cir. 1980).

2. *The narcotics broker.* In *United States v. Manzella*, 791 *F.*2d 1263 (7th Cir. 1986), the court held that one who acts as a "finder" or "broker" between a buyer and seller does not constructively possess the drugs ultimately sold and purchased. *Id.* at 1266. Comparing the situation to that of the real estate broker, the court reasoned that the broker of real estate does not possess the house he is trying to sell. Just as the real estate broker knows where the house is, defendant Manzella knew where the cocaine was. He arranged for the get-together between buyer and seller, but he never, according to the court, had individual or joint control over the cocaine. Nor could defendant assure the cocaine's delivery. Constructive possession requires the defendant to have "the ultimate control over the drugs. He need not have them literally in his hands or on premises that he occupies but he

must have the right (not the legal right, but the recognized authority in his criminal milieu) to possess them, as the owner of a safe deposit box has legal possession of the contents even though the bank has actual custody." *Id.* Here, defendant had no right to possess the drugs. His role was merely that of "a finder, a broker, a bringer together of seller and buyer." *Id. See also United States v. Gallagher,* 565 *F.*2d 981 (7th Cir. 1977); *United States v. Jackson,* 526 *F.*2d 1236 (5th Cir. 1976).

3. *Stepping over the line between the broker and the seller. See United States v. Esdaille,* 769 *F.*2d 104 (2d Cir. 1985), where the defendant was introduced to the buyer of cocaine as a supplier, led the buyer to an apartment, and emerged a short time later with the cocaine; this evidence, according to the court, was held sufficient to establish the defendant's constructive possession of the cocaine in the apartment. *Id.* at 105, 108-109. *See also United States v. Davis,* 679 *F.*2d 845, 848, 852-853 (11th Cir. 1982) (evidence supported constructive possession where defendant was a part of a group of conspirators who jointly controlled a quantity of cocaine); *United States v. Weisser,* 737 *F.*2d 729, 732 (8th Cir. 1984) (defendant's ability to assure delivery of the drug in combination with association with the actual possessors sufficient to convict for constructive possession).

UNITED STATES v. JAMES
United States Court of Appeals
764 *F.*2d 885 (D.C. Cir. 1985)

QUESTION: In the proper set of circumstances, may an individual's close proximity to the location where illegal narcotics are found establish his constructive possession of the contraband ?

ANSWER: YES. "[P]roximity may, under certain circumstances, amount to constructive possession." *Id.* at 889. The circumstances must clearly show that the defendant "was knowingly in a position to exercise dominion or control over the drugs." *Id.*

RATIONALE: During the course of a narcotics investigation, police developed probable cause to believe that Jerry James was selling cocaine from his Washington D.C. residence. A search warrant was secured and entry was attempted at approximately one o'clock in the afternoon. As the officers knocked on the door, they heard someone inside the house running down the back stairs. The door was forced and once inside the officers spread out to search different parts of the home.

Officer Stumbo ran down a hallway to the rear of the house and down stairs into a dark basement. "After a few moments searching in the dark, one of the two officers who had followed Stumbo to the basement found and switched on an overhead light. * * * Stumbo saw a bookcase with a curtain hanging behind it and an arm reaching from behind the bookcase." *Id.* at 887. Stumbo drew his revolver and told

889

the individual, later identified as Jerry James' brother, Thomas, to put his hands up. Rather than following the officer's instructions, Thomas grabbed for Stumbo's gun, pulled down on it and caused it to discharge. Thomas was quickly subdued. At the time, Thomas was dressed in his underwear. "When asked to get dressed, he put on clothes taken from a rack of clothes on the other side of the room. After taking Thomas James to the first floor where the other officers were assembling all the persons found in the house, the police began a search of the basement." *Id.*

The basement consisted of two distinct areas; a laundry area and a sleeping area. The laundry area contained a washer, a dryer, and a sink. The officers described the sleeping area as containing a bookcase and curtain, and behind the curtain, a bed which had been recently slept in and a nightstand. On top of the nightstand was a toothbrush, toothpaste, a razor, and an alarm clock. Opposite the bed was the metal clothing bar from which Thomas had selected his clothing. Several items of men's clothing of similar size hung there. Initially, the officers searched the clothing and discovered "a plastic bag containing 10,780 milligrams of marijuana laced with PCP in one of the jackets, and in another seven tin foil packets containing a total of 2,420 milligrams of marijuana laced with PCP." *Id.*

"When the officers first entered the basement they heard water running. In the sink was found a jar with water from the spigot running into it. On the walls of the jar and around the base of the sink there remained flecks of a material that resembled marijuana. * * * When tested[,] the flecks proved to be marijuana laced with PCP." *Id.*

"In several holes in the basement ceiling, running generally from the area of the sink to that of the bed, were found two bags of cocaine, several bags of marijuana, marijuana seeds, and marijuana laced with PCP. * * * Also in the ceiling holes were procaine and mannitol [substances used to dilute cocaine], starch, syringes, a cut card used to mix cocaine, and a spoon with a white powder residue." *Id.* at 887-888.

"Partially partitioned off from the rest of the basement, but without a door, was a small room in which the officers found a variety of drug processing and user materials including mannitol, measuring spoons, pipes used to 'free base' cocaine, glassine bags with a white powder residue, the tops of acetylene torches, * * * a triple beam Ohaus scale used to measure weight to within a tenth of a gram, sheets of plastic, and a heat sealer * * *." *Id.* at 888.

In this appeal, Thomas James "contends that because the government showed him only to be in 'proximity' to the contraband he could not be convicted as a possessor." *Id.* at 889. *Judge Bork, writing for the District of Columbia Circuit, could not agree.*

According to the court, "proximity may, under certain circumstances, amount to constructive possession."

"Possession of a narcotic drug may be either actual or constructive. . . . Constructive possession may be shown through direct or circumstantial evidence of dominion and control over the contraband . . ., and may be found to exist where the evidence supports a finding that the person charged with possession was knowingly in a position, or had the right to exercise 'dominion or control' over the drug."

Id. (quoting *United States v. Lawson*, 682 *F.*2d 1012, 1017 (D.C.Cir. 1982)). The evidence presented by the government in this case "was clearly adequate to show that [Thomas James] was knowingly in a position to exercise dominion or control over the drugs. Thomas [] was found in a basement that [clearly appeared to be] an operating drug-processing factory. The spigot water running into a jar that still contained flecks of illegal narcotics indicated that the destruction of evidence of narcotics had just been attempted by somebody in the basement. There was nobody in the basement but [Thomas]. Moreover, Thomas James was not simply standing in the room or passing through. He was in his underwear, hiding behind a bookcase, and the evidence indicates he tried to disarm the arresting officer. These facts alone, which indicate consciousness of guilt, * * * would seem to be amply sufficient to sustain the conviction for possessing drugs, but there was more." *Id.*

Not only was Thomas James found in his underwear, but next to where he was found was a bed which had been recently slept in. "On the nightstand were articles showing that somebody regularly used the basement as a bedroom. [Thomas] dressed himself in clothing hanging in the room and the remaining clothing, according to a police witness, appeared also to be of the size that fit [Thomas]. Two of the jackets contained large amounts of marijuana laced with PCP. The drugs and paraphernalia in the small room without a door were only a short distance from the bed and were within view." *Id.* In light of this evidence, it would be entirely reasonable to conclude that Thomas James "often slept in the bedroom and, quite aside from the evidence of his consciousness of guilt, could not have been unaware of the narcotics and processing equipment around him." *Id.*

"The only contraband not in plain sight was that in the holes in the ceiling, though the holes themselves were clearly visible. Given the clear pattern revealed by the evidence, it [is] entirely reasonable * * * to infer possession of that contraband as well. [Thomas James'] apparent use of the basement as a residence, the fact that the basement was an operating drug-processing factory, that he had tried to destroy evidence of narcotics possession, and that he had demonstrated consciousness of guilt so clearly tied him into the entire drug operation that it would be idle to speculate that he might not have known of a particular quantity of narcotics merely because it was not in plain view. Were [this court] to rule otherwise, narcotics dealers and possessors could always avoid responsibility for illegal drugs hidden from sight on their premises." *Id.* 890.

Accordingly, defendant Thomas James' conviction was based on sufficient evidence of guilt. His proximity to the illegal drugs, when combined with the other evidence against him, clearly support the finding that he was in constructive possession of the contraband seized.

NOTE

1. *Constructive possession—not a "legal fiction."* In *United States v. Disla*, 805 *F.*2d 1340 (9th Cir. 1986), the court emphasized that "constructive possession" is not a legal fiction. "Rather, the term simply reflects the common sense notion that an individual may possess a controlled substance even though the substance is not on his person at the time of arrest." *Id.* at 1350. "[C]onstructive possession may be demonstrated by direct or circumstantial evidence that the defendant had the power to dispose of the drug, * * * or 'the ability to produce the drug * * *,' or that the defendant had the 'exclusive control or dominion over property on which contraband narcotics are found[.]' " *Id.* [Citations omitted.] The ultimate question is whether "the evidence establishes a sufficient connection between the defendant and the contraband to support the inference that the defendant exercised a dominion and control over the substance." *Id.* " '[M]ere proximity to the drug, mere presence on the property where it is located, or mere association, without more, with the person who does control the drug or the property on which it is found, is insufficient to support a finding of possession.' " *Id.* at 1351. [Citations omitted.]

But see United States v. Manzella, 791 *F.*2d 1263 (7th Cir. 1986), where the court explained that the doctrine of constructive possession, under which a person can be convicted for possessing contraband though he does not possess it in a literal sense, "creates a legal fiction to take care of such cases as that of a drug dealer who operates through hirelings who have physical possession of the drugs." *Id.* at 1266. Whether legal fiction or not, this court is correct in its observation: "It would be odd if a dealer could not be guilty of possession, merely because he had the resources to hire a flunky to have custody of the drugs." *Id.*

2. *Joint ventures.* It has been held that constructive possession may be established by the participation of two or more defendants in a "joint venture" to possess a controlled dangerous substance. Thus, in *United States v. Valentin*, 569 *F.*2d 1069 (9th Cir. 1978), defendant's conviction for knowingly possessing cocaine with the intent to distribute was upheld where the evidence revealed that defendant and his brother had participated in a "joint venture" to obtain and distribute cocaine. Peter Valentin, defendant's brother, delivered a package containing cocaine to an airline freight office in Los Angeles and addressed the parcel to "John Valencia" at Fairbanks, Alaska. Drug inspectors intercepted the package but sent it on to Fairbanks. Officials at Fairbanks observed defendant pick up the package, signing 'J. Valencia' on the receipt for it. Prior investigation uncovered telephone records which indicated that defendant had made several calls to his brother's residence, and that he and his brother had traveled to various parts of South America earlier in the year. Several officers followed defendant to his home, arrested him, and confiscated the package of cocaine.

In the appeal following his conviction, defendant argued that the government had failed to demonstrate that he had possessed the cocaine with the intent to distribute. The Ninth Circuit, however, held that the government presented more than sufficient evidence to support the conviction. Defendant and his brother entered into a "joint venture" for the purpose of obtaining and distributing cocaine. "[T]hey both shared knowing dominion and control over a large quantity of cocaine," and according to the court, defendant was in constructive possession of it at the time when his brother delivered it to the air freight office in Los Angeles and addressed it to defendant. *Id.* at 1071.

But see United States v. Penagos, 823 *F.*2d 346 (9th Cir. 1987), where the court made it clear that a "joint venture" in the absence of "knowing" possession is not enough. Here, defendant's alleged role as a "look-out" was insufficient to establish his constructive possession of cocaine in a set of circumstances in which the government could not establish that he ever had control over the cocaine, that he ever handled any of the boxes or packages of cocaine, or that he had any knowledge of the existence of the drug. *Id.* at 350-351.

MARYLAND v. PRINGLE
Supreme Court of the United States
540 *U.S.* 366, 124 *S.Ct.* 795 (2003)

QUESTION: In the below circumstances, did the officer have probable cause to arrest Pringle for possession of the controlled dangerous substance?

CIRCUMSTANCES: At 3:16 a.m. on August 7th, an officer stopped a Nissan Maxima for speeding. There were three occupants in the car: Donte Partlow, the driver and owner, defendant Joseph Pringle, the front-seat passenger, and Otis Smith, the back-seat passenger. "The officer asked Partlow for his license and registration. When Partlow opened the glove compartment to retrieve the vehicle registration, the officer observed a large amount of rolled-up money in the glove compartment. The officer returned to his patrol car with Partlow's license and registration to check the computer system for outstanding violations. The computer check did not reveal any violations. The officer returned to the stopped car, had Partlow get out, and issued him an oral warning." *Id.* at 798.
  "After a second patrol car arrived, the officer asked Partlow if he had any weapons or narcotics in the vehicle. Partlow indicated that he did not. Partlow then consented to a search of the vehicle. The search yielded $763 from the glove compartment and five plastic glassine baggies containing cocaine from behind the back-seat armrest. When the officer began the search, the armrest was in the upright position flat against the rear seat. The officer pulled down the armrest and found the drugs, which had been placed between the armrest and the back seat of the car." *Id.*

"The officer questioned all three men about the ownership of the drugs and money, and told them that if no one admitted to ownership of the drugs he was going to arrest them all. The men offered no information regarding the ownership of the drugs or money. All three were placed under arrest and transported to the police station." *Id.* Later that morning, Pringle waived his rights and gave an oral and written confession in which he acknowledged that the cocaine belonged to him.

ANSWER: YES. "[T]he officer had probable cause to believe that Pringle had committed the crime of possession of a controlled substance." *Id.* at 802.

RATIONALE: In the circumstances presented, it is clear that the officer, upon recovering the five plastic glassine baggies containing suspected cocaine, had probable cause to believe a crime had been committed. "The sole question is whether the officer had probable cause to believe that Pringle committed that crime." *Id.* at 799.

The probable-cause standard "deals with probabilities and depends on the totality of the circumstances. * * * 'The substance of all the definitions of probable cause is a reasonable ground for belief of guilt,' [ ] and that the belief of guilt must be particularized with respect to the person to be searched or seized." *Id.* at 800. [Citations omitted.]

To determine whether an officer had probable cause to arrest an individual, courts will "examine the events leading up to the arrest, and then decide 'whether these historical facts, viewed from the standpoint of an objectively reasonable police officer, amount to' probable cause[.]" *Id.* [Citation omitted.]

In this case, the Court found that:

> Pringle was one of three men riding in a Nissan Maxima at 3:16 a.m. There was $763 of rolled-up cash in the glove compartment directly in front of Pringle. Five plastic glassine baggies of cocaine were behind the back-seat armrest and accessible to all three men. Upon questioning, the three men failed to offer any information with respect to the ownership of the cocaine or the money. We think it an entirely reasonable inference from these facts that any or all three of the occupants had knowledge of, and exercised dominion and control over, the cocaine. Thus a reasonable officer could conclude that there was probable cause to believe Pringle committed the crime of possession of cocaine, either solely or jointly.

Id. at 800-01.

Accordingly, the Court held that Pringle's arrest did not violate the Fourth and Fourteenth Amendments. *Id.* at 802.

UNITED STATES v. MASSEY
United States Court of Appeals
687 *F*.2d 1348 (10th Cir. 1982)

QUESTION: In the below set of circumstances, may defendant Massey be deemed to have been in constructive possession of the marijuana at the time of his arrest ?

CIRCUMSTANCES: Three women, two men, and Massey made a round-trip from Oklahoma to Missouri in mid-July. The purpose of the trip was to pick marijuana from an area in Missouri where some members of the group knew it was growing wild. Unbeknownst to the others, one of the women acted as a police informant, alerting the state authorities when the trip was to take place and maintaining contact with officers who followed the group to Missouri. The group traveled in two cars equipped with CB radios, one of which was driven by Massey.

"After two nights of picking, the group had accumulated six large burlap sacks of marijuana. The sacks were loaded into the car that Massey was not driving, and the group headed back toward Oklahoma, still under surveillance. The automobiles were stopped at a roadblock in Muskogee County, Oklahoma, and five of the group were arrested. Warrants to search the two automobiles were obtained, and the marijuana was discovered and seized."

ANSWER: YES. The evidence set forth is legally sufficient to demonstrate Massey's constructive possession of the marijuana at the time he was placed under arrest. *Id.* at 1354.

RATIONALE: "Constructive possession is possession in law but not in fact. A person in constructive possession of an item knowingly holds the power and ability to exercise dominion and control over it." *Id.* Moreover, "[c]onstructive possession may be joint among several individuals and may be established by circumstantial evidence." *Id.*

The circumstances of this case demonstrate that "the trip was a cooperative venture, that Massey helped pick and load the marijuana, and that he was to receive a one fourth share. Even though he was not driving the car in which the marijuana was found, the two vehicles were traveling together and maintained communication by CB radio. The evidence was [therefore] sufficient to permit the inference that a working relationship existed among the group members by which Massey had 'some appreciable ability to guide the destiny of the drug.'" *Id.* (quoting *United States v. Staten*, 581 *F*.2d 878, 883 (D.C.Cir. 1978)). "Therefore, the evidence of constructive possession was legally sufficient[.]" *Id.*

UNITED STATES v. BRETT
United States Court of Appeals
872 F.2d 1365 (8th Cir. 1989)

QUESTION: May the Government establish an individual's constructive possession of contraband found in a "crack house" when, upon arrival of the police, the individual is (1) observed fleeing from the area of the house, and (2) found to be in possession of a key to the house ?

ANSWER: YES. Under the circumstances of this case, "proof of possession of the key to the front door of the [crack] house [was] sufficient to prove the 'knowing [constructive] possession'" of the contraband found inside. *Id.* at 1369. "[E]very other circuit to address this issue agrees that the holder of the key, be it to the dwelling, vehicle or motel room in question, has constructive possession of the contents therein." *Id.* 1369 n.3.

RATIONALE: In early November, Kansas City Police Detective Rosilyn Morrison, while working in an undercover capacity, went to a house at 4039 Park Avenue and purchased crack cocaine from two unknown males. On the basis of this purchase, Morrison obtained a warrant to search the 4039 premises. When the search team arrived at the premises, one officer observed a black male, later identified as defendant Gray, run out the back of the building and head north. The officer immediately entered the rear of the house, arrested and secured the two other occupants (defendants Williams and Brett), and then went searching for Gray. Two houses north of the 4039 Park Avenue residence, Gray was found hiding under a porch. Also found under the porch next to Gray was $300 in currency. Gray was placed under arrest and a subsequent search of his person disclosed $3,746 in additional currency and the key to the front door of 4039 Park Avenue.

"A search of 4039 Park Avenue revealed the existence of a fortified drug house. While the utilities were on, the house did not appear to be lived in. It had no refrigerator, no stove, no food, no telephone, and there was no clothing present. The windows were covered and the doors were reinforced. The back door was reinforced with plywood and had two locks on it as well as a chain lock at the top. The front door had metal brackets on either side of the frame which were fitted with a two-by-four board across the door." *Id.* at 1368.

Defendant Williams was found to be in possession of a 9 millimeter pistol with thirteen rounds of ammunition in the magazine and one round in the chamber, $1,465 in cash, and a large plastic bag, later determined to contain 82 small ziplock bags of crack cocaine totaling 46.66 grams in weight. Brett was found to be in possession of $1,300 in currency.

After his arrest, Gray told the officers that his name was "James Monroe," and that he did not work at the crack house. He stated that he was unemployed, but maintained that the $4,046 seized from him was "not drug money."

In this appeal, defendant Gray contends, among other things, that the Government did not present sufficient evidence to prove his possession of the contraband. *The Court of Appeals for the Eighth Circuit could not agree.*

"Proof of constructive possession is sufficient to satisfy the element of knowing possession under 21 *U.S.C.* §841(a)(1)." *Brett* at 1369. "A person has constructive possession of contraband if he has 'ownership, dominion or control over the contraband itself, *or dominion over the premises in which the contraband is concealed.'* " *Id.* [Emphasis in original; citations omitted.] Moreover, "constructive possession may be joint among several defendants; it need not be exclusive." *Id.*

The circumstances in this case, according to the court, sufficiently demonstrate Gray's constructive possession of the evidence seized from Williams and Brett during the course of their arrest at the crack house. It is undisputed that Gray (1) fled from the scene at the time police officers initially approached the house; (2) falsely identified himself at the time of arrest; (3) had in his possession $3,746 at the time of his arrest and claimed ownership to an additional $300 recovered from the location where he was apprehended; and (4) stated that he was unemployed, but would not explain how he obtained the money which he claimed was his. "While it may be that, standing alone, each piece of this evidence would perhaps be insufficient to convict, its cumulative effect cannot be ignored." *Id.*

Perhaps the most "significant link" showing Gray's participation in the criminal possession of the evidence "was his possession of a key to the front door of 4039 Park. This house was a fortified, operational crack house where over 46 grams of cocaine, large amounts of cash, a gun and ammunition were concealed." *Id.* And in this respect, the court finds Gray's argument—that Brett and Williams were the ones in control of the contraband—"unpersuasive." *Id.* "[C]onstructive possession," reiterates the court, "may be joint among several defendants; it need not be exclusive." *Id.*

Accordingly, the Government's proof of Gray's "possession of the key to the front door of the [crack] house * * * sufficient[ly] established Gray's] 'knowing possession' " of the evidence seized from Williams and Brett at the house. *Id.*

NOTE

The court in *Brett* noted that "every other circuit to address this issue agrees that the holder of the key, be it to the dwelling, vehicle or motel room in question, has constructive possession of the contents therein." *Id.* at 1369 n.3. *See e.g., United States v. Zabalaga,* 834 *F.*2d 1062 (D.C.Cir. 1987) (keys to locked car where drugs were found); *United States v. Perlaza,* 818 *F.*2d 1354 (7th Cir. 1987) (key to motel room where drugs were seized); *United States v. Gaviria,* 740 *F.*2d 174 (2d Cir. 1984) (keys to apartment and box where cocaine was found); *United States v. Damsky,* 740 *F.*2d 134 (2d Cir. 1984) (key to camper where hashish was located); *United States v. Martorano,* 709 *F.*2d 863 (3rd Cir. 1983) (keys to van and to padlock on van where contraband was found); *United States v. Martinez,* 588 *F.*2d 495 (5th Cir. 1979) (key to trunk of car sufficient even when defendant was not the owner of the car nor in the car at the time contraband was found).

COMMONWEALTH v. KITCHENER
Superior Court of Pennsylvania
351 *Pa.Super.* 613, 506 *A*.2d 941 (1986)

QUESTION: May more than one person have possession of an illegal substance at the same time ?

ANSWER: YES. " 'Possession of an illegal substance need not be exclusive; two or more can possess the same drug at the same time.' " *Id.* at 620. [Citation omitted.]

RATIONALE: While in the course of executing an arrest warrant for a New Jersey fugitive from justice, police observed, in plain view, a small amount of marijuana in an ashtray in the fugitive's and defendant's living room. Based on this finding, a search warrant issued for the fugitive's and defendant's residence, and the search uncovered contraband in the living room, in the bedroom under the bed, and in the freezer. Since the controlled substances were not found on the person of either defendant or her "boyfriend, the fugitive," the court required that "constructive possession" be proved.

Constructive possession may be proved by showing joint possession. " 'Possession of an illegal substance need not be exclusive; two or more can possess the same drug at the same time.' " *Id.* at 620. (quoting *Commonwealth v. Macolino*, 503 *Pa.* 201 (1983)). Here, the evidence clearly supports the finding that defendant was in joint constructive possession of the controlled substances. "The drugs were found in a dwelling where defendant and her boyfriend were the sole adult residents[, and in specific locations] which would be particularly within the access and knowledge of the residents." *Kitchener* at 620. Therefore, this court finds that "it was reasonable for the fact finder to conclude that defendant knowingly or intentionally possessed [the] controlled substances." *Id.*

Significantly, the locations in which the contraband was discovered were peculiarly within the control of defendant and her boyfriend—the methamphetamine discovered in a mason jar and in a briefcase under the bed where both occupants were found, the controlled substances discovered in the freezer and under a living room chair—all lending additional support for the conclusion that each occupant or resident intended to jointly possess the substances.

Accordingly, this court concludes that there was sufficient evidence on the record to find the defendant in constructive possession of the contraband found in plain view and seized pursuant to the warrant.

---

§14.3. Distribution.

§14.3(a). Introduction.

Once a defendant is charged with possession of a particular controlled dangerous substance with the intent to distribute, the Government bears the burden of establishing sufficient proof of the possessor's "specific intent" to distribute the contraband, and it may do so "by either direct or circumstantial evidence." *United States v. Brett*, 872 *F*.2d 1365, 1370 (8th Cir. 1989). *See also United States v. Matra*, 841 *F*.2d 837, 841 (8th Cir. 1988). In the absence of direct evidence of distribution, a court must infer a possessor's intent to distribute from the circumstantial evidence produced by the prosecution which tends to demonstrate an inference of such an intention. *United States v. Franklin*, 728 *F*.2d 994, 998 (8th Cir. 1984).

ESTABLISHING AN INTENT TO DISTRIBUTE

[I] QUANTITY

Quantity is perhaps the foremost indicator; the intent to distribute may, in some cases be inferred "solely" from the possession of a large quantity of drugs. *United States v. LaGuardia*, 774 *F*.2d 317, 320 (8th Cir. 1985). *See also United States v. Koua Thao*, 712 *F*.2d 369, 371 (8th Cir. 1983) (154.74 grams of opium); *United States v. Vergara*, 687 *F*.2d 57, 62 (5th Cir. 1982) (intent to distribute found from defendant's possession of five ounces of heroin, valued at that time at $8,500); *United States v. DeLeon*, 641 *F*.2d 330, 335 (5th Cir. 1981) (294 grams of cocaine); *United States v. Love*, 599 *F*.2d 107, 109 (5th Cir. 1979) (26 pounds of marijuana); *United States v. Edwards*, 602 *F*.2d 458, 470 (1st Cir. 1979) (200 grams of heroin); *United States v. Muckenthaler*, 584 *F*.2d 240, 247 (8th Cir. 1978) (147.09 grams of cocaine); *United States v. Echols*, 477 *F*.2d 37, 40 (8th Cir. 1973) (199.73 grams of cocaine); *United States v. Mather*, 465 *F*.2d 1035, 1037-38 (5th Cir. 1972) (197.75 grams of cocaine).

When dealing with a drug such as LSD (lysergic acid diethylamide), the United States Supreme Court has explained that it is "such a powerful narcotic that the average dose contains only 0.05 milligrams of the pure drug. The per-dose amount is so minute that in most instances LSD is transferred to a carrier medium and sold at retail by the dose, not by weight. In the typical case, pure LSD is dissolved in alcohol or other solvent, and the resulting solution is applied to paper or gelatin. The solvent evaporates; the LSD remains. The dealer cuts the paper or gel into single-dose squares for sale on the street. Users ingest the LSD by swallowing or licking the squares or drinking a beverage into which the squares have been mixed." *Neal v. United States*, 516 *U.S.* 284, 116 *S.Ct.* 763, 764 (1996); *See also Chapman v. United States*, 500 *U.S.* 453, 111 *S.Ct.* 1919, 1926, 1929 (1991) (when calculating the weight of LSD for punishment purposes, the weight of the blotter paper or other carrier medium used to distribute the drug is included in the calculation of the total weight of the drug; defendant's mandatory minimum sentence of five years affirmed where, even though weight of the pure LSD was under the statutory requirement (50 milligrams), the combined weight of the LSD and blotter paper (5.7 grams) triggered the mandatory minimum sentence).

The absence of the requisite intent may at times be inferred where only a small amount of the controlled substance is discovered. *See e.g., Commonwealth v. Gill*, 490 *Pa.* 1, 415 *A.2d* 2, 4 (1980) (small amount of controlled substance held consistent with personal use, not distribution). In fact, it has been held that "[p]roof of possession of a small amount of a controlled substance, standing alone, is an insufficient basis from which an intent to distribute may be inferred." *United States v. Washington*, 586 *F.*2d 1147, 1153 (7th Cir. 1978) (possession of 1.43 grams of cocaine). *See also Turner v. United States*, 396 *U.S.* 398, 422-23, 90 *S.Ct.* 642, 655-656 (1970) (possession of 14.68 grams of 5% pure cocaine held insufficient to demonstrate an intent to distribute); *United States v. Bailey*, 691 *F.*2d 1009, 1019 n.13 (11th Cir. 1982) (possession of 3.4 grams of cocaine held insufficient to raise an inference of intent to distribute); *United States v. Oliver*, 523 *F.*2d 1252, 1253 n.1 (5th Cir. 1975) (possession of 1.84 grams of 16.8% pure cocaine held to be too small an amount to demonstrate an intent to distribute); *Bentley v. Cox*, 508 *F.Supp.* 870, 877 (E.D. Va. 1981) (possession of 73 grams of marijuana held consistent with possession for personal use).

[II] PARAPHERNALIA

The presence or absence of drug paraphernalia can be significant. While the presence of a razor, mirror and straw along with a small amount of cocaine would certainly be indicative of personal use, a larger amount of the drug and no paraphernalia could suggest possession for the purpose of distribution. On the other hand, possession of a small amount of the drug together with a substantial quantity of paraphernalia, such as boxes of new vials, scores of new plastic baggies or sensitive weighing scales may suggest the presence of an intent to distribute. *See e.g., United States v. Staten*, 581 *F.*2d 878, 886 (D.C.Cir. 1978) ("intent to distribute may be inferred from possession of drug-packaging paraphernalia"); *United States v. Fitzgerald*, 719 *F.*2d 1069, 1072 (10th Cir. 1983) (possession of 33 grams of 70% pure amphetamine and 25 grams of 47% pure cocaine, found along with sensitive weighing scales supported an inference of an intent to distribute); *United States v. Burns*, 624 *F.*2d 95, 102 (10th Cir. 1980) (possession of 100% pure cocaine along with weighing equipment supported inference of an intent to distribute); *United States v. Hollman*, 541 *F.*2d 196, 199 (8th Cir. 1976) (possession of heroin packaged in 127 separate foil packets held consistent with an intent to distribute).

The presence of cutting agents coupled with the possession of a controlled substance whose physical characteristics permit dilution in this way leads to a reasonable inference that the drug is not merely possessed for personal use. *United States v. Franklin*, 728 *F.*2d 994, 999 (8th Cir. 1984). *See also United States v. Marszalkowski*, 669 *F.*2d 655, 662 (5th Cir. 1982) (possession of 38.2 grams of at least 84% pure cocaine along with cutting substance, a large amount of cash and a weapon justified inference of intent to distribute); *State v. Binns*, 222 *N.J.Super.* 583, 593 (App.Div. 1988) (baking soda and gram scale seized along with 62.96 grams of cocaine, 22.91 grams of which were free base, found indicative of distribution); *United States v. James*, 494 *F*.2d 1007, 1030 (D.C.Cir. 1974) (possession of significant amounts of glassine bags, assorted cutting and weighing paraphernalia, and address books containing notations in terminology used in the drug-trafficking trade supported an inference of an intent to distribute).

[III] PURITY

"Purity level is another factor properly considered with respect to intent to distribute." *Brett, supra*, 872 *F*.2d at 1370. *See also Burns, supra*, 624 *F*.2d at 102; *United States v. Blake*, 484 *F*.2d 50, 58 (8th Cir. 1973) (possession of 14.3 grams of 17.3% pure heroin, a bottle of quinine, a mirror, two playing cards, and testimony that the purity level exceeded the average street purity level supported an inference that the drug was not possessed merely for personal use); *State v. Perez*, 218 *N.J.Super*. 478, 482 (App.Div. 1987) (possession of 124.6 grams of 56% pure cocaine, 70 grams of which were free base supported inference of intent to distribute).

[IV] PRESENCE OF LARGE SUMS OF CASH

The unexplained presence of large sums of cash in connection with other evidence of drug dealing has been considered as probative of prior drug sales. *See e.g., United States v. Tramunti*, 513 *F*.2d 1087, 1105 (2d Cir. 1975); *Marszalkowski, supra*, 669 *F*.2d at 662. In order to successfully present this indicator of an intent to distribute, the prosecution must demonstrate a sufficient nexus between the money and the controlled substance.

[V] LOCATION

At times, smaller quantities of a controlled substance may still sustain an inference of the intent to distribute when the quantity of drug possessed is "highly unusual" in the context of the location at which the possessor is found. *See e.g., United States v. Ramirez-Rodriquez*, 552 *F*.2d 883 (9th Cir. 1977) (prison inmate's possession of 10 grams of cocaine, calibrated at its pure level, supported inference of an intent to distribute when that quantity of cocaine was "very unusual" in the context of the prison setting and prison authorities on prior occasions almost never found any narcotics in that quantity).

[VI] PRESENCE OF FIREARMS

"[T]he presence of a firearm, generally considered a tool of the narcotics dealer's trade, also is evidence of an intent to distribute." *Brett, supra*, 872 *F*.2d at 1370; *Marszalkowski, supra*, 669 *F*.2d at 662; *United States v. Moses*, 360 *F.Supp*. 301, 303 (W.D.Pa. 1973) (possession of weapon and heroin packaged in a manner commonly used in street distribution sustained an inference of an intent to distribute).

[VII] POSSESSOR ADDICTED TO SAME OR DIFFERENT DRUG

The question whether the possessor is addicted to the drug found in his possession is another consideration in determining whether there is sufficient evidence of an intent to distribute. On the one hand, "[a] finding of addiction may support an inference that a larger quantity of the drug may be kept for personal use." *Ramirez-Rodriquez* at 885. On the other hand, evidence that demonstrates that a defendant is addicted to a substance other than the one found in his possession may support an inference that the drug possessed was for distribution.

[VIII] EXPERT TESTIMONY

Expert testimony on the subject of a defendant's possession with the intent to distribute is permitted so long as the testimony relates information that is not within the common knowledge of the average lay person and is helpful in assisting the trier of fact to understand the evidence or determine a fact in issue. Persons permitted to testify as expert witnesses about controlled dangerous substances and narcotics activities will usually have several years of experience in drug-related fields and advanced training in the detection and recognition of controlled substances. *United States v. Franklin*, 728 *F*.2d 994, 998 n.8 (8th Cir. 1984); *United States v. Pugliese*, 712 *F*.2d 1574, 1581 (2d Cir. 1983); *United States v. Carson*, 702 *F*.2d 351, 369 (2d Cir. 1983).

Once the expert witness is properly qualified, many courts will permit the witness to testify about the characteristics, processing and packaging of narcotics, their street value, average dosage unit, usage and whether the circumstances surrounding a particular individual's possession demonstrate possession for sale rather than personal use. *See e.g., State v. Keener*, 520 *P*.2d 510 (Ariz. 1974) (en banc); *State v. Carreon*, 729 *P*.2d 969 (Ariz.Ct.App. 1986); *People v. Douglas*, 193 *Cal.App*.3d 1691, 239 *Cal.Rptr*. 252 (Ct.App. 1987); *State v. Avila*, 353 *A*.2d 776, 780-781 (Conn. 1974); *Hinnant v. United States*, 520 *A*.2d 292, 293 (D.C. 1987); *State v. Olsen* 315 *N.W*.2d 1, 6-7 (Iowa 1982); *State v. Montana*, 421 *So*.2d 895 (La. 1982); *Commonwealth v. Nichols*, 356 *N.E*.2d 464, 468-469 (Mass. 1976); *State v. Odom*, 116 *N.J*. 65, 78-79 (1989); *Commonwealth v. Johnson*, 517 *A*.2d 1311 (Pa.Super. 1986).

Expert testimony that a defendant fits the "drug courier profile." The use of "drug courier profiles" as substantive evidence that a defendant possessed a quantity of drugs with the intent to distribute has been "severely criticized." *United States v. Belton-Rios*, 878 *F*.2d 1208, 1210 (9th Cir. 1989). Where the prosecution engages in a point-by-point examination of an expert, with specific references to the defendant's characteristics as fitting the typical "drug courier profile," for the purpose of offering such testimony as substantive evidence of the defendant's guilt (*i.e.*, because the defendant fits the profile he must have possessed the drugs for distribution purposes rather than personal use), the tactic has been held to be error. *See United States v. Quigley*, 890 *F*.2d 1019, 1023-24 (8th Cir. 1989) (while the expert "did not directly say that he thought Quigley was guilty of the offense charged because he fit the profile, that was the clear implication of his testimony[, and t]his use of drug courier profile evidence was error"); *United States v. Hernandez-Cuartas*, 717 *F*.2d 552, 555 (11th Cir. 1983) ("Although this information is valuable in helping drug agents to identify potential drug couriers, we denounce the use of this type of evidence as substantive evidence of a defendant's innocence or guilt.").

But see United States v. Belton-Rios, supra, where the court held that such testimony could be used in rebuttal to refute specific attempts by the defense to suggest innocence based on the particular characteristics described in a drug courier profile. *Note also* that in *Quigley* and *Hernandez-Cuartas,* both defendants' convictions were affirmed; in *Quigley* because "the error, in the context of all the evidence, was harmless," *id.* at 1024, and in *Hernandez-Cuartas* because the testimony admitted was used "purely for background material" on how and why the defendant was stopped and searched. *Id.* at 555.

[IX.] MEDICAL NECESSITY NO DEFENSE

In *United States v. Oakland Cannabis Buyers' Cooperative,* 532 *U.S.* 483, 121 *S.Ct.* 1711 (2001), the United States Supreme Court held that "medical necessity is not a defense to manufacturing and distributing marijuana." *Id.,* 121 *S.Ct.* at 1719. Consequently, evidence that some people have "serious medical conditions for whom the use of cannabis is necessary in order to treat or alleviate those conditions or their symptoms" is irrelevant. *Id.* at 1722.

---

§14.3(b). **Cases and materials.**

UNITED STATES v. FRANKLIN
United States Court of Appeals
728 *F.*2d 994 (8th Cir. 1984)

QUESTION: Does the below set of circumstances support an inference of possession of cocaine *with the intent to distribute?*

CIRCUMSTANCES: At about 6:50 a.m., on August 31, Officer Steven Olish was on patrol in the City of St. Louis, Missouri. At the time, Olish was a ten-year veteran of the St. Louis Police Department. "While in his patrol vehicle at the intersection of Hodiamont, Skinker and Horton Streets, Officer Olish observed a 1960 Thunderbird drive through a red light traffic signal." Officer Olish activated his overhead lights and signaled the vehicle to stop.

Franklin, the driver of the Thunderbird, got out of his car and immediately walked toward the officer's patrol car. "He was dressed in his St. Louis City Fire Department uniform. Franklin apologized to Officer Olish, explaining that he was in a hurry and would get in trouble if he was late for work." A check of Franklin's driving credentials revealed an expired driver's license with the photograph completely burned off. Franklin could not produce another license or a registration. Additionally, the Thunderbird exhibited Kentucky license plates and did not have a Missouri inspection sticker or an appropriate St. Louis City or County permit. Olish placed Franklin under arrest.

A search incident to the arrest produced two clear plastic bags containing white powder, which later proved to be 35 grams of 42% pure cocaine (14 grams of 100% pure cocaine). A complete search of Franklin's vehicle produced no additional evidence. At trial, a narcotics officer testified that the average dosage unit of cocaine was approximately one-quarter of a gram. Further, it was stipulated that the amount of cocaine seized had an approximate street value of $3,000.00.

ANSWER: NO. The amount of cocaine possessed by Franklin, without more, constitutes insufficient evidence from which an intent to distribute can be inferred. Consequently, this court holds that the circumstances surrounding Franklin's possession were "insufficient as a matter of law" to demonstrate his possession of the drug with the intent to distribute. *Id.* at 1000.

RATIONALE: In order to establish a violation of 21 *U.S.C.* §841(a)(1), the Government must prove, in addition to defendant's knowing possession, that he "had the 'specific' intent to distribute the controlled substance." *Franklin* at 998. In this case, the prosecution offered no direct evidence of distribution. Intent to distribute, therefore, must be inferred from the facts and circumstances surrounding Franklin's possession. *Id.*

While it is clear that an intent to distribute a controlled substance may, in many cases, be inferred solely from the possession of a large quantity of the substance, it is equally clear that " '[p]roof of possession of a small amount of a controlled substance, standing alone, is an insufficient basis from which an intent to distribute may be inferred.' " *Id.* at 999. [Citation omitted.] "Admittedly, courts have sustained the inference of intent to distribute in cases involving quantities of drugs comparable to the amount found in Franklin's possession at the time of his arrest. However, in each case the government's proof included additional circumstances or evidence consistent with an intent to distribute narcotics." *Id.*

Here, "the cocaine was not packaged in a manner consistent with distribution. Further, despite a complete search of Franklin[and his automobile], the government offered no evidence of distribution paraphernalia, amounts of cash, weapons, or other indicia of narcotics distribution." *Id.* at 1000. The search of authority conducted by this court "fails to reveal a single case in which the amount of cocaine possessed by Franklin, without more, constitutes sufficient evidence from which intent to distribute can be inferred. Thus, [this court holds] the evidence that Franklin possessed the cocaine with the requisite intent to distribute it insufficient as a matter of law." *Id.*

PART IV

LIABILITY

CHAPTER 15

LAW ENFORCEMENT LIABILITY

Section
15.1   Introduction
15.2   Cases and materials

§15.1. Introduction.

When a civil law suit is brought against a law enforcement officer for actions taken in the course of his or her employment, the officer may be protected by the doctrine of "qualified immunity." Procedurally, qualified immunity is deemed to be an "affirmative defense" that the officer must establish by the "preponderance of the evidence." Qualified immunity, also referred to as "executive or good faith immunity, is generally raised by a law enforcement official in defense of a suit brought by a plaintiff under 42 *U.S.C.* §1983, alleging a constitutional or statutory violation. In pertinent part, Section 1983 provides:

> Every person who, under color of any statute, ordinance, regulation, custom, or usage, of any State . . . subjects, or causes to be subjected, any citizen of the United States . . . to the deprivation of any rights, privileges, or immunities secured by the Constitution and laws, shall be liable to the party injured in an action at law, suit in equity, or other proper proceeding for redress.

In general, this statute provides a cause of action for a citizen claiming to have been deprived of his or her well-established federal constitutional or statutory rights by any person acting under the color of state law. *Gomez v. Toledo*, 446 *U.S.* 635, 640, 100 *S.Ct.* 1920, 1923 (1980). *Harlow v. Fitzgerald*, 457 *U.S.* 800, 818, 102 *S.Ct.* 2727, 2738 (1982).

Courts stress that the resolution of immunity issues should occur "at the earliest possible stage in litigation." *Hunter v. Bryant*, 502 *U.S.* 224, 227, 112 *S.Ct.* 534, 536 (1991). In fact, it is improper for a court to routinely submit the issue of qualified immunity to a jury. "Immunity ordinarily should be decided by the court long before trial," *id.* at 228, 112 *S.Ct.* at 537, with the trial judge generally using the summary judgment standard.

To determine whether a law enforcement officer has a qualified immunity defense against a §1983 lawsuit, a court will look to see if the officer violated "clearly established statutory or constitutional rights of which a reasonable person would have known." *Harlow* at 818, 102 *S.Ct.* at 2738. If the police official did not violate clearly established constitutional or statutory law, he or she should have immunity. On the other hand, if the official did violate "clearly established law," the focus then shifts to a consideration of "extraordinary circumstances" that require the official to prove that he or she neither knew nor should have known of the relevant legal standard. *See Harlow* at 819, 102 *S.Ct.* at 2738). The "clearly established law" requirement also has a time component that requires a court to judge an officer's conduct based on the state of the law and facts that existed at the time of the alleged violation. *Anderson v. Creighton*, 483 *U.S.* 635, 639, 107 *S.Ct.* 3034, 3038 (1987).

In *Anderson*, the Court explained that the standard for determining whether qualified immunity exists is an "objective (albeit fact-specific) question whether a reasonable officer could have believed" the action taken was proper, "in light of clearly established law and the information the" the officer possessed at the time. *Id.*, 483 *U.S.* at 641, 107 *S.Ct.* at 3040. Therefore, an officer's "subjective beliefs" about the arrest, search or seizure "are irrelevant." *Id.*

Thus, to determine if law enforcement officer is entitled to qualified immunity, a two-part inquiry must be made:

(1) Was the law governing the officer's conduct clearly established?

(2) Under that law, could a reasonable police officer believe his conduct lawful?

In cases alleging that a police officer engaged in an unlawful arrest, search or seizure, the police officer will be entitled to qualified immunity if the officer can successfully prove: (1) that he or she acted with probable cause; or (2) even if probable cause did not exist, that a reasonable police officer could have believed in its existence. The latter inquiry consists of "a standard of objective reasonableness," which is interpreted as a lesser standard than that required for probable cause. Generally, the only time when that standard is not satisfied is when, on an objective basis, "it is obvious that no reasonably competent officer would have concluded" that the action taken was proper. *See Malley v. Briggs*, 475 *U.S.* 335, 341, 106 *S.Ct.* 1092, 1096 (1986)).

When a search or seizure, or both, is performed under the authority of a warrant, the existence of probable cause will be presumed to exist for purposes of a Section 1983 cause of action based on an alleged Fourth Amendment violation. A plaintiff seeking recovery must then prove by a preponderance of the evidence that probable cause did not exist. If probable cause is found to have existed, then judgment should be entered for the law enforcement official as a matter of law. If probable cause did not exist, however, a court must then decide whether a reasonable police official could have believed in its existence.

§15.2. Cases and materials.

HOPE v. PELZER
Supreme Court of the United States
536 *U.S.* 730, 122 *S.Ct.* 2508 (2002)

QUESTION: In order for a plaintiff to defeat a government officer's "qualified immunity" defense, must the plaintiff show that the preexisting law on the subject was "clearly established" by cases having facts that are "materially similar" to the plaintiff's case?

ANSWER: NO. Although earlier cases involving "materially similar" facts can provide especially strong support for a conclusion that the law was "clearly established" at the time of an officer's conduct, such cases are not necessary for such a finding. Rather, for a constitutional or statutory right to be clearly established, it need only be shown that the contours of the right were "sufficiently clear that a reasonable official would understand that what he is doing violates that right." *Id.* at 2515.

RATIONALE: When a law enforcement or corrections officer is sued under 42 *U.S.C.* §1983, a court is required to make a threshold inquiry as to whether the plaintiff's allegations, if true, establish a constitutional violation. Even if the officer's conduct is determined to be constitutionally impermissible, the officer may nevertheless be shielded from liability for civil damages if the officer's "actions did not violate 'clearly established statutory or constitutional rights of which a reasonable person would have known.' " *Id.* (quoting *Harlow v. Fitzgerald*, 457 *U.S.* 800, 818, 102 *S.Ct.* 2727 (1982)). This standard is sometimes referred to as the "fair warning" standard, or the "*Harlow* test."
    In this case, in assessing whether the constitutional violation here met the *Harlow* test, the court below took the approach that the facts of previous cases must be "materially similar" to the facts of the case at hand. This approach makes the plaintiff's case dependent on the existence of previously-decided, nearly identical cases. According to the United States Supreme Court, however, this rigid approach to the qualified immunity standard was improper. *Id.* The Court explained:

> [Q]ualified immunity operates "to ensure that before they are subjected to suit, officers are on notice their conduct is unlawful." * * * For a constitutional right to be clearly established, its contours "must be sufficiently clear that a reasonable official would understand that what he is doing violates that right. This is not to say that an official action is protected by qualified immunity unless the very action in question has previously been held unlawful * * *; but it is to say that in the light of pre-existing law the unlawfulness must be apparent."

Id. [Citations omitted.]

Naturally, there may be some cases—for example, where the earlier case law on the subject expressly leaves open whether a general rule applies to the particular conduct at issue—when a very high degree of prior factual similarity may be necessary. " 'But general statements of law are not inherently incapable of giving fair and clear warning, and in other instances a general constitutional rule already identified in the decisional law may apply with obvious clarity to the specific conduct in question, even though the very action in question has [not] previously been held unlawful.' " *Id.* at 2516. [Citations and internal quotes omitted.]

Thus, law enforcement and corrections officials "can still be on notice that their conduct violates established law even in novel factual circumstances." *Id.* Although earlier cases involving "materially similar" facts "can provide especially strong support for a conclusion that the law is clearly established, they are not necessary to such a finding." *Id.* In the final analysis, the main question is whether the state of the law at the time of the challenged actions gave the law enforcement officials "fair warning" that their alleged conduct was unconstitutional. *Id.*

In this case, Larry Hope sued several prison officials employed by the Limestone Prison in Alabama, alleging that he was subjected to cruel and unusual punishment, in violation of the Eighth Amendment, when prison guards twice handcuffed him to a hitching post to punish him for disruptive conduct. In the second, more serious situation, Hope fell asleep during the morning bus ride to the chain gang's worksite, and when it arrived, he was less than prompt in responding to an order to get off the bus. "An exchange of vulgar remarks led to a wrestling match with a guard. Four other guards intervened, subdued Hope, handcuffed him, placed him in leg irons and transported him back to the prison where he was put on the hitching post. The guards made him take off his shirt, and he remained shirtless all day while the sun burned his skin. He remained attached to the post for approximately seven hours. During this 7-hour period, he was given water only once or twice and was given no bathroom breaks. At one point, a guard taunted Hope about his thirst." *Id.* at 2512.

Preliminarily, the Court determined that the use of the hitching post unnecessarily and wantonly inflicted pain, and thus was a clear violation of the Eighth Amendment. Arguably, the violation was so obvious that the Supreme Court's own Eighth Amendment cases gave these prison officials "fair warning that their conduct violated the Constitution." *Id.* at 2516. More directly, however, the earlier cases decided in this jurisdiction dictate the conclusion that the prison officials' conduct violated "clearly established statutory or constitutional rights of which a reasonable person would have known." *Id.* For example, in one of those cases, decided in 1974, the Court of Appeals "squarely held" that " 'handcuffing inmates to the fence and to cells for long periods of time, . . . and forcing inmates to stand, sit or lie on crates, stumps, or otherwise maintain awkward positions for prolonged periods' " constitutes cruel and unusual punishment under the Eighth amendment. *Id.* (quoting *Gates v. Collier*, 501 *F*.2d 1291, 1306 (5th Cir. 1974)). For purposes of providing "fair notice to reasonable officers administering punishment for past misconduct," the Supreme Court could find no "reason to draw a constitutional distinction between a practice of handcuffing an inmate to a fence for prolonged periods and handcuffing him to a hitching post for seven hours." *Id.* at 2517. Indeed, " '[n]o reasonable officer could have concluded that the constitutional holding of *Gates* turned on the fact that inmates were handcuffed to fences or the bars of cells, rather than a specially designed metal bar designated for shackling.' " *Id.* [Citation omitted.]

Accordingly, the Limestone Prison officials violated clearly established law. They should have realized that the use of the hitching post under the circumstances alleged by Hope violated the Eighth Amendment prohibition against cruel and unusual punishment. It was not necessary that the prior cases in this area of law be nearly identical on their facts in order to meet the "fair warning" standard.

> The obvious cruelty inherent in this practice should have provided [these officials] with some notice that their alleged conduct violated Hope's constitutional protection against cruel and unusual punishment. Hope was treated in a way antithetical to human dignity—he was hitched to a post for an extended period of time in a position that was painful, and under circumstances that were both degrading and dangerous. This wanton treatment was not done of necessity, but as punishment for prior conduct. [The prior case law in this jurisdiction] put a reasonable officer on notice that the use of the hitching post under the circumstances alleged by Hope was unlawful. The "fair and clear warning," * * * that [this law] provided was sufficient to preclude the defense of qualified immunity at the summary judgment stage.

Id. at 2518.

NOTE

See also *Willingham v. Loughnan*, 261 *F.*3d 1178 (11th Cir. 2001), a case in which police officers were granted qualified immunity from liability for shooting the plaintiff eight times after she lunged at a fellow officer with a knife. The United States Supreme Court granted certiorari in *Willingham*, vacated the judgment and remanded the matter for reconsideration in light of *Hope v. Pelzer*.

MALLEY v. BRIGGS
Supreme Court of the United States
475 *U.S.* 335, 106 *S.Ct.* 1092 (1986)

QUESTION: May a police officer be sued for money damages by the victim of an unlawful arrest, when that officer's complaint and supporting affidavit, which gave rise to a judicially issued warrant, failed to establish probable cause for the arrest?

ANSWER: YES. A police officer may be sued civilly for money damages by the victim of an unlawful arrest. The test is whether a reasonably well-trained officer, under the same circumstances, "would have known that his affidavit failed to establish probable cause and that he should not have applied for the warrant." *Id.* at 1098.

RATIONALE: Rhode Island State Troopers were conducting a narcotics investigation which gave rise to a reasonable suspicion that the defendant (and others) were in possession of marihuana. On the basis of this "suspicion," the state trooper in charge of the investigation drew up felony complaints charging the defendant (and the others) with conspiracy "to violate the uniform controlled substance act of the State of Rhode Island by having (marihuana) in their possession[.]" *Id.* at 1094. The trooper's complaints, supporting affidavits, and arrest warrants were presented to a judge who signed the warrants [authorizing the arrest of the defendant and the others].

The defendant and the others were arrested at their homes, brought to the police station, booked, arraigned, and released. However, all charges were dropped when the grand jury failed to return an indictment.

The persons arrested then brought a civil action under 42 *U.S.C.* §1983 for damages, asserting that the Rhode Island state trooper violated their Fourth and Fourteenth Amendment rights by applying for, obtaining, and executing an arrest warrant without probable cause.

In a seven-to-two decision, the United States Supreme Court held that the same standard of reasonableness set forth in *United States v. Leon*, 468 *U.S.* 897, 104 *S.Ct.* 3405 (1984), "defines the qualified immunity accorded an officer whose request for a warrant allegedly caused an unconstitutional arrest." *Malley* at 1098. In *Leon*, the objective reasonableness test was presented in the context of whether evidence obtained pursuant to a defective search warrant should be suppressed when police officers act in good faith and objectively and reasonably rely upon a warrant issued by a detached and neutral magistrate.

The state trooper argued that a police officer, in these circumstances, is like a prosecutor, and should have the same absolute immunity from such a civil action. If not, "the officer may not exercise his best judgment if the threat of retaliatory lawsuits hangs over him." *Id.* at 1096.

The Court rejected this argument and emphasized that police officers have never been accorded an absolute immunity. Absolute immunity is only given to those functions "intimately associated with the *judicial* phase of the criminal process." *Id.* at 1097. [Citations omitted;

emphasis in original.] The act of a police officer applying for a warrant is much further removed from the "judicial phase" of a criminal proceeding than the actions of the prosecutor who maintains a central role in the continuing judicial process. Additionally, the American Bar Association has developed and presently enforces professional standards for prosecutors which lessen the danger of prosecutorial misconduct. "The absence of a comparably well developed and pervasive mechanism for controlling police misconduct weighs against allowing absolute immunity for the officer." *Id.* at 1097 n.5.

In the alternative, the state trooper argued that he should at least be shielded from liability for damages in this case for he presented his complaints and supporting affidavits to a judge who signed the arrest warrants, and, "the act of applying for a warrant is *per se* objectively reasonable, provided that the officer believes that the facts alleged in his affidavit are true." *Id.* at 1098.

The Court rejected this argument also, holding that the proper test in this case and cases similar "is whether a reasonably well trained officer in [the trooper's] position would have known that his affidavit failed to establish probable cause and that he should not have applied for the warrant. If such was the case, the [trooper's] application for a warrant was not objectively reasonable, because it created the unnecessary danger of an unlawful arrest." *Id.*

If our criminal justice system operated perfectly, "an unreasonable request for a warrant would be harmless, because no judge would approve it. But ours is not an ideal system, and it is possible that a magistrate, working under docket pressures, will fail to perform as a magistrate should." *Id.*

As a result, police officers must "minimize this danger by exercising reasonable professional judgment." *Id.* An officer "cannot excuse his own default by pointing to the greater incompetence of the magistrate." *Id.* at 1098-99 n.9.

NOTE

1. Although *Malley* only involved an objectively unreasonable "arrest," police officers should take note that they are subject to the same civil liability standards for objectively unreasonable searches and seizures. *Malley* at 1097 n.6. However, the professional officer should not allow this case to deter performance of official duties. The officer who properly builds his case, and in good faith constructs an affidavit containing the requisite probable cause will be shielded from liability by the qualified immunity accorded police officers who act objectively and reasonably in the good faith performance of their official duties. At most, this case should cause those officers to take an extra few minutes to reflect upon their affidavits to ensure the existence of probable cause as mandated by the Fourth Amendment.

2. *Absolute immunity for officers effecting arrests at the direction of a judge.* In *Valdez v. City and County of Denver*, 878 F.2d 1285 (10th Cir. 1989), plaintiff, Robert Valdez, was present as a spectator in state traffic court. During the course of the proceedings, when the judge said something to a defendant with which Valdez disagreed,

Valdez exclaimed, "bullshit," and exchanged words with the judge. Thereafter, Valdez was held in contempt and the judge ordered several deputies from the sheriff's department to take him into custody.

After his release from custody, Valdez brought an action for damages under 42 *U.S.C* §1983, alleging, among other things, false arrest and imprisonment against the officers (in their individual capacities) who arrested him. Concluding that the complaint should be dismissed, the Tenth Circuit held that "an official charged with the duty of executing a facially valid court order enjoys absolute immunity from liability for damages in a suit challenging conduct prescribed by that order." *Valdez* at 1286.

Generally, " 'immunity is justified and defined by the *functions* it protects and serves, not by the person to whom it attaches.' " *Id.* at 1287 (quoting *Forrester v. White*, 484 *U.S.* 219, 108 *S.Ct.* 538, 542, 544 (1988) (emphasis in original)). In the context of judicial proceedings, courts have long recognized an absolute immunity " 'for *all* persons—governmental or otherwise—who were integral parts of the judicial process.' " *Id.* [Citations omitted; emphasis in original.] Thus, "the Supreme Court has recognized not only the absolute civil immunity of judges for conduct within their judicial domain, * * * but also the 'quasi-judicial' civil immunity of prosecutors, * * * grand jurors, * * * witnesses, * * * and agency officials * * * for acts intertwined with the judicial process." *Id.*

According to the *Valdez* court, "[e]nforcing a court order or judgment is intrinsically associated with a judicial proceeding." *Id.* at 1288.

> If losing parties were free to challenge the will of the court by threatening its officers with harassing litigation, the officers might neglect the execution of their sworn duties. As the Ninth Circuit aptly reasoned: 'The fearless and unhesitating execution of court orders is essential if the court's authority and ability to function are to remain uncompromised.' * * * Absolute immunity for officials who carry out a judge's orders is necessary to insure that such officials can perform their function without the need to secure permanent legal counsel. A lesser degree of immunity could impair the judicial process.

Id. at 1288 (quoting *Coverdell v. Department of Social and Health Services*, 834 *F.*2d 758, 765 (9th Cir. 1987)).

Moreover, "[t]o force officials performing ministerial acts intimately related to the judicial process to answer in court every time a litigant believes the judge acted improperly is unacceptable. Officials must not be called upon to answer for the legality of decisions which they are powerless to control." *Id.* at 1289. In this respect, the court concluded:

> [I]t is simply unfair to spare the judges who give the orders while punishing the officers who obey them. Denying these officials absolute immunity for their acts would make them a "lightning rod for harassing litigation aimed at judicial orders." * * *

Tension between trial judges and those officials responsible for enforcing their orders inevitably would result were there not absolute immunity for both. * * *

Absolute immunity will ensure the public's trust and confidence in courts' ability to completely, effectively and finally adjudicate the controversies before them. * * *

Because the record viewed as a whole indicates that every action of the defendant[officers] to which Valdez objects was taken under the direction of a state court judge, * * * this ca[se is] remanded with instructions to dismiss the complaint as to [each of the officers] in their individual capacities on the basis of absolute immunity.

Id. at 1289-90. [Citations omitted.]

See also Coverdell v. Department of Social and Health Services, 834 *F.*2d 758, 764-65 (9th Cir. 1987) (social worker accorded absolute quasi-judicial immunity from suit arising out of worker's apprehension of child pursuant to court order); *Henry v. Farmer City State Bank*, 808 *F.*2d 1228, 1238-39 (7th Cir. 1986) (sheriff acting under a court order directing enforcement of judgment accorded absolute immunity); *Tymiak v. Omodt*, 676 *F.*2d 306, 308 (8th Cir. 1982) (sheriff accorded absolute immunity from suit for eviction of plaintiff from home in compliance with court order); *Tarter v. Hury*, 646 *F.*2d 1010, 1013 (5th Cir. 1981) (absolute immunity accorded court clerks in actions for damages based upon ministerial conduct required by court order); *Slotnick v. Garfinkle*, 632 *F.*2d 163, 166 (1st Cir. 1980) (state hospital superintendent acting at the direction of a judge accorded judicial immunity); *Waits v. McGowan*, 516 *F.*2d 203, 206 & n.6 (3rd Cir. 1973) (judicial immunity accorded to police officers engaged in ministerial functions under court's direction); *Fowler v. Alexander*, 478 *F.*2d 694, 696 (4th Cir. 1973) (sheriff and jailer who confined plaintiff pursuant to a court order accorded absolute immunity from suit).

3. *Whether a reasonable officer could have believed the arrest to be lawful.* In *Hunter v. Bryant*, 502 *U.S.* 224, 112 *S.Ct.* 534 (1991), James Bryant delivered two photocopies of a handwritten letter to two administrative officers at the University of Southern California. "The rambling letter referred to a plot to assassinate President Ronald Reagan by 'Mr. Image,' who was described as 'Communist white men within the National Council of Churches.' The letter stated that 'Mr. Image wants to murder President Reagan on his up and coming trip to Germany,' that 'Mr. Image had conspired with a large number of U.S. officials in the plot to murder President Reagan' and others, and that 'Mr. Image (NCC) still plans on murdering the President on his trip to Germany in May of 1985.' * * * President Reagan was traveling in Germany at the time." *Id.*, 112 *S.Ct.* at 535.

"A campus police sergeant telephoned the Secret Service, and agent Brian Hunter responded to the call. After reading the letter, agent Hunter interviewed University employees. One identified James Bryant as the man who had delivered the letter and reported that Bryant had 'told her "[h]e should have been assassinated in Bonn."' 'Another employee said that the man who delivered the letter made statements about ' "bloody coups" ' and ' "assassination," ' while moving his hand horizontally across his throat to simulate a cutting action." *Id.*

"Hunter and another Secret Service agent, Jeffrey Jordan, then visited a local address that appeared on the letter. Bryant came to the door and gave the agents permission to enter. He admitted writing and delivering the letter, but refused to identify ' "Mr. Image" ' and answered questions about ' "Mr. Image" ' in a rambling fashion. Bryant gave Hunter permission to search the apartment, and the agent found the original of the letter. While the search was underway, Jordan continued questioning Bryant, who refused to answer questions about his feelings toward the President or to state whether he intended to harm the President." *Id.*

Hunter and Jordan arrested Bryant for making threats against the President, contrary to 18 *U.S.C.* §871(a), and a magistrate ordered him held without bond. Ultimately, the criminal complaint against Bryant was dismissed on the Government's motion.

Bryant subsequently sued agents Hunter and Jordan, the United States Department of the Treasury, and the Director of the Secret Service. The only issue before the Supreme Court was whether the agents, as a matter of law, were entitled to a qualified immunity on the claim that they had arrested Bryant without probable cause. Rejecting the Ninth Circuit's conclusion that the agents "had failed to sustain the burden of establishing qualified immunity because their reason for arresting Bryant—their belief that the ' "Mr. Image" ' plotting to kill the President in Bryant's letter could be a pseudonym for Bryant—was not the most reasonable reading of Bryant's letter," the Court explained:

> Our cases establish that qualified immunity shields agents Hunter and Jordan from suit if "a reasonable officer could have believed [Bryant's arrest] to be lawful, in light of clearly established law and the information the [arresting] officers possessed." * * * Even law enforcement officials who "reasonably but mistakenly conclude that probable cause is present" are entitled to immunity. [] Moreover, because "[t]he entitlement is an *immunity from suit* rather than a mere defense to liability," * * * we repeatedly have stressed the importance of resolving immunity questions at the earliest possible stage in litigation.

Id. at 536. [Citations omitted; emphasis in original.]

According to the Court, the decision of the Ninth Circuit Court of Appeals "ignores the import" of the principles set forth above. That court should have asked "whether the agents acted reasonably under settled law in the circumstances, not whether another reasonable, or more reasonable, interpretation of the events can be constructed five years after the fact." *Id.* at 536-37. "Under settled law, Secret Service agents Hunter and Jordan are entitled to immunity if a reasonable officer could have believed that probable cause existed to arrest Bryant." *Id.* at 537.

> Probable cause existed if "at the moment the arrest was made . . . the facts and circumstances within their knowledge and of which they had reasonably trustworthy information were sufficient to

warrant a prudent man in believing" that Bryant had violated 18 U.S.C. §871. * * *

When agents Hunter and Jordan arrested Bryant, they possessed trustworthy information that Bryant had written a letter containing references to an assassination scheme directed against the President, that Bryant was cognizant of the President's whereabouts, that Bryant had made an oral statement that " 'he should have been assassinated in Bonn,' " [] and that Bryant refused to answer questions about whether he intended to harm the President. On the basis of this information, a magistrate ordered Bryant to be held without bond.

These undisputed facts establish that the Secret Service agents are entitled to qualified immunity. Even if we assumed, *arguendo*, that they (*and* the magistrate) erred in concluding that probable cause existed to arrest Bryant, the agents nevertheless would be entitled to qualified immunity because their decision was reasonable, *even if mistaken*. * * *

The qualified immunity standard "gives ample room for mistaken judgments" by protecting "all but the plainly incompetent or those who knowingly violate the law." * * * This accommodation for reasonable error exists because "officials should not err always on the side of caution" because they fear being sued. * * * Our National experience has taught that this principle is nowhere more important than when the specter of Presidential assassination is raised.

[T]he judgment of the Court of Appeals is reversed.

Id. at 537. [Citations omitted; emphasis added.]

4. *Civil actions against state officials.*

(a) In their "official capacities." For §1983 purposes, a State, or an official of the State acting in his or her official capacity, is not considered a "person" within the meaning of that section. *Will v. Michigan Dept. of State Police*, 491 *U.S.* 58, 109 *S.Ct.* 2304, 2312 (1989).

In pertinent part, section 1983 provides:

> Every person who, under color of any statute, ordinance, regulation custom, or usage, of any State * * * subjects or causes to be subjected, any citizen * * * to the deprivation of any rights, privileges, or immunities secured by the Constitution and laws, shall be liable to the party injured in an action at law, suit in equity, or other proper proceeding for redress.

"Section 1983 provides a federal forum to remedy many deprivations of civil liberties, but it does not provide a federal forum for litigants who seek a remedy against a State for alleged deprivations of civil liberties. The Eleventh Amendment bars such suits unless the State has waived its immunity." *Will* at 2309. It is a well-established rule of "sovereign immunity" that "a State cannot be sued in its own courts without its consent." *Id.* at 2309-2310. Thus, it cannot be concluded that the enactment of "§1983 was intended to disregard the well-established immunity of a State from being sued without its consent." *Id.* at 2310.

According to the Court, this ruling should not be read to "cast any doubt" on *Monell v. New York City Dept. of Social Services*, 436 *U.S.* 658, 98 *S.Ct.* 2018 (1978). Municipalities are still "persons" within the meaning of §1983. The holding in *Will*, however, merely determines that States or governmental entities that are considered "arms of the State" for Eleventh Amendment purposes, including state officials acting in their official capacities, are not "persons" within the meaning of that section. Ironically, the State and its officials *are* considered persons when the relief sought is prospective in nature, *e.g.*, an injunction. *Id.* at 2311 n.10.

(b) *In their "individual capacities."* In *Hafer v. Melo*, 502 *U.S.* 21, 112 *S.Ct.* 358 (1991), the Court rejected the argument that *Will v. Michigan Dept. of State Police, supra*, should be interpreted to disallow *all* suits against state officers for damages arising from official acts. The Court declared: "We reject this reading of *Will* and hold that state officials sued in their individual capacities are 'persons' for purposes of §1983." *Hafer*, 112 *S.Ct.* at 360. According to the Court, state officers may be held personally liable for damages under §1983 based upon actions taken in their official capacities.

Here, in *Hafer*, the Court distinguished between "official-capacity" suits and "personal-capacity" suits.

> A suit against a state official in her official capacity [] should be treated as a suit against the State. * * * Indeed, when an official sued in this capacity in federal court dies or leaves office, her successor automatically assumes her role in the litigation. * * * Because the real party in interest in an official-capacity suit is the governmental entity and not the named official, "the entity's 'policy or custom' must have played a part in the violation of federal law." * * * For the same reason, the only immunities available to the defendant in an official-capacity action are those that the government entity possesses. * * *
>
> Personal-capacity suits, on the other hand, seek to impose individual liability upon a government officer for actions taken under color of state law. Thus, "[o]n the merits, to establish *personal* liability in a §1983 action, it is enough to show that the official, acting under color of state law, caused the deprivation of a federal right." * * * While the plaintiff in a personal-capacity suit need not establish a connection to governmental "policy or custom," officials sued in their personal capacities, unlike those sued in their official capacities, may assert personal immunity defenses such as objectively reasonable reliance on existing law.

Id. at 361-62 (quoting *Kentucky v. Graham*, 473 *U.S.* 159, 165-67, 105 *S.Ct.* 3099, 3104-06 (1985)). [Emphasis in original.]

Will held that state officials, sued in their official capacities, are not "persons" under §1983. An "official-capacity suit against a state officer 'is not a suit against the official but rather is a suit against the official's office. As such it is no different from a suit against the State itself.'" *Hafer* at 362. [Citation omitted.] The phrase "acting in his or her official capacity," therefore, "is best understood as a reference to the capacity in which the state officer is sued, not the capacity in which the officer inflicts the alleged injury." *Id.*

As a result, the *Hafer* Court concluded that because a state officer sued in his or her "personal capacity" comes to court as an "individual," such an officer, "in the role of personal-capacity defendant thus fits comfortably within the statutory term 'person.'" *Id.* Consequently,

> state officials, sued in their individual capacities, are "persons" within the meaning of §1983. The Eleventh Amendment does not bar such suits, nor are state officers absolutely immune from personal liability under §1983 solely by virtue of the "official" nature of their acts.

Id. at 365.

5. *Acting under color of state law.* In pertinent part, 42 *U.S.C.* §1983 provides:

> Every person who, *under color of any statute, ordinance, regulation, custom, or usage of any State* * * *, subjects, or causes to be subjected, any citizen of the United States or other person within the jurisdiction thereof to the deprivation of any rights, privileges, or immunities secured by the Constitution and laws, shall be liable to the party injured in an action at law. * * * (emphasis added).

In a civil rights lawsuit brought under §1983, the person suing must, in addition to alleging a violation of a right secured by the Constitution and laws of the United States, "show that the alleged deprivation was committed by a person *acting under color of state law.*" *West v. Atkins*, 487 *U.S.* 42, 48, 108 *S.Ct.* 2250, 2254-55 (1988). [Emphasis added.]

"The traditional definition of acting under color of state law requires that the defendant in a §1983 action have exercised power 'possessed by virtue of state law and made possible only because the wrongdoer is clothed with the authority of state law.'" *Atkins* at 49, 108 *S.Ct.* at 2255 (quoting *United States v. Classic*, 313 *U.S.* 299, 326, 61 *S.Ct.* 1031, 1042-43 (1941)). In this respect, acts of state or local law enforcement officers in their official capacities "will generally be found to have occurred under color of state law," *Barna v. City of Perth Amboy*, 42 *F.*3d 809, 816 (3rd Cir. 1994), even when an officer oversteps the bounds of his or her authority. *Screws v. United States*, 325 *U.S.* 91, 111, 65 *S.Ct.* 1031, 1040 (1945).

Under "color" of law also means under "pretense" of law. *Screws* at 111, 65 *S.Ct.* at 1040. "Thus, one who is without actual authority, but who purports to act according to official power, may also act under color of state law." *Barna* at 816. For example, in *Griffin v. Maryland*, 378 *U.S.* 130, 84 *S.Ct.* 1770 (1964), the Supreme Court held that a deputy sheriff employed as a private security guard by a private park operator acted under color of state law when he ordered the plaintiff to leave the park, escorted him off the premises, and arrested him for criminal trespass. While the deputy sheriff was actually acting as an agent of the private park operator rather than as an agent of the state, he nonetheless "wore a sheriff's badge and consistently identified himself as a deputy sheriff rather than as an employee of the park," and consequently "purported to exercise the authority of a deputy sheriff." *Id.* at 135, 84 *S.Ct.* at 1772. Finding that the deputy was acting under color of state law, the Court stated:

> If an individual is possessed of state authority and purports to act under that authority, his action is state action. It is irrelevant that he might have taken the same action had he acted in a purely private capacity.

Id.

Similarly, "off-duty police officers who purport to exercise official authority will generally be found to have acted under color of state law. Manifestations of such pretended authority may include flashing a badge, identifying oneself as a police officer, placing an individual under arrest, or intervening in a dispute involving others pursuant to a duty imposed by police department regulations." *Barna* at 816.

"On the other hand, a police officer's purely private acts which are not furthered by any actual or purported state authority are not acts under color of state law." *Id. See e.g., Delcambre v. Delcambre,* 635 *F.*2d 407, 408 (5th Cir. 1981) (alleged assault by on-duty police chief at police station held not to occur under color of state law because the altercation with the plaintiff, the chief's sister-in-law, arose out of a personal dispute and the chief neither arrested nor threatened to arrest the plaintiff).

Even an officer's use of a department-issue weapon in pursuit of a private activity may not be enough indicia of state authority to conclude that the officer acted under color of state law. *Compare Bonsignore v. City of New York,* 683 *F.*2d 635 (2nd Cir. 1982) (officer who used police-issue handgun to shoot his wife and then commit suicide did not act under color of state law even though he was required to carry the handgun at all times); *Barna v. City of Perth Amboy, supra* at 817-19 (off-duty police officers intervening in a family altercation involving one officer's sister, outside their official jurisdiction, where neither officer identified himself as a police officer, held not to be conduct "under color of state law," notwithstanding the unauthorized use by one officer of a police-issue nightstick) *with United States v. Tarpley,* 945 *F.*2d 806, 809 (5th Cir. 1991) (off-duty deputy sheriff acted under color of state law when the deputy assaulted his wife's alleged ex-lover in a private vendetta but identified himself as a police officer, used his service revolver, and intimated that he could use police authority to get away with the paramour's murder).

6. *Establishing probable cause; suspect denying incident.* In *Brodnicki v. City of Omaha,* 75 *F.*3d 1261 (8th Cir. 1996), nine-year-old Meaghan reported to the police that she had been approached and followed by a man who tried to coax her into his car. "She stated that the man had dirty-blonde hair, a moustache, wore glasses, a black hat and black shirt, and drove a white car with license plate number

1-AA864." *Id.* at 1263. According to Meaghan, the man opened his car door and said, "Your mother's going to be late at work, and she told me to pick you up." *Id.* When she refused to get into the car with the man, he allegedly followed her for about two blocks, repeating his request for her to get into his car. The police traced the license plate to Edward Brodnicki's car.

Several officers brought Meaghan and her father to Brodnicki's home, where Meaghan identified Brodnicki's car as the one that followed her. An officer obtained Brodnicki's consent for a "showup," and arranged the procedure with Brodnicki standing in his front yard so that Meaghan could observe him from the police car. The officers cautioned Meaghan about "the serious nature of her allegations and the importance of accuracy." *Id.* She positively identified Brodnicki as the driver of the car that had followed her.

Thereafter, the officers secured Brodnicki's consent to search his car, where they found sunglasses, a baseball cap similar to the one described by Meaghan, and a stocking cap. Brodnicki was then taken to police headquarters for questioning. He said that he was home alone on the afternoon in question. When given an opportunity to confront Meaghan about the allegation, he declined. Consequently, the officers charged Brodnicki with attempted kidnapping. Ultimately, the County Prosecutor dismissed the charge when it was learned from a witness (one of Meaghan's friends) that Brodnicki never approached Meaghan.

In the lawsuit that followed, Brodnicki claimed, among other things, that the Omaha police officers violated his Fourth and Fourteenth Amendment rights by arresting him without probable cause. The Eighth Circuit Court of Appeals rejected Brodnicki's claims.

Brodnicki contended that the police were not justified in believing Meaghan's story when confronted with his denial of the alleged incident. According to Brodnicki, the officers "had a duty to investigate his alibi before making their probable cause determination." *Id.* at 1264. The court held:

> The officers were not required to conduct a mini-trial before arresting Brodnicki. * * * Probable cause is to be determined upon the objective facts available to the officers at the time of the arrest. [] Moreover, the officers' reliance on [Meaghan's] story of her near-abduction was not objectively unreasonable. [She] appeared to be a credible witness. She gave the police a specific description of the car, its license plate number, and a detailed account of the incident. This information led police to identify Brodnicki's car, which matched [the] description. Brodnicki's car then was found in the immediate vicinity where, according to [Meaghan], she was accosted while on her way home after playing with her friends. [Her] mother made statements to the officers attesting to her daughter's truthfulness. [Meaghan] identified Brodnicki in a showup. Upon this evidence, a reasonable police officer could conclude that probable cause existed to arrest Brodnicki.

Id. at 1264-65.

ANDERSON v. CREIGHTON
Supreme Court of the United States
483 *U.S.* 635, 107 *S.Ct.* 3034 (1987)

QUESTION: May a law enforcement officer who participates in a search that violates the Fourth Amendment be held personally liable for money damages if a reasonable officer could have believed that the search was consistent with the Fourth Amendment ?

ANSWER: NO. A law enforcement officer who participates in a search that is ultimately found to violate the Fourth Amendment may not be held personally liable for money damages so long as "a reasonable officer could have believed" the "search to be lawful, in light of clearly established law and the information the searching officers possessed." *Id.* at 3040.

RATIONALE: FBI Agent Russell Anderson, along with other state and federal officers, conducted a warrantless search at the Creighton home because Anderson believed that a man suspected of a bank robbery committed earlier that day, might be found there. Anderson believed that probable cause and exigent circumstances permitted the search he undertook. The suspect was not found.

The Creightons later filed suit against Anderson, asserting, among other things, a claim for money damages under the Fourth Amendment. For summary judgment, Anderson argued that such a lawsuit was barred by his qualified immunity from civil damages liability. While the trial court granted Anderson's motion, finding the search to be lawful, the Circuit Court of Appeals for the Eighth Circuit reversed, refusing to permit Anderson to argue the lawfulness of his warrantless search on his motion for summary judgment.

The United States Supreme Court held that if Anderson could establish that a reasonable officer could have believed the search to be lawful, this qualification would immunize him from civil liability and he would be entitled to summary judgment in his favor as a matter of law. Id. at 3040.

"When government officials abuse their offices, 'action(s) for damages may offer the only realistic avenue for vindication of constitutional guarantees.' * * * On the other hand, permitting damage suits against government officials can entail substantial social costs, including the risk that fear of personal monetary liability and harassing litigation will unduly inhibit officials in the discharge of their duties." *Id.* at 3038 (quoting *Harlow v. Fitzgerald*, 457 *U.S.* 800, 814, 102 *S.Ct.* 2727, 2736 (1982)). To accommodate these conflicting concerns, government officers performing discretionary functions are provided with "a qualified immunity, shielding them from civil damages liability as long as their actions could reasonably have been thought consistent with the rights they are alleged to have violated." *Id.* at 3038. In other words, whether a law enforcement officer will be protected from suit by a qualified immunity or held personally liable for an alleged unlawful official action "generally turns on the 'objective legal reasonableness' of the action, * * * assessed in light of the legal rules that were 'clearly established' at the time it was taken[.]" *Id.* [Citations omitted.] The "contours" of the "clearly established" right the officer is alleged to have violated "must be sufficiently clear that a reasonable official would understand that what he is doing violates that right[;]* * * that in light of preexisting law the unlawfulness must be apparent." *Id.* at 3039.

Whether Anderson possessed the requisite probable cause and exigent circumstances is an issue he should be permitted to argue. Conversely, the trial court should "consider the argument that it was *not* clearly established that the circumstances with which Anderson was confronted did not constitute probable cause and exigent circumstances." *Id.*

"[I]t is inevitable that law enforcement officials will in some cases reasonably but mistakenly conclude that probable cause is present, and * * * in such cases those officials * * * should not be held personally liable. * * * The same is true of their conclusions regarding exigent circumstances." *Id.*

Thus, the relevant objective, fact-specific question in this case is "whether a reasonable officer could have believed Anderson's warrantless search to be lawful, in light of clearly established law and the information the searching officers possessed. Anderson's subjective beliefs about the search are irrelevant." *Id.* at 3040.

Accordingly, "[t]he principles of qualified immunity * * * require that Anderson be permitted to argue that he is entitled to summary judgment on the ground that, in light of the clearly established principles governing warrantless searches, he could, as a matter of law, reasonably have believed that the search of the Creighton's home was lawful." *Id.*

NOTE

Prosecutorial liability:

(a) *For providing improper legal advice.* In *Burns v. Reed,* 500 *U.S.* 478, 111 *S.Ct.* 1934 (1991), the United States Supreme Court held that a prosecuting attorney is not absolutely immune from liability for damages under 42 *U.S.C.* §1983 for giving improper legal advice to the police. According to the Court, "advising the police in the investigative phase of a criminal case is [not] so 'intimately associated with the judicial phase of the criminal process' * * * that it qualifies for absolute immunity." *Id.,* 111 *S.Ct.* at 1943 (quoting *Imbler v. Pachtman,* 424 *U.S.* 409, 430, 96 *S.Ct.* 984, 995 (1976)).

Historically, "prosecutors were immune from suits for malicious prosecution and for defamation, and [] this immunity extended to the knowing use of false testimony before the grand jury and at trial." *Id.* at 1938. The interests supporting the grant of absolute immunity have been "held to be equally applicable to suits under §1983." *Id.* Like the immunity granted to judges and grand jurors, prosecutorial immunity "was viewed as necessary to protect the judicial process." *Id.*

Specifically, there was "concern that harassment by unfounded litigation would cause a deflection of the prosecutor's energies from his public duties, and the possibility that he would shade his decisions instead of exercising the independence of judgment required by his public trust." * * *

[Moreover,] potential liability "would prevent the vigorous and fearless performance of the prosecutor's duty that is essential to the proper functioning of the criminal justice system[.]"

Id. at 1938-39 (quoting *Imbler* at 423, 427-428, 96 *S.Ct.* at 991, 993-994).

As a result, prosecutors presently enjoy an absolute immunity from civil liability under §1983 "for their conduct in 'initiating a prosecution and in presenting the State's case,' * * * insofar as that conduct is 'intimately associated with the judicial phase of the criminal process[.]' " *Id.* at 1939 (quoting *Imbler* at 430-431, 96 *S.Ct.* at 995).

According to the Court here in *Burns*, the prosecutorial function of giving legal advice to the police is not "so 'intimately associated with the judicial phase of the criminal process' * * * that it qualifies for absolute immunity." *Id.* at 1943. [Citation omitted.] Rather, the "qualified" immunity defense " 'provides ample support to all but the plainly incompetent or those who knowingly violate the law.' " *Id.* at 1944. [Citation omitted.] In this respect, the Court observed:

> Although the absence of absolute immunity for the act of giving legal advice may cause prosecutors to consider their advice more carefully, " "[w]here an official could be expected to know that his conduct would violate statutory or constitutional rights, he *should* be made to hesitate.' " * * * Indeed, it is incongruous to allow prosecutors to be absolutely immune from liability for giving advice to the police, but to allow police officers only qualified immunity for following the advice. * * * Ironically, it would mean that the police, who do not ordinarily hold law degrees, would be required to know the clearly established law, but prosecutors would not.

Id. [Citations omitted; emphasis in original.]

The Court in *Burns* also addressed the question whether a prosecutor should be protected by an absolute immunity for his or her participation in a probable cause hearing which leads to the issuance of a search warrant. Writing for the Court, Justice White concluded:

> The prosecutor's actions at issue here—appearing before a judge and presenting evidence in support of a motion for a search warrant—clearly involve the prosecutor's "role as advocate for the State," rather than his role as "administrator or investigative officer[.]" Moreover, since the issuance of a search warrant is unquestionably a judicial act, * * * appearing at a probable cause hearing is "intimately associated with the judicial phase of the criminal process." * * * It is also connected with the initiation and conduct of a prosecution, particularly where the hearing occurs after arrest, as was the case here.

As this and other cases indicate, pretrial court appearances by the prosecutor in support of taking criminal action against a suspect present a substantial likelihood of vexatious litigation that might have an untoward effect on the independence of the prosecutor.

Therefore, absolute immunity for this function serves the policy of protecting the judicial process * * *.

Accordingly, we hold that [the prosecutor's] appearance in court in support of an application for a search warrant and the presentation of evidence at that hearing are protected by absolute immunity.

Id. at 1942. Significantly, *Burns* only challenged the prosecutor's participation at the probable cause *hearing.* Burns did not challenge the prosecutor's "motivation in seeking the search warrant or his conduct outside the courtroom relating to the warrant." *Id.* at 1940. Consequently, the Court's majority did not address whether, or what type of an immunity defense might be available to a prosecutor for an alleged "malicious procurement of a search warrant." *Id.* at 1941 n.5. *But see id.* at 1948-49, where Justice Scalia, dissenting in part, would "find no absolute immunity" for the wrongful initiation of the search-warrant process.

(b) *For conduct in obtaining an arrest warrant. See Kalina v. Fletcher,* 522 *U.S.* 118, 118 *S.Ct.* 502, 510 (1997) (There is absolute immunity for a prosecutor's "decision to seek an arrest warrant after filing an information, but only qualified immunity for testimony as a witness in support of that warrant.") (Scalia, J., concurring).

OSABUTEY v. WELCH
United States Court of Appeals
857 *F.2d* 220 (4th Cir. 1988)

QUESTION: In the below set of circumstances, will Officers Welch and Kearney be entitled to a qualified immunity from §1983 civil liability with respect to the warrantless searches conducted ?

CIRCUMSTANCES: In the third week of February, Narcotics Officer Welch received a telephone call from a confidential informant at about 11:15 a.m. The informant reported that a red Ford Granada would be arriving at 827 Merrimon Avenue at approximately 12:00 noon that day. According to the informant, the Ford's passenger-side window was broken but covered with plastic. The informant also reported that in the vehicle would be a black male who was approximately 6'1" to 6'2" tall, about 230 pounds, dark complected, and he would be wearing a cream-colored shirt, blue jeans and white tennis shoes. This male, stated the informant, would be in possession of cocaine. Additionally, the informant stated that he/she had observed this black male in possession of approximately one and one half ounces of cocaine just fifteen minutes before the phone call, and the informant observed the male enter the Ford for the purpose of going to the Merrimon address. According to Officer Welch, the informant had provided information on more than 100 occasions during a three-year period preceding this incident and the information previously supplied had been reliable.

Welch advised Officer Kearney of the information received, and together they drove in an unmarked police vehicle to the address, "a known site for drug trafficking." The officers arrived at about 11:30 a.m. and parked about a half block away. At approximately 12:00 noon, as scheduled, the vehicle that had been described to Officer Welch arrived at the address. The vehicle fit the description provided by the informant in all respects. As soon as the car stopped, a black male, also fitting the description given by the informant, got out from the passenger side and approached the house in a hurried manner. A black female remained in the car, in the driver's seat. The presence of the female (plaintiff Beverly Osabutey) was not forecast by the informant.

Welch and Kearney approached the vehicle, identified themselves as police officers, and told Mrs. Osabutey of the information related to them by the informant. The officers then advised Osabutey of their intention to search her and the automobile. As Osabutey stood outside the car, Kearney and Welch searched the passenger compartment and trunk. No contraband was found. During the search, the vehicle's other occupant, Ulysses Gaither, came out of the house and approached the officers. The officers identified themselves and advised Gaither of their intention to search him. After completing the vehicle search, the officers searched Osabutey's purse and conducted a pat-down of her outer clothing. Gaither was also subjected to a pat-down. "Then, shielded behind the car door from spectator view, Gaither was instructed to loosen his belt and unbutton his pants. While Welch held Gaither's pants up, Gaither pulled his underwear outward, away from his body, in order to permit the officers to conduct a visual check inside Gaither's underwear, the purpose of which was to ascertain if the cocaine had been secreted therein. At no time were Gaither's private parts exposed nor did the officers do anything more intrusive than conduct a visual search. * * * No contraband was discovered as a result of these searches." *Id.* at 222-223. No arrests based on the informant's information were made.

ANSWER: YES. According to the court, it is not readily apparent that the actions of Officers Welch and Kearney violated any clearly established constitutional principles. They are entitled to a "qualified immunity" from suit because the circumstances demonstrate that the officers held a "reasonable belief," based on legal rules which were clearly established at the time of the search, that the search was supported by "probable cause and exigent circumstances." *Id.* at 223-224.

RATIONALE: The standard which applies to the circumstances of this case "is one of the 'objective legal reasonableness' of official conduct, 'assessed in light of the legal rules that were "clearly established" at the time it was taken.'" *Id.* at 223 (quoting *Anderson v. Creighton,* 483 *U.S.* 635, 107 *S.Ct.* 3034, 3038 (1987)). "It is the right which is alleged to have been violated that must be 'clearly established.' It must be sufficiently clear so ' . . . that in the light of pre-existing law the unlawfulness must be apparent.'" *Id.* [Citation omitted.]

In this appeal, plaintiffs contend, among other things, that Officers Welch and Kearney violated their right to be "free from unreasonable searches and seizures," and their right to be "free from the deprivation of liberty without due process." *Id.* According to the court, "[s]imply alleging violation of such general rights, however, does not meet the test articulated in *Anderson.*" *Welch* at 223. Rather, the inquiry is "whether it was 'clearly established that the circumstances with which [Welch and Kearney were] confronted did not constitute probable cause and exigent circumstances.'" *Id.* (quoting *Anderson,* 107 *S.Ct.* at 3039).

"Unconstitutional conduct does not by itself remove the immunity. * * * *Anderson* requires the application of qualified immunity to law enforcement officers who act in ways they reasonably believe to be lawful, even in cases where they reasonably, but mistakenly, believe that probable cause or exigent circumstances exist." *Id.*

As a result, the court states that it "cannot conclude that the conduct of Welch and Kearney contravened any constitutional principles so 'clearly established' that they as reasonable officers 'would understand that what [they] . . . were doing violate[d the rights secured by those principles].'" *Id.* [Citation omitted.] "Officer Welch had received a tip from a known, reliable informant. Subsequent surveillance corroborated every facet of the information given him. The only variance from the information provided by the confidential source * * * was the presence of the black female in the vehicle. Except for the presence of Mrs. Osabutey, the informant's descriptions of (1) the vehicle; (2) Gaither; (3) Gaither's presence in the vehicle; (4) the destination of the vehicle, *i.e.,* the address; and (5) the time of arrival, were corroborated in every respect. Especially since the officer, Welch, had personally verified all of the information given him by the informant, he could reasonably believe that he had probable cause to arrest the suspects. * * * Rather than arresting plaintiffs, Welch and Kearney first conducted the searches, which produced no contraband, and thereafter decided not to make an arrest. While fortuitous for the plaintiffs, the decision not to arrest does not extinguish or qualify the reasonable belief, held by the officers, that they were acting within constitutional limits." *Id.* at 223-224.

Consequently, the searches were supported by probable cause and the search of the vehicle was valid under the automobile exception to the written warrant requirement. *Id.* at 224. Moreover, under the facts of this case, the officers could have reasonably believed that exigent circumstances, coupled with the personal corroboration of a tip from a known and reliable informant, provided a sufficient basis for the personal searches of the plaintiffs.

The case is remanded with instructions to enter summary judgment in favor of the defendants.

VATHEKAN v. PRINCE GEORGE'S COUNTY
United States Court of Appeals
154 *F*.3d 173 (4th Cir. 1998)

QUESTION: Will a police canine handler's failure to give a verbal warning prior to deploying a police dog to seize a suspected burglar subject the officer to civil liability for any injuries caused by the dog's actions ?

ANSWER: YES. It is clearly established that "failing to give a verbal warning before deploying a police dog to seize someone is objectively unreasonable and a violation of the Fourth Amendment." *Id.* at 179. "An attack by an unreasonably deployed police dog in the course of a seizure is a Fourth Amendment excessive force violation." *Id.* at 178.

RATIONALE: "Esther Vathekan was mauled and disfigured by a police dog when a canine unit searched her house as she slept. She sued Corporal Jeffrey Simms, the officer conducting the search, and Prince George's County (Maryland) under 42 *U.S.C.* §1983, contending that the dog's attack constituted excessive force in violation of her Fourth Amendment rights." *Id.* at 175.

On the day in question, the plaintiff, Esther Vathekan, lived in a one-story house with a furnished basement. The basement apartment, which had a separate door to the outside, was rented to two students. "A staircase led from the basement to Vathekan's residence on the ground floor, and a door at the top of the stairs separated the two living units." *Id.* at 176. As Esther slept in her bedroom, one of her tenants, Jonathan Lopez, returned home to find that the door to his basement apartment was ajar and that its glass had been broken. Lopez immediately called the police, suspecting that a burglary had occurred. Shortly thereafter, officers from the Takoma Park Police Department arrived on the scene. These officers established a perimeter around the house and called the Prince George's County canine unit for assistance. At the time, Lopez told the officers that "there shouldn't be" anyone in the house. *Id.*

Upon the arrival of Corporal Simms and his canine partner, Castro, Simms was told that "no one was home." *Id.* "Simms was ready to unleash his dog for a search of the house. At this point, Simms should have given a loud verbal warning that he was about to release the dog." *Id.* In this respect, the written Standard Operating Procedures for the Prince George's County canine unit provide:

> A canine will not be committed until an amplified announcement has been given. This will enable innocent persons to exit the area and afford suspects an opportunity to surrender.... It will be the canine handler's responsibility to ensure that the announcement is made.

Id. Esther did not hear any warning. In addition, Lopez insisted that he did not hear any announcement or warning from his position just across the street.

Corporal Simms then released the dog into the house at the basement entrance. He followed the dog and issued the command, "Find him!", "which signaled the dog to begin the search *and to bite* whomever it found in the house." *Id.* [Court's emphasis.] After finding no one in the basement, the dog ran to Esther's room and signaled that there was a "human presence" on the other side of the door. Without making an announcement at this interior door, Corporal Simms allowed the dog to go through the interior door. ["Standard police procedure would have been to give a warning at that point in order [to] allow any [person therein] an opportunity to surrender prior to being bitten by the dog." *Id.*]

> Once through the door, the dog fixed on the target whose presence he had indicated to Simms moments before: that turned out to be Esther Vathekan. The dog bounded to the bed where Vathekan slept and bit into the left side of her skull. She struggled in vain to escape as the dog shook her violently. Suddenly, the dog let go of Vathekan's skull and then clamped its jaws firmly onto the right side of her face. Vathekan was now wide awake and fully conscious of the cracking sound of the bones in her face being crushed under the dog's vise-like grip. * * *

Id. at 176-77.

Simms got to the bedroom within seconds and called off the dog. Vathekan was carried from the scene in an ambulance. She sustained deep lacerations to her head and face, fractured facial bones, and a permanently damaged tear duct in her right eye, and spent six days in the hospital. To date, her face remains scarred and disfigured.

In the lawsuit that followed, Vathekan argued that the police canine was deployed in an unreasonable manner and, as a result, Corporal Simms violated her Fourth Amendment right to be free from excessive force during a seizure.

"A Fourth Amendment seizure occurs whenever there is a governmental termination of freedom of movement *through means intentionally applied.*" *Id.* at 178 (quoting *Brower v. County of Inyo*, 489 *U.S.* 593, 597, 109 *S.Ct.* 1378 (1989)). [Emphasis in original.] Moreover, " '[a] seizure occurs even when an unintended person or thing is the object of the detention or taking.' " *Id.*

"By giving the command 'Find him!', Simms intended the dog to find anyone in the house. It is undisputed that once that command was given, the dog would bite *anyone* it found. In other words, a police dog cannot discriminate between a criminal and an innocent person. Moreover, Simms admits that once the order to search is given, the dog is trained to 'go in and bite someone,' even if the person is asleep." *Id.* at 178. [Emphasis in original.]

"Since Simms intended the dog to seize Vathekan because he thought she might be a burglar, he seized her for Fourth Amendment purposes even though she turned out to be innocent." *Id.*

"An attack by an unreasonably deployed police dog in the course of a seizure is a Fourth Amendment excessive force violation. Because Simms deployed the dog to find, bite, and detain the person who turned out to be Vathekan, she was seized under the Fourth Amendment." *Id.*

The court then went on to consider whether Corporal Simms was entitled to "qualified immunity." Vathekan's claim "is based on her Fourth Amendment right to be free from excessive force in the course of a Fourth Amendment seizure brought about by a police dog that was deployed without a verbal warning." *Id.* at 179.

"In evaluating whether an officer is entitled to qualified immunity on an excessive force claim, the question is 'whether a reasonable officer could have believed that the use of force alleged was objectively reasonable in light of the circumstances.'" *Id.* [Citation omitted.] At the time of this incident, however, it was clearly established law that "failure to give a warning before releasing a police dog is objectively unreasonable in an excessive force context." *Id. See e.g.*, *Kopf v. Wing*, 942 *F.*2d 265, 268 (4th Cir. 1991) (improper deployment of a police dog that mauls the target constitutes excessive force in violation of the Fourth Amendment).

During the hearing on this matter, Vathekan asserted that "Simms failed to give a verbal warning before releasing the dog into the house. Simms, by contrast, says that he gave a 'very loud' warning, and his fellow officers also say that they heard a warning." *Id.* at 180. In light of this genuine issue of fact, the court determined that Corporal Simms should not have been awarded summary judgment on qualified immunity grounds. It therefore remanded the matter for further proceedings.

COOPER v. DUPNIK
United States Court of Appeals
963 *F.*2d 1220 (9th Cir. 1992)

QUESTION: Can police coercion of a statement from a suspect in custody amount to a full-blown constitutional violation sufficient to support a federal civil rights cause of action under 42 *U.S.C.* §1983 ?

ANSWER: YES. The plaintiff in this case, Cooper, has adequately "stated a cause of action under §1983 for a violation * * * of his clearly established Fifth Amendment right against self-incrimination. [The officers] conspired not only to ignore Cooper's response to the advisement of rights pursuant to *Miranda*, but also to defy any assertion of the Constitution's Fifth Amendment substantive right to silence, and to grill Cooper until he confessed. * * * [The officers] refused to honor Cooper's rights when Cooper asserted them, and simply continued questioning him as if no request for counsel had been made." *Id.* at 1242-43. The conduct of the officers in this case "shocked the conscience"; they deliberately chose to ignore the law and the Constitution, and as a result, subjected themselves to civil liability under §1983. *Id.* at 1252.

RATIONALE: "Michael Cooper was arrested for rape. Pursuant to a preexisting interrogation plan, members of the Tucson Police Department and the Pima County (Arizona) Sheriff's Department ignored Cooper's repeated requests to speak with an attorney, deliberately infringed on his Constitutional right to remain silent, and relentlessly interrogated him in an attempt to extract a confession." *Id.* at 1223. The officers' plan was to purposely ignore the suspect's constitutional right to remain silent as well as any request he might make to speak with an attorney, to hold the suspect incommunicado, and to pressure and interrogate him until he confessed. "Although the officers knew any confession thus generated would not be admissible in evidence in a prosecutor's case in chief, they hoped it would be admissible for purposes of impeachment if the suspect ever went to trial. They expected that the confession would prevent the suspect from testifying he was innocent, and that it would hinder any possible insanity defense."* *Id.* at 1224. As one officer testified:

> There was an agreement * * * that when we identified the Prime Time Rapist, that we would *not honor an assertion of counsel or silence.* * * * [T]he profile that I had was that he would immediately ask for an attorney. I knew he would, whoever he was. * * *

> [This plan] should be used only in two situations: Number one, where the [] evidence is overwhelming and the [] proof is evident and/or when you think you've got the wrong guy.

Id. at 1224. [Court's emphasis.]

"Eventually the evidence against Cooper began to disintegrate. Cooper's interrogators concluded that he was not guilty, and so advised Peter Ronstadt, Chief of the Tucson Police Department. Nonetheless, Ronstadt subsequently told the media that Cooper properly had been identified and arrested. Further investigation fully exonerated Cooper, and he was released. Two months later, the Tucson Police Department publicly cleared him of all charges." *Id.* at 1223.

Cooper sued the officers of the Pima County Sheriff's Department and the Tucson Police Department, as well as the agencies and municipalities for which they worked. Among the federal civil rights claims in his complaint, Cooper contended that the officers in this case did more than merely violate the procedural safeguards provided by *Miranda.* He charged that the officers violated his substantive constitutional rights to silence and counsel. The officers, on the other hand, argued that "this case clearly presents a situation in which they are entitled as a matter of law to a complete defense of qualified immunity." *Id.* at 1235. The officers "characterize[d] their conduct as simply 'continuing with custodial interrogation after a request for counsel.' At most, they concede a violation of *Miranda* safeguards." *Id. The Court of Appeals for the Ninth Circuit rejected the officers' contentions.*

---

* The officers miscalculated. Because the interrogation violated Cooper's "substantive Fifth Amendment right to remain silent, rather than just the *Miranda* rules designed to safeguard that right, Cooper's statements would not have been admissible for *any* purpose." *Id.* at 1225. [Court's emphasis.]

"Section 1983 imposes civil liability on any person who, acting under color of state law, deprives a United States citizen of his federal constitutional or statutory rights." *Id.* at 1236. Cooper's lawsuit "hinges on whether the [officers] deprived him of a constitutional right." *Id.* The *Miranda* warnings and rights are not themselves constitutionally mandated, but rather are procedural safeguards, or prophylactic measures, designed to ensure that the Fifth Amendment right against compulsory self-incrimination is safeguarded. Yet, to characterize the officers' conduct in this case as a "mere violation of *Miranda's* prophylactic advisement requirements is to see a hurricane as but a movement of air." *Id.* at 1237. The officers in this case "engaged in the premeditated elimination of Mr. Cooper's substantive Fifth Amendment rights, not merely the disposal of the procedural safeguards designed to protect those rights. Thus, Cooper's statements were 'compelled' and 'coerced.'" *Id.*

"By the same reasoning, Cooper's Fourteenth Amendment rights also were violated. It is irrelevant that Cooper's coerced statements were never introduced against him at trial. The [officers'] wrongdoing was complete at the moment [they] forced Cooper to speak." *Id.*

The court also determined that the officers were "not protected by the doctrine of qualified (good-faith) immunity. Qualified immunity protects officials from suits under §1983 for violations of rights which are not 'clearly established at the time of the challenged actions * * *.'" *Id.* But this case, emphasized the court, does not involve any borderline constitutional violations. "There is no question that the constitutional holding in *Miranda* is 'clearly established' law; similarly, there is no question that the [officers'] conduct violate[d] both the Fifth Amendment itself (as opposed to just the *Miranda* rules designed to protect it), and the Fourteenth Amendment. [The officers] knew they were violating the Constitution." *Id. See Malley v. Briggs,* 475 *U.S.* 335, 341, 106 *S.Ct.* 1092, 1096 (1986) (qualified immunity not available to officials who "knowingly violate the law").

Although Cooper, an innocent man, was never actually coerced into a confession, he nonetheless made statements which the prosecution might have used at trial. "Cooper admitted that he had slapped his wife, and that he often left his home, unaccompanied, at night, sometimes for hours at a time." *Cooper* at 1237-38. Such statements, concluded the court, support a constitutional violation—they are "sufficient to constitute a breach of his right to remain silent." *Id.* at 1238. The court elaborated:

> [W]e conclude that Cooper adequately has stated a cause of action under §1983 for a violation * * * of his clearly established Fifth Amendment right against self-incrimination. [The officers] conspired not only to ignore Cooper's response to the advisement of rights pursuant to *Miranda*, but also to defy any assertion of the Constitution's Fifth Amendment substantive right to silence, and to grill Cooper until he confessed. * * * The clear purpose of these tactics was to make Cooper talk, and to keep him talking until he confessed. [The officers] refused to honor Cooper's rights when Cooper asserted them, and simply continued questioning him as if

no request for counsel had been made. This tactic was designed to generate a feeling of helplessness, and we are sure it succeeded. * * * With his requests to see a lawyer disregarded, Cooper was a prisoner in a totalitarian nightmare, where the police no longer obeyed the Constitution, but instead followed their own judgment, treating suspects according to their whims.

If the evisceration of *Miranda* warnings and the indifference to repeated requests for counsel were not enough, the police continuously badgered Cooper for four hours in an attempt to [obtain] a confession. * * * The questioning was harsh and unrelenting. At one point, Cooper stated, "I'm breaking down," but the questioning continued. Cooper told [one of the officers], "you're making me sick, sir," but the questioning continued. * * * Cooper was reduced to sobbing and pleading his innocence, but still the questioning continued. * * *

Although Cooper did not retreat from his protestations of innocence, he did make a lengthy statement, and it is our view that every word he uttered after he was taken to the sheriff's department was compelled. Cooper's treatment presents a *prima facie* case of law-enforcement behavior that violates the Fifth Amendment's privilege against self-incrimination.

Id. at 1242-43.

The court further ruled that the due process violation caused by the coercive behavior of the interrogating officers in pursuit of a confession was "complete with the coercive behavior itself." *Id.* at 1245. "The actual use or attempted use of that coerced statement in a court of law is not necessary to complete the affront to the Constitution. * * * Hence, the fact that Cooper never formally was charged in court and that none of his statements ever were offered in evidence to his potential detriment is relevant only to damages, not to whether he has a civil cause of action in the first place." *Id.*

Finally, as a matter of substantive due process, the court ruled that the officers' conduct in this case "shocked the conscience." *Id.* at 1249. By forcing Cooper to talk, "the officers hoped to prevent him from being able to do so in the courtroom. [T]heir purpose was not just to be able to impeach him if he took the stand and lied, but to keep him off the stand altogether." *Id.* There is, however, no "impeachment exception" to the *Miranda* rule for compelled, coerced, or involuntary statements. *Id.* at 1250. Moreover, the officers' unlawful plot to deprive Cooper of his right to present an insanity defense, if one was available, had an underlying purpose to deprive him of the defense altogether, not just to defeat it with the facts or the truth. All in all, the court concluded, based on the totality of the facts and circumstances, that the conduct of the officers was nothing less than shocking to the conscience. *Id.*

In sum, it is "clearly established" law that

the Fifth and Fourteenth Amendments forbid the use of compulsion and coercion by law enforcement in pursuit of a confession. As far as the police are concerned, any violation is complete at the time of the offending behavior. Behavior like the [officers' in this case] shocks the conscience; it deprived Cooper of "one of our Nation's most cherished principles—that the individual may not be compelled to incriminate himself." * * * Indeed, one would have thought it unnecessary to spend so much time reiterating the settled law in an appellate opinion. Yet the facts of this case indicate that these law-enforcement officers resist that message. It is this stubborn resistance that has generated this lawsuit, not any lack of clarity as to the law.

This case is an example of officials who deliberately choose to ignore the law and the Constitution in favor of their own methods. For victims caught in their snare, the Constitution of the United States becomes a useless piece of paper. When law-enforcement officials act this way, they invite redress under §1983.

Id. at 1251-52.

NOTE

1. During the course of its opinion in *Cooper v. Dupnik*, the court emphasized that the case did not deal with a product of police interrogation that was just technically involuntary, or presumptively involuntary, as those terms are used in *Miranda* and the cases applying *Miranda*. Rather, the case dealt with a statement that was involuntary *"because it was actively compelled and coerced* by law-enforcement officers during in-custody questioning[.]" *Id.*, 963 *F.*2d at 1243. [Court's emphasis.] Thus, this case should not be read as creating a Fifth Amendment cause of action under Section 1983 for conduct that merely violates *Miranda*'s prophylactic safeguards. To maintain such a cause of action, the plaintiff would need to establish, in addition, that the police officials violated the actual constitutional right against self-incrimination that the *Miranda* safeguards are designed to protect. *See id.* at 1243-44. *See also id.* at 1252 ("our decision in this case does not expand liability under 42 *U.S.C.* §1983 to include ordinary *Miranda* rights advisement violations") (WIGGINS, Circuit Judge, concurring).

2. In *Chavez v. Martinez*, 538 *U.S.* 760, 123 *S.Ct.* 1994 (2003), the United States Supreme Court was presented with a case involving a single police interrogation which prompted two critical issues: First, whether a police officer's failure to administer Miranda warnings during custodial interrogation is itself a completed constitutional violation which may support civil liability under 42 *U.S.C.* §1983; and second, whether, in this case, the law enforcement officials should be held civilly liable under the Due Process Clause of the Fourteenth Amendment when the interrogating officer may have used compulsion or extraordinary pressure in an attempt to elicit a confession.

In this case, during the course of a narcotics investigation, Martinez approached investigating officers, interfered with the investigation and grabbed an officer's gun. As a result of this conduct, an officer shot Martinez several times, causing severe injuries. Martinez was then placed under arrest.

A short time after the shooting, a patrol supervisor arrived on the scene and accompanied Martinez to the hospital. As Martinez was receiving treatment from medical personnel, the police supervisor questioned him, with the interview lasting a total of about 10 minutes, over a 45-minute period, with the officer stopping at times to permit medical personnel to administer emergency aid. During the course of the interview, Martinez admitted that he took the gun from the officer's holster and pointed it at the police. He also admitted that he used heroin regularly. At one point, Martinez said, "I am not telling you anything until they treat me," yet the officer continued the interview. *Id.*, 123 *S.Ct.* at 1999. At no point during the interview, however, was Martinez given *Miranda* warnings. As a result of his injuries, he was permanently blinded and paralyzed from the waist down.

Martinez was never charged with a crime, and his answers were never used against him in any criminal prosecution. Nevertheless, he filed suit under 42 *U.S.C.* §1983, maintaining that the interrogating officer's actions violated his Fifth Amendment right not to be "compelled in any criminal case to be a witness against himself," as well as his Fourteenth Amendment substantive due process right to be free from coercive questioning.

To determine if a police officer is entitled to qualified immunity, courts must first decide whether the officer's conduct "violated a constitutional right." *Id.* at 2000. If not, the officer is entitled to qualified immunity, and there is no need to determine if the asserted right was "clearly established." *Id.*

Preliminarily, the Court found that *the mere "failure to give a Miranda warning does not, without more," establish a substantive constitutional violation sufficient to establish a ground for a civil action against the interrogating law enforcement officials. Id.* at 2004-04. [Emphasis added.] In this regard, statements obtained in the absence of the administration of the *Miranda* warnings are inadmissible in a criminal trial by virtue of the "prophylactic rules" established in *Miranda v. Arizona. Miranda's* "prophylactic" exclusionary rule is designed to safeguard constitutional rights; its violation does not, however, provide a basis for civil liability. Accordingly, in this case, the Court held that the officer's failure to read the *Miranda* warnings to Martinez did not rise to the level of a direct violation of Martinez's constitutional rights, and therefore "cannot be grounds for a Section 1983 action." *Id.* at 2004.

Regarding the second issue, the justices were not wholly in agreement as to whether Martinez demonstrated a violation of his constitutional rights by virtue of the coercive nature of the officer's interrogation. A plurality of the Court, led by Justice Thomas, could not see how, based on the text of the Fifth Amendment, Martinez can allege a violation of this right, since Martinez "was never prosecuted for a crime, let alone compelled to be a witness against himself in a criminal case." *Id.* at 2000.

Here, Martinez was "never made to be a 'witness' against himself in violation of the Fifth Amendment's Self-Incrimination Clause because his statements were never admitted as testimony against him in a criminal case." *Id.* at 2001. Accordingly, "the mere use of compulsive questioning, without more," did not violate the Constitution, "absent use of the compelled statements in a criminal case against the witness." *Id.* at 2001-02.

The Court did pause to add, however, that such a ruling does not mean that "police torture or other abuse that results in a confession is constitutionally permissible so long as the statements are not used at trial; it simply means that the Fourteenth Amendment's Due Process Clause, rather than the Fifth Amendment's Self-Incrimination Clause, would govern the inquiry in those cases and provide relief in appropriate circumstances." *Id.* at 2004.

The Due Process Clause of the Fourteenth Amendment protects citizens from police methods that are "so brutal and so offensive to human dignity" that they "shock the conscience." *Id.* at 2005. Although several of the justices in this case were satisfied that the officer's interrogation did not violate Martinez's Due Process rights, finding an absence of "egregious" or "conscience-shocking" behavior, a majority of justices concluded that the case should be remanded to the trial court to permit Martinez to pursue his claim of civil liability for the possible substantive due process violation. In this respect, Justices Kennedy, Stevens and Ginsburg observed:

> A constitutional right is [violated] the moment torture or its close equivalents are brought to bear. Constitutional protection for a tortured suspect is not held in abeyance until some later criminal proceeding takes place. * * * In a case like this one, recovery should be available under §1983 if a complainant can demonstrate that an officer exploited his pain and suffering with the purpose and intent of securing an incriminating statement. * * *

Id. at 2013.

COUNTY OF SACRAMENTO v. LEWIS
Supreme Court of the United States
523 *U.S.* 833, 118 *S.Ct.* 1708 (1998)

QUESTION: Will an officer be held civilly liable for harm caused by a high-speed motor vehicle pursuit when that officer did not intend to physically harm the fleeing suspect or to worsen his legal plight ?

ANSWER: NO. Officers who engage in high-speed motor vehicle chases "with no intent to harm suspects physically or to worsen their legal plight" will not be civilly liable under the Fourteenth Amendment's Due Process Clause. *Id.* at 1720. Civil liability will only arise in those cases where the officer's conduct reflects "a purpose to cause harm unrelated to the legitimate object of arrest[.]" *Id.* at 1711. ***The police conduct must be so egregious that it constitutes an abuse of official power that "shocks the conscience,"*** a necessary prerequisite for a due process violation. *Id.* at 1712.

RATIONALE: At about 8:30 p.m., Sheriff's Deputy James Smith and Officer Murray Stapp responded to a fight call. After handling the call, Officer Stapp returned to his patrol car, and as he did so, he observed a motorcycle approaching at high speed. Brian Willard, an 18-year-old, was operating the cycle. Seated behind him was his passenger, 16-year-old Philip Lewis.

"Stapp turned on his overhead rotating lights, yelled to the boys to stop, and pulled his patrol car closer to Smith's, attempting to pen the motorcycle in." *Id.* at 1712. Instead of pulling over, Willard maneuvered the cycle between the two patrol cars and sped away. Deputy Smith "immediately switched on his own emergency lights and siren, made a quick turn, and began a pursuit at high speed. For 75 seconds over a course of 1.3 miles in a residential neighborhood, the motorcycle wove in and out of oncoming traffic, forcing two cars and a bicycle to swerve off of the road. The motorcycle and patrol car reached speeds of up to 100 miles an hour, with Smith following at a distance as short as 100 feet; at that speed, his car would have required 650 feet to stop." *Id.*

"The chase ended after the motorcycle tipped over as Willard tried a sharp turn. By the time Smith slammed on his brakes, Willard was out of the way, but Lewis was not. The patrol car skidded into him at 40 miles an hour, propelling him some 70 feet down the road and inflicting massive injuries. Lewis was pronounced dead at the scene." *Id.*

In the lawsuit that followed, Philip Lewis' parents and the representatives of his estate brought the action under 42 *U.S.C.* §1983, against Sacramento County, the Sacramento County Sheriff's Department and Deputy Smith, alleging a deprivation of Philip's Fourteenth Amendment substantive due process right to life.

Determining that no civil liability should attach to Deputy Smith's conduct, the United States Supreme Court, in this appeal, resolved a conflict over the standard of culpability on the part of a law enforcement officer for violating substantive due process during the course of a motor vehicle pursuit.

Preliminarily, the Court ruled that the Lewis claim was not "covered by" the Fourth Amendment, which governs only "searches and seizures." *Id.* at 1715. The Court said:

> No one suggests that there was a search, and our cases foreclose finding a seizure. We held in *California v. Hodari D.* * * * that a police pursuit in attempting to seize a person does not amount to a "seizure" within the meaning of the Fourth Amendment. And in *Brower v. County of Inyo,* * * * we explained that a Fourth Amendment seizure does not occur whenever there is a governmentally caused termination of an individual's freedom of movement (the innocent passerby), nor even whenever there is a governmentally caused and governmentally *desired* termination of an individual's freedom of movement (the fleeing felon), but only when there is a "governmental termination of freedom of movement *through means intentionally applied.*" We illustrated the point by saying that no Fourth Amendment seizure would take place where a "pursuing police car sought to stop the suspect only

by a show of authority represented by flashing lights and continuing pursuit," but accidentally stopped the suspect by crashing into him. * * * This is exactly this case.

Id. at 1715. [Citations omitted; Court's emphasis.]

This case is governed by the Due Process Clause of the Fourteenth Amendment, which guarantees more than just "fair process." In addition, it contains "a substantive sphere as well, 'barring certain government actions regardless of the fairness of the procedures used to implement them[.]' " *Id.* at 1713. [Citations omitted.] The Due Process Clause is intended to prevent government officers from abusing their power or using it as an instrument of oppression. *Id.* at 1716. [Citation omitted.] In this regard, courts will focus on a "level of executive abuse of power as that which shocks the conscience." *Id.* at 1717. This was made clear in *Rochin v. California*, 342 *U.S.* 165, 72 *S.Ct.* 205 (1952), where the Court "found the forced pumping of a suspect's stomach enough to offend due process as conduct 'that shocks the conscience' and violates the 'decencies of civilized conduct.' " *Lewis* at 1717 (quoting *Rochin* at 172-73, 72 *S.Ct.* at 209-10). *See also Breithaupt v. Abram*, 352 *U.S.* 432, 435, 77 *S.Ct.* 408, 410 (1957) (conduct that " 'shocked the conscience' and was so 'brutal' and 'offensive' that it did not comport with 'traditional ideas of fair play and decency' would violate substantive due process").

In this case, the Court emphasized that "the Constitution does not guarantee due care on the part of state officials; liability for negligently inflicted harm is categorically beneath the threshold of constitutional due process." *Id.* at 1718. In addition, the Court explained that the standard of fault must be above that of "deliberate indifference" or "reckless disregard," before an officer will be liable for harm caused in a vehicular pursuit. *Id.* at 1720, 1721. To support civil liability, and a substantive due process claim, the constitution should be interpreted to focus in on behavior that is at the other end of the culpability spectrum—"on conduct intended to injure in some way unjustifiable by any government interest[.]" *Id.* at 1718. This is the type of official action "most likely to rise to the conscience-shocking level." *Id.*

> Like prison officials facing a riot, the police on an occasion calling for fast action have obligations that tend to tug against each other. Their duty is to restore and maintain lawful order, while not exacerbating disorder more than necessary to do their jobs. They are supposed to act decisively and to show restraint at the same moment, and their decisions have to be made "in haste, under pressure, and frequently without the luxury of a second chance." * * * A police officer deciding whether to give chase must balance on one hand the need to stop a suspect and show that flight from the law is no way to freedom, and, on the other, the high-speed threat to everyone within stopping range, be they suspects, their passengers, other drivers, or bystanders.

Id. at 1720. [Citation omitted.]

Accordingly, "high-speed chases with no intent to harm suspects physically or to worsen their legal plight do not give rise to liability under the Fourteenth Amendment, redressible by an action under §1983." *Id.* The Court concluded, therefore, that Deputy Smith's conduct "fail[ed] to meet the shocks-the-conscience test." *Id.*

Smith was faced with a course of lawless behavior for which the police were not to blame. They had done nothing to cause Willard's high-speed driving in the first place, nothing to excuse his flouting of the commonly understood law enforcement authority to control traffic * * *. Willard's outrageous behavior was practically instantaneous, and so was Smith's instinctive response. While prudence would have repressed the reaction, the officer's instinct was to do his job as a law enforcement officer, not to induce Willard's lawlessness, or to terrorize, cause him harm, or kill. * * *

Regardless whether Smith's behavior offended the reasonableness held up by tort law or the balance struck in law enforcement's own codes of sound practice, it d[id] not shock the conscience * * *.

Id. at 1721.

CITY OF CANTON, OHIO v. HARRIS
Supreme Court of the United States
489 *U.S.* 378, 109 *S.Ct.* 1197 (1989)

QUESTION: May a municipality ever be held civilly liable (under 42 *U.S.C.* §1983) for constitutional violations resulting from its failure to adequately train its police officers or other municipal employees?

ANSWER: YES. There are certain "circumstances in which an allegation of a 'failure to train' can be the basis for liability under §1983." *Id.* at 1204. "[T]he inadequacy of police training may serve as the basis for §1983 liability *only* where the failure to train amounts to *deliberate indifference to the rights of persons with whom the police come into contact.*" *Id.* [Emphasis added.]

RATIONALE: Geraldine Harris was arrested by several officers of the Canton Police Department, and thereafter transported to the police station in a patrol wagon. Upon arrival at the station, Harris was found sitting on the floor of the wagon. When asked if she needed medical attention, she responded in an incoherent manner. Once brought inside for processing, Mrs. Harris "slumped to the floor" on several occasions. "Eventually, the police officers left Mrs. Harris lying on the floor to prevent her from falling again. No medical attention was ever summoned for Mrs. Harris. After about an hour, Mrs. Harris was released from custody, and taken by an ambulance (provided by her family) to a nearby hospital." *Id.* at 1200. Thereafter, she was hospitalized for one week and received subsequent outpatient treatment for a year for severe emotional ailments.

In this appeal, Harris argues that the city should be held civilly liable under 42 *U.S.C.* §1983 for its violation of her right, under the Due Process Clause of the Fourteenth Amendment, to receive necessary medical attention while in police custody. It is contended that the constitutional violation resulted from the failure to adequately train the Canton shift commanders to make a determination as to when to summon medical care for an injured detainee.

Monell v. New York City Dept. of Social Services, 436 *U.S.* 658, 98 *S.Ct.* 2018 (1978), held "that a municipality can be found liable under §1983 only where the municipality *itself* causes the constitutional violation. * * * It is only where the 'execution of the government's policy or custom . . . inflicts injury' that the municipality may be held liable under §1983." *Harris* at 1203. [Citations omitted; emphasis added.] Moreover, there must be "a direct causal link between a municipal policy or custom, and the alleged constitutional deprivation." *Id.* The pivotal question then becomes: "Under what circumstances can inadequate training be found to be a 'policy' that is actionable under §1983 ?" *Id.* at 1202.

In this case, the Court concludes that there are limited circumstances in which an allegation of a "failure to train" can form the basis for liability under 42 *U.S.C.* §1983; that case where a clearly valid policy is unconstitutionally applied by a police officer or other municipal employee because that employee has not been adequately trained and the constitutional wrong has been *caused by* that failure to adequately train. *Id.* at 1203-1204.

For the *degree of fault* to be applied, the Court holds that:

> the inadequacy of police training may serve as the basis for §1983 liability only where the failure to train amounts to *deliberate indifference to the rights of persons with whom the police come into contact.*

Id. at 1204. [Emphasis added.] "Only where a municipality's failure to train its employees in a relevant respect evidences a 'deliberate indifference' to the rights of its inhabitants can such a shortcoming be properly thought of as a city 'policy or custom' that is actionable under §1983." *Id.* at 2105. This conclusion is consistent with the established rule that " 'municipal liability under §1983 attaches where—and only where—a deliberate choice to follow a course of action is made from among various alternatives' by city policy makers. * * * "

Thus, where a failure to adequately train the city's police force reflects a "deliberate" or "conscious" choice by the city (*i.e.*, municipal "policy"), civil liability will lie for such a failure under §1983. In this respect, the Court points out that a §1983 violation will not be made out "merely by alleging that the existing training program for a class of * * * police officers[] represents a policy for which the city is responsible. * * * The issue * * * is whether that training program is adequate; and if it is not, the question becomes whether such inadequate training can justifiably be said to represent 'city policy.' " *Id.* It is possible "that in light of the duties assigned to specific officers or employees the need for more or different training is so obvious, and the inadequacy so likely to result in the violation of constitutional rights, that the policy makers of the city can reasonably be said to have been deliberately indifferent to the need. In that event, the failure to provide proper training may fairly be said to represent a policy for which the city is responsible, and for which the city may be held liable if it actually causes injury." *Id.*

To determine the issue of a city's liability in these circumstances, the "focus must be on the adequacy of the training program in relation to the tasks the particular officers must perform." *Id.* at 1205-1206. Liability will not be placed on the city, however, merely by showing that one particular officer was unsatisfactorily trained. The officer's shortcomings "may have resulted from factors other than a faulty training program." *Id.* at 1206. Moreover, liability will not be placed on the city when it is merely shown that an otherwise sound police training program has occasionally been negligently administered. "Neither will it suffice to prove that an injury or accident could have been avoided if an officer had had better or more training, sufficient to equip him to avoid the particular injury-causing conduct." *Id.* While such a claim could be made about almost any police-citizen encounter resulting in injury, it does not, however, establish a police training program so inadequate as to warrant §1983 liability. Naturally, "adequately trained officers occasionally make mistakes; the fact that they do says little about the training program or the legal basis for holding the city liable." *Id.*

In order for liability to attach, therefore, "the identified deficiency in a city's training program must be closely related to the ultimate injury." *Id.* The injured individual must ultimately "prove that the deficiency in the police training program actually caused the police officer's [clearly inappropriate response]." *Id.* In this case (on remand), Ms. Harris must prove that the alleged deficiency in the police training program actually caused the police officer's indifference to her medical needs; questioning whether the injury would "have been avoided had the police officer been trained under a program that was not deficient in the identified respect." *Id.*

Accordingly, a citizen may bring a §1983 civil action against a municipality for its failure to provide adequate training to its police officers or other employees when that citizen suffers injury at the hand of one or more of those employees. The constitutional deprivation will only produce civil liability against the municipality, however, where that "city's failure to train reflects a *deliberate indifference to the constitutional rights of its inhabitants.*" *Id.* [Emphasis added.]

NOTE

1. *Failure to train on the subject of strip/body cavity searches.* Since the Supreme Court's decision in *City of Canton, Ohio v. Harris,* it has been well settled that administrators and department chiefs in charge of municipalities and law enforcement agencies may incur civil liability for the failure to provide their police officials with sufficient, up-to-date training. Whenever that failure amounts to a " 'deliberate indifference' to the rights of its inhabitants" with whom their police come into contact, civil liability will likely ensue.

Thus, in *DiLoreto v. Borough of Oaklyn*, 744 *F.Supp.* 610 (D.N.J. 1990), the court held that Oaklyn Borough's failure to provide its police officers with formal training on (1) the subject of strip searches and (2) whether officers were routinely permitted to accompany detainees to the bathroom and observe their use thereof, constituted "deliberate indifference" to the rights of persons arrested or detained at the Borough's police department. The *DiLoreto* court elaborated:

> As can be seen from the large number of cases discussing the issue, strip searching by police and accompanying detainees to the bathroom is not an uncommon occurrence. *It is something that the police must confront daily and an area in which they should receive training.* Police officers should be aware of the limits placed on their actions by the Constitution. *The Borough has the responsibility to implement policies that are consistent with the Constitution and to train its officers accordingly.* * * * By not creating and implementing a policy and not training its employees regarding [strip searches and] accompanying detainees to the bathroom, the Borough has expressed deliberate indifference to the fourth amendment rights of detainees[.]* * *
>
> The court is dismayed that there has been so little progress in educating police officers as to the constitutionality of strip searching detainees and arrestees * * *. It is unfortunate that so many boroughs in this state appear to have adopted a policy of non-acquiescence to the constitutionally mandated norms. * * *

Id. at 621 n.7, 623-24. [Emphasis added.]

Regarding the claim of the particular police officer involved— that she should be accorded a "qualified immunity" based on the good-faith performance of her duties—the court ruled that the qualified immunity defense is not available to her

> because the law concerning the unconstitutionality of such searches was so clearly established that no reasonable officer could have believed that [her] conduct was constitutional. * * *
>
> [T]he actions of [this officer] obviously constitute[d] a violation of the fourth amendment's protection against unreasonable searches and seizures. In *Wilkes v. Borough of Clayton*, 696 *F.Supp.* 144 (D.N.J. 1988), [the court] clearly established that * * * "arrestees may reasonably expect to defecate, urinate and change sanitary napkins or tampons without direct visual observation by law enforcement officers, unless some justification for the intrusion is demonstrated." * * *
>
> An additional factor supports the conclusion that the law concerning the action involved here was clearly established by June of 1987. *Davis v. [City of] Camden*[, 657 *F.Supp.* 396 (D.N.J. 1987),] was published before the events in this case occurred and thus placed the defendant on notice as to the unconstitutionality of unreasonable strip searches. * * * The *Davis* court held that in order for a strip search to be constitutional there must be reasonable suspicion that the arrestee is concealing weapons or contraband;

such suspicion could arise either from the specific circumstances of the [arrest, or the] arrestee, or from the nature of the offense charged. The law was clearly established in June of 1987 such that reasonable officials would have realized that the conduct here was unconstitutional. Qualified immunity is not available as a defense based on the undisputed facts of this case.

DiLoreto at 618-20.

2. *Failure to adequately train on the subject of deadly force.* In *Zuchel v. City and County of Denver, Colo.,* 997 F.2d 730 (10th Cir. 1993), the court identified four elements that a plaintiff must prove under *City of Canton, Ohio v. Harris,* to support a §1983 claim that a municipality's failure to adequately train its police officers on the subject of deadly force constituted deliberate indifference to the constitutional rights of its citizens.

First, the plaintiff must establish that the officer's use of deadly force was unconstitutional. This determination must be made from the perspective of a reasonable officer on the scene at the time of the event. *Id.* at 735.

Second, the plaintiff must prove that the circumstances giving rise to the shooting "represented a usual and recurring situation with which police officers were required to deal." *Id.* at 737.

Third, the plaintiff must show that the municipality's police training program was inadequate, and the inadequacy of the training was directly linked to the officer's unconstitutional use of excessive force. *Id.* at 738. In this case, the *Zuchel* court agreed with the plaintiff's experts that the City's "police use of deadly force" training program was inadequate because of the absence of periodic, live "shoot-don't shoot" range training. *Id.* at 738-40.

Finally, the plaintiff must demonstrate that the municipality "was deliberately indifferent to the rights of persons with whom the police come in contact." *Id.* at 740.

3. *Abandoning a citizen in a "high crime area."* In *Hilliard v. City and County of Denver,* 930 F.2d 1516 (10th Cir. 1991), plaintiff alleged in her Section 1983 suit that several officers of the Denver Police Department violated her rights under the Colorado "emergency commitment statute," *Colo.Rev.Stat.* §25-1-310 (1989), by failing to take her into protective custody. Plaintiff was a passenger in an automobile driven by an individual who was arrested by the defendants for drunk driving. At the time plaintiff's companion was taken into custody, the defendants also determined that plaintiff was too intoxicated to drive and ordered her not to do so. The car was impounded and plaintiff was left by defendants to fend for herself in a location described by the district court as "a high crime area." Some time after the defendants left the scene, plaintiff was robbed and sexually assaulted. Later the next morning, she was found "stripped naked, bleeding and barely conscious." *Id.* at 1518.

In the appeal which followed the district court's denial of defendants' motion for summary judgment on qualified immunity grounds, defendants argued that, at the time of the incident, the Colorado "emergency commitment statute" created no "constitutionally protected liberty interest," and even if it did, it was not "clearly established." The Tenth Circuit agreed.

In *Harlow v. Fitzgerald*, 457 *U.S.* 800, 102 *S.Ct.* 2727 (1982), the Supreme Court set forth the standard by which claims of qualified immunity are to be evaluated. "This standard provides that '[w]hen government officials are performing discretionary functions, they will not be held liable for their conduct unless their actions violate "clearly established statutory or constitutional rights of which a reasonable person would have known."'" *Hilliard* at 1518. [Citations omitted.] "In determining whether the law involved was clearly established, the court examines the law as it was at the time of defendants' actions." *Id.*

> It is the plaintiff's burden to convince the court that the law was clearly established. * * * In doing so, the plaintiff cannot simply identify a clearly established right in the abstract and allege that the defendant has violated it. Instead, the plaintiff "must demonstrate a substantial correspondence between the conduct in question and prior law allegedly establishing that the defendant's actions were clearly prohibited." * * * While the plaintiff need not show that the specific action at issue has previously been held unlawful, the alleged unlawfulness must be "apparent" in light of preexisting law. * * * The " 'contours of the right must be sufficiently clear that a reasonable official would understand that what he is doing violates that right.' " * * * If the plaintiff is unable to demonstrate that the law allegedly violated was clearly established, the plaintiff is not allowed to proceed with the suit.

Id. [Citations omitted.]

In this case, the district court "identified the plaintiff's interest as a liberty interest in personal security protected by the [F]ourteenth [A]mendment," *id.* at 1519, relying largely on *Ingraham v. Wright*, 430 *U.S.* 651, 674-75, 97 *S.Ct.* 1401, 1414-15 (1977). The Tenth Circuit, however, rather than expressly finding that the Colorado statute creates such a constitutionally protected liberty interest—which would be a necessary basis for plaintiff's Section 1983 claim—held that "even if such a constitutional right exists, it was not clearly established in the law at the time of the defendants' actions thus entitling them to immunity from suit." *Hilliard* at 1519.

According to the court, the *Ingraham* right to personal security attaches when there is some element of state-imposed confinement or custody. It is, however, less than clear whether such a right to personal security would apply in the absence of such confinement or custody. *Hilliard* at 1520. As a result, the court concluded that "it was not clearly established in 1988 that someone whose person was not under some degree of physical control by the state or who was not involved in a [F]ourth [A]mendment search or seizure would have a clearly established, constitutionally protected liberty interest." *Id.*

Notwithstanding its conclusion, the court did pause to observe:

> While we are appalled by the conduct of the defendants in this case, we note the danger of confusing the question of whether the plaintiff has state tort remedies with whether the plaintiff has stated a claim amounting to the deprivation of a constitutional right. The district court's opinion makes a persuasive case * * * that state tort remedies may exist under these facts. We are not persuaded, however, that the plaintiff here has articulated the deprivation of a constitutional right, much less a "clearly established" constitutional right.

Id. at 1521. [Citation omitted.]

4. *Failure to provide adequate protective services.* In *DeShaney v. Winnebago County Department of Social Services*, 489 *U.S.* 189, 109 *S.Ct.* 998 (1989), the United States Supreme Court held that the failure of a state or local municipality or its agents to provide an individual with adequate protective services will not constitute a violation of the individual's due process rights. In this appeal, arising from a 42 *U.S.C.* §1983 action, 4-year-old Joshua and his mother (plaintiffs) allege that defendants Winnebago County, its Department of Social Services, and various individual employees deprived Joshua of his liberty without due process of law, in violation of his rights under the Fourteenth Amendment, by failing to intervene to protect him against a risk of "known" violence at the hands of his father. The last beating inflicted by Joshua's father caused the 4-year-old to fall into a life-threatening coma which ultimately caused brain damage so severe that he is expected to spend the rest of his life confined to an institution for the profoundly retarded.

Because the government agencies here involved knew of the family's case history, and in fact investigated past instances of suspected child abuse, plaintiffs contend that the government agencies deprived Joshua of his Fourteenth Amendment liberty interest to be free from unjustified intrusions on personal security, "by failing to provide him with adequate protection against his father's [known] violent propensities." *Id.*, 109 *S.Ct.* at 1003. The United States Supreme Court disagreed.

According to the Court, "nothing in the language of the Due Process Clause itself requires the State to protect the life, liberty, and property of its citizens against invasion by private actors. The Clause is phrased as a limitation on the State's power to act, not as a guarantee of certain minimal levels of safety and security." *Id.* While the Due Process Clause prohibits the State from depriving its citizens of life, liberty, or property without "due process of law," it does not, however, "impose an affirmative obligation on the State to ensure that those interests do not come to harm through other means. * * * Like its counterpart in the Fifth Amendment, the Due Process Clause of the Fourteenth Amendment was intended to prevent government 'from abusing (its) power, or employing it as an instrument of oppression[.]' " *Id.* [Citations omitted.] *Its purpose was to protect the people from the*

State, not to ensure that the State protected them from each other." Id. [Emphasis added.]

Since "the Due Process Clause does not require the State to provide its citizens with particular protective services, it follows that the State cannot be held liable under the Clause for injuries that could have been averted had it chosen to provide them." *Id.* at 1004. ("The State may not, of course, selectively deny its protective services to certain disfavored minorities without violating the Equal Protection Clause." *Id.* at 1004 n.3). "As a general matter, then, [the Court holds] that a State's failure to protect an individual against private violence simply does not constitute a violation of the Due Process Clause." *Id.*

A State may, however, under its own tort law, address such a problem by imposing liability upon State officials in situations where they voluntarily undertake to protect or render services to a particular individual but do so negligently.

Cf. Collins v. City of Harker Heights, Texas, 503 *U.S.* 115, 112 *S.Ct.* 1061 (1992) ("the Due Process Clause does not impose an independent federal obligation upon municipalities to provide certain minimum levels of safety and security in the workplace").

BD. OF CO. COM'RS. OF BRYAN COUNTY, OKL. v. BROWN
United States Supreme Court
520 *U.S.* 397, 117 *S.Ct.* 1382 (1997)

QUESTION: May a municipality or its chief of police, or a county or its sheriff, be held liable for injuries caused by an officer on the basis of an isolated inadequate hiring decision ?

ANSWER: GENERALLY NO. In order for an inadequate screening/background investigation to give rise to civil liability, a plaintiff must demonstrate that the hiring decision "reflects deliberate indifference to the risk that a violation of a particular constitutional or statutory right will follow the decision. Only where adequate scrutiny of an applicant's background would lead a reasonable policymaker to conclude that the plainly obvious consequence of the decision to hire the applicant would be the deprivation of a third party's federally protected right can the official's failure to adequately scrutinize the applicant's background constitute 'deliberate indifference.' " *Id.* at 1392. In this case, the plaintiff failed to establish that the sheriff's background investigation revealed that the reserve officer, if hired, would use excessive force.

RATIONALE: Plaintiff, Jill Brown, brought a claim for damages under 42 *U.S.C.* §1983, against Bryan County and its Sheriff. Brown contended that "a county police officer used excessive force in arresting her, and that the county itself was liable for her injuries based on its sheriff's hiring and training decisions." *Id.* at 1386.

At the hearing, the evidence established that in the early morning hours of May 12th, plaintiff Jill Brown and her husband were driving from Grayson County, Texas, to their home in Bryan County, Oklahoma. "After crossing into Oklahoma, they approached a police checkpoint. Mr. Brown, who was driving, decided to avoid the checkpoint and return to Texas. After seeing the Browns' truck turn away from the checkpoint, Bryan County Deputy Sheriff Robert Morrison and Reserve Deputy Stacy Burns pursued the vehicle. Although the parties' versions of events differ, at trial, both deputies claimed that their patrol car reached speeds in excess of 100 miles per hour. Mr. Brown testified that he was unaware of the deputies' attempts to overtake him. The chase finally ended four miles south of the police checkpoint." *Id.* at 1386.

"After he got out of the squad car, Deputy Sheriff Morrison pointed his gun toward the Browns' vehicle and ordered the Browns to raise their hands. Reserve Deputy Burns, who was unarmed, rounded the corner of the vehicle on the passenger's side. Burns twice ordered [] Jill Brown from the vehicle. When she did not exit, he used an 'arm bar' technique, grabbing [her] arm at the wrist and elbow, pulling her from the vehicle, and spinning her to the ground. [Brown's] knees were severely injured, and she later underwent corrective surgery." *Id.* at 1386-87.

Brown sued to recover compensation for her injuries from Burns, Bryan County Sheriff B. J. Moore, and the County itself, claiming, among other things, that the County "was liable for Burns' alleged use of excessive force based on Sheriff Moore's decision to hire Burns, the son of his nephew." *Id.* at 1387. Specifically, Brown claimed that "Sheriff Moore had failed to adequately review Burns' background. Burns had a record of driving infractions and had pleaded guilty to various driving-related and other misdemeanors, including assault and battery, resisting arrest, and public drunkenness. Oklahoma law does not preclude the hiring of an individual who has committed a misdemeanor to serve as a peace officer." *Id.* "At trial, Sheriff Moore testified that he had obtained Burns' driving record and a report on Burns from the National Crime Information Center, but had not closely reviewed either. Sheriff Moore authorized Burns to make arrests, but not to carry a weapon or to operate a patrol car." *Id.*

In this appeal, the Court determined that the County was not liable for Brown's injuries "based on Sheriff Moore's single decision to hire Burns." *Id.* According to the Court, "in enacting §1983, Congress did not intend to impose liability on a municipality unless deliberate action attributable to the municipality itself is the 'moving force' behind the plaintiff's deprivation of federal rights." *Id.* at 1386 (citing *Monell v. New York City Dept. of Social Servs.*, 436 U.S. 658, 694, 98 S.Ct. 2018, 2027 (1978)).

Under *Monell*, "a municipality may not be held liable under §1983 solely because it employs a tortfeasor." *Id.* at 1388. Instead, in *Monell* and subsequent cases, the Court has "required a plaintiff seeking to impose liability on a municipality under §1983 to identify a municipal 'policy' or 'custom' that caused the plaintiff's injury." *Id.* In this respect, the identification of a "policy" ensures that "a municipality is held liable only for those deprivations resulting from the decisions of its duly constituted legislative body or of those officials whose acts may fairly be said to be those of the municipality. * * * Similarly, an act performed pursuant to a 'custom' that has not been formally approved by an appropriate decisionmaker may fairly subject a municipality to liability on the theory that the relevant practice is so widespread as to have the force of law." *Id.*

The critical issue in this case was whether a single hiring decision by a county sheriff or other chief executive of a law enforcement agency can be a "policy" that triggers municipal liability. The plaintiff contended that "a single act by a decisionmaker with final authority in the relevant area constitutes a 'policy' attributable to the municipality itself." Id. Under the plaintiff's theory, the "identification of an act of a proper municipal decisionmaker is all that is required to ensure that the municipality is held liable only for its own conduct." Id. The United States Supreme Court disagreed.

According to the Court, "it is not enough for a §1983 plaintiff merely to identify conduct properly attributable to the municipality. *The plaintiff must also demonstrate that, through its deliberate conduct, the municipality was the 'moving force' behind the injury alleged.* That is, a plaintiff must show that the municipal action was taken with the requisite degree of culpability, *and must demonstrate a direct causal link between the municipal action and the deprivation of federal rights.*" *Id.* [Emphasis added.]

In this case, the sheriff's hiring decision was itself legal. Moreover, at no time did Sheriff Moore authorize Burns to use excessive force. *Id.* at 1389. Merely because a plaintiff has suffered a constitutional injury "at the hands of a municipal employee will not alone permit an inference of municipal culpability and causation; the plaintiff will simply have shown that the *employee* acted culpably." *Id.* [Court's emphasis.] These difficulties were recognized in *City of Canton, Ohio v. Harris,* 489 *U.S.* 378, 109 *S.Ct.* 1197 (1989), where the Court addressed a claim that inadequate training of shift supervisors at a city jail led to a deprivation of a detainee's constitutional rights. The Court held that "a plaintiff seeking to establish municipal liability on the theory that a facially lawful municipal action has led an employee to violate a plaintiff's rights must demonstrate that the municipal action was taken with 'deliberate indifference' as to its known or obvious consequences. * * * A showing of simple or even heightened negligence will not suffice." *Id.* at 1390. [Citations omitted.]

The Court concluded in *Canton* that "an 'inadequate training' claim could be the basis for §1983 liability in 'limited circumstances.'" *Id.* (quoting *Canton* at 387, 109 *S.Ct.* at 1204). The *Canton* Court spoke, however, "of a *deficient training 'program,' necessarily intended to apply over time to multiple employees. * * * Existence of a 'program' makes proof of fault and causation at least possible in an inadequate training case. If a program does not prevent constitutional violations, municipal decisionmakers may eventually be put on notice that a new program is called for.* Their continued adherence to an approach that they know or should know has failed to prevent tortious conduct by employees may establish the conscious disregard for the consequences of their action—the 'deliberate indifference'—necessary to trigger municipal liability." *Id.* [Emphasis added.] *See also Canton* at 390 n.10,

109 *S.Ct.* at 1205 n.10) ("It could . . . be that the police, in exercising their discretion, so often violate constitutional rights that the need for further training must have been plainly obvious to the city policymakers, who, nevertheless, are 'deliberately indifferent' to the need"). "In addition, the existence of a pattern of tortious conduct by inadequately trained employees may tend to show that the lack of proper training, rather than a one-time negligent administration of the program or factors peculiar to the officer involved in a particular incident, is the 'moving force' behind the plaintiff's injury." *Id.*

In this case, Brown has not claimed that she can identify any pattern of injuries linked to Sheriff Moore's hiring practices. Nor has she contended that Sheriff Moore's hiring practices are generally defective. Rather, she seeks to "trace liability to what can only be described as a deviation from Sheriff Moore's ordinary hiring practices." *Id.* In this regard the Court cautioned:

> Where a claim of municipal liability rests on a single decision, not itself representing a violation of federal law and not directing such a violation, the danger that a municipality will be held liable without fault is high. Because the decision necessarily governs a single case, there can be no notice to the municipal decision-maker, based on previous violations of federally protected rights, that his approach is inadequate. Nor will it be readily apparent that the municipality's action caused the injury in question, because the plaintiff can point to no other incident tending to make it more likely that the plaintiff's own injury flows from the municipality's action, rather than from some other intervening cause.

Id. at 1390.

In *Canton*, the Court "did not foreclose the possibility that evidence of a single violation of federal rights, accompanied by a showing that a municipality has failed to train its employees to handle recurring situations presenting an obvious potential for such a violation, could trigger municipal liability." *Id.* at 1391. *See Canton* at 390, & n.10, 109 *S.Ct.* at 1205 & n.10 ("[I]t may happen that in light of the duties assigned to specific officers or employees the need for more or different training is so obvious . . . that the policymakers of the city can reasonably be said to have been deliberately indifferent to the need"). And in this case, Brown purports to rely on *Canton*, "arguing that Burns' use of excessive force was the plainly obvious consequence of Sheriff Moore's failure to screen Burns' record. In essence, [she] claims that this showing of 'obviousness' would demonstrate both that Sheriff Moore acted with conscious disregard for the consequences of his action and that the Sheriff's action directly caused her injuries, and would thus substitute for the pattern of injuries ordinarily necessary to establish municipal culpability and causation." *Id.* The Court rejected this contention as well, finding unpersuasive the proffered analogy between "failure to train" cases and "inadequate screening" cases.

"In leaving open in *Canton* the possibility that a plaintiff might succeed in carrying a 'failure to train' claim without showing a pattern of constitutional violations, [the Court] hypothesized that, in a narrow range of circumstances, a violation of federal rights may be a highly predictable consequence of a failure to equip law enforcement officers with specific tools to handle recurring situations. The likelihood that the situation will recur and the predictability that an officer lacking specific tools to handle that situation will violate citizens' rights could justify a finding that policymakers' decision not to train the officer reflected 'deliberate indifference' to the obvious consequence of the policymakers' choice—namely, a violation of a specific constitutional or statutory right. The high degree of predictability may also support an inference of causation—that the municipality's indifference led directly to the very consequence that was so predictable." *Id.*

"Where a plaintiff presents a §1983 claim premised upon the inadequacy of an official's review of a prospective applicant's record, however, there is a particular danger that a municipality will be held liable for an injury not directly caused by a deliberate action attributable to the municipality itself. Every injury suffered at the hands of a municipal employee can be traced to a hiring decision in a 'but for' sense: But for the municipality's decision to hire the employee, the plaintiff would not have suffered the injury." *Id.*

"Unlike the risk from a particular glaring omission in a training regimen, the risk from a single instance of inadequate screening of an applicant's background is not 'obvious' in the abstract; rather, it depends upon the background of the applicant. A lack of scrutiny may increase the likelihood that an unfit officer will be hired, and that the unfit officer will, when placed in a particular position to affect the rights of citizens, act improperly. But that is only a generalized showing of risk. The fact that inadequate scrutiny of an applicant's background would make a violation of rights more likely cannot alone give rise to an inference that a policymaker's failure to scrutinize the record of a particular applicant produced a specific constitutional violation. After all, a full screening of an applicant's background might reveal no cause for concern at all; if so, a hiring official who failed to scrutinize the applicant's background cannot be said to have consciously disregarded an obvious risk that the officer would subsequently inflict a particular constitutional injury." *Id.* at 1391-92.

While Sheriff Moore's assessment of Burns' background may have been inadequate, that is not the total inquiry. Rather, a plaintiff must demonstrate that the hiring decision reflected a "deliberate indifference to the risk that a violation of a particular constitutional or statutory right will follow the decision. Only where adequate scrutiny of an applicant's background would lead a reasonable policymaker to conclude that the plainly obvious consequence of the decision to hire the applicant would be the deprivation of a third party's federally protected right can the official's failure to adequately scrutinize the applicant's background constitute 'deliberate indifference.'" *Id.* at 1392.

The lower courts in this matter did not directly "test the link" between Burns' actual background and the risk that, if hired, he would use excessive force. "As discussed above, a finding of culpability simply cannot depend on the mere probability that any officer inadequately screened will inflict any constitutional injury. *Rather, it must depend on a finding that this officer was highly likely to inflict the particular injury suffered by the plaintiff. The connection between the background of the particular applicant and the specific constitutional violation alleged must be strong." Id.* [Emphasis added.] To adequately "test the link," between the sheriff's hiring decision and the plaintiff's injury, the relevant question is whether, in full view of Burns' background, the sheriff "should have concluded that Burns' use of excessive force would be a plainly obvious consequence of the hiring decision." *Id.* This, of course, presupposes that "proof of a single instance of inadequate screening could [] trigger municipal liability." *Id.* "On this point," the Court concluded, the plaintiff's "showing was inadequate." *Id.* at 1392-93. In this case, the Court was not convinced that Burns' use of excessive force was a plainly obvious consequence of the hiring decision.

"Cases involving constitutional injuries allegedly traceable to an ill-considered hiring decision pose the greatest risk that a municipality will be held liable for an injury that it did not cause. In the broadest sense, every injury is traceable to a hiring decision." *Id.* at 1393-94. "Congress did not, however, intend that municipalities be held liable unless deliberate action attributable to the municipality directly caused a deprivation of federal rights." *Id.* at 1394.

Accordingly, "Bryan County is not liable for Sheriff Moore's isolated decision to hire Burns without adequate screening, because [the plaintiff] has not demonstrated that his decision reflected a conscious disregard for a high risk that Burns would use excessive force in violation of [her] federally protected right." *Id.*

TOWN OF NEWTON v. RUMERY
Supreme Court of the United States
480 *U.S.* 386, 107 *S.Ct.* 1187 (1987)

QUESTION: Are "release-dismissal" agreements, whereby a criminal defendant releases his right to sue public officials in return for the dismissal of charges pending against him, always invalid as against public policy ?

ANSWER: NO. "Release-dismissal agreements * * * further legitimate prosecutorial and public interests," and are not "invalid *per se*." *Id.* at 1195. In this case, the "agreement was voluntary, there was no evidence of prosecutorial misconduct, and * * * enforcement of this agreement would not adversely affect the relevant public interests." *Id.*

RATIONALE: Defendant, Rumery, and his defense attorney entered into an agreement with the county prosecutor whereby the prosecutor would dismiss the criminal charges against Rumery in exchange for Rumery agreeing not to sue the Town of Newton, its officials, or the victim (the release-dismissal agreement). The prosecutor drafted the agreement, Rumery's attorney approved the form, and, after three days of contemplation, Rumery signed it.

Ten months later, Rumery filed a federal civil rights suit under 42 *U.S.C.* §1983 in the Federal District Court for the District of New

Hampshire, alleging that the Town and its officers violated his constitutional rights by arresting him, defaming him, and imprisoning him falsely. The Town and its officers filed a motion to dismiss the suit, relying on the release-dismissal agreement as an affirmative defense. Rumery contends that the release-dismissal agreement is unenforceable and that such agreements are void as against public policy.

The Federal District Court disagreed with Rumery and concluded that a "release of claims under section 1983 is valid * * * if it results from a decision that is voluntary, deliberate and informed." *Id.* at 1192. *The United States Supreme Court agreed.*

As a preliminary matter, the Court held that an agreement to waive a right to sue conferred by federal statute "is a question of federal law." *Id.* "The relevant principle is well established: a promise is unenforceable if the interest in its enforcement is outweighed in the circumstances by a public policy harmed by enforcement of the agreement." *Id.* While release-dismissal agreements in some cases "may infringe important interests of the criminal defendant and of society as a whole * * * the mere possibility of harm to these interests" does not call "for a *per se* rule" of invalidation. *Id.* It is true that some release-dismissal agreements may not be the product of an informed and voluntary decision, but there is no reason to believe that all such agreements are inherently coercive. These agreements, when properly entered, pose no more of a coercive choice than other situations adopted by the Court as acceptable (*e.g.*, plea bargaining).

"In many cases, a defendant's choice to enter into a release-dismissal agreement will reflect a highly rational judgment that the benefits of escaping criminal prosecution exceed the speculative benefits of prevailing in a civil action. Rumery's voluntary decision to enter this agreement exemplifies such a judgment." *Id.* at 1193. He considered the agreement for three days before signing it, and "[t]he benefits to him are obvious: he gained immunity from criminal prosecution in consideration of abandoning a civil suit that he may well have lost." *Id.*

"Because Rumery voluntarily waived his right to sue under §1983, the public interests opposing involuntary waiver of constitutional rights is no reason to hold this agreement invalid. Moreover * * * the possibility of coercion in the making of similar agreements [is] insufficient by itself to justify a *per se* rule against release-dismissal agreements." *Id.* "No one suggests that all such suits are meritorious. Many are marginal and some are frivolous. Yet even when the risk of ultimate liability is negligible, the burden of defending such lawsuits is substantial. * * * This diversion of officials from their normal duties and the inevitable expense of defending even unjust claims is distinctly not in the public interest." *Id.* at 1194.

Accordingly, "this agreement was voluntary, * * * there is no evidence of prosecutorial misconduct, and * * * enforcement would not adversely affect the relevant public interests." *Id.* at 1195.

PART V

ADDENDA

As a complement to the materials presented in the main text, the following Addenda has been included:

(1)   The Constitution of the United States.

(2)   Current Justices of the Supreme Court of the United States.

(3)   Glossary of Terms Frequently used in Case Law Analysis.

THE CONSTITUTION OF THE UNITED STATES

Preamble

We the People of the United States, in Order to form a more perfect Union, establish Justice, insure domestic Tranquility, provide for the common defence, promote the general Welfare, and secure the Blessings of Liberty to ourselves and our Posterity, do ordain and establish this Constitution for the United States of America.

ARTICLE I

Section 1. All legislative Powers herein granted shall be vested in a Congress of the United States, which shall consist of a Senate and House of Representatives.

Section 2. [1] The House of Representatives shall be composed of Members chosen every second Year by the People of the several States, and the Electors in each State shall have the Qualifications requisite for Electors of the most numerous Branch of the State Legislature.

[2] No Person shall be a Representative who shall not have attained to the Age of twenty five Years, and been seven Years a Citizen of the United States, and who shall not, when elected, be an Inhabitant of that State in which he shall be chosen.

[3] Representatives and direct Taxes shall be apportioned among the several States which may be included within this Union, according to their respective Numbers, which shall be determined by adding to the whole Number of free Persons, including those bound to Service for a Term of Years, and excluding Indians not taxed, three fifths of all other Persons.[1] The actual Enumeration shall be made within three Years after the first Meeting of the Congress of the United States, and within every subsequent Term of ten Years, in such Manner as they shall by Law direct. The Number of Representatives shall not exceed one for every thirty Thousand, but each State shall have at Least one Representative; and until such enumeration shall be made, the State of New Hampshire shall be entitled to chuse three, Massachusetts eight, Rhode-Island and Providence Plantations one, Connecticut five, New York six, New Jersey four, Pennsylvania eight, Delaware one, Maryland six, Virginia ten, North Carolina five, South Carolina five, and Georgia three.

[4] When vacancies happen in the Representation from any State, the Executive Authority thereof shall issue Writs of Election to fill such Vacancies.

---

[1] Affected by the 14th Amendment, §2 and the 16th Amendment.)

[5] The House of Representatives shall chuse their Speaker and other Officers; and shall have the sole Power of Impeachment.

² **Section 3.** [1] The Senate of the United States shall be composed of two Senators from each State, chosen by the Legislature thereof, for six Years; and each Senator shall have one Vote.

[2] Immediately after they shall be assembled in Consequence of the first Election, they shall be divided as equally as may be into three Classes. The Seats of the Senators of the first Class shall be vacated at the Expiration of the second Year, of the second Class at the Expiration of the fourth Year, and of the third Class at the Expiration of the sixth Year, so that one third may be chosen every second Year; and if Vacancies happen by Resignation, or otherwise, during the Recess of the Legislature of any State, the Executive thereof may make temporary Appointments until the next Meeting of the Legislature, which shall then fill such Vacancies.

[3] No Person shall be a Senator who shall not have attained to the Age of thirty Years, and been nine Years a Citizen of the United States, and who shall not, when elected, be an Inhabitant of that State for which he shall be chosen.

[4] The Vice President of the United States shall be President of the Senate, but shall have no Vote, unless they be equally divided.

[5] The Senate shall chuse their other Officers, and also a President pro tempore, in the Absence of the Vice President, or when he shall exercise the Office of President of the United States.

[6] The Senate shall have the sole Power to try all Impeachments. When sitting for that Purpose, they shall be on Oath or Affirmation. When the President of the United States is tried, the Chief Justice shall preside: And no Person shall be convicted without the Concurrence of two thirds of the Members present.

[7] Judgment in Cases of Impeachment shall not extend further than to removal from Office, and disqualification to hold and enjoy any Office of honor, Trust or Profit under the United States: but the Party convicted shall nevertheless be liable and subject to Indictment, Trial, Judgment and Punishment, according to Law.

³ **Section 4.** [1] The Times, Places and Manner of holding Elections for Senators and Representatives, shall be prescribed in each State by the Legislature thereof; but the Congress may at any time by Law make or alter such Regulations, except as to the Places of chusing Senators.

[2] The Congress shall assemble at least once in every Year, and such Meeting shall be on the first Monday in December, unless they shall by Law appoint a different Day.

Section 5. [1] Each House shall be the Judge of the Elections, Returns and Qualifications of its own Members, and a Majority of each shall constitute a Quorum to do Business; but a smaller Number may

---

² (Affected by the 17th Amendment.)

³ (Affected by the 20th Amendment.)

adjourn from day to day, and may be authorized to compel the Attendance of absent Members, in such Manner, and under such Penalties as each House may provide.

[2] Each House may determine the Rules of its Proceedings, punish its Members for disorderly Behaviour, and, with the Concurrence of two thirds, expel a Member.

[3] Each House shall keep a Journal of its Proceedings, and from time to time publish the same, excepting such Parts as may in their Judgment require Secrecy; and the Yeas and Nays of the Members of either House on any question shall, at the Desire of one fifth of those Present, be entered on the Journal.

[4] Neither House, during the Session of Congress, shall, without the Consent of the other, adjourn for more than three days, nor to any other Place than that in which the two Houses shall be sitting.

Section 6. [1] The Senators and Representatives shall receive a Compensation for their Services, to be ascertained by Law, and paid out of the Treasury of the United States. They shall in all Cases, except Treason, Felony and Breach of the Peace, be privileged from Arrest during their Attendance at the Session of their respective Houses, and in going to and returning from the same; and for any Speech or Debate in either House, they shall not be questioned in any other Place.

[2] No Senator or Representative shall, during the Time for which he was elected, be appointed to any civil Office under the Authority of the United States, which shall have been created, or the Emoluments whereof shall have been increased during such time; and no Person holding any Office under the United States, shall be a Member of either House during his Continuance in Office.

Section 7. [1] All Bills for raising Revenue shall originate in the House of Representatives; but the Senate may propose or concur with Amendments as on other Bills.

[2] Every Bill which shall have passed the House of Representatives and the Senate, shall, before it become a Law, be presented to the President of the United States; If he approve he shall sign it, but if not he shall return it, with his Objections to that House in which it shall have originated, who shall enter the Objections at large on their Journal, and proceed to reconsider it. If after such Reconsideration two thirds of that House shall agree to pass the Bill, it shall be sent, together with the Objections, to the other House, by which it shall likewise be reconsidered, and if approved by two thirds of that House, it shall become a Law. But in all such Cases the Votes of both Houses shall be determined by Yeas and Nays, and the Names of the Persons voting for and against the Bill shall be entered on the Journal of each House respectively. If any Bill shall not be returned by the President within ten Days (Sundays excepted) after it shall have been presented to him, the Same shall be a Law, in like Manner as if he had signed it, unless the Congress by their Adjournment prevent its Return, in which Case it shall not be a Law.

[3] Every Order, Resolution, or Vote to which the Concurrence of the Senate and House of Representatives may be necessary (except on

a question of Adjournment) shall be presented to the President of the United States; and before the Same shall take Effect, shall be approved by him, or being disapproved by him, shall be repassed by two thirds of the Senate and House of Representatives, according to the Rules and Limitations prescribed in the Case of a Bill.

Section 8. [1] The Congress shall have Power To lay and collect Taxes, Duties, Imposts and Excises, to pay the Debts and provide for the common Defence and general Welfare of the United States; but all Duties, Imposts and Excises shall be uniform throughout the United States;

[2] To borrow Money on the credit of the United States;

[3] To regulate Commerce with foreign Nations, and among the several States, and with the Indian Tribes;

[4] To establish a uniform Rule of Naturalization, and uniform Laws on the subject of Bankruptcies throughout the United States;

[5] To coin Money, regulate the Value thereof, and of foreign Coin, and fix the Standard of Weights and Measures;

[6] To provide for the Punishment of counterfeiting the Securities and current Coin of the United States;

[7] To establish Post Offices and Post Roads;

[8] To promote the Progress of Science and useful Arts, by securing for limited Times to Authors and Inventors the exclusive Right to their respective Writings and Discoveries;

[9] To constitute Tribunals inferior to the supreme Court;

[10] To define and punish Piracies and Felonies committed on the high Seas, and Offences against the Law of Nations;

[11] To declare War, grant Letters of Marque and Reprisal, and make Rules concerning Captures on Land and Water;

[12] To raise and support Armies, but no Appropriation of Money to that Use shall be for a longer Term than two Years;

[13] To provide and maintain a Navy;

[14] To make Rules for the Government and Regulation of the land and naval Forces;

[15] To provide for calling forth the Militia to execute the Laws of the Union, suppress Insurrections and repel Invasions;

[16] To provide for organizing, arming, and disciplining, the Militia, and for governing such Part of them as may be employed in the Service of the United States, reserving to the States respectively, the Appointment of the Officers, and the Authority of training the Militia according to the discipline prescribed by Congress;

[17] To exercise exclusive Legislation in all Cases whatsoever, over such District (not exceeding ten Miles square) as may, by Cession of particular States, and the Acceptance of Congress, become the Seat of the Government of the United States, and to exercise like Authority over all Places purchased by the Consent of the Legislature of the State in which the Same shall be, for the Erection of Forts, Magazines, Arsenals, dock-Yards, and other needful Buildings;—And

[18] To make all Laws which shall be necessary and proper for carrying into Execution the foregoing Powers, and all other Powers

vested by this Constitution in the Government of the United States, or in any Department or Officer thereof.

Section 9. [1] The Migration or Importation of such Persons as any of the States now existing shall think proper to admit, shall not be prohibited by the Congress prior to the Year one thousand eight hundred and eight, but a Tax or duty may be imposed on such Importation, not exceeding ten dollars for each Person.

[2] The Privilege of the Writ of Habeas Corpus shall not be suspended, unless when in Cases of Rebellion or Invasion the public Safety may require it.

[3] No Bill of Attainder or ex post facto Law shall be passed.

[4] No Capitation, or other direct, Tax shall be laid, unless in Proportion to the Census or Enumeration herein before directed to be taken.[4]

[5] No Tax or Duty shall be laid on Articles exported from any State.

[6] No Preference shall be given by any Regulation of Commerce or Revenue to the Ports of one State over those of another: nor shall Vessels bound to, or from, one State, be obliged to enter, clear, or pay Duties in another.

[7] No money shall be drawn from the Treasury, but in Consequence of Appropriations made by Law; and a regular Statement and Account of the Receipts and Expenditures of all public Money shall be published from time to time.

[8] No Title of Nobility shall be granted by the United States: And no Person holding any Office of Profit or Trust under them, shall, without the Consent of the Congress, accept of any present, Emolument, Office, or Title, of any kind whatever, from any King, Prince, or foreign State.

Section 10. [1] No State shall enter into any Treaty, Alliance, or Confederation; grant Letters of Marque and Reprisal; coin Money; emit Bills of Credit; make any Thing but gold and silver Coin a Tender in Payment of Debts; pass any Bill of Attainder, ex post facto Law, or Law impairing the Obligation of Contracts, or grant any Title of Nobility.

[2] No State shall, without the Consent of the Congress, lay any Imposts or Duties on Imports or Exports, except what may be absolutely necessary for executing its inspection Laws: and the net Produce of all Duties and Imposts, laid by any State on Imports or Exports, shall be for the Use of the Treasury of the United States; and all such Laws shall be subject to the Revision and Controul of the Congress.

[3] No State shall, without the Consent of Congress, lay any Duty of Tonnage, keep Troops, or Ships of War in time of Peace, enter into any Agreement or Compact with another State, or with a foreign Power, or engage in War, unless actually invaded, or in such imminent Danger as will not admit of delay.

---

4 (Affected by the 16th Amendment.)

ARTICLE II

Section 1. [1] The executive Power shall be vested in a President of the United States of America. He shall hold his Office during the Term of four Years, and, together with the Vice President, chosen for the same Term, be elected, as follows:

[2] Each State shall appoint, in such Manner as the Legislature thereof may direct, a Number of Electors, equal to the whole Number of Senators and Representatives to which the State may be entitled in the Congress: but no Senator or Representative, or Person holding an Office of Trust or Profit under the United States, shall be appointed an Elector.

[3]⁵ The Electors shall meet in their respective States, and vote by Ballot for two Persons of whom one at least shall not be an Inhabitant of the same State with themselves. And they shall make a List of all the Persons voted for, and of the Number of Votes for each; which List they shall sign and certify, and transmit sealed to the Seat of the Government of the United States, directed to the President of the Senate. The President of the Senate shall, in the Presence of the Senate and House of Representatives, open all the Certificates, and the Votes shall then be counted. The Person having the greatest Number of Votes shall be the President, if such Number be a Majority of the whole Number of Electors appointed; and if there be more than one who have such Majority, and have an equal Number of Votes, then the House of Representatives shall immediately chuse by Ballot one of them for President; and if no Person have a Majority, then from the five highest on the List the said House shall in like Manner chuse the President. But in chusing the President, the Votes shall be taken by States, the Representation from each State having one Vote; A quorum for this Purpose shall consist of a Member or Members from two thirds of the States, and a Majority of all the States shall be necessary to a Choice. In every Case, after the Choice of the President, the Person having the greatest Number of Votes of the Electors shall be the Vice President. But if there should remain two or more who have equal Votes, the Senate shall chuse from them by Ballot the Vice President.

[4] The Congress may determine the Time of chusing the Electors, and the Day on which they shall give their Votes; which Day shall be the same throughout the United States.

[5] No person except a natural born Citizen, or a Citizen of the United States, at the time of the Adoption of this Constitution, shall be eligible to the Office of President; neither shall any Person be eligible to that Office who shall not have attained to the Age of thirty five Years, and been fourteen Years a Resident within the United States.

[6] In Case of the Removal of the President from Office, or of his Death, Resignation, or Inability to discharge the Powers and Duties of the said Office, the same shall devolve on the Vice President, and the Congress may by Law provide for the Case of Removal, Death, Resignation or Inability, both of the President and Vice President,

---

⁵ (Affected by the 12th Amendment.)

declaring what Officer shall then act as President, and such Officer shall act accordingly, until the Disability be removed, or a President shall be elected.

[7] The President shall, at stated Times, receive for his Services, a Compensation, which shall neither be encreased nor diminished during the Period for which he shall have been elected, and he shall not receive within that Period any other Emolument from the United States, or any of them.

[8] Before he enter on the Execution of his Office, he shall take the following Oath or Affirmation:—"I do solemnly swear (or affirm) that I will faithfully execute the Office of President of the United States, and will to the best of my Ability, preserve, protect and defend the Constitution of the United States."

Section 2. [1] The President shall be Commander in Chief of the Army and Navy of the United States, and of the Militia of the several States, when called into the actual Service of the United States; he may require the Opinion, in writing, of the principal Officer in each of the executive Departments, upon any Subject relating to the Duties of their respective Offices, and he shall have Power to grant Reprieves and Pardons for Offences against the United States, except in Cases of Impeachment.

[2] He shall have Power, by and with the Advice and Consent of the Senate to make Treaties, provided two thirds of the Senators present concur; and he shall nominate, and by and with the Advice and Consent of the Senate, shall appoint Ambassadors, other public Ministers and Consuls, Judges of the supreme Court, and all other Officers of the United States, whose Appointments are not herein otherwise provided for, and which shall be established by Law: but the Congress may by Law vest the Appointment of such inferior Officers, as they think proper, in the President alone, in the Courts of Law, or in the Heads of Departments.

[3] The President shall have Power to fill up all Vacancies that may happen during the Recess of the Senate, by granting Commissions which shall expire at the End of their next Session.

Section 3. He shall from time to time give to the Congress Information of the State of the Union, and recommend to their Consideration such Measures as he shall judge necessary and expedient; he may, on extraordinary Occasions, convene both Houses, or either of them, and in Case of Disagreement between them, with Respect to the Time of Adjournment, he may adjourn them to such Time as he shall think proper; he shall receive Ambassadors and other public Ministers; he shall take Care that the Laws be faithfully executed, and shall Commission all the Officers of the United States.

Section 4. The President, Vice President and all civil Officers of the United States, shall be removed from Office on Impeachment for, and Conviction of, Treason, Bribery, or other high Crimes and Misdemeanors.

ARTICLE III

Section 1. The judicial Power of the United States, shall be vested in one supreme Court, and in such inferior Courts as the Congress may from time to time ordain and establish. The Judges, both of the supreme and inferior Courts, shall hold their Offices during good Behaviour, and shall, at stated Times, receive for their Services, a Compensation, which shall not be diminished during their Continuance in Office.

[6] **Section 2.** [1] The judicial Power shall extend to all Cases, in Law and Equity, arising under this Constitution, the Laws of the United States, and Treaties made, or which shall be made, under their Authority;—to all Cases affecting Ambassadors, other public Ministers and Consuls;—to all Cases of admiralty and maritime Jurisdiction;— to Controversies to which the United States shall be a Party;—to Controversies between two or more States;—between a State and Citizens of another State;—between Citizens of different States;—between Citizens of the same State claiming Lands under the Grants of different States, and between a State, or the Citizens thereof, and foreign States, Citizens or Subjects.

[2] In all Cases affecting Ambassadors, other public Ministers and Consuls, and those in which a State shall be a Party, the supreme Court shall have original Jurisdiction. In all the other Cases before mentioned, the supreme Court shall have appellate Jurisdiction, both as to Law and Fact, with such Exceptions, and under such Regulations as the Congress shall make.

[3] The Trial of all Crimes, except in Cases of Impeachment, shall be by Jury; and such Trial shall be held in the State where the said Crimes shall have been committed; but when not committed within any State, the Trial shall be at such Place or Places as the Congress may by Law have directed.

Section 3. [1] Treason against the United States, shall consist only in levying War against them, or, in adhering to their Enemies, giving them Aid and Comfort. No person shall be convicted of Treason unless on the Testimony of two Witnesses to the same overt Act, or on Confession in open Court.

[2] The Congress shall have Power to declare the Punishment of Treason, but no Attainder of Treason shall work Corruption of Blood, or Forfeiture except during the Life of the Person attainted.

ARTICLE IV

Section 1. Full Faith and Credit shall be given in each State to the public Acts, Records, and judicial Proceedings of every other State. And the Congress may by general Laws prescribe the Manner in which such Acts, Records and Proceedings shall be proved, and the Effect thereof.

---

[6] (Affected by the 11th Amendment.)

Section 2. [1] The Citizens of each State shall be entitled to all Privileges and Immunities of Citizens in the several States.

[2] A Person charged in any State with Treason, Felony, or other Crime, who shall flee from Justice, and be found in another State, shall on Demand of the executive Authority of the State from which he fled, be delivered up, to be removed to the State having Jurisdiction of the Crime.

[3] No Person held to Service or Labour in one State, under the Laws thereof, escaping into another, shall, in Consequence of any Law or Regulation therein, be discharged from such Service or Labour, but shall be delivered up on Claim of the Party to whom such Service or Labour may be due.[7]

Section 3. [1] New States may be admitted by the Congress into this Union; but no new State shall be formed or erected within the Jurisdiction of any other State; nor any State be formed by the Junction of two or more States, or Parts of States, without the Consent of the Legislatures of the States concerned as well as of the Congress.

[2] The Congress shall have Power to dispose of and make all needful Rules and Regulations respecting the Territory or other Property belonging to the United States; and nothing in this Constitution shall be so construed as to Prejudice any Claims of the United States, or of any particular State.

Section 4. The United States shall guarantee to every State in this Union a Republican Form of Government, and shall protect each of them against Invasion; and on Application of the Legislature, or of the Executive (when the Legislature cannot be convened) against domestic Violence.

ARTICLE V

The Congress, whenever two thirds of both Houses shall deem it necessary, shall propose Amendments to this Constitution, or, on the Application of the Legislatures of two thirds of the several States, shall call a Convention for proposing Amendments, which, in either Case, shall be valid to all Intents and Purposes, as Part of this Constitution, when ratified by the Legislatures of three fourths of the several States, or by Conventions in three fourths thereof, as the one or the other Mode of Ratification may be proposed by the Congress; Provided that no Amendment which may be made prior to the Year One thousand eight hundred and eight shall in any Manner affect the first and fourth Clauses in the Ninth Section of the first Article; and that no State, without its Consent, shall be deprived of its equal Suffrage in the Senate.

---

[7] (Affected by the 13th Amendment.)

ARTICLE VI

[1] All Debts contracted and Engagements entered into, before the Adoption of this Constitution, shall be as valid against the United States under this Constitution, as under the Confederation.

[2] This Constitution, and the Laws of the United States which shall be made in Pursuance thereof; and all Treaties made, or which shall be made, under the Authority of the United States, shall be the supreme Law of the Land; and the Judges in every State shall be bound thereby, any Thing in the Constitution or Laws of any State to the Contrary notwithstanding.

[3] The Senators and Representatives before mentioned, and the Members of the several State Legislatures, and all executive and judicial Officers, both of the United States and of the several States, shall be bound by Oath or Affirmation, to support this Constitution; but no religious Test shall ever be required as a Qualification to any Office or public Trust under the United States.

ARTICLE VII

The Ratification of the Conventions of nine States, shall be sufficient for the Establishment of this Constitution between the States so ratifying the Same.

ARTICLES IN ADDITION TO, AND AMENDMENT OF, THE CONSTITUTION OF THE UNITED STATES OF AMERICA, PROPOSED BY CONGRESS, AND RATIFIED BY THE LEGISLATURES OF THE SEVERAL STATES, PURSUANT TO THE FIFTH ARTICLE OF THE ORIGINAL CONSTITUTION.

AMENDMENT I [1791]

Congress shall make no law respecting an establishment of religion, or prohibiting the free exercise thereof; or abridging the freedom of speech, or of the press; or the right of the people peaceably to assemble, and to petition the Government for a redress of grievances.

AMENDMENT II [1791]

A well regulated militia, being necessary to the security of a free State, the right of the people to keep and bear arms, shall not be infringed.

AMENDMENT III [1791]

No Soldier shall, in time of peace be quartered in any house, without the consent of the owner, nor in time of war, but in a manner to be prescribed by law.

AMENDMENT IV [1791]

The right of the people to be secure in their persons, houses, papers, and effects, against unreasonable searches and seizures, shall not be violated, and no Warrants shall issue, but upon probable cause, supported by Oath or affirmation, and particularly describing the place to be searched, and the persons or things to be seized.

AMENDMENT V [1791]

No person shall be held to answer for a capital, or otherwise infamous crime, unless on a presentment or indictment of a Grand Jury, except in cases arising in the land or naval forces, or in the Militia, when in actual service in time of War or public danger; nor shall any person be subject for the same offence to be twice put in jeopardy of life or limb; nor shall be compelled in any criminal case to be a witness against himself, nor be deprived of life, liberty, or property, without due process of law; nor shall private property be taken for public use, without just compensation.

AMENDMENT VI [1791]

In all criminal prosecutions, the accused shall enjoy the right to a speedy and public trial, by an impartial jury of the State and district wherein the crime shall have been committed, which district shall have been previously ascertained by law, and to be informed of the nature and cause of the accusation; to be confronted with the witnesses against him; to have compulsory process for obtaining witnesses in his favor, and to have the Assistance of Counsel for his defence.

AMENDMENT VII [1791]

In Suits at common law, where the value in controversy shall exceed twenty dollars, the right of trial by jury shall be preserved, and no fact tried by a jury, shall be otherwise re-examined in any Court of the United States, than according to the rules of the common law.

AMENDMENT VIII [1791]

Excessive bail shall not be required, nor excessive fines imposed, nor cruel and unusual punishments inflicted.

AMENDMENT IX [1791]

The enumeration in the Constitution, of certain rights, shall not be construed to deny or disparage others retained by the people.

AMENDMENT X [1791]

The powers not delegated to the United States by the Constitution, nor prohibited by it to the States, are reserved to the States respectively, or to the people.

AMENDMENT XI [1798]

The Judicial power of the United States shall not be construed to extend to any suit in law or equity, commenced or prosecuted against one of the United States by Citizens of another State, or by Citizens or Subjects of any Foreign State.

AMENDMENT XII[8] [1804]

The Electors shall meet in their respective states, and vote by ballot for President and Vice-President, one of whom, at least, shall not be an inhabitant of the same state with themselves; they shall name in their ballots the person voted for as President, and in distinct ballots the person voted for as Vice-President, and they shall make distinct lists of all persons voted for as President, and of all persons voted for as Vice-President, and of the number of votes for each, which lists they shall sign and certify, and transmit sealed to the seat of the government of the United States, directed to the President of the Senate;—The President of the Senate shall, in the presence of the Senate and House of Representatives, open all the certificates and the votes shall then be counted;—The person having the greatest number of votes for President, shall be the President, if such number be a majority of the whole number of Electors appointed; and if no person have such majority, then from the persons having the highest numbers not exceeding three on the list of those voted for as President, the House of Representatives shall choose immediately, by ballot, the President. But in choosing the President, the votes shall be taken by states, the representation from each state having one vote; a quorum for this purpose shall consist of a member or members from two-thirds of the states, and a majority of all the states shall be necessary to a choice. And if the House of Representatives shall not choose a President whenever the right of choice shall devolve upon them, before the fourth day of March next following, then the Vice-President shall act as President, as in the case of the death or other constitutional disability of the President.—The person having the greatest number of votes as Vice-President, shall be the Vice-President, if such number be a majority of the whole number of Electors appointed, and if no person have a majority, then from the two highest numbers on the list, the Senate shall choose the Vice-President; a quorum for the purpose shall consist of two-thirds of the whole number of Senators, and a majority of the whole number shall be necessary to a choice. But no person constitutionally ineligible to the office of President shall be eligible to that of Vice-President of the United States.

---

[8] (Affected by the 20th Amendment, §3.)

AMENDMENT XIII [1865]

Section 1. Neither slavery nor involuntary servitude, except as a punishment for crime whereof the party shall have been duly convicted, shall exist within the United States, or any place subject to their jurisdiction.

Section 2. Congress shall have power to enforce this article by appropriate legislation.

AMENDMENT XIV [1868]

Section 1. All persons born or naturalized in the United States, and subject to the jurisdiction thereof, are citizens of the United States and of the State wherein they reside. No State shall make or enforce any law which shall abridge the privileges or immunities of citizens of the United States; nor shall any State deprive any person of life, liberty, or property, without due process of law; nor deny to any person within its jurisdiction the equal protection of the laws.

Section 2. Representatives shall be apportioned among the several States according to their respective numbers, counting the whole number of persons in each State, excluding Indians not taxed. But when the right to vote at any election for the choice of electors for President and Vice President of the United States, Representatives in Congress, the Executive and Judicial officers of a State, or the members of the Legislature thereof, is denied to any of the male inhabitants of such State, being twenty-one years of age, and citizens of the United States, or in any way abridged, except for participation in rebellion, or other crime, the basis of representation therein shall be reduced in the proportion which the number of such male citizens shall bear to the whole number of male citizens twenty-one years of age in such State.

Section 3. No person shall be a Senator or Representative in Congress, or elector of President and Vice President, or hold any office, civil or military, under the United States, or under any State, who, having previously taken an oath, as a member of Congress, or as an officer of the United States, or as a member of any State legislature, or as an executive or judicial officer of any State, to support the Constitution of the United States, shall have engaged in insurrection or rebellion against the same, or given aid or comfort to the enemies thereof. But Congress may by a vote of two-thirds of each House, remove such disability.

Section 4. The validity of the public debt of the United States, authorized by law, including debts incurred for payment of pensions and bounties for services in suppressing insurrection or rebellion, shall not be questioned. But neither the United States nor any State shall assume or pay any debt or obligation incurred in aid of insurrection or rebellion against the United States, or any claim for the loss or emancipation of any slave; but all such debts, obligations and claims shall be held illegal and void.

Section 5. The Congress shall have power to enforce, by appropriate legislation, the provisions of this article.

AMENDMENT XV [1870]

Section 1. The right of citizens of the United States to vote shall not be denied or abridged by the United States or by any State on account of race, color, or previous condition of servitude.

Section 2. The Congress shall have power to enforce this article by appropriate legislation.

AMENDMENT XVI [1913]

The Congress shall have power to lay and collect taxes on incomes, from whatever source derived, without apportionment among the several States, and without regard to any census or enumeration.

AMENDMENT XVII [1913]

[1] The Senate of the United States shall be composed of two Senators from each State, elected by the people thereof, for six years; and each Senator shall have one vote. The electors in each State shall have the qualifications requisite for electors of the most numerous branch of the State legislatures.

[2] When vacancies happen in the representation of any State in the Senate, the executive authority of such State shall issue writs of election to fill such vacancies: *Provided,* That the legislature of any State may empower the executive thereof to make temporary appointments until the people fill the vacancies by election as the legislature may direct.

[3] This amendment shall not be so construed as to affect the election or term of any Senator chosen before it becomes valid as part of the Constitution.

AMENDMENT XVIII[9] [1919]

Section 1. After one year from the ratification of this article the manufacture, sale, or transportation of intoxicating liquors within, the importation thereof into, or the exportation thereof from the United States and all territory subject to the jurisdiction thereof for beverage purposes is hereby prohibited.

Section 2. The Congress and the several States shall have concurrent power to enforce this article by appropriate legislation.

Section 3. This article shall be inoperative unless it shall have been ratified as an amendment to the Constitution by the legislatures of the several States, as provided in the Constitution, within seven years from the date of the submission hereof to the States by the Congress.

---

[9] (Repealed by the 21st Amendment.)

AMENDMENT XIX [1920]

[1] The right of citizens of the United States to vote shall not be denied or abridged by the United States or by any State on account of sex.

[2] Congress shall have power to enforce this article by appropriate legislation.

AMENDMENT XX [1933]

Section 1. The terms of the President and Vice President shall end at noon on the 20th day of January, and the terms of Senators and Representatives at noon on the 3d day of January, of the years in which such terms would have ended if this article had not been ratified; and the terms of their successors shall then begin.

Section 2. The Congress shall assemble at least once in every year, and such meeting shall begin at noon on the 3d day of January, unless they shall by law appoint a different day.

Section 3. If, at the time fixed for the beginning of the term of the President, the President elect shall have died, the Vice President elect shall become President. If a President shall not have been chosen before the time fixed for the beginning of his term, or if the President elect shall have failed to qualify, then the Vice President elect shall act as President until a President shall have qualified; and the Congress may by law provide for the case wherein neither a President elect nor a Vice President elect shall have qualified, declaring who shall then act as President, or the manner in which one who is to act shall be selected, and such person shall act accordingly until a President or Vice President shall have qualified.

Section 4. The Congress may by law provide for the case of the death of any of the persons from whom the House of Representatives may choose a President whenever the right of choice shall have devolved upon them, and for the case of the death of any of the persons from whom the Senate may choose a Vice President whenever the right of choice shall have devolved upon them.

Section 5. Sections 1 and 2 shall take effect on the 15th day of October following the ratification of this article.

Section 6. This article shall be inoperative unless it shall have been ratified as an amendment to the Constitution by the legislatures of three-fourths of the several States within seven years from the date of its submission.

AMENDMENT XXI [1933]

Section 1. The eighteenth article of amendment to the Constitution of the United States is hereby repealed.

Section 2. The transportation or importation into any State, Territory, or possession of the United States for delivery or use therein of intoxicating liquors, in violation of the laws thereof, is hereby prohibited.

Section 3. This article shall be inoperative unless it shall have been ratified as an amendment to the Constitution by conventions in the several States, as provided in the Constitution, within seven years from the date of the submission hereof to the States by the Congress.

AMENDMENT XXII [1951]

Section 1. No person shall be elected to the office of the President more than twice, and no person who has held the office of President, or acted as President, for more than two years of a term to which some other person was elected President shall be elected to the office of President more than once. But this Article shall not apply to any person holding the office of President when this Article was proposed by the Congress, and shall not prevent any person who may be holding the office of President, or acting as President, during the term within which this Article becomes operative from holding the office of President or acting as President during the remainder of such term.

Section 2. This article shall be inoperative unless it shall have been ratified as an amendment to the Constitution by the legislatures of three-fourths of the several States within seven years from the date of its submission to the States by the Congress.

AMENDMENT XXIII [1961]

Section 1. The District constituting the seat of Government of the United States shall appoint in such manner as the Congress may direct:

A number of electors of President and Vice President equal to the whole number of Senators and Representatives in Congress to which the District would be entitled if it were a State, but in no event more than the least populous State; they shall be in addition to those appointed by the States, but they shall be considered, for the purposes of the election of President and Vice President, to be electors appointed by a State; and they shall meet in the District and perform such duties as provided by the twelfth article of amendment.

Section 2. The Congress shall have power to enforce this article by appropriate legislation.

AMENDMENT XXIV [1964]

Section 1. The right of citizens of the United States to vote in any primary or other election for President or Vice President, for electors for President or Vice President, or for Senator or Representative in Congress, shall not be denied or abridged by the United States or any State by reason of failure to pay any poll tax or other tax.

Section 2. The Congress shall have power to enforce this article by appropriate legislation.

AMENDMENT XXV [1967]

Section 1. In case of the removal of the President from office or of his death or resignation, the Vice President shall become President.

Section 2. Whenever there is a vacancy in the office of the Vice President, the President shall nominate a Vice President who shall take office upon confirmation by a majority vote of both Houses of Congress.

Section 3. Whenever the President transmits to the President pro tempore of the Senate and the Speaker of the House of Representatives his written declaration that he is unable to discharge the powers and duties of his office, and until he transmits to them a written declaration to the contrary, such powers and duties shall be discharged by the Vice President as Acting President.

Section 4. Whenever the Vice President and a majority of either the principal officers of the executive departments or of such other body as Congress may by law provide, transmit to the President pro tempore of the Senate and the Speaker of the House of Representatives their written declaration that the President is unable to discharge the powers and duties of his office, the Vice President shall immediately assume the powers and duties of the office as Acting President.

Thereafter, when the President transmits to the President pro tempore of the Senate and the Speaker of the House of Representatives his written declaration that no inability exists, he shall resume the powers and duties of his office unless the Vice President and a majority of either the principal officers of the executive department[10] or of such other body as Congress may by law provide, transmit within four days to the President pro tempore of the Senate and the Speaker of the House of Representatives their written declaration that the President is unable to discharge the powers and duties of his office. Thereupon Congress shall decide the issue, assembling within forty-eight hours for that purpose if not in session. If the Congress, within twenty-one days after receipt of the latter written declaration, or, if Congress is not in session, within twenty-one days after Congress is required to assemble, determines by two-thirds vote of both Houses that the President is unable to discharge the powers and duties of his office, the Vice President shall continue to discharge the same as Acting President; otherwise, the President shall resume the powers and duties of his office.

AMENDMENT XXVI [1971]

Section 1. The right of citizens of the United States, who are eighteen years of age or older, to vote shall not be denied or abridged by the United States or by any State on account of age.

Section 2. The Congress shall have power to enforce this article by appropriate legislation.

AMENDMENT XXVII[11] [1992]

No law, varying the compensation for the services of the Senators and Representatives, shall take effect, until an election of Representatives shall have intervened.

Proposed September 25, 1789, ratified May 7, 1992.

---

[10] *So in original. Probably should be "departments"*

[11] (Originally "Article the second.")

CURRENT

JUSTICES OF THE SUPREME COURT

OF

THE UNITED STATES OF AMERICA

CHIEF JUSTICE

JOHN G. ROBERTS, JR.

ASSOCIATE JUSTICES

JOHN PAUL STEVENS

ANTONIN SCALIA

ANTHONY M. KENNEDY

DAVID H. SOUTER

CLARENCE THOMAS

RUTH BADER GINSBURG

STEPHEN G. BREYER

SAMUEL A. ALITO, JR.

GLOSSARY OF
TERMS FREQUENTLY USED IN
CASE LAW ANALYSIS

ACQUITTAL
Verdict in a criminal trial representing a formal and legal certification of the absence of guilt of a person charged with a crime.

AFFIANT
The individual who makes and subscribes to an affidavit.

AFFIDAVIT
A statement or declaration of facts, written or printed, sworn to by the maker, and presented to a person having official authority to administer the oath or affirmation.

AFFIRMED
Approved, ratified, or confirmed. Generally represents the determination of an appellate or higher court that the judgment or decision of the lower court should stand.

APPEAL
A formal process through which a party resorts to a superior (or higher) court to review the decision or judgment of the inferior (or lower) court or administrative agency.

APPELLANT
Generally, the unsuccessful party in the lower court (or administrative agency) who requests that a higher court review the lower court's (or administrative agency's) action, determination, or judgment. The party who brings the appeal.

APPELLEE
Usually (but not always) the successful party in the lower court (or administrative agency). Represents the party against whom the appeal is taken. In contrast to the appellant who attacks the lower court's (or administrative agency's) ruling, the appellee generally defends the lower court's ruling. Note that the party's status as appellant or appellee in the higher court bears no relation to the party's status as plaintiff or defendant in the lower court (or administrative agency).

ARRAIGNMENT
Proceeding conducted in open court consisting of a reading of the indictment or information to the defendant or stating to the defendant the substance of the charge and calling on the defendant to plead thereto. Prior to being called upon to enter his plea, the defendant is given a copy of the indictment or information. *Fed.R.Crim.Pro.* 10.

ARREST

A substantial physical interference with the liberty of a person, resulting in his apprehension and detention. It is generally effected for the purpose of preventing a person from committing a criminal offense, or calling upon a person to answer or account for an alleged completed crime.

BORN ALIVE RULE

The "born alive" rule, recognized by most jurisdictions by 1850, provides that only one who has been born alive can be the victim of a homicide. If, however, the fetus was born and then died of injuries inflicted prior to birth, a prosecution for homicide could be maintained. Today, however, with the vast strides in fetal medicine and neonatology that have occurred in recent decades, the continuing viability of the "born alive" rule has been called into question.

CASE LAW

The law of reported judicial opinions or decisions as distinguished from statutory or administrative law.

CERTIORARI

Literally (Latin term meaning) "to be informed." A discretionary device or vehicle most commonly used by the Supreme Court of the United States to choose the cases most deserving of review. The party requesting certiorari will present his or her request in a formal writ or petition explaining the reasons why the High Court should hear the case; specifically outlining the major questions of significant interest and importance to the general public.

CLEAR AND CONVINCING EVIDENCE

A burden of proof standard that is greater than the preponderance of the evidence, but less than proof beyond a reasonable doubt. Clear and convincing evidence is evidence that is "so clear, direct, weighty and convincing" as "to enable either a judge or jury to come to a clear conviction, without hesitancy, of the precise facts in issue." *Matter of Seaman*, 133 *N.J.* 67, 74, 627 A.2d 106 (1993). Clear and convincing evidence should produce in the mind of the judge or jury a firm belief or conviction as to the truth of the matter sought to be established.

CODE JURISDICTION

A state which does not recognize "common law" crimes.

COMPLAINT

A written statement, made upon oath, of the essential facts constituting the offense charged. *Fed.R.Crim.Pro.* 3.

CORPUS DELICTI

A Latin phrase meaning "the body of the crime." The *corpus delicti* consists of two elements: (1) the occurrence of a loss or injury; and (2) some person's criminal conduct as the source of that loss or injury. The identity of the person responsible for the criminal act is not part of the *corpus delicti.*

CORPUS DELICTI RULE

A rule standing for the proposition that a criminal conviction may not be based on the extra-judicial confession or admission of the defendant, unless it is corroborated by independent evidence establishing the *corpus delicti.* The purpose of the rule is to safeguard against criminal convictions being obtained solely on the out-of-court confession of one accused of a crime, and thus, a case may not go to the trier of fact where independent evidence does not suggest that a crime has occurred.

DEFENDANT

The individual against whom a criminal or civil action is brought.

E.G.

Abbreviation for "exempli gratia," meaning: "For Example."

ET SEQ.

Abbreviated form of *et sequentes.* Literally (Latin term meaning) "and the following." Most commonly used to denote inclusive references to pages or statutory sections; *e.g.*, The New Jersey Criminal Statutes encompassing Theft may be found in *N.J.S.* 2C:20-1 *et seq.* (Such a citation may also be represented as *N.J.S.* tit. 2C, §§20-1 to 20-34 for additional clarity.)

EXEMPLAR

Any type of physical object of "known" authorship or origin which may be used by the investigator or detective for purposes of comparison to an object of "questionable" authorship or origin. The exemplar—as a "model"—is a standard; it constitutes the "typical" or "representative" article with which a questioned article may be compared.

The exemplar may be a standard of writing or typing, stamp or seal impression with which a questioned writing, typing, stamp or seal impression may be compared. It may also be a standard of fingerprints, palm prints, footprints, physical measurements, blood, urine or saliva samples, fingernail scrapings, hair samples, voice samples, photographs (for use in lineups), or display of one's bodily characteristics (for in-person lineups or photographs), which may be used either by an expert or laywitness, the jury, or by the victim of the crime for comparison purposes.

FALSUS IN UNO, FALSUS IN OMNIBUS

Literally (Latin phrase meaning) "false in one, false in all." When given as a jury charge, the maxim means that if the jury believes a witness deliberately lied about a material issue, the jury may, for that reason alone, choose to disbelieve the rest of the witness's testimony.

FRUIT OF THE POISONOUS TREE

Receiving most notable mention in the case of *Wong Sun v. United States*, 371 *U.S.* 471, 83 *S.Ct.* 407 (1963). The poisonous tree doctrine displays the notion that evidence obtained after illegal government action will be excluded from evidence. This pertains not only to physical or tangible materials generally subject to the Exclusionary Rule, but also intangibles such as subsequent confessions, admissions, identifications, and testimony obtained as a result of the primary taint (or initial unlawful activity).

GRAND JURY

Body of 16 to 23 citizens who sit to decide whether there is sufficient evidence in a criminal prosecution to warrant further action by the State. Generally, attendance at the grand jury will be comprised of the 16-23 jurors, the prosecutor, the clerk of the grand jury, the grand jury stenographer, and the witness.

HABEAS CORPUS

Literally (Latin term meaning) "you have the body." Name given to a variety of writs, most commonly consisting of a written order directing one in authority to produce the body of another before the issuing court. It is a collateral civil proceeding whereby a person presently incarcerated seeks to obtain his release from custody, generally naming his custodian as defendant. The purpose of the writ is not to determine the prisoner's innocence or guilt, but to determine the constitutionality of his imprisonment. Issuance of the writ does not necessarily result in the prisoner's discharge; in fact, the majority are issued on the condition that the prisoner be retried. The Writ of habeas corpus, today, is still one of the unique instruments in our legal system which allows a method to gain access to the courts by one who believes he or she has been unjustly incarcerated.

ID.

Abbreviated form of *Idem.* Literally (Latin term meaning) "the same." Indicates a reference previously made. Used when citing to the immediately preceding case or other authority. [See READING GUIDE for more extensive explanation and modified use of *id.*]

INFRA

Literally (Latin term meaning) "below or beneath." "Shorthand" way to refer the reader *ahead* to the fully cited authority appearing subsequently in the text. [See READING GUIDE for more extensive discussion on the use of *Infra.*]

INTERLOCUTORY ORDER

A provisional, temporary, or nonfinal order. Although it does not dispose of the case, it decides some point or matter in controversy or affords some sort of temporary relief. *E.g.*, a temporary restraining order.

JUDGMENT

The official legal decision of a court of law which resolves the dispute and settles or determines the rights and obligations of the parties to the legal proceeding.

JURISDICTION

The authority or power of a court to hear and determine a case. The authority is established with reference to the particular parties before the court as well as the particular subject matter. To validly exercise jurisdiction, the parties to the action must be accorded fair notice of the proceeding and an opportunity to be heard. If jurisdiction is lacking, the court's judgment is void.

JURISPRUDENCE

Science or philosophy of law.

MOTION

Formal request made to a court relating to any issue arising during the pendency of a legal proceeding.

MOTION TO SUPPRESS

Formal request made to a court to eliminate unlawfully seized evidence from a criminal trial which has been obtained in violation of the Fourth Amendment (search and seizure), Fifth Amendment (privilege against self-incrimination) or the Sixth Amendment (right to assistance of counsel, right of confrontation, etc.), or under parallel provisions of a state constitution.

OPINION

Expression of the reasons why a certain decision (the judgment) was reached in a case.

Majority opinion is usually written by one judge and represents the rules of law which a majority of his associates on the court believe operative in a given decision. Has more precedential value than any other type of opinion, unless, of course, it is a unanimous opinion of the entire Court.

Separate opinion may be written by one or more judges in which he, she, or they concur in or dissent from the majority opinion.

Concurring opinion agrees with the result reached by the majority but for different reasons. Many times written by a particular judge to express a different view of the subject matter discussed, or expound upon his particular views on the matter.

Dissenting opinion disagrees with the result reached by the majority, and as such, disagrees with the reasoning or rules of law used by the majority in deciding the case.

Plurality opinion (in a judgment by the United States Supreme Court) is agreed to by less than a majority as to the reasoning of the decision, but is agreed to by a majority of the Court as to the result. For example a plurality opinion would be one in which the opinion of the Court was delivered by one justice in which two other justices joined, with two different justices concurring for different reasons, and four justices dissenting.

Per curiam opinion is an opinion "by the court" which expresses its decision in the case but withholds the identity of the author.

Memorandum opinion is a holding of the whole court which is generally very short and concise.

OVERRULE

To overturn, invalidate, reject, or negate the ruling of a prior case. Decisions may only be overruled by the same court or higher court within the same jurisdiction.

PEN REGISTER

"[A] device which records or decodes electronic or other impulses which identify the numbers dialed or otherwise transmitted on the telephone line to which such device is attached, but such term does not include any device used by a provider or customer of a wire or electronic communication service for billing, or recording as an incident to billing, for communications services provided by such provider or any device used by a provider or customer of a wire communication service for cost accounting or other like purposes in the ordinary course of its business." 18 *U.S.C.* §3126(3).

PETITION

A formal written application requesting some form of relief. Most commonly presented to a court requesting judicial action on a particular matter.

PETITIONER

Similar to the *appellant*. Generally, the unsuccessful party in the lower court who brings his or her appeal by way of petition for writ of *certiorari* to the United States Supreme Court.

PLAINTIFF

The party who initiates or brings an action against another in a court of law. In a criminal case the plaintiff is generally the State or United States Government.

POISONOUS FRUIT DOCTRINE

See FRUIT OF THE POISONOUS TREE

PROMULGATE

To publish or announce officially. The formal act of announcing a statute written by a legislative body or a decision handed down by a court.

REMAND

To send back. Generally used by a higher court which sends the case back to the lower court with directions for the taking of specified further action.

RESPONDEAT SUPERIOR

"Let the master answer." A maxim meaning that a master or employer is responsible or liable in certain cases for the wrongful acts of his servant or employee. Generally, in order for an employer to be held vicariously liable for the torts of an employee, the conduct of the employee must have some relationship to his employment.

RESPONDENT

Similar to the *appellee* in the appellate court. Generally represents the successful party in the lower court and is the party against whom the petition for *certiorari* or certification is brought. When the case comes to the higher court by petition for *certiorari* or certification, the parties are generally referred to as the petitioner and respondent as distinguished from a case which comes to the higher court by appeal where the parties are referred to as appellant and appellee. Here, as in the case of appeal, the party's status as petitioner or respondent bears no relationship to their former status as plaintiff or defendant in the trial court.

REVERSE

To void, set aside, annul, or change to the contrary or former state. As to reverse the judgment of a lower court or administrative agency.

SUBPOENA

A formal written command directed to a witness ordering him to appear at a certain time and place and to give testimony upon a certain matter and/or produce certain evidentiary documents pursuant to a certain matter in a legal proceeding.

Subpoena duces tecum requires the recipient to produce specific evidentiary documents and/or things at the legal proceeding.

Subpoena ad testificandum compels the attendance of the witness to give testimony at a legal proceeding. Is the technical or descriptive term for the ordinary subpoena.

SUPRA

Literally (Latin term meaning), "above." "Shorthand" way to refer the reader *back* to the fully cited authority previously appearing in the text. [See READING GUIDE for more extensive discussion on the use of *supra*.]

SUSTAIN

To affirm, approve, establish, or uphold in evidence. As when an appellate court sustains or affirms the lower court's ruling. In the context of an objection at trial court, when a judge sustains such an objection to testimony or evidence offered, the judge agrees with the objection and gives it effect by ruling in its favor.

TORT

A private, personal, or civil wrong or injury, other than a breach of contract, for which the law will provide a remedy in a form of an action for money damages. In order to maintain a tort action, the plaintiff must establish (1) the existence of a legal duty owed to plaintiff by defendant, (2) the breach of that duty, and (3) damage or injury to plaintiff as a proximate result of that breach.

TORTFEASOR
One who commits or is guilty of a tort; a civil wrong-doer.

VERDICT
Has origin from the Latin term, "veredictum," literally meaning "a true declaration." Represents the formal decision or finding of a properly impaneled and sworn jury. In criminal cases the verdict shall generally consist of a declaration of "guilty" or "not guilty."

TABLE OF CASES

References are to pages in this volume. Principal cases are in **bold** type. Page numbers of extended discussions of cases are in *italic* type. For In re _____, and In the Matter of _____, see the name of the party. For Commonwealth v. _____, People v. _____, State v. _____, and United States v. _____, see the name of the other party. Where a case is discussed in another case, reference is made only to the first page at which it is cited.

INDEX

All References are to Sections

I

Notes

Notes

Notes

Notes

Notes

Notes